child&adolescent development

an integrated approach

David F. Bjorklund
Florida Atlantic University

Carlos Hernández Blasi
University Jaume I

WADSWORTH
CENGAGE Learning™

Australia • Brazil • Japan • Korea • Mexico • Singapore • Spain • United Kingdom • United States

Child and Adolescent Development:
An Integrated Approach
David F. Bjorklund and Carlos Hernández Blasi

Senior Publisher: Linda Schreiber-Ganster

Senior Acquisitions Editor: Jaime Perkins

Senior Developmental Editor: Renee Deljon

Assistant Editor: Paige Leeds

Editorial Assistant: Phillip Hovanessian

Media Editor: Mary Noel

Senior Marketing Manager: Jessica Egbert

Marketing Assistant: Janay Prior

Marketing Communications
  Manager: Laura Localio

Senior Content Project Manager: Christy Frame

Creative Director: Rob Hugel

Senior Art Director: Vernon Boes

Senior Print Buyer: Mary Beth Hennebury

Rights Acquisitions Account Manager, Text
  and Images: Dean Dauphinais

Production Service: Mandy Walden,
  Lachina Publishing Services

Text Designer: Jeanne Calabrese

Photo Researcher: Roman Barnes

Copy Editor: Ginjer Clark,
  Lachina Publishing Services

Cover Designer: Jeanne Calabrese

Cover Image: Eric Meola/Getty Images

Compositor: Lachina Publishing Services

For product information and technology assistance, contact us at
Cengage Learning Customer & Sales Support, 1-800-354-9706.

For permission to use material from this text or product,
submit all requests online at **www.cengage.com/permissions**.
Further permissions questions can be emailed to
permissionrequest@cengage.com.

Library of Congress Control Number: 2010934027

ISBN-13: 978-0-495-09563-7

ISBN-10: 0-495-09563-X

Wadsworth
20 Davis Drive
Belmont, CA 94002-3098
USA

Cengage Learning is a leading provider of customized learning solutions with office locations around the globe, including Singapore, the United Kingdom, Australia, Mexico, Brazil, and Japan. Locate your local office at **www.cengage.com/global**.

Cengage Learning products are represented in Canada by Nelson Education, Ltd.

To learn more about Wadsworth, visit **www.cengage.com/wadsworth**.

Purchase any of our products at your local college store or at our preferred online store **www.CengageBrain.com**.

Printed in Canada
1 2 3 4 5 6 7 14 13 12 11 10

To Brendan and Shayne, for all the inspiration they have given me.
David F. Bjorklund

To my parents, Elisa and José María, with love and gratitude.
Carlos Hernández Blasi

Brief Contents

Contents

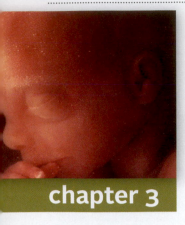

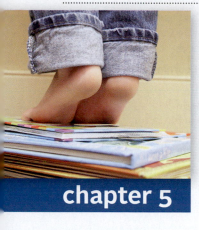
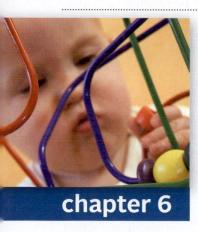

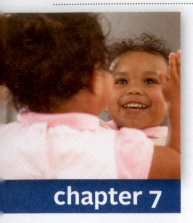
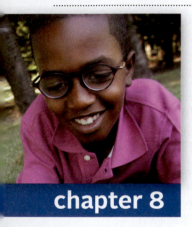
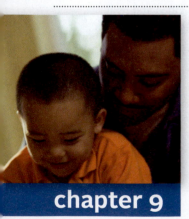

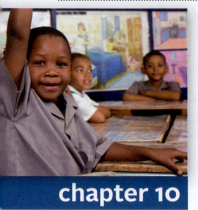

PART THREE : SOCIAL DEVELOPMENT: BECOMING A SOCIAL BEING 434

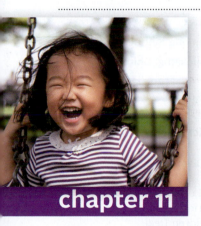

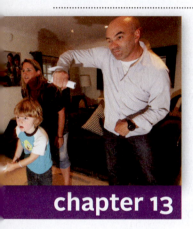

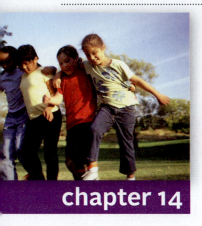

Features

evolution in action

food for thought

socioculturally speaking

About the Authors

DAVID F. BJORKLUND, PH.D., is a Professor of Psychology at Florida Atlantic University, where he has taught graduate and undergraduate courses in developmental psychology since 1976. He received a B.A. degree in Psychology from the University of Massachusetts in 1971, an M.A. degree in Psychology from the University of Dayton in 1973, and a Ph.D. degree in Developmental Psychology from the University of North Carolina at Chapel Hill in 1976. He has received numerous teaching and research awards from Florida Atlantic University, and is the recipient of an Alexander von Humboldt Research Award. He served as Associate Editor of *Child Development* (1997–2001) and is currently serving as Editor of the *Journal of Experimental Child Psychology*. He has served on the editorial boards of *Developmental Psychology, Developmental Review, Cognitive Development, Educational Psychology Review, Evolutionary Psychology, Journal of Comparative Psychology, Journal of Cognition and Development, Journal of Experimental Child Psychology*, and *School Psychology Quarterly*, and has also served as a contributing editor to *Parents Magazine*. He has published more than 150 scholarly articles on various topics relating to child development and has received financial support for his research from the National Science Foundation, the Spencer Foundation, and the German Research Foundation. His other books include *Children's Thinking: Cognitive Development and Individual Differences*, now in its fifth edition; *Why Youth Is Not Wasted on the Young; Looking at Children: An Introduction to Child Development* (with Barbara Bjorklund); *Parents Book of Discipline* (with Barbara Bjorklund); *Applied Child Study* (with Anthony Pellegrini); *The Origins of Human Nature: Evolutionary Developmental Psychology* (with Anthony Pellegrini); *Children's Strategies: Contemporary Views of Cognitive Development; False-Memory Creation in Children and Adults: Theory, Research, and Implications*; and *Origins of the Social Mind: Evolutionary Psychology and Child Development* (edited with Bruce Ellis). His current research interests include children's cognitive development and evolutionary developmental psychology. He lives in Jupiter, Florida, with his wife, Barbara, and enjoys traveling, cooking, playing basketball, and kayaking.

CARLOS HERNÁNDEZ BLASI, PH.D., earned his undergraduate degree in psychology from the Universitat de Barcelona in 1986 and his Ph.D. from the Universidad Autónoma de Madrid in 1993. Since 1997, he has been Associate Professor at the University Jaume I in Castellón, Spain, where he teaches developmental psychology through the Department of Psychology and the College of Education. His primary field of research is cognitive development, particularly memory development in children, although his interests have become increasingly focused on how contemporary biological approaches (neurosciences, behavioral genetics, and, especially, evolutionary theory) can improve our understanding of psychological development. Professor Hernández Blasi has been a visiting professor and invited lecturer at different U.S. and European research institutions, including Florida Atlantic University, the Max Planck Institute in Munich, Germany, and Aalborg University in Denmark. He has been awarded several research grants in Spain and currently serves as an Associate Editor of *Infancia y Aprendizaje*, the leading Spanish-language journal on child development. His other books (all in Spanish) include *Contexts for Psychological Development and Education* (edited with Rosana Clemente) and *Developmental Psychology: An Historical and Conceptual Approach*. He lives in Castellón, on the Mediterranean coast, and loves the arts, especially film and music, as well as traveling, swimming, and watching sports.

Barbara Bjorklund

Carlos Hernández Blasi and David Bjorklund

In 1975 Hetherington and Parke published a bold new topical approach to the study of development. This was an excellent beginning. The text was cutting edge, emphasized process over description, and was heralded as a crowning achievement and integration of the then-rising field of experimental child psychology. While paying good homage to this tradition, we soon came to the conclusion that this older approach often makes it difficult for students to integrate many of the new approaches and findings that have occurred in the field in the last 40 years. Times change, and so must textbooks.

In recent years, developmental scientists have made great strides in a number of areas, including an understanding of infant development; increased attention to experimental research in socioemotional development; advances in biomedical science, particularly neuroscience, genetics, and evolution; and the recognition of the important role of social context and culture in shaping development. Our field has been greatly enriched by these advances, and over the last half century child and adolescent development textbooks have faithfully presented the basic facts of development, along with the traditional theories about how development progresses—Freud and Erikson's theories of psychosexual development, Piaget's theory of cognitive development, Bandura's theory of social development—integrating new research findings and theories alongside the more traditional ones. But when presenting new research and theories to students, textbook writers have had a tendency to emphasize one perspective over another (for example, biological vs. sociocultural), or to present as fairly as possible multiple perspectives of development as contrasting points of views. These tendencies often result in an overly eclectic and atheoretical approach, telling students, essentially, "Here's the evidence, you choose which approach you think makes the most sense." The result is a book that provides students all the facts and up-to-date accounts of development, but often leaves them without a coherent picture of what development is and how contemporary scientists actually view infants, children, adolescents, and the process of human development.

The field of developmental psychology has changed drastically over the past two decades, and the older piecemeal approach does not work to explain more modern viewpoints of the discipline. As a result, we have taken a different tact. We have organized this book using what we see as three overarching perspectives that guide today's researchers and practitioners of developmental psychology, and we use them not as contrasting and sometimes contradictory ways of looking at development, but rather as viewpoints that must be integrated in order to truly understand infants, children, and adolescents and how they develop. These three perspectives are *developmental contextualism*, a *sociocultural perspective*, and *evolutionary theory*.

A Closer Look at Developmental Contextualism

The first modern perspective that has become axiomatic in most contemporary journals, *developmental contextualism*, emphasizes that development should be viewed as the continuous and bidirectional interaction between an active organism and a changing environment, at all levels of organization from the molecular (What causes genes to be turned on and off? What are the effects of hormones on physical and psychological development?) to the cultural (How do societal traditions influence the development of self-esteem? How might culture interact with infant temperaments to produce adaptive or maladaptive behavior?), and everything in between (How does children's physical health affect their mother's behavior, and how does her behavior, in turn, affect the children's emotional and intellectual development?). Development always occurs in a *context*, of which the child is a contributing part. From this viewpoint, one cannot ask "how much" of any trait—intelligence or personality, for example—is due to genetics and how much is due to environment. Rather, one must ask how biologic and environmental factors interact over time to produce developmental outcomes.

A Closer Look at the Sociocultural Perspective

The second complimentary modern perspective, the *sociocultural perspective*, recognizes the centrality of the social environment for human development. We are a social species, and human development can be properly understood only when the influences of social relations and the broader social/cultural environment are considered. How do parent-child relationships vary in different cultures, and how do these differences affect children's social, emotional, and psychological development? How does being raised in a schooled versus nonschooled society influence how parents interact with children and the cognitive abilities that children acquire? How might a culture's names for its numbers affect how children learn arithmetic? Culture counts, and this in no way contradicts the recent discoveries about and emphasis on the biological bases of development. Biological development also occurs within a social context, which can influence the course of a child's life (How does a culture contribute and respond to pubertal changes?). Even if one were to eliminate the influence of "culture" on development by raising a child in total social isolation, it would not reveal a child's "true" nature. Development always occurs within a social context, culturally shaped and historically conditioned, although the specific details of a child's social environment can vary widely.

A Closer Look at Evolutionary Theory

The third complimentary perspective, *evolutionary theory*, helps us to better understand "why" children and adolescents behave as they do, which we believe will help us to better understand the "hows" and the "whats" of development, as well as help us apply knowledge of child and adolescent development to everyday problems. Theodosius Dobzhansky famously said, "Nothing in biology makes sense except in the light of evolution." We make the same argument for psychology, particularly for the understanding of infants, children, adolescents, and their development.

The Benefits of Integrating These Perspectives

Together, these perspectives are even better than the sum of their parts. That is, the three perspectives serve as complementary agents in modern developmental psychology and represent a dynamism and specificity that goes well beyond the old "description versus process" debates of the 1970s. These three approaches also represent three different levels of analysis.

Developmental contextual models examine the development of psychological processes over an individual's lifetime, beginning prenatally; sociocultural models also look at the immediate causes of behavior, but additionally take into account the impact of humans' 10,000-year cultural history on development; and evolutionary theory takes a truly long view of human history, examining the role that natural selection has had on shaping human development, particularly since the emergence of *Homo* as a genus, about two million years ago. By integrating these three perspectives, this book provides a truly comprehensive and realistic look at child and adolescent development, covering all the "regular" contents (following a traditional topical approach) but doing so from the vantage point of the major overarching viewpoints in the field of modern developmental psychology.

Consider, for example, the phenomenon of puberty, discussed in all child and adolescent development textbooks, usually in the chapter on physical development. We do the same, examining the role of hormones in producing secondary sexual characteristics in boys and girls, for example. We also examine, however, historical changes and cultural differences in the attainment of menarche (a girl's first menstrual period) and environmental factors in modern societies that contribute to accelerated pubertal development in some girls and even the development of female secondary sexual characteristics in some boys! In addition, we look at how different cultures view the transition to puberty, as well as puberty's relation to falling in love and the development of romantic relationships in adolescence (Chapter 15: *The Development of Sexuality and Gender Identity*). We also examine research based on evolutionary theory that predicts that a girl's early home environment can affect the age at which she reaches puberty and her subsequent "mating" and parenting strategies (Chapter 4: *Physical Development*). This attempt to reflect and integrate modern perspectives of development allows us to go beyond "process versus description" debates characteristic of most other textbooks and provide a more integrated and coherent view of development.

Our integrated and science-based approach also helps us to emphasize applied issues. Most students take a child and adolescent development course because of what it can teach them about how to deal with children, sometimes as professionals (a police office, nurse, teacher, or therapist, for example), but usually as parents (or parents-to-be). We agree with the adage that the best science is science that helps people, and this is true not only of disciplines such as physics, chemistry, and biology, but also psychology, perhaps especially developmental psychology. To this end, we have included many "applied" topics throughout this book, tying them to theory and basic research whenever we can. We have also tried to make the writing accessible to students, to provide examples and stories that make sometimes-difficult concepts clear, and to relate theory and research to the "real world."

Some of the "real world" topics we cover involve practical advice for parents and other people who deal with typically developing children on a regular basis—for example, how do you deal with an unruly child, what do you do when babies won't sleep, or how can reading to young children enhance their language and school performance? Other applied topics are concerned with *atypical development* and *developmental psychopathology*. Rather than having a separate chapter on these issues, as is done in many textbooks, we incorporate discussion of these topics in the appropriate content chapters, integrating some topics into text and presenting others in boxes. For example, we discuss: pathologies and atypical development due to chromosomal abnormalities (such as Down syndrome) in Chapter 3: *Genetics, Prenatal Development, and the Neonate*; ADHD as it relates to executive function in Chapter 8: *Becoming Self-Directed Thinkers: Problem Solving and Memory*; Williams syndrome and specific language disabilities in Chapter 9: *Language Development*; and intellectual disabilities and savants in Chapter 10: *Intelligence and School Achievement*, among others. Where possible, we illustrate how a particular pathology may provide insight into what underlies typical development and vice versa (for example, autism with respect to theory of mind and how deficits in theory of mind are at the bottom of some significant developmental problems in social relations and understanding).

Finally, a developmental contextual/sociocultural/evolutionary approach to child and adolescent development inherently requires attention to diversity. One important source of information about whether a feature of childhood is universal and a likely product of evolution by natural selection, for example, is whether (and how) it is expressed in different cultures. In this vein, for instance, we discuss different patterns across cultures (and subcultures) of physical development, including the attainment of puberty, in Chapter 4: *Physical Development*; the development of ethnic identity for minority youth in Chapter 7: *Understanding Self and Others*; and differences in attachment patterns and their consequences in different cultures in Chapter 12: *Attachment and Early Parent-Child Care*, among others. In most cases, we integrate discussions of cultural diversity within the text, because cross-cultural comparisons will often be central to the main arguments of a chapter. In some cases, we discuss aspects of cultural diversity in boxes.

Organization of the Book

This text includes the core topics covered in traditional child and adolescent development texts, and like many other textbooks, ours is organized into three parts: *The Foundations of Development*; *Cognitive Development: Becoming a Problem Solver*; and *Social Development: Becoming a Social Being*.

Part One begins with an introductory chapter that provides a brief overview of the history of research in child and adolescent development, a history of childhood, core issues in the field, and a review of the basic research methodologies of child development. The second chapter reviews traditional theories of child and adolescent development, but focuses mainly on contemporary theoretical approaches, specifically the three integrated throughout the text: *developmental contextualism*, a *sociocultural perspective*, and *evolutionary developmental psychology*. Chapters 3 and 4 (usually considered to be the "biology" chapters in a child and adolescent development textbook) examine genetics, prenatal development, and the neonate (Chapter 3), and physical development, including a section on brain development (Chapter 4). We also discuss relevant aspects of brain/neurological development in specific content chapters where it is most relevant and where we have found it to make most sense to students.

Part Two focuses on cognitive development. Intelligence, or cognition, is essentially used to solve problems. Individuals change in order to solve problems associated with their local environment. Those problems may involve understanding the social world–getting along with other people–or understanding the physical world–comprehending the nature of objects, or using tools to gain resources. Humans' problem-solving abilities are perhaps unique in the animal world in that they involve *symbolic* and *explicit* (that is, self-aware) cognition. Much cognition, however, is based on *implicit* (that is, out of conscious awareness) processes; both implicit and explicit processes develop, and we address both types of cognition throughout the chapters that comprise Part Two.

Chapter 5 (*What Do Infants Know and When and How Do They Know It?*) looks at infant perception and cognition, while Chapter 6 explores the development of symbolic representation, focusing primarily but not exclusively on Jean Piaget's historically important and highly influential account of cognitive development. This is followed by Chapter 7 (*Understanding Self and Others*), which looks at the development of *social cognition*–how children come to think about their own thoughts, feelings, motives, and behaviors as well as those of other people. In Chapter 8 (*Becoming Self-Directed Thinkers: Problem Solving and Memory*), we explore how children become self-directed thinkers through examining the development of problem solving, executive function, strategies, and memory. Chapter 9 follows to present students with an overview of and provide insights into language development. Part Two concludes with Chapter 10 (*Intelligence and School Achievement*), in which we examine applied cognitive development—the meaning and measurement of "intelligence," the many factors that influence a child's IQ, and the development of perhaps the three most important academic skills for children in schooled cultures: reading, writing, and arithmetic.

In Part Three we explore important aspects of social development. Humans are social animals, and one can only understand human behavior and development within the social contexts in which we live. From this perspective, a significant part of becoming fully human has to do with becoming a social being.

Accordingly, we start this section with Chapter 11 focusing on emotion, temperament, and personality development. Chapter 12 (*Attachment and Early Parent-Child Care*) addresses infant-parent attachment as well as examines childcare through an evolutionary lens (for example, looking at factors that influence how much care parents, grandparents, stepparents, and adoptive parents provide to children). Chapter 13 (*The Family and Other Contexts for Socialization*) follows to provide a thoughtful look at the role of family, particularly parents, in child development, and also to examine two other important socializing agents in children's lives: school and the media, including television, computer games, and the Internet. The part's last two chapters are devoted to helping students understand the development of social relationships in the context of peers (Chapter 14, *Competing and Cooperating with Peers*), and the development of sexuality, gender differences, and gender identity (Chapter 15, *The Development of Sexuality and Gender Identity*).

Pedagogical Features

In addition to its topical organization, integrated approach, and emphasis on applications, this text offers a select set of pedagogical features to keep student readers engaged and help them learn the concepts covered. In particular, this text's pedagogy is designed to support students' reading without interrupting it and to guide their study while engendering genuine understanding.

High-Interest Boxes

Six types of boxes appear in rotation throughout the chapters to add both depth and dimension to the presentation of the text's comprehensive core content and featured perspectives: The Biopsychology of Childhood, Child Development in the Real World, Evolution in Action, Food for Thought, Big Questions, and Socioculturally Speaking.

The Biopsychology of Childhood boxes examine different aspects of biopsychological development (for example, *Brain Development and the Development of Declarative Memory in Infancy* in Chapter 5; *Hormonal and Neural Development and Changes in Risk-Taking in Adolescence* in Chapter 14).

Child Development in the Real World boxes focus on applied issues (for example, *To Sleep, Perchance to Be Psychologically Healthy* in Chapter 4; *Children's Memory and Testimony in the Real World* in Chapter 8).

Evolution in Action boxes deal with adaptations evolved over our species' history (for example, *An Evolutionary Approach to Emotions and Emotional Development* in Chapter 11; *The Case of Incest Avoidance* in Chapter 15).

Food for Thought boxes deal with provocative, counterintuitive, or just-plain-interesting topics (for example, *Case Studies of Growing Up in Extreme Conditions: Wild and Feral Children* in Chapter 1; *Can You Ever Be Too Rich or Too Thin?* in Chapter 4).

Big Questions boxes address big questions related to child and adolescent development (for example, *Where Do Babies Come From?* in Chapter 6; *Are People Getting Smarter? The Flynn Effect* in Chapter 10).

Socioculturally Speaking boxes examine issues dealing with culture (for example, *Culture, Symbols, and Development* in Chapter 6; *China's One-Child Policy* in Chapter 13).

Concept Review Tables

About three concept review tables are provided within each chapter, periodically summarizing information and giving students a snapshot of key principles.

Running Glossary Terms

Located in the margin throughout a chapter, the "running" glossary terms provide concise definitions right where they're needed, a convenient complement to the complete listing of terms and definitions collected in the full glossary at the back of the book.

Purposeful and Engaging End-of-Chapter Resources

These resources comprise the following elements:

- **The Summary**, a longer version of the overview that opens each chapter, highlights the main points of each section in each chapter.
- **Key Terms and Concepts** lists are handy reference tools that indicate the page on which each term is covered. (In addition to the key term definitions running throughout each chapter, full definitions are also provided in the Glossary at the back of the book.)
- Two sets of study questions are provided for homework or classroom use. The first set, called **Ask Yourself . . . ,** poses ten relatively straightforward questions about important issues in the chapter that permit students to evaluate how well they have mastered the material. The second set of prompts does not really consist of questions, but three intellectual exercises that we call **Exercises: Going Further.** These exercises provide students the opportunity to use the knowledge they have acquired in reading each chapter in applied and creative ways, as well as to reflect on some contemporary and controversial issues linked to modern developmental science, encouraging them to do more than memorize basic facts and theories.
- Three categories of **Suggested Readings** that pertain to the topics in each chapter are given. Classic Readings include foundational books and articles for an area of inquiry (for example, for Chapter 6: *The Symbolic Child,* Piaget and Inhelder's classic text, *The Psychology of the Child*). Scholarly Works list several cutting-edge research papers, books, or review articles on topics discussed in the chapter (for example, for Chapter 6, Kayoko Inagaki and Giyoo Hatano's article, "Young Children's Conception of the Biological World" from *Current*

Directions in Psychological Science). Finally, Readings for Personal Interest include mainly current books and magazine articles written for the educated layperson (for example, for Chapter 6, Alison Gopnik's book, *The Philosophical Baby: What Children's Minds Tell Us About Truth, Love, and the Meaning of Life*).

We have devoted much time and effort in writing this book, attempting to describe how children and adolescents grow up in our contemporary world, as well as to provide an appreciation for the process of development. In so doing, we hope we have at least approached our goal of presenting a coherent picture of child and adolescent development that reflects the current state of the field as reflected in the research literature, and one that is accessible to a diverse undergraduate audience. By organizing material around traditional content (for example, physical, cognitive, and social development) and in terms of integrative theory, we have tried to present an up-to-date account of development, matching what developmental psychologists are currently talking about. As one reviewer during the development of the text described it, this is "a new generation of text for undergraduates that speaks to the increasingly complex models that frame our understanding of human development in an accessible way." That was our intention, and we hope readers find that we have succeeded, at least in part.

Comprehensive Supplements Package

A wide array of supplements developed to create the best teaching and learning experience inside as well as outside the classroom accompanies *Child and Adolescent Development: An Integrated Approach*. We invite you to start taking full advantage of the teaching and learning tools available to you by reading this overview of supplements provided by Cengage Learning.

Instructor's Manual with Test Bank

978-0-495-91685-7

Streamline and maximize the effectiveness of your course preparation using such resources as Chapter Outlines, Lecture Topics, and more! This time-saving resource also includes a Test Bank that offers multiple-choice and essay questions.

PowerLecture with JoinIn™ and Examview®

978-0-495-91686-4

This one-stop lecture and class preparation tool contains ready-to-use PowerPoint® slides that allow you to assemble, edit, publish, and present custom lectures for your course. PowerLecture lets you bring together text-specific lecture outlines and art from Bjorklund and Hernández Blasi's text along with videos or your own materials, culminating in a powerful, personalized media-enhanced presentation. The DVD also includes the JoinIn™ Student Response System that lets you pose book-specific questions and display students' answers seamlessly within the PowerPoint® slides of your own lecture in conjunction with the "clicker" hardware of your choice, as well as the ExamView® assessment and tutorial system, which guides you step-by-step through the process of creating tests.

WebTutor™ on WebCT™/ BlackBoard®

978-0-8400-6096-9 / 978-0-8400-6077-8

Jump start your course with customizable, rich, text-specific content within your Course Management System. Whether you want to Web-enable your class or put an entire course online, Web-Tutor™ delivers with a wide array of resources including quizzing, videos, and more. Visit **webtutor.cengage.com** to learn more.

Psychology CourseMate

978-0-8400-6647-3

Cengage Learning's Psychology CourseMate for this text brings course concepts to life with interactive learning, study, and exam preparation tools that support the printed textbook. In addition to **an ebook version of the text,** this interactive resource has an extensive library of observational videos that span early childhood through adolescence, many accompanied by questions that will help foster critical thinking and **reinforce students' understanding** of the core concepts being covered. For instructors, this text's CourseMate also includes **Engagement Tracker,** a first-of-its-kind tool that monitors student engagement in the course. Go to login.cengage.com to access these resources.

Study Guide

978-0-495-89706-4

Created by Gabie Smith, the Study Guide for this text helps students prepare for exams, build problem-solving skills, and get the grade they want through easy access to Chapter Outlines, Key Terms, practice test items, and more.

CengageNow with eBook

978-0-8400-6714-2

CengageNOW is an online teaching and learning resource that gives you and students more control in less time and delivers better outcomes—NOW.

These resources are available to qualified adopters, and ordering options for student supplements are flexible. Please consult your local Cengage Learning sales representative or visit **www.cengage.com** for more information, including additional ISBNs, or to receive examination copies of any of these instructor or student resources, or for product demonstrations. All text purchase and rental options as well as supplemental materials are available to students at **www.cengagebrain.com**.

Acknowledgments

Anyone who writes a book such as this does so with much help from many people. We would like to thank our Editor, Jaime Perkins, and many other specialty editors and support people at Cengage for making this book possible. We want to thank our students and colleagues for their comments on earlier versions of chapters, including Kayla Causey, Amy Gardiner, Jason Grotuss, Virginia Periss, and Adriana Csinady. Our special thanks goes to Marc Lindberg for his constructive criticism, constant support, and unflagging enthusiasm for our project. He was our muse. David Bjorklund's greatest gratitude goes to his wife Barbara who provided constructive comments on many chapters, while working on a textbook of her own—all in addition to being a supportive and understanding spouse. Carlos Hernández Blasi would like to thank his university and the Ministry of Education and Science in Spain for providing him with the adequate conditions to develop this project (SEJ2004-06683/ EDUC, PR2006-0224, PSI2009-13724), as well as to all of his former professors in Barcelona and Madrid, particularly Angel Rivière, whose expertise and spirit are at the heart of this book.

Finally, we would like to thank the conscientious professional reviewers for their consistently constructive comments:

Daisuke Akiba, City University of New York
Melissa Atkins, Marshall University
Lynne Baker-Ward, North Carolina State University
Stephanie Berk, Chatham University
Margaret Bierly, California State University, Chico

Belinda Blevins-Knabe, University of Arkansas at Little Rock
Gloria Boutte, University of South Carolina
Cornelia Brentano, Chapman University
Leilani M. Brown, University of Hawaii at Manoa
Catherine Chambliss, Ursinus College
Pedro "Peter" Cosmé, Union County College
Jessica Dennis, California State University, Los Angeles
Trina Diehl-Cowan, Northwest Vista College
Rachel Dinero, Cazenovia College
Bruce Ellis, University of Arizona
Staussa Ervin, Tarrant County College
Cheryl R. Every-Wurtz, Suffolk Community College
David Geary, University of Missouri
Vicki S. Gier, Mississippi State University/ Meridian
George Hollich, Purdue University
Farrah M. Hughes, Francis Marion University
Kristy Huntley, Briarwood College
Cheri L. Kittrell, Manatee Community College
Dawn Kriebel, Immaculata University
Mary B. Lewis, Oakland University
Hung-Chu Lin, University of Louisiana at Lafayette

Marc A. Lindberg, Marshall University
Francesca Lopez, Marquette University
Kevin MacDonald, California State University-Long Beach
Elizabeth Mazur, Penn State
Ashley Maynard, University of Hawaii
John Opfer, Ohio State University
Roger Page, Ohio State University
Patricia K. Prunty, Mount Olive College
Glenn I. Roisman, University of Illinois at Urbana-Champaign
Jane A. Rysberg, California State University, Chico
Eileen Smith, Fairleigh Dickinson University
Hallie Gammon Speranza, University of Texas at Austin
Michael M. Steele, Washington State University
Lorraine C. Taylor, University of North Carolina at Chapel Hill
Kristie Veri, William Paterson University
Jaime Vitrano, Queensborough Community College
Jamie L. Walter, Albion College
Judy M. Watkinson, Arizona Western College
Lori Werdenschlag, Lyndon State College
Ric Wynn, County College of Morris
Fatemeh Zarghami, St. Cloud State University

David F. Bjorklund
Jupiter, Florida, USA

Carlos Hernández Blasi
Castellón, Spain

child&adolescent
development

an integrated approach

We begin our investigation by providing a brief overview of the history of research in child and adolescent development, a history of childhood, core issues in the field, and a review of the basic research methodologies of child development. In Chapter 2 we sketch some of the major theoretical perspectives that have influenced the field of child and adolescent development (for example, learning theory, information-processing approaches, Piaget's theory, psychoanalytic theories), but the bulk of the space is devoted to more modern approaches that we describe as *developmental-contextual theories*. More specifically, in this chapter we introduce three overarching approaches to the study of child and adolescent development that we attempt to integrate throughout the book: *developmental contextualism*, a *sociocultural perspective,* and *evolutionary developmental psychology.*

The first approach, *developmental contextualism*, emphasizes that development should be viewed as the continuous and bidirectional relationship between an active organism and a changing environment. Asking "how much" of any trait is due to genetics or environment is the wrong question. Rather, one must ask how biological and environmental factors interact over the course of development to produce some outcome. A *sociocultural perspective* emphasizes that children's development always occurs within a social context, with that context having a cultural history that can also influence how children are treated and thus their course of development. Finally, the third approach, *evolutionary developmental psychology*, takes a truly long view of human history and at the role that natural selection has had on shaping human

development. It examines how patterns of development and children's behavior and thinking may have (or may have had in ancient environments) adaptive value. By incorporating these three perspectives, our goal is to provide a truly integrative look at child and adolescent development.

Chapters 3 and 4 examine what are usually considered to be the "biology" chapters in a child and adolescent development textbook. As we make clear in Chapter 2, it is not possible to truly separate biological from environmental factors in explaining development. Genes and other biological agents are in continuous interaction with outside agents and events, requiring that the whole organism be studied in context in order to understand its behavior and development. That notwithstanding, it is often convenient to look at some factors as *foundational* to development, and these include genetics, prenatal development, and aspects of physical growth. In these chapters we aim to provide you not only with a tutorial of how genes work or a description of physical development, but also to address the issue of the relation between the physical "stuff" of an organism and its behavior, a theme that will run through the rest of the chapters of the book. We devote only a portion of the *Physical Development* chapter to brain development, a topic that surely deserves more extensive coverage given the explosion of information that has occurred in recent years. The reason for this is that we discuss relevant aspects of brain/neurological development in specific content chapters.

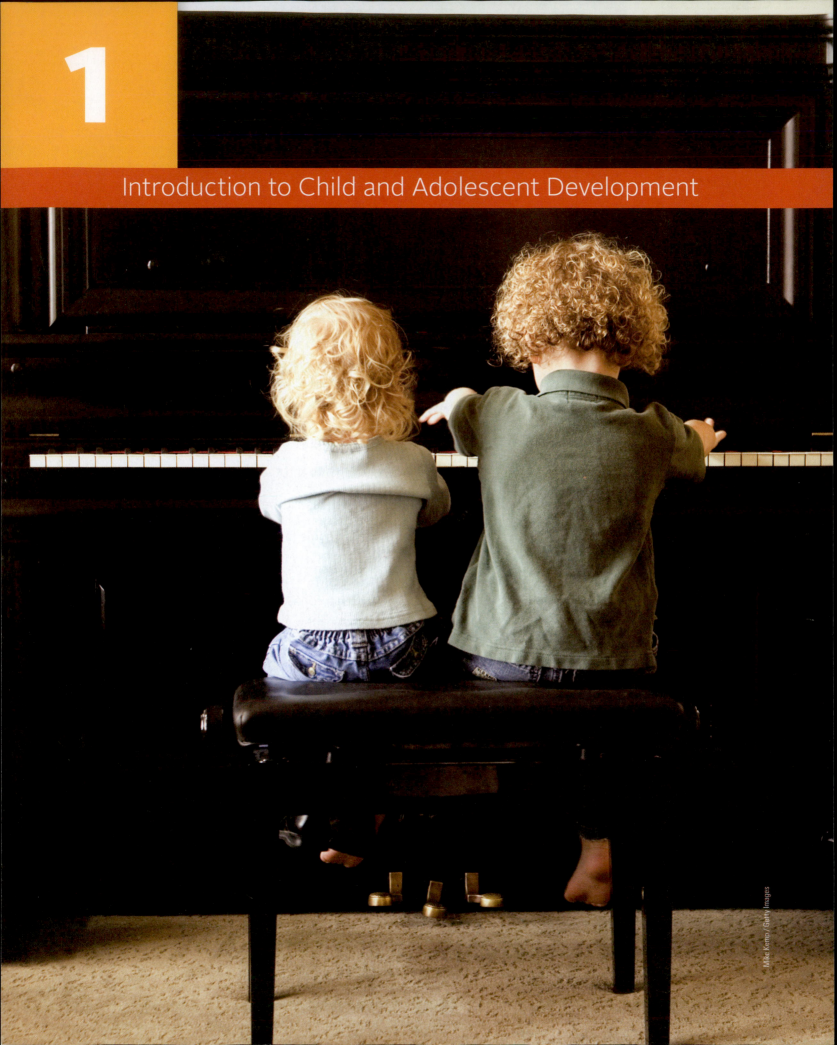

1

Introduction to Child and Adolescent Development

Mika Kemp/Getty Images

In this chapter we introduce the modern field of child and adolescent development. We define some basic concepts of developmental psychology, examine the field's history, and identify some of the core issues in the discipline. Among these issues are:

- The degree to which behavior and cognition are stable over time, versus the degree to which behavior, once established, can be changed:

- Whether developmental change is smooth and continuous, or relatively abrupt and discontinuous, reflecting stages

- How much emphasis one gives to general patterns of development that typify all typically developing children, versus individual differences and the factors that cause children to differ from one another

- The extent to which development is influenced by biological (nature) and environmental (nurture) factors

We also examine some methods of collecting data and research designs with children and adolescents and discuss some of the challenges of conducting research with children.

The "hawk game" is a favorite of the Canela Indian children of the Amazon rain forest. One child is designated as "the hawk." The others stand in line, from tallest to short-est, and each holds tightly to the next child in line. The hawk then screams "I'm hungry," and the first child in line bends down and looks back through parted legs and yells, "Do you want this?" Each child in turn yells back "No," except the last child who yells "yes," at which point the hawk begins to chase the child. The group, while still holding on to one another, tries to trap the hawk. The hawk takes captured children to his or her nest, and the game continues until all children are captured (Gosso et al., 2005).

This game, played by children from a traditional culture, may be similar to games many of you played as children. One of the authors recalls fondly summer evenings playing "wolves and pigs," in which one child was designated the wolf and ran after and caught the other children by tagging them. Once a child was caught, he or she also became a wolf, and the chase continued until all children were caught.

The point we wish to make here is that, despite some obvious differences, children around the globe are similar in many ways and have been for eons. There are clearly differences in how children growing up in different cultures think, what material resources they have available to them, what social norms they will be expected to follow, and what they will do when they grow up. Despite these often substantial differences, children share a common human nature, and this nature develops, nurtured and shaped by family, friends, and community.

We do not want to give the impression, however, that children's common biological inheritance means that the course of development simply follows some genetic plan. It does not. The path to adulthood is influenced by a host of factors—from the genetic through the cultural—and in order to understand

adults, one must understand development. Nothing arises fully formed, first blossoming in adolescence or young adulthood. Everything develops, and in order to understand adult behavior, one must understand the route traveled through childhood.

Concepts in Developmental Psychology

Why Study Development?

So one reason for studying development is to understand adults, including ourselves. There are others. Some are a bit more philosophical. To understand human nature or the underlying mechanisms that produce human behavior, one must study its development. Are people products of their environment? Are they merely a reflection of their genes? These are extreme philosophical positions, but the factors that make us the people we become have long interested scholars and laypeople alike, and these can only be assessed by examining development.

Knowledge of children and their development is not only of interest to philosophers and the theoretically minded among us, but also to real people in everyday situations. Parents are the first group that comes to mind. At one level, parents have been rearing children without the help of psychologists for untold generations. But the demands of modern society are substantial and variable and quite different from the demands faced by our ancestors. Parents who have an understanding of typical infant, child, and adolescent development can better deal with their offspring and hopefully guide them to successful futures. Teachers need knowledge of child development as well. What's the best way to teach children to read? When should instruction start? Do the same practices work best in all environments with all children? How does one deal with aggression on the schoolyard? What's normal rough-and-tumble play and what's bullying?

A wide range of professionals who deal with children even on an irregular basis can benefit greatly from knowledge of development. These include nurses, physicians, and others in the medical profession, as well as social workers, police officers, attorneys and people in the legal system. For instance, children get involved in the legal system as perpetrators of crimes. How responsible are children at different ages for their actions? To what extent can children of different ages understand the consequences of their behavior? What type of punishment or rehabilitation should be meted out for a crime? Children are also victims and witnesses of crimes. What's the best way to interview

Children across the world have much in common, such as playing chase games, much like the game of tag many American children play growing up.

© Finbarr O'Reilly/Reuters/Corbis

children? Are young children more or less believable, more or less suggestible than older children? What are the long-term effects of early trauma, such as physical or sexual abuse, on children? Children are also victims of poverty, divorce, accidents, and a host of other ills that befall people of all ages. Do children of different ages recover particularly well or particularly poorly from such experiences? Entire journals and many books are devoted to such topics. Experts in these areas consult with legislators and policy makers about issues related to children's well-being and write books and give numerous talks to community groups about their areas of expertise. In short, knowledge of children and their development is important for improving the lives of the youngest members of our society, and this will be one of the focuses of this book.

We are admittedly biased in our opinion, but we believe that understanding development is the key to acquiring an understanding of human behavior. This is true regardless of what topic one is studying, from how the brain works or the effects of culture on stereotypes, to the effects of poverty on mental health or ways of enhancing education. Development matters.

What Is Development?

Before getting too caught up with why we study development or how knowledge of development may be important for certain professions, we first need to define it. At its most basic, development refers to change over time. The focus of developmental psychology is changes in psychological characteristics occurring over a lifetime (as well as the physical changes associated with them). The emphasis in this book is on changes between conception and adolescence. The technical term for this type of development—changes in the *individual* over the course of his or her lifetime—is ontogeny. This is what most people mean when they use the word *development*, and it is how the term is used in this book (at least most of the time).

Development is rooted in biology, so its general course is known for all biologically normal members of the species in all but the most atypical of environments. Despite this predictability, there is also variability. Individual differences exist among children at any age, and these differences will affect how infants, children, and adolescents make sense of their environments and how others perceive and respond to them, making the outcome of development a function of many interacting factors.

Development not only occurs for us as individuals, but also for humans as a species. Human beings have a long history as a species. *Homo sapiens* developed from earlier ape-like animals, which evolved from earlier animals. This type of develop-

ment is called evolution, or **phylogeny,** and occurs over thousands and millions of years. Evolution and its relation to developmental psychology will be examined in Chapter 2.

What Do Developmental Psychologists Study?

The focus of most developmental psychological inquiry can be divided into three major areas:

1. *Physical and psychomotor development*, which includes examination of changes in sensory systems (vision, audition), the control over our bodies (for example, learning to crawl, walk, or throw), body proportions (such as changes evident during puberty), and development of the brain;
2. *Cognitive development*, which includes changes in all processes involved with thinking or knowing, such as perception, attention, consciousness, memory, intelligence, problem solving, and language;
3. *Socioemotional development*, which includes changes in processes related to our affective (emotional) world, such as self-esteem, love, temperament, personality, and morality, and our interactions with and relationships to other people.

In focusing on these changes, developmental psychologists typically divide the life span into distinct time periods: infancy (0–2 years old), early childhood (2–7 years old), middle childhood (7–12 years old), adolescence (12–18 years old), young adulthood (18–40 years old), middle adulthood (40–65 years old), and older adulthood (older than 65 years). People who study older adulthood often make even finer distinctions (B. Bjorklund & Bee, 2008).

Although researchers may focus on a particular aspect of development (for example, cognitive development), we must keep in mind that the whole child is developing, not just his or her memory, self-esteem, intelligence, or whatever a researcher is interested in. In fact, development of any characteristic must be viewed from the broader perspective of a child's surroundings. Development always occurs in a context, and for a social species like humans, that context is among other people and the culture that people construct. True human nature cannot be found by raising a child independent of

development Predictable changes that occur in structure or function over the life span.

developmental psychology The scientific discipline that examines changes in psychological characteristics occurring over a lifetime (as well as the physical changes associated with them).

ontogeny Development of the individual over his or her lifetime.

phylogeny Evolution of the species.

culture and the influence of other people; human nature develops in human environments. This theme is emphasized throughout this book.

The task of developmental psychologists of describing and explaining psychological changes over time is not always an easy one. For example, some sorts of changes are easier to identify and observe than others. Physical changes in the body or increases in the number of words in a child's vocabulary are more readily recognized than are changes in memory, intelligence, or personality. The former examples can be directly observed by anyone who knows what he or she is looking for, whereas the latter examples leave no easily identifiable mark but must be inferred from numerous assessments of a child's behavior.

Moreover, just because one charts change in some important psychological characteristic over time does not mean that one has explained anything. Chronological age is not by itself what causes development. As the behaviorist B. F. Skinner wisely pointed out in 1971, "changes are not produced by the passing of time, but rather because of what happens while time is passing by" (p. 131). In the same way that people do not die because they are old, but rather because of a deterioration of their bodies associated with age, children's intelligence, language, social skills, or physical prowess do not improve because they get older, but because of what transpires during the passage of time. And what transpires during time are interactions between changes in the physical body (including the brain) and the environment (both physical and social) that surrounds it. This is sometimes expressed in terms of the interaction between nature (genes, biology) and nurture (experience, environment, learning, culture), which is further discussed later in this book.

The process of development is a call to order. From two elementary cells, the egg and sperm, a multicellular organism grows. Cells divide and differentiate, producing bone, muscle, gut, and brain. The process is not random or chaotic, but highly organized. After birth, development continues to be orderly. From a mass of sensations and experiences, from consumption of foods from mother's milk to sushi, mind and body develop in a relatively predictable fashion.

A Brief History of Childhood

Biologists and physical anthropologists have long recognized different stages in the life of an animal, and these biological life stages in humans are examined in Chapters 3 and 4. But biological stages of childhood are only partly related to the *sociological* meaning of childhood—how people in a society view children at different times in their development. Children in developed countries across the world today are accorded special status (if nothing else, they are the ones who attend school). Children were likely always recognized as distinct in some way and treated differently from adults, but these distinctions were not always as clear-cut as they are today.

For instance, archaeological evidence dating back thousands of years indicates that children were killed as religious sacrifices and sometimes buried in walls of buildings to "strengthen" the structures. In 1999 the mummified remains of a 15-year-old girl were found in the mountains of Argentina (see Photo). Anthropologists called her "La Doncella" (The Maiden), and she and two younger children were apparently sacrificed in an annual Inca corn-harvest ceremony about 500 years ago. The children had apparently been given alcohol to put them to sleep and then left to freeze to death. During Greek and Roman times, children were sold into slavery for domestic work or as prostitutes, and they were used as collateral for loans. *Infanticide,* the killing of an infant, was a common, and legal, practice in Europe if a child was sickly, deformed, one of twins, illegitimate, a girl, or otherwise unwanted. The Romans outlawed this practice in 374 A.D., but for the next thousand years or more, parents simply abandoned their unwanted infants to die outside the city gates (de Mause, 1974).

Child abandonment was outlawed in Europe in the 1600s, and foundling homes were established, where mothers could bring their unwanted

Development through childhood is orderly and (generally) predictable, not random and chaotic

© David Young-Wolff/PhotoEdit

infants and have them cared for by the Church. Women could leave their infants at these homes anonymously, believing that their babies would be well cared for. In the 1700s, one-quarter of the infants born in Paris became foundlings (Katz, 1986). Unfortunately, wet nurses (lactating women who would nurse babies for a fee) were rare, and in the days before baby formula, infants were fed mainly a diet of porridge, and death rates exceeded 60% (Hrdy, 1999).

The Invention of Childhood

Some historians have argued that the concept of childhood is a truly modern one (Ariès, 1962; de Mause, 1974). This position was made popular by Philippe Ariès (1962), who examined documents and portraits from Middle Ages Europe and concluded that the concept of childhood did not exist—that before 1600, children from the age of 7 or so were viewed as miniature adults. In medieval England, for example, children as young as 7 could be hanged for relatively minor offenses, such as stealing a pair of boots.

Ariès' extreme interpretation has been rejected by more contemporary historians (Orme, 2001). For example, children's special status was recognized in law, as well as by the Catholic Church, which dominated social life in medieval Europe. Children were not viewed as being as responsible for their actions as adolescents and adults were, and there were sanctions against harming or imprisoning children. Nonetheless, children during the Middle Ages were treated more like adults than they are today. Many worked alongside their parents doing farm work; others became apprentices. They shared in the social intercourse of adult life; they ate what adults ate, dressed like adults, and were privy to adult conversations and sexual activity. Although medieval Europe may not have literally viewed children as miniature adults, the life and lot of children was very different than what it would become.

As health conditions in Europe improved during the 1700s, the death rate for infants and young children declined; and as the probability of living increased for children, so did their quality of life. By 1800, conditions had improved so that an infant born in London had a better than 50% chance of living to celebrate his or her fifth birthday (Kessen, 1965).

The intellectual climate of the 18th and early 19th centuries also contributed to a more "enlightened" view of children. John Locke in England viewed a child's mind as a blank slate, or *tabula rasa*, and believed that children came to understand the world through experience. It was the parents' responsibility to see that children's minds were filled appropriately. (Locke's ideas are discussed

AP Photo/Natacha Pisarenko

Children were sometimes used as sacrifices. This nearly perfectly preserved mummy of a 15-year-old girl, called *La Doncella* ("The Maiden"), was found on a platform on top of a 22,000-foot mountain in the Andes. The child still had red pigment around her mouth and was adorned with fine bone and metal ornaments.

in greater detail later in this chapter.) The French Enlightenment philosopher Jean-Jacques Rousseau was perhaps the most ardent advocate of childhood, believing that children are important in their own right and are not merely a means to an end (that is, adulthood). It is somewhat ironic then, that Rousseau placed all of his five children in foundling homes so they would not interfere with his work.

Lewis W. Hine/Contributor/Getty Images

During the Industrial Revolution, and extending into the 20th century, many children in the United States and Europe worked full time in factories.

BOX 1.1 **socioculturally speaking**

Secrets of Adulthood and the Appearance and Disappearance of Childhood

Although parents see children as more competent in many respects, they typically restrict their freedom when it comes to exploring their world outside of the home.

One interesting speculation about the underlying cause of the appearance of childhood in the Renaissance, which has some implications for society's changing views of childhood today, is related to "secrets." Neil Postman (1982) argued that to have a concept of childhood requires that there must be some important aspects of society that children are not privileged to. This was not the case for the most part in the Middle Ages, as children witnessed or partook in most of their parents' activities. What changed this, claimed Postman, was the invention of moveable type in the 1440s by Johannes Gutenberg. Before Gutenberg, it was impossible to mass-produce the written word, and as a result, literacy was limited to the elite. With the invention of the printing press, first the Bible and later other books, newspapers, and pamphlets became commonplace. This gave a new importance to literacy and afforded greater status to those who could read. It also marked a distinction between literate adults and illiterate children.

The process of becoming an adult (that is, a literate member of society) was now viewed as one requiring years of study accomplished through formal schooling. This separated children from adults, and with the separation highlighted the uniqueness of children. In addition to not knowing how to read, other differences between children and adults became more apparent. They had different sensibilities and drives than adults. Aspects of adult language were deemed inappropriate for children, as were aspects of adult behavior (especially sexual). These were the secrets of adulthood, which were kept from children until they had the physical, emotional, and intellectual maturity to deal with them.

Postman and others (Bjorklund, 2007a; Elkind, 1998) have proposed that childhood in contemporary society has moved backward, viewing children as increasingly competent and making them privy to what were once secrets of adulthood. The principal cause of this, Postman argues, is the speed with which information is transmitted, mainly via television. With the advent of television, it became increasingly difficult to protect children from adult knowledge. For example, even parents wishing to keep knowledge of adult sexuality from children have a difficult time censoring television commercials for the latest undergarments from *Victoria's Secret* or explaining ads about drugs for erectile dysfunction. As a result, knowledge that was once the privilege of adults is accessible at ever-earlier ages.

Many changes have occurred in society over the past 50 years or so other than television that have also contributed to a change in childhood. These include an increasing divorce rate, women more frequently working outside of the home, and young children spending more time in daycare, preschool, and after-school programs. As a result of these and other factors, parents have developed new views of childhood. David Elkind (1998) suggested that Americans in particular have moved from the modern view of childhood to a *postmodern* one. We are less likely to view children as innocent and in need of protection and more likely to view them as *competent*. Many children are required to cope for themselves more so than children in past decades were. Latchkey kids, for instance, come home to an empty house and use the microwave to prepare snacks for themselves. Elkind (1998, p. 15) argues that this new view of childhood "developed because postmodern families need competent children. We need children who can adapt to out-of-home parenting, and who will not be unduly upset by the graphic violence and lurid sexuality so prominent on our television screens."

At the same time that parents expect children to be more independent around the house, they limit their freedoms outside of the home, fearful of neighborhood crime or child predators. A minor controversy erupted in 2008 when a New York columnist wrote that she let her 9-year-old son take the New York City subway alone (Crawford, 2008). How much independence is too much seems to depend on the context (preparing meals at home is okay, but riding the subway is not), as well as how dangerous one perceives the outside world to be for children.

The concept of childhood has continued to evolve as society changes. Children in the United States and many other countries lead busier lives than children did in past generations. More of their play is sedentary than physical; middle-class children are increasingly involved in adult-directed after-school activities, from team sports and gymnastics to music lessons and tutoring. The concept of childhood does not remain static, even in the most enlightened of societies.

Economics played a part in changing how adults viewed children, as children became more valuable as farm laborers or factory workers. The industrial revolution made use of children's unskilled labor, and many children in the 18th and 19th centuries spent their short lives working long hours in factories, mills, and mines (Somerville, 1982).

By the early decades of the 20th century in Europe and America, children's lots were increasingly improving. Child labor laws were passed in most states (although the first U.S. federal law regulating the minimum age of employment and hours of work per week for children was not passed until 1938). More children attended school for more years. By the middle of the 20th century, universal education in America and Europe had been realized, and with it the modern conception of childhood. Children were seen as being innocent and helpless, who needed to be protected and nurtured, ideally in a two-parent family with a stay-at-home mom.

In many countries around the world, children are recruited or kidnapped and forced to serve as soldiers.

Children in the 21st Century

Many who recount the historical development of adults' perception of children use it as an introduction to today's literature of developmental psychology as though all children are now living happily ever after. We must make it clear that the modern conception of childhood we are talking about is a Western invention, characterizing countries in the developed world today (although see Box 1.1 for a discussion of the proposal that childhood is disappearing today).

In poverty-stricken countries, children join their parents in the fields or beg on the streets to make a living; as many as 10 million young girls work as prostitutes to support themselves and their families (Willis & Levy, 2002). In Asia and Africa today, millions of children have been born into slavery or sold into servitude to pay their families' debts (King, 2004). In some South American cities, "street children" roam in gangs trying to stay alive. Where there is war, children are recruited (often abducted) to serve as soldiers. It is estimated that tens of thousands of children younger than age 18 bear arms around the world each year, and children were involved in conflicts in at least 21 countries between 2001 and 2004 (Coalition to Stop the Use of Child Soldiers, 2004). Even in affluent countries such as the United States, millions of children are "food insecure" and nearly as many are homeless (Nord, Andrews, & Carlson, 2004).

Despite the discrepancy in how children around the globe are treated, the view of childhood that evolved in the West over the past 500 years has been accepted by the United Nations, which in 1989 approved *The Convention on the Rights of the Child* (www.unicef.org/crc). It has since been ratified by all but two of the 192 members of the United Nations (the United States and Somalia being the exceptions). This international treaty

recognizes the human rights of children, defined as persons up to the age of 18 years. . . . [I]t establishes in international law that States Parties must ensure that all children—without discrimination in any form—benefit from special protection measures and assistance; have access to services such as education and health care; can develop their personalities, abilities and talents to the fullest potential; grow up in an environment of happiness, love and understanding; and are informed about and participate in, achieving their rights in an accessible and active manner.

Such treaties are difficult if not impossible to enforce, but they do acknowledge the specialness of childhood and the need to foster children's development to produce effective adults.

A Brief History of Developmental Psychology as a Science

Although interest in child development is not new, developmental psychology is a relative newcomer to the field of science. However, it is also one of the most user-friendly of the sciences. Although most of the general population is not very concerned with the latest findings in astrophysics or polymer chemistry, new trends in developmental psychology are met with wide interest and become popular topics not only in research laboratories and university classes, but also in magazines and on TV talk shows.

The Emergence of Developmental Psychology

Developmental psychology has gone through a series of changes in its brief history (see Cairns, 1998). The foundational period extends from the end of the 19th century to the early decades of the 20th century. This period is characterized by important contributions made by a small group of influential scientists from different fields (from philosophy to medicine), both in theoretical and methodological terms, for the establishment of a science of child psychology. Major figures during this foundational period include Alfred Binet (1857–1911), G. Stanley Hall (1844–1924), James

Mark Baldwin (1861–1934), Sigmund Freud (1856–1939), and John B. Watson (1878–1958). Some of the contributions of these pioneers are discussed in later chapters.

Following World War I, two major traditions in developmental psychology were established. The first is sometimes referred to as the "child psychology" tradition, and involves the systematic description of child development, often with little concern for theory. This was represented in the Unites States by the work of Arnold Gesell and Myrtle McGraw, who focused their careers on the detailed description of motor development and other aspects of behavior believed to be under strong maturational control. But description was not the only concern in this tradition. Developmental psychology was viewed as a discipline that could be applied to *help* children. This is reflected in the Child Study Movement, which had its origins in the ideas of G. Stanley Hall, who believed that the findings of developmental psychology should be applied to children in a very immediate, practical way. While the child psychology tradition exemplified American developmental psychology, a different tradition—more theoretically oriented and more focused on explaining or understanding child development—emerged in Europe. This was represented by Jean Piaget in Switzerland, Lev Vygotsky in the Soviet Union, Henri Wallon in France, and Heinz Werner in Germany.

Despite its growing influence, developmental psychology remained out of the mainstream of academic psychology in the first half of the 20th century. The study of children was viewed as not possessing the rigor that behavioral scientists could bring to the study of laboratory rats or college sophomores. In an effort to gain academic respectability, beginning in the middle of the 20th century, scientists studying child development began applying increasing rigor in their research, using laboratory techniques that afforded greater experimental control relative to naturalistic observations of children's behavior. This brought the study of children and their development into the academic mainstream and made developmental psychology a first-level discipline within university psychology programs (McCall, 1977). This greater rigor had its costs, however. The emphasis on experimental control sometimes meant that the behavior under study had little ecological (that is, real-world) validity. In the words of Urie Bronfenbrenner (1977, p. 513), developmental psychology had become the "science of behavior of children in strange situations with strange adults for the briefest possible period of time."

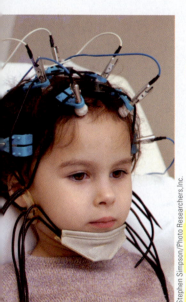

Research in developmental science often involves examining the neural correlates of behavior. Here we see a young child wearing a cap with sensors used to measure brain activity.

Stephen Simpson/Photo Researchers, Inc.

The Modern Era: Toward an Integrative Perspective

The last two decades or so (1990–2010) have seen a maturing of developmental psychology, we believe. This period is characterized by a greater focus on socioemotional development (in contrast to the greater focus on cognitive development that dominated the decades between 1960 and 1990), on the importance of context in development (versus a narrower way of looking at the environment), and on the contributions of biology to development, versus earlier perspectives, which saw biological knowledge as essentially unimportant for the understanding of development) (Hernández Blasi, 1998, 2000).

Developmental psychologists continue to be interested in applied issues, from the effects of poverty on children's developing social and intellectual abilities, and the social and biological underpinnings of developmental disorders such as autism, to factors that influence child abuse and neglect. Developmental psychology is also becoming less insulated from other scientific disciplines. This is particularly true with respect to biology, with developmental psychologists developing expertise in and/or collaborating with researchers in fields such as genetics, ecology, evolutionary biology, and especially neuroscience. In fact, many contemporary developmental psychologists identify their field as *developmental science*, reflecting the multidisciplinary approach that is typical of the modern era. Although we review important research from all periods of developmental psychology, most of the findings reported in this book are from the last two decades, the modern era of developmental psychology.

Although the biologizing of development has led to many advances in our understanding of children and how they change over time, knowing the genes a person possesses or which areas of the brain "light up" when children perform some cognitive task will not in itself provide an understanding of that person's behavior. Nor does having a theory of the brain make it unnecessary to have a theory of the mind. In all cases, body, behavior, and mind develop, requiring that psychologists understand the complex interactions between biological and environmental processes responsible for the emergence of behavior over time. To do this requires a perspective that integrates biological and environmental factors into a coherent framework. In this book we reflect this modern multidisciplinary perspective of development by attempting to integrate three overarching approaches in the study of child and adolescent development: *developmental contextualism*, a *sociocultural perspective*, and *evolutionary theory*.

Most central to modern developmental psychology and to this book is *developmental contextual-*

Child Study Movement Social movement begun in the United States around 1900 that proposed the systematic application of science principles to the study of children.

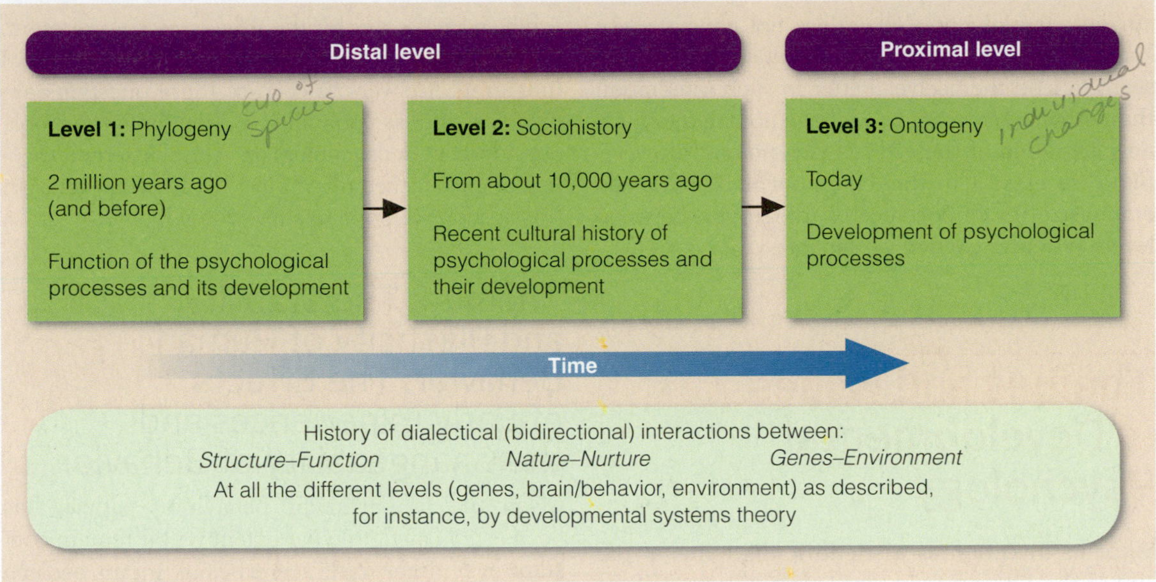

FIGURE 1.1 The different levels of analysis of developmental phenomena.

ism. Developmental contextualism emphasizes that development occurs as a result of the continuous interaction between a child and all levels of his or her environment. Children's thoughts and behaviors are affected by their genes and by other biological factors, but these thoughts and behaviors in turn influence how their nervous system develops. Likewise, children's actions influence others in their environment, and how others react to children in turn affects children's subsequent actions. From this perspective, development should be viewed as the continuous and *bidirectional* (two-way) relationship between an active organism and a changing environment. From this viewpoint, one cannot ask how much of any trait (for example, intelligence or personality) is a result of genetics and how much is a result of the environment. Rather, one must ask *how* biologic and environmental factors interact over time to produce developmental outcomes.

The second approach, a *sociocultural perspective*, recognizes the centrality of the social environment for human development. We are a social species, and human development can only be properly understood when the influences of social relations and the broader sociocultural environment are considered. Development always occurs within a social context, culturally shaped and historically conditioned, although the specific details of a child's social environment can vary widely.

The third approach we take in this book, *evolutionary theory*, helps us better understand *why* children and adolescents behave as they do. We believe that a better understanding of the "whys" of development will help us to better understand the "hows" and the "whats" of development, as well as help us apply knowledge of child and adolescent development to everyday problems. Theodosius Dobzhansky famously said, "nothing in biology makes sense except in the light of evolution." We make the same argument for psychology, particularly for the understanding of infants, children, adolescents, and their development.

These three approaches also represent three levels of analysis (see Figure 1.1). Developmental contextual models examine the development of psychological processes over an individual's lifetime, beginning before birth; sociocultural models also look at the immediate causes of behavior, but in addition take into account the impact of humans' 10,000-year cultural history on development; and evolutionary theory takes a truly long view of human history, examining the role that natural selection has had on shaping human development, particularly since the emergence of humans as a species, about 2 million years ago. Each of these approaches will be examined in greater detail in Chapter 2, although, because of its centrality to the current book, we will look at a specific developmental contextual model (developmental systems theory) later in this chapter in the context of the nature versus nurture debate in developmental psychology.

We do not see developmental contextualism, a sociocultural approach, and evolutionary theory as alternative and competing theories of development, but rather viewpoints that reflect three different but compatible levels of analyses, each of which is necessary to obtain a full understanding of development. This book attempts to show whenever possible how these three levels of analysis can be integrated. It is worth noting, however, that the current state of knowledge does not always make such an integration easy, and that some topics seem to lend themselves better to such integration than others. Accordingly, we have not tried to force an integration of these three viewpoints for *everything* we present in this book, but nonetheless do emphasize the importance of integration between levels of analysis wherever tenable.

Themes and Issues in Developmental Psychology

Since its inception as a scientific discipline at the end of the 19th century, developmental psychology has made great progress describing and explaining a wide range of psychological processes in children and adolescents, ranging from changes in neural structures during prenatal development to physical aggression in the schoolyard. For all developmentalists, however, a set of underlying questions is never far from the surface, which our research, directly or indirectly, strives to answer. Most of these questions are concerned with describing and understanding the principal characteristics of development:

- What are the effects of early experience on behavior? Is behavior basically stable over time, or is there a great deal of *plasticity*; that is, once established, can a behavioral pattern be easily changed later on?
- Which aspects of development are universal and which vary among individuals and/or cultures?
- Do developmental changes emerge gradually and continuously over time or do they materialize abruptly, or discontinuously, in stages?

In addition to these questions, developmentalists must deal with one overarching question: What is the nature of development? That is, what *causes* people, or animals, to develop, and how do we explain developmental outcomes, either for specific individuals or for members of the species in general? Although there are many different ways to explain development, most explanations boil down eventually to examining the interacting roles of biology and experience. This is usually expressed as the *nature/nurture issue*. Is development primarily the product of genetics and other internal, or *endogenous*, causes (nature), or is it produced basically by the effects of environment, or *exogenous*, causes, external to the individual (nurture)? Answers to each of these questions are complex, and, as you will see throughout this book, developmental psychologists from different theoretical approaches often vary in their opinions. In this section we hope to show you why.

Theme 1: The Stability and Plasticity of Human Behavior: The Effects of Early Experiences and the Changeability of Behavior

Given that a particular behavioral pattern has been established, to what extent will it remain constant over time? Will a precocious infant become a bright 3-year-old and later a talented adult? Will an abused child recover from his maltreatment to become a well-adjusted and productive member of society? Will a "difficult" infant become a difficult child and a difficult adult, or are such difficult periods merely transitory stages children grow out of? Once patterns have been established, what does it take to change them? In short, is human behavior characterized by stability or plasticity?

Stability refers to the degree to which children maintain their same rank order in comparison to other children with respect to some characteristic. The behavior in question itself may change—for example, a highly intelligent 10-year-old knows more and thinks differently than a highly intelligent 3-year-old—but, if a characteristic is stable, a child's rank in relation to his or her peers stays essentially the same over time. *Plasticity*, in contrast, refers to the ability to change as a result of experience.

For the better part of the 20th century, individual differences in intelligence and emotionality were believed to be relatively stable over time and not likely to be strongly modified by later environments. Many scientists believed that experience early in life played a critical and nonreversible role in establishing certain aspects of social and intellectual behavior. Jerome Kagan (1976) referred to this view as the *tape recorder model* of development. Every experience was seen as being taped for posterity, without the opportunity to rewrite or erase something once it had been recorded. Evidence for this view came from studies of children reared in nonstimulating institutions (Skeels & Dye, 1939; Spitz, 1945). Infants receiving little in the way of social or physical stimulation showed signs of mental, social, and motor retardation as early as 3 or 4 months of age. These deleterious effects became intensified the longer children remained institutionalized and were maintained

---

stability In developmental psychology, the degree to which a person maintains over time the same rank order in comparison with peers for a particular characteristic.

plasticity The extent to which behavior or brain functioning can be changed.

BOX 1.2 child development in the real world

Does Adversity in Early Childhood Leave Irreversible Effects in Adulthood?

This is the interesting question that H. Rudolph Schaffer (2000) addressed in a paper on the widespread (but not well-documented) assumption that early childhood experiences determine personality formation. Does early deprivation, maltreatment, or sexual abuse leave irreversible effects? According to available research on these and other similar issues, Schaffer, like many other child and adolescent developmental psychologists (Kagan, 1984, 1998), thinks that it is not possible to give a simple yes-or-no answer. Rather, the answer must be "it depends." It depends on (1) the various dimensions of the adverse experience, such as the child's age at the beginning and end of the negative experience; (2) the total duration of the experience; (3) the severity of adversity; and (4) the specific components that define the experience. But it also depends on many other important variables, such as the child's individuality, the child's subjective interpretation of the experiences, the social context in which the child lived before and after the adverse experience, the life opportunities provided to the child subsequently (and those finally chosen), and the specific psychological outcomes one is talking about.

Regarding child individuality, for example, it has been well documented that some children are more resilient and able to bounce back from adverse experiences than are others (Masten & Coatsworth, 1998). For instance, in a longitudinal study examining the psychological outcomes of children reared in seriously disadvantaged environments, most children displayed multiple behavior problems when they were adolescents, including psychological maladjustments and delinquency (Fergusson, Horwood & Lynskey, 1994). However, the

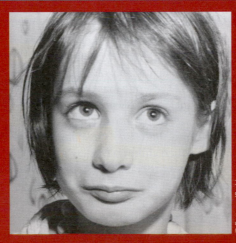

Genie had limited cognitive and motor skills when she was rescued at age 13.

© Bettmann/Corbis

researchers reported that 13% of the teenagers in this sample were completely problem-free. This phenomenon is known in the research literature as "resiliency." Why do some children from the worst environments make it while others flounder? Perhaps the single most important factor is competent parenting, starting early in life (Bugental et al., 2006; Kim-Cohen et al., 2004). However, Ann Masten and J. Douglas Coatsworth (1998) point out that it does not take extraordinary efforts to raise a competent child, even in disadvantaged environments. "Through the process of evolution, parenting has been shaped to protect development; nature has created in ordinary parents a powerful protective system for child development" (p. 213).

In a similar vein, Schaffer believes that certain adverse experiences could have substantially different effects depending on which behavioral systems are affected (MacDonald, 1985). For example, sensorimotor intelligence and perceptual-motor skills

seem to be less vulnerable than language to the effects of adverse experiences, developing pretty much according to schedule under a wide range of rearing conditions, including some of the most adverse. Even some aspects of language development, such as comprehension, seem to be less vulnerable than others, such as expressive speech (Scarr, 1976; Skuse, 1993). Also, recovery of physical functions seems to occur more quickly than recovery of psychological functions. For example, Genie, a severely deprived child who was confined to her room and chained to a chair by her schizophrenic father until the age of 13, made rapid gains in height and weight once she was rescued, but she remained intellectually impaired in all aspects of social adjustments and language development (Curtiss, 1977). Something similar has been reported by Michael Rutter and his colleagues (1998) for a group of extremely deprived Romanian orphans who were removed from stifling institutions and placed in adoptive homes.

Schaffer speculates that one possible reason that some functions are more robust than others might have to do with how old, evolutionarily speaking, they are. The more ancient the behavioral systems, the more critical they may be for survival (or were for the survival of our ancestors), and these systems are less affected by adverse early living conditions. An alternative hypothesis is that the difference in rate of recovery is related to the degree of social context required to function properly (Skuse, 1993). For example, perceptual-motor skills rely less on interpersonal exchanges than does language development for their proper development and expression. We might hypothesize that perhaps both positions have some truth to them.

long after children left the orphanages (Dennis, 1973; Goldfarb, 1947). Research in the 1960s and 1970s, using both children and animals as subjects, showed that the harmful effects of early experience were not always permanent—that, under some conditions, drastic reversals in behavior could be realized (Kagan, 1998; Skeels, 1966; Suomi & Harlow, 1972; see Chapters 10 and 12 and Box 1.2).

It is apparent today that development is more plastic, or changeable, than we once thought. We realize that although early experience is impor-

tant in influencing development, later experience plays a role as well. Moreover, we are also aware that some behaviors are more easily modified than others. One of the chores of the developmentalist is to determine which aspects of development can be modified through experience and which are likely to remain constant despite changes in the environment. As should be apparent by now, there is not a single answer to all developmental questions, and the important issue of the stability and plasticity of development is a complicated one.

Theme 2: Continuity vs. Discontinuity: The "Stages Debate," or Understanding How Development Progresses

When speaking of children, we often refer to stages. The "Terrible Twos" is reserved for 2-year-olds, and we may speak of a stubborn 4-year-old who insists on wearing his snorkel, diving mask, and fins everywhere he goes (including tricycle rides around the neighborhood) as being "in a stage." In everyday language, we use the term "stage" to refer to a period of time in which children display a certain type of behavior. Stages are transitory, with children eventually growing out of them, possibly into another.

Developmental psychologists think of stages in a similar way. For a developmental psychologist, children are said to be in a stage when their behavior is *qualitatively different* from the behavior of children in earlier or later stages. The best examples of qualitative changes in development come from species that *metamorphose*, or go through radical changes in appearance over time. For example, butterflies start life as fertilized eggs that hatch into caterpillars. These worm-like creatures usually eat leaves, and after some time spin a cocoon, or chrysalis. Weeks or months later, they emerge as butterflies. One could not know just by looking at a caterpillar and a butterfly that they were the same animal. They look radically different, have different diets, different predators, different physiology, and different ways of getting around (the caterpillar crawls, whereas the butterfly flies). The caterpillar and butterfly represent qualitatively different stages in the life of a single animal.

In comparison to the butterfly, mammal development is quite boring. Mammals experience a radical change in some aspects of their behavior and biology at birth (for example, from living in a liquid to an air environment, from getting food through the placenta versus through the mouth), but, after birth, physical development, although not always smooth (there are growth spurts in development, particularly at puberty), is qualitatively similar over time. Of course, some of the processes underlying physical or psychological development may be stage-like, such as the changes in hormone production associated with puberty.

Qualitative changes may be seen in other aspects of human development, particularly cognition. This is best depicted in Jean Piaget's theory of cognitive development, in which children during infancy are said to understand the world by their physical actions on objects (see Chapter 6), which develop through a series of six substages. For instance, according to Piaget, children much younger than 6 months old believe that an object, such as their bottle, no longer exists when it is out of their sight. When they are sitting in front of an object and a cloth covers it, they do not try to retrieve it but act as if it no longer exists. Out of sight is out of mind. They lack what Piaget called *object permanence.* By 8 months or so, infants understand that the covered object continues to exist in time and space even if it is out of their immediate perception. Now when the cloth covers the object, babies will remove the cloth to get the object. (It is not until about 18 months that Piaget believed that infants have a fully developed concept of objects.) For Piaget, this transition in understanding the nature of physical objects represents a qualitative change in knowledge and occurs abruptly, or discontinuously.

Piaget similarly saw changes from infancy to early childhood as being qualitative in nature. Unlike the preverbal infant, 2- or 3-year-olds can understand the world in terms of symbols, such as language. However, these young children still lack the mental tools of logic, making their understanding of the world different from that of an older child or adult. The point in stage theories is that behavior or thought at any one stage is of a different type than the behavior or thought at another stage. The 4-year-old is not just a smaller-sized version of the 12-year-old, but rather is a qualitatively different person who understands the world in a different way than the older child. Stage theorists hold that changes from one stage to another are discrete, reflecting **discontinuity of development**. This means that the change from one style of behaving or thinking to another is relatively abrupt. Figure 1.2 (panel a) illustrates the step-like nature of developmental change postulated by stage theorists.

A contrasting belief is that developmental changes are mainly *quantitative* in nature. That is, as children get older, the types of things they do do not differ greatly, but they are able to do things more skillfully. For example, with cognitive development, it is possible that as children age they are able to hold more things in memory, know the meaning of more words, and process information faster (Bjorklund, 2005). These are quantitative, or countable, changes. Developmental changes of quantitative abilities are said to exhibit **continuity of development**, with development occurring gradually. Figure 1.2 (panel b) illustrates the smooth nature of developmental change postulated by non-stage theorists.

There has been much debate concerning the nature of developmental change (see Kagan, 2008,

discontinuity versus continuity of development The scientific debate over whether developmental change is gradual (continuous) or relatively abrupt (discontinuous).

and commentaries). One reason why whether development is stage-like or not is important is because it is related to the underlying mechanisms and causes of development. Developmental psychologists are not only interested in describing how children change with age, but they are concerned with the processes that underlie such changes. And whether these changes are discontinuous and qualitative (stage-like) or continuous and quantitative (nonstage-like) is at the center of many controversies about the nature of development.

Theme 3: Normative vs. Idiographic Approaches: Developmental Function and Individual Differences

We have defined development as being characteristic of the species—of human beings, in general. This does not mean, however, that developmental psychology is concerned only with things that do not vary from individual to individual. If that were the case, this would be a very short book. No two children are alike in terms of physical abilities, rate of growth, intelligence, personality, temperament, social responsiveness, or any other dimension you can think of. Nonetheless, most children of a particular age share certain things in common, and the factors that promote change and the consequences of such change are also highly similar among children.

Developmental psychologists sometimes refer to research that focuses on commonalities of children at a given age as the **normative** (or **nomographic**) **approach**. They are studying **developmental function**, the typical, or normative, form or pattern that occurs over time. These changes may be in physical characteristics, such as body size and proportion, motor abilities, or the organization of neurons in the brain; in social characteristics, such as children's relationships with significant others, from infant-mother attachment, to friendships, to romantic partners; or in cognitive characteristics, such as children's understanding of numbers and arithmetic concepts, logical reasoning, and the number of items one can keep in mind at a time. People who do normative research are usually interested in universals—what is true about the course and causes of development for all members of the species. This does not mean that people who study normative development are unaware of individual differences. Development is a process of change, and although the basic direction of change and the features of body, behavior, and mind may be highly similar among children at any given age, no one can deny the substantial variability among people at all ages, beginning in

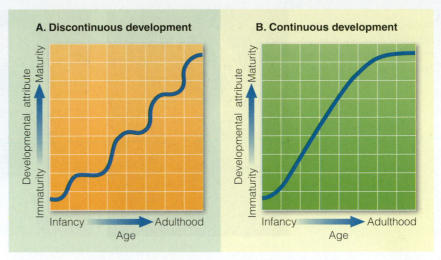

FIGURE 1.2 Stage (discontinuity) versus nonstage (continuity) approaches to development.

Stage, or discontinuity, theorists propose that development proceeds in a step-like fashion (a), with qualitative changes from one stage to the next occurring abruptly. Nonstage, or continuity, theorists propose that development proceeds in a continuous fashion (b), with quantitative changes occurring gradually over time. SOURCE: From Bjorklund, D. F. (2005). *Children's thinking: Cognitive development and individual differences*, 4th ed., Fig. 1.2, p. 12. Copyright © 2005 Wadsworth, a part of Cengage Learning, Inc. Reproduced by permission. www.cengage.com/permissions.

infancy and actually before. But the description of normative development—what the typical pattern of development is for children in all cultures in all but the most atypical of environments—is the focus.

This is contrasted with researchers whose principal concern is with *individual differences*—factors that make children distinct from one another. Developmental psychologists sometimes refer to this type of research as the **idiographic approach**. Variation among people is as universal as is the general course of development, and describing these differences, explaining their origins, and sometimes discovering ways to alter the course of atypical development has long been a focus of developmental psychologists. Developmental psychologists must identify these individual differences, while still acknowledging the commonalities among people at a particular time in life and the factors that influence change over time.

Individual differences can result from many interacting factors. For example, we know that, other than identical twins, no two people have the

normative approach Approach in psychology concerned with features that all people have in common.

developmental function The form that development takes over time.

idiographic approach Approach to psychology that is concerned with individual differences among people, as opposed to concern with features that all people have in common.

There are many causes for individual differences in patterns of development, with culture being a major one.

same set of genes, making genetic differences a major source of variation. Experiences, beginning in the womb, also vary among people and interact with genetic differences to produce individual differences in all aspects of development. Most psychologists who adopt an idiographic approach do not deny that there are some universals that typify human development; they just are not as interested in them as they are in the individual differences among children.

Culture is often viewed as a major source of individual differences in children's behavior. The values and intellectual tools (such as books, abacuses, or computers, for instance) of a culture greatly influence how a child develops (Vygotsky, 1978). Other factors must be responsible for individual differences among children *within* a culture, but one should not assume that just because all (or most) children in one's own culture behave or think in a certain way, that this is true for *all* children across the globe. We believe that there are many universals in development, but how these universal aspects of behaving, thinking, and socializing develop depends in large part on the culture in which a child grows up.

There is also substantial variability in functioning *within* any particular child. A given 8-year-old will often show a wide range of behaviors on very similar tasks, depending on the context that he or she is in. For instance, a child who is struggling with multiplication and long division in school may be able to compute baseball batting averages and pitchers' earned-run averages with

relative ease. Increasingly, developmental psychologists have come to realize the significance of individual differences and variability in psychological performance among and within people of a given age and to see these variations as providing interesting and important information about developmental outcomes (Coyle, 2001).

Most developmental psychologists take either a normative or idiographic approach in their research, but one approach should not be thought of as being the antithesis of the other. One needs to be aware both of universal psychological changes over time and what varies among individual children and when, and recognize that the normative and idiographic approaches, both alone and in combination, can contribute important information about children and their development.

Theme 4: Nature vs. Nurture: About the Role of Genetics and Environment in Human Development

Perhaps the central issue of all psychology, including developmental psychology, has been that of nature/nurture. To what extent is development a function of nature (that is, biology, genetics) or nurture (that is, learning, experience, culture)? At one extreme we have the philosophical position of empiricism. This position assumes a nearly infinite ability to change mind and behavior, or *plasticity*. At the other extreme is the philosophical camp of nativism, which holds that important aspects of behavior are programmed into the brain and inherited from generation to generation.

John Locke is the philosophical grandfather of empiricism. He proposed that children are born as blank slates, or *tabula rasa*, and experience serves as the chalk that writes on and fills the board. The human nervous system has certain limitations (for

nature/nurture Debate concerning the degree to which biology ("nature") and experience ("nurture") influence the development of any psychological characteristic and its development.

empiricism Philosophical perspective that nature provides only species-general learning mechanisms, with cognition arising as a result of experience.

nativism Philosophical perspective that human intellectual abilities are innate.

example, we cannot hear sounds in the same range that dogs can), but, outside of these extremes, children are born with no dispositions to make some types of learning easier than others, for example, or preferences that may influence how they learn and develop. From this perspective, there is no human nature other than a propensity to adapt one's behavior to the demands of the environment (Moore, 2001). Locke's basic empiricist position held sway in the behavioral sciences until quite recently. Evolutionary psychologists John Tooby and Leda Cosmides (1992) proposed that the behavioral and social sciences were dominated by the *Standard Social Science Model* throughout most of the 20th century, holding that the culture one grows up in (or the experiences one has within the family) determine all important psychological features of a person.

Nativists, in contrast, believe that animals, including humans, have many complex instincts that are activated when the proper environment is encountered. Perhaps most evident today is the idea that one's genes *determine* one's behavior, a position known as **genetic determinism**. A week rarely goes by without a newspaper story of scientists announcing the discovery of a gene for some disease, such as diabetes, some physical characteristic, such as obesity, some mental disorder, such as schizophrenia, or some aspect of so-called normal behavior, such as shyness. The public often gets the idea that this gene determines a particular physical, behavioral, or mental outcome. In actuality, the story is more complicated. A closer look at the news report, or the scientists' published article, usually indicates that the gene is merely associated with some characteristic, and it is assumed that other genes, plus people's experiences, interact with this newfound slice of DNA to produce behavior.

One rarely encounters either of these extreme positions today; nearly everyone is an *interactionist*, believing that both nature and nurture interact to produce development. There is really no other alternative. However, there remains considerable debate about *how* biological factors interact with environmental ones to produce patterns of behavior. The approach we favor, that of *developmental contextualism*, is discussed in Chapter 2, and we provide some examples of gene–environment interaction in Chapter 3. But let us first provide a few examples of how biological and environmental factors, as traditionally thought of, interact to produce patterns of development.

Development Systems Theory and Epigenetic Development

With respect to the central issue of gene–environment interaction and development, advocates of the **developmental systems theory** (Gottlieb, 2000,

2007; Oyama, 2000) hold that development occurs via a process known as **epigenesis**. From this perspective, development is not simply produced by genes, nor constructed by the environment, but emerges from the continuous, bidirectional interaction between all levels of biological and environmental factors.

This all may seem quite complicated, but it has its roots in some very basic ideas about where babies come from. Historically, epigenesis was contrasted with **preformationism**, the idea that structures in development appear fully formed. For instance, with the invention of the microscope, 16th-century scientists identified male sperm and female eggs and correctly postulated that the joining of these two cells started a new life. But how? One preformationist camp (oovists) held that every egg contained a fully formed infant, and the sperm was needed to provide the "spark of life." The other camp (spermists) held that the fully formed little person was in the head of the sperm, with the egg providing the environment necessary for growth to commence. Epigenesis, in contrast, holds quite correctly that development is not preformed but emerges over the course of development (see Gottlieb, 1992, for the history of this controversy). Until relatively recently, however, the processes involved in the emergence of new structure and function over the course of life remained something of a mystery.

For modern epigenesists, all **structure** (parts of the body) and **function** (behavior) emerge as a result of the bidirectional (that is, two-way) interaction of genes and environment, such that the actions of genes both influence and are influenced by structural maturation. That is, the changing nature of the body is bidirectionally related to function and activity—what a particular part of the body does. Gilbert Gottlieb (1991) described this relationship as follows:

genetic activity (DNA $\leftrightarrow$ RNA $\leftrightarrow$ proteins) $\leftrightarrow$ structural maturation $\leftrightarrow$ function, activity.

Although genetic factors certainly influence a child's (or adult's) behavior (in fact, gene expression

---

genetic determinism The idea that one's genes determine one's behavior.

developmental systems theory The perspective that development is not simply "produced" by genes, nor constructed by the environment, but emerges from the continuous, bidirectional interaction between all levels of biological and environmental factors.

epigenesis The emergence of new structures and functions during the course of development.

preformationism The idea that development is just the expression of previously fully formed structures.

structure In developmental psychology, a substrate of the organism that develops, such as muscle, nervous tissue, or mental knowledge.

function In developmental psychology, action related to a structure, such as movement of a muscle, nerve firing, or the activation of a mental representation.

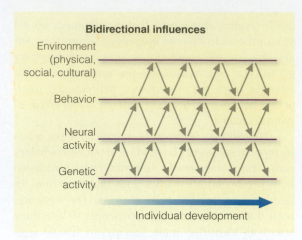

Bidirectional influences

Environment (physical, social, cultural)

Behavior

Neural activity

Genetic activity

Individual development

FIGURE 1.3 A simplified schematic of the developmental systems approach.

The figure shows a hierarchy of four mutually interacting components. Activity at one level influences activity at adjacent levels. For instance, genetic activity (DNA → RNA → proteins) may affect the generation or activity of neurons, which in turns influences how a person behaves. That behavior then has some outcome on the environment. The response of environment (for example, how people respond to a child's action), in turn, influences behavior, which affects brain activity, which itself alters genetic activity (turns on or off a particular gene, for example). SOURCE: Gottlieb, G. (1991). Experiential canalization of behavioral development: Results. *Developmental Psychology, 27,* 35–39. Copyright © 1991 by the American Psychological Association. Reprinted by permission.

is involved in *all* aspects of human functioning), their effects are always mediated by the environment. From this perspective, there are no pure biological or environmental effects; all development is the product of epigenesis, with complex interactions occurring among multiple levels. This bidirectional approach to development is expressed in Figure 1.3. This somewhat complicated figure reflects the complex nature of development and suggests that we can never understand development merely by looking for genetic effects or for environmental effects alone. To understand development, we must look at the relationship between the organism and its environment, broadly defined. Developmental neuroscientist Mark Johnson (1998, p. 4) makes this point especially clear: "Since it has become evident that genes interact with their environment at all levels, including the molecular, there is no aspect of development that can be said to be strictly 'genetic,' that is, exclusively a product of information contained in the genes."

From this perspective, nothing is preformed, including behavioral "instincts" that arise shortly after birth when an animal is presented with the proper stimuli. But aren't animal instincts well

documented? Take the classic example of *imprinting* in early-developing birds such as geese and ducks. Hours after hatching, ducklings will follow the first moving thing they encounter (usually their mother) and stick with her for the remainder of their infancy. In fact, these young birds are especially sensitive to the sound their mothers make. If a duckling is placed in a circular container hours after hatching and the maternal call of its species is played from one speaker and the call of another species is played from an opposite speaker, the duckling will reliably approach the call of its own species (Gottlieb, 1997). This looks like an instinct—a complex behavior displayed early in life that requires no prior experience.

But is this claim of "no experience necessary" true? Is this complex and adaptive behavior preformed and expressed instinctively at the right time in development, as was suggested by the ethologist Konrad Lorenz? Gottlieb (1991, 1997) recognized that ducklings in these situations are not without experience. What kinds of experience might ducklings have before hatching that could influence auditory imprinting? Ducklings can hear before hatching, and in the wild the mother duck vocalizes while sitting on the eggs, particularly during the last few days before hatching. The ducklings also peep, so ducklings hear their mothers' vocalizations, the peeping of other chicks in the clutch, and their own peeps.

In a series of experiments, Gottlieb prevented the pre-hatchlings from hearing the maternal call by placing the eggs in an incubator. After hatching, the ducklings were tested, and they still approached the maternal call of their own species, which they had never heard. He then placed a single egg in an incubator so that the embryo did not hear its mother or its clutch mates. Still, when tested, the ducklings approached the maternal call. He then developed a procedure in which he opened the egg, made an incision at the neck of the duckling, and put some glue on the vocal cords of the bird that prevented it from producing any sound. (This wears off several days after hatching.) The duckling was then tucked back into its shell, placed alone in an incubator, and hatched several days later. We now have an animal with no auditory experience other than the whirring of the incubator. What happens now when tested? These inexperienced ducklings were just as likely to approach the call of a chicken as they were the maternal call of their own species. What was once thought to be an instinct and the pure product of genetic inheritance actually requires experience and is an example of epigenetic development. The tendency to approach the maternal call, which is an important adaptive behavior displayed by nearly all members of the species, is not preformed but emerges from the interaction of biological (clearly involving the expression of genes) and experiential factors.

Although experience is necessary for auditory imprinting to occur, it is a type of experience that almost all members of the species will get (unless one is unfortunate enough to be hatched in Gottlieb's laboratory). This is why so much animal (and human) behavior appears "instinctive," or "innate"; organisms, be they ducks, chimpanzees, or humans, inherit not only a species-typical genome but also a species-typical environment. For mammals, this includes a prenatal environment and all the experiences associated with it, a lactating mother, and, for social species, members of one's own species to interact with over the course of development. Gene expression and experiences are typically highly coordinated, so the proper environmental event (auditory stimulation or the movement of a developing limb) occurs at a time when genes are ready for them. Genes, in turn, are activated (or deactivated) by these experiences, and development proceeds normally.

Although ducklings will follow their mother shortly after hatching, a seeming example of an "instinct," research by Gilbert Gottlieb showed that prenatal auditory experience was necessary for them to display this behavior.

© First-Light/Alamy

What Does It Mean to Say Something Is Innate?

As you might have gathered from the discussion of epigenesis, many developmental psychologists avoid the word "innate." When they do use it, they often put it in quotes as we do here. Why such an aversion? The primary reason is that this term implies *genetic determinism*, which is the antithesis of a truly developmental (that is, bidirectional) perspective. A more lenient definition of "innate" may be "based in genetics." However, this is meaningless, for every action of every living being is based in genetics. Some people equate the concept "innateness" with "instinct." The problem here is that instinct is not easily defined. This is made clear by Patrick Bateson (2002, p. 2212), who wrote

> Apart from its colloquial uses, the term instinct has at least nine scientific meanings: present at birth (or at a particular stage of development), not learned, developed before it can be used, unchanged once developed, shared by all members of the species (or at least of the same sex and age), organized into a distinct behavioral systems (such as foraging), served by a distinct neural module, adapted during evolution, and differences among individuals that are due to their possession of different genes. One does not necessarily imply another even though people often assume, without evidence, that it does.

Many developmental psychologists are just as uncomfortable with the term "instinct" as they are with "innate" and for the same reason: its association with genetic determinism; and, as Bateson's quote illustrates, it is not always clear which definition of instinct one is talking about.

The term "innate" however, is not without its usefulness. Usually, when developmental psychologists use the term "innate," they mean that there are some genetically based *constraints* on behavior or development. Constraints place restrictions or limitations on learning. The brain can only process (identify, classify, learn about, remember) certain types of information in certain ways, or can process some forms of information more readily than others. Such constraints, rather than making learning more difficult, actually make learning ecologically relevant and species-typical content easier (Gelman & Williams, 1998).

The world that children (or the young of any species) are born into is amazingly complex. How are infants to know what is important to attend to and what is irrelevant? Some types of learning (for example, language, social relations leading to attachment, the ability to identify and remember faces) are critical for survival. Constraints imply that some stimuli, such as faces or language sounds, are easily or at least specially processed. The same brain/learning mechanisms cannot be used to learn other things. Specific parts of the brain are constrained, or limited, to processing a narrow range of information. This means that an infant or child will easily make sense of faces or language sounds, for example, but may not be as flexible at learning other things, such as arbitrary lists of words, propositional logic, or algebra.

For example, the architecture of a particular area of the brain might be best suited for processing a certain type of information (for instance, face processing), but the architecture will change as a function of the information it receives. Structures in the brain are not preformed to know human faces, for example, but are biased toward processing information about faces and developing the skill of identifying and remembering faces as a result of interactions with the world. For

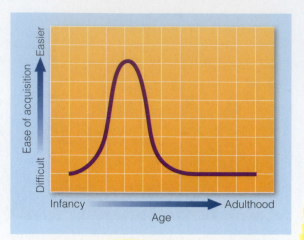

FIGURE 1.4 Some abilities, such as language, are more easily acquired during a sensitive time in development.

SOURCE: From Bjorklund, D. F. (2005). *Children's thinking: Cognitive development and individual differences*, 4th ed., Fig. 2.4, p. 37. Copyright © 2005 Wadsworth, a part of Cengage Learning, Inc. Reproduced by permission. www.cengage.com/permissions.

instance, human adults and 9-month-old infants process upright human faces more effectively than upside-down human faces, as reflected by how quickly they can make decisions about faces and the activation of different neural pathways. They treat upright faces as special stimuli, recognizing and remembering them better than upside-down faces, which are processed much as other visual stimuli are.

But this special status is limited to faces from their own species; adults and 9-month-olds show no such behavioral or neural differences when processing upright and upside-down monkey faces. In contrast, 6-month-old infants process upright faces differently than upside-down faces for both humans and monkeys. This suggests that the brain of young infants is biased to process faces, an important stimulus in the world of a young animal highly dependent on care from others; however, at 6 months they do not give special privilege to human faces, suggesting that brain processing of human faces becomes more specialized with age and experience (Johnson & de Haan, 2001; Pascalis, de Haan, & Nelson, 2002). Olivier Pascalis and his colleagues (2002, p. 1321) proposed "that the ability to perceive faces narrows with development, due in large measure to the cortical specialization that occurs with experience viewing faces. In this view, the sensitivity of the face recognition system to differences in identity among the faces of one's own species will increase with age and with experience in processing those faces." (The development of face processing will be discussed

in greater detail in Chapter 5.) Such findings are consistent with the position that human infants are born with biases to process some information more effectively than others, but that such biases become modified with experience (Johnson, 2000; Nelson, 2001).

Similarly, the brain may be prepared or ready to process some type of information at certain times in development, and the same experience at earlier or later times may have minimal consequences. This is related to a concept central to developmental psychology, that of **sensitive periods** (Thomas & Johnson, 2008). A sensitive period is the time in development when a skill is most easily attained and a person is especially receptive to specific environmental influences.

The time boundaries for a sensitive period are wider than for a *critical period,* which postulates a relatively narrow window of opportunity for a particular experience to affect the organism. Critical periods are more likely to be found in early prenatal development, when specific body parts (for example, arms and legs) are generated at specific points during the embryonic period and can be adversely affected by exposure to teratogens, external agents that can alter the course of development (see discussion of the effects of teratogens on prenatal development in Chapter 3).

The timing of a sensitive period will depend on the specific ability that is developing. For example, exposure to patterned light during the first several months of infancy is important for the development of vision (Maurer, Mondloch, & Lewis, 2007; see Chapter 4). In contrast, the sensitive period for the easy acquisition of a first or second language extends from early childhood to the onset of adolescence (Lenneberg, 1967; Newport, 1991). For example, both a first and second language are more easily acquired before puberty. Adolescents and adults are capable of learning a second language, although it is usually only with great difficulty and typically with a heavy accent. More will be said about a sensitive period for language acquisition in Chapter 9. Figure 1.4 presents the idea that an ability, such as language, can be more easily acquired when the relevant experiences (here, exposure to spoken language) are had during a sensitive time in development.

Experience does not start at birth, however, and many sensitive periods for a late-developing ability such as language may extend back to prenatal development. This is most readily seen in the development of bodily structures such as arms and legs, or hands and feet. For instance, in the 1960s, the drug Thalidomide was prescribed to women to combat pregnancy sickness. Unfortunately, when taken early in pregnancy, the drug interfered with the formation of limbs, resulting in babies with

sensitive period The time in development (usually early in life) when a certain skill or ability can be most easily acquired.

arms emanating directly from their shoulders or feet from their hips. If the drug was taken after the arms and legs had already formed—after the sensitive period for the formation of the limbs—there were no ill effects. (Thalidomide was not approved for use in the United States, so most cases of Thalidomide babies were from Canada, Japan, and some European countries, which did not have as tight government regulations over drug companies.)

Modern science recognizes that there are multiple causes of development and that one cannot partition nature and nurture into neat little boxes and attribute so much influence to one, so much influence to the other, and the rest to their interaction. In fact, some people argue that it is impossible to state where nature ends and nurture begins, making any distinction between the two arbitrary and inappropriate (Oyama, 2000). This may be so at a deep theoretical level, but most psychologists—and we would bet nearly all laypeople—make a distinction between factors internal to the organisms (genes, hormones, neurotransmitters) and factors external to the organisms (social and physical experience). However, rather than asking "How much of a particular developmental outcome (intelligence or personality, for instance) is a result of nature and how much is a result of nurture?", a better question is: "How do factors endogenous (internal) and exogenous (external) to the organism interact to produce patterns of development?" Developmental psychologists do not necessarily agree on how best to answer this question, but it is a central one to the field, and it is discussed frequently in this book.

Research Methods in Child and Adolescent Development

As part of a requirement for a seminar, two first-year graduate students in developmental psychology designed a simple study of social interactions between mothers and their toddlers. They watched through a one-way mirror as mothers and their young children interacted in a toy-filled room. They developed a coding scheme that included 42 separate categories of mother-toddler interaction, which they recorded every 30 seconds over a 15-minute interval. By the end of the semester, they had 18 mother-toddler pairs and loads of data. Being novices at scientific research, they approached the resident methodologist/statistician for advice on how to analyze their data.

"What you have here," the statistician said, "is what we call a Polynesian Island Study. It's like you

measured everything you could possibly think of about the handful of natives on a small Polynesian island. You have more measures than participants, you don't have a central question, and you don't have a way of organizing your measures to make any statement about your results. Your original idea may have been very interesting, but the way you've collected the data, I can't help you make any sense out of what you've got."

Being a scientist means doing research, and doing research means formulating hypotheses and developing techniques to test them. This is where methodology comes in. What most people are really interested in are the results or interpretations of a study, but coherent results and interpretations can be achieved only when the study was designed properly. How we design our studies determines how (or whether) we can analyze the results and what sense we can make of them. A study may produce provocative findings, but depending on how the study was conducted, the results may be of limited application.

In this section, we explore the scientific study of child and adolescent development. We first discuss what it means to be a science, giving examples from the field of child and adolescent development. We next explore several methods of collecting developmental data and then look at the basic research designs of developmental psychology. We conclude with a discussion of some of the problems of doing research with children.

The Science of Developmental Psychology

What is science? How does a scientific explanation differ from a nonscientific one? The science of developmental psychology describes development and behavior; it also explains the causes of development and patterns of behavior. One purpose of science is to get a better understanding of nature, or to discover regularities in the natural world. What makes this scientific is the descriptions are based on objective and reliable observations, and the explanations are based on a possible chain of physical or psychological (that is, "natural") causes.

Describing Behavior

To be described scientifically, a behavior must be *objective*; that is, it must be clearly observable, irrespective of the observer's emotion, prior expectation, or personal belief. This is sometimes more easily said than done. Much of what is of interest to psychologists cannot be observed and measured directly. How strong is the attachment of an infant to its mother? How is information stored in memory? Can infants recognize familiar faces? How distressed are adolescents when they get into disagreements with their parents or their friends? It is one thing to measure how many inches a baby crawls in a 3-minute period; it is quite another to measure something like "quality of attachment."

What psychologists who are interested in these phenomena do is find some evidence from children's observable behavior that will provide them with clues to the underlying concepts they are interested in. Thus, for example, psychologists interested in infant-mother attachment may look at how many seconds it takes for an infant to be soothed by its mother following a brief separation; psychologists interested in memory development may examine how many items children remember from a list of familiar words compared to how many items they remember from a list of unfamiliar words; psychologists interested in infants' recognition of faces may record the number of seconds babies spend looking at a picture of a face they have seen frequently versus one they have never seen before; and researchers interested in adolescents' distress as a result of conflict may develop a rating scale and have participants evaluate the degree of stress they felt for specific events during the past week. In each case, some overt and measurable action of a child is used as an indication of some covert construct. The measure may or may not be the most appropriate, but it is objective and expressed in terms of quantifiable (countable) data, such as the number of seconds a baby looks at a picture or the score an adolescent gets on a personality test. Such objective and quantifiable measures permit others to examine the same behavior. Other scientists can then discuss whether the particular measure chosen is the best one for studying the behavior of interest.

Making a behavior objective is only the first step in scientific description; its measurement must also be valid. **Validity** refers to the extent to which a measurement accurately assesses what it purports to measure. Validity comes in various forms, the two most basic being internal validity and external validity.

Internal Validity. *Internal validity* concerns the extent to which the design of one's experiment permits one to make cause-effect statements about the variables under study. For instance, a researcher interested in the effects of exercise on school performance may assign one group of third-grade children to an "exercise condition," in which children spend half an hour on the playground between 10:00 and 10:30 every morning, and another to a

"no-exercise condition," in which children remain in their classroom reading stories. After several weeks, children's performance on a standardized math test is given, and the researcher finds that children in the exercise group perform better than children in the no-exercise group. Is the researcher able to state that it was daily exercise that is responsible for children's enhanced performance? Probably not, at least as the study was described. Maybe it was not the exercise, but just the time-out from schoolwork. What would have happened if a group of children stayed indoors and participated in sedentary play activities? Might they, too, have improved their math performance? Did children in the exercise group really exercise? Maybe some sat under a tree on most days and talked, or played videogames, or sat on benches and read books. Was there any measurement of children's math performance *before* the experiment started? Perhaps, just by chance, children in the exercise group had higher math scores to begin with than children in the no-exercise group. The bottom line is that researchers must be careful in designing their studies to insure that their experimental measurements assess what they purport to measure.

External Validity. *External validity* refers to the extent to which the findings of a particular study can be generalized to other people and contexts. For example, can the findings of a study about the relationship between instruction in the phonics method of reading and reading comprehension be generalized to children who speak different languages? Can they be generalized to Chinese children who learn to read ideograms? What about to children who speak languages that have different degrees of correspondence between spoken sounds and written letters? The relationship between spoken and written English is very irregular, for example, with a single letter having multiple pronunciations depending on what word it is in (take for instance, the letter "c" in cat, ice, children, science); will findings on phonics instruction performed with English-speaking children generalize to children speaking a language like Spanish, where the letter-sound correspondence is more regular?

This brings up the issue of the relevance of one's findings to children and adolescents around the globe. Are your findings restricted to a small sample of middle-class children in one developed nation? Although you can only test the children you have access to, researchers need to be mindful of the extent to which their findings are generalizable to other groups of children. This is where cross-cultural studies come in handy. Children from different cultures can be tested on the same or similar tasks, and assessments can be made

validity The extent to which a measurement accurately assesses what it purports to measure.

about the extent to which one's culture affects patterns of behavior or development. Most developmental psychologists live in developed countries, but research in less-developed countries, or those done with traditional groups, usually studied by anthropologists, can be of great importance in getting the big picture of development.

There are other forms of validity that researchers must be concerned with, some of which are described briefly in Table 1.1.

Reliability. One's observations not only must be valid, but they also must be reliable. Reliability also comes in several types, two of which concern us here. The first is *interobserver reliability*: the same behavior seen by one observer is also seen by a second observer. This requires that the behavior in question be carefully defined ahead of time. For example, if two observers are sent to a school playground to observe aggression in children, they must first know what constitutes aggression. Clearly, a right cross to the nose is an aggressive act, but what about the friendly shove, the headlock during a playground wrestling match, or the verbal taunt that starts a scuffle? Even when definitions are agreed upon, will different people record the behaviors similarly? To ensure interobserver reliability, most investigations require at least two independent observers to record the target behavior. If they generally agree with one another—say, 90% of the time—the data are considered reliable and worthy of further analysis. If not, it's back to the drawing board.

The second type of reliability is *replicability*. If we observe some behavior in our laboratory, will another scientist be able to replicate it—observe the same thing under the same conditions in his or her laboratory? Or, even more basic, if we observe some behavior in our lab this week, will we find the same thing if we repeat our observations three weeks from now? The goal of science is to obtain some broad truths that will hold regardless of who is doing the observing and when. Phenomena that can be found only in one person's laboratory, or only once, are curiosities, not scientific data. They may have resulted from unrecognized quirks in the lab procedures, a special sample of children selected as participants, or simply chance. Good scientists and good scientific procedures sometimes produce unreplicable findings. However, when research is reported in the scientific literature, the methods used to obtain the findings are included, and the replicability of the research can then be assessed. Thus, even after a scientific project has been completed and the results published, judgments of scientific merit must wait, for only if a finding is replicable can it be judged an important step in science.

table 1.1 Various Forms of Validity Important to Developmental Psychologists

Internal validity	The extent to which the design of one's experiment permits one to make cause-effect statements about the variables under study.
External validity	The extent to which the findings of a particular study can be generalized to other people and contexts.
Face validity	The extent to which a test or measurement "looks like" what it is supposed to measure. For example, does a test of infant-mother attachment "look like" (on the face of it) it reflects such attachment?
Content validity	The extent to which a measure represents all facets of a given concept. For example, does a test of impulsivity measure both cognitive and behavioral impulsivity, or only one?
Construct validity	The extent to which a measure relates to a theorized psychological construct (such as "intelligence" or "personality").

Scientific Explanations

Science does more than describe behavior; it also attempts to explain it. After an experiment has been designed, performed, and the data analyzed, the results need to be explained in natural cause-and-effect terms. Thus, concluding that a child behaves in a certain way because of experiences in a previous life does *not* qualify as a scientific explanation. Even if the child's behavior is described in objective, valid terms, is reliably recorded and replicable, this explanation of the behavior goes beyond the natural world and is not within the realm of science.

Does this mean that we can only explain behavior in terms of what we already know scientifically—that we cannot discover new patterns of cause and effect that go beyond our current understanding? Not at all. It does mean that we should be pragmatic, sticking close to simple and conventional explanations whenever we can. To suggest a complex, extraordinary explanation of some behavior requires that all simple and conventional explanations be considered first and judged inadequate. Moreover, the simpler the explanation is, the better it tends to be. This is called **parsimony**. Basically, when two explanations are equally able to account for a phenomenon, the simplest explanation is preferred.

reliability The trustworthiness of a research finding; includes interobserver reliability and replicability.

parsimony Preference for the simplest scientific explanation for a phenomenon.

Some methods of collecting data in developmental psychology with their strengths and weaknesses

	Definition	Strengths	Weaknesses
Structured interviews	Children are interviewed under conditions in which the researcher can control extraneous factors that may influence a child's behavior.	The researcher can control many factors in the interview session that may influence children's performance.	Structured interviews may have poor "ecological validity," and their results may not be generalized to real-world contexts.
Clinical interviews	Clinical interviews are conversations in which the examiner probes a child's knowledge about certain topics.	When performed by a skilled interviewer, such as Jean Piaget, researchers can gain much insight into development and generate hypotheses for later experimental testing.	It is difficult to generalize findings, and bias in the interview process is likely.
Questionnaires and standardized tests	Children are asked to answer a series of questions about themselves or perhaps other children. Questionnaires are a form of self-report.	Children can reveal information about themselves.	Self-reports may be biased, and children's memory may be incomplete or incorrect.
Observational studies	Children's behaviors are observed and recorded in either structured or naturalistic settings.	More naturalistic behavior can be observed, and, in structured settings, children's behavior can be compared in the same context.	Some behaviors may never be emitted, and the researcher has less control over the situation, especially in naturalistic observations.
Case studies and diaries	A case study is a detailed description of an individual made by an expert observer. A diary study is a particular type of case study.	Case studies are very useful for collecting information that would be difficult to get at otherwise.	Case studies are not representative of the general population, have questionable reliability, and no experimental control.

Methods of Collecting Developmental Data

Developmental psychologists use different methods for collecting data depending on whom they study and what they want to measure. For example, developmental psychologists typically study infants, children, and adolescents directly. Sometimes careful observation is involved. Other times, children are tested for specific behaviors under controlled conditions. (How many randomly presented numbers can 6-, 8-, and 10-year-olds remember in exact order?) Depending on the research question, psychologists may want to interview parents, peers, or teachers about children, or perhaps even measure the behavior of adults as they interact with children. Sometimes developmental psychologists measure physical or physiological responses, such as heart rate; other times they get self-reports from children or answers to questionnaires. Some of the methods of collecting data in developmental psychology, along with their respective strengths and weaknesses, are summarized in the accompanying Concept Review 1.1.

Interviews

Interviews refer to one-on-one interactions with children and researchers. In **structured interviews**, children are asked a set of standardized questions, so that all children receive the same questions. For example, in one study, 5- to 11-year-old English children were questioned individually about their

structured interviews Interviews in which participants are asked a set of standardized questions under conditions in which the researcher can control extraneous factors that may influence a child's behavior.

identification with the England soccer team (this was several weeks before the June 2002 World Cup Finals) (Abrams, Rutland, & Cameron, 2003). On a scale from 1 (*not at all*) to 5 (*very much*), they were asked: "How much do you like the England soccer team?" "Do you like to watch England games on TV?" and "Do you cheer for England in soccer?" They were then asked about how they felt about supporting the England soccer team and the German soccer team. Children were then read a story about two boys. In one version of the story, the boys were described as fans of the England team and in the other as fans of the German team. The children were then asked some questions about the two boys in the story.

The researchers reported that nearly all children showed in-group bias (they favored the England over the German team), and they rated the boys in the story differently depending on whether they were England or German fans. When the story character showed deviant behavior (for example, saying something nice about the opposing team), it was regarded more critically if it came from an in-group member (a supporter of the England team) than if it came from an out-group member (a supporter of the German team). This is the so-called *black-sheep effect*, when a deviant member of an out-group (here the German fan) is rated more highly than a deviant member of an in-group (here the England fan; see Chapter 14 for a discussion of in-group favoritism and out-group discrimination).

In other interviews, children are seen one-on-one by an experimenter who gives them one or several tasks to perform, and their responses are carefully recorded and compared to children who may have slightly different experiences. For example, Andrea Follmer Greenhoot and Patricia Semb (2008) read stories to preschoolers either with or without illustrations. For some children, the illustrations were relevant to the story, and for others the illustrations were irrelevant to the story. Other children saw the pictures only without being read the story. How would having the illustrations affect children's recollection of the story, both immediately and one week later? Having the relevant pictures helped children remember the central aspects of the story, especially for the older preschoolers. Many studies in cognitive development use interviews of this kind, where different children are given slightly different experiences on some cognitive task.

In contrast to structured interviews, **clinical interviews** are conversations in which the examiner probes a child's knowledge about certain topics. Unlike naturalistic studies, the clinical interview requires an intense relationship between examiner and child. Jean Piaget used this technique extensively in his studies of children's cognitions, questioning his own children and others.

Here, for example, is an excerpt of an interview with a child concerning the common belief of young children that the moon follows them when they are walking (from Piaget, 1969, p. 218):

Interviewer: What does the moon do when you are out walking?

Child: It follows us.

Interviewer: Why?

Child: Its rays follow us.

Interviewer: Does it move?

Child: It moves, it follows us . . .

Interviewer: Has it ever happened to you that it couldn't follow you?

Child: Sometimes when one runs.

Interviewer: Why?

Child: One's going too fast.

Interviewer: Why does it follow us?

Child: To see where we are going . . .

Interviewer: When there are lots of people in town what does it do?

Child: It follows someone . . . Several people . . . With its rays. [The moon] stays still and its rays follow us.

Such interviews can provide insights into the thoughts of children, and although they are not used widely today, they continue to be useful for some research questions (see Ginsburg, 1997). However, there are problems associated with the clinical method. Unlike structured interviews, in which each child receives the same set of instructions, each child in a clinical interview will have a different experience, making it difficult to generalize the findings. Also, it would be relatively easy for an interviewer to bias a child's responses or to get off track. Piaget, acknowledging the difficulty of doing clinical interviews, stated that to become a skilled interviewer required daily practice for a year (Flavell, 1963).

Questionnaires and Standardized Tests

Many issues in developmental psychology can be addressed by giving children **questionnaires**. These are essentially self-reports, in which children respond to a series of questions designed to get at some specific aspect of children's behavior, thinking, or feelings (for instance, "Some kids are happy with themselves as a person": (a) True of me, (b) Sort of true of me, (c) Not true of me). For example, in a study by Pol van Lier and his colleagues (2005), Dutch and Canadian schoolchildren filled

clinical interviews Interviews, used extensively by Piaget, in which the examiner probes a child's knowledge about a given topic.

questionnaires A form of self-reports, in which participants respond to a series of questions designed to get at some specific aspect of people's behavior, thinking, or feelings.

out a series of questionnaires. Some were *peer nominations* of antisocial behavior. Children were given a set of descriptions such as *starts fights, angers easily, says mean things to peers,* and *is disruptive* and were asked to list all of their classmates who fit each description. Children also completed questionnaires that asked about their own externalizing behaviors (for example, fighting, theft, vandalism) over the past two months. Only boys followed what the researchers called a "high trajectory of increasing antisocial development." Boys who followed such an antisocial trajectory tended to have more deviant friends and were more likely to be rejected by their peers than other children. A few girls followed a "moderate antisocial behavior trajectory." Although these girls did not tend to have more deviant friends than most other groups of children, they were frequently rejected by their peers. Results from these questionnaires pointed to the influence that friends and poor social relations with peers plays in the development of antisocial behavior.

Standardized tests are special types of questionnaires that are administered following consistent, standardized instructions. Norms for these tests have typically been obtained by testing many children, producing reliable indications of a typical score. For example, the *Wechsler Intelligence Scale for Children* (*WISC*) is standardized on thousands of children at different ages and produces an IQ score. An average IQ is 100, making it easy to know where a child stands with respect to intelligence from a single score. (We will discuss how IQ tests are constructed as well as how to interpret them in Chapter 10.) Although standardized tests are used frequently to assess intellectual abilities or academic achievement (for example, the SAT [Scholastic Aptitude Test] or ACT [American College Test]), other standardized tests assess a wide range of psychologically relevant factors.

Some standardized instruments even evaluate the quality of children's environment. For instance, the *Home Observation for Measurement of the Environment* (*HOME*) scale (Caldwell & Bradley, 1978) evaluates the quality of the home environment for young children by examining six general aspects of the home: (1) emotional and verbal responsivity of the mother; (2) avoidance of restriction and punishment; (3) organization of the physical and temporal environment; (4) provision of appropriate play materials; (5) maternal involvement with the child; and (6) opportunities for variety in daily stimulation. Scores on this instrument can be used to compare the quality of households and to relate the home environment to aspects of children's psychological functioning.

Observations

In contrast to interviews, in observational studies researchers identify a type of behavior they are interested in and watch children in specific situations for the incidence of those behaviors. For example, what do toddlers do in a preschool classroom when they are on their own? Do they play alone, interact with other toddlers, and if they do, what exactly do they do? We mentioned previously when discussing reliability that researchers must carefully define what constitutes a target behavior. Is name-calling an example of aggressive behavior? What about a dirty look or a friendly shove when children are smiling? Will different observers see the same thing and code it in the same way? Will two observers classify the same dirty look as an aggressive action, or is one observer more apt to code such behavior as aggressive than the other?

Observational studies can be naturalistic or structured. In *naturalistic observations*, the researcher attempts to intervene as little as possible, observing what goes on in a natural environment. Naturalistic studies are the favorite tool of *ethologists*, who study the behavior of animals in their natural habitats. Such work is important in child development as well. For example, Roger Barker (1965) provided detailed descriptions of school-age children as they went about their daily routines, believing that we must begin with an understanding of how children interact in their natural environments before proceeding further. In a more recent example, Laura Berk (1986) observed first- and third-grade children during daily math periods and related their behavior during these times (particularly the incidence of talking to themselves) to their school performance. Berk reported interesting relationships among age, the nature of the problems, and children's performance on math tests that would have been difficult to assess in a laboratory situation (see Chapter 8).

Naturalistic observations can get at important behaviors that are difficult to assess in interviews or through questionnaires. For example, Anthony Pellegrini and Jeffrey Long (2003) observed "poke and push courtship" and peer-group integration in a group of middle-school children over a two-year period and related these behaviors to other aspects of children's social lives. Each participant was observed at least once per week over the course of the school year. Most observations took place in the hallways and the cafeteria. "Poke and push courtship" was defined as rough play with a member of the opposite sex and involves playfully hitting, pushing, grabbing, and teasing. These behaviors can be viewed as friendly overtures to a member of the opposite sex. If they are greeted positively, a new romance (or flirtation, anyway) may begin; if they are rejected, the initiator can save face because the bout can be viewed as playful and not serious.

Pellegrini and Long argued that middle school is a time when children's social lives and interests are beginning to change, and this should be captured not simply from their answers to questionnaires but also in their everyday behaviors. The researchers reported that peer-group integration—the proportion of boys and girls interacting in the same group together—varied with dating behavior, and that "poke and push courtship" did not seem to influence either peer-group integration or dating in this group of young adolescents. Perhaps different patterns would be found if older children were observed, but the significant point here is that children's real behaviors, and not just what they say about themselves or other people say about them, are being assessed, reflecting important aspects of their social development.

At other times, *structured observations* are used in which researchers set up situations, often in a laboratory or a school classroom, where they control certain aspects of the situation and look for specific behaviors. The description of two graduate students studying mother-toddler inter-

"Push and poke courtship" during middle school can best be evaluated by observing real behavior in naturalist settings.

action that opened the methodology section is an example of a structured observation conducted in a laboratory (albeit one that did not produce worthwhile results). A context was established (a small, toy-filled room in which mother and toddler were the only people present); a time limit was set (15 minutes); different aspects of social interaction were identified and measured following specific guidelines (code behavior every 30 seconds); and the graduate students were careful not to let their presence influence the behavior of mothers and children (they observed behind a one-way mirror). Perhaps an even better method would have been for the researchers to videotape the 15-minute interaction and then separately code for *all* behavior (not just what happened every 30 seconds) from the tapes.

Many observational studies are structured, with experimenters setting up a context, such as this toy-filled room, and seeing what children (and their mothers) do. Many structured observational studies today involve the use of video, so that the interaction can be coded at a later time.

BOX 1.3 food for thought

Case Studies of Growing Up in Extreme Conditions: Wild and Feral Children

There have long been stories of children being raised by wolves or other animals. Mowgli, the protagonist in Rudyard Kipling's *The Jungle Book*, was raised by wolves, as were Romulus and Remus, the supposed founders of Rome. These tales are works of fiction, but throughout history there have been stories of children raised in the wild by wolves, monkeys, and other animals, some of which have been well documented. (For a listing of cases, go to www.feralchildren.com.)

Take, for example, Saturday Mthiyane, a South African boy who roamed with a troop of monkeys. Saturday Mthiyane was named after the day of the week when he was found and the school he attended. A local newspaper that followed up on the child 10 years after his discovery reported that at an estimated age of 15 he had learned to walk, but he still did not talk. He refused cooked food, preferring raw vegetables and fruits.

The cases of Amala and Kamala are particularly well documented. These girls were estimated to be about 3 and 5 years of age when they were found in a wolf's den, along with two wolf cubs, in India in 1920. The girls could not speak, refused to wear clothes, walked on their hands and feet, and would eat only raw meat. Amala died shortly after being discovered. Kamala learned to walk, was toilet trained, mastered a small vocabulary, and eventually was able to speak

in short, broken sentences. Kamala was examined by the prominent developmental psychologist Arnold Gesell, who concluded that, after nearly 10 years since leaving the wild, she had the mind of a 3 1/2-year-old. She died of typhoid in 1929.

One can never know whether these children were truly raised by animals or merely living in the company of animals, and one must interpret such tales with a healthy dose of skepticism. However, it seems clear that these children were in fact living in the wild, and their behavior upon being discovered and attempts to rehabilitate such children can provide insight into the flexibility of human nature. Moreover, it is only through case studies such as these that scientists can investigate the effects of extreme deprivation on children.

Most case studies do not document children living in such extreme conditions. We present these examples here to show how case studies can be used to address questions that experimental science cannot. What questions do these case studies address? The plasticity of human development, for one thing. These cases indicate that human nature develops within human culture. Children who somehow survive living with animals (or perhaps on their own) during their early years do not show behaviors typical of human children. Humans did not evolve for lives with wolves or monkeys or in isolation,

© Mary Evans Picture Library/The Image Works

Although Kamala eventually learned to walk and developed a small vocabulary, she continued to display many animal-like behaviors.

but with our own kind. The fact that children can survive under such bizarre conditions is a testament to human resiliency. The fact that they do not subsequently resort to human ways reflects the limits of human plasticity.

Case Studies

A **case study** is a detailed description of an individual made by an expert observer. It may involve interviews, structured and naturalistic observations, as well as rely on information from other informants (parents, for instance). Usually, the details of the history or reactions of a particular person are recorded by a clinical psychologist and serve as the raw data for building a theory. Sigmund Freud's entire theory of psychosexual development was based on case studies of his patients—most of them adults recalling childhood experiences.

Some data can be collected ethically only by the case-study method. For example, several case

studies document the behavior and development of children raised in highly unusual early environments (Curtiss, 1977; Koluchova, 1976). Perhaps the most famous is that of a boy thought to be raised in the wild, first published in 1806 by Jean-Marc Itard (1962). Itard recorded the behavior and development of Victor, the *Wild Boy of Aveyron*, providing interesting and important data about the child's adjustment to human society after an early life of deprivation. When Victor was discovered at about 12 years of age, he could not speak, and he had numerous scars, suggesting that he had been living in the woods for some time. After five years of attempting to "civilize" the boy, Victor was able to speak and read a few words, he displayed affection for his caretakers, and he could carry out simple tasks.

case study Detailed description of a single individual made by an expert observer.

There are, of course, great limitations of case studies such as this. Was Victor's retardation caused by living in the wild, or was he retarded or autistic before he was abandoned and took up life in the woods? One can never know. Further, the number of children involved is so small, and their experiences so different from one another, that no group study could be done. Nonetheless, case studies of children living in extreme or unusual situations can be informative for the unique opportunities they afford for examining development in conditions that could never be duplicated ethically in a laboratory. Box 1.3 summarizes a few other case studies of children living in extreme conditions.

Another particular form of case study is the diary. Much can be learned from careful, up-close observation, and a great deal of the influential work of the Swiss psychologist Jean Piaget (1952) was based on the careful observation and recording of the development of his three children over their first two years of life.

Diaries can also be kept by parents or by children at the request of researchers for specific behaviors. For example, Donald Roberts, Ulla Foehr, and Victoria Rideout (2005) asked 694 7th- to 12th-grade children to keep diaries of their media use (for example, watching television, playing video games, listening to MP3 players). Combined with data from a total sample of more than 2,000 children who completed a single questionnaire, the researchers reported that American teenagers spend, on average, more than 8 hours a day involved with media. The rates are so high because about 2 of these 8 hours children are multitasking, using two types of media simultaneously. In contrast, adolescents spend on average about 2 hours a day hanging out with their friends (and about as much time with their parents), and about 1 hour each, give or take, talking on the phone, involved in physical activity, and doing homework. We will discuss the role of media on development in Chapter 13.

Case studies and diaries are very useful for collecting information that would be difficult to get at otherwise, but there are limits to what one can learn from this approach. How do we know that what we observe for one or two children holds true for children in general? Also, how reliable are the observations, or people's own recollections? The investigator has only one person's interpretation of the events—sometimes that of a proud parent or the participant him- or herself. Would another observer see the same thing? Despite these problems, the case-study method has produced important data for developmental psychologists, and these findings can serve as the basis for more systematic studies of child development and behavior.

Interviewing and Observing Parents and Teachers

Although our interest is in gaining knowledge about infants, children, and adolescents, we can sometimes do this by interviewing or observing important people in children's lives, usually their parents and sometimes their teachers. As we will see in Chapter 12, how mothers respond to their infants' signals of physical and social need is related to the quality of infant-mother *attachment*. To assess this, researchers must observe how mothers interact with their infants, possibly in structured settings such as feeding time (Britton, Britton, & Gronwaldt, 2006) or simply over the course of an afternoon in their home (Schaffer & Emerson, 1964).

Alternately, parents can fill out questionnaires about certain aspects of their children's behavior. For instance, Jamie Ostrov and Christa Bishop (2008) gave questionnaires to the parents and teachers of preschoolers that dealt with the adults' relationship to their children. Parent-child conflict was evaluated using a five-point scale ranging from 1 (*not at all true*) to 5 (*always true*) ("I get mad at my child"; "My child gets made at me"; "My child annoys me"). Other questions asked parents to rate how aggressive they thought their children were toward them ("When my child gets mad at me, s/he hits and kicks me"). Parents were also given questionnaires about how frequently their children engage in aggressive

Many American teenagers uses several forms of media simultaneously, something that can be discovered by asking the teens to keep diaries of their media use, as well as through questionnaires.

Different research designs in developmental psychology with their strengths and weaknesses

	Definition	Strengths	Weaknesses
All research designs			
Correlational	Correlational studies examine relations between two or more factors (for example,, age, weight, vocabulary, socioeconomic status).	Can often identify relations between two variables quickly.	Correlations do not imply causality, so it is not possible to determine what causes what (for example, do aggressive children like to watch violent video or does watching violent video cause children to be aggressive?)
Experimental	Experimental studies involve the manipulation of one or more factors and observation of how these manipulations change the behavior under investigation.	If conducted properly, results from experimental studies can point to causality (for example, samples of children who watched violent video were subsequently more aggressive than children in a control group who watched nonviolent video).	Some factors cannot be ethically manipulated. For instance, one cannot assign one group of children to an intellectually "deprived" environment and another to an "enriched" environment and see the consequences on subsequent intelligence.
Developmental designs			
Cross-sectional	Cross-sectional studies assess different individuals at different ages.	Information about changes in average abilities over broad age ranges can be obtained quickly and economically.	Cross-sectional studies do not measure change within individuals, making any definitive statement about the mechanisms of development tentative.
Longitudinal	Longitudinal studies assess the same people over an extended period of time.	Longitudinal studies measure "true" developmental (change over time within single individuals).	Longitudinal studies can be costly to run, take a long time to get meaningful results, and can suffer from subject loss and cohort effects.
Cross-sequential	In cross-sequential studies, groups of children at different ages are tested, and each group of children is then followed longitudinally.	This approach combines the strengths of the longitudinal and cross-sectional studies: information about change over time can be obtained quickly, and true developmental change can be assessed.	Like longitudinal designs, it can take many years before all data are collected.
Microgenetic	Microgenetic studies involve assessing children repeatedly over relatively short intervals, usually days or weeks.	Details of change can be assessed for behaviors and cognitions that change over brief periods of time.	Microgenetic studies are not useful for assessing characteristics of development that change over longer periods of time.

("He hits or kicks other kids") and prosocial ("He says supportive things to other kids") behaviors outside of the home. Teacher-child conflict was also assessed using a questionnaire ("This child and I always seem to be struggling with each other"; "This child easily becomes angry with me"), and teachers completed a checklist that assessed levels of children's aggression in school. The researchers reported that parents and teachers generally agreed with one another on how aggressive children were (their ratings were significantly correlated), and that parent-child conflict was significantly related with teachers' ratings of children's aggression.

But what makes this study innovative is that the researchers also *observed* children's aggressive behavior during school and related it to the parent and teacher ratings. Each child was observed for eight separate 10-minute sessions over the course of 8 weeks. The researchers identified specific behaviors that would constitute both direct aggression (hitting, kicking, taking objects) and indirect aggression (malicious gossiping, spreading rumors, ignoring). Interobserver reliability was obtained. They reported that levels of observed indirect aggression were *not* significantly related with either the parents' or teachers' ratings. In contrast, levels of observed direct aggression were significantly correlated with teachers' ratings but not with parents' ratings of physical aggression. There were thus cases of both agreement and disagreement between the various raters when it came to children's aggression and what else it was related to, causing the authors to state, "The best practice may be to use multiple informants, multiple methods, and (when possible) observational methods" (p. 319).

Research Designs in Developmental Psychology

The term *research* in psychology typically refers to the empirical study of some topic, endeavors that involve the collection of data—whether observations of children in a natural setting, children's responses to problems in a laboratory task, high school students' scores on an achievement or IQ test, or the ratings given by teachers on some dimension of a child's personality. These data are then analyzed, often using statistics, to find out something about the nature of children's behavior or development. Besides collecting and analyzing data, scientists may also review and interpret earlier research and theory or construct a theory independent of new data. These endeavors are also in the realm of science, but they are not empirical research.

Many of the research methods used and the research problems encountered by child and adolescent psychologists are the same as those in other areas of psychology. However, because developmental psychologists study change over relatively long periods of time, some methods are unique to this field. And because the participants we study are infants and children, some research problems arise that are not usually encountered by psychologists who study college sophomores or laboratory rats. In this section we examine basic research designs. Some, such as correlational and experimental studies, are used by researchers in all fields. Others, such as longitudinal, cross-sectional, and cross-sequential approaches, are specific to studying developmental issues. The various research designs in developmental psychology, along with their respective strengths and weaknesses, are summarized in the accompanying Concept Review 1.2.

Correlational Studies

In **correlational studies**, the relation between two or more factors of interest is assessed. After the data have been collected, a statistical test, called a correlation (represented by *r*), is performed, and the magnitude of the correlation is measured to determine if the relationship is greater than would be expected by chance. Correlations can range from –1.0 to +1.0, with zero reflecting a lack of any systematic relationship between two factors. A zero correlation, for example, would be expected between shoe size and IQ: the size of one's foot should not be related to one's general intellectual ability. A positive correlation would be expected between height and weight (in fact, it's about .65): the taller a person is, the heavier one is apt to be. A negative correlation would be expected between a student's grade-point average and the number of errors made on a midterm exam: better students (as reflected by GPA) are likely to make fewer errors on tests than less-proficient students.

The idea of correlation can be represented visually by *scatter plots*, as shown in Figure 1.5. In Figure 1.5a, the relationship between a score on an exam (factor Y) and the number of hours people studied for that exam (factor X) is presented as a perfect *positive* relationship (*r* = +1.0). In this example, each point on the graph corresponds to a certain number of hours studied and a certain score on the exam. As can be seen, people who studied very little received the lowest grades, people who studied a lot received the highest grades, and people who studied some intermediate amount received intermediate grades. Figure 1.5b shows a perfect *negative* correlation (*r* = –1.0) between the number of hours of sleep an infant gets and a score of irritability. The less sleep infants get, the

---

correlational studies Type of study that examines two or more factors to determine if changes in one are associated with changes in another.

FIGURE 1.5 Examples of scatter plots of different degrees of relationship between two factors, X and Y.
Perfect relationships are shown in a. (r = +1.0) and b. (r = −1.0). More realistic relationships are shown in c. (r = .65) and d. (r = −.80). Figure e. shows no relationship between the two factors (r = 0.0).

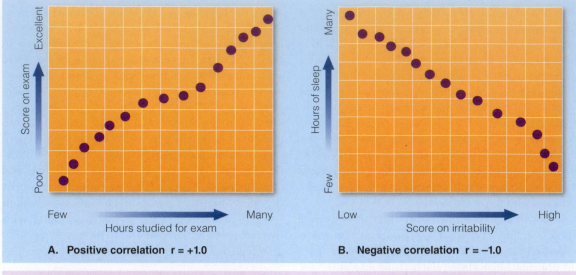

A. Positive correlation r = +1.0

B. Negative correlation r = −1.0

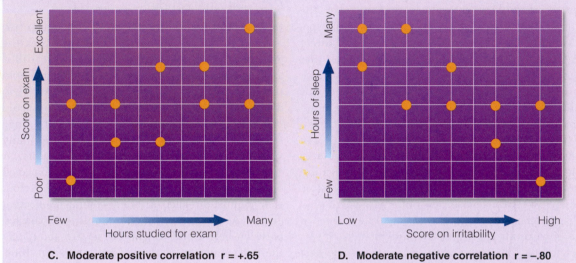

C. Moderate positive correlation r = +.65

D. Moderate negative correlation r = −.80

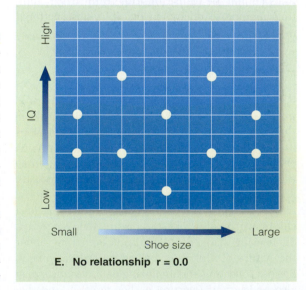

E. No relationship r = 0.0

more irritable they are. We should note that perfect correlations are seen only (or almost only) in textbooks. In real life there is nearly always enough noise to prevent even two strongly related factors to achieve a perfect correlation. Figures 1.5c and 1.5d show more moderate correlations (of about .65 and −.80, respectively). Figure 1.5e shows what a scatter plot looks like when there is no relationship between two factors (r = 0.0). In this case, knowing the value of one factor (shoe size) would not help at all in predicting the second factor (IQ).

Correlational studies are used frequently in developmental research. For example, if one were interested in the relationship between children's viewing filmed aggression and engaging in aggressive behavior, one would first need to identify measures of aggression in film and of children's aggressive behavior in some context. The next step would be to see if changes in one measure (viewing filmed aggression) are associated with changes in the other measure (aggressive behavior). This is what Mark Singer and David Miller (1999) did in their study of 2,245 third- through eighth-grade children. Children completed surveys about how much TV viewing they do, including television with violent content, and how much violent behavior they engaged in during the past year ("threatening others; slapping, hitting, or punching someone before the other person hit them;

slapping, hitting, or punching someone after the other person hit them; beating someone up; and attacking someone with a knife," p. 880). Singer and Miller reported that high exposure to violence on TV was associated with a higher rate of self-reported violent behavior.

Given this finding, it would be tempting to conclude that watching violent television *causes* children to be aggressive. However, the correlational nature of this study precludes such an interpretation. A correlation tells us about the strength of a relationship, but not about which factor caused which. In this example, although the interpretation that watching aggressive television leads to aggressive behavior makes intuitive sense, it is also possible that children who are aggressive tend to select violent television programs. Does violent TV cause kids to be aggressive, or do aggressive children choose to watch more violent TV? This issue cannot be resolved through correlational methods, which can only establish a relationship between the two factors. Correlation does not imply causality.

Experimental Studies

Experimental studies involve the manipulation of one or more factors, or variables (called **independent variables**), and observation of how these manipulations change the behavior under investigation (called **dependent variables**). To investigate the relationship between viewing violent television and behaving aggressively, for example, we could manipulate the TV viewing of children and assess the consequences. Many such experiments have been conducted (see Anderson et al., 2003) with children of various ages and from a variety of backgrounds. One of the first studies to do this was conducted by Lynette Friedrich and Aletha Stein (1973) with a sample of preschool children. After recording the level of aggressive behavior during school hours for three weeks, they divided the children into three groups. Each group viewed one of three types of television shows during the first half-hour of the school day: aggressive programs (such as "Batman" and "Superman"), prosocial programs ("Mister Rogers' Neighborhood"), and neutral programs (such as Disney nature films). Aggressive behavior during school was assessed again during the four-week period when children watched the programs and the two-week period afterward. The independent variable in this study was the type of program children watched, and the dependent variable was aggressive behavior (actually changes in aggressive behavior from baseline).

Friedrich and Stein reported that viewing aggressive television did result in increased aggressive behavior, *but only for those children who were high in aggression to begin with.* The experimental manipulation of TV viewing permitted Fried-

Picture Partners/Photo Researchers, Inc.

Aggression in preschoolers is related to how much violent TV they watch, a finding derived from correlational studies. However, viewing violent film only tends to affect children who are high in aggression to begin with, a finding derived from experimental studies.

rich and Stein to state that watching aggressive programs *caused* aggressive behavior. However, their careful measurement of aggression before classroom TV viewing allowed them to determine exactly which children were most influenced by the aggressive content of the programs.

True experiments require that participants be randomly assigned to the different experimental conditions. So, for example, in the Friedrich and Stein study, preschool children were randomly assigned to the "aggressive film" and the "prosocial film" conditions. However, true random assignment is often not possible. For instance, when looking at differences in aggression in groups of 4-, 6-, and 8-year-old boys and girls, one cannot randomly assign someone to the "4-year-old group" or to the "boys" group. These are preexisting characteristics of children. Such studies are called **quasi-experimental designs**, and researchers must be more cautious in making causal inferences about their results than in a true experiment.

experimental studies Type of studies in which a researcher manipulates one or more factors, then observes how these manipulations change the behavior under investigation.

independent variables In experimental studies, the factors, or variables, that are modified to see their effect on the dependent, or outcome, variables.

dependent variables The "outcome" variable, or behavior, that is being studied.

quasi-experimental studies Studies in which assignment of participants to conditions is not made at random (for example, males vs. females).

table 1.2 Differences between Longitudinal and Cross-sectional Studies

In longitudinal studies, the same children are tested repeatedly. In the following example, children born in 2000 were tested in 2004, 2006, 2008, and 2010, when they were 4, 6, 8, and 10 years old, respectively. In cross-sectional studies, different children are tested at each age. In the next example, children born in 2006, 2004, 2002, and 2000 were tested when they were 4, 6, 8, and 10 years old, respectively.

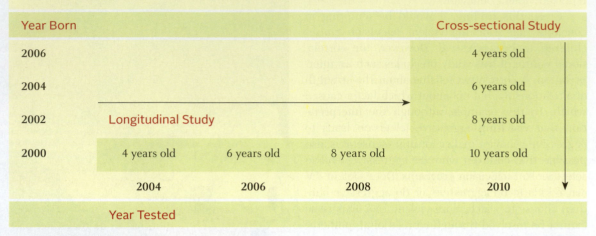

Year Born				Cross-sectional Study
2006				4 years old
2004				6 years old
2002	Longitudinal Study			8 years old
2000	4 years old	6 years old	8 years old	10 years old
	2004	2006	2008	2010
Year Tested				

One type of quasi-experimental design involves what are called naturalistic studies. (Naturalistic studies can be correlational as well.) We previously described naturalistic observations and commented how they can be valuable in getting information that would be difficult or impossible to get otherwise. Other studies take advantage of naturally occurring situations that may have important psychological consequences on children's lives but could not be conducted ethically through experimentation. In a sense, these can be thought of as group case studies, in that groups of children who go through a specific type of experience are observed or interviewed to see if there is anything special about their psychological development. For example, early in the 20th century, children were placed in overcrowded and understaffed orphanages and as a result experienced less-than-supportive care (Spitz, 1949, see Chapter 12). How did the lack of social interaction during their first year of life affect their later social and intellectual development? The answer to such a question can give psychologists great insight into the role of social support for both typical and abnormal development, but such studies could not be done experimentally. (Unfortunately, such conditions still exist in the world, as new findings from children living in stultifying orphanages in Romania testify; Nelson et al., 2007; see Chapter 10). Other studies have examined the effects on children of experiencing natural disasters, such as hurricanes and tornados (Ackil, Van Abbema, & Bauer, 2003) or the consequences of sexual child abuse (Cicchetti & Toth, 2006). Obviously, it is important to understand how these experiences affect children, but it is equally obvious that one cannot use true experiments to get at these answers.

Longitudinal and Cross-sectional Designs

By definition, developmental psychology is concerned with change over time. Perhaps the most obvious way to assess developmental change is to follow a person or group of people over an extended period, documenting the changes as they age. This approach describes longitudinal studies. An alternative approach is to look for differences among people of different ages. Thus, for example, instead of testing the same children at ages 4, 6, 8, and 10 (the longitudinal approach), one can examine four different groups of children at each of these four ages and note the differences in their behavior. This approach is used in cross-sectional studies. Differences between the longitudinal and cross-sectional approaches are displayed in Table 1.2.

Each method has its inherent strong and weak points. Longitudinal designs represent a true developmental approach, in that they record change over time within the same person. This cannot be said for cross-sectional studies. Although a group of 6-year-olds may show greater social skills than a group of 4-year-olds, for example, one does not know, using a cross-sectional design, whether the 6-year-olds with the most social skills were also the most socially skilled at age 4. We know that social skills improve with age, but we do not know the pattern of change within individual children. Without that knowledge, we are limited in what

naturalistic studies Studies in which the researcher observes individuals in their own environments, intervening as little as possible.

longitudinal studies Type of developmental studies that assesses developmental change by following a person or group of people over an extended period of time.

cross-sectional studies Type of developmental studies that compares different individuals of different ages at the same point in time.

we can say about the mechanisms of developmental change. Thus, the major strength of the longitudinal method—its ability to assess change within individuals over time—represents the major weakness of the cross-sectional approach. The major weakness of the longitudinal method is that it is expensive and time consuming.

There is another potential weakness with longitudinal studies, and that is participant loss. A study that starts out with 100 participants at age 5 may have only a fraction of that amount when children are age 10 or 15. Families move, parents and children become busy and decide they have better things to do with their time than take part, again, in a research project. Also, one cannot be sure if the children who drop out are similar to the ones who continue to participate in the study. Perhaps the dropouts are children who have lower IQs, a more irritable disposition, or whose parents are more permissive than children who stay in the program.

Not surprisingly, most research that finds its way into child and adolescent development journals is cross-sectional in nature. However, major longitudinal studies, following people from birth to adulthood, have been conducted, and the data from these studies are valuable. Several longitudinal studies were begun in the 1920s or 1930s and followed people into adulthood and old age. For example, in the Fels Longitudinal Study, begun in 1929, participants entered the program as infants or young children and were followed through adulthood, being assessed for a broad range of physical and psychological features. Other longitudinal projects are a bit more focused in what they study. For example, the Minnesota Longitudinal Study of Parents and Children recruited 267 first-time mothers in 1975 and continues to follow them today, assessing the continuity and long-term consequences of infant-mother attachment and related issues (Reis & Collins, 2004; Carlson, Sroufe, & Egeland, 2004; Sroufe et al., 2005). Focusing mainly on cognitive development, researchers at the Max Planck Institute for Psychological Research in Munich, Germany, instituted the Longitudinal Study on the Genesis of Individual Competencies (LOGIC) in 1984. They began with more than 200 kindergarten children and followed them through age 21, documenting changes in basic cognitive abilities such as memory, as well as aspects of social and personality development (see Schneider & Bullock, 2009; Weinert & Schneider, 1999).

Researchers also conduct short-term longitudinal studies, following children over the course of months or several years, as opposed to a lifetime. For example, Catherine Haden and her colleagues (2001) were interested in the relationship between how mothers talk to their toddlers and their children's subsequent memory ability. They

table 1.3 Cross-sequential Design

Children born in different years are tested longitudinally. In the following example, children are tested every two years, some beginning when they are 2 years old, some when they are 6 years old, and others when they are 10 years old.

Year Born				
2002	2 years old	4 years old	6 years old	8 years old
1998	6 years old	8 years old	10 years old	12 year old
1994	10 years old	12 years old	14 years old	16 years old
	2004	**2006**	**2008**	**2010**
		Year Tested		

observed 21 mother-child pairs when the children were 30, 36, and 42 months old as they took part in specially constructed activities in their homes. For instance, during one visit, mother and child engaged in a pretend camping trip and during another a pretend bird-watching trip (all while never leaving their living rooms). The researchers then tested the children for their memories of these events and found relations between how mothers and children interacted during the events and later recall. For example, aspects of the activities that were jointly handled and talked about by mothers and children (for instance, both holding the binoculars and talking about seeing a bird) were remembered better than activities that were not jointly handled and talked about. The question these researchers were asking required a longitudinal approach to answer, but not one that spanned 20 years; 18 months was enough.

It is possible to combine cross-sectional and longitudinal approaches, and one such technique is called the **cross-sequential approach** (see Table 1.3). In cross-sequential studies, groups of children at different ages are tested, just as in a normal cross-sectional study. Each group of children is then followed longitudinally. For example, the Longitudinal Study of Australian Children (Australian Institute of Family Studies, 2008; Sanson et al., 2002) plans to assess a broad range of physical and psychological characteristics of children from more than 10,000 families over 6 years using a cross-sequential design. In 2004, groups of infants and 4-year-olds began the study, and they have been assessed every 2 years at least through 2010.

One important aspect of using a cross-sequential design is that it permits one to evaluate

cross-sequential approach Type of developmental studies that combines aspects of cross-sectional and longitudinal designs; groups of participants at different ages are tested, and then followed longitudinally.

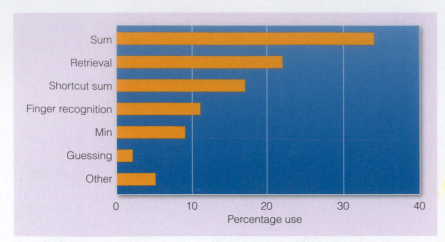

FIGURE 1.6 Percentage use for each arithmetic strategy: The results of a microgenetic study.

Many 4-year-old children who did not use the min strategy spontaneously did so after repeated sessions solving simple arithmetic problems. Most children used a variety of different strategies to solve the different problems. SOURCE: From Siegler, R. S., & Jenkins, E. (1989). *How children discover new strategies*. Hillsdale, NJ: Lawrence Erlbaum and Associates. Reprinted by permission.

cohort effects. A *cohort* refers to a group of people who are living in a culture at the same time and are thus influenced by the same historical events. Societal attitudes, medical care, climate, a country's economy, means of communication, and a host of other factors can change in a culture, and these changes may influence important aspects of children's (or adults') behavior and development. By using a cross-sequential design, one can separate the effects of development ("This is what 8-year-olds are like") from the effects of being in a particular cohort ("This is what 8-year-olds are like at this time in history versus at another time in history, such as before and after the wide availability of video games").

Microgenetic Studies

The study by Catherine Haden and her colleagues described earlier shows that the amount of time you need to follow children or the interval between assessments varies depending on what you are looking for. It would have made little sense for Haden and her associates to follow these children until they were 21 years old, or to test them at weekly intervals. What they were interested in should develop gradually over the course of months. Testing once a year may cause them to miss an important transition in verbal memory in children who are just beginning to talk. Likewise, memory abilities change gradually over this time,

meaning that they would probably see little change worth talking about from session to session if they tested children every week.

This would not be so for other abilities, or perhaps even for the same ability (memory) for older children. Some abilities emerge, often as the result of practice, over relatively brief periods of time, and for such abilities **microgenetic studies** are called for. The microgenetic method involves assessing children repeatedly over relatively short intervals, usually days or weeks (Miller & Coyle, 1999; Siegler, 2000). Many, perhaps most, aspects of development do not lend themselves to such repeated testing over closely separated intervals, but some behaviors do. This would be most evident when a child is in the process of making a transition from one form of thinking or behaving to another.

Let us provide an example from the work of Robert Siegler and Eric Jenkins (1989), who were interested in how children made the transition from using one simple arithmetic strategy to a more complicated and efficient one. When children first start to add two numbers together (for example, 3 + 2 = ?), they do so by counting the first addend ("1, 2, 3") and then counting the second addend ("4, 5"). This is called the *sum strategy*, and although it usually results in the correct answer for small quantities, it is very time consuming. A more sophisticated strategy involves starting with the first addend ("3") and counting up from there ("4, 5"). This is called the *min strategy*, because it involves counting the minimum number of elements. (Children's math strategies will be discussed in Chapter 10.)

Siegler and Jenkins tested eight 4- and 5-year old children, all of whom were using the sum strategy but none of whom were using the min strategy at the beginning of the study. They gave them a series of simple addition problems to solve for 11 consecutive weeks and examined when and how children switched from using the sum strategy most of the time to using the min strategy most of the time. Although no child was using the min strategy at the beginning of the study, six of eight were by week 11. The percentage of the strategies most frequently used by children in this study is shown in Figure 1.6. Different children used different combinations of the strategies, so that any particular child used a unique mixture of the strategies in his or her solutions. Over the course of the 11 weeks, children's strategies became more sophisticated, so that the children who started mainly by guessing or using the sum strategy progressed to using the min or fact-retrieval strategy more often.

Siegler and Jenkins also observed that children took longer to solve a problem the first time they used the min strategy and the problems *before* they first used it. Why the longer solution time? Siegler

cohort effects The psychological effects associated with being a member of a group born at a particular time (for example, a generation) and place; the fact that people who are living in a culture at the same time are influenced by the same historical events.

microgenetic studies Studies assessing some target behaviors of participants repeatedly over relatively short intervals of time, usually days or weeks.

and Jenkins speculated that children were experiencing conflict, or interference, from alternate strategies, and that new strategies require more mental effort than previously established ones. Thus the children required more time and did some hemming and hawing before arriving at an answer.

The microgenetic method can be very useful in assessing behaviors that show relatively rapid change over brief periods of time, and they have been used extensively, mainly to investigate aspects of cognitive development, including memory strategies (Schlagmüller & Schneider, 2002), spelling (Rittle-Johnson & Siegler, 1999), and changes in how parents instruct children in the use of arithmetic strategies (Bjorklund, Hubertz, & Reubens, 2004), among others (see Miller & Coyle, 1999; Siegler, 1996).

Problems Doing Research with Children

Obtaining Children to Serve as Research Participants

For all their delightfulness, children can cause problems for researchers. Difficulties arise in simply obtaining children to use as research participants. Laboratory rats can be ordered by telephone and delivered UPS for $9.50 apiece, and college sophomores are typically willing to perform in experiments in exchange for course credit. Although most children will gladly comply with the requests of a researcher, the problem is obtaining a large source of willing participants.

When dealing with children between the ages of about 5 and 18 years, the best source is the schools. Often, participation in research projects must be approved by school boards, principals, teachers, children's parents, and the children. Once approval has been obtained, the next problem is finding a place to conduct the study. Schools often provide small rooms suitable for testing, but much improvisation may be required to make the testing environment appropriate to the specific project. Because researchers are guests of the schools, they must comply with school schedules. This often means suspension of testing during certain hours of the day and limited access to the testing rooms, not to mention the problems of fire drills, Valentine's Day parties, and field trips. Principals, teachers, and parents are reluctant to have children miss too much class instruction for the sake of an experiment, meaning that most studies must be designed to be run as quickly as possible.

Working with preschoolers presents similar opportunities and problems. Although many children younger than age 5 remain at home with a parent, many more children today (at least in the United States and Europe) spend a significant portion of their early years in some institutional setting, be it a daycare center or educational preschool. Some research is done in an investigator's laboratory, where one has greater experimental control. This presents the problem of getting children and their parents to the lab.

Work with newborns is often done in hospitals shortly after delivery, making the newborn, like the college sophomore, a captive audience. Once babies leave the hospital, however, finding them as research participants can be difficult. Many scientists conduct research in the babies' homes. Others transport babies and mothers to their labs, or bring the labs to them, using mobile trailers and renovated recreational vehicles. Still other research is done at daycare centers.

Working with children can also require more effort, social skill, and time than working with rats or college students. An experimenter needs to establish a positive rapport with a child, putting the child at ease and generating a comfortable atmosphere so that the child will likely comply with the adult's requests. Interviewers have to speak on the children's level, being certain that the children understand instructions, and they must be sensitive to children's feelings and interests while they are being tested. Although a good experimenter or interviewer must be aware of these things when testing adults, they are especially important when working with children.

The Problem of Subject Loss

Once a suitable sample of children has been found, the next step is getting them to cooperate. In any study, a few children will be unable or unwilling to complete the testing. Are those children who complete testing different in any way from those who do not? For example, in a study by Steven Friedman (1972), newborn infants demonstrated memory for a visual pattern over a brief interval. However, of 90 infants who began the study, 50 were excluded for reasons such as crying or falling asleep. Of the remaining 40 babies, memory was indicated in 29. What do these results say about the memory abilities of newborns? As Friedman noted, that depends on the characteristics of the 50 babies who never completed the task. If they are different from those infants who completed testing, it can affect the interpretation of the results of the experiment. Investigators have shown that, in some cases, this appears to be true, with cooperative children showing different patterns of performance than less cooperative children, for example (Bathurst & Gottfried, 1987). This means that developmental psychologists must keep in mind the children who do *not* complete their projects as well as those who do.

table 1.4 Ethical Standards for Research with Children

Doing research with children involves all the same ethical considerations when one does research with adults, plus some additional ones. The principles listed below are a subset of those published in the 1990–91 *Directory of the Society for Research in Child Development* (SRCD).

Non-harmful procedures	The investigator should use no research operation that may harm the child either physically or psychologically. The investigator is also obligated at all times to use the least stressful research operation whenever possible . . .
Informed consent	Before seeking consent or assent from the child, the investigator should inform the child of all features of the research that may affect his or her willingness to participate and should answer the child's questions in terms appropriate to the child's comprehension. The investigator should respect the child's freedom to choose to participate in the research or not by giving the child the opportunity to give or not give assent to participation as well as to choose to discontinue participation at any time . . .
Parental consent	The informed consent of parents, legal guardians or those who act in loco parentis (for example, teachers, superintendents of institutions) similarly should be obtained, preferably in writing.
Additional consent	The informed consent of any persons, such as school teachers for example, whose interaction with the child is the subject of the study should also be obtained . . .
Incentives	Incentives to participate in a research project must be fair and must not unduly exceed the range of incentives that the child normally experiences . . .
Jeopardy	When, in the course of research, information comes to the investigator's attention that may jeopardize the child's well-being, the investigator has a responsibility to discuss the information with the parents or guardians and with those expert in the field in order that they may arrange the necessary assistance for the child.
Unforeseen consequences	When research procedures result in undesirable consequences for the participant that were previously unforeseen, the investigator should immediately employ appropriate measures to correct these consequences, and should redesign the procedures if they are to be included in subsequent studies.
Confidentiality	The investigator should keep in confidence all information obtained about research participants. The participants' identity should be concealed in written and verbal reports of the results, as well as in informal discussion with students and colleagues . . .

SOURCE: From *Directory of the Society for Research in Child Development, 1990–1991*. Principles 15 and 16 first published in the Fall 1991 SRCD Newsletter. Reprinted by permission.

A related problem concerns securing a representative sample. Are the various socioeconomic classes in a school represented in your study? Is the rate of boys and girls who return permission slips comparable? Middle-class parents, for example, may be more likely to consent for their children to participate in psychological studies than are parents from lower socioeconomic homes. Perhaps boys are less likely to bring permission slips home to their parents, or girls are more likely to request that parents sign such slips, resulting in gender inequality in the sample. Investigators must take such possibilities into consideration and describe carefully who their participants were when they write up the results of their study.

Ethical Guidelines of Doing Research with Children

Conducting behavioral research requires following certain ethical guidelines. This is true regardless if one's participants are white rats, college sophomores, or kindergarten children. University-based research must be approved by Internal Review Boards, most of which follow guidelines established by the federal government. People doing research with infants, children, and adolescents have additional responsibilities. Table 1.4 presents some of the Ethical Standards for Research with Children published by the Society for Research in Child Development, the leading organization of child developmental researchers.

summary

The study of development can help us understand adults, including ourselves; can provide insights into the origins of human nature; and can help us better deal with children in everyday situations. **Developmental psychology** is concerned with changes in physical and psychological characteristics occurring over a lifetime. **Ontogeny** refers to the development of the individual, whereas **phylogeny** refers to the development of the species, or evolution.

Some have argued that the concept of childhood is a modern one that did not exist in medieval Europe. Although this may be an exaggeration, children were increasingly afforded special status in Europe and America throughout the 19th and 20th centuries, brought about in part by the need for formal education. Some believe that in the United States we have entered a postmodern view of childhood, being less likely to see children as innocent and in need of protection and more likely to view them as competent.

Developmental psychology has gone through a series of changes in its brief history. The **Child Study Movement** was spurred by G. Stanley Hall, based on his belief that the findings of developmental psychology should be applied to children in a very immediate, practical way. Developmental psychology was out of mainstream psychology until the middle of the 20th century, when it brought increasing experimental rigor to the study of children. In recent decades, developmental psychology has expanded its boundaries and is becoming integrated with other scientific disciplines, particularly biology, causing some developmental psychologists to identify their field as *developmental science*. In this book, we reflect this modern multidisciplinary perspective of development by attempting to integrate three overarching approaches in the study of child and adolescent development: **developmental contextualism**, a **sociocultural perspective**, and **evolutionary theory**.

Issues relating to the **stability** and **plasticity** of behavior have been a focal point for developmental theory and research, with evidence accumulating that although early experiences are important in influencing behavior, later experiences play an important role as well. The question of how stage-like human development is centers around the issue of whether age-related changes are **discontinuous** and abrupt (stage-like), reflecting qualitative changes, or are **continuous** and gradual, reflecting quantitative changes. Developmental psychologists differ in their emphasis on **normative** patterns of development, the typical form that development takes over time (**developmental function**), or idio-graphic patterns, individual differences among children at a given age.

Perhaps the most prominent issue in developmental psychology is that of **nature/nurture**, the extent to which patterns of development are a function of biology versus experience. At one extreme is the philosophical position of **empiricism** (individuals are shaped by experience) and at the other is **nativism** (individuals are shaped by their innate biology, or genes, **genetic determinism**). **Developmental systems theory** centers around the concept of **epigenesis**, a bidirectional relationship between all levels of biological and experiential variables, such that genetic activity both influences and is influenced by structural maturation, which is bidirectionally related to function and activity. Historically, epigenesis was contrasted with **preformationism**, the idea that structures in development appear fully formed. Organisms inherit not only a species-typical genome but also a species-typical environment, and species-typical experiences early in life can greatly influence the course of development. **Sensitive periods** refer to times in development when a skill is most easily attained and a person is especially receptive to specific environmental influences.

The scientific study of development requires the objective and reliable observation of children's behavior. **Validity** refers to the extent to which a measurement accurately assesses what it purports to measure. **Reliability** refers to (1) interobserver reliability and (2) replicability. Scientific explanations are based on natural cause and effect, without the intervention of magical or supernatural agents. Preference is given to the simplest explanation for a phenomenon, a concept known as **parsimony**.

In **structured interviews**, children are interviewed under conditions in which the researcher can control extraneous factors that may influence a child's behavior. **Clinical interviews** (or the clinical method) involve an intense relationship between an examiner and a child. When researchers use **questionnaires**, children are asked to answer a series of questions about themselves or perhaps other children. **Standardized tests** are a special type of questionnaire. In **observational studies**, researchers watch children in specific situations for the incidence of specific behaviors. Observational studies can be naturalistic or structured. **Case studies** and diaries are used by clinicians and other researchers and involve a detailed description of a single individual. They can be useful for generating hypotheses and examining conditions that would be unethical to examine experimentally. **Naturalistic studies** evaluate children in their natural habitats.

In **correlational studies**, the relationship between two or more factors is assessed. In **experimental studies**, the researcher manipulates one or more factors (**independent variables**) and assesses the effects on some behavior (**dependent variables**). In **quasi-experimental studies**, assignment to groups cannot be made randomly (for example, age, sex), so researchers must be more cautious about making cause-effect interpretations.

Two techniques for studying change over time are **longitudinal studies** and **cross-sectional studies**. In longitudinal studies, the same children are tested over an extended period of time, whereas in cross-sectional studies, different children are tested at each age of interest. These methods can be combined, producing **cross-sequential designs**, which can separate developmental effects from **cohort effects**. **Microgenetic studies** evaluate changes in behavior over relatively short periods of time, such as days or weeks, as opposed to months or years.

Obtaining children as research participants and getting them to cooperate entail complications not faced by psychologists who study college students or laboratory animals. Doing research with children presents ethical considerations that are somewhat different from those faced by researchers doing research with animals or adults. Most child developmentalists follow the ethical standard of the Society for Research in Child Development.

Key Terms and Concepts

development (p. 7)
developmental psychology (p. 7)
ontogeny (p. 7)
phylogeny (p. 7)
Child Study Movement (p. 12)
stability (p. 14)
plasticity (p. 14)
discontinuity versus continuity
   of development (p. 16)
normative approach (p. 17)
developmental function (p. 17)
idiographic approach (p. 17)
nature/nurture (p. 18)
empiricism (p. 18)

nativism (p. 18)
genetic determinism (p. 19)
developmental systems theory (p. 19)
epigenesis (p. 19)
preformationism (p. 19)
structure (p. 19)
function (p. 19)
sensitive period (p. 22)
validity (p. 24)
reliability (p. 25)
parsimony (p. 25)
structured interviews (p. 26)
clinical interviews (p. 27)
questionnaires (p. 27)

standardized tests (p. 28)
observational studies (p. 28)
case studies (p. 30)
correlational studies (p. 33)
experimental studies (p. 35)
independent variables (p. 35)
dependent variables (p. 35)
quasi-experimental studies (p. 35)
naturalistic studies (p. 36)
longitudinal studies (p. 36)
cross-sectional studies (p. 36)
cross-sequential approach (p. 37)
cohort effects (p. 38)
microgenetic studies (p. 38)

Ask Yourself . . .

1. What is meant by "development" in psychology, and what actually "develops"?
2. What are some of the reasons for studying development, and what psychological fields study it?
3. How have the ways adults perceive children and childhood changed throughout history? How is childhood viewed today?
4. When did the scientific study of children and adolescents begin, and what have been the major accomplishments in the field?
5. What is meant by "an integrative approach to development," and what are the three levels of analysis proposed in this textbook?

6. What are the main themes and issues in developmental psychology? Why are they important?
7. What is the distinction between the concepts of **epigenesis** and **preformationism**? How is the concept of epigenesis incorporated into modern developmental psychology?
8. What does it mean to say something is "innate"?
9. What are the various methods of empirical research in developmental psychology?
10. What are some of the problems of doing research with infants, children, and adolescents?

Exercises: Going Further

1. Imagine that you are a developmental psychologist and you see a 6-year-old child whose parents say he is having "psychological problems." What aspects of this child's development and his social environment would you want to know about in order to get a better idea of what is going on in this child's life? Make a short list and tell why you think each item would be helpful.

2. Think about yourself when you were 5, 10, and 15 years old. Which aspects of your psychological development do you feel are the same now as they were then (that is, are stable), and which have changed somehow? Did the changes you experienced happen gradually or abruptly? Do you think what has happened to you over your lifetime is essentially the same as for your classmates (or not)? And what about people in other cultures (for example, Chinese people at 5, 10, 15, and 18 years old)? Do you think changes over development would be essentially the same as for you?

3. You are hired to perform a study assessing developmental changes in intelligence from 2 to 20 years old. Suggest to your employers different designs or ways in which this study could be done, and let them know about the advantages and disadvantages of each proposal.

Suggested Readings

Classic Works

Postman, N. (1982). *The disappearance of childhood*. **New York: Vintage Books**. This book presents the provocative proposal that the invention of the printing press in the 1400s and the subsequent importance of literacy and schooling was the impetus for the "invention of childhood" in Renaissance Europe, and that television was the primary impetus for its disappearance in the late 20th century.

Flavell, J. H. (1971). Stage-related properties of cognitive development. *Cognitive Psychology*, 2, 421–453. This article presents one of the most articulate discussions of the role of stages in cognitive development.

Scholarly Works

Orme, N. (2001). *Medieval children*. **New Haven, CT: Yale University Press.** This book provides a scholarly overview of what children and childhood were like in medieval Europe. It dispels the myth that medieval Europeans had no sense of childhood, while revealing that children were not judged or treated the same as they are today.

Elman, J. L., Bates, E. A., Johnson, M. H., Karmiloff Smith, A., Parisi, D., & Plunkett, K. (1996). *Rethinking innateness: A connectionist perspective on development*. **Cambridge, MA: MIT Press**. This book discusses issues related to the concept of innateness as it relates to developmental psychology. Although numerous aspects of development are discussed, most discussion is related to brain and language development. The authors present a connectionist (computer modeling) perspective, but the book is valuable even for those who want to avoid such approaches.

Readings for Personal Interest

Elkind, D. (1998). *Reinventing childhood: Raising and educating children in a changing world*. **Rosemont, NJ: Modern Learning Press**. David Elkind discusses the lives of children in contemporary culture and compares them to the lives of children in decades past. He proposes that we have a *postmodern* view of childhood, in which we see children as competent and less in need of protection than we did in the past.

Kagan, J. (1984). *The nature of the child*. **New York: Basic Books.** Jerome Kagan, a leading researcher and theorist in developmental psychology for more than 40 years, presents a provocative account of human development, addressing some of the basic assumptions we hold about development, including the continuity of change and the role of early experience on later development.

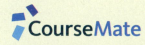

Cengage Learning's **Psychology CourseMate** for this text brings course concepts to life with interactive learning, study, and exam preparation tools, including quizzes and flashcards for this chapter's Key Terms and Concepts (see the summary list on page 42). The site also provides an **eBook** version of the text with highlighting and note taking capabilities, as well as an extensive library of observational videos that span early childhood through adolescence. Many videos are accompanied by questions that will help you think critically about and deepen your understanding of the chapter topics addressed, especially as they pertain to core concepts. Log on and learn more at **www.cengagebrain.com**.

2

© Blend Images/SuperStock

In this chapter we explore the multiple contexts in which infants, children, and adolescents live and develop. These contexts include the evolutionary and sociohistorical contexts, as well as children's immediate physical and social environments. The role of theories in understanding psychological development is discussed. We then examine briefly some classical theories of development, including mechanistic and organismic theories, followed by a discussion of more contemporary frameworks that take a developmental contextual perspective. Specifically, we examine Vygotsky's sociocultural theory, Bronfenbrenner's ecological systems theory, and evolutionary developmental psychology.

The famous child-development theorist lost his temper and yelled unkind things at the child who was leaving her handprints and footprints in his newly poured concrete driveway. Shortly later, the child's mother confronted the theorist about the tongue-lashing he had given her daughter.

"What's the matter with you?" she said. "You're supposed to like children."

"My dear woman," the theorist replied, "I like my children in the abstract, not in the concrete."

We imagine that if we conducted a survey among undergraduate students taking a child and adolescent development course, most would see theories as not-too-useful abstractions that ignore the real (concrete) stuff of our lives; but for some unknown reason, university professors love theories and accordingly put them regularly on academic tests,

with the seeming purpose of making their students' lives more complicated. We admit that some theories can seem a bit removed from the happenings of everyday life. But in actuality, as social psychologist Kurt Lewin (1952, p. 169) said, in science "there is nothing more practical than a good theory." As we will see later, one of the virtues of theories is that they give us a forest (versus a trees) view of a topic.

Developmental psychologists are a varied lot, and there is no one-size-fits-all theory of human development. Most contemporary developmental psychologists do hold a few views in common, however (see Table 2.1). They realize that it is impossible to understand development out of context. Development happens while children are interacting with others—in families, schools, or neighborhoods, and within a larger cultural and historical context. Development always occurs within a context, and for humans this includes a

table 2.1 Some Views about Development Shared by Most Developmental Psychologists

- Development always occurs within a context (family, school, peers).
- Children and adolescents are biological creatures.
- Multiple perspectives are needed to acquire a full understanding of human development:
  1. A proximal or more immediate one (here and now)
  2. A distal or more remote one taking into account the
     - Sociohistorical context of development
     - Evolutionary or phylogenetic context of development
- The relationship between organism and environment is bidirectional across levels and life periods.
- A holistic view of children and adolescents must be sustained in developmental analyses.

social environment, although the specific details of a child's social environment can vary widely.

Developmental psychologists also realize that children are biological creatures, endowed by their inheritance with behaviors, perceptions, emotions, and cognitions that, in many respects, are unique to *Homo sapiens* and are shared by all typically developing members of the species. This is seen in increased research in the area of developmental neuroscience (see Chapter 4), as well as in research that examines children's physiological reactions to different environments, such as changes in levels of cortisol in response to stressful experiences (see Chapter 11).

Multiple perspectives are needed to acquire a full understanding of human development. Most theories focus on the immediate, or *proximal*, causes of development. Children's learning, thinking, social behavior, and emotional responding require explanations at the immediate level (for instance, history of reinforcement, how information is processed, interactions with parents, effects of diet on brain growth). In addition, development must be viewed within a **sociohistorical context**, which reflects the values, tools, and institutions found in one's society. It must also be viewed from an evolutionary, or phylogenetic, context, which attempts to explain the adaptive value that certain behaviors, cognitions, or patterns of development may have had for our ancestors and continue to have for us today (see Figure 1.1 in Chapter 1). These are *distal* causes of development.

Although sociohistorical and evolutionary factors, by themselves, cannot *explain* development, they provide the necessary backdrop for understanding how and why more proximal, or immediate, causes affect the course of developing children

as they do (see Bjorklund & Hernández Blasi, 2005; Cole, 2006; Hernández Blasi & Bjorklund, 2003). As an example, consider reading. Literacy is critical in modern society, but reading and writing are new to our species. Human beings did not evolve to read. Our ancestors did not sit by the campfire in the evenings, squinting to read letters delivered from their friends living in distant caves. But they possessed language and the basic cognitive abilities used for other tasks of daily living that enabled them to learn to read once that technology was invented. However, given the evolutionary novelty of reading, it should not be surprising that many children have difficulty learning to read (Geary, 1995, 2007a).

In addition to these distal evolutionary and sociohistorical factors, we need to examine more proximal explanations for learning to read. These include the language and literacy environment in children's homes, the type of reading instruction they receive, cognitive factors such as children's abilities to focus their attention and to hold ideas in their minds for brief periods of time, and perhaps neurological factors, among others (Adams, Trieman, & Pressley, 1998; see Chapter 10). Although it is unusual for any researcher to focus on all of these levels of analysis in a single study, we hope it is clear that a consideration of both the multiple distal and proximal influences on behavior enhances our understanding of important aspects of development. This is consistent with the integrative approach to development we introduced in Chapter 1, particularly explaining development by integrating developmental contextual, sociohistorical, and evolutionary approaches.

Most developmental psychologists also assume a *holistic* view of children and adolescents; this means that although we know that it is necessary to examine different aspects of child and adolescent development separately (for example, physical, socioemotional, and cognitive development) in order to provide a comprehensible picture, we see children as whole and complete beings, producing behaviors within certain environments. In addition, as we mentioned in Chapter 1, developmental psychologists see the relation between organism and environment as *bidirectional*, characterizing all levels and periods of development, from the time of conception through death.

In this chapter we examine more generally the role of theories in child and adolescent development. We then provide a brief description of some of the classic theories of child and adolescent development. We feel it is helpful for students to get the lay of the theoretical landscape before delving too deeply into the nuts and bolts of developmental psychology. However, we also believe that theories are most useful when they

---

sociohistorical context The values, tools, and institutions found in one's society.

are discussed with their relevant content (theories of cognitive development with the phenomena associated with children's thinking, for instance), and we provide more detailed descriptions of these theories in the appropriate content chapters. We then examine in greater detail contemporary approaches to development, specifically frameworks following, implicitly or explicitly, a developmental contextual perspective, described briefly in Chapter 1. We devote more space to these more modern perspectives, because we believe that they capture the essence of development. We use concepts from these theories throughout the remainder of the book.

Why Theorize about Development?

Theories are like noses: everybody has one. Theorizing is not something that only men and women in lab coats sitting in ivory towers do. Theorizing is something that comes quite naturally to people in everyday life. For example, when we are introduced to someone (a new roommate, a new professor), we have no real knowledge of the person, but, based on what little we observe (for example, she smiled a couple of times, made some jokes, and used "please" regularly while talking), we theorize about what type of person we think she is ("This is probably a nice person, worth getting to know"). The same thing happens when we experience something new: the first time we fly, sail, or make contact with an unfamiliar animal. We generate theories about these novel things or events based on what we know of the world in general and what we witness of the new person, event, or thing. We keep the theory, change it, or get rid of it depending on how our new experiences fit with our previous view. From this perspective, theories help us organize facts—they help us figure out what is related to what and how (for example, the boat moves in a systematic way when I move the rudder), and distinguish what is relevant (the direction the wind is blowing when sailing) from what is irrelevant (the family relationship between the captain and the passengers of the sailboat).

Theories are important not only for organizing facts but also for directing research. The theories we hold help determine the types of questions we ask. For example, if we believe that development occurs in stages, the research questions we ask will be different than if we believe that development is continuous. Without theories, facts are merely isolated bits of information. Theories permit us to explain known phenomenon and, even more important, make predictions.

In our view, theories are basically simplified representations of reality that, if used properly, help us make practical decisions. In this sense, a theory is similar to a road map. On the one hand, a road map is not reality but a simplified representation of it: the size and the colors of the map are not the size and the colors of the real roads, and we would be extremely surprised if we found a driver astonished because there is no red or blue road in front of him. (However, we know of at least one child who was expecting to see a large brown mark when crossing the state line from Florida to Georgia.) On the other hand, this simplified representation of roads provides us information to practically decide if making a right or left turn at the next intersection will be the best way to get to our desired destination.

However, like road maps, not all theories are equally useful. In the same way that there are good and not-so-good road maps, there are also good and not-so-good theories. Normally, the theories we find in textbooks on developmental psychology are the good ones, in that they have influenced research and how people think about children and development. The not-so-good theories were rejected, we hope, and never made it into the textbooks. Moreover, the more general a theory is, the less useful it is, in a similar way that a U.S. road map is of little use if one never expects to leave the state of Florida. As a result, most theories of development focus on a specific aspect of reality (for example, Piaget's account of the development of intelligence or Freud's theory of psychosexual development). They are not useful for everything, but only for those aspects of psychological development they represent. Eventually, if theories want to be really useful, they must keep up-to-date, modified by new data. So, in the same way that a 40-year-old roadmap of Florida is useless to navigate on present-day Florida roads, we should not be surprised that older theories of development may also not be so useful, unless they take into consideration new findings. Sometimes it is enough simply to make some additions to old theories, like adding lines on a map to reflect new roads. Other times the theory needs to be drastically changed or even put aside in favor of a new theory (or an updated road map).

Scientific theories are different from our personal theories. An important feature of any scientific theory is that it can be disproved. A theory is not a statement about the world that relies solely on opinion or faith; rather, it is a statement about known facts that can be potentially disproved by new facts. If a theory is found to be incorrect because of new discoveries, these findings do not contradict the previous facts, only how they are explained. For example, the theory that birth defects are caused by experiences of the mother (such as being frightened by an elephant) has been replaced by the theory that birth defects are caused by genetic abnormalities or external agents the fetus is exposed to (such as drugs ingested by the mother). The fact of birth defects remains.

To sum up, theories of development are extremely useful for people who are interested in understanding and working with children, because they summarize and connect in an effective way the facts we know about different aspects of child and adolescent development (physical, cognitive, and socioemotional). In doing so, they provide a useful framework for generating fruitful research questions and also for making decisions regarding children's care, education, and general well-being. Most of the research presented in this book has been motivated by theory. As a colleague of ours likes to say, "Science walks on two legs—theory and data."

Classical Theories of Development

There have been several major theoretical approaches to the study of children, with hundreds of variations on these major theories. Classical theories are those that widely caught the attention of mainstream developmental psychologists for a significant part of the 20th century: behaviorism (Pavlov, Skinner, and Bandura's theories), psychoanalysis (Freud and Erikson's theories), Piaget's theory of cognitive development, and the information-processing approach, for example. Most of these theories can be organized into two big families of theories, or models: mechanistic and organismic (Reese & Overton, 1970). **Mechanistic theories** liken people to machines, such as the mind-as-a-computer model of information-processing approaches. They see people as composed of parts (behaviors) that can be broken down, or decomposed, into more basic parts. They view people as being relatively passive, changing as a result of external stimulation and fall more on the empiricist (nurture) side of the nature-nurture debate (see Chapter 1). Mechanistic theories also tend to view development as occurring gradually and continuously over time, rather than as occurring abruptly and discontinuously. **Organismic the-**

ories, in contrast, take a more biologic (nature) view of development, seeing people as whole beings who cannot be understood by decomposing them into their constituent parts. Children are seen as playing an active role in their own development, influenced as much by internal as by external forces. Organismic theories also tend to view development as occurring discontinuously in stages. In the following sections, we look at major classical mechanistic and organismic theories of development.

Mechanistic Theories

Mechanistic theories include (1) learning theories of development, (2) Bandura's social learning/social cognitive theory, and (3) information-processing approaches to development.

Learning Theories of Development

Among the more influential mechanistic theories are the various *learning theories*, collectively known as **behaviorism**, which emphasized that psychological development is primarily the result of changes brought about by classical or operant conditioning. *Classical conditioning* is illustrated by the work of the Russian physiologist Ivan Pavlov (1849–1936), who discovered the conditioned reflex. We imagine that every reader is probably familiar with Pavlov's famous experiments with salivating dogs: Dogs who initially salivated in anticipation of receiving food soon salivated to buzzers and bells that had been associated with food. The initial behavior (unconditioned response) is elicited by the unconditioned stimulus (food), and once-neutral stimuli (the conditioned stimulus, here bells and buzzers) soon elicited the behavior because of their association with the unconditioned stimulus. The early-20th-century American behaviorist John Watson argued that emotional responses to various stimuli are learned via classical conditioning, beginning early in infancy.

Operant conditioning, as articulated by the American psychologist B. F. Skinner (1904–1980), is based on the behaviors an animal emits and the consequences to the animal as a result of emitting those behaviors. Essentially, behaviors that are followed (or reinforced) by positive outcomes (or removal of negative outcomes) increase in frequency, whereas behaviors that are followed by negative outcomes decrease in frequency. Skinner and his followers attributed nearly all complex behaviors in animals and humans, including infants and children, to mechanisms of operant, or instrumental, conditioning.

For example, Alexia may perform well on spelling tests because of a history of positive reinforcements by her teacher. Her teacher may tell

mechanistic theories Theories of development that liken people to machines, such as the mind-as-a-computer model of information-processing approaches..

organismic theories Developmental theories that take a holistic (organism-like) view of development, seeing people as whole beings who cannot be understood by decomposing them into their constituent parts.

behaviorism Theory popular in the United States throughout the middle of the 20th century, holding that behavior and development are shaped by environmental influences

The ideas of Pavlov (classical conditioning) and Skinner (operant conditioning) assumed that principles of learning discovered for animals could be applied to humans, including infants and children.

her how well she did on her previous tests, or may allow her extra time at recess for her good performance, increasing the probability of high performance on subsequent tests. Alternatively, Alexia's teacher may punish her when she does poorly on a spelling test, such as making her stay indoors at recess time. Note that punishments can diminish the probability of a certain behavior but do not necessarily guide children toward a better alternative. That is, punishment of an undesirable behavior, such as poor performance on a spelling test, does not tell children what they should be doing, only that what they are doing now is not working. In other words, from an educational point of view, reinforcements are generally (but not always) more effective than punishments, as they orient the child toward what to do instead of only what not to do.

According to learning theorists such as Skinner (1938, 1953), real scientific psychology should focus only on the study of observable behaviors (that is, those that one can see and touch, such as physical movements or sounds). Psychologists should not spend their time studying things that they cannot directly observe, such as consciousness, mind, feelings, love, plans, purposes, attitudes, and so forth.

Behaviorism is no longer in vogue in academic psychology, and particularly not in contemporary developmental psychology. Yet, although reinforcement is much more complicated and works differently than Skinner suggested, the patterns of behavior change that behaviorism describe have been useful for controlling children's behavior at home and school (for example, time-out, the extinction of undesired behaviors in the classroom), for dealing with some clinical problems such as phobias (for example, behavior modification), and for educating children with special needs (for example, behavioral techniques used with children with autism and intellectual impairments). This is best illustrated by the field

of applied behavioral analysis (Bijou & Baer, 1961), which is discussed in Box 2.1.

Bandura's Social Learning/ Social Cognitive Theory

Albert Bandura's (1925–) social learning theory is another mechanistic approach that has been influential in child-development research. Bandura's early theorizing was based on the application of traditional learning theory to the social behavior of children (Bandura & Walters, 1963). Basically, Bandura argues that children learn important social behaviors from observing others. This is illustrated by Dorothy Law Nolte's (1998) poem, "Children Learn What They Live," which is found on the refrigerator doors of many parents:

If children live with criticism, they learn to condemn.

If children live with hostility, they learn to fight.

If children live with fear, they learn to be apprehensive.

If children live with pity, they learn to feel sorry for themselves.

If children live with ridicule, they learn to feel shy.

If children live with jealousy, they learn to feel envy.

If children live with shame, they learn to feel guilty.

If children live with encouragement, they learn confidence.

If children live with tolerance, they learn patience.

If children live with praise, they learn appreciation.

If children live with acceptance, they learn to love.

If children live with approval, they learn to like themselves.

applied behavioral analysis Extension of B. F. Skinner's behaviorism to practical settings.

social learning/social cognitive theory Bandura's theory of how individuals operate cognitively on their social experiences and how these cognitive operations influence behavior and development.

BOX 2.1 child development in the real world

Applied Behavioral Analysis and Developmental Psychology

Applied behavioral analysis (often abbreviated as ABA) is based on B. F. Skinner's research on operant conditioning. **Operant**, or **instrumental**, **conditioning** occurs when the frequency of a certain response (for example, a baby turning her head toward the left side) increases or decreases as a consequence of what happens afterward (for example, giving the baby a taste of a sweet drink or a bitter drink). The first step in applied behavioral analysis is to define precisely some socially significant behaviors that may be in need of changing. These target behaviors may be tantrums by a 2-year-old, brushing one's teeth for a child with intellectual impairment, head banging by an autistic child, or completing homework assignments for a fourth-grade student. Next, some schedule of reinforcement or implementation of other techniques from behavioral theory is implemented to increase, decrease, or maintain the targeted behavior (Baer, Wolf, & Risley, 1968).

Applied behavioral analysis techniques are widely used in several different settings. For example, many of the techniques recommended by child-care experts to take care of unruly children use ideas based on behaviorism. Jo Frost, the star of ABC television's *Supernanny*, shows parents how to gain control over some amazingly difficult children using, among other things, age-appropriate techniques developed by behavioral psychologists. For example, Supernanny instructs parents to establish rules and enforce them consistently. When putting children in "the naughty corner," for instance, she emphasizes persistence, making certain children spend their full 5 minutes of time-out in the corner. To do this, parents must sometimes chase fleeing children and return them to the corner, often dozens of times, until the children finally give in. Left to their own, parents often

return a wayward child to the corner several times, then finally give up, letting the child eventually escape the punishment. By giving in after repeated escapes, children learn that persistence counts and are more likely to obstinately continue their attempts to avoid punishment. By enforcing the 5-minute time-out, even if it takes over an hour to do so, children's escape behavior becomes extinguished, and coupled with warmth and perhaps something to distract children from the offending behavior, discipline becomes easier.

Teachers are taught to use behavioral techniques as a way of managing their classrooms (Alberto & Troutman, 2005). For instance, experienced teachers know that when a student is trying to get a teacher's attention by exhibiting some minor disruptive behavior (for example, making loud comments in the middle of a lesson), to reduce this behavior it is sometimes effective to use an extinction technique, consisting of removing all possible reinforcements contingent to the target behavior (that is, doing and/or saying nothing in this case). Other times, however, desirable behavior can be modeled or shaped through a series of reinforcements (*successive approximations*), initially providing praise when a child reduces his or her spelling errors from 10 to 8, for example ("That's great! Much better than before!"), then requiring improved performance before the reinforcement (in this case, social praise) is given (only 5 errors), until eventually all (or most) spelling errors are eliminated.

One program based on applied behavioral analysis used in some schools to control behavior and aid in instruction is the *Good Behavior Game* (Embry, 2002). In the Game, teachers first help students generate rules that would make the classroom (or any context) a good place to learn and that would be more enjoyable. These are labeled "good things we all want." Teachers

then get children to provide descriptions of behaviors that would interfere with desirable outcomes, called "fouls." Teachers and students then generate examples, physically and in words, of both "good things we all want" and "fouls." The Game is then played in intervals during the day, like innings in a baseball game, never for the whole day. The class is then divided into teams, and teachers explain that the team with the fewest fouls "wins" for that day or for a specific activity. Teachers then construct a scoreboard placed in a conspicuous place in the classroom, listing fouls and wins (with "wins" being more prominent than "fouls"). More than 20 independent studies have shown that school-age and teenage children enjoy the Good Behavior Game and that it is associated with reductions in impulsive and disruptive behaviors, as well as reductions in substance abuse and serious antisocial behaviors (see Embry, 2002).

Behavioral techniques have been especially useful for working with children with certain developmental disabilities, including intellectual impairment, attention-deficit with hyperactivity disorder (ADHD), and autism. For instance, children and adolescents with severe intellectual impairments can be taught many of the basic activities of everyday life, such as grooming, toileting, eating, and dressing, using consistently applied behavioral techniques. Similarly, parents can be taught how to manage their sometimes out-of-control intellectually impaired children. This often involves a careful charting of their children's behavior. For example, what, exactly, are children doing, what events precede an undesired behavior, and how do children react to parents' responses? Parents can be taught to model desired behavior and to break down complex tasks into their component parts, reinforcing each part (for exam-

---

If children live with recognition, they learn it is good to have a goal.

If children live with sharing, they learn generosity.

If children live with honesty, they learn truthfulness.

If children live with fairness, they learn justice.

If children live with kindness and consideration, they learn respect.

If children live with security, they learn to have faith in themselves and in those about them.

If children live with friendliness, they learn the world is a nice place in which to live. [SOURCE: Dorothy Law

operant (instrumental) conditioning Learning procedure where behavior is shaped through rewards and punishment

Applied behavioral analysis has been widely used with children with developmental disabilities, such as autism.

....

ple, putting toothpaste on the toothbrush, brushing one's teeth, washing the toothpaste off the brush) and then chaining the various parts into a whole activity (see Hodapp & Dykens, 2006).

Token economies have also been used with children with intellectual impairment. Briefly, this technique consists of delivering a series of tokens, or artificial reinforcers, to children (for example, a "gold" coin) upon performing a target behavior, such as making their beds, making eye contact with a teacher, or picking up trash on the floor in front of their desks. The tokens can later be used to purchase products or privileges (for instance, a pencil = 3 gold coins; an ice-cream cone = 6 gold coins; an excursion out of school = 20 gold coins).

One of the areas in which applied behavioral analysis has been used extensively is treating children with autism. Autism is a serious developmental disorder, characterized by minimal emotional attachment, absent or abnormal speech, low IQ, ritualistic behaviors, aggression, and self-injury. (The severity of disabilities in people with autism can vary widely, however. See Chapter 7 for a more in-depth discussion of the social-cognitive abilities of children with autism.) UCLA psychologist Ivar Lovaas and his colleagues developed behavioral methods for teaching children with autism (Lovaas, 1987, 2003; McEachin, Smith & Lovaas, 1993). In his seminal research, Lovaas provided intensive (40 hours per week), one-on-one behavioral therapy to 19 severely impaired children with autism over the course of two years. He reported that 47% of children receiving the behavioral intervention attained first-grade level academic performance and a typical level of IQ by 7 years of age. In contrast, only

2% of autistic children in a control group attained this level of intellectual proficiency. Another 42% of the children were classified as mildly retarded and assigned to special education classes. Only 11% of the children were classified as profoundly retarded. When the children in this study were 12 years old, eight of nine children who had shown the best results immediately after intervention continued to do well, being undifferentiated from same-age children with respect to intelligence and social adjustment.

Applied behavioral analysis is widely used for treating autism in the United States. Although there have been many examples where applied behavioral analysis has been effective for children with autism (Sallows & Graupner, 2005), there are other examples where the effects are negligible or even harmful, making the therapy controversial (see Dawson, 2004). Because of the controversies, many insurance companies consider applied behavioral analysis to be an "experimental procedure" and do not cover the expenses. Some states have passed laws requiring that insurance providers cover such therapy, and in 2007 the New Jersey Supreme Court ruled in favor of a father who sued to require that his insurance company pay for his son's treatment.

Although most psychologists no longer view behaviorism as a theoretical approach useful for explaining the complexities of human behavior and development, it has generated some useful techniques for dealing with serious developmental disabilities. More generally, applied behavioral analysis provides an excellent framework for assessing and treating many aspects of problem behaviors, ranging from the everyday difficulties of parents dealing with an unruly child, to the often self-destructive behaviors associated with children with severe developmental disabilities.

Nolte, "Children learn what they live," Workman Publishing Co., New York, 1998. Reprinted by permission.]

The 1960s saw the advent of the *cognitive revolution*, in which behaviorism was replaced as the major paradigm of psychology with one that viewed children (and adults) as thinking beings, with minds that could not always be directly assessed through observation. In the spirit of this new wave of theorizing, Bandura proposed that observational learning involved a set of cognitive processes, each of which changed with age, thus affecting how well children of different ages learned. Accordingly, the theory was renamed as **social cognitive theory**.

Basically, according to Bandura (1989), children learn proper (and sometimes improper) social

According to Bandura, children learn new behaviors by watching the reinforcement other children get for their actions. If they observe a child getting rewarded for aggression, for example, they will learn to behave aggressively.

positive outcomes. Bandura referred to this ability to learn from the consequences of others' actions as **vicarious reinforcement**.

However, observing and imitating others is not a reflexive, or automatic, reaction, but rather involves a set of cognitive capabilities and learning processes (see Table 2.2). In addition to vicarious reinforcement, Bandura proposed that social learning involves:

- *Symbolization*, the ability to mentally represent social behavior in words or images (for example, "Twila's smile means she likes me")
- *Forethought*, the ability to anticipate the consequences of one's actions and the actions of other people (for example, "When I smile back at Twila, she'll know I like her, too")
- *Self-regulation*, the adoption of standards of acceptable behavior for oneself (for example, "Don't hit other children")
- *Self-reflection*, the ability to analyze one's thoughts and actions (for example, "I think what I said to Jeremy yesterday may have hurt his feelings")

behavior by watching others. If they view a peer, for example, getting praise from a teacher for sharing her toys, they recognize the benefits of such actions and may be more likely to share themselves; similarly, if they see a child forcefully taking toys away from another child, they recognize that aggressive behavior can sometimes lead to

Bandura also proposed four subprocesses involved in observational learning: attentional processes, retention processes, production processes, and motivational processes. Children must first attend to a model or event, remember central features of the behavior, produce that behavior at the appropriate time, and have the motivation to display

table 2.2 Capabilities Involved in Bandura's Social Cognitive Theory and the Four Subprocesses of Observational Learning

Key Cognitive Capabilities	
Symbolization	The ability to think about social behavior in words and images
Forethought	The ability to anticipate the consequences of our actions and the actions of others
Self-regulation	The ability to adopt standards of acceptable behavior for ourselves
Self-reflection	The ability to analyze our thoughts and actions
Vicarious reinforcement	The ability to learn new behavior and the consequences of one's actions by observing others

Subprocesses of Observational Learning	
Attentional processes	Children must attend to a model or event if they are to imitate it.
Retention processes	Children must be able to remember the modeled behavior.
Production processes	Children must have the physical ability to reproduce an observed behavior.
Motivational processes	Children must have the motivation to display an observed behavior.

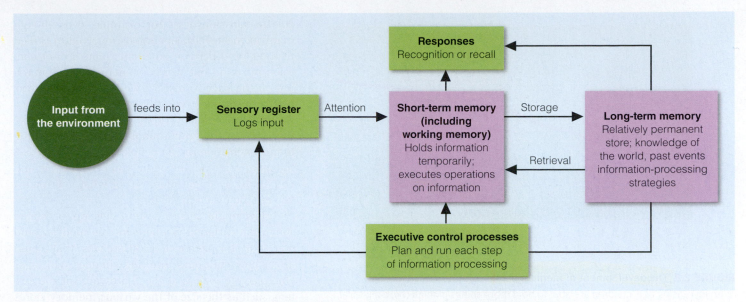

FIGURE 2.1 The flow of information through the memory system.

SOURCE: Based on Shaffer, D. R. (1996). *Developmental psychology: Childhood and adolescence* (4th ed.). Pacific Grove, CA: Brooks/Cole.

the behavior. Each of these processes changes with age and influences the likelihood of children learning something from observing a model.

In later formulations of his theory, Bandura (1989) emphasized the role of children in affecting their own development. Bandura proposed the concept of **reciprocal determinism**, which refers to children influencing how others respond to them, just as others influence them. Bandura's theory evolved over the course of more than 40 years, adapting to new findings and new views of human behavior, particularly advances made in cognitive psychology as reflected by the popularity of information-processing approaches, beginning in the 1960s.

Information-Processing Approaches to Development

Bandura borrowed many ideas from information-processing theory, which continues to be the most currently influential approach from a mechanistic perspective in developmental psychology. Information-processing approaches view children (or their minds) as developing computers, taking information in, doing something with it, and then making some response. Information is taken in through the senses and then processed (for example, compared with existing information, organized, repeated), with children eventually making some decision or response (recalling a phone number, recognizing a face). Both the hardware (for example, memory capacity, speed of processing) and the software (for example, the programs, or strategies, that the

computer/child can run) change with age. These theories are concerned with both so-called lower-level, or basic, processes, such as how many items one can keep in mind at once or how quickly one can process information (see Chapter 8), as well as higher-level processes, such as those involved in reasoning, language, or reading.

Central to such theories is the assumption that information flows through a limited-capacity system, as illustrated in Figure 2.1. *Limited capacity* refers to the fact that people can deal with only so much information at any single time. As can be seen from the figure, information flows through a series of stores, or memories. The *sensory register* logs information into the system, which is then sent to the *short-term*, or *working*, *memory*, where that information may be subject to conscious awareness. From here, information may be acted upon, or thought about (using executive control processes, or strategies), responded to (for example, coming up with the solution to a problem, such as the differences between 23 and 17), or sent to *long-term memory* for (potentially) permanent storage. Note that information from long-term memory can be sent to the short-term store, providing the person with past knowledge that may help interpret some new piece of information or solve a problem.

---

vicarious reinforcement In Bandura's social cognitive theory, learning from observing others' behaviors and their consequences, without the need to receive specific reinforcement for one's behavior.

reciprocal determinism In Bandura's theory, the belief that children have as much of an effect on their environment as their environment has on them.

FIGURE 2.2 The development of memory span.

With increasing age, children are able to hold more things in mind (here digits) at once, and this affects their ability to perform more complicated tasks. SOURCE: From Dempster, F. N. (1981). Memory span: Sources of individual and developmental differences. *Psychological Bulletin, 89,* 63–100. Copyright © 1981 by the American Psychological Association. Reprinted by permission.

An important distinction of the information-processing approach concerns how much of one's limited capacity is needed to execute a cognitive operation. Cognitive psychologists often assume that mental operations can be placed on a continuum reflecting how effortful the process is (that is, how much of one's limited capacity an operation takes). At one extreme are *automatic processes* that require no effort, and at the other extreme are *effortful processes* that require substantial effort. Truly automatic processes are hypothesized (1) not to interfere with the execution of other processes; (2) not to improve with practice; (3) not to be influenced by individual differences in intelligence, motivation, and education; and (4) to occur without intention and without conscious awareness (Hasher & Zacks, 1979). For instance, even though you have not been keeping track of how many points you won from the left versus the right side of the tennis court, if you were asked to tell on which side you won more points, you would likely be right. People are able to keep track of the relative *frequency of occurrence* of events with surprising accuracy, even though they have little or no explicit recollection of the events and they are performing other cognitive tasks (like deciding where your opponent is going to hit the ball) in the meantime.

In comparison, effortful processes are hypothesized to (1) interfere with the execution of other effortful processes; (2) improve with practice; (3) be influenced by individual differences in intelligence, motivation, and education; and (4) be available to consciousness. For example, even though many of the specific operations involved in skilled reading have become automatic (you do not consciously sound out words or analyze every marking on the page to discern what letter it denotes), getting meaning from print is an effortful process. Reading rate will slow down if you try to do something else at the same time (for example, listening to a conversation of the people next to you). Also, the more you read, the better you become at it, and you are likely to get more out of what you read if you are interested in the topic.

How might such a system develop, or, stated somewhat differently, where in this model would you look for age-related differences that could affect how children's thinking changes with age? One place to look is at the "hardware" of the system, such as the size of the various memory stores (for example, how much information can be held in the short-term store), or, relatedly, at the speed with which information can be moved through the system (that is, how fast can children process, or think about, information). Keeping with our computer metaphor, another place to look for developmental differences is in the "software" children use—the strategies, or programs, they use to think about information.

Take, for example, the case of *digit span*—the number of randomly presented digits people can recall in exact order. Digit span is an indication of how many things someone can hold in consciousness at any one time, which, from an information-processing perspective, should influence one's ability to solve problems. Not surprisingly, digit span increases with age. Figure 2.2 presents the average digit span for people ranging in age from 2 to adulthood (Dempster, 1981). As you can see, the average digit span of 2-year-old children is just a little more than two items, with this value increasing steadily to about seven items in adulthood. Many studies have been conducted examining the relationship between measures of memory capacity such as the digit span and other cognitive abilities, and the connection is often quite substantial (Fry & Hale, 2000; Miller & Vernon, 1996; see Chapter 8).

Although they are both mechanistic approaches, information-processing theories are, in some ways, the antithesis, or opposite, of learning theories. The mind-as-a-computer metaphor is the backbone of most theories of cognition and cognitive development, investigating topics that were off-limits to learning theories. Information-processing perspectives have been extremely influential in developmental psychology, and we will examine these approaches in more detail in later chapters.

Organismic Theories

As we mentioned earlier, the major difference between mechanistic and organismic theories is that the former see people as composed of parts (behaviors) that can be broken down into more basic parts, whereas the latter take a more biologic and holistic view of development, seeing people as whole beings who cannot be understood by decomposing them into their constituent parts. Among classic organismic theories in developmental psychology, two of the most influential have been Jean Piaget's theory of cognitive development and Sigmund Freud's psychoanalytic theory. Although Piaget's theory has been eclipsed by more contemporary views of cognitive development, his ideas continue to be influential and to serve as the basis for much contemporary research in child and adolescent development. Freud's psychosexual ideas about development, in contrast, are generally out of favor among today's developmental theorists. However, his influence continues to be felt, especially in research and theorizing about infant-mother attachment (see Chapter 12) and sexuality (Chapter 15). The theorizing of other psychoanalytic thinkers, particularly Erik Erikson, is still followed by many modern developmental psychologists.

Piaget's Theory of Cognitive Development

We think it is fair to say that Jean Piaget (1896–1980) has had the greatest lasting impact on developmental psychology of any theorist, and the specifics of his theory and findings will be discussed in several chapters of this book, most notably in Chapter 6. According to Piaget, children pass through four stages of intellectual development (see Table 2.3 and Concept Review 2.1), the final stage reflecting mature, adult thinking. Piaget was a classic stage theorist, believing that each stage represented a qualitatively different way of thinking and that changes from one stage to the next were relatively abrupt and discontinuous. (See our discussion of the issue of the continuity/discontinuity nature of development in Chapter 1.) Each stage of development reflects a different level of the inner construction of a child's world. Moreover, Piaget described children's thinking as being relatively *homogeneous*, or consistent, at any one time. That is, a 4-year-old thinks like a 4-year-old in everything she says or does. Her thinking is characteristic of her stage of development. According to Piaget, children are consistent in how they interpret the world from one time and context to another. As children's thinking changes from one stage to another, the change is relatively abrupt

table 2.3 Characteristics of Major Periods in Piaget's Theory

Period and Approximate Age Range	Major Characteristics
Sensorimotor: birth to 2 years	Intelligence is limited to the infant's own actions on the environment. Cognition progresses from the exercise of reflexes (for example, sucking, visual orienting) to the beginning of symbolic functioning.
Preoperations: 2 to 7 years	Intelligence is symbolic, expressed via language, imagery, and other modes, permitting children to mentally represent and compare objects out of immediate perception. Thought is intuitive rather than logical and is egocentric, in that children have a difficult time taking the perspective of another.
Concrete operations: 7 to 11 years	Intelligence is symbolic and logical (for example, if A is greater than B and B is greater than C, then A must be greater than C). Thought is less egocentric. Children's *logical* thinking is applied to concrete objects and events (that is, thinking is not abstract).
Formal operations: 11 to 16 years	Children are able to make and test hypotheses; possibility dominates reality. Children are able to introspect about their own thought processes and, generally, can think abstractly.

SOURCE: From Bjorklund, D. F. (2005). *Children's thinking: Cognitive development and individual differences,* 4th ed., p. 85. Copyright © 2005 Wadsworth, a part of Cengage Learning, Inc. Reproduced by permission. www.cengage.com/permissions.

and influences the whole child, not just a portion of his or her thinking.

According to Piaget, intelligence is initially practical ("I see and touch it, therefore it is") during the **sensorimotor period** (0–2 years); it becomes symbolic and intuitive ("I can think with my head, without my hands, but logic escapes me and appearance *is* reality") during the **preoperational period** (2–7 years); thinking becomes logical, although restricted to concrete entities ("I can do it without hands and with logic, but my logic fails a bit if problems are not touchable") during the **concrete operational period** (7–11 years); and eventually thinking becomes logical and abstract ("I can

sensorimotor period In Piaget's theory, the first major stage of cognitive development (birth to approximately 2 years), in which children understand their world through sensory and motor experiences.

preoperational period In Piaget's theory, the second major stage of cognitive development (approximately ages 2 to 7), characterized by prelogical, intuitive thought.

concrete operational period The third major stage of cognitive development in Piaget's theory, in which children can decenter their perception, are less egocentric, and can think logically about concrete objects.

FIGURE 2.3 Piaget's conservation-of-liquid task.

SOURCE: From Bjorklund, D. F. (2005). *Children's thinking: Cognitive development and individual differences*, 4th ed., Fig. 4.2, p. 94. Copyright © 2005 Wadsworth, a part of Cengage Learning, Inc. Reproduced by permission. www.cengage.com/permissions.

Is there the same amount of water in the two glasses, or does one have more?

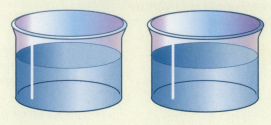

Water is poured from one of the original glasses to a taller, thinner glass.

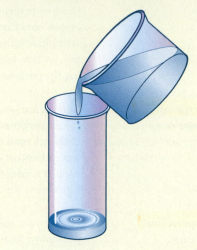

Is there the same amount of water in the two glasses now, or does one have more? Why?

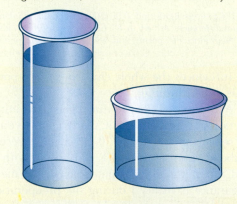

think and solve problems proficiently without the need of concrete stuff, and I can even imagine many other possibilities") during the **formal operational period** (11–16 years).

Let us provide one classic example of Piagetian research. Among other things, Piaget was concerned with how children come to understand their physical world. How do children develop an intuitive understanding of physics? One basic concept of intuitive physics is what Piaget referred to as *con-*

formal operational period In Piaget's theory, the final stage of cognitive development, in which children are able to apply abstract logical rules.

servation—knowledge that a substance remains the same despite some changes to the appearance of the substance. Any substance that can be quantified can be conserved—number, mass, space, matter, liquid. Consider the conservation-of-liquid task, illustrated in Figure 2.3. A child is shown two identical glasses with equal amounts of water in them. Once the child agrees that the two glasses contain the same amount of water, the water in one glass is poured into a taller, thinner glass, all while the child watches. The child is then asked if the amount of water is still the same in the two glasses or if one glass has more.

Most school-age children answer correctly that the amount is the same and explain that it's the same water that was in the original glass, that the greater height of the water in the taller glass is compensated by the greater width in the shorter glass, and that you could prove the amount is the same by pouring the water back into the original glass. In contrast, most preschool children insist there is now more water in the taller glass. When asked why this is so, they will point to the difference in height, ignoring the fact that the taller glass is also thinner. For Piaget, this reflects qualitative differences in thinking about the physical world. Children are not taught to conserve, but they come to have different mental representations of the world as a result of maturation and active interaction with the environment. We will discuss conservation and other aspects of children's thinking in Chapter 6.

Freud and Erikson's Psychoanalytic Theories of Development

Whereas Piaget dealt with children's thinking, Freud (1856–1939) focused on children's feelings and personalities. Freud's five stages of psychosexual development are likely well known to most readers: oral, anal, phallic, latency, and genital. Freud (1938) proposed that the sex drive is a primary instinct, expressed at all stages of life. The main source of pleasure satisfaction, or tension reduction, is centered on specific bodily zones, called *erogenous zones.* (We should note that Freud used the word "sexuality" in a broader sense than laypeople do, often as a synonym for "looking for pleasure.") These zones change throughout the course of development, with erogenous centers shifting from the oral to the anal area over the course of early childhood, and then eventually to the genitals. According to Freud, how parents deal with their children's sexual impulses has significant consequences for their later development. Aspects of Freud's theory are discussed in several chapters of this book, notably Chapter 15 on sexual development.

Erik Erikson (1902–1994) adopted many of the ideas of his mentor, Freud, including stages of psychosexual development, the three-part structure of the mind (id, ego, and superego), and the importance of the unconscious. However, Erikson (1950, 1968) also recognized a shortcoming in Freud's theory, namely the absence of a progression of *psychosocial development*, which he believed paralleled psychosexual development. Erikson also acknowledged the role that society plays in shaping a child's personality and behavior. As children gain in competence, society makes new demands on them. How children respond to those demands affects their current thinking and later development. Moreover, Erikson believed that important developmental milestones extended past childhood and adolescence, so he postulated stages of development covering the entire life span.

Erikson postulated eight stages of psychosocial development. During these stages, children face conflicts, or *crises*, in their relationship with the outside world. The first five stages correspond roughly with Freud's psychosexual stages, with the final three stages describing development over the adult years. Erikson described the crisis at each stage in terms of a continuum, with positive and negative outcomes. Although Erikson believed that inborn laws of development guided these stages, and thus these conflicts, how a child handled a conflict at one stage would influence how he or she would deal with crises at later stages. Whereas Freud's emphasis was on people's control of unpleasant tensions, Erikson was primarily concerned with how people develop a sense of *identity*. For Erikson, identity referred to an understanding and acceptance of one's self and one's society. Erikson's theory deals with people coming to understand who they are. The answer one gets to the question "Who am I?" is a function of which stage of psychosocial development one is in and how one resolved the conflicts that each stage presented. We will discuss Erikson's ideas with respect to identity in Chapter 8.

One thing that Piaget, Freud, and Erikson had in common was the belief that development progresses in stages—that there are qualitative differences in children's thinking, feeling, or personality over time. We briefly contrast the stage progression of the three major organismic theorists in the accompanying Concept Review.

Contemporary Approaches to Development

Developmental psychology has many theories, designed to describe and explain a host of relatively specific phenomena, from how babies learn to recognize faces and the factors that account for the attachment between infants and their mothers, to risk-taking in adolescence and the relationship between self-esteem and academic achievement. Such theories can help us get a better understanding of infants, children, adolescents, and their development and give us insight into how we can best foster development. We discuss many of these theories throughout this book. The theories discussed in this section, however, are broader in their reach. In fact, it may be more appropriate to call them "meta-theories," for they are actually broad, overarching ways of viewing development. More specific theories are then formulated within these larger frameworks.

We start with developmental contextual theories, introduced briefly in Chapter 1, which is, in our opinion, the central meta-theory of developmental psychology. We then examine several theories that emphasize sociocultural perspectives (Vygotsky's and Bronfenbrenner's), and conclude by examining evolutionary developmental psychology. As mentioned in Chapter 1, these three perspectives (developmental contextual, sociocultural, and evolutionary theories) do not reflect alternative approaches to development, but compatible perspectives that need to be integrated to obtain a more complete view of human development.

Developmental Contextual Approaches: Development as a Dynamic System

As stated in Chapter 1, modern theories argue that development should be viewed as the continuous and bidirectional relationship between an active organism and a changing environment. From this viewpoint, one cannot ask how much of any trait (for example, intelligence or personality) is the result of genetics and how much is the result of environment. Rather, we must look at *how* biologic and environmental factors interact over time to produce any particular outcome if we truly want to understand development. We classify such theories as **developmental contextual approaches.** Terms such as *dialectical, transactional, relational, contextual,* and *dynamic interactional* have been used to describe these theories (Lerner, 2006; Riegel, 1976; Sameroff, 2009). Developmental systems theory, discussed in Chapter 1, is an example of a developmental contextual approach. From these perspectives, all parts of the organism (such as genes, cells, tissues, and organs), as well as the whole organism, interact dynamically with "the contexts within which the organism is embedded" (Lerner, 1991,

....

developmental contextual approaches Perspective that views development as the result of bidirectional interaction between all levels of biological and experiential variables.

Contrast of the stages in Freud's, Erikson's, and Piaget's theories with approximate ages

Freud's Psychosexual Stages	Erikson's Psychosocial Stages	Piaget's Cognitive Stages
Infancy		
Oral Stage (birth to 1 year)	*Basic Trust vs. Mistrust* (birth to 1 year)	*Sensorimotor Period* (birth to 2 years)
Anal Stage (1 to 3 years)	*Autonomy vs. Shame & Doubt* (1 to 3 years)	
Early Childhood		
Phallic Stage (3 to 6 years)	*Initiative vs. Guilt* (3 to 6 years)	*Preoperational Period* (2 to 7 years)
Middle Childhood		
Latency Stage (6 years to puberty)	*Industry vs. Inferiority* (6 years to puberty)	*Concrete Operational Period* (7 to 11 years)
Adolescence		
Genital Stage (adolescence and adulthood)	*Identity vs. Identity Confusion* (12 to 18 years)	*Formal Operational Period* (11 to 16 years)
Young Adulthood		
	Intimacy vs. Isolation	
Middle Adulthood		
	Generativity vs. Stagnation	
Late Adulthood		
	Integrity vs. Despair	

p. 27). This requires always treating the organism-context as a unit, or a **dynamic system**, and realizing that there are multiple interacting levels of context.

A dynamic system is defined as a set of elements that undergoes change over time as a result of interactions among the elements within the system. Those elements can be molecules, neu-rons, attitudes, or even groups within a society (Lewis, 2000; Thelen & Smith, 2006). The system is dynamic because it is constantly changing. Changes in one part of the system—a child's brain, the length of a child's legs, or some aspect of the physical environment—disrupts the current child–environment relationship, causing the child to reorganize his or her behavior so the various parts fit together again, this time in a more sophisticated or effective manner. From this perspective, new patterns of behavior are not dictated simply

dynamic sytstem A set of elements that undergoes change over time as a result of inter-actions among the elements. Dynamic systems theories propose that developmental dif-ferences emerge as a result of the self-organization of lower-level elements.

by genes or by environment but *emerge* as a result of changes in the system.

Dynamic systems are perhaps most easily demonstrated with examples from motor development. Consider the loss of a neonatal reflex—the stepping reflex. When newborn infants are held upright so that their legs touch a surface, they make stepping motions. This reflex typically disappears around 2 months of age. The conventional interpretation was that the brain has matured, with the area controlling this reflex being inhibited by higher-cortical areas.

As it turns out, the explanation is not that simple. Early research questioning this interpretation showed that when 2-month-old infants were given practice exercising their stepping reflex, the age at which the reflex faded was delayed (Zelazo, Zelazo, & Kolb, 1972). But these results did not provide an explanation for the typical pattern of the disappearing reflex (Thelen, 1995). Esther Thelen and her colleagues provided an explanation, demonstrating that an important factor influencing whether babies show the stepping reflex is the weight of their legs. Babies will continue to step if their legs and hips are submerged in water (Thelen & Fisher, 1982). Why? Because infants' bodies are buoyant in water, effectively making them weightless. The extra weight of the legs in an air environment inhibits the reflex, not just some factor of brain maturation.

This interpretation was further supported in a study in which the stepping reflex disappeared at an earlier-than-usual age when researchers placed weights on the legs of young infants (Thelen, Fisher, & Ridley-Johnson, 1984). It is not that maturation does not play a role in the disappearance of the stepping reflex, but rather that the developmental pattern is a result of the dynamic interaction between maturation, the increasing weight of an infant's body, and gravity. Modifying the effects of gravity on an infant's body (increasing its effects by putting weights on babies' legs, or decreasing its effects by submerging infants in water) affects whether and when the stepping reflex will be observed. Other aspects of motor development are discussed from a dynamic systems perspective in Chapter 4.

In the remainder of this chapter, we discuss three theoretical approaches, each of which takes an explicitly contextual (and dynamic) perspective of development: Vygotsky's sociocultural theory, Bronfenbrenner's ecological systems theory, and evolutionary developmental psychology. Although at first blush, these approaches may seem to be at odds with one another, they share much in common in addition to a developmental contextualist perspective. All emphasize the importance of the social environment in development. This may be self-evident for sociocultural and ecological sys-

tems theory, but it is also true for evolutionary developmental psychology. Moreover, although Vygotsky and Bronfenbrenner did not write much about evolution, it is not contradictory to their viewpoints, and other scientists working within these traditions have incorporated evolutionary perspectives into their theories (Gauvain, 2001, 2009, 2011). Before discussing these theories, however, we say a few words about culture and development.

Culture and Development

The traditional dichotomy of the nature-nurture debate (see Chapter 1) pitted culture *against* biology: How much of a child's development is governed by biology versus how much is shaped by culture? Modern theorists view the relationship between biology and culture very differently. Culture is seen as being as much a part of human nature as is upright walking. Our species' cognitive and physical abilities—evolved to deal with recurrent problems in ancestral environments—influenced how we made a living, which created culture. The effects of culture, in turn, influenced our behavior that served as pressures for natural selection and subsequent biological evolution (Cole, 2006; Rogoff, 2003). In the words of Henry Plotkin (2001, p. 93), "biology and culture relate to each other as a two-way street of causation." Or, as Michael Cole (2006, p. 659) wrote: "Culture is, quite literally, a phylogenetic property of human beings."

It may appear to be trivial to state that culture influences development. Different cultures have different values, religions, languages, family structures, and educational systems, to name a few of the more obvious differences. Children growing up in different cultures cannot help but be different from one another in many ways. But what do we mean by *culture*, and *how* is it that culture influences children? How do the people and institutions in a child's culture result in different ways of thinking and socializing?

At its simplest, culture involves the traditions, artifacts, values, tools, and beliefs that are transmitted from one generation to the next. When we define culture this way, it is not unique to humans. For example, researchers have shown that chimpanzees, orangutans, and dolphins pass on forms of grooming, foraging, and greeting from one generation to the next (Whiten et al., 1999). Human culture, however, is infinitely more complex than that of any other animal, as is the fidelity with which information is transmitted across generations. Cultures have long histories, traditions, values, institutions, and ways of thinking that differ from other cultures in the world, and these differences surely influence child development.

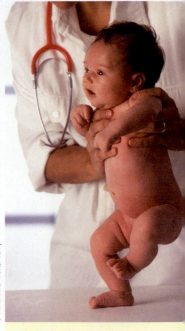

It was once thought that infants lose their stepping reflex as a result of brain maturation. In actuality, the developmental pattern of the stepping reflex is a result of the dynamic interaction between maturation, the increasing weight of an infant's body, and gravity.

table 2.4 A Chronology of Some Human Cultural Inventions

(a) Cultural Inventions prior to the 20th Century

Invention	Invented	Invention	Invented
boomerang	c. 15,000 yrs. ago	stove, gas	1826
beer	before 6000 B.C.	matches, friction	1827
wheel	about 3500 B.C.	locomotive	1829
candle	c. 3000 B.C.	motor, electric	1834
glass	c. 2500 B.C.	plow, steel	1836
ink	c. 2500 B.C.	photography	1837
alphabet	c. 1700–1500 B.C.	Morse code	1838
coins	c. 650 B.C.	stamps, postage	1840
paper	c. 105 A.D.	sewing machine	1841
money, paper	late 900s	refrigerator	1842
gunpowder	c. 10th century	dry cleaning	1855
printing press	c. 1450	steel, mass-production	1856
toothbrush	1498	tissue, toilet	1857
pocket watch	c. 1500	engine, internal-combustion	1859
pencil	1565	dynamite	1867
calendar (Gregorian)	1582	telegraph	1832–35
toilet, flush	c. 1591	typewriter	1868
microscope	c. 1600	periodic table	1871
telescope	1608	telephone, wired-line	1876
engine, steam	1698	phonograph	1877
balloon, hot-air	1783	light bulb, incandescent	1879
bifocal lens	1784	film, photographic	1884
oil lamp	1784	rayon	1884
cotton gin	1793	motorcycle	1885
metric system	1795	dishwasher	1886
vaccination	1796	contact lenses	1887
battery, electric storage	1800	automobile	1889
steamboat, successful	1807	jukebox	1889
American Sign Language	1817	tractor	1892
bicycle	1818	X-ray imaging	1895
stethoscope	1819	radio	1896
Braille system	1824	stove, electric	1896
cement, Portland	1824	aspirin	1897

(b) Cultural Inventions in the 20th and early 21st Centuries

Invention	Invented	Invention	Invented
Bakelite	1907	computer, personal	1974
condom, latex	c. 1930	DNA fingerprinting	1984
Teflon	1938	digital videodisc (DVD)	1995
microwave oven	1945	Viagra	1997
contraceptives, oral	early 1950s	iPod, MP3	1997
pacemaker, cardiac	1952	water purifier	2003
calculator, handheld	1967	camera cell phone	2003
automatic teller machine (ATM)	1968	iTunes Music Store	2003
video games	1972	Twitter	2006
genetic engineering	1973	iPhone	2007

SOURCE: Adapted from the *Britannica Encyclopedia Almanac*, 2003.

Humans have had culture as long as there have been humans on the Earth, but the complexity, and presumably the diversity, of human culture increased drastically with the advent of a sedentary lifestyle and civilization. About 40,000 years ago in Europe, Cro-Magnons, named after the region in France where their fossils were first discovered, developed new, complex stone technologies, painted grand scenes on cave walls, buried their dead, and made statues exaggerating the female form (likely fertility symbols). They, like their predecessors, lived as hunter-gatherers during the last ice age. With the end of the ice age about 10,000 years ago, they settled down, domesticated plants (wheat, barley) and animals (cattle, sheep), and began a life leading to civilization. Modern bodies and brains are nearly identical to those of our ancestors 40,000 years ago (actually, Cro-Magnons had slightly larger brains than modern people), but the way we make a living today and the conditions in which most people live would be unrecognizable to our ancestors.

Much has happened to our species since some humans settled down. Agriculture spread from the fertile crescent of Mesopotamia to modern-day Europe, Asia, Africa, and the Americas. A sedentary lifestyle based around agriculture permitted (perhaps demanded) that people specialize. Not everyone had to acquire expertise in hunting or gathering but could develop skills in support of the farmers and herders, such as making tools, clothes, or pottery, building structures, serving as defenders of the town, or as political and spiritual leaders. As people settled in different areas of the globe, technological changes occurred rapidly, driven, in part, by the availability of natural resources, including, for example, the presence of wild crops and animals that could be easily domesticated (Diamond, 1997). Ideas also surely spread, including those related to religion, forms of government, commerce, and morality. Although culture was not new to *Homo sapiens*, with specialization and a stable population, innovations could spread quickly, increasing the cultural differences among people in different parts of the world. Although we may think of humankind as going through a cultural revolution beginning with the advent of agriculture, more recent changes in public health, medicine, and societal care of the least fortunate in a community has more than doubled the life expectancy of people, representing, perhaps, a second cultural revolution for our species.

Table 2.4 lists some of the important cultural inventions and the approximate dates they were invented. The upper part of the table lists inventions prior to the 20th century, and the lower part lists inventions in the 20th and 21st centuries. As you can see, although technology has been on a constant march at least since the invention of the boomerang, the rate of technological, and thus cultural, change has been especially rapid over the last century or two, changing substantially the world in which children develop.

Two of the three contemporary approaches discussed here have as their primary focus the influence of culture on child development. We first examine the *sociocultural approach*, originally formulated by the Russian psychologist Lev Vygotsky (1978), which examines how children's cognition is shaped by social forces and how children, in interaction with more knowledgeable members of their society, learn to think. According to Vygotsky, one's culture not only shapes *what* children think about but also *how* they think. We then look at *ecological systems theory* proposed by Urie Bronfenbrenner (1979a), which examines how the many influences *within* a child's culture—from the child's unique biology to family, school, the neighborhood, and cultural institutions such as churches, law enforcement, and forms of government—interact to produce patterns of behavior and development.

Although culture is the focus of both Vygotsky's and Bronfenbrenner's theories, neither takes the

The technological tools available to a culture, or the tools of intellectual adaptation, affect how children learn to think.

Tools of intellectual adaptation	Tools a culture provides it members to guide thinking and problem solving. These tools can be physical implements such as books or computers, methods of transmitting information, such as reading or the base-10 number system, and even the characteristics of the language spoken.
The social construction of mental functioning	Children's thinking develops (or is constructed) through interactions with more competent members of their society. Adults foster children's cognitive development by working within children's *zone of proximal development* and by *scaffolding* their problem solving.
Sociohistorical influences	Historical changes in a culture influence higher psychological processes, and if these changes are sustained over many generations (reading, writing, and formal school, for example, are not about to disappear from the modern world), then cognitive development, and thus eventually how adults think, will change as well.

extreme environmentalist approach that culture causes behavior and is independent of biological factors. Each theorist recognizes that children are active participants in their own development, with unique biologies that influence how they view the world and how others perceive and respond to them. Each theory can be described as a developmental contextual theory, with an emphasis on the social environment as the primary influence on development. Bronfenbrenner makes explicit the different levels of children's social environment that affect their development, whereas Vygotsky places greater emphasis on the tools a culture provides its members and how specific interactions between children and more experienced members of their societies shape children's thinking. Both theorists acknowledged that development involves interactions between different levels of organization (brain, behavior, genes, environment) and that development has been shaped by evolutionary and sociocultural histories. We follow the discussion of these two cultural approaches with a look at evolutionary developmental psychology and see how this more biological approach similarly emphasizes the importance of the social environment in human development.

Vygotsky's Sociocultural Theory

Lev Semenovich Vygotsky (1896–1934) was a Russian psychologist who led a movement in the first half of the 20th century that later became known as **sociocultural theory**. Contrary to the behavior-ism of his day, Vygotsky thought that scientific psychology should focus primarily on those processes that are specific to humans instead of *only* those more basic processes that humans have in common with other species. He called these *higher psychological processes*, what we today identify as cognitive processes: perception, attention, memory, language, and thinking. Vygotsky's revolutionary idea was that historical changes in a culture influence higher psychological processes, and if these changes are sustained over many generations (reading, writing, and formal school, for example, are not about to disappear from the modern world), cognitive development, and thus eventually how adults think, will change as well.

Some readers may be asking themselves "Why is Vygotsky's theory being discussed as a contemporary approach to development?" After all, he died more than 75 years ago. The reason is that Vygotsky's work was originally published in Russian in the 1920s and '30s and not translated into other languages until the 1960s and '70s. Although Vygotsky's ideas were influential in the former Soviet Union throughout the 20th century, it was only relatively recently that his ideas became known in the West, where they have since substantially influenced the thinking of developmental psychologists.

Vygotsky believed that the ways in which higher psychological processes become shaped through development are social and cultural in nature. From his perspective, the environment is not simply the place where development occurs but rather *the main source* of development (Vygotsky, 1962). Yet, despite Vygotsky's belief that the environment plays a significant role in shaping development, he was not a behaviorist. On the contrary, he believed that there is always both "a natural line of development" and "a cultural line of develop-

sociocultural theory A perspective of cognitive development that emphasizes that individual development is socially mediated, and historically and culturally conditioned.

ment," whose permanent dialectical (bidirectional) interplay is ultimately responsible for children's, and later adults', cognition and behavior. To put it simply, Vygotsky believed that "we are our brain" in the sense that all of our behaviors and cognitions are based on neurological processes, but the way in which our brains eventually become organized depends critically on the social environment that surrounds us from birth through adulthood. Some of the major concepts in Vygotsky's sociocultural theory are presented in the accompanying Concept Review 2.2.

Alexander Luria (1979), one of Vygotsky's most famous followers and a pioneer of neuropsychology, described Vygotsky's views in terms of the relevance that he gave to three issues: (1) tools, (2) the social origins of individual mental functioning, and (3) the role of history and culture in the shaping of mind. In fact, Vygotsky emphasized that cognitive development cannot be understood without considering the cultural context in which a child lives, including other people, tools of intellectual adaptation, and societal values and institutions (see Figure 2.4).

Tools of Intellectual Adaptation

Regarding the first issue, Luria pointed out that for Vygotsky human action is always mediated by tools. Each culture provides its members with tools of intellectual adaptation. Some of these are technical tools, such as hammers, screwdrivers, pencils, tractors, or desktop computers. Other tools of intellectual adaptation can be thought of as psychological tools, and these may be more important than the technical tools in affecting how children learn to think. These include signs or symbolic systems such as language, methods of counting, mnemonic techniques, algebraic symbol systems, works of art, writing, diagrams, maps, and so forth (Vygotsky, 1981; Wertsch & Tulviste, 1992). These psychological tools alter the way people think, and children growing up in different cultures with different sets of psychological tools will learn to think differently. Box 2.2 presents some research illustrating how something as simple as the names a language uses for its number words can influence mathematical development.

The Social Construction of Mental Functioning

How do children learn to use the tools that their culture provides them? The simple answer is they learn through the assistance of other people. Vygotsky viewed cognitive development as involving the child actively trying to know the world, but also involving at least one more competent person, often a parent or teacher, who mediates between the child and the things the child is trying to know.

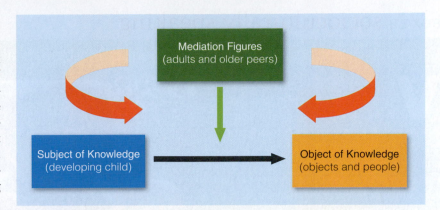

FIGURE 2.4 **The social mediated nature of cognitive development.**
According to Vygotsky, cognitive development can only be properly understood in terms of a triadic relationship, where the developing child (*Subject of Knowledge*) gets to know a world of objects and people (*Object of Knowledge*) through the mediation of adults and more competent peers (*Mediation Figures*), who know him, know the world of objects and people, and actively mediate relationships between them. For example, a child's first encounter with a frog can result in greater understanding of the animal if a parent guides the child's exploration of the new object.

For example, adults usually do not permit children to play with dangerous objects; they help children complete tasks, such as tying their shoes or putting puzzles together; they tell them some stories but not others; and they teach them the values and technological skills of their culture.

Vygotsky's ideas about the social construction of mental functioning are reflected in two of his better-known concepts: the **general genetic law of cultural development** and the **zone of proximal development**, which are closely related. According to the general genetic law of cultural development,

> Any function in the child's cultural development appears twice, or on two planes. First it appears on the social plane, and then on the psychological plane. First it appears between people as an interpsychological category, and then within the child as an intrapsychological category. This is equally true with regard to voluntary attention, logical memory, the formation of concepts, and the development of volition. (Vygotsky, 1981, p. 163)

For example, adults show children how to count on their fingers, and later children count by themselves; we prompt children to recall events that happened earlier in the day, and in the

Adults or other more competent peers help children complete complex tasks, and in the process foster cognitive development.

tools of intellectual adaptation Vygotsky's term for tools a culture provides for thinking and problem solving.

general genetic law of cultural development In Vygotsky's theory, the idea that cognition occurs on two planes: first the social, between individuals, and later the psychological, as it is internalized by the child.

zone of proximal development In Vygotsky's theory, the difference between a child's actual level of ability and the level of ability that he or she can achieve when working under the guidance of a more qualified instructor (adult or older child).

BOX 2.2 **socioculturally speaking**

Language, Numbers, and the Development of Mathematical Thinking

Vygotsky (1962) placed great emphasis on the role of language in organizing children's thinking. Just as a plow permits farmers to prepare their land for seeding, language serves to prepare children's minds for thinking. Different languages express things differently, and even subtle differences in this all-important tool of intellectual adaptation can influence cognitive development. Consider the words a culture has for representing numbers and quantities. Western number systems, for example, permit enumeration of an infinite number of entities (1 – ∞), the concept of zero, and even negative numbers. The languages of some cultures, however, have a limited way of expressing quantities (for example, having number words for "one, two, many"), and this affects how these people perform basic arithmetic operations. For example, researchers examined basic arithmetic and number abilities of adult speakers of two Amazonia languages (Pirahã and Mundurukú) that have no number words for quantities larger than five (Gordon, 2004; Pica et al., 2004). The adults performed tasks involving small quantities easily, but their performance deteriorated rapidly when

Differences in how the Chinese and English languages name the numbers from 11 to 19 affect how quickly children in the two cultures learn to count to 20.

attempting tasks with larger quantities. However, unlike their parents, Pirahã children who learn Portuguese are capable of performing arithmetic calculations with larger quantities, bolstering the interpretation that the language's ability to represent numbers is responsible for the pattern of numerical thinking in these cultures (Gordon, 2004).

Even more subtle differences in the number names that a language uses can affect children's mathematics. In all languages, the first 10 digits are arbitrary and must be learned by rote (*one, two, three*, in English;

yee, uhr, sahn in Chinese; *uno, dos, tres* in Spanish). Some languages take advantage of the base-ten counting system and name subsequent numbers accordingly. In English, we do this beginning with the number 20 (twenty-one, twenty-two, and so on). But for the numbers 11 to 19, some of the names are again arbitrary. Eleven and twelve are arbitrary. The base-ten counting system begins at 13, (three + ten = "thirteen") and continues to 19, but even here some of the numbers do not follow the basic pattern of "digit + ten." "Fourteen," "sixteen," "sev-

---

process show them how to tell a story and to remember and report on events in their lives. All of this occurs smoothly and unconsciously in the course of daily living, usually without explicit planning or self-awareness. Nevertheless, the social activities serve as the basis of a child's developing intellect and can vary greatly among cultures.

Vygotsky emphasized the importance of cooperative, or collaborative, *dialogues* between a child and a skillful tutor. During these dialogues, the tutor might demonstrate competent behavior and provide verbal instructions, which the child would eventually internalize and use to regulate his or her own behavior. For instance, consider 4-year-old Julie, working on a jigsaw puzzle with her mother's help. Julie struggles in her early attempts to put pieces together, but her mother sees this and suggests that she look for corner pieces. Julie finds several, and her mother helps her place them appropriately. Julie's mother then suggests that her daughter look for pieces with straight edges, which she does, and then suggests that Julie put the pieces

with the same color or pattern side by side. "Do any of these pieces fit together?" Julie's mother asks. Julie shrugs, but she then finds two that go together. Her mother moves other pieces close to one another, and Julie notices pieces that fit together. Julie finds more pieces that fit together, and her mother helps less, occasionally turning a piece to make the relationship between two pieces more obvious and providing praise when Julie puts pieces together.

Vygotsky proposed that these types of interactions promote cognitive development. Julie and her mother are operating in what Vygotsky called the *zone of proximal development*, defined as the difference between a child's "actual developmental level as determined by independent problem solving and the level of potential development as determined through problem solving under adult guidance or in collaboration with more capable peers" (Vygotsky, 1978, p. 86). Intelligence for Vygotsky is not something that is simply inherent in the child, but in how children are able to take advantage of the support provided by others.

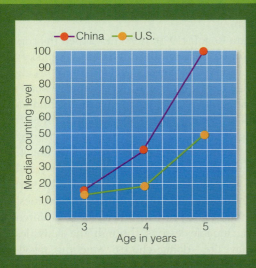

for 10 is "shi," and the numbers 11 through 19 are made by taking "shi" and adding the appropriate digit (11 = "shi yee," or "ten one"; 12 = "shi uhr," or "ten two"; 13 = "shi shan," or "ten three," and so on).

Might this difference in how a language names its numbers affect how children learn to count? Kevin Miller and his colleagues (1995) investigated this by asking Chinese and American preschool children to count as high as they could. The highest level of counting for 3-, 4-, and 5-year-old Chinese and American children is shown in the accompanying figure. As you can see, although there were no cultural differences at age 3, the Chinese children outcounted the American children at ages 4 and 5. Subsequent examination of the data indicated that the cultural difference was limited to the teen decade (that is, the numbers 11 to 19). Greater than 90% of all children in the sample, both Chinese and American, could count to 10. However, whereas 74% of the Chinese children could count to 20, only 48% of the American children could. Once children could count to 20, there were no cultural differences for counting to 100. These results demonstrate the subtle difference in how a

language names its numbers can have on the acquisition of an early cognitive ability. It is also possible that this early difference associated with a *tool of intellectual adaptation* might contribute to later differences in mathematical abilities found between Chinese and American children (see Chapter 10).

And it is not just English versus Chinese where language differences affect early mathematical competence. For instance, unlike English or Chinese, some languages invert the ones and tens decade position when stating numbers between 21 and 99. For example, in German, "27" is said "sieben-undzwanzig," literally "seven and twenty," and so on. This is in contrast to the way English and Chinese form two-digit numbers (past the teen decade, anyway), with the decade name said first ("twenty-seven"). As a result of this inversion, German-speaking children have difficulty when learning how to convert spoken numbers (for instance, "zweiundvier-zig," or "two-and-forty") to numerals, with many inverting the order of the numerals (for example, writing "24" instead of "42") (Zuber et al., 2009).

enteen," "eighteen," and "nineteen" do, but "thirteen" and "fifteen" do not and must be memorized. Moreover, rather than following the model that begins at 20 of stating the decade number first (*twenty*-one; *thirty*-two; *forty*-three), the teen decade states the digit first followed by the decade name (*six*teen, *seven*teen). It can be a bit confusing. In contrast to English, Chinese (among other languages) uses the base-ten system beginning with 11. For example, the Chinese word

According to Vygotsky, in a social world where everything depends on other people, real cognitive abilities are better described as the capability that children have in taking advantage of more competent adults or peers than as the capability of solving problems independently (see Figure 2.5a).

Related to the concept of zone of proximal development is the concept of *scaffolding* (Wood, Bruner, & Ross, 1976). In the construction industry, scaffolding refers to the temporary framework used to support people while they work on a building. In psychological parlance, scaffolding occurs when experts are sensitive to the abilities of a novice and respond contingently to the novice's responses in a learning situation so that the novice gradually increases his or her understanding of a problem. Scaffolding obviously will be most effective when done within the zone of proximal development. Scaffolding occurs not just in formal educational settings but any time a more expert person tailors his or her interactions to guide children to a level near the limits of their abilities. The

interaction of Julie and her mother described previously is an example of scaffolding.

All of the responsibility for determining the extent of adult involvement is not on the adult. Both adults and children jointly determine the degree to which children can function independently. For example, children who are less able to solve problems on their own will elicit more support from adults than will more capable children. More skilled children need less adult support, or scaffolding, to solve a problem (Plumert & Nichols-Whitehead, 1996).

According to Vygotsky, higher psychological processes, such as memory, develop from such interactive dialogues. The first step involves thinking in the social realm (*interpsychological processes*), for instance, an adult showing the different ways in which something can be remembered. Eventually, through repeated interactions, children come to internalize these experiences and are able to perform the cognitive activities on their own (*intrapsychological processes*). As this new level of competency is achieved, a new zone

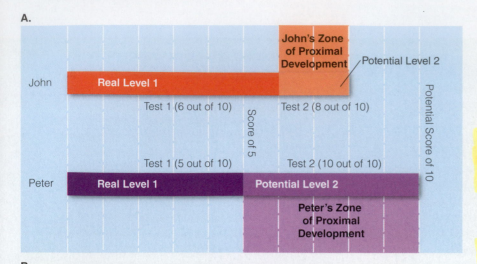

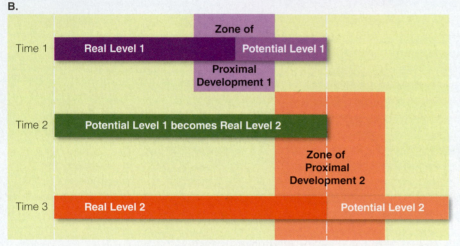

FIGURE 2.5 Zone of proximal development: An example and the typical progression.
(a) *An example*: John and Peter are both 8 years old. Their teacher gives them both an exam in math. John gets a better score (6 of 10) than Peter (5 of 10) when tested individually (left bar: "real level of development"). But after a math specialist trains John and Peter intensively for a month, Peter gets a better score (10 of 10) than John (8 of 10) (right bar: "potential level of development"). Why? Vygotsky would say that this is because Peter's zone of proximal development was broader than John's. That is, the distance between what Peter can do by himself and what he can do when supported by others is broader than John's distance. In other words, Peter is able to get more benefit from his interaction with a proficient adult than John.

(b) *The typical progression*: According to Vygotsky, development proceeds in this way: Adult interacts with a child within the child's zone of proximal development at *time 1* in order to improve child's performance (for example, pronouncing properly the word "potato"); but the child performs only part of the task well (for example, pronounces properly only the first segment, and the adult has to say the rest: **"PO**-TA-TO"). Later on, as a result of social interaction with the adult, the child will perform the whole task alone (for example, the child will also pronounce the second segment, **"PO-TA-**TO" and eventually the whole word, **"PO-TA-TO"**). Therefore, in *time 2*, the former potential level of development at *time 1* becomes the real level of development. In *time 3*, the adult and the child get involved in another more complicated developmental task (for example, pronouncing well the word "handkerchief").

guided participation The process and system of involvement of individuals with others as they communicate and engage in shared activities.

apprenticeship in thinking Routine transactions between children and adults, with novice children improving their skills and understanding through participation with more skilled partners in culturally organized activities.

of proximal development can be established, with children capable of doing more on their own than previously, with adults continuing to support children to achieve more advanced performance (see Figure 2.5b).

Barbara Rogoff (1990, 1998) developed the concept of **guided participation** to extend Vygotsky's idea of the zone of proximal development. Working within the zone of proximal development usually meant that adults were explicitly teaching children some skill or helping them solve some task. Rogoff argued, however, that much learning occurs during the more routine activities of everyday life. Rogoff defined guided participation as "the process and system of involvement of individuals with others, as they communicate and engage in shared activities" (Rogoff et al., 1993, p. 6). In other words, children can learn valuable lessons through the activities of everyday life—doing chores, watching television, playing in the backyard, casual conversations with parents—in addition to during more deliberate teaching episodes. Rogoff (1990) views some transactions between children and adults as reflecting an **apprenticeship in thinking**, with novice children improving their "skills and understanding through participation with more skilled partners in culturally organized activities" (1990, p. 39).

Consider the phenomenon of *shared memory*, for example. It is quite common in Western cultures to see mothers asking children to remember important aspects of a recent event. ("Where did we go today? What did we see? What else did we see? Did it scare you? No? Who else was there?") The older the children are, the more information they are apt to provide to their mothers' questions, eventually needing only a general prompt ("What did you do today?") to be able to tell a story of events during their day. Table 2.5 lists some of the functions of shared remembering in fostering children's memory development. Parents also frequently discuss future events with children (for example, an upcoming trip to the zoo), and when they do, particularly when they include photographs of what they may see (such as pictures of zoo animals), they later remember more about the event (Salmon et al., 2008).

There are individual differences in how mothers (and probably fathers, but they have not usually been studied) engage their children in shared remembering. For example, some mothers have been described as *elaborative*. These mothers often expand on what children have to say, adding new information, and confirming or negating a child's statement (such as "That's right," "Yes," or "No"). The children of such mothers tend to have better memories for events than children whose mothers are less elaborative (Cleveland & Reese, 2005; Fivush, Haden, & Reese, 2006; Wenner et al., 2008).

There are also some differences in how children in different cultures come to remember events and form narratives. For example, American mothers talk about the past with their 3-year-old children nearly three times as often as Korean mothers (Mullen & Yi, 1995). This is consistent with reports that American children talk about past events more than Korean children do (Han, Leichtman, & Wang, 1998) and that American adults report earlier childhood memories than do Korean adults (Mullen, 1994). This suggests that early language experience contributes to the onset of autobiographical memory, a topic discussed in Chapter 8.

Sociohistorical Influences

In addition to the tools of intellectual adaptation and the social construction of meaning, the third important issue in Vygotsky's theory has to do with the role of history and culture in the shaping of the mind. The tools and people that mediate higher psychological processes in development are not the same across cultures or during different historical periods. So, for example, writing systems differ between Western countries that use an alphabetic system and China, for example, that uses an ideographic system. Differences are even greater between literate cultures that may also have books, newspapers, and computers, and illiterate cultures where reading and writing are not practiced. The same contrast could be made between Western Europe today and 600 years ago, before the printing press, calculators, personal computers, the iPod, compulsory education, and laws limiting child labor. The difference in genes between people in hunter-gatherer societies today and contemporary Europeans is inconsequential, as are the genetic differences between Europeans of the early 21st century and those of the early 15th century. But because of differences in the tools of intellectual adaptation that different cultures at different historical times provide, and the values and institutions in these cultures, children learn to think differently.

Moreover, sociocultural influences do not reflect merely history. Rather, they represent dynamic forces at work in the here and now (Greenfield, 2009). For instance, significant changes in the economy, such as the world financial crisis beginning in 2008, an influx of immigrants to a community, or a natural disaster such as Hurricane Katrina to the people of New Orleans in 2005 can affect people and thus children's development in significant ways, influencing the structure of the local community, educational and economic opportunities, and how people interact with one another.

It is easy to think of intellectual development as something that just happens exactly the same

way for children worldwide. After all, evolution has provided humans with a unique nervous system, and the center of our flexible intelligence is the brain. Yet intelligence is also rooted in the environment, particularly in the culture. Understanding how cultural beliefs and technological tools influence cognitive development through child-rearing practices helps us better comprehend the process of development and our role as adults in fostering that process. In the chapters to follow, we will provide other examples of cultural influence on cognitive development. Keep in mind, however, that these examples are not intended to provide an *alternative* interpretation to those based on biology (neurological factors, for instance) or specific experience (for example, how mothers talk to their babies); rather, cognitive development must be seen as the result of interacting factors, with the social environment being a critical ingredient to this mix.

Vygotsky died at 38 from tuberculosis and actually focused on psychological issues for only the last 10 years of life. As a result, his theory was not as well articulated as those of other theorists such as Piaget or Freud. His work was continued in the Soviet Union and championed much later by West-

table 2.5 Some Functions of Shared Remembering in Children's Memory Development

- Children learn about memory process (for example, strategies).
- Children learn ways of remembering and communicating memories with others (for example, narrative structure).
- Children learn about themselves, which contributes to the development of the self-concept.
- Children learn about their own social and cultural history.
- Children learn values important to the family and the community (that is, what is worth remembering).
- Shared memory promotes social solidarity.

SOURCE: Gauvain, M. (2001). *The social context of cognitive development.* New York: Guilford, p. 111.

Much learning occurs during the more routine activities of everyday life, termed guided participation.

© Bob Torrez/PhotoEdit

Children in more traditional cultures, such as the Mayans of Guatemala or the Efe of Africa, see first-hand what their parents and other adults do for a living. In contrast, many children from Western cultures do not know what their parents do for a living.

ern psychologists. Vygotsky's ideas have had a significant influence not only in the area of cognitive development, but also in the field of education, with his emphasis on collaborative learning and on the relationship between language and thought (Berk, 1992, see Chapter 9). They were also the basis of the influential neuropsychological tradition of Luria. Perhaps Vygotsky's greatest contribution, however, was in showing how biology, social interactions, culture, and history interact to influence cognitive development, anticipating some of the contextualist and dynamic systems perspectives that currently dominate theorizing in developmental psychology.

Bronfenbrenner's Ecological Systems Theory

Urie Bronfenbrenner (1917–2005) believed that "we know much more about children than about the environments where they live or the processes through which those environments affect the course of development" (1979a, p. 844). Like Vygotsky, he was aware of how variable development could be depending on the culture and the historical epoch in which one grew up. This conviction caused him to be an active proponent of the Head Start Program, the most ambitious compensatory preschool education program ever run in the United States.

Bronfenbrenner first articulated **ecological systems theory** in 1979 and expanded the theory several times in subsequent decades (Bronfenbrenner, 1979a, 1979b, 1989, 2000; Bronfenbrenner & Ceci, 1994; Bronfenbrenner & Morris, 2006). He viewed development as involving "changing individuals in changing environments," meaning that development is the result of a progressive and continuous interaction between an active and changing child and the active and changing

environments in which that child is embedded. However, Bronfenbrenner emphasized that the objective environment is not as important as the subjective environment (that is, how the child perceives the environment). Therefore, in the same way that people with claustrophobia will perceive the dimensions of a train car differently than people without it, he believed that children would behave according to their subjective, or phenomenological, perception of the world. That is, Bronfenbrenner believed that "If man defines situations as real, they are real in their consequences" (Bronfenbrenner, 1979b, p. 42). For example, if an 8-year-old boy perceives children as being unfriendly and mean to him, he will behave as he typically does toward unfriendly peers, even if their actual behavior from the point of view of an objective observer is friendly.

Bronfenbrenner described children's ecological environment in terms of four basic systems, or levels: the *microsystem*, *mesosystem*, *exosystem*, and *macrosystem*, which are embedded one inside the other like a Russian doll (see Figure 2.6). He later introduced a fifth system, the *chronosystem*, which reflects the fact that the child and these systems change with time.

The **microsystem** is composed of all the different social systems in which a child is an active participant (for example, a child's family, school, and peer group). Bronfenbrenner pointed out that to understand children's microsystems, one must properly described three main features: the activities, relationships, and roles that are exhibited in the systems. *Activities* refer to what children do during a typical day. Does a 9-year-old spend time with his family after school, regularly play outside with neighborhood children, or does he come home to an empty house and watch television until a parent returns from work? *Relationships* refer to the number of people and the quality of the links that the child maintains with those people. Does a 12-year-old have positive interactions with her father, mother, and siblings, or does she have little interactions and substantial conflicts with members of her family? How does the marital relationship affect children's day-to-day functioning? For instance, 8- and 9-year-old children have disruptions in both the quantity and quality of their sleep as a result of marital conflict, which in turn can affect how they perform in school (El-Sheikh et al., 2006). *Roles* refer to the different social functions that a child assumes in the different systems (for example, in the family—daughter, granddaughter, big sister, little sister; a student; a friend; a member of a church youth group). According to Bronfenbrenner, assuming many different roles forces children to adapt their behavior to different situations, which fosters development.

ecological systems theory Bronfenbrenner's theory that views development as occurring within embedded spheres: *microsystem*, *mesosystem*, *exosystem*, and *macrosystem*, and the *chronosystem*.

microsystem In Bronfenbrenner's ecological systems theory, all of the different social systems in which a child is an active participant (for example, a child's family, school, and peer group).

A child's **mesosystem** is composed of all the possible microsystems in interaction. For instance, when we talk about an elementary school child's behavior as it relates to interactions between the family and the school, we are dealing with the mesosystem, as are interactions between family and peers, school and peers, or the more complex interactions between family, school, and peers. For example, examining the intelligence of 12-year-old children based on experiences in the family, in the school, or with peers independently, would likely produce a very different picture than when considering family-school-peer interaction effects on intelligence. Bronfenbrenner assumed that the effects on behavior of experiences in the various microsystems were not simply added together or averaged. Rather, these effects interact dynamically, making analysis at the mesosystem more complicated, but a necessary level of analysis to evaluate the real influences on a child's behavior and development.

The **exosystem** is composed of all the social systems in which children are *not* regularly part of, but which nonetheless influence their lives. These would include the extended family, neighbors, family friends, where one's parents work, and other important institutions in the local community, such as the school board and law enforcement agencies. Although children may not be actively involved in these systems, these systems can have a substantial indirect effect on them. For example, a parent's work environment can impact a child. Do a child's parents work long hours? Are they happy in their jobs? Researchers have found that parents who are more satisfied with their work engage in more positive parenting behaviors (for example, display greater warmth) than parents who are unhappy in their jobs (Greenberger, O'Neil, & Nagel, 1994). The idea that there are levels of the environment that are apparently far removed from children's worlds that can yet have a powerful influence on their lives is one of the innovative proposals of Bronfenbrenner's theory.

The **macrosystem** is composed of all the values, attitudes, laws, ideology, and so forth of the culture in which children and adolescents live. This is reminiscent of Vygotsky's proposal that the broader culture has a significant impact on development. Bronfenbrenner points out that the culture one grows up in affects each of the previous three levels of the ecology. For example, cultural differences between Japan and the United States go a long way toward explaining different patterns of child and adolescent development in the two countries. Japanese parents stress academic excellence beginning very early in school more so than do American parents; personal independence is stressed to a much greater degree in the United States than it is in Japan, whereas cooperation, both among family members and peers, is emphasized

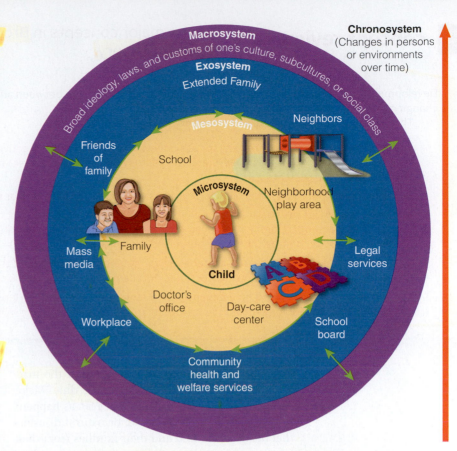

FIGURE 2.6 **Bronfenbrenner's ecological systems theory.**
Bronfenbrenner described children's ecological environment in terms of four basic systems, or levels: the microsystem, mesosystem, exosystem, and macrosystem, which are embedded one inside the other like a Russian doll. The *chronosystem* emphasizes the fact that both the child and his or her four levels of ecology change over time. SOURCE: From Shaffer and Kipp, *Developmental psychology: Childhood and adolescence*, 8th ed., Fig. 2.2, p. 64. Copyright © 2010 Wadsworth, a part of Cengage Learning, Inc. Reproduced by permission. www.cengage.com/permissions.

in Japan; and being a loyal employee and staying with a single company has been the tradition in the Japanese labor market, whereas Americans are more likely to emphasize entrepreneurship and moving up by changing jobs. As we mentioned in Chapter 1, cultural values can affect how much a society invests in children, such as money the state provides for education or health care, which in turn influences how children develop.

The **chronosystem** represents the time dimension in the theory, emphasizing the fact that both the child and his or her four levels of ecology—

---

mesosystem In Bronfenbrenner's ecological systems theory, all the possible *microsystems* in interaction.

exosystem In Bronfenbrenner's ecological systems theory, all of the social systems in which children are *not* regularly part of, but which nonetheless influence their lives.

macrosystem In Bronfenbrenner's ecological systems theory, all the values, attitudes, laws, ideology, and so forth of the culture in which children and adolescents live.

chronosystem In Bronfenbrenner's ecological systems theory, the system that reflects the fact that the child and the other systems change with time.

Development is the result of a progressive and continuous interaction between an active and changing child and the active and changing environments in which that child is embedded.

There are five interacting levels of children's ecological environment:

1. **Microsystem**: All of the different social systems in which a child is an active participant (for example, a child's family, school, and peer group). To understand the microsystem, one must describe children's activities, relationships, and roles displayed in the systems.

2. **Mesosystem**: All of the possible microsystems in dynamic interaction (for example, family, peers, and school).

3. **Exosystem**: All of the social systems which children are *not* regularly part of, but which nonetheless influence their lives, such as the extended family, neighbors, family friends, where one's parents work, and other important institutions in the local community, such as the school board and law enforcement agencies.

4. **Macrosystem**: All of the values, attitudes, laws, ideology, and so forth of the culture in which children and adolescents live. The culture one grows up in affects each of the previous three levels of the ecology.

5. **Chronosystem**: This is the time dimension in Bronfenbrenner's theory, emphasizing the fact that both the child and his or her four levels of ecology—from the various microsystems through the macrosystem—are subject to change over time.

from the various microsystems through the macrosystem—are subject to change over time. Major changes may involve societal upheaval, as happens in war-torn parts of the world, or natural disasters that displace children and their families from their usual environments and disrupts their micro- and macrosystems, as happened in the United States with Hurricane Katrina in 2005 or the Christmas tsunami that hit south Asia in 2004.

Less radical changes can be thought of as *cohort effects* (see Chapter 1), in which cultural tools and values change over relatively brief periods of time, as happened in the latter part of the 20th century in the United States and much of Europe. For instance, in the middle part of the 20th century, mothers were less likely to work outside the home, the divorce rate was lower, and young children spent less time in daycare than in the decades that followed. Add to this VCRs, DVDs, videogames, MP3 players, and the personal computer (see lists of 20th-century cultural inventions in Table 2.4 presented earlier), and the microsystems, mesosystems, and possibly even the exosystems and the macrosystem, are quite different for children today than they were for children just 50 years ago (see discussion of the postmodern view of childhood in Chapter 1, Box 1.1). The addition of a temporal dimension also adds the necessary developmental component to Bronfenbrenner's model. Children change as they grow up. They influence their immediate environments (microsystems) as much as their environments influence them, and this impact will change with age. Children become more independent and seek their own friends, activities, and niches to experience life as they grow up, which will affect how their family and friends respond to them (see Scarr, 1993, Chapter 3).

Ecological systems theory as proposed by Bronfenbrenner and his colleagues has served as a useful framework for looking at development,

Natural or man-made disasters can greatly affect the people who live through them and influence their subsequent development.

AP Photo/David J. Philip, Pool

© Sean Adair/Reuters/Corbis

recognizing that children cannot be studied out of context, but that their development must be considered within the various environments in which they live. It has much in common with Vygotsky's ideas about the role that culture plays in shaping children's behavior and minds.

Evolutionary Developmental Psychology

Lady Ashley, a pillar of 19th-century London high society, on hearing Darwin's theory that humans descended from apes, is purported to have said, "Let's hope it's not true; but if it is true, let's hope that it does not become widely known." Lady Ashley would be much disappointed today. Darwin's theory is widely known and is the only scientifically valid theory of how life originated on Earth.

Evolutionary thinking has invaded the social and behavioral sciences in the past few decades. Most of the attention has been on explaining adult behavior. How, for instance, has our evolutionary history affected our mating strategies or the way we relate to one another, including prosocial aspects of human behavior such as empathy and cooperation, but also the darker side of human actions such as homicide and war (Buss, 2005, 2009; Daly & Wilson, 1988a)?

Scientists have slowly begun to realize that an evolutionary perspective can also benefit the study of children and development. By considering the possible evolutionary influences on child development, we add a new and important dimension to developmental psychology. It provides the possible whys for patterns of behavior and causes us to look at how aspects of development or of children's behaviors may be adaptive, or were adaptive for children in ancient environments. Evolutionary thinking is also useful in that it can provide insights into the causes of some real-world problems facing children and their possible solutions. These include infant-mother attachment, child abuse, the use of aggression, the promotion of prosocial and moral behavior, teenage sexuality, incest avoidance, and education, to name just a few.

Evolutionary theory does not replace traditional or alternative theoretical accounts of development, but rather provides an overarching framework under which other more specific theoretical accounts can be applied. Moreover, evolutionary *developmental* psychology adopts an explicit developmental contextualist perspective (Bjorklund & Hernández Blasi, 2005; Bjorklund & Pellegrini, 2002), emphasizing the bidirectional relationship between children and their evolved natures and their immediate physical and social environments.

Evolution by Natural Selection

Most readers will be familiar with the basic principles of evolutionary theory, originally formulated by Charles Darwin (1809–1882) in his 1859 book *The Origin of Species*. Darwin did not invent the concept of evolution. Several earlier scholars had considered the possibility that species evolved from earlier species, but no one could come up with a good mechanism for how it happened. Darwin discovered the mechanism for how complex designs in nature come about: **natural selection**.

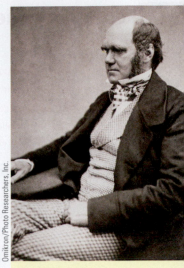

Charles Darwin discovered the concept of evolution by natural selection, which greatly influenced how scientists understood life. Darwin also believed that, eventually, his theory would be applied to psychology, writing "In the distant future . . . psychology will be based on a new foundation, that of the necessary acquirement of each mental power and capacity by gradation."

> **Natural selection in Darwin's own words** (from Introduction to *The Origin of Species*):
>
> As many more individuals of each species are born than can possibly survive; and as, consequently, there is a frequently recurring struggle for existence, it follows that any being, if it vary however slightly in any manner profitable to itself, under the complex and sometimes varying conditions of life, will have a better chance of surviving, and thus be naturally selected. From the strong principle of inheritance, any selected variety will tend to propagate its new and modified form.

The concept of natural selection is a simple one, having four core concepts:

1. More individuals are born in a generation than will survive (that is, there is overproduction of offspring, or *superfecundity*).
2. Not all members of a generation are the same—there is variation in features or traits.
3. These individual differences are inherited, passed from one generation to the next.
4. Individuals with collections of traits that fit well with the local environment are more apt to survive or have more offspring than individuals whose traits do not fit as well with the local environment. In the language of evolutionary biology, such traits are selected by the environment because they result in more or better-adapted offspring.

Let us provide an example of natural selection in action. Peter and Rosemary Grant (B. R. Grant & Grant, 1989, 1993; P. R. Grant & Grant, 2002, 2006) studied finches on the Galápagos Islands and noted a relationship between beak size, availability of resources, and survival. Beak size varies among one species of Galápagos finches (*Geospiza fortes*). Large beaks are better suited to cracking large seeds, whereas small beaks are better suited to handle small seeds. In a period of drought, there were fewer small-seed plants,

natural selection Primary mechanism for species evolution described by Darwin that, in which some members of a species are more fit than others and thus more likely to survive and reproduce.

- There is overproduction of offspring, or *superfecundity*, in each generation.
- There is *variation* in features or traits within members of a generation.
- Individual differences are inherited from one generation to the next.
- Individuals with collections of traits that fit well with the local environment are more apt to survive or have more offspring than individuals whose traits do not fit as well with the local environment.

giving the larger-beaked birds an advantage over the smaller-beaked ones. Even those small-beaked birds that survived were at a mating disadvantage to their bigger-beaked cousins, however. Small-beaked males were less healthy, weaker, and less vigorous in their courtship displays than large-beaked males, and, as a result, attracted fewer females. Over the period of the drought, the number of large-beaked birds increased and the number of small-beaked birds decreased.

Several years later, however, the climate changed, and small plants with small seeds proliferated, giving the foraging advantage to the small-beaked birds. Over several generations, the distributions changed, and small-beaked birds outnumbered the large-beaked ones. As you see here, natural selection did not favor large beaks over small ones, or vice versa. Whichever feature was best adapted to the local environment and associated with greater survival was passed on to more offspring and eventually led to changes in average beak size in a population.

Natural selection is truly a simple idea. After learning of Darwin's theory, the prominent biologist Thomas Henry Huxley is purported to have said, "How extremely stupid not to have thought of that!" This simple idea is also an elegant one. It can be applied to all aspects of life, from bacteria through humans.

Since the publication of Darwin's groundbreaking book, scientists have applied the theory of natural selection to the evolution of *behavior*. Beginning in the 1980s and 1990s, a small group of psychologists began to combine principles of evolutionary biology and cognitive psychology in an attempt to explain human behavior (Barkow, Cosmides, & Tooby, 1992; Buss, 1995; Daly & Wilson, 1988a). This was the discipline of evolutionary psychology, and we discuss briefly the central principles of this field in the next section, followed by a look at the principles of evolutionary developmental psychology.

Principles of Evolutionary Psychology

Evolutionary psychology applies the principles of modern evolutionary biology to explain human behavior. Central to evolutionary psychology is the assumption that adaptive behavior is predicated on adaptive thought, which in turn is predicated on the organization and functioning of the brain. What this means is that how an animal behaves is based on how that animal processes information. What an animals knows, what it perceives, what it can and does learn, how it interprets a particular context, how it feels, and what it expects to happen in a specific situation influences its behavior. This is true for all animals with complex nervous systems and behaviors. Cognition in this context is not limited to the thoughtful processes we humans sometimes engage in ("Should I ask Jessica out on Saturday night, or is Madison more likely to accept my invitation?"), but also involves unconscious processes of identifying other members of one's species, for example, or in remembering that eating a particular type of berry made one sick.

The core concept of evolutionary psychology is **evolved cognitive mechanisms** (Tooby & Cosmides, 1992). These are information-processing mechanisms shaped by natural selection during the **environments of evolutionary adaptedness** to deal with specific and recurrent problems faced by our ancestors, such as getting food, avoiding predators, and finding and keeping a mate. These are ancient environments, during which human nature was shaped. There is not a single environment of evolutionary adaptedness, for some aspects of our thought and actions have their roots in our vast mammalian past. But much of what makes us distinct from chimpanzees, for example, evolved in the last 5 to 7 million years, and given the dif-

evolutionary psychology The application of the principles of modern evolutionary biology to explain human behavior.

evolved cognitive mechanisms Information-processing mechanisms shaped by natural selection during the *environments of evolutionary adaptedness* to deal with specific and recurrent problems faced by our ancestors, such as getting food, avoiding predators, and finding and keeping a mate.

environment of evolutionary adaptedness Ancestral environments during which human nature was shaped.

hominids Group of animals in the line that led to *Homo sapiens*.

domain-specific mechanisms Cognitive abilities specific to one cognitive domain under control of a specific mind/brain function.

BOX 2.3 # evolution in action

A Sketch of Human Evolution

Where did humans come from? All living species can trace their ancestry back to earlier species, most of which have long gone extinct. No one kept records of what animals were around millions of years ago and which species evolved into which other species, so the task of constructing an evolutionary tree is not an easy one. What we can do is examine the fossil records and infer from the bones which species roamed the Earth when and who likely begat whom. We can also look at the relations between modern animals, particularly their DNA.

Humans are mammals, more specifically primates. We are in the same biologic group as monkeys, gorillas, and chimpanzees. In fact, we are actually *great apes*, as are chimpanzees (*Pan troglodytes*), bonobos, or pygmy chimpanzees (*Pan Paniscus*), gorillas (*Gorilla gorilla*), and orangutans (*Pongo pygmaeus*). We are closest genetically to chimpanzees and bonobos, sharing nearly 99% of our DNA with both of these species (The Chimpanzee Sequencing and Analysis Consortium, 2005).

These great apes, including *Homo sapiens*, are all fully modern species; one did not evolve from another. For example, it is often heard that humans evolved from chimpanzees. We did not (nor did chimpanzees evolve from us). Rather, based on fossil and DNA evidence, chimpanzees and humans last shared a common ancestor between 5 and 7 million years ago. At that time, there was an animal that lived in the jungles of Africa (for that is where both humans and chimpanzees originated) that diverged and gave rise to the lines that led, eventually, to both humans and chimpanzees. Based on what we can infer from the fossil evidence, that common ancestor was probably chimplike in many ways, making chimpanzees the best model we have for what our ancient ancestor may have been like.

Humans did not emerge as an identifiable species for some time after separating from the line that eventually led to chimpanzees. Rather, between 4 and 7 million years ago,

several short (3 to 4 feet tall), small-brained animals that apparently walked upright lived in Africa. They have been given such tongue-twister names as *Orrorin tugenensis*, *Sahelanthropus tchadensis*, *Ardipithecus kadabba*, and *Ardipithicus ramidus* (Balter, 2001; Galik et al., 2004). These were the links (no longer missing) between our common great-ape ancestor and the evolutionary path that would lead to humans. Which, if any, of these were our ancestor we do not know for sure, but they belong to a group of animals called **hominids** (or sometimes *hominins*) that represent species in the *Homo sapiens* line. (For descriptions of human evolution, see Olson, 2002; Tattersal, 1998; and Springer & Andrews, 2005.)

The earliest member of the *Homo* line was *Homo habilis*, first seen in the fossil record about 2.5 million years ago. *Homo habilis* had a bigger brain than earlier hominids, about 650 cc, and apparently made the first systematic stone tools, thus the name, "handy man." *Homo habilis* was replaced by *Homo erectus* and a variety of other larger-brained hominids, who made more advanced tools and apparently controlled fire. Our own kind, *Homo sapiens*, appeared in Africa as recently as 160,000 years ago, with a brain capacity of about 1300 cc (McDougall, Brown, & Fleagle, 2005). Some of these *Homo sapiens* left Africa and populated the Old World, replacing the other human populations they found there (*Homo erectus* or Neanderthals), either by outcompeting them or killing them (Johanson & Edgar, 1996; Wood, 1994). We continued to live as hunter-gatherers until about 10,000 to 12,000 years ago, when some humans formed permanent settlements, domesticated plants and animals, and began a sedentary life leading to civilization. (See our earlier discussion of *Culture and Development*.)

How did our ancestors live before they settled down? Although we cannot know for certain, we can make some educated guesses based on the lives of modern hunter-gatherers, fossil evidence, and the social organization of our close genetic relatives,

chimpanzees and bonobos (see Bjorklund & Pellegrini, 2002). First, they likely lived in small social groups ranging between 30 and 60 people, but interacted with other social groups from time to time, trading goods and spouses. Cooperation and competition were likely a part of everyday life, including warfare. Our ancestors made their living on the savannas of Africa, gathering fruits, nuts, vegetables, and tubers (most likely the work of women), scavenging food left by other predators, and hunting game, likely in small groups (most probably the work of men).

Women likely first gave birth in their late teens or early 20s and nursed their offspring for 2 to 3 years (perhaps more). Mothers were the primary caretakers of their children during the first 4 or 5 years, with help from other women in the community, most probably relatives (grandmothers, aunts, sisters). Fathers likely provided food and protection for their mates and children, but did little direct childcare (Kaplan et al., 2000). Women likely gave birth every 3 to 5 years, with the infant mortality rate being about 50%, much lower than in chimpanzee populations. Mortality rates during childhood and adolescence were likely much higher than today, with few people living past 40 years. However, there were probably always some people who lived to old age (Austad, 1997). Some men likely had multiple wives (polygamy), whereas other men had none.

We do not want to give the impression that there was only one lifestyle among ancient humans. As today, there was surely cultural variation. Yet, despite such diversity, some aspects of ancient human life were surely stable from generation to generation: a complex social organization involving cooperation and competition both between and within groups; sexual division of labor and child-rearing; dependency on tools; and a nomadic lifestyle. Such stability permitted the evolution of a common human nature that still influences our behavior today.

---

ference in brain size between early **hominids** and later members of our genetic line (see Chapter 4), it is likely that the last 2 million years (referred to as the *Pleistocene*) was an important time in shaping human nature (see Box 2.3).

Emphasis on domain-specific mechanisms. A central thesis of evolutionary psychology is that evolved cognitive mechanisms are domain-specific in nature. **Domain-specific mechanisms** are essentially just what they sound like: cognitive

- Adapted behavior is based on adaptive thought.
- What evolved are cognitive mechanisms (*evolved cognitive mechanisms*).
- These mechanisms were shaped by natural selection in the *environments of evolutionary adaptedness* to help solve recurrent problems faced by our ancestors.
- Evolved cognitive mechanisms are not available to conscious awareness (that is, they are implicit).
- Evolved cognitive mechanisms are relatively independent *domain-specific modules*.
- There is an emphasis on *adaptationist thinking*, which stresses the function of a behavior or trait.

mechanisms shaped to solve specific problems. These mechanisms are sometimes referred to as *modules*, in that they are viewed as self-contained units. John Tooby and Leda Cosmides (1992), architects of modern evolutionary psychology, liken the human mind to a Swiss Army knife, consisting of a set of specialized tools, each designed to perform a specific function. The difference is that whereas the Swiss Army knife was designed by people, the human mind was designed by natural selection. Domain-specific mechanisms are contrasted with **domain-general mechanisms**, which are cognitive abilities that can be applied across domains. A domain here refers to some content of thought or behavior, such as language, face recognition, tool use, or understanding the thought and behavior of others (theory of mind). Some of these evolved cognitive mechanisms are quite ancient and shared by all mammals, such as basic sensory abilities and fight-or-flight responses. Others evolved to deal with avoiding predators, eating the right food, forming alliances and friendships, providing help to children and other relatives, reading other people's minds (or trying to, anyway), communicating with others, and attaining and maintaining a mate, all in our species' more recent past. Note that in a social species like ours, dealing with the social environment is as important (if not more so) as dealing with the physical environment.

A functional analysis: Adaptationist thinking. Evolutionary psychology places an emphasis on *adaptationist thinking*, which stresses the function of a behavior or trait. **Adaptations** are universal and reliably developing inherited features that arose as a result of natural selection and helped solve some problem in the environment of evolutionary adaptedness. As an example of adaptationist thinking, let us look at the phenomenon of pregnancy sickness (Flaxman & Sherman, 2000; Profet, 1992). Pregnancy sickness is indeed a sickness—just ask any woman who's experienced it. It is associated with nausea, vomiting, and food aversion. It is counterintuitive, then, to think of it as an adaptation. What adaptive problem might it have solved? First, it is important to know that early in prenatal development the human fetus is especially susceptible to *teratogens*—agents that may interfere with development, resulting in birth defects or miscarriages. These may include disease, such as rubella (German measles), or some things that the mother eats or drinks. By about 8 to 12 weeks after conception, major organs are formed (although not fully developed, see Chapter 3), and external agents will have less of an impact, if any, on development. So one possible function of pregnancy sickness is preventing a pregnant woman from ingesting something that may be harmful to her fetus during a critical time in development.

Research from a variety of sources suggests that this interpretation is correct. For example, the timing of pregnancy sickness corresponds to the period in prenatal development when the fetus is most susceptible to the effects of teratogens; pregnancy sickness is universal; women develop aversions to foods that are high in toxins, and thus potentially deleterious to their developing fetus; and women who experience pregnancy sickness have a lower incidence of spontaneous abortions than women who do not (see Flaxman & Sherman, 2000 and Profet, 1992 for reviews). It is somewhat ironic, then, that the drug Thalidomide, which was given to pregnant women to reduce nausea, resulted in deformities of the limbs, with some infants born with hands growing directly from their shoulders. The drug only had this negative effect when taken early in pregnancy. (See the topic of Thalidomide in Chapter 1 when discussing the concept of sensitive period.) For now, it is sufficient to note that by taking a functional perspective, an

domain-general mechanisms General, underlying cognitive abilities that influence performance over a wide range of situations (or domains).

adaptations In evolutionary theory, universal and reliably developing inherited features that arose as a result of natural selection and helped to solve some problem in the environment of evolutionary adaptedness.

adaptive role can be discerned for a phenomenon that has obvious negative immediate effects (it's a sickness, after all).

We should emphasize that evolutionary psychologists do not believe that all aspects of modern behavior or thinking are adaptations. Some universal characteristics may be *by-products* of adaptations, such as the belly button is a by-product of having an umbilical cord—the umbilical cord is the adaptation, not the belly button. Alternately, some outcomes are just noise, random effects that may be attributed to mutations, changes in the environment, or deviations of development, such as the shape of one's belly button (Buss et al., 1998).

It is also important to point out that evolved (and adaptive) cognitive mechanisms did not evolve to deal with problems of modern life, such as driving cars, reading, programming a computer, or Internet dating. What was adaptive to our ancestors may or may not be adaptive to contemporary people. Remember, natural selection adapts individuals to current and local environments; it does not anticipate future ones. So, for example, behaviors that may have been adaptive to early humans, such as a fondness for foods that are high in fats and sugars (both signals of foods high in calories and thus energy), may be associated with high blood pressure, obesity, and diabetes in some cultures today where fast food is available on every corner. Likewise, a polar bear's heavy coat of fur evolved to adapt the animal to the frigid Arctic weather. In an age of global warming, such a coat may be maladaptive and lead to the species' extinction.

Evolutionary psychology has gained in popularity among academics and caught the attention of the general public as well (see Wilson, 2007); however, it has its critics (Buller, 2005). Some argue that an evolutionary approach justifies some less savory aspects of human behavior such as sexism, racism, and a propensity for violence. This is a misunderstanding and misuse of evolutionary theory and is addressed in Box 2.4. For us, the most significant shortcoming of evolutionary psychology is its failure to explain how genetically inherited dispositions get expressed in the behavior of adults: how does one get from genes to behavior? Although evolutionary psychologists emphasize that their approach is *not* one of genetic determinism, they have been less than successful in convincing many of their detractors of this, largely because of an absence of a developmental model. For us, evolutionary psychology makes sense only when it explains how evolved characteristics develop. Natural selection has influenced not only the evolution of adults but also of embryos, infants, children, and adolescents. And importantly, the very nature of development

Early in pregnancy, some modern women acquire aversions to foods that are high in toxins (for example, meat, coffee, alcohol).

evolved, affecting the adults we become (see discussion of the evolution of childhood in Chapter 4). Therefore, we believe that an understanding of human evolution can help us better understand human development, which in turn, is crucial for understanding contemporary adult behavior and its evolution.

Principles of Evolutionary Developmental Psychology

Evolutionary developmental psychology is an examination of human development from an evolutionary perspective. Evolutionary developmental psychology is not a single theory of development but an approach for studying and understanding development. As such, there is not a single set of principles or assumptions that everyone agrees upon. We discuss as follows what we see as the basic principles of evolutionary developmental psychology, realizing that other scientists may see things a bit differently. (For a more in-depth examination of the principles of evolutionary developmental psychology, see Bjorklund & Ellis, 2005; Bjorklund & Hernández Blasi, 2005; Bjorklund & Pellegrini, 2000, 2002; Geary & Bjorklund, 2000; Hernández Blasi & Bjorklund, 2003; Hernández Blasi, Bering, & Bjorklund, 2003; and MacDonald & Hershberger, 2005.)

evolutionary developmental psychology The application of the principles of modern evolutionary biology to explain human development.

Mark Weiss/Getty Images

John A. Rizzo/Getty Images

Spencer Jones/Getty Images

BOX 2.4 **food for thought**

Misuses of Evolutionary Ideas in Human Psychology and Development

One frequent criticism of evolutionary approaches to behavior is that they necessarily imply that if a certain pattern is "natural," it is also "normal," or justifiable in some other way. But the idea that something is good because it is natural, the so-called **naturalistic fallacy**, is precisely that, a fallacy. It is one thing to *understand* the past and the evolutionary influences on contemporary behavior, but it is quite another thing to *justify* that behavior or to propose its inevitability or social desirability. So, for example, understanding the evolutionarily based factors that contribute to patterns of child abuse, male-on-male aggression, some gender differences, or spousal abuse in no way implies that these behaviors are acceptable in contemporary society. Natural selection shaped human behavior for success in a very different environment from the one in which most members of our species now live, making many products of natural selection actually maladaptive for modern life. Furthermore, perhaps the single defining feature

of *Homo sapiens* is our flexible intelligence, meaning that we are able to adapt to a wide range of environments and are not destined to repeat the actions of our phylogenetic or sociocultural ancestors. Evolution is not destiny. But knowing that past, the social and information-processing biases we have inherited, and their development, can help us not only better understand human behavior but also, perhaps, provide insights for dealing with our baser tendencies.

Unfortunately, some evolutionary theorists in the late 19th and early 20th centuries adopted positions that promoted racism, sexism, and discrimination against minorities and socially disadvantaged groups (see Shipman, 1994). For example, *social Darwinists* assumed that the current social status quo, with them at the top, was the result of the application of natural selection to human affairs. It would be against "natural law," the social Darwinists argued, to provide assistance for the poor. They were poor for a reason (based on the notion of survival of the fittest), and providing

social services to help the poor was not in the best interest of society or the human race. Given this history, it is understandable that many people are reluctant to adopt an evolutionary perspective to explain human behavior and development.

Yet, these earlier evolutionary proposals were not simply politically incorrect, but the assumptions underlying them were scientifically unfounded or based on a misreading of the basic biological literature (see Lickliter & Berry, 1990; Morss, 1990). Given the potential implications of an evolutionary-based theory of psychological development, certainly we must be cautious not to repeat the mistakes of our scientific predecessors. But we emphasize that to understand is not to justify, and we strongly believe that conceptualizing human development from the perspective of an evolutionary approach has great potential for furthering our knowledge about development, informing us about our evolutionary past, and potentially helping to ameliorate some problem behaviors in modern societies.

Natural selection works at all stages of development, but especially during early development. Natural selection has operated as much, if not more, on the early stages of life as it has on adults. Surviving infancy and childhood is no mean feat. While the likelihood of death before adolescence in developed countries today is less than 1%, that rate is closer to 50% in traditional cultures today and for human cultures in the not-too-distant past, and was surely even higher for our hunter-gatherer ancestors (Volk & Atkinson, 2008). Thus, anything that can promote the survival of a young animal would be favored by natural selection. This can be easily seen when looking at some of the physical and behavioral characteristics of infancy. For example, infants' large heads relative to body size, large eyes, flat noses, and rounded cheeks gives babies a look that most adults find cute, prompting nurturing and likely reducing feelings of anger toward often-difficult infants (Lorenz, 1943, see Chapter 12). Infant reflexes such as sucking insure that helpless babies will be able to acquire nutrition, and their tendency to orient toward faces enhances the likeli-

hood that they will become attached to their mothers or to other attachment figures (see Chapter 12). These and many other evolved features of infancy increase the chances that they will survive their early years, moving into childhood where other evolutionarily influenced characteristics (such as affiliating with peers, see Chapter 14) will affect their behavior, their course of development, and eventually how they function as adults.

All evolved characteristics develop via continuous and bidirectional gene–environment interactions that emerge dynamically over time. Consistent with the developmental contextual approach discussed in this chapter, evolutionary developmental psychologists argue that everything develops from the continuous and bidirectional interaction of biologic and environmental factors at all levels, beginning with the genes and extending through the culture. "Environment" is defined very broadly here, and includes not only events external to the individual, such as perceptual stimulation and social interaction (*macroenvironments*), but also events internal to the individual, such as hormones, the presence of neurotransmitters, and even the firing of one neuron as it affects its neighbors and even itself (*microenvironments*).

naturalistic fallacy The erroneous idea that something is good because it is natural.

We have provided several examples of the bidirectional relationship between the child, his or her biology, and the environment in this and the previous chapter, and we will encounter other examples throughout this book. For example, Gottlieb's (1997) work discussed in Chapter 1 on the role of prehatching auditory experience on imprinting in ducks contradicted the prevalent view that such behavior was hardwired into the brain and required no experience for its expression. Similarly, in Chapter 1, we saw that babies seem specially prepared to make sense of faces, but this at first extends to monkey faces as well as to human faces. By 9 months of age, infants' experience with human faces results in their special face-processing abilities being limited to people's faces, as they now treat monkey faces as just regular stimuli (Pascalis, de Haan, & Nelson, 2002). In other words, babies' brain organization at birth interacts with their visual experiences and changes how they process faces.

Development is constrained by both genetic and environmental factors. The world that infants are born into is amazingly complex. How are infants to know what is important to attend to and what is irrelevant? Some types of learning (for example, language, social relations leading to attachment, the ability to identify and remember faces) are critical for survival. When both the genes and environments children inherit are similar to those of their ancestors, children can be said to expect certain stimulation (for instance, patterned light) and be prepared for certain experiences (for example, a lactating mother) (Bjorklund, 2003; Bjorklund, Ellis, & Rosenberg, 2007). From this perspective, one can talk of infants and children inheriting biases that increase the likelihood of their developing adaptive responses to their environment.

The biases and constraints with which infants enter the world *enable* learning. It is not that infants are born with innate knowledge, but rather they are biased to attend to and/or learn some types of information more readily than others. For example, at birth and shortly thereafter, infants show decided preferences in what they like to look at and listen to (see Chapter 5). There are some things that infants and children learn easily and other things that are very difficult for them to learn. Of course, some of these biases are the result of prenatal experiences and not just genes. For instance, babies at birth prefer the voices of women to those of men (DeCasper & Fifer, 1980) and prefer to listen to the language that their mothers speak rather than to other languages (Mehler et al., 1988); these biases are surely the result of prenatal auditory experiences (in interaction with genes, of course). We would not want to call them "innate," but see them as nearly inevitable outcomes that are constrained by the ways genes and experience interact in a species-typical way during early development.

An extended childhood is needed in which to learn the complexities of human social communities. Humans spend more times as "prereproductives" than any other mammal. Waiting so long before one reproduces is risky. The chance of death before having offspring can leave one out of the Darwinian game completely. In evolutionary biology, when there are great costs associated with a trait (here, a prolonged juvenile period), there should also be great benefits. These benefits, many believe, are in developing a large brain capable of acquiring the skills necessary to navigate the social world (Bjorklund, Cormier, & Rosenberg, 2005). Ancient children may have also used this time to acquire complicated technological skills (as children do today) associated with tool use or acquiring food (hunting and gathering) (Kaplan et al., 2000). Social sophistication cannot be acquired without substantial time and effort (it is certainly not "innate"), and our extended period of childhood, coupled with a big brain that permits social learning ability unsurpassed in the animal world (see Chapter 7), allows us to become as socially adept as we are.

The importance of the social world in human evolution and development is consistent with Vygotsky's ideas about the social construction of cognition. Children learn to think like members of their social group through both direct tutelage and the routine social interactions of daily life. Cultural practices vary so much around the world that children could not be hardwired to know how best to relate to other people. Children are biased from infancy to orient to other people and to form relationships with their mothers, other family members, and peers. These skills are critical for survival but variable. It makes sense that children's cognition should be greatly influenced by the specific cultural milieu in which they find themselves, and also, given the subtleties and complexity of social life, that they have a long time to develop their social skills.

Many aspects of childhood serve as preparations for adulthood and were selected over the course of evolution (deferred adaptations). Most people, psychologists included, believe, at least implicitly, that childhood is preparation for adulthood. That's what childhood is *for*. "The child is the father to man," as the old saying goes (and the "mother to woman" as well). **Deferred adaptations** refer to

....

deferred adaptations Aspects of childhood that serve as preparations for adulthood and were selected over the course of evolution.

Peter Cade/Getty Images

John Brown/Getty Images

Girls worldwide are more apt to show an interest in babies and childcare than are boys, something that is also seen in some nonhuman primates. This pattern suggests that such a bias may represent a deferred adaptation, preparing girls for the roles they will play (or likely would have played in traditional environments) as adults.

the idea that aspects of children's learning or social behavior have been shaped by natural selection to make such preparations easier (Hernández Blasi & Bjorklund, 2003). This is most apt to occur when environmental or social conditions remain relatively stable over time, as would likely be the case, for example, of children from hunter-gatherer groups interacting with the same set of peers both as juveniles and as adults.

Some sex differences in cognition or social behaviors are good examples of such adaptations. One sex difference that is found in early childhood is an interest in infants, with girls from cultures across the world showing more interest in nurturing babies than boys (see Maestripieri & Pelka, 2002). A similar sex difference is seen in many primates (Maestripieri & Roney, 2006). Might this childhood bias have a long-term adaptive value for girls? Females of nearly all mammal species are the primary caretakers for young offspring. This was certainly true for our hunter-gatherer foremothers and is true for most women today, even in egalitarian societies such as ours (see Chapter 12). Experience taking care of infants provides girls with the skills they will need as mothers in the years ahead, or certainly would have needed in traditional environments. The fact that this tendency is found universally and also in related species suggests that it is not a quirk of socialization but an evolved adaptation—one that has little consequence for children's current functioning, but rather prepares them for the future.

ontogenetic adaptations Behaviors that play a specific role in survival for an individual at one time only and then disappear when they are no longer needed.

Note that these sex differences are not inevitable or genetically determined. Boys and girls may begin life with different biases for certain behaviors, but experience supports, or perhaps fails to support, those biases and is responsible for adult functioning.

Some characteristics of infants and children were selected to serve an adaptive function at specific times in development and not as preparations for adulthood (ontogenetic adaptations). Many features of infancy and childhood serve to adapt children to their immediate environments and not to prepare them for a future one. These are referred to as **ontogenetic adaptations** (Bjorklund, 1997; Oppenheim, 1981). Perhaps some of the most straightforward examples of ontogenetic adaptations come from prenatal anatomy and physiology. In mammals, fetuses get their nutrition and oxygen from the placenta. Fetuses do not eat or breath in utero but are specially adapted to life in the womb. After birth, the placenta is discarded, and wholly new mechanisms kick in for getting food and oxygen. One such mechanism is the sucking reflex, which makes nursing possible but which disappears months later, after infants gain greater intentional control of their own behavior.

Once we acknowledge that some aspects of early life are adaptations for surviving the niches of infancy and childhood, it causes us to look at children's immature cognitions and behaviors a bit differently. Some features of children's immaturity may not simply be incomplete versions of adult behavior that need to be overcome as soon as possible—necessary evils on the way to maturity—but may reflect adaptations suited to the particular contexts of infancy and childhood. For instance, young infants' poor perceptual abilities might protect them from overstimulation and competition between developing senses (Turkewitz & Kenny, 1982); infants' slow information processing might prevent them from establishing intellectual habits early in life that will be detrimental later on when their life conditions are considerably different (Bjorklund & Green, 1992; Bjorklund, Periss, & Causey, 2009); and preschool children's tendencies to be overly optimistic about their physical and cognitive abilities might bolster their self-esteem and result in their persisting at tasks that children with more realistic self-evaluations would cease (Shin, Bjorklund, & Beck, 2007). Such a perspective may also have important consequences for education and remediation. Beginning formal education before children are ready, or expecting children who are developmentally delayed or who have learning deficits to master age-appropriate skills might be counterproductive, even if possible (Bjorklund, 2007a; Goodman, 1992).

Children show a high degree of plasticity, or flexibility, and the ability to adapt to different contexts. Although infants and children are constrained in how they learn and the type of information they are attentive to, this does not mean that their thinking is inflexible; in fact, human cognition and behavior is the most flexible of any species on the planet. *Homo sapiens* inhabit nearly every possible environment on Earth, and although there are many commonalities to human culture, there are also many differences. Children's learning could not be overly constrained if they have to adjust to the wide range of environments and lifestyles that they do (Geary, 2005a; 2007a).

For example, because the environments children grow up in vary, there is not a one-size-fits-all approach to finding a mate and rearing children. For instance, children growing up in homes with both parents present, economic stability, warm and supportive relationships, and relatively little stress can anticipate that such supportive and stable environments will typify their adult years. A good reproductive strategy for such children would be to reach sexual maturity late, have relatively few children, but invest heavily in each child. Based on their childhood environments, it is likely they will have the resources to invest heavily in a few "high-quality" offspring when they become parents. In contrast, children growing up in father-absent homes lacking emotional support with relatively few reliable resources and high levels of stress can anticipate similar conditions as adults. A good strategy for these children ("good" from a Darwinian perspective) would be to reach sexual maturity early, have many children, but invest relatively little in them. By having many children in a resource-poor environment, parents can increase their chance that at least one of their offspring will be successful. (Such strategies do not involve conscious decisions, of course, but reflect implicit learning/cognition, see Chapter 8.) This hypothesized pattern has been found by several researchers, at least for girls (see Ellis, 2004 for a review), and is discussed in greater detail in Chapter 4. What such patterns reflect is that children are sensitive to the conditions of their early environment and have the plasticity to adjust important aspects of their development in adaptive ways, as predicted by evolutionary theory.

As we have stressed repeatedly, although the minds, bodies, and behaviors of our forechildren may have been shaped by natural selection, this in no way means the paths of development for individual children are predetermined. Rather, natural selection has resulted in the evolution of certain biases or dispositions in children, causing them to expect some forms of stimulation (for example, language) and to be able to respond to some environments (for instance, those including a lactating mother) in adaptive ways. Evolutionary theory does not replace other more proximal accounts of development but should be viewed as an overarching perspective that can help further our understanding of infants, children, and adolescents and their journey to adulthood.

Understanding the Contexts of Development

We have tried to emphasize in this chapter the importance of viewing development within context. Taken broadly, context can refer to the physical environment of a child, beginning in the womb, the social environment, extending to culture, and sociohistorical and evolutionary contexts. This means that we must examine the whole child and look for interactions between various levels of influence, from the genetic through the cultural (Cole, 2006; Sameroff, 2009; 2010; Konner, 2010;

---

concept review | 2.6 Some basic assumptions of evolutionary developmental psychology

1. Natural selection works at all stages of development, but especially during early development.

2. All evolved characteristics develop via continuous and bidirectional gene–environment interactions that emerge dynamically over time.

3. Development is constrained by both genetic and environmental factors.

4. An extended childhood is needed in which to learn the complexities of human social communities.

5. Many aspects of childhood serve as preparations for adulthood and were selected over the course of evolution (*deferred adaptations*).

6. Some characteristics of infants and children were selected to serve an adaptive function at specific times in development and *not* as preparations for adulthood (*ontogenetic adaptations*).

7. Children show a high degree of plasticity, or flexibility, and the ability to adapt to different contexts.

To understand a behavior, such as an infant's smile, one must ask at least four different questions: (1) What is its immediate benefit? (Does it influence the feelings of others?) (2) What are the immediate causes? (Does it represent the feeling of joy or "just gas"?) (3) How does it develop within the species? (When is it first seen in development?) and (4) How did it evolve across species? (Do other species "smile"?)

JGI/Jamie Grill/Getty Images

Tinbergen's first question a bit to ask about the immediate benefit of some behavior to a child *at a particular point in development*. For example, how might an infant's smile influence the feelings and actions of his or her mother? Might smiling result in the infant being played with, spoken to, fed, or otherwise cared for?

The second question relates to the immediate causes for a behavior. These may include factors internal, or endogenous, to a child, such as patterns of neural firings or the effects of hormones, as well as factors external, or exogenous, to a child, such as diet or, especially, the social environment. Is the infant's smile the result of feeling joy, perhaps as the result of being held or smiled at, or is it merely a response to internal physiological states?

The third and fourth questions—ontogeny and phylogeny—simply reiterate the importance of understanding the development of a behavior, both in the individual and in the species. For example, when is smiling first seen in development, and how does its frequency and causation change over time? (Smiling in infants will be discussed in Chapter 11.) And when did smiling likely evolve? Is smiling something that is seen in our genetic relatives, the great apes, and thus something that our common ancestor also likely did? Does smiling have the same benefits, consequences, and follow the same developmental sequences in our ape relatives as it does in humans?

Our aim is to present a truly integrated perspective of development in this book, following Tinbergen's four questions and an explicitly developmental contextual view. Essentially, this integrative approach recognizes that human behavior is based in biology and emerges in social contexts via complex interactions between the individual and his or her environment that have evolved over geological time (see Hebb, 1974). We should always keep this big picture in mind when evaluating the merit of scientific research, or just when thinking about children.

see Figure 1.1 in Chapter 1). It is our goal to show how understanding these biological, cultural, social, cognitive, and emotional interactions can help promote the welfare of children in general and help you become a better teacher, nurse, police officer, social worker, lawyer, psychologist, physician, parent.

For scientists and students to achieve this goal, it is useful to have a road map of sorts for how such research should be done and interpreted. A good place to start is with the ethologist Nikolaas Tinbergen's "four questions." Tinbergen (1963) stated that we must ask four questions to understand the behavior of an animal: (1) What is the immediate benefit to the organism? (2) What are the immediate causes? (3) How does it develop within the species (ontogeny)? (4) How did it evolve across species (phylogeny)?

The first question about immediate benefits relates to the function of a behavior. This takes an explicitly adaptationist viewpoint, central to evolutionary theory. For our purposes, we can alter

Developmental psychologists recognize the importance of evaluating development in context, including cultural, sociohistorical, and evolutionary contexts.

A theory is a form of explanation that organizes specific facts. Scientific theories make predictions, generate research, and are modified or rejected as demanded by data. Classical theories can be divided into two broad groups: mechanistic and organismic theories. Mechanistic theories liken people to machines and emphasize learning. It is seen in learning theories, collectively known as behaviorism, based on classical and operant, or instrumental, conditioning, and in developmental psychology exemplified by applied behavior analysis. Bandura's social cognitive theory stressed that social behavior is acquired via vicarious reinforcement, and that children influence how others respond to them, just as others influence them (**reciprocal determinism**). Information-processing approaches liken the mind to a computer and emphasize the flow of information through a *limited-capacity* processing system.

Organismic theories are more biologic in nature and view the organism as a whole that cannot be broken down into its constituent parts. Piaget proposed that children progress through four stages, or periods, of development: **sensorimotor, preoperational, concrete operational**, and **formal operational.** Freud and Erickson's psychoanalytic theories similarly proposed stages of psychosexual and psychosocial development.

Culture involves the traditions, artifacts, values, tools, and beliefs that are transmitted from one generation to the next. Human nature and development can only be interpreted within human culture.

Developmental contextual approaches take seriously the interaction of genes and environment, and that development should be viewed as the continuous and bidirectional relationship between an active organism and a changing environment at multiple levels of organization (from the molecular through the cultural). **Dynamic systems** theories propose that there are multiple interacting levels of context. As such, development is viewed not as the product of learning or of innately specified information in the genes, but as the process of *emergence*.

Vygotsky's **sociocultural theory** holds that the social environment constructs a child's cognition. Each culture transmits beliefs, values, and preferred methods of thinking or problem solving—its **tools of intellectual adaptation**—to each successive generation. According to the **general genetic law of cultural development**, cognitive function occurs on two planes, first on the social, between individuals, and only later is internalized by the child. Children acquire cultural beliefs and problem-solving strategies in the context of collaborative dialogues with more skillful partners as they gradually internalize their tutor's instructions to master tasks within their **zone of proximal development** and through **guided participation** and an **apprenticeship in thinking.** This is reflected by how parents in developed societies talk and read to children.

Bronfenbrenner's **ecological systems theory** views development as occurring within four embedded spheres. The **microsystem** consists of all the social systems in which a child is an active participant (for example, the family, school, peer group); the **mesosystem** consists of all the possible microsystems in interaction; the **exosystem** consists of all the social systems in which children are not regularly part of but which nonetheless influence their lives (for example, the

extended family, neighbors, family friends); and the **macrosystem** consists of all the values, attitudes, laws, ideology, and so forth of the culture. A fifth system, the **chronosystem**, represents the time dimension in the theory.

There are four core principles to Darwin's concept of **natural selection**: (1) more offspring in a generation are produced than can survive (*superfecundity*); (2) there is *variation* among individuals; (3) this variation is inherited; and (4) individuals with characteristics that fit well with the local environment are more likely to survive or have more offspring than are less-fit individuals.

Humans last shared a common ancestor with chimpanzees between 5 and 7 million years ago. A variety of **hominid** species lived in Africa, with *Homo sapiens* emerging as a unique species about 160,000 years ago. Ancient humans likely lived in small groups as hunters and gatherers.

Evolutionary psychology integrates evolutionary biology with cognitive psychology. Its core principle is that of **evolved cognitive mechanisms**, based on the premise that adapted behavior is predicated on adaptive thought. Natural selection yields at least three products: **adaptations**, by-products, and noise. The human mind and behavior evolved to deal with recurrent problems in our **environments of evolutionary adaptedness.** Most cognitive and behavioral characteristics unique to humans likely evolved within the past 2 million years or so. Evolutionary psychology further assumes that evolved cognitive mechanisms are implicit, **domain-specific mechanisms**, in contrast to **domain-general mechanisms**. Evolutionary psychology takes an *adaptationist view*, which stresses the function of a behavior or trait.

Evolutionary developmental psychology examines human development from an evolutionary perspective. Seven basic principles of evolutionary developmental psychology were proposed: (1) natural selection works at all stages of development, but especially during early development; (2) all evolved characteristics develop via continuous and bidirectional gene–environment interactions that emerge dynamically over time; (3) development is constrained by both genetic and environmental factors; (4) an extended childhood is needed in which to learn the complexities of human social communities; (5) many aspects of childhood serve as preparations for adulthood and were selected over the course of evolution (**deferred adaptations**); (6) some characteristics of infants and children were selected to serve an adaptive function at specific times in development (**ontogenetic adaptations**); and (7) children show a high degree of plasticity, or flexibility, and the ability to adapt to different contexts.

In decades past, evolutionary theory was misapplied to social problems. The **naturalistic fallacy** is the erroneous idea that something is good because it is natural. Tinbergen's four questions are a useful guide for directing research: (1) What is the immediate benefit (internal and external) of the behavior to the organism? (2) What are the immediate causes? (3) How does it develop within the species (ontogeny)? (4) How did it evolve across species (phylogeny)?

Key Terms and Concepts

sociohistorical context (p. 46)

mechanistic theories (p. 48)

organismic theories (p. 48)

behaviorism (p. 48)

applied behavioral analysis (p. 49)

social learning/social cognitive theory (p. 49)

operant (instrumental) conditioning (p. 50)

vicarious reinforcement (p. 53)

reciprocal determinism (p. 53)

sensorimotor period (p. 55)

preoperational period (p. 55)

concrete operational period (p. 55)

formal operational period (p. 56)

developmental contextual approaches (p. 57)

dynamic system (p. 58)

sociocultural theory (p. 62)

tools of intellectual adaptation (p. 63)

general genetic law of cultural development (p. 63)

zone of proximal development (p. 63)

guided participation (p. 66)

apprenticeship in thinking (p. 66)

ecological systems theory (p. 68)

microsystem (p. 68)

mesosystem (p. 69)

exosystem (p. 69)

macrosystem (p. 69)

chronosystem (p. 69)

natural selection (p. 71)

evolutionary psychology (p. 72)

evolved cognitive mechanisms (p. 72)

environment of evolutionary adaptedness (p. 72)

hominids (p. 72)

domain-specific mechanisms (p. 72)

domain-general mechanisms (p. 74)

adaptations (p. 74)

evolutionary developmental psychology (p. 75)

naturalistic fallacy (p. 76)

deferred adaptations (p. 77)

ontogenetic adaptations (p. 78)

Ask Yourself . . .

1. What are the three main levels of analyses that, according to your textbook, are necessary for a proper understanding of human development?

2. Why are theories useful for understanding child and adolescent development?

3. What is a classical theory of development, and which are the most important ones?

4. What is the distinction between mechanistic and organismic theories of development?

5. What is a developmental context approach to human development? How does this approach relate to the nature/nurture issue discussed in Chapter 1?

6. Why is it important to consider culture to understand human development?

7. What are the main assumptions of Vygotsky's sociocultural and Bronfenbrenner's ecological systems theories of development?

8. What is meant by the naturalistic fallacy, and how does it relate to theories of development?

9. What are the basic principles of an evolutionary approach to human development?

10. What is meant by "an integrative view of development" and why it is important?

Exercises: Going Further

1. On the basis of some of the theories described in this chapter (namely, behaviorism, social learning theory, information processing, Piaget's theory, and Vygotsky's theory), what suggestions could be given to parents and teachers about how children and adolescents learn, and therefore how they should be taught/approached by adults?

2. According to stage theorists (for example, Piaget, Freud, and Erikson), what should we expect from children at about 1, 5, 8, and 14 years of age with respect to major aspects of their psychological development?

3. Think about when you were a child, and describe the number and composition of your principal microsystems. Then describe in terms of activities, relations, and roles a typical day in your life at that time, beginning when you got up in the morning until the end of the day. (You might want to use a chart like the following.) What do you think about all this now?

Day Time	Place to Stay	Activity Made	People Present	Role Assumed
8 a.m.	Home kitchen	Having breakfast	Mom and my little sister	Son
9 a.m.	School-Classroom A	Explaining about weekend	18 children and one teacher	Student

Suggested Readings

Classic Work

Vygotsky, L. S. (1978). *Mind in Society: The development of higher psychological processes.* **Cambridge, MA: Harvard University Press**. This is an edited volume of Vygotsky's essays, presenting his seminal ideas, including the zone of proximal development.

Bronfenbrenner, U. (1979). *The ecology of human development.* **Cambridge, MA: Harvard University Press**. Bronfenbrenner introduces his ecological systems theory.

Dawkins, R. (1976). *The selfish gene.* **New York: Oxford University Press**. Richard Dawkins' book provided a gene's-eye view of evolution and the concept of inclusive fitness. It, perhaps more than any other book, brought the research and theories of sociobiologists to a broader audience and spawned the field of evolutionary psychology.

Scholarly Work

Bergen, D. (2008). *Human development: Traditional and contemporary theories.* **Upper Saddle River, NJ: Prentice Hall**. This textbook presents the major historical plus contemporary theories of development in a more thorough way than we can do in a single chapter. What makes this book different from other similar textbooks is the inclusion at the end of original papers written by many of the major theorists discussed in the book, including B. F. Skinner, Sigmund Freud, Erik Erikson, Albert Bandura, Lev Vygotsky, and Urie Bronfenbrenner, among others.

Cole, M. (2006). Culture and cognitive development in phylogenetic, historical, and ontogenetic perspective. In W. Damon & R. M. Lerner (Gen. Eds.), *Handbook of Child Psychology* (6th ed.), D. Kuhn & R. S. Siegler (Vol. Eds.), Vol. 2, *Cognition, perception, and language* (pp. 636–683). **New York: Wiley**. This chapter takes into consideration both the evolutionary and sociohistorical contexts in explaining human development.

Bjorklund, D. F., & Pellegrini, A. D. (2002). *The origins of human nature: Evolutionary developmental psychology.* **Washington, DC: American Psychological Association**. This was the first book-length treatment of evolutionary developmental psychology, and it presents theory and research on a broad range of topics while introducing the discipline. For a much briefer introduction, see Geary, D. C., & Bjorklund, D. F. (2000). Evolutionary developmental psychology. *Child Development, 71,* 57–65.

Konner, M. (2010). *The evolution of childhood: Relationships emotions, mind.* **Cambridge, MA: Belknap Press**. This highly readable and ambitious book, written by an eminent anthropologist, looks at childhood from multiple perspectives, from genetics and neuroscience through cross-cultural and cross-species comparisons. Among its many conclusions: life *is* development, nothing in childhood makes sense except in the light of evolution, and both genetic determinism and environmental determinism are dead.

Reading for Personal Interest

Gauvain, M. (2001). *The social context of cognitive development.* **New York: Guilford**. This book presents an authoritative yet highly readable account of research and theory from the sociocultural perspective. The first set of chapters discusses mainly theory, whereas the second set of chapters presents sociocultural research in areas of higher mental functions, including the acquisition of knowledge, memory, problem solving, and planning.

Bjorklund, D. F. (2007). *Why youth is* not *wasted on the young: Immaturity in human development.* **Oxford: Blackwell**. This book takes an explicitly Darwinian view of childhood, arguing that humans' extended youth played an important role in evolution and continues to play a role in children's development today. It also argues against the contemporary trend of rushing children through childhood.

Gladwell, M. (2008). *Outliers: The story of success.* **New York: Little, Brown, & Company**. Popular writer Malcolm Gladwell explains how success is as much a function of a person's cultural heritage and time in history as it is of natural intelligence or hard work. Although never mentioning Vygotsky or the sociocultural approach to development, Gladwell's book provides many examples of how a child's social surroundings and cultural traditions interact with other aspects of their personalities and intellects to produce successful people, from Bill Gates to the Beatles to professional hockey players.

CourseMate

Cengage Learning's **Psychology CourseMate** for this text brings course concepts to life with interactive learning, study, and exam preparation tools, including quizzes and flashcards for this chapter's Key Terms and Concepts (see the summary list on page 82). The site also provides an **eBook** version of the text with highlighting and note taking capabilities, as well as an extensive library of observational videos that span early childhood through adolescence. Many videos are accompanied by questions that will help you think critically about and deepen your understanding of the chapter topics addressed, especially as they pertain to core concepts. Log on and learn more at **www.cengagebrain.com**.

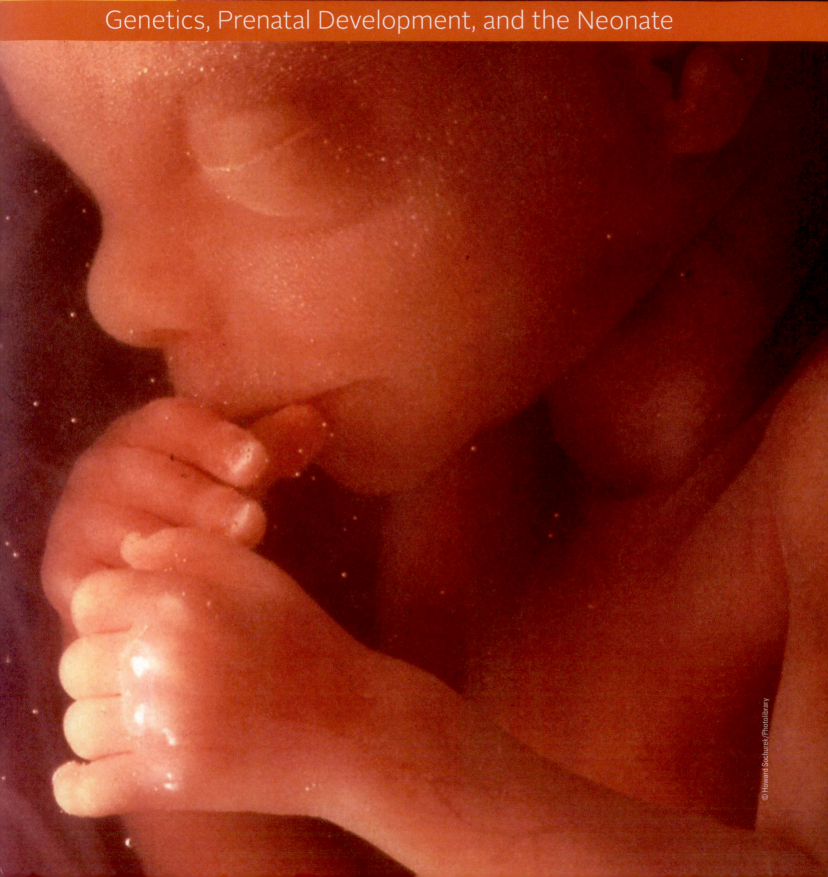

In this chapter we examine the biological foundations of development. We begin with a primer on genetics, including a look at behavioral genetics. We next examine the course of prenatal development, including factors that can influence the developing child while still in the womb. We then discuss the birth process, followed by a look at what neonates, or newborn children, actually do.

On a tour of the Galápagos Islands, we had the opportunity to visit a field of Galápagos giant turtles, some who may have been the grandchildren or great-grandchildren of the same turtles Charles Darwin saw when he visited the islands in the 1820s (they can live to be more than 100 years old). Our guide told the group that, unlike humans and other mammals, male and female Galápagos turtles are *not* genetically different. For these turtles, as well as for other reptiles including alligators and crocodiles, sex is not determined by differences in genes, but by differences in the temperature at which the eggs are incubated. We could, theoretically, have genetically identical twin turtles, one a male and one a female. The guide told us the mnemonic he uses to remember the relationship between incubation temperature and sex for Galápagos giant turtles: "Hot chicks and cool dudes."

Schafer & Hill/Getty Images

Like some other reptiles, sex determination in Galápagos giant turtles is determined by the temperature at which the eggs are incubated, not differences in genes as in mammals. A mnemonic for remembering what temperature produces which sex in these animals is "Hot chicks and cool dudes."

Since 10th-grade biology class, if not before, we have been told that being male or female is a matter of which pair of chromosomes you have and which genes are on those chromosomes. If you have two X chromosomes you are a female, and if you have an X and a Y you are a male—plain and simple. As it turns out, sex determination is not that simple. Genes are still critically important in sex determination of Galápagos turtles. At certain temperatures, genes are activated that set in motion the construction of a female body ("hot chicks"), and at another temperature, genes are activated that set in motion the construction of a male body ("cool dudes"). It still shakes our intellectual foundation a bit, however, when we think of males and females being the result of different *incubation temperatures* and not different *genes*.

Obviously, we do not mean to imply that humans are like turtles or that important psychological features of children and their development are uninfluenced by genes. In fact, genes and other biological agents are in continuous interaction with outside agents and events, requiring that the whole organism be studied in context in order to understand its behavior and development. In this example, genetically identical animals can develop into very different creatures (one a male and one a female) based on the early context (here, the temperature at which the eggs are incubated) in which they develop. As discussed later, although being a male or female in humans is associated with different sets of genes (on different chromosomes), the route from genes to a male or a female body is cluttered with context. As demonstrated throughout this chapter, context influences the development of several biological features, beginning at conception, progressing through the prenatal period, and continuing after birth.

We hope we have made clear in the first two chapters that it is not possible to truly separate biological from environmental factors in explaining development. However, differences in context notwithstanding, it is often convenient to look at some factors as *foundational* to development, and these include genetics and the mechanisms of biological inheritance, prenatal development, birth, the physical and behavioral characteristics of newborns, and aspects of physical growth. We examine the first four topics in this chapter and devote a separate chapter to physical growth (Chapter 4).

The Basics of Genetics

With the mapping of the **human genome**, first announced in 2001 (see later discussion), the popular press has been filled with reports of genes associated with specific physical (for example, obesity) or psychological (for example, intelligence) characteristics. There has developed what might be called "genomicophilia," or a love affair with all things genetic and what it can tell us about the human condition—and possibly how to cure what ails us. There is no doubt that genes play a central role in determining who we are and how we develop, but to attain a proper appreciation of that role, one must have a little knowledge of what genes are and how they work. Most critically, genes are the basic unit of biological inheritance.

The Study of Inheritance: A Little History

Although the term *gene* was not coined until 1909, humans have long been aware of heredity and have used its principles for more than 10,000 years to improve the quality of domesticated plants and animals. The early understanding of heredity was simple: "Like produces like." The seedlings of tall wheat plants will be tall, and the pups of gentle dogs will be gentle. However, this rule did not always work in the laboratory.

The key to understanding inheritance was found in the research of a Moravian monk, Gregor Mendel, who spent years growing pea plants and recording the traits that appeared in successive generations. In 1865, Mendel presented a research report to the National Science Society of Brunn, Moravia, detailing his findings. Surprisingly, few took notice of the article.

Mendel's findings were the basis for two laws. The first was the **law of segregation**, which states that for each inherited trait there are two elements of heredity. These elements segregate clearly during reproduction, so that an offspring receives either one element or another, never some blend of both. Due to this law, inherited traits are passed down in segregated, unblended form from generation to generation. Second was the **law of independent assortment**, which states that when two traits of a parent are considered (such as the height of a plant and the color of its flowers), each trait is inherited independently. In other words, inheritance of one trait does not affect inheritance of another.

Mendel's work was ignored until 1900, when it was rediscovered independently by three scientists and produced a new scientific industry. During the first half of the 20th century, geneticists worked on a variety of organisms to demonstrate the functions

human genome A description of all of a human's genetic material.

law of segregation Mendel's law stating that for each inherited trait there are two elements of heredity that segregate clearly during reproduction so that an offspring receives either one element or another, never some blend of both.

law of independent assortment Mendel's law stating that different traits are inherited independently, so that the inheritance of one trait does not affect inheritance of another.

of genes in inheritance. It was found that each cell nucleus contained a collection of rod-shaped bodies and that the number of bodies, or **chromosomes**, was constant in all cells of an individual organism. But it was not until 1953 that the chemical nature of chromosomes, and thus heredity, was revealed. American postdoctoral student James Watson and English graduate student Francis Crick proposed that each chromosome is made of long strands of the self-replicating molecule deoxyribonucleic acid, or **DNA**, and that DNA played the central role in heredity. Their model was confirmed through subsequent research, and the field of molecular genetics was born.

In a little more than half a century, scientists have examined the genetic basis of inheritance and found that it is much more complex than Mendel could ever have imagined. To truly understand modern genetics requires a Ph.D. in biochemistry or other esoteric disciplines. However, the basics of how genes work can be understood by the educated layperson, and such knowledge serves to demystify the process of genetic inheritance. Genes do not directly determine our behavior but are subject to effects of the environment. In the next section, we provide what we believe are the basics for an understanding of human genetics and how it relates to human development and behavior.

The Genetic Code and What Genes Do

DNA is made up of chains of nucleotide pairs, coiled up around itself within the chromosome, "like a mass of barbed wire" (Pierce, 1990) (see Figure 3.1). Humans have 46 chromosomes that contain 3 billion nucleotide pairs. The nucleotides of DNA come in four types: adenine, thymine, guanine, and cytosine (abbreviated A, T, G, and C, respectively).

Protein Production

Combinations of nucleotide pairs, depending on their order, code for, or determine, the production of amino acids, which in turn combine in different assortments and amounts to form the thousands of proteins that make up a living organism. Proteins are used to build the tissues of a body. A **gene** is simply a segment of DNA that codes for a particular protein. There is no set number of nucleotides that determine a gene. Some genes have only a few pairs of nucleotides, whereas others have thousands, with the average gene being made up of several hundred nucleotide pairs. It is estimated that humans have between 20,000 and 25,000 genes, far fewer than was once proposed (Pennisi, 2005). Genes, then, direct the production of proteins, which in turn affect our development,

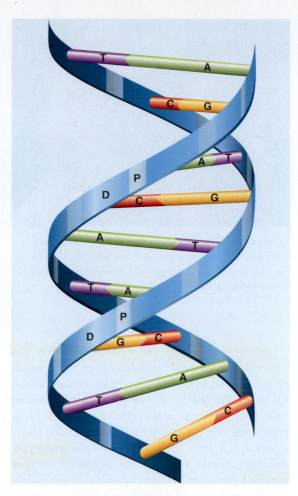

FIGURE 3.1 DNA.

The DNA (deoxyribonucleic acid) molecule consists of two long chains of nucleotides twisted into a double helix, and joined by bonds between adenine and thymine or cytosine and guanine.

(A = adenine; T = thymine; C = cytosine; G = guanine; D = deoxyribose; P = phosphate)

our health, and our behavior through normal biological pathways.

Genotypes and Phenotypes

Basically, pairs of genes determine our inherited traits, one member coming from our mother and the other from our father. (The process whereby parents produce sex cells with their particular sets of genes to pass on to their children will be discussed when we examine the "behavior" of chromosomes later in this chapter.) Most inherited human traits are determined by more than one pair of genes, but in order to simplify the explanation, we will consider hair color (red versus nonred), which may be influenced by one gene pair. The term **monogenic inheritance** is used to refer to traits that are influenced by only a single pair of genes. This is also sometimes referred to as *Mendelian inheritance*, because Mendel's original observations were for traits in pea plants that were influenced by a single pair of genes.

---

chromosomes The rod-shaped strands of DNA found in the nucleus of cells that contain genetic information.

DNA Deoxyribonucleic acid, the self-replicating molecule of which chromosomes are made.

gene The basic unit of heredity; segment of DNA that codes for a particular protein.

monogenic inheritance Traits that are influenced by only a single pair of genes.

Genes associated with red hair are recessive, so that the only way someone can have red hair (phenotype) is if he or she has two genes, one from mother and one from father (genotype).

table 3.1 Genotype versus Phenotype for Red versus Nonred Hair

Both mother and father have nonred hair (phenotype) but carry the recessive genes for red hair. They can expect three-fourths of their offspring to have nonred hair and only one-fourth (those with two recessive alleles, rr) to have red hair.

		Father	
		N	r
Mother	N	NN*	Nr*
	r	Nr*	rr

N = Dominant gene for nonred hair
r = Recessive gene of red hair
* = Nonred hair in the phenotype

Different versions of the same gene are referred to as **alleles**. For instance, in our example of red and nonred hair, there may be two alleles for hair color, one for red hair and one for nonred hair. Although each person has two genes for hair color, only one color will be expressed. The genes a person has for a trait are termed the **genotype**, and the expression of that trait is termed the **phenotype**. For example, any particular individual may have two genes for red hair color, two genes for nonred hair, or one of each, constituting his or her genotype for hair color. The phenotype may be either red or nonred hair (see Table 3.1).

It is easy to predict that individuals with the genotype of red/red (rr in Table 3.1) will have the phenotype of red hair and that individuals with the genotype of nonred/nonred (NN in the Table 3.1) will express the phenotype of nonred. But what happens when the genotype is mixed, when one allele is for red hair and one is for nonred hair? The answer is that one of the members of the genotype will be *dominant* and one will be *recessive*, and the dominant trait will be expressed in the phenotype. In the case of hair color, nonred is the dominant trait, and when an individual has the genotype of red/nonred, the nonred allele will dominate the red allele, and the phenotype will be nonred. The only way a recessive trait such as red hair can be expressed in the phenotype is if a person has two recessive genes. (An exception to this is sex-linked inheritance, discussed later in the chapter.)

One simple behavior that is governed by a single dominant gene is the ability to curl one's tongue. Try it. If you cannot curl your tongue, you have inherited two recessive genes associated with control of your tongue. If you can curl your tongue, you inherited at least one dominant gene for this ability, possibly two.

Several diseases are transmitted via monogenic inheritance, with people who have two recessive genes being afflicted by the disease. As an example, consider *Tay-Sachs disease*. Infants with Tay-Sachs disease appear normal at birth but fail to develop muscle control or intellectual ability. After the first year, they lose any developmental progress they have made, become blind and deaf, are unable to eat, and die before the age of three.

Tay-Sachs disease is transmitted genetically from parent to child by a single gene, much as the red hair trait or tongue-curling ability in the previous examples. The alleles can either be for Tay-Sachs or non-Tay-Sachs. Because the non-Tay-Sachs allele is dominant, only the genotype of two Tay-Sachs alleles will result in the Tay-Sachs phenotype. Other examples of traits that are transmitted through recessive patterns of inheritance are shown in Table 3.2.

Most debilitating inherited disorders are transmitted by recessive genes, making it unlikely that they will be passed on to the next generation in great numbers. (Although there is evidence that some advantages may be associated with possessing one recessive allele, which may keep the recessive gene in the population. See Box 3.1.) First, if neither parent or only one parent carries the gene, the child will not be afflicted. If both parents carry the recessive gene, the child has only a 25% chance of inher-

alleles Different versions of the same gene.

genotype An individual's entire genetic endowment.

phenotype The actual expression of a genetic trait.

mutations Irregularities in the DNA duplication process that result in an altered genetic message.

sickle-cell anemia A disease associated with two recessive genes that causes malformations of the red blood cells; however, carriers of a single recessive gene have heightened resistance to malaria.

iting both genes and expressing the disorder, a 25% chance of not inheriting either gene, and a 50% chance of not having the disorder but becoming a carrier (that is, inheriting only one recessive gene).

Few debilitating disorders are transmitted on dominant genes, because any individual who has the dominant gene present in his or her genotype will have the disorder and will usually not live to pass it on to the next generation. The exception to this is when the fatal disease is not expressed until later in adulthood. To illustrate this point, consider two fatal genetic diseases, each associated with the inheritance of a single dominant gene: *Huntington's disease* and *progeria.* In both cases, a person inherits two genes associated with the disease (or its absence). Progeria, which causes premature aging and an early death, is extremely rare, occurring in about 1 in every 8 million births. Huntington's disease, in contrast, causes a deterioration of the central nervous system and death in middle age and is about 500 times more frequent than progeria (Austad, 1997). The difference in frequency between these two fatal genetic diseases is that one has its fatal effects before a person has had a chance to reproduce (progeria), and the other one kicks in later in life, after a person may have had children (Huntington's disease). Natural selection weeds out the early-acting progeria gene (it is produced only via mutation) but has no effect on the late-acting Huntington's gene. (Tests are now available to determine if an individual has the Huntington's gene, and counseling is given both before and after the tests. Hopefully new techniques will lead to an intervention in the disease process.)

As we are confident most readers know, genetic abnormalities can also occur from mutations. Mutations refer to a change in the chemical structure or arrangement of a gene. As a result, the function of a gene is changed and in some cases can have negative effects on the developing individual. When those genes are in the sex cells (ova and sperm), the faulty gene can be passed along to the next generation. We just discussed the rare disease progeria, which occurs only as a result of a mutation. Mutations can be caused by random copying errors when DNA is replicating itself, or as a result of events in the environment, such as exposure to radiation or toxic chemicals.

Mutations are the principle way in which genetic changes are transmitted from parent to offspring, and thus are important in evolutionary change. If the mutant gene causes a change in individuals that is associated with a greater chance of survival or reproductive success, it will be favored by natural selection. That is, individuals who possess the mutated gene will have more offspring, and thus more copies of those genes will be in future generations than will nonmutated copies of the

© Michael Newman / PhotoEdit

The ability to curl one's tongue is governed by a single dominant gene. If you can't curl your tongue, you have inherited two recessive genes.

gene. Although mutations are the engine of evolutionary change, most are associated with negative outcomes, as reflected by our example of progeria. However, mutations must sometimes result in positive outcomes, at least in some environments. Box 3.1 discusses a genetic disease, sickle-cell anemia, which apparently arose in human history as the result of a genetic mutation of a gene that influences blood-cell shape. As you will see, the negative outcome of having two copies of this gene is balanced when a person has only a single copy. As a result, this gene, associated with a genetic disease, remains in the gene pool.

table 3.2 Some Traits Associated with Having Two Recessive Genes

Albinism: lack of skin pigmentation

Alopecia: general loss of body hair

Baldness: pattern baldness (head only) in females

Blood type: RH positive; Type O blood

Cretinism: some types caused by lack of thyroid enzymes

Cystic fibrosis: metabolism disorder of mucous-producing glands

Deafness: some types that are present at birth

Dwarfism: some types

Galactosemia: lack of enzyme to digest milk

PKU: lack of enzyme to neutralize digestion waste in blood

Sickle-cell anemia: defect in blood hemoglobin

Tay-Sachs disease: Failure to develop muscle control or intellectual ability, leading to death by age 3.

Thalassemia major: various defects in blood hemoglobin

Wilson's disease: inability to metabolize copper

BOX 3.1 evolution in action

Natural Selection's Cruel Deal: The Double-edged Sword of Sickle-cell Anemia

Genetic diseases such as Tay-Sachs lead to an early death. So do many of the other genetic diseases listed in Table 3.2. Infants who are unfortunate enough to inherit two recessive genes for Tay-Sachs do not grow up to reproduce, and it has only been in the 20th century with the help of modern medicine that children afflicted with diseases such as sickle-cell anemia or thalassemia were likely to live to adulthood. The question that many people have asked themselves is "Why haven't these death-dealing genes disappeared?" Natural selection is supposed to favor characteristics that enhance the chances of an individual surviving. Obviously, genes that lead to early death do not do much for the survival of the individual who possesses them, meaning that they do not get passed on to the next generation. Why, then, do they persist?

One possibility is that they arise anew in every generation through mutations. This is not the case, however. We know the inheritance pattern of most genetic diseases—they run in families. They rarely happen "out of the blue," as would be expected if they were the result of random mutations. Also, known mutations are relatively rare and could not account for the high frequency with which genetic diseases occur. A more likely possibility is that some survival advantage is associated with having these disease-causing genes, either for the person with the disease or, more likely, for people who are carriers of the disease. That is, having the gene for the disease may convey some benefit that offsets its harmful effects.

There is at least one genetic disease for which there is good evidence that this is so: sickle-cell anemia. Sickle-cell anemia, like Tay-Sachs, occurs only when a person has two recessive genes for the disease. The disease interferes with the transport of oxygen in the blood. The red blood cells that carry the oxygen are usually disk shaped. In sickle-cell anemia, the blood cells are distorted, shaped like a sickle, or half-moon. This is most apt to occur upon exposure to low levels of oxygen. Because of their shape, the sickled cells tend to pile up and block small blood vessels, resulting in pain and destruction of tissue (Desai & Dhanani, 2004).

Sickle-cell anemia is found primarily among people of central African or Indian descent. Among African Americans, about 1 in every 625 children is born with the sickle-cell trait. It has been estimated that nearly 10% of African Americans carry the sickle-cell gene (that is, have one recessive sickle-cell allele and one dominant normal allele) (Pierce, 1990). In some parts of Africa, the frequency of carriers is as high as 40% (Diamond, 1989). Although having two recessive sickle-cell genes means having the disease—and in the past the probability of an early death—having just one recessive gene provides some benefit. People with a single sickle-cell gene have a significant advantage over people who have no sickle gene where malaria is common. They are less likely to die of the disease, because their red blood cells are poor at supporting the growth of the malaria parasite. Carriers (people who possess one recessive gene) in these areas are thus more likely to live to reproduce than noncarriers, keeping the recessive and potentially deadly gene in the gene pool. The benefit is not to those who have the disease, but to those who are carriers.

There has been speculation that other genetic diseases may afford some advantages to carriers, keeping the recessive genes from going extinct (Diamond, 1989). For example, being a carrier for thalassemia,

People who have one recessive gene for sickle-cell anemia are more resistant to malaria than people with two genes that code for the normal cell shape. This is why sickle-cell anemia is more common in people who live (or have ancestors who lived) in areas where malaria is common, such as central Africa.

a blood disease that occurs predominantly in people of Mediterranean, African, and Asian descent, may also provide some protection against malaria. Having a single recessive gene for Tay-Sachs disease may have helped fight against tuberculosis, a leading killer centuries ago, especially in the urban ghettos where many European Jews (the main target of Tay-Sachs) were confined. The gene for cystic fibrosis, the most common recessive genetic disease among Caucasians, may protect carriers against bacterial infections that cause diarrhea, once a major childhood killer (and continues to be in parts of the underdeveloped world).

Genetic diseases, particularly those that strike children, seem cruelly unfair. Some of these diseases may reflect a grim deal evolution has made with us. The genes responsible for these calamities may have helped our ancestors or our current relatives survive, even if they resulted in the early death of others.

Mendelian genetics describes well how genes interact to produce a particular outcome. It describes how a single set of genes affects the phenotype, such as hair color and some inherited diseases. Most physical and psychological characteristics are not under the influence of a single pair of genes, however. Rather, our intelligence, personalities, and even our height and weight are influenced by many different genes (that is, **polygenic inheritance**), and, in addition, are also influenced by the environments in which they are expressed. This type of influence is the rule rather than the exception.

polygenic inheritance Inherited traits that are determined by multiple genes.

How Do Genotypes Become Phenotypes?

Geneticists have been identifying genes (or specific versions of a gene, or alleles) associated with important physical and behavioral outcomes for some time; the rate at which new genes are being identified has skyrocketed in recent decades (Plomin & Schalkwyk, 2007). When such genes are found, it is tempting to state that a gene for aggression (or anxiety, or obesity, or diabetes, etc.) has been identified. Geneticists rarely actually say this (it is more likely to be said by reporters or laypeople who hear of the discovery), because, for the most part, it is not true. Rather, genes are found that are *associated* with some specific outcome. As geneticists know quite well, specific genes get expressed in specific environments, and the simple possession of a gene does not necessarily mean that a person will have a particular trait.

There are many cases in nature in which a single genotype can produce drastically different phenotypes depending on the (usually early) environment the organism is exposed to. Sex determination in some reptiles, described earlier in this chapter, is one (Bull, 1980). Other animals develop radically different bodies depending on their early diet. For example, the moth *Nemoria arizonia* lays its eggs on oak trees. Based on its diet during the first few days after hatching, the caterpillars develop one of two forms, or morphologies. When moths lay their eggs in the spring, the caterpillars feed on oak catkins and quickly come to resemble the catkins. In contrast, when moths lay their eggs in the summer, the newly hatched caterpillars feed on oak leaves and come to resemble oak twigs (see Photo). In each case, their morphology helps them blend in with their surroundings, protecting them from predators (Greene, 1996).

Let us provide what would appear to be a straightforward case of a human genetic disease caused by the possession of a specific pair of genes (see Widaman, 2009). Phenylketonuria, or PKU, is a classic example of a genetically caused disease. Infants who are born with two recessive genes that normally are involved in the processing of the amino acid phenylalanine end up having the amino acid accumulate in their brain, which can lead to intellectual impairment. However, the disease has its detrimental effects only when infants and children eat foods that contain phenylalanine. (Phenylalanine is found in many foods and is one of the principal ingredients in some artificial sweeteners made with Aspartame.) Newborns are now routinely screened for the ability to process phenylalanine, and when babies having the defective genes are placed on a phenylalanine-free diet they do not experience any negative effects. Moreover, by adulthood, people with the defective genes

 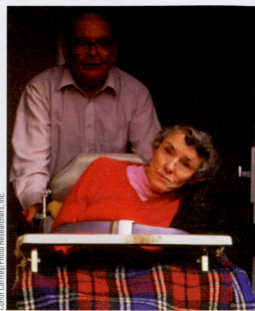

Both progeria (left) and Huntington's disease (right) are caused by a single dominant gene. Progeria is rare, because people with the disease die before having children. Huntington's is more common, because it does not strike its victims until middle adulthood, after the time many have reproduced.

can consume phenylalanine without any ill consequences. Genes themselves, then, do not "cause" PKU; rather, excessive phenylalanine in the diet does. However, the inability to process phenylalanine is "caused" by defective genes. Thus, even in this prototypical case of a genetic disease, genes and environment clearly interact.

In general, a child's environment will interact with a child's genotype to produce the phenotype. This is expressed by the idea of a **norm of reaction** (Dobzhansky, 1955), which refers to all the possible phenotypes that could result from a single genotype, given all the possible environments an organism could be exposed to (see Figure 3.2). Obviously, the range of actual environments children are exposed to is limited, and we will never know all possible outcomes associated with a single genotype. We will provide specific examples of gene–environment interactions for some psychological characteristics later in this chapter.

The "Behavior" of Chromosomes

Before discussing any further what genes do, we are going to examine the "behavior" of chromosomes—the long strands of DNA, segments of which are protein-coding genes. (Much of the DNA, and thus much of the content of chromosomes, does not code

norm of reaction All of the possible phenotypes that could result from a single genotype, given all of the possible environments an organism could be exposed to.

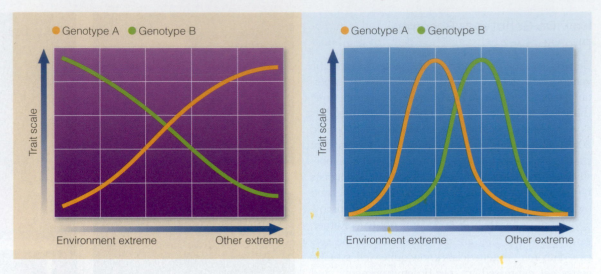

FIGURE 3.2 Norm of reaction.

Different genotypes (A and B) can result in similar or different phenotypes, reflected by how much of a trait individuals express, depending on the environments they experience. The first example reflects nearly opposite outcomes for two different genotypes in extreme environments (for example, a highly supportive versus a highly nonsupportive home environment). The second example reflects greater potential overlap between individuals with different genotypes as a function of different environments, with the different genotypes peaking for a trait (for example, aggressiveness) under different environmental conditions.

for anything specific and is sometimes referred to as junk DNA.) As we noted, humans possess 46 chromosomes in each cell in their bodies (the exception being the sex cells, or gametes, which we will discuss shortly). These chromosomes come in 23 pairs—one member from each chromosome pair coming from one's mother and the other from one's father.

Chromosomes and the Generation of Genetic Variability

When we begin life at conception as a single-celled zygote, we have only 46 chromosomes total. As we develop into a multicelled embryo, our chromosomes duplicate and divide within the nucleus of each of those cells, giving us a complete set of 46 chromosomes in each cell of our developing bodies. During *mitosis*, chromosomes duplicate themselves exactly. Each new cell has a set of chromosomes that are perfect copies of the original. Deviation does not occur under normal conditions. Many cells go through this duplication process daily, whereas others seldom do (nerve cells, liver cells). Cancer cells divide much more rapidly than healthy cells.

Critical for transmitting genetic information between generations (that is, for inheritance) is the process of meiosis. Meiosis occurs when germ, or

sex, cells (ova in females, sperm in males) are being formed and plays a central role in heredity. During meiosis, chromosomes duplicate themselves and the cell divides once; but instead of stopping there as in mitosis, the cells divide again. However, the chromosomes do not duplicate themselves during this second division. The result is four cells with 23 single chromosomes each (see Figure 3.3).

Meiosis takes place in different locations in males than in females and also at different times of development. Ova (eggs) are formed in the ovaries of females while they are still fetuses, and at sexual maturity only slight finishing touches are necessary each month for an ovum to "ripen" and be released for possible fertilization. Sperm, on the other hand, are formed in the testes of sexually mature males, and this process takes place on an as-needed basis. When conception takes place, the sperm is one to five days old, and the egg is the mother's age plus a few months. (This is one reason why the mother's age is a bigger factor in some birth defects than the father's age. Ova are older and have been exposed to more environmental agents than have sperm.)

The process of meiosis gives two guarantees for inherited variability, and variability is what sexual reproduction is all about (see Chapter 15). First, chromosomes in the germ cells are shuffled so that different combinations of the 1st through 23rd chromosomes occur. During the second division, the chromosomes shuffle themselves again and, although each germ cell ends up with one

meiosis The type of cell division that occurs when sperm and ova are being formed, resulting in half the number of chromosomes in each gamete compared to body cells.

from each of the 23 pairs, maternal and paternal members of each chromosome pair are combined randomly. With 23 pairs, the possible combinations from random selection are about 8 million for any particular individual. This number represents the vast variety of chromosome arrangements each pair of individuals can pass on to their offspring and gives an indication of why siblings are different from one another even though they are products of the same parents.

A second key element for genetic variability is the process of crossing over, which takes place during meiosis before the first cell division. As chromosomes duplicate themselves but before they completely divide, they exchange pieces of genetic material. Not only do we give our children a potpourri of chromosome selection from our own mothers and fathers, but we also pass on a patchwork arrangement of genetic material within each chromosome itself.

Two Types of Chromosomes

The 23 human chromosome pairs are grouped into two major classifications: autosomes and the sex chromosomes. Autosomes are pairs 1 through 22, and sex chromosomes are the 23rd pair only (see Photo). All autosomes are essentially the same size and shape as their matching partner, which is not always the case with sex chromosomes.

The two sex chromosomes determine an individual's genetic sex. In females, the two sex chromosomes are the same size and are labeled "XX." In males, the two sex chromosomes are different sizes. One is large and identical to the female sex chromosome, X; the other is about one-fifth the size of the first and is called "Y."

Because all males have XY sex chromosomes and all females have XX sex chromosomes, it is easy to see how parents determine their offspring's gender. The child receives one member of each chromosome pair from each parent. Because the mother only has X chromosomes, that is what she contributes to any child she bears. The father, on the other hand, can give a child an X or a Y. If he gives the child an X, it will be added to the mother's X, and the child will be female (XX). If the father gives a Y, it will be added to the mother's X, and the child will be male (XY) (see Table 3.3).

In actuality, however, there are about 105 boys born for every 100 girls (expressed as 1.05). The sex ratio at birth varies somewhat worldwide (ranging from 1.0 to 1.17, CIA World Factbook, 2006) and over historical time, with environmental factors believed to be responsible for these differences (Davis et al., 1998). When miscarriages and spontaneous abortions are considered, the estimates for males and females *conceived* range from

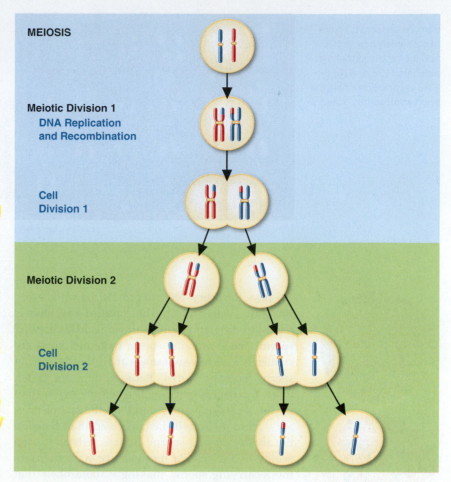

FIGURE 3.3 Meiosis.
During meiosis, after the germ cells (ova in females and sperm in males) duplicate once (as in mitosis), the cells divide a second time. However, the chromosomes do not duplicate themselves during this second division. The result is four cells with 23 single chromosomes each.

table 3.3 Sex Determination

The sex of a fetus is determined by which chromosome it gets from its father. If the fetus receives an X chromosome, a female develops. If the fetus receives a Y chromosome, a male develops. The mother provides the fetus with one of her two X chromosomes.

		Father	
		X	Y
Mother	X	XX	XY
	X	XX	XY

XX = Female
XY = Male

crossing over A process of genetic exchange that occurs during meiosis, when two corresponding chromosomes exchange pieces of DNA.

autosomes Chromosome pairs 1 through 22.

sex chromosomes In humans, the 23rd chromosome pair that determines gender.

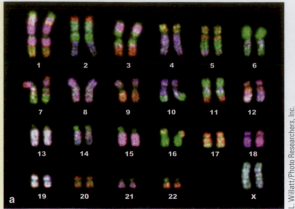

Humans possess 23 pairs of chromosomes, shown at right: (a) the autosomes, numbers 1–22, and (b) the 23rd chromosome pair, the sex chromosomes, X and Y.

L. Willatt/Photo Researchers, Inc.

Biophoto Associates/Photo Researchers, Inc.

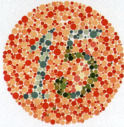

© Prisma/SuperStock

FIGURE 3.4 Color blindness.

What do you see? The first image (top) serves as a control. Everyone should see the number "12." For the second image, people with normal color vision will see the number "15." People with color vision (mostly males) will see only the "1," only the "5," or no numbers at all.

116 boys for every 100 girls to 160 boys for every 100 girls (Volpe, 1971). The lopsided sex ratio is related to differences in X-carrying and Y-carrying sperm. The Y-carrying sperm (potential boys) are smaller and faster swimmers than the X-carrying sperm (potential girls). Because they are faster, more Y-carrying sperm will reach the ovum than slower X-carrying sperm and, by the law of averages, more males will be conceived than females. But the Y-carrying sperm are less resistant to the acidity of the female reproductive tract than are the X-carrying sperm, making it more likely that the slower X-carrying sperm will survive. To make matters more complicated, the reproductive tract becomes less acidic (more alkaline) closer to the time of ovulation, again affording an advantage to the Y-carrying sperm.

One factor recently shown to affect the ratio of girl to boy babies is the mother's diet. In a recent study of 740 pregnant British women, the sex of their child was related to their diet at time of conception (not during pregnancy), with women having the best nutrition having 56% male fetuses, and women with the worst nutrition having only 45% male fetuses (Mathews, Johnson, & Neil, 2008).

Sex-linked Inheritance: The Case of Color Blindness

Earlier in the chapter, we discussed inheritance of recessive and dominant characteristics. We stated that a recessive trait is expressed in the phenotype only if a person has two genes for that trait. There is at least one common exception to this rule, and it relates to genes carried on the 23rd chromosomes. Some genetically determined charac-

teristics appear more frequently in males than in females. The most serious genetic diseases to follow this pattern are Duchenne muscular dystrophy and a form of hemophilia. The most common (and benign) phenomenon to show this pattern is color blindness (see Figure 3.4). Each of these three characteristics is passed on via the sex chromosomes.

Recall that for the 22 autosomal pairs, the two chromosomes are alike. If there is a point on chromosome number 6 that codes for hair color, for instance, then there will be a corresponding point on its pair that codes for the same trait. This is not necessarily so for the sex chromosomes. In males, the X member of the pair is about five times larger than the Y. The smaller Y chromosome carries less genetic information than the larger X chromosome. Traits that are inherited through the sex chromosomes are said to reflect **sex-linked inheritance**.

As with the autosomes, sex-linked genes may be dominant or recessive. What is unusual about sex-linked inheritance, however, is that a single recessive gene on the X chromosome in the male can be expressed in the phenotype when there is no corresponding gene on the Y chromosome to counteract its effect. Thus, for a recessive trait, such as Duchenne muscular dystrophy, hemophilia, and color blindness, females, having two Xs, will not express the trait if only one recessive gene for the disorder is inherited. This is precisely the way things happen for the autosomes. Males, in contrast, will express the trait if only one recessive gene is present on the X, because they have no dominant gene on the Y chromosome to be expressed instead. This means that recessive sex-linked characteristics are passed along from mothers to their sons. The only way a daughter can express the recessive trait is if she has a recessive gene on both of her X chromosomes. Table 3.4 shows the typical inheritance pattern of color blindness, from a carrier mother to a color-blind son. For more examples of diseases transmitted by sex-linked patterns, see Table 3.5.

sex-linked inheritance Recessive traits that are inherited by way of a single gene on the sex chromosomes, usually the X chromosome; also called X-linked inheritance.

table 3.4 Genetic Transmission of Color Blindness, a Sex-linked Trait

Because the gene for color vision (and color blindness) is carried on the X chromosome only, males (XY) get their only gene for color vision from their mothers. If a male receives a single recessive gene for color blindness from his mother (X^b), he will be color blind, because there is no corresponding gene of the Y chromosome to counteract the effect. Females, in contrast, require two recessive genes, one from each parent, to be color blind.

		Father with normal color vision	
		X^N	Y
Mother with normal color vision but who carries a gene for color blindness (X^b)	X^b	$X^b X^N$	$X^b Y^*$
	X^N	$X^N X^b$	$X^N Y$

N = dominant gene for color vision
b = recessive gene for color blindness
* = color blind in phenotype

table 3.5 Some Traits That Follow a Sex-linked Hereditary Pattern

Color blindness (red/green): defects in the red receptors

Deafness: 2% of cases at birth

Dwarfism (a variety of growth-related syndromes all involving short stature): some types

Hemophilia: problems with blood clotting

Hunter syndrome: enzyme deficiency that causes neural destruction

Lesch-Nyhan syndrome: fatal enzyme deficiency

Muscular dystrophy (Duchenne's): missing protein important to muscle function

Chromosomal Abnormalities

We can learn much about how chromosomes function by studying their dysfunctions. During the process of meiosis, accidents sometimes happen. Parts of a chromosome can break off and become attached to another chromosome, producing germ cells with missing pieces or germ cells with extra pieces. Other times, something goes wrong with the chromosome duplication and it fails to divide properly, producing germ cells with only 22 chromosomes or with 24 chromosomes. We do not know how often this happens during meiosis, because many of these defective germ cells fail to join with others at conception, and we do not know how many typically developing babies may have unknown chromosomal abnormalities that have little effect on their health and behavior. At birth, about 1 in every 200 babies has obvious chromosomal abnormalities, and some of these die soon after birth. About half of the abnormalities involve the 22 pairs of autosomes and half involve the one pair of sex chromosomes.

The following are two examples of chromosome abnormalities. One involves the autosomes and one involves the sex chromosomes.

Down syndrome, an abnormality of the autosomes. This is probably the most familiar chromosome abnormality. Once called "mongolism," it is now known by the name of its discoverer, John Langdon Down. Down noticed that about 10% of his patients were very similar in appearance, although they were not related. He carefully described the traits these children had in common—a broad, flat face, thick tongue, small nose, and Asian-like eyes resulting from epicanthal folds of the eyelids. In 1959, a chromosome abnormality was discovered in Down syndrome individuals, the first abnormality found in the autosomes. Instead of having 46 chromosomes, individuals with Down syndrome have 47 chromosomes, the extra being a third member of the 21st pair, giving the disorder its technical name, *trisomy 21*, or third body on the 21st pair.

The incidence of Down syndrome births is related to the mother's age. Once a woman reaches 35 years of age, the chances of her giving birth to a Down syndrome child increase substantially to about 1 in every 350 births compared to a rate of about 1 in every 1,200 births for younger women. Apparently, the older the egg, the greater the chances that it has been exposed to environmental agents resulting in chromosomal abnormalities. For women 45 years and older, the chance of giving birth to a Down syndrome infant is 1 in 25.

Down syndrome Chromosome abnormality, in which individual has an extra 21st chromosome; also known as *trisomy 21*.

table 3.6 Some Abnormalities of the Autosomes (Body Chromosomes)

Anomaly	Type and Location	Incidence per Live Births	Symptoms
Edward's syndrome	Trisomy 18	1:6000	Multiple congenital problems; early death
D-trisomy (Patau syndrome)	Trisomy 13	1:12,000	Multiple congenital problems; early death; severe intellectual impairment for those who survive infancy
Cri du chat (cat cry)	Missing short arm of chromosome 5	1:15,000 to 1:50,000	High-pitched cry; slow or abnormal physical growth; developmental delays
Down syndrome	Trisomy 21	1:600	Intellectual impairment; poor muscle tone; distinctive facial features; heart abnormalities
Prader-Willi syndrome	Missing part of chromosome 15	1:10,000 to 1:15,000	Poor muscle tone and color; small hands and feet; obesity at 2 or 3 years of age
Wolf-Hirschorn syndrome	Missing part of chromosome 4	1:50,000	Severe delays in cognitive and physical growth; facial anomolies; seizures; early death
Partial trisomy 3q syndrome	Extra piece of chromosome 3	rare	Severe delays in cognitive and physical growth; head and chest deformities; early death

Because of the known relationship between maternal age and Down syndrome, many pregnant women over age 35 have prenatal screening to detect chromosomal abnormalities in the fetus (see discussions of prenatal screening techniques later in this chapter). A woman can thus know relatively early in pregnancy if she is carrying a Down syndrome child and use this information in her decision whether or not to take the pregnancy to term. Because of this, the incidence of Down syndrome births has decreased, dropping from 1 in 600 births 40 years ago to 1 in 1,000 today (Plomin et al., 2008). For other abnormalities of the autosomes, see Table 3.6.

The most common abnormality associated with the autosomes is Down syndrome, or trisomy 21. People with Down syndrome have distinctive facial features and usually display intellectual impairment.

Lauren Shear/Photo Researchers, Inc.

Turner syndrome, an abnormality of the sex chromosomes. This disorder was first identified in 1938 by Henry Turner, who had seen seven female patients with similar traits that he believed were caused by hormone deficiencies. The women were all in their late teens or early twenties but had not matured sexually. They had extra connecting tissue on the neck, low hairlines on the back of their heads, and deformed elbows. In 1959, improved equipment and techniques showed that Turner syndrome females were lacking a second X chromosome. Turner syndrome is designated as "XO," meaning that one X chromosome is present and one is absent, giving affected women only 45 chromosomes.

Because, early on, the only women diagnosed with Turner syndrome were those whose symptoms were extreme enough to seek medical help, it was considered a seriously debilitating disorder. More recently, by screening healthy members of the population, researchers have found that the vast majority of Turner syndrome cases are less

table 3.7 Some Abnormalities of the Sex Chromosomes (23rd Pair)

Anomaly	Type and Location	Incidence per Live Births	Symptoms
Turner's syndrome	XO	1:2,500 girls	Some physical abnormalities including short stature, broad chest, low-set ears; specific deficits in spatial cognition
Triple X syndrome (trisomy X)	XXX	1:1,000 girls	No distinguishable differences to XX females
Klinefelter's syndrome	XXY	1:500 boys	For some, abnormal development of secondary sexual characteristics; tall, lanky body; many are indistinguishable from XY males
XYY syndrome	XYY	1:1,000 boys	Typically no unusual physical or medical problems; accelerated early growth and taller-than-average adult height
Fragile X syndrome	Fragile site on X chromosome resulting in failure to produce a specific protein	1:1,000 boys; 1:2,500 girls	Intellectual impairment

severe and respond well to hormone replacement treatment. However, by studying the traits found in Turner syndrome women, such as poor spatial ability and directional sense, researchers have gained information about what role the second X chromosome plays in the development of typically developing females (Berch & Bender, 1990).

Turner syndrome occurs in 1 of every 2,500 live births and is neither connected to mother's age nor does it run in families. Ninety-eight percent of conceptions resulting in XO fetuses are spontaneously aborted (Plomin et al., 2008). For other examples of abnormalities of the sex chromosomes, see Table 3.7.

Behavioral Genetics

Genes are obviously involved in all aspects of development and of life itself. Researchers have long wanted to understand the connection between genes and behavior, specifically how individual differences in people's biological inheritance influence their behavior and thought. In recent years, advances in technology have permitted scientists to identify variants of specific genes and associate those genes with psychological characteristics. In many cases, geneticists know what these genes do (that is, what proteins they produce and what the proteins do in the body) and thus have a clue as to how they affect behavior.

More common, however, are studies that examine behavioral or cognitive similarities among people as a function of their genetic similarity. In this section we examine the field of **behavioral genetics**, starting with a look at research that focuses on family similarities, followed by research that examines the association between individual genes, children's rearing environment, and behavioral outcomes.

Family Studies

Most research in behavioral genetics has inferred about the role of genes on behavior by studying how traits vary within families. More specifically, people with varying degrees of genetic relationships (for example, siblings, identical twins) are examined for some particular trait, and degree of similarity in the trait is compared as a function of degree of genetic relatedness. If genes play an important role in influencing a specific trait, people who share a greater percentage of genes (siblings) should be more alike in terms of this trait than people who are less closely related (cousins). These are referred to as *family studies* and represent the vast majority of research from a behavioral genetics perspective.

> **Turner syndrome** A chromosomal disorder in females in which one X chromosome is missing, resulting in a total complement of only 45 chromosomes.
>
> **behavioral genetics** Discipline that focus on the study of genetic effects on behavior.

Identical (maternal, monozygotic) twins (left) share 100% of their genes, whereas nonidentical (fraternal, dizygotic) twins (right) are as genetically similar as regular siblings, sharing 50% of their genes, but, like identical twins, grow up in the same household together. Behavioral genetic studies make great use of identical and nonidentical twins in trying to decide the influence of genes on behavior.

We should note at the outset that about 99.9% of the genome is exactly the same for all people (International Human Genome Sequencing Consortium, 2001). These genes make humans distinct from other species. The remaining 0.1% of the genome still represents millions of nucleotide base pairs, and differences in this part of the genome (essentially different alleles for the same genes) constitute genetic differences among people. When we refer to percentage of genes that people of different degrees of genetic relatedness share (for example, twins, siblings), we are referring to this 0.1%.

One way of assessing genetic influence on some behavior is to assess the **concordance rates** of some characteristics. *Concordance rate* refers to the percentage of genetic relatives (for example, siblings, twins) who exhibit a particular trait or characteristic. For instance, identical (maternal, or monozygotic) twins share 100% of their genes, whereas nonidentical (fraternal, or dizygotic) twins share 50% of their genes, just as regular siblings do. So, for example, if genetics was all that mattered in determining a trait, the concordance rate for that trait would be 100% for identical twins (if one twin had the trait, there would be a 100% probability that the other twin would have it) and 50% for nonidentical twins and regular siblings (if one sibling had the trait there would be a 50% probability that the other sibling had the trait). Of course, factors other than genes affect the expression of traits, but if genes play an

important role in some trait, one would expect pairs of identical twins to be more likely to share that trait than pairs of nonidentical twins.

This is indeed the case for some forms of mental disorders. For schizophrenia, for example, the concordance rate for identical twins is between 41% and 65%, whereas the concordance rate for nonidentical twins is between 0% and 28% (Cardno & Gottesman, 2000). Similar average differences in the concordance rates between identical and nonidentical twins have been reported for major depression (about 40% versus 20%, The National Institute of Mental Health, 2007) and juvenile crime (about 80% versus 69%, Ishikawa & Raine, 2002), to name just a few. In each case, the likelihood of one twin exhibiting a characteristic, such as depression, given that his or her twin has the characteristic, is greater for identical than nonidentical twins. Results such as these clearly indicate a significant role of genes in these outcomes. However, in all cases, the concordance rates for identical twins is less than perfect (in most cases, substantially less than 100%), suggesting that environment must also be playing a significant role in the expression of these traits.

Another technique that is used more frequently in behavioral genetics research is to compute correlations of some trait (for example, height, weight, or intelligence as measured by IQ) between people of different degrees of genetic relatedness. At one extreme we have pairs of unrelated people chosen at random from a large sample—"two strangers who pass on the street." Next in line would be distantly related individuals such as second cousins, and then more closely related individuals such as cousins and siblings, and finally identical twins. In addition, we can assess people who share environments but not genes, such as adopted siblings who grow up in the same house together but are genetically unrelated to one another. As we saw when looking at concordance rates, comparisons between identical and nonidentical twins can be particularly useful. Although nonidentical twins share 50% of their genes just as normal siblings do, they are born at the same time and thus experience a family environment similar to that experienced by identical twins. Finally, we have identical twins who were separated early in life and reared apart. Here we have children who are genetically identical but who experienced different environments (Bouchard et al., 1990).

Correlational analyses permit us to evaluate the similarity of people with different degrees of genetic relatedness for traits that vary continuously, like height, weight, or IQ. With concordance rates, either two people share the trait (for example, schizophrenia) or they do not. With correlations, one can assess the extent to which two people (or two sets of people, really) share a characteristic. For example, for the trait of height, the

concordance rates The probability that one member of a pair of individuals (for example, identical or fraternal twins) will display a trait possessed by the other member.

heritability The extent to which differences in any trait within a population can be attributed to inheritance.

correlation between identical twins is about .90 (1.0 is perfect). This means that if you know the height of one twin, you can predict very accurately the height of the second twin. The correlation between nonidentical twins for height is about .50. This means you could predict reasonably well the height of one twin by knowing the height of his or her sibling, but not nearly so well as you could for identical twins. The correlation for height between randomly selected, unrelated people is 0. Height is a good example of a trait that is substantially influenced by heredity, and this is reflected by the pattern of correlations obtained between people of different degrees of relatedness.

As we mentioned, one particularly interesting group of people is identical twins who were separated early in life and reared apart. Thomas Bouchard and his colleagues (1990) identified more than 100 reared-apart identical twins and compared correlations between them and sets of identical twins who were reared together as children. Table 3.8 presents the correlations for a selection of physical and psychological characteristics for reared-apart and reared-together identical twins. As you can see, the correlations were quite high for both sets of twins, with the reared-apart twins typically having only slightly lower correlations than the reared-together twins, suggesting to Bouchard and his colleagues that there are only small effects of being reared together on most characteristics.

Let's look at the research findings on the genetic effects on IQ and the personality measure of neuroticism based on family studies. Table 3.9 shows the average correlations of IQs and scores on a measure of neuroticism for people of different degrees of genetic relatedness. As can be seen, as genetic relatedness increases, so do the average correlations, although this effect is stronger for IQ than for neuroticism. However, note that environment also plays a role: adopted siblings share no genes, yet there is a correlation of .32 between their IQs and .11 for measures of neuroticism. In fact, the correlations for neuroticism between adopted siblings are actually slightly higher than that for biological siblings reared together.

Heritability

Data such as these are used to generate estimates of **heritability**. Heritability refers to the extent to which differences in any trait within a population are attributed to inheritance. Heritability is expressed as a statistic that ranges from 0 (none of the differences in a trait are attributed to inheritance) to 1.0 (100% of the differences in a trait are attributed to inheritance). The easiest way to compute a heritability coefficient (H) is by using data from twin studies. The correlation (denoted as r)

table 3.8 Correlations for Identical Twins Reared Apart and Reared Together for a Variety of Physical and Psychological Characteristics

Characteristic	Identical Twins Reared Apart	Identical Twins Reared Together
Height	.86	.93
Weight	.73	.83
Speed of responding	.56	.73
Adult IQ	.69	.88
Psychological interests	.39	.48
Personality	.50	.49

SOURCE: Adapted from Bouchard, T. J., Jr., Lykken, D. T., McGue, M., Segal, N. L., & Tellegen, A. (1990). Sources of human psychological differences: The Minnesota study of twins reared apart. *Science, 250,* 223–228.

table 3.9 Average Correlations of IQ and Neuroticism as Function of Genetic and Environmental Relatedness

	IQ	Neuroticism
Identical twins reared together	.86	.46
Identical twins reared apart	.78	.38
Fraternal twins reared together	.60	.20
Siblings reared together	.47	.09
Biological parents and offspring	.42	.13
Adoptive parents and offspring	.19	.05
Adopted siblings	.32	.11

SOURCE:Data adapted from Plomin, R., DeFries, J. C., McClearn, G. E., & Rutter, M. (1997). *Behavioral genetics* (3rd ed.). New York: Freeman.

based on data from nonidentical twins is subtracted from the correlation based on data from identical twins, and the difference is doubled, or,

$$H = (r\ identical\ twins - r\ nonidentical\ twins) \times 2$$

If you take the correlation for the IQs of identical twins reared together shown in Table 3.9 (.86) and those of nonidentical twins reared together (.60), the resulting computation is $H = (.86 - .60) \times 2 = .52$. This means that the heritability of intelligence (at least based on this data set) is .52, or that 52% of the differences in intelligence between people can be attributed to genetics. Despite the lower overall correlations, heritability is the same for neuroticism [$H = (.46 - .20) \times 2 = .52$].

Heritability is a population statistic, in that it describes average differences among people within a population. It does not refer to how much of any one person's intelligence or height or personality characteristics can be attributed to genetic factors (that is, how much of one's height is inherited). Rather, it refers only to what percentage of the difference in a trait within a specific population can be attributed to inheritance, on average. This is not always an easy concept to grasp, but it is a very important one.

For the purpose of illustration, assume that individual differences in height are related to two factors and two factors only: inheritance and diet. On an isolated island, every person receives 100% of his or her nutritional needs (no one receives more or less). The average height of men on the island is 6 feet. If you were to meet two men from this island, one being 6 feet 1 inch tall and the other being 5 feet 11 inches tall, 100% of the 2-inch difference in their height would be attributed to inheritance. Heritability would be 1.0. The reason is because environments (diets in this case) are homogeneous, or perfectly identical—no differences in environments exist. Thus, any difference in height between people must be attributed to inheritance.

What would happen if a famine hit the island, changing the diet of the people and thus the average height (from 6 feet to 5 feet 10 inches, say)? If the dietary change were uniform (for example, everyone getting 75% of his or her nutritional needs) the heritability would still be 1.0. Although the environment changed drastically, it changed equally for everyone. Thus, because the environments remained homogeneous, 100% of the differences in height between people would still be attributed to inheritance. If the effects of the famine were not uniform, however, the picture would change. If some people still received 100% of their nutritional needs, others 75%, and still others only 50%, when you meet two men who differ by 2 inches in height you know that, on average, some proportion of this difference must be attributed to differences in diet. That is, heritability has changed to something less than 1.0, say .80. The more heterogeneous, or different, the environments are, the lower heritability will be. Heritability is thus relative, varying with the environmental conditions in which people within the population live.

If heritability for height were .80 (which it approximately is in European populations, although it tends to be lower, about .65, in Asian populations; Lai, 2006), this would *not* mean that 80% of one's height was inherited, or, to provide a concrete example, that, for a person who is 5 feet tall, four of those feet were inherited while one foot resulted from diet. It means, rather, that, on average, 80% of differences in height between people are related to inheritance.

If heritability for IQ is approximately .5, what accounts for the other 50% of differences? The simple answer is the environment and gene x environment interactions (see Moffitt, Caspi, & Rutter, 2006). When behavioral geneticists look at environmental effects, they typically divide them into two types: shared and nonshared environments. A shared environment is an environment shared by different family members. Thus, twins, for instance, living in the same home at the same time, share the same family environment. Nontwin siblings growing up in the same family at different times do not share the same environment to the extent that twins do. Similarly, twins reared apart do not share any common environment. A nonshared environment is an environment unique to an individual, not shared by a sibling, for instance. Table 3.10 provides the formulas for

table 3.10 Computing Heritability

Computing heritability, nonshared environmental effects, and shared environmental effects for a trait is relatively straightforward, once some basic facts are known. All you need are two pieces of information: the correlations of identical twins (reared together) and the correlations of nonidentical twins (reared together) (see Plomin et al., 1990). For an example, we will use the trait of IQ. The critical correlations (r) are:

Correlation of IQs for identical twin (reared together) = .86

Correlation of IQs of nonidentical twins (reared together) = .60

The formula for heritability is:

$$Heritability = (r\ identical\ twins - r\ nonidentical\ twins) \times 2$$

or

$$Heritability\ of\ IQ = (.46 - .20) \times 2 = .52$$

The formula for nonshared environmental effects is:

$$Nonshared\ environmental\ effects = 1.00 - r\ (identical\ twins\ reared\ together)$$

or

$$Nonshared\ environmental\ effects\ of\ IQ: 1.0 - .86 = .14$$

The formula for shared environmental effects is:

$$Shared\ environmental\ effects = 1.00 - (Heritability + Nonshared\ environmental\ effects)$$

or

$$Shared\ environmental\ effects\ of\ IQ = 1 - (.52 + .14) = .34$$

computing shared and nonshared effects for the trait of IQ.

For measures of cognitive abilities, about 50% of the variance in performance is attributed to genetics and about half of the remaining difference is split between shared and nonshared environment, although this varies some as a function of which specific abilities are tested and when (in childhood or adulthood) (Plomin et al., 2008). But what about the interaction of genes and environment? Perhaps genetic effects would be larger in some environments and smaller in others, with shared and nonshared environmental effects showing similar trends. This was investigated in a study that examined the genetic and shared-environmental contributions to IQ as a function of the education level of children's parents (Rowe, Jacobson, & der Oord, 1999). The sample consisted of 3,139 adolescent sibling pairs, including sets of identical and nonidentical twins, and adopted siblings. David Rowe and his colleagues reported that heritability of IQ for the overall sample was .57, and the effect of shared environment was .13.

The patterns were much different, however, when analyses were done separately for children from high-education homes (greater than high-school education) and children from low-education homes (high-school education or less). For children in the high-education group, the heritability coefficient was .74, and the effect of shared environment was 0. In contrast, for children in the low-education group, the heritability coefficient was .26, and the effect of shared environment was .23. In other words, the heritability of IQ increased from about 25% for children of parents with less than a high-school education to about 75% for offspring of parents with greater than a high-school education, with a corresponding decrease in the effects of shared environment (from about 25% to about 0%) (see also Turkheimer et al., 2003, for similar findings).

What findings like this suggest is that heritability varies with environmental conditions, and specifically that when environments are positive, reflected here by high levels of parent education, heritability is particularly high (Bronfenbrenner & Ceci, 1994; Scarr, 1992). In other words, when children grow up in enriched and supportive environments, individual differences in genes will account for more of the individual differences in some trait, here IQ. The environments are good enough to support development, making individual differences in them relatively unimportant and thus increasing the influence of individual differences associated with genes. However, when environments are below average, individual differences in children's experiences will increase in influence and match or possibly exceed the effects of individual differ-

ences in genes in affecting individual differences in a trait.

Although we have said it before, it bears repeating: heritability is a population statistic and varies with environmental conditions. Intelligence, personality, and other complicated psychological characteristics are the products of genes and environment interacting over time and cannot be reduced to a single number. Behavioral genetics give us a general idea of the role of genetics on the development of psychological traits. But genes never act out of context. We have to ask, "*How* do genes influence behavior?", and we turn now to this topic.

How Do Genes Influence Behavior?

Genotype → Environment Theory

An influential behavioral genetics theory of development was presented by Sandra Scarr and Kathleen McCartney (1983; see also Scarr, 1992, 1993). Their **genotype → environment theory** (read as "genotype influences environment") holds that one's genotype (one's actual genetic constitution) influences which environments one encounters and the type of experiences one has (see also Plomin, DeFries, & Loehlin, 1977). Their basic contention is that *genes drive experience.* Thus, experience *does* play a significant role in shaping personality and intellect, but a person's inherited characteristics largely determine what those experiences are and how they are perceived.

Scarr and McCartney proposed three types of *genotype → environment effects* that vary in influence over the course of development: *passive, evocative,* and *active. Passive effects* occur when genetically related parents provide the rearing environment of the child. It is termed "passive" because children are passive recipients of both the genes and the environment provided by their parents. When biological parents rear a child, the effects of genetics and environment cannot be separated, because the people who provide the genetic constitution for a child also provide the environment. The influence of passive effects is proposed to decline with age.

---

shared environment An environment shared by different family members (for example, two siblings).

nonshared environment An environment that is unique to an individual, not shared by a sibling, for instance.

genotype → environment theory Scarr and McCartney's theory that one's genotype (genetic constitution) influences which environments one encounters and the type of experiences one has, or that genes drive experience.

Passive	Biological parents provide both genes and environment for child. Children are passive recipients of genes (and the environment) provided by their parents. Passive effects *decrease* with age.
Evocative	Temperamental characteristics of the child evokes responses from others. For example, a child with an irritable temperament will be treated differently than a child with a more easygoing temperament. Evocative effects remain *constant* with age.
Active	Children seek out environments consistent with their genotypes. For example, children interested in sports will seek out different environments than children who are more interested in sedentary activities, such as playing computer games. The experiences children have in these environments will shape their behaviors, personalities, and thinking. Active effects *increase* with age.

Evocative effects refer to characteristics of children that evoke responses from other people. Aspects of children's temperament (for example, degree of sociability or irritability) are believed to be primarily under genetic influence, and these characteristics affect how people view and respond to children. (Temperament will be discussed in Chapter 11.) For example, a well-tempered child is responded to differently than is an irritable child, and the type of attention received by an infant who likes to cuddle is different from that received by an infant who does not want to be held. Because temperament is believed to be relatively stable over a person's lifetime, evocative effects presumably remain constant throughout development.

Active effects occur when a child's genotype influences the type of environments he or she chooses to experience. People actively select environments in which they feel comfortable. For instance, children interested in playing computer games seek other like-minded children to play with and will likely have very different playmates than children interested in competitive sports. Accordingly, people with different genotypes choose to interact in different environments, selecting or creating niches in which to experience the world, and thus have different experiences that influence their development. Active effects increase with age as children become increasingly independent of their parents and able to select their own environments.

The increasing role of active genotype → environment effects accounts for the fact that siblings become *less* alike the longer they live together (Plomin & Daniels, 1987; McCartney et al., 1990), a somewhat counterintuitive finding. As children grow up, they gain greater independence as they increasingly search for their own niche in the world. For example, Sandra Scarr and Richard Weinberg (1978) reported that the average correlations for the IQs of adopted siblings measured in childhood ranged from .25 to .39, reflecting a moderate degree of shared-environmental effects. However, when the IQs of adopted siblings were measured in adolescence, the correlation fell to zero! The longer these genetically unrelated siblings lived together, the less alike in terms of IQ they became. A similar pattern has been found for brothers: the older they get, the lower is the correlations of their IQs (Sundet, Eriksen, & Tambs, 2008). Presumably, this pattern is the result of the decreasing influence of passive genotype → environment effects and the corresponding increasing influence of active genotype → environment effects.

Such a view suggests that environment plays a critical role in shaping the personalities and intellects of children, much as proposed by the radical behaviorists of years gone by. What is different about today's proposal is that *genes* influence which experiences a child will have. From this perspective, it is clear that the issue is not nature versus nurture; nor is it appropriate to ask how much is nature versus how much is nurture. Rather, following Thomas Bouchard and his colleagues (1990), the correct formula is *nature via nurture.* Such a perspective acknowledges the important role that genetics plays in every aspect of our being, but it also acknowledges the equally significant role of environment and the possibility of remedial intervention even for highly heritable traits.

Genes, Environment, and Behavior

Family studies do not actually study genes, but genetic relations, as inferred by family relations. With the advancement of technology, however, behavioral geneticists have been able to identify genes that are associated with specific behavioral outcomes and to examine the conditions under which these genes influence children's behavior and development. For example, researchers working both with people and nonhuman animals have identified a ==gene located on the X chromosome that is associated with antisocial and violent behavior.== The gene is involved with the ==production of an enzyme called monoamine oxidase== A (*MAOA*) that metabolizes several types of neurotransmitters, chemicals that foster the transmission of signals between neurons in the brain (see Chapter 4). When the gene responsible for production of *MAOA* is "knocked out" (that is, it does not function), animals display elevated levels of aggression. Some people naturally have higher levels of *MAOA* than others, and it is believed that these different levels are influenced by different versions of this gene, or different alleles. Moreover, low levels of *MAOA* (or low *MAOA* activity) have been shown to be associated with elevated levels of aggression in people.

Avshalom Caspi and his colleagues (2002) analyzed data from a longitudinal study in New Zealand assessing the relationship between *MAOA* activity (low versus high), childhood rearing environment, and antisocial behavior in adolescent boys. Children's environments were grouped into three categories in terms of maltreatment (abuse): none, probable, and severe.

Figure 3.5 shows levels of antisocial behavior for groups of boys with low versus high *MAOA* activity as a function of degree of childhood maltreatment. As you can see, ==boys who experienced severe maltreatment *and* had low *MAOA* activity displayed the highest levels of antisocial behavior.== Severely maltreated boys with high *MAOA* activity also showed the next highest levels of antisocial behavior, but much below that of maltreated boys with low *MAOA* activity. But more important, *MAOA* activity itself did not predict (or did not cause) antisocial behavior, nor did the child's rearing environment. Levels of antisocial behavior were comparable between low- and high-*MAOA*-activity boys when there was either no maltreatment or only probable maltreatment. Thus, both the genes associated with *MAOA* activity level *and* child-rearing environment clearly contribute to antisocial behavior, but a child's behavior (in this case, antisocial behavior) is expressed differently in different environments, *in interaction with specific genes.* (Recall our discussion earlier of norm of reaction.) Similar findings have been reported for a sample of American males from the National Longitudinal Study of Adolescent Health (Guo, Roettger, & Cai, 2008).

Although not all cases of the interactions between genes and environment are as clear-cut

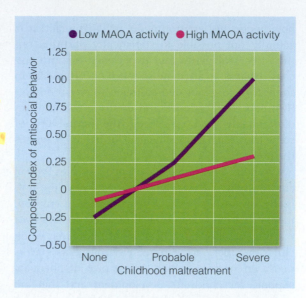

FIGURE 3.5 Relationship between childhood maltreatment (none, probable, severe) and *MAOA* activity (low versus high) on antisocial behavior. Adolescent boys with a genetic disposition toward aggression (those having low-*MAOA* activity) were significantly more likely to display antisocial behavior than those without such a disposition (those with high-*MAOA* activity), *but only when they grew up experiencing severe maltreatment*. There were no differences in antisocial behavior between the low- and high-*MAOA*-activity boys growing up in other environments. This reflects an interaction between having specific genes (in this case associated with levels of *MAOA*) and environment (childhood maltreatment) on behavior. SOURCE: From Caspi, A., McClay, J., Moffitt, T. E., Mill, J., Martin, J., Craig, I. W., Taylor, A., & Poulton, R. (2002). Role of genotype in the cycle of violence in maltreated children. *Science, 297* (2 August), 851–854. Reprinted by permission of AAAS.

as this one, the general message is that ==genes are always expressed in an environment, and this interaction of genes and environments shape behavior== (see Rutter, 2006, 2007). Caspi and his colleagues have reported similar patterns between genes and behavior for depression (Caspi et al., 2003; see also Haeffel et al., 2008 and Chapter 11) and the benefit of breastfeeding on children's IQs (Caspi et al., 2007), the latter of which we will discuss briefly later in this chapter.

Is Behavioral Genetics the Answer to Explain Gene–Environment Interaction?

Although behavioral genetics has produced some important findings and insights into how genes and environment interact in development, not all scientists see the approach as useful. For example, advocates of the developmental systems approach argue that behavioral geneticists misrepresent how genes and environments really interact. It is actually not possible to statistically partition out the effects of genes and experience for any outcome (that is, to attribute so much of differences in some trait to genes and so much to environment) (Gottlieb, 2007). Genes and environment interact dynamically, and specifying the heritability of some trait, such as intelligence, for instance, misses the point.

When children experience species-typical environments, they can expect to develop normally, because genes will be expressed in environments that have been typical for their species over many generations. All bets are off, however, when children experience extreme environments, particularly environments that do not provide adequate support for children's development and that are evolutionarily novel (that is, unlike the environments experienced by one's ancestors). Fortunately, most children develop normally in a wide range of environments, and as such the estimates of genetic and environmental effects provided by behavioral genetics analysis can provide a helpful heuristic to understanding how nature and nurture interact in development.

Prenatal Development

Almost everyone knows where babies come from, but the actual process of conception is a complicated one. Each month, beginning some time after menarche and ending with menopause, a woman releases an ovum from one of her ovaries. All the ova that a woman will ever have are present at birth, although these ova will not be ready for fertilization until years later, when they are released and find their way down the **fallopian tube**, where conception occurs.

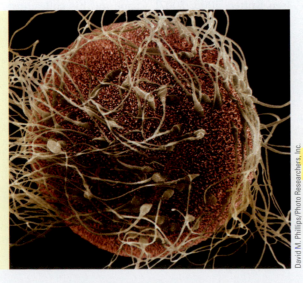

Dozens of sperm may reach the ovum (egg), but only one can impregnate it.

David M. Phillips/Photo Researchers, Inc.

In contrast to the one egg that females release each month, males release approximately 250 million sperm in each ejaculation (Baker & Bellis, 2007). Most of these sperm will die and never reach the fallopian tubes, and of the several hundred or so that do make it to the ovum, only one can impregnate it (see Photo). As you can see in the photograph, each sperm consists of a bulbous head and long, slender tail. The tail is in continuous motion, propelling the sperm into the uterus and up the fallopian tube to the ovum. The ovum is about the size of the period at the end of this sentence, just barely visible to the naked eye, whereas sperm are microscopic.

The Course of Prenatal Development

When fertilization occurs, the **prenatal period** officially begins. The typical newborn has spent 38 weeks developing inside the mother's reproductive system, beginning at conception and ending at birth. This time period can be divided into three phases: the germinal phase (sometimes referred to as the "period of the zygote"), the embryonic phase, and the fetal phase. (See photos of embryos and fetus at different stages of prenatal development. For a more detailed set of illustrations from conception to birth, go to: http://www.youtube.com/watch?v=RS1ti23SUSw.)

Germinal Phase

conception – 3wks

The **germinal phase** begins when the ovum is penetrated by a sperm in the fallopian tube and begins its journey, as a **zygote**, down to the uterus. Once a sperm and ovum have joined, a chemical barrier is set up, preventing entrance of any additional sperm. If a second sperm should enter the egg, the resulting embryo will not survive. (Twins are *not* the result of two sperm impregnating the same ovum.) The zygote then begins a process of growth, with cells duplicating by mitosis. Occasionally during these early cell divisions, the cells separate into two unique clusters, and each cluster continues to grow independently. This is how identical twins are produced (also known as maternal, or *monozygotic, twins*). The result is two individuals who are genetically identical, although they can experience different conditions in the uterus. Identical twins occur in about 1 of every 250 births. Nonidentical twins result when a woman produces two viable ova in a month and each is fertilized (also known as fraternal, or *dizygotic, twins*). The result is twins who are as similar to one another genetically as two siblings. Fraternal twins may be both boys, both girls, or one of each. It is even possible for fraternal twins to have different fathers—one supermarket tabloid story that has some scientific basis. Some women produce two ova every month, making it likely that each pregnancy they have will result in fraternal twins. Nonidentical twins occur in about 1 of every 150 births.

During this trip from the fallopian tube to the uterus, the zygote begins dividing and forms into a hollow sphere called a **blastocyst**. This phase ends about two weeks later when the blastocyst becomes implanted in the uterine wall. This may sound like a simple process, but, although it is difficult to establish with great accuracy, it is estimated that 40% of zygotes do not survive this phase of prenatal development, and as many as one-third of those that do become implanted are lost in later phases by spontaneous abortions, also known as miscarriages (O'Railly & Müller, 2001).

Embryonic Phase 3rd wk – 8th wk

The second phase of the prenatal period is the **embryonic phase**. During this time, which extends from about the third to the eighth week after conception, most of the basic organ systems are formed, a process known as *organogenesis*. During this phase, the outer layer of the blastocyst gives rise to the nervous system, the sensory organs (such as eyes and ears), and the skin. The middle layer of the blastocyst becomes muscles, bones, and the circulatory system. The inner layer develops into the digestive and respiratory systems. Growth is rapid during the embryonic phase. At the beginning, the embryo is a thin disk that is about 2 mm in length (less than 1/10th of an inch) with a vague head and tail structure, similar to the embryo of a fish, chicken, or dog (Carmichael, 1970). At the end of this phase, it will be 3 cm in length (over an inch) and have a fully human appearance (see Photos).

The embryo is nourished by nutrients from its mother's bloodstream that are transmitted from the **placenta**, an organ that develops in the uterus during pregnancy, via the umbilical cord. The placenta also exchanges wastes, oxygen, and antibodies between the mother and embryo. Embryos are cushioned by the *amniotic* and *chorionic sacs*. The amniotic sac (or amnion) is a fluid-filled membrane that forms around the embryo about two weeks after conception and remains until birth. The chorionic sac (or chorion) surrounds the amnion and eventually becomes part of the placenta. (When women speak of "their water breaking," it is these sacs that rupture at the beginning of labor.)

During the second month, facial features begin to develop. The ears, nose, mouth, and external portions of the eyes are apparent, making it clear, by the seventh week, that the embryo is human. Arms, legs, and toes are formed, the circulatory system is working, and the digestive and respiratory systems are fully formed but not yet functioning (Moore & Persaud, 2003; O'Railly & Müller,

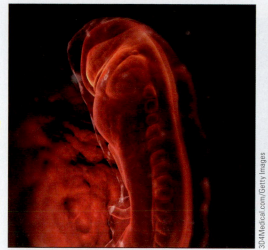
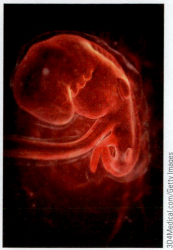
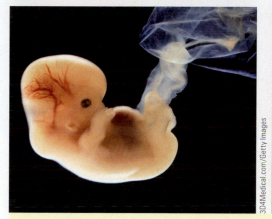
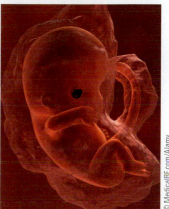

Development proceeds rapidly during the embryonic period, and by the end of the period the embryo is recognizable as human.

2001). By the eighth week, the kidneys are functioning and excreting urine. The embryo is capable of movement by the eighth week, although the movements are jerky and uncoordinated, with the whole body or large segments of the body reacting in a general way to stimulation (Hoffer, 1981). Finer muscle control and voluntary movement must wait until the next period of development.

fallopian tube The tubes through which mature ova travel from the ovaries to the uterus, and where conception takes place.

prenatal period The 38 weeks the embryo/fetus spends developing inside the mother's reproductive system, beginning at conception and ending at birth.

germinal phase Earliest phase of prenatal development, beginning when the ovum is penetrated by a sperm in the fallopian tube and starts its journey, as a *zygote*, down to the uterus.

zygote The single-celled organism formed from the union of egg and sperm at the earliest phase of prenatal development.

blastocyst Early stage in prenatal development, in which the zygote begins dividing and forms into a hollow sphere.

embryonic phase The prenatal period from approximately 2 to 8 weeks after conception, during which organs are formed and begin to function.

placenta The organ along the uterine wall of a pregnant woman that serves as the transport system between mother and fetus.

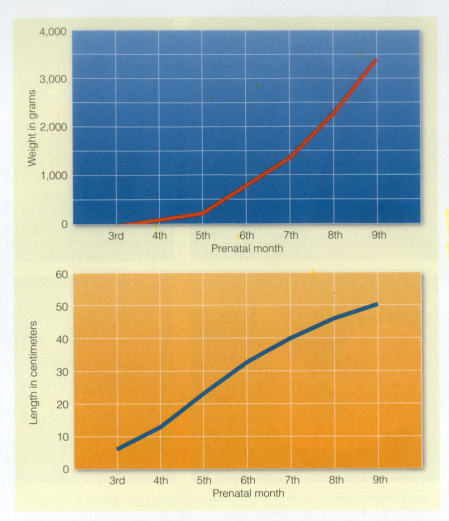

FIGURE 3.6 Average weight (in grams) and length (in centimeters) of fetus from the third to ninth prenatal month.

The Fetal Phase

The third phase of the prenatal period is called the **fetal phase**, and it extends from about the 9th week after conception to the 38th week. During this phase, there is dramatic growth of the organs and body structures, especially from the 9th to the 20th week. Interestingly, at the end of the 12th week after conception, all the organs of the fetus are formed and are in proportion to each other as in a full-term newborn, just smaller. They are not, however, functioning perfectly and could not sustain life were an infant to be born at this time. Around the 12th week, there is a significant increase in the activity and mobility of the fetus, and this is when the mother might feel slight kicking and fluttering of the infant, although most mothers begin to feel this movement around the fourth or fifth month of pregnancy (Fifer, 2005). This is referred to as *quickening* and in the past

Fetal 9wks – 38wks

Movement

was used as an indication that the baby is a living being. This is not the first movement for the fetus, however, who has shown signs of activity since late in the embryonic period. Earlier movements were not noticed by the mother because the embryo/fetus was so small.

During the fetal period, ultrasounds of infants have shown them sucking their thumbs. They also develop their sense of touch. This is the phase of development in which genitals begin to differentiate, forming different structures for males and females. The external genitalia begin to differentiate between males and females around the 9th week but are not fully differentiated until about the 12th week.

The most obvious change during the fetal period is physical growth. The 3-month-old fetus is about 2.5 inches (6.35 cm) long and weighs only about half an ounce (14 grams); by the time of birth, the fetus is about 20 inches long (50 cm) and weighs about 7.5 pounds (3400 grams). Average changes in weight and height over the fetal period are shown in Figure 3.6.

Although many functions such as eating and hearing will not be necessary until the child is born, they get a start during the fetal phase. For example, during the third month, a fetus can swallow amniotic fluid and excrete it through its bladder. In the fourth month, the fetus inhales the amniotic fluid, which is thought to increase the sense of smell. During this time the mother's diet can modify the taste and smell of the amniotic fluid, and the fetus is sensitive to the change. For example, if the mother's sugar intake is increased, the fetus will ingest some of it (Fifer, 2005). In the sixth month, the fetus responds to the mother's heartbeat, digestive sounds, and sounds from outside the womb. These responses of the fetus include changes in heart rate and movement. Vision is the last sense to develop. Although fetuses cannot see in utero (there's no light, making vision impossible), 7-month-old fetuses have a protective blink reflex. Pain is apparently a late-developing sense. According to Susan Lee and her colleagues (2005), awareness of pain requires functional connections in the thalamocortical regions of the brain, and these do not begin to appear until between the 23rd and 30th week and are not fully developed before the 29th or 30th week of gestation. It is unlikely then that the fetus would feel any pain before the third trimester of the prenatal period.

During the last two months or so before birth, development consists mainly of growth, as no new structures develop during this time. The sensory systems steadily mature and are ready to function at birth, although not all perfectly. For example, as we will see later in this chapter, vision in newborn infants is not highly developed and improves

fetal phase The prenatal period from approximately 8 weeks after conception to birth.

substantially in the 6 months following birth. In contrast, the development of the auditory system exhibits an especially high level of functioning, which explains the child's preference for his or her mother's voice immediately after birth (DeCasper & Fifer, 1980; Kisilevsky et al., 2003).

Although a full-term delivery is considered to be 38 weeks from conception (40 weeks from a woman's last menstrual period), infants have a reasonable chance of living, under highly protective environments, if they are born as early as the 23rd week. An infant born much earlier than this would not likely live because of the immaturity of its respiratory system. The lungs are able to exchange limited amounts of gases beginning between the 26th and 29th weeks, and, if infants weigh greater than 1,000 grams (about 2.2 pounds), they have a good chance of survival (Hoekstra et al., 2004; Moore & Persaud, 2003). We will have more to say about premature infants later in this chapter.

At the end of the eighth month of gestation, fetuses show two types of sleep: a quiet sleep that they engage in 20% to 30% of the time, and an active sleep with rapid eye movements (REM sleep) for the remainder of the time. The first waking component is added to the sleep cycle during the ninth month (Fifer, 2005).

As can be seen from the photographs, the heads of fetuses are disproportionately large relative to the rest of their bodies. This reflects a pattern that will characterize children throughout their growth, which is that development proceeds from head to foot. This head-downward developmental trend is referred to as **cephalocaudal development** and characterizes both prenatal and postnatal growth. Cephalocaudal development characterizes all mammals but is especially prominent in humans, whose large brain (relative to body size) needs to develop early (and continue late) in order to promote survival. We will discuss cephalocaudal development further in Chapter 4 on physical development.

Risk Factors during Prenatal Development

Typical development during the prenatal period can be affected by four major types of problems: (1) chromosomal disorders; (2) maternal risk factors, or conditions of the mother that adversely affect the developing child; (3) environmental agents that cause harm to the developing child, which are known as **teratogens**; and, somewhat ironically, (4) the fetus itself. We discussed chromosomal disorders in the previous sections, so the following paragraphs focus on mother's risk factors, teratogens, and how the fetus can jeopardize the pregnancy.

Maternal Risk Factors

Mother's age. One of the most obvious risk factors during pregnancy is the mother's age. Considering health alone, the optimal age for a woman to have a baby is between about 20 and 35 years (James et al., 1999). Pregnancy after 35 or during adolescence increases significantly the risk of atypical prenatal development, and both younger and older women are more likely to give birth prematurely. The incidence of miscarriages is also greater in these (especially older) women (James et al., 1999; Smith & Buyalos, 1996). For example, as we noted earlier, the risk of having a child with Down syndrome increases greatly with maternal age.

Fetal malnourishment. Another important maternal risk factor is malnutrition. Ideally, pregnant women should eat a diet of 2,700 to 3,000 calories a day that contains adequate amounts of vitamins and minerals to ensure the development of a healthy child (Fifer, 2005), and most pregnant women in developed countries today follow these recommendations. However, at times in the past when achieving this goal was not possible, such as during wars or famine, studies of pregnant women have shown that malnutrition has serious and long-term negative effects on children. For example, a study of pregnant women in the Netherlands who lived through the Dutch Hunger Winter during World War II showed that those who were malnourished during the first 6 months of pregnancy (that is, eating fewer than 1,000 calories a day) were more likely to give birth to children with symptoms of fetal brain disorganization, including higher rates of schizophrenia and antisocial personality behaviors. They also had higher rates of premature and low-weight births than similar women who were not malnourished during that time (Fifer, 2005; Stein et al., 1975). It is also interesting that these effects extended to the next generation, with the offspring of women who were fetuses during the Dutch Hunger Winter having smaller babies (Lumey, 1992).

Fetal malnourishment produces infants who are often lethargic, have aversive cries, and are slow to develop. Such a combination of characteristics can make infants difficult to deal with, particularly for families living in stressful conditions, and this can have lasting effects on children's development, even after the effects of fetal malnourishment have disappeared. This is illustrated in a classic study by Philip Sanford Zeskind and Craig Ramey (1978, 1981). In their

cephalocaudal development The head-to-foot sequence of physical growth.

teratogens External agents, such as drugs and radiation, that can have harmful effects on a developing embryo or fetus.

table 3.11 Mean Stanford-Binet Scores at 36 Months for Children in the Zeskind and Ramey Study

A mean of 100 reflects "average" intelligence.

	Biologically Typical	Fetally Malnourished
Experimental (daycare) group	98.1	96.4
Control group	84.7	70.6

SOURCE: Zeskind, P. S., & Ramey, C. T. (1981). Sequelae of fetal malnutrition: A longitudinal, transactional, and synergistic approach. *Child Development, 52*, 213–218.

table 3.12 List of Major Known Teratogens

Drugs	Medicines/Prescriptive Drugs	
	Antibiotics (for example, streptomicin)	Sex hormones (for example, birth control pills)
	Antiepileptics (for example, *Dilantin*)	Sedatives/antidepressives (for example, lithium)
	Analgesics (for example, aspirin/ibuprofen)	Vitamins (for example, Vitamin A derivative, *Accutane*)
	Illegal Drugs	
	Cocaine	Marijuana
	Heroin	Methadone
	Addictive Substances	
	Alcohol	Caffeine
	Amphetamines	
Diseases	**Viruses**	
	AIDS	Influenza (flu)
	Chicken pox	Mumps
	Cytomegalovirus	Rubella (German measles)
	Herpes simplex (genital herpes)	
	Bacteria	
	Chlamydia	Parasitarian
	Gonorrhea	Toxoplasmosis
	Syphilis	Malaria
	Tuberculosis	
	Other Complications	
	Diabetes	Rh factor incompatibility
	Hypertension	
Environmental pollutants	Mercury	Lead
	Policarburs (PCBs)	Nicotine
	Radiation	

study, infants from poor, rural environments who had been classified as high risk for intellectual impairment were assigned to one of two caregiving environments. Infants in one group received medical care and nutritional supplements and participated in an educationally oriented daycare program beginning at approximately 3 months of age (experimental group). Infants in a control group received the medical care and nutritional supplements but did not partake in the daycare program. As it turned out, fetal malnourishment was common in this population of infants, and within each group, approximately one-half of the infants were classified as being fetally malnourished at birth, whereas the remaining infants were described as being biologically typical.

Perhaps not surprisingly, both the biologically typical and fetally malnourished infants who attended the experimental daycare had higher IQs when tested at 24 and 36 months of age (see Table 3.11). As you can see in Table 3.11, the IQs of the once–fetally malnourished infants (babies had been given nutritional supplements after birth) were especially low for children in the control group. Why this difference? When looking at how mothers interacted with their children, Zeskind and Ramey reported that by 24 months, fetally malnourished infants in the control group received less attention from their mothers than did typical control children. In contrast, there were no differences in mothers' behaviors between those experimental infants who were initially diagnosed as fetally malnourished and those who were biologically typical. They proposed that the increased responsivity of fetally malnourished infants receiving the educational daycare resulted in increased attention from their mothers and a generally positive developmental outcome. That is, the stimulation these infants received in the educational daycare made them more alert and accelerated their early development. These infants brought home their more outgoing behaviors, which influenced how their mothers responded to them. In contrast, the continued withdrawn and sickly behavior of the fetally malnourished infants in the control group resulted in less maternal attention, exaggerating the injurious effects of their biological impairment, even after the children began receiving healthy postnatal diets.

Maternal stress. A third maternal risk factor is psychological stress. Women who experience high levels of stress during pregnancy are more apt to have premature births and low-weight babies (Mulder et al., 2002). It is important to note that stress is not some phantom effect but quite real in its

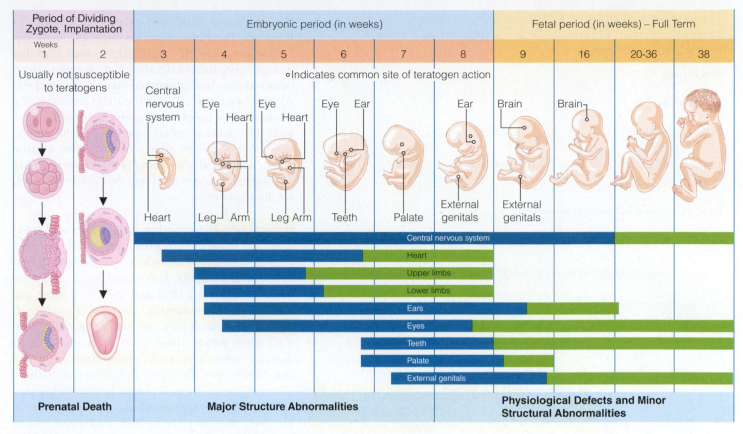

FIGURE 3.7 Phases of prenatal development and sensitivity to teratogenic effects.

As you can see, the developing child is most sensitive to the effects of teratogens during the embryonic phase of prenatal development. The green bars reflect periods that are somewhat less sensitive to teratogens, although damage can still occur. SOURCE: From *Essentials of embryology and birth defects*, 6th ed., by K.L. Moore and T.V.N Persaud, 2003. Reprinted by permission of Elsevier.

physical effects; it causes decreased nutrients and oxygen to the fetus and weakens the mother's immune system, making the fetus more vulnerable as well. Stress in the mother can cause hormone imbalances in the placenta. In addition, women with high levels of stress are more apt to engage in behaviors that are harmful to the fetus, such as tobacco and alcohol use (DiPietro, 2004; Huizink, Mulder, & Buitelaar, 2004). There is also some evidence that women who experienced extreme stress during pregnancy have an increased likelihood of having sons who as adults identify themselves as homosexual (Ellis et al., 1988; see further discussion of factors associated with sexual orientation in Chapter 15).

Environmental Risk Factors

Birth defects occur in 3% to 5% of all newborns, and about 10% of those are caused by *teratogens* (Fifer, 2005), substances that come into contact with the fetus through the mother that interfere with typical development (see list in Table 3.12). The effects of teratogens vary with the phase of prenatal development (see Figure 3.7 and Table

3.13). Teratogens can be legal or illegal substances, addictive or not. They can even be medications that would be safe and helpful except during pregnancy. The effects of teratogens depend on several interacting factors, including the amount of the agent the fetus is exposed to, the health of the mother and the fetus, the amount of other teratogens the fetus is exposed to during the prenatal period, and the phase of prenatal development (Moore & Persaud, 2003). For example, because the zygote (blastocyst) is "free floating" (that is, not yet connected to the mother), its sensitivity to environmental factors is limited. Nevertheless, factors such as maternal diet, stress, or infection can affect a zygote's trip down the fallopian tube and even kill it (Fifer, 2005).

The developing organism is most susceptible to teratogens during the embryonic period, primarily because this is the time when all major organ systems are forming, and any interference with the course of development can have drastic effects (for example, deformation of the limbs, see Moore & Persaud, 2003). Recall from our discussion in Chapter 2 of *sensitive periods*, that some experiences will affect the child only at certain times in

table 3.13 List of Most Common Consequences of Teratogens and Maternal Risk Factors during Prenatal Development

Miscarriage

Low birth weight

Premature birth

Physical malformations (internal: for example, brain; and external: for example, limbs)

Damage to visual and/or audition systems

Delay or damage of physical development (for example, slow growth)

Delay or damage of cognitive development (for example, mental retardation)

Higher vulnerability of regulatory systems (for example, attention, arousal level, mood)

development. During the fetal phase, minor structural abnormalities and physiological defects can still occur as a result of exposure to teratogens, although these are typically less severe compared to the major structural abnormalities that can occur during the six-week embryonic phase (see Figure 3.7).

The concept of teratogens in human development is fairly new. Scientists once thought that

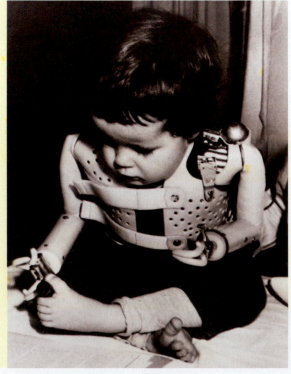

Pregnant women who took the drug Thalidomide early in pregnancy, before the end of the sensitive period for the formation of limbs, gave birth to babies with deformations of the arms and/ or legs.

Omikron/Photo Researchers, Inc.

the developing child was safely tucked away in the mother's womb, protected from all harm. But certain events in the mid-1900s showed that this was not true, specifically the identification of birth defects caused by thalidomide in the 1960s and Fetal Alcohol Syndrome (FAS) in the 1970s (see following discussion). It quickly became a topic of interest, both for developmental scientists and parents-to-be. Although the effects of teratogens can be tragic, they are also preventable, and an active field of research was quickly instituted, some of which we discuss here.

Medications. Perhaps the best-known and most dramatic incident of a prescription drug causing birth defects is *thalidomide*, which was prescribed in Canada, Australia, Japan, and many European countries between 1956 and 1962 as a sleep aid and to combat morning sickness in pregnant women. The result was approximately 10,000 children born during these years with severe birth defects, such as abnormally short or missing limbs (see Photo). We discussed the effects of thalidomide on prenatal development briefly in Chapter 1. The drug was not tested adequately, and many families paid the price for this negligence, not to mention the now-many middle-aged people who were thalidomide babies.

Legal drugs taken during pregnancy can sometimes have delayed effects. Perhaps the best-known example of this is the aftereffects of treatment with the drug DES (diethylstilbestrol), a synthetic hormone routinely given to women from the 1940s to the 1970s to prevent premature labor and miscarriage. Although infants exposed to this drug prenatally did not show any effects at birth, problems with their reproductive systems sometimes emerged in adolescence. Females who had been exposed to DES had greater risks of developing a rare form of vaginal and cervical cancer (Hatch et al., 1998), and males had greater risk of noncancerous cysts in their reproductive system. Malformations of the uterus were found in females, as well as malformations of the genital structures, later fertility problems, and premature labor and miscarriages during their pregnancies (Giusti, Iwamoto, & Hatch, 1995; Hammes & Laitman, 2003).

Illegal drugs. When pregnant women use illegal drugs, it can result in harm to their fetus. For example, marijuana—the illegal drug most often used by pregnant women in the United States—has been found recently to produce problems in fetal cognitive development, although the precise nature of those problems is still in question. Some studies have found that marijuana affects attention, others that it is more generalized, but the consensus is that the use of marijuana by pregnant women is harmful to the development of the fetus (Mereu et al., 2003; Fried & Smith, 2001). This is an interesting finding, because for many years the thought was that marijuana use by pregnant women was not a problem.

The opposite change has occurred in the case of cocaine use (including crack cocaine) by pregnant women. The former way of thinking was that the use of this illegal drug was extremely damaging to the fetus. In fact, some states imprisoned pregnant women who used crack cocaine, believing that such women put their unborn children at significant risk for later developmental disabilities, which would end up being expensive for the state after these children were born. More recent studies have shown that the effects, though damaging, are not as extreme as once thought (Brown et al., 2004; Tronick et al., 2005) and often not as serious as those brought about by alcohol use. Women who use cocaine during pregnancy have a greater chance of giving birth to a low-weight infant with signs of retarded growth (Chiriboga et al., 1999). These babies may also have other problems, but they are related to factors surrounding the cocaine use, such as malnutrition, poverty, sexually transmitted diseases, and other drugs, not the cocaine per se (see National Institute of Drug Abuse [2006], http://www.nida.nih.gov/ResearchReports/Cocaine/cocaine4.html).

Legal but addictive substances. The last group of teratogens that often is underestimated by nonscientists are addictive, but legal substances, such as alcohol and tobacco. Women who drink high levels of alcohol during pregnancy have an increased risk of giving birth to children with **Fetal Alcohol Syndrome (FAS)**, which involves symptoms such as intellectual impairment, slow growth rate, deformities of the face, and attention deficit disorders (Jacobson & Jacobson, 2002; Sood et al., 2001; see Photo). A milder but also serious form of this disorder is *Fetal Alcohol Effects (FAE)*, which involves some but not all of the features of FAS (Vorhees & Mollnow, 1987).

How much is *too much* alcohol for pregnant women to drink? It has been estimated that one glass of beer or wine per day, or regular episodes of binge drinking (defined as more than five drinks per episode) can produce FAE (Jacobson & Jacobson, 2002; Sokol, et al., 2003). However, recent research indicates that pregnant women who have one to two drinks per week are at no greater risk of having children with significant problems than are women who abstain from drinking (Kelly et al., 2009).

Tobacco use is related to several problems for newborns. Although smoking is becoming less popular in the United States, about 18% of American women continue to smoke, and it is still popular in both sexes in Europe and Asia. The health hazards to smokers are well known, and the hazards to unborn children are also becoming well publicized, as reflected by the warning on packs of cigarettes sold in the United States.

Children with fetal alcohol syndrome often have distinctive facial features, including small heads and upper jaws, short upturned noses, smooth and thin upper lips, and narrow, small eyes with large epicanthal folds.

Babies of women who smoke weigh 100 to 200 grams less at birth, on average, than babies of nonsmoking women. They have greater incidence of slower-than-average growth, premature births, detached placentas, and respiratory and vascular problems. In addition, some later cognitive and behavioral problems have been linked to mothers smoking during pregnancy (Moore & Persaud, 2003; Wakschlag et al., 2006). Even when mothers do not smoke, the effects of passive smoke exposure increases the probability of low birth weight (40 to 50 grams, or about 2 ounces, less) and Sudden Infant Death Syndrome (SIDS) (see Box 3.5, later in this chapter) (Fifer, 2005; McKenna, 2005). Cigarette smoking during pregnancy has also been associated with children's later IQs, with children of smoking mothers having, on average, lower IQs (about 4 points, on average) than children of women who did not smoke when they were pregnant (Olds, Henderson, & Tatelbaum, 1994).

The detrimental effects of smoking are related to the gases carried in cigarette smoke, including nicotine, carbon monoxide, and cyanide compounds. These gases pass through the placenta to the fetus and prevent the absorption of oxygen. The high amounts of carbon monoxide gases in smoke are particularly deleterious to proper growth (Bureau et al., 1983).

Another legal but addictive substance that can cause harm to the developing fetus is caffeine, which is found in coffee, tea, and many soft drinks.

Fetal Alcohol Syndrome (FAS) Syndrome characterized by a set of symptoms that occur in children as a result of alcohol consumption by the mother during pregnancy, including physical abnormalities and intellectual deficits.

When pregnant women have more than two to three cups of coffee, tea, or caffeine-containing soft drinks per day, they run a greater risk of miscarriage and having babies born at low birth weight and high irritability levels (Fernandez, et al., 1998; Gilbert-Barness, 2000).

Toxic substances and products. Another group of teratogens involves exposure to toxic substances over an extended period, such as hormone treatments and radiation, either in the form of medical treatment or in the workplace. In the case of radiation, high doses can produce severe damage to a developing embryo and fetus, including microcephaly (abnormally small brain), physical deformities, and miscarriages. This was perhaps most dramatically seen in pregnant women and their babies in Japan who were exposed to excessive levels of radiation as a result of the atomic bombs dropped on Hiroshima and Nagasaki during World War II. However, pregnant women can also be exposed to radiation through routine medical tests and dental examinations. As a precaution, women of childbearing age (and sometimes older) are asked to sign waivers when X-rays are taken, whether dental X-rays, mammograms, or other imaging that could be harmful to the fetus. In addition, women who are X-ray technicians or radiation therapists are required to monitor their exposure level to be sure no harm is done if they become pregnant.

Other ways that dangerous substances can enter a pregnant woman's body are through the food she eats and the air she breathes. A good example of the first case was seen in Minimata, Japan, in the late 1950s, when women gave birth to a greater than average number of children with intellectual impairment and brain damage as a result of high levels of mercury in the water and in the fish they ate (Reuhl & Chang, 1979; Vorhees & Mollnow, 1987). Another chemical that can have a teratogenic effect is lead, previously found in gasoline and some paints. (You may recall the discovery of lead paint on some toys exported to the United States from China in 2007 that caused quite an uproar.) Large quantities of lead exposure for pregnant women can result in delayed cognitive development in their children (Bellinger et al., 1987; Dietrich et al., 1993). In addition to mercury and lead, trace elements of other metals (including manganese and cadmium) found in the physical environment and many consumer products are associated with lower childhood IQs, and these effects are magnified when exposure is continued after birth (Hubbs-Tait et al., 2005). Recent research has even reported a connection between exposure to air pollution during pregnancy and lower IQ during childhood (Perera et al., 2009).

Infectious diseases. Another group of teratogens is infectious diseases, mostly from viruses that infect the mother during pregnancy and then are passed on to the developing fetus, causing miscarriage, intellectual impairment, low birth weight, and other deficits. Examples of these are diseases that were once considered harmless childhood illnesses. For instance, the relatively mild disease of rubella, or German measles, if contracted by the mother during the first two months of pregnancy, can result in blindness, deafness, and other deformities in her offspring (Gregg, 1942). Chicken pox can result in defects of muscles and bones if the embryo/fetus is exposed to it in the first trimester (March of Dimes Birth Defects Foundations, 1989). However, when the mother contracts rubella or chickenpox after the third month of pregnancy, the chances of any birth defects occurring are minimal (remember the concept of sensitive periods).

Other infections that can harm the embryo/fetus and potentially lead to miscarriages are sexually transmitted diseases such as syphilis, gonorrhea, herpes, and human immunodeficiency virus (HIV), which can lead to acquired immune deficiency syndrome (AIDS). Perhaps the most common infectious disease that is passed along to a developing fetus is *cytomegalovirus*, a form of herpes that affects the salivary glands. Cytomegalovirus can also be transmitted to the infant during birth and in breast milk, as can its close relative, herpes simplex 2, the most common sexually transmitted disease in the United States. The herpes viruses can cause a range of deformities and also death. Because the virus is most easily passed on

Although AIDS has seemingly come under control in the United States and most of the developed world, in some African countries about one-quarter of newborns are infected with HIV.

AFP/Getty Images

to the child during vaginal birth, women who have the disease are advised to have Cesarean-section deliveries to prevent infecting the baby (Visintine, Nahmias & Josey, 1978).

Although AIDS has seemingly come under control in the United States and most of the developed world, its incidence is climbing in many developing countries. For example, in the African countries of Botswana, South Africa, and Lesotho during the first decade of the 21st century, between 28% and 38% of pregnant women visiting medical clinics were infected with HIV. Women pass HIV to their fetuses about 20% to 30% of the time, and most infants born with HIV die within the first year of life (United Nations, 2006).

At least one infectious disease that acts as a teratogen is caused by a parasite—*toxoplasmosis*. Pregnant women who eat meat that is not cooked enough or who are near feces from an infected cat are at risk for this infection, which can damage the visual system and brain of their developing child (Gagne, 2001).

Might the Fetus Be a Risk Factor to Itself?

Perhaps somewhat surprisingly, the fetus itself can also be a source of complication for a woman's pregnancy. For instance, the Rh blood factor may be different between mother and fetus (**Rh factor incompatibility**). If the mother lacks the Rh protein (is Rh negative) and the fetus inherited the protein from the father (is Rh positive), then complications can occur if some of the fetal blood crosses the placenta into the mother's bloodstream. The Rh proteins will be identified as foreign bodies, and the mother will begin to make antibodies to combat them. If these antibodies enter the fetus's blood system, they will destroy blood cells, depriving the fetus of oxygen, which can lead to miscarriage, intellectual impairment, or heart damage. It is typically only later-born infants who are susceptible to this problem. A first pregnancy essentially primes the mother's system, and she does not produce enough antibodies to result in any harm to her fetus. If subsequent fetuses are also Rh incompatible, however, the antibodies will be produced in high numbers, and the fetus will be at risk. The good news is that Rh-negative women can receive a vaccine after each birth of an Rh-positive baby that prevents the buildup of antibodies.

The incompatibility between mother and fetus extends beyond different blood types, however (Haig, 1993; Trivers, 1974). Remember that the fetus is a foreign body to the mother, with 50% of its genes coming from another being. As a result, the mother's body may attempt to abort any fetus.

Her efforts may be particularly vigorous if the fetus has chromosomal or other abnormalities. The fetus in turn tries to remain in the womb by producing a hormone that prevents the mother from shedding her uterine lining along with the newly implanted embryo. The fetus also sends projections into the mother's arteries that supply nutrients to the placenta that prevent the arteries from constricting, ensuring a healthy flow of blood to the fetus. Once the fetus controls the blood flow to the placenta, it releases a hormone to decrease the effects of insulin in the mother's blood. This maintains high levels of glucose (fuel) available to itself, even though it may have deleterious effects on the mother, causing *gestational diabetes*. In effect, the fetus has strong-armed the mother into providing adequate resources to ensure its healthy development, even though these fetal manipulations may be harmful, in some cases, to the mother and thus the fetus itself.

We do not want to give the impression that pregnancy is a dangerous time, resembling a walk through a jungle full of predators. This is simply not the case. Pregnancy is usually a period of joy and deep satisfaction for both mothers- and fathers-to-be, eagerly awaiting the birth of their children. Our point here is that this time of life is a particularly sensitive one for negative environmental factors, and even for some factors that would be harmless to a fetus at other times. Almost all pregnancies progress normally and result in healthy newborns. Parents are aware that they need to be concerned for the safety of their children once they are born, but it is worth a reminder that those concerns begin some months earlier.

Prenatal Diagnostic Procedures

Unlike any time in history, we have knowledge and technology today that make it easier to prevent, control, and even intervene with problematic prenatal development. Even as we write this chapter, new ideas and technology are being introduced to increase the chances that the prenatal period will result in a healthy newborn child. These methods include a variety of prenatal diagnostic techniques, some of which are summarized in Table 3.14. Modern technology has also made it possible for once-infertile couples to conceive and have children, and some of these techniques are discussed in Box 3.2.

Rh factor incompatibility Mismatch between the mother's and the fetus's Rh type (a blood protein). Namely if Rh of the fetus is positive, and Rh of its mother is negative, complications can occur because of the production of antibodies in the mother that can attack red blood cells in the fetus.

BOX 3.2 # the biopsychology of childhood development

The ART of Making Babies

Modern biological and medical science has devoted millions of hours and dollars investigating the secrets of reproduction. Some of that knowledge has led to technologies to enhance fertility for couples who have difficulty conceiving. The rate of infertility in the United States is estimated as about 7% of married couples (Stephen & Chandra, 2006). For them, the new technologies, called **assisted reproductive techniques (ART)**, are their best chance to become parents (Sher & Davis, & Stoess, 2005). These technologies have become widespread since the first baby was born using assisted reproductive techniques (Louise Brown on July 24, 1978). It is estimated that 1% of all infants born in the United States in 2004 were conceived via ART (Wright et al., 2004).

At the heart of the new technologies is **in vitro fertilization (IVF)**, which refers to fertilization of the egg by the sperm outside of the woman's body. More specifically, fertilization takes place in a test tube or other suitable laboratory container, where the resulting embryo is nurtured for a few days until it is returned to the mother's body.

The standard IVF procedure involves the use of conventional fertility drugs to stimulate ovulation. Once the eggs are ripe, the woman is anesthetized and a small incision is made near her belly button. Using an ultrasound probe, the eggs are located, and the surgeon uses another instrument to suck out the eggs (usually 6 to 8 per procedure). The man's sperm is prepared by separating the semen from the sperm and washed in a special liquid that simulates the chemical action that occurs naturally in a woman's body. A high concentration of sperm is then obtained, and several drops, containing about 50,000 sperm, are added to each egg in a Petri dish. Alternatively, a single sperm can be injected into an egg under a microscope (intracytoplasmic sperm injection), a method that increases the chances of fertilization for men with low sperm counts. According to Geoffrey Sher and his colleagues (2005), in about 70% of the cases, the inseminated egg will become fertilized.

Embryos are placed in the uterine cavity with the guidance of an ultrasound device.

Using this technique, the likelihood that an embryo will implant in IVF is about the same as in natural conceptions (about 25% to 35%), although this varies with the mother's age. Because of this relatively low implantation rate and the expense of a single procedure (ranges from $7,000 to $15,000), several embryos are usually transplanted, which increases the chance of multiple births. About one-third of all live births resulting from ART are twins, triplets, or more, and because of the widespread use of ART in recent years, the number of multiple births has increased substantially (Reynolds et al., 2003; Wright et al., 2004).

The eggs implanted in a woman do not necessarily have to be hers. For women who have healthy uteruses but who cannot produce their own eggs, *embryo transfer* is a possibility. This involves finding a woman to donate an egg. The only thing different from the standard IVF procedure is that the woman providing the egg and the woman implanted with the embryos are not the same (Sher et al., 2005).

Somewhat controversial is the use of donor embryos with postmenopausal women. Eggs from a younger woman are extracted and fertilized with the sperm from the older woman's husband. The new technology allows women in their late forties and fifties (and theoretically even later) to carry a pregnancy to term and may have significant implications for a generation of couples who have postponed starting a family. It may also have implications for the generation to follow, who will be teenagers when their parents are ready for retirement. As of this writing, several women over 60 years of age have given birth through ART with donor eggs, the oldest being a 66-year-old Spanish woman, who died of undisclosed causes three years later.

A variant on embryo transfer occurs when a woman can produce eggs but has no uterus or the eggs will not successfully implant in her uterus. In this case, the egg and sperm from a couple can be fertilized using standard IVF procedures but implanted in the uterus of another woman. In this case, the pregnant woman is genetically unrelated to the child she is carrying, and is referred to as a *gesta-*

"Let me get this straight. One bouquet goes to the mother who donated the egg. A second goes to the mother who hosted the egg for insemination. A third goes to the mother who hosted the embryo and gave birth to the child. A fourth goes to the mother who raised it, and a fifth goes to the mother with legal custody."

© Nick Downes

Modern fertility technology can result in some unusual Mother's Days.

tional surrogate. It should not be surprising that such arrangements can sometimes lead to problems. Some states have enacted surrogacy laws, making clear if gestational surrogacy is legal or not, if legal who can engage in it (in some states, only married couples), and the rights of the various people involved (see *http://www.allaboutsurrogacy.com/surrogacylaws.htm*). However, at least one study has found that the mothers and fathers of infants born through surrogacy showed *better* psychological adjustment to parenthood than mothers and fathers of children conceived naturally (Golombok et al., 2004).

Despite the controversies, most Americans favor basic IVF and related procedures and believe that infertile couples who want a child should have access to the techniques that can help them. The new technologies, however, must be administered ethically, with further advances (particularly in the area of genetic engineering) made cautiously.

Birth and the Neonate

As Wenda Trevathan (2005) has pointed out, birth is a critical event for two individuals: the newborn and the mother. We also would add that it is an important event for fathers and older siblings, for grandparents, and for the extended family and the community. In fact, in most cultures, the birth of an infant is surrounded by rituals in which different members of the family and the community are involved. The biological aspects of childbirth do not differ much from one culture to another, but the variety of social practices that surround it emphasizes the vast differences in cultural meaning for this event. For example, in many Christian cultures, newborns undergo the rite of baptism in which the parents, the family, and the church community commit to the child's religious upbringing. In Jewish cultures, the birth of a boy is followed by (ritual) circumcision and the acknowledgment of the family and community that this boy is a member of the group.

The father's role in the birth of a child depends on cultural practices of the group. Perhaps the most intense involvement is found in some tribal societies in which gender roles are flexible and females have high status. Fathers-to-be in these groups may exhibit symptoms of pregnancy, such as weight gain, indigestion, cravings, swollen breasts, and insomnia (Mead & Newton, 1967; Whiting, 1974). This condition is known as *Couvade syndrome,* or sympathetic pregnancy. It has appeared in the medical literature throughout history and was written about by Marco Polo during his travels to Asia. Lesser forms of this phenomenon are found in other societies. In one study of Italian fathers-to-be, between 11% to 65% reported some of these symptoms (nausea, insomnia, and weight gain) before the birth of their child (Masoni et al., 1994). Today's medical researchers speculate that this could result from hormone shifts men experience when living with a pregnant woman, anxiety surrounding the impending childbirth, or some sort of pseudo-sibling rivalry or envy of the woman's ability to bear children (Klein, 1991).

On the opposite pole from Couvade syndrome is the father's lack of involvement in childbirth. For example, for the Nigoni in east Africa, the practice is often for men to move away from home until the child is born, because of suspicion of the mother and her family that the father, who is not part of their kinship group, might have some harmful influence on the unborn child (Read, 2003).

There is also a wide range of differences in family and community involvement in the birth of a child. For example, in Panama, the Cuna Indians give birth in secret, as though it is something

table 3.14 Some Diagnostic Prenatal Techniques

Ultrasound, or sonography: This technique uses high-frequency sounds—sonar—to produce a visual image of the fetus (see Photos), permitting a physician to determine the precise age, shape, and size of a fetus as well as uterine position. Ultrasound can be informative beginning about 15 weeks after conception. New versions can provide three-dimensional (3D) images, allowing physicians and parents to really see the developing fetus.

Alpha-fetoprotein (AFP): If high levels of alpha-fetoprotein are found in a pregnant woman's blood, it could signal an open neural-tube defect in the fetus, a condition in which the tissue surrounding the developing spinal cord does not close properly and leaves the spinal cord unprotected by the vertebrae. One of these conditions, *spina bifida*, is one of the most common birth defects, occurring in 1 to 2 cases for each 1,000 births worldwide.

*Amniocentesis: This test is done by removing a small amount of fluid from the amniotic sac between the 12th and 16th weeks of pregnancy in order to examine the fetal cells that are present in the fluid. Because the genetic markers for the fetus are contained in these cells, it is possible to identify chromosomal abnormalities, as well as the sex of the fetus.

*Chorionic biopsies: This is similar to amniocentesis, but this procedure can be done earlier, during the 6th to 8th week after conception. These tests involve examining fetal cells in the chorionic membrane.

*Fetoscopy: This is a way to actually examine the fetus using a thin needle with a small camera attached that is inserted through a small incision in the mother's abdomen. This is usually done after the 18th week of pregnancy, when the fetus and placenta are well developed.

Preimplantation genetic diagnosis: After in vitro fertilization (see Box 3.3), once egg and sperm have joined and the zygote has reached the eight-cell phase, one cell is removed and checked for genetic abnormalities. Only zygotes that are free from apparent abnormalities are selected for implantation in the women. This technique can screen for approximately 90% of known genetic disorders (Adams, 2003; Moore & Persaud, 2003).

* Although risks are still low, the chances of miscarriage as a result of these procedures are greater than for the other techniques.

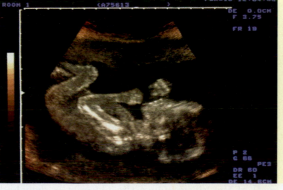

Hugh Burden/Getty Images

Sonograms, also known as ultrasound, provide a picture of the developing fetus and allow physicians to determine if a fetus is developing properly. Parents can often know the sex of the child based on a sonogram.

assisted reproductive techniques (ART) Technologies, most including *in vitro fertilization*, that facilitate couples to become parents.

in vitro fertilization (IVF) Fertilization of the egg by the sperm outside of the woman's body.

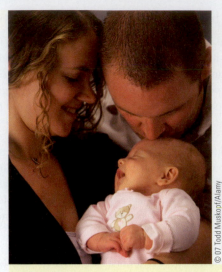

The birth of a child is an important event not just for the mother and the infant, but for the community as well, although the extent to which fathers, other family members, and the community at large participate in the birthing process varies across cultures.

strange or abnormal (Fogel, 1997), whereas in other groups, such as the Balinese in the South Pacific and the Jarara in South America, women give birth during public celebrations (Diener, 2000).

The Birth Process

The end of pregnancy usually occurs about 38 weeks after conception (40 weeks after a woman's last menstrual period), and results in the birth of a human infant. The date of birth is determined by the fetus, which releases a stream of hormones into the mother's blood system that begins the birth process. The process is described in three stages (see Figure 3.8). The first stage is *labor*, a period of time during which the cervix begins to open (dilate), the birth canal softens (effaces), and the uterus undergoes rhythmic contractions that become increasingly stronger. If it is a woman's first child, this period of labor can last from 12 to 14 hours; for subsequent children, it can last as little as 4 to 6 hours. Labor intensifies into harder, more frequent contractions as the infant's head is pushed lower and lower until it begins to emerge from the cervix. At this point, the second stage begins, which is referred to as *delivery*. Normal delivery is relatively quick, usually taking 1 to 2 hours for first births and 20 minutes or so for subsequent births. The third stage, *afterbirth*, follows delivery and lasts about 15 minutes. This stage involves the expulsion of the placenta as it separates from the wall of the uterus. Once the placenta is detached, the uterus contracts where the placenta separated to stop the bleeding. The times for these stages are

all averages, and many of us have heard tales (perhaps from our mothers) of labors and deliveries that lasted many hours.

Birth can be a difficult process for women (and their babies), primarily because the human infant's head is about as big as it can be and still pass through the birth canal. This is largely a result of bipedalism (walking on two feet): Women's hips can only get so large and still permit upright walking (Rosenberg & Trevathan, 2001). In fact, this tight fit is in contrast to that of chimpanzees, whose pelvises are much wider compared to the head of the neonate and permit a less painful and safer passage through the birth canal. Beyond this, human fetuses are larger and heavier than those of other primates. If humans were like other primates, a 140-pound (65 kilogram) woman would give birth to a 4.8-pound (2.2 kilogram) baby. Instead, she actually gives birth to a 7.25-pound (3.3 kilogram) infant (Trevathan, 2005).

One occasional complication of the birth process is *anoxia*, or the infant being deprived of oxygen. This sometimes occurs when infants are delivered in the *breech position*—exiting the womb feet or buttocks first as opposed to head-first. Newborns can experience periods of oxygen deprivation without harm longer than adults can by lowering their metabolism and thus conserving oxygen. However, significant brain damage can occur if newborns are deprived of oxygen for more than 10 minutes (Parer, 1998).

Childbirth has likely always been difficult for women, and practices vary across cultures and have changed in Western culture as both technology and values changed. We examine briefly some of these changes in Box 3.3, *Childbirth through the Ages* (pp. 118–119).

Cesarean section (C-section) Delivery of a baby through a surgical incision in the abdomen.

Cesarean Delivery

Most births in the United States and other developed countries follow this description and take place in a hospital with a doctor or midwife present. However, there are many exceptions to this rule. One frequent exception to the norm is babies who do not pass through the birth canal in the typical process of labor and delivery. Instead, they are removed surgically in a procedure called a **Cesarean delivery/Cesarean section**, or **C-section**. (This procedure got its name because, according to legend, Julius Caesar was delivered in this fashion.) The incidence of births using this procedure has increased over the last few decades and now accounts for more than 30% of all births in the United States. Why would a woman need a C-section? One set of reasons is the baby's size and position as it begins the delivery stage of birth. If the baby is too large for the mother's pelvic structure or is turned so the shoulder or the buttocks enter the birth canal instead of the head (that is, in the breech position), then a C-section is often called for. Another set of reasons involves the mother's health. If she has diabetes or high blood pressure, hours of labor may be too difficult for her. And if she has HIV or genital herpes, it is safer for the baby to be delivered surgically to avoid contagion. Other reasons include the position of the placenta and the umbilical cord, multiple births, and fetal distress. C-sections are also easier for the physician and can avoid some birth defects associated with difficult delivery and can be scheduled by the mother so she knows for certain on which day her child will be born.

The Mother during Pregnancy and at Birth

Our discussion of the birth process so far has been a bit technical, investigating the biological mechanics of birth and the history of birth procedures. But we do not want to forget the mother, for being pregnant, giving birth, and dealing with a new baby, especially for a first-time mother, can be life-changing experiences. Although our focus is on child development in this book, we think it is worthwhile to spend a little time looking at the mother during pregnancy and childbirth.

Pregnancy brings changes to women that have implications for the yet-to-be-born infant. For example, we mentioned earlier that the embryo/fetus is especially susceptible to the effects of teratogens during the first 8 to 12 weeks of pregnancy (see Figure 3.7). It appears that pregnant women have evolved a mechanism to combat the many environmental agents that can potentially harm a fetus at this time, but it comes at a personal expense. The mechanism is *pregnancy sickness.*

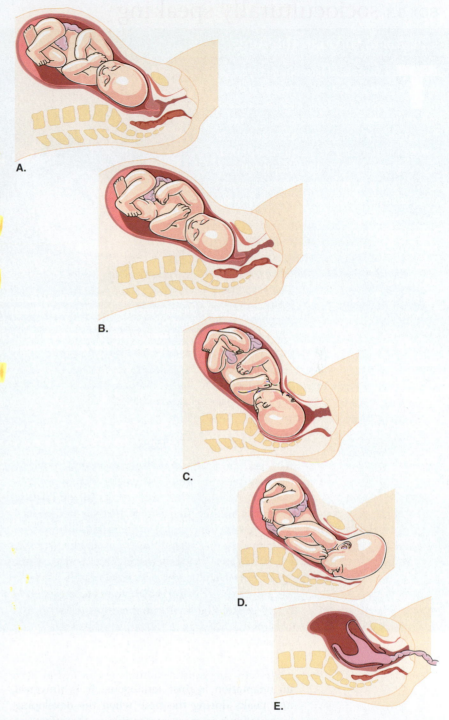

FIGURE 3.8 The three stages of the birth process.
Figure (a) shows the baby in the uterus before the onset of *labor*; Figure (b) shows the early phase of labor; Figure (c) shows later labor with the cervix completely dilated and baby ready for birth; Figure (d) shows the beginning of *delivery*, as the baby's head emerges; and Figure (e) shows the *afterbirth*. SOURCE: Bjorklund, D. F., & Bjorklund, B. R. (1992). *Looking at children: An introduction to child development.* Pacific Grove, CA: Brooks/Cole.

Usually between about 4 and 12 weeks postconception, women experience nausea, often with vomiting, and develop aversions to food that they once liked (and will again). We mentioned in Chapter 2 that pregnancy sickness might have evolved as

BOX 3.3 socioculturally speaking

Childbirth through the Ages

The process of birth for humans has undergone many changes in human history, and these changes probably mirror the changing attitudes society has had about family in general, and women and children in particular. The earliest recorded accounts of childbirth, dating back to the second century A.D., attest to it being an event presided over by women. The mother-to-be was usually assisted by other women, some being family members and friends who were there for moral support and others being older women who were valued for their own experiences in childbirth and also for assisting others. These experts became known as *midwives*, and they were the main characters in the history of childbirth assistance until the 1900s, when doctors took over the business of delivering babies.

Childbirth has changed considerably over the centuries, and while we cannot point to any single reason for the change, we can look at some of the factors that have had an effect.

Disease and Infection

Death of the mother caused by infection was common in the 19th century. A major source of infection was the use of instruments and unwashed hands by physicians and midwives working at hospitals and in the home. Birth attendants felt compelled to routinely examine the prospective mother's cervix to see "how things were doing," even though this procedure was more for their own curiosity

In traditional societies, and in Western societies in past centuries, midwives had the main responsibility for birthing babies. Midwives are being increasingly used by women in modern societies, sometimes in collaboration with physicians.
....

National Geographic/Getty Images

(and that of the awaiting family) than for any reason relevant to the birth. Because antiseptic procedures were not widely known until 1867, centuries of childbirth-related infections had their origins this way (Shorter, 1982). Relatedly, bacteria in the home or hospital invaded mothers after childbirth, passed along in the air, on clothing, or on bathroom or bedroom surfaces. Between 1870 and 1939, the rate of death from infection for new mothers declined dramatically, in both home births and hospital births.

The Use of Anesthesia

Anesthesia had been used for childbirth since 1847, when ether and chloroform were discovered, and as childbirth became safer and concern for the infant shared the stage with concern for the mother, new pain relievers were found. In 1902, *Twilight Sleep* was introduced in Freiberg, Germany, and soon was made available to physicians in the United States and Europe. This mixture of morphine and scopolomine allowed women to drift through labor in a semiconscious state. The effect this movement had on childbirth practices was to move birth from the home to the hospital and to give priority to medical staff—physicians and nurses—rather than midwives, at least in middle- and upper-class urban areas. Because the mother was often unconscious, more medical intervention and use of instruments was needed to deliver the child. Childbirth was no longer *assisted* by others; it was *performed* by others, much like an appendectomy. The downfall of anesthetized childbirth was the discovery of its harm to the child. Science was investigating the effects of different factors on the developing fetus, and an important one was the effect of drugs given to the mother.

Not long after physicians had adjusted their obstetrical procedures to fit anesthetized childbirth, a new movement began. Grantly Dick-Read (1944), a British obstetrician, believed that women had been subjected to a fear of childbirth from childhood and that

an adaptation against teratogens. It is universal and peaks during the time when the developing embryo/fetus is most susceptible to the effects of external agents. The aversions women develop are for foods that may be toxic to their fetus, and women who have more extreme pregnancy sickness have a lower incidence of miscarriages than those who have little or no pregnancy sickness (Flaxman & Sherman, 2000; Profet, 1992). This accumulation of data does not definitively prove that pregnancy sickness is an evolved adaptation, the product of natural selection operating over the course of evolution (Hernández Blasi & Bjorklund, 2003); however, the confluence of evidence from a variety of sources makes the evolutionary hypothesis seem very plausible.

As discussed in Box 3.3, the birth process has traditionally been women's work, with the delivering mother being assisted by other women in her social group, often close kin. Nowadays, fathers and older offspring are often involved in the birth of a baby. It is interesting to note that, beyond the lower risk of death due to the support of other people at birth, emotional and social support to the mother during labor seems to be important for mother-infant primary relationships, extending some weeks after birth (Trevathan, 2005). For example, in one study, mothers who received extra socioemotional support at birth showed a higher involvement in breastfeeding, exhibited less anxiety and depressive symptoms after birth, devoted more time to their infants, had a higher level of this deep-seated fear caused muscular tension during childbirth, which, in turn, made labor painful. His solution was to educate women (and society in general) so that childbirth could be seen as a joyous and satisfying event. Dick-Read also made popular the view that primitive women who gave birth naturally had no fear of childbirth and as a result experienced no pain (Sandelowski, 1984). Initially, the trend was for women to have hospital births free of medication, but in a stark, clinical hospital environment, without family members present. Assistance during labor consisted of the floor nurses, who would come and go with their appointed shifts so that no one person would stay with the mother-to-be during the entire period. And to top it off, not many of these fearless women found childbirth to be so painless. Only 2% in a 1949 study of 400 women reported that their experience had been painless (Goodrich, 1950).

Natural, or **prepared, childbirth**, much as advocated by Dick-Read and French physician Ferdinand Lamaze (1958), remains a popular option for contemporary women. Expectant mothers and their partners usually attend a series of classes where they learn about the birth process and are taught relaxation and breathing exercises to counteract the pain of labor. The woman's partner serves as the labor coach, whose job it is to remind the mother to relax and breathe properly, massage her back, support her body, and, in

Many of today's parents-to-be take a team approach to childbirth preparation.

general, offer social support. Women who attend such classes and have natural childbirth with a coach often report experiencing less pain during delivery, use less medication, and generally have a more positive experience about their baby and the birth process than do other women (Wilcock, Kobayashi, & Murray, 1997).

The Modern Era

The 1980s brought new economic factors into the arena of childbirth. Hospitals overbuilt and medical costs soared. To keep their obstetrical patients using hospital facilities, birthing centers were created, where couples could attend prenatal classes on childbirth preparation, and siblings of the expected baby could tour the facility before the baby came so they would know "where Mommy will be." This practice is generally followed today in the United States, with labor and birth taking place in a cozy bedroom-type setting with the father present and any other attendants the mother wants. Once the baby is delivered, it is immediately handed to the wide-awake mother and kept in the room with the mother until she is stabilized and moved to a conventional room. There the options continue, with the mother deciding between rooming-in (having the baby with her in her room) or nursery care—or any combination of the two. Many hospital birthing centers continue the perks for couples who choose them, including champagne dinners for the new parents, family parties for all the relatives, and "birth day" parties for the other children in the family. Understandably, these perks sometimes cost more than routine service, and the result is women with greater economic means may receive better medical treatment than women with less economic clout, a trend that begins with prenatal care.

self-esteem, and had more positive feelings about their partners and their babies than did mothers in a control group (Klaus et al., 1992).

Immediately following birth, the mother's relationship with her new baby begins in earnest, and we will examine this in some detail in Chapter 12 on "Attachment and Early Parent-Child Care." Not everyone gets off to a good start, however, as about 10% of new mothers experience **postpartum depression**, strong feelings of sadness or resentment shortly after giving birth. About half of all women experience milder forms of this, sometimes called *maternity blues* (Kessel, 1995), which usually pass within a week or so. Postpartum depression, however, can persist for several months and can have harmful and long-

term effects on the parent-child relationship (Dawson et al., 2003; Jones, Fields, & Davalos, 2000). Depressed mothers are often passive, rarely interact with their infants in an animate way, and frequently view their children negatively. This can lead to a parent-child interaction style that is associated with poor psychological adjustment in children (see Chapter 13 for a discussion of parenting styles and child adjustment).

natural (prepared) childbirth Method of labor and childbirth that does not involve anesthetics, in which a woman and her partner/coach receive education in areas such as relaxation and breathing.

postpartum depression A mother's strong feelings of sadness or resentment shortly after giving birth.

FIGURE 3.9 Neonate's skull.

Because the sutures between the various head plates are not fully formed, the plates can shift during birth, sometimes leaving the newborn's head misshapen. The anterior fontanelle, or soft spot, doesn't close until about age 2 and is not fully closed until puberty.

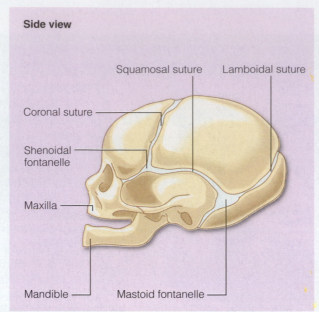

Side view

Squamosal suture — Lamboidal suture

Coronal suture

Shenoidal fontanelle

Maxilla

Mandible — Mastoid fontanelle

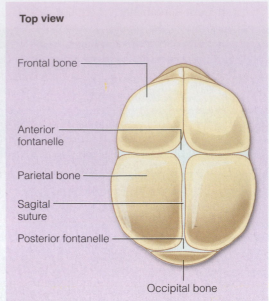

Top view

Frontal bone

Anterior fontanelle

Parietal bone

Sagital suture

Posterior fontanelle

Occipital bone

What are the reasons for postpartum depression? At least the milder forms seem to be associated with hormonal changes surrounding birth (Hendrick & Altshuler, 1999). More severe forms are associated with a history of depression as well as a history of substance abuse, including cigarettes and alcohol (Brockington, 1996), as well as lack of social support to care for the new baby (Field et al., 1988). The substantial effort, disruption of established family routines, and lack of sleep associated with introducing a baby to the household can also exaggerate the effects of postpartum depression. Additionally, before birth much focus is on the mother and meeting her needs, and then almost immediately the focus shifts away from her and to the infant. These factors can aggravate predispositions to depression or other mood disorders. Given the potential long-term negative consequences on child development of maternal depression, women who experience postpartum depression should seek medical help.

The Baby at Birth

The average newborn is about 50 cm (20 inches) long and weighs about 3400 grams (about 7.5 pounds). Like any human trait, however, there is substantial variability, with full-term infants from Europe and North America varying in length between 48 cm to 56 cm and in weight from 2500 to 4000 grams or more (O'Railly & Müller, 2001). In the United States, about 97% of babies are born healthy, without major developmental problems or abnormalities (Simpson & Elias, 2003). However, worldwide about 8 million children are born with birth defects each year, about 6% of all births (March of Dimes, 2006).

Infant mortality, the number of children out of every 1,000 births who die during the first year of life, is relatively low in modern societies (usually less than 5 per 1,000; the U.S. infant mortality rate is 6.37 per 1,000 births), although in some areas of the world it is still high, with a global average of 43.5 deaths per 1,000 births (CIA World Facts Book, 2007). The highest rates tend to be in Africa, with many countries having rates in excess of 100 deaths per 1,000 births. Infant mortality rates were much higher in the past, primarily because of the dangers surrounding birth and the vulnerability of infants to infectious diseases that are now (mostly) under control (Volk & Atkinson, 2008).

The term **neonate** is used to describe babies from the time of their birth until they are 1 month of age. Full-term neonates enter the world with an appearance that is far removed from the pretty pictures seen in baby food commercials. Instead, they are usually extremely pink in color and covered in a thin layer of a white, fatty substance called *vernix caseosa* that protected their skin from contact with the amniotic liquid in the womb, and white downy hair called *lanugo* that helps the vernix caseosa stick to the skin. Neonates' heads are often misshapen because of compression of the skull during the birth process. Fortunately, the bones of their skulls are flexible, and their heads will shortly settle into a more pleasing shape (see Chapter 4 for a discussion of skeletal development). At birth, the bones of the skull are separated by six *fontanelles,* which are gaps filled by fibrous tissue. The

neonate An infant from birth through the first month of life.

Apgar scale A test that evaluates a baby's biological fitness at birth.

largest of these fontanelles is found on the top of the head (anterior fontenelle); it can be felt easily in infants and is sometimes referred to as the *soft spot* (see Figure 3.9). This gap closes by the child's second birthday, although all of the fontanelles do not fully close until puberty. In addition to having slightly misshapen heads, newborns' faces may be distorted and they may even have suffered bruises, both conditions that change within days of birth. Birth can be difficult, because the pelvic structure of women and the size of the birth canal are small relative to the size of an infant's head.

A newborn's appearance improves over the first days of life, but of greater significance is not how the baby looks but its health. The transition from life in the uterus to life in the outside world is a drastic one. Infants must for the first time breathe for themselves rather than receive oxygen through the placenta. They must adjust from a cozy world of 98.6 degrees to one that is in all likelihood much cooler (mid-70s for most hospital births). They will soon need to get nourishment from eating, replacing the automatic delivery of nutrition through the umbilical cord. The changes are substantial indeed. Birth represents an unquestionable discontinuity, with many physiological systems changing drastically and abruptly. It is understandable that not all infants make the transition easily.

With respect to the newborn's appearance, an interesting phenomenon, predicted by evolutionary theory, is that the mother and her family are more likely to state that the newborn resembles the father than the mother (Daly & Wilson, 1982; McLain et al., 2000). For example, in the first study to report this, Canadian mothers were four times more likely to say to their husbands that the baby looked like them ("He looks like you, honestly he does") than themselves. This pattern has been shown in other cultures (Regalski & Gaulin, 1993), and occurs even though newborns do *not* actually resemble their fathers more than their mothers (Brédart & French, 1999; McLain et al., 2000). Why should mothers and their kin say this? Mothers are always certain that a baby is theirs, whereas there is always some uncertainty about the parentage of fathers. These assertions by the mothers and her relatives might serve to assure the domestic father that he is indeed the genetic father, increasing the chances that he will care for and invest in the new baby.

Newborns' physical health is usually measured by one of several scales, including the Brazelton Neonatal Assessment Scale (Brazelton & Nugent, 1995), and the most frequently used instrument, the **Apgar scale** (Apgar, 1953). The Apgar test evaluates a baby's biological fitness, giving scores of 0, 1, or 2 for each of five areas: heart rate, breathing (or respiration), reflex irritability, muscle tone, and color (see Table 3.15). The test is given immediately

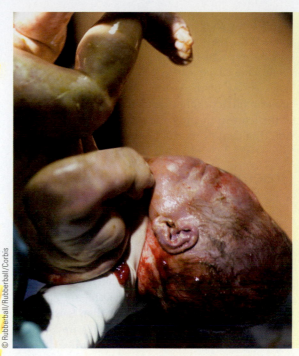

Newborn infants are not always that attractive, sometimes having misshapen heads, distorted facial features, and being covered with a thin layer of a white, fatty substance. They get cuter, however.

© Rubberball/Rubberball/Corbis

after birth and then 4 minutes later, with a score of 7 indicating that the infant is in good health (a score of 10 is perfect). Scores between 4 and 6 indicate that the infant may require special help establishing breathing or other vital signs, while a score of 3 or lower reflects serious danger and calls for emergency intervention.

table 3.15 Apgar Test

Sign	Score		
	0	1	2
Heart rate	No heart beat	Under 100 beats per minute	100 to 140 beats per minute
Breathing (respiratory effort)	No breathing	Irregular, shallow breathing	Strong breathing and crying
Reflex irritability	No response	Weak reflexive response	Strong reflexive response (sneezing, coughing, grimacing)
Muscle tone	Limp	Weak flexion of arms and legs	Strong flexion of arms and legs
Color	Blue body and extremities	Body pink, extremities blue	Completely pink

SOURCE: From Apgar, V. (1953). A proposal for a new method of evaluation in the newborn infant. *Anesthesia & Analgesia*, 32, 260–267. Reprinted by permission of Lippincott, Williams & Wilkins.

Infants who "pass" their Apgar test usually go home with their parents in a few days, but those who have problems stay in the hospital for treatment. One major cause of extended care for neonates is low birth weight. This can be caused by preterm birth or other factors that slow the growth of the fetus in the uterus, such as placenta dysfunction (Hadders-Algra, 2005) or multiple fetuses.

Preemies: Babies Born Too Soon

A large number of babies (about 2% in the U.S.) are born between 23 and 37 weeks of gestational age and are called *preterm infants*, or preemies. Most spend time in the hospital Neonatal (or Newborn) Intensive Care Unit (NICU) after their mothers leave the hospital, usually staying until their scheduled birthdates. Some preemies are the appropriate size and weight for their gestational age, whereas *small-for-date infants* are smaller and weigh less than expected for their age. Infants below 2500 grams (about 5.5 pounds) are labeled *low birth weight* (LBW), below 1500 grams (about 3.3 pounds) as *very low birth weight* (VLBW), and below 1000 grams (about 2.2 pounds) as *extremely low birth weight* (ELBW). With today's technology, about 90% of infants who weigh less than 2 pounds (about 900 grams) survive, and about 50% of those who weigh around 1 pound (about 450 grams) at birth survive, although there are greater chances of problems than there are with full-term, normal birth-weight infants. For example, many

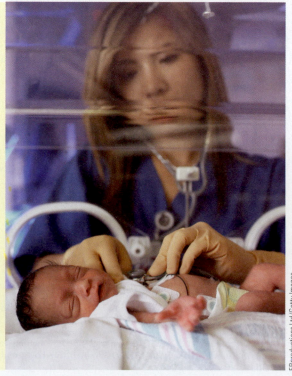

Many premature infants spend time in a neonatal intensive care unit. Advances in medical technology have resulted in many more such infants surviving than in decades past.

preterm infants have trouble breathing and suffer from *respiratory distress syndrome*, characterized by irregular breathing and possible cessation of breathing altogether.

The incidence of premature births has increased in recent decades partly because of improved medical resources that enhance the probability of very low birth-weight infants surviving. This increase is also a consequence of the more extended use of artificial reproductive techniques that increase the possibility of multiple births and the higher rate of women over 34 years old getting pregnant (Hadders-Algra, 2005; Lumley, 2003; see discussion of artificial reproductive techniques in Box 3.2).

Why do some babies enter the world before their due dates? Some causes are infections in the mother's birth canal and structural abnormalities of the cervix. Mothers who are older than 35 and younger than 19 are also at greater risk of having a preemie, as are mothers with multiple fetuses (that is, twins or triplets). Other causes reflect the mother's lifestyle choices during pregnancy: smoking, drinking alcohol, using drugs, eating poorly, not gaining enough weight, exposure to physical stress, and poor prenatal care all contribute to preterm delivery.

The main problem of premature infants is that their organs are not mature enough to adapt to extrauterine life, and they often experience respiratory and cardiovascular problems that can result in lack of oxygen to the brain and improper brain development. For example, between 2.4% and 9% of infants weighing 1500 grams or less experience some degree of cerebral palsy; between 2% and 38% show visual impairment; between 2% and 44% exhibit hearing loss; and between 7% and 27% have intellectual impairment (Ornstein et al., 1991).

This immature development, jointly with poor physical conditions and the chronic stress of their neonatal life, is also partly responsible for some problems that preterm children can experience, even years later as adolescents and adults. For example, examination of data from more than 1 million births in Norway between 1967 and 1988 indicated that individuals born prematurely had an increased risk of dying during childhood and lower fertility rates as adults, and women who were born prematurely had a greater chance of having preterm infants themselves, all relative to individuals born full term (Swamy, Ostbye, & Skjaerven, 2008). Children and adolescents who were born prematurely are more prone than children born full term to show some minor motor development problems (for example, fine motor skills, coordination and balance, muscle tone), some behavioral disorders (attention deficit with hyperactivity disorder [ADHD]), and some enduring learning difficulties (for example, in mathematics, reading, spelling, and writing) (Botting et al., 1997, 1998; Hadder-Algra, 2002, 2005). It is worth noting, however, that the specific relations between brain and behavior in the case of preterm infants remain unclear (Steward et al., 1999), and many factors, including characteristics of children's mothers and the home environment, interact with neonatal condition to influence social and cognitive outcomes.

Beyond the prevalence of the problems described previously, preterm infants tend to increase the level of stress their parents experience, which in turn can negatively affect parent-child interactions. To begin with, parents are less likely to hold or otherwise have body contact with premature babies relative to full-term infants (Hadder-Algra, 2005). Moreover, relative to full-term babies, premature infants are not as cute, are slower to develop endearing behaviors such as smiling and making eye contact, have greater difficulty regulating their behavior, are more demanding, and require significantly more attention and effort from parents. Given these characteristics, it should not be surprising that premature infants are at greater risk of suffering maltreatment some time during their lives than are full-term infants (Mann, 1992).

Therapeutic Touch and Kangaroo Care

Over the course of several decades, advances in medical technology have made it possible for infants born as early as 22 or 23 weeks to survive and often go on to lead normal lives. It is somewhat ironic then that some of the more successful therapies for premature infants involve the very low-tech approach of increasing skin-to-skin contact between these babies and their caretakers. Maternal touch has been shown to help regulate infants' physiology and bio-behavioral development (Field et al., 2004), including brain activity (Jones et al., 1998).

Throughout most of the 20th century, premature babies in most NICUs received little touching. However, research began to show that premature infants who were stroked or touched by parents, nurses, or other caregivers gained weight faster, stayed awake longer, scored better on developmental scales, were released from the hospital sooner, and developed better mother-infant interactions than infants who were not systematically touched (see Jones & Mize, 2007). For example, in one study, 16 preterm neonates (average gestational age = 30.1 months; average weight = 1359 grams) received massage therapy for 15 minutes three times per day for five days (Dieter et al., 2003). These infants showed 53% greater gain in weight compared to a

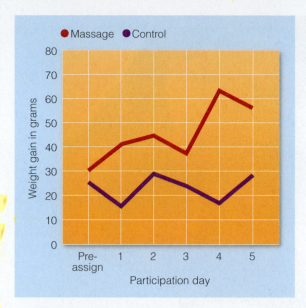

FIGURE 3.10 Weight gain between massage therapy and control infants.

Premature infants who received daily massage therapy gained weight faster than did premature infants in a control (no message therapy) group. SOURCE: From Dieter, J. N., Field, T., Hernandez-Reif, M., Emory, E. K., & Redzepi, M. (2003). Stable preterm infants gain more weight and sleep less after five days of massage therapy. *Journal of Pediatric Psychology, 28*, 403–411. Reprinted by permission of Oxford University Press.

group of comparably premature infants over the course of the study (see Figure 3.10).

One technique that has proved surprisingly successful in dealing with the effects of prematurity is called kangaroo care (sometimes kangaroo mother care). It began in 1978 in Bogota, Columbia, in response to overcrowding in NICUs. Premature babies were placed naked (sometimes with a diaper) between the mother's breasts to facilitate nursing and to keep the baby warm. This was done around the clock, as much as possible, with fathers and other family members cradling infants on their chests part of the day (Charpak, Ruiz-Pelaz, & Figueroa, 2005). Since that time, numerous studies of the effects of kangaroo care have been conducted, with consistently positive results (see Charpak et al., 2005 and Feldman, 2007 for reviews). Premature infants who receive kangaroo care in the hospital and continue the practice in the home after hospital release gain more weight, regulate their body temperature, attention, emotions, and other physiological/psychological functions better, and develop better relationships with their mothers than do control infants. A longitudinal study that has followed premature infants until the

----

kangaroo care A practice that has been found to improve premature infants' development, consisting of putting them between the mother's breasts to facilitate nursing and to keep the baby warm.

Premature infants who receive kangaroo care gain more weight; regulate their body temperature, attention, emotions, and other physiological/psychological functions better, and develop better relationships with their mothers than do control infants.

age of 9 years has shown that many of the positive effects of kangaroo care persist long past infancy (see Feldman, 2007).

Why do simple procedures such as touch therapy and kangaroo care have such substantial benefits on premature infants? Touching between young babies and their mothers releases hormones and neurotransmitters that facilitate brain development in infants (Feldman & Eidelman, 2003) and mother-infant bonding. For example, skin-to-skin contact increases levels of *oxytocin*, the so-called love hormone, in mothers, which promotes mother-infant bonding (see Chapter 12) and reduces maternal stress and depression (Carter, 1998). This can result in faster neurobehavioral development for premature infants and greater ability to regulate their own behavior, such as controlling their arousal and paying attention to the mother (for example, making eye contact, being soothed by the mother). This, coupled with a mother who is less stressed and is hormonally prepared to bond with her infant, can result in increased breastfeeding and a more responsive relationship between the developing baby and the mother (Feldman, 2007). In other words, the simple act of increasing skin-to-skin contact between premature infants and their mothers can set in motion transactions that can foster neurological, physiological, and behavioral development, resulting in a more positive outcome.

The various touch therapies used with premature infants are in part a reaction to the often-harsh environment of the NICU. Preemies are pricked and poked and exposed to auditory and visual stim-

ulation that they would not typically receive until months later. When other animals received stimulation earlier than is typical for their species, they often developed deficits in some areas but accelerated development in others. For example, bobwhite quail that receive visual stimulation while still in the egg show detriments in auditory imprinting (they fail to approach the maternal call of their species) but display greater visual discrimination abilities than do normal hatchlings (Lickliter, 1990). Something similar may happen to human premature infants. Neonatologist Heidelise Als (1995) proposed that the stimulation that premature infants sometimes receive in hospitals interferes with brain development (particularly the frontal cortex) during sensitive periods, often causing problems in speech, eye-hand coordination, attention, and lowered IQ. Yet, these deficits are often accompanied by accelerated development or enhanced abilities in other areas, such as mathematics (see also Lickliter, 2000). According to Als, advances in medical technology permit infants with very immature nervous systems to survive. However, these medical environments are no substitutes for the womb, and they provide inadequate support for immature nervous systems "leading to maladaptations and disabilities, yet also to accelerations and extraordinary abilities" (Als, 1995, p. 462).

Neonate Behaviors: What Do Newborns Do?

If you have been around a newborn for any length of time, you may think that "neonate behaviors" is a strange term for the limited range of activity observed during this time. Their main activity is sleeping, and when they are not sleeping, they are eating, crying, or needing their diapers changed. Although these behaviors are enough to keep parents sleep deprived, less apparent activities are also taking place.

In this section we first focus on how infants and their parents establish progressively regular patterns of sleep-awakeness and eating (and also on some practical problems that parents have to face regarding this). We then examine the three adaptive behavioral systems proposed by Spanish psychologist Juan Delval (1994) available when an infant is awake, namely: (1) systems for receiving information (sensory systems), (2) systems for transmitting information (crying and basic emotions), and (3) systems for acting (reflexes).

Regulation of Sleep-Awake Cycles

Sleep is a very complex behavior, even in a neonate. For example, Peter Wolff (1987, 2005) described six basic states of arousal in neonates (active sleep, quiet sleep, drowsiness, alert awake, active awake, and crying), based on the use of four behavioral criteria (eyes status: closed vs. open; respiration status: regular vs. irregular; amount of movements; and vocalizations). The distribution of these various stages of arousal over the course of a regular 24-hour day is described in Table 3.16, although it should be noted that there may be, as usual, significant individual differences among children.

Interestingly, as you can see from Table 3.16, part of a neonate's sleeping time has been described as an active sleep, characterized by the presence of rapid eye movements (REM) and high levels of electrical activity in the brain. Another part has been described as quiet sleep, characterized by the absence of REM and reduced electrical brain activity (Wolff, 1987; Prechtl & O'Brien, 1982). The distribution of these two types of sleep changes dramatically over time (see Figure 3.11). For example, a newborn sleeps about 16 hours a day, and half of that is REM sleep. The percentage of REM sleep to total sleep decreases to about 35% by 6 months and to 20% by the preschool years and stays relatively constant into adulthood (de Weerd & can den Bossche, 2003; Roffwarg, Muzio, & Dement, 1966). REM sleep is even more frequent during the late prenatal period and for premature infants; about 90% of the sleep of 28-week-old fetuses is REM.

It is worth noting that infants and children, like adults, are more easily wakened during the active, or REM, phase than the quiet, or non-REM, phase of sleep. (We will discuss the importance of sleep to psychological functioning during child-

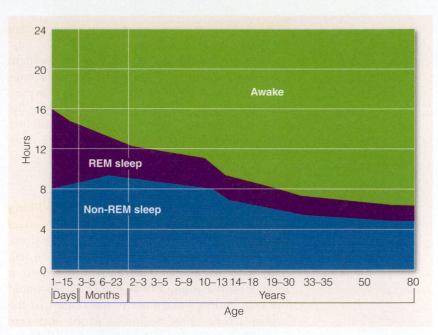

FIGURE 3.11 Changes in sleep patterns over development.
Half of a newborn's sleep (8 of 16 hours) is REM sleep. The proportion of REM to non-REM sleep decreases with age, so that by adulthood only about 20% of sleep is REM sleep. SOURCE: Adapted from Roffwarg, H. P., Muzio, J. N., & Dement, W. C. (1966). Ontogenetic development of the human sleep-dream cycle. Science, 152, 604–619. Reprinted by permission of AAAS.

hood in Chapter 4.) As can be seen from Figure 3.11, a substantial portion of infants' and preschool children's sleep is spent in the active phase, and this has given rise to the hypothesis that the high levels of brain activity during active sleep must be critical for brain development. More specifically, the *autostimulation theory* emphasizes the importance

table 3.16 Infant States of Arousal

State	Description	Number of Hours per Day in Newborn
Quiet sleep	Baby is at rest and shows little movement. Breathing is slow and regular.	8–9 hours
Active sleep	Baby's eyes are closed but moving under eyelids (rapid eye movement [REM] sleep). Baby occasionally stirs and makes facial grimaces. Breathing may be irregular.	8–9 hours
Drowsiness	Baby is either falling asleep or waking up. Eyes open and close with a glazed look when opened. Breathing is regular, but more rapid than in quiet sleep.	Varies from half an hour to 3 hours
Alert awake	Baby is awake, attentive, but relatively inactive. Breathing is even.	2–3 hours
Active awake	Baby is awake, breathing is irregular. Baby may become fussy and show bursts of uncoordinated motor activity.	1–3 hours
Crying	Baby is awake and crying, which maybe difficult to stop.	1–3 hours

SOURCE: Adapted from Wolff, P. H. (1966). The causes, controls and organization of behavior in the neonate. *Psychological Issues, 5* (1, Serial No. 17).

of REM sleep for development of the visual system (Roffwarg et al., 1966; Boismeyer, 1977).

Most children begin to sleep through the night by about 4 months of age and have daily naps until they are 4 years old (Stores, 1999). However, some babies (and some parents, as establishing the infant's sleep/wake cycle is a shared responsibility between baby and parents) can experience problems with this pattern.

Eating

Humans are mammals, and one of the defining characteristics of mammals is that mothers nurse their young. Until relatively recently, breastfeeding was the only way that infants could be fed, baby formula being a modern invention. If a mother with a young infant should die, so would her baby unless some other women breastfed the orphan (Hrdy, 1999). Beginning in the 20th century, advances in technology in the food industry made it possible for babies to be bottle-fed using artificial milk. Specially prepared solid foods are added to milk or formula beginning usually about 5 to 6 months of age.

Whether a neonate is breast- or bottle-fed, it usually needs to be fed about five or six times per day, with an average feeding lasting about 20 minutes. Babies will typically become drowsy and fall asleep shortly after feeding (sometimes dur-

ing). Feeding times are distributed throughout the 24-hour day, making late-night feedings inevitable for parents, usually until the baby gets on a schedule by about 4 months of age. And, of course, what goes in must come out, and neonates can eliminate liquids between 15 to 20 times per day and feces about 7 to 8 times, requiring numerous diaper changes. For many traditional groups, breastfeeding will continue until a child is 2 or 3 years old (sometimes older), whereas most women in contemporary society stop breastfeeding by 1 year of age (Li et al., 2003) and wean babies off the bottle before their second birthdays.

The use of artificial milk and bottle-feeding was well received by physicians and parents alike. It permitted greater freedom to mothers, who could return to work knowing that their infants would be well fed. It permitted fathers and other family members to partake in infant feeding, and it was a godsend to women who had difficulty nursing. In the middle portions of the 20th century, physicians routinely gave new mothers shots to discontinue their milk supply, with bottle-feeding being the preferred way of feeding infants. However, there has been a trend in recent decades for women to nurse their babies, at least for several months after birth, in the belief that mother's milk provides protective and preventive components (for example, antibodies), and fosters both cognitive development and the mother-infant social relationship (American Academy of Pediatrics, 1997; Blum, 2002).

Several studies have found a relationship between breastfeeding and later IQ, with children, adolescents, and adults who were breastfed as babies having higher IQs than those who were bottle-fed (Anderson et al., 1999; Mortensen et al., 2002). One hypothesis for this effect is that breast milk provides fatty acids (not found in cows' milk) that foster brain development early in life (Institute of Medicine, 2004). In addition, the *act* of breastfeeding has been implicated in the higher IQs of breastfed infants: The greater skin-to-skin contact between mothers and breastfed babies promotes better mother-infant relationships, which serve to foster enhanced cognitive development over childhood (Feldman & Eidelman, 2003).

Recent evidence has shown that the benefits to IQ of breastfeeding are related to a specific gene, with infants who have one version of the gene experiencing a benefit in later IQ due to breastfeeding, whereas infants with different versions of the gene experience no IQ-advantage from breastfeeding (Caspi et al., 2007). Avshalom Caspi and his colleagues (2007) identified a gene located on chromosome 11 involved in processing fatty acids. In two large samples, one from New Zealand and

Infants who are breastfed have slightly higher IQs than do bottle-fed infants, although this effect is found only for infants who have a particular version of a gene associated with processing fatty acids.

Nancy Ney/Getty Images

the other from Great Britain, they reported that children who had either of two versions of this gene and were breastfed as infants had significantly higher IQs (approximately 104) relative to children who were not breastfed (approximately 97). In contrast, children with a third version of the gene showed no effect on IQ of being breastfed (both groups had IQs of about 100). This finding reflects the often-complex interactions between specific genes and environment that researchers are increasingly discovering (see discussions earlier in the genetics portion of this chapter).

The Neonate's Adaptive Behavioral Toolkit

Neonates are born with a toolkit that allows them to communicate basic information with the world around them, especially through social interactions. Many of the abilities in this toolkit are socially oriented reflexes that permit infants to begin learning about the world and communicating with people. We look at three systems in infants' toolkit: systems for receiving information (sensory systems), systems for transmitting information (crying and basic emotions), and systems for acting (reflexes), following the classification of Delval (1994).

Systems for receiving information: Sensory systems. Vision, perhaps the most dominant sense in adults, is the least developed of the senses at birth. The focusing, or accommodation, of the lens of the eye is poor at birth, and most of what newborns see is fuzzy (Banks, 1980; Tondel & Candy, 2008). Newborns can see objects most clearly that are about 20 to 25 cm, or 8 to 10 inches, from their eyes, which corresponds to the distance between an infant's face and that of his or her mother during nursing. Newborns are apparently able to discriminate between various facial expressions denoting emotion and to imitate some of those expressions (Field et al., 1982), a phenomenon known as *neonatal imitation*. We will discuss some of this research in Chapters 5 and 11, but in general, neonates have limited *visual acuity*. Other visual abilities that are not well developed in neonates are depth and color perception. Despite this slow beginning, the visual system is mature and efficient by about 6 months of age (Slater, 1995).

The sense of touch, as mentioned before, develops early in prenatal life. Touch is tremendously important for mammals, especially species that lick their offspring to regulate their temperature, respiration, and digestion (Trevathan 2005). Although licking neonates is not a typical practice with humans, analogous behaviors can be seen in touch—rubbing and stroking the baby with the

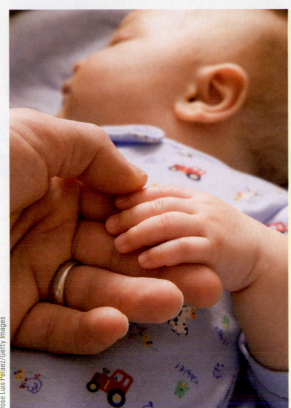

Parents hold, massage, and explore their infants' faces, fingers, and toes. Newborns are sensitive to touch, and this may help them regulate their temperature, respiration, and digestion.

Jose Luis Pelaez/Getty Images

hands. This is thought to help regulate respiratory and cardiovascular functions, and, as mentioned previously, infant massage has been shown to have positive effects on the development of premature babies (Dieter et al., 2003; Feldman, 2007). Typically, mothers embrace their babies, hold them and cradle them against their left side (regardless of handedness), and explore their babies' fingers, hands, face, and limbs with their fingertips (Klaus, Kennell, & Klaus, 1995; Trevathan, 2005).

Newborns are also sensitive to pain (Delevati & Bergamasco, 1999), and some animal research suggests that painful experiences during the fetal period can have long-term consequences after birth by organizing how the brain interprets painful stimuli. This was investigated in a study with neonatal rats (Ruda, et al., 2000). Neurons in the spinal cords of rats develop during embryonic and early postnatal times, typically when rat pups are protected by their mother from painful experiences. When newborn rats (who are maturationally much like human fetuses) were exposed to painful stimulation, the nerve circuits that respond to pain were altered, making the rats more sensitive to pain as adults. There is also evidence that extremely low birth weight (ELBW) infants' response to pain is influenced by repeated painful episodes, which are often necessary for preterm babies. When ELBW infants were tested at 8 months of age, the number

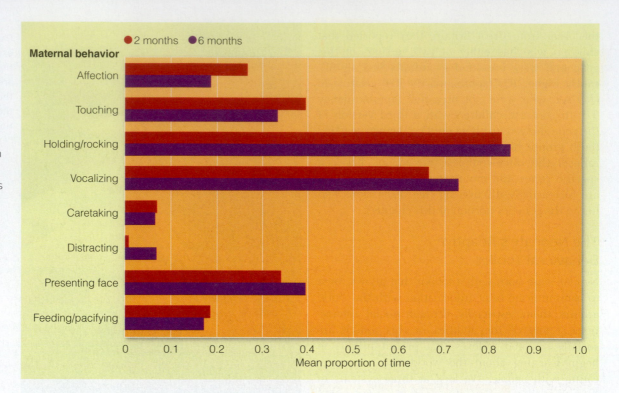

FIGURE 3.12 Mean proportion of time that various soothing techniques were used by mothers with their infants when they were 2 and 6 months old. Mothers use a variety of soothing techniques with their infants that change somewhat as their babies get older. SOURCE: Jahromi, L. B., Putnam, S. P., & Stifter, C. A. (2004). Maternal regulation of infant reactivity from 2 to 6 months. *Developmental Psychology*, 40, 477–487. Copyright © 2004 by the American Psychological Association. Reprinted by permission.

of invasive procedures infants had had from birth was related to their facial and heart rate reactions to pain (blood collection) (Grunau et al., 2001). It has been only within the past 25 years that physicians bothered giving human infants anesthesia for some medical procedures, believing that their perception of painful stimuli was minimal. These findings suggest that such unanticipated stimulation, even if the infants seem not to perceive it as acutely painful, can adversely alter the species-typical course of development.

Taste and olfaction are two senses that develop before birth. Infants develop a clear preference for sweet tastes, even while in the womb, and reject bitter tastes at birth. In fact, a pregnant woman's diet can influence taste preferences in her newborn. This was illustrated in a study in which some women consumed anise-flavored food during pregnancy while others did not. At birth and 4 days later, infants born to anise-consuming mothers showed a preference for anise odor, whereas those born to non-anise-consuming mothers displayed aversion or neutral responses to anise (Schaal, Marlier, & Soussignan, 2000). Young infants can also tell the difference among a wide range of odors early in life (Steiner, 1979) and develop preferences for certain odors within the first week. For example, in one study, 6-day-old nursing babies were able to discriminate the odor of their mothers from those of other women (Macfarlane, 1975). Mothers wore breast pads in their bras between nursings. Infants were placed

between two breast pads—one from the baby's mother and the other from another woman. These 6-day-old babies turned to their own mother's pad more often than to the pad of another woman (there was no differential turning at 2 days of age). Thus, not only can neonates discriminate odors, but they also quickly learn to associate odors with people and to modify their behavior accordingly. More recently, researchers reported that infants develop a preference for the odor of milk versus amniotic fluid (which they had been living in for 9 months) by 4 days (Marlier, Schaal, & Soussignan, 1998) and that bottle-fed, 2-week-old infants prefer the breast odor of a lactating woman to that of a nonlactating woman (Makin & Porter, 1989; Porter & Winberg, 1999).

The sense of hearing is also well developed at birth and even before. It should be no surprise that neonates recognize their mothers' and fathers' voices, given that they were exposed to those sounds when in the womb. They also prefer women's voices over those of men (DeCasper & Fifer, 1980), again, not surprising given that they had been hearing their mother's voice ever since their hearing was well-enough developed to perceive voices from outside the womb. In a much-cited study, newborns showed a preference for listening to a story their mothers had read aloud frequently during the last weeks of pregnancy relative to another story (DeCasper & Spence, 1986). In this study, pregnant women read aloud passages from one of two stories (*The Cat in the Hat* or *The*

King, the Mice, and the Cheese) twice a day during the last 6 weeks of their pregnancies. Shortly after birth, babies were fitted with headphones and heard either the passage their mothers had read to them or the other passage. Babies sucked on a pacifier and could change the passage they heard by changing their rate of sucking (for instance, some could hear the passage their mothers read by increasing their sucking rate, others by decreasing their sucking rate).

The main finding was that newborns changed their sucking rate in order to hear the passage their mothers had read during their last weeks of pregnancy. This finding not only indicates that hearing is functioning well during the final weeks of pregnancy, but that neonates and fetuses learn some of the auditory characteristics of the sounds they hear and develop preferences for those sounds. (Some of those preferences are for the language their mothers speak, which we discuss in Chapter 9.) It is also impressive, we believe, that newborns can demonstrate this knowledge in a learning paradigm (in this case, by changing their sucking rate), indicating that babies from birth are able to adjust their behavior as a result of environmental reinforcements.

Systems for transmitting information: Crying. Although children do not produce their first words until they are nearly 1 year old, they are still able to communicate, and this ability begins at birth. The earliest form of communication is crying. This may not be the most elegant communication system (it is noisy, disturbing, imprecise, and limited to negative expressions), but it works pretty well. Crying serves as a sort of alarm system for adults, particularly the infants' caregivers, and quite soon parents learn to interpret some of the specific types of crying. Peter Wolff (1987) described at least four different types of cries neonates use to communicate: one that is very strong for expressing pain; another that is weaker and rhythmic for expressing hunger; a third cry that expresses anger; and a fourth type, seen about the third or fourth week of life, simply calling for attention. Some researchers are reluctant to accept that infants' crying provides any specific information about the causes of distress, just that it is a graded signal that expresses different levels of distress (Gustafson, Wood, & Green, 2000).

In any case, crying is the first significant sound produced by babies at birth, and, on average, neonates cry for about 2 hours per day. Crying bouts are typical during the first 3 months of life, peaking around 5 to 6 weeks and then diminishing in healthy infants (St. James-Roberts, 2005). However, there are individual differences in the amount of crying babies do. Some show a higher level of reactivity than others (see Chapter 11), and some parents are more proficient at soothing their infants or preventing their crying (Jahromi & Stifter, 2007). What do mothers do to soothe their infants and stop them from crying? That depends somewhat on the child's age, but most mothers do a combination of things, such as holding or rocking their babies, talking to them, and looking right at them (see Figure 3.12). In fact, using a combination of different techniques simultaneously (for example, holding/rocking and vocalizing) rather than a single technique is most effective in soothing a crying infant (Jahromi, Putnam & Stifter, 2004). And the techniques that are used will depend on how stressed the infant is. For example, distracting a baby or giving the baby a pacifier can be very effective when his or her level of stress is low, but ineffective when stress is high.

Although techniques that promote continuous and rhythmic stimulation, such as rocking or sucking on a pacifier, tend to be quite effective and used by mothers everywhere, some soothing techniques differ across cultures. For example, the Hopi and Navajo Indians of North America, and Quechua Indians of South America, swaddle infants to soothe them, wrapping them tightly in a blanket so that their limbs are immobile, often on a cradleboard or in a pouch (Chisholm, 1963; Tronick, Thomas, & Daltabuit, 1994). Infants are then either carried or can be stood upright so they have a view of their surroundings. It is believed that swaddling stabilizes body temperature and can result in infants getting more external (visual) stimulation, in comparison with infants lying horizontally in a cradle (Tronick et al., 1994; Shonkoff & Phillips, 2000). This may also be a reason why babies who are carried on a shoulder or placed upright in a parent's lap are less fussy—there is more for them to see than when they are lying on their backs (Korner & Thoman, 1970).

Systems for acting: Neonatal reflexes. At birth, infants lack control over their bodies. They move their legs, arms, and heads in what seem to be a random fashion, and they sometimes squirm, particularly when they are distressed. However, they do have available to them several prewired responses to certain stimuli—automatic responses called *neonatal reflexes*. The presence of these reflexes makes possible certain important behaviors in response to environmental input. Some of these reflexes are described in Table 3.17. Pediatricians

Kristin Duvall/Getty Images

Neonates cry about two hours per day, and crying usually peaks between 5 and 6 weeks of age. Parents use a variety of techniques to soothe infants, some of which vary among cultures.

table 3.17 Neonatal Reflexes

Most neonatal reflexes disappear within the first six months. Some disappear later, whereas others are permanent.

Reflex	Eliciting Stimulus	Response	Approximate Course of Development
Moro	Loud sound, loss of support, sudden movement	Extension of forearms and fingers followed by return to chest	Disappears within 3 months
Palmar	Pressure against palm	Grasping	Disappears within 4–6 months
Plantar	Pressure to balls of feet	Flexion of toes (toe grasping)	Disappears within 10 months
Walking	Upright position and feet touching level surface	Walking movements	Disappears within 2 months
Righting of head and body	Head or leg turning	Trunk or head movement in the same direction	Disappears within 1 year
Withdrawal	Painful stimulus	Limb withdrawal	Permanent
Rooting	Stimulation around mouth region	Head movement toward stimulus	Disappears within 4–6 months
Sucking	Object inserted into mouth	Sucking	Disappears within 4–6 months
Crawling	Prone position and pressure applied alternately to soles of feet	Crawling pattern	Disappears within 4–6 months
Swimming	Placed in water with head supported	Swimming movements	Disappears within 5 months
Climbing	Held in horizontal position	Climbing movements	Disappears within 6 months

SOURCE: From Bjorklund, D. F., & Bjorklund, B. R. (1992). *Looking at children: An introduction to child development.* Copyright © 1992 Wadsworth, a part of Cengage Learning, Inc. Reproduced by permission. www.cengage.com/permissions.

use the presence and strength of an infant's reflexes at birth as an indication of neurological development. However, most of these reflexes disappear over the first four months or so, and if they are still present later in infancy, they are an indication of impaired neurological development.

Some neonatal reflexes have obvious survival values. For instance, infants will turn their heads away from an object that obstructs their breathing. The survival value for such a reflex is self-evident, as is the reflex for sucking. An infant who had to learn to suck would have a very difficult time obtaining nutrition, and thus would not be likely to live. Related to nursing is the *rooting reflex*, whereby infants turn their heads in the direction of stimulation when they are stroked on the cheek or corner of the mouth. The *palmar grasp*, or *grasping reflex*, consists of the infant spontaneously grasping an object (such as a finger) that is pressed into his or her hand. The survival benefits of this reflex may not be as obvious as the sucking or rooting reflex, but the value of this reflex may have been much greater for our distant ancestors who needed occasionally to cling to tree branches or to the hair on their mothers' backs.

One way to classify reflexes is to describe them in terms of how they develop (see for example, Delval, 1994). Some reflexes are permanent, because they do not disappear over time and remain relatively the same throughout life, such as the eye-blink reflex, the knee-jerk reflex, and the sneeze reflex. Others disappear some time after birth (most around the third or fourth month, but some disappear later, during the second half of the first year of life), and never come back again, such as the Moro, or startle, reflex and the tonic neck reflex. Finally, a third group of reflexes is composed of behaviors that become voluntary with time, some of them in an apparently easy and fast way, such as the sucking and grasping reflexes, and others that involve a longer relearning period following their disappearance as reflexes, as in the walking, or stepping, reflex and the swimming reflex (see Chapter 4).

Sudden Infant Death Syndrome (SIDS) The death of a seemingly healthy infant during sleep for no apparent reason during the first year of life.

BOX 3.4 **food for thought**

Sudden Infant Death Syndrome (SIDS)

One of the most perplexing questions to medical science has been the cause of **Sudden Infant Death Syndrome (SIDS)**, which is defined as the sudden and unexplained death of an apparently healthy infant that occurs between one week and one year of age. One of every 2,000 infants born each year succumbs to this tragedy, and it remains a mystery despite years of research into its cause and its prevention.

Several prenatal risk factors have been identified, including low birth weight, premature birth, inadequate prenatal care, mother's use of tobacco, alcohol, and heroin during pregnancy, and being male (more than 60% of the SIDS cases are male babies). Factors in the infant's environment after birth have been investigated, such as secondhand smoke, sleeping face-down, sleeping with excess clothing and bedding, not being breastfed, and co-sleeping (sleeping together with parents or other family members). Although none has been identified as the cause of SIDS, this research has led to several recommendations on reducing the risk of SIDS.

The best-known method to reduce the chances of SIDS is for parents to put babies on their backs instead of on their tummies to sleep, which was the standard practice until two decades ago. In 1992, the American Academy of Pediatrics began recommending this change, and in 1996, the National Institute of Child Health and Human Development (NICHD) began an educational campaign called "Back to Sleep" (Lipsitt, 2003). Since that time, the percentage of infants who sleep on their backs has increased, and the rate of SIDS has decreased (see Photo). Today about 75 percent of all infants in the United States sleep on their backs, compared to 13 percent in 1992, and the SIDS rate has been cut in half during that same time. Similar results have been found in other countries that followed this practice, such as New Zealand (see McKenna, 2005). Although the mechanism for SIDS has still not been identified, most pediatricians agree that this sleep position is a good way to lower the chances of an infant dying from SIDS. Physicians recommend that infants be placed on their stomachs for playtime, which allows crawling to develop on time.

Another way to lower the chance of SIDS is to protect infants from secondhand smoke. The U.S. Surgeon General reported in 2006 that infants who are exposed to secondhand smoke have a greater incidence of SIDS, and also that autopsies of infants who have died of SIDS show a higher concentration of nicotine in their lungs and higher levels of nicotine in their blood than healthy infants, which are markers for exposure to secondhand smoke. The Surgeon General also stated that there is no risk-free level of exposure to secondhand smoke and strongly recommended smoke-free environments for pregnant women, infants, and children (U.S. Department of Health and Human Services, 2006).

Early speculation that breastfeeding helped reduce the chances of SIDS has not been supported by research, and other speculation that co-sleeping increased the chances of SIDS has been met with mixed findings (McKenna & McDade, 2005; American Academy of Pediatrics Task Force on Sudden Infant Death Syndrome, 2005). Other recommendations to reduce the chance of SIDS are for parents to make sure that the baby's mattress is firm and that

there are no blankets, toys, or other bedding in the crib that could interfere with breathing. Some researchers have shown that the use of pacifiers seems to reduce the risk of SIDS, probably because it keeps the baby's face away from the mattress. Using a sleep sack has also been shown to be useful in some studies, because it keeps the baby on his or her back during sleep and also controls the body temperature in cold weather.

Most research on biological mechanisms involved in SIDS has centered on problems with babies' respiratory control, for example, disturbance in the brain mechanisms that regulate breathing, a fast-acting bacteria that attacks the infant's respiratory muscles, or sleep apnea (sudden cessation of breathing while sleeping). A gene has been identified, 5-HTT, that is linked to serotonin regulation in the brain. Research has shown that this gene is more prevalent in populations that have a high level of SIDS and almost nonexistent in populations that have low levels (Weese-Mayer et al., 2007; McKenna, 2005).

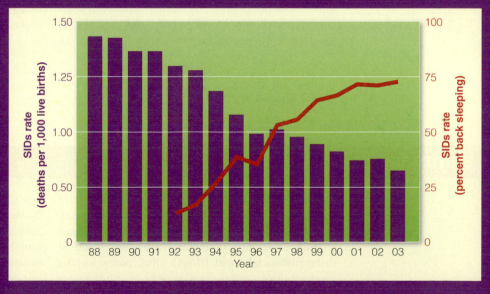

The percentage of infants who sleep on their backs has increased since the 1990s (purple line), and the rate of SIDS has decreased (red line). SOURCE: National Center for Health Statistics, CDC, www.nichd.nih.gov/sids/upload/SIDS_rate_backsleep_03.pdf, Downloaded July 20, 2009.

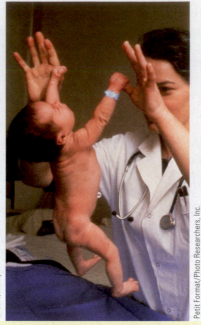

© Caro/Alamy

Petit Format/Photo Researchers, Inc.

Petit Format/Photo Researchers, Inc.

Babies display a number of basic reflexes at birth including (from left) the sucking reflex, grasping reflex, and Moro reflex.

Given developmental psychologists' emphasis on studying thought and behavior, it is understandable that they tend to focus on infants, children, adolescents, and adults of various ages more so than on fetuses and newborns. After all, fetuses and newborns do not behave much, and there is certainly not much thought going on in their heads, at least as conventionally understood. But the actions and cognitions that characterize infants, children, adolescents, and even adults have their origins in the genes they inherit at the moment of conception and their experiences while still in the womb and during their first days of life. We do not want to give the impression that either genes or prenatal experiences destines one's life, but they undeniably serve as a foundation for later development, as do the experiences of the neonate. The bidirectional relationship between child and environment, which will shape the course of development, begins before birth and continues uninterrupted throughout life.

summary

Gregor Mendel is credited as being the father of genetics with his discovery of the **laws of segregation** and **independent assortment**. **Chromosomes** contain thousands of **genes**, which are made of deoxyribonucleic acid (**DNA**). DNA codes for the production of amino acids, which, in combination with one another, form proteins. Modern science has mapped the **human genome**, a description of all of a human's genetic material.

Monogenic inheritance refers to traits that are influenced by only a single pair of genes. Different versions of a single gene are referred to as **alleles**. **Polygenic inheritance** refers to the inheritance of traits that are influenced by many different genes. Modern genetics makes a distinction between **genotype** (the actual genes one inherits) and **phenotype** (one's observed characteristics) and between dominant and recessive traits. The **norm of reaction** refers to all the possible phenotypes that could result from a single genotype, given all the possible environments an organism could be exposed to.

Chromosomes divide during the process of **meiosis** to form sperm in males and ova in females. Genetic variability is further increased by **crossing over**, which takes place during meiosis before the first cell division. Humans have 23 chromosome pairs—22 **autosomes** and a single pair of **sex chro-**

mosomes (XX in females and XY in males). The male determines the sex of a child, in that he provides either an X (eventual female) or Y (eventual male) chromosome to an offspring, whereas the female always provides an X. Most **sex-linked inheritance** characteristics are passed along from mothers to sons and are caused by the fact that there is no gene on the Y chromosome to counteract the effect of a single recessive gene on the X chromosome. About half of all chromosomal abnormalities are related to the autosomes (as in **Down syndrome**) and half to the sex chromosomes (as in **Turner syndrome**).

Behavioral genetics refers to the study of the genetic basis of behavior and psychological characteristics, such as intelligence and personality. Twin and adoption studies have shown that intelligence, personality, and psychopathology are highly heritable, as reflected by **concordance rates** and estimates of **heritability**. Shared and nonshared environments also influence psychological traits. According to contemporary theory, one's genes influence which environments a person will experience, with environment playing a major role in shaping psychological characteristics, as expressed by **genotype → environment theory**.

Prenatal development is divided into three periods. **The germinal phase** begins with conception in the **fallopian tube**, forming the **zygote**, and ends with the **blastocyst** implanting in the wall of the uterus. Beginning in the **embryonic phase**, the embryo gets its nutrition through the **placenta**. The **fetal phase** begins at about 9 weeks and continues until birth, with the fetus perfecting its organs and gaining in weight and size. During the prenatal period, development is most rapid in the head area relative to the rest of the body, which is known as **cephalocaudal development**.

Teratogens are external agents that adversely affect the developing embryo/fetus and are apt to have the most severe effect during the embryonic and early fetal phases. A variety of factors can adversely affect the developing fetus, including maternal health, environmental toxins, including medications and illegal drugs, smoking, maternal alcohol consumption (which can lead to **fetal alcohol syndrome**, or **FAS**), infectious diseases, and **Rh factor incompatibility** between the mother and the fetus. Prenatal diagnostic testing includes ultrasound, alpha-fetoprotein testing, amniocentesis, chorionic villous sampling, fetoscopy, and preimplantation genetic diagnosis. Infertility is relatively common in the United States, and **assisted reproductive techniques** (**ART**) using **in vitro fertilization** (**IVF**) have revolutionized the treatment of infertility.

Childbirth occurs in three stages: labor, delivery, and afterbirth. Childbirth practices have gone through substantial changes over the centuries, with women and families taking more control of childbirth and having a broader range of options. When birth complications occur, a **Cesarean delivery/Cesarean section**, or **C-section**, is often required, with the infant being removed through a surgical incision in the mother's abdomen. Some women experience **postpartum depression** that can last several months and adversely affect the mother-child relationship. Childbirth practices have changed through the years, but many women today opt for **natural**, or **prepared**, **childbirth**.

Neonates' physical health is usually measured by the **Apgar scale**, a test of five indicators of a neonate's physical condition. Infants born prematurely can benefit from therapeutic touch therapy and **kangaroo care**, which involves prolonged skin-to-skin contact between infant and mother.

Newborns spend a disproportionate amount of time sleeping. They possess several reflexes, some of which have obvious survival value, such as rooting and sucking. All of an infant's sensory systems are functioning at birth, although some, such as vision, function poorly but develop rapidly over the following months. Neonates' primary means of communication is through crying

Several prenatal risk factors are associated with **Sudden Infant Death Syndrome** (**SIDS**), including low birth weight, premature birth, inadequate prenatal care, mother's use of tobacco, alcohol, and heroin during pregnancy, and being male (more than 60 percent of the SIDS cases are male babies).

Key Terms and Concepts

human genome (p. 86)

law of segregation (p. 86)

law of independent assortment (p. 86)

chromosomes (p. 87)

DNA (p. 87)

gene (p. 87)

monogenic inheritance (p. 87)

alleles (p. 88)

genotype (p. 88)

phenotype (p. 88)

mutations (p. 89)

sickle-cell anemia (p. 89)

polygenic inheritance (p. 90)

norm of reaction (p. 91)

meiosis (p. 92)

crossing over (p. 93)

autosomes (p. 93)

sex chromosomes (p. 93)

sex-linked inheritance (p. 94)

Down syndrome (p. 95)

Turner syndrome (p. 96)

behavioral genetics (p. 97)

concordance rates (p. 98)

heritability (p. 99)

shared environment (p. 101)

nonshared environment (p. 101)

genotype → environment theory (p. 101)

Ask Yourself . . .

1. What are genes and how do they operate? How do genes influence human behavior and development?
2. What are some of the chromosomal abnormalities associated with the sex chromosomes? How do these abnormalities come about? How are sex-linked characteristics transmitted?
3. What are concordance rates and heritability coefficients, and what they are useful for?
4. What are the ways that children's genotypes and environments influence their development, according to Scarr and McCartney's genotype → environment theory?
5. How does development proceed from conception to birth?
6. What are the most significant risks during prenatal development? In what ways can development be altered between the time of conception and birth?
7. What are the primary diagnostic techniques for assessing the status of the fetus and newborn, and how do they work?
8. How does birth proceed, and what are some of the most frequent complications?
9. What are some of the problems of premature infants, and how can they be managed?
10. What are the main challenges that newborns face to become adapted to life outside the womb? What behavioral devices do they have available to help them cope with their new environment?

Exercises: Going Further

1. Your father tells you he read in the newspaper that a recent Harvard study of colleague graduates reported the heritability of intelligence is about .74. This means, as far as he understands, that genes are what really matters with respect to intelligence and that environment plays an insignificant role. How would you explain this finding to him?
2. A friend has recently found out that she is pregnant. What concrete suggestions would you give her so that she can prevent some potential problems during pregnancy and birth?
3. A couple of acquaintances are going to be parents soon, and they tell you they feel worried because they have been told that, for the first several months after birth, many infants stay awake all night, cry a lot, and are even at risk of "dying all of a sudden." They also are concerned about whether to breastfeed or not, because the mother-to-be has to return to her job as soon as possible after giving birth. They also feel insecure about their interactions with their future baby, because they have heard that infants are essentially blind at birth and socially incompetent. What would you tell them to ease their fears a bit, and what recommendations, if any, would you give them to help them avoid some of the problems they anticipate?

Suggested Reading

Classic Works

Scarr, S., & McCartney, K. (1983). How people make their own environments: A theory of genotype → environment effects. *Child Development, 54,* 424–435. This article introduces the genotype → environment model of development, proposing that "genes drive experience." This model has had a profound effect on how psychologists view the interactions of genes and environment over the course of development.

Plomin, R., & Daniels, D. (1987). Why are children in the same family so different from one another? *Behavioral and Brain Sciences, 10,* 1–15. In this article, Plomin and Daniels make the critical distinction between shared and nonshared environmental effects, showing, contrary to conventional thinking in psychology at that time, that the effects of nonshared environment within the same family on siblings for personality, psychopathology, and cognitive abilities are more important than the shared effects.

Scholarly Works

Caspi, A., McClay, J., Moffitt, T. E., Mill, J., Martin, J., Craig, I. W., et al. (2002). Role of genotype in the cycle of violence in maltreated children. *Science, 297,* 851–854. This is the first of several studies from Caspi and his colleagues examining how specific genes in interaction with rearing environments can result in patterns of behavior, here violence.

Moore, K. L., & Persaud, T. V. N. (2003). *The developing human: Clinically oriented embryology* **(7th ed.). Saunders: Philadelphia**. This book, with hundreds of animations, will tell you more about embryological development than you need to know. It provides information clearly about both typical and abnormal prenatal development. A shorter version, distilling the detailed information in this text can be found in the authors' 2007 book, *Before we are born: Essentials of embryology and birth defects* (6th ed.). Saunders: Philadelphia.

Plomin, R., DeFries, J. C., McClearn, G. E., & McGuffin, P. (2008). *Behavioral genetics* **(5th ed.). New York: Worth Publishers**. This is an authoritative textbook on behavioral genetics, including the most up-to-date research and theory in the field.

Reading for Personal Interest

Rutter, M. (2006). *Genes and behavior: Nature-nurture interplay explained.* **Malden, MA: Blackwell**. This book provides a highly readable and up-to-date account of research in behavior genetics, written by one of the leaders of the field who also knows a thing or two about development. We were tempted to include this in the category *Scholarly Works* because it is so thorough, but it is written so it can be understood by the educated layperson.

Nilsson, L., & Hamberger, L. (2004). *A child is born* **(4th ed.). New York: Delta**. Lennart Nilsson's photographs of prenatal development have fascinated scientists, parents-to-be, and just about everyone else who has looked at them. They turn the cold, technical details of prenatal development into something rich and alive.

Karmiloff, K., & Karmiloff-Smith, A. (2004). *Everything your baby would ask you if only he or she could ask.* **Buffalo, NY: Firefly Books**. This book answers a series of questions that a hypothetical baby asks about itself, providing easy-to-understand, scientifically based answers, beginning first with life in the womb.

Blumberg, M. S. (2009). *Freaks of nature: What abnormalities tell us about development and evolution.* **New York: Oxford University Press**. Developmental neuroscientist Mark Blumberg examines the genetic and environmental causes of freaks of nature, from two-headed sisters growing up in Minnesota to people (and animals) born without limbs, and how individuals with such abnormalities develop ways to function normally. In the process, we learn a great deal about the processes of typical development and evolution.

Cengage Learning's **Psychology CourseMate** for this text brings course concepts to life with interactive learning, study, and exam preparation tools, including quizzes and flashcards for this chapter's Key Terms and Concepts (see the summary list on pages 133–134). The site also provides an **eBook** version of the text with highlighting and note taking capabilities, as well as an extensive library of observational videos that span early childhood through adolescence. Many videos are accompanied by questions that will help you think critically about and deepen your understanding of the chapter topics addressed, especially as they pertain to core concepts. Log on and learn more at **www.cengagebrain.com**.

In this chapter we examine physical development over infancy, childhood, and adolescence. We begin by looking at changes in size and proportions and factors that affect physical growth. We devote considerable space to development in adolescence, in part because both the physical changes and the psychological consequences are so substantial. We then discuss both gross and fine motor development. We conclude by exploring the evolution and development of the brain.

Fourth-grader Tanya came home one day with an unusual story. She had been standing in the lunch line when the girl in front of her confided in a whisper, "I hope they don't pop out while we're up here." Tanya asked what "they" were, and her classmate replied, "You know," and pointed to either side of her chest. Later at recess, Tanya's friend explained that she had recently asked her mother when she would have breasts. Her mother laughed and said, "Don't worry about it, they'll just 'pop out' someday." Instead of laying her daughter's worries to rest, her mother's answer had only added to her anxiety. Pop out? When? Where? Would it happen at school when she was in the lunch line? Would people be able to hear it? Do other girls worry about this, too? Tanya told her she didn't think it would happen that way, but she would ask her mother to be sure.

Physical growth often takes a back seat in developmental psychology to social, cognitive, and emotional development—topics that are seemingly more complex, variable, and interesting than physical development. But as this young girl's story reminds us, physical development involves more than just predictable changes in a child's size, shape, and motor control. Those changes affect the way adults view children, the way children view themselves, and the type of experiences they have. Physical changes underlie all aspects of a child's being and

BOX 4.1 evolution in action

Slow Growth and Human Development: The Evolution of Childhood

We humans take many years before we reach adulthood. We spend a greater proportion of our lives in childhood than any other mammal. For example, among primates, sexual maturity is achieved in lemurs at approximately 2 years, in macaque monkeys at approximately 4 years, in chimpanzees at approximately 8 years, and in humans at approximately 15 years or longer (Poirier & Smith, 1974). In fact, based on historical data and data from traditional cultures (Hill & Hurtado, 1996; Kaplan et al., 2000), it is likely that our ancient ancestors were closer to 18 to 20 years of age before being fully reproductive.

Development is also slow in a less obvious way, and that is from the perspective of evolution. Many of the adult characteristics of humans are actually embryonic or neonatal characteristics of our distant ancestors. Using the chimpanzee as a model for what our distant ancestors may have been like, we find many features in *adult* humans that resemble those of *infant* chimps. What happens in development is that chimps outgrow these features. The face is a case in point. At birth, the faces of a human infant and an infant chimpanzee or orangutan are remarkably similar (see Photos this page). The proportions of the chimp's face change drastically with age, however. Prominent brow ridges develop, and both the upper and lower jaws jut out (see Photos next page). The facial proportions change in humans in these same directions but

The faces of infant humans and apes (here, a baby orangutan) are very similar.

not nearly as drastically as for chimpanzees (with men showing more apelike change than women). The tendency toward slow development in general and the retention of infantile characteristics of an evolutionary ancestor has been termed **neoteny** (de Beer, 1958; Gould, 1977), which literally means "holding youth."

But perhaps the most obvious difference in development between humans and other mammals is the length of time it takes to reach sexual maturity and adulthood. Is this merely an extension of the typical primate pattern, or is there something new in the way humans make their way to adulthood? Zoologists generally recognize three postnatal stages in mammal development: *infancy*, the *juvenile period*, and *adulthood*.

Infancy begins at birth and continues until weaning. The juvenile period comes next and describes young animals that are basically fending for themselves but are not yet ready to reproduce, which is followed by the period of adulthood. The physical anthropologist Barry Bogin (2001, 2003) proposed that over the course of human evolution, *Homo sapiens* did not simply extend the infancy and juvenile periods to postpone reaching adulthood, but rather developed two new developmental stages: *childhood* and *adolescence*.

In everyday parlance, we think of childhood as the time between infancy and adolescence, but Bogin defines it a bit more precisely. Childhood for Bogin begins with the cessation of weaning, about 3 years old

---

in some cases can have profound effects on school performance, relationships with family members, choice of after-school activities, and choice of friends. Physical development reflects the biological changes that underlie psychological development; there is no psychology without biology. This means that knowledge of physical development is an important component in our attempt to understand the development of the whole child.

We begin the chapter with Box 4.1, which looks at our species' slow journey to adulthood and the possible invention of new developmental stages

in our ancestors that led to the evolution of modern human beings. We then provide an overview of the major changes in physical size and the nature of developmental changes in physical growth. We also examine factors that influence growth and discuss the problem of childhood obesity as well as eating disorders. We then shift our focus to one of the most important and drastic periods of change in the life span—adolescence and the onset of sexual maturity. We next look at aspects of children's motor development, examining both gross and fine motor changes in children's abilities to control their bodies. We then devote a relatively large section to the development of perhaps the body's most important organ—at least from a psychological perspec-

---

neoteny Retention of the infantile characteristics of an evolutionary ancestor.

Chimpanzee faces show substantial change with age, including the development of prominent brow ridges and the jutting out of both the upper and lower jaws. Humans, in contrast, show much less facial development, retaining many of their juvenile facial features.

in traditional cultures, until 6 or 7 years of age. During this time, young humans cannot remotely fend for themselves. They still have their baby teeth, with their first permanent teeth coming in sometime during their seventh year. Not only do 3- to 6-year-old children lack the teeth, strength, and motor coordination to survive on their own, but they also lack the intellectual wherewithal to function independently. As we mentioned briefly in Chapter 2, Jean Piaget described the thinking of preschool children as *preoperational*. Their thinking is symbolic (they use language quite successfully, after all), but it lacks logic, or mental operations in Piaget's terminology. (See more in-depth discussion of preoperational thinking in Chapter 6.) It is likely no coincidence that many societies begin formal education, religious training, or the establishment of new responsibilities around the end of this childhood period.

It is nearly inconceivable to imagine children much before the age of 7 making their way successfully on their own. We do not expect too much more of 8- or 9-year-old children, but they seem to have both the minimal physical (for example, teeth) and intellectual abilities to survive (if marginally) in a social group without substantial dependency upon adults. Think of the Artful Dodger from Dickens' *Oliver Twist*, and the millions of street children around the world today, who eke out an existence, often despite the actions of adults. (See Del Giudice, Angeleri, & Manera, 2009 for a discussion of the significance of the juvenile period to human development.)

Concerning adolescence, it is defined by a growth spurt and by the development of sec-ondary sexual characteristics (see discussion later in this chapter). Although adolescents may look like mature adults and are capable of mature sexual behavior, there is a period of low fertility. These features, too, Bogin states, are unique to humans.

Bogin argues based on fossil evidence that the stages of childhood and adolescence evolved over the past 2 million years or so. According to Bogin, the age of reaching adulthood and reproductive maturity increased gradually in the hominid lineage, ranging from about 12 to 13 years for *Australopithecine afarensis* (about 3 million years ago) and *Homo habilis* (about 2.5 million years ago), to 14 or 15 years for *Homo erectus* (about 1 million years ago), to the late teens and early twenties for modern *Homo sapiens*. Childhood is first seen in the fossil record in *Homo habilis* and got continually longer over the many millennia. Adolescence, in contrast, is truly modern, being observed only in our own species (see also Gibbons, 2008).

Not all anthropologists agree with Bogin's model. For example, female chimpanzees also display a period of low fertility following menarche, and chimpanzee mothers continue to provide some help to their juvenile offspring after they get their permanent teeth. Nonetheless, no other mammal develops so slowly, and the life stages of childhood and adolescence, if not unique to humans, are at least expressed in *Homo sapiens* to a far greater extent than in any other species.

tive—the brain. The brain is behind the developing psychological functions that will be the focus of Parts II and III of this book, and we provide here an overview of its development, which will be expanded in later chapters.

Changes in Physical Growth

Changes in Body Size

Perhaps the first thing worth noting about growth is that all parts of the body do not grow at the same rate. Figure 4.1 shows **growth curves** for vari-ous organ systems. As can be seen from the figure, there is a sharp increase in height over infancy; this is followed by slow growth over middle childhood, ending with a growth spurt during the teen years into early adulthood. The brain and head, in contrast, grow rapidly over the preschool years, continuing the rapid rate of growth of the prenatal period. Changes in the reproductive system (including both internal and external genitals) follow an almost opposite pattern of changes from the brain and head, showing virtually no change over childhood and then rapid maturation beginning around

growth curves Graphic representation of the growth rate of an organism.

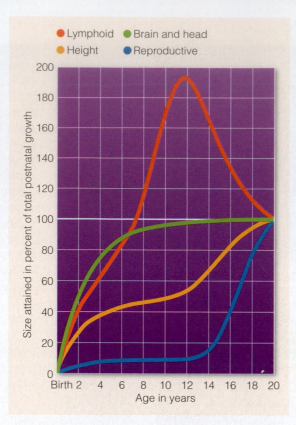

FIGURE 4.1 Growth curves for different parts of the body, expressed in terms of percentage of eventual adult growth.

Different organ systems and parts of the body develop at different rates. SOURCE: Adapted from Scammon, R. E. (1930). The measurement of the body in childhood. In J. A. Harris, C. M. Jackson, D. G. Paterson, & R. E. Scammon (Eds.), *The measurement of man.* Minneapolis: University of Minnesota Press.

12 or 13 years of age. Finally, the lymphoid system, which includes the thymus and lymph glands, develops quickly over childhood, greatly exceeding adult dimensions, until about 12 years of age, when it just as quickly declines to adult levels.

The curves in Figure 4.1 are averages. Some children not only grow taller or have bigger heads than other children but grow at different rates. One factor that is a reliable predictor of differences in rate of growth is sex. In general, girls reach maturity earlier than boys. Although boys are slightly larger than girls at birth and maintain this small advantage until girls reach puberty, girls attain 50% of their adult height about 1.75 to 2 years sooner than boys, enter puberty earlier, and stop growing sooner. This difference in rate of growth (that is, how fast one grows, as opposed to how big one becomes) is seen even during the prenatal period. Girls' skeletons are three weeks more advanced than those of boys midway through the fetal period, and girls have a four- to six-week advantage in skeletal development at birth. By the beginning of puberty, this advantage is a full two years. Girls also develop permanent teeth before boys (but not baby, or milk, teeth). Girls are also physiologically more mature in other organ systems at birth (for example, the respiratory system), which may account in part for their greater survival rate in the early months (Tanner, 1990).

Skeletal and Dental Development

An important indication of physical age is the skeleton. When we think of the skeleton, we think of bones. But the skeleton starts as *cartilage*, a soft, pliable tissue that, in adults, serves to cushion joints. (Many athletes have had cartilage damage to knees or other joints and as a result are more susceptible to arthritis and related problems later in life.) As we mentioned in the previous chapter, bone tissue begins to replace cartilage beginning about the sixth week of prenatal development, a process known as *ossification* that continues throughout childhood and adolescence (Hall, 2005).

Unlike some reptiles, human growth (and that of mammals in general) is limited. People do not keep getting taller every year; eventually skeletal development reaches a maximum, usually in late adolescence or early adulthood. Such development is governed by growth plates at the ends of most bones in the body (Bogin, 1999). These plates produce cartilage, which separates the growing part of the bone from the rigid part (the "real bone"). These growth plates increase in size over childhood, then eventually thin out and disappear, as cartilage is replaced by bone.

Figure 4.2 shows X-rays of the hands of children of different ages (Gilsanz & Ratib, 2005). Note in the X-ray for the 2-year-old child there are wide gaps in the bones of the wrists and at the ends of the fingers. These gaps are smaller for the 6-year-old child, smaller yet for the 10-year-old, and essentially disappear in the X-ray of the 14-year-old. Although there are substantial individual differences in height, *skeletal maturity*, or *bone age*, is an accurate measure of physical development. As we mentioned previously, it also differs between boys and girls, with girls' skeletal development being four to six weeks more advanced than boys at birth, with this difference increasing over childhood (Fitzpatrick, 2004).

It is easy to think of skeletal development as being directed solely by genes, afforded by an adequate diet, but not as being an active process, as described by developmental contextual accounts. But even skeletal development progresses as a result of the bidirectional interaction between an active organism and its environment. For example, while still in the egg, chicken embryos move

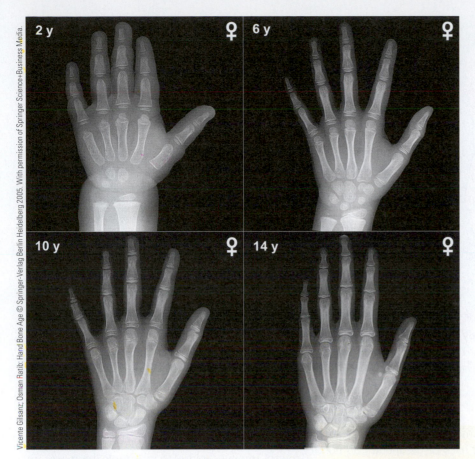

2 y ♀ 6 y ♀

10 y ♀ 14 y ♀

FIGURE 4.2 Bone development of the hand. X-rays of the hands of children of different ages reveal differences in bone age, or skeletal maturity. Note that the gaps between bones get smaller as children age. The disappearance of growth plates at the ends of bones signals the end of skeletal growth.

their legs before muscle and skeletal development is complete. The ability to move is a result of the maturation of the muscles and bones, which is clearly influenced by specific genes. But genes are not enough for proper limb development to occur. Self-generated movement is also necessary.

If chick embryos are given a drug that prevents them from moving their not-yet-fully-formed legs for as little as one to two days, deformations of the joints of the legs, toes, and neck develop, which in turn affect the subsequent movement of the limbs (Drachman & Coulombre, 1962). The spontaneous activity of moving the legs provides critical feedback to the genes, which, in normal circumstances, leads to a properly developed skeleton (Müller, 2003). But without that self-generated activity, the genes alone cannot provide instructions to create a perfect limb and spine. Development proceeds as a result of interaction of genes with events and agents external to the genes, including functioning of the body itself, all in feedback loops that, when all goes right, produces a species-typical body.

Dental development is another reliable measure of physical age. Both *primary teeth* (also called baby, deciduous, or milk teeth) and *secondary teeth* (also called permanent, or adult teeth) begin to develop prenatally. An infant's first primary teeth typically erupt, or break through the gum, beginning as early as 7 months after birth, and the last of the 20 primary teeth typically do not erupt until sometime after a child's second birthday. Teething can be painful for infants, and parents can ease the pain some by rubbing babies' gums with their finger or the back of a small, cool spoon, or by applying some over-the-counter medicine recommended by their dentist, doctor, or pharmacist.

Children typically get their first secondary teeth sometime after their sixth birthday. The gap-toothed grins of many 7- and 8-year-olds reflect the rapid loss of baby teeth and eruption of permanent teeth during the early school years, although children typically do not lose all of their primary teeth until they are about

Children begin to lose their primary, or baby, teeth and to get their secondary, or permanent, teeth beginning around 6 years of age. This leaves many 7- and 8-year-old children with characteristic gap-toothed smiles.

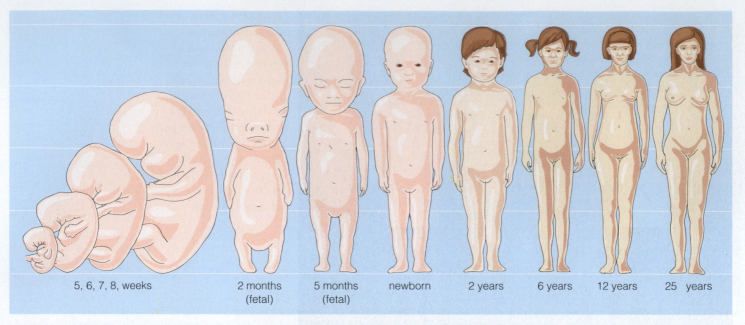

FIGURE 4.3 Changes in proportions of the human body from the fetal period through adulthood.

Note how the head becomes proportionally smaller relative to the rest of the body with age, reflecting the cephalocaudal principle of development. SOURCE: Bjorklund, D. F., & Bjorklund, B. R. (1992). *Looking at children: An introduction to child development.* Pacific Grove, CA: Brooks/Cole.

| 5, 6, 7, 8, weeks | 2 months (fetal) | 5 months (fetal) | newborn | 2 years | 6 years | 12 years | 25 years |

12 years old. Some permanent molars (the large teeth for grinding food in the back of the mouth) do not erupt until early adolescence, with third-year molars, or *wisdom teeth*, often not erupting until late adolescence or early adulthood, if at all. Wisdom teeth often become *impacted*, meaning that they adversely affect other teeth, and must be extracted.

You may question the wisdom of having wisdom teeth. Many people never develop them, and others have serious problems with them. (At least one of the authors had to have all four pulled—two while conscious and two while unconscious.) Wisdom teeth are sometimes referred to as *vestigial third molars*. Vestigial structures refer to those that have no apparent function but may have had some function in our ancestors. Human jaws have become smaller over the course of hominid evolution as brain size increased, making the jaw often too small to easily accommodate 32 teeth. The result is often impacted wisdom teeth (Schissel, 1970). We should also realize that tooth loss was common for our ancestors (and is still common for people who do not get modern dental care), and wisdom teeth had the potential to fill the gap left by a lost tooth, making the problem of wisdom teeth the product, in large part, of modern dental practices (Goldberg, 2003).

cephalocaudal development The head-to-foot sequence of physical growth.

proximodistal development Pattern of development in which body grows from the center to the periphery.

Changes in Proportions

Growth involves more than simple increases in size but also changes in proportion. In the previous chapter we commented that embryonic development spreads from head to foot, referred to as **cephalocaudal development** (literally, head to tail). This process continues postnatally and is graphically reflected in Figure 4.3. In this figure, the absolute size of the individual is held constant, so one can see the proportions of the different parts of the body relative to total size. As can be seen, at 2 months post conception, the head constitutes 50% of the entire body. By the time of birth, the head accounts for about 20% of the body and is about 70% of its eventual adult size, making newborns quite brainy creatures from at least one perspective. Although the head continues to grow over the course of postnatal development, it constitutes proportionally less of a person's total body size, representing about 12% by adulthood (Tanner, 1990). Cephalocaudal development characterizes all mammals but is especially prominent in humans, whose large brains (and thus heads) relative to body size need to develop early and continue to develop for an extended period to promote survival.

As the body is growing from head to foot, it is also growing from its center to the periphery, referred to as **proximodistal development**. Beginning during the prenatal period, development is most rapid toward the center of the body. For instance, the chest and the internal organs form and increase in size first, followed by the arms and legs and then the hands and feet. Infants and later toddlers seem to be all head and body, with short arms and legs. This also gives them a lower center of gravity, which accounts in part for their often unbalanced form of locomotion, termed, quite appropriately, toddling. Over childhood, arms and legs grow rapidly, catching up to the torso and head. This process continues throughout infancy and childhood until adolescence, when the hands and feet show a growth spurt, becoming the first body parts to reach adult proportions.

The Renaissance artist Michelangelo captured these proportions in his famous statue of the teenage David, whose oversized hands hold the sling and the stone that slew Goliath (see Photo). The changing proportions of adolescents account for their sometimes awkward appearance and clumsy actions, as they adjust to adult-sized hands and feet (and arms and legs), waiting for the rest of their body to catch up (Tanner, 1990). By the end of adolescence, most girls have attained their adult physical status and will show little or no subsequent increase in height. Boys, in contrast, are likely to grow another inch or so after 18 years of age.

Related to changes in proportion are changes in the distribution of muscle and body fat. Infants are not very muscular creatures. In fact, the classic baby is one with puffy cheeks and rolls of baby fat, most of it located just beneath the skin. The amount of fat increases during the last few weeks of prenatal development and peaks around 9 months of age. As noted in Chapter 3, babies have a difficult time regulating their temperature, which the presence of baby fat helps them maintain. Infants typically begin to lose their baby fat during their second year as they become more mobile, a trend that continues into middle childhood (Fomon & Nelson, 2002). Girls are born with slightly more fat than boys, with this difference increasing in childhood and throughout puberty. In contrast to fat, muscle mass increases gradually over childhood and then increases substantially in adolescence (see later discussion).

Factors Influencing Growth

A host of factors influence individual differences in growth, both rate and eventual size. Perhaps most obvious is genetics. Tall parents, for instance, typically have tall children, and although they also usually share a similar environment, individual differences in genetics surely play an important role. This is illustrated by behavioral genetics studies that show greater similarity in height and timing of puberty in identical versus fraternal twins (Bouchard et al., 1990).

Babies are born with appreciable body fat, which they typically begin to lose during their second year as they become more mobile

The Endocrine System

The **endocrine system** is perhaps the most significant biological system with respect to growth. The endocrine system is a collection of glands that produce **hormones**, many of which are directly responsible for orchestrating growth. Hormones are released into the blood stream and thus can potentially reach any cell in the body. Hormones are like chemical messengers, sent through the blood stream with instructions from one part of the body to another. A colleague of ours refers to hormones as "blood-borne neurotransmitters," reflecting a connection between the brain and body tissue through the circulatory system. Certain cells are sensitive to certain hormones, making the hormonal communication system a very specific one (Ulijaszek, Johnston, & Preece, 1998).

Dozens of hormones are produced in different glands throughout the body (Ulijaszek et al, 1998). Central control of hormone production is governed by the *hypothalamus* (see discussion of brain development later in this chapter), which exerts its influence on the pituitary gland located nearby (see Figure 4.4). Acting as a master gland, the pituitary releases hormones that can directly influence a particular body tissue (and thus cause growth) or can cause other glands to release hormones, which will also affect growth. As a hormone circulates through the body, specialized cells detect its concentration, and, when it reaches a certain level, the pituitary will send out another hormonal signal to reduce or stop its production. Thus, the endocrine system works by way of a feedback loop, much

Michelangelo's statue of the teenage David shows the overly large hands and feet, often typical in early adolescence.

endocrine system A system of glands that produces hormones, many of which are responsible for directing growth.

hormones Chemical substances produced by the endocrine glands and sent through the bloodstream transporting instructions from one part of the body to another.

pituitary gland The master gland that produces hormones that influence growth

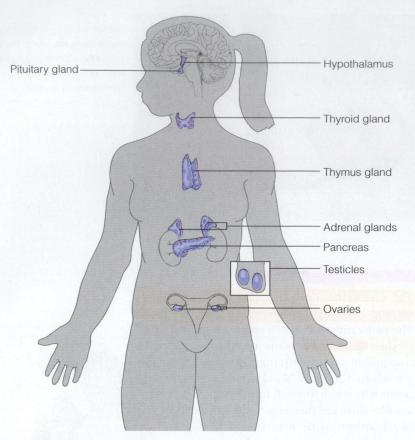

Pituitary gland

Hypothalamus

Thyroid gland

Thymus gland

Adrenal glands

Pancreas

Testicles

Ovaries

FIGURE 4.4 The endocrine system.

The endocrine system includes a collection of glands that produce hormones that regulate growth, metabolism, and sexual development and function. Central control of hormone production is governed by the *hypothalamus* in the brain, which exerts its influence on the *pituitary gland*, the master gland.

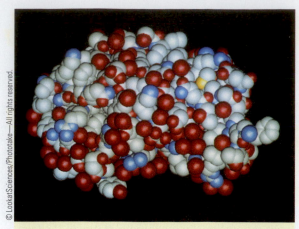

Human growth hormone (HGH), shown here in molecular form, is produced directly by the pituitary gland.

like a thermostat. You can use a thermostat to raise or lower the temperature in a room. It detects when the room reaches the desired temperature and reduces the heat to maintain that temperature. Similarly, the endocrine system triggers the production of hormones, monitors the amount of those hormones in the blood, and reduces or stops hormone production when they reach the appropriate level.

One hormone that is produced directly by the pituitary is **human growth hormone**, which stimulates the replication of most body cells and thus affects growth. Children who do not produce adequate amounts of human growth hormone grow slowly, attaining an adult height of slightly over 4 feet, despite having typical proportions. This condition can be diagnosed and treated with supplemental doses of human growth hormone (Vance, Mauras, & Wood, 1999).

The pituitary also influences the gonads (testes and ovaries), the thyroid, and the adrenal glands. The ovaries produce **estrogen** and **progesterone**, and the testes produce **testosterone** (a form of **androgen**), hormones that promote sexual maturation and also activate portions of the brain that control sexual arousal. (More will be said about the role of sex hormones later in this chapter, and the development of sexuality is examined in Chapter 15.) The *thyroid gland*, located in the neck, also plays a critical role in growth. It produces **thyroxine** beginning early in the fetal period, which influences brain development. Children born with a thyroxine deficiency can become intellectually impaired unless treated immediately, while thyroxine deficiencies later in childhood result in slow body and skeleton growth but no brain damage. The *adrenal glands*, located on top of the kidneys, produce adrenalin, which has little to do with growth, and also androgens, which play an important role in growth for both boys and girls. In boys, androgen joins with testosterone to foster physical growth (including muscle bulk) and the development and maintenance of secondary sexual characteristics. In girls, androgen is primarily responsible for the adolescent growth spurt and the growth of pubic hair.

Environmental Factors Influencing Growth

Although physical growth shows a species-typical pattern, suggesting that it is greatly influenced by endogenous (internal) biological factors, environ-

human growth hormone Pituitary hormone that stimulates duplication of most body cells, affecting growth.

estrogen Hormone produced primarily by the ovaries that regulates female sexual development during puberty.

progesterone A hormone produced by the ovaries that promotes sexual development.

testosterone A form of androgen or male hormone, produced primarily by the testes, that promotes sexual maturation.

androgen A class of hormones, including testosterone, that are found at higher levels in males than females and that influence physical growth and sexual development.

thyroxine A hormone produced by the thyroid gland that influences growth and prenatal brain development.

mental factors also contribute to rate of maturation and eventual size. One factor that has been found to result in a slower rate of growth is *psychological stress*. Children living in environments of constant stress produce lower levels of human growth hormone. When the stress is removed, human growth hormone production increases and typical growth resumes. The physical anthropologist James Tanner (1978) cited several interesting examples of the effects of stress on children. For instance, children living in an orphanage under the direction of a particularly sadistic schoolteacher showed slow growth despite adequate food. Other case studies have shown that when children who have stopped growing are removed from a chronically stressful home and are placed in supportive foster homes, they quickly catch up with their peers in height. The change in height for such a child is similar to that of a child who is deficient in human growth hormone and is given replacement therapy with that hormone. Stress does not have to be extreme to affect growth. For example, a large-scale study examining the physical growth of 6,574 British children revealed that, at 7 years of age, significantly more children who experienced chronic family conflict were small in stature (defined as being among the lowest one-fifth of the height distribution) compared to children living in less-stressful homes (Montgomery, Bartley, & Wilkinson, 1997).

Perhaps the most obvious environmental influence on physical growth is nutrition. One statement about nutrition and growth can be made unequivocally: malnutrition delays growth. At the extreme, malnutrition can lead to death. Although one cannot experimentally deprive children of adequate nutrition and see the consequences on growth as one can with animals, real-world evidence shows that children who do not get enough to eat grow more slowly. For example, marasmus is a wasting away of the body that results when infants receive a diet low in all essential nutrients, often because their mothers are too malnourished to provide adequate breast milk. Other children suffering from Kwashiorkor receive just enough calories to survive, usually from starches, but do not receive adequate amounts of proteins. These children develop distended bellies (see Photo), lose their hair, and become listless and irritable. If malnourishment is prolonged, children have smaller statures as adults than those children who eat well. This has been clearly demonstrated by the effects of war and famine on children's physical development (see Susser & Stein, 1994). The effects of malnutrition on growth are apt to be most severe for children younger than 5 years of age, particularly when accompanied by infection or disease.

Malnutrition is also associated with lower levels of intelligence, presumably by affecting brain

AFP/Getty Images

Children suffering from Kwashiorkor, caused by a lack of protein in their diets, develop distended bellies, lose their hair, and become listless and irritable.

development. Tanner (1978) points out, however, that poor nutrition can have an indirect effect on intelligence by reducing activity level. A malnourished infant is lethargic, and this will lead to less exploration, less play, and less social interaction that "may be a more potent cause of delay in intellectual and emotional development than any nutritional effect on the nervous system" (Tanner, 1978, p. 129). It is worth noting that children subjected to brief periods of starvation typically recover. When nutrition is poor, children grow more slowly, but they retain the ability to catch up when good nutrition is resumed, so-called *catch-up growth*.

Although malnutrition is a serious problem worldwide, most children get enough food to sustain growth. Yet, poor nutrition short of malnourishment can also affect physical growth. The effects of improving nutrition on growth can be seen by looking at secular trends from historical records. Although the diets of children in Western countries today are far from perfect (see discussion on obesity), most children get more than enough calories to promote growth. This was not

---

marasmus A nutritional condition, in which the body wastes away when infants receive a diet low in all essential nutrients, often because their mothers are too malnourished to provide adequate breast milk.

Kwashiorkor Nutritional condition in which children receive just enough calories to survive, usually from starches, but do not receive adequate amounts of proteins. These children develop extended bellies, lose their hair, and become listless and irritable.

always the case. The diets of most Americans, Europeans, and other groups of people living in industrialized societies have improved considerably over the past 150 years or so, and as a result the average height of people in these cultures has increased (Komlos & Lauderdale, 2007; Ulijaszek et al., 1998). For example, the average heights of men in both Denmark and the Netherlands in 1850 were about 5 feet 5 inches; by the year 2000, the average heights in both countries had increased to slightly over 6 feet, a 7-inch difference. Differences in men's heights in most European countries over this time span increased 5 to 6 inches, with similar trends for women. American men were, on average, about 3 inches taller than most European men in 1850 (about 5 feet 9 inches) and increased another 2 inches in the following 150 years (to about 5 feet 11 inches), a trend that has reversed in recent decades (Komlos & Lauderdale, 2007). Some have speculated (Komlos & Lauderdale, 2007) that the relative decline in height for Americans relative to Europeans in the second half of the 20th century is related to the lack of universal health care in the United States.

Differences in childhood diets contribute to some of the cultural differences in height. Children from developed countries tend to receive the best nutrition and to be the tallest, and those from undeveloped countries where there is widespread poverty tend to receive the poorest nutrition and to be the shortest (Bogin, 2001). The effects of nutri-

tion on growth are nicely illustrated in a study that contrasted the heights of 5- to 12-year-old Mayan children whose families had immigrated to the United States from Guatemala with those of Mayan children who remained in Guatemala (Bogin et al., 2002). The Mayan-American children were, on average, 4.5 inches taller than their Guatemalan peers, with about 60% of the height difference being in leg length (about 2.7 inches). The improved diet of the Mayan-American children occurred at a time when their legs were growing particularly fast (recall that legs tend to grow more rapidly than the torso during childhood), accounting for the more leggy proportions of the American versus the Guatemalan children.

All ethnic and cultural differences in growth cannot be attributed to diet, however. Genetic differences predispose some groups of people to different average heights and body proportions than others. Some of these differences may be evolutionary adaptations to local climate and ecology. For example, people living in hot tropical climates, such as the Masai of Kenya and Tanzania, are often tall and lean, which facilitates cooling the body. In contrast, people living in cold climates, such as the Inuit who live in the northern regions of Canada, are often short and stocky, an ideal body build for conserving heat (Raff, 1996). These are ancient adaptations, and, as the research with Mayan immigrants to the United States indicates, surely interact with diet.

Some cultural and ethnic differences in body size and shape may be influenced by evolutionary adaptations to climate. For instance, the lean and lanky bodies of Masai children of eastern Africa are well suited for the hot tropical climate, whereas the stockier bodies of Inuit children are well suited for the cold climate of the Arctic.

Psychological Consequences of Physical Growth

Children's growth is associated, at least in a general way, with other aspects of development. Changes in children's height, weight, and body proportions serve as external signals for changes in social, emotional, and intellectual functioning. As such, adults believe that children who *look* older should *act* older.

Adults may treat children who are big or mature-looking for their age as if they were older, whereas the reverse may be true for children who look young for their age. This was illustrated in a study in which parents were shown photographs of mature- and immature-looking 4- and 11-year-olds and asked a series of questions about these hypothetical children (Zebrowtiz, Kendall-Tackett, & Fafel, 1991). The adults were more likely to assign cognitively demanding tasks to mature-looking than to immature-looking 11-year-olds and judged misdeeds of mature-looking 11-year-old children as more likely being intentional than those of their baby-faced peers (at least for children of the parent's opposite sex). In a second study, misdeeds committed by immature-looking preschoolers were viewed as less serious and adults recommended less severe punishment than when the misdeeds were committed by more mature-looking children.

The psychological consequences of physical development are likely most profound at adolescence, and we will examine the effects of these changes on teenage boys and girls later in this chapter. But first we discuss obesity in childhood and its effects on children's psychological development.

Childhood Obesity

Although lack of adequate nutrition has likely been a serious issue for humans historically and continues to be an issue for many children today, a different type of problem tends to plague children from industrialized societies, and that is obesity. Obesity among children in the United States has been increasing over the last two to three decades (Institute of Medicine of the National Academies, 2005). Based on the body mass index (BMI), a measure of weight in relation to height, the National Health and Examination Survey in 2004 reported that 31% of American children 6 to 19 years of age were overweight or at risk of becoming overweight (Hedley et al., 2004). This represents more than a doubling of pediatric obesity in two decades. This trend extends down to preschoolers, with a 2009 study reporting that 18.4% of 4-year-olds in the United States were obese (Anderson & Whitaker, 2009). Moreover, this is not just an American problem, but also one that faces most developed nations.

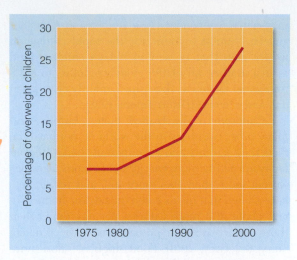

FIGURE 4.5 Age trends in percentage of overweight children in England, 1975–2000. Adapted from International Task Force on Obesity (2004). SOURCE: Adapted from T. Lobstein, L. Baur and R. Uauy, International Task Force on Obesity. Obesity in children and young people: A crisis in public health, *Obesity Reviews*, Vol. 5 Issue 1, p. 4–85. Reprinted by permission of the International Task Force on Obesity, www.iotf.org.

For example, it is estimated that, worldwide, there are 22 million severely overweight children under the age of 5 and 155 million severely overweight school-age children. This includes approximately 14 million children in the European Union (British Medical Association, 2005). The change in childhood obesity between the 1970s and 2000 in England is shown in Figure 4.5, a pattern that is repeated in many nations in the world, including the United States.

Body mass index (BMI) is the ratio of one's weight in kilograms relative to one's height in meters, squared (kg/m^2). Using American measurements, it is one's weight in pounds divided by one's height in inches, squared, with the entire equation multiplied by 703 (BMI = [weight in pounds ÷ height in inches^2] (703). There are easy-to-use BMI calculators on the Internet (for example, www.nhlbisupport.com/bmi/). The BMI range for typical weight is 18.5 to 24.9. People with BMIs below 18.5 are judged to be underweight. People are said to be overweight who have BMIs in the range of 25 to 29.9, and people with a BMI of 30 or greater are said to be obese. Although the BMI is a useful index for assessing obesity, it does not take into account body shape or muscularity, and thus can produce inaccurate ratings of obesity, especially in adolescence.

Causes of Increasing Childhood Obesity

What are the reasons for this sudden change in weight among many of the world's children? The simple answer is modern life. Individual differences

obesity A body weight that is 20% or more higher than normal for the person's height, age, sex, and stature.

body mass index (BMI) A measure of weight in relation to height.

in genetics influences one's weight and BMI, but genetics cannot account for the rapid change in weight gain that is seen in today's children (and adults). Rather, all of the evidence points to environmental factors as the culprit, mainly changes in diet and exercise (Hill & Peters, 1998).

Children in the United States, Europe, and many other countries in the world do not have the diets their parents and grandparents had. Children today are eating more energy-dense foods. Families eat out more than they once did, and researchers have shown that meals eaten outside the home contain about 200 more calories per day than when those same foods are prepared at home (French, Story, & Jeffrey, 2001). Foods high in calories are frequently advertised to children on television, and children in turn influence their parents' purchases (see Krishnamoorthy, Hart, & Jelalian, 2006).

Children's increasing caloric consumption over the years has been paired with a decrease in physical exercise. Schools have been cutting back on both recess and physical education in recent decades (Nestle & Jacobson, 2000; Pellegrini,

Poor diet and lack of exercise is resulting in many adolescents having poor cardiorespiratory fitness.

2005), and outdoor play in general has decreased. There are several reasons for the decline in outdoor play. For one, children are engaging in increasing amounts of sedentary activities in their free time, especially watching television, but recently also playing video and computer games (Nunez-Smith et al., 2008; Rideout, Vandewater, & Watella, 2003; see Chapter 13). Richard Louv (2005), author of *The Last Child in the Woods*, attributes some of the decrease in outdoor play to adults declaring many outdoor areas off-limits to children. There are several reasons adults give for limiting children's outdoor play, including protection against injuries (and lawsuits), fear for children's safety, and aesthetics (torn-up baseball fields or tree forts can be an eyesore for a community park). That safety is a concern for parents is revealed in a study that looked at rates of overweight children as a function of how safe parents believed their neighborhoods to be (Lumeng et al., 2006). Only 4% of children were overweight at the age of 7 for parents who rated their neighborhoods as most safe. In contrast, 17% of children were overweight for parents who perceived their neighborhoods to be the least safe.

Some children are obviously more likely to become overweight than others, and it is tempting to attribute such a tendency to genes. Although the heritability of body weight is high (about .70, Plomin et al., 2008), prenatal nutrition is also implicated in later obesity. Women who experience poor nutrition when pregnant have children who are more likely to be overweight. Although such babies are born lighter than babies with better prenatal nutrition, most eventually catch up and show elevated levels of the appetite-regulating hormone *leptin*. They develop "thrifty phenotypes," storing more fat than children whose prenatal diets were more nutritious. This makes good sense if you consider that one's prenatal environment is an indication of what one's postnatal environment will be like. Natural selection has made fetuses sensitive to their level of nutrition. When nutrition in the womb is good, brain circuitry that controls appetite and metabolism develops as if food resources will be plentiful after birth; when nutrition in the womb is poor, brain circuitry develops differently, causing individuals to hold on to as many calories as they can in anticipation of limited food resources (see Gluckman & Hansen, 2005). Peter Gluckman and Mark Hanson (2005) refer to fetuses responding to current conditions (in this case poor nutrition) not for immediate advantage but in anticipation of later advantage after birth as *predictive adaptive responses*. The result of this strategy with respect to poor fetal nutrition for people in modern cultures is often obesity.

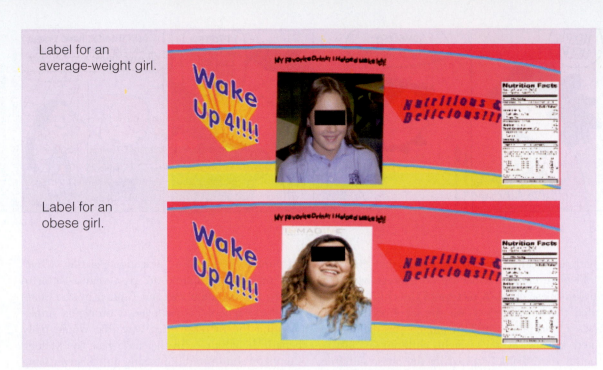

Label for an average-weight girl.

Label for an obese girl.

FIGURE 4.6 Example of labels used for soft drinks, one for an average-weight child and one for an obese child. Children judged the drinks created by the average-weight children as tasting better than drinks created by the obese children, and also stated that drinks created by the obese children were more likely to cause sickness. SOURCE: From Klaczynski, P. (2008). There's something about obesity: Culture, contagion, rationality, and children's responses to drinks "created" by obese children. *Journal of Experimental Child Psychology, 99,* 58–74.

Consequences of Obesity

Obesity in children and adolescents is associated with a host of medical problems, as well as being a predictor of medical problems later in adulthood. Some of these medical problems include hypertension, insulin resistance, sleep apnea, asthma, non-insulin-dependent diabetes, and orthopedic and metabolic diseases (British Medical Association, 2005; Must & Strauss, 1999).

The lack of exercise and increased caloric consumption of American youth is not only affecting their weight but also their more general physical fitness. In a 2005 study, Mercedes Carnethon and her colleagues examined the cardiorespiratory fitness of more than 3,000 adolescents 12 to 19 years of age. The teenagers ran on an inclined treadmill with the goal of achieving at least 75% to 90% of their maximum age-predicted heart rate. Slightly more than one-third of the adolescents were rated as displaying "low fitness" on this measure, a risk factor for cardiovascular disease. This is in contrast to about 14% of adults, aged 20 to 49.

There are also significant psychological risks associated with obesity. These include lowered self-esteem, poor body image, increased symptoms of depression, decreased perceived quality of life (Israel & Ivanova, 2002; Puhl & Latner, 2007), and difficulties with peers, including being teased

and marginalized (Neumark-Sztainer et al., 2002; Strauss & Pollack, 2003). Children develop obesity stereotypes early (by age 3), and unlike other stereotypes they become stronger with age (Klaczynski & Daniel, 2008; Musher-Eizenman et al., 2004). Children view their overweight peers negatively, and rather than decreasing as obesity has become more common over the decades, the stigmatization of obese children has actually increased over this same time (Latner & Stunkard, 2003).

What can account for the strength and persistence of obesity stereotypes? Paul Klaczynski (2008) has suggested that children associate obesity with illness (see also Park, Schaller, & Crandall, 2007). Overweight children and adults often display medical problems, are less vigorous, prone to orthopedic problems, sweat more, and miss school more often than do average-weight children and adults. Children develop early in life "intuitive theories" of biology (Inagaki & Hatano, 2006, see Chapter 6) that, in part, help them understand the causes and consequences of illness. Perhaps, based on these intuitive theories, children associate obesity in other children with contagious illness, accounting for the early development and the robustness of their obesity stereotypes.

To test this, Klaczynski (2008) presented 7- and 10-year-old American and Chinese children

Many American children spend many hours watching television or engaging in other sedentary activities and play outdoors less than children did in the past.

with identically flavored soft drinks that they were told were created either by an average-weight or by an obese child. A picture of the child who created the beverage was on the label of the drink (see Figure 4.6). Children judged the drinks created by the average-weight children as tasting better than drinks created by the obese children, and also stated that drinks created by the obese children were more likely to cause sickness. Children's association of the drink's creator and sickness is an example of *magical thinking*—believing some magical connection between characteristics of a person (here, illness associated with obesity) and the product they designed. Such thinking can account, in part, for the strong negative stereotype associated with being overweight, even in a society such as the United States where being overweight is increasingly common.

What Can Be Done to Deal with the Problem?

The increase in obesity and the associated medical and psychological consequences of being overweight have been recognized as a major health crisis worldwide (Krishnamoorthy et al., 2006; Puhl & Latner, 2007). What can and is being done about it? There have been numerous school-, home-, and community-based programs aimed at altering children's diets and the amount of exercise they get. The results of such programs have been mixed, with some, but not others, producing changes in eating or exercise habits and short-term weight loss (see Krishnamoorthy et al., 2006; Stice, Shaw, & Marti, 2006).

A consensus is emerging that many levels of society need to become involved to stem the tide of increasing childhood obesity (British Medical Association, 2005; Krishnamoorthy et al., 2006). Schools are being encouraged to offer a healthier choice of foods and drinks to children and to increase the amount of exercise they receive during the day. For example, in 2007, the governor of Florida mandated that every elementary-school child in the state have

30 minutes of physical education per day, a five-fold increase compared to past years. Unfortunately, the mandate was not funded by the State, and local school districts faced problems implementing the increase in a way that would truly benefit the children. In the same year, the Kellogg Company committed to phasing out its advertising of high-caloric food to children younger than 12 years of age. If they cannot reduce the sugar or salt content of some of their best-selling child-oriented foods, including *Froot Loops*, *Rice Krispies*, and *Apple Jacks* cereals and *Pop-Tarts*, they will not be advertised to young children.

In 2007, *The Learning Channel* began a television program called "Honey, We're Killing the Kids" about the causes and consequences of childhood obesity. A nutrition expert evaluated a family's eating and exercise habits, provided the family with new guidelines for a healthier lifestyle, and then followed them for three weeks to see if they could reverse the years of poor eating and other lifestyle choices. In another television program, "Shaq's Big Challenge," basketball star Shaquille O'Neill took six overweight teens and developed a program with a group of experts to help the kids lose weight and start following a healthy lifestyle. These latter two shows make for good Reality TV, but it is not known the impact that such television programs have on the dietary and exercise habits of children.

There is no debate that childhood (and adult) obesity is approaching epidemic proportions and that its cause is life in modern society. Parents want what is best for their children, but the lure of fast (and high-caloric) food is strong, both among adults and children, as is the lure of sedentary activities such as watching television and playing video games. It is not possible to turn back the clock to the middle of the 20th century and our eating and exercise habits with it. (Americans smoke less now than they did 50 years ago, so not all health habits have gotten worse.) The concerted efforts of government, medical, business, and community interests, both in the United States and elsewhere,

BOX 4.2 food for thought *Anorexia & Bulimia*

Can You Ever Be Too Rich or Too Thin?

Wallis Simpson, the American-born Duchess of Windsor and wife of the once King of England Edward VIII, made the claim that "You can never be too rich or too thin." Although her statement was intended to describe the ideal state for aristocratic women of the 1920s and '30s, many teenage girls have taken her sentiment to heart, at least the part about being thin. It is ironic that as much of the world's BMI is increasing, the ideal of young womanhood in much of the Western world, and especially in the United States, is trending toward slimness. A look at top fashion models, magazines for teens such as *Seventeen* and *Sassy*, tabloids at the grocery checkout, and female stars on television and in movies makes it clear that "thin is in." It is little wonder that a majority of American adolescent girls are dissatisfied with their bodies (Rosenblum & Lewis, 1999) and that most engage in some form of dieting to lose weight during their teen years. In fact, in one study, more than half of high-school girls interviewed were engaged in some form of unhealthy behavior in an effort to lose weight, including smoking, fasting, vomiting after eating, or using diet pills (Croll et al., 2002).

Given the increasing body mass of the average person over the last several decades, is it so unusual for teenage girls to be dieting? Dieting seems to be an American obsession, an attempt to at least not gain any *more* weight. Yet, teenage girls are especially prone to engage in unhealthy eating behaviors, and these are associated with psychological and medical problems, some of which can persist into adulthood. In addition to having poor body images, adolescents with eating disorders are more likely to experience a variety of stress-related symptoms, including depression, tobacco and alcohol use, and poor interpersonal relationships (Graber et al., 1994; Neumark-Sztainer et al., 1998). Whether eating disorders are the cause of the psychological stress, its consequence, or part of a more general underlying psychological problem is not certain.

Although it seems clear that a fixation with thinness and constant dieting to keep one's weight down are maladaptive, some evidence shows that adolescent girls' preoccupation with thinness has some immediate benefits for them. It is not only girls who are influenced by societal ideals of the feminine physique, but also boys. One study that examined the frequency of dating in teenage girls as a function of their body mass index (BMI) reported that the heavier they were, the less likely they were to date (Halpern et al., 2005). Given how important having a boyfriend and dates are to teenage girls (see Chapter 15), it is little wonder that they are sometimes obsessed with their weight.

Although many adolescents occasionally display unhealthy eating behaviors, only a minority develops the more serious eating disorders of **anorexia nervosa** and **bulimia**. Anorexia nervosa is characterized by severe, self-induced weight loss, in which adolescents starve themselves in an effort to be thin. In bulimia, people will sometimes eat excessively and then force themselves to vomit to avoid weight gain. These disorders are seen disproportionately in females, with the female-to-male ratio being about 10 to 1 in adolescence (Jacobi et al., 2004), although the sex differences are smaller for less serious eating problems (Muise, Stein, & Arbess, 2003). Although anorexia is not an exclusively teenage problem, adolescent females are between 5 and 10 times more likely to be diagnosed for anorexia than are adult women (Pawluck & Gorey, 1998). The overall incidence of these serious eating disorders is relatively low, however. For adolescent girls, the incidence of anorexia is about three-tenths of 1% (0.3%), whereas the incidence of bulimia for this group is about 1% (Hoek & van Hoeken, 2003).

Although death can result from anorexia, it is relatively rare. However, a host of medical problems is associated with starvation, including compromised thyroid function, damage to the heart, loss of bone mass, and amenorrhea, the cessation of menstrual periods (Olivares et al., 2005). About half of a person's bone mass is laid down during adolescence, and a diet deficient in calcium can result in reduced bone mass, which can have serious repercussions later in life (Stoffman et al., 2005). Anorexic young women have an increased incidence of fractures and are susceptible to developing osteoporosis early in life (Gordon et al., 2002). These effects need not be permanent; typical physiological functioning can resume with a healthy diet, so long as there has been no permanent heart damage (Olivares et al., 2005).

Fortunately, most adolescents with severe eating disorders do not continue their unhealthy behavior into adulthood, although a small percentage do. A variety of therapies have been successful at treating anorexia and bulimia, including antidepressant medication and individual, group, and family therapy (Killian, 1994). Interventions that involve the teen's family seem to be particularly effective (Krautter & Lock, 2004). The sooner an adolescent's parents become involved in treatment, the quicker and more complete is the recovery (Woods, 2004). Consistent with the importance of the family in treating eating disorders, teenage girls who have three or four meals with their families per week show fewer unhealthy weight-control behaviors than girls who eat with their family less often (Eisenberg et al., 2004).

Perhaps you can never be too rich, but one can certainly be too thin. Although obesity may be a more prevalent problem for modern children and teens, society's standard of female beauty has promoted unhealthy eating behaviors in many adolescent girls, resulting in potentially serious medical problems in many teenagers.

---

will be needed to stem the tide of childhood obesity. Although obesity is the most prevalent eating problem for children and adolescents, others suffer from under-eating in a quest to be thin, and this is discussed in Box 4.2.

anorexia nervosa An eating disorder characterized by excessive dieting and weight loss that affects adolescents and young adults, especially girls.

bulimia Eating disorder in which people will sometimes eat excessively and then force themselves to vomit to avoid weight gain.

© Tetra Images/Alamy

Chronological age tells us only part of the story of physical development. Two children with the same birthdays can vary considerably in physical development, particularly during the transition to adolescence.

Adolescence, Puberty, and Sexual Development

Physical development follows a slow and continuous path over childhood, but this changes with the onset of puberty. **Puberty** refers to the life stage when the glands associated with the reproductive system begin to enlarge, bringing about changes in **primary sexual characteristics** (those associated directly with reproduction, such as maturation of the gonads and anatomy of the genitals) as well as **secondary sexual characteristics** (those not directly related to reproduction, for example, pubic and underarm hair, breasts in girls, changes in the voice and shape of the face in boys). Tables 4.1 and 4.2 present secondary sexual characteristics and the age sequence of events at puberty, separately for boys and girls. As you can see, there is substantial variation in the onset of these developmental milestones, with the various pubertal events occurring at different times. The ages provided are only averages. There is substantial variability in the onset and completion of each pubertal event in both boys and girls.

The terms *puberty* and *adolescence* are typically used interchangeably today, although they do not refer to exactly the same phenomenon. As we noted earlier, puberty refers to the physical changes that all humans experience sometime between about 10 and 18 years of age. These are

puberty Period in life in which children attain adult size and physical characteristics, including sexual maturity.

primary sexual characteristics Characteristics associated directly with reproduction, such as maturation of the gonads and anatomy of the genitals.

secondary sexual characteristics Physical characteristics developed in puberty that signal sexual maturity but are not directly related to changes in reproductive organs (for example, pubic and underarm hair, breasts in girls, changes in the voice and shape of the face in boys).

table 4.1 Secondary Sexual Characteristics and Sequence of Pubertal Events in Males

Secondary Sexual Characteristics in Males
Pubic, axillary (under arm), and facial hair
Increase in muscle mass
Increase in size of the larynx with deepening of the voice
Acceleration of linear growth
Stimulation of libido

Sequence of Pubertal Events in Males	
Event	Average Age in Years
Initial testicular growth	11.75
Early growth of pubic hair	12
Enlargement of penis begins	13
Temporary breast development	13
Voice cracking begins	13
Growth spurt	13.5
Hair in armpits	14
Nocturnal emissions	14
Adult voice attained	15
Moustache begins to appear	15
Whiskers appear	16

the changes that we mostly describe in this chapter. In contrast, adolescence more properly refers to the psychological traits that characterize people during puberty.

Puberty is marked by the activation of the *hypothalamus-pituitary-gonadal system*, which results in the production of a series of hormones that promote sexual maturity (Bogin, 1999). Rising hormone levels in both males and females during adolescence support the development of both primary and secondary sexual characteristics. In males, *androgens*, especially *testosterone*, are important in the maturation of the penis and testes, and they enhance sexual feelings. *Estrogens* are especially important for maturation of the uterus, ovaries, and fallopian tubes in females, as well as the onset of menstruation. Another hormone, *progesterone,* plays an important role in regulating menstruation and preparing the uterus for a fertilized egg.

Before the gonads begin producing hormones, the adrenal glands in both boys and girls begin to produce a form of androgen called dehydroepiandrosterone (DHEA). This is not the more potent testosterone but a precursor of both testosterone and estrogen. This onset of androgen production is known as **adrenarche** and has been referred to as the awakening of the adrenal glands and the beginning of *adrenal puberty.* Adrenarche typically occurs between 6 and 8 years of age for both boys and girls (Ellis & Essex, 2007; Del Giudice, Angeleri, & Manera, 2009). Adrenal puberty so far has been observed only in humans, chimpanzees, and gorillas, three species with extended juvenile periods. Adrenal androgens seem to have only minimal physical effects, being related to the initial growth of underarm and pubic hair, oily skin, and a slight acceleration of skeletal growth. However, preliminary evidence suggests that adrenal androgens are related to aggression in middle childhood, with high levels being associated with conduct disorder in boys. There is some speculation that adrenarche may be responsible for the first romantic/sexual feelings occurring between 7 and 10 years of age (see Del Giudice et al., 2009).

Puberty is not a single phenomenon, but a series of physiologically related events that occur at different times and vary between boys and girls. Among the physical changes is the **growth spurt,** which typically begins earlier in girls than boys. During puberty, boys' chests and shoulders grow. This is a result of male sex hormones (androgens) stimulating the cartilage in these bones. In girls, a widening of the hips takes place. This is the result of cartilage cells being sensitive to the female sex hormone (estrogen). Other skeletal changes involve the bones of the face in boys. The forehead becomes more prominent because of a growth of brow ridges, and the jaw grows forward (Tanner, 1990).

Related to skeletal differences between the sexes are differences in fat and muscle. Girls acquire more body fat than boys, with fat constituting slightly more than 30% of body weight for the average young adult female and slightly less than 20% for the average young adult male. Muscle takes an opposite developmental course, with boys developing more muscle (and strength) during their adolescent growth spurt than girls. Girls, too, increase in muscle strength during their growth spurt, and because they start their spurt a couple of years earlier than boys, there is a period of about two years (between 10 and 12 years) where girls are actually more muscular (and stronger) than boys (Tanner, 1990).

table 4.2 Secondary Sexual Characteristics and Sequence of Pubertal Events in Females

Secondary Sexual Characteristics in Females
Breast development
Pubic and axillary (under arm) hair
Increase in body fat mass
Stimulation of skeletal growth

Sequence of Pubertal Events in Females	
Event	Average Age in Years
Initial breast development	11
First wisps of pubic hair	11.25
Growth spurt	12.25
Breast growth midway	12.25
Breast growth mostly completed	13
First menstruation (menarche)	13
Pubic hair adult distribution	14.25
Skeletal growth completed	14.25
Final breast development	15.25

Pubertal Changes for Boys

For boys, the first sign of puberty is usually enlargement of the testes followed by the appearance of pubic hair and enlargement of the penis. Acceleration of penis growth typically begins at about 12.5 to 13 years and is complete by about 14.5 years. But this development may begin as early as 10.5 years or as late as 14.5 years and still be within the typical range (Tanner, 1990).

The presence of facial hair begins above the lips, starting typically around 15 years of age. Growth of body hair increases gradually and usually continues into young adulthood. Boys' voices become deeper during adolescence as their vocal chords lengthen. An adolescent's voice sometimes breaks, although not all boys experience voice breaking.

....

adrenarche The onset of androgen production by the adrenal glands.

growth spurt Rapid change in growth of body occurring during puberty, which typically begins earlier in girls than boys.

Boys' prostate glands and seminal vesicles enlarge during puberty. The prostate gland makes most of the seminal fluid, and the seminal vesicles add substances that aid in sperm mobility, thus increasing the likelihood that conception will occur. Although the neural paths underlying orgasm are present from infancy, there is no true ejaculation until puberty (see Chapter 15). The first ejaculation, called **spermarche**, usually occurs about a year after the beginning of the growth of the penis, often during sleep (called *nocturnal emissions*, or "wet dreams"), and is often accompanied by erotic dreams.

Boys begin producing viable sperm by about 13.5 years, but fertility for boys younger than 15 years of age is exceptionally low, both in developed and traditional societies (see Bogin, 2001). There are likely several related reasons for this period of low fertility. Boys of this age are only just beginning their growth spurt, levels of male hormones are still relatively low, and they have the appearance of juveniles more than of men. As they continue through puberty, hormonal and physical changes cause them to be more interested in sex and cause females to be more interested in them, resulting in an increased likelihood of becoming fathers (see Bogin, 2001).

Pubertal Changes for Girls

Girls show the same variability of growth as do boys, but they usually enter puberty earlier. Breast development usually begins at about age 11 in North American and European girls, but the typical range extends from 9 to 13 years of age. Pubic hair usually appears after the beginning of breast development, but the two events (breast development and pubic hair) are relatively independent (Tanner, 1990).

Perhaps the clearest sign of womanhood is the first menstrual period, called **menarche**. This occurs relatively late in puberty, usually between the ages of 12.8 and 13.2 years for girls of European descent. Again, there is substantial variability, with 95% of all girls having their first menstrual period between the ages of 11 and 15 years.

There is some cultural variation in the average age of menarche, however. James Tanner (1990) reviewed the data of the average age of first menstrual period from 49 different cultural/ethnic groups and reported a range between slightly over 12 years (affluent girls of European descent in Spain, Brazil, and Venezuela) to 15.5 years and 18.0 years for two ethnic groups from New Guinea. Despite the broad range, one is impressed with how little variability there is in average age of menarche.

Of the 49 populations studied, only two had an average age of menarche of 14 years or greater, with 41 groups (84%) having an average age between 12.5 and 13.5 years.

Although menarche represents mature development of the uterus, it does not necessarily reflect full reproductive capability. There is a period of between two and three years when fertility is low. Most girls experience one to three years of menstruation that is not accompanied by ovulation, meaning that they cannot become pregnant. Although this is typical, it does not happen in all girls (Bogin, 1999), and girls can become pregnant during the year following menarche.

Historical Trends in Attainment of Puberty

There has been a great deal of coverage in the popular press over the last several years, noting that children, especially girls, are attaining puberty earlier than in years past. There is some truth to this, although it depends on how many years past (several decades or several centuries) and which aspects of puberty one is talking about.

Let's start with the big picture, going back about 150 years. The easiest and most reliable measure of puberty is menarche, which obviously tells us something about pubertal development only in girls. Data on age of girls' first menstrual period date back to the 1830s in parts of Europe. One must be cautious in interpreting these older data sets, but the historical trend is clear. As you can see in Figure 4.7, the average age of menarche has declined in Europe and the United States over the past 150 years, from between 14 to 16 years in the 19th century to between 12 and 13 years in 1960 (Bullough, 1981; Tanner, 1981).

Age of menarche has remained relatively constant over the past 50 years or so. The average age of menarche in the United States for Caucasian females is 12.6 years and for African American females is 12.1 years (Steingraber, 2007). The drastic decline in average age over the 19th and early 20th centuries apparently was the result of improved nutrition.

However, other pubertal events have been occurring earlier relative to the middle of the 20th century. For example, Marcia Herman-Giddens and her colleagues (1997) studied pubertal development in more that 17,000 American girls between the ages of 3 and 12 years. They reported that although the age of menarche was unchanged relative to earlier generations, girls were developing breasts (called *thelarche*) and growing pubic hair (called *pubarche*) earlier since the 1950s. For the most part, average ages, although earlier than in decades past, remain within the typical range. For instance,

---

spermarche A male's first ejaculation.

menarche A woman's first menstrual period.

Herman-Giddens and her colleagues reported that the average age for breast development was 8.87 years for African American girls and 9.96 years for Caucasian girls. However, many girls show signs of puberty very early. For example, 3% of African American girls and 1% of Caucasian girls show signs of breast development by 3 years of age (see Steingraber, 2007).

Several candidates have been suggested for these changes. Tops on the list is obesity. For instance, girls who are overweight experience menarche sooner than other girls, and diet may be associated with other signs of earlier puberty. Another candidate for early puberty is environmental contaminants. Exposure to insecticides, passive tobacco smoke, arsenic, polybrominated biphenyls (a fire retardant), and chemicals used in common plastics have all been shown to be associated with pubertal onset. Also indicated are estrogen-related hormones/chemicals. For instance, some hair products contain estrogen, and repeated exposure to these may accelerate aspects of puberty (Blanck et al., 2000; Herman-Giddens et al., 1997). Relatedly, atypical breast development in prepubertal *boys* has been found to be associated with the use of certain lavender and tea tree oil body creams that contain estrogen (Henley et al., 2007).

In addition to the physical environment, aspects of children's social environment have been shown to be associated with earlier pubertal development and sexual activity. For example, exposure to sexually explicit contexts, either in real life or on television, has been hypothesized to be related to sexual development in girls. Recently, researchers have examined in some detail the relationships between psychological factors such as economic and social stress, father absence, and maternal depression and pubertal timing, specifically from the viewpoint of evolutionary theory, and we look at some of these findings in greater detail in the following section.

Psychological Factors, Pubertal Timing, and Children's Evolved Sensitivity to Rearing Environments

The attainment of puberty would seem to be a biological thing, influenced more by genetics and diet than psychological factors. In fact, the age of attaining puberty is moderately heritable; for example, there is a significant relationship in the age of menarche between mothers and their daughters (Belsky et al., 2007; Ellis & Graber, 2000), and the decline in the age of menarche over the last 150 years is associated primarily with changes in diet (Hofferth, 1990). Also, adolescent girls who are physically active and

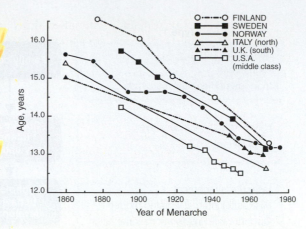

FIGURE 4.7 Historical trends in menarche. Average age of menarche decreased sharply from the middle of the 19th to the middle of the 20th century. The average age of menarche has not changed appreciably in the past 50 years. SOURCE: From Tanner, J. M. (1990). *Foetus into man: Physical growth from conception to maturity*, p. 160. Cambridge, MA: Harvard University Press. Reprinted by permission.

have a low amount of body fat can experience a delay of menarche, or a cessation of menstruation once it has begun (Warren & Brooks-Gunn, 1989).

But psychological factors have also been shown to have a significant impact on pubertal timing, particularly age of menarche. Jay Belsky, Lawrence Steinberg, and Patricia Draper (1991) proposed that aspects of the rearing environment bias children, particularly girls, toward developing a reproductive strategy that emphasizes either mating opportunities over investment in children or the reverse. According to Belsky et al. (1991, p. 650),

a principal evolutionary function of early experience—the first 5 to 7 years—is to induce in the child an understanding of the availability and predictability of resources (broadly defined) in the environment, of the trustworthiness of others, and of the enduringness of close interpersonal relationships, all of which will affect how the developing person apportions reproductive effort.

Belsky et al. proposed that children evolved mechanisms that are sensitive to features of the early childhood environment that influence rate of pubertal maturation and reproductive strategies. Homes characterized by inadequate resources, high stress, insecure attachment, and father absence tend to accelerate pubertal development in girls, lead to early sexual activity, and encourage a mating strategy that emphasizes short-term bonds and limited parental investment (that is, have many children but invest little in each). This is reflected as the Type 1 strategy in Figure 4.8. In contrast, homes that are characterized by adequate resources, low stress, father presence, and secure attachment are associated with slower pubertal development in girls, delayed sexual activity, and a reproductive strategy that emphasizes long-term pair bonds and greater parental investment in children (that is, have fewer children and invest heavily in each). This is reflected as the Type 2 strategy in Figure 4.8. Basically, Belsky and his colleagues argued that children's early environments are good predictors of what their later environments will be

FIGURE 4.8 Two developmental pathways of reproductive strategies. The type of home environment children experience influences their rate of attaining puberty and their adult mating/parenting styles. These effects are particularly strong for girls. SOURCE: From Belsky, J., Steinberg, L., & Draper, P. (1991). Childhood experience, interpersonal development, and reproductive strategy: An evolutionary theory of socialization. *Child Development*, *62*, 647–670. Reprinted by permission of John Wiley & Sons, Inc.

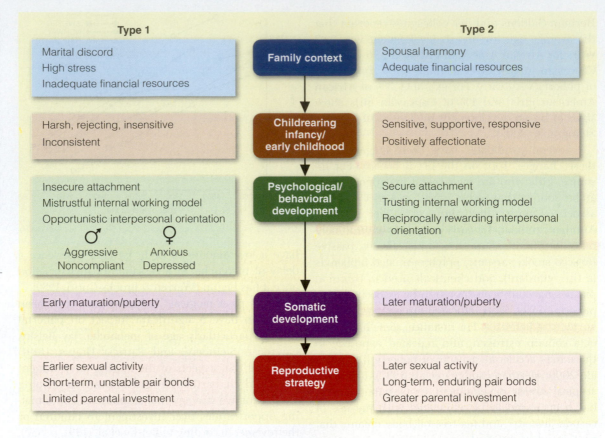

like. An adaptive reproductive strategy (adaptive from an evolutionary perspective, not necessarily from the point of view of mainstream society) for children growing up in high-stress, low-resource, and unpredictable homes is to reproduce early and often, because it is unlikely that any one child will have the requisite resources to succeed. The opposite pattern would develop for children from more predictable and supportive homes, with their most adaptive strategy being to postpone reproduction and to invest heavily in children.

Although boys from high-stress, father-absent homes tend to be noncompliant and aggressive (Draper & Harpending, 1987), differences in rates of pubertal maturation are essentially limited to girls (Kim, Smith, & Palermiti, 1997). This sex difference makes sense, given the greater investment in offspring by females. Because females' investment in any pregnancy is greater than males', they should be more sensitive than males to environmental factors that may influence the rearing of offspring (such as malnutrition, stress, or lack of resources) (Surbey, 1998).

What factors have researchers uncovered that affect rate of pubertal maturation in girls? Girls who experience socioemotional stress during childhood attain menarche earlier than girls who experience less stress (Ellis et al. 1999; Graber et al., 1995), as do girls whose mothers have depression (Ellis & Graber, 2000) or practice harsh control (Belsky et al., 2007; Belsky et al., 2010). Family stress has also

been found to be related to production of adrenal hormones in girls, which typically occurs between 6 and 8 years of age (*adrenarche*) and are necessary for the development of secondary sexual characteristics (Del Giudice, 2009; Ellis & Essex, 2007). Several studies have reported a significant relationship between father absence and accelerated pubertal development in girls (Quinlan, 2003; Tither & Ellis, 2008; see Mustanski et al., 2004, who also reported an effect in boys), and increased sexual activity and adolescent pregnancy (Ellis et al., 2003; Belsky et al., 2010; see Belsky, 2007; Del Giudice, 2009; Ellis, 2004 for reviews). Moreover, the earlier a father leaves the family, the earlier his daughters reach puberty (Moffitt et al., 1992; Surbey, 1990). In one study, father absence was associated not only with an earlier menarche but also with greater interest in infants, suggesting that such girls are becoming prepared for early reproduction and parenting (Maestripieri et al., 2004). Other research in father-intact homes has shown that the quality of the father-daughter relationship impacts age of puberty: the better the father-daughter relationship, the later girls reach puberty (Ellis et al., 1999).

One interesting line of research has shown that the age of menarche is associated with the presence of a stepfather or mother's boyfriend in the home, at least in high-stress environments (Ellis & Graber, 2000). For girls living in high-stress environments, the younger she was when an unrelated adult male joined the household, the earlier she tended to have her first menstrual period. This effect may be influenced by chemical signals, possibly from sweat glands, given off by men, often referred to as pheromones.

This line of research makes it clear that psychological factors, particularly those associated with family life, can influence the rate of the attainment of puberty, at least in girls, and associated adult behaviors (specifically sexual activity). Children appear to be sensitive to family conditions during their early years of life, and this affects their trajectory of physical development in adaptive ways. Children growing up in stable, low-stress, supportive homes can likely expect similar environments when they grow up, making it adaptive for them to delay puberty and parenthood and to invest heavily in a few offspring. In contrast, children growing up in unstable, high-stress, and nonsupportive homes may find that the best strategy (best from an evolutionary perspective, not the perspective of adjusting to contemporary society) is to mature early, anticipate unreliable partners, and have many children but invest relatively little in them. None of this behavior is conscious, but reflects how the rate of physical development in humans has been influenced by our evolutionary past.

Psychological Consequences of Physical Growth during Adolescence

As we noted earlier, the psychological consequences of physical growth are likely most profound at adolescence, both because of the physically transforming nature of the changes that take place and the cognitive, emotional, and social sophistication of the young people who are experiencing those changes. Because of changes in cognitive abilities that occur at this time (see Chapters 6 and 8), adolescents are particularly self-conscious, and this makes them feel awkward about changes in their bodies. They are also aware of changes taking place in the body proportions of others and compare their own development with that of their peers.

Adolescents' reactions to physical changes will depend largely on their expectations. Changes in height, strength, and body size are obvious, and all children anticipate them, but young adolescents may not be prepared for other changes. For example, menstruation in girls and nocturnal emissions in boys can be disturbing if they have not been prepared for these changes. This is reflected by one young adolescent's comments about menstruation:

> I didn't know about it. She (mother) never told me anything like that. I was scared. I just started washing all my underclothing hoping that my mother won't find out but she came and caught me, she caught me washing it, and she started laughing at me (Konopka, 1976, p. 47).

Few adolescent girls in developed societies today are surprised by their first menstrual period, and most view it as a memorable event, although often with mixed emotions (Zani, 1991). In contrast, many adolescent boys are not prepared for their first ejaculation, and unlike girls, who often tell their mothers and friends about their first menstrual period, boys rarely tell others about their first ejaculation (Stein & Reiser, 1994; Zani, 1991).

Puberty is a big deal. The physical changes that occur over the course of a few years in adolescence are drastic, changing the child into a young woman or man. Substantial behavioral and psychological changes occur with this transformation, and even when children are not alarmed by the changes in their bodies' function and proportions, the changes have important consequences for social development. Many children experience some degree of distress in dealing with these changes, which are discussed in various chapters in this book. However, the impact of these changes is also influenced by *when* children experience them. Most research has focused on the effects of early maturation on adolescent adjustment, with effects tending to vary between boys and girls.

The Impact of Timing of Puberty on Girls

Girls, in general, begin puberty earlier than boys. As a result, early-maturing girls are about two years more advanced than other girls their age and about four years ahead of the boys in their peer group. This can make an early-maturing 9- or 10-year-old girl feel conspicuous. As a result, early-maturing girls experience more emotional problems than their peers; they have lower self-esteem and higher rates of anxiety, depression, and eating disorders, all relative to girls who mature on time (Mendle, Turkheimer, & Emery, 2007; Stice, Presnell, & Bearman, 2001). One possible reason for this is that early-maturing girls produce increasing amounts of sex hormones that may heighten their sensitivity to their social environment, causing them to be disproportionately distressed about negative exchanges with peers or adults (Warren & Brooks-Gunn, 1989). The picture is not all bad for early-maturing girls; they tend to be more popular than later-maturing girls, especially with (older) boys (McCabe & Ricciardelli, 2004).

Much of early-maturing girls' problems stems from their concerns about their increasing weight and the increased fat deposits that adolescence brings. Adolescent girls in the United States aspire to achieve the feminine ideal of a slim body, and, compared to the girlish figures of their peers, their own bodies seem to be moving away from this ideal. The influence of peers and media (for example, television) on the importance of thinness in girls is seen as early as 5 years of age (Dohnt &

FIGURE 4.9 The effect of age of menarche on teenage smoking. Early-maturing girls are more likely to be frequent users of alcohol, tobacco, and other drugs than girls who mature on time or later. SOURCE: Adapted from Dick, D. M., Rose, R., Viken, R. J., & Kaprio, J. (2000). Pubertal timing and substance use: Associations between and within families across late adolescence. *Developmental Psychology*, *36*, 180–189. Copyright © 2000 by the American Psychological Association. Reprinted by permission.

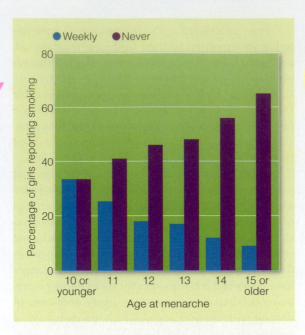

Tiggerman, 2006). Adolescent girls in general have negative body images, which become more negative from early to late adolescence (Rosenblum & Lewis, 1999), and the body images of early-maturing girls tends to be worse than those of girls who mature on time (Ohring, Graber, & Brooks-Gunn, 2002). As a result, eating disorders are relatively common among adolescent girls, as discussed in Box 4.2.

It is worth noting that the lower self-esteem that characterizes early-maturing girls is not inevitable. In fact, substantial cultural variability exists. For example, in Germany, where there is less of an emphasis on slimness and attitudes about adolescent sexuality are more open, early-maturing girls actually have higher self-esteem than other girls (Silbereisen et al., 1989). There is also evidence that African American girls are less apt to experience the negative effects of early maturation than are Caucasian American girls. For example, some studies show that early-maturing African American girls are no more likely to have eating disorders, depression, elevated levels of anger (Michael

Early-maturing boys often excel in sports, and their greater height and strength often causes others to perceive them as more responsible and as having interests different from those of their less-mature peers.

& Eccles, 2003), or to engage in sexual intercourse (Cavanagh, 2004) than girls who mature later.

Early-maturing girls are also more likely to engage in problem behavior relative to other girls. For instance, they are more likely to be involved in drug and alcohol use, have school problems, exhibit delinquency, and experience sexual intercourse at an earlier age (Mendle et al., 2007; Stice et al., 2001). This pattern has been found in different subcultures within the United States (Deardoff et al., 2005) and in different countries (Silbereisen et al., 1989; see Mendle et al., 2007). Figure 4.9 presents the percentage of girls who smoked cigarettes weekly or not at all as a function of their age at menarche (Dick et al., 2000). As you can see, girls who matured early were more likely to be frequent smokers than girls who matured on time or late. Similar patterns were found for alcohol and drug use.

What is the reason for this relationship? Most likely it can be attributed to early-developing girls spending time with older adolescents and getting into situations they are not emotionally or cognitively able to handle. It is important to take context into consideration here. For example, in a study of New Zealand girls who attended all-female schools, early-maturing girls were no more likely to get into trouble than other girls, presumably because the negative influence of older boys was minimized in the same-sex school environment (Caspi et al., 1993).

It is important to keep in mind that problems associated with adolescence are not limited to early-maturing girls. In fact, the overall differences in the extent to which early-maturing versus other girls engage in risky behaviors are small: maturational time accounts for just 2% of the differences for eating disorders, 4% for delinquency, and 6% for sexual activity (see Mendle et al., 2007). Many factors affect psychological adjustment during adolescence, with early maturation being only one of them.

The Impact of Timing of Puberty on Boys

There are both positive and negative immediate consequences for early maturation for boys. On the positive side, research dating back more than 60 years reports a social advantage for early-maturing boys (Graber et al., 1997; Jones & Bayley, 1950). Unlike their female counterparts, early-maturing boys are not overly conspicuous, because many girls have already begun their adolescent growth spurt. Their greater height and strength and other aspects of their masculine physique serve as social signals, both to themselves and to others, and most adolescent boys view this positively. Early-maturing boys are more likely to excel in sports, which plays an important role in their social world, and their burst into manhood causes them and others to perceive them as more responsible and as having interests different from those of their less-mature peers. It is little wonder then, that, in comparison to late-maturing boys, early-maturing boys are more popular, self-assured, sociable, and have higher achievement aspirations (Graber et al., 1997; McCabe & Ricciardelli, 2004).

Like their female counterparts, early-maturing boys are more likely to become involved in anti-social activities, including delinquency, school problems, and drug and alcohol use (Duncan et al., 1985; Wichström, 2001). These effects are especially large for adolescents living in disadvantaged neighborhoods or whose parents use harsh and inconsistent discipline (Ge et al., 2002). As with early-maturing girls, these boys may make friendships with older boys and become involved in activities for which they are not emotionally or cognitively prepared.

We have focused so far on children who experience early puberty. What about children who are late maturers? One early longitudinal study reported that as adults, late-maturing males were more insightful, inventive, and creative than their early-maturing peers, who were more responsible, cooperative, and self-controlled, although also more conforming, conventional, and humorless (Jones, 1965). The early-maturing boys, because of their more adultlike appearance, may have adopted adult roles and behaviors early, possibly stifling their creativity and risk-taking. Late-maturing boys, in contrast, had additional time to develop their social and intellectual skills during adolescence. Slow growth is a characteristic of our species (see Box 4.1), and boys who take extra time to reach adulthood may hone some of their social skills to a greater extent than early-maturing boys, and as a result end up with a competitive advantage.

Motor Development

As children's bones and muscles grow, they become more willing and able to move their bodies. Children progress from sitting to standing to walking to running, all in a relatively brief period. By early childhood, they cannot only run well, but they also have enough coordination to climb trees, keep their balance while walking along a curb, and swing hand-to-hand on a set of monkey bars. At the same time that such **gross motor behaviors** are developing, children are also perfecting their fine motor capabilities. Most **fine motor behaviors** have to do with control of the hands. During infancy, newborns' reflexive grasp becomes refined, so that by the end of the first year they can pick up Cheerios with their fingers and guide them quickly and accurately into their mouths. It is not until years later that children develop the fine-motor coordination necessary for precise writing, and many years must pass before they can type proficiently or dash off a quick signature at the bottom of a check.

Motor development proceeds on a species-typical course, because it is substantially influenced by maturation of the brain. Yet events in the outside world, and feedback from children's own actions, also affect motor development, and children's motor abilities have a great impact on their social and cognitive development. The 12-month-old who can walk (or run) is treated differently than the 12-month-old who is still limited to a less-efficient mode of locomotion, such as crawling. Older children who have the coordination to excel in sports and games will find themselves in different social situations with their peers than less well-coordinated children. In short, changes in motor development have greater consequences for children than simply giving them an increased ability to move about.

Motor development in children is regulated by some of the same principles that regulate physical growth: the *cephalocaudal principle* and the *proximodistal principle*, which we discussed earlier in this chapter with respect to physical growth and in Chapter 3 concerning prenatal development. According to these principles, voluntary motor control progresses from head to toe and from the interior (for example, shoulders) to the exterior (for example, fingers) of the body. In addition, children display increasing *lateralization* of motor ability, showing a decided preference, for example, for handling, throwing, or kicking things with the hand, arm, or foot on one side of their body (usually the right) than the other.

Gross Motor Development

Before discussing children's control of their legs, arms, and hands, we should mention another aspect of motor control that is important to many parents, and that is development of voluntary control of the muscles that regulate bodily eliminations. Children begin to gain control of these muscles sometime during their second year of life, and toilet training typically begins between 18 and 24 months of age. Usually children gain control of the anal sphincter, which regulates feces elimination, before they gain bladder control. Children typically achieve bladder control during the daytime before they are able to spend dry nights. There are substantial individual differences in when children gain control of their bodily elimination functions. While some are able to regulate their anal sphincters when they are

Toilet training is an important milestone in a child's life, and children usually gain control of the anal sphincter between 2 and 3 years of age. Control of urination usually develops later.

---

gross motor behaviors Motor behaviors associated with large muscles, such as arms and legs.

fine motor behaviors Motor behaviors having to do with control of the hands.

BOX 4.3 child development in the real world

To Sleep, Perchance to Be Psychologically Healthy

All animals with brains sleep. Sleep is necessary to restore the brain and seems to be important in consolidating memories from experiences had during waking hours (Prehn-Kristensen et al., 2009; Stickgold et al., 2001). The amount of sleep people require changes with age. As noted in Chapter 3, newborns spend an average of 16 hours per day sleeping, although this can range from about 11 to 18 hours. As children age, the amount of sleep they need declines: about 12 to 14 hours for toddlers, 11 to 13 hours for preschoolers, 10 to 11 hours for school-age children, and about 9 hours for teenagers (National Academy of Sciences, 2000; National Sleep Foundation, 2007). Teenage girls tend to get less sleep than boys, getting up earlier in the mornings than boys (Fredriksen et al., 2004). One hypothesis for this difference is that girls require more time to groom themselves to get ready for school than boys and have more household chores than boys, illustrating an unanticipated consequence of gender stereotyping (Lee, McEnany, & Weekes, 1999).

Not only does the number of hours children sleep change, but so too does the *pattern* of sleep. Beginning as early as 8 or 9 years of age, children's sleep-wake cycles shift to later bedtimes and earlier wake-up times, at least when left to their natural schedules (Snell, Adam, & Duncan, 2007).

There is real concern today that children are not getting enough sleep. Inadequate sleep is associated with poor school performance, fatigue during the day, depressive mood, and lower self-esteem in teenagers

High-school students' natural sleep-wake cycle makes it likely that they will be tired at school.

Image Source/Getty Images

(Buckhalt et al., 2009; Wolfson & Carskadon, 1998), as well as memory deficits in school-age children (Steenari et al., 2003) and behavior problems in preschoolers (Bates et al., 2002). Children who go to bed late and get little sleep are also more likely to be overweight than are children with better sleeping habits (Snell et al., 2007).

Why are so many children not getting the sleep they need? There are surely many reasons. Young children may want to stay up to watch favorite television shows and play with older siblings or adults, not wanting to miss any fun activities. These same children will likely be reluctant to get out of bed the next morning. Teenagers may want to spend time talking with their friends or staying

online, extending their wake time until sleep overtakes them. But most of the problem of sleepy children seems to be a result of the requirements of formal schooling. Emily Snell and her colleagues (2007) collected sleep diaries from more than 2,000 children, completed by the children or by their parents. The accompanying figure displays the average number of hours children between the ages of 3 and 18 reported sleeping, separately for weekdays and weekends. The first thing to note is that at every age, children get more sleep on weekends than on weekdays, with the difference generally increasing as children get older. In fact, the age differences in the amount of sleep children get varied only slightly for weekends: 3-year-olds

1 year old, most gain such control between 2 and 3 years. Control of urination, both day and night, usually develops later (for example, in the United States, 3 years is the expected age; Charlesworth, 1996), although some children will not be toilet trained until 5 or 6 years.

From Lifting Their Heads to Hopping and Skipping

Babies do not do much in terms of motor behavior at birth. They are born with well-developed reflexes such as grasping and sucking (see discussion of neonatal reflexes in Chapter 3). Their motor abili-

ties increase gradually but steadily over the course of the first year. Most (90%) infants are able to lift their heads while lying on their stomachs by 3.2 months, can roll over by 4.7 months, can sit up when propped by 4.2 months, and can sit without support by 5.5 months (Frankenburg & Dodds, 1967). However, during their first 6 months of life, when infants are put somewhere, for the most part, that is where they will stay until someone moves them.

This immobile period does not last long, however. By 6 or 7 months, many infants are able to move from place to place by lying on their stomachs and pulling themselves along with their arms. This

slept only 40 minutes more on average than 17-year-olds. In contrast, the difference in sleep between 3- and 17-year-olds during weekdays was about 2.5 hours. Most of this difference is because older children and adolescents go to bed later during the week than younger children. Weekday wake-up times varied little with age and averaged between 6:45 a.m. and 7:00 a.m. for children between the ages of 6 and 15.

You may note a bit of a reversal in sleep trends at age 18. Eighteen-year-olds tended to sleep a bit less than 17-year-olds on weekends but slept about 45 minutes *more* on weekdays. This was apparently because many of these 18-year-olds left high school and were able to determine their own sleep-wake cycles.

Are teenagers destined to spend their early school hours with their eyes half-opened? High school students in most of the United States begin school before middle-school students, who begin before elementary-school children. It seems that, if alertness were the only factor to consider, this is exactly the opposite pattern that would make the most sense based on children's natural sleep-wake cycles. In fact, researchers have concluded that current school schedules are causing sleep deprivation in high-school students (Hansen et al., 2005). Some school districts have recognized this and have changed school starting times to better match the sleep-wake cycles of their students. Changing school hours can be a politically charged issue. Starting school later means ending it later, which can

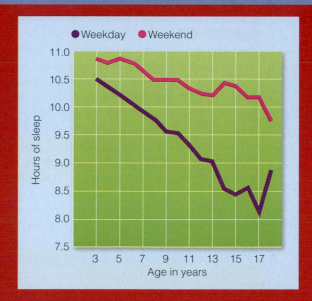

Average number of weekday and weekend hours of sleep for children between 3 and 18 years of age. Children sleep more during the weekends at all ages, with this difference increasing with age. SOURCE: Snell, E. K., Adam, E. K., & Duncan, G. J. (2007). Sleep and body mass index and overweight status of children and adolescents. *Child Development, 78,* **309–323.**

interfere with school sports programs and other school-sponsored activities, as well as with teenagers' after-school jobs. Although solid research on the effects of changing school starting time is meager, some preliminary results from a Minnesota school system showed that changing the start of high school from 7:15 a.m. to 8:40 a.m. resulted in increased school attendance, less depression, and a small positive change in school grades (Walhstrom, 2003).

The obligations and busy and complicated life of today's children (and adults) make it difficult for them to get all the sleep they ideally should. In literate societies such as ours, formal schooling is a must, and it is impossible for a school system to adjust its schedule to accommodate all children and their parents. But daily sleep is a vital bodily function that is as important as eating. Just as we do not want to provide children with chronically poor diets, we should be mindful not to deprive them of the necessary rest they need to be at their psychologically best.

is not a very efficient form of locomotion, and few infants who move in this way travel far, but within several months most infants are on their hands and knees, crawling to where they want to go. Before too long, crawling is followed by walking, which brings new freedom to the toddler. Figure 4.10 presents some of the developmental milestones in early gross motor development, as well as the typical age range in which each milestone is achieved (Franenburg et al., 1981).

Gross motor development is not complete with baby's first steps, however. Jane Clark (2005) lists six important developmental milestones typically linked to human locomotion, all but two of them acquired *after* children learn to walk: crawling, walking, running, galloping, hopping, and skipping. Although most children are walking shortly after their first birthdays, they do not run or gallop until about 18 and 22 months, respectively. Hopping and skipping require even more coordination and are typically acquired when children are about 3 (hopping) and 5 (skipping) years old. It is important to note that substantial variability occurs in when children achieve these milestones, so that a child who walks at 11 months and one who does not take her first steps until 14 months are both well within the typical range of motor development.

Travel Broadens the Mind

Being able to move around in the world signals a major life transition in early development and affects infants' physical, social, emotional, and cognitive growth. It also affects how parents relate to their babies. Mother can no longer set little Joey on a blanket in the middle of the living-room floor and expect that he will be there when she returns from a quick trip to the bathroom. This influences not only what infants see, but also *how* they see things, what they physically can interact with, and whom they interact with. Children who crawl and walk can actually travel toward people of interest and can share experiences with these people in ways that sitting infants cannot. The transitions from sitting to crawling and crawling to walking correlate with changes in children's understanding of their physical and social worlds.

As discussed in later chapters, children begin to understand other people as social agents beginning around 9 months of age, looking where they look or point, as if they know that the other person sees something that they too should see (*shared attention*, see Chapter 7). Most infants are crawling by this time, and babies improve in their shared-attention abilities considerably by 14 or 15 months, when most are walking. Researchers have proposed that the advent of crawling and then walking provides infants with new experiences that influence how they view and interact with their physical and social worlds, which in turn sets in motion a host of psychological processes, leading inevitably to advances in children's socioemotional and intellectual development (Campos et al., 2000).

Locomotion and the Development of Spatial Abilities

Several studies have examined the effect of locomotor experience on young children's visual/spatial abilities. For example, research assessing infants' depth perception used the *visual cliff*, which consists of a glass-topped table with a board across its center (Walk & Gibson, 1961). On the shallow side of the board, infants see a checkerboard pattern placed directly under the glass; on the deep side the checkerboard pattern is several feet below the glass (see Photo). Infants who can crawl are placed on the center board and called by their mothers from either side of the cliff. Infants who crawl to their mothers on the shallow side but not on the deep side are said to be able to discriminate depth. By the time babies can crawl, they rarely go to their mothers on the deep side, suggesting to some that little or no learning is necessary to discriminate depth (Walk & Gibson, 1961). However, the likelihood of showing fear on the visual cliff is related to the amount of locomotive experience children have. In a series of studies, children with more experience crawling or walking were more likely to display fear on the visual cliff than were children with less locomotor experience, suggesting that early locomotor experience influences depth perception, or at least the knowledge that a fall could hurt (Bertenthal, Campos, & Barrett, 1984; Bertenthal, Campos, & Kermoian, 1994).

FIGURE 4.10 Some developmental milestones in gross motor abilities.
Note that there is substantial variability in acquiring each of these skills. SOURCE: Adapted from Franenburg, W. K., Fandal, A. W., Sciarillo, W., & Burgess, D. (1981). The newly abbreviated and revised Denver Developmental Screening Test. *Journal of Pediatrics, 99,* 995–999. Reprinted by permission of Elsevier.

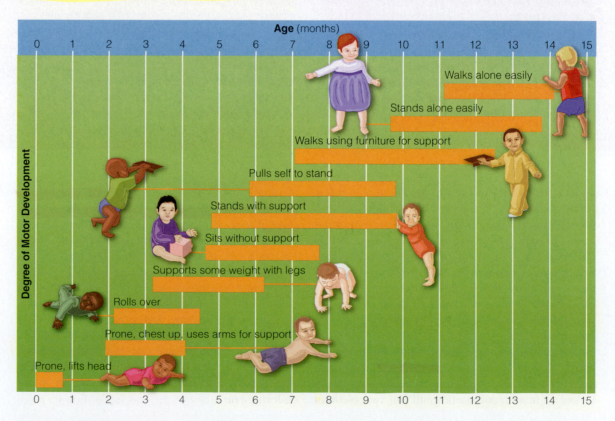

Walks alone easily
Stands alone easily
Walks using furniture for support
Pulls self to stand
Stands with support
Sits without support
Supports some weight with legs
Rolls over
Prone, chest up, uses arms for support
Prone, lifts head

Age (months)

Degree of Motor Development

Most children take their first tentative steps around their first birthdays. It will be several more months before they run, hop, or skip.

An infant on a visual cliff. Infants who can perceive depth will crawl to their mothers across the shallow side but not across the deep side. Infants' performance on this task is related to their amount of locomotive experience.

In other research, infants' locomotive experience was related to their ability to retrieve an object hidden under a cloth. For example, in one study, 8.5-month-old infants were divided into three groups: (1) locomotive (that is, crawling), (2) prelocomotive (that is, not yet crawling), or (3) prelocomotive but with walker experience (Kermoian & Campos, 1988). Walkers are essentially wheeled seats in which infants can push themselves around the floor (see Photo). Babies with locomotive experience, either by crawling or in a walker, showed more advanced performance on the object-retrieval task than did the noncrawlers. Moreover, there were no differences in performance between the crawlers and those in the walkers, suggesting that the locomotor experience and not maturation is responsible for the advanced spatial memory (see also Arterberry, Yonas, & Bensen, 1989; Bai & Bertenthal, 1992). In other words, infants who get around their environment on their own develop more advanced spatial cognition than infants who do not. This is consistent with the idea that cognitive development is not the simple unfolding of a genetic plan or brain maturation, but proceeds as a result of an active child in physical interaction with his or her environment. Related work with 9-month-old infants has shown that those who could crawl showed enhanced spatial memory abilities relative to those who could not, suggesting that independent locomotion is associated with better and more flexible memory early in life (Herbert, Gross, & Hayne, 2007).

(We should note that the American Academy of Pediatrics recommends against the use of walkers for infants, noting that they do not result in children walking sooner and their use is associated with increased injuries, mainly caused by falling down stairs. Between 1973 and 1998, 34 infants died in walker-related accidents in the United States [American Academy of Pediatrics, Committee on Injury and Poison Prevention, 2001]).

Some physical tasks may need to be relearned as infants make the transition from crawling to walking. For instance, in one study, infants were

Babies in walkers show faster development of visual/spatial abilities than nonwalking children without walker experience; however, they are also more prone to injuries.

© David Young-Wolff/PhotoEdit

placed on inclines of various steepness and encouraged to crawl down them. Experienced crawlers were able to judge quite well which inclines they could manage and which they could not. However, when these same infants began to walk, they would topple down the slopes headfirst. Their new mode of locomotion apparently required them to re-learn some basic skills (Adolph, 1997).

Locomotion and Changes in Social Relations

Perhaps less obviously, self-locomotion also changes infants' social relations and understanding. When children begin to crawl, and especially walk, the nature of the mother-child relationship must change. Walking, in particular, brings with it new freedoms and potential dangers that parents must deal with. The early teen months, when most infants begin to walk, correspond to a stage in Piaget's theory of sensorimotor development in which he described infants as "little experimenters," trying to figure out how things work (see Chapter 6). This can result in a test of wills between parent and child, as parents must child-proof their house and be continually on-guard for things their toddler may get into. (It may not be a coincidence that one of children's first words is "No," often used when a parent is preventing a child from engaging in some interesting task, like putting the cat food into the water dish, or worse yet, eating it.) This advent of the testing of wills between mothers and their children seems to begin not at a particular age, but when infants start to walk, regardless of age. In one study, walkers, more so

than crawlers of comparable age, were more apt to continue a behavior after being told repeatedly by their mothers to stop it. In addition, although infants tended to express more positive emotion once they started walking, this was not how their mothers saw it. Mothers actually perceived that their infants were emotionally more negative, perhaps a result of the frequent battle of wills (Biringen et al., 1995). Some longitudinal research indicates that crawling infants will look at adults when they are talking with one another, whereas once they start walking, they look at adults to try to engage them in social interaction. In other words, changes in form of locomotion results in a switch in forms of *social looking*, from "watching others communicating" to making "bids for social attention" (Clearfield, Osborne, & Mullen, 2008).

Taken together, the research clearly indicates that self-locomotion changes infants' relationships with their physical and social worlds and instigates changes in how babies think about things and other people. This was stated elegantly by Joseph Campos and his colleagues (2000, p. 151): "Locomotion is a setting event, a control parameter, and a mobilizer that changes the intrapsychic states of the infant, the social and nonsocial world around the infant, and the interaction of the infant with that world." The relations between physical, cognitive, and social development are surely transactional, and we cannot be sure what, if any of these, is the motivating factor. Perhaps getting around on their own may motivate infants to engage in more social interactions, or perhaps the desire for social interactions may push infants to learn to walk (Clearfield et al., 2008). Regardless, crawling, and especially walking, changes more than simply how infants get around, but also how they interact with the people and things that surround them.

Fine Motor Development

Fine motor movements are those using individual body parts to control small objects. Although some people are quite proficient at picking up objects with their toes, fine motor control in humans is typically expressed in terms of manual (hand) skills. Infants come into the world with a reflexive grasp. Over the course of the first year, this grasp becomes less reflexive and more under an infant's intentional control.

Becoming "Handy"

From an evolutionary perspective, precise hand control was probably the main advantage derived from bipedal (upright) walking. The possibility of using four fingers precisely with an opposable thumb has permitted humans to construct and use tools to an extent not achieved by any other animal. Moreover, we are able to use both hands in a coordinated manner. If you are unsure about the importance of this, try to imagine doing routine activities during the course of a day with your fingers tied together and without the use of your thumb. You could still grasp some objects, but you would find that many of the tasks of daily living, from buttoning a shirt to using a knife and fork, would be very difficult indeed.

Children's control of their arms and hands shows a species-typical pattern. Although newborns have a grasping reflex, and some can get their hands or fingers to their mouths and suck on them, neonates can do little else other than to make a series of repetitive movements of their heads, torsos, and limbs (Vereijken, 2005). These movements constitute about 5% of babies' waking time and have been linked to the development of neuromuscular coordination (Thelen, 1979, 1981). Infants within the first month of life make swipes or swings toward objects, most often with their right hand, termed *pre-reaching* (Harris, 2005). Voluntary arm and hand movements improve over the early months of life, and by 4 or 5 months of age, most infants can reach and grasp objects within an arm's length. Frequently, this first *directed reaching* is bimanual, with babies launching both hands toward the objects instead of only one (see Photo). Reaching becomes primarily unimanual (one-handed) by about 9 to 10 months (Harris, 2005).

Infants' early grasping is not very precise, with the thumb not always being in opposition to the fingers. By 9 to 12 months, infants can make a *pincer grasp*, picking up objects with their thumb and a single finger, usually the index finger (von Hofsten, 2005). From 13 to 25 months old, hand skills continue to improve. According to Lauren Harris (2005, pp. 322–323), "among other accomplishments, infants can eat with a spoon, draw with crayons, put pegs in a pegboard, bang with a hammer, and use their fingers like pincers to pick up small objects." Definite handedness is often observable by this time, with most toddlers showing a distinct preference for their right hand (Harris, 2005; see section on lateralization later in this chapter).

The key to fine motor control is getting the hands to move in coordination with incoming visual information—or **eye-hand coordination**. Eye-hand coordination, which is quite sophisticated by 1 year of age, has its origins in early infancy. During the first month, infants will follow a moving object with their eyes and may thrust a hand out to attempt to grab it, although such attempts are rarely successful. Within the first couple of months, infants discover their hands and will spend much time staring at them or looking back

By 4 or 5 months of age, most infants can make directed reaching movements, usually with two hands.

Late in the second year of life, most children have enough fine motor control to handle a spoon. Most also show a decided hand preference by this time (usually the right hand).

and forth between their hands and some object (Williams, 1983).

Infants are able to visually inspect objects before they are able to pick them up. Stated another way, following the cephalocaudal principle, the muscles controlling infants' eye movements develop before the muscles controlling their fingers and hands. However, the rudiments of visually guided reaching can be found in the first few months of life. Three-month-olds can reach for and grasp an object if it is presented on the same side as the reaching hand, and 6-month-olds are able to reach for objects presented in front of them or on the opposite side of the reaching hand. Thus, at about the time most infants can sit unaided, they are able to visually direct their hands to reach for objects in front of them or to either side. This permits them to grasp a second object if one hand is already busy and to begin to explore objects with two hands (Provine & Westerman, 1979).

eye-hand coordination Moving the hands in coordination with incoming visual information.

table 4.3 Goodenough's Stages of Design Copying

Stage	Age	Description
I	1 yr.	Scribbling. Motor actions unrelated to any goal and undirected by visual schema.
II	2 yrs.	Scribbling. Spontaneous production but child now is visually responsive to the scribbles and gives them post hoc meaning.
III	2-1/2 yrs.	Child's preponderant response to any request to copy and/or draw is to scribble with inclusion of closed loops and parts of loops.
IV	3 yrs.	Copying. The child begins to pay attention to characteristics of visual model presented to her or him to be copied.
	4 yrs.	Copying. The child begins to make differential drawings that involve *angular* as well as smooth contours.
	5 yrs.	Copying. There is a definite organization of drawing in relationship to the visually presented model. but copying is still being refined.

SOURCE: Goodenough, F. L. (1926). *The measurement of intelligence through drawing.* Yonkers-on-the-Hudson, NY: Holt.

Eye-hand coordination continues to improve, but before the end of the first year, infants have acquired the basics of this important skill that they will use continually throughout the rest of their lives (Williams, 1983). Children's increasing ability to use their hands, especially in coordination with their vision, affords them the opportunity to use tools effectively. According to Jeffrey Lockman (2000, p. 137) "the origins of tool use in humans can be found during much of the first year of life, in the perception-action routines that infants repeatedly display as they explore their environments." The development of tool use is examined in Chapter 8.

Although eye-hand coordination is necessary for most important manual activities that children (or adults) do, vision is not absolutely necessary for successful reaching. For example, 4- to 8-month-old infants can reach and grasp invisible objects in a dark room guided only by sound (Clifton et al., 1991; Robin, Berthier & Clifton, 1996). Blind infants can find objects based on sound and learn to reach and grasp those objects, but they do not usually do so until about 10 to 12 months of age, about 6 months later than sighted infants (Adelson & Fraiberg, 1974).

cerebral lateralization (cerebral dominance) Functional specialization of the two hemispheres of the brain.

Fine motor skills must develop beyond simple visually guided reaching if a child is to become a proficient member of society. In some cultures, motor abilities involved in weaving, carving, sculpting, or creating stone tools are valuable skills that children must master on the way to adulthood. In schooled societies such as ours, the fine motor skills involved in drawing or writing are critical to adult functioning. Florence Goodenough (1926) studied these skills extensively early in the 20th century. Table 4.3 presents the ages and stages of children's abilities for copying a design. As can be seen from the table, the earliest stages reflect unstructured and apparently non-goal-directed movements. Gradually over the preschool years, children's copying becomes goal directed as they begin to pay attention to the stimulus and attempt to re-create what they see. However, even by age 5, children's copying skills are not complete. This difficulty with coordinating the muscles used in copying carries over into writing. In the early school years, children's writing is typically limited to learning how to form letters and copying words written by adults (see Chapter 10).

Lateralization: Focusing on One Side of the Body

Between 85% and 90% of the adults in the world are dominantly right-handed, meaning that they prefer and are more proficient at using their right hand instead of their left to perform daily tasks such as writing, throwing a ball, or opening a door. True *ambidextrism*, exhibiting no hand preference and being equally proficiently in the use of both, is quite exceptional (Harris, 2005). It seems that our ancestors also shared this right-handed bias, based, in part, on ancient cave paintings showing people using their right hands to hold weapons as well as analysis of tooth wear (Lozano et al., 2009).

The hands are controlled by the brain, and the decided preference for one hand over the other is a result of **cerebral lateralization** or **cerebral dominance**, which refers to one hemisphere being dominant relative to the other. The brain is composed of two connected parts, or hemispheres (see discussion of brain development later in this chapter), with the left hemisphere receiving information from and controlling the right side of the body, and the right hemisphere controlling the left side. Thus, the left hemisphere is dominant in right-handed people.

This right-hand preference seems to develop quite early and reflects a general bias toward the right side of the body. For example, infants and young children show a right-side bias for head turning, visually directed hand reaching, and manipulating objects (Corballis, 1990). In one study, 75% of 9- to 10-week-old fetuses showed systematically more right arm than left arm movements, with 12.5% showing the reverse pattern and 12.5% showing no bias (Hepper, McCartney, & Shannon, 1998). These differences tended to remain stable over the prenatal period (McCartney & Hepper, 1999). At 15 to 18 weeks of uterine life, fetuses who suck their thumbs show a preference for the right thumb over the left one (Harris, 2005) (see Photo). Neonates continue to show some signs of a side preference, with a clear bias to turn their heads to the right side (Johnson, 1997; van Gelder et al., 1989).

This does not necessarily mean that children's hand (or side) preference is set at birth or in early infancy. For example, although young children show a distinct preference for their left or right hands, these preferences increase over childhood, becoming highly stable by the early school years (Harris, 2005; Merola & Liederman, 1985). For instance, about 97% of children in one study who exhibited a right-hand preference when they were 5 years old continued exhibiting it when they were about 11 years old. This stability was lower, however, for left-handed children, with only 74% of left-handed 5-year-olds also being left-handed when they were 11 (Fennell, Satz, & Morris, 1983). In general, when children switch dominant hands, it is usually from an early left-hand preference to a later right-hand preference and rarely the reverse (Harris, 2005).

Where do these hand preferences come from? One obvious possibility is genes (Annett, 1985; McManus & Bryden, 1993). Until recently, evidence of genes for handedness was indirect. However, in 2007, British researchers identified a gene that increases the likelihood of being left-handed (Francks et al., 2007), which was also associated with an increase in the incidence of dyslexia and schizophrenia. Other genetic explanations propose that a second, sex-linked gene might be involved in handedness, which can explain the fact that more females than males are left-handed, as well as the fact that left-handed mothers have more left-handed offspring than do left-handed fathers (McManus & Bryden, 1993).

A more environmental explanation of handedness comes from the so-called *uterus hypothesis* (Hopkins, 1993). According to this view, the way most fetuses are situated in the womb late in prenatal development greatly restricts their ability to move the left sides of their bodies. As a result, fetuses make more body and head movements with the right sides of their bodies, with this prenatal experience establishing a side preference that continues after birth.

Because of the prevalence of right-handers in the population, there are also social and educational pressures to be right-handed. In fact, most human environments in most cultures implicitly

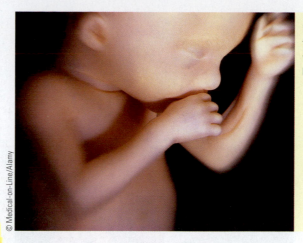

Fetuses who suck their thumbs show a preference for the right thumb over the left one.

favor the use of the right instead of the left hand. If you are right-handed and have some doubts about this, try to open a regular door, cut paper with a pair of scissors, or play the strings of a guitar with your left hand instead of your right one. In any case, most experts agree that the origins of handedness are likely the result of multiple factors—genetic, prenatal experience, and postnatal experience—all interacting in a dynamic way (Johnson, 1997; Harris, 2005).

Sex and Cultural Differences in Motor Development

As we noted earlier, there are substantial individual differences in when children attain the various developmental milestones of motor development. Take crawling, for instance. Some infants are quite conventional, moving on their hands and knees. Others, however, scoot, propelling themselves as they sit upon the floor, others roll, and still others ambulate on hands and feet, not letting their knees or elbows touch the floor (Adolph, Vereijken, & Denny, 1998). However, some reliable sex differences in motor development have been found, as well as differences as a function of cultural practices.

Sex Differences in Motor Development

There are few sex differences in the early milestones of motor development, such as reaching, sitting, crawling, and walking. However, some sex differences in motor abilities begin to appear in the second year of life (Ruble, Martin, & Berenbaum, 2006). Boys, for example, are typically able to throw overhand sooner than girls and from the very beginning are able to throw objects farther and with greater velocity than girls (Blakemore et al., 2008). Boys also seem to be better than girls in tasks requiring rapid movements (Largo et al., 2001a, 2001b).

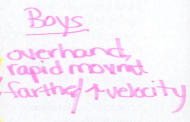

Boys overhand, rapid movmnt farther & velocity

Boys are able to throw overhand sooner and farther than girls at an early age. This is the exception, however. Girls exhibit earlier development of most gross and fine motor skills relative to boys.

Girls, in contrast, are able to hop and skip sooner than boys (Malina, 2005; Seefeldt & Haubernstricker, 1982) and surpass boys in fine motor skills involving eye-hand coordination (Largo et al., 2001a, 2001b; Blakemore et al., 2008). Females are more apt to be left-handed than males, with this difference being seen as early as 4 to 5 years old. Girls also show, on average, an earlier and more stable hand preference pattern than boys (Harris & Carlson, 1993; Humphrey & Humphrey, 1988).

One reason for girls' superior motor performance on some tasks, particularly during infancy and the preschool years, is their faster rate of neurological development (see further discussion). Boys' typically greater athletic ability in later childhood and adolescence is likely related, in part, to their increased strength (at least in adolescence) and to cultural factors that place greater value on athletic skills for boys than for girls (Blakemore et al., 2008; Kimura, 1999).

Cultural Variability in Motor Development

Although there is a species-typical pattern of motor development, there are also substantial cultural differences, indicating quite clearly that motor development is not simply a matter of maturation. For example, in some West African groups, such as the Kipsigis, mothers encourage their infants' motor development, placing babies in holes in the ground so they can sit with their backs supported (Super, 1976); in Mali, mothers stretch and massage infants to foster their physical development (Bril & Sabatier, 1986). Such practices are associated with an advance in early motor development by about 2 to 3 months. In comparison, in China infants are often placed on beds surrounded by pillows to keep them from crawling on dirty floors (Campos et al., 2000). In some traditional groups, such as the Ache from Paraguay, infants are car-

Cultures differ in ways in which babies are carried and encouraged (or discouraged) to exercise their motor abilities, which can affect their rate of motor development, although these practices seem to have no effect on mature motor functioning.

ried everywhere by their mothers, and their feet rarely touch the ground until the age of 3 (Kaplan & Dove, 1987), whereas other traditional groups wrap babies in cloth for most of their first year, providing them with little opportunity for exercising their large muscles (Greenfield & Childs, 1991). Not surprisingly, motor development is slowed in these cultures. Despite these extremes, it is noteworthy that these practices do not delay or accelerate motor development by much and seem not to affect mature motor functioning.

Even some recent child-rearing practices in the United States have had an unintended effect on motor development. There has been a public campaign beginning in the 1990s to prevent Sudden Infant Death Syndrome (see Box 3.4 in Chapter 3) by recommending that parents put young infants in a supine position (on their backs) when placing them in a crib. This practice has resulted in infants crawling later or not at all (Davies et al., 1998). It seems lying on their back is more stimulating for infants than lying on their stomachs, but does not create conditions that promote crawling.

Motor development appears to most people to be a simple process, with children mastering new physical tasks following a biologically based schedule. However, as the patterns of sex, cultural, and individual differences reflect, it is not that simple. In fact, new research is showing that motor development is highly dependent not only upon one's inherited biology, but also upon experience and one's own actions in interaction with physical structure, such as bones and muscle. If this statement reminds you of developmental contextual theory as discussed in Chapter 2, it is not a coincidence. Contemporary theorists interpret motor development following an explicitly developmental systems model, and this approach to motor development is examined in Box 4.4.

BOX 4.4 big questions

How Do Babies Learn to Walk?

Psychologists' descriptions of motor development in the early days of developmental psychology gave the impression that children's increasing control of their bodies was a product of maturation, with experience having little influence (Gesell, 1933; McGraw, 1943). But recall our discussion in Chapters 1 and 2 of contemporary approaches to development and the emphasis on the complex interaction of environmental and biological factors in explaining change over time. This perspective was made most explicitly by developmental systems theorists (Gottlieb, 2007) and has been applied to understanding motor development (Adolph, 2008; Adolph & Berger, 2006; Thelen, 1995).

We provided an example of an aspect of motor development from a dynamic systems perspective in Chapter 2—the loss of the stepping reflex. Recall that newborns will make stepping movements when they are held upright, but that this behavior disappears around 2 months of age. Research showed, however, that more was involved in this pattern than just maturation of the nervous system. Rather, the increasing weight of the infants' legs was responsible for the disappearance of the reflex at 2 months; babies would display the reflex when their legs were submerged in water (their legs becoming effectively weightless), and babies who typically showed the reflex

would not do so when weights were placed on their legs (see Thelen, 1995). The presence or absence of the stepping reflex resulted from the dynamic interaction among gravity, maturation, and the increasing weight of the baby's body.

Crawling, walking, balancing, reaching, and running are even more complex than neonatal reflexes, and research has shown that these abilities are also the result of a dynamic interaction among a host of factors (Adolph & Berger, 2006; Garciaguirre, Adolph, & Shrout, 2007). Successful walking requires the child to overcome the force of gravity, which is three times stronger than the infant experienced while in the womb (Clark, 2005). This requires not only staying upright while standing on two feet, but also holding one's entire weight on one foot while the other is in the air moving forward. It also requires getting control of several different body parts (arms, legs, hips, torso) and coordinating those different body parts while moving. When children first begin to walk, they are only able to move their heads, necks, and trunks together, holding their arms next to their bodies without any movement, in what has been called the "high guard" position (Clark, 2005).

Infants and toddlers learn to walk (and run) by making adjustments as they attempt to move from one place to another. As their limbs and muscles grow and strengthen, they get

sensory feedback as they try different movements on different surfaces. As a result of their attempts at walking in different contexts, new patterns of locomotion emerge (Thelen & Smith, 1994). Such a pattern was revealed by Karen Adolph and Anthony Avolio (2000) as they watched 14-month-old toddlers walking down a slope. Toddlers walked down slopes of different degrees of incline while wearing weighted vests that shifted the children's centers of gravity, simulating weight gains as infants grow. Infants adjusted their movements, both to changing weights and different slopes, much as adults do when they carry a heavy load or traverse novel spaces. The toddlers would bend their knees, keep their upper bodies stiff to maintain balance, and sometimes refused to attempt to make their way down the slope when it appeared too steep.

Children do not learn to walk or crawl or run as a result of a simple reading of the genetic code or maturation of brain, bone, and muscle. All of these factors contribute to motor development, but children learn to walk, for instance, by adjusting their behavior to different contexts, including their own weight, as well as the landscape they are trying to traverse. Motor development proceeds progressively as children find, little by little, different satisfactory motor solutions for the different challenges that the environment presents to them.

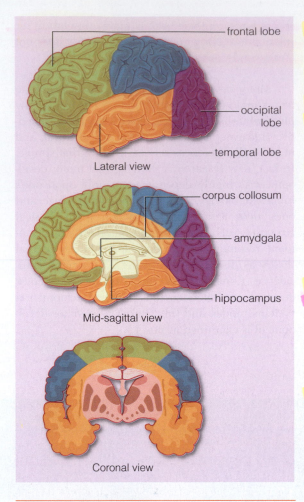

FIGURE 4.11 Lateral, mid-sagital, and coronal view of human brain.

frontal lobe

occipital lobe

temporal lobe

Lateral view

corpus collosum

amydgala

hippocampus

Mid-sagittal view

Coronal view

The Evolution and Development of the Brain

The adult human brain weighs between 1300 and 1400 grams and is divided into two parts, or hemispheres, connected by a thick bundle of nerves called the *corpus callosum*. As described by Rita Carter (1999, p. 6) "the human brain is as big as a coconut, the shape of a walnut, the color of uncooked liver, and the consistency of chilled butter." Figure 4.11 provides three different views of the adult brain.

The human brain is the most complex organ in the known universe, and thus it defies a simple description. However, for our purposes, we can divide the brain into four hierarchically organized, interacting levels: the brain stem, the hypothala-

brain stem The evolutionarily oldest part of the brain that contains cells that control relatively primitive responses associated with defense and attack behavior, feeding, freezing, sexual behavior, and facial expressions.

hypothalamus Part of the brain that controls most body systems by regulating the production of hormones in response to both internal and environmental events.

limbic system Part of the inner brain that mediates learning, memory, and emotion.

cerebral cortex (neocortex) The outer layer of the brain that gives humans their highly developed intelligence.

mus, the limbic system, and the cortex (see Lewis, 2005; see Figure 4.12).

The brain stem is the evolutionarily oldest structure and contains cells that control relatively primitive responses associated with defense and attack behavior, feeding, freezing, sexual behavior, and facial expressions. Many of these responses date back to our reptilian ancestors. The brain stem also contains circuits for many emotions, including anger, fear/anxiety, love/attachment, sadness, joy, and sexual excitement (Lewis, 2005).

In humans and other mammals, many of the actions of the brain stem are influenced by the hypothalamus, which we encountered earlier in our discussion of the endocrine system. The hypothalamus controls most body systems by regulating the production of hormones in response to both internal and environmental events.

Little learning, as conventionally understood, is needed for the brain stem and hypothalamus to do their jobs. They respond to events in the environment in pretty much the same way across the life span. It is the job of the limbic system to mediate learning, memory, and emotion. According to Marc Lewis (2005, p. 258), "limbic and higher structures may be considered 'open' in that they change with development on the basis of experience, whereas lower structures [such as the brain stem and hypothalamus] are considered 'closed' because they change little or not at all."

The limbic system contains several structures, including the *amygdala* and the *hippocampus*. The amygdala helps generate associations between experiences and emotions, although such processing does not necessarily become conscious. Events that generate emotions need to be remembered with their emotions, so that the individual can know how to respond to similar events in the future. How we respond and think about things, and our decisions to act in relation to experience, are dependent on the emotions associated with previous similar events. Was this an experience that felt good, that resulted in a good meal, or a loving touch? Or was this an experience that produced fear or pain? Located near the amygdala, the hippocampus plays an important role in organizing and storing memories for events (episodic memory, see Chapter 8). The amygdala and hippocampus seem to work together, so that emotions associated with past experiences influence the storage and retrieval of specific memories, helping individuals to plan and achieve goals.

The newest part of the brain is the cerebral cortex, sometimes referred to as the neocortex. *Neo* means "new," reflecting that this part of the brain is a relative latecomer, evolutionarily speaking, and is particularly prominent in primates and especially humans (MacLean, 1990). The cor-

table 4.4 Some Techniques for Studying the Brain and Its Development

Analyzing Electrical Brain Activity

Electroencephalography (EEG): Recording of the electrical activity of the cortex using multiple scalp electrodes.

Event-Related Potentials (ERPs): An encephalographic measure of local changes in the brain's electrical activity in response to specific stimuli.

Magnetoencephalography (MEG): Detects the magnetic field changes produced by the cortical electrical activity.

Transcranial Magnetic Simulation (TMS): The localization of a brain function by temporarily blocking the electrical activity of an area by exposure to a magnetic field.

Analyzing Anatomical Structure

Magnetic Resonance Imaging (MRI): High-resolution image of brain anatomy measuring energy changes of brain tissue after an exposure to a strong magnetic field.

Diffusion Tension Imaging (DTI): Measures the diffusion of water in the brain tissue, permitting the imaging of the white matter tracts.

Analyzing Functional-metabolic Activity

Positron Emission Tomography (PET): Assesses the metabolic activity of glucose or oxygen in the brain by following the path of a radioactive tracer injected intravenously.

Functional Magnetic Resonance Imaging (fMRI): Assesses indirectly the metabolic activity of the brain through measuring the changes of the blood flow.

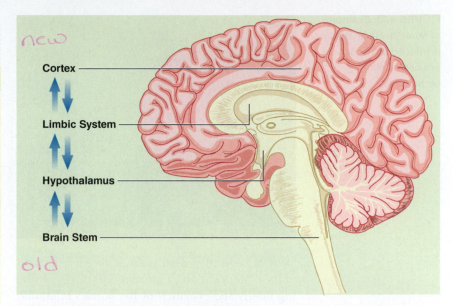

new

Cortex

Limbic System

Hypothalamus

Brain Stem

old

FIGURE 4.12 Hierarchical levels of the brain.
The brain can be divided into four hierarchically arranged levels, with lower levels being evolutionarily older and less advanced than adjacent higher levels. As reflected by the arrows, information flows between the various levels. SOURCE: From Lewis, M. D. (2005). Bridging emotion theory and neurobiology through dynamic systems modeling. *Behavioral and Brain Sciences*, 28, 169–245. Reprinted by permission of Cambridge University Press.

---

tex consists of a series of six extremely thin layers of cells. Different parts of the cortex, sometimes described as *lobes*, are associated with different psychological functions. For example, the *occipital lobe* is involved in processing visual information, some *temporal lobe* areas are involved in language (for example, Wernicke's and Broca's areas), and the **frontal lobe** is implicated in human thinking, including the planning of voluntary behaviors.

Although it has long been known that the brain is the source of human thought, until relatively recently scientists were limited in their ability to evaluate how brains worked, what parts were associated with what behavioral and intellectual functions, and how they developed. This has changed in recent years with the advent of **neuro-**

imaging techniques, which permit scientists to get a glimmer of how the brain works (Amos & Casey, 2006; Johnson, 2005; Lenroot & Giedd, 2007). The oldest of these techniques is *electroencephalography* (EEG) measurements, in which electrodes are placed on the scalp and electrical activity of the brain is measured. In some studies, *evoked potentials* are examined, with the electrical reactions of specific brain areas being measured in response to a specific stimulus (for example, the image of a face). More detailed information about the structure and function of brains can often be obtained using newer imaging techniques. These include *functional magnetic resonance imaging* (fMRI), which is a noninvasive technique that measures blood flow to the brain while people are performing cognitive tasks, and *positron emission tomography* (PET), in which radioactive materials are injected into participants, and changes in radioactivity are used to reflect glucose consumption or oxygen use in specific areas of the brain. Table 4.4 provides a partial list of some of the imaging techniques in use today, and Figure 4.13 displays some of the brain images produced by these techniques. These and other imaging techniques are still limited, but these new technologies afford us a better understanding of how brains work and develop.

frontal lobe Part of the brain that is implicated in human "thinking," including the planning of voluntary behaviors.

neuroimaging techniques Technologies that permit imaging of brain activities, including high-density event-related potentials, positron emission tomography (PET), and functional magnetic resonance imaging (fMRI).

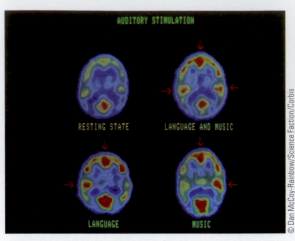

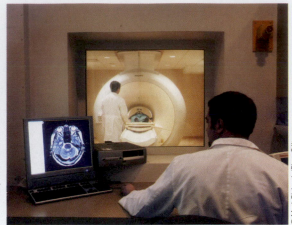

We begin our discussion of the development of the brain by taking a broad perspective, examining briefly the evolution of the human brain and how it made us the species we are. After briefly discussing brain development from a phylogenetic perspective, we focus more attention on the ontogeny of brain development, beginning with the building block of the nervous system, the *neuron*. We next look at developmental differences in the degree to which the two hemispheres are specialized for carrying out certain functions. We then examine briefly the relationship between brain development and behavior and the role of experience in brain development and plasticity. This will not be the last chapter in which brain development and the relationship between children's brain and behavior is examined; many chapters will devote space to this topic, as research in developmental neuropsychology and developmental cognitive neuroscience has expanded over the past decade.

The Evolution of the Human Brain

What distinguishes human beings from all other animals? Although there are surely several candidates, we believe that most people would concur that it is our intelligence, whether as reflected by language, tool manufacture and use, the invention of art, science, and religion, or our ability to live in complex social environments. Humans are unique in other ways (we are the only bipedal primate, and we have a distinct digestive system, for instance), but our intelligence sets us apart from other animals. Modern scientists clearly concur that the brain is the seat of human intelligence, making a look at the evolution of the brain a topic of some interest and import.

The most notable feature of the human brain is its size. When compared to other mammals, the human brain is much larger than expected for body size (Jerison, 1973; Rilling & Insel, 1999). This is a trend seen among primates in general, but it is exaggerated in humans. When did human brains get so big? As it turns out, hominid brains became progressively larger over the past 2 to 3 million years.

Although size does matter, there are other differences between the brains of humans and chimpanzees that relate to differences in the species' intelligence. For example, humans have more cortical neurons than any other mammal (including much larger whales) and nearly twice as many as chimpanzees (see Roth & Dicke, 2005). Moreover, the substantial increase in brain size has been somewhat selective, with some parts of the brain showing greater increases in size relative to other primates than other parts. The human cortex, which plays a central role in complex human cognition, has been estimated to be about 200% larger than expected for an ape of comparable body size (Barton & Harvey, 2000; Deacon, 1997). Although other areas of the human brain are larger than expected for an ape of comparable body size, none is as large as the cortex, and other areas actually display a decrease in size (for example, the olfactory cortex, some areas related to vision and motor control). Importantly, substantial evolutionary changes in the genes affect the *rate* of brain development (Somel et al., 2009). Brain development is extended from the prenatal period into infancy in humans more so than in other primates, and genetic differences between humans and chimpanzees have been identified associated with this delayed brain development.

The Development of the Brain
Neuronal Development

There are different types of brain cells, but the ones that have received the most attention and are responsible for transmitting electrical and neural information are **neurons**. It has been estimated that the adult brain has up to 100 billion neurons

neuron Nervous system cell through which electrical and chemical signals are transmitted.

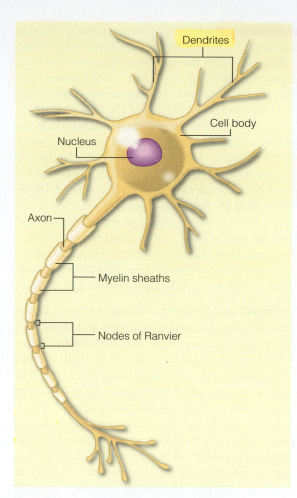

FIGURE 4.14 Primary structures of the neuron.

SOURCE: From Bjorklund, D. F. (2005). Children's thinking: cognitive development and individual differences, 4th ed., Fig. 2.10, p. 45. Copyright © 2005 Wadsworth, a part of Cengage Learning, Inc. Reprinted by permission.

(Kolb, Gibb, & Robinson, 2003). (Table 4.5 presents some facts about neurons and their development.) A mature neuron is composed of a cell body, which contains its nucleus, and an **axon**, which carries messages away from the cell body to other cells (see Figure 4.14).

The basic structure of the neuron. As can be seen in Figure 4.14, many fibers, called **dendrites**, extend from the cell body. Dendrites receive electrochemical messages from other cells and transfer them to the cell body. Dendrites do not actually come in physical contact with other dendrites (or with dendrite-like branches on axons, called *axon terminals*) when receiving messages. Rather, there are small spaces between dendrites called **synapses**, through which messages are passed. The result is many billions of connections among neurons. Like the two poles of a battery (positive and negative), the dendrites get neural impulses, or messages, *from* other neurons, while the axon terminals send the neural impulses *to* other neurons.

What is the nature of these messages that are passed from one neuron to the next? They are electrical, with messages traveling down the axon of one cell and causing the release of certain chemicals, called **neurotransmitters**, into the synapse. Neurotransmitters, which include dopamine, acetylcholine, serotonin, and GABA, among others, move across the space between the cells and are read at the dendrites of the adjacent cell, which convert the message back to an electrical signal and pass it on to its cell body. Some neurotransmitters excite the activation of a neuron, causing it to fire, whereas others inhibit activation, causing it *not* to fire.

Fully developed axons are covered by sheaths of **myelin**, a fatty substance produced by supportive brain cells called *glial cells*. Like the plastic cover of an electric wire, myelin protects and insulates axons, speeding the rate at which nervous impulses can be sent and reducing interference from other neurons. When brains are stained with a chemical so that scientists can get a better look at their structure, myelinated areas appear white, whereas cell bodies and dendrites appear slightly pink or gray. This is a source of the terms *white matter*, reflecting mainly myelinated axons mostly beneath the surface of the brain, and *gray matter*, reflecting mostly cell bodies in both cortical and subcortical (below the cortex) regions.

axon The long fiber of a neuron that carries messages from that cell to another.

dendrites The numerous fibers of a neuron that receive messages from other neurons.

synapses The tiny spaces between the dendrite of one neuron and the axon of another through which chemical messages are passed; the structures through which neurons communicate.

neurotransmitters Chemicals that move across synapses and are "read" at the dendrites of adjacent cells, which convert the message back to an electrical signal and pass it on to its cell body.

myelin (myelination) A sheet of fatty substance that develops progressively around the neurons to promote faster transmission of electrical signals through the nervous system.

Stages of neural development. The first stage of neuronal development is referred to as **neuralation**, in which the neural tube develops, which is the source of the central nervous system (Lenroot & Giedd, 2007; Nelson, Thomas, & de Haan, 2006). This is usually completed by 3 to 4 weeks of gestation (see Chapter 3).

Neurons then go through at least three stages of development (Lenroot & Giedd, 2007; Spreen, Risser, & Edgell, 1995). Phase one is referred to as **proliferation**, or *neurogenesis* (literally the "birth" of neurons), and occurs during the first 20 weeks after conception, peaking in the third and fourth months of gestation. During its peak, several hundred thousand neurons are generated *each minute* (Nelson et al., 2006). Although *most* neurons that a person will ever have are produced at this time, neuroscientists have discovered that neurons in some parts of the brains continue to be generated throughout life, specifically the dentate nucleus of the hippocampus, which is involved in forming new memories (Eriksson et al., 1998). New neurons are also produced throughout life in the olfactory bulbs, involved in the sense of smell, and there is some speculation that neurogenesis might occur after birth in several other brain areas (see Nelson et al., 2006). In general, unlike other cells of the body, new neurons are typically not produced after birth. So, with a handful of exceptions, a person has all the neurons he or she will ever have at birth.

Once neurons are produced, they must move to their permanent position in the brain, a process known as **migration** (Aylward, 1997; Lenroot & Giedd, 2007). Different sets of neurons migrate at different times, but most neurons are in their final location by approximately the seventh month of gestation (Johnson, 1997; Nelson et al., 2006). Errors in neural migration have been associated with several developmental problems, including cerebral palsy, epilepsy, intellectual impairment, and learning disorders (Aylward, 1997).

The final phase of neurogenesis begins at about 20 weeks of prenatal life and is referred to as **differentiation**. During this time, neurons increase in size, increase the numbers of dendrites and axon terminals, as well as the number of synapses they form (**synaptogenesis**, or the "birth" of synapses). Most brain areas associated with the sensory systems are fully myelinated by the end of the first year, which corresponds to the well-developed sensory abilities of human infants. This is followed by myelination of the motor areas of the brain, and finally the integrative areas, which correspond to brain areas that are involved in complex cognition (see Lenroot & Giedd, 2007; Yakovlev & Lecours, 1967).

It is important to point out that differentiation does not stop at birth. In fact, most neuronal differentiation takes place *after* birth, particularly synaptogenesis and myelination (see de Haan & Johnson, 2003; Lenroot & Giedd, 2007; Nelson et al., 2006).

Cell death and synaptic pruning. Although it may seem obvious that brains get bigger and better with age, the actual process is not that simple. Brains do indeed get larger with age. At birth an infant's brain is only 25% of its eventual adult weight, but only two years later it increases to up to 75%. The brain is 95% of its adult volume by age 6 (Lenroot & Giedd, 2007). But this rapid increase is caused primarily by the increasing size of individual neurons and myelination of axons, not by the generation of new neurons. In fact, both the number of neurons and the number of synapses actually *decrease* over early development. At its peak during prenatal development, up to 250,000 synapses are being formed per minute. Yet, between 40% to 50% of these synapses will be lost, or pruned.

Not only are synapses lost, but so too are neurons in a process known as **selective cell death**, or **apoptosis**. Selective cell death begins prenatally and continues after birth, well into the teen years (see Huttenlocher, 1979; Lenroot & Giedd, 2007; Spear, 2007). Thus, rather than thinking of brain development as simple increases in size and complexity, a better metaphor may be that of sculpting. The brain first overproduces neurons and synapses, but then, just as a sculptor chisels away at superfluous stone to produce his or her work of art, so too do experience, hormones, and genetic signals shape the brain, producing an amazing product of a different kind (Kolb, 1989).

Rises and declines in brain development. Cell death and synaptic pruning occur at different rates for different parts of the brain. For example, the adult density of synapses for the visual cortex is attained between 2 and 4 years of age; in contrast, children continue to have more neurons and synapses than do adults in the frontal areas well into their teen years (Huttenlocher & Dabholkar, 1997, see Figure 4.15). In fact, the pattern of changes during adolescence often mirrors those found in early

---

neuralation The first stage of neuronal development, in which the neural tube develops, which is the source of the central nervous system.

proliferation The process of nerve-cell division by mitosis.

migration (of neurons) The movement of neurons in the brain to their permanent positions in the brain, most of which is completed during the prenatal period.

differentiation (of neurons) The final stage of neuronal development, in which neurons gain in size, produce more dendrites, extend their axons farther away from the cell body, and form new synaptic connections.

synaptogenesis The process of synapse formation.

selective cell death (apoptosis) Early developmental process in which neurons that are not activated by sensory and motor experience die.

childhood. For example, white matter increases throughout childhood and adolescence, not being complete until sometime during the third decade of life or beyond. These changes in myelination of axons are linear in nature, increasing in a straight line, so to speak, from infancy to maturity. The most substantial changes in white matter from adolescence to adulthood are in the frontal cortex, the so-called thinking part of the brain (Giedd et al., 1999; Sowell et al., 1999). In contrast, gray matter (neuronal cell bodies, Giedd et al., 1999) and synaptic connections (see Spear, 2007) display declines in adolescence into adulthood, particularly in the frontal lobes. Thus, by their middle to late teens, adolescents have fewer but stronger and more effective neuronal connections than they did as children. Interestingly, children with exceptionally high IQs tend to display an initial acceleration of growth in gray matter followed by a rapid (and equally early) loss of neurons by early adolescence. Adolescents with average IQs show the same pattern of development but at later ages (Shaw et al., 2006).

Similar rise-and-decline changes occur for energy consumption. For example, the basic metabolism of the brain (as measured by the amount of glucose uptake in the resting brain) increases sharply after the first year of life and peaks at about 150% of the adult rate between the ages of 4 and 5 years, dropping to adult levels at about age 9 (Chugani, Phelps, & Mazziotta, 1987). Thus, not only do infants and children have more neurons and synapses than adults, but their brains are also working harder (or at least using more calories) than those of adults. There is also evidence of increases followed by decreases for some neurotransmitters in development (Johnson, 1998).

What might be the function of these increases and decreases in brain development? One possibility is that the high rate of metabolism and elevated levels of neurons, synapses, and neurotransmitters seen during the preschool years might be necessary for the rapid learning that occurs during this time (Elman et al., 1996). For instance, children learn language rapidly, speaking only single words at 10 or 12 months, to delivering speeches by 3 or 4 years of age. Others have speculated that these rising and falling patterns may be related to some interesting developmental phenomena, such as infantile amnesia (difficulty remembering events that happened before 3 to 5 years of age; see Chapter 8) and the loss in infancy of the ability to discriminate sounds of languages other than those found in one's native tongue (see Chapter 5) (Huttenlocher, 2002; Kolb, 1989). Although it may seem that slowing down the processes of synaptic pruning and cell death would afford children some advantages (more neurons and synapses can presumably do more learning), the failure to display such losses has been linked to

Visual cortex ● **Prefrontal cortex**

intellectual impairment, schizophrenia, and other developmental disorders (Feinberg, 1982, 1983).

A brief description of the major features of neuron development is presented in Concept Review 4.1.

Sex Differences in Brain Development

To the extent that there are sex differences in psychological characteristics between males and females (see Chapter 15), we should not be surprised to find corresponding sex differences in brain structure or function. First, in adulthood, male brains are larger than female brains (as are their bodies). However, more interesting are the sex differences in gray and white matter: females have proportionally more gray matter (neurons) than males, and males have proportionally more white matter (mostly myelinated axons) than females. One major exception to this pattern is that females have more white matter in the corpus callosum, the large bundle of neurons that connect the two hemispheres (Gur & Gur, 1990). Female brains are also more lateralized than male brains, meaning that gray matter is more evenly distributed across the two hemispheres in females than males (Gur et al., 1999). Males and females also seem to approach problems differently, in that females show greater use of language-related brain areas, whereas males show greater use of visuospatial-related brain areas when solving similar complex problems (Haier et al., 2005).

Although there has been relatively little research on the development of sex differences in brain structure or function, both sexes seem to display the same general pattern of gray- and white-matter development. However, the volume of gray

FIGURE 4.15 Age differences in synapse production and pruning in the prefrontal and visual cortex.

The number of synapses show sharp increases early in development but then experience pruning as the brain gets sculpted to its eventual adult form. Note the particularly sharp decline in synapses in the prefrontal cortex in adolescence. SOURCE: From Huttenlocher, P., & Dabholkar, A. S. (1997). Regional differences in synaptogenesis in human cerebral cortex. *Journal of Comparative Neurology, 387*, 167–178. Reprinted by permission of John Wiley & Sons, Inc.

Developmental event	Timeline	Brief description
Neuralation	18–24 prenatal days	The neural tube develops, which will serve as the source of the central nervous system.
Proliferation (neurogenesis)	First 20 weeks after conception	Neurons are born from neural stem cells. This peaks in the third or fourth month of gestation.
Neural migration	6–24 weeks after conception	Neurons move, or migrate, to their adult location in the brain.
Differentiation/ synaptogenesis	3rd trimester through adolescence	Neurons extend their dendrites and axonal terminals, forming synapses with other neurons.
Postnatal neurogenesis	Birth–adulthood	New neurons develop in some parts of the brain, including the dentate gyrus of the hippocampus and the olfactory bulb.
Myelination	3rd trimester to adulthood	Neurons become coated by a fatty tissue that results in faster transmission of nervous signals and a reduction of interference.
Selective cell death (apoptosis)	3rd trimester to adulthood	Neurons die.
Synaptic pruning	infancy through adulthood	The number of synapses per neuron is greatest between 4 and 8 months of life and decreases with age.

matter development in the frontal cortex peaks earlier in girls than in boys, and peaks earlier for boys than for girls in the temporal cortex. In some parts of the brain, gray matter does not peak for boys until the early twenties, whereas it peaks for girls around 13 years of age. White matter shows an opposite trend, peaking sooner in males than in females (Giedd et al., 1999). Males, then, display an extended developmental period for brain development. This makes male brains more susceptible to environmental influences (there's more time to affect the adult structure of the brain) than female brains. Because of this, males are more vulnerable to poor environments (poor health or nutrition) than females, and this, in part, may account for the greater variability seen for many traits in males than in females (Halpern et al., 2007; see Chapter 15).

The Relationship between Brain Development and Behavior

In recent years there has been substantial research demonstrating the connection between brain development and children's behavior and cognition (see Coch, Fischer, & Dawson, 2007; Nelson et al., 2006). We will discuss some of this research throughout the book when we discuss specific topics (such as the role of mirror neurons in social learning in

Chapter 7, brain development and risk-taking behavior in adolescence in Chapter 14, and the development of the hippocampus in children's memory in Chapter 8). In the next sections we provide just a few examples of research findings examining the link between infants', children's, and adolescents' thought and behavior and brain development.

The Role of the Frontal Cortex in Knowing That Objects Are Permanent in Time and Space

One much-studied accomplishment of infancy is that of *object permanence,* as initially described by Jean Piaget (1954). Object permanence refers to the knowledge that objects continue to exist even when they can no longer be seen. Infants only gradually come to understand this. (Object permanence is discussed in more detail in Chapter 5.) One often-used test of object permanence is the *A-not-B task* (see Photo). On this task, infants watch as a toy is hidden in one of two locations. They are briefly distracted and then allowed to retrieve the toy. After the infant has retrieved the toy successfully at one location (Location A), the toy is then hidden at location B, all while the infant watches. Piaget reported that infants much younger than 12 months have great difficulty performing this latter task, typically looking for the hidden object at the A location, where they successfully retrieved it previously.

One factor that may be important in solving the A-not-B task is memory. Recall that there is a delay between the time the toy is hidden and when infants are permitted to search for it (Diamond, 1985). In support of these hypotheses, Adele Diamond (1985) tested infants between 7 and 12 months of age on the A-not-B task and reported that the delay between hiding and searching necessary to produce the A-not-B error increased at a rate of about 2 seconds per month. That is, 7.5-month-old infants would search for the hidden object at the erroneous A position following only a 2-second delay. By 12 months of age, infants made the error only if approximately 10 seconds transpired between the hiding of the object and the beginning of the search.

But more than memory is involved. Diamond (1991) proposed that young infants' difficulty in searching at the proper location on the critical B trials was caused by their inability to inhibit a previous behavioral response, in this case, reaching to the previously correct location A. Infants had learned a response, but before they can learn a new one, they must inhibit the old one. This ability develops over the first year, with girls showing faster progress than boys (Diamond, 1985). There is substantial research with adults (Luna et al., 2001), older children (Barkley, 1997), and infants (Bell, Wolfe, & Adkins, 2007) that points to the frontal lobes as the locus of inhibitory control, and Diamond suggested that slow frontal lobe maturation was the source of infants' errors.

Support for this claim comes from a study showing significant relationships between performance on the A-not-B task and scores on a task of inhibitory ability in 9-month-olds (Holmboe et al., 2008) and neuroimaging studies that show connections between infants' performance on A-not-B tasks and frontal lobe activity (Baird et al., 2002; Segalowitz & Hiscock, 2002). For example, Martha Bell and Nathan Fox (1992) recorded EEG activity from the frontal lobes of 7- to 12-month-old infants performing the A-not-B task. Consistent with Diamond's hypothesis, they reported systematic changes in EEG patterns as a function of age and length of delay.

Changes in Executive Functioning in Adolescence

As noted earlier, substantial changes in brain development occur during adolescence. There is an increase in white matter as a result of myelination, reflecting faster and more efficient neural processing, as well as a decrease in gray matter (cell bodies) and synaptic connections, reflecting more fine-tuned sculpting of the brain. Moreover, these changes are most prominent in the frontal lobes, the area of the brain associated with higher-level

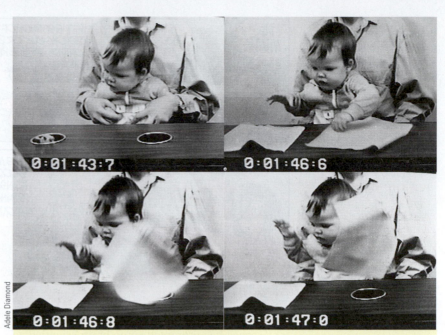

Adele Diamond

Piaget's A-not-B task. After babies retrieve an object several times hidden at one location (A), they watch as the item is hidden at another location (B). After a brief delay, babies are permitted to search for the hidden object. Infants much younger than 12 months have great difficulty performing this latter task, typically looking for the hidden object at the A location, where they successfully retrieved it previously. Part of their difficulty seems to be related to their inability to inhibit their previous response (reach to location A), which is related to the development of the frontal lobes.

cognition. In particular, the frontal lobes have been associated with *executive functioning*, a term that reflects a suite of abilities associated with planning, inhibiting inappropriate responses, decision making, and monitoring one's behavior (see Kuhn, 2006). (Executive functioning will be discussed in greater detail in other chapters of this book, particularly Chapter 8.)

Deanna Kuhn (2006) has argued that adolescents display improvements in various areas of executive functioning and that these cognitive and behavioral improvements are associated with neurological changes occurring at this same time. In support of this, Beatriz Luna and her colleagues (2001) gave participants between 8 and 30 years of age tasks that assessed inhibition abilities. The ability to inhibit inappropriate responses developed gradually into adulthood and was related to patterns of brain activity. Luna and her colleagues reported that the frontal cortex was more active on these inhibition tasks in adolescents than in either children or adults. Thus, age-related changes in task performance were not related to underlying brain activation in a straightforward, linear way. Task performance increased gradually with age, whereas brain activation in the frontal cortex on this task increased sharply between childhood and adolescence, only to decrease again in adulthood. This sensitive period of cortical development in

Brain development, particularly of the frontal cortex, is not fully developed until young adulthood and can account for some of the behaviors characteristic of adolescents.

adolescence has prompted some brain scientists to suggest that drinking alcohol to excess can have the most deleterious effects during late adolescence and early adulthood (Volkow, 2007).

As the examples provided here demonstrate, age-related changes in brain development are associated with important changes in infants', children's, and adolescents' thinking and behavior, and many more such examples are provided throughout this book. Having an idea of the neural causes of behavior and development helps psychologists ask better research questions and achieve a better understanding of development. For example, knowledge of the developmental relationship between brain and behavior has important implications for many societal practices. How flexible is human intelligence? At what ages can children most benefit from certain educational experiences? Is earlier always better, or are there certain sensitive periods for particular experiences distributed throughout development?

No one today questions that behavior, thought, and their development are governed by the brain, but we must not be fooled into thinking that a knowledge of brain development will tell us all we need to know about the development of the mind and behavior. We should not be surprised, for example, to learn that the brains of children with schizophrenia are different from the brains of children without schizophrenia, or that the brains of children growing up in extreme deprivation are different from the brains of children growing up in more enriched circumstances. We have long known that the brain is the seat of consciousness and thought, as well as the underlying cause of

behavior; having images to prove it may help us understand the process of development, but alone it is only part of the picture. Although the concepts of psychology must be consistent with those of biology, they represent a different level of analysis. Having a theory of the brain and its development is important, but it is not enough. Having a theory of the brain does not make it unnecessary to have a theory of the mind and of behavior.

Neural Plasticity and the Role of Experience in Brain Development

The description provided in the previous sections may give the impression that brains mature following a species-typical pattern and determine the behavior and cognition of children. We can only be as smart, social, or emotional as our brains permit us to be. Or, as reflected by a frequent statement of one 5-year-old we know, "My brain told me to do it." Such an account leaves little room for experience. Yet we know that humans and their brains show substantial changes as a result of experience and that such **plasticity** is especially apparent in children. Plasticity, the ability to change, seems to be a property of complex nervous systems (Huttenlocher, 2002), causing the British developmental neuroscientist Mark Johnson (1997, p. xiii) to state "plasticity is a fundamental property of brain development, and not just a specialized response to injury."

However, just as different structures and substructures of the brain show different developmental timing, they also show different levels of plasticity (Huttenlocher, 2002; Neville, 2007). For example, it has been argued that some evolutionarily older parts of the brain, such as the brain stem, are less plastic than younger parts of the brain, specifically the cortex (Aylward, 1997).

plasticity The extent to which behavior or brain functioning can be changed.

Experience-expected and Experience-dependent Synaptogenesis

In fact, the process of synaptogenesis in the cortex is highly dependent upon experience. For example, William Greenough and his colleagues (Black et al., 1998; Greenough, Black, & Wallace, 1987) suggested that the brains of most of mammals, including humans, have been shaped through evolution to use two different processes in synaptogenesis: *experience-expectant synaptogenesis* and *experience-dependent synaptogenesis*. (For similar arguments, see Johnson, 2007; Nelson, 2001). **Experience-expectant synaptogenesis** describes the process in which synapses are formed and maintained when an animal has species-typical experiences. For example, the experience of viewing or hearing a normal world would result in the visual and auditory cortices developing typically. Generations of an organism's ancestors had received such stimulation, and as a result, brains evolved to expect it; when they get this species-typical experience, development proceeds normally. However, experience is still necessary. Even highly predictable outcomes (for example, seeing and hearing) are not the inevitable product of maturation but require specific experiences.

The way to assess experience-expectant synaptogenesis is to restrict an animal from receiving species-typical experiences. This was done in experiments in which rats and cats were raised in total darkness. Upon entering a lit world, these animals had great difficulty making even simple visual discriminations. Because they were not exposed to light early in life, their vision developed abnormally once they were exposed to light (Crabtree & Riesen, 1979).

Such experiments cannot be done with humans, but Daphne Maurer and her colleagues have followed infants who had cataracts at birth, some of whom had them removed shortly after birth and others not until several years later (Le Grand et al., 2001; Maurer, Mondloch, & Lewis, 2007; Maurer et al., 1999; see also Ostrovsky, Andalman, & Sinha, 2006). Maurer and her colleagues reported that the visual development of infants who had cataracts removed and new lenses placed within several months of birth was generally positive. The longer the delay in removing the cataracts, the poorer vision was. Moreover, even for those infants who had cataracts removed early and developed normal vision, some aspects of *face* processing were impaired (Le Grand et al., 2001). This finding suggests that there may be different sensitive periods for the brain areas associated with visual acuity and those associated with processing faces. It also points to the importance of identifying and correcting visual problems early to minimize their long-term effects.

In contrast to experience-expectant synaptogenesis, **experience-dependent synaptogenesis** refers to synapses that are formed as a result of unique experiences of the individual, rather than experiences that all members of a species can expect to have. In both cases, the overproduction of neurons enables an individual to make connections (and thus store information) that reflect his or her particular environment. When certain experiences are not had—when the world does not cause certain neurons to be activated and synapses to form—synapses can disappear and neurons die. This is captured by Bennett Bertenthal and Joseph Campos's (1987, p. 560) summary of Greenough's research: "What determines the survival of synaptic connections is the principle of use: Those synapses activated by sensory or motor experience survive; the remainder are lost through disuse. For Greenough et al., then, experience does not create tracings on a blank tablet; rather experience erases some of them."

To sum up, the combination of different levels of plasticity for different neural systems and subsystems (some more open to experiences; some more constrained) across brain development seems to be the norm in human ontogeny. Neural plasticity is definitely an advantage, but not an absolute one. One purpose of experience is to train the brain to process efficiently some types of information that will likely be encountered repeatedly. For example, as discussed in Chapter 9, although people can acquire any language with relative ease early in childhood, this ability declines with age. Although you may think it would be wonderful to have the neural plasticity to learn a new language with the ease that children learn their first (or even second and third) language, a little thought shows the problems such a brain and the person who possessed it would face. Our ancestors, as well as most people today, were exposed to only a single language for most of their lives, and it made sense for them to devote some of their brain cells to processing that language efficiently. Perhaps they could learn a second language more easily by keeping their neural options open, but this would be at the cost of neural efficiency in processing one's first language. The same could be said for any dedicated brain system (for example, face processing) (see Chapter 5). Yet, for a species that earns its living to a large extent by being clever, mastering new environments, and learning things one's ancestors never experienced, neural plasticity is a must (Geary, 2005a).

experience-expectant synaptogenesis Processes whereby synapses between neurons are formed and maintained when an organism has species-typical experiences; as a result, functions (such as vision) will develop for all members of a species given a species-typical environment.

experience-dependent synaptogenesis Processes whereby synapses between neurons are formed and maintained as a result of the unique experiences of an individual.

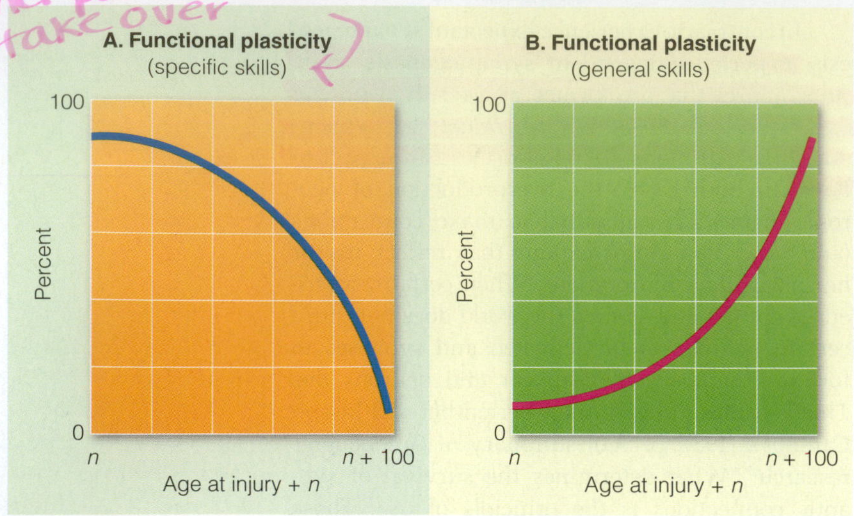

Other parts of brain take over

A. Functional plasticity (specific skills)

Percent

100

0

n   n + 100

Age at injury + n

B. Functional plasticity (general skills)

Percent

100

0

n   n + 100

Age at injury + n

FIGURE 4.16 Theoretical relationship between age (represented by *n*) when brain damage is suffered and recovery of function depending on whether the brain injury affects a specific skill (such as language) or a more general skill (such as intelligence or planning).

SOURCE: Adapted from "Neurobiological aspects of language in children," by S. F. Witelson, 1987, *Child Development, 58*, 653–688. Copyright © 1987 The Society for Research in Child Development, Inc. Reprinted by with permission of John Wiley & Sons, Inc.

Brain Injury during Development

Sometimes nervous systems become unforeseeably injured, and this has often been an important source of information about how the brain works, develops, and is able to change. In fact, perhaps the best evidence for the plasticity of the human nervous system comes from studies examining the recovery of function from brain damage in people of different ages. For example, Margaret Kennard, a pioneer in early studies of recovery of function from brain damage, proposed that the earlier in life brain injury occurs, the greater the chance that the corresponding functions may be successfully assumed by other parts of the brain (the *Kennard effect*) (Kolb, 1989). This thesis received additional support from the work of Eric Lenneberg (1967) on children's recovery of function from damage to language areas of the brain. This pattern is also seen for milder forms of brain injuries, such as concussion. Children tend to recover from the effects of concussion (for example, headaches, memory loss) faster than do adolescents and adults (see Yeates & Taylor, 2005). However, newer research has shown that the Kennard effect does not hold for all types of brain injuries, and recovery depends rather on a wider series of variables than previously considered (de Haan & Johnson, 2003; Kolb, 1989).

The sort of function that is affected seems to be particularly important. Some suggest that perhaps the Kennard effect can explain brain damage associated with specific skills such as language, but not when the injured area controls more general cogni-

tive abilities. When an area dedicated to a specific function is damaged, other areas can more easily assume that function, at least when damage occurs early in life before the function fully develops. The opposite, however, seems to be true for brain damage associated with more general skills, such as intelligence or planning, where the functional plasticity seems to be higher in adulthood, once those functions have been already successfully wired (Kolb & Whishaw, 1990; Stiles et al., 2005; Witelson, 1987; see Figure 4.16).

There is debate today about the degree to which different areas of the cortex are *equipotential*. That is, can any neuron initially assume different psychological functions (equipotentiality), or, rather, are neurons limited to some degree in the functions they can perform? Some research demonstrates that brain cells destined for one type of function can be put into service for another function if the switch is made early enough. For example, researchers have shown that if sensory input from the eyes is sent to the auditory cortex in young ferrets, the animals come to see with a part of their brain that customarily processes auditory stimulation (Sur & Leamey, 2001). Thus, even if the neurons are not infinitely plastic in their early days, neither are they innately prespecified.

Research in developmental brain science is still in its infancy, but we have learned much about how infants', children's, and adolescents' brains develop and how such development is related to both typical and atypical behavior. One point we hope is clear in our presentation is that brain development is a dynamic process, the result of interactions between genes, neurons, behavior, cognition, and environment (Marshall, 2009). Such a dynamic perspective is sometimes referred to as **neuroconstructivism**, in which the multiple factors listed previously interact over the course of development to produce a functioning brain and mind (Karmiloff-Smith, 2009). Brains do not develop via the simple "reading of the genetic code," although genes are essential for the development of brains. And once established, structures and functions of brains do not remain unchanged. Rather, brains, as other aspects of development, are the product of multiple factors, with new structures and functioning emerging as a result of the dynamic interactions among them.

neuroconstructivism Theoretical perspective in which brain development is viewed as a dynamic process, the result of interactions among genes, neurons, behavior, cognition, and environment.

Humans' extended rate of growth provides greater time to learn the many complexities of human culture and greater plasticity of the brain early in life. **Neoteny** refers to the retention of infantile characteristics of an evolutionary ancestor. Many characteristics of humans have been described as neotenous, such as the way the spine connects to the skull that permits bipedality. According to some anthropologists, humans evolved two new life stages: childhood and adolescence.

Different organ systems grow at different rates, with **growth curves** reflecting that the head and brain grow most rapidly early in life and the reproductive system takes the longest to reach maturity. Physical growth proceeds from head to foot (**cephalocaudal development**) and from the center of the body to the extremities (**proximodistal development**).

The **endocrine system** produces **hormones** that greatly influence growth. The hypothalamus signals the **pituitary gland**, which in turn releases **human growth hormone**, which influences growth directly, and sends messages to other endocrine glands. The gonads produce **estrogens**, **proestrogens**, and **testosterone** (a form of **androgen**), which play an important role in growth at puberty. The thyroid gland produces **thyroxine**, which influences growth primarily during the prenatal period. Stress can affect growth, although the single most important environmental influence on growth is nutrition. Malnourished children grow more slowly, although they retain the ability for normal growth when good nutrition is resumed. Children are growing taller sooner than in generations past, effects that can be attributed to better nutrition and disease control.

Growth is affected by several factors, notably malnutrition. Infants whose mothers lack adequate breast milk can suffer from **marasmus**, a wasting away of the body, whereas others who receive just enough calories to survive may suffer from **Kwashiorkor**.

Obesity in children, as measured by the **body mass index** (**BMI**), is associated with a host of psychological and health problems and is increasing in the United States and in other parts of the world. Many adolescent girls display various degrees of eating disorders, with the more serious disorders of **anorexia nervosa** and **bulimia** occurring infrequently.

Puberty refers to the life stage when the glands associated with the reproductive system begin to enlarge, bringing about changes in both **primary** and **secondary sexual characteristics**. Puberty is preceded by **adrenarche**, occurring between 6 and 8 years of age for both boys and girls, when the adrenal glands start producing androgens. Puberty usually begins earlier in girls than in boys. Other changes include, for boys, adolescent **growth spurt**, presence of pubic and facial hair, enlargement of the penis, first ejaculation (**spermarche**), and deeper voices, and for girls, adolescent growth spurt, presence of pubic hair, breast development, and beginning of the menstrual period (**menarche**). Different aspects of puberty have been occurring earlier, especially in girls, than in previous generations. Pubertal timing is influenced by hormones produced at adolescence but is also affected by environmental/family factors. The timing of puberty affects psychological development, with early-maturing boys generally showing good psychological adjustment and early-maturing girls generally showing more adjustment problems than children who experience puberty on time.

Both **gross motor** and **fine motor** development improve with age. Crawling and walking change infants' relationships with their physical and social worlds and affect their cognitive and social development. Much of fine motor development involves improved **eye-hand coordination**, with visually guided reaching being observed in the first months of life. **Cerebral lateralization** (or **cerebral dominance**) refers to one hemisphere being dominant relative to the other, and is reflected by favoring one side of the body (usually the right) over the other. A right-side preference is observed prenatally and increases in strength over childhood. Contemporary theories of motor development emphasize the dynamic nature of change rather than seeing motor development as the product of maturation.

Brains became increasingly larger over the course of hominid evolution. The human brain is the largest relative to body size of any animal. A large brain is important for learning in a long-lived animal that is likely to encounter a wide range of environments.

The brain can be thought of as consisting of four hierarchically organized interacting levels: the **brain stem**, the **hypothalamus**, the **limbic system**, and the **cerebral cortex** or **neocortex**. The cerebral cortex is divided into lobes, one of which, the **frontal lobes**, is implicated in high-level cognition. **Neuroimaging** techniques, such as event-related potentials, positron emission tomography (PET), and functional magnetic resonance imaging (fMRI), are providing new knowledge about brain functioning and development.

The nervous system consists of **neurons**, which transport chemical and electrical signals. Neurons consist of a cell body, an **axon** that carries messages away from the cell body to other cells, and **dendrites**, which receive messages from other cells. Electrical messages travel down the axon of one cell and cause the release of **neurotransmitters** into the **synapse**. Axons are coated with **myelin**, fatty tissue that promotes faster transmission of electrical signals. The first stage of brain development is referred to as **neuralation**, in which the neural tube develops. Neurons go through at least three phases of development, which are **proliferation** (**neurogenesis**), **migration**, and **differentiation**. The formation of synapses (**synaptogenesis**) occurs during this last stage. Myelination begins prenatally for some parts of the brain but is not complete for other parts until adulthood. Synapse formation is rapid during prenatal development and continues to be rapid during the early months of life. A complementary process of **selective cell death** (**apoptosis**) also occurs, with many neurons dying.

Brain development has been shown to be related to cognitive development, including object permanence in infancy and executive functioning in adolescence.

With age, the **plasticity** needed to form new synapses declines, but it does not disappear. Some neural connections are made by all members of a species given typical experiences (**experience-expectant synaptogenesis**), whereas other connections are made because of the unique experiences of an individual (**experience-dependent synaptogenesis**). Examination of the recovery of function from brain damage shows that, at least for damage to areas of the brain that control specific abilities such as language, plasticity is greater the earlier the damage occurs. Brains develop as a result of interactions among genes, neurons, behavior, cognition, and environment, a perspective referred to as **neuroconstructivism**.

Key Terms and Concepts

neoteny (p. 138)

growth curves (p. 139)

cephalocaudal development (p. 142)

proximodistal development (p. 142)

endocrine system (p. 143)

hormones (p. 143)

pituitary gland (p. 143)

human growth hormone (p. 144)

estrogen (p. 144)

progesterone (p. 144)

testosterone (p. 144)

androgen (p. 144)

thyroxine (p. 144)

marasmus (p. 145)

kwashiorkor (p. 145)

obesity (p. 147)

body mass index (BMI) (p. 147)

anorexia nervosa (p. 151)

bulimia (p. 151)

puberty (p. 152)

primary sexual characteristics (p. 152)

secondary sexual characteristics (p. 152)

adrenarche (p. 153

growth spurt (p. 153)

spermarche (p. 154)

menarche (p. 154)

gross motor behaviors (p. 159)

fine motor behaviors (p. 159)

eye-hand coordination (p. 165)

cerebral lateralization (cerebral dominance) (p. 166)

brain stem (p. 170)

hypothalamus (p. 170)

limbic system (p. 170

cerebral cortex (neocortex) (p. 170)

frontal lobe (p. 171)

neuroimaging techniques (p. 171)

neuron (p. 172)

axon (p. 173)

dendrites (p. 173)

neurotransmitters (p. 173)

myelin (myelination) (p. 173)

neuralation (p. 174)

synapses (p. 174)

proliferation (neurogenesis) (p. 174)

migration (p. 174)

differentiation (p. 174)

synaptogenesis (p. 174)

selective cell death (apoptosis) (p. 174)

plasticity (p. 178)

experience-expectant synaptogenesis (p. 178)

experience-dependent synaptogenesis (p. 179)

neuroconstructivism (p. 180)

Ask Yourself . . .

1. What two principles govern physical growth and motor development?

2. What are the main changes in physical growth, and what factors can influence them?

3. Which developmental problems have been identified as a result of improper nutrition during childhood and/or adolescence, and what are their consequences?

4. What historical, social-environmental, and physical-environmental factors influence the timing of puberty in girls? What consequences do differences in rate of pubertal development have on girls' psychological development?

5. How do developmental differences in physical growth (other than brain development) influence psychological development, particularly during adolescence?

6. What are major milestones in motor development? What factors influence the rate at which motor development proceeds?

7. How can motor development influence the development of other psychological processes, such as spatial cognition?

8. How do babies learn to walk?

9. What are major milestones in brain development? What factors can influence brain development? How "plastic" is the brain at different times in development?

10. How does brain development relate to the development of behavior and cognition? How and to what extent can environment influence this relationship?

Exercises: Going Further

1. As a child psychologist, you have been asked to speak to a group of parents about the developmental risks of childhood obesity and how to prevent them. What principal ideas and issues would you focus on in your talk?

2. A group of high-school teachers notice that some of their students are concerned that they are developing more slowly (or more rapidly) than many of their classmates. What would you tell the teachers about adolescent physical development, and what suggestions would you give them for managing their students' stress?

3. After a bike accident, 6-year-old Trevor is suspected to have suffered an injury to the language area of his brain. His parents have been told that he should get a neuropsychological assessment, as well as an fMRI, to know what's going on. How would you describe to them what those techniques are, and, in the case that an injury to the language area was found, what would the probability be of Trevor recovering his language abilities?

Suggested Readings

Classic Works

Tanner, J. M. (1990). *Foetus into Man: Physical growth from conception to maturity* (revised and enlarged edition). Originally published in 1978, this classic review of human physical growth by one of the pioneers in the field provides a comprehensive look at research over the 20th century.

Greenough, W. T., Black, J. E., & Wallace, C. S. (1987). **Experience and brain development.** *Child Development*, *58*, 539–559. This early article by William Greenough and his colleagues introduced to a wider audience of developmental psychologists the concept of experience-expected and experience-dependent synaptogenesis, which has had substantial influence on how scientists understand brain development.

Thelen, E. (1995). **Motor development: A new synthesis.** *American Psychologist*, 50, 79–95. Although not yet 20 years old, we think this article by Esther Thelen warrants the label "classic." It introduced much of psychology to the dynamic systems perspective of motor development, a view that has continued to dominate the field.

Scholarly Works

Bogin, B. (2001). *The growth of humanity.* New York: Wiley. Physical anthropologist Barry Bogin provides an updated account of research and theory of human growth, including the evolution of growth patterns and the "invention" of the life span stages of *childhood* and *adolescence*.

Herman-Giddens, M. E., Slora, E. J., Wasserman, R. C., Bourdony, C. J., Bhapkar, M. V., Koch, G. G., & Hasemeir, C. M. (1997). **Secondary sexual characteristics and menses in young girls seen in office practice: A study from the pediatric research in office settings network.** *Pediatrics 99*, 505–512. This influential paper brought the accelerated rate at which some girls were attaining some aspects of puberty to the public's attention.

Lenroot, R. K., & Giedd, J. N. (2007). **The structural development of the human brain as measures longitudinally with magnetic resonance imaging.** In D. Coch, K. W. Fischer, & G. Dawson (Eds.), *Human behavior, learning, and the developing brain: Typical development* (pp. 50–73). New York: Guilford. This chapter by leading researchers in the field of developmental neuroimaging provides an up-to-date review of structural changes in the brain based on longitudinal data.

Reading for Personal Interest

Healy, J. (2006). *Your child's growing mind: Brain development and learning from birth to adolescence.* New York: Broadway. Jane Healy, educational psychologist turned science writer, presents a well-written and authoritative book about brain development and learning that is accessible for the educated layperson.

Koop, C. N. (2003). *Baby steps: A guide to your child's social, physical, mental and emotional development in the first two years* (2nd ed.). New York: Holt. This book by developmental psychologist Claire Koop provides a month-by-month description of children's physical, motor, social, emotional, and cognitive development, with "the goal of helping parents better understand the meaning and significance of the first two years."

Gibbons, A. (2008). **The birth of childhood.** *Science, 322* (14 November), 1040–1043. This brief article presents a summary of some of the latest research investigating the evolution of human childhood.

CourseMate

Cengage Learning's **Psychology CourseMate** for this text brings course concepts to life with interactive learning, study, and exam preparation tools, including quizzes and flashcards for this chapter's Key Terms and Concepts (see the summary list on page 182). The site also provides an **eBook** version of the text with highlighting and note taking capabilities, as well as an extensive library of observational videos that span early childhood through adolescence. Many videos are accompanied by questions that will help you think critically about and deepen your understanding of the chapter topics addressed, especially as they pertain to core concepts. Log on and learn more at **www.cengagebrain.com.**

An animal's intelligence, or cognition, is essentially used to solve problems. Individuals change in order to solve problems associated with their local environment. Those problems may be in terms of understanding the social world—getting along with other people—or understanding the physical world—comprehending the nature of objects, or using tools to gain resources. Humans' problem-solving abilities are perhaps unique in the animal world in that they involve *symbolic* and *explicit* (that is, self-aware) cognition. Much cognition, however, is based on *implicit* (that is, out of conscious awareness) processes, and both implicit and explicit processes develop.

We begin this section with a chapter titled *What Do Infants Know and When and How Do They Know It?* As the title reflects, this chapter examines the development of perception and cognition in infancy, examining, among other topics, infants' attraction to and processing of human faces, the coordination of their senses, their understanding of the physical world (for example, that objects continue to exist even when out of their sight), and memory.

We then explore the development of symbolic representation, particularly as presented in Jean Piaget's theory. In addition to describing and critiquing Piaget's highly influential account of cognitive development, we examine an alternative approach to Piaget's account of cognitive development, *theory theories*, particularly as it relates to children's development of biological knowledge. We also examine the development of several aspects of "the symbolic function," including symbolic (or pretend) play, drawing, storytelling, and children's ability to distinguish between real and imaginary beings.

This is followed by a chapter looking at the development of *social cognition*—how children come to think about their own thoughts, feelings, motives, and behaviors and those of other

people. As children become aware of themselves as thinking beings, it changes how they see themselves and how they are able to compete, cooperate, and learn from others. Some have suggested that becoming self-aware was a major step in the evolution of the modern human mind. Our topics include, among others, the development of self-concept, theory of mind, and social learning.

We then explore how children become self-directed thinkers by examining the development of problem solving, executive function, strategies, and memory. The chapter includes a look at some important basic-level abilities, such as speed of processing, working memory, and inhibition, as well as higher-level cognitive abilities, such as autobiographical memory, including an examination of children as eyewitnesses.

We devote a separate chapter to language, exploring both its relatively rapid development over childhood and prominent theories about the mechanisms underlying this uniquely human ability. We also examine bilingualism, language in atypical populations, including children with specific language disabilities, and the developmental relation between language and thought.

The section concludes with a chapter on applied cognitive development, *Intelligence and School Achievement*. We first examine the psychometric approach, which gave us IQ tests, as well as alternative approaches to intelligence, and the many interacting factors that influence a child's level of intellectual functioning. We then look at the development of perhaps the three most important academic skills for children in schooled cultures: reading, writing, and arithmetic.

In this chapter we first examine methods based mostly on infants' looking behavior that revolutionized the study of infant perception. We then look at the development of infant vision, including face perception, audition (including speech perception), and intermodal (between senses) perception. We next explore methods used to study infant cognition and then examine some of the cognitive accomplishments of infancy. We begin with a look at infant categorization, followed by an examination of the core-knowledge approach, including infants' understanding of objects, neonatal imitation, and their knowledge of numbers. We conclude the chapter with a look at the development of memory in infancy.

Andrea, a woman with plenty of experience with babies, sat in front of her 7-month-old grandson, Fletcher, covering her face with her hands, then quickly removing them and saying "boo" followed by a big smile, which caused Fletcher to laugh. She and Fletcher repeated the routine for several minutes. When Andrea delayed the "boo" for too long, Fletcher would vocalize, lean forward, and swat at her hands. Then he reacted with a startle followed by a laugh when Andrea finally lowered her hands and delivered the "boo." After the game, as grandmother and grandson were both calming down, Andrea said out loud, to no one in particular, "Wouldn't it be just lovely to know what he's thinking?

Wouldn't it be great if babies could tell us what was on their minds?"

If you have ever held a baby in your arms, you have probably asked yourself these or similar questions. In fact, one of the things that makes babies both mysterious and fascinating to adults is that, because they cannot yet speak, it seems impossible to know how they feel, what they perceive, and what (or if) they think about the different people, things, and events that surround them.

However, Andrea's questions—ones she assumed had no answers—have also been asked by scientists, and until the latter part of the 20th century, they also assumed that the mind of the preverbal infant was generally unknowable. That began to change when researchers realized that babies, even very young babies, had control over some simple behaviors, such as sucking, turning their heads, kicking, and looking, and that they could use these behaviors to gaze into infants' minds to get a glimpse of what they perceived, thought, and felt. How all of these simple behaviors are used to that purpose is described in this chapter.

Chapter 3 provided a short summary of some basic abilities of newborns. For example, from the first days of life, babies have available some primitive systems to (1) receive information (sensory systems); (2) transmit information (crying and basic emotions); and (3) act (reflexes) (Delval, 1994). These primitive systems are critical for survival, as well as getting them started on the long road of becoming progressively adapted to life outside of the womb. Chapter 4 provided some specific data about infant brain and motor development. This chapter first focuses on infants' *perception*, starting with a look at methods that have provided psychologists with insights into what babies perceive, mainly what they see and hear. We then examine several aspects of infant visual perception, including visual preferences, depth perception, and face perception. We follow this with a brief look at infant auditory perception and then intermodal (between senses) perception, focusing mainly on the integration of vision and hearing.

Our discussion then turns to topics of infant *cognition*. As in our review of infant perception, we start with some of the methodologies used to assess infant cognition. We follow this with a discussion of how infants form categories about the different things the world is composed of. We then look at the concept of *core knowledge*, followed by reviews of research on object representation, neonatal imitation, and infants' abilities to make sense of quantitative information. We then examine infants' memory skills. The chapter concludes with a short discussion about the role of experience regarding infant perceptual and cognitive development. Other aspects of infant cognition, including some specifics on problem solving and social cognition, are discussed in Chapters 6 and 7.

The distinction between perception and cognition in infancy is often a difficult and arbitrary one, even among experts (see, for example, Cohen & Cashon, 2006, for a review). Some would say that perception has more to do with the organization of the sensations that come to our different senses, whereas cognition has more to do with what we do with those perceived sensations (see Figure 5.1 and Table 5.1). But this is only one possible view. In fact, for many people there is no distinct boundary between one and the other. However, from a practical point of view, and for the sake of improving communication, most scientists would agree that perception has to do more with a series of mental activities that occupy a lower level in the informa-

table 5.1 Distinctions between Sensation, Perception, and Cognition

Here we provide some basic definitions of these terms as we use them in this and other chapters. We realize that the distinction between cognition and perception (and between perception and sensation) is subtle and perhaps arbitrary in some cases, but making these imprecise distinctions helps psychologists and students organize the many knowledge-acquisition and manipulation processes that people, beginning in infancy, engage in.

Term	Definition
Sensation	The process or experience of perceiving through the senses. It is the result of stimulation of a sensory receptor (for example, the rods or cones of the eyes for vision) and the resulting activation of a specific area of the brain, producing an awareness of sight, sound, odor, taste, etc.
Perception	The process of becoming aware of objects, relations, and events by way of the senses, including mechanisms such as discrimination (distinguishing one sensation from another) and recognition (identifying a sensation as one that has been previously experienced). Unlike sensation, which involves generally disorganized input, perception involves organized input, in that it enables the individual to organize and interpret events into meaningful knowledge.
Cognition	The processes or faculties by which knowledge is acquired and manipulated. These include perceiving, remembering, reasoning, imaging, and problem solving. Perception, then, is a form of cognition. However, when we contrast perception with cognition, as we do in this chapter on "what infants know," we use perception to refer to what are generally viewed to be lower-level processes, such as discriminating two sights or sounds. Cognition is used to refer to higher-level processes, such as remembering an experience, realizing that objects continue to exist even when they are out of one's immediate perception (for example, a toy still exists when it is covered by a cloth), and copying the behavior of another person.

tion-processing flow, such as seeing and hearing, whereas cognition has to do more with a series of higher-level mental activities, such as solving problems and memorizing.

Infancy is usually considered to span the first two years of life, but distinctions are sometimes made between children in their first year and toddlers, children in their teen months and beyond, who, while still mostly nonverbal, are able to walk. Although toddlers will not be ignored in this chapter, most of the perceptual and cognitive abilities we discuss here will deal with infants in their first year of life.

Why Study Infant Perception and Cognition?

Infant perception and cognition have been much-studied topics in psychology for several reasons. One is very practical: Knowing what infants perceive and think can be very helpful in dealing with them on a day-to-day basis. They cannot directly tell us what they experience, so we need to develop techniques to infer what they perceive and know. Such techniques are also very useful for detecting sensory disabilities and correcting some problems if possible. A second reason why infant perception and cognition have been hot topics is because they provide a window into the nature of human knowledge and thinking. Because of newborns' limited experience, psychologists can address some questions that philosophers have been asking for centuries (for example, the role of experience on perception and the degree to which infants are prepared by biology to make sense of their physical and social worlds).

Let us provide a couple of examples. When a baby girl first experiences a new stimulus (for instance, a cat), what does she actually see and hear? Is her experience a "blooming, buzzing confusion" of visual and auditory sensations (like pioneer of psychology William James suggested more than 100 years ago), or does she see a perfectly integrated and organized image, with sound ("meowing") coordinated with sight, much as adults do? In a similar vein, when a baby boy realizes that an object he pushes falls off the table, what does he think happened? Is he surprised because the object fell to the floor? Perhaps he expected that the object would float in the air, like an astronaut's tool on the Space Shuttle? In other words, do babies understand gravity?

If young babies see and hear things in the world much as adults do, and think that objects pushed off a hard surface fall, for example, we might be tempted to infer that the role of experi-

ence in infant perception and cognition is minimal and that infants are somehow prepared by biology to interpret events in their world (or to learn about them very early). However, if what babies see, hear, and think is quite different from what older children and adults see, hear, and think, we might propose that the role of experience in infant perception and cognition is very important, with biological preparedness playing less of a role. We now know that phrasing the question like this (that is, nature versus nurture) does not get us very far, but nonetheless, understanding what the perceptual and cognitive abilities of infants are at birth, what they are prepared to perceive and understand, the biases they have, if any, and how these early biases interact with experience give us powerful insights into the very nature of human knowledge and thinking.

Related to the practical and philosophical reasons for studying infant perception and cognition, such abilities are critical for solving some basic problems that humans have to deal with at the very beginning of life, as well as in subsequent months and years. These include recognizing people and objects; understanding language (for example, by distinguishing organized sound sequences and intonations); integrating information from various senses about people and objects (for example, by connecting visual images and sounds); distinguishing among different sorts of things (for example, between inanimate and animate objects, or the different types of animate beings); understanding how objects and people behave in a natural environment (for example, what causes an object to move); and recognizing and recalling information. Along these lines, the distinguished infant researcher, Marshall Haith (1993), pointed out long ago how important it is to take a more functional approach to infant perception: Describing a perceptual ability is certainly important, but this tells us nothing about its impact on an infant's everyday life.

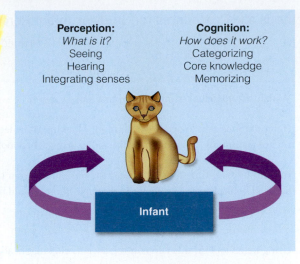

Perception: *What is it?* Seeing Hearing Integrating senses

Cognition: *How does it work?* Categorizing Core knowledge Memorizing

Infant

FIGURE 5.1 Infant perceptual and cognitive development has become a fascinating and much-studied topic in contemporary developmental psychology. Design of new and highly creative methods to measure what babies perceive and know has been responsible for this burst of knowledge. In this figure, we characterize the main topics described in this chapter. We should note that the distinction between perception and cognition is made more for practical than scientific reasons. For many scientists, these concepts are difficult, if not impossible, to distinguish.

table 5.2 Some Methods and Procedures for Studying Infant Perception and Cognition

Method	Procedure
Looking Measures	
Visual preference	Which of two visual stimuli do infants look at more?
Habituation/ dishabituation	Habituation is said to occur when infants' looking time decreases significantly as a result of repeated presentation of a stimulus. Dishabituation is said to occur when looking time increases when a new stimulus is presented.
Violation-of-expectation	Infants' looking time will increase if they see some event that violates what they expected to see (for example, one doll behind a screen when they thought there should be two).
Other Measures	
Operant conditioning	Using behaviors infants can control, such as sucking, head turning, and kicking, researchers can condition infants to indicate memory or an ability to discriminate between two stimuli.
Facial expressions	Emotional expressions can be used to indicate recognition of stimuli.
Reaching	This can be an indication of interest toward a certain perceived stimulus.
Deferred imitation	Infants' ability to copy behaviors they witnessed some time earlier is an indication of memory.
Heart rate	Variations of heart rate can reflect variations in interest to new stimuli. Increases in heart rate are associated with fear, whereas decreases in heart rate are an indication of interest, or attention.
Respiration	Variations in breathing rate can be used to reflect interest in new stimuli.
Brain activation (such as EEG)	Identification of some specific brain activity can serve as an indicator that infants recognize and/or distinguish between some stimuli.

How Can We Know What Babies Perceive?

When I (DB) was a young graduate student, teaching my first child development course in the early 1970s, I told my class that all of a baby's senses were working at birth—not very well, mind you, but they were able to make some limited sense of

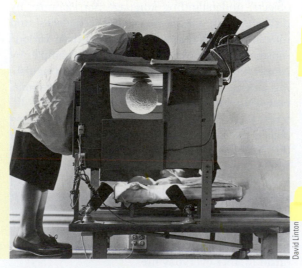

Fantz's original looking chamber. SOURCE: Fantz, R. L. (1961). The origin of form perception. *Scientific American, 204, 66–72.*

their surroundings. A middle-aged woman immediately informed me that I was wrong. She had had four children and her doctors told her, for each one, that babies are blind at birth. Judging by her age, my guess is that she had had most of her children a decade or two earlier, and her physicians were giving her the best scientific knowledge of the day. Newborns certainly do not look like they are capable of much in the way of thought or even perception, but there was really no way to tell. This changed when researchers realized that babies could control some behaviors, such as sucking, turning their heads, and looking, and that these behaviors could be the windows to their minds. It was primarily looking behavior that drove the revolution in infant perception and provided scientists a glimpse of what babies perceive.

Table 5.2 lists some of the behaviors researchers have used over the last half-century to assess what infants perceive, think, and know. The two most widely used looking methods are the *visual preference* and *habituation/dishabituation paradigms*, which we examine in this section. We look at the other methods of evaluating what infants know later in the chapter in the section on infant cognition.

Visual Preference Paradigm

Sometimes the simplest ideas are the best. Robert Fantz (1958, 1961) wanted to know if 2- and 3-month-old infants could tell the difference between, or *discriminate*, two visual stimuli. To do this, he developed the **visual preference paradigm**. Babies were placed in a looking chamber (see Photo) and shown a series of visual stimuli in random order. These could be pictures of a human face or geometric patterns, such as a bull's eye or a checkerboard. A researcher, peeking through a hole in the chamber above the infant, would then record where the baby was looking. If groups of babies looked significantly longer at one pattern (the bull's eye, for instance) relative to another (the checkerboard), one could say that the infants could tell the difference between the two patterns and had a preference for the bull's eye over the checkerboard. If infants could not tell the difference between the two, or had no preference for one versus the other, there would be no difference in looking time.

Figure 5.2 shows the results of one of Fantz's (1961) early studies. As you can see, babies as young as 2 to 3 months old preferred to look at schematic faces rather than other stimuli, and preferred stimuli with some pattern (for example, newsprint or a bull's eye) relative to simpler stimuli. Using this technique, Fantz showed that babies younger than 1 week old can tell the difference between stimuli such as a schematic face, a bull's-eye pattern, and a solid-colored disk. Modern versions of Fantz's procedure use computers to present stimuli and record infants' looking behavior using cameras, but the basic procedure has not changed much from that developed by Fantz more than half a century ago.

We use the term *preference* here not in the same way that adults may have a preference for impressionist versus abstract art, but merely that infants look more at one object than another. In this sense, *preference* is synonymous with *perceptual bias*. Showing a bias to look at one object more than another tells us that infants are not responding randomly and that something must be going on in their heads to produce that bias. However, we must be cautious and not attribute too much in terms of higher-order thought to such preferences.

Note, however, that infants may look equally long at two stimuli, and this would not necessarily mean that they could not tell them apart. Perhaps both are equally appealing. If babies have no preference for one stimulus over another, how can you tell if they can discriminate them? One technique is the habituation/dishabituation paradigm, which we now describe.

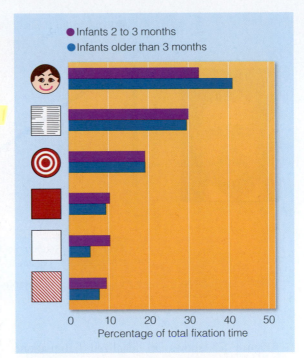

Courtesy of David Lewkowicz

Although new technology permits far more control of stimuli and measurement of infants' behaviors, the basic idea of seeing where infants are looking hasn't changed much from Fantz's original research.

Habituation/Dishabituation Paradigm

A related procedure takes advantage of the fact that infants, like older children and adults, get bored of, or used to, seeing (or hearing or feeling) the same old thing. When infants are repeatedly shown a visual stimulus, this boredom is reflected by a decrease in looking time, or habituation. **Habituation** occurs when there is a decrease in responding as a result of the repeated presentation of a stimulus. In this case, it is looking at a visual stimulus, perhaps a picture of something, say a photograph of Brad Pitt. When a new stimulus is presented, such as a photograph of Zack Efron, infants increase their attention to the new stimulus. This increase in attention to a novel stimulus is **dishabituation**, sometimes referred to as *release from habituation*.

---

visual preference paradigm In research with infants, observing the amount of time infants spend looking at different visual stimuli to determine which one they prefer (i.e., look at more often); such preferences indicate an ability to discriminate between stimuli.

habituation Decrease in the response to a stimulus that has been presented repeatedly.

dishabituation The tendency to show renewed interest in a stimulus when some features of it have been changed.

FIGURE 5.3 Habituation/dishabituation paradigm. Looking time decreases with repeated presentation of the same stimulus (habituation, here a photo of Brad Pitt) but increases after the presentation of a new stimulus (dishabituation, here, a photo of Zack Efron). SOURCE: From Bjorklund, D. F. (2005). *Children's thinking: Cognitive development and individual differences,* 4th ed., Fig. 7.2, p. 187. Copyright © 2005 Wadsworth, a part of Cengage Learning, Inc. Reprinted by permission.

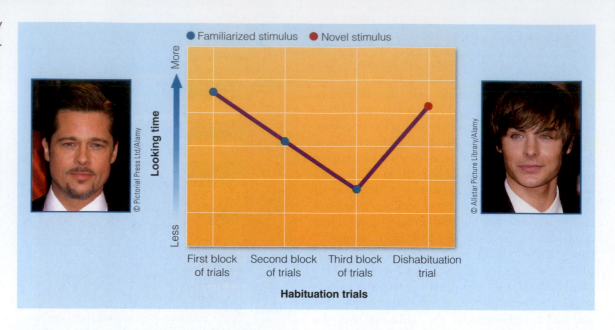

Infants initially look intently at a new stimulus (a), but they lose interest in it as it is presented repeatedly (b). This reduction in looking time as a result of repeated presentation of a stimulus is called *habituation*.

Figure 5.3 shows an idealized habituation/dishabituation curve. Looking time decreases the longer the familiarized stimulus (the photo of Brad Pitt) is shown (trial blocks 1 to 3 in the figure). Habituation is usually said to occur when a baby's looking time is 50% of what it was initially. Then a new, or novel, stimulus is shown (the dishabituation trial, the photo of Zack Efron), and looking time increases, often to what it was originally.

What does such a pattern tell us about infant perception? First, this informs us that infants can tell the difference between the two stimuli.

Reducing their looking time as a result of seeing the same stimulus over and over again means that babies are familiar with or know the first stimulus (that is, Brad Pitt), and their increase in looking time at the novel stimulus (Zack Efron) indicates that they realize that this is different from the earlier one. As with the visual preference paradigm, if infants could not tell the difference between the two stimuli, there would be no increase in looking time during the dishabituation trial. But this pattern tells us more than that babies can tell the two stimuli apart. Infants are discriminating between one stimulus that is physically present (the novel stimulus, Zack Efron) and one that is present only in their memories (the familiarized stimulus, Brad Pitt). That is, habituation/dishabituation reflects a very basic form of recognition memory.

How do we know that babies may not just think Zack Efron is more interesting to look at than Brad Pitt? To make sure, experiments like this *counterbalance* the presentation of the stimuli. This means that half of the babies would first see Brad Pitt and then see Zack Efron, whereas the other half would be habituated to the photo of Zack Efron, and a photo of Brad Pitt would be used as the novel stimulus. If infants show the habituation/dishabituation pattern under both conditions (that is, Brad Pitt followed by Zack Efron and vice versa), the results cannot be attributed to a preference for one face over the other.

At what age do babies show this pattern? As it turns out, even newborns display habituation/dishabituation (and thus evidence of memory) for vision (Friedman, 1972) and also for touch (stroking their skin; Streri, Lhote, & Dutilleul, 2000); and fetuses as young as 30 weeks habituate and later dishabituate (as demonstrated by their movement) to vibrations delivered via sound waves through the mother's abdomen (Dirix et al., 2009; Sandman et al., 1997).

There are other ways to know what infants perceive. For example, a sour or a sweet substance can be placed on babies' tongues, and their facial reactions to each substance can be recorded. However, the new and simple techniques of assessing infants' visual preferences and the extent to which they get bored with a stimulus and then recover when a new stimulus is presented set the stage for a revolution in our knowledge of what babies perceive, know, and think. We discuss other techniques and more advanced forms of infant cognition later in this chapter. In the next section, we stick close to basic perception, looking at the development of visual perception, including the things that infants like to look at.

The Development of Visual Perception

Humans, like our primate cousins, are a visual species (Gómez, 2004). Given the importance of vision to normal human functioning, it is not surprising that it has been the most investigated of all the senses, and this includes its development. Seeing involves an amazing coordination of sense organs, muscles, and neurons. The eyes are sophisticated devices, and all of their components must work together in harmony to produce clear vision. This involves, for example (1) regulating the amount of light that comes into the eyes; (2) focusing the lens to get a clear view of objects and people at different distances from the eyes; (3) processing color information; (4) coordinating both eyes' movements to integrate their different images into a single one; and (5) tracking moving targets. The eyes are connected directly to the brain through the optic nerve, and aspects of brain development also play an important role in seeing. For instance, areas of the visual cortex become more richly interconnected as a result of receiving information from the eyes, which in turn facilitates faster and more precise visual processing.

In the following sections, we first describe some basic properties of infants' visual system and its development. We then look at some of the things infants like to look at, followed by discussions of the development of depth perception, and conclude with an examination of babies' processing of particularly important visual stimuli—human faces.

The Development of Basic Visual Abilities

We briefly discussed vision in newborns in Chapter 3. Contrary to what many people believed not too long ago, babies can see at birth. (Babies are not born with their eyes closed like puppies and kittens, either, which is something one of my (CHB) students found out to his embarrassment when he asked at the beginning of an infant perception lecture, "But how can you test them so early? How old are they when their eyes open?") Newborns' pupils constrict when light is bright and expand when light is dim. There is also little focusing, or **accommodation**, of the lens at birth, meaning that most of what they see is out of focus. They can see objects most clearly about 8 to 10 inches away (25 cm)—about the distance of their mothers' faces when they are being fed. By the time infants are 3 to 4 months old, their accommodation is as good as that of adults (Banks, 1980; Tondel & Candy, 2008).

Many objects that people attend to do not remain stationary but move, and this requires following objects with one's eyes. Newborns are able to follow a moving object with their eyes (**visual tracking**), although not very smoothly at first. In fact, it is not until about 2 months that infants show **binocular convergence**, the ability of *both* eyes to focus together on the same object, which is necessary for depth perception (see later discussion), and it is not fully functioning until months later (Aslin, 1977).

Newborns also have poor **visual acuity**, the ability to see something sharply and clearly (see

FIGURE 5.4 Infants' visual acuity, how clearly they can see objects, is poor at birth but improves substantially over the course of the first year.

The 6-by-6 and 16-by-16 checkerboard patterns on the top appear quite differently to young infants. SOURCE: Adapted from *Carmichaels, Manual of Child Psychology,* Vol. 2, 4th ed. Reprinted by permission of John Wiley & Sons, Inc.

What we see

Moderately complex 6x6 — Highly complex 16x16

What the young infant sees

---

accommodation (of the lens) The process of adjusting the lens of the eye to focus on objects at different distances.

visual tracking The ability to follow a moving object with one's eyes.

binocular convergence The ability of *both* eyes to focus together on the same object, which is necessary for depth perception.

visual acuity The ability to see something sharply and clearly. *poor in newborns*

Although newborns can see, their visual acuity, or how clearly they see images, is not well developed. Even when an object, like their mother's face, is in clearest focus, about 9 or 10 inches from their face, the image they see is fuzzy (photo a) compared to what an adult would see (photo b).

Figure 5.4 and Photo). When you read the letters on the eye doctor's chart, the optometrist is measuring your visual acuity—how well you can distinguish, for example, between the "F" and "E" or the "F" and "P." How clearly can newborn infants see? To determine this, infants are shown high-contrast patterns of various sizes, such as the pattern of stripes shown in Figure 5.5. If they look at the striped pattern longer than at a plain gray one, we know that they can see the lines. When they can no longer tell the difference between the gray pattern and the striped pattern, this reflects the narrowest width of stripes that an infant can discriminate, and this is used to determine their visual acuity. With normal acuity for adults being 20/20 (one can see at a distance of 20 feet what a person with normal vision can see at 20 feet), estimates of newborn acuity range from 20/400 to 20/600 (Slater, 1995), making the neonate legally blind in most states. Acuity improves substantially during the first year of life, although does not reach adult levels until 6 years of age (Skoczenski & Norcia, 2002; Kellman & Arterberry, 2006).

We do not want to forget an important aspect of vision, and that is seeing color. It was once believed that newborns and young infants saw the world only in black and white. Research has shown that although newborns do not see the world as if it's a black-and-white photograph, their color vision is greatly limited. They can distinguish very dark colors (like deep red) from very light colors (like white), but that is about it. However, by about 4 months of age, their color perception has improved greatly and is similar to that of adults (see Kellman & Arterberry, 2006).

Although being perhaps the least-well-developed sense at birth, the visual skills of infants improve considerably with time, and by 6 to 8 months of age, their visual systems works just about as well as those of adults. Concept Review 5.1 presents a summary of some of the visual abilities (and disabilities) of newborns.

Infant Visual Preferences

Think about the basic visual preference paradigm. In addition to informing us that infants can discriminate between two stimuli, the very existence of preferences tells us something important about babies; they come into the world, or develop shortly thereafter, *preferences*, or perceptual biases. They look at some things more than others. This in itself was quite a revelation to psychologists and indicated that babies are not blank slates, as proposed by the philosopher John Locke and an earlier generation of psychologists. Rather, they come into the world with perceptual biases, their attention being drawn to some stimuli more than to others. Many of these preferences can be seen from the first month or two of life.

Some of these preferences are based on the *physical characteristics* of stimuli. Infants look more at stimuli that (1) move versus those that are stationary (Haith, 1966), (2) have a certain level of complexity (Fantz, 1961, see Figure 5.1 presented earlier in this chapter), and (3) have high contrast (for example, dark lines on a light background, Banks & Salapatek, 1983; see Photo). Although this ability is not present at birth, infants in their first year also look longer at stimuli that are *vertically symmetrical* (that is, the left and right halves are alike, Bornstein, Ferdinandsen, & Gross, 1981).

---

concept review | 5.1   Some visual abilities of newborns

- They are very sensitive to changes in light intensity as reflected by the pupillary reflex.
- They can see items most clearly at a distance of about 25 cm (9 or 10 inches) from their eyes.
- They can track moving objects, although not smoothly.
- They cannot accommodate (focus) the lenses of their eyes well.
- They cannot coordinate movements of the two eyes.
- They cannot perceive objects clearly; that is, they have poor visual acuity.
- They can distinguish white from red, but they cannot distinguish the full range of colors.

All other things being equal, infants (usually) prefer to look at:

- Moving stimuli
- Complex stimuli (versus stimuli with few elements in them)
- Stimuli with areas of high contrast
- Vertically symmetrical stimuli

- Curvilinear (curved) stimuli
- Face-like stimuli
- Stimuli with a moderate degree of novelty
- Attractive faces versus less-attractive faces

Infants by 3 or 4 months old also look more at stimuli that are *curvilinear* (curved lines) versus linear (straight lines). Babies' perceptual biases for curved and vertically symmetrical forms make good evolutionary sense (Bornstein et al., 1981). Arguably the most important visual stimuli in the world of infants are the faces of their caretakers, and these faces are both concentric and have vertical symmetry (that is, the left and right sides are nearly mirror images). Faces, in fact, also move (the whole head moves, as do individual components such as eyes and the mouth), have areas of high contrast (for example, the whites versus iris of the eyes, the forehead against the hair line), and certainly present at least a moderate degree of complexity. Not surprisingly, infants from early on are attracted to faces, and we will discuss the development of infants' face processing later in this chapter.

Other research has shown that infants between 2 and 4 months old begin to prefer stimuli that are moderately novel. Thus, some biases seem to be based on the *psychological significance* of the stimulus rather than its physical characteristics. For example, infants (usually) look longer at stimuli that are slightly different from what they are already familiar with (McCall, Kennedy, & Appelbaum, 1977). For instance, for an infant around 6 months of age, a stimulus that differs slightly from what he or she already knows (for example, a bearded face when the infant is familiar with nonbearded faces) is likely to maintain attention, whereas a highly familiar stimulus (a nonbearded face) or a highly discrepant one (a model of a face with its features scrambled) is likely to receive less of an infant's attention (Kagan, 1971). The fact that a stimulus's familiarity or novelty influences infants' attention implies some sort of recognition memory for the stimulus event. For a stimulus to be regarded as familiar, it must be contrasted with some previous mental representation of that stimulus; that is, it must be contrasted with a stimulus that was previously known. Similarly, to be novel, a stimulus has to be slightly different from something that the perceiver already knows (Rheingold, 1985). We will discuss infant memory later in this chapter. Concept Review 5.2 presents some basic infant visual biases, or preferences.

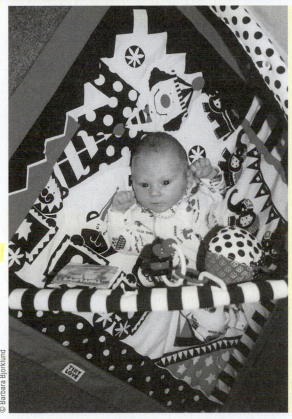

© Barbara Bjorklund

Young children's attention is attracted by high contrast.

Depth Perception

When we look at pictures or a video, we see objects much differently than we do in real life. There is the obvious difference in size, but there is also a difference in *depth*. Depth perception, or the ability to discriminate visual patterns denoting depth, is important. Without it we would not know that stairs require careful footing, that people at a distance can be as tall as people nearby, and that the soccer ball we see growing larger in size is going to hit us if we do not move out of the way. We could not gauge distance or navigate successfully in our environment without depth perception.

We discussed the relationship between depth perception and locomotion in Chapter 4. As you

depth perception The ability to discriminate visual patterns denoting depth.

may recall, when placed on a visual cliff—a glass-topped table with a shallow side with no drop-off and a deep side that has a checkerboard pattern 3 feet below the see-through surface (Walk & Gibson, 1961; see photo in Chapter 4)—most 7- to 8-month-old infants will gladly crawl to their mothers over the shallow side, but most will not cross over to the deep side, despite their mothers' encouragement and the feel of a solid surface (the glass top). This refusal to cross the visual abyss despite having such a motivating stimulus waiting for them has been interpreted as a strong indication that infants at this age do have depth perception.

Can noncrawling infants discriminate depth on the visual cliff? Some evidence suggesting that they can comes from a study that placed 2- and 3-month-old infants on the deep side of the visual cliff. These babies showed significant changes in their heart rates, suggesting that they can tell the difference between the deep and shallow sides. However, unlike older infants, who show an *increase* in heart rate when placed on the deep side of a visual cliff indicating fear, 2- to 3-month-old infants show a *decrease* in heart rate, indicating attention or interest (Campos, Langer & Krowitz, 1970). In other words, infants from 2 months of age seem to be able to perceive the cues denoting depth, but their reactions differ from those of older infants. Younger infants can tell the difference between the deep and shallow side and find the deep side interesting instead of dangerous or fearful. Such an interest, however, would not prevent them from avoiding a fall off the side of the bed. The older infants, presumably with some crawling experience, realized that what they were seeing was associated with danger and responded accordingly, physiologically.

More contemporary research has shown that depth perception does not emerge suddenly between 6 and 8 months of life, but rather involves a series of components that infants progressively acquire over the course of their first year: *kinetic cues, stereoscopic cues*, and *monocular*, or *pictorial, cues.*

Kinetic cues refer to information associated with the movement of objects we are watching. For example, if I take an apple in my hand and I watch it while I move it across my visual field, I pick up information related to the three-dimensional nature of the fruit. The image of the apple on my retina changes as I have slightly different views of it, providing information about its three-dimensional shape. Infants are sensitive to

kinetic-depth cues when they are about 2 months old and probably earlier (Johnson, Hannon & Amso, 2005). This has been shown, for example, by 1-month-old infants' reflexive blink, as they close their eyes defensively when an object in the distance approaches suddenly toward them (Ball & Tronick, 1971; Nanez & Yonas, 1994).

Stereoscopic, or binocular, cues serve to integrate the images provided by each eye into a single, richer one. In this way, new cues for depth, particularly in the case of reaching nearby objects, are incorporated. Stereoscopic vision requires the ability of both eyes to focus together on the same object (binocular convergence), which, as mentioned previously, does not develop until about 2 months. Stereoscopic vision emerges between the third and fifth months of life, becoming adult-like by about six months (Johnson et al., 2005).

Monocular, or pictorial cues, basically have to do with understanding *visual perspective.* For example, realizing that a railroad track visually fades, converging to a far point in the distance, requires perspective. It is called pictorial because it permits us to perceive three dimensions from a two-dimensional target, as in a picture or a painting. It is called monocular because these depth cues can be perceived even with one eye closed. Typically, infants develop such perspective between 5 and 7 months of age (Johnson et al., 2005). Visual perspective is illustrated in infants' preference for M. C. Escher-like impossible figures (see Figure 5.6). For example, in a set of studies, 4-month-olds looked significantly longer at the impossible than the possible figures, indicating an ability to use pictorial cues earlier than previously thought (Shuwairi, 2009; Shuwairi, Albert, & Johnson, 2007).

Using the visual preference, the habituation/dishabituation, and other simple techniques, researchers have discovered that infants experience a rich visual world. They can tell the differences between two visual patterns, such as a bull's eye and a checkerboard pattern, shortly after birth. (It will be a few months more before they can discriminate the photographs of Brad Pitt and Zack Efron.) As their visual system matures, they increasingly see things as older children and adults do, such as depth. And perhaps most important, they enter the world with preferences, spending more time looking at some stimuli than others. This suggests that infants are not blank slates but are prepared by their biology to make sense of their physical world. Some aspects of visual stimuli they are biased to look at—curvature, high contrast, concentricity, and vertical symmetry—are characteristics of the human face. We turn now to infants' perception of perhaps the most important visual stimulus in the life of an infant, human faces.

kinetic cues Information about depth of objects associated with the movement of objects we are watching.

stereoscopic (or binocular) vision The ability to integrate the images provided by each eye into a single, richer one.

monocular (or pictorial) cues Cues used to understand visual perspective; such cues permit the perception of three dimensions from a two-dimensional target, as in a picture or a painting.

Perception of Human Faces

For a social animal who will be dependent for years on the care of others, learning to recognize and read faces may mean the difference between life and death. Faces provide a lot of information about other people, and, particularly in the case of babies, about their caregivers. As we will see in this section, infants seem to be very proficient in face processing from an early age, and this has raised two important questions: Is there a specific mechanism in humans for processing information about faces different from the mechanisms used in the perception of objects? And, if so, is this mechanism innate? Modern research seems to answer "Yes" to the first question and "No" to the second.

Many authors point to research indicating that adults process human faces more effectively than any other type of stimuli (Maurer et al., 2002; Bruce et al., 1991), and neuropsychological evidence from both human and nonhuman animals shows that specific areas of the brain are activated when looking at faces (Nelson, 2001, 2005; Morris et al., 1996). For example, *prosopagnosia*—the inability to recognize familiar faces despite being able to perceive other visual stimuli—is associated with lesions in specific areas of the brain (the fusiform gyrus in the temporal lobe and the amygdala). This is reflected by the case of L.H., a 37-year-old man with brain damage to the temporal lobe who could not recognize his wife and their children, not even himself, although he was able to solve other visual-perception tasks where faces were not involved (Farah, Levinson, & Klein, 1995).

But what about infants? Do they also process faces differently than other visual stimuli, and, if so, how does this develop? As we noted earlier, even newborns prefer face-like to nonface-like stimuli (Johnson et al., 1991; Mondloch et al., 1999) and show a preference for familiar faces, looking longer, for example, at their mothers' faces than at those of other women (Bushnell, Sai, & Mullin, 1989; Walton, Bower, & Bower, 1992). Newborns also pay more attention to faces whose eyes are open and gazing directly at them than to faces where eyes are averted (Farroni et al., 2003, 2006).

Beginning at about 2 months of age, infants change *how* they look at faces. Specifically, whereas 1-month-old babies scan mostly the outside of a face (termed the **externality effect**), by 2 months old most of infants' attention is focused on internal features (Salapatek, 1975; Turati et al., 2006). Figure 5.7 provides an example of the scanning patterns of a typical 1- and 2-month-old infant. Note that even 1-month-olds, although spending most of their time looking at the outline of the face, still spend some time looking at the eyes.

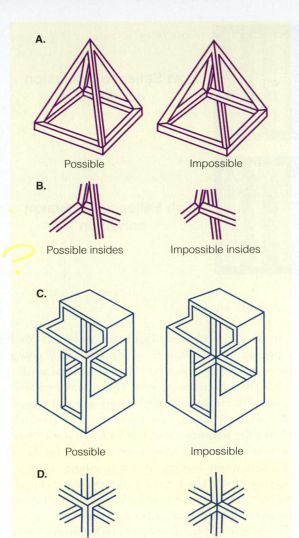

FIGURE 5.6 Some possible and impossible figures. Four-month-old infants looked longer at the impossible than the possible figures, indicating that they can use pictorial cues to discriminate between visual stimuli. SOURCE: From Shuwairi, S. M. (2009). Preference for impossible figures in 4-month-old infants. *Journal of Experimental Child Psychology, 104*, 115–123. Reprinted by permission of Elsevier.

A.
Possible   Impossible

B.
Possible insides   Impossible insides

C.
Possible   Impossible

D.
Possible insides   Impossible insides

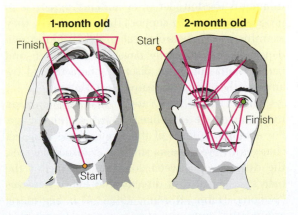

FIGURE 5.7 Externality effect. One-month-old infants explore the contour of faces, called the externality effect, while 2-month olds spend more time looking at the internal features of faces. SOURCE: From Schaffer, D. R. (1993). *Social and personality development* (3rd ed.). Copyright © 2005 Brooks/Cole, a part of Cengage Learning, Inc. Reproduced by permission. www.cengage.com/permissions.

1-month old   2-month old
Finish   Start
Start   Finish
Start

The Eyes Have It

In fact, it seems that infants and adults pay special attention to the eyes. For instance, Lucia Gava and her colleagues (2008) showed newborns (43.5 hours old on average) faces that were partially covered, or occluded. Some faces hid the eyes and others

externality effect The tendency of young infants (1-month-olds) to direct their attention primarily to the outside of a figure and to spend little time inspecting internal features.

Low Salience Occlusion condition

High Salience Occlusion condition

FIGURE 5.8 An example of the stimuli used by Gava et al. (2008). Using a visual preference paradigm, these researchers found that newborns who could see the eyes of a person showed a stronger preference toward the upright (vs. the upside-down) face, as is typically found in research using faces without occlusions. In contrast, newborns showed *no* preference for either the upside-down or right-side-up faces in the condition in which the eyes were covered. SOURCE: Gava, L., Valenza, E., Turati, C., & de Schonen, S. (2008). Effect of partial occlusion on newborns' face preference and recognition. *Developmental Science, 11,* 563–574.

left the eyes visible (see Figure 5.8). Infants looked longer at the right-side-up versus the upside-down faces, a pattern shown by older infants and adults, when they could see the eyes. They showed no preference for either the right-side-up or upside-down face when the eyes were covered. Other research shows the importance of *eye gaze* to infants' face processing. For example, babies' attention to faces declines when looking at a face whose eyes are averted rather than looking directly at them, or, worse yet, to a face whose eyes are closed (Batki et al., 2000; Farroni et al., 2002).

In this vein, developmental neuroscientists Teodora Gliga and Gegerly Csibra (2007) have suggested that the bias toward eye gaze beginning in infancy is the foundation of humans' expertise in processing faces. To support this hypothesis, they examined both neurological and behavioral evidence in both typically developing children and people with autism, a disorder characterized by, among other things, impaired social cognition.

Gliga and Csibra noted that eye-detection mechanisms are adult-like by 4 to 5 months of age. For example, infants of this age are able to detect changes in eye gaze as small as 5 visual degrees, the difference between someone looking at the baby's ear instead of directly into his or her eyes (Symons, Hains, & Muir, 1998). Also beginning around this time, the eyes evoke a stronger electrical response in the brain than do other facial features, as reflected by electroencephalography (EEG) measurements (see Chapter 4), a pattern that persists across development (Gliga & Dehaene-Lambertz, 2007; Taylor et al., 2004). Infants are also better able to recognize faces that are gazing at them versus faces whose gazes are averted, with the former again evoking a stronger neurological electrical response than the latter (see Farroni et al., 2002, 2004, 2006).

Some differences in face processing between typically developing and autistic children have been related to differences in brain development, pinpointing a possible neurological source for aspects of face processing. For instance, whereas typically developing children pay more attention to the eyes than the mouth, children and adults with autism do the reverse, attending more to the mouth than the eyes (Dalton et al., 2005; Klin et al., 2002). And, unlike typically developing children, children with autism are better able to discriminate faces using the bottom part of the face (mouth but no eyes) than the top part of the face (eyes but no mouth) (Joseph & Tanaka, 2003). Consistent with these findings, people with autism typically show an indifference toward mutual eye gaze, and faces in general, beginning in infancy (Dalton et al., 2005; Klin et al., 2002).

But why are the eyes, and eye gaze particularly, so important in face processing? Gigla and Csibra think that there are at least two important factors involved. First, the eyes are an area of high contrast, particularly in direct gaze (versus averted gaze), a feature that attracts infants' attention. Second, eyes play an important role in communication. For example, sustained mutual gaze within mother-infant interactions is associated with positive emotions; eye gaze helps infants interpret reactions to strangers and other novel events via social referencing in which babies look to their parents' reactions to an event; and eye gaze is important in shared attention, in which infants learn to look at objects that their parent is also looking at. In other words, babies may start life with a bias to attend to eyes, but this bias develops as a result of infants' interactions with their mothers and other important people.

However, understanding eyes is not all there is to understanding face processing. In fact, one very important aspect of face processing has little to do with the eyes—smiling (although the appearance of the eyes does change when someone smiles). Yet, it seems that understanding faces starts with the eyes, and eyes continue to provide important cues for what another person is thinking and feeling throughout life.

Is Beauty in the Eye of the Beholder?

Infants look longer at faces that adults find attractive (Slater et al., 1998; Langlois et al., 1987). In initial research, adults rated the attractiveness of the photographs of Caucasian women. The photos were then divided into "more attractive" and "less attractive" groups (Langlois et al., 1987). Two- to 3-month-old and 6- to 8-month-old infants then saw pairs of more attractive and less attractive photographs and consistently looked longer at the more attractive faces. This bias for attractive faces has been extended across the sex, race, and age of the modeled faces (Langlois et al., 1991).

Why should infants, even newborns, show a preference for adult-defined attractive faces? One possibility is that attractiveness is not an arbitrary phenomenon as many people think, but has some universal characteristics. For example, adults across the globe (and across animals species as well) find faces that are highly symmetrical to be more attractive than less symmetrical faces (Gangestad & Thornhill, 1997). Recall that vertical symmetry is one feature that attracts infants' attention. Evolutionary psychologists have found that symmetry, both in the face and the body in general, is a sign of physical (Gangestad & Thornhill, 1997) and psychological (Shackelford & Larsen, 1997) health and suggest that facial symmetry may have been selected in evolution in selecting mates. The greater the degree of asymmetry, the more susceptible the individual was to genetic or environmental (mostly prenatal) factors that caused the individual to develop away from the symmetrical norm (Gangestad & Thornhill, 1997). Although mate selection is surely not on the minds of infants, the preference may be a general one that is weak early in life but becomes stronger with experience. However, infants also show a preference for attractive versus less attractive faces of cats and tigers (as judged by an independent sample of adults), suggesting that this preference is not specific to human faces (Quinn et al., 2008).

Development of Face Perception over Infancy

From the third to the ninth month of life, face perception seems to become increasingly specialized. For example, by 3 or 4 months of age, infants find it easier to distinguish among female than male faces and generally prefer to look at females, unless their primary caregiver was their father (Quinn et al., 2002). They also are increasingly able to make more subtle distinctions among faces, using spatial relations, such as the distance between the eyes, in differentiating faces (Bhatt et al., 2005). Infants now begin to show the adult pattern of processing upright faces more effectively than upside-down faces, again suggesting that faces have special status compared to other visual stimuli (de Haan, Olivier, & Johnson, 1998). For example, 4-month-old infants spend more time exploring internal facial features, especially the nose and mouth, when looking at upright versus upside-down faces (Gallay et al., 2006).

However, as we noted in Chapter 1, this ability gets refined with time and experience. As you

may recall, although adults process upright human faces differently (and more effectively) than upside-down human faces, they process upright and upside-down *monkey* faces just like they do other visual stimuli. In other words, what is special for adults is *human* faces, not faces in general (see Photo). This is also true for 9-month-old babies, but not for 6-month-olds. These young infants show the same processing bias for upright monkey faces as they do for upright human faces (de Haan et al., 1998; Pascalis, de Haan, & Nelson, 2002). It takes them another 3 months before monkey faces lose this special status that is reserved only for human faces, which, unlike monkey faces, they see everyday.

In other words, even if infants develop very early an ability for processing faces that is different from how they process other visual stimuli (which they do), this ability gets refined with experience. Their increasing specialization at making distinctions between faces of different sexes and species clearly shows the importance of experience in processing this most important of social stimuli (Nelson, 2005; Ramsey-Rennels & Langlois, 2006; Turati, 2004). Moreover, although infants are quite adept at face perception by the end of their first year, the ability to process faces continues to develop into adolescence (de Haan, 2001; Mondloch et al., 2004).

Infants also develop an increasing ability to discriminate between faces of their own race rather than other races, termed the *other-race effect*. For example, researchers habituate infants to faces from a particular ethnic group, and later show them photos of people from their own ethnic group and others (for example, Caucasian versus Asian). David Kelly and his colleagues (2007, 2009) reported similar patterns for both British and Chinese infants. At 3 months old, infants showed no other-race effect but were equally skilled at recognizing faces from all ethnicities tested (Caucasian, Chinese, and African, as well as Middle Eastern for the British infants). At 6 months old, infants could recognize faces in their own race plus one other (Chinese and Caucasian), and at 9 months old, infants could recognize only faces in their own race (Chinese or Caucasian). This effect is *not* an example of implicit racism in the crib, but rather a reflection of the role of familiarity in shaping infants' perceptual abilities.

In summary, the research shows that the system for processing faces is initially very general, making no distinctions, for example, among different races, genders, species, or orientations of the faces (upright versus upside-down). With experience, the ability to process faces is refined. As it does, however, the system loses a bit of its plasticity.

Adults process right-side-up human faces more efficiently than upside-down human faces. However, they show no distinction in processing right-side-up and upside-down monkey faces. This is also true for 9-month-old infants, but not for 6-month-olds, who show the right-side-up bias for both human and monkey faces.

Concept Review 5.3 presents 10 interesting findings about infants' perception of faces.

In general, the consensus among researchers seems to be that (1) there are dedicated and complex areas of the brain for processing faces; (2) these are evolutionarily old abilities, found in humans' primate cousins; and (3) they develop as a result of experience over infancy and childhood (Pascalis & Kelly, 2009).

Like other primates, humans are visual animals, and although an infant's vision is one of the least mature senses at birth, it develops rapidly over the first year. Infants not only come to see things with more acuity but also come to understand how the things they see in their everyday world function. They learn to perceive and fear depth, and they develop a seemingly special ability to process faces, getting especially efficient at the types of faces they see most frequently. These and other basic perceptual abilities serve as the foundation for later advances in visual cognition, some of which we discuss later in this chapter. But first we examine briefly the development of auditory perception in infancy, followed by a look at the development of intermodal perception.

The Development of Auditory Perception

Although humans, like all primates, are heavily dependent on vision, the role of hearing, or *audition*, should not be underestimated, particularly when considering that one of the more distinctive human traits is language. In fact, children with hearing impairments (about 2 to 3 in every 1,000 births) often experience significant handicaps in a variety of areas of cognitive development, particularly if the loss is detected late (Saffran, Werker, & Werner, 2006). Unfortunately, most cases of hearing loss are not discovered until children are about 2.5 years old, although most could be identified in neonates with appropriate screening (Norton et al., 2000). As we pointed out in Chapter 3, auditory perception is far more mature than vision at birth and is functioning relatively well even before birth.

Despite the head start that hearing has over vision, newborns are often described as being a bit hard of hearing (Trehub & Schellenberg, 1995), and despite showing marked improvements over the first year, adult-like auditory abilities are not

concept review | 5.3 — Ten interesting findings about infants' perception of faces

Newborns (to 1 month)	Prefer face-like more than non-face-like stimulus
	Prefer familiar faces, like their mothers' faces
	Prefer attractive faces more than less-attractive faces
	Prefer faces with eyes open and gazing at them
1-month-olds	*Externality effect*: Explore the contours of faces more than the inside of faces
2-month-olds	Explore the inside features of the face (for example, mouth, nose)
3-month-olds	Process female faces better than male faces
6-month-olds	Process faces from their own race better than those from other races
	Process upright faces better than upside-down or inverted faces
9-month-olds	Process faces from their own species better than other species' faces (for example, monkeys)

Infants around the world are able to discriminate the sounds (phonemes) found in all languages when they are about 6 months old, but they lose this ability by their teen months, when they become increasingly skilled at discriminating the sounds found in their own language.

achieved until about 10 years of age (Johnson et al., 2005; Saffran et al., 2006). At birth, babies require a louder level of sound than do adults in order to hear clearly, about 15 decibels louder than for adults. (A decibel is a measure of sound intensity. For example, a typical conversation is about 60 decibels, a train about 90 decibels, and conversation in a library about 30 decibels.) Newborns are relatively good at identifying where a sound comes from, called *auditory localization*, as shown by turning their heads toward the source of sound. Not surprisingly, their ability to localize sound is initially limited (for example, distinguishing between left versus right or near versus far) but improves substantially by the end of the first year (Johnson et al., 2005; Morrongiello et al., 1994).

As in vision, infants enter the world with some auditory biases. For example, they prefer high-pitched sounds relative to low ones. In fact, they are less sensitive to low-pitched sounds at birth and remain so until about 2 years of age (Saffran et al., 2006; Saffran & Griepentrog, 2001). This auditory profile might explain, at least in part, why babies are more attentive to infant-directed speech, or motherese, spoken with a high pitch (along with exaggerated emphasis and much repetition), than adult-directed speech, which is typically spoken in a lower pitch (Kuhl et al., 1997).

Speech Perception

As we noted in Chapter 3, speech perception actually begins prenatally, as fetuses hear their mothers' voices as well as other sounds produced in the immediate environment. This explains why newborns prefer to listen to the sound of their mother's voice compared to that of another woman and also to listen to the language that was being spoken during their time in the womb (Jusczyk, 1997). Newborns also prefer to listen to language relative to comparably complex nonlanguage sounds, suggesting that human infants begin life with a bias for listening to speech, thus providing an advantage

for acquiring language (Vouloumanos & Werker, 2007).

Beginning early in life, babies are able to tell the difference between phonemes, the individual sounds that make up words. This ability changes over the course of the first year or so but not necessarily in a straightforward way. For example, in a classic study using the habituation/dishabituation paradigm by Peter Eimas and his colleagues (1971), 1-month-old infants listened repeatedly to a single phoneme (for example, "pa") until they decreased the rate at which they sucked on a pacifier. This is a form of habituation. The infants were then presented with a similar phoneme, in this case "ba." If infants recognize this as different from the previous stimulus (that is, "pa"), they should increase their sucking rate (that is, show *dishabituation*). If they cannot tell the difference between "pa" and "ba," they should continue their low rate of sucking. Babies increased their sucking rate when they shifted from "pa" to "ba," indicating that even 1-month-old infants can discriminate between two similar phonemes and seem to classify language sounds much as adults do (see Saffran, Werker, & Werner, 2006 for some more recent examples of young infants' abilities to discriminate phonemes).

Other research has shown that from the first months of life, babies are able to discriminate most, if not all, of the phonemes of all the world's languages—some 600 consonants and 200 vowel sounds (Aslin, Jusczyk, & Pisoni, 1998; Tsao, Lui, & Kuhl, 2004). This fact suggests that infants enter the world prepared to discriminate between the speech sounds of human languages, causing Patricia Kuhl (2007) to describe young infants as "citizens of the world," in that they seem equally ready and able to acquire any of the world's 6,000 languages.

Infants' abilities to tell the difference between the sounds of human languages do not persist, however. Beginning around the middle of their

phonemes Individual sounds that are used to make up words.

BOX 5.1 evolution in action

Let the Music Play, Baby

The young parents had planned to fill the nursery with classical music for their new son, but a premature birth and a month in the neonatal intensive care unit postponed this. When they finally brought their baby home, they found that the only thing that would soothe him when he became restless was country music, just like the kind they played every night while he was in the hospital.

Babies seem no different from adults in that they enjoy music, and, if you can believe this tale told by two classical music fans, they appear to develop a preference for certain types of music early. Music has always been a bit of a puzzle to evolutionists. Charles Darwin (1871) himself pondered humans' musical skills: "As neither the enjoyment nor the capacity of producing musical notes are faculties of the least use to man in reference to his daily habits of life, they must be ranked among the most mysterious with which he is endowed" (p. 878). Like language, music is universal and also rule-based. But what's it for? Some have hypothesized that it served to help ancestral men impress women (Miller, 2000), others that it served to coordinate the movements and emotions of large groups of people (McNeill, 1995), and still others that it is only a by-product of humans' perceptual systems—simply "auditory cheesecake"—coincidently pleasant to listen to but of no adaptive

purpose (Pinker, 1997). Despite the debates concerning the natural-selective history of music, one fascinating thing about it is that infants have some extraordinary musical talents, suggesting to many that, like language, human infants are predisposed to be musical.

Infants display some surprising adult-like musical abilities (see Trehub, 2003 for a review). For instance, infants respond to changes in rhythmic pattern, melody, and redundancy much the same way adults do and seem to be able to distinguish "good" from "bad" melodies (see Trehub, Trainor, & Unyk, 1993; Schellenberg & Trehub, 1999). "Good" melodies are those that are *consonant*—for adults this means two or more sound frequencies played together to produce a pleasing sound; in contrast, "bad" melodies are dissonant and produce unpleasing sounds. Several studies have shown that, like adults, infants prefer consonant versus dissonant melodies. For example, in one study, 4-month-old infants heard either consonant or dissonant melodies coming out of speakers decorated with visual patterns (Zentner & Kagan, 1996). Infants looked longer at the speakers playing the consonant melodies and showed less motor activity when they heard the consonant versus the dissonant melodies (see similar results by Trainor & Heinmiller, 1998 with 6-month-olds).

In other research, 4.5- and 6-month-old infants listened to segments of Mozart minuets (Krumhansl & Jusczyk, 1990). Some of the segments had pauses inserted at the end of each musical phrase (natural), whereas others had pauses inserted in the middle of phrases (unnatural). The infants could determine which music they heard—natural or unnatural—by turning their heads in the direction of the speaker. Infants of both ages showed a clear preference for listening to the natural segments, with 92% of the 6-month-olds and 83% of the 4.5-month-olds turning more to the speaker playing the natural rather than the unnatural patterns. Although these infants had surely heard music in their homes, given their tender age, their experience with music was limited. Despite this, the findings of these studies suggest that music appreciation might not require a college class but is a basic characteristic of the human nervous system.

Like speech perception, infants seem able to appreciate music from a variety of cultural traditions early in life and lose this ability as they age and become specialized in the music of their culture. For example, in one study (Lynch et al., 1990), 6.5-month-old infants and adults heard a series of notes based on Western scales and Javanese pelog scales, the latter being an example of a nonharmonic musical scale. (To listen to some pelog music,

---

first year of life, infants begin to specialize, as they are exposed to the sounds of the language (or languages) being spoken around them. For example, 6- to 8-month-old babies from English-speaking homes were able to discriminate the sounds found in English but not those found in Spanish; the opposite pattern was found for babies from Spanish-speaking homes (Eilers, Gavin, & Wilson, 1979; see also Kuhl et al., 2006; Saffran et al. 2006). At the same time that infants are losing their abilities to discriminate among foreign phonemes, they are able to make increasingly fine discriminations between the phonemes in their mother tongue (Kuhl et al., 2006).

Why do children lose the ability to discriminate among foreign phonemes? One reason could be that it is not adaptive to maintain a full range of

speech flexibility once children learn their mother tongue. Maintaining neural flexibility to discriminate a large variety of phonemes requires the commitment of neurons that could be used for other important functions in life. Although it makes it more difficult for us to learn new languages later in life, our ancestors probably had little need for learning a second language once the first one was acquired. Infants who are exposed to more than one language are an interesting exception to this general trend. For example, bilingual children show the ability to discriminate among a wider range of phonemes than monolingual children (see Bosch & Sebastián-Gallés, 2001; MacWhinney, 2005).

Infants also show a somewhat surprising ability to make sense of music early in life, and their talents for music appreciation are examined in Box 5.1.

Mothers use music to soothe and regulate their babies' behavior and mood, which may be the original function of music for our ancestors.

go to YouTube, Javanese Gamelan: Lancaran Ora Jamu (pelog nem), http://www.youtube.com/watch?v=YfolcuvNOLO.) Infants and adults heard both well-tuned (consonant to the Western or Javanese ear) or out-of-tune (dissonant to the Western or Javanese ear) patterns of both types of music and were asked to distinguish between the two. For infants, this involved an operant-conditioning paradigm, in which they were rewarded for turning their heads to the out-of-tune series. In contrast, adults simply raised their hands for an out-of-tune series. The adults, who came from a Western culture, were better able to discriminate the in-tune versus out-of-tune segments for the Western than for the Javanese music. The infants, however, distinguished between the in-tune versus out-of-tune series equally well for both the Western and Javanese patterns, "suggesting that infants may be born with an equipotentiality for the perception of scales from a variety of cultures" (Lynch et al., 1990, p. 275). That is, just as children are capable of and biologically prepared to acquire any human language, they seem also to be prepared to acquire any system of music. By 4 months of age, infants display a preference for the music of their own culture relative to that of another culture (Soley & Hannon, 2010).

As mentioned previously, one hypothesis about the evolutionary origins of music concerns its social function. This may stem from humans' ability to synchronize body movements to an external beat, which permits dancing and music-making. The social origin of music is supported in a study that found that 2.5-year-old children were better able to synchronize their body movements to a beat in a social situation (a person drumming to create the beat) versus a nonsocial situation (the drumming was done by a machine) (Kirschner & Tomasello, 2009).

However, the social origins of music are found even earlier. Mothers around the world sing to their babies, and babies prefer the types of songs mothers sing to their infants—lullabies, sung in an expressive and highly ritualized manner—rather than non-maternal versions of the same songs (see Masataka, 1999; Trainor, 1996). Like infant-directed speech, or "motherese," the sing-songy, highly expressive speech mothers around the world use to talk to their babies (see Chapter 9), lullabies serve to regulate infants' attention and emotion (see Trehub, 2003). Although infants are highly attentive to infant-directed speech, they are even more attentive to maternal singing (Trehub & Nakata, 2001, 2002).

We may never know the origins of music. The ability to process music is based in part on the structure of our perceptual systems that we share with other primates (see Hauser & McDermott, 2003; Masataka, 2007), and thus not totally unique to *Homo sapiens*. However, no other primate produces music like humans do, and once music caught hold in human groups, it became socially important. Through song and dance, music served as a way to organize and coordinate group members, and possibly as a technique to woo a mate. But regardless of what it was (and is) used for in adulthood, its origins lie in infancy. Babies are prepared to make sense of music, and music may have had its beginnings as a way for mothers to control and soothe their infants.

Intermodal Perception

To this point we have been writing as if infants use one sense at a time, but this is not the case. Rather, the environment for infants and adults is "intrinsically multimodal" (Bahrick, Lickliter, & Flom, 2004). That is, most of the objects and events we experience in the world are perceived simultaneously through different senses, or modes. For example, a dog can be identified by sight, by listening to its bark, by touching its skin, and even by its smell. Depending on the context, we may experience any number of these sensations (for example, when playing Frisbee with your pet in the park). The same is true for inanimate objects, like a basketball, or events, such as attending a rock concert. Real-world stimuli from different sensory modalities present systematically overlapping information that infants must be able to associate and interconnect. The ability to associate and interconnect information provided by different senses about a certain experience (like a dog or a basketball) is called **intermodal perception**.

As with unimodal (one-sense) perception, infants seem well prepared to attend, process, and *integrate* multimodal (multiple-senses) information. For example, Andrew Meltzoff and Richard Borton (1979) reported that infants younger than 1 month old were able to integrate visual and tactile information. Babies were given one of two

intermodal perception The ability to associate and interconnect information provided by different senses about a certain experience.

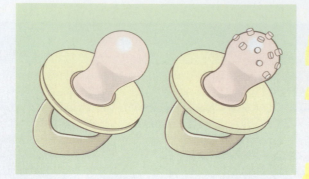

different shaped pacifiers to suck on, but not to see. One pacifier was smooth and the other had knobs on it (see Figure 5.9) After this period of "tactile familiarization," the pacifiers were removed from their mouths and they were shown both pacifiers. Babies looked longer at the pacifier they had held in their mouths, suggesting that they recognized it as familiar, even though they had never seen it before. They must have been able to integrate the earlier tactile experience with the subsequent visual experience. Other research confirmed these results (Gibson & Walker, 1984; but see Maurer, Stager, & Mondloch, 1999 for a failure to replicate), and similar results have been found in 4- to 6-month-old babies (Rose, Gottfried & Bridger, 1981; Streri & Spelke, 1989).

The most studied form of intermodal integration is between vision and audition. Like visual-tactile integration, rudiments of audiovisual integration are seen at birth. For example, newborns can move their heads and eyes in the direction of a sound, and some early research reported that the presence of sound increases neonates' visual attention (Mendelson & Haith, 1966). Audiovisual integration seems well established by the middle of the first year of life. For example, 6- to 9-month-old infants are able to associate images of someone hitting a drum two or three times with their corresponding sound (that is, two or three drum beats, Starkey, Spelke, & Gelman, 1990).

The area where infants seem to exhibit the most impressive audiovisual intermodal competence is visual identification of speech (that is, the association of sound patterns to the face patterns and movements that produce them). For instance, 4- to 5-month-old infants can associate lip movements congruent with the speech they are hearing (Spelke & Cortelyou, 1981) or with the utterance of specific phonemes, like "i" and "a" (Kuhl & Meltzoff, 1982). They are also able to associate a certain intonation pattern of sounds with their corresponding emotional facial expressions (Walker-Andrews, 1997).

This precocious ability to interconnect visual and auditory information becomes more specific with experience. For example, infants can reliably associate female voices to specific female faces when they are about 9 months old, but they do not make matches reliably for male voices and faces until they are about 18 months old, and even at that later age they continue to match female voices to faces better than those of males (Poulin-Dubois et al., 1994, 1998). This superiority of matching the voices and faces of females is likely a result of babies having more experience interacting with women than with men (Ramsey-Rennels & Langlois, 2006).

As noted earlier when discussing auditory perception, infants initially are able to tell the difference between a wide range of language sounds but lose this ability as they become more proficient in discriminating the sounds of their own language (Kuhl et al., 2006). Something similar seems to be happening for intermodal perception. For example, infants as young as 2 months of age will look longer at a human face that corresponds to a sound (for instance, seeing a face saying "ah" and hearing the sound "ah") than at a face that does not correspond to a sound (for example, a face saying "ah" and the sound "ee"), and this ability improves with age (Kuhl & Meltzoff, 1982; Patterson & Werker, 2003).

How general is this ability, and do children always get better at it with age? In one study, 4-, 6-, 8-, and 10-month-old infants watched the face of a monkey as it made one of two sounds, a coo or a grunt (see Photo; Lewkowicz & Ghazanfar, 2006). Sometimes the infants heard a sound that corresponded with the face (for example, the coo face with the coo sound), and other times the sound and face mismatched (for example, the coo face with the grunt sound). Four- and 6-month-old infants looked significantly longer at the faces that matched the sounds, but the 8- and 10-month-old infants did not. A subsequent study found that even newborns looked significantly longer at the faces that matched the sounds (Lewkowicz, Leo, & Simion, 2010). Much like unimodal perception of language sounds, intermodal perception also shows a loss, or narrowing, of ability with age and experience. What begins as a general ability to match sounds and faces becomes specialized to the types of faces (humans) and sounds (native language) one hears (for similar results, see Pons et al., 2009; Weikum et al., 2007).

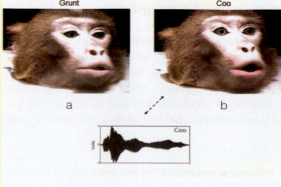

Vision	*1–2 months*: Infants pass from exploring the borders of a face to exploring internal features of face (for example, eyes, nose, mouth).
	3–9 months: Face perception becomes progressively specialized in terms of gender, race, and species, depending on how frequently infants are exposed to some types of faces (for example, male versus female faces).
	6–8 months: Infants' visual system works just about like that of adults.
Audition	Newborns prefer to listen to language relative to comparably complex nonlanguage sounds.
	During the first months, infants can distinguish among phonemes of all human languages; however, beginning at 6 to 8 months, infants begin to specialize, as they are exposed to the sounds of the language (or languages) being spoken around them.
	Infants show a similar pattern for their ability to differentiate well-formed versus poorly formed music from different cultures.
Intermodal perception	Rudiments of visual-tactile integration and audiovisual integration are seen at birth.
	Audiovisual integration seems well established by the middle of the first year of life and becomes more refined with experience (for instance, infants can associate female voices to female faces when they are about 9 months, but they are not able to make this association for male voices until much later).

We have learned a lot about infant perception in the last 40 years (see Concept Review 5.4). However, as Marshall Haith (1993) pointed out some time ago, we should not become too complacent with existing knowledge or attribute too much in terms of intellectual abilities to infants based on sucking rate or looking time (see also Hood, 2004; Keen, 2003). For example, we should avoid the tendency to view an infant's perceptual skills as fully developed the first time we witness them. Like most aspects of development, perceptual development is highly sensitive to context, and an infant's response can be highly variable from one time or situation to the next. Haith argued that we should focus more on how and under which conditions perceptual development takes place, as well as its impact on infants' everyday lives, rather than on when exactly a certain skill emerges.

How Can We Know What Babies Know and Think?

As mentioned earlier in this chapter, the distinction between perception and cognition in infancy is often a difficult and arbitrary one. Most—some would say all—of an infant's cognition is implicit, that is without conscious awareness, at least to the point they cannot tell us in words what they know. In any case, cognition is what problem solving is all about, and becoming a problem solver starts in infancy. We will examine aspects of infant cognition in other chapters of this book: Piaget's account

of sensorimotor development in Chapter 6, social cognition in Chapter 7, and certain aspects of problem solving in infancy in Chapter 8.

In this section, we begin with a brief description of some procedures that researchers have created to assess infant cognition. We then examine three critical issues of infant cognition: (1) how infants learn there are different *kinds*, or *categories*, of things in the world and how they come to organize their experiences in terms of these kinds (*category representation*); (2) to what extent infants are ready to make some simple inferences regarding some of those kinds of things or categories (*core knowledge*), namely regarding object representation, people (through neonatal imitation), and quantities; and (3) how much and for how long infants are able to remember their actions and experiences.

Measuring Infant Cognition

The Violation-of-Expectation Method

The **violation-of-expectation method** uses infants' looking behavior, much as in the visual preference and habituation/dishabituation procedures, to assess infants' reaction to unexpected events. The logic is simple: If infants see an event that deviates from what they expect—that violates their expectation—they should look longer at that event than at an expected event. Consider a study designed

---

violation-of-expectation method Based on habituation/dishabituation procedures, techniques in which increases in infants' looking time at impossible events are interpreted as reflecting a violation of what they expected to see.

FIGURE 5.10 Sequence of events for the 1 + 1 = 2 (possible) outcome and the 1 + 1 = 1 (impossible) outcome from the experiment by Wynn (1992).

Five-month-old infants looked longer at the impossible than the possible outcome, suggesting that they had some understanding of rudimentary arithmetic.

SOURCE: "Addition and Subtraction by Human Infants," by K. Wynn, 1992, *Nature, 358*, 749–750. Reprinted by permission of Macmillan Publishers Ltd.

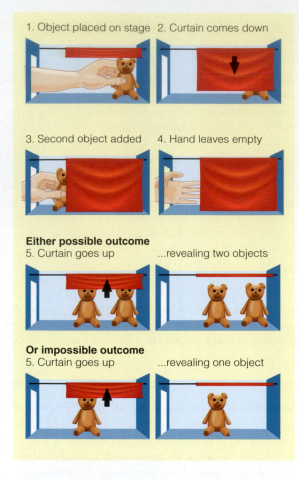

1. Object placed on stage   2. Curtain comes down

3. Second object added   4. Hand leaves empty

Either possible outcome
5. Curtain goes up   ...revealing two objects

Or impossible outcome
5. Curtain goes up   ...revealing one object

In violation-of-expectation experiments, infants look longer at and act surprised when they see an unexpected or impossible event.

to determine whether infants can add and subtract small quantities (Wynn, 1992). Five-month-old babies watched as dolls were placed behind a screen. Two of these sequences are shown in Figure 5.10. In one sequence a doll was placed in a box, a screen came up, and then babies saw a hand place a second doll in the box. Then the screen was raised revealing either two dolls (a "possible outcome") or one (an "impossible outcome"). If babies understood that 1 + 1 = 2, they should expect to see two dolls when the screen is raised. The presence of only one doll should therefore be an unexpected outcome and result in surprise and increased looking time. This was exactly what happened, both for the addition problem shown in Figure 5.10 and for a simple subtraction problem (2 − 1 = 1). As you can see, the violation-of-expectation method does more than simply inform researchers that infants "can tell the difference between two stimuli," and variants of this method have been frequently used to provide insights into the infant mind (see Aslin, 2007; Baillargeon, 2008, and discussion later in this chapter).

Other Methods for Assessing Infant Cognition

How else can infant cognition be measured? Remember that the key is to use some behavior that infants can control to give us some insight into what they know. What else can babies do? Once infants are about 5 or 6 months old, they can reach for objects they want, but this is not a reliable measure for younger infants. Three simple behaviors that even young infants have some control over are sucking, turning their heads, and kicking. Couple this with infants' ability to learn via operant conditioning, and the clever researcher can design experiments to test some basic cognitive abilities in babies.

We described a famous study that used sucking and conditioning to investigate auditory learning in fetuses in Chapter 3 (DeCasper & Spence, 1986). As you may recall, pregnant women read one of two stories to their unborn babies the last 6 weeks before birth. At birth, the babies were fitted with headphones and given a pacifier; the researchers then played one of the stories, either the one the newborns had heard in the weeks immediately before their birth or a novel one. Infants could control what they heard, however, by changing the rate at which they sucked on the pacifier, some by increasing their rate and others by decreasing it. The newborns altered their sucking rate to hear the stories their mothers had read to them, even if another woman read the story. This indicates prenatal auditory learning (infants preferred to hear the stories their mothers had read) using a simple behavior (sucking) that infants could control.

Head turning is another simple behavior that researchers can use to assess infant cognition and learning. For instance, the Czech psychologist Hanus Papousek (1977) conditioned infants to turn their heads to a buzzer or a bell. Milk was delivered through a nipple when they made the right response (for example, turning left when they heard the buzzer, turning right when they heard the bell). Some infants began the task at birth and others when they were 31 or 44 days old. Using this simple technique, Papousek discovered, somewhat surprisingly, that the earlier infants started training, the longer it took them to master the task. Figure 5.11 shows the average age in days when infants reached criterion on this task as a function of how old they were when they started. As you can see, newborns were 128 days before they reached criterion, nearly twice as old as infants who had started a month or more later. This somewhat unexpected finding, using a simple head-turning response, reflects that fact that earlier is not always better, and in the words of Papousek (1977), "beginning too early with difficult learning tasks, at a time when the organism is not able to master them, results in prolongation of the learning process."

Another behavior infants can control is kicking. Caroline Rovee-Collier developed the **conjugate reinforcement procedure**, which takes advantage of the fact that infants beginning around 3 or 4 months of age will associate some

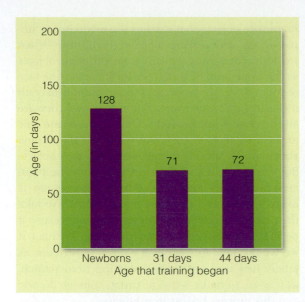

FIGURE 5.11 **Average age at which infants reached the criterion on the conditioning task as a function of when training was begun.**
As you can see, perhaps somewhat counterintuitively, the earlier training began, the older infants were before they mastered the task. SOURCE: Adapted from Papousek, H. (1977). The development of learning ability in infancy (Entwicklung der Lernfähigkeit im Säuglingsalter). In G. Nissen (Ed.), *Intelligence, learning, and learning disabilities (Intelligenz, Lernen und Lernstörungen)*. Berlin: Springer-Verlag.

An infant connected to a mobile in an experiment using the conjugate reinforcement procedure to assess memory.

of their actions to some environmental outcome (Rovee-Collier, 1999). In this procedure, which can be used with infants as young as 2 to 3 months old, researchers tie a ribbon to an infant's ankle that is connected to a mobile suspended over a crib (see Photo). It does not take long for infants to learn that the mobile moves when they kick their feet, and they soon make repeated kicks, controlling the movement of the mobile overhead. In a typical experiment, the ribbon is not connected to the mobile for the first 3 minutes, providing a baseline for kicking rate (that is, how much do infants kick when nothing happens?). For the next 9 minutes, the ribbon is tied to the mobile, and infants learn to kick to make the mobile move. Sometime later, perhaps several hours or several days, infants are returned to the crib, but the ribbon around their ankle is no longer tied to the mobile. Will the babies resume kicking, reflecting that they remember the connection between being in the crib, their actions, and the movement of the mobile (even though the mobile is not moving when they kick now), or will their kicking rate return to baseline, indicating that they have forgotten that kicking produced an interesting outcome? Rovee-Collier and her colleagues have made great use of this procedure to assess the development of memory across infancy, and this work is discussed later in the section on infant memory development.

Another clever technique for assessing infant memory takes advantage of their ability to copy the actions of others. If infants or toddlers observe someone engage in some behavior and copy that behavior, not immediately but some significant time later, it indicates that they remembered the actions over the delay interval. This is **deferred imitation**. In deferred imitation, infants watch as a model performs some novel action (for example, pressing his head against a panel to make a light turn on). Sometime later, infants are given the materials and have the opportunity to replicate the actions they had witnessed earlier. If they perform the novel behavior at rates greater than during a baseline procedure or than that of a group of infants who had not seen the novel behavior, it is an indication of memory. Although deferred imitation has been used with infants under 1 year of age, most studies of deferred imitation have been done with preverbal toddlers (see Bauer, 2007; Meltzoff, 1995).

Once psychologists figured out how to use the behaviors that babies could control, they developed a series of simple techniques for inferring what

conjugate reinforcement procedure Conditioning procedures used in memory research with infants, in which children's behaviors, for example, kicking, control aspects of a visual display.

deferred imitation Imitation of a modeled act some time after viewing the behavior. Deferred imitation is a reflection of memory.

infants know and how they think. In fact, the field of infant cognition has been one of the great success stories of developmental psychology. In a very short time, infants went from being viewed as mindless creatures to little people whose cognitive abilities were far more advanced than we had ever imagined. As early as 1973, a group of researchers put together a volume of scientific papers titled *The Competent Infant* (Stone, Smith, & Murphy, 1973) that described infants not as the mindless beings we had long thought them to be, but as intellectually and socially "competent." Since that time methodologies have improved, theories have changed, and we have acquired an ever-expanding warehouse of knowledge about infant cognitive abilities.

We must keep in mind, however, not to get too carried away with what these simple techniques tell us about what babies know. Does the 5-month-old who looks longer when one versus two dolls appear from behind a screen have the same understanding of addition that a 4-year-old does who notices that one of the cookies she had put aside on the counter is gone? Do simple experiments using looking time or head turning tell us how babies apply their abilities to the real world? Maybe not (Haith, 1993; Hood, 2004). Nonetheless, the infant mind is no longer off-limits to scientists, and although we may never be certain what babies are thinking, these research technologies are allowing us to make some educated guesses about what is going on in their heads.

Category Representation in Infancy

As the research we have reviewed to this point makes clear, infants are able to make sense of their world from an early age. They are prepared by natural selection to process some information more readily than others and to acquire some abilities more easily than others. Essentially, infants are discovering, or creating, meaning from the sensations and experiences that surround them. One important way in which meaning is acquired is through the process of **categorization**. Infants learn there are different *kinds* of things in the world, and they come to organize their experiences in terms of these kinds, or categories. For example, infants must be able to distinguish animate from inanimate objects, people from other living beings, edible from inedible objects, and among the host of

inanimate objects that exist in the world (for example, shoes, cars, eating utensils, furniture). When we form categories we can treat different objects as the same kind of thing. So, for instance, the face of Mom, Dad, big sister, and the babysitter may all differ in significant ways, but at one level they are all the same—human faces. Once children are able to form categories, they can use what they know about similar objects to make sense of new objects (for example, another face is likely someone I can become socially engaged with; another spoon is likely something I can feed myself with). We take the process of categorization for granted because it permeates all aspects of our thinking. Without it we would have to treat every novel experience as totally new and unfamiliar, starting from scratch, as it were, to make sense of things. But we do not, and this process begins in infancy.

How can we know the categories that infants form? Variants of the same procedures used to assess other aspects of infant perception and cognition can be used to determine whether infants form categories, particularly the habituation/dishabituation paradigm. For example, in one study, 3- and 4-month-old infants saw a series of pictures of either horses or cats (Eimas & Quinn, 1994). Once they became habituated to one category of items (that is, reduced their looking time to horses, for example, relative to what it had been on early trials), they were shown pairs of new pictures: another horse that they had not seen before (new item, old category) and one from a different but related category, a zebra, for example (new item, new category). If infants now spend more time looking at the zebra than the horse, neither of which they had seen before, it would mean that they realize that is it different from the horse—a member of a different category. This is indeed what they did, showing that they had formed a category of horse, and they recognized that the similar-looking zebra was not a horse but something distinct. This research indicates that young infants are able to form distinct perceptual categories of natural objects (here, animals) based on relatively brief exposure to them.

Infants seemingly construct their categories in a similar way as adults and children do, by forming **category prototypes** (see, for example, Mervis & Rosch, 1981; Rosch, 1975). A category prototype is an abstract representation that reflects the best example of that category. For example, a dog is a prototypical example of mammals, particularly if compared with, for instance, a platypus or a whale. By comparing a horse or a cat to a dog, for instance, infants might infer that cats and horses are mammals, too (but quite probably not a platypus or a whale, at least initially, which are atypical examples of the category mammal).

categorization The process of treating different objects as members of the same category.

category prototype The central tendency, "best example," of a cognitive category.

Infants seem to form categories based on typicality. For instance, if habituated to examples of category-typical birds (for example, blue jay, robin, and sparrow), they will later dishabituate (increase looking time) to a picture of a nonbird, demonstrating that they formed a bird category. However, they will not dishabituate to a picture of a nonbird if they were initially habituated to photos of category-atypical birds (for example, ostrich, chicken, and turkey).

Several studies, using both natural (for example, birds) and artificial (for example, patterns of dots) stimuli have documented category-prototype formation in infants. For example, in one study, 9-month-old infants were able to generate a category for the concept bird if they were habituated to a series of prototypical, or good, examples of birds (for instance, robin, sparrow, and blue jay), but not if they were habituated to atypical category examples (for instance, ostrich, chicken, and turkey) (Roberts & Horowitz, 1986; see Photos). Similarly, infants seem to develop a prototype for female faces before male faces (Rubenstein et al., 1999; Ramsey et al., 2005) as a by-product of their wider experience with women beginning early in life. As you may recall, infants generally prefer to look at female faces more than male faces and are better able to distinguish among female than male faces (Quinn et al., 2002).

Infants' categories get more complicated as the distinctions they need to make become more difficult. For example, infants begin to distinguish between animate and inanimate objects around 6 months of age, using movement as a principal cue, but it will be another several years before they have an adult classification of the animate-inanimate distinction, based on physical and psychological causality (that is, animate beings cause things to happen, whereas inanimate objects do not) (Cohen & Cashon, 2006; Rakison & Poulin-Dubois, 2001).

And as you will learn in Chapter 11 on emotions, 10-month-old babies seem to form categories of potentially dangerous animals (spiders and snakes) versus animals that would have been less likely to harm our ancestors (rabbits and frogs) (Rakison, 2005a, 2005b), even though they do not necessarily fear them.

We do not mean to claim that the categories infants form or how they form them are identical to those of adults. Nonetheless, the process of categorization, which is so central to everyday psychological functioning, is seen early in infancy and develops with time and experience. We know that infants within their first year of life form categories based on perceptual similarity, that the categories they form are based on their experiences (for instance, babies develop categories of female faces before male faces), and, like adults, they form categories based on category typicality. Overall, it seems that the basic process of forming categories of objects is essentially the same in infants as it is in adults.

Core Knowledge

We have learned over the past 20 years or so that infants know much more about objects, people, and the physical world in general than we once thought. How do scientists make sense of this new

table 5.3 Four Core-knowledge Systems

According to the core-knowledge systems perspective, human infants are endowed with at least four core-knowledge systems, three that develop during infancy, to represent and make inferences about relevant aspects of their surrounding environment. Core-knowledge system 4, geometry of the environment, does not develop until childhood and is not discussed in this chapter.

Core knowledge system 1: Inanimate objects and their mechanical interactions	1. *Cohesion* (objects have boundaries and their components are connected to each other) 2. *Continuity* (objects move along unobstructed paths and cannot be in the same place) 3. *Contact* (one object must contact another to make it move) 4. *Number limitation* (infants cannot represent more than about three objects at a time)
Core knowledge system 2: Persons and their actions	1. *Goal-directness* (intentional human actions are directed to goals) 2. *Efficiency* (goals are achieved through the use of effective means) 3. *Contingency* (means are not applied rigidly but adjusted to the conditions found) 4. *Reciprocity* (such as turn-taking in conversation) 5. *Gaze direction* (the direction of a gaze is used to interpret social and nonsocial actions)
Core knowledge system 3: Numbers representation	1. *Abstractness* (number representations are abstract: they apply to different entities or things, from different sensory modalities; for example, sets of objects, or set of sounds) 2. *Comparability and combinability* (number representations are comparable and can be combined by addition and subtraction operations)
Core knowledge system 4: Geometry of the environment (not realized until after infancy)	Infants are sensitive to geometric information from the spatial layout, basically: distances, angles, and sense relations among surfaces.

SOURCE: Adapted from information in Spelke, E. S., & Kinzler, K. D. (2007). Core knowledge. *Developmental Science, 10*, 89–96.

evidence of precocious abilities in young infants? Elizabeth Spelke and her colleagues (Spelke, 1991, 2000; Spelke & Kinzler, 2007), among others (for example, Baillargeon, 2008), argue that babies possess **core knowledge** about several different domains from birth. Basically, the core-knowledge perspective suggests that humans are born with a small set of distinct systems of knowledge that have been shaped by natural selection over evolutionary time and upon which new and flexible skills and belief systems (such as reading, navigating by maps, mathematic skills, reasoning about other peoples' thoughts) are later built.

Spelke and her colleagues argue that there is strong evidence for the existence of at least three core-knowledge systems in infancy (see Table 5.3). The first and most investigated system deals with infants' knowledge of inanimate objects and their mechanical interactions, or *object representation*. The second system concerns knowledge of people and their actions. Infants see people, and animate beings in general, as behaving intentionally, and they are biased to understand some basic notions about social interaction. We saw some evidence for this system when looking at the development of face perception, and we will examine infants' emerging social cognition in greater detail in Chapter 7. We will also see that one interpretation of newborns' ability to mimic the facial expressions of an adult model, to be discussed later in this chapter, is consistent with this second core-knowledge system. A third system concerns infants' abilities to represent numbers, or quantities. We discussed a pioneering study of infants' simple arithmetic ability earlier (Wynn, 1992), and we will examine these abilities in more detail later in this chapter.

Core-knowledge theorists share much with the thinking of David Geary (2005a, 2007a), who assumes that infants are born with a small set of *skeletal competencies* specialized to process information relating to the physical world (intuitive physics), the biological world (intuitive biology), and people (intuitive psychology). These skeletal abilities become fleshed out with time and experience, enabling children to deal efficiently with a wide range of objects, events, and relationships as they develop. Infants thus enter the world prepared to learn and understand some things better than others, but such biases are modified, in a species-typical way, as a result of experience.

The core-knowledge perspective has served as a useful approach for understanding infant cognition. It was fostered by findings from researchers using the violation-of-expectation methodology, revealing that infants seemed to know far more than we had previously thought. In two of the following three sections, we examine research on aspects of infant cognition that have made great use of the violation-of-expectation method—object representation and infants' understanding of quantitative relations. Between these two sections we examine a third topic that, when it was discovered, also made obvious that there was much more to infant cognition than we had once believed—neonatal imitation.

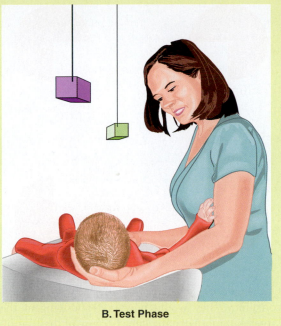

A. Habituation Phase　　　　　**B. Test Phase**

FIGURE 5.12 Size constancy experiment. After becoming used to looking at a small cube at different distances (habituation to changes in retinal image), infants are presented a second larger but more distant cube (same retinal image for both cubes). If infants pay more attention to the larger than the smaller cube, researchers conclude that the infants are distinguishing the cubes on the basis of their actual, not retinal, size. That is, they are demonstrating size constancy. SOURCE: Adapted from Slater, A. M., Mattock, A., Brown, E., & Bremner, G. J. (1991). Form perception at birth: Cohen and Younger (1984) revisited. *Journal of Experimental Child Psychology*, *51*, 395–406. Reprinted by permission of Elsevier.

Object Representation

Infants have to recognize at least three features related to objects: object constancy, object continuity and cohesion, and object permanence. To understand what these mean, think of a restaurant table arranged for lunch. One thing we all understand implicitly is, first, the soup bowl does not change size or shape regardless of the position it is placed upon the table or the angle at which you view it. This reflects object constancy. Second, we see the horizontal surface of the table and the table legs as a part of the same object, but we do not perceive the soup bowl as part of the table, or the knife as a part of the bowl or the table. This reflects object continuity and cohesion. We also do not think that the knife ceases to exist when we place our napkin over it. That is, we think that objects continue to exist whether we are currently perceiving them or not. This reflects object permanence. We discuss the development of each of these aspects of object representation in this section.

Object constancy. Object constancy refers to the knowledge that an object remains the same despite changes in how it is viewed. This seems to be an early-developing ability in infants. For example, in one experiment, newborns saw a small cube placed at different distances from their eyes (Slater, Mattock, & Brown, 1990). After habituating to the cube (that is, once their looking time to the cube declined to about half of what it had been originally), babies were shown this same small cube and a larger cube, but at a distance so that the image of the larger cube was the same as the small cube (see Figure 5.12).

© W. Hanenberg/Corbis

We see the objects in this photo as remaining the same in size and shape despite viewing them from different angles (object constancy), and realize that each object in the photo is distinct from one another (object continuity and cohesion). Infants seem to develop similar knowledge over the first 6 months of life.

core knowledge Expression used by some infant researchers to refer to the set of knowledge that young infants possess in certain domains, including objects, people and social relations, numbers and quantities, and geometry.

object constancy The knowledge that an object remains the same despite changes in how it is viewed (for example, from a different perspective, or distance).

object permanence The knowledge that objects have an existence in time and space independent of one's own perception or action on those objects.

object continuity and cohesion The knowledge that objects are cohesive entities and move continuously through space.

FIGURE 5.13 Subjective (illusory) contour.

What do you see here at first glance? If you're like most people, you see a square, although actually this is only an illusory square. Infants also see a square sometime between 7 and 8 months of age. SOURCE: Bertenthal, B. I., Campos, J. J., & Haith, M. M. (1980). Development of visual organization: The perception of subjective contours. *Child Development*, 51, 1072–1080. Reprinted by permission of John Wiley & Sons, Inc.

One would expect that, if newborns possess object constancy, they would now prefer looking at the larger, but more distant, cube because of their familiarity with looking at the small cube. This would indicate that they realize that the two cubes are actually different sizes, although the images projected onto their retinas are the same. If newborns do not possess object constancy, they should look at the two cubes equally often, because they produce identical images on the back of the babies' eyes. The researchers reported that newborns looked longer at the large cube, indicating that infants possess the rudiments of object constancy shortly after birth.

Object cohesion and continuity. As adults we understand that objects have boundaries. This is sometimes referred to as the *principle of cohesion*. The soup bowl, knife, and napkin that are lying on the table are separate entities, distinct from one another and from the table on which they lie. We use an object's contour to differentiate, or segregate it, from other objects in the same perceptual field. This is not something that is necessarily obvious to young infants, but it develops over the course of the first 6 months of life.

One source of evidence that infants perceive boundaries comes from research on *subjective*, or *illusory, contours*. Figure 5.13 presents an example of

an illusory contour. If you are like most people, you see a square, even though a square does not exist. It is an illusion, produced by the perceptual system filling in the missing details, resulting in the impression of a square. It is not until between 4 and 7 to 8 months that infants also see a square in this image, as reflected by their patterns of looking time (Bertenthal, Campos, & Haith, 1980; Ghim, 1990).

We also see objects as being unified, or possessing what the Gestalt psychologists called *continuation*, or the *principle of continuity*. This is illustrated in research using the violation-of-expectation paradigm. For instance, Renée Baillargeon and her colleagues (see Baillargeon 2004, 2008) have conducted experiments assessing the concepts of *occlusion* (events in which an object goes behind—that is, is occluded by—another object, while moving), *containment* (events in which an object is put into a container), *covering* (events in which an object is covered by another), *collision* (events in which an object hits another), and *support* (events in which an object exhibits different degrees of physical support regarding the surface that is beneath it), each of which provides particularly compelling evidence for the principle of continuity.

For example, in an occlusion experiment, infants as young as 2.5 months of age seem to realize that objects cannot disappear at one point and then magically appear at another. They must travel through space to get from point A to point B. This is revealed in a study in which 2.5-month-old infants watched as a toy mouse disappears behind one screen on the left side of a display and then reappears seconds later from behind another screen on the right side of the display without appearing in the gap between the two screens (Aguiar & Baillargeon, 1999; see Figure 5.14). Infants looked longer at the magically appearing mouse than at the expected events, indicating that they were puzzled about how the mouse could have made the trip from one side of the display to the other without passing through the middle.

In other research reflecting the concept of collision, 2.5-month-old infants increased their looking time when a toy bug on wheels remained stationary after being hit by a cylinder rolling

FIGURE 5.14 An example of an impossible occlusion event.

A toy mouse disappears behind a first screen and appears later on behind a second screen, without appearing in the gap between them. Infants as young as 2.5 months of age seem to realize that objects cannot disappear at one point and then magically appear at another. SOURCE: Adapted from Baillargeon, R. (2004). Infants' physical world. *Current Directions in Psychological Science*, 13 (3), 89–94; p. 90. Reprinted by permission of Sage Publications.

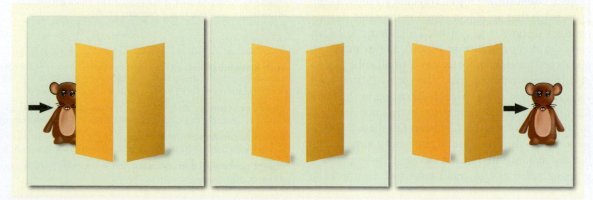

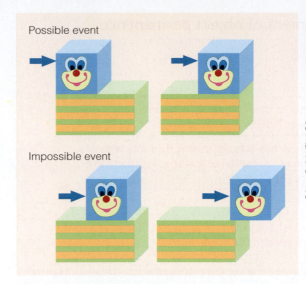

Possible event

Impossible event

FIGURE 5.15 **Example of possible and impossible events for object support.**
Although 3-month-old infants were not surprised by the impossible event, by 4.5 months of age, infants begin to understand that the *amount* of contact between the box and the platform is important. SOURCE: From Baillargeon, R., Kotovsky, L., & Needham, A. (1995). The acquisition of physical knowledge in infancy. In G. Lewis, D. Premack, & D. Sperber (Eds.), *Casual understandings in cognition and culture.* Reprinted by permission of Oxford University Press.

down a ramp, or, conversely, when the bug moved in the absence of contact (Kotovsky & Baillargeon, 1994, 2000; Wang, Kaufman, & Baillargeon, 2003). Based on looking time, young infants behave as if they understand that objects are solid and move only when contacted by some outside force.

Another interesting expectation of infants is that objects require support: An object cannot remain suspended in midair or it will fall, and this, too, develops gradually over infancy. Baillargeon and her colleagues (1995) showed infants possible and impossible events reflecting the principle of support (see Figure 5.15). As you can see in Figure 5.15, a hand would push a box with a clown face painted on it across a platform. In the *possible event* the box stopped situated firmly on the platform. In the *impossible event* the hand continued to push the box, stopping when only 15% of it rested on the platform. Perhaps somewhat surprisingly, 3-month-old infants were not surprised by the impossible event, apparently believing that so long as the box maintained some contact with the platform (or the hand), it should not fall. By 4.5 months of age, infants begin to understand that the *amount* of contact between the box and the platform is important, and by 6.5 months, infants expect that the box will fall unless a significant portion of it is in contact with the platform.

Six-month-old infants will retrieve a partially covered object, and by 8 months they will retrieve a fully hidden object.

Object permanence. Object permanence refers to the belief that objects exist independent of one's perceptions or actions on them. This has been the most investigated aspect of infants' understanding of objects and was brought to light by Piaget (1954) early in the 20th century. Piaget argued that infants much younger than 8 months of age believe that objects exist only when they are acting upon them, including perceptual action (for example, seeing the object). Out of sight (and touch) is literally out of mind. Object permanence is actually related to the old philosophical question, "If a tree falls in the middle of the forest, and no one is there to hear it, will it make any noise?" According to Piaget, for young infants the answer, assuming they could talk, would be "no"; if they are not there to hear the noise, it cannot exist. Moreover, neither the tree nor the forest exists if they do not perceive them!

Piaget's account of the development of object permanence. The classic demonstration of object permanence (or actually the lack thereof) involves playing a hiding game with a 5- or 6-month-old infant. (You can try this one at home.) Most babies of this age love to play "get this" games, in which an adult shows an infant an interesting object (for example, a jingling set of keys) and places it just out of his or her reach, saying, "You get 'em," which most babies will happily do. The adult then takes the keys away from the infant, jiggles them while smiling, and places them just out of reach again. This can continue for some time (most adults will tire of this game before babies will), but one time, as the adult places the keys just out of baby's reach, she covers them with a cloth, all while the infant watches. There the keys sit, bulging beneath the cloth, but the 6-month-old, although possibly staring at the cloth, will not reach for them. It is as if they cease to exist.

Some infants may get distressed, others look puzzled, and still others just look away unperturbed, but few at this age will remove the cloth and retrieve the keys. In two short months, however, this is just what most infants will do, no longer being fooled by the cover-up. Piaget actually noted 5- or 6-month-old infants show a glimmer

Birth–4 months	No evidence of object permanence.
4–8 months	Infants will retrieve a hidden object if it is partially visible to them. They will retrieve a fully hidden object if they were moving toward the object when it was hidden.
8–12 months	Infants will retrieve a hidden object, but they still fail the *A-not-B tasks*, in which infants who retrieved an object repeatedly at one location (A) continue to search for it at that location even though they watched it being hidden in a different place (B).
12–18 months	Infants can now solve the A-not-B task.
18–24 months	Infants can now understand *invisible displacement*, in which they retrieve an object hidden in a container that is then placed, unbeknownst to the child, in a second container.

of object permanence in that they will remove the cloth and grab the keys if they were moving in the direction of the keys when they were hidden. They will also retrieve the keys if they are only partially hidden, something that infants much younger than 4 months will not—or perhaps, cannot—do.

Eight-month-old infants do not have an adult notion of object permanence, however, for Piaget observed that they continue to fail more complicated object-retrieval tasks. For example, it is not until about 12 months that most babies are able to solve the **A-not-B task**. We described this task briefly in Chapter 4, and it is basically an extension of the "get the keys" game. If we play the "get the keys" game with a 9-month-old infant, she will not be fooled and will remove the cloth and retrieve the keys repeatedly. After successfully doing this several times at one location (to the baby's right side, for example), the adult takes the keys and, right before her eyes, places them to her left side and covers them with a second cloth. Piaget observed that infants of this age will reach for the cloth where the keys were originally hidden and where they had successfully retrieved them several times before (the A location), despite seeing them hidden in the new (B) location. According to Piaget, infants knew the object from their previous actions on it (reaching toward location A and uncovering the object), and they trust their prior actions more than their immediate perception. Let us provide a real-life example (from Bjorklund, 2005, p. 90):

> At approximately 10 months, my daughter Heidi was seated in her high chair, having just completed lunch. She was banging her spoon on the tray of the chair when it fell to the floor to her right. She leaned to the right, saw the spoon on the floor, and vocalized to me; I retrieved it for her. She began playing with the spoon again, and it fell to the right a second time. She again leaned to the right, saw the spoon on the floor, and vocalized until I returned it to her. Again, she played with the spoon, and again it fell to the floor, but this time to her left. After hearing the clang of the spoon hitting the floor, Heidi leaned to the right to search for the spoon, and she continued her search for several seconds before looking at me with a puzzled expression. Heidi had been watching the spoon at the time it fell. Thus, when it fell the third time, she had both visual and auditory cues to tell her where it must be. But she searched where she had found the vanished object before. She trusted her past experience with the fallen spoon more than her perceptions.

Object permanence is not fully acquired, Piaget asserted, until about 18 months old, when infants can understand **invisible displacements**, in which an object is hidden in one container and then hidden under another container out of the sight of the observer. Piaget (1954) provided an example in which his 16-month-old daughter, Jacqueline, watched as Papa Piaget placed a potato in a box, placed the box under a rug, turned the box over, depositing the potato under the rug, and then removed the empty box. When Piaget asked his daughter to "Give papa the potato," Jacqueline looked at the box, the bump in the rug, and her papa, but never lifted the rug to retrieve the potato.

Piaget's basic observations of the development of object permanence have been replicated in both large- and small-scale studies, using variants of the procedures he described and almost always with greater experimental control than in the original studies (Kopp, Sigman, & Parmelee, 1974; Uzgiris & Hunt, 1975). However, researchers using some of the new techniques developed to study infant cognition believe that babies possess knowledge of the permanency of objects at earlier ages than Piaget proposed. A summary of Piaget's account of the development of object permanence is presented in Concept Review 5.5.

A-not-B task Object permanence task, in which the infant has to retrieve a hidden object at one location (B), after having retrieved it several times previously from another one (A).

invisible displacements An object permanence task in which an object is hidden first in one container and then under another container out of the sight of the observer. Infants typically pass this task around 18 months.

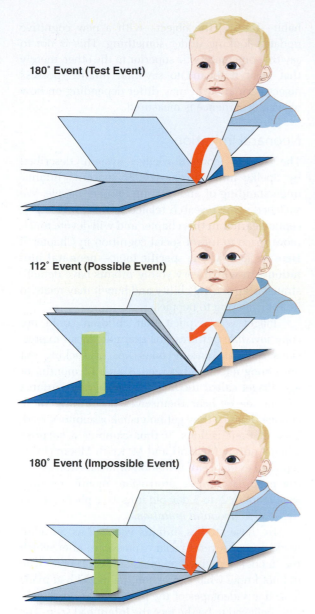

180° Event (Test Event)

112° Event (Possible Event)

180° Event (Impossible Event)

FIGURE 5.16 The design of Baillargeon's (1987) object-permance experiment.

Infants watch as a screen is repeatedly rotated from front to back until they habituate. Some infants then see an impossible event, with the screen rotating through a block the infants saw placed toward the back of the screen. Other infants see a possible event, with the screen stopping at the point it reaches the block. Infants in a control condition see the screen move without the block. SOURCE: From Baillargeon, R. (1987). Object permanence in 3 1/2- and 4 1/2-month-old infants. *Developmental Psychology, 23,* 655–664. Copyright © 1987 by the American Psychological Association. Reprinted by permission.

A new look at object permanence. One of the first studies to call into question Piaget's developmental time table of object permanence was performed by Reneé Baillargeon (1987) using the violation-of-expectation method. In this study, 3.5- and 4.5-month-old infants watched as a moving screen was rotated 180 degrees from a flat-forward to a flat-

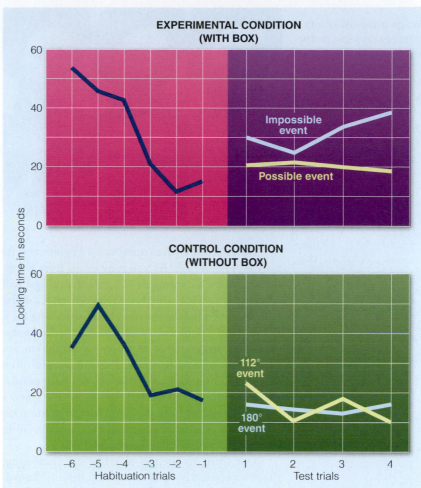

FIGURE 5.17 Looking times of infants in the Experimental and Control conditions during habituation and test trials in Baillargeon's study.

Note the increased looking time for the infants in the experimental condition during the test trials for the impossible event. SOURCE: From Baillargeon, R. (1987). Object permanence in 3 1/2- and 4 1/2-month-old infants. *Developmental Psychology, 23,* 655–664. Copyright © 1987 by the American Psychological Association. Reprinted by permission.

backward position in front of the infants (see Figure 5.16). Once infants habituated to the screen (that is, looked significantly less than they had initially), they saw a wooden block with a clown face painted on it that was placed to the rear of the flat screen. In the *possible condition*, the screen rose upward, occluded the infant's view of the block, and stopped at the point where it made contact with the block. In the *impossible condition*, the screen rose and continued downward until it lay flat. If infants understood that the block was permanent in time and space (and solid), they should have expected the screen to hit the block, making the 180-degree trip impossible. As such, they should look more at the impossible event than the possible event, and also more than children in a control condition who were not shown the block. This, in fact, is what infants did. As you can see in Figure 5.17, infants who saw the impossible event increased their looking time relative to infants who saw the possible event or those in a control condition. Other studies using this (Baillargeon & De Vos, 1991) and similar (Baillargeon, 2004; Newcombe, Huttenlocher, & Learmonth, 1999) methods have produced similar results. This does not necessarily mean that Piaget was wrong, but rather that infants' understanding of the permanence of objects varies with the type of task used to assess it.

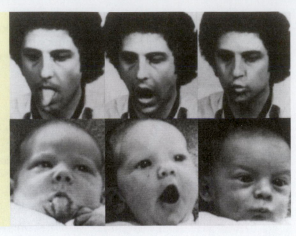

Two- to 3-day-old infants imitating (a) tongue protrusion; (b) mouth opening, and (c) lip protrusion, demonstrated by an adult experimenter. SOURCE: Meltzoff, A. N., & Moore, M. K. (1977). Imitation of facial and manual gestures by human neonates. *Science, 198*, 75–78.

Other research has questioned Piaget's results for the A-not-B task. As you may recall from Chapter 4, infants as young as 7.5 months of age will sometimes reach correctly on the "B" trials if the delay between hiding the object and searching for it is very brief (Diamond, 1985). This has caused some people to propose that memory or inhibition are involved in solving this task. It is not so much that infants fail to understand that objects have permanence in time and space, but they forget the object's location or do not have the neurological maturation to inhibit a previously practiced behavior (reaching to the correct A location; Diamond, 1991).

One thing to keep in mind before concluding that Piaget greatly underestimated infants' knowledge of objects is that infants' and young children's performance is highly dependent on the context in which they are tested, in this case the measure used to assess object permanence. Piaget used more demanding reaching measures, whereas Baillargeon and colleagues used looking time. When a slightly more complicated retrieval task is used (for example, showing a toddler where a toy is hidden in a sandbox and then having the child move to the other end of the box before retrieving it), 21-month-old children perform poorly (Newcombe et al., 1998). We would not want to say that 4-month-old infants possess the notion of object permanence, whereas 21-month-old toddlers do not.

One possibility is that different types of knowledge are tapped by these different tasks: violation-of-expectation tasks rely on implicit (unconscious) knowledge, whereas the various retrieval tasks rely more on explicit knowledge, or knowledge in consciousness (Bremner & Mareschal, 2004; Newcombe, 2002; Karmiloff-Smith, 1992). That is, the violation-of-expectation paradigm taps perceptual knowledge, whereas the reaching task taps self-aware thought, the ability to combine an old habit—finding the object—with a new cognitive update—looking under something. This is not to say that one method is superior to the other, merely that what it means to say that infants "possess object permanence" may differ depending on how object permanence is measured.

Neonatal Imitation

The second core-knowledge system described by Spelke and Kinzler (2007) concerns infants' understanding of and relating to other people. We sketched some research related to this on face perception earlier in this chapter and will devote much more space to infant social cognition in Chapter 7. Here we look at one specific topic—neonatal imitation—in which very young infants have demonstrated a surprising ability and how it may relate to infants' relating to people.

Piaget was explicit that children could not copy *invisible gestures* (for example, facial expressions such as pursing one's lips or sticking out one's tongue) until between 8 and 12 months of age. Piaget called them "invisible" because infants cannot see or hear themselves performing these actions. That is, they get no visual or auditory feedback of their actions. It thus came as a surprise when Andrew Meltzoff and M. Keith Moore (1977) reported evidence of imitation of facial expressions (for example, tongue protrusion, mouth opening, see Photo) in 2- to 3-day-old infants, a phenomenon they called *neonatal imitation*.

In these studies, infants watched as an adult made one of several facial expressions, after which the model remained expressionless. People who did not know what expression the model had made looked at videotapes of the infants and coded what they believed to be the face the infant had seen. The coders observed the same expressions in the infants as those made by the model significantly greater than expected by chance, providing evidence of imitation. Further research demonstrated neonatal imitation in newborns (Field et al., 1982; Vinter, 1986), although this ability usually disappears around 2 months of age (Abravanel & Sigafoos, 1984; Jacobson, 1979). Not everyone who has looked for neonatal imitation has found it, but it seems clear that, under the right conditions, many newborns will mimic the facial expressions of an adult model.

How can one explain this seemingly advanced behavior in newborns and its developmental pattern? It seems unlikely that it could be the result of learning, given that it is seen immediately after birth. Meltzoff and Moore (1977, 1985) proposed that infants were displaying "true imitation," mentally mapping the expression they see with their own facial expression.

An alternative explanation, and one we think is more likely, is that neonatal imitation is not

neonatal imitation The ability of newborns to reproduce some specific behaviors, such as certain facial expressions, that they have seen in others.

related to the later imitation seen in infancy and childhood but has a different function in early infancy. Several functions have been suggested, among them the facilitation of nursing (Jacobson, 1979) and enhancing communication and social interaction between infants—who have little intentional control over their actions (for example, arms, legs, eye gaze)—and their mothers (Bjorklund, 1987a; Byrne, 2005; Legerstee, 1991). These explanations are consistent with the observation that imitation of facial expressions disappears around 2 months of age, when infants are gaining increasing intentional control over their own behavior.

From this perspective, neonatal imitation is an example of an *ontogenetic adaptation*, discussed in Chapter 2, which serves a function at a specific time in development but does not necessarily prepare the child for later life and disappears when it is no longer needed. Consistent with this interpretation, individual differences in neonatal imitation predict the level of social interaction infants have with their mothers 3 months later: The more infants copy facial expressions at birth, the greater sophistication is their social interaction with their mothers at 3 months (Heimann, 1989).

More recently, researchers have reported that humans are not the only animal to display neonatal imitation; it has been observed in several species of nonhuman primates including chimpanzees (Bard, 2007; Myowa-Yamakoshi et al., 2004) and rhesus monkeys (Ferreri et al., 2006). As with human babies, chimpanzee infants show a decline in copying facial expressions around 2 months of age (Myowa-Yamakoshi et al., 2004). These behaviors are also more frequently seen in the context of more natural social communication as opposed to more formal (and unnatural) settings, causing some primate researchers to argue for a communicative and/or affiliative function of neonatal imitation (Bard, 2007; Ferreri et al., 2006), similar to what has been argued for human infants (Bjorklund, 1987a; Byrne, 2005).

Understanding Quantities: Infants Love Numbers

A third proposed core-knowledge system is an understanding of quantities and numbers. David Geary (1995, 2005a) proposed that infants and young children possess skeletal competencies in four abilities related to mathematics: numerosity, ordinality, counting, and simple arithmetic (see Table 5.4).

Numerosity refers to the ability to determine quickly the number of items in a set without counting them. To do this, one does not necessarily have to understand the concept of "three" or "four." Rather, infants display numerosity by consistently being able to differentiate between two arrays with

table 5.4 Potential Skeletal Mathematical Abilities

Numerosity	The ability to accurately determine the quantity of small sets of items or events without counting. In humans, accurate numerosity judgments are typically limited to sets of four or fewer items.
Ordinality	A basic understanding of *more than* and *less than* and, later, an understanding of specific ordinal relationships. For example, understanding that $4 > 3$, $3 > 2$, and $2 > 1$. For humans, the limits of this system are not clear, but it is probably limited to quantities < 5.
Counting	Early in development there appears to be a preverbal counting system that can be used for the enumeration of sets up to three, perhaps four, items. With the advent of language and the learning of number words, there appears to be a pan-cultural understanding that serial-ordered number words can be used for counting, measurement, and simple arithmetic.
Simple arithmetic	Early in development there appears to be sensitivity to increases (addition) and decreases (subtraction) in the quantity of small sets. This system appears to be limited to the addition or subtraction of items within sets of three, perhaps four, items.

SOURCE: From D. C. Geary, (1995). Reflections of evolution and culture in children's cognition: Implications for mathematical development and instruction. *American Psychologist, 50*, 36.

different numbers of items in them. For example, by 6 months of age, infants can tell the difference between arrays containing different numbers of items, so long as the quantities do not exceed three or four (Starkey, Spelke, & Gelman, 1990; van Loosbroek & Smitsman, 1990). Slightly older infants demonstrate knowledge of numerosity using more explicit search measures. For example, in one study, 10- and 12-month-old infants watched as different numbers of crackers were placed inside two boxes (Feigenson, Carey, & Hauser, 2002). The boxes were then separated, and infants could crawl to retrieve the crackers in whichever box they pleased. Infants consistently crawled to the box that contained the larger number of crackers when the boxes contained 1 versus 2 and 2 versus 3 crackers, but responded indiscriminately when the larger quantity was 4 or greater (for example, 3 versus 4; 2 versus 4; and 3 versus 6).

Related to the concept of numerosity is **ordinality**, which refers to a basic understanding that one array has more (or fewer) items in it than does another array. For instance, in one study, 16-month-old infants viewed screens consisting of arrays of dots that varied in number. The infants were then conditioned to point to either the smaller or larger of the arrays (Strauss & Curtis, 1984). For example, an infant might view arrays of three and four dots

numerosity The ability to determine quickly the number of items in a set without counting.

and be reinforced for touching the smaller array. After training, babies saw arrays with different numbers of dots, in the present example, two versus three dots. Which array will they point to? If they had learned merely to point to the absolute number of dots in an array, they should continue to point to the array with three dots in the transfer phase, but if they instead had learned an ordinal relationship (select the array with the smaller number of dots), they should point to the array consisting of two dots. Infants did the latter, suggesting they had learned an ordinal relationship.

We will discuss the development of counting and arithmetic, abilities that develop in early childhood, in Chapter 10. However, some provocative research suggests that the roots of understanding (very) simple arithmetic may lie in infancy. This is best illustrated in the study by Karen Wynn (1992) discussed earlier in this chapter. Using the violation-of-expectation paradigm, 5-month-old babies looked longer at impossible outcomes $(1 + 1 = 1)$ than possible outcomes $(1 + 1 = 2)$. Others have replicated these results (Simon, Hespos, & Rochat, 1995), and although the interpretation of these findings is not without debate (Clearfield & Westfahl, 2006; Moore & Cocas, 2006), this and other research suggests that young infants do develop an early understanding of quantitative relations. Recent research using methods much like those used with human infants have shown that 3- and 4-day-old chicks show similar quantitative abilities (Rugani et al., 2009), suggesting that such basic computation is not unique to humans.

As the research reviewed here indicates, infants are not born with an advanced knowledge of numbers, but they possess some basic abilities that permit them to distinguish between larger and smaller quantities and to recognize simple increases and decreases in those quantities (that is, simple addition and subtraction). Whether those abilities are based in perception or reflect innate ideas is a matter for debate. In fact, we are not comfortable posing this as a problem of nature versus nurture, for, as we have argued throughout this book, development proceeds as a result of the interaction of one's biology with experience at all phases of life, beginning prenatally (see Spencer et al., 2009 for a discussion of this issue with respect to core knowledge). But regardless of the origin, infants' quantitative abilities improve in effectiveness with experience and serve as the basis for the more advanced mathematical abilities that preschool and school-age children acquire, both in schooled and nonschooled societies.

Memory Development in Infancy

We rarely think of infants as mental giants, but the research we have reviewed in this chapter suggests that a lot of thinking is going on in infancy, even if it is not always qualitatively the same as it is in older children and adults. Almost all forms of cognition involve some type of memory process, and infants from early on are able to remember things and events that have happened to them, if sometimes only briefly. We saw in Chapter 3 that even fetuses develop memories for their experience, specifically for the language they hear during the last weeks before their birth. Recall that newborns will modify their behavior (in this case, how rapidly they suck on a pacifier) in order to hear a story (for example, *The Cat in the Hat*) their mothers had read during the final weeks of their pregnancy (DeCasper & Spence, 1986). How much infants can remember and how long those memories last increases with time, and they continue to improve over childhood. In this section, we examine several aspects of infant memory, beginning in the first hours of life and continuing into the toddler years.

Using Looking to Assess Memory

How do you determine whether a young infant can remember something? As mentioned earlier in this chapter, when infants display dishabituation, they are demonstrating a basic form of perceptual memory. The increase in looking time on the dishabituation trials indicates not only that infants can tell the difference between the new and former stimuli, but also that they are discriminating between one stimulus that is before their eyes and one that is in their mind (that is, in their perceptual memory system). Thus, infants' increased attention for the new stimulus indicates a perceptual (visual) memory. We noted earlier that some research suggests that newborns will show habituation and dishabituation to visual stimuli, making basic visual memory an early-developing ability, certainly within the capacity of most infants within their first months of life.

This, however, is only a single technique that contains some problems (Bahrick & Pickens, 1995; Courage & Howe, 2001) and tests only a limited range of memory capabilities. Researchers have developed other techniques for evaluating infant memory, and we look at a couple of them in the following sections.

Kicking Up Their Heels

One technique that has been used to assess infants' memory for their actions is based on operant conditioning and is called the *conjugate reinforcement procedure*, which we discussed briefly earlier in

---

ordinality A basic understanding of *more than* and *less than* relationships.

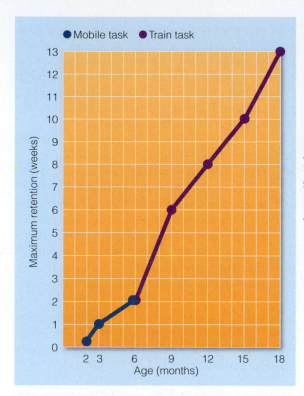

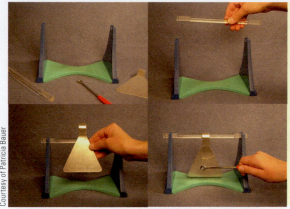

The "gong" task. Infants watched as a model performed a three-step sequence: placing the bar across two posts, hanging a plate on the bar, and striking the plate with a mallet. Infants were later given the opportunity to reproduce the sequence, demonstrating evidence of deferred imitation, and thus memory.

FIGURE 5.18 Maximum duration of retention from 2.5 to 18 months of age.
Blue circles show retention on the mobile task, and purple circles show retention on the train task; 6-month-olds were trained and tested on both tasks. As you can see, the duration of infants' memories for their actions increased steadily over infancy. SOURCE: From Rovee-Collier, C. (1999). The development of infant memory. *Current Directions in Psychological Science, 8*, 80–85. Reprinted by permission of John Wiley & Sons, Inc.

this chapter (see Rovee-Collier, 1999; Rovee-Collier & Gerhardstein, 1997 for reviews). As you may recall, infants' rate of kicking to make a mobile over their head move is evaluated days, weeks, or months after the original experience, when the mobile is no longer attached to their leg. If kicking rates remain high, it indicates that infants remembered the early association (that is, kicking makes the mobile move). Results from studies using this procedure have shown that 3-month-olds can remember their actions for up to 8 days, with some showing no forgetting for a full 2 weeks (Sullivan, Rovee-Collier, & Tynes, 1979).

Older infants, who can sit on their own, crawl, or walk, often do not cooperate with a researcher who wants them to lie quietly in a crib and watch a mobile overhead. However, they will sit in front of a miniature train set and watch as a train goes around. This is what older infants do in the *train task*. They learn to move the train around the set by pressing a lever in front of them, and memory is tested as it is in the mobile task. With infants sitting in front of the display after a delay, the rate that

they press the lever (when it is now not connected to the train) is measured (Rovee-Collier, 1999).

When we combine data from the mobile task with young infants and the train task with older infants, we can get an idea of age changes in the duration of infants' memories. Figure 5.18 summarizes results from studies using both the mobile and train tasks, illustrating the maximum duration of memories (in weeks) for infants between the ages of 2.5 and 18 months (from Rovee-Collier, 1999). As you can see, the duration of infants' memories shows gradual but steady increases with age, reflecting a continuously developing memory system.

Baby See, Baby Do

The conjugate reinforcement technique has been successful in developing a picture of how long infants can remember their actions and some of the factors that affect the length of time these memories will last. But infants remember more than can be assessed by hooking their ankles to a mobile in a crib or from pushing a lever to make a train travel around a set. Infants still cannot speak, so asking them to tell us in words, as we do for older children, is out of the question. As we mentioned earlier, deferred imitation can be used as a measure of memory in infancy. If infants, after watching a model perform some novel action, repeat that action some time later, it indicates memory.

At what age do infants display deferred imitation? Although the results one finds vary with the specific task that is used, infants as young as 9 months old will imitate simple actions for up to 5 weeks later (Carver & Bauer, 1999), and 6-month-olds have been shown to imitate simple behaviors after a 24-hour delay (Collie & Hayne, 1999).

Once infants observe an action, how long do those memories last? The answer depends primarily on the infant's age, with older infants being able to remember more complicated sets of behaviors over longer periods. For instance, Patricia Bauer and her colleagues (Bauer, 2002, 2007; Bauer et al., 2000, 2001) showed infants a series of three-step sequences. In the "gong task," the model placed a

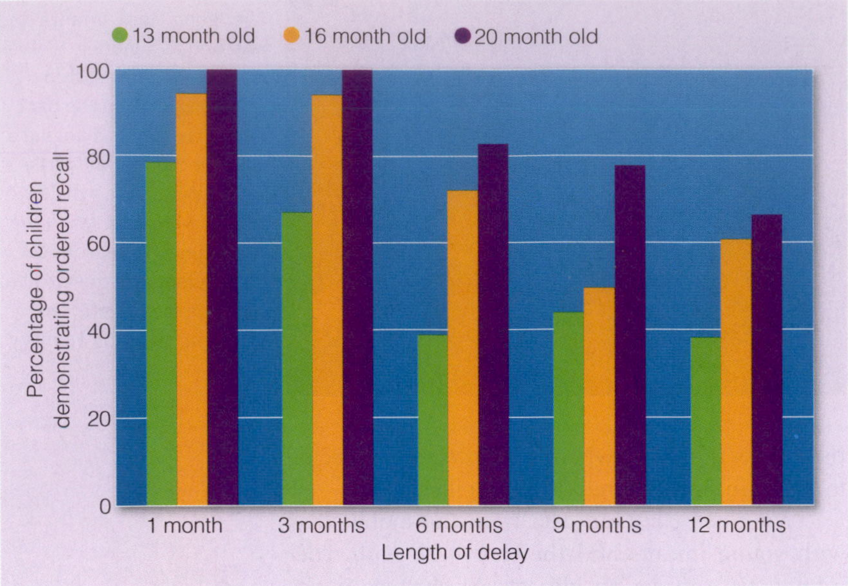

FIGURE 5.19 Percentage of 13-, 16-, and 20-month-old infants displaying deferred imitation of three-step sequences as a function of length of delay.

SOURCE: Data from Bauer, P. J., Wenner, J. A., Dropik, P. L., & Wewerka, S. S. (2000). Parameters of remembering and forgetting in the transition from infancy to early childhood. *Monographs of the Society for Research in Child Development, 65* (Issue no. 4, Serial No, 263). Figure from Bauer, P. J. (2002). Long-term recall memory: Behavioral and neuro-developmental changes in the first 2 years of life. *Current Directions in Psychological Science, 11*, 137–141. Reprinted by permission of Sage Publications.

bar across two posts, hung a plate from the bar, and then struck the plate with a mallet (see Photo). Beginning around the time of their first birthdays, infants were able to imitate the three-sequence actions over delays, with older babies showing higher levels of deferred imitation during each delay interval than younger babies (Bauer et al., 2000). The results of successful deferred imitation over various delay intervals (from 1 to 12 months) for 13-, 16-, and 20-month-old infants are shown in Figure 5.19. As you can see, the results from deferred-imitation tasks are similar to those using operant conditioning procedures (the mobile and train tasks, Rovee-Collier, 1999): The duration of preverbal memory for actions or events increases steadily over the course of infancy.

Some researchers believe that deferred imitation is a nonverbal form of *explicit*, or *declarative*, *memory*. In older children and adults, declarative memory refers to memory you can talk about (declare); it is available to conscious awareness and is seen in our memory for events. In contrast, *implicit*, or *procedural*, *memory* is memory for actions or procedures, such as learning to tie a knot, and is not available to conscious awareness.

The ability to form explicit memories has been tied to specific areas of the brain. For example, adults with hippocampal damage are unable to acquire new explicit memories, although they can acquire new implicit memories. This is demonstrated in a classic study in which a patient with hippocampal damage was given a mirror-drawing task over several days in which he had to trace figures while watching his hand in a mirror (Milner, 1964). The patient's performance was initially very poor but improved over several days of practice, although he had no recollection of ever performing the task. The enhancement of performance as a result of practice is a reflection of intact implicit (procedural) memory, whereas the failure to recall previously performing the task is a reflection of a lack of explicit (declarative) memory.

How do adults with hippocampal damage perform on deferred-imitation tasks similar to the gong task? They fail them (McDonough et al., 1995), just as they do the more conventional verbal recall and recognition tasks. These findings suggest that deferred-imitation tasks tap the same memory system as do declarative tasks used with older children (for example, "Tell me what you had for breakfast this morning"), and that the neurological structures necessary for declarative memory are in place, at least in rudimentary form, by children's first birthdays. We discuss some of the things we know about neurological systems underlying memory in infancy in Box 5.2 and the extent to which the neurological and behavior data tell the same story.

Infants certainly do not have the memories attributed to elephants—they forget, and the younger they are the more likely they are to forget. However, infants store memories from their earliest months of life. Initially, these seem to be perceptually based memories that can be assessed using looking-time tasks. But by 2 or 3 months, infants are able to form memories for their actions, remembering, for example, the crib they were in when a mobile was tied to their ankles and that their kicking made a mobile move. By 9 months, and perhaps as early as 6 months, infants can form memories of actions they see and later reproduce those actions. Such deferred imitation may reflect a sophisticated representational system (explicit memory), similar to the type of memory system that typifies older children and adults. Children's memory abilities become more sophisticated, especially once they are able to talk, but the more sophisticated forms of remembering shown by verbal children have their basis in the memories of infants, which are surprisingly (to many of us) quite well developed.

Blank Slates, or Ready to Learn?

It has become increasingly obvious over the past several decades that human infants are not the blank slates that philosophers and psychologists once thought they were. Rather, infants enter the world ready to learn, with predispositions to attend to some stimuli more than others (faces, for instance) and an ability to acquire some knowledge

dentate gyrus Part of the hippocampus that continues to develop after birth and plays an important role in memory.

BOX 5.2 the biopsychology of childhood

Brain, Behavior, and Memory Development

Over the past couple of decades, we have learned more and more about brain development, while also learning more about memory development. One of the central tenets of modern psychology is that theories about psychological development must be consistent with what we know about biological development. Let's see if what we know about brain development during infancy tells the same story as infants' memory behavior does.

From the research with amnesic patients, we know the hippocampus is involved in establishing long-term declarative memories, and if deferred imitation is a form of declarative memory, as the research of McDonough and her colleagues (1995) suggests, the hippocampus should be relatively well developed in infants by their first birthdays or so. Most parts of the hippocampus develop early and are adult-like in structure before birth. But the hippocampus has several parts to it, an important one being the **dentate gyrus**, which continues to develop after birth (Richmond & Nelson, 2007). In fact, at birth, one layer of the dentate gyrus includes only about 70% of the number of cells it will have in adulthood (Seress, 2001). This means that about 30% of the cells in this layer will be generated after birth. As mentioned in Chapter 4, although it was believed not too long ago that no new neurons were generated after birth, we now know that neurogenesis continues throughout life in the hippocampus, particularly the dentate gyrus. Once neurons are generated, synapses between neurons need to be formed, and this reaches its peak in the dentate gyrus in the fourth or fifth months after birth; synapses are then pruned to adult levels by about 10 months.

Other areas of the brain are involved in forming and retrieving declarative memories, most importantly the frontal cortex, which develops more slowly than the hippocampus and related areas (Monk, Webb, & Nelson, 2001). For example, synaptic density does not reach its peak in the frontal cortex until between 15 and 24 months after birth, and significant pruning takes place during childhood (Huttenlocher, 1979). In fact, frontal lobe development, which is important in most types of higher-level cognition includ-

ing declarative memory, continues well into childhood and adolescence (see discussion in Chapter 4).

Infants as young as 2 and 3 months old demonstrate some long-term memory using the conjugate reinforcement procedures (Rovee-Collier, 1999), and even newborns display brief memories using the habituation/dishabituation procedure (Freidman, 1972). But the memories tapped by these procedures do not seem to require the involvement of the hippocampus (at least not critically so). Preference for novelty in young infants may be a reflexive response to infrequently presented stimuli, and the operant conditioning that is at the heart of the conjugate reinforcement procedure is likely mediated primarily by the cerebellum (see C. Nelson, 1997). Although infants as young as 6 months old display deferred imitation for periods up to 24 hours (Collie & Hayne, 1999), their ability to remember sequences of actions over longer delays improves substantially around their first birthdays (see Bauer, 2007). This corresponds with the increases in synaptogenesis in both the dentate gyrus of the hippocampus and the frontal cortex, providing at least a strong correlation between brain and memory development.

Further evidence that early brain development influences early memory development comes from studies of premature infants. In one study, groups of 19-month-olds were given a series of imitation tasks, some involving the immediate imitation of some actions and others involving a 10-minute delay before they were given an opportunity to imitate (de Haan et al., 2000). One group of babies had been born full term (38 to 40 weeks' gestation), another had been born premature (35 to 37 weeks' gestation) but were physiologically healthy, and a third had been born premature (27 to 34 weeks' gestation) and were physiologically immature. The assumption was that the preterm infants, particularly the physiologically immature ones, were also neurologically immature. When tested at 19 months, all groups of babies showed high and comparable levels of immediate imitation. Differences were found, however, on deferred-imitation tasks, with the preterm infants, especially those who were physiologi-

cally immature, having significantly lower levels of memory. These findings suggest that the declarative memory system of these preterm infants was adversely affected by depriving them of the last several weeks of their prenatal environment.

Not only can being born too soon adversely affect memory development, but so too can an abnormal postnatal environment. This was shown in another study that examined the imitation abilities of 20-month-old infants, some of whom had been adopted about 8 months earlier from a Romanian orphanage, where they experienced extreme deprivation (Kroupina et al., 2010). The patterns were much like those for the prematurely born infants: Children who had lived their first year or so in conditions of extreme deprivation displayed immediate imitation comparable to that of home-reared children. The difference was in deferred imitation, with the adopted children having significantly poorer memories than the home-reared children. As we noted in Chapter 4, postnatal experience is of vital importance in getting the brain wired properly, and, as this study shows, when infants receive less-than-optimal experiences during their first year of life, their brains and the memory behavior their brains influence suffer.

So how does brain development correspond to memory development? Brain and behavior are generally telling the same developmental story, at least across infancy. There are sure to be some surprises as we learn more about how the brain works and develops, but for the most part psychologists and biologists are on the same page.

Categorization	*From 3–4 months*: Infants can form perceptual categories of natural objects (for example, animals).
	By 6 months: Infants can distinguish between animate and inanimate objects.
	By 9 months: Infants can form categories based on category-prototypes.
Core knowledge	Rudiments of object-property representation (object constancy, coherence, continuity, and permanence) are seen in infants 4 months old and younger; however, a full understanding of objects does not develop until the end of the first year, if not later.
	Neonatal imitation is present at birth but disappears when infants are about 2 months old.
	Even 5- to 6-month-old infants seem to know that 3 > 1 and that 1 + 1 = 2 (and not = 1).
Memory	Perceptual memory is present at birth and even before (last months of gestation).
	By 3 months: Infants can remember their own actions (for example, kicking associated with moving a mobile overhead) up to 8 days later.
	By 6–9 months: Infants can imitate other people's actions after a 24-hour delay (indicating long-term memory) as early as 6 months and reliably by 9 months, and for up to 5 weeks when they are about 9 months old.

(the sounds of one's mother tongue, for example) more easily than others.

Not surprisingly, contemporary views see infant perception and cognition as involving both biological readiness and learning (Kellman & Arterberry, 2006). The biological basis of perception is seen in the typical pattern of development that most members of the species follow, including infants' typical biases for some sensory stimuli over others (for example, toward attractive faces and speech). But these dispositions are only the foundation, and perceptual and cognitive abilities are modified by experience throughout development (for example, face perception becomes specialized by gender and race by 3 to 6 months). Moreover, research on perceptual deprivation in different species clearly shows that a significant lack of sensory stimulation during early stages of development can have serious and permanent consequences (see Huttenlocher, 2002), indicating that species-typical perceptual development requires a species-typical perceptual environment to actually work out.

Although infants seem prepared to understand how the physical world works, experience in that world, both with people and objects, is necessary for them to develop an adult appreciation of basic physics and social relations, and this will continue to develop with experience over childhood. This contemporary view of perceptual and cognitive development is consistent with both developmental systems (Lewkowicz, 2000; Bahrick, Lickliter & Flom, 2004) and evolutionary approaches to development (see Chapters 1 and 2), both viewpoints widely supported in this textbook. However, for the most part, aspects of infant perception and cognition have been studied in isolation from other aspects of their cognition and from their social environment. A task for the next generation of developmental psychologists is to deal with the "Humpty Dumpty problem," and "put the developing cognitive system (and the infant) back together again," looking at the whole child (Oakes, 2009, p. 352).

Despite infants' considerable sophistication, as stated earlier in this chapter, we should be cautious and not overinterpret the findings of recent research. Developmental science's new techniques may have revealed abilities that were previously unknown, but they have not changed the nature of infants, who have been developing pretty much the same way for tens of thousands of years. We provide this cautious assessment in part because of a trend, particularly apparent in the United States, of beginning formal education in the crib. Box 5.3 takes a brief look at this phenomenon and provides a preliminary assessment of its success.

BOX 5.3 # child development in the real world

Educating Baby

It seems clear that babies are a whole lot smarter than scientists used to think they were. They develop early many abilities related to intuitive physics, for example, an understanding of the physical properties of objects (solidarity, continuity; Spelke & Kinzler, 2007) and intuitive psychology, such as neonates' ability to match the facial expressions of adults (Meltzoff & Moore, 1977). They are also able to learn, even in the womb, as shown by research in which newborns will prefer to listen to a story that their mothers had read during the last weeks of pregnancy (DeCasper & Spence, 1986). Given these remarkable abilities, some parents and educators have argued that formal instruction should not wait until kindergarten, or even for when children learn to speak, but should begin as early as possible.

For example, BabyPlus® (*www.babyplus.com*) is a "fetal enrichment technology" that fits around a pregnant mother's belly and plays sounds to her fetus (Logan, 1991). The reasoning behind this is that prenatal brain stimulation can prevent the usual pattern of brain-cell death that occurs before birth, increasing the number of neurons and synapses a baby has when it enters the world. This presumably would set the stage for better learning and greater intelligence. Yet, as we noted in Chapter 4, selective cell death during the prenatal and postnatal months is the species-typical pattern, and preventing such cell loss (if that is what BabyPlus® would actually do) may have unintended consequences. According to neuroscientist Peter Huttenlocher (2002, p. 214): "One has to consider the possibility that very ambitious early enrichment and teaching programs may lead to crowding effects and to an early decrease in the size and number of brain regions that are largely unspecified and that may be necessary for creativity in the adolescent and adult."

Educators have been publishing books and developing programs for accelerating infant learning for decades (for example, *How to Multiply Your Baby's Intelligence*, Doman, 1984), but new technologies have brought about an explosion of ways to teach your baby (see Wartella, Richert, & Robb, 2010). For instance, computer programs designed for infants and toddlers as young as 6 months

"They grow up too fast."

Although baby DVDs are intended to enhance infants' cognitive development, there is limited evidence that the more infants watch such videos, the slower they are to acquire new vocabulary.

old, called *lapware*, can be played with while the infant is sitting in Mom or Dad's lap. These programs are promoted as educational software, designed to teach babies a host of concepts, presumably faster or better than would be the case if computers were not involved. For example, the *ToddlerToons* website states that "ToddlerToons allows babies and toddlers to build language skills and to learn concepts such as cause and effect, big and little, up and down, happy and sad, colors and shapes, body parts, and more."

Although the intent of the developers of these products is surely to enhance cognitive development, do the products work? There is surprisingly little scientific research on this topic. Some studies (Zimmerman & Christakis, 2007), but not others (see Courage & Setliff, 2009), report that children under 3 years of age who watch fast-paced television, often including violence, are at risk for subsequent attentional problems. The claims that watching baby videos enhances cognitive development has also been questioned. In one recent study that investigated vocabulary development in 12- to 24-month-old infants, there was no evidence that watching baby DVDs enhanced infants' word learning (Richert et al., 2010). In other research, the amount of time children 8 to 16 months old

spent watching baby DVDs/videos, such as *Baby Einstein®* and *Brainy Baby®*, was *negatively* related to the size of their receptive vocabularies (words they understand): Each hour children watched baby DVDs/videos was associated with 6 to 8 *fewer* vocabulary words (Zimmerman, Christakis, & Meltzoff, 2007).

Even having a TV playing in the background can adversely affect infant and young children's behavior. For instance, 12-, 24-, and 36-month-old children were observed playing both with and without television broadcasting in the background (Schmidt et al., 2008; see also Courage et al., 2010). The quality of children's play and their focused attention was negatively affected by having the TV on in the background, even if they paid little attention to it.

Although these studies are preliminary, they suggest that a heavy exposure to television and use of lapware do not enhance young children's intellectual development, as many parents believe, but may actually be detrimental (see also Bjorklund, 2007a). This is reminiscent of the finding of Hanus Papousek (1977), discussed earlier in the chapter, in which infants who began a simple learning procedure at birth were nearly twice as old as children who started at 1 month of age before they mastered the task.

Infants need stimulation—interesting objects and especially responsive people to speak to and interact with them. However, stimulation can be excessive, can distract infants and young children from other tasks, and may replace activities, such as social interaction, that are vital to their development. We in no way are advocating a hands-off policy toward educating infants and young children. However, just because research indicates that infants are smarter than we once thought they were does not mean they are ready for stimulation and instruction that is more appropriate for older children.

The study of infant perception and cognition expanded with the development of new methods based on simple infant behaviors. In the **visual preference paradigm**, infants' ability to tell the difference between two stimuli is based on how much they attend to each stimulus. In the *habituation/dishabituation paradigm*, looking time decreases as a result of repeated presentation of a stimulus (**habituation**) and increases with the presentation of a new stimulus (**dishabituation**). Habituation and dishabituation to visual stimuli are found for some newborns and reflect both discrimination and memory.

Accommodation, or focusing, of the lens is poorly developed at birth but improves rapidly during the first 6 months. Newborns are able to follow a moving object with their eyes (**visual tracking**), but they do not show **binocular convergence**, the ability of both eyes to focus together on the same object, until about 2 months. Newborns have poor **visual acuity** and have limited color vision.

From birth, infants look longer at some stimuli than others, indicating that they can discriminate between the stimuli and have perceptual biases, or preferences. Among the physical characteristics of a stimulus that attracts infants' visual attention are movement, contour and contrast, certain levels of complexity, vertical symmetry, and curvature.

Depth perception is the ability to discriminate visual patterns denoting depth. Infants' perception of depth is affected by different types of depth cues that develop over the first year: **kinetic cues** (information associated with the movement of objects), **stereoscopic**, or **binocular**, **vision** (the ability to integrate the images provided by each eye from their particular angle into a single image), and **monocular**, or **pictorial cues** (understanding *visual perspective*).

From shortly after birth, infants seem to have a bias toward attending to the human face, with the eyes in particular being important in processing faces. Over the first year, face processing becomes increasingly specialized, as infants come to process faces more as adults do. During the first month of life, infants tend to direct their attention to the outside of a figure, including faces, which is referred to as the **externality effect**.

Infants' hearing, or audition, is relatively good at birth but improves over infancy. Newborns are relatively good at identifying where a sound comes from, called *auditory localization*. Early in the first year, infants can tell the difference between **phonemes** (the individual sounds that make up words) from all human languages, but they lose this ability later in the first year of life as they become specialized in processing the sounds from their own language. Similarly, infants seem prepared to process music. Musicality may have its origins in mothers trying to regulate their infants' behaviors and emotions.

Intermodal perception refers to the coordination of information from two or more sensory modalities and may be present at birth or shortly thereafter.

In the **violation-of-expectation paradigm**, infants' attention to an unexpected, often impossible, event increases relative to baseline. Other techniques for assessing infant cognition involve the use of operant conditioning for behaviors infants can control themselves, such as sucking and head turning.

Using the habituation/dishabituation technique, researchers have been able to demonstrate **categorization** in infants and conclude that infants form categories in much the same way that older children and adults do. Infant categories are formed around **category prototypes**, which are abstract representations reflecting the central tendency, or best example, of a category.

Core knowledge refers to the idea that infants possess a small set of domain-specific systems of knowledge that have been shaped by natural selection upon which new and flexible skills are built. Three core-knowledge systems have been proposed to be present during infancy: knowledge of inanimate objects and their mechanical interactions, or object representation; knowledge of people and their actions; and the ability to represent numbers, or quantities.

Infants from birth seem to have a rudimentary understanding of **object constancy**, the knowledge that an object remains the same despite changes in how it is viewed. Infants' understanding of **object cohesion and continuity** (understanding that objects have boundaries) develops over the first year, reflected in their ability to perceive subjective, or illusory, contours. Research using the violation-of-expectation method has tested infants' understanding of the continuity of objects in a variety of experiments and finds that infants have some notion of the continuity of objects early in life, which develops with experience. However, in some cases, using tasks tapping explicit cognition, older children fail to show the same knowledge displayed by infants using looking time, challenging the nature of early object knowledge.

Object permanence refers to the belief that objects exist independent of one's perceptions or actions. Piaget was the first to describe the development of object permanence and proposed that infants could not retrieve a hidden object until about 8 months old, did not solve the **A-not-B task** until about 12 months, and cannot understand **invisible displacements** until about 18 months. By using variations of the violation-of-expectation method, researchers have demonstrated evidence of object permanence earlier than Piaget had proposed.

Neonatal imitation of facial gestures has been interpreted by some as a reflection of symbolic functioning. However, others have found that neonatal imitation typically disappears by about 2 months, suggesting that it may reflect an *ontogenetic adaptation*, serving a specific function at a particular time in development, rather than a reflection of symbolic ability.

By using variations of the violation-of-expectation method, researchers have demonstrated evidence for simple quantitative abilities in infants. Among these are **numerosity** (the ability to determine quickly the number of items in a set without counting), **ordinality** (a basic understanding of more than and less than relationships), and simple arithmetic, although there is some debate about the interpretation of these latter findings.

Infants display memory in habituation/dishabituation procedures shortly after birth. Techniques such as **conjugate reinforcement procedure** and **deferred imitation** tasks have shown that older infants can retain information over relatively long periods. There is some evidence that the deferred imitation displayed by infants is a nonverbal form of declarative/explicit memory. Recent research has examined the relationship between early memory and brain development. Maturation of an area of the hippocampus, the **dentate gyrus**, as well as maturation of the frontal cortex, is associated with infants' ability to display deferred imitation.

Although research has shown that infants have far more abilities than we previously believed, there is debate about the wisdom of accelerating the education of infants, with some evidence pointing to detrimental effects of providing infants with learning experiences before they are ready for them.

Key Terms and Concepts

visual preference paradigm (p. 191)

habituation (p. 191)

dishabituation (p. 191)

accommodation (p. 193)

visual tracking (p. 193)

binocular convergence (p. 193)

visual acuity (p. 193)

depth perception (p. 195)

kinetic cues (p. 196)

stereoscopic (or binocular) vision (p. 196)

monocular (pictorial) cues (p. 196)

externality effect (p. 197)

phonemes (p. 201)

intermodal perception (p. 203)

violation-of-expectation paradigm (p. 205)

conjugate reinforcement procedure (p. 207)

deferred imitation (p. 207)

categorization (p. 208)

category prototype (p. 208)

object constancy (p. 211)

object continuity and cohesion (p. 211)

objects permanence (p. 211)

core knowledge (p. 211)

A-not-B task (p. 214)

invisible displacements (p. 214)

neonatal imitation (p. 216)

numerosity (p. 217)

ordinality (p. 220)

dentate gyrus (p. 216)

Ask Yourself . . .

1. What is the difference between infant perception and infant cognition, and why do people believe that it is important to study them?

2. How can we know what babies perceive and what they are thinking about? What are some of the more frequently used methods to assess infant perception and cognition?

3. What are the basic visual and auditory abilities in newborns? How do these abilities develop over infancy?

4. What visual and auditory preferences, or perceptual biases, have been found in infancy? How are these preferences explained from an evolutionary perspective?

5. Describe the development of depth perception and intermodal perception. Why are these abilities important for infants?

6. What are the major milestones in the development of face processing and speech perception? What do the development of these abilities have in common, if anything?

7. How do infants categorize things in the world?

8. What is meant by the core-knowledge approach to infant cognition? What are the main findings regarding infants' understanding of objects, people, and quantitative relations?

9. What types of memory do infants exhibit and when? How much can they remember and for how long?

10. Are infants born as blank slates? What does modern research in infant perception and cognition contribute to this issue?

Exercises: Going Further

1. Let's do a play. Pretend that you are a baby, and write how you would describe to an adult how you perceive and think about the world. You can choose to be a newborn, a 4- to 8-month-old infant, or an 8- to 12-month-old. (Obviously you can try to be each of them!)

2. In a recent family gathering, the question was raised whether your sister's 4-month-old daughter, Martha, could tell the difference between spoons and forks. How would you design a simple experiment you could do at home to provide a tentative answer to this question?

3. One of your former classmates from high school has begun medical school. You run into him accidentally at the university, and while talking about the different things you are studying in your respective schools, there is a point where he lets you know that he does not believe that environment or learning are particularly important processes in infancy. He thinks most of what happens to babies is genetically driven. What would you reply, and what list of examples, if any, would you give him?

Suggested Readings

Classic Work

Haith, M. M. (1993). **Preparing for the 21st century: Some goals and challenges for studies of infant sensory and perceptual development.** *Developmental Review, 13,* 354–371. Haith briefly reviewed the state of the art in infant perceptual development, circa 1990, and suggested directions for the future. These included taking a more continuous, developmental perspective of infant perception, integrating ideas about infant perception with those about older children, looking more at the brain basis of perceptual development, and increasing the emphasis on applying research findings to at-risk populations. The field has moved in some of these directions since this article was published, and his advice is as relevant today as it was in 1993.

Piaget, J. (1954). *The construction of reality in the child.* **New York: Basic.** This is one of the core books of Piaget's account of sensorimotor development in which he described some of his early studies of the development of object permanence.

Scholarly Work

Baillargeon, R. (2008). **Innate ideas revisited: For a principle of persistence in infants' physical reasoning.** *Perspectives on Psychological Science, 3,* 2–13. This article reviews research by Reneé Baillargeon and her colleagues on object representation in infants using the violation-of-expectation method. She proposes the principle of persistence, in which babies seem to know something about the continuity of objects from birth.

Spelke, E. S., & Kinzler, K. D. (2007). **Core knowledge.** *Developmental Science, 10,* 89–96. Elizabeth Spelke and Katherine Kinzler present evidence for the core-knowledge perspective of infant cognition, listing several areas in which core knowledge is proposed to exist.

Bauer, P. J. (2007). *Remembering the times of our lives: Memory in infancy and beyond.* **Mahwah, NJ: Erlbaum.** This book, by one of the leading researchers in infant memory, provides an up-to-date review of research and theory of memory development in infancy and early childhood and includes several chapters on the neurological basis of memory development. A concise summary of this work can be found in Bauer, P. J. (2002). Long-term recall memory: Behavioral and neuro-developmental changes in the first 2 years of life. *Current Directions in Psychological Science, 11,* 137–141.

Reading for Personal Interest

Dobbs, D. (2005). **Big answers from little people.** *Scientific American Mind, 16 (3).* This article, written for the layperson, examines the latest research into infants' cognitive abilities, focusing on the work of Harvard developmental psychologist and advocate of the core-knowledge approach, Elizabeth Spelke.

Rochat, P. (2004). *The infant's world.* **Cambridge, MA: Harvard University Press.** Developmental psychologist Philippe Rochat examines the development of infant social cognition, taking an ecological perspective that is somewhat different from the core-knowledge perspective as advocated by Elizabeth Spelke and her colleagues.

Field, T. (2007). *The amazing infant.* **Malden, MA: Wiley-Blackwell.** In this book, infant researcher Tiffany Field examines the wonders of the infant's developing mind.

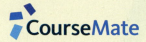
CourseMate

Cengage Learning's **Psychology CourseMate** for this text brings course concepts to life with interactive learning, study, and exam preparation tools, including quizzes and flashcards for this chapter's Key Terms and Concepts (see the summary list on page 225). The site also provides an **eBook** version of the text with highlighting and note taking capabilities, as well as an extensive library of observational videos that span early childhood through adolescence. Many videos are accompanied by questions that will help you think critically about and deepen your understanding of the chapter topics addressed, especially as they pertain to core concepts. Log on and learn more at **www.cengagebrain.com**.

In this chapter we examine Piaget's theory of cognitive development, the most influential in the history of developmental psychology. We look at the assumptions of the theory, describe stages of cognitive development, and briefly assess the state of Piaget's theory today. We discuss theory theories as a neo-Piagetian approach to cognitive development and examine mostly theory-theory-based research on children's development of biological knowledge. We then look at several everyday expressions of children's developing symbolic functions: symbolic play, drawing, storytelling, and children's belief in fantasy characters.

Four-year-old Hilary was patiently waiting for her father to fix her favorite lunch, a peanut-butter-and-jelly sandwich. Dad placed the sandwich, cut in quarters, before her. Hilary looked at the sandwich and then immediately looked at her father and said, "Oh, Daddy. I wanted you to cut it into only two pieces. I'm not hungry enough to eat four!"

What in the world is Hilary talking about? Isn't it obvious that it makes no difference how many pieces the sandwich is cut into? It is still the same sandwich, regardless if it is cut into two pieces or four. But that is not the way that Hilary and most other 4-year-olds see it. For this preschool child, the appearance of "more sandwich," as reflected by the four pieces, translates into more food to eat (and she's just not that hungry!).

Four-year-olds really think this way, and 8-year-olds do not. In fact, if you described the episode of Hilary and her sandwich to 8-year-olds and asked them if they ever thought that way, most would say no, they never did, and they may suggest that there must be something wrong with Hilary's thinking. What is wrong with her thinking is that it has not developed to understand the distinction between appearance and reality, at least in the way that an 8-year-old's has. This topic, and many others, was investigated by the Swiss psychologist Jean Piaget, who believed that the way children represent the world changes systematically between infancy and adolescence. We have discussed Piaget's theory in several chapters in this book already, and here we examine in greater detail some of his ideas about how children come to use symbols in their thinking.

Assumptions of Piaget's Theory of Cognitive Development

In Chapter 2, we mentioned that if we had to choose the most influential theory in the history of developmental science, our choice would be that of Piaget. Jean Piaget (1896–1980) was a Swiss developmental psychologist, initially trained as a biologist, who devoted his life to studying the development of knowledge in human beings. In the process, Piaget proposed a theory of cognitive development that changed radically how psychologists, educators, and many parents view children. Rather than seeing children as shaped by their environments or destined by their genes, Piaget viewed children as playing an active role in shaping their own development. Children do not merely perceive reality, they construct it.

Piaget proposed four major stages of development—sensorimotor, preoperational, concrete operational, and formal operational—with children in each stage having a particular way of understanding the world. For Piaget, thought is initially practical ("I see and touch, therefore I know") during the sensorimotor period (0–2 years); it becomes symbolic and intuitive ("I can think with my head, without my hands—but logic escapes me and appearance *is* reality") during the preoperational period (2–7 years); at the stage of concrete operations (7–11 years) thinking becomes logical, although restricted to concrete entities ("I can do it without hands and with logic, but my logic fails a bit if problems are not touchable"); and eventually thinking becomes logical and abstract ("I can think and solve problems proficiently without the need of concrete stuff, and I can even imagine many other possibilities") during formal operations (11–16 years). However, before describing these four types of thought, it is necessary to explain some important assumptions Piaget made about children and the nature of cognitive development.

According to Piaget (1983; Piaget & Inhelder, 1969), children enter a chaotic world at birth. They are faced with the monumental task of making sense of a world that bombards them with stimulation. Given this situation, the top priority of infants is to organize the world in their minds, or, as Piaget said, to "construct" it in their minds: Children must get to know that on Earth objects fall when they are dropped, that a toy covered by a blanket continues to exist even if it is out of one's sight, that a person or an animal is the same whether you view it from the front or from the side, and that the amount of sandwich one has to eat does not change when it is cut into four versus two pieces. Underlying his constructivist point of view, reality does not exist independent of the mind of the person who constructs it. Does the real world have eight dimensions instead of three, or 1,200 different colors? We simply do not know; we only know that human minds perceive basically three dimensions, as well as a limited number of colors. In other words, following German philosopher Immanuel Kant's ideas, what we call "reality" is actually what is "inside me" (mentally constructed), not what is "really" in the external world.

Schemes and Operations

But how do children construct the world in their minds? Piaget proposed that infants initially come to know objects by physically acting on them: watching, touching, listening, licking, everything! (But especially touching. According to Piaget, "intelligence begins with the hands.") He called organized and sequential series of actions *action schemes*, as, for example, when an infant sucks everything that comes in contact with her mouth (sucking scheme) or voluntarily grasps things with her hands (grasping scheme). A **scheme** is the basic unit of knowledge for Piaget. Later in development, children internalize these actions so they can "think without hands," that is, mentally manipulate the things they perceive (like we do, for example, when thinking of the different possible arrangements for furniture in a living room). Piaget called these internalized actions **operations**, or *operational schemes*. As we will see later, operations are organized and follow a system of logical rules.

Children must learn to coordinate independent schemes; here, a grasping scheme is coordinated with a sucking scheme as the infant brings the object to her mouth.

Stockbyte/Getty Images

Schemes are systematic patterns of actions or mental operations that reflect children's current state of understanding of the world. Children systematically apply each of these schemes to all of the objects they encounter in order to know them better. For example, an infant who is limited to sucking and grasping schemes will apply these schemes to any object that comes near his lips or hands. An older child may apply her counting scheme to the small set of rocks she has collected, the M&Ms she has poured on the table, or the members of her kindergarten class. The nature of schemes varies over development. Roughly speaking, they correspond to the four stages in the development of thought described later in this chapter.

Organization and Adaptation

But how do schemes change? That is, what are the mechanisms for cognitive development? Piaget believed that two basic processes characterize all biological systems, including thought: **organization** and **adaptation**. Organization refers to the fact that intellectual operations are integrated with one another in a hierarchical nature. For instance, a newborn baby has one scheme for sucking his thumb and another for moving his arms. Before too long, these schemes become coordinated so that the infant moves his arm so that his fingers are in his mouth. Children are not born with a thumb-sucking scheme, but they develop one from the coordination of two independent, lower-order schemes.

Piaget's second mechanism, adaptation, refers to the tendency of children to modify their behavior (actually their schemes) in order to adjust to, or make use of, new information. Piaget proposed two complementary operations of adaptation: **assimilation** and **accommodation**. Assimilation refers to the incorporation of new information into already existing schemes, whereas accommodation refers to changing one's schemes in order to incorporate the new information. Let's look at an example.

When a new object can be understood thanks to a previously existing pattern of actions/operations (for example, a child who has previously grasped and held a rattle discovers that spoons can also be grasped and held with one hand), Piaget said that the child is assimilating this new object into a preexisting scheme, in this case a one-hand grasping scheme. However, if the child realizes that, after her efforts, it is not possible to make sense of this new object with a previously existing scheme (for example, a child cannot hold onto a balloon with only one hand), she must modify her schemes ("holding on to a balloon requires two hands") if she is to incorporate this new piece of world knowledge (here, balloons) into her repertoire of "things I understand/can control." In

Infants need to accommodate, or change, aspects of their previous behavior in order to incorporate new objects or events into their behavioral repertoire. Here, the infant has to learn to use both hands to prevent the balloon from escaping his grasp.

this case, the child is accommodating this novel object in order to understand a new property that could not be assimilated into a preexisting scheme. Accommodation involves modifying existing schemes as a result of those schemes' interactions with the environment. Both assimilation and accommodation are active, as opposed to passive, processes, requiring children to act on their physical (or social) world in order to understand new information. Children's cognition develops little by little, achieving a more enriched comprehension of the world through the continuous and complementary processes of assimilation and accommodation.

For Piaget, it is actually children's schemes that develop, changing as a result of four factors: (1) maturation, (2) children's self-generated activity (that is, children "exercising their schemes"),

---

scheme An abstract representation of an object or event.

operations In Piaget's theory, types of cognitive schemes that are mental (that is, require symbols), derive from action, exist in organized systems, and follow a set of logical rules, most importantly that of reversibility.

organization The cognitive mechanism that keeps the different mental schemes integrated with one another in a hierarchical nature.

adaptation The process of adjusting one's cognitive structures to meet environmental demands; includes the complementary processes of *assimilation* and *accommodation*.

assimilation The process of incorporating information into already existing cognitive structures.

accommodation The process of changing a mental structure to incorporate new information.

(3) information from the physical and social world, and (4) **equilibrium**. You probably had no trouble understanding the first three factors, but the concept of equilibrium is unique to Piaget's theory. According to Piaget, equilibration is an inner tendency of an organism to keep its cognitive schemes in balance. When we encounter information that is inconsistent with our current understanding of reality (that cannot be assimilated into existing schemes), this results in a state of *disequilibrium*, and our minds look for a response for this cognitive discomfort. The response is accommodation, changing schemes to fit with the new information, which results in a new, more advanced state. For Piaget, equilibration is what motivates development. Having our cognitive structures out of whack, so to speak, is inherently displeasing, and we (or, more properly, our cognitive system) strive to put things back in balance. In the process, cognitive development happens.

To summarize the main ideas in this section (see Concept Review 6.1), Piaget believed that children mentally construct their world through their actions and operations on it. This makes children an active force in their own development. Children (and schemes) do not wait for events in the environment to stimulate them to action, but rather they are active forces seeking interaction with the world around them. Children organize their existing schemes and use assimilation and accommodation to develop new, more advanced schemes, which develop from earlier, less sophisticated ones.

Equilibrium is what motivates development. [handwritten margin note]

Stages of Development

As mentioned in Chapter 2, Piaget was a classic stage theorist, believing that each stage reflected a qualitatively different way of making sense of the world. According to Piaget, children pass through four stages, or periods, of intellectual development: *sensorimotor, preoperational, concrete operational,* and *formal operational* (see Table 6.1), the final stage reflecting mature, adult thinking. Piaget also believed that a child's thinking was relatively even, or *homogeneous*, within a stage. That is, children did not show more advanced thinking for one content (thinking about the physical world, for instance) and less advanced thinking for another (thinking about social relations), but rather they thought about different things in generally the same way, applying the same set of mental schemes.

Piaget also emphasized that development of intelligence was *epigenetic* in nature; that is, later developments were based on earlier accomplishments. This means that stages progress in a constant, or invariant, order; children cannot skip stages, because the accomplishments of one stage are necessary steps for later accomplishments. Children can go through stages at different rates—the ages we provide are only approximate—and some may never progress past a certain level; but all children must pass through the same stages in a single, invariant order.

The Sensorimotor Period (Birth to 2 Years)

Piaget called the first stage of development, beginning at birth and lasting until about 2 years, the **sensorimotor period**. Infants enter the world with a suite of reflexes, such as sucking and grasping,

---

equilibration The process by which balance is restored to the cognitive structures.

sensorimotor period In Piaget's theory, the first major stage of cognitive development (birth to approximately 2 years), in which children understand their world through sensory and motor experiences.

table 6.1 Main Traits and Accomplishments of the Four Stages of Cognitive Development in Jean Piaget's Theory

Stage of Cognitive Development	Traits and Accomplishments
Sensorimotor stage (0 to 2 years old)	*Cognition is practical.* ("I see and touch, therefore I know") Object permanence Deferred imitation Mean-Goals mental coordination
Preoperational stage (2 to 7 years old)	*Cognition is symbolic and intuitive.* ("I can think with my head, without my hands, but logic escapes me and appearance is reality") Expression of the symbolic function (for example, images, language, drawing, symbolic play) Magical thinking (for example, animism, finalism, artificialism, realism)
Concrete operational stage (7 to 11 years old)	*Cognition becomes logical, although restricted to concrete entities.* ("I can do it without hands and with logic, but my logic fails a bit if problems are not touchable") Conservation Classification Seriation
Formal operational stage (11 to 16 years old)	*Cognition becomes logical and abstract.* ("I can think and solve problems proficiently without the need of concrete stuff, and I can even imagine many other possibilities") Hypothetico-deductive thinking Abstract thinking

or following a moving object with their eyes, and they apply these reflexes to objects they encounter. Infants come to know the world by their actions on it. It is for this reason that Piaget labeled thought during this period "practical" (that is, children think about things only when they physically act on them). This is why in Chapter 2 we suggested that infants' motto for this period could be: "I see and touch it, therefore it is." In other words, infants' thought is in terms of their sensations of and motor actions on the world, thus the label *sensorimotor*.

Piaget (1952, 1954, 1962) proposed six substages of the sensorimotor period, each one building on the previous. Piaget investigated many aspects of sensorimotor cognition. We examined Piaget's description of object permanence in Chapter 5, and here we focus on Piaget's account of how infants solve problems, especially the extent to which they display intentionality, or *goal-directed behavior*.

According to Piaget, during the first substage, *the use of reflexes* (birth to 1 month), infants apply the set of reflexes they are born with to objects and events they encounter. Piaget used the term "reflex" very broadly, including typical reflexes such as grasping and sucking, but also some other subtle behaviors such as eye movements, vocalizing, and orienting to sound. (Piaget viewed perception as action, so the act of seeing or hearing an object counted as acting on that object.) Accordingly, during this time, behaviors are mostly automatic, reactive, and not intentional. By this Piaget meant that infants do not have some goal in mind and then

intentionally, or purposively, act to achieve that goal. Rather, they respond reflexively to stimuli.

During the second substage, *primary circular reactions* (1 to 4 months), reflexes continue to dominate, but a new mechanism for knowing emerges: the *circular reaction*. A circular reaction is simply a repetitive behavior, and *primary circular reactions* are the first class of repetitive behaviors that focus around infants' bodies. For example, Piaget described how his 1-month-old son, Laurent, learned to suck his thumb. Initially, Laurent's hand

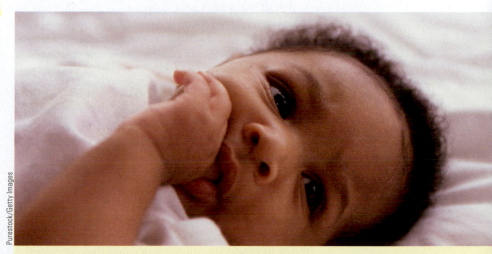

Infants do not instinctively know how to suck their thumbs, but rather they discover this ability by coordinating what were once two independent actions centered around their own bodies: moving their arm and sucking. Piaget referred to this as a primary circular reaction.

made it to his mouth only by chance, as Laurent seemingly moved his arms randomly. When his hand did contact his mouth, it activated his sucking reflex, which produced a pleasurable outcome. After several such accidental experiences, Laurent tried to re-create the event, coordinating his arm, hand, and finger movements with his mouth until he was able to suck his thumb whenever he pleased.

Piaget also observed primary circular reactions for grasping, hearing, vision, and vocalizations. Note that once infants acquire a circular reaction, they can activate it intentionally to achieve some outcome. But the initial occurrence of the interesting event was by chance. Babies this age do not set out to find a way to get their thumbs to their mouths; the initial contact was unintentional, with babies trying to re-create the pleasurable event via primary circular reactions.

Repeating continues to be an infant's dominant form of knowledge acquisition during the next substage, *secondary circular reactions (4 to 8 months)*. However, this time repetitions are not focused on babies' bodies, but rather on objects and external events. Let me (DB) provide a personal observation:

> My daughter, Heidi, at 4 months of age, was lying in her playpen. She did not seem particularly interested in any of the toys that surrounded her, although she was awake, alert, and active. Strung over her head was a crib gym, a complex mobile with parts that spin when they are hit. I had spun the objects for her on several occasions, and when I did, Heidi seemed to like it. But today was to be different. While flailing her arms and legs, she hit the mobile, causing it to spin. She happened to be looking at the mobile, and its movement caught her attention. She suddenly stopped and stared intently at the moving object over her head. It ceased moving, and she began to shake her arms and legs, to squirm, and finally to cry. Again she hit the mobile, and again she froze and quieted, staring straight ahead at the wonderful event she had caused. (Bjorklund, 2005, p. 87)

This is called a secondary circular reaction. It is a circular reaction because, like that seen in the previous stage, it is a repetitive behavior. It is secondary because it does not focus on an infant's body, but on objects and events external to the child. But note that although these behaviors are clearly not reflexes, there is still no intention before the fact. The original source of the interesting event is again random movements of the infant. The intention comes only later, as babies try to repeat the interesting event they (accidently) caused. Yet, thanks to secondary circular reactions,

infants begin to increasingly exert control over their external world.

The next substage, *coordination of secondary circular reactions* (8 to 12 months), marks the arrival of intentional, or **goal-directed, behavior**. Infants now act in order to achieve a specific goal. Rather than stumbling onto some interesting event by chance, as do infants in substages 2 and 3, infants now set out to achieve a specific goal. As you can infer from the title of this substage, they do this by coordinating two previously acquired secondary circular reactions. For example, infants may pull on a blanket (one secondary circular reaction) to reach a desired object (a second secondary circular reaction). One behavior (pulling the blanket) is now used in the service of another (retrieving a desired object). This is seen in the classic object permanence task in which an infant will now remove the cloth that covers an object in order to reach and grasp that object (see Chapter 5), something that is achieved during this substage.

Infants continue to behave intentionally during the next substage, *tertiary circular reactions* (12 to 18 months), initiating a phase of active experimentation over the world of people and things. Like a scientist (Piaget recurrently used the metaphor of the child as a young scientist trying to understand the rules and principles of how the world worked), infants can repeat the same action (for example, dropping something to the floor, but every time from a different height, to see the consequences). Circular reactions are now characterized by slight variations among them, intentionally directed toward testing all possible outcomes (the child seems to be asking: "Will this toy break if I drop it from this stair?" or "What if I throw it out the window?"). These repeated actions permit the child to discover new solutions for a problem, such as getting a long stick through the bars of a playpen (Piaget, 1952).

Infants at this stage are walking and become active experimenters, explorers, and adventurers. What happens when you pour the dog food into the water dish? How can one climb onto the counter and reach the kitchen faucet? This is the time when parents need to childproof their house, putting locks on cabinets, covering up electrical sockets, and putting breakables out of harm's way. However, the toddler's experimentation is a trial-and-error process. According to Piaget, all of a child's thinking at this stage is overt. A child has to physically attempt to fit her brother's tricycle under the coffee table to see if it will fit. She cannot make a mental comparison of the heights of the tricycle and table and determine the feat is not possible. That awaits the next substage.

The final substage of the sensorimotor period, *invention of new means through mental combina-*

---

goal-directed behavior Means-ends (that is, intentional) problem solving, first seen in the latter part of the first year.

Deferred imitation: Imitation of a modeled act following a delay after viewing the behavior.

Symbolic play: Pretending. Early in development, this may be expressed as using one object to represent another (for example, pretending a shoe is a phone), while a bit later it may involve playing different roles ("You be the baby, and I'll be the mommy.").

Mental imagery: The internal representation of an external event. Although we usually think of mental images in terms of vision, mental images can be formed for any sensory modality.

Language: Language is viewed not only as a communication system, but also as a mean of representing objects and events in an abstract way.

---

tions (18 to 24 months), marks the transition from the hands-on sensorimotor infant to the symbolic child capable of mental representation. Beginning around 18 months, children begin to show evidence of the *symbolic function*, which finds its expression in a variety of modes. Concept Review 6.2 presents some expressions of the symbolic function, including language (children begin to put their first words together into sentences around this time), deferred imitation (copying a behavior after some significant delay), symbolic, or fantasy, play, graphic representations such as drawing, and imagery. We discuss some aspects of the symbolic function in more detail later in this chapter.

Piaget's description of development through the sensorimotor period was based primarily on the observations of his own three children. Needless to say, he was an excellent observer of children, and his observations have stood the test of time. This does not mean that Piaget had everything right. For example, new techniques for doing research with infants have revealed abilities in object permanence beyond those described by Piaget (see Chapter 5). However, Piaget's account of the development of goal-directed behavior, or intentionality, seems for the most part right on target with new research on the topic that focuses on infants' social understanding, reflected by shared attention (discussed in Chapter 7). It is not so much that Piaget was right about everything but that he was the first to see and describe important aspects of infant cognition so elegantly and set the stage for future generations of psychologists to plumb the infant mind.

The Preoperational Period (From 2 to 7 Years)

Piaget referred to the second major stage of cognitive development, occurring between the ages of 2 and 7 years, as the **preoperational period**. During this time, children's thinking is symbolic; they are no longer limited to understanding their world in terms of their perceptions and actions on it but can mentally represent objects and events (see Box 6.1). However, the symbolic thought of the 2-year-old is not on par with that of the older child or adult. In fact, children at this stage lack true cognitive operations, defined as thought governed by rules of logic. This stage is called *preoperational* because children's thinking is not logical, at least not in the way it is for older children. Rather, Piaget described the symbolic thought of the preschool child as *intuitive* rather than logical. That is, thought is driven by perception, or the appearance of things. Children seem much more sensitive to the physical characteristics of objects ("what it looks like") than to their real characteristics ("what it actually is").

Take, for example, the attainment of **conservation**, the ability to realize that changes in the physical appearance of things have no influence on changes in their substantial, real properties, such as number, length, area, mass, liquid, weight, or volume (see Figure 6.1). We provided an example of conservation of liquid in Chapter 2 and conservation of sandwich in the opening of this chapter. For instance, if you present two small but equal balls of clay to a 4-year-old child, and then you roll one ball into a sausage shape, the child will be convinced that there is now more clay in the sausage than in the ball. If you ask why, the child will likely say because the sausage is now so much longer than the ball. If you then roll the sausage into a ball again, all while the child watches, the 4-year-old is likely to say "now there is the same amount of clay in both." Nothing is wrong at all with this child. Quite simply, children in the preoperational period believe that because the sausage looks like it has more clay in it than the ball, then it must actually *have* more clay in it than the ball. They are insensitive to the logical contradiction.

Young children's dependence on the appearance of things is reflected by research examining

---

preoperational period The second major stage of cognitive development (approximately ages 2 to 7), characterized by prelogical, intuitive thought

conservation The knowledge that the quantity of a substance remains the same despite changes in its form..

BOX 6.1 food for thought

A Picture's Worth a Thousand Words

Not all things in the physical world are as they appear. Sometimes one thing stands for, or represents, another, and children must learn when a physical entity is a thing worthy of attention itself or merely a representation of something else. In everyday life, pictures, particularly photographs, are ubiquitous examples of such representations. Photographs are everywhere, and we easily understand that a photograph is a representation (a symbol) for the person, object, or event it depicts. The knowledge that one entity can stand for something other than itself is called *representational insight* (DeLoache, 1987; DeLoache & Marzolf, 1992). When can children use external forms of representation, such as pictures and models, to stand for other things? What does such ability tell us about children's cognitive development, particularly their representational abilities?

But pictures are actually an evolutionary novelty. Cave paintings date back only tens of thousands of years, and it was very recently, in historical terms anyway, that pictures and photographs of things became widespread. Given the relative newness of pictures for humans, it should not be surprising that it takes a while before children treat pictures and photographs, not as real objects themselves, but as representations of things. For instance, in one study, researchers gave pictures of objects to children between 9 and 19 months of age in the United States and the Ivory Coast (DeLoache et al., 1998).

Children in both countries behaved similarly. The youngest children touched the pictures as if they were real objects, sometimes even trying to pick them off the page. By 19 months, children realized that the pictures represented something else. They pointed at the depicted objects rather than trying to manipulate them.

In other studies, researchers asked 2- and 3-year-old children to find a toy hidden in a room. Before searching for the toy, however, children were given some hints about where the toy was hidden. In some studies, children saw a scale model of the room—a smaller version of the real room—and were shown where the toy was hidden (DeLoache & Marzolf, 1992; Kuhlmeier, 2005). In other studies, children saw a photograph of the room, along with the location of the hidden toy (DeLoache, 1987, 1991; Suddendorf, 2003). Children were then asked to enter the real room and find the toy. Later, children were asked to locate the toy in the model or picture they had seen earlier. If they find the toy in the latter conditions, it means that they can remember what they were shown.

Somewhat surprisingly, children had the most difficulty using the scale model as a symbol to find the toy. For example, most 2.5-year-old children could find the toy when a picture was used as a hint, although 2-year-olds generally could not. However, 2.5-year-olds failed to find the toy when the scale model was used, although most 3-year-olds were successful. The accompanying figure

Infanes and young toddlers often treat pictures as if they were the real thing, sometimes even trying to pick them off the page.

Vanessa Davies/Getty Images

presents the results for groups of older (3-year-olds) and younger (2.5-year-olds) children on the scale-model task. Retrieval 1 presents the number of errorless trials when searching for the toy in the real room, and Retrieval 2 presents performance for the children's memory for the location of the toy in the model. As you can see, both groups of children remembered where the toy had been hidden in the model (performance was

the development of the appearance/reality distinction. In some pioneering work by Rheta De Vries (1969), 3- to 6-year-old children were familiarized with a trained cat named Maynard. After the children pet Maynard, he was fitted with a realistic dog mask. (Did we mention he was a trained cat?) The children were then asked some questions about Maynard. "What kind of animal is it now? Would this animal eat dog food or cat food? Does it bark or meow?" Most 3-year-olds said that the mask had actually changed the identity of the animal, whereas most 5- and 6-year-olds believed that changes in the appearance of the animal had not altered its identity. More recent research has confirmed young children's confusion between appearance and reality (Deák, Ray, & Brenneman, 2003; Flavell, Green, & Flavell, 1986).

Here is an anecdote to illustrate young children's thinking about how appearance can influence reality (from Bjorklund, 2005, p. 245):

Three-year-old Nicholas sometimes spent the night with his grandparents, who would take him to preschool the following morning. Nicholas especially liked to ride with his grandfather because he drove a somewhat battered, stick-shift Chevy, which Nicholas called "Papa's car." Nicholas's grandmother, however, drove only cars with automatic transmissions, and thus she was unable to take Nicholas to school in Papa's car. One morning when Grandma was about to drive Nicholas to school, he said, "Grandma, dress up like a man this morning. Put on Papa's shirt and wear his hat." When asked why he wanted her to do that, he responded, "Then you can take me to school in Papa's car." Nicholas had a problem and attempted to solve it by changing

The number of errorless retrievals (correctly locating the hidden toy) for 2.5- (younger) and 3-year-old (older) children on a model task. Retrieval 1 involved locating the real toy in the real room; Retrieval 2 involved locating the miniature toy in the scale model. Although the younger children remembered where the toy in the scale model was hidden, they were not able to use the model to guide their search in the real room. SOURCE: "Rapid Change in the Symbolic Functioning of Very Young Children," by J. S. DeLoache, 1987, *Science, 238,* 1556–1557. Copyright © 1987 American Association for the Advancement of Science. Reprinted with permission.

about 80%), but only the older children were able to find the toy at its corresponding location in the real room.

At first blush, this pattern does not make sense. The results should be just the opposite: The model, which looks a lot more like the real room, should be easier to use than the photograph. Why did children have an easier time with the less-realistic photograph? Judy DeLoache (2000; DeLoache, Pierroutsakos, & Uttal, 2003) proposed that one reason for the pattern of results was because children have difficulty thinking about an entity in two different ways at the same time, or what she called *dual representation* (or *dual orientation*). A model is an object worthy of attention all by itself. A picture, in comparison, is itself uninteresting, with its primary purpose being to represent something else. When models are made less interesting and less concrete, or when pictures are made more salient, performance should change.

In a series of experiments, this is exactly what was found. For example, when 2.5-year-old children looked at models through a window, their performance improved relative to when the model was right in front of them. By making the model less salient for these young children, they were more likely to see the model as a symbol rather than an interesting object itself. Likewise, when 3-year-olds were allowed to play with the model before the hiding task, making it more interesting as an object, their performance significantly *decreased* (DeLoache, 1991). Other studies have shown that under favorable conditions, even 2-year-olds can appreciate that a picture can relate both to something else and be an object itself (Preissler & Bloom, 2007; Suddendorf, 2003; Troseth, 2003). This is a reminder that we should not think of children as necessarily either having or not having certain cognitive abilities at any one time. Rather, children's skill at expressing these abilities, or to deal with different forms of representation, increase with age and are influenced by the amount of support they have in their immediate environment, much as reflected by Vygotsky's principle of the *zone of proximal development.*

With a little reflection, it seems obvious that most 2-year-old children display some symbolic abilities. They use words, for example, to represent real objects, and during play they will use one object to stand for another, such as an 18-month-old holding a shoe to her ear and pretending it's a phone. But this is only the beginning of symbol use. To be a truly effective symbol user, a child must understand that the object can be both a symbol (for example, a representation of a room) and an object (for example, a model) *at the same time*, and this takes time to develop. According to DeLoache and Donald Marzolf (1992, p. 328), "Young children are capable of responding to a single entity either concretely, as an object itself, or abstractly, as a representation of something else. It is very difficult for them to do both at once, that is, to achieve dual representation."

his grandmother's appearance, which he believed would transform her temporarily into a man and give her the ability to drive a stick-shift car.

What is the basis for this way of understanding? One of the most distinctive characteristics of the preoperational period is egocentrism. According to Piaget, children at this stage are so cognitively focused on themselves that they have trouble understanding that other people could see or understand things differently than they do. Egocentrism can be seen in many aspects of young children's everyday functioning. For example, young children assume that if they see something, another person will see the same thing. Consider a study by John Flavell and his colleagues (1981) in which preschool children were familiarized with a card having a different picture on each side (for example, a dog and a cat). An experimenter held the card up between the child and the experimenter and asked what the experimenter saw. Children as young as 2.5 years old were able to say that the experimenter saw a different picture than the child (a cat versus a dog, for example), but it was not until 4 or 5 years old that children could say *how* the experimenter saw the picture (right-side-up versus upside down, for example).

Preschool-age children's egocentrism is also seen in social perspective-taking. For instance, 5-year-old Derek asks Emily how old her parents are. Emily says she doesn't know, but that her mother is older than her father. Derek immediately

egocentrism In Piaget's theory, the tendency to interpret objects and events from one's own perspective.

FIGURE 6.1 Sample of typical Piagetian conservation tasks.

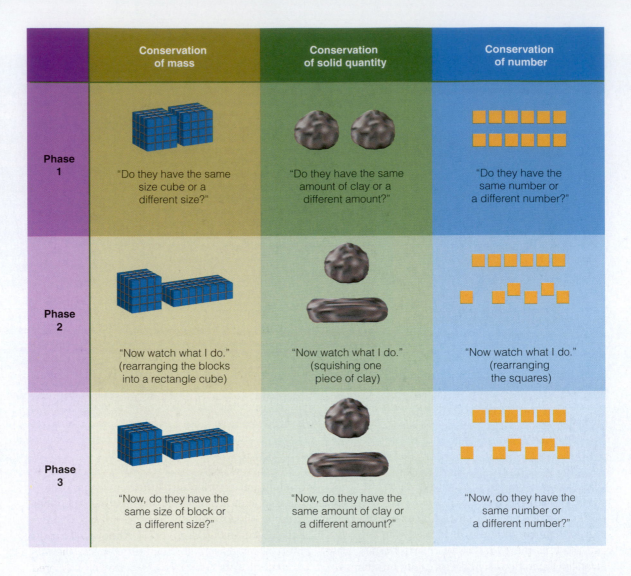

says that that is not possible: Daddies are *always* older than mommies. That's the way it is in Derek's family, and that's the way it must be in all families. Other research has shown that preschool children are not as egocentric as Piaget thought (Borke, 1975; Newcombe & Huttenlocher, 1992). Yet, preschool children are more egocentric than older children, and their self-focused tendency is responsible in part for much of the often-amusing things that young children do and say.

Another factor that influences the thinking of preoperational children, according to Piaget, is that they lack the logical rules associated with cognitive operations, the most important of which is reversibility. **Reversibility** permits children to mentally undo an operation. For example, in simple arithmetic, subtraction is the inverse (or reverse) of addition. If 3 plus 2 equals 5, then, logically, 5 minus 3 must equal 2. In conservation, reversibility means

that a child understands that one operation (rolling a ball of clay into a sausage) can be reversed (the sausage can be rolled back into a ball). Relatedly, children with the concept of reversibility understand that a difference in one dimension (the length of the sausage versus the ball) can be compensated by a difference in another dimension (the thickness of the sausage versus the ball). Reversibility is something that concrete operational children possess but preoperational children do not.

Another aspect of preoperational children's thinking that affects their thought is **perceptual centration**, which refers to young children's difficulties in considering all factors of a situation when making a decision. Piaget described the thinking of preschool children as *stimulus bound*, with their attention, and thus their thinking, confined, or centered, to literal perceptual properties of objects. For example, in the classic conservation-of-liquid task, where a liquid is poured from a tall container into a shorter but wider container, children are so focused on differences in the height of the glasses that they ignore differences in their width, concluding that there is more liquid in the taller, skinnier glass.

reversibility In Piaget's theory, the knowledge that an operation can be reversed, characteristic of the concrete operational period.

perceptual centration In Piaget's theory, the tendency of preoperational children to attend to one aspect of a situation to the exclusion of others.

Perceptual centration can be seen in young children's everyday thinking. For example, Piaget (1969) observed that children often judge age on the basis of height—taller people are older than shorter people. This brings to mind the 5-year-old child who believed that his 4-foot 11-inch mother was the youngest mother of all the children in his class, when in reality she was only the shortest. Empirical research has confirmed that young children do judge people's age by height but that they can make relatively accurate judgments of age when not distracted by differences in height (Kratochwill & Goldman, 1973; Montepare & McArthur, 1986). When faced with the discrepancy in an obvious physical dimension, they cannot ignore it and make their assessment of age based on how many feet a person's head is above the floor.

We should comment that in the world of 4- and 5-year-olds, this practice of judging age by height often produces generally accurate results. Children during these years usually get taller as they age, so first graders are both older and taller than kindergarteners, and adults are all taller and older than children, so it likely makes no difference in a child's world the age of any particular adult—they are all tall and old.

Adults often view the thinking of preschool children as cute. They make cognitive errors that catch adults by surprise, such as thinking that the amount of clay in a ball changes when it is rolled into a sausage, or believing there is more sandwich when it is cut into four pieces rather than two. Despite these errors, preoperational children's cognition shares the important trait of mental representation with that of adults. The advent of symbolic thought truly transforms children's thinking. Despite the difference in age, a 3-year-old child is more like an adult than he or she is like a 1-year-old, intellectually speaking. Yet, children's thinking becomes more sophisticated, and a big jump occurs sometime between 5 and 7 years of age and the advent of what Piaget described as concrete operations.

The Concrete Operational Period (From 7 to 11 Years)

Piaget called the third stage of cognitive development, occurring between 7 to 11 years, the **concrete operational period**. Thought is now not only symbolic but also logical, and most importantly, children possess the logical rule of reversibility discussed earlier. That is, in this period, logic instead of perception drives thought. Now children no longer think that, for example, there is more clay in the sausage than in the ball (they have become "conservers" in Piagetian terms). But, as the stage name suggests, children's thinking is generally limited to concrete entities; they have trouble thinking in a systematic and logical way about abstract information. So, for example, something like $5 + 2x = y$ is still difficult to understand, as is the concept of infinity. Like a plane while it is taking off, their thinking is already flying, but it is still too close to the runway. However, children at this stage have already overcome their intellectual egocentrism (that is, they are better able to see things from others' perspectives) and perceptual centration (that is, they are able to *decentrate*, to combine different dimensions of a perceptual field, like height and width, at once).

As a consequence of these shifts, children at this period exhibit substantial progress in several areas of knowledge, among them conservation, as discussed previously. Yet it is important to note that conservation of all those properties shown in Figure 6.1 is not accomplished at once but gradually. For example, most 7-year-olds conserve number and mass, but they do not conserve weight or volume, which most children will not master until between 9 and 11 years of age. Piaget called this progressive acquisition of a certain skill, in this case conservation, within the same intellectual stage **horizontal décalage** (in French, *décalage* refers to a time lag).

Conservation is also attained at different rates for children in different cultures, with children in schooled cultures generally displaying an understanding of conservation before children from nonschooled cultures (Dasen, 1977). Although there are surely many reasons for such differences, one may be attributed to how such tests are administered. For instance, in one study in Canada, the conservation abilities of English-speaking children of European origin and a group of Native American Indians were assessed following standard Piagetian procedures (Nyiti, 1982). All of the European children were tested in English by a person of European descent. Half of the Indian children were tested in English, the language they use in school, by a European-Canadian interviewer, and the other half were tested in Micmac, the language they speak at home, by a Micmac Indian. Performance of the European and Indian children was the same when they were tested in their home languages—English for the European children and Micmac for the Indian children. However, when the Indian children were tested in English by a European interviewer, their performance was significantly worse. These findings suggest that although the timetable for the

concrete operational period The third major stage of cognitive development in Piaget's theory, in which children can decenter their perception, are less egocentric, and can think logically about concrete objects.

horizontal décalage The progressive acquisition of a certain skill within the same intellectual stage.

FIGURE 6.2 A typical Piagetian class-inclusion problem.

Are there more daisies or more flowers? School-age children can generally answer this correctly, realizing that daisies are a subset of the larger category of flowers. Younger children, however, have a difficult time with this problem, usually stating that there are more daises than flowers, being unable to ignore the more numerous daises relative to roses.

development of certain aspects of thought may be universal, their assessment can be affected by the cultural contexts in which they are measured.

Piaget also noticed a change in children's ability to classify objects during the concrete operational period. For example, children now understand that the same set of objects can be classified according to different criteria (for example, being able to switch from classifying on the basis of shape to size). This affords children increased cognitive flexibility to think in terms of different dimensions (for example, shape and size). Piaget observed that younger children tend to think that if something is labeled on the basis of one dimension, you cannot classify it simultaneously on the basis of another one. For instance, preschool children think that if someone is a Bostonian, she cannot simultaneously be an American, and a father cannot simultaneously be a son. The ability to classify objects simultaneously on two dimensions (size and shape, for instance) is referred to as **multiple classification**.

The epitome of classification is reflected by children being able to perform class-inclusion problems. **Class inclusion** refers to the knowledge that a class, or category, must always be smaller than any more-inclusive class in which it is contained. Consider a typical Piagetian class-inclusion problem: Children are shown an array of 10 pictures of flowers (7 daisies and 3 roses) (see Figure 6.2) and are asked if there are more flowers or more daisies in the array. Preschool children usually say there are more daisies, not getting the idea that flowers is a higher-level, or superordinate, category that includes both daisies and roses, which are more specific, or subordinate, categories.

Children during this period are not just able to classify objects according to a certain criteria (for example, long versus short things), but they are also able to order objects according to the quantitative dimension of a certain trait, or perform **seriation**. For example, they can order a ruler, a pencil, and a rubber band by length (the ruler is longer than the pencil, and the pencil is longer than the rubber band). Preoperational children have difficulty performing such tasks. This was brought to our attention recently when a group of 5- to 7-year-old children on a soccer team were asked to line up by height, shortest to tallest, so uniforms could be passed out. Most children initially placed themselves on the tall end of the line (perhaps reflecting some egocentricity—they all saw themselves as tall), and there was quite a bit of shuffling and confusion going on, until half a dozen mothers finally managed to arrange the children by height and got them to stand still.

It is important to note that beneath a skill such as seriation, there is a logical thinking ability, which Piaget called *transitive inference*, that permits children to draw conclusions without the need to double-check them through perception. For example, if a child of this age is told that a ruler is longer than a pencil (statement 1), and later that a pencil is longer than a rubber band (statement 2), she easily and automatically concludes that the ruler is longer than the rubber band, without any need to measure or visually confirm any of these objects. (If A > B, and B > C, then A must be > C. There is no need to actually check the difference in length between A and C.) If the first two statements are true, the logical conclusion will necessarily be true as well. The motto for a concrete operational child could be: "In logic we trust!"

By the time children wind their way through the concrete operational period, they are impressive thinkers. Their thinking is not only symbolic but also logical. They do not know as much as adolescents or adults, but, in truth, most of the thinking that adults do on a day-to-day basis can be done with the abilities Piaget attributed to the concrete operational child. However, human thought extends beyond concrete operations. Despite its logic, such thinking is still performed on concrete

multiple classification The ability to classify items in terms of more than one dimension simultaneously, such as shape and color.

class inclusion The knowledge that a subordinate class (for example, dogs) must always be smaller than the superordinate class in which it is contained (for example, animals).

seriation The ability to order objects according to the quantitative dimension of a certain trait.

objects. The thought of the 10-year-old rarely drifts to abstractions or hypothetical situations, but all this changes, at least for some children, with the advent of formal operations.

The Formal Operational Period (From 11 to 16 Years)

Piaget called the fourth and final stage of thought, typically occurring between 11 to 16 years of age, the **formal operational period**, and, according to Piaget, this is the upper level of intelligence in the human species. Some people can make better use of it (as Einstein did) than others, but, according to Piaget, it cannot be qualitatively improved upon once acquired. Its main feature is the addition of abstract reasoning to concrete operational abilities, permitting adolescents to comprehend such complex concepts as infinity or variables in a scientific experiment. With formal operations, adolescent thinkers can ponder not just things that are (that is, concrete entities) but also things that might be, such as world peace, universal religion, or an extended curfew ("Why I should have to be at home at midnight? Why not at 2 a.m., or even 4 a.m.?"). Adolescents can now solve real-world or hypothetical problems using reasoning, and they can think about thinking; they can reason in a systematic way about the hypothetical as well as the concrete.

Let's start with **hypothetico-deductive reasoning**. Piaget used this term to refer to any reasoning that goes beyond everyday experiences to things that have not been experienced. Deductive reasoning, which involves going from the general to the specific, can be done by concrete operational children. In fact, even preschool children can engage in deductive reasoning in some situations. However, the reasoning of preadolescent children is limited to events and objects with which they are already familiar. Formal operational children, in contrast, are not restricted to thinking about previously acquired facts but can generate hypotheses—what is possible is more important than what is real.

According to Piaget, the formal operational child can now think based solely on abstract symbols, requiring no referents in real life. For Piaget, this did not mean someone who is detached from reality, but rather a person who can postulate what might be as well as what is. Formal operational thinkers can formulate ideas of things not yet experienced, accounting for the novel (to the child) and often-grand ideas adolescents generate concerning morality, ethics, justice, government, and religion. The formulations of most teenagers are naive because of their limited knowledge, but Piaget believed these adolescents are flexing their mental muscles, using their newly acquired symbolic skills to deal with ideas rather than with things.

© Bob Daemmrich/PhotoEdit

By late in the concrete operational period, children are able to think logically, allowing them to perform many of the tasks that adults do.

Teenagers' ability to go beyond what is real and imagining what might be is very important in many practical senses. For example, adolescents can now appreciate in history class that although Columbus discovered America, many others could have done so if circumstances (that is, all of the other variables involved: political, technical, etc.) had been different. Before this period, history is often understood in terms of entertaining battles and life destinies, as often depicted in films, instead of understanding its core issues.

Adolescents cannot only reason hypothetically, but inductively, like a scientist, going from specific observations to broad generalizations. Let us provide an example of **inductive reasoning** based on a classic formal operational task, the pendulum problem (Inhelder & Piaget, 1958).

Children's task is to discover what factor or combination of factors causes differences in the rate that the pendulum oscillates, or swings. The factors they can consider include the weight of the object, the height from which the object is dropped, the force of push, and the length of the string. Think about this yourself: What factors do you think cause the pendulum to swing at different rates,

formal operational period In Piaget's theory, the final stage of cognitive development, in which children are able to apply abstract logical rules.

hypothetico-deductive reasoning A formal operational ability to think by generating and testing hypothesis.

inductive reasoning The type of thinking that goes from specific observations to broad generalizations, characteristic of formal operational thought.

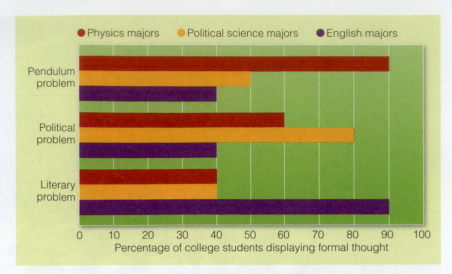

 shows a horizontal bar chart.

Legend: ● Physics majors ● Political science majors ● English majors

Categories (top to bottom): Pendulum problem, Political problem, Literary problem

X-axis: Percentage of college students displaying formal thought (0 to 100)

FIGURE 6.3 Percentage of college students displaying formal thought. College students perform best when formal operational tasks are in their area of expertise. SOURCE: Adapted from De Lisi, R., & Staudt, J. (1980). Individual differences in college students' performance on formal operations tasks. *Journal of Applied Developmental Psychology, 1*, 163–174. Reprinted by permission of Elsevier.

and if you were given the pendulum to experiment with, how would you test your hypothesis? Let's make the problem a bit simpler and assume that there are only two levels for each factor: the weight can be heavy or light, it can be dropped from a high versus a low point, the force of the push can be easy or hard, and the string can either be short or long. This leaves us with 16 alternatives, and if you tested them all, you would discover that only one factor made a difference: pendulums on short strings oscillate fast and those on long strings oscillate slowly. Adolescents are able to generate hypotheses (maybe it's the weight that makes the pendulum swing fast) and then test those hypotheses empirically, either confirming or disconfirming them (no, it's not the weight that makes a pendulum vary in speed), something that children who are not yet in formal operations have a difficult time doing.

Also developing during adolescence is the ability to think about thinking, or examine the content of one's own thought. Although concrete operational thinkers have some powerful problem-solving skills available to them, they are not able to reflect on the content of their thinking to arrive at new insights. Accordingly, while concrete operational thinkers are able to learn from their real-life experiences, formal operational thinkers are also able to learn by contemplating their own thoughts, and, as a result, generate new knowledge, a process Piaget called **reflective abstraction**. For example, a teenage basketball player can mentally analyze some aspects of a previous game, realizing that by

moving a different way he can avoid the defense of an opponent and be in a better position to make a basket. Reflective abstraction is linked to the "A-ha!" experience, or, if you prefer, insight.

Another characteristic often attributed to adolescents is self-centeredness. Piaget described adolescents as exhibiting a sort of egocentrism different from the egocentrism seen during the preoperational period. Adolescents' increased ability to reflect on their own thinking results in an extreme self-consciousness at a time when they are attempting to develop an adult identity. They believe, mistakenly, that everyone's attention is focused on them, and that everybody is as concerned about their feelings, behaviors, and thoughts as they are. David Elkind (Elkind, 1967; Elkind & Bowen, 1979) described adolescents as acting as if they are constantly on stage playing to an **imaginary audience**. This self-centeredness is also the basis for what Elkind called the **personal fable**—that is, the belief that one is unique and invulnerable—and contributes to adolescents' often-reckless behavior. (This is reflected by the statement of one teenager familiar to one of the authors: "I can drive 100 miles per hour on the highway. It's the old farts who don't have good reflexes who need to get off the road.") Our point here is that cognitive and socioemotional development are deeply related, with changes in one influencing changes in the other.

Piaget saw adolescence as a time of great intellectual awakening rather than a time of emotional storm and stress. Given that Piaget's theory was one of cognitive development and not of socioemotional development, this is reasonable. However, many scientists have questioned whether the thinking of the 16-year-old reflects the epitome of cognition available to our species, and some have proposed post-formal operational stages of cognitive development (see, for example, Commons & Richard, 1984; 2003). Moreover, Piaget's picture of adult intelligence is one of a reasonable, systematic, and logical thinker. This, however, is a picture that is shared by few psychologists who study adult cognition. Adults in general are not nearly as logical in their thinking as Piaget would have them be. We take mental shortcuts, make estimations, and arrive at conclusions before exhausting all possibilities. In fact, formal operational thinking does not seem to be typically used by adults in daily life (Capon & Kuhn, 1979), it is rare in cultures where formal schooling is not the norm (Cole, 1990; Dasen, 1977), and it may be used in some contexts but not others. For example, when groups of college students were given a series of formal-operational problems to solve, they tended to perform best when the problems were in their area of expertise—physics majors on physics problems (the pendulum problem), political science majors on political problems,

---

reflective abstraction The ability to reflect upon knowledge one already possesses, and without the need of additional information from the external environment, to arrive at new knowledge; characteristic of adolescent thought.

imaginary audience Expression of adolescent egocentrism, with adolescents feeling that they are constantly "on stage," or playing to an imaginary audience.

personal fable A belief in one's uniqueness and invulnerability, which is an expression of adolescent egocentrism.

and English majors on literary problems (De Lisi & Staudt, 1980, see Figure 6.3).

Piaget's description of formal operations may reflect the best adults can do, but it fails to capture how grown-ups deal with real-world problems on a daily basis. To quote Peter Wason and Philip Johnson-Laird (1972, p. 245): "At best, we can all think like logicians: At worst, logicians all think like us." Despite its shortcomings, Piaget's account of adolescent thought captures some of the uniqueness of adolescence and has provided insight to psychologists, educators, and parents about the teenage mind.

Let us summarize briefly the basic pattern of cognitive development as proposed by Piaget. Children enter the world armed with basic reflexes, and for about 2 years their thought is based primarily on action, including perceptual action. Around 2 years of age, with the advent of the symbolic function, children represent their world symbolically, reflected by deferred imitation, symbolic play, language, and imagery. However, such thinking, although symbolic, is intuitive, with appearance being more important than reality. Beginning sometime around when Western children begin school at 5 years of age, thinking becomes logical, although limited to concrete objects. Sometime in the early teen years, children's thinking becomes abstract, as they are able to reason both deductively and inductively and to create new knowledge simply by reflecting on their own knowledge. According to Piaget, each of these four stages (sensorimotor, preoperational, concrete operational, and formal operations) reflects qualitatively distinct ways of understanding the world, with accomplishments at one stage serving as the basis for future intellectual feats.

Piaget's Theory Today

Piaget has been dead for nearly a third of a century, and much of the research for his theory was done in the early part of the 20th century. Why does he warrant so much space in a 21st-century textbook compared to other 20th-century theorists, and what do modern developmental psychologists think of his theory? Much has changed since Piaget first (and last) wrote about children and their development, but his ideas and the phenomena he brought to light are still discussed today and serve as the foundation of contemporary cognitive development. Piaget essentially founded the modern field of cognitive development, and, as one scholar put it, "assessing the impact of Piaget on developmental psychology is like assessing the impact of Shakespeare on English literature or Aristotle on philosophy—impossible" (Beilin, 1992, p. 191).

Contributions of Piaget's Theory

First, Piaget provided a relatively accurate description of how children of different ages think. Piaget may have overestimated children's abilities in some cases and underestimated them in others, but his overall description of changes in thinking rings true. Moreover, the influence of Piaget's ideas has been enormous, not just in psychology, but also in education. Most teachers are well aware of Piaget's ideas of an active child and that children of different ages and stages are capable of understanding information in different ways. In this sense, it is interesting to note how, roughly speaking, educational levels in most schools throughout the West are organized in a way reminiscent of Piaget's stages: preschool education (preoperational stage), primary school (concrete operational stage), and secondary school (formal operational stage). In fact, one of us (CHB) often uses students' own transitions through the educational system before entering university as an aid for remembering Piaget's stages. In addition, Piaget's ideas have been at the heart of some modern psycho-pedagogical strategies, particularly "discovery learning," in which children are encouraged to discover important aspects of an educational curriculum through active experimentation. This is in opposition to traditional approaches in which teachers directly instruct children. According to Piaget (1972, p. 27), "Children should be able to do their own experimenting and their own research. Teachers, of course, can guide them by providing appropriate materials, but the essential thing is that in order for a child to understand something, he must construct it for himself; he must reinvent it."

Criticisms of Piaget's Theory

Despite this achievement and many other merits of the theory, it is also clear that Piaget's is not the last word on cognitive development. Contemporary research has shown that some important aspects of cognitive development are not adequately captured by his theory, while others were simply wrong (see Table 6.2). Basically, two important sources of criticism have emerged: one, focused on the timing and skills exhibited by children at different stages, and a second focused on the relevance of the concept of stage.

Regarding the timing of skills at certain ages, it has been generally found that children are more competent in cognitive terms than Piaget suggested. Starting with the sensorimotor period, other researchers, often using better-controlled procedures than those used by Piaget, have replicated the major sequence of events he described. For example, the sequence of infants' progression through

BOX 6.2 **evolution in action**

Piaget and the Animals

Piaget proposed that his theory described the universal course of cognitive development. Some children may go through stages faster than others, and some may not achieve the higher intellectual levels, but because the accomplishments of the earlier stages serve as the foundation for later stages, children go through them in the same constant order. Might Piaget's stages of cognitive development be even more universal than he proposed? Might Piaget's description of intellectual accomplishment also describe the cognitive development of nonhuman animals? Applying aspects of Piaget's theory to other animals would seem particularly appropriate for humans' genetic cousins, monkeys and apes, whose cognition, in many ways, seems like our own. Although this may appear like an obvious thing to do, according to Juan Carlos Gómez (2004), it took primatologists about 40 years to take Piaget seriously.

If you have been paying attention up to this point in the book, you may recognize that there are some substantial limitations in applying Piaget's theory to nonhuman animals, the most obvious being that three of four Piaget's stages involve mental representation, something that may be unique to humans, or at least greatly limited in other species. But Piaget also provided detailed descriptions of the progression through the

Developmental Sensorimotor Substages in Object Permanence in Monkeys, Great Apes, and Humans

The numbers refer to the age range in months that object permanence is attained for each species.

Species	Age in Months				
	Stage 2	Stage 3	Stage 4	Stage 5	Stage 6
Humans	2	4 to 8.5	7 to 8	7 to 10	11 to 21
Chimpanzees	3	6	9	12	18
Gorillas	1.5	3.5	7.5	7 to 9	9 to 10
Macaques	0.75	1 to 1.5	1.75	3.5	none or partial
Capuchins	1	2 to 3	3 to 7.5	8 to 12	none

SOURCE: Adapted from Parker, S. T., & McKinney, M. L. (1999). *Origins of intelligence: The evolution of cognitive development in monkeys, apes, and humans.* Baltimore: The Johns Hopkins University Press, p. 42.

substages of his nonverbal *sensorimotor period*, spanning from birth to about 2 years of age for human children, and comparative psychologists have examined some of the accomplishments nonhuman animals make in nonlinguistic sensorimotor intelligence in terms of these substages.

For example, Piaget's progression of the development of object permanence has been investigated in a wide range of species and extensively studied in a variety of primates, using many of the same tasks and procedures Piaget used with human infants and toddlers. Sue Taylor Parker and Michael

McKinney (1999) summarized data from a variety of monkey (macaques and capuchins) and ape (chimpanzees, gorillas) species on the development of object permanence following the substages of Piaget's sensorimotor period. The accompanying table shows the average age in months when each substage is achieved for each species. Included in this table are the average ages that human infants achieve each substage.

A look at this table reveals several interesting facts. First, each primate species shows the same order of attaining the various accomplishments of object permanence

the sensorimotor substages is much as Piaget described them (Uzgiris & Hunt, 1975; Uzgiris, 1983). However, as we saw in Chapter 5, infants possess a more sophisticated knowledge about objects (for example, object permanence) and the physical world than Piaget proposed, at least when using some of the new methodologies (for example, the violation-of-expectations paradigm; Baillargeon, 2004; Reznick, Fueser & Bosquet, 1998). Infants display deferred imitation earlier than Piaget proposed (although only for simple actions), and they may even possess some rudimentary symbolic abilities in their first year, as reflected, for example, by their ability to perform simple arithmetic (Wynn, 1992; see Gelman & Williams, 1998; Spelke & Kinzler, 2007). In fact, evidence of symbolic competencies in infancy, some of them described in Chapter 5, caused Andrew Meltzoff (1990, p. 20) to conclude that *"in a very real sense, there may be no such thing as an exclusively 'sensorimotor period' in the normal human infant"* (italics in the original).

Regarding preoperations, preschool children generally have greater competency than Piaget proposed. For example, children as young as 4 years old and children with intellectual disabilities can be trained to conserve (Brainerd & Allen, 1971; Gelman, 1969; Hendler & Weisberg, 1992). Piaget believed that training should only be effective when children are "on the cusp," ready to make the transition between two stages. In general, Piaget's theory was one of *competence*—what he believed children of a certain age or stage were *capable* of doing. When infants fail to retrieve a hidden object, for instance, it is because they do not have the underlying cognitive structures (that is, the competence) to execute the task. Yet, his descriptions are better thought of as reflecting *performance*—what children usually do under typical situations (but as human children do. That is, monkeys and apes go through the same sensorimotor stages in the same order as their *Homo sapiens* cousins.

Second, some species go through the stages faster than do human children. For example, gorilla babies attain each of the object permanence stages sooner than human children, mastering stage 6 (invisible displacement), on average, about 6 months earlier than children. Macaques develop even faster, attaining stage 4 (retrieving hidden objects) four times faster than human children do. Other animals, such as cats, develop stage-4 object permanence even sooner than macaques, by about 2 weeks (Gómez, 2004). Humans' slower rate of development should really not be surprising. Recall that humans have an extended period of immaturity and that our species' relatively slow rate of growing up, in part, permits us to develop our advanced brain and mind (Bjorklund, 1997, 2007a).

Third, the highest level of achievement varies with species. Chimpanzees and gorillas, which are closer genetically to humans than macaques and capuchins, attain substage-6 object permanence, whereas the monkey species do not.

The fourth fact cannot be discerned solely from this table but involves the acquisition of the suite of sensorimotor accomplishments at each stage. In general, there seems to be greater homogeneity, or evenness, in the accomplishments of sensorimotor intelligence in humans than in the other primate species. For example, capuchins monkeys acquire stage 4 of object permanence significantly earlier (3 to 7.5 months) than do human infants (7 to 8 months), but it takes them about 4 months more than humans to master the coordination of secondary circular reactions, an acquisition that also takes place in stage 4 (8 months in humans vs. 12 months in capuchin monkeys) (Parker & McKinney, 1999). In other words, cognitive development during the sensorimotor period seems to be much more synchronous and well coordinated in humans than in other species.

What, if anything, does this tell us about the development of thought in children? Although it is difficult to summarize briefly, we think that a comparison of human and primate thought from a Piagetian perspective tells us at least two things. First, and most obvious, some aspects of thought are shared with closely related species, implying a common evolutionary origin. Developmental primatologists Parker and McKinney (1999) suggest that, in primate cognition, the more advanced species might have added new abilities to the end states of their ancestors. This appears wholly reasonable and is consistent with other research showing that humans seem to possess representational abilities that their ape and monkey relatives do not.

The second thing we learn from this research is that many of the phenomena described by Piaget are involved in solving real-world problems facing most animals with a brain, not just young humans. To quote primatologist Juan Carlos Gómez (2004, p. 58) regarding object permanence,

> objects are not an invention of humans: the world is full of natural objects—stones, water, trees, sand, leaves, fruits, mud, branches, carcasses, and finding hidden objects (sensorimotor stage 4) is not just a refined Piagetian task performed to amuse developmental psychologists, but a critical survival skill for tasks such as finding food, and keeping track of predators, prey, or conspecifics (members of one's own species).

Not surprisingly then, a vast range of species, from insects to birds to primates, possess at least rudimentary object-permanence abilities (Etienne, 1976; Gómez, 2004).

Certainly, primatologists and comparative animal psychologists have investigated many aspects of cognitive development beyond those studied by Piaget (see, for example, Hernández Blasi & Bjorklund, 2003, p. 271), revealing what children's cognition has (or does not have) in common with other species. Together, along with investigations of children's thinking, we gain greater insight into the nature and origins of human cognitive development.

see Lourenço & Machado, 1996). From a performance perspective, children of different ages have basically the same underlying concept (of object permanence, for example), but younger children lack the supporting skills (for example, eye-hand coordination, ability to inhibit previous responses) to pass the test. Much as Vygotsky proposed, children's cognitive performance can vary considerably depending on the context and how much support they have from more capable others.

Formal operations, as mentioned earlier, are not achieved by all people, probably not even *most* people in the world, vary with context and the demands of one's culture (see Box 6.3, on pp. 248-249), and do not describe well the way most adults think. On the other side of the coin, concrete operational children can be trained to solve formal operational tasks after only brief instruction (Adey & Shayer, 1992; Stone & Day, 1978), although the effectiveness of such training is debatable (see Adey & Shayer, 1994).

The concept of stage has also been questioned. Although most of a child's cognitive functioning may occur within a relatively narrow range, children show more variability in their thinking than suggested by Piaget's stage theory (see Brainerd, 1978; Flavell, 1978). However, others claim that Piaget's stage concept has been misunderstood, and that he did not insist on the high degree of "cognitive evenness" that most contemporary scholars assume (Lourenço & Machado, 1996). Other theorists assume that infants bring more knowledge into the world than Piaget proposed (for example, the core-knowledge approach described in Chapter 5 and theory theories to be discussed in the following section), making Piaget's constructivist view (at least an extreme version of it) not tenable. Generally speaking, most modern theories of cognitive

table 6.2 Main Criticisms (and Alternatives) to Piaget's Theory

On Stages of Cognitive Development

The timing of the stage progression is more variable than Piaget proposed.

Piaget believed he was describing children's cognitive competence (the limits of their abilities), whereas he was actually describing their performance (what a child usually does under certain circumstances)

Piaget underestimated the abilities of sensorimotor children, including object permanence, deferred imitation, and their problem-solving skills.

Preoperational children are not as egocentric as Piaget proposed, with magical thinking being restricted to unfamiliar contexts.

Preoperational children can learn some concrete operational concepts (for example, conservation), and concrete operations children can be taught some formal operational contents.

Adults frequently fail to use formal operations in daily life. Not all adults in all cultures exhibit formal operations. Formal operations can also be domain-specific (that is, they can be successfully applied to certain contexts, but not to others).

On Mechanisms of Cognitive Development

Stage is not a worthy concept; many scientists think there is no real proof that stages actually exist, at least as described by Piaget. (*Information-processing Approaches*)

Stage can be a useful concept if used more liberally than Piaget did. (*Neo-Piagetian Theories*)

Social environment and culture play a more significant and crucial role than Piaget proposed. (*Sociocultural Approach*)

Evolved dispositions play a more significant role in early development than Piaget proposed. (*Theory Theories* and *Core-Knowledge Approaches*)

---

development use Piaget as a starting point, and in this sense, it is fair to say that Piaget's influence seems to be everywhere.

Cognitive Development in the Post-Piaget Era

If Piaget's theory no longer dominates cognitive development, what, if anything, has taken its place? Some neo-Piagetian theorists take a more flexible interpretation of stages and apply concepts of information processing to explain some of the transitions between stages that Piaget observed. For example, both Juan Pascual-Leone (1970, 2000) and Robbie Case (1985, 1992) proposed that increases in children's limited capacity to hold information in memory can explain the changes that Piaget uncovered between preoperational and concrete operational children. For instance, in conservation problems, preoperational children typically make their judgments based on a single dimension ("The sausage is so long, there must be more clay in it"). Once children have the mental capacity to keep two dimensions in mind at once (the difference in length is compensated by the difference in width), they are able to solve these problems. This occurs not because of changes in underlying cognitive structures as Piaget proposed, but because of increases in working-memory capacity.

In general, information-processing accounts dominated the field of cognitive development in the latter part of the 20th century, with researchers essentially viewing children's minds as analogous to developing computers, with age-related changes in speed of processing, the capacity of the various stores, and the software, or strategies, children had available to them (see Chapter 8 for examples of research findings primarily from the information-processing tradition). However, despite the recognition by nearly all developmental psychologists of the importance of aspects of information processing to explain cognitive development (the role of executive function, for example), many have not abandoned Piaget's central belief of the significance of underlying changes in conceptual development in children's thinking. This is reflected by the view of Alison Gopnik (1996), who argued that, in the same way that technological advances facilitate changes in science but do not generate scientific changes themselves (she ironically observes, "buying a telescope does not make you Galileo," p. 224), advances in information processing can certainly facilitate children's conceptual changes, but they do not fully explain them.

Piaget's account of cognitive development has often been contrasted with Vygotsky's sociocultural approach, which was described in some detail in Chapter 2. Consistent with other contemporary approaches to development, Vygotsky emphasized that cognitive development is mediated through culture. Further, Vygotsky argued that Piaget's account of cognitive development often did not pay enough attention to the "real child," but rather emphasized the "child as a thinker," or the "epistemic child." Piaget tended to see the child as a sort of Robinson Crusoe abandoned on an island, surrounded only by physical objects, ignoring that in real life cognitive development always takes place in a world filled with objects *and* people. Vygotsky, and sociocultural theorists in general (as well as developmental contextual theorists), emphasize children's cognition as developing in the context of their daily lives, with other people, as well as objects, being important components of the context. From this perspective, and counter to classic Piagetian theory, culture reflects more than interesting variation that makes children from different societies think a bit differently from one another, but rather *how* they think, beginning in infancy (Rodríguez, 2007).

Consistent with the criticisms of Piaget's theory discussed in the previous section, Gopnik (1996) argued that most experts today, regardless of their own specific theoretical orientation, believe that cognitive development consists of advances in a series of different domains of knowledge (for example, physical knowledge, biological knowledge, and psychological knowledge) rather than in general changes applied simultaneously to all the domains of children's knowledge. In other words, cognitive development does not consist of changes in a single domain-general mechanism, as Piaget proposed, but in terms of a series of domain-specific mechanisms.

Gopnik and others have modified Piaget's ideas and developed a new approach for studying important aspects of children's physical, biological, and social worlds, termed **theory theories**, and we examine this neo-Piagetian approach briefly here.

Theory Theories

In many ways, theory theories of cognitive development continue where Piaget left off. They are called "theory theories" because they hold that children form "theories" about how aspects of their psychological, physical, and biological worlds work. Modifications in children's intuitive theories are often described as reflecting *conceptual change*, with the implication that cognitive advancements in understanding the world require a radical change in children's naïve theories (see, for example, Carey, 1985; Vosniadou & Brewer, 1992). The idea of conceptual change is similar to the idea of a transition from one *stage* of thinking to another, as Piaget's theory proposed. It reflects the belief that changes in conceptual structures underlie changes in cognitive development. For example, in Piaget's account of the development of object permanence, infants' understanding of objects changes from one in which objects exist only when they are acting upon them to one in which objects are conceived of as being permanent in time and space, regardless of whether they are acting on them or not.

Essentially, theory theorists see children as little scientists, much as Piaget did. Children test theories about how different aspects of the world work, and when their experiences contradict their existing theories, they eventually change them (that is, make a conceptual change), and as a result develop a more reliable mental map to navigate in the real world. In fact, Alison Gopnik and Andrew Meltzoff (1997, p. 32) turn this idea on its head, stating, "It is not that children are little scientists but that scientists are big children. Scientific progress is possible because scientists employ cognitive processes that are first seen in very young children."

Theory theories have much in common with core-knowledge theories discussed in Chapter 5, in that each assumes that children possess rudimentary ideas about how a specific segment of their world works, yet each also assumes that these naïve theories are modified by experience (Gopnik & Meltzoff, 1997; Karmiloff-Smith, 1992). They tend to differ in terms of the degree to which knowledge is viewed as being innate versus constructed by experience, á la Piaget (see Siegal, 2008). Both approaches assume that infants' and children's cognition is *constrained* in that they are not able to process all information equally well, but they are especially able to make sense of some information, particularly those in *core domains* (for example, psychological, physical, and biological information). According to Rochel Gelman and Earl Williams (1998, p. 600), "From an evolutionary perspective, learning cannot be a process of arbitrary and completely flexible knowledge acquisition. In core domains, learning processes are the means to functionally defined ends: acquiring and storing the particular sorts of relevant information which are necessary for solving particular problems."

Much research has been done over the past several decades exploring children's developing knowledge of their physical, biological, and psychosocial worlds, often on the assumption that such knowledge is based on some intuitive understanding children have in each of these domains that changes with experience. We discussed some aspects of intuitive physics in Chapter 5, and much of Chapter 7 will be devoted to children's intuitive psychology, or their social cognition. The following section examines the topic, originally investigated by Piaget, of the development of children's biological knowledge, most of which has been approached from a theory theory perspective.

theory theories Approach to cognitive development that combines neonativism and constructivism, proposing that cognitive development progresses by children generating, testing, and changing their naïve theories about the physical and social world.

BOX 6.3 **socioculturally speaking**

Culture, Symbols, and Development

One of the major themes of this book is that culture counts; that is, a child's social environment, including the broader culture, influences not only what a child thinks about but also *how* he or she thinks. However, the variations we witness caused by cultural differences are not infinite: children the world over inherit species-typical nervous systems and possess the same basic mechanisms to acquire the skills and knowledge important to their local ecology. Children the world over develop symbolic abilities, much as Piaget described, beginning around their second birthdays, with these skills improving with age. Yet, although children around the globe are born with the same nervous system and are prepared to make sense of their social and physical worlds in similar ways, the problems they face can differ greatly depending if they grow up, for example, in the jungles of South America versus the deserts of North Africa; on an equatorial island in the Pacific versus the Arctic tundra; or even in a rural area versus a city. Human beings have inhabited nearly every ecological niche on dry land at one time or another, and each ecology provides a unique set of problems that must be faced, calling for different types of cognition, including different expressions of the symbolic function.

As an example, consider the expression of formal operations in Piaget's theory. As mentioned in the text, formal operations are not universally acquired (in fact, not all people in any culture display formal operational thought), and when people do think formally, their thoughts are frequently applied to some contents (for example, developmental psychology) but not to others (for example, automobile mechanics). For instance, preliterate Bushman hunters from Africa do not solve standard problems of formal operational thinking like the pendulum problem, but they do display formal thought while tracking prey (Tulkin & Konner, 1973). The ability is present, but, just as for people in Western societies, it is expressed only under supportive conditions.

For a second example, consider classification abilities. In the 1930s, the Russian neuropsychologist Alexander Luria (1976) evaluated the cognitive styles of inhabitants from a remote area in the former Soviet Union (Uzbekistan) and reported that, unlike Westerners, most of the adults he studied did not develop a conceptual, or taxonomic, way of classifying objects. Rather, they used a more functional approach, perhaps better suited for their ecology. Consider the following example from Rakmat, a 38-year-old illiterate peasant (from Luria, 1976, pp. 56–57):

He is shown drawings of the following: *hammer-saw-log-hatchet.*

"They're all alike. I think all of them have to be here. See, if you're going to saw, you need a saw, and if you have to split something you need a hatchet. So they're all needed here."

We tried to explain the task by another, simpler example: "Look, here you have three adults and one child. Now clearly the child doesn't belong in this group."

"Oh, but the boy must stay with the others! All three of them are working, you see, and if they have to keep running out to fetch things, they'll never get the job done, but the boy can do the running for them. . . . The boy will learn; that'll be better, then they'll be able to work well together." [p. 55]

Subject is then shown drawing of: *bird-rifle-dagger-bullet.*

"The swallow doesn't fit here. . . . No . . . this is a rifle. It's loaded with a bullet and kills the swallow. Then you have to cut the bird up with the dagger, since there's no other way to do it. . . . What I said about the swallow before is wrong! All these things go together."

In a similar vein, Scott Atran (1994, 1998) reported that, among Itza-Maya hunters of Central America, taxonomies regarding mammals are not very different from those made by American college students. However, like Uzbekistani peasants, the Itza make greater use of functional classifications than Americans do. For example, they include in the same group of arboreal (tree-dwelling) animals monkeys (primates), raccoons (tree-dwelling procyonids), and squirrels (rodents). Itza hunters are also more likely to consider large predators, such as jaguars, to be typical representatives of the mammal category,

Children's Development of Biological Knowledge

Children of all ages and all cultures are particularly interested in animals, as witnessed by the many pets children have, from dogs and cats to hamsters, turtles, and goldfish. As discussed in Chapter 5, infants as young as 3 and 4 months old can form categories of different animals, differentiating horses from cats, zebras, and giraffes, for example (Eimas & Quinn, 1994). Some have suggested that this early and persistent interest in animals has an evolutionary basis, with specific areas of the brain devoted to processing information about animals (see, Geary, 2005a, for a review). It would seem to go without saying that biological knowledge would have been important for the survival of our ances-

tors in a natural environment (see, for example, Barrett, 2005; Medin & Atran, 1999).

Is It Alive?

Piaget (1929) was one of the first to investigate systematically children's development of biological knowledge. This is perhaps best seen in young children's beliefs that some inanimate things act as if they are alive, termed **animism.** Piaget observed that preschool children often attribute human properties, like hopes, feelings, and thoughts, to inanimate things ("The sun didn't come out today because it's angry" or "I lost a lot of races because my sneakers didn't want to run. Please, Daddy, buy me new ones.") However, more contemporary research has found that preschool children often have more knowledge about living things than Piaget initially proposed (Inagaki & Hatano, 1991).

Yet, older children, adolescents, and even college-educated adults continue to persist in some

animism Attributing human properties, like hopes, feelings, and thoughts, to inanimate things.

Children's drawings vary depending on the culture in which they grow up. Here you have an example of the typical "pen-head" human figure drawn by Bemba children in the former Rhodesia (Zimbabwe). SOURCE: From Paget, G.W. (1932). Some drawings of men and women made by children of certain non-European races. *Journal of the Royal Anthropological Institute, 62*, **127–144.**

prototype with which to compare other animals is shaped according to current ecological needs and circumstances (see also Geary, 2005a).

When we look at the way illiterate Uzbekistani peasants or Itza-Maya hunters classify objects, we might feel tempted to evaluate them as being less cognitively advanced than the classifications used by Western people. (In fact, a functional type of classification is typical in many 5-year-old children in developed societies.) However, this would be a mistake, for these differences in classification style are well suited to the local environments. Moreover, cognitive differences are also found among children in developed countries as a function of schooling or tradition. For example, Australian children, because of their early familiarization with cosmology (study of the universe), tend to have a more advanced understanding of how the Earth is structured than do British children (Siegal, Butterworth, & Newcombe, 2004), and Indian children seem to be more prone to see the Earth as a big flat disc floating on water, in agreement with their own traditional cultural cosmology (Samarapungavan, Vosniadou, & Brewer, 1996).

Children's expressions of the symbolic function also are deeply affected by the ecological conditions in which they grow up. Imitation, drawing, symbolic play, and storytelling

are always about something (that is, produced by the mind of children), but within their immediate environment, and these immediate environments, and thus children's expressions of the symbolic function, can vary widely. For example, in an extensive collection of about 60,000 drawings from non-Western children (Paget, 1932), many African children drew human figures with a typical pin-head shape, in agreement with their cultural standards to represent human figures, which are very different from Western ones (see accompanying Figure). In the case of symbolic play, we also know that it is seriously influenced by which activities occur frequently in the ecology where children grow up. For example, in the Marquesas Islands in Polynesia, children's symbolic play focuses on activities such as fishing, hunting, and preparing feasts (Martini, 1994), instead of driving cars, flying planes, or playing cops and robbers, common themes in the play of Western children.

Culture certainly counts in shaping children's thinking. However, children around the globe possess the same set of symbolic abilities that develop in much the same fashion. What differs is how children in different cultures express their symbolic abilities, not the abilities themselves.

whereas Americans are more likely to select smaller animals (for example, dogs) as typical representatives of this category. Thus, the selection of the animal that is used as the

aspects of animistic thinking. In their extensive review, William Looft and Wayne Bartz (1969) stated that between 50% and 75% of adults tested displayed some animistic thinking. For example, some college students claimed that a lighted match was alive because "it has a flame which indicates life," or the sun is alive "because it gives off heat." Looft and Bartz believed that the animism shown by adults was qualitatively different from that shown by children; nonetheless, the high frequency of adults, even those with college educations, who attribute life characteristics to inanimate objects indicates that this tendency extends beyond early childhood. This, along with newer research (for example, Goldberg & Thompson-Schill, 2009; Reuven et al., 2010), suggests that adults retain some of the same biases about living things as do children, but overcome these biases, for the most part, as they learn the scientific way to classify living and nonliving things.

Self-propelled motion is perhaps the best cue to determine if an object is animate or not, something even infants seem to be aware of (Schlottmann & Ray, 2010). For example, infants are able to recognize biological motion as young as 3 months of age. In these studies, infants watch a human figure walking with 10 to 12 light patches at the joints, as well as other displays with randomly moving patterns of light (see Figure 6.4). (This is really better appreciated when seen in motion.) Typically, 3- to 5-month-old infants recognize the pattern of lights as something special, looking at it longer than a random pattern of moving lights, although they do not seem to recognize the same walking figure if it is presented upside down (panel B in Figure 6.4; Bertenthal, Proffitt, & Cutting, 1984). However, although infants spend more time looking at displays showing biological motion, they do not seem to treat it as a person until about 9 months (Bertenthal, 1996; Bertenthal, Proffitt & Kramer, 1987; see also Yoon &

1. Children all over the world are fascinated by other living beings, particularly animals.

2. Infants are able to distinguish inanimate from animate beings based on movement.

3. Children do not see plants as living organisms until they are about 7 to 9 years old.

4. Verbal preschool children (3 to 6 years old approximately) seem to know a lot of things about biology, but the depth and degree of organization of this knowledge may vary depending on culture and ecological circumstances, as, for example, growing up in urban versus rural areas, or living in traditional societies versus technological societies.

5. Some verbal preschool children, in some cultures in some contexts, *can* use what they know about themselves and other people to make inferences about the biological world.

6. Knowledge about the biological world improves substantially when children are about 7 to 10 years old, already resembling the sort of understanding typically exhibited by adults

Johnson, 2009). Some recent research suggests that even newborns may be able to recognize biological motion (Bardi, Simion, & Regolin, 2009).

Recent research has shown that toddlers with autism spectrum disorder fail to recognize biological motion (Klin et al., 2009). In adults and neurotypically developing children, biological motion is associated with activation of an area in the temporal lobe of the brain (the superior temporal sulcus). It is interesting that children with autism show a different pattern of brain activation in this area in response to biological motion (see Pelphrey & Carter, 2008). People with autism have particular difficulty with social relations (see Chapter 7). These findings suggest that the deficit shown by children with autism in detecting biological motion may contribute to their deficits in intuitive psychology (see Frith & Frith, 1999).

What Young Children Know and Don't Know about Biology

How do children organize their understanding of the biological world, and how does it develop? Pioneering research by Susan Carey and her colleagues (Carey, 1985, 1999; Slaughter, Jaakkola, & Carey, 1999) set out to answer these questions. Carey (1985, 1999) argued that children much before the age of 7 do not have an organized understanding of the natural world, but rather possess a series of isolated pieces of knowledge. For example, Carey proposed that preschool children generalize what they know about people to animals. As evidence for this, 4- and 5-year-old children attribute human properties such as having bones, a heart, sleeping, and thinking to different species, depending on their similarities to humans (Carey, 1985). A major conceptual change occurs sometime between 7 and 10 years as a consequence of acquired experience, which makes their understanding of biological issues more coherent and similar to that of adults.

Despite research over the past 20 years or so that has shown that preschool children sometimes display quite sophisticated knowledge of the biological properties of life, other research reveals that they have much to learn (see Inagaki & Hatano, 2006; Siegal, 2008). (Concept Review 6.3 lists some conclusions about the development of children's biological knowledge.) For example, on the negative side, 4-year-old children initially believe that the inheritance of some physical traits (eye color, for instance) depends on environmental factors, such as the family children are living with, regardless of whether children live with their biological or adoptive parents (Solomon et al., 1996). It is not until children are about 7 years old that they understand that some traits are linked to one's biological family, whereas others are not (for example, beliefs). This phenomenon is not limited to children in Western cultures but has also been reported for Vezo children from Madagascar (Astuti, 2001; Astuti, Solomon, & Carey, 2004). In other research, children in preschool through the second grade believe that you are less apt to catch a cold from a relative or friend than from a stranger (Raman & Gelman, 2008). Other studies demonstrated that young children often think that dead people retain some biological properties of life, like eating and breathing (Slaughter et al., 1999).

Other research suggests that some aspects of young children's biological knowledge are relatively sophisticated. For example, Inagaki and Hatano (1993, 2002) reported that 4- and 5-year-old Japanese children understand that eye color, breathing, and one's heartbeat are not under voluntary control, and that if children are not well nourished, they are more susceptible to illness (see Figure 6.5, p. 252). Other research has shown that most 4- to 5-year-old children:

1. Are able to grasp some apparently complex biological phenomena, such as reproduction

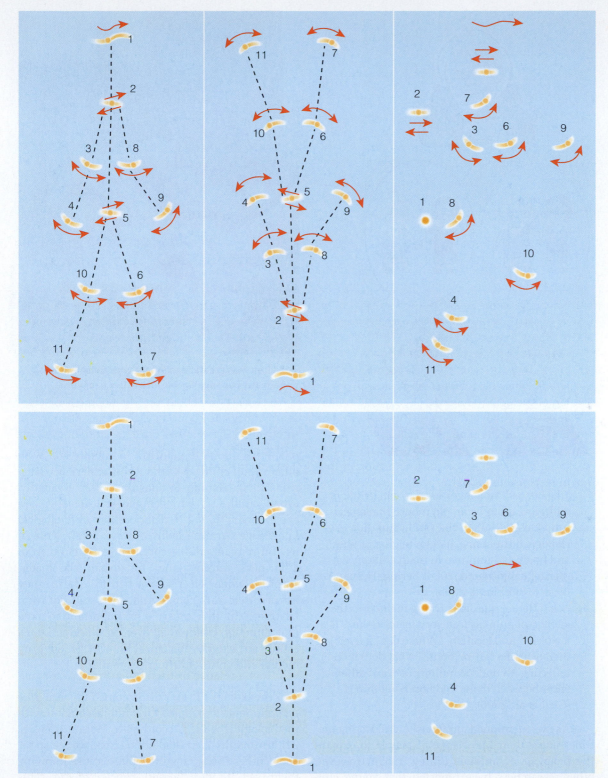

FIGURE 6.4 **Biological motion.**
Three- to 5-month-old babies look longer at the first panel of moving lights—that is, one depicting biological (here, specifically human) motion—than at the other patterns of moving lights or patterns of nonmoving lights (bottom panel). SOURCE: From Bertenthal, B. I., Proffitt, D. R., & Kramer, S. J. (1987). Perception of biomechanical motions by infants: Implementation of various processing constraints. *Journal of Experimental Psychology: Human Perception & Performance, 13*, 577–585. Copyright © 1987 by the American Psychological Association. Reprinted by permission.

(that babies grow inside their mothers, and seeds of a certain species of plant produce a new plant of the same species; Springer, 1999; Hickling & Gelman, 1994) and contamination (for example, if a cockroach is in a glass of orange juice, the juice should not be drunk, even if the cockroach is removed; Siegal & Share, 1990).

2. Can distinguish between dead and sleeping animals, not confusing these apparently similar states, and making clear that they know that dead animals cannot exhibit living functions, such as moving, while sleeping animals can once they awake (Barrett & Behne, 2005).

3. Know, after watching a puppet show, that an anthropomorphized mouse eaten by an

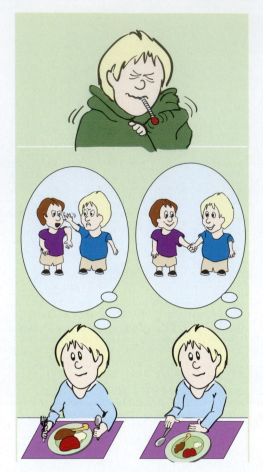

FIGURE 6.5 Most 5-year-old children seem to know that a deficit in nutrients can be a factor contributing to poor health. They also seem to know that the origin of disease has to do with biological/physical reasons, not moral/psychological reasons. Here is an example of a stimulus used in a study about children's understanding of illness. Children were asked, "When playing with a child who has a cold and is coughing a lot, who is more likely to catch cold: boy A, who often hits and pinches his friend on the back but eats a lot at meals every day, or boy B, who is a good friend, but eats only a little?" Most 5-year-olds choose boy B. SOURCE: From Inagaki, K., & Hatano, G. (2006). Young children's conception of the biological world. *Current Directions in Psychological Science, 15* (4), 177–181. Reprinted by permission of Sage Publications.

Children with greater experience with animals are less apt to attribute human-like properties to animals.

alligator will no longer need to eat, drink, or will grow up to be an old mouse (biological functions), although they still think that psychological functions, like loving his mother and hoping to improve in math, still persist (Bering & Bjorklund, 2004; Bering, Hernández Blasi, & Bjorklund, 2005).

4. Ask different questions trying to discover the identity of animals (category membership, "Is it a bear?" and location, "Where does it live?") than of artifacts (functions, "What does it do?"), reflecting an understanding of critical differences between living and nonliving things (Greif et al., 2006).

As we mentioned previously, children sometimes apply their knowledge of people to explain the behavior of animals (Carey, 1985). However, other researchers have reported that young children, although perhaps preferring to use their knowledge about people to think about animals, can indeed reason about plants and animals without making reference to the psychological (that is, people) domain (Keil, 2007). One reason why children frequently apply their psychological knowledge to the biological domain may be because of a lack of knowledge of animals. For example, urban children who have had experience caring for goldfish at home do not make anthropomor-

phic attributions to goldfish, in comparison with other urban children without this experience (Inagaki, 1990; Hatano & Inagaki, 1992). Relatedly, urban children from technological societies are experiencing today a deterioration of biological knowledge (Atran, Medin, & Ross, 2004). (One of us still remembers the comments of a child from a farmer's family about his urban classmates' surprise, when, on a school trip to a farm, they learned that milk comes from cows and not from factories.) In this sense, it is important to note that, although children all over the world are powerfully attracted by biological knowledge, environmental and cultural influences matter.

The biologist E. O. Wilson coined the term *biophilia* to refer to people's love and fascination with the biological world. According to Wilson (1984, p. 22), "Humanity is exalted not because we are so far above other living creatures, but because knowing them well elevates the very concept of life." This fascination with the biological world begins early. Children seem to be biased to attend to and learn about the natural (biological) world, although it takes them some time before they have the understanding that adults do. One important thing that children learn is about reproduction, reflected by the question that causes many parents to squirm when asked by their young children, "Where do babies come from?" We look at children's knowledge and thinking about reproduction in Box 6.4.

table 6.3 Types of Play, Typical Developmental Patterns, and Possible Adaptive Functions

	What Is It? (Examples)	How Does It Develop?	What Is It (Possibly) For?
Object-oriented play	Object manipulation (banging); Construction of things (blocks tower)	Starts in infancy. Declines about 6 years	Acquisition of skills for survival; related to tool use
Symbolic (fantasy/pretend) play	Using objects "as if they were other things" (riding a broom like it's a horse); Imitating actions "as if they were real" (pretending to sleep on the ground)	Starts about 15 months. Declines about 6 years	Understanding and practicing adult behaviors
Sociodramatic play	A form of symbolic play; representation of social dynamics and roles (playing school, house, or doctor)	Starts about 3 years. Declines about 6 years	Understanding and practicing social adult behaviors and roles
Physical activity play A. Rhythmic stereotypies b. Exercise play c. Rough & tumble play (R&T)	Body is used as a main play component Repetitive movements of arms; running; climbing Simulated fighting and chasing	a. More typical in infancy b. Toddler age to about 8 years old c. Toddler age to adolescence	In general, neuromuscular maturation, and psychomotor coordination. *R&T*: Acquisition of fighting and hunting skills; Identification of social signs; Establishment and maintenance of social dominance
Games (rules play)	Predetermined rules must be respected (tag; basketball; Monopoly)	Starts about 6 years old. Interest in games remains relatively stable across life	Fosters cognitive, social, and moral development

Everyday Expressions of the Development of the Symbolic Function

In this section we provide a more detailed look at four aspects of the symbolic function that reflect not just what children say and do when being interviewed by psychologists, but how their developing symbolic abilities are expressed in their daily activities. These are activities that parents, teachers, and older siblings also partake in, such as symbolic, or fantasy, play, drawing, and telling stories. These topics, and children's belief in fantasy characters, will be our focus here.

Symbolic Play

Play is usually seen as a purposeless activity, in that it is done voluntarily without any obvious immediate function (Rubin, Fein, & Vandenberg, 1983). Children play for the sake of playing. Yet most people who have given the topic serious thought believe that play serves several functions.

Table 6.3 provides a brief overview of the different types of play. Physical-activity play builds stronger bodies, rough-and-tumble play provides boys with the competitive skills they may need for fighting as adults, and play with other children prepares both boys and girls for the roles they will likely play (or would have played in ancient environments) as adults, the latter of which we examine in Chapter 14. In this section we discuss one very special type of play that may be unique to humans (but see Gómez & Martín-Andrade, 2005)—**symbolic**, or **fantasy play** (also called *pretend* or *make-believe play*), including sociodramatic play.

The Development of Symbolic Play

Symbolic play includes an "as if" orientation to objects, actions, and peers. It involves a child taking a stance that is different from reality and using a mental representation of the situation as part of the enactment (Lillard, 2001; Pellegrini & Bjorklund, 2004). At its simplest, symbolic play involves substituting one thing for another in a playful setting. For example, a child may place a broom between his legs and pretend he is riding on a horse, use a banana as if it is a telephone, or put a napkin on her head and pretend she is wearing a hat. More sophisticated forms of symbolic play include role playing, in which children pretend they are some other person—a teacher, a race-car driver, Mommy,

---

symbolic (fantasy) play Pretending; it involves an 'if-then' orientation to objects, actions, and peers..

BOX 6.4 **big questions**

Where Do Babies Come From?

In the 1920s, Jean Piaget was interested in the development of children's thinking about reproduction. However, he was well aware of the problems involved in interviewing children directly about these matters. "To solve this problem," he wrote, "it would be well to know children's ideas on the birth of babies. But it goes without saying that there are grave moral and pedagogic reasons for not pursuing such an investigation directly" (1969, p. 360). During the next half-century, although morality changed somewhat, few researchers took advantage of the more open atmosphere to follow up on Piaget's suggestion. Exceptions to this were studies by Anne Bernstein and Philip Cowan (1975) and Ronald and Juliette Goldman (1982), who examined children's understanding of "where babies come from" from an explicitly Piagetian perspective.

Bernstein and Cowan (1975) interviewed 30 boys and 30 girls ranging in age from 3 to 12 years to demonstrate that knowledge of the origin of babies develops in stages and that those stages follow the same general blueprint of Piaget's stages of cognitive development. A description of the stages children pass through while learning the origin of babies is presented in the accompanying table. As you can see from the table,

many preschool children think that babies have always existed and were somehow given to their mothers (Level 1). Parents in generations past have supported this type of thinking by telling children, for example, that the stork brings babies.

Other preschoolers understand that babies must be made, but they do not understand the process (Level 2). For example, 4-year-old Hector's mother had just given birth to a new sister, and he was preoccupied about where babies come from. Out of the blue one afternoon, he stated that his mother had gone to the paint store, drew a picture of a baby, and then she "popped" out of his mother's tummy.

Children in Level 3 realize the importance of mothers and fathers to produce a baby, but the process is unclear to them. For example, we recall a third-grade boy being excited that he was going to have a baby sister but confused about how his divorced mother could be pregnant. Didn't she have to be married to get pregnant? The presence of her live-in boyfriend did not seem to make a difference. Another young child, when hearing his parents speak of a childless couple, asked, "Why don't they have any children? Don't they love each other enough?" Children at this stage understand that a special relation-

ship between a man and a woman is needed for reproduction, but they do not understand the nature of that relationship.

Children seem to understand the basic facts of reproduction during concrete operations, between 7 and 11 years of age (Level 4), but it takes them some time to fully understand the biology of the process. For example, much as the preformationists of centuries past (see Chapter 2), preadolescents in Level 5 often believe that babies exist in the egg fully formed, waiting for the sperm to initiate growth.

Bernstein and Cowan concluded that children actively construct their notions about babies rather than waiting to be told. These self-constructed ideas reflect their present cognitive structures and often are based on information they have received but were unable to comprehend until they transformed it in some way to fit their cognitive level. In other words, parents could give the same talk about the origin of babies to their children every few years, and each time their children would learn something different—not just bits and pieces of the talk, but qualitatively different versions.

In a more extensive study, Goldman and Goldman (1982) interviewed 838 children in four countries to compare not only devel-

Fantasy play starts with children using some object as a substitute for another object, such as pretending that a shoe is a phone. The fantasy play of slightly older children involves taking on roles, such as Mommy and Daddy, often with other children.

or Daddy—and engaging in behaviors, perhaps with another child or adult, that act out pretend events (for example, racing a car, feeding a baby, playing school).

Consistent with Piaget's (1962) observations, symbolic play is first seen late in the second year of life, usually between 15 to 18 months of age. In the earliest types of symbolic play, children substitute perceptually similar objects for the real thing. For instance, a shoe may be used as a telephone, or children may take an empty teacup, put it to their lips, and make drinking noises. As children get older, the physical similarity between the objects they use in play and the real things diminishes. For example, a 3-year-old child may take a baby bottle and comb her doll's hair with it (Ungerer et al., 1981).

Although symbolic play can be solitary (for example, a child pretending she is feeding her doll or flying a plane), most symbolic play, especially for children beyond 3 years of age, occurs in a social setting (for example, playing house, school, opmental differences but also cultural differences in children's thinking about reproduction. Similar to the findings of Bernstein and Cowan (1975), they reported several well-defined levels of understanding that followed Piaget's stages of cognitive development. When asked about the origin of babies, Swedish children progressed through these levels of thinking well ahead of Australian and English children, with North American children being the slowest. More recent research has confirmed that preschool children know little about procreation and also have little knowledge of adult sexual behavior (Volbert, 2000).

Children's basic biological knowledge of reproduction is related to their general cognitive ability but also to the degree of societal (and family) openness regarding sexuality. Thus, it is not surprising that Goldman and Goldman found that Swedish children, whose parents are generally open about sexuality, showed more sophisticated understanding of reproduction than Australian, English, or American children, whose parents are typically more reserved about informing their children about the "birds and the bees."

Development of Children's Thinking about Reproduction

Level	Piagetian Stage	Ages	Description	Example
1	Preoperational	3–7	Babies have always existed in completed form; need to be aquired (bought, found, ordered, delivered).	Mommy got me at the hospital
2	Preoperational	4–8	Babies haven't always existed in completed form; need to be assembled.	Mommy made me out of blood and bones she had left over from my brother.
3	Transitional	5–10	Babies need two parents in special relationship, sexual intercourse, sperm and egg; process is unclear.	Doctor put a seed in Mommy, and Daddy put some stuff in to make the seed grow.
4	Concrete operations	7–12	Know the basic facts but don't speculate on why; only accuracy counts.	Daddy puts sperm in Mommy, and the baby starts growing. (Why?) I guess it loosens up the egg or something.
5	Transitional	10–13	Know basic facts and basic why's; don't understand that eggs and sperm can join to produce a third entity.	Baby is in the egg, and the sperm makes it start growing.
6	Formal operations	14–adult	Know that two distinct entities, sperm and ovum, can become one qualitatively different entity, the embryo.	The male injects sperm into the female's womb and fertilizes the egg and it grows into a fetus, and nine months later a baby is born.

SOURCE: From *The Flight of the Stork* by Anne C. Bernstein. Copyright © 1978 by Anne C. Bernstein. Used by permissions of Dell Publishing, a division of Random House.

or store with other children) (Rubin et al., 1983). Mothers in particular promote symbolic play in their preschool children (Bornstein et al., 1999; Youngblade & Dunn, 1995). One social form of symbolic play that is not seen until about 3 years of age is called **sociodramatic play**, in which children take on different roles and follow a story line as if they were in a theatrical performance. For instance, children may play doctor, taking turns as the doctor, nurse, and patient, and following a script that involves what children think goes on during a visit to the doctor's (for instance, asking a patient what's wrong, listening to the patient's heart, making a diagnosis, giving the patient some pills or a shot). Sociodramatic play requires not only that children imagine that some object is something that it is not (a shoe is a phone, for instance) or that they are someone they are not (a mommy or race-car driver), but they must also be able to represent the actions and thoughts of other people. (If I'm a pretend doctor, you're a pretend patient.) Students can likely easily recall popular themes of symbolic play

from their childhoods, perhaps playing school, cops and robbers, firefighters, or astronauts. (Some students' more recent bouts of fantasy may involve being rock stars or developmental psychologists.)

Like most types of play, symbolic play follows an inverted-U developmental pattern, being essentially nonexistent until about 15 months of age, peaking between 5 and 7 years, and decreasing thereafter (Rubin et al., 1983; Smith, 2005). When measured while children are attending preschool or in their homes, symbolic play accounts for between 10% and 33% of children's waking time, making it one of the most frequent behaviors that children of this age engage in (Fein, 1981; Haight & Miller, 1993). Part of the decline in symbolic play during the school years may involve parents and, especially teachers, discouraging such play, as well as the increase in other types of playful activities, such as games. Yet, older children continue to

sociodramatic play Play in which children take on different roles and follow a story line as if they were in a theatrical performance.

Children in traditional cultures often include real or toy tools in their symbolic play, frequently imitating adult work.

©Frans Lanting/Corbis

engage in symbolic play from time to time, such as building Lego monsters and other characters and inventing make-believe scenarios in which they interact.

We should note that symbolic and sociodramatic play are strongly influenced by culture, in that different cultures provide different roles and activities for children to incorporate into their play (Smith, 2005). In all cultures, children's symbolic play is based on the materials they have available (various toys, or cardboard boxes that can be used as spaceships) and the activities and roles of adults in their culture that they can emulate during play. Although some adult roles are truly universal, such as mommy or daddy, others are tied to specific cultures. Thus, it is not surprising that the sociodramatic play of children growing up in developed countries often involves occupations such as doctor, teacher, police officer, or astronaut. It should also not be surprising that children from traditional cultures include different objects and roles (such as hunter and gatherer) in their fantasy and sociodramatic play.

For example, children from traditional cultures are more likely to include real or toy tools and imitation of real adult work in their symbolic play than are children from developed countries. This is because children from hunter-gatherer or horticultural societies are more apt to observe adults at work on a daily basis than are children in schooled cultures. In some traditional societies, children are given toy tools, often made by their parents, to use in play. For instance, among the Parakanãs of the Amazon rain forest, fathers give their sons toy

bows and arrows, and mothers give their daughters small baskets, both tools that adult men and women use and that children then incorporate into their play. Four- to 6-year-old Parakanã girls make small baskets with palm leaves imitating their mothers' activities, although the baskets are not strong enough to be useful. By 8 years of age, most girls are making functional baskets. Parakanã parents do little direct teaching of hunting or gathering skills and seem to put no pressure on their children to engage in sex-appropriate play, but merely provide their children with traditional toys, which the children use in sociodramatic play much as they see their elders do in their work (Gosso et al., 2005).

Other observations of children from traditional cultures indicate that they spend significantly more time in play activities related to specific tasks associated with their subsistence economy than in other play activities, consistent with the idea that play is preparation for adult work (Bock & Johnson, 2004; Lancy, 1996). For example, David Lancy (1996) observed that most of the symbolic play of 4- to 11-year-old Kpelle children from Liberia involved children reenacting the chores and behaviors of adults in work-related situations, which adults encouraged. In general, in cultures that lack industry, play tends to evolve into work as children grow into adults.

Like other types of play, symbolic play, in one form or another, is not restricted to children but characterizes adult thinking as well. Professional actors make a living engaging in sociodramatic play, and many adults rarely spend a day without pretending, although strictly in their thoughts, that they are someone else, perhaps a celebrity, a professional athlete, one's boss, or just the attractive person sitting beside them in class. The ability to engage in such play involves using symbols—to let one thing stand for another—and may be important in developing an understanding of the beliefs and feelings of other people. And in addition to its significance for cognitive development, it is just plain fun to do and amusing to watch as children construct a fantasy world to play out their dreams.

The Development of Drawing

Piaget listed "graphical representations" as one form of the symbolic function, the simplest form of which is drawing, or the pictorial representation of some object (other important ones being writing and numerical notation). Drawing is a uniquely human activity. Although some captive chimpanzees and elephants have been known to draw (go to the You Tube site and type in "Elephant drawing" to see an amazing video, http://www.youtube.com/watch?v=Cy9kKxJJpug), no other animal in the wild makes pictorial representations. As a form of

table 6.4 Children's Drawing Progresses Gradually from Scribbles to Accurate Representations of Objects

Age	Drawing Type
1 to 2 years	Children produce scribbles, most of which are not representations of objects. By about 2 years old, children can complete drawings with another person (adding eyes to a face, for example).
3 to 4 years	Children first draw identifiable objects. Their depictions of people have the shape of tadpoles—a circle representing the head, facial features such as eyes, mouths, or hair, and arms and legs attached to the head.
5 to 8 years	Children's drawings become more realistic. By 5 years old, their depictions of people have a trunk. Their drawings are based more upon what they know (for example, what a cup, in general, looks like) rather than what they see (for example, the cup that is in front of them), termed *intellectual realism*.
9 years and older	Children increasingly draw what they see, relying less upon what they know, termed *visual realism*.

representation, drawing is far older than writing, as revealed by paintings of hunting scenes found in caves going back at least 32,000 years (Golomb, 2002; Guthrie, 2005).

Learning to Draw

Table 6.4 presents a summary of the progression of children's basic drawing skills. Children seem to know what drawing is about before they can draw. For example, Maureen Cox (2005) noted that 12- to 15-month-old children ask their mothers to draw with them or to draw something for them. Around 18 months, children even suggest the topic of the drawing to their mothers (for instance, saying "horse," while handing a crayon to their mothers). Beginning around 22 months, children can complete a shared drawing (for example, by adding eyes to a face that the mother neglected to draw). Thus, like most human activities, drawing is, in part, a social activity, with young children, who can only scribble at best, understanding that the marks people make on paper are supposed to mean something.

Children in developed cultures begin drawing when they are 1 to 2 years of age, making *scribbles*, or marks made with some implement (crayons, pencils, brushes, lipstick) on a surface (paper, coloring book, table top, bedroom wall). Are these scribbles the antecedents or prerequisites of drawings? Probably not. In cultures that do not have a tradition of pictures, children who are shown how to draw figures are able to do so after a few attempts, even though they had not scribbled at all before that time (Harris, 1971).

When young children are engaged in scribbling, adults often ask them what they are drawing, and children usually give an answer, but it is doubtful whether these representations are in the child's mind while they are scribbling or if they produce them in response to the adult's questions. Most 2- and 3-year olds do not talk about what they are drawing unless an adult asks, and then they generate an after-the-fact response about what

their scribbling represents ("That's a horse"), often pointing out fortuitous resemblances to the object they name ("See the tail!") (Golomb, 2002).

There is some recent evidence that scribbles may be representing more in children's minds than was once thought (Golomb, 2002; Winner, 2006). For example, scribbles may not represent objects as much as they represent actions (Matthews, 1999). A child may make circular scribbles that represent the flight of a plane (see Figure 6.6) or make dots on paper that represent the hopping of a bunny. Children often accompany these scribbles

Most young children don't identify what they're drawing unless asked to do so by an adult, and their responses seem to be after the fact, identifying something in their drawing that reminds them of something else ("Yeah, that's a horse.").

© Craig Holmes/Alamy

FIGURE 6.6 Do children's scribbles mean anything?
Traditionally it has been thought not, but some authors nowadays think that they might be action representations, that is, representation of an object's motion. Above you see an action representation of a plane scribbled by a child who was 2 years and 2 months old. SOURCE: From Matthews, J. (1999). *The art of childhood and adolescence: The construction of meaning.* Reprinted by permission of the Taylor & Francis Group.

a   b   c

FIGURE 6.7 Children like drawing pictures of the human figure.
When they are about 3 years old, children typically draw what has been called "tadpoles" to represent people (a and b). Before they begin to draw a complete human figure, at about 5 years of age (c), they often go through a transitional period where, for example, arms may be attached to the head (b). SOURCE: From Golomb, C. (2004). *The child's creation of a pictorial world* (2nd ed.). Mahwah, NJ: Erlbaum. Reprinted by permission of the Taylor & Francis Group.

intellectual realism In children's drawing, children's tendency to draw what they know rather than what they see.

*what they know
not see*

with appropriate sounds, such as the "zoom" of an airplane or the words "hop, hop, hop" (Wolf & Perry, 1988).

Children produce their first drawings of easily identifiable objects between 3 and 4 years of age (Golomb, 2004; Winner, 2006). These objects are often human figures, and at the earliest ages they have the shape of tadpoles—a circle representing the head, facial features such as eyes, mouths, or hair, and arms and legs attached to the head (Golomb, 2004; Cox & Parkin, 1986). It is not until they are about 5 years old that they add a trunk to the human figures they draw, and this only occurs after a transition period (see Figure 6.7).

Why do children draw such incomplete versions of a human figure? There are several hypotheses. One explanation is that young children are not fully aware of the composition of the human body so they just draw parts; they really think that people look that way! This seems not to be the case. When children who draw tadpole people are asked to add other body parts, or are given cutouts of body parts, they are able to arrange them into a complete human figure (Golomb, 2004; Cox, 2005) (see Figure 6.8). Rather, tadpole people seem to be the result of young children lacking a schema for representing the trunk of the body. That is, young children do not know how to draw a trunk properly and/or how to incorporate it into their mental scheme for drawing a body (Cox, 2005; Karmiloff-Smith, 1990).

From the age of 5 to 7 or 8, children's drawings become more representational, meaning they look more like what children intend them to represent, including more details, more technical features, and more precision. Children at these ages assess their drawing skill according to how realistic the drawings are, as do their parents and teachers. However, drawing at this age seems to be driven more by the internal models or representations that children have about real things than by reality (Cox, 2005). In other words, children do not draw so much what they see, but rather what they know (Piaget & Inhelder, 1956). This has been referred to as **intellectual realism**. For example, in one study (Freeman & Janikoun, 1972), children from 5 to 9 years of age were asked to draw a cup without having a specific model to refer to. Most children drew a cup with a handle. The children were then asked to draw a real cup that was in front of them on the table. This cup had a flower on it, and it was turned so the handle was out of view. The younger children (5 to 7) drew a cup with a handle and without a flower (similar to the cup they drew from their imagination). The older children (8 and 9) drew a cup without a handle and with a flower (similar to the cup that was before their eyes). When the younger children were asked why they drew a

FIGURE 6.8 Lack of knowledge about the human body does not seem to be the reason why young children draw tadpoles to represent human figures. In fact, it has been shown that about 50% of children who draw tadpole people can form a conventional human figure with the pieces on the left side, 80% of children can do it with the pieces put in the middle, and all of them can do it with the pieces on the right side. SOURCE: From Cox, M. V. (2005). *The pictorial world of the child*. New York: Cambridge University Press, p. 83. Reprinted by permission of Cambridge University Press.

handle on the cup when they could not see it, they expressed ideas such as "If you turned it round, it would be there" (p. 1121). And others who had not drawn the handle said, "Well, without the handle, it looks like a pot. Shall I put it on to make it a cup?" (p. 1120). In other words, this research shows that young children's drawings may be influenced by their mental models of things, although they are not unaware of reality.

Children older than 9 or so increasingly rely less on what they know about an object in drawing figures but draw what they actually see, referred to as **visual realism**. Surprisingly enough, just as their drawing abilities improve, children draw less often and in a less playful manner, unless they are particularly proficient at or fond of drawing (Gardner, 1980). It is not until adolescence that this playful and aesthetic interest returns. For example, when 6- to 12-year-old children were asked to complete a realistic and an abstract drawing (for example, a realistic picture of an arm or a less-realistic picture by Picasso), 6- and 12-year olds each performed well, completing the drawings in the appropriate styles. But the 8- and 10-year-olds did not; they completed all the drawings in the same realistic way (Winner et al., 1983).

Cultural and Historical Influences in Children's Drawings

Cultural factors seem to be at work in a number of aspects of children's drawings. Depending on the culture, children will use different themes, prefer different drawing tools, and be schooled in different art lessons (Cox, 2005; Golomb, 2002). For example, Claire Golomb (2002) points out that cultures that have long artistic traditions, such as China, begin systematic drawing instruction at an early age, and that it is difficult to find children who are not skilled at drawing the major themes of the art tradition, such as goldfish, birds, and flowers. Another example comes from Japan, where the drawing style of *anime* found in Japanese comic books (called *manga*, literally translated as "whimsical pictures") is very popular. Children's drawings follow this form, having many figures in each drawing, very dynamic themes, and the distinct perspective found in Japanese comic books and cartoons (Wilson, 1997; Wilson & Wilson, 1987). As another example, in drawings by European children collected more than a century ago, some pictorial devices, such as the two-eyed profile, which were typical in 70% of the drawings of Italian children, were found in only 50% of the drawings of English children and 5% of American children (see Wilson & Wilson, 1981). This is similar to other features that were common in the drawings of children in decades past but have since all but disappeared, such as ladder mouths, milk-bottle-shaped bodies, and garden-rake hands (Wilson & Wilson, 1981). Like other aspects of development, the development of drawing cannot be understood without considering the culture in which it takes place and appreciating that cultures change over time.

In any case, the strong influence of culture on drawing and art should not cause us to conclude these variations are infinite. Beyond the fact that cultures in contemporary times are becoming increasingly homogeneous across the globe, some typical features in drawing and art development seem to remain constant, including, for example, children's skills to generate spontaneously and proficient representations of human figures without previous experience or instruction, as well as to easily identify objects and figures drawn by other humans (Cox, 2005; Golomb, 2005; Winner, 2006).

visual realism In children's drawing, children's tendency to draw what they actually see.

What they see

Some scientists believe that many ancient cave paintings were made by children and adolescents, based, in part, on the size and dimensions of the handprints found on the cave walls.

© Barry Lewis/In Pictures/Corbis

In Western countries, parents usually relate stories to young children by reading picture books to them.

Cecilia Magill/Photo Researchers, Inc.

Children around the world learn to draw, and this tendency apparently goes back thousands of years. In fact, some experts of paleolithic art believe that much, if not most, of the art found in ancient caves was drawn by adolescents and children (Guthrie, 2005). What and how well children draw is a reflection of their motor skills but also of their ability to represent something they see or know in a graphic form. A drawing is not the real thing, but a representation of something else. As children develop, their drawings become more accurate and artistic.

Storytelling

Language is by far the most distinctive form of the symbolic function. Children begin to recognize a few words before their first birthdays and start speaking individual words by 10 or 12 months. It is not until about 18 months or a bit later when children start to put words together into sentences. Once children begin this process, it is off to the races, with children becoming expert users of their culture's language by 4 or 5 years of age. We devote an entire chapter to language (Chapter 9), and here wish to focus only on one aspect of language that we believe is an important reflection of the symbolic function—*storytelling*.

What do a Steven Spielberg movie, a J. K. Rowling novel, a Shakespeare play, and an article in *People* magazine have in common? They all tell a good story, and everyone loves a good story. We are all interested in what is happening to other people and what is going on in their lives, and this has been a trait of our species since the time of our primitive ancestors. Stories support a key function of social meaning-making (Bruner, 1990). They "make sense of the social world by interpreting human actions and intentions, organize everyday experience, and seek plausibility and internal consistency that is lifelike" (Genereux & McKeough, 2007, p. 850). And this love of stories begins in childhood.

Preschool children love to be told tales by their parents (most frequently their mothers). In Western countries, this is often done in the context of picture books, small in size with lots of pictures and few words. (Some of the functions of picture-book reading are discussed in Chapter 10.) Other countries use the oral tradition of storytelling.

Sometimes these tales are told during the day; other times they serve as bedtime stories. A good story told by a loving person makes it easier for children to fall asleep. Children in Western cultures also enjoy puppet shows, TV cartoons, and feature films made for children by Disney or Pixar. The technology may change across cultures and time, but children across the world and from early in development love a good story.

The form and content of the stories are culturally influenced. For example, European American children's stories typically focus on a single topic, explained in three steps—beginning, middle, and end—and storytelling is valued as a path to literacy (see Chapter 10). In contrast, African Americans often tell stories that move from one topic to another and value other qualities, such as oral virtuosity and emphasis on moral education (Bloome et al., 2001). There are also cultural differences in the interactions between the storyteller and the listening child. For example, European American storytelling tends to be monologic—the storyteller tells the story and the children listen; in contrast, for African Americans and Native Americans, storytelling tends to be dialogic—the storyteller and the children speak back and forth during the story (Stadler & Ward, 2005).

As these cultural differences indicate, there is not a universal way of telling a story, although some people within every culture are better at storytelling than others. The quality of a story is influenced by a host of factors, including the immediate storytelling environment, cultural values and norms, and the historical context (Banks-Wallace, 2002). Accordingly, within each cultural oral tradition and depending on specific social features, certain storytelling styles seem to be promoted over the others (Champion, 1998; Wang, Leichtman, & Davies, 2000).

What's in a Story?

What constitutes a story, and what differentiates a good one from a poor one? The technical definition of a story is a portrayal of "sequences and actions that are temporally and causally related" (Nicolopoulou & Richner, 2007, p. 412). In the Western world, a basic story episode is composed of six elements, organized sequentially (McKeough, Genereux, & Jeary, 2006, p. 204): A story has a(n)

1. Beginning (the initiating event for the protagonist's reaction)
2. Simple reaction (the protagonist's emotional or cognitive reaction)
3. Goal (the protagonist's intentions in terms of dealing with the initiating event)
4. Attempt (the protagonist's attempt to achieve the goal)
5. Outcome (the result of the attempt)
6. Ending (the characters' reactions to the outcome and/or the long-term consequences of the episode events)

More complex stories include several of these story episodes.

In other words, stories are not just a narration of a sequence of events and actions, but also a narration of the mental, or internal, states of some characters that, particularly in good stories, are coordinated with the mental states of others (Bruner, 1986, 1990; Nicolopoulou & Richner, 2007). As Jerome Bruner (1986) pointed out, good stories involve simultaneously two "landscapes"—the *landscape of action* (related to events and actions in the external physical world) and the *landscape of consciousness* (related to characters' thoughts, intentions, feelings, beliefs, and so forth). If these two landscapes are not present, it is difficult to tell and to understand a story. In addition, good stories must be both coherent—that is, meaningfully integrated around a plot (Shapiro & Hudson, 1991)—and cohesive—that is, properly constructed in linguistic terms, linking effectively the different units and sentences that compose those stories (Hoff, 2009).

The Development of Children's Understanding and Production of Stories

Children can understand the basic story structure described in the last section around the age of 6 to 8 years, with children approaching 9 being able to understand more complex structures involving different episodes and more complex characters (Genereux & McKeough, 2007; Stein & Glenn, 1979; see Table 6.5). Most researchers have found that preschool children do a good job following physical aspects of a story, as well as the physical description of the characters, but do less well understanding characters' mental states (Stein & Glenn, 1979). In other words, preschool children have access to the "landscape of action" but not the "landscape of consciousness," in Bruner's terms.

Some recent research suggests that preschool children know more about the landscape of consciousness than earlier researchers believed. Most 4-year-olds, and many 3-year-olds, for example, seem to be able to track the mental states of others in a story, with 5-year-olds showing an adult-like level of inferences about mental states (Nicolopoulou & Richner, 2007; O'Neill & Shultis, 2007). Girls tend to show more advanced abilities to track the mental states of others than do boys (Nicolopoulou & Richner, 2007; O'Neill & Shultis, 2007), consistent with other research on stories and language development (see, for example, Nicolopoulou,

table 6.5 Developmental Pattern of Social-Psychological Understanding in Children's and Adolescents' Stories

Some recent research suggests that "intentional understanding of human actions" might start earlier, when children are about 4 to 5 years old.

Very young children (up to 4 years of age)	**Action/event knowledge of human experience** Descriptions based on physical/external events and states *For example*: "She was blind"; "The boy had a dog"
Middle childhood (6 to 10 years old)	**Intentional understanding of human actions** Descriptions in terms of immediate feelings, thoughts, and goals *For example*: "She was really *sad*"; "He then *decided* to do it"
Adolescence (12 to 18 years old)	**Interpretative understanding of human actions** Intentional states are taken as an object of reflection by the narrator *For example*: "Mary loved children because her parents were teachers"; "John would not have behaved that way if he had imagined what was going to happen"

SOURCE: Based on McKeough, A. (1992). A neo-structural analysis of children's narrative and its development. In R. Case (Ed.), *The mind's staircase: Exploring the conceptual underpinnings of children's thought and knowledge* (pp. 171–188). Hillsdale, NJ: Erlbaum; and Genereux, R., & McKeough, A. (2007). Developing narrative interpretation: Structural and content analyses. *British Journal of Educational Psychology, 77*, 849–872.

Scales, & Weintraub, 1994; Richner & Nicolopoulou, 2001).

Let's look at an example of this early ability in preschoolers by examining the narration of Edgar, a 5-year-old who tells about Robin Hood's false belief and later change of mind (from Nicolopoulou & Richner, 2007, p. 426):

> Once there was Robin Hood. Then a bear came. But the bear was nice. And Robin Hood thought the bear was evil so he shot an arrow at the bear. But the bear knocked the arrow out of the way. The bear didn't fight Robin Hood. So he shot another arrow at the bear. But the bear again knocked the arrow out of the way. After that the bear didn't run at Robin Hood. Bear was a nice bear. So then that told Robin Hood that the bear was a nice bear. So they were friends. Then a bad guy came. The bear and Robin Hood fighted the bad guy. And the bad guy died. And Robin Hood and the bear won the fight. The End. (Edgar, 5–8)

Between the ages of 2 and 6 years, the sophistication of children's stories develops substantially (Eisenberg, 1985; McCabe & Peterson, 1991). According to Nancy Eisenberg (1985), children go through three stages when talking about a past event, such as a visit to the zoo. During the first stage, children depend on adults to scaffold their stories, for example, introducing new topics ("What about the lion?") and cuing them to continue ("What happened then?"). Children in the second stage tell their stories without help, but they first focus on general aspects of the event ("We went to McDonald's and ordered Happy Meals"), then the more specific ones ("McDonald's was almost empty" and "The guy at the counter mixed up the order"). In the third stage, children include more specific information as the event unfolds.

Other developmental changes in children's stories concern the linguistic structures they use

(Peterson & McCabe, 1983, 2004). Around the age of 4, children typically produce leapfrog narratives, jumping from one topic to another, often randomly and requiring a lot of inference (and patience) on the part of the listener. When Western children from the majority culture are about 5 years old, they tend to produce stories that follow a chronological sequence of events and have a distinct, high-interest ending (Nelson & Gruendel, 1981). Eventually, around the age of 6, children can tell classic, adult-like stories, with beginnings, middles, and endings. Over the next few years, they produce more complex stories with multiple events and several points of view (Hoff, 2009).

It is difficult to minimize the importance of language as a symbolic tool. How children use language to tell and understand stories, whether fiction or nonfiction, develops with age and with children's increasing facility to understand and manipulate words and ideas. It is related to their ability to understand their own minds and those of others and influences how well they are able to interact with other language-using people, including parents and peers.

Distinguishing between Imagined and Real Events: Children's Belief in Fantasy Characters

One of the expressions of the symbolic function for Piaget was mental imagery, the ability to generate an internal image of some object or event. Certainly by late in the preschool years, children are able to generate such images, and can, in fact, create images of things they have never experienced before. As we saw when discussing the appearance/reality distinction, preschool children often have a difficult time distinguishing what is real from what appears before their eyes.

Distinguishing the Imagined from the Real

Related to this is children's ability to distinguish what they imagine from what they experience. Do children realize that thinking or imagining something is distinct from actually doing or experiencing something? At one level, this seems to be an ability possessed by most 3- and 4-year-olds. For instance, it is clear that even young children know the difference between imagining and doing. For example, although dreams can seem quite real to people of any age, apparently even 3- and 4-year-olds know the difference between dreams and reality, although many 3-year-olds seem to falsely believe that the same dream is experienced by different people (Woolley & Wellman, 1992) and that dreams are highly controllable (Woolley & Boerger, 2002).

Young children often have difficulty identifying the source of something they know—did they experience it or just imagine it? The awareness of the origins of one's memories, knowledge, or beliefs is called **source monitoring**. When children are asked to perform certain actions (for example, "touch your toes") or to imagine performing certain actions (for instance, "imagine touching your toes"), the ability to distinguish imagined from real actions at a later time improves gradually with age. Older preschoolers perform better than younger preschoolers (Sussman, 2001; Welch-Ross, 1995), but even 6- and 7-year-olds have greater difficulty making such distinctions than older children or adults do (Foley & Ratner, 1998; Parker, 1995). Most of children's errors involve claiming that they had performed an action they had actually only imagined. Thus, for young children, imagination can easily be remembered as reality. Children also have difficulty knowing if they witnessed an event or experienced it second-hand (for example, were told about it or saw it on television), or if they performed a behavior or watched someone else perform it (Ackil & Zaragoza, 1995; Foley, Ratner, & Passalacqua, 1993). This may make young children more susceptible to suggestion, something that is important when they serve as witnesses (Ceci & Bruck, 1995).

Believing in Fantasy Beings

Believing in fantasy beings requires a relatively sophisticated cognitive system. We saw earlier that by about 3 years of age, children's symbolic play becomes more complicated, involving other children in sociodramatic play. At about this same time, many children create **imaginary friends**. By 3 or 4 years of age, children endow these invisible agents (usually make-believe children but some-

Preschool children are encouraged to believe in fantasy characters, such as Santa Claus, the Easter Bunny, and the Tooth Fairy, and they do so readily.

times talking animals or beings from another planet) with ideas, motivations, personalities, and feelings of their own (Taylor, 1999). In other words, they treat them as intentional agents who act purposely based on what they know and what they want, much as they treat real people. Having imaginary friends is quite common. In one study, 65% of children up to age 7 had had an imaginary friend sometime in their lives (Taylor et al., 2004). There may be some cognitive advantage to having imaginary friends. Recent research has found that 5-year-old children with imaginary friends tell more detailed stories than do children without such friends (Trionfi & Reese, 2009).

Young children seem ready to believe in fantasy characters. Adults encourage the belief in some fantasy characters, such as Santa Claus, the Easter Bunny, and the Tooth Fairy, and children who express strong belief in the Tooth Fairy, for instance, are more likely to provide fictitious reports about the Tooth Fairy (for example, "I saw her come through my window") (Principe & Smith, 2008). Others fantasy beings, however, such as the monster under the bed, the bogeyman, and dragons, are actively discouraged by parents, but children believe in them anyway (or act as if they are real, even if they may profess that there is no such thing as monsters that hide under beds).

source monitoring The awareness of the origins of one's memories, knowledge, or beliefs..

imaginary friends Make-believe friends.

WHEN A KID LOSES A TOOTH IN THE DOMINICAN REPUBLIC, THEY THROW IT ON THE ROOF.

THEY BELIEVE THAT A MOUSE WILL TAKE THE OLD TOOTH AWAY AND BRING THEM A BETTER ONE.

HA! HA! HA! THAT'S THE SILLIEST THING I'VE EVER HEARD!

NOW QUIT READING AND PUT YOUR TOOTH UNDER YOUR PILLOW SO THE TOOTH FAIRY CAN LEAVE YOU MONEY.

Baby Blues, 10/5/2007 © Jerry Scott and Rick Kirkman. Baby Blues Partnership—King Features Syndicate

Courtesy of Jacqueline Woolley

Older preschoolers (5-year-olds) were more likely than younger preschoolers (3-year-olds) to believe that the Candy Witch was real, suggesting that a certain level of cognitive development is necessary to believe in fantasy characters.

Young children's tenuous grasp of the distinction between fantasy and reality is seen in studies by Paul Harris and his colleagues (1991). These researchers demonstrated that 4- and 6-year-olds could easily distinguish between real and imagined objects. For example, when asked to imagine that there was either a bunny or a monster in a box on a table in front of them, few children had any difficulty with the task; most stated quite clearly that the bunny or the monster was pretend and not real (see also Woolley & Cox, 2007). But this knowledge was not well established for many of the children. For example, after asking children to imagine a bunny or a monster in the box, the experimenter said she had to leave the room for a few minutes. Twenty-five percent of 4-year-olds who had imagined a monster in the box became frightened and would not let the experimenter leave. No child who was asked to imagine a bunny became frightened. When the experimenter returned and questioned the children, nearly half of both the 4- and 6-year-olds admitted to wondering whether there was indeed a monster or a bunny in the box. Perhaps imagining made it so. That is, although nearly all of the children admitted that the bunny or the monster was make-believe at the beginning of the experiment, many had second thoughts at the end.

Many children develop a fear of the dark during the late preschool and early school years, based, in part, on their ability to generate ideas about what might be lurking in the dark. For instance, one 6-year-old told us, when asked why he's afraid of the dark, "Because I can, like, imagine things and see it, when it's not really there." Like Harris's 4-year-olds who do not believe in monsters in boxes, many children do not believe that scary things lurk in the dark, but they can imagine that they do, and that is enough to warrant a night-light.

Does belief in fantasy characters represent immature cognition? At one level it would seem so. But just as understanding the actions of real people improves with age, perhaps a certain level of cognitive development is necessary for children to appreciate the behaviors of fantasy creatures. In one study, researchers evaluated age differences in children's tendencies to believe in a new fantasy character, the Candy Witch (Woolley, Boerger, & Markman, 2004; see Photo at left). The Candy Witch was introduced as someone who, on Halloween night, comes into children's homes and replaces candy she finds under children's pillows with a toy. Children were shown a doll representing the Candy Witch but were not told anything about whether she was real or not. The parents of some of the children exchanged a toy for candy after their children were asleep. When they were later interviewed, older preschool children (average age = 5.3 years) were more likely to express belief in the Candy Witch relative to younger children (average age = 3.7 years). In other words, for children who had actually been visited by the Candy Witch (much as they are visited by the Tooth Fairy), the older and presumably more cognitively advanced ones were more likely to believe in the Candy Witch, not the younger children.

Adults often describe children as being more imaginative than older people. This may be true, but it is likely so not because adults lack the ability to be imaginative, but rather that the constraints of making a living and the knowledge of how the world actually works give adults less motivation to take flights of fancy than children. Imagination actually requires a sophisticated representational system, and this develops over the preschool and school-age years. Although children become increasingly able to distinguish fantasy from reality with age, their ability to extend their imagination to the unreal or supernatural also increases. Imagination may be a characteristic of childhood, but it is based on a developing symbolic system that becomes more sophisticated over the course of development.

summary

Jean Piaget's theory of intellectual development has had a profound impact on how we view children, their thinking, and their development. Piaget believed that **schemes** are systematic patterns of actions or mental **operations** that reflect children's current state of understanding. Piaget proposed two governing principles of cognitive development: **organization**—an organism's tendency to integrate structures into higher-order systems or structures—and **adaptation**—the adjustment the organism goes through in response to the environment. This process has two complementary components: **assimilation**, the structuring of environmental input to fit a child's current schemes, and **accommodation**, the structuring of the child's schemes to match environmental data. Piaget proposed **equilibration** as a mechanism for development, in which children resolve cognitive incongruity.

Piaget postulated four major stages, or periods, of cognitive development. During the **sensorimotor period** (from birth to about 2 years), children's thinking is limited to their own actions on objects. Piaget described six substages during the sensorimotor period. During the earliest substages, cognition is limited to inherited reflexes and simple extensions of these reflexes. **Goal-directed behavior** is seen first in substage 4. Infants become capable of mentally representing environmental events in the final substage of the sensorimotor period.

Piaget described the thoughts of children in the **preoperational period** (2 to 7 years) as being symbolic but intuitive, in contrast with the logical thought of children in the **concrete operational period** (7 to 11 years). Preoperational children fail **conservation** tasks (knowing that a substance remains the same despite a perceptual transformation of that substance), confusing appearance with reality. They lack the logical rule of **reversibility**. Piaget described the perception of preoperational children as being **centered** on the most salient aspects of a perceptual array, in contrast with the decentered perception of children in the concrete operational period. Preoperational children are said to be **egocentric**, in that they have a difficult time seeing the perspective of another. The acquisition of similar skills (for example, conservation for different types of materials) does not occur all at once, but in an invariant order, and is referred to as **horizontal décalage**.

Piaget noted age-related differences in classification, including **multiple classification**, the ability to classify objects simultaneously on two dimensions, and **class inclusion**, the knowledge that any subordinate category (dogs, for example) can be no larger than its superordinate category (animals, for example). Concrete operational children are able to perform **seriation**, ordering objects according to the quantitative dimension of a trait.

The **formal operational period** (11 to 16 years) involves the advent of **hypothetico-deductive reasoning**, so that thinking can be done solely in terms of symbols. Piaget described the formal operational child as being able to think like a scientist, or to use **inductive reasoning**, and to reflect on the outcome of their own thought (**reflective abstraction**). Adolescents display a form of egocentrism, reflected in their feelings that they are constantly "on stage" or playing to an **imaginary audience**, and a belief in their uniqueness and invulnerability, referred to as the **personal fable**. Piaget's theory has been applied to nonhuman animals, particularly acquisitions during the sensorimotor period, such as object permanence.

More recent research indicates that children are typically more competent than Piaget proposed, and numerous studies have demonstrated that children can be easily trained to display both concrete and formal operational abilities. Aspects of Piaget's stage concept have also been criticized, with children being less homogeneous in cognitive functioning than Piaget proposed.

Theory theories extend Piaget's ideas, assuming that children possess some rudimentary naïve theories to represent and reason about the principal domains of knowledge. Theory theories have been used to explain children's development of biological knowledge. Children in all cultures are interested in animals and biological life. Children have a tendency toward **animism**, attributing human properties to inanimate things. Movement is a key component in whether children think something is alive or not. Children's understanding of intuitive biology becomes more adult-like with age and is affected by culture and children's experience with animals. Children's knowledge about sexuality and reproduction follows a developmental course similar to that suggested by Piaget.

Children use their symbolic abilities in everyday interactions with family members and peers. **Symbolic**, or **fantasy, play** involves an "as if" orientation to objects, actions, and peers. **Sociodramatic play** is first seen at about 3 years of age and involves children playing roles, usually with parents or peers. Symbolic play is based on the materials children have available and the activities and roles of adults in their culture. In cultures that lack industry, play tends to develop into work as children grow into adults. Symbolic play has been proposed to facilitate cognitive development.

Drawing is the oldest form of graphic representation. Children's earliest drawings are scribbles. Children's drawings of the human figure begin with a head with limbs attached to it, but drawings become more person-like, including a trunk, at about 6 years of age. Early school-age children draw what they know, rather than what they see, referred to as **intellectual realism**, whereas children 9 years and older tend to draw what they actually see, referred to as **visual realism**.

Children enjoy stories from an early age, but they cannot understand the basic structure of stories until about 6 to 8 years of age. Children's storytelling improves with age, as they are increasingly able to take the perspective of other people.

Preschool children have difficulty distinguishing real from imaginary events. They have problems with **source monitoring**, distinguishing between things they experienced versus things they imagined. Most children have **imaginary friends** sometime during childhood and believe in fantasy characters, such as Santa Claus or the Easter Bunny. Although belief in such fantasy characters decreases with age, a certain level of cognitive development is required for them.

Key Terms and Concepts

scheme (p. 231)
operations (p. 231)
organization (p. 231)
adaptation (p. 231)
assimilation (p. 231)
accommodation (p. 231)
equilibration (p. 232)
sensorimotor period (p. 232)
goal-directed behavior (p. 234)
preoperational period (p. 235)
conservation (p. 235)
egocentrism (p. 237)

reversibility (p. 238)
perceptual centration (p. 238)
concrete operational period (p. 239)
horizontal décalage (p. 239)
multiple classification (p. 240)
class inclusion (p. 240)
seriation (p. 240)
formal operational period (p. 241)
hypothetical-deductive reasoning (p. 241)
inductive reasoning (p. 241)
reflective abstraction (p. 242)
imaginary audience (p. 242)

personal fable (p. 242)
theory theories (p. 247)
animism (p. 248)
symbolic (fantasy) play (p. 253)
sociodramatic play (p. 255)
intellectual realism (p. 258)
visual realism (p. 259)
source monitoring (p. 263)
imaginary friends (p. 263)

Ask Yourself . . .

1. What are the critical concepts necessary to understand Piaget's description of cognitive development? Provide examples.
2. What are the most distinctive characteristics of thinking at each of Piaget's four major stages of cognitive development?
3. What are the major contributions and criticisms of Piaget's theory of cognitive development?
4. What are some of the alternative theories to Piaget's account of cognitive development?
5. In what ways is the theory-theory approach similar and different to both the core-knowledge approach discussed in Chapter 5 and to Piaget's theory?

6. What do young children know and not know about biology, and how does their knowledge of the biological world develop?
7. When and how is symbolic play exhibited by children? How is symbolic play affected by culture?
8. How do drawing skills develop in children, and how are they influenced by one's culture?
9. What is a story composed of? How do children's storytelling abilities develop? How can storytelling be shaped by social and cultural differences?
10. When are children able to distinguish real from imagined events, and how can we know this? To what extent is it correct to state that "the belief in fantasy characters represents immature cognition"?

Exercises: Going Further

1. Based on Piaget's findings about cognitive development, make a list of main facts and possible recommendations you would give to teachers working in preschool, primary, and secondary education, respectively. They should be useful in order to improve their students' understanding and learning. Make a distinction between general recommendations and age-specific recommendations.

2. As you have read in this chapter, one criticism made against Piaget was that he talked "only" about children's cognition and paid little or no attention to socioemotional development. However, if you recall from Chapter 2, contemporary views of development believe that everything in development is interconnected. Provide some concrete examples of how the principle traits exhibited at each stage of cognitive development might influence children's social interactions and emotions.

3. Ask children at several different ages (for example, 4, 6, 8, and 10 years old) about three things: draw a person, tell a story, and comment about what they like to play the most. Then write a summary about what the information tells you about each child's thinking and developmental differences you found among children. Does what you found from your interviews support what you have read in this chapter about drawing, storytelling, and play?

Suggested Readings

Classic Work

Piaget, J., & Inhelder, B. (1969). *The psychology of the child.* **New York: Basic Books.** This book by Piaget and his long-time collaborator presents a brief overview of Piaget's theory in Piaget's own words. One word of caution: It is difficult to read works by Piaget before reading works written by others about Piaget.

Flavell, J. (1963). *The developmental psychology of Jean Piaget.* **Princeton, NJ: Van Nostrand.** Both scholarly and well written, this book was the first exposure to Piaget's work for many students and psychologists for decades. Piaget wrote the prologue and recognized the extraordinary effort made by Professor John Flavell.

Brainerd, C. J. (1978). *Piaget's theory of intelligence.* **Englewood Cliffs, NJ.** This remains perhaps the most thorough critical evaluation of research on Piaget's theory.

Scholarly Work

Brainerd, C. J. (1996). Piaget: A centennial celebration. *Psychological Science, 7,* 191–195. This is the introductory article to a special issue of *Psychological Science* devoted to commemorating the centennial of Piaget's birth. Piaget's many contributions are summarized in the articles in this issue, written by prominent cognitive developmental psychologists, documenting that Piaget's influence and legacy lives on.

Winner, E. (2006). Development in the arts: Drawing and music. In W. Damon & R. Lerner (Gen Eds.) & D. Kuhn & R. S. Siegler (Vol. Eds.), *Handbook of child psychology: Vol. 2. Cognition, perception, and language* **(6th ed., pp. 859–904). New York: Wiley.** This review of theory and research on children's drawings and musical skills reminds us of the importance of the arts in children's development.

Inagaki, K., & Hatano, G. (2006). Young children's conception of the biological world. *Current Directions in Psychological Science, 15,* 177–181. In this short paper, Kayoko Inagaki and Giyoo Hatano, two pioneers in the study of the development of children's biological knowledge, propose that preschool children possess a naïve understanding of biology before such knowledge is formerly taught in schools. The authors show how this naïve biology might be at the basis of children's performance and learning in some relevant sociocultural areas of their lives (for example, health practices and biological instruction).

Reading for Personal Interest

Lenox, M. F. (2000). Storytelling for young children in a multicultural world. *Early Childhood Education Journal, 28* (2), 97–103. This short paper provides resources related to storytelling for young children, particularly in the context of Asian American, African American, Hispanic, and Native American heritages.

Paley, V. G. (2004). *A child's work: The importance of fantasy play.* **Chicago, IL: University of Chicago Press.** This book, by well-known preschool educator and researcher Vivian Gussin Paley, tells us about the importance of storytelling and fantasy play in children's development in contemporary societies, describing their positive effects on children's academic and social development.

Gopnik, A. (2009). *The philosophical baby: What children's minds tell us about truth, love, and the meaning of life.* **New York: Farrar, Straus, and Giroux.** In this delightfully written book, developmental psychologist Alison Gopnik examines how babies and young children form and test theories, how they use their imagination, and generally what it's like to be a baby.

CourseMate

Cengage Learning's **Psychology CourseMate** for this text brings course concepts to life with interactive learning, study, and exam preparation tools, including quizzes and flashcards for this chapter's Key Terms and Concepts (see the summary list on page 266). The site also provides an **eBook** version of the text with highlighting and note taking capabilities, as well as an extensive library of observational videos that span early childhood through adolescence. Many videos are accompanied by questions that will help you think critically about and deepen your understanding of the chapter topics addressed, especially as they pertain to core concepts. Log on and learn more at **www.cengagebrain.com.**

In this chapter we explore the development of children's understanding of the self and of others as psychological beings. We begin by looking at the development of self-concept from infancy through young adulthood, the development of self-esteem and self-efficacy, and identity formation in adolescence, including the development of ethnic identity. We next look at the development of theory of mind—children's developing concepts of mental activity—beginning in infancy with the importance of seeing other people as intentional agents, perspective taking, and progressing through passing false-belief tasks. We conclude by examining the development of various forms of social learning.

Six-year-old Tyson and his 10-year-old brother Jefferson were negotiating a trade of some Yu-Gi-Oh cards. Tyson especially wanted a King Pumpkin card that would permit him to double the power of some of his attack cards. Jefferson had two such cards, and surely, Tyson reasoned, he'd be willing to trade one to him. Jefferson, however, was not making it easy for Tyson. He wanted three cards in exchange for his King Pumpkin card, including Tyson's Crush Card Virus card. Moreover, unbeknownst to Tyson, Jefferson had a defense card that could combat the King Pumpkin card that Tyson wanted so badly. Tyson was in tears for a short time over his brother's reluctance to make a trade, and Tyson eventually agreed to the deal his brother proposed. Although both seemed happy at the conclusion of the negotiation, Jefferson later confided to his father that he had really taken advantage of Tyson,

but he remarked, "Hey, he's the one who wanted to trade. It's not like I made him do it or anything!"

This example of an older sibling taking advantage of a younger sibling illustrates the importance of knowing how to deal with other members of our species to get what we want. Jefferson did not strong-arm his younger brother to make the trade—as he pointed out, it was Tyson's idea in the first place. He did not get his way by physical force or intimidation but by talking a good game and taking advantage of his greater knowledge of the value of the various Yu-Gi-Oh cards under consideration and his knowledge of his brother's strong desire to trade for one particular card.

Making deals is something that humans do all the time. Evolutionary psychologists Leda Cosmides and John Tooby (1992) suggested five specific cognitive abilities needed to make deals and to avoid

FIGURE 7.1 Social cognition: Understanding self, understanding others.

The arrow originating from the "Self" and circling back onto the "Self" represents self-reflection. What does a person know about his or her own beliefs, mental states, or other psychological processes? The arrow pointing to "Others" represents what one infers about the beliefs, mental states, and psychological processes of *other* people, individually considered. We refer to this ability to understand the psychological processes of others as *theory of mind*. The arrow pointing to "Group" indicates how individuals mentally represent the "Social World," which involves different types of social interactions and group phenomena.

Understanding self
(self-concept, self-esteem, self-efficacy, identity)

Self

Understanding others
(Theory of Mind)

Others

Group

Understanding social world
(for example human relations, moral values, gender roles, sociocultural traditions and organizations)

being cheated: (1) recognize many different people; (2) remember one's past interactions with people; (3) communicate one's beliefs and desires to others; (4) understand the beliefs and desires of others; and (5) represent the costs and benefits of items or services that are being exchanged. As you will see in this chapter, all of these abilities improve with age, experience, and knowledge, so it is not surprising that adults make better deals than children, and that 10-year-olds make better deals than 6-year-olds.

As we have just seen in the preceding chapter, the development of symbolic representation has been an important and much-studied topic in psychology, with Jean Piaget and his followers leading the way. Most of Piaget's theorizing, as well as the research and theorizing of most people who followed the great Swiss psychologist (Case, 1992; DeLoache, 1995; Fischer, 1980) emphasized children's symbolic representation of the *physical world*—of thinking about things. This is nonsocial cognition, and it has been a major focus of child development research (see Bjorklund, 2005; Flavell, Miller, & Miller, 2002; Siegler & Alibali, 2004). This emphasis on cognition caused some researchers with an interest in social development to posit that understanding children's thinking may be important in understanding their *social* behavior (Brooks-Gunn & Lewis, 1978; Damon, 1978). From this perspective, social behavior is predicated on social thought. Children can only be as social as their ability to think about social relations permits them to be.

Thinking about one's own thoughts, feelings, motives, and behaviors and those of other people is referred to as **social cognition,** and it is every bit as symbolic as nonsocial cognition, with infants and children mentally representing first their own

minds and then other people's minds, in order to make sense of their social world (Olson & Dweck, 2008). In reality, social cognition involves at least three critical tasks: understanding the self, understanding others' minds, and understanding the social world in which one lives (see Figure 7.1). The latter includes issues such as the nature of gender roles, cultural traditions and organizations, moral values, and how human relations are conceived in one's society, among others, topics examined in later chapters of this book.

Interestingly, many scholars who ponder the evolution of human intelligence believe that our species' intellectual claim to fame came about because of our ability to represent the self, which then permitted us to deal more effectively with other members of our own kind (Alexander, 1989; Dunbar, 2010; Humphrey, 1976; Tomasello & Moll, 2010). More specifically, as humans became self-aware, they also became other-aware, which led to new ways of cooperating and competing with one another that transformed human societies as well as the course of human evolution. Box 7.1 investigates a bit further the evolutionary origins of self- (and other) awareness and the advantages it may have afforded our ancestors.

In this chapter, we examine the foundations for the development of social cognition—how children come to understand themselves and others. We begin by looking at the development of the *self*. We next discuss the development of *theory of mind*, that is, how children come to understand that people's behavior is influenced by their beliefs and desires. We also look at how children sometimes extend theory of mind to fantasy characters and supernatural beings. We then examine the development of *social learning*, the acquisition of social information and behavior from observing others, which is responsible for humans' ability to transfer information with such fidelity from one person (and generation) to another.

The Development of Self

The Development of a Concept of Self

Before we delve into the development of self, we would like you to engage in a simple exercise. Write down (or at least think about) how you would describe yourself to someone of your same age and sex. What aspects of *you* do you think are important to mention? Would your description change if you were writing to someone of the opposite sex (perhaps for an eHarmony posting), a distant relative whom you did not know well, or a person from another culture? Now write down areas of

social cognition Thinking about the self, other people, and social relationships.

BOX 7.1 **big questions**

Did Self-awareness Make Us Human?

Robots have long been a topic of science fiction, and recent technical advances are making them a reality. In the near future, it looks like we'll have robots that will be able to obey many simple commands, from opening the windows and putting dishes away in the dishwasher to vacuuming the floor. But such robots will lack at least one thing that (nearly) every human possesses, and that is *self-awareness*—an awareness of one's self.

What advantages did self-awareness provide our ancestors, how did it come about, and why are humans the only species that seem to possess it, or at least to make the most use of it? One popular theory about the advantages of self-awareness was first articulated by the psychologist Nicholas Humphrey (1976), who postulated that self-awareness was mainly useful in dealing with other members of the species. Although some of the most impressive feats of human intellect may involve the construction of pyramids and space shuttles, Humphrey noted that little of that technological brilliance is witnessed for most people most of the time. Where our intellectual genius is displayed on a daily basis is in dealing with our fellow human beings. In all societies, from the high society of Fifth Avenue, New York, to the hunter-gatherer societies of the San !Kung in the Kalahari Desert, social interactions and relations are complex and the basis of human life. From this perspective, human intellect evolved to solve social problems, with civilization and advanced technology being by-products.

This means that there were strong selection pressures on social cognition. Individuals who could anticipate what others were going to do, cooperate with others, and learn from others were also likely to be able to successfully compete with others, all of which would be to their advantage. Individuals who lacked self-awareness presumably could not as easily plan their own action ("Should I save this tool for future use?"), anticipate the actions of others ("Will he retaliate if I take his food?"), and cooperate and compete successfully, and such individuals would be at a decided disadvantage when living among individuals who possessed self-awareness.

In other words, we became the thoughtful creatures we are in order to cope with one another (Alexander, 1989; Flinn, Geary, & Ward, 2005).

Two other factors presumably evolved along side of (co-evolved with) social complexity: big brains and an extended juvenile period (Bjorklund, Cormier, & Rosenberg, 2005). As noted in Chapter 4, humans have the largest brain relative to body size of any animal. This large brain is likely necessary for self-awareness, in addition to other impressive cognitive abilities that humans display. This large brain also takes a long time to reach maturity. The frontal cortex, the so-called thinking part of the brain, continues to develop into early adulthood, with adolescents' brains being noticeably different from the brains of young adults in the distribution of white and gray matter. This slow rate of neural development is likely necessary in order for children to master the complexities of the social group. Human cultures and social relations are complicated, and children need substantial time and a flexible intelligence to learn to navigate the social terrain. Humans do not reach sexual maturity until the middle teen years, and some anthropologists suggest that this was likely closer to 20 years of age for our ancestors (Bogin, 1999; Kaplan et al., 2000). Ancient humans' advanced technological skills, such as those involved in tool making, hunting, and foraging, also required a long time to master (Kaplan et al., 2000).

Evidence for the relationship between social complexity, big brains, and an extended juvenile period comes from studies comparing each of these factors in various primate groups. For instance, researchers have found a significant relationship between measures of brain size and social complexity among primates (correlation between size of neocortex and group size = .76; see Dunbar, 1992, 2001), and primate species with larger brains have, on average, the longest juvenile periods (Bonner, 1988). In other research, Tracey Joffe (1997) compared social complexity, measured in terms of size of the group, the length of the juvenile period, and the size of the neocortex (the thinking part of the brain) for 27 different primate species, including

Children need to understand what is involved in making deals, who can be trusted, and when a social contract is being honored or broken.

humans. Joffe reported a significant relationship among these three factors: the bigger the brain, the larger the social group, the longer the juvenile period tended to be. These findings suggest that both brain size and delayed development are important, interdependent factors that are related to success in complex social groups.

Humans have the biggest brains, longest juvenile period, and live in the most socially complex environments of any animal. However, our ancestors had the beginnings of these three characteristics at least 6 million years ago, if modern chimpanzees are any indication of what our common ancestor was like. Chimpanzees have the largest brain relative to body size of any land mammal other than humans, have a prolonged juvenile period, and live in socially complex groups, at least relative to other nonhuman primates. So our common ancestor with chimpanzees surely also had the preconditions necessary for evolving human intelligence.

We will likely never know for certain all of the factors that contributed to the modern human mind, but we feel confident that the evolution of self-awareness was an important event in the transition from ape to human. Its development from infancy to childhood is equally important in the life of the individual.

Self-concept	A person's awareness (and potentially definition) of one's self, including physical and psychological characteristics and skills. At its most basic, this involves knowledge of the self, as reflected in toddlers by visual self-recognition.
Self-esteem	The evaluative component of the self. The judgments people make of their general worth as a person and the feelings associated with those judgments. Researchers have identified at least five areas of self-esteem: scholastic competence, social competence, behavioral conduct, athletic competence, and physical appearance.
Self-efficacy	The extent to which a person views him or herself as an effective individual; the confidence one has in being able to control events in one's surroundings. Self-efficacy develops with experience, but young children believe that they are more competent (efficacious) than they actually are, frequently overestimating their abilities.
Identity formation	A self-portrait of the different pieces of the self integrated in a coherent way (including physical, sexual, ideological, intellectual, relational, vocational, and cultural/ethnic aspects). Erik Erikson believed that adolescents grapple with their developing adult identity, asking seriously, "Who am I?" and "What do I want to be?" for the first time.

your life in which you think you excel. For example, are you good at sports (in general or only specific activities), academics, or social relationships (both with family and with friends)? How about areas of your life that you are not so good at? And now write down a general appraisal of yourself. Do you like yourself now? What, if anything, would you like to change about yourself? Do you see yourself being the same person in another 5 or 10 years?

If you have taken this exercise seriously, you now likely have an idea about some of the central concepts that we examine in this section, including self-concept, self-esteem, self-efficacy, and identity. We provide a brief definition of each of these concepts in Concept Review 7.1. Although distinctions among these various forms of self are sometimes difficult to make (their close relationships make their borders a bit fuzzy and imprecise, making some confusion among them almost inevitable), it is worth noting here that they are not interchangeable.

We do not think it is possible to overstate the significance of a sense of personal self, or **self-concept**. Although one could seemingly perform many everyday tasks without the conscious knowledge that *you* are performing these tasks, a sense of self also implies a sense of others, and this affects greatly how people of all ages go about their business. Many years ago, Charles Cooley (1902) used the term *looking-glass self* to capture the idea that our concept of who we are is a reflection of how other people see and respond to us. According to

Philippe Rochat (2009, p. 3), "self-consciousness stands for the representation we hold of ourselves through the eyes of others."

Early Signs of Self-awareness

Early self-concept comes in two types: the *implicit self*, sometimes referred to as the *I-self*, and the *explicit self*, sometimes referred to as the *me-self* (Case, 1991; Lewis, 1991). The implicit self typifies infants from birth to about 15 to 18 months old and reflects what Michael Lewis (1991) termed the "machinery of the self." Infants of this age have no self-awareness and are only able to make a distinction between the self and others and a realization that "I can cause things to happen." In contrast, the explicit self involves a conscious (explicit) awareness of the self, or, as Lewis stated, the "idea of me."

How can one tell if an infant has an explicit self rather than an implicit self? One technique that some people think captures the idea of an explicit self (or the me-self) is visual self-recognition. For example, infants as young as 2 months old often have daily exposure to their images from mirrors (Bahrick, 1995). But how do we know that babies understand that the image looking back at them is their own? To assess this, researchers place a mark on a child's body unbeknownst to the child (usually on the forehead) and then observe the child's reaction to his or her image in a mirror. By 18 months old, most children show signs of self-recognition by touching the mark on their face rather than touching the mirror (Brooks-Gunn & Lewis, 1984; Nielsen, Suddendorf, & Slaughter, 2006). That is, they act as if they know the face looking back at them is their own. Younger infants,

self-concept The way a person defines himself or herself.

visual self-recognition The ability to recognize oneself in a mirror; a form of self-recognition.

in contrast, do not seem to realize that the image facing them is theirs and will touch the mirror. It is as if there is another person looking back at them with a strange mark on his or her face. Visual self-recognition is also found in the great apes—chimpanzees, orangutans, and a few gorillas (Gallup, 1979; Suddendorf & Whiten, 2001)—dolphins (Reiss & Marino, 2001), elephants (Plotnik, de Waal, & Reiss, 2006), and magpies (Prior, Schwarz, & Güntürkün, 2008), but not in any other animals so far tested (but see Northoff and Panksepp [2008] for a proposal that a sense of self is shared by most mammals).

However, the development of a sense of self is more complex than just an ability to recognize one's own reflection as self. Several different measures point to the fact that a sense of self develops slowly and includes several different aspects. For example, when do children recognize themselves in pictures or videos? In one set of studies, researchers videotaped or took Polaroid photos of preschool children while they played (Povinelli, Landau, & Perilloux, 1996; Povinelli & Simon, 1998). Without the children knowing it, researchers placed large stickers on children's heads. How would children react when they saw themselves in the photos or on the video with stickers on their heads? Most 2- and younger 3-year-old children did not reach for the stickers, whereas most older preschoolers did. All children, however, removed the sticker when they looked at themselves in a mirror (Povinelli et al., 1996). These results suggest that children's sense of self develops gradually over the preschool years, as their ability to deal with different modes of representation (mirrors, photos, videos) develops (see also Zelazo, Sommerville, & Nichols, 1999; Skouteris, Spataro, & Lazarid, 2006).

Other indices of self-awareness can be observed late in the second year. For example, around this time many children begin using the personal pronouns *I*, *me*, *my*, and *mine*, thereby indicating a distinction between themselves and others (Lewis & Brooks-Gunn, 1979; Lewis & Ramsay, 2004). They also begin to display secondary, or self-conscious, emotions, such as embarrassment (Lewis et al., 1989). As Piaget (1962) noted many years ago, children around 2 years of age begin to display new symbolic, or representational, abilities, and self-concept seems to be one important product of the symbolic function. Given the significance of other people in the lives of children, possessing a sense of self has great impact on their lives. Neuroscience research has discovered a connection between the onset of these early signs of self-awareness and brain development. For example, the degree of self-representation that 15- to 30-month-old children show, as reflected by mirror self-recognition, use

Children beginning around 18 months of age will recognize themselves in a mirror. Such mirror self-recognition is also shown by some great apes.

of personal pronouns, and pretend play, is related to maturation of a portion of the left hemisphere (Lewis & Carmody, 2008).

Self-concept in Childhood and Adolescence

Once children realize they are distinct from other people and objects, how can we determine how they think about themselves? One way of gaining some insight into children's self-concepts is simply to ask them to describe themselves. Preschool children generally describe themselves in terms of physical characteristics ("I'm strong," "I have brown hair," "I have blue eyes"), by their actions ("I run real fast," "I play baseball," "I walk my dog"), where they live, and who is in their family (Keller, Ford, & Meachum, 1978; Livesley & Bromley, 1973). Rarely do preschool children provide psychological descriptions of themselves (for example, "I'm happy," "I'm smart," "I'm friendly"). Below is a composite self-description typical of a 3- to 4-year-old child (from Harter, 1999, p. 37):

> I'm three years old and I live in a big house with my mother and father and my brother, Jason, and my sister, Lisa. I have blue eyes and a kitty cat is orange and a television in my room. I know all of my ABCs, listen: A, B, C, D, E, F, G, H, I, J, K, L, M, N, O, P, Q, R, S, T, U, V, W, X, Y, Z. I can run real fast. I like pizza, and I have a nice teacher at preschool. . . . I love my dog Skipper. I can climb to the top of the jungle gym—I'm not scared! I'm never scared! . . . I'm really strong. I can lift this chair, watch me!

This self-definition by physical characteristics is consistent with Piaget's idea that preschool children's thinking is concrete and tied to specific

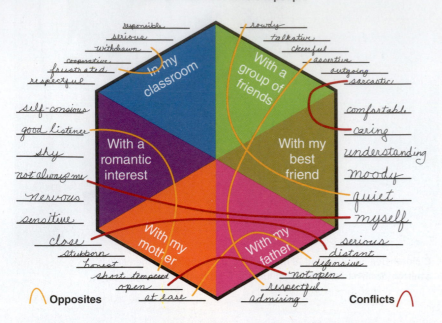

What I am like with different people

responsible
serious
withdrawn
cooperative
frustrated
respectful

In my classroom

rowdy
talkative
cheerful
assertive
outgoing
sarcastic

self-conscious
good listener
shy
not always me
nervous
sensitive
close
stubborn
honest
short-tempered
open
at ease

With a romantic interest

With a group of friends

With my best friend

comfortable
caring
understanding
moody
quiet
myself
serious
distant
defensive
not open
respectful
admiring

With my mother

With my father

⋀ **Opposites**   **Conflicts** ⋀

FIGURE 7.2 "What I Am Like with Different People."

Multiple selves of a prototypical 15-year-old girl. SOURCE: Adapted from Harter, S. (1999). *The construction of the self: A developmental perspective.* Reprinted by permission of Guilford Publications.

experiences, as discussed in Chapter 6. This picture does not change substantially during the early school years. As children approach adolescence, their thinking becomes more abstract, and so does the way they view themselves. Children are now more likely to define themselves in terms of psychological qualities—things they like and personality characteristics (Montemayor & Eisen, 1977).

The sense of self for adolescents becomes increasingly differentiated. Adolescents realize that there are multiple aspects of their personalities and that they posses multiple selves that vary with social context ("I'm an extrovert with my friends: I'm talkative, pretty rowdy, and funny. . . . With my parents, I'm more likely depressed. I feel sad as well as mad and also hopeless about ever pleasing them," from Harter, 1999). This can lead to confusion, however, as adolescents grapple with the fact that they sometimes think of themselves in diametrically opposing terms: they are sometimes outgoing and sometimes introverted, sometimes happy and sometimes depressed, sometimes responsible and sometimes irresponsible. Susan Harter and her colleagues (1999, 2006; Harter et al., 1997) found that the number of opposing attributes adolescents use in describing themselves, as well as the expression of conflict in dealing with these opposing selves, increases between early and middle adolescence. This is related in part to adolescents' increasing abilities for introspection and a self-centered perspective that results in the mistaken belief that other people are as concerned with their feelings and behavior as they are, which only enhances their self-consciousness.

self-esteem The judgments people make of their general self-worth and the feelings associated with those judgments.

By late adolescence and early adulthood, preoccupation with what others think decreases. Adolescents are also becoming aware that possessing different attributes of the self in different contexts is not necessarily a contradiction, all while they are integrating different aspects of themselves into a coherent identity (see discussion to follow). In other words, a mature sense of self is developing, one that recognizes that people behave differently in different contexts and at different times, and that such variability is not a reflection of a fractured self, but, in fact, the norm. ("You have to be adaptive around other people. It would be weird to be the same kind of person on a date and with my friends at a football game," Harter, 2006, pp. 546, 547). Figure 7.2 presents a diagram of a prototypical 15-year-old girl and how she views her multiple selves (from Harter, 1999). Generally, as children's abilities to mentally represent themselves and others change with age, so too does their sense of self.

The Development of Self-esteem

Self-esteem is an evaluative component of the self and refers to the judgments people make of their general worth as a person and the feelings associated with those judgments. For example, people with high self-esteem believe they are generally competent and take pride in their accomplishments, whereas people with low self-esteem regard themselves as less competent and often express shame, despair, or uncertainty in the things they do. It is important to note that these evaluations of self may or may not correspond with actual competencies that other people perceive as real. Self-esteem can be viewed as a product of two internal assessments: (1) the discrepancy between the *perceived self* and the *ideal self*, and (2) support from social others.

Self-esteem refers to a person's beliefs about his or her global worth, although there are more domain-specific elements to a child's sense of self-esteem. For example, Susan Harter (1999) proposed that preschool children distinguish two general categories of self-esteem: their physical and cognitive competence (for example, "I'm strong"; "I'm smart") and their general social competence (for example, "Other kids like me"). By the third or fourth grade, researchers have identified five categories of self-esteem: scholastic competence, social competence, behavioral conduct (that is, do they stay out of trouble?), athletic competence, and physical appearance (see Figure 7.3). Children now have relatively well-defined ideas of their abilities in these various areas and are able to differentiate among them ("I'm really good in math, don't get into trouble much at school, but I'm too skinny and I'm not too good at kickball"). Note that Harter does not view self-esteem as being hierarchical in nature (one dimension is not more important than another) nor as additive (overall self-esteem is not the result of adding the self-perceptions in each of these dimensions), but views a person's self-esteem as the product of the relationship among perceptions of adequacy across domains and of each domain's personal importance. Table 7.1 presents some sample items from a self-perception scale used to assess children's self-esteem (Harter, 1985).

Preschool children's self-esteem tends to be overly positive (Harter & Pike, 1984), but they become more accurate (that is, reflect their actual abilities) beginning around 8 years of age. Self-esteem usually remains relatively high and stable until about early adolescence, when it typically declines a bit, often associated with the transition to high school. Self-esteem tends to become increasingly positive over adolescence and into young adulthood, with most teenagers feeling considerable pride and self-confidence (Trzesniewski, Donnellan, & Robins, 2003). Not all adolescents feel good about themselves, however. In most cases, feelings of low self-esteem during adolescence are transitory, reflecting temporary periods of discomfort that are soon overcome.

It may strike some of you as odd to say that self-esteem stays "relatively high and stable" over adolescence. Most of us can recall episodes from our adolescence when we felt anything but high self-esteem. Such low levels of self-esteem reflect what researchers call *barometric self-esteem*, which reflects feelings about ourselves that fluctuate from moment to moment. This is contrasted with *baseline self-esteem*, which reflects a less transitory and more stable assessment of our self-esteem (Rosenberg, 1986) and remains "relatively high and stable" over adolescence and into young adulthood.

However, persistent low self-esteem has been linked to more serious problems. For example, there is a strong relationship between a low global self-esteem, induced in part by perceived physical appearance or attractiveness, and eating disorders such as anorexia and bulimia, particularly in girls (Harter, 1999; see discussion of eating disorders in Chapter 4). Similarly, there is a relationship between low self-esteem and depression, suicide, and violent and maladjusted behaviors (Fenzel, 1994; Harter, 2006). For instance, long periods of peer rejection and humiliation are associated with violent ideation and action during adolescence. This is expressed at the most extreme in teenagers who bring guns to school and murder their classmates (Harter, 2004, 2006; Harter & McCarley, 2004).

There is a sex difference in self-esteem beginning in middle childhood, with boys reporting higher self-esteem than girls, although the absolute magnitude of this difference is small, and average levels of self-esteem for both boys and girls are generally high (see Kling et al., 1999). Several reasons have been hypothesized for this difference. Decreases in self-esteem are more likely to occur in adolescence, when youth face multiple stressors, such as going through puberty, changing schools, and beginning to date. Girls mature faster than boys and are thus more likely to experience more of these stressors than boys do during early adolescence (see Shaffer, 2009). Also, girls are more apt than boys to be dissatisfied with their bodies, and Western culture places greater emphasis on physical appearance for young women than it does for young men. The

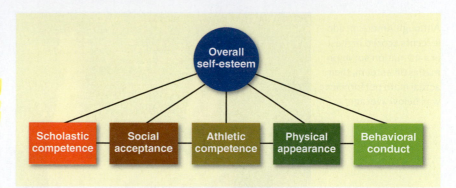

FIGURE 7.3 The multidimensional nature of self-esteem.

According to Harter, self-esteem is composed of a series of possible dimensions, with overall self-esteem based on individuals' perceptions of their competence in those domains they view as important. The relationship among perceptions across domains and their personal importance determines a person's overall self-esteem. SOURCE: Adapted from Harter, S. (1996). Historical roots of contemporary issues involving self-concept. In B. A. Bracken (Ed.), *Handbook of self-concept: Developmental, social, and clinical considerations.* Reprinted by permission of John Wiley & Sons, Inc.

table 7.1 Some Examples of Items on Susan Harter's *Self-Worth Profile for Children*

For each question, children first decide which statement is more true of them, the one on the right or the left. They then indicate whether that statement is "sort of true" or "really true" of them.

Really true of me	Sort of true of me				Sort of true of me	Really true of me
❑	❑	Some kids are *not* very happy with the way they do things.	BUT	Other kids think the way they do things is *fine*.	❑	❑
❑	❑	Some kids are *happy* with themselves as a person.	BUT	Other kids are often *not* happy with themselves.	❑	❑
❑	❑	Some kids *don't* like the way they're leading their life.	BUT	Other kids *do* like the way they're leading their life.	❑	❑
❑	❑	Some kids like the kind of person they are.	BUT	Other kids often wish they were someone else.	❑	❑

SOURCE: From Harter, S. (1985). *Manual for the self-perception profile for children.* Denver, CO: University of Denver. Reprinted by permission.

Although American adolescents scored highest in a 40-nation survey in math self-esteem, their actual math performance was below average.

Dimitri Vervitsiotis/Getty Images

female icons of Western culture tend to be unrealistically attractive and thin, which makes it nearly impossible for girls and young women to attain the perceived standard. Alternately, girls may be more realistic than boys in their self-appraisal. For example, although boys express higher scholastic self-esteem than girls do, they perform more poorly in school than girls do at all levels.

Children's self-esteem varies with their experiences. Children who have experiences of success in academics, for example, appropriately develop a high sense of scholastic self-esteem, and as a result, are more apt to enjoy school, try harder, and perform well in academics, although the overall effects of self-esteem on academic achievement tend to be small in magnitude (Valentine, DuBois, & Cooper, 2004).

Parents can have a significant influence on their children's self-esteem, beginning early in life. According to Harter (2006, p. 518), early in development, "soothing positive affect, interest in the infant's activities, support for mastery attempts, praise, and (nonintrusive) encouragement all lay the groundwork for a healthy sense of self during toddlerhood and early childhood." Children and adolescents whose parents are warm and have reasonable expectations for them generally display high levels of self-esteem (Feiring & Taska, 1996). In contrast, children whose parents repeatedly discourage or disapprove of their actions tend to have lower levels of self-esteem. Such parents make their children feel inadequate, and children are constantly seeking approval, often looking to their peers rather than their parents as a source of self-worth (DuBois et al., 2002; Lamborn et al., 1991). Not surprisingly, young children who are victims of abuse develop more negative self-evaluations than their well-treated peers do (see Cicchetti & Rogosch, 2001; Toth et al., 2000). At the other extreme, children of permissive parents, who demand little of their children but frequently indulge them, often have unrealistically high levels of self-esteem. Such overblown feelings of self-worth can cause children to feel superior to others and entitled, and they often have adjustment prob-

lems, including school misconduct and substance abuse (Lamborn et al., 1991).

Although relatively few children have what we would call an overinflated sense of self, some researchers report that the levels of self-esteem that most American adolescents display have increased over the decades. Since the mid-1970s, American adolescents have been expressing increasingly positive views of themselves, promoted by a societal emphasis on building self-esteem (Twenge, 2006; Twenge & Campbell, 2001). Although others refute these claims (Trzesniewski, Donnellan, & Robins, 2008), all seem to agree that higher self-esteem does not always translate into better achievement or psychological adjustment. Perhaps somewhat surprisingly, this increase in self-esteem over recent decades has been accompanied by some *declines* in academic achievement and increases in adjustment problems, including depression (see Berk, 2005). For example, in an international comparison of 40 developed nations, American adolescents scored below the average in mathematics achievement, but they ranked first in math self-concept (OECD, 2004).

High self-esteem needs to be based on real achievement. There is a bidirectional relationship between self-esteem and performance: good performance fosters a positive sense of self-esteem, which in turn fosters good performance (Guay, Marsh, & Boivin, 2003). According to Martin Seligman (1998), the self-esteem movement in American homes and schools has produced children who feel good about themselves often without the accomplishments to justify their feelings. This is an unstable edifice on which to build a personality and can lead to depression when bad things happen.

This problem of an overinflated sense of self seems to be especially prominent in children from more affluent homes. According to clinical psychologist Madeline Levine (2006), many affluent parents want to protect their children from feelings of failure, which may, they believe, harm their children's self-esteem. They sometimes go to great lengths to achieve this goal. Levine tells of a baseball league for young children in her community with a rule they call "good-enough catch." If a child is anywhere near a ball that is hit and not too far away from a base, it counts as an out. (This may prevent feelings of inadequacy for the fielder, but we are not sure what it does for the kid who hit the ball.) Levine states that many affluent parents expect great things of their children and let their children's teachers and coaches, as well as their own colleagues and next-door neighbors, know how special their children are. It is not surprising that the children come to believe they are extraordinary and as a consequence experience adjustment problems when they face challenges they cannot handle (and their parents can't fix) and

Self-concept	*By 18 months old*: Most children recognize themselves in a mirror (for example, they touch a mark on their face rather than touching the mirror).
	Preschool age: Children typically describe themselves in terms of their physical features ("I have blue eyes"), things they do ("I play baseball"), where they live ("I live in a small house"), or who is in their family ("I have a big sister").
	Childhood to adolescence: Children's self-descriptions in psychological terms increase and differentiate ("I'm smart," "I'm friendly," "I am good at math but not at baseball").
	Early and middle adolescence: Adolescents develop different selves that vary with social context. They often feel confused about these opposing selves ("I'm an extrovert with my friends: I'm talkative, and funny. . . . With my parents, I'm more likely depressed"). They feel extremely concerned about what others think about them.
	Late adolescence and early adulthood: Preoccupation with what others think decreases, and the different attributes of the self in different contexts are not seen as opposing ("You have to be adaptive around other people. It would be weird to be the same kind of person on a date and with my friends at a football game").
Self-esteem/self-worth	*Preschool children*: Children distinguish two categories of self-esteem: their physical and cognitive competence (for example, "I'm strong"; "I'm smart") and their general social competence (for example, "Other kids like me"). They overestimate their competences.
	By the third/fourth grade: Children differentiate among five categories of self-worth: scholastic competence, social competence, behavioral conduct, athletic competence, and physical appearance. They become more realistic about their own competences.
	Adolescence: At the beginning of adolescence, children's self-esteem typically declines some, often associated with the transition to high school. Self-esteem then increases again in most (but not all) adolescents. Many adolescents experience temporary periods of discomfort that are soon overcome.

SOURCE: Some examples taken or adapted from Harter, S. (1999). *The construction of the self: A developmental perspective.* New York: Guilford Press; and Harter, S. (2006). The self. In W. Damon (Gen Ed.) & N. Eisenberg (Vol. Ed.), *Handbook of child psychology: Vol. 3. Social, emotional and personality development* (5th ed., pp. 505–570). New York: Wiley.

encounter others who do not view them as the entitled people they view themselves to be.

Parents should promote their children's self-esteem by giving them praise when they really accomplish a difficult task and encouragement when they find them struggling with a tough problem. However, false praise does not help children determine what they are good at and what they are not, what they need to practice, or the value of persistence in completing difficult tasks. The trick is not to paint an either unjustly rosy or dour picture for children about their skills, but to promote their self-esteem based on accomplishments that are appropriate for their age and ability levels.

Self-esteem is a complicated phenomenon. In many ways, it can be seen as a personality characteristic, having a moderate degree of heritability (Neiss, Sedikides, & Stevenson, 2002). Yet, it varies between domains (for example, scholastic, social), over time (it generally increases into young adulthood), is related to some personality characteristics and measures of psychological adjustment, and is influenced by parents and, especially it seems, peers. Self-esteem is a reflection of a person's developing concept of self—the type of person one is and the type of things one is good and not so good at doing. Children's and adolescents' views of themselves are affected by how others see them as well as how they view their own accomplishments. This, in turn, influences how they behave—what types of tasks they attempt and who they interact with—which often serves to confirm their sense of self. Concept Review 7.2 lists some of the milestones in the development of self-concept.

The Development of Self-efficacy

Related to the concept of self-esteem is **self-efficacy**, defined "as people's beliefs about their capabilities to produce designated levels of performance that exercise influence over events that affect their lives" (Bandura, 1994, p. 71), or the confidence one

self-efficacy The extent to which a person views him- or herself as an effective individual.

Infants whose parents respond contingently to their behavior develop a sense of prediction and control, the beginning of a positive sense of self-efficacy.

Young children tend to overestimate their physical, social, and intellectual abilities.

others, and are told by others the degree to which their behavior meets certain standards. Children who believe they are competent (even if they are not) develop feelings of positive self-efficacy and behave effectually. Conversely, when self-efficacy is poor, children tend to behave ineffectually, regardless of their actual abilities (Bandura, 1997).

The development of self-efficacy begins early, as infants learn that they can exert some control over their environment. Beginning around 3 or 4 months, babies learn that their actions have consequences. If they kick their feet, the mobile over the crib will move, and if they smile and coo, their parents will smile and talk back to them. Infants who have experienced some control over their environments are better able to learn new behaviors (Finkelstein & Ramey, 1977). Mary Ainsworth and her colleagues (1978) proposed that parents' responsiveness to their infants' attempts to communicate their needs gives the infants some sense of control over their parents and is related to later social and cognitive development.

With the development of language and other symbols, children are able to reflect on their new social and intellectual abilities and evaluate what others tell them about their skills. Initially, the family provides children with feedback on their effectiveness. As children approach school age, their peer group becomes a valuable source of information, and school is a potent agent in forming children's self-efficacy. Children learn through daily experience with teachers and peers that they are good at some things and not so good at others (Bandura, 1997).

The Optimistic Child

Although children learn self-efficacy through experience, developing a positive sense of self-efficacy is facilitated by a generally optimistic (and often unrealistic) opinion of their own abilities that children across the globe seem to have. Preschool children think that they can remember more items, communicate more effectively, imitate a model more accurately, and perform a host of tasks better than they actually can (Lipko, Dunlosky, & Merriman, 2009; Plumert, 1995). Young children's beliefs that they know more than they actually do and can do more than they actually can provides them with positive perceptions of their own skills.

This point was made by Deborah Stipek and her colleagues (Stipek, 1984; Stipek & Daniels, 1988), who found that young children can make relatively accurate predictions of how *other* children are likely to perform on school-like tasks but are overly optimistic in predicting their *own* future performance. Stipek suggested that this overly optimistic self-perception is due to *wishful thinking*, a concept originally introduced by Piaget (1930):

has in being able to control events in one's surroundings (Harter, 1998). However, unlike self-esteem, which relates to a person's global worth, self-efficacy relates to a person's perception of his or her ability to reach a specific goal. Children evaluate the effectiveness of their own actions in specific contexts, compare it with the actions of

Children wish for *A*s on their report cards; therefore, they expect *A*s. By the third or fourth grade, children's assessments of their abilities move closer to reality, and they are able to tell the difference between what they wish would happen and what they can reasonably expect to happen.

Stipek believes that children's tendency to overestimate their abilities enhances their self-efficacy and gives them the confidence to attempt things they would not otherwise try (see also Bjorklund, 1997a; Bjorklund & Green, 1992). Some evidence indicates that brighter 3- and 4-year-olds overestimate their abilities on an imitation task more than less-bright 3- and 4-year-olds do, suggesting an adaptive value of overestimation in young children (Bjorklund et al., 1993). Stipek proposed that rather than trying to make young children's self-assessments more accurate, we should "try harder to design educational environments which maintain their optimism and eagerness" (1984, p. 53). This would involve the inclusion of age-appropriate tasks on which children can show improvement with practice, making their initial overly optimistic assessments of their performance a reality.

The positive consequences of overestimation is shown, for example, in a study that demonstrated that 8- to 11-year-old children who overestimated their capabilities had better school performance than did less-optimistic children (Lopez et al., 1998). These children may not have been quite as good as they thought, but their school performance was better than that of their more-accurate peers. In other research, kindergarten, first-, and third-grade children who overestimated their memory abilities showed greater subsequent memory improvement than did more-accurate children (Shin, Bjorklund, & Beck, 2007).

Children overestimate not only their intelligence, problem-solving, and memory abilities but also their social standing. Social (or dominance) hierarchies are found at all ages, from preschool through adolescence (see Hawley, 1999; Weisfeld & Janisee, 2005). Given the importance of social status, even for young children, it should not be surprising that children tend to overestimate their place in social hierarchies. For example, children from 3 years through early adolescence tend to rate themselves as tougher and stronger (factors important in children's dominance hierarchies, especially for boys), and generally as more popular than teachers or their peers rate them. This effect is sometimes greater for boys than for girls, but not always (Boulton & Smith, 1990).

The overall picture is one of young children having an overly positive opinion of their physical, social, and cognitive abilities. Over the school years, children's self-assessments become more realistic, but an overly positive sense of self-efficacy is associated with generally positive outcomes. Although there may be some benefits to children overestimating their abilities, there are also some obvious potential problems for children who think they are more skilled than they really are. Concept Review 7.2 lists some of the milestones in the development of self-esteem.

The Possible Pitfalls of Overestimating One's Abilities

One relatively minor problem of overestimating one's talents can be embarrassment that comes from publicly displaying the skills that you do not actually have. One of us (DB) recalls vividly the end of a school day in first grade, when the teacher decided to fill the time with some entertainment. "Can anyone sing a song for us?" she asked, and several children complied. "Can anyone dance?" she asked, and I, feeling it was my time to shine, blurted out "I can tap dance!" I walked to the front of the room and proceeded to shuffle my feet, trying my best to imitate the dancers I had seen on television. The result *was* entertainment, but strictly comedy. My classmates roared with laughter, and even the teacher was unable to hide a smile. Fortunately, the bell rang soon and the children lined up to go home, so my embarrassment was short lived, although I still remember it more than 50 years later. (It is not just children who overestimate their abilities, as reflected by some singers and dancers who appear on reality-TV shows and are shocked to be told that their talent must lay elsewhere.)

Children who overestimate their singing or dancing talents may experience embarrassment, but they are not likely to injure themselves. This is not necessarily the case for children who believe they can skateboard down a steep hill, cross a busy street, or climb a tree. Jodie Plumert and her colleagues have studied children's evaluations of their physical skills and related them to their history of accidents. In a series of experiments, 6- and 8-year-old children performed a variety of physical tasks (Plumert, 1995; Plumert & Schwebel, 1997). For instance, one task involved reaching an object on a shelf and another doing the limbo by sliding under a wooden bar attached to two posts. Children were first tested for their abilities to perform the tasks (for instance, how high they could reach and how low they could go). They were then asked to perform tasks that were well within their ability (for example, reaching an item on a shelf 13% below their ability), just at their ability, slightly beyond their ability (reaching an item on a shelf 8% above their ability), and well beyond their ability (reaching an item on a shelf 13% above their ability). They were first asked if they thought they could do each task, and if they said "yes," they were given the

— Embarrassment
— Injury

TALES OF THE OVERLY OPTIMISTIC...

I THINK I CAN
I THINK I CAN
I THINK I CAN
I THINK I CAN
I THINK I CAN...

Non Sequitur, © 1999 Wiley Miller/Universal UClick

opportunity to try. If they succeeded they would get a point toward a prize. If they failed, however, they would lose a point, and if they thought they could not do it, they would not perform the task and they would neither gain nor lose points. Most children overestimated their likelihood of performing tasks both just beyond and well beyond their ability. What is interesting is that 6-year-olds' estimation accuracy was related to the number of accidents they had had in their lifetimes that required medical attention. Children, especially boys, who overestimated their physical abilities made more trips to the emergency room than their more-accurate peers. By age 8, however, the relationship between estimation ability and accident proneness was no longer significant.

As children age, they continue to overestimate their physical abilities at some potential peril. For instance, Plumert and her colleagues (Plumert, Kearney, & Cremer, 2004, 2007) asked 10- and 12-year-old children and adults to determine when it was safe to ride their bikes across a busy street. (They did not actually cross streets. Judgments were made on a virtual street.) They found that the children were less accurate than the adults in making safety judgments. Children took longer to get moving, so the gap between cars that they judged to be safe turned out to result in more close calls than when adults made judgments.

Childhood by its very nature involves reaching beyond one's current abilities. As Harriet Rheingold (1985) said, the child's task in development is to "render the novel familiar," and this means exploring the unfamiliar, which may sometimes involve attempting new and perhaps somewhat dangerous tasks. Without such motivation, development would be short-circuited, with children engaging in easily performed and safe activities, showing little change from one day to the next, and even from one year to another. As Plumert (1995, p. 875) wrote, "The developmental dilemma, therefore, is to continually aspire to trying new and difficult things but not to try things that might have dangerous consequences." Parents must guide this development, monitoring their children's behavior, encouraging some activities, discouraging others, and scaffolding still others.

Building an Identity

The self, as we've described it, is a complicated concept with many different components, and it clearly develops over infancy and childhood. One of the main psychological challenges in adolescence is to establish an **identity**—a self-portrait of the different pieces of self in a coherent and integrated mode (including, for example, physical, sexual, ideological, intellectual, relational, vocational, and cultural/ethnic aspects). In this section, we first examine the process of identity formation in adolescence and then look at the formation of ethnic identity. Although in the past, one's ethnic identity was never in question, in modern times, when people immigrate and assimilate into very different societies, ethnic identity becomes a topic of great significance.

On Adolescent Identity

Erikson and the adolescent identity crisis. Erik Erikson (1950, 1968) was the first modern psychologist to emphasize the importance of identity formation in psychological development in general, and particularly during adolescence. Erikson believed that each stage of development centered on resolving an age-specific crisis. According to Erikson, the crisis in adolescence focused on developing a sense of adult identity; during this time, a person first seriously searches for answers to questions such as "Who am I?" and "What do I want to be?"

Erikson saw children's identity as being composed of individual pieces of a puzzle that were put together in adolescence. According to Erikson (1968, p. 345), "From among all possible and imaginable relations, [adolescents] must make a series of ever-narrowing selections of personal, occupational, sexual, and ideological commitments." How do adolescents do this? Certainly by reflection, but

---

identity The process of forming a coherent identity. A self-portrait of the different pieces of the self integrated in a coherent mode/way (including, for example, physical, sexual, ideological, intellectual, relational, vocational, and cultural/ethnic aspects).

also by interacting with others and responding to the reactions of other people to them. Other people reflect back to adolescents information about who they are and ought to be. Over the course of adolescence and young adulthood, young people try out different identities and eventually settle on a relatively stable sense of who they are. However, recall from Chapter 2 that Erikson was one of the first life span developmental psychologists, and he believed that a person's identity continued to change throughout adulthood.

We often think of adolescence as the time between the onset and completion of puberty. However, if instead we view it as the societal transition between childhood and adulthood, we can see that the quest to form an adult identity can extend for quite a while, at least in comparison to previous historical times. Erikson argued that in modern societies there is a need for a **psychosocial moratorium**, a time when the young person can put on hold the quest for a permanent identity and taking on adult responsibilities. In Western societies today, adolescents can take a time-out in their search for an adult identity. Many will attend college, join the military, or even travel for an extended time before settling down. There is also a tendency in Western culture for people to postpone marriage and have children later relative to decades past, which in essence postpones entry into adulthood (see Arnett, 2004).

It was not long ago that eight years of school made you an educated person. As jobs became more technologically demanding, more people needed more schooling. In most developed countries, the best jobs require some postsecondary education. About half of American young people attend some college, and the most intellectually demanding jobs are reserved for people with postgraduate education. Physicians, for example, complete four years of college, four years of medical school, and several years of internships and residencies before they have their own practice. The authors of this book were both in their late twenties before getting a "real" job, something that was brought to our attention by younger siblings and cousins.

Children from Western societies, particularly among middle- and upper-class families, are more likely to be afforded a psychosocial moratorium than are children from traditional societies or children who must make early decisions about their marital and vocational futures. Many parents provide some support for their college-age offspring, often well past the four years it takes to get a college degree. In general, contemporary society is functionally prolonging adolescence (at least for a large segment of society) and thus the need to resolve the identity crisis traditionally associated with the teenage years.

In many societies, older adolescents or young adults are encouraged to take time off to explore the world.

Allan Danahar/Getty Images

Differences in how societies relate to teenagers and their search for identity were made apparent to one of us (CHB) while visiting a Danish university. I was told that it was quite usual for young people to take one or two years off after completing high school. During this time, adolescents are encouraged to travel or work at a variety of jobs before starting university. There is also a tradition in New Zealand in which many adolescents, either before or after college, go on their "Big OE." OE stands for "overseas experience," and many New Zealand youth spend a year or more seeing the world before returning to their island country to settle down.

According to Erikson, if adolescents resolve the crisis successfully, they develop a sense of identity; if not, *role confusion* is established, which, if it continues, will have a negative impact on psychological development.

Marcia's identity status approach. James Marcia (1980, 1994) extended Erikson's ideas and developed the **identity status approach**, which pays special attention to occupational and ideological (for example, politics, religion) aspects of identity. Marcia classified adolescents' identity status based on their responses from interviews with respect to two dimensions of identity: *crisis* (or *exploration*) and *commitment*. First, is the adolescent facing an identity crisis? Is the person actively involved in a

---

psychosocial moratorium A sort of time-out period when, where possible, young people have a chance to explore who they are and what they want to be, in both the near and distant future.

identity status approach Marcia's extension of Erikson's theory of adolescent identity that pays special attention to occupational and ideological (for example, politics, religion) aspects of identity.

concept review | 7.3

The four identity statuses in Marcia's theory and prominent psychological characteristics of people in each status classification

Identity diffusion status	No crisis; no commitment	Apathy; at risk for drug use; lack of intimate relationships with peers: *Example*: "I haven't given much thought to what I want to be when I grow up. I've got plenty of time to decide."
Identity foreclosure status	No crisis; commitment	Conformity to authority; rely on others to make important decisions for them: *Example*: "I'm going to law school and become a lawyer. That's what men in my family do, and that's what I see myself doing in the years ahead."
Identity moratorium status	Crisis; no commitment	Highly anxious; unhappy; reject authority: *Example*: "My parents and all my family are Baptists, but I just don't know if I believe all the things they do. I don't think I'm an atheist, but I just don't know. My parents would be so unhappy with me if I rejected my religion and experimented with Buddhism, or even if I tried Catholicism. But I just don't know what's right for me."
Identity achievement status	Crisis overcome; with commitment	Socially mature; high in achievement motivation; more involved in careers: *Example*: "I really like cooking, and I loved the summer job I had as a cook. I've spoken with the owner of the restaurant, and I'm going to continue to work there part time and go to culinary school to become a chef."

personal search among different identity alternatives, or has the person resolved his or her crisis? Second, has the person already made a commitment to a particular identity, and is he or she showing a personal investment in that identity? Combining these two dimensions, Marcia described four possible identity statuses:

1. *Identity diffusion* (no crisis; no commitment), in which adolescents lack intimate relationships with peers and show a general apathetic attitude toward life
2. *Identity foreclosure* (no crisis; commitment), in which adolescents are happy to go along with authority and let others make decisions for them, such as going to college or not
3. *Identity moratorium* (crisis; no commitment), in which adolescents reject authority and are highly anxious
4. *Identity achievement* (crisis overcome with commitment), in which adolescents have overcome their identity crisis and are ready to take on adult responsibilities

Subsequent research has shown that most movement across adolescence and young adulthood is in the direction from identity diffusion to identity achievement, with the percentage of youth in the diffusion (no crisis, no commitment) and foreclosure (no crisis; commitment) statuses decreasing with age, and the percentage

in the achievement status increasing (Berzonsky & Adams, 1999; Waterman, 1999). This is illustrated in a cross-sectional study that examined the percentage of males at five different ages (12, 15, 18, 21, and 24 years) who were classified in each of Marcia's four statuses (Meilman, 1979). As you can see in Figure 7.4, most 12- and 15-year-old boys were classified as being in the identity diffusion status, with many 18-year-olds (48%) also being so classified. Changes in identity achievement status showed the opposite trend, with nearly no 12- and 15-year-olds being so classified and percentage of achievement identity status increasing into young adulthood. However, note that fewer than 60% of the 24-year-olds were classified in the achievement status, meaning that many young adults had still yet to resolve their identity crisis and make a commitment (see Kroger, 2005). In general, over the course of adolescence and into young adulthood, people in the diffusion and moratorium statuses tend to make a commitment, and move into identity achievement status. Many adolescents in the foreclosure status, who experience no crisis, tend to remain in this state into young adulthood.

Although there is much variability, researchers have reported different patterns of psychological adjustment for children and adolescents in these various classifications (Damon, 1983; Meeus et al., 1999) (see Concept Review 7.3). Not surprisingly, adolescents and young adults who are in the identity achievement or identity moratorium statuses tend to have higher self-esteem, are more apt to engage in critical thinking, and display greater similarity between their ideal and real self relative to adolescents and young adults who spend substantial time in the foreclosure and diffusion statuses (Kroger, 2005).

Particularly surprising is identity foreclosure status, where the adolescent, according to Marcia, does not actually experience a personal searching period and choice of an identity, but rather assumes other people's occupational and ideological identity. This may happen in traditional societies where limited adult identities are available to adolescents, or when children are raised by authoritarian parents who may restrict options for their children (for instance, deciding to be a lawyer in a family of lawyers), or when there is a codependent-preoccupied attachment to the parent.

Factors influencing identity formation. According to David Shaffer (2009), at least four factors influence an adolescent's identity formation: level of cognitive development, relationship with parents, education, and cultural-historical influences.

We noted earlier in our discussion of self-concept how adolescents' increasing cognitive abilities causes them to become preoccupied with themselves and what others think of them—a form of adolescent egocentricity. As they pass through adolescence, they come to realize they can, and often times should, display different aspects of their self in different contexts (in school versus on a date, for example). As adolescents become more capable of abstract thinking, they are better able to imagine future identities for themselves. As a result, they are more likely than their less-cognitively-mature peers to resolve identity issues (Boyes & Chandler, 1992).

Adolescents' relationship with their parents is related to their identity status. For example, adolescents who have a warm and stable relationship with their parents find it easier to move into the moratorium and achievement statuses than do adolescents with less-secure relationships (Grotevant & Cooper, 1998). Attending college also affects an adolescent's path toward identity formation, but not necessarily in a simple way. For example, adolescents and young adults who attend college are more likely than their noncollege peers to be advanced with respect to setting career goals and making stable occupational commitments (Waterman, 1982). However, adolescents and young adults who do not attend college often establish their religious and political identities earlier than same-age college attendees (Munro & Adams, 1977).

Identity formation is also greatly influenced by the broader culture. In some traditional societies, and certainly for our ancestors just several generations ago, one's adult identity could almost be predicted from birth. People living in a community had few options

for "what they will be when they grow up." Everyone follows the same religion, and one is expected to marry, have children, and do the same kind of work as one's mother or father (and their mothers and fathers before them) did. The soul-searching that characterizes many adolescents and young adults from developed societies today is unknown for people growing up in more traditional cultures.

The Development of Ethnic Identity

In nearly all cultures for most of human history, major aspects of adult identity were integrated. People living in the same culture spoke the same language, had the same religion, were of the same ethnic group, and shared the same cultural history. Differences among people within a society still existed—some were rich, others were poor; some were members of the elite classes, others were peasants—but one never had to question his or her cultural identity.

Life has changed in the modern world. The United States, for example, has always been a pluralistic society, with people from different parts of the globe immigrating to the New World and bringing with them their own religions, languages, and traditions. Pluralism is not unique to the United States but is seen in other North and South American countries and is increasingly seen in Europe, with an influx of immigrants from Asia and Africa, most occurring since the middle of the 20th century. How do minority adolescents and young adults develop a sense of ethnic identity? Are they able to meld the values and traditions of the majority culture with those of their parents and grandparents—keeping a foot in two cultural worlds, so to speak—or do the cultures clash, and as a result must they choose one identity over the other?

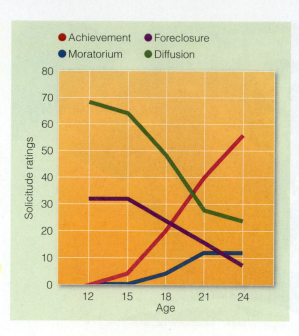

FIGURE 7.4 Percentage of 12-, 15-, 18-, 21-, and 24-year-old males in each of Marcia's Identity Statuses. Movement across adolescence and young adulthood is in the direction from identity diffusion to identity achievement, with the percentage of youth in the diffusion and foreclosure statuses decreasing with age, and the percentage in the achievement status increasing. SOURCE: From Meilman, P. W. (1979). Cross-sectional age changes in ego identity status during adolescence. *Developmental Psychology, 15*, 230–231. Reprinted by permission.

Adolescents from minority backgrounds who develop a strong sense of ethnic identity show healthy psychological development.

Although even youngsters from the majority culture (White, or Euro-Americans in the United States) have a sense of their ethnic background and traditions, ethnic identity becomes especially important for children from minority groups. Martha Bernal and her colleagues (1993) identified five aspects of ethnic identity:

1. *Ethnic self-identification*. Children identify themselves as a member of their ethnic group.
2. *Ethnic constancy*. Children realize that important aspects of their ethnic group are constant over time and situations and that they will always be a member of their ethnic group.
3. *Ethnic-role behaviors*. Children engage in behaviors or take on roles that characterize their ethnic group.
4. *Ethnic knowledge*. Children become aware that their ethnic group has certain features, such as customs, types of food, language, that distinguish it from other groups.
5. *Ethnic feelings and preferences*. Children have positive feelings about and preferences for characteristics of their ethnic group.

These aspects of ethnic identity develop over childhood, but ethnic identity becomes especially salient in adolescence (Marks et al., 2007), often because of an increasing realization of differences between members of their ethnic group and the majority culture. Adolescents may become aware of negative stereotypes associated with their ethnic group and experience overt or covert discrimination. Parents who maintain ethnic traditions may foster stronger feelings of ethnic identity for their children (Phinney, Romero et al., 2001a).

What are the consequences of developing an ethnic identity for adolescents from minority groups? First, in studies with minority adolescents from a variety of backgrounds (African American, Hispanic American, and Asian American), developing a strong sense of ethnic identity is associated with healthy psychological development. This includes high levels of self-esteem, optimism, mastery over their environment, and general psychological well-being (Phinney, Horenczyk et al., 2001; Smith et al., 1999). This, at first, may seem counterintuitive, particularly for youths from ethnic minorities associated with discrimination and lower socioeconomic status, such as African Americans. In fact, research and theorizing in the middle part of the 20th century had suggested that African American children had lower self-esteem than White children. Much of this was based on research by Kenneth and Mamie Clark, who, in a series of studies spanning more than 30 years, asked children to choose which of two dolls they preferred: a dark-skinned versus a light-skinned one. Across the many studies, White children were more likely than African American children to select a doll of their own skin color (see Banks [1976] for a review). This was interpreted as reflecting a racial self-esteem advantage for White relative to African American children. However, the racial differences in doll choice were strongest early in childhood and disappeared by adolescents, when both African American and White children showed a same-race preference. More recent work, using more sophisticated measures of self-esteem, has shown that the White self-esteem advantage is a myth: African American youth consistently score *higher* on measures of self-esteem than do Euro-American youth, who in turn score higher than other minorities (Asian, Hispanic, and American Indians). The differences are relatively small in magnitude but are consistently found across studies (Gray-Little & Hafdahl, 2000; Twenge & Crocker, 2002).

How does one explain this counterintuitive advantage for African American youths' self-esteem? Bernadette Gray-Little and Adam Hafdahl (2000) suggested that African Americans do not use the majority culture as their reference group but rather look to the Black community as a source of values and opinions. Similarly, by developing a positive ethnic identity, African Americans (and surely other minority groups) can attribute negative outcomes such as underemployment or poverty to prejudice. In a sense, they devalue the majority culture by enhancing their identification with their ethnic minority group.

There can be some negative consequences of a strong ethnic identity, however, when it is perceived as being at odds with some positive aspects of the majority culture. For example, some African American and Hispanic American youth see doing well in school as a capitulation to the majority culture—or "acting White" (Ogbu, 2003). Not surprisingly, this can result in poorer academic performance, higher school dropout rates, lower rates of college attendance, and limited access to the economic benefits that education provides people in the developed world. For many minorities, adopting values and behaviors associated with the majority culture is viewed as a rejection of one's ethnic identity.

Many minority children are able to integrate their ethnic identity with that of the majority culture, a phenomenon termed **bicultural identity**. In fact, although the research on this topic is relatively meager, what has been done shows that adolescents with bicultural identity score higher than minority children without bicultural identity on measures of psychological well-being (LaFromboise, Coleman, & Gerton, 1993; Phinney, Horenczyk, et al., 2001).

Self-concept clearly develops over childhood, into adolescence, and beyond. At its simplest, it involves distinguishing oneself from others, realizing that the child staring back from the mirror is you. It gets far more complicated, however. Children's sense of who they are is related to their ethnic or cultural group, but also to what they do and how well they do it, both from their own perspective and from that of others. Merely having a self-concept is a requirement for understanding other people and affects how children interact with others. As a result of such social interaction, children's self-concept develops along with other social skills, which is the hallmark of our species.

Children's Theory of Mind: Understanding Others

As self-aware adults, we understand the distinction between the *public self*, the me that other people see, and the *private self*, the I that represents one's inner self, which is available only to the self and not to others (Shaffer, 2009). We are also aware of this distinction in other people; that is, that they have a private self to which we are not privy. If we are to deal successfully with other people, we need to develop an understanding not only of ourselves but also of others, and accept that other people's public selves may not be identical to their private selves. This begins with the realization that, like us, other people have beliefs, feelings, thoughts, desires, emotions, and knowledge that drive their behavior. Sometimes their beliefs and desires may be much like our own;

other times, they may be quite different. How we interact with other people changes drastically when we understand how their minds work.

This is true not only for people living in complex, technologically sophisticated nation-states but also for people living in small hunter-gatherer communities. Some of the most complicated mental calculations people make on a regular basis have to do with dealing with other people. Because we are thinking animals, cooperating, competing, and generally getting along with other people requires that we have some idea of how *they* think. This has its origins in understanding how *we* think. We must first recognize that how we think influences how we act. What motivates my behavior? How do I make the decisions that I do? Once children develop a basic understanding of what motivates them to action, they can begin to get an idea of why other people behave the way they do. This requires developing what has been called a **theory of mind**.

In general, the phrase *theory of mind* refers to children's developing concepts of mental activity. Having a theory of mind implies that children have some coherent framework for organizing facts and making predictions about how minds work, both one's own mind and, importantly, the minds of other people (that is, to explain why someone behaves the way he or she does). Henry Wellman (1990) proposed that adults' theory of mind is based on **belief-desire reasoning**. Basically, we explain and predict what people do based on what we understand their desires and beliefs to be—that is, by referring to their wants, wishes, hopes, and goals (their desires) and to their ideas, opinions, suppositions, and knowledge (their beliefs). For example, if Samantha knows that there is only one cookie left in the cookie jar, and she knows (or thinks she does) that Kayla also wants a cookie, she may be less apt to divulge the location of the cookie jar than when she knows there are two cookies in the jar. Such belief-desire reasoning is depicted in Figure 7.5. Basically, this is what researchers mean when they talk about children developing a theory of mind: To what extent do children have a coherent explanatory theory to understand, predict, and explain both their behavior and the behavior of other people?

Children's representation of others and of themselves as thinkers is vitally important to our species' way of life. Cooperation, competition, and

....

theory of mind A person's concepts of mental activity; used to refer to how children conceptualize mental activity and how they attribute intention to and predict the behavior of others.

bicultural identity The ability of people to integrate their ethnic identity with that of the majority culture in which they are living.

belief-desire reasoning The process whereby we explain and predict what people do based on what we understand their desires and beliefs to be.

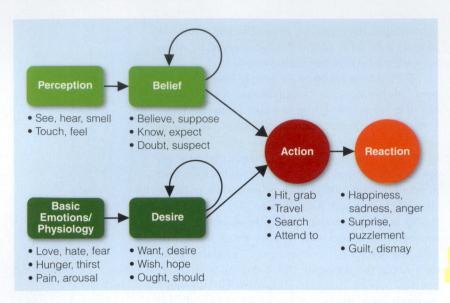

FIGURE 7.5 A simplified scheme depicting belief-desire reasoning.

People's perception of the world affects their knowledge, or beliefs, and their emotions influence their wants and desires. Beliefs and desires, in turn, motivate one's actions. Children learn that such belief-desire reasoning describes not only their own behavior but also that of other people. SOURCE: From *The child's theory of mind*, by H. M. Wellman. Copyright © 1990 Massachusetts Institute of Technology Press. Reprinted with permission.

social interaction in general as we know it would be radically different if we did not develop a theory of mind and the ability to read the minds of others.

Basic Social-Cognitive Skills Underlying Theory of Mind

A sophisticated theory of mind, capable of making simple deals (like trading Yu-Gi-Oh cards as we discussed in the opening lines of this chapter), takes some time to develop. Many skills must be acquired before someone is ready to negotiate peace between Israel and Palestine, mediate a strike between the United Auto Workers and Ford Motor Company, or, more realistically, negotiate turn-taking on the playground swings or the distribution of Halloween candy.

What are the most elementary social-cognitive abilities required for theory of mind, and when do they develop? First, as mentioned earlier and discussed in Box 7.1, it requires self-awareness—an ability to differentiate oneself from other people. Second, at its most basic, social cognition involves seeing oneself and other individuals as intentional agents—viewing oneself and others as individuals who *cause* things to happen and whose behavior is designed to achieve some goal (that is, people do things on purpose and for a reason; see Bandura, 2006; Harris, 2006; Tomasello, 1999; Woodward, 2009). This may not seem like much of an intellectual accomplishment, but it is the basis of all advanced forms of social cognition and of successful cooperation and competition among

people. For instance, the concept of intentionality goes to the heart of our legal system and our sense of morality. Did someone commit an act on purpose that led to an undesirable outcome, such as breaking a dish, missing an appointment, or hitting a pedestrian with a car? We assume the outcome had a cause, and how we interpret that cause (Was the act intentional or accidental? Was she in her right mind when she took the money?) determines how we view the individual who was responsible for the outcome. What we consider to be legally and morally right is based on our sense of intentionality.

A third basic component of our social cognition is perspective taking, the ability to take the point of view of others. At its most rudimentary, this can mean understanding that another person knows things that you do not know, or even sees things that he or she is looking at. This may bring to mind Piaget's concept of *egocentrism*, preschoolers' tendency to assume that other people see and understand the world as they do. However, even infants are able to take the perspective of others in some contexts, expressing empathy, for example, for another child's distress. Perspective taking is critical for social interactions. Appreciating that another person has knowledge, motivations, and feelings that may (or may not) be different from one's own (and, of course, being aware of one's own knowledge and motivations) affects how we think about and interact with that person. Perspective taking is also important in teaching, where both student and teacher have to be able to take the point of view of the other and to adjust their behavior to maximize learning.

Infants are not born with these abilities, but they develop over the first two years of life, beginning in infancy with shared attention (sometimes called *joint attention*) (Carpenter, Nagell, & Tomasello, 1998; Tomasello & Carpenter, 2007). Shared attention is exactly what it sounds like: two people both attending to the same thing or event and sharing that experience. Such a sharing of an experience implies that person A understands that person B sees the same things and has essentially the same experience as he or she does. For example, if Molly is looking across the room at her cat batting a toy mouse, and Molly's mother is nearby and looking at the same cat and mouse, *and* if Molly and her mother can see each other watching this event, the two are sharing attention. Note that shared attention is more than a two-way (or dyadic) relationship, but involves at least two people and a third object (which can be another person). This is a three-way, or *triadic*, relationship, reflecting the interaction between two social partners (for example, Molly and her mother) and a third object (in this case, Molly's cat; see Figure 7.6).

intentional agents Individuals who cause things to happen and whose behavior is designed to achieve some goal.

perspective taking The ability to take the point of view of others.

shared attention (joint attention) Two people both attending to the same thing or event and sharing that experience.

Shared attention is not something babies come into the world knowing how to do, although they do seemed biased toward social stimuli from birth. For example, neonates orient to the human face and quickly learn to seek their mothers' faces (Feldman & Eidelman, 2004), and by 2 or 3 months (or earlier) they can recognize self-produced, biological motion and soon turn to look in the same direction of another person (Tomasello et al., 2005). However, they do not engage in shared attention for many months, despite repeated attempts by their parents.

Beginning around 9 months of age, infants will gaze in the direction adults are looking or pointing, engage in repetitive interaction with an adult and an object, imitate an adult's action, and point or hold up objects to another person (see Carpenter et al., 1998; Tomasello, 1999). These abilities increase over the next year (see Tomasello, 1999; Tomasello, Carpenter, & Liszkowski, 2007). For example, 12-month-olds will point to objects to let others know about events they do not know—a cookie that fell off a table and onto the floor, for example (Liszkowski, Carpenter, & Tomasello, 2007). These findings indicate that infants now view other people as *intentional agents*. Using our example of Molly, her mother, and the cat, when both Molly and her mother are looking at the cat, Molly understands that they both see the same thing, and if Mom is not looking at the cat, Molly understands that the two of them see different things. Molly also understands that if Mom calls her name and points in the direction of the cat, Mom sees something that Molly does not and is signaling Molly to share an experience. Mom is acting intentionally—for a reason—to point something out to her daughter. Mom also sees Molly as an intentional agent and treats her accordingly.

Is there other evidence, independent of shared attention, that infants and toddlers view others as intentional agents? In one interesting study, 18-month-olds could tell the difference between intentional and unintentional actions of another person when deciding whether to provide help (Warneken & Tomasello, 2006). The toddlers sat across a table from an adult who performed a series of tasks. The adult had difficulty performing the tasks, and in some cases it was obvious that the adult was trying to achieve a specific outcome (the intentional condition). For instance, in one task, the adult accidentally dropped a marker on the floor and reached unsuccessfully to retrieve it. In a control condition, the adult deliberately threw the marker on the floor. In another task, the adult attempted to place a book on a stack of other books, but it slipped and fell beside the stack. This was contrasted with a control condition in which the person simply placed the book beside the stack. In 6 of 10 tasks, children helped the adult (for example,

Beginning around 12 months, infants will point out things to an adult that the adult doesn't see.

retrieved the marker, placed the book on top of the stack) more in the experimental than in the control condition, reflecting not only an understanding of another person's intention, but a willingness to help.

Sharing attention and experiences may not seem like such a great cognitive feat. Yet, almost all forms of complex human social interaction rest on the premise that the people we are dealing with are intentional agents: they do things on purpose, and

FIGURE 7.6 **The concept of shared attention featuring Molly, her mother, and a cat batting a toy mouse.** Molly and her mother share a visual experience. Each is aware that the other is seeing a cat batting a toy mouse. This is an example of *shared attention*.

That is, when the marble is moved to a different location while Sally is out of the room, will the child understand that Sally still believes, incorrectly, that the marble is in the basket, where she last saw it?

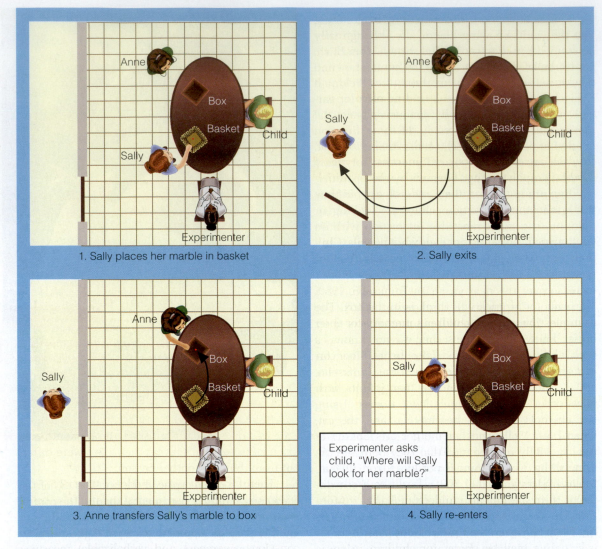

1. Sally places her marble in basket

2. Sally exits

3. Anne transfers Sally's marble to box

4. Sally re-enters

Experimenter asks child, "Where will Sally look for her marble?"

they see us the same way. Human social interaction requires more than shared attention. One central skill has been referred to as *mind reading*—putting yourself in another person's shoes (or mind), and trying to figure out what he or she is thinking. We do this all the time, it is the basis of most social interaction, and this skill develops over childhood.

The Development of Mind Reading

Displaying shared attention may be a good beginning, but engaging in triadic interaction is a far cry from the social-cognitive skills shown by most 8-year-old children, to say nothing of adults. We mentioned earlier that true theory of mind requires belief-desire reasoning. When and how do children come to appreciate that other people have beliefs and desires, often different from their own, which motivate their behavior? To assess

this question, researchers have developed tasks in which children must predict what another person will do or say, or what another person thinks, in an effort to determine what young children know about the minds of others. **False-belief tasks** are the gold standard of mind-reading tasks, and it is not until about 4 years of age when children typically solve them.

Solving False-belief Tasks

Basically, false-belief tasks assess the extent to which children understand that someone else can believe something that is not true. In a standard false-belief task (Baron-Cohen et al., 1985; Wimmer & Perner, 1983; see Figure 7.7), children watch as a marble is hidden in a special location (in a basket, for example). Two other people, Sally and Anne, are present when the marble is hidden. Sally then leaves the room. While Sally is gone, Anne moves the marble from the basket to another container. When Sally returns, will she know where the marble is hidden? The results of using variants of this standard task are relatively straightforward. Most

false-belief tasks A type of task, used in theory-of-mind studies, in which the child must infer that another person holds a belief that is false.

4-year-old children can solve the problem, stating that Sally will look where the marble was originally hidden. That is, they understand that Sally will have a false belief. Most 3-year-olds, in contrast, generally cannot solve the problem, stating that Sally will look for the marble in the new hiding place, apparently not realizing that Sally does not possess the new knowledge (Wellman et al., 2001).

In another frequently used false-belief task, children are shown a box of Smarties (a type of candy in a distinctive box, with which British children are highly familiar) and asked what they think is in the box (Hogrefe, Wimmer, & Perner, 1986). Naturally, they say "Smarties." The box is then opened, revealing not candy but pencils. Children are then asked what they originally thought was in the box before being shown the contents, as well as to predict what another child who was not privy to the trick will think is in the box. The first question assesses children's memory for their initial belief, whereas the second question assesses their ability to understand false belief. The correct answer to both of these questions is "Smarties," but most 3-year-olds say "pencils" to both questions.

The developmental patterns observed in variants of the "Sally-Anne" and "Smarties" tasks are not limited to European and North American children but have been found for children from all continents (Sabbagh et al., 2006; Tardif & Wellman, 2000), even among the children of Baka pygmies living in the rain forests of Cameroon (Avis & Harris, 1991). However, the timetable for passing false-belief tasks may be slower for children in some cultures than others (see Lillard, 1998; Liu et al., 2008; Wellman et al., 2006 for a discussion of cultural variations in theory of mind).

Despite the impressive evidence that most 3-year-old children cannot solve false-belief tasks, they seem to have some understanding that other people have desires and knowledge different from their own (see Caron, 2009). For example, in one study (Repacholi & Gopnik, 1997), 14- and 18-month-old infants were first tested for their preference for two types of food (Pepperidge Farm Goldfish and raw vegetables). They then watched as a woman tasted the two types of food. She expressed disgust for one type and happiness for the other. The woman then placed her hand, palm up, between the two bowls of food and said, "Can you give me some?" What did the toddlers do? The 14-month-olds gave the woman the type of food *they* liked, regardless of what food the woman liked. In contrast, the 18-month-olds were more likely to give the woman the food she had expressed a preference for, independent of whether it was what they liked best. That is, whereas the 14-month-olds responded as if the woman's prefer-

When most 3-year-old children are asked what they think is inside a Smarties box, they say "Smarties." When they are then shown that it actually contains pencils, they say that another child, unaware of the switch, will also think that there are pencils in the box and that they originally thought that there were pencils in the box.

ence was the same as their own, the 18-month-olds did not but recognized that their likes were different from those of another person.

There is even some evidence that 2.5- and 3-year-old children can pass standard false-belief tasks, but only when *implicit* (unconscious and not verbalizable) as opposed to *explicit* (available to conscious awareness and verbalizable) measures are considered. Wendy Clements and Josef Perner (1994) told children ranging in age from 2 years 5 months to 4 years 6 months a story about a mouse named Sam who had placed a piece of cheese in a specific location (Location A), so that he could get it later when he was hungry. While Sam was sleeping, Katie the mouse found the cheese and moved it to another place (Location B). When Sam

Although 18-month-old children understand that another person can have likes different from their own, 14-month-olds will offer an adult a food they like, such as these Goldfish, even if the adult had earlier expressed dislike for them.

Beginning around *9 months of age*, infants:

Will gaze in the direction that adults are looking or pointing

Engage in repetitive interaction with an adult and an object

Imitate an adult's actions

Point or hold up objects to another person

These abilities increase over the *second year* of life. For example:

By 12 months, infants will point to inform others about events they do not know (for example, a cookie that fell off a table and onto the floor).

By 18 months, and possibly earlier, infants can tell the difference between intentional and unintentional actions of another person (for example, to provide help to retrieve an accidentally dropped marker that an adult unsuccessfully reaches for).

Most *3-year-old* children cannot solve false-belief tasks; however, they have some understanding that other people have desires and knowledge different from their own.

Most *4-year-old* children can pass false-belief tasks. They are capable of mind reading (that is, adopting others' perspective and realizing that other people's feelings, thoughts, beliefs, and knowledge can be different from their own).

---

woke up, he said, "I feel very hungry now. I'll go get the cheese." Children were then asked, "I wonder where he's going to look?" The answer most older children should give is Location A, where he originally hid it, whereas most younger children should say Location B, reflecting their lack of understanding of false belief. This is the standard, or *explicit*, false-belief task, and this was the pattern of results that Clements and Perner found. However, Clements and Perner also recorded where children *looked*, at Location A or Location B. This is an *implicit task*, requiring no verbal response and presumably no conscious awareness. Now, all but the youngest children showed high levels of cor-

FIGURE 7.8 Average implicit and explicit understanding scores on false-belief task by age. Although most children much under 4 years of age could not correctly say where Sam the mouse would look to find the piece of cheese he had hidden earlier (explicit false-belief task), 3-year-old children *looked* in the proper location (implicit false-belief task), suggesting that they have greater knowledge of false beliefs than they can verbalize. SOURCE: From Clements, W. A., & Perner, J. (1994). Implicit understanding of belief. *Cognitive Development, 9*, 377–395. Reprinted by permission of Elsevier.

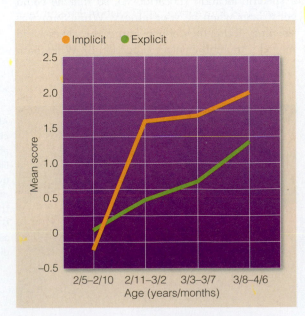

rect responding (that is, they looked at Location A). Figure 7.8 shows the average explicit and implicit understanding scores, based on children's performance on the tasks in this experiment (see also Clements, Rustin, & McCallum, 2000; Garnham & Ruffman, 2001; Low, 2010, for replications of this finding). Other studies, using looking time and the violation-of-expectations paradigm, have suggested that infants as young as 15 months may have an implicit understanding of false belief (Onishi & Baillargeon, 2005; Song & Baillargeon, 2008).

What these findings imply is that by about 3 years of age, and perhaps earlier, children have a well-developed *implicit* understanding of false belief that exceeds their explicit (verbalizable) knowledge. In other words, although children may not be able to pass standard false-belief tasks until about 4 years of age, they show greater understanding of other people's beliefs and desires when simpler tasks are used (such as the "Goldfish versus vegetables" task discussed previously or the implicit false-belief task). Concept Review 7.4 lists some of the developmental milestones in children's understanding of other people's beliefs and desires.

Influences on Children's Performance on False-belief Tasks

Although the development of theory of mind, as reflected by solving false-belief tasks, shows a regular developmental pattern, a host of factors has been found to predict children's performance on these tasks. Among them are quality of attachment, parenting styles, parent-child communica-

Theory of mind gets more complicated than simply solving false-belief tasks, as children come to understand what other people know and don't know.

tion (Carpendale & Lewis, 2004), language skills (Lockl & Schneider, 2007; Milligan, Astington, & Dack, 2007), maternal warmth, and the extent to which mothers use mental state talk (that is, talking about what they and their children are thinking) (Ruffman et al., 2006), among others. One factor that has received substantial attention of late is *executive function*, which refers to the basic cognitive abilities involved in planning, executing, and inhibiting actions, which are discussed in greater detail in Chapter 8.

In essence, the idea is that children need basic-level information-processing abilities to regulate their own behavior—to hold several ideas in mind for a short time and to resist saying or doing the first thing that pops into their heads—if they are going to be able to pass false-belief tasks. In other words, before children can display advanced levels of theory of mind, they must first develop some requisite lower-level information-processing skills. This hypothesis finds support in a study in which 3-year-old children were tested on a battery of false-belief and executive-function tasks once every 4 weeks for six phases (24 weeks in all) (Flynn, O'Malley, & Wood, 2004). The researchers reported that most children performed well on the executive-function tasks *before* they performed well on the false-belief tasks. That is, having good executive control preceded and was necessary for successful performance on false-belief tasks (see also Hughes & Ensor, 2007).

One interesting finding is that 3- and 4-year-old children's performance on false-belief tasks is related to family size and structure (Perner, Ruffman, & Leekam, 1994; Jenkins & Astington, 1996). Specifically, having an older, but not a younger, sibling is associated with better theory of mind (Ruffman et al., 1998). Why should this be so? One explanation is based on social dominance theory (Cummins, 1998). Siblings are always competing with one another, with older siblings typically having the advantage because of their greater size and mental abilities. Younger children would be motivated to develop whatever latent talents they have to aid them in their social competition with their older siblings, and developing an understanding of the mind of their chief competitor sooner rather than later would certainly be to younger children's advantage.

Another interesting finding about theory of mind is that advanced forms of mind reading are typically absent or significantly delayed in one particular class of developmental disability, **autism**, which is characterized by severe social and communication disabilities. Many of you may have seen the classic film *Rain Man*, in which Dustin Hoffman played the role of a high-functioning autistic adult. In addition to displaying some impressive abilities (he was fascinated by numbers and could keep track of all the cards played in a game of Black Jack and knew the history of plane crashes for all airlines), he also showed substantial difficulties relating to other people. Not all people with autism function as well as Dustin Hoffman's character did in the movie, but difficulties in understanding social relations characterizes nearly all people with autism.

Recent estimates of the incidence of autism spectrum disorder in the United States range between about 1 in 1,000 children to 1 in 110 children, with most (about 80%) being boys (Center for Disease Control and Prevention, 2009; National Institute of Child Health and Development, 2005; Rice et al., 2009). These children (and later adults) often seem to be in a world of their own and have a difficult time with most forms of social interaction. Table 7.2 presents some warning signs for parents that their toddler may have autism spectrum disorder (from Wetherby et al., 2004). Researchers have identified nearly 30 genes associated with autism, but it seems that no single gene or set of genes causes autism, but rather autism can have many different causes (Sutcliffe, 2008). One hypothesis is that genes that are normally activated by neuronal activity after birth malfunction, resulting in errors in synaptogenesis or other aspects of neu-

autism A developmental disorder characterized by severe social and communication disabilities.

table 7.2 Some Red Flags of Autism Spectrum Disorder

Although there are no definitive signs that all children with autism spectrum disorder show, if children in the second year of life show two or more of the signs listed below, parents are encouraged to ask their pediatric health-care provider for an immediate evaluation.

Impairment in social interaction	Lack of appropriate eye gaze Lack of warm, joyful expressions Lack of sharing interest or enjoyment Lack of response to name
Impairment in communication	Lack of showing gestures Lack of coordination of nonverbal communication Unusual prosody (little variation in pitch, odd intonation, irregular rhythm, unusual voice quality)
Repetitive behaviors and restricted interests	Repetitive movements with objects Repetitive movements or posturing of body, arms, hands, or fingers

SOURCE: Wetherby, A., Woods, J., Allen, L., Cleary, J., Dickinson, H., & Lord, C. (2004). Early indicators of autism spectrum disorders in the second year of life. *Journal of Autism and Developmental Disorders, 34,* 473–493.

ronal functioning (Morrow et al., 2008). Developmental neuroscience research has identified a part of the brain, the superior temporal sulcus, which is involved in the dynamic processing of emotion, as functioning abnormally in adults and children with autism when processing social stimuli such as eye gaze (Pelphrey & Carter, 2008).

Simon Baron-Cohen (1995, 2005) claims that the primary deficit of children with autism is an inability to read minds, or what he calls **mindblindness**. Evidence for this comes from studies in which children with autism are presented with false-belief and other theory-of-mind tasks and consistently fail them, despite performing well on other, nonsocial tasks. This is in contrast to children with intellectual deficits, such as Down syndrome, who perform the theory-of-mind tasks easily despite often doing poorly on other tasks that assess more general intelligence (Baron-Cohen, Leslie, & Frith, 1985; Peterson, Wellman, & Liu, 2005). However, it is not just the more advanced forms of theory-of-mind abilities that children with autism lack. For example, 3- and 4-year-old children with autism are significantly worse than neurotypical children in social orientation, shared attention, and attending to the distress of another (Hobson et al., 2006; Dawson et al., 2004). According to Baron-Cohen, autistic children are unable to understand other people's different feelings and beliefs, and as a result, the world consisting of humans must be a confusing and frightening one, even for those children who are functioning at a relatively high intellectual level (see Baron-Cohen, 2005).

Extending Theory of Mind: Children's Belief in Fantasy Beings

As we hope we have made clear, children use their theory of mind to help them navigate their social world and to explain and predict the behavior of other people. However, children (and many adults) extend their theory-of-mind abilities to help explain some natural phenomena not commonly associated with social partners. For example, as discussed in Chapter 6, preschool children tend to treat inanimate objects as if they were alive, termed *animism*. In a related vein, they tend to attribute intention to natural events, much as they attribute intention to people's behavior. This latter phenomenon was first brought to light by Piaget (1929), who observed that preschool children tend to believe there is a purpose for everything, even events that adults would interpret as accidental. Piaget referred to this tendency to attribute human causes to natural events as **finalism**. For example, 4- and 5-year-old children will say that mountains are "for climbing," clouds are "for raining," pointy rocks are "so animals could scratch on them when they get itchy." Deborah Kelemen (2004) refers to such thinking as **promiscuous teleology**. *Teleology* refers to the tendency to reason about events and objects in terms of purpose—what they are for.

How can such magical thinking be explained? One possibility is that children learn that people do things for a reason—that is, they are intentional beings. They then extend such logic to explain natural phenomena. Everything happens for a reason, and someone (or something) must be the cause for objects (for example, pointy rocks) and events (for example, the rain, or Hurricane Katrina) (Bering, 2006; Evans, 2001; Kelemen, 2004).

promiscuous teleology Children's tendency to reason about events and objects in terms of purpose.

finalism Young children's tendency to attribute human causes to natural events.

mindblindness Expression used to describe the difficulty that people with autism typically show in "reading" other people's minds.

The Intentions of Supernatural Beings

We saw in Chapter 6 that young children often have make-believe friends and believe in supernatural beings, such as Santa Claus, the Tooth Fairy, and perhaps the monster under the bed. Do children attribute intention and theory of mind to such supernatural beings as they do with people? Given that preschool children attribute meaning and intention to natural phenomena, are they also likely to see purpose in the behavior of supernatural beings? Recall from Chapter 6 the study about the Candy Witch, in which older preschoolers (5.3 years) were more likely than younger preschoolers (3.7 years) to believe in the reality of the Candy Witch (Woolley, Boerger, & Markman, 2004). This finding suggests that believing that supernatural beings act as intentional agents may require more cognitive abilities than displayed by most 3- and 4-year-old children.

This is illustrated in a study by Jesse Bering and Becky Parker (2006), who asked three groups of children (ages 3 to 4 years; 5 to 6 years; and 7 to 9 years) to perform a task in which they had to guess in which of two boxes a prize was hidden. They were to place their hand on one of the boxes, and whichever box their hand was on at the end of each of four 15-second trials, they would get whatever was in the box (a prize or nothing). Children in an experimental condition were also shown a picture of Princess Alice. They were told that Princess Alice was invisible, was in the room, and would like to help them win the prize. They were told, "Princess Alice will tell you when you pick the *wrong* box." Children in a control condition were told nothing of Princess Alice. On two of the trials, unexpected events happened: either a table lamp flashed on and off in rapid succession, or the picture of Princess Alice fell from the wall. Would children move their hand from one box to the other after receiving these perceived clues, and if so, how would they explain the messages they received (that is, the flashing light or the falling picture)?

As you can see in Figure 7.9, compared to children in the control condition, who were told nothing about Princess Alice, only the oldest children tested moved their hand from one box to the other significantly greater than expected by chance. When children were later asked what they thought the unexpected events meant, the youngest children tended to invoke strictly physical causes (for example, "The picture fell because it wasn't sticking very well"). The most frequent type of answer provided by the 5- and 6-year-olds attributed the unexpected events to Princess Alice, but it had nothing to do with helping them win the prize (for example, "Princess Alice did it because she wanted to"). Only the oldest children attributed the unexpected events to Princess Alice behaving

in a way that was intended to communicate to the child (for example, "Princess Alice did it because I chose the wrong box"). Thus, like the findings in the study about children's belief in the Candy Witch, only the older children attributed intention to Princess Alice, suggesting that mature and not immature cognition, specifically theory of mind, is associated with how imaginary (and supernatural) agents function. Before children can appreciate how a fantasy character might behave on their behalf, they must first be able to represent the minds and motivations of others, even imaginary others.

How different are 8- and 9-year-old children from adults regarding such magical thinking? Jacqueline Woolley (1997) thinks not too much. The belief systems of most cultures include supernatural beings who intervene in the physical world on a regular basis and who can be beseeched to intercede on people's behalf. Many adults are highly superstitious. They believe that blowing on dice before a roll will produce a good outcome, knocking on wood will prevent a bad outcome, and breaking a mirror will result in bad luck. Adults in all cultures attribute human characteristics, including emotions, motivation, and knowledge, to real-world entities, such as automobiles, computers, clouds, and weather ("If I want it to rain, all I have to do is wash my car") (Guthrie, 1993). Belief in the paranormal approaches 50% among American adults, including faith healing, demonic possession, and astrology. Thus, the tendency to provide a magical explanation for phenomena for which we have no known physical explanation is not unique to children. One likely reason for children's greater tendency to believe in fantasy is knowledge, or the lack thereof. Older children and adults know more about how the physical world works and know the domains in their culture

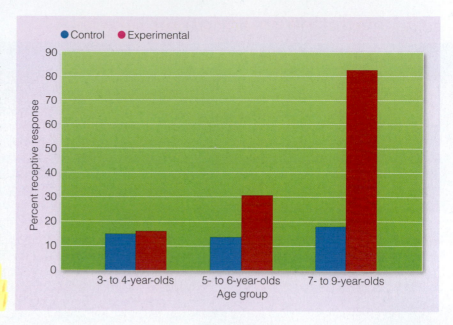

FIGURE 7.9 Percentage of children who moved their hands from the box (receptive responses). Only older children who were told that "Princess Alice wants to help you win the prize" were more likely than children who did not hear the story about Princess Alice to move their hand from one box to the other when Alice gave them a signal (that is, make a "receptive response").

SOURCE: From Bering, J. M., & Parker, B. D. (2006). Children's attributions of intentions to an invisible agent. *Developmental Psychology, 42*, 253–262. Copyright © 2006 by the American Psychological Association. Reprinted by permission.

BOX 7.2 *evolution in action*

Do Chimpanzees Have a Theory of Mind?

Dating back at least to Darwin, there has been a persistent debate among scientists concerning how much humans' close genetic relative, chimpanzees (*Pan troglodytes*), are like us. At times, chimpanzees have been viewed simply as clever animals—good learners, but with a cognitive system that is light years away from anything humans possess. At other times, and in the minds of other scientists, chimpanzees and humans have been seen to differ not in quality of mind but only in degree. Humans have been described as "the naked ape" and "the third chimpanzee," reflecting the closeness between us and them. Darwin believed that there must be continuity between modern species and their ancestors, and this was true for mind as well as body. Although humans did not evolve directly from chimpanzees, because we shared a common ancestor with them between 5 and 7 million years ago, we should find some signs of intellectual similarity between the two living species. This has been a hot topic of research in the past decade, with the focus being on social cognition. How much are chimps like us in terms of how they understand social relations and operate in a social world? Do chimpanzees have a theory of mind?

First, we should note that chimpanzees are a social species, living in complex groups with well-defined though fluctuating social hierarchies. They possess culture in that they transmit specific forms of greetings, grooming, foraging, and tool use from one generation to the next via social learning (Whiten, 2010; Whiten et al., 1999). So they are no slouches when social cognition is concerned, but to what extent does their social cognition reflect theory of mind as used by our own species?

Let's start with the basics of theory of mind: seeing others as intentional agents, as reflected by shared attention. Like human infants and toddlers, chimpanzees, and even some monkeys, will follow the gaze of another individual in some contexts (Bräuer, Call, & Tomasello, 2005; Pitman & Shumaker, 2009). However, most researchers believe there is no evidence of shared attention in chimpanzees (Herrmann et al., 2007; Tomasello & Carpenter, 2005). Mother chimps and their babies do not engage in triadic interactions, pointing out objects for the other to attend to. However, others note that chimpanzees, especially those raised by humans as if they were children (Povinelli, Nelson, & Boysen, 1992), will point out things for others to attend to, for instance, pointing to food only in the presence of a caretaker (Leavens, Hopkins, & Bard, 2005).

An important ability seemingly needed for shared attention is understanding that seeing is knowing. For example, if Juan looks at Miguel as Janice watches, she understands that Juan sees Miguel. That is, the eyes possess knowledge. Human children seem to understand this before their first birthdays (see Baron-Cohen, 1995), but do chimpanzees? In studies by Daniel Povinelli and his colleagues (Povinelli & Eddy, 1996), a treat was placed on a table between two caretakers, and chimpanzees had to make a begging gesture (that is, extend their hand) to one of the two caretakers, one of whom could see the treat and the other who could not (for example, wearing a blindfold or having a bucket over her head, see Photo). They reported that the chimpanzees chose randomly, suggesting an ignorance of the role of seeing (and eyes) in knowing. Yet, in other research, Brian Hare and his colleagues (Hare et al., 2000; Hare, Call, & Tomasello 2001) found that chimpanzees of lower social rank would retrieve a treat only if a more dominant chimpanzee could not also see it, but would forego the treat if the more-dominant chimp could see the food. This suggests that in a more naturalistic food-competition task, chimpanzees do understand that if another individual is looking at something, they see it and use this information adaptively (see also Melis, Call, & Tomasello, 2006). However, the contradictory evidence in chimpanzees by Povinelli and his colleagues suggests that this ability is not one that chimpanzees use

where belief in supernatural explanation is accepted (for example, religion) and where it is not (for example, David Blaine's or Chris Angel's illusions). Much of the knowledge about the natural world comes from formal education. For example, in a study that assessed teleological thinking (for example, mountains are "for climbing," clouds are "for raining," pointy rocks are "so animals could scratch on them when they get itchy") in groups of schooled and nonschooled Romanian Romani (Gypsies), schooled adults gave answers similar to those given by Western adults. In contrast, the nonschooled adults gave answers more similar to preschool children (Casler & Kelemen, 2008).

Are Children Intuitive Theists?

All cultures have religion and a belief in some supernatural beings or powers. Might a belief in supernatural agents be a by-product of our developing symbolic system (Atran, 2002; Bering, 2006; Bloom, 2004; Boyer, 2001)? As we have just seen, young children believe that things occur for a reason, and they endow fantasy creatures with opinions, desires, and knowledge. This, according to Deborah Kelemen (2004), makes them susceptible to cultural beliefs of the supernatural, particularly to the idea of God or gods. Kelemen refers to children as *intuitive theists*. They believe in the existence of fantastic individuals, attribute human-like motivation to such fantasy characters, and assume that everything happens for a reason. Children do not come into the world with a concept of God, but their symbolic system develops over the preschool years to make it likely that they will acquire the supernatural beliefs of their culture. Kelemen (2004, p. 297) argues that

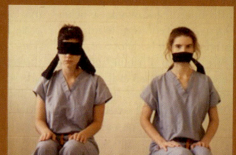

Povinelli, D.J., & Eddy, T.J. (1996). What young chimpanzees know about seeing. Monograph of the Society for Research in Child Development, 61, No. 3, serial no. 247.

across social settings, as human children do, but one that is more limited in application.

What about false-belief tasks, which human children pass around 4 years of age? Nonverbal forms of the false-belief task have been developed, which children pass around 5 years of age (Krachun et al., 2009). (Actually, the first false-belief task, as well as the term "theory of mind," was developed by primatologists David Premack and Guy Woodruff [1978] in their research with chimpanzees, although methodological problems with this first experiment make it difficult to interpret the findings.) When these nonverbal tasks are used with chimpanzees or bonobos, there is no evidence that they can pass them (Herrmann et al., 2007; Krachun et al., 2009). However, chimpanzees in the wild and in captivity have sometimes displayed behavior suggestive of theory of mind. For example, there have been numerous examples

of *deception* in chimpanzees (see Byrne & Whiten, 1988). Jane Goodall (1986) relates accounts of male chimpanzees inhibiting their distinctive cry while copulating with a favorite female so not to alert a more dominant male, who might put an end to the coupling. Emil Menzel (1974) described the actions of Belle, who was shown the hiding place of some food and quickly retrieved it when given the opportunity. However, when the more-dominant chimpanzee Rock was around, he would follow Belle and take the food for himself. Belle quickly learned to wait until Rock was out of sight before getting the food, and even led Rock to a wrong location and then double-backed to the food cache while Rock was busy looking in the wrong place. These are sophisticated social behaviors that require substantial control of one's actions. However, these apes could have learned the proper response simply by keeping track of the behavior of the

other animals. "When I go directly to the food, Rock gets it and I don't. When I wait until I don't see Rock before going to the food, I get to eat it." This demonstrates a sophisticated learning ability, but such learning does not necessarily require an understanding of what another individual knows, only an appreciation of past behavior and its consequence.

It seems clear that the social-cognitive abilities of chimpanzees are less than those of human preschool children. However, it also seems clear that chimpanzees have some understanding of the psychological states of others. The task of researchers is to determine which states and the extent of their understanding (Tomasello, Call, & Hare, 2005; Tomasello & Herrmann, 2010). These findings also suggest that our common ancestor with chimpanzees also likely possessed the social-cognitive abilities that would one day lead to human theory of mind.

children make sense of the world in a manner superficially approximating adult theism, by forming a working hypothesis that natural phenomena derive from a nonhuman 'somebody' who designed them for a purpose—an intuition that may be elaborated by a particular religious culture but derives primarily from cognitive predispositions and artifact knowledge.

Paul Bloom (2004) has made similar arguments about children's natural tendencies to believe in supernatural agents. He argued that children's distinction between social and nonsocial phenomenon, seen early in infancy, sets the stage for humans' natural distinction between body and soul. The 18th-century French philosopher René Descartes formalized this distinction, referring to nonhuman animals as "beast-machines," or *automata*, without minds or souls. Humans, in contrast,

have both bodies and minds/souls. Although modern science clearly points to the fact that the mind is the product of the very physical brain, Bloom claims (and we agree) that the mind-body distinction feels right to all of us. This stems, according to Bloom, from the early distinction that children make between social beings who intentionally cause things to happen and physical objects that do not do things themselves but obey the laws of physics (for example, unsupported objects will fall). As children's representational abilities increase in sophistication, they realize that people's behaviors are based on their thinking—their unseen (and unseeable) desires and knowledge—further solidifying the distinction between body and soul.

We do not believe we can emphasize enough how important theory of mind is to human social functioning. The rudiments of theory of mind are seen in infancy, with shared attention and infants and toddlers seeing other people as intentional agents. Theory-of-mind abilities develop over the preschool years, until children can solve false-belief tasks around 4 years of age, and continue to improve as their cognitive abilities grow. Is theory of mind unique to humans? We tend to attribute intention to our pets and other animals in general. Do they see us (and other members of their own species) the same? Of particular interest, to what extent do our close genetic relatives, chimpanzees, possess theory of mind? How much like us are they, and what type of social cognition might our common ancestor with these animals have had? We investigate these controversial issues briefly in Box 7.2 , p. 294.

The Development of Social Learning

Two-year-old Shayne and his father walked hand-in-hand from the car to the supermarket. As they approached the automatic door, Shayne raced into the store and stepped onto the scale in the lobby. Once on the scale, he stood very still, his arms to his side and his head pointed upward, staring at the face of the scale. After a few moments he looked at his father, smiled, and stepped down. His father then repeated the same routine.

Who's imitating whom here? As it turns out, Shayne has accompanied his father to the grocery store on many occasions, and his father usually sees how his latest diet and exercise regime is working. Shayne, who does not yet speak in sentences, cannot read numbers, and has no idea what a scale is for, has watched his father and now copies his dad's routine every time he goes into the supermarket, regardless of whom is with him. Shayne is a social creature, and he is mimicking an action he has seen his beloved father do repeatedly. He was not encouraged to do this, although his actions usually bring smiles from the adults who are with him, which likely reinforce him. Shayne is demonstrating a form of social learning—not a very sophisticated one, but it is only one of many ways that Shayne and children around the globe learn from other people in their lives.

What's so special about social learning? As it turns out, it was very likely humans' ability to learn from one another that permitted our ancestors to attain ecological dominance to, essentially, be the masters of all they surveyed. Throughout history (and prehistory), people acquired knowledge through their own experience, much as other animals do today. But we also learned from one another, and we do this better than any other animal on the planet. We can also deliberately teach other people. This means that each generation does not have to reinvent the accomplishments of the past; each generation begins where the last left off, which is a tremendous advantage and results in the rapid accumulation of cultural knowledge (Richerson & Boyd, 2005; Tomasello, 2000). We are not the only animal that learns from one another, but we do it better and pass on information with greater fidelity than any other species, and this is afforded by our social cognition, specifically theory of mind. Because we can read the minds of other people, we can understand what they are trying to accomplish, match their goals with our own, make their actions our own to achieve these goals, and perhaps even actively instruct others to attain similar goals.

At its simplest, *social learning* refers to the acquisition of social information and behavior. A narrower definition of social learning refers to "situations in which one individual comes to behave similarly to others" (Boesch & Tomasello, 1998, p. 598). Learning from others does not necessarily require shared attention or mind reading, but, as we will see shortly, more advanced forms of it apparently do.

Most research on children's social learning throughout the latter part of the 20th century followed Albert Bandura's social learning/social cognitive theory (Bandura, 1977, 1986, 1989), which we discussed in Chapter 2. Basically, Bandura proposed that children observe the behavior of others and, through vicarious reinforcement (learning from the consequences of others' actions), they come to incorporate some of the model's actions in their behavioral repertoire.

Types of Social Learning

Bandura and most other child developmentalists assumed that if children acquire some behavior by observation it was through the mechanism of imitation. However, imitation is only one rather sophisticated form of social learning, and it is worthwhile distinguishing among the various forms. One relatively simple form of social learning is mimicry, which occurs when a child duplicates a behavior relatively exactly but without any understanding of the goal of that behavior. The behavior of 2-year-old Shayne in the story that opened this section is an example of mimicry. Shayne would step on the scale, look up at the face of the scale, and then step off, just like his father did, despite not understanding the purpose of such actions. Three more advanced types of social learning, which require

mimicry A form of social learning that involves the duplication of a behavior without any understanding of the goal of that behavior.

Mimicry	The duplication of a behavior without any understanding of the goal of that behavior. *Example*: A 2-year-old child steps on a scale, looks at the scale face, and steps off, just like Dad does.
Emulation	One individual observes another interacting with an object to achieve a specific goal. The first individual then interacts with the object attempting to attain the same end but does not duplicate the same behavior as the model to achieve that goal. *Example*: A child watches someone sifting sand through her fingers to get seashells, then tosses sand in the air to find seashells.
Imitative learning	Reproduction of observed behavior to achieve a specific goal. This requires an understanding of the goal that the model had in mind, as well as the reproduction of important components of the observed behavior. *Example*: Child watches an adult open a latch and push a button to open a box to get a piece of candy, and repeats the same actions with the same result.
Teaching (instructed learning)	Actor A modifies his or her behavior only in the presence of another, Actor B, without attaining any immediate benefits. As a result of encouraging or discouraging B's behavior, B acquires a new skill. To be done effectively, teaching requires that both the instructor and student take the perspective of the other. *Example*: An adult shows a child how to make actions to open a box, perhaps making slow and deliberate motions, molding the child's fingers, and the child, not the adult, gets the candy inside.

understanding the goal, or intentions, of the model, are *emulation, imitative learning,* and *teaching,* or instructed learning (Tomasello, 2000) (see Concept Review 7.5).

Emulation is said to occur when a child understands the goal of the model but does not use the same behavior that the model did to achieve that goal (Horner & Whiten, 2005; Tomasello, 2000). For example, Amy may observe Brittany sifting sand through her fingers to search for seashells. Amy may then start searching through sand with her hands, tossing handfuls of sand to separate the shells from the sand. Amy identified Brittany's goal and worked to achieve it herself, but she did this through a trial-and-error process in which she used different actions to achieve her goal.

In contrast to emulation, **imitative learning** requires that the observer take the perspective of the model, understand the model's goal, and reproduce important portions of the model's behavior (Tomasello, 2000; Tomasello, Kruger, & Ratner, 1993). At least some social learning of infants and toddlers is accomplished via imitative learning. For example, in one study, 18-month-old infants watched as an adult performed actions on objects both successfully and unsuccessfully (Meltzoff, 1995). For one task, a model picked up a dumbbell-shaped object and made deliberate movements to remove the wooden cube at the ends of the dumbbell (*successful condition*). In the *unsuccessful condition,* toddlers watched as the model pulled on the ends of the dumbbell, but her hand slipped off the cubes and they stayed on the dumbbell. When

they were later given the dumbbell, babies who had watched both the successful and unsuccessful demonstrations removed the ends of the dumbbell significantly more often than did infants in control conditions. They seemed to understand what the model in the unsuccessful condition *intended* to do and imitated her behavior to achieve an inferred (but not witnessed) goal (see also Carpenter, Akhtar, & Tomasello, 1998). One study even suggests that infants understand and selectively imitate a model's goal as young as 7 months (Hamlin, Hallinan, & Woodward, 2008).

Teaching is even more complicated. In teaching (or **instructed learning,** Tomasello, 2000; Tomasello et al., 1993), a more accomplished person instructs a less accomplished person. For teaching to be successful, both the instructor and the learner must have some understanding of what the other has in mind. Instructed learning requires that "children learn about the adult, specifically, about the adult's understanding of the task and how that compares with their own understanding" (Tomasello et al., 1993, p. 499).

---

emulation A form of social learning that refers to understanding the goal of a model and engaging in similar behavior to achieve that goal, without necessarily reproducing the exact actions of the model.

imitative learning A form of social learning that requires that the observer take the perspective of the model, understand the model's goal, and reproduce important portions of the model's behavior.

teaching (instructed learning) A form of social learning in which a more accomplished person intentionally conveys his or her knowledge and/or skills to a less accomplished person.

BOX 7.3 # the biopsychology of childhood

Mirror, Mirror (Neurons) in My Brain: Looking for the Biological Basis of Social Learning and Cognition

The neurobiology of social learning and its development is complicated, to say the least. No single brain area is responsible for social learning, and learning is accomplished through many neural pathways. This fact makes all the more impressive the findings by Giaccamo Rizzolatti and his colleagues of individual neurons in the frontal lobes of monkeys that respond both when monkeys are performing certain actions *and* when they observe others execute those actions (Rizzolatti & Craighero, 2004; Rizzolatti et al., 1996). These **mirror neurons** were initially observed to fire when a monkey performed a specific goal-directed act with its hands, such as grasping a piece of food, or when it watched a human grasp the food. The neurons did not fire when a monkey watched a hand making grasping movements without something to grasp, only when the actions were *goal-directed*, in this case grasping a piece of food. The implication of this was that monkeys had specific neurons that were sensitive to the actions of others when they corresponded to actions the monkey could make. These neurons may allow monkeys to perform basic actions without having to think about them, as well as to comprehend such actions without the need of explicit reasoning. Such neurons, it was proposed, may serve as a basis for imita-

tion. A monkey sees an action and neurons associated with motor areas of the brain are activated, providing a neurological system underlying imitation. Neurons in other parts of monkey brains were later discovered that had mirror properties, associated with the mouth, for instance (for example, responding when a monkey sees food being ingested or when another individual makes a species-typical lip-smacking response, see Rizzolatti & Craighero, 2004).

This finding is made all the more provocative by the fact that monkeys are not known to display imitative learning. What, then, are these neurons doing in monkeys' heads? Although such neurons were initially dubbed "monkey see, monkey do" neurons, later research has shown that their purpose in monkeys is not to *reproduce* observed behavior, but to *recognize* when another individual's behavior matches its own. For example, in research by Annika Paukner and her colleagues (2005), both monkeys and humans manipulated small cubes with either their hands or their mouths. In some instances, the human copied the exact actions of a monkey, whereas other times the person merely engaged in monkey-like actions, just not the same actions that the monkey was currently doing. Paukner et al. reported that, in most cases, the monkeys preferred to look at the

human who was imitating them, seemingly recognizing that another individual is displaying the same, or similar, behavior as they were. More generally, mirror neurons reflect an individual being "able to recognize when another is doing something that the self can do" (Byrne, 2005, p. R499).

In a similar vein, Rizzolatti and Craighero (2004) argued that mirror neurons reflect *action understanding*. For instance, when monkeys watch a person reaching for and grasping an object, or when they reach for and grasp objects themselves, mirror neurons are activated. What would happen if they watch someone begin to execute the task but the final actions are hidden from their sight behind a barrier? If the monkeys in such a hidden condition expected that the person would indeed grasp an object, for example, the same set of mirror neurons should become activated as in the full-view condition (Umiltà et al., 2001). This was exactly what the researchers found. In other words, the monkeys' mirror neurons were triggered both by watching a goal-directed action and by the mental representation of that action. This suggests that there is a link between organization of motor actions and the ability to understand the intentional actions of others. In other words, mirror neurons may provide a means for the under-

According to Michael Tomasello and his colleagues, *self-regulation* is the best evidence of instructed learning. Self-regulation in this context refers, basically, to self-control—a person's ability to purposefully direct his or her own behavior in the pursuit of some goal. Tomasello and his colleagues (1993) proposed that such self-regulation is not present until about the age of 4. Not coincidentally, this is the age when children can solve false-belief tasks, demonstrating that they realize that other people can have different knowledge and a different perspective from their own. This last point is critical, for true instructed learning requires that the learner appreciate the perspective of the teacher. But effective teaching also requires that the teacher be sensitive to the knowl-

edge, motivations, and emotions of the learner. Instructed learning is truly a bidirectional relationship involving sophisticated perspective-taking on both the part of the student and the teacher.

Children are not only learners but also sometimes serve as teachers. Recent research with 3.5- to 5.5-year-old children showed that children with higher levels of theory of mind were more effective teachers than children whose theory-of-mind abilities were less well developed (Davis-Unger & Carlson, 2008).

What Kind of Social Learning Do Children Engage in and How Does It Develop?

As we have seen, even infants engage in imitative learning, at least on some occasions. Yet, at least when direct attempts at teaching are not involved, young children seem to be natural mimics (Nagell,

mirror neurons A neuron, found in both monkeys and humans, that fires both when an individual acts and when an individual observes the same action performed by another.

standing of intentional actions in others without the need for sophisticated cognition (for example, perspective taking). Such intentional understanding may be related to sets of specific behaviors in monkeys, but it may serve as the foundation for the more complex social learning displayed by people.

What about humans? There are no experiments recording electrical activation from single mirror neurons in humans as there are in monkeys, but brain-imaging studies indicate that humans, and presumably other great apes, also have mirror neurons. There are some differences between the mirror-neuron systems of monkeys and humans, however. First, when people observe another person experience an emotion, such as disgust as a result of smelling something foul or pain as a result of being shocked, the same mirror neurons are activated in their brains as when they experience the emotion themselves (see Rizzolatti, Fogassi, & Gallese, 2006). Second, whereas mirror neurons in monkeys will activate only to goal-directed behaviors (such as grasping an object), in humans they will also become activated to meaningless actions, such as random finger movements. Third, human mirror neurons, unlike those of monkeys, seem to code for movements *forming* an action and not only for the action itself (see Rizzolatti &

Craighero, 2004). This suggests that mirror neurons are important in imitative learning, where the specific behaviors a model performs (the means) are as important as the goal the model attains (the ends).

The potential role of mirror neurons in imitative learning was illustrated in a study by Giovani Buccino and his colleagues (2004), in which people watched an expert as he played guitar chords. Mirror neurons became activated when participants watched the expert play chords, but became even more active when they tried to imitate the movements. The research on human mirror neurons has been performed mostly with adults, although brain-imaging studies with infants suggests that they, too, likely possess a mirror-neuron system similar to those of adults, although this still needs to be confirmed (Nagy, 2006; Southgate et al., 2009).

What implications do mirror neurons have for understanding social learning and its development? The neuroscientist V. S. Ramachandran (2000; Ramachandran & Oberman, 2006) proposed that these neurons provide the brain-based mechanisms for identifying with others, which is the basis of empathy, imitative learning, perspective taking, mind reading, and even language. When you observe another person doing something, or even attempting to do something,

mirror neurons in your cerebral cortex fire. This may permit you to understand another's intentions, which, as we have seen, is the basis of all advanced forms of social learning. Some have argued that the social-learning deficits in people with autism are associated with defects in the mirror-neuron system (Ramachandran & Oberman, 2006; Williams et al., 2001). For example, using neural imaging techniques, several studies have found decreased mirror-neuron activity in people with autism relative to control participants (Oberman et al., 2005). One provocative idea is that changes in the mirror-neuron system permitted greater social-learning abilities in our hominid ancestors and set the stage for the revolutionary changes in thinking and lifestyle that occurred over relatively brief periods of evolutionary time (Ramachandran & Oberman, 2006; Rizzolatti & Craighero, 2004).

As of now, there is as much speculation about mirror neurons as there are hard data about them. However, this relatively recent discovery may lead the way to important insights about human social cognition, the development of social learning in infants and children, and perhaps even human intellectual evolution.

Olguin, & Tomasello, 1993; Horner & Whiten, 2005). In other words, like the boy in the opening story of this section, young children copy the often-arbitrary behaviors of adults (such as standing on scales in grocery stores), without any external motivation or true understanding of the intentions of the model.

This is illustrated in a study in which an experimenter displayed one of two sets of actions to 2-year-old children using a rake to retrieve an out-of-reach object. The children copied the actions of the adults, even when a more effective way of solving the problem was possible (Nagell et al., 1993). In contrast, chimpanzees given the same task achieved the goal not by copying the often-inefficient behaviors of the model but by using more straightforward and effective actions to attain the goal (see also Whiten et al., 1996). This suggests that the children may not understand the intention of the adults for using tools but were merely mimicking the modeled behavior. What

this and similar research seems to suggest is that young children are motivated to mimic the actions of others to maintain a social interaction (something chimpanzees seem not inclined to do), and that such social motivation may be as important, or more so, as an understanding of intentions in some contexts of social learning. In fact, 2-year-old children are more apt to copy the exact actions of a live, socially responsive person than a person in a video display, and they are more likely to imitate the behavior of a person they could communicate with via a closed-circuit TV system than a videotape of a person who could not provide feedback (Nielsen, Simcock, & Jenkins, 2008). Two- and 3-year-old children also learn about the properties of a tool on simple problem-solving tasks more readily by watching a model than by actually manipulating the materials themselves (Gardiner, Gray, & Bjorklund, 2009).

Others have proposed that young children's *overimitation* can be attributed to their beliefs

Young children tend to copy exactly the behaviors of adults, even if they do not understand the actual goal of the behavior.

perfect, in that it can result in children executing irrelevant actions, even though such actions would seem to be obviously unnecessary from the point of view of an objective observer.

Humans are not the only species that possess sophisticated social-learning abilities. Our close genetic relatives, chimpanzees (*Pan troglodytes*), are socially sophisticated animals and display impressive social-learning abilities. For example, they have been shown to possess a form of culture, passing along behavioral traditions from one generation to the next, such as styles of greeting, grooming, or food gathering (nut cracking or termite fishing, for example) (Whiten et al., 1999). This can only be done by socially intelligent animals. However, the ways in which chimpanzees do this seem not to be the same ways that humans transmit social information. Stated succinctly, unlike human 4-year-old children, chimpanzees and all other nonhuman primates do not possess theory of mind sufficient to pass false-belief tasks (Herrmann et al., 2007; Krachun et al., 2009; see Box 7.3, p. 298).

that all of an adults' actions to achieve some goal are causally related to that goal, making imitation of all of those actions the best course to take (Gardiner, Greif, & Bjorklund, 2011; Lyons, Young, & Keil, 2007; McGuigan & Whiten, 2009; McGuigan et al., 2007). For example, in a series of studies by Derek Lyons and his colleagues (2007), preschool children observed adults perform a series of actions on an object in order to open that object and get a toy locked inside. Some of the actions were seemingly irrelevant to opening the object, but the children copied them anyway, even when they were warned to avoid silly, unnecessary actions. This nearly automatic imitation of all the behaviors of a model is typically adaptive, in that it results in children copying key parts of actions that result in achieving a goal. However, such an approach is not

Human social cognition, and the symbolic system that underlies it, has permitted our species to cooperate and compete with one another with remarkable effectiveness and to learn from one another with astonishing efficiency. This has permitted the high-fidelity transmission of information from one person to the next, and from one generation to the next, resulting in a vast material culture and humans' domination of the world. However, the social-cognitive skills associated with social cognition are not inborn but develop over infancy and childhood. The outcome may seem inevitable, but children require responsive social partners in order to develop a proper social cognition. Fortunately, human families and human societies are structured in such a way that makes it almost certain that children will receive the experience they need to become socially competent members of their species.

summary

Social cognition refers to one's own thoughts, feelings, motives, and behaviors and those of other people. The evolution of *self-awareness* played an important role in the emergence of human intelligence. The confluence of enlarged brains, an extended juvenile period, and a complex social environment has been proposed to be responsible for the evolution of human social intelligence.

Self-concept refers to the way a person defines him- or herself. One demonstration that a child

has an explicit sense of self is through visual self-recognition, which is seen in most children by 18 months of age. Young children describe themselves mainly in terms of physical characteristics, whereas older children use more psychological descriptions of themselves.

Self-esteem refers to judgments people make of their general worth and the feelings associated with those judgments. Self-esteem is high in early childhood, decreases some in early adolescence, and increases over adolescence and into young adulthood. There is a consistent, though small, sex difference in self-esteem favoring boys. Self-esteem has increased over recent decades for American youth.

Self-efficacy refers to the extent to which a person views him- or herself as an effective individual and is specific to a domain or task. Young children tend to overestimate their abilities, which encourages them to attempt things that they would not try if they had a more realistic idea of their abilities.

During adolescence and young adulthood, the sense of self becomes more differentiated, and teenagers and young adults build an **identity**—a self-portrait of the different pieces of the self—in a coherent and integrated fashion. Marcia's **identity status approach** provides four possible identity statuses: *identity diffusion, identity foreclosure, identity moratorium,* and *identity achievement.* Many teens experience a **psychosocial moratorium**, a sort of time-out period when they have a chance to explore who they are and what they want to be, in both the near and distant future. Ethnic identity becomes a central issue in adolescence and is associated with psychological well-being. Children in pluralistic societies who form **bicultural identities** are often the best adjusted.

At the core of human social intelligence is viewing other people as **intentional agents**—as beings who are goal-directed and do things on purpose—and **perspective taking**. **Theory of mind** refers to children's developing concepts of mental activity, including the understanding that people's behavior is motivated by what they know, or believe, and what they want, or desire (**belief-desire reasoning**). In infancy, the beginnings of theory of mind are seen in **shared attention**, which is reflected in gaze following, pointing, and other forms of triadic interaction, as well as infants seeing others as being intentional agents.

Concerning children as mind readers, 3-year-olds usually fail **false-belief tasks.** Some explanations for young children's poor performance on false-belief tasks are that they have **poor** *executive function*. Children with **autism** are particularly deficient in mind-reading skills and have been described as having **mindblindness**. Chimpanzees and other great apes show only limited evidence that they possess components of theory of mind.

Children tend to extend their theory of mind to nonsocial (natural) phenomena. Preschool children have a tendency toward **finalism**, believing that natural objects and events must have a specifiable cause, with some people describing such thinking as **promiscuous teleology**. Some scientists have described children as *intuitive theists,* arguing that their belief in supernatural agents is a by-product of humans' developing symbolic system.

There are different forms of social learning, including **mimicry, emulation, imitative learning**, and **teaching**, or **instructed learning**, the latter three requiring that the observer understand the intention of the model. Although even infants display imitative and emulative learning in some situations, young children tend to mimic the behavior of adults. **Mirror neurons** have been identified in the brains of monkeys and humans that may play an important role in social learning.

Key Terms and Concepts

social cognition (p. 270)

self-concept (p. 272)

visual self-recognition (p. 272)

self-esteem (p. 274)

self-efficacy (p. 277)

identity (p. 280)

psychosocial moratorium (p. 281)

identity status approach (p. 281)

theory of mind (p. 285)

bicultural identity (p. 285)

belief-desire reasoning (p. 285)

intentional agents (p. 286)

perspective taking (p. 286)

shared attention (p. 286)

false-belief tasks (p. 288)

autism (p. 291)

promiscuous teleology (p. 292)

finalism (p. 292)

mindblindness (p. 292)

mimicry (p. 296)

teaching (instructed learning) (p. 293)

emulation (p. 292)

imitative learning (p. 292)

mirror neurons (p. 298)

Ask Yourself . . .

1. What is social cognition (as opposed to nonsocial cognition)? What three areas are typically involved in social cognition, and why is it important from both developmental and evolutionary perspectives?

2. What is meant by *self-concept, self-esteem, self-efficacy,* and *identity* (provide examples)? What do these different concepts share in common, and, conversely, how do they differ?

3. What is the difference between the I-self and the Me-self of self-concept, and how do they develop? What is meant by "a sense of self implies a sense of others"?

4. What are the two main sources of self-esteem? How many types of self-esteem are there? What is known about the development of self-esteem in childhood and adolescence?

5. What are the major milestones in self-efficacy development, and how does the concept of self-efficacy relate to social-learning theory? How do children's tendencies to overestimate their abilities relate to the development of self-efficacy?

6. What are some of the important ideas in both Erikson's and Marcia's theories of identity formation in adolescence? What factors have been found to contribute to identity formation, particularly the development of one's ethnic identity?

7. What is meant by theory of mind, and what basic skills underly it? What are false-belief tasks (provide examples), and how do they relate to theory of mind and mind reading? How does theory of mind relate to the development of self?

8. Why are issues related to theory of mind so often associated with children with autism spectrum disorder?

9. Why do some authors think that children's beliefs in fantasy and supernatural beings are an extension of theory of mind, and what evidence do they present to support their claims?

10. What is social learning? What are four types of social learning (provide examples)? Why is social learning important for development and evolution?

Exercises: Going Further

1. Based on evidence found in this chapter, write about 5 to 10 recommendations to parents and teachers to foster both positive self-esteem and identity in children and adolescents. Be concrete and provide specific examples.

2. As a child psychologist, you consult with a couple of parents who are deeply concerned about whether their 2-year-old son William suffers from autistic spectrum disorder. Some friends have told them that autistic children communicate poorly, and they feel William does not communicate well with them. What questions would you ask them, and what specific areas would you screen in William in order to see if his parents' concerns might be warranted?

3. Based on evidence found in this chapter (as well as in other chapters of this book that you might want to look up), write a short essay titled "Social cognition in nonhuman primates: Some basic data and some current debates." In this essay, you should check evidence and controversies on the development of the self, theory of mind, and social learning in different types of primates, and then write a summary, including your own conclusions and their potential implications.

Suggested Readings

Classic Work

Erikson, E. (1968). *Identity: Youth and crisis.* London: Faber & Faber. This is Erik Erikson's classic work on identity formation in adolescence. Of all the psychoanalysts, Erikson is the one whose ideas remain most influential among contemporary child developmental psychologists.

Wimmer, H., & Perner, J. (1983). Beliefs about beliefs: Representation and constraining function of wrong beliefs in young children's understanding of deception. *Cognition, 13,* 103–128. This was the first research paper to study theory of mind in children, introducing the false-belief task. Despite an earlier paper by Premack and Woodruff investigating false belief in chimpanzees, Wimmer and Perner's work spawned a cottage industry of research that is still continuing more than a quarter century later.

Scholarly Work

Tomasello, M. (2000). Culture and cognitive development. *Current Directions in Psychological Science, 9,* 37–40. This paper presents a brief summary of Tomasello's ideas on the social origins of human cognition and a discussion of some of the different forms of social learning. For a more in-depth discussion, read his 1999 book *The Cultural Origins of Human Cognition* (Cambridge, MA: Harvard University Press).

Harter, S. (2006). The self. In W. Damon (Gen Ed.) & N. Eisenberg (Vol. Ed.), *Handbook of child psychology: Vol. 3. Social, emotional, and personality development* (5th ed., pp. 505–570). New York: Wiley. Harter presents a thorough review of research and theory on the development of self-concept from infancy through adolescence.

Kelemen, D. (2004). Are children "intuitive theists"? Reasoning about purpose and design in nature. *Psychological Science 15,* 295–301. This paper presents the argument that young children's tendencies to see purpose in all things makes them susceptible to cultural beliefs of the supernatural, particularly to the idea of God or gods.

Reading for Personal Interest

Arnett, J. J. (2004). *Emerging adulthood: The winding road from late teens through the twenties.* New York: Oxford University Press. Jeffrey Jensen Arnett discusses a new period of development, emerging adulthood, a period from the late teens through the twenties, during which young people spend their time in self-focused exploration of self-identities, as they try out different possibilities in their careers and relationships.

Seligman, M. E. P. (with Reivich, K., Jaycox, L., & Gillham, J.) (1995). *The optimistic child.* Boston: Houghton Mifflin. Martin Seligman describes children as being inherently optimistic and provides some ideas of how to promote such optimism and turn optimistic kids into optimistic and psychologically healthy adults.

Robison, J. E. (2007). *Look me in the eye: My life with Asperger's.* New York: Random House. This is an autobiography of a high-functioning Asperger's man growing up in a dysfunctional family. John Elder Robison tells what it's like growing up with Asperger's at a time before anyone had heard of the syndrome. The author reads the audio-book version, and listening to his accounts of how he navigated childhood, adolescence, and the business world, as well as his descriptions of his thought processes, provides real insight into Asperger's syndrome.

Bloom, P. (2004). *Descartes' baby: How the science of child development explains what makes us human.* New York: Basic Books. In this highly readable account, Paul Bloom explains how children are natural dualists, believing in the distinction between body and soul, and how this affects their thinking.

 CourseMate

Cengage Learning's **Psychology CourseMate** for this text brings course concepts to life with interactive learning, study, and exam preparation tools, including quizzes and flashcards for this chapter's Key Terms and Concepts (see the summary list on page 301). The site also provides an **eBook** version of the text with highlighting and note taking capabilities, as well as an extensive library of observational videos that span early childhood through adolescence. Many videos are accompanied by questions that will help you think critically about and deepen your understanding of the chapter topics addressed, especially as they pertain to core concepts. Log on and learn more at **www.cengagebrain.com**.

8

© David Deas/Photolibrary

In the last two chapters we examined symbolic development and the development of some critical aspects of social cognition. In this chapter we focus on the cognitive processes underlying these and other forms of cognition, particularly processes that lead children to become self-directed thinkers. We first look at the development of problem solving, including tool use and reasoning. We then examine some of the basic-level mechanisms that underlie children's increasing abilities to control their thoughts and actions, collectively known as executive function. This is followed by an examination of strategy development. In the final section we examine the development of memory, including the development of implicit/procedural memory, explicit/declarative memory, and autobiographical memory, including children's eyewitness testimony.

Ten-month-old Sergio wanted to get his stuffed elephant that had slipped out of his hands and fallen behind a pillow on the couch. At first, Sergio simply stared at his hand and then the pillow where he had last seen his favorite toy. After a few seconds he slapped at the pillow, which produced no results. He paused again, and this time gripped the edge of the pillow and moved it aside, revealing the trunk of his elephant. He released the pillow, grabbed the trunk of the elephant and pulled, but the elephant would not budge. He looked again at the pillow, grasped it with both hands, and pulled it off his toy. He then returned his attention to his toy, grabbing it with his right hand and pulling it from under the now-dislodged pillow.

Life never runs smoothly. There are always obstacles in our way and problems we must solve. When you think about it, solving problems is what cognition is for. We use our symbolic abilities not simply for their own sake, but to solve everyday problems. An important part of solving problems is becoming able to intentionally regulate our actions and thoughts (becoming *self-directed thinkers*). This is what this chapter is all about. After reviewing the development of problem solving, including tool use and reasoning, we focus on some basic-level processes involved in problem solving (the development of executive function), the development of strategic thinking in children, and finally, the development of memory, a crucial element to both preserving knowledge to solve new problems and activating old solutions once they are learned.

The Development of Problem Solving

We stated in the opening pages of the cognitive section that cognition is essentially used to solve problems, and, in one way or another, the previous three chapters have dealt with problem solving. For instance, infants retrieving covered objects, preschool children making decisions about whether there is more lemonade in a tall, skinny glass than a short, stout glass, and children trying to figure out what another person is thinking all involve cognitions aimed at solving some problem. However, in cognitive psychology problem solving is usually defined a bit more precisely. Specifically, problem solving involves having a goal, determining obstacles to that goal, developing strategies for overcoming the obstacles, and evaluating the results (DeLoache, Miller, & Pierroutsakos, 1998). In this section we describe the basic phenomenon of problem solving, starting in infancy, examine how children come to use tools to solve problems, and then look at a special type of problem solving that involves reasoning.

Goals, Obstacles, and Strategies

Problem solving begins in infancy, as we saw in Chapter 5. But properly speaking, infants cannot be said to solve problems until they demonstrate goal-directed behavior. Recall our discussion of Piaget's theory of infancy from Chapter 6. According to Piaget, it was not until about 8 months that infants intentionally set out to achieve a goal, using one behavior in the service of another. Consider, for example, the behaviors of 6-, 7-, and 8-month-old infants who were faced with the problem of retrieving an out-of-reach toy. The toy was resting on a cloth, which was within the infants' reach (Willatts, 1990). The goal (the toy), the obstacle (the toy was out of reach), and the strategy (pull on the cloth to bring the toy to them) all seem quite obvious, but would they to the infants? Many 6-month-olds retrieved the toy, but

their behavior did not look intentional. They rarely simply pulled the cloth toward them but instead played with the cloth, which often by chance eventually put the toy within their reach. In contrast, the 8-month-olds seemed to size up the problem instantly. They kept their eyes on the toy, grabbed the cloth, and immediately pulled the toy toward them. Seven-month-olds showed a combination of the haphazard and intentional behaviors of their younger and older peers.

Children's ability to identify a goal, determine its obstacles, derive strategies for achieving those goals, and evaluate the outcome of their actions increases over infancy and childhood (see DeLoache et al., 1998). Sometimes children must solve real-world problems, with obvious goals, such as how to get out-of-reach cookies from the kitchen shelf or how to avoid being seen by the neighborhood bully while walking home from school. Other problems children are asked to solve have goals that may seem arbitrary to a child. Children solve a problem because a teacher (or less often, an experimenter) asks them to do so, and one of the things children in schooled societies learn early is to solve such problems without asking too many questions. Some of the problems children face, both real-world and arbitrary, involve the use of tools.

Learning to Use Tools

Humans are not the only animal to make and use tools (see Box 8.1), although no other species comes close to *Homo sapiens* in our mastery of tools. Human children seem biased to understand that some objects can be used to affect changes in other objects, which serves as the foundation for learning about tools (Casler & Kelemen, 2005).

The Development of Tool Use in Young Children

Five-year-old Shawn sat down to a family Sunday dinner of sweet-and-sour chicken when his grandfather asked, "Does anyone else want chopsticks?" To everyone's surprise, Shawn blurted out, "Yeah, I do!" His grandfather showed him how to hold them, then molded his hands around the chopsticks and helped him pick up his first several pieces of chicken. After that, Shawn insisted he could do it himself, but little food made it to his mouth. He modified his grip, then put one stick in each hand to capture a piece of chicken and maneuvered it to his mouth, and then managed to stab several pieces of chicken with a stick, as if he were spearing a fish. He never tried to eat any of his rice with the chopsticks. After several minutes and as much chicken on the floor as in his mouth, Shawn put the chopsticks down and finished eating dinner with his more-familiar fork.

problem solving Process in which someone has a specific goal in mind that cannot be attained immediately because of the presence of one or more obstacles; problem solving involves a goal, obstacles to that goal, strategies for overcoming the obstacles, and an evaluation of the results.

goal-directed behavior Means-end (that is, intentional) problem solving, first seen in the latter part of the first year.

By 5 years of age, children around the world have mastered the use of some of the basic tools of their culture.

Life is full of problems, some of them we bring on ourselves. Shawn's problem here was how to feed himself with implements used by millions of children in some parts of the world, but that were novel to him. He watched a more proficient member of his species use the simple tool, was physically guided in the tool's use, and then tried to use it on his own. After several failures, he approached the task in new ways (the two-handed chopstick move, followed by the "stick the stick in the chicken" move), then fell back to a familiar strategy with a different, well-practiced tool. Shawn may be a novice at using chopsticks, but he already has a long history of tool use, one that he shares with nearly every other 5-year-old child on the planet.

Although the tools older children and adolescents use, such as toasters, calculators, and computers, may seem far distant from anything infants can understand, children's eventual use of tools to solve problems have their origins in infants' manipulation of their physical world (Lockman, 2000). Tool use develops from infants' interactions with objects in everyday life (for example, seeing what objects do, hitting two objects together), often to obtain some perceptual outcome, such as noise. In the process, children learn how objects relate to each other and learn, often through trial and error, how best to manipulate one object (a spoon, for example) in relation to other objects (various types of food, for instance) in order to achieve specific goals (eating).

Although Piaget (1954) proposed that children did not start to use tools until their first birthdays, later research showed that infants as young as 9 and 10 months of age will use a properly-shaped stick

to retrieve a toy, although it helps if the tool is in close proximity to the toy, making the relationship between the potential tool and the desired object obvious (Bates, Carlson-Luden, & Bretherton, 1980).

In a study with slightly older youngsters, 1.5- and 2.5-year-old children were shown an out-of-reach toy and a set of toy tools, only one of which could be used to get the toy (Chen & Siegler, 2000). As you can see in Figure 8.1, only one tool, the rake, was both long enough and had the appropriate shape to retrieve the toy. Children sat with their parents and were urged to get the toy. If they did not retrieve the toy after three trials, some children were told that they could use one of the tools to help them get the toy (hint condition), whereas others saw the experimenter retrieve the toy with the appropriate tool (model condition). Children were then given a second and third set of trials using different tools and toys. Most children failed to use a tool to retrieve the toy initially, but, following the hint or modeling, even the youngest group of

FIGURE 8.1 Example of the lure-retrieval task used by Chen and Siegler. The child needed to choose the appropriate tool (here, the rake) to retrieve the toy (here, the duck). SOURCE: Chen, Z., & Siegler, R. S. (2000). Across the great divide: Bridging the gap between understanding of toddlers' and older children's thinking. *Monographs of the Society for Research in Child Development 65* (Issue no. 2, Serial No. 261).

BOX 8.1 evolution in action

Tool Use: Not Just for Humans Anymore

It was not all that long ago that some anthropologists believed that tool use was a defining characteristic of *Homo sapiens*—something we did that others species did not, at least in the wild. As it turns out, humans are far from alone in their use of tools, although we are without a doubt the world champions when it comes to tool use. Sea otters crack open mollusks by smashing them against stones they place on their bellies; song thrushes drop snails onto rocks to crack them open; and New Caledonian crows construct one of two types of hooked twigs to extract insects from trees (Hauser, 2000). Perhaps not surprisingly, the champion tool users of the animal world, other than humans, are chimpanzees.

The list of tools wild chimpanzees use is quite long and can be divided into several broad functional categories. Chimpanzees use tools to obtain out-of-reach objects, usually food; to amplify force to open objects, again usually food; to sponge up liquids; as weapons; and for personal grooming (McGrew, 1992; Tomasello & Call, 1997). One of the most widely cited examples of tool use in chimpanzees is termite fishing (Goodall, 1986). Chimps will select a stick of an appropriate size, strip off the leaves, and insert it into a

termite mound. With a little patience, termites climb onto the stick, and, upon extraction, the chimps have a tidy meal (see Photo).

A seemingly more complicated task involves using large branches or stones as hammers and anvils to crack nuts (Boesch-Achermann & Boesch, 1993). Once the appropriate tools are in place, the chimps will put a nut on the anvil stone and strike it with the hammer, either a branch or another stone. Their choice of tools appears to be deliberate. They rarely use a branch to open particularly hard nuts but select a stone hammer, and once they have found effective stone tools, they leave them by a fruiting tree to use in the future. Opening nuts this way is a difficult task for chimpanzees and often takes years to master (Boesch-Achermann & Boesch, 1993; Matsuzawa & Yamako-shi, 1996). Chimpanzees will also crumble up leaves and stick them into a crevice to extract water, throw sticks and stones at an opponent, and use leaves to clean themselves or as rain hats.

On the personal grooming side, one of the most impressive uses of tools is for dental hygiene (McGrew & Tutin, 1973). A captive adult female, Belle, was observed using a twig as a dental pick. The fascinating thing was

Chimpanzees use simple tools to solve problems, such as fishing for termites, a skill that youngsters apparently learn from their mothers.

© DLILLC/Corbis

children was successful. Children also tended to transfer their tool-use strategies to new tools and toys and showed a general improvement in their ability to retrieve the toy with a tool over the three problems they received.

The Design Stance

It is remarkable how easily humans recognize what a tool can be used for. They assume tools are designed for an intended function, something that has been called the **design stance** (Dennett, 1990). Thus, pens are for writing, hammers for hammering, and objects that resemble pens and hammers were likely made for writing and hammering, respectively. This makes selecting tools very efficient, although it sometimes results in *functional fixedness*, the tendency not to identify alternative uses for familiar objects (German & Johnson, 2002). Children as young as 3 years tend to believe that an object designed for one purpose (catching bugs, for instance) is indeed a bug catcher, even

though it can be successfully used for another function (collecting raindrops) (Bloom & Markson, 1998; German & Johnson, 2002).

Young children will apparently treat a novel tool as having a special function after only limited experience. This was investigated in a study in which 2- and 3-year-old children were shown a box with a slot in it and two similar objects (see Figure 8.2), both of which could fit into the slot (Casler & Kelemen, 2005, Experiment 2). An adult then took one of the objects (tool i in Figure 8.2B), placed it into the slot of the box, which turned on a light. The children were told that they could do the task themselves if they wanted, and the experimenter handed them both tools. The adult even inserted the alternative object (tool ii) into a case similar to the slot on the box (although there was no light show for this action). The adult also pointed out how similar the bottoms were for the two objects ("Hey, I noticed something. These look really different, but at the bottom, they're exactly the same size. Wow! See that?"). Children were later given both tools (sometimes of different colors) and

design stance The assumption that tools are designed for an intended function.

that Belle did not use it on herself, but on a juvenile male, Bandit. Bandit was losing his baby teeth, and in the process of normal social grooming (for example, picking off insects from another animal's body), Belle inspected Bandit's teeth with her fingers. On several occasions she used a nearby twig to help her probe, and in one instance stripped the leaves off a twig to create a dental tool.

Other great apes rarely use tools in the wild, although they seem comparably proficient to chimpanzees at tool use in captivity. In fact, some suggest that orangutans, that seldom use tools in the wild (van Shaik, Fox, & Sitpmpul, 1996), are the most adept and creative great-ape tool users in captivity (Byrne, 1995). Tool use by monkeys is also limited in their natural habitats, although some, especially South American capuchin monkeys, are quite skilled at tool use in laboratory settings (Visalberghi & Limongelli, 1996).

Why all the interest and fuss about tool use in chimpanzees, and primates in general? In part, it tells us something about the origin of human intellect. The intelligence required for effective tool use, and especially for tool construction, is quite sophisticated. It involves an understanding of cause-and-effect relationships as they relate to the use

of objects to solve problems, something that human children seem to understand at an early age. Some argue that this means that chimpanzees, and other great apes if you consider their behavior in captivity, are able to symbolically represent objects and how their actions on objects can produce meaningful results (Byrne, 1995). Most great apes, however, seem not to develop the design stance with respect to tools that young children do. For example, unlike 14-month-old toddlers, who are more likely to use a tool that a model freely chose to use to solve a task rather than a tool she was obligated to use, apes generally show no such preference (the exception is orangutans). Unlike children, they seem not to view a person's use of a specific tool as reflecting an intentional choice, and thus, likely the most effective means of solving a problem (Buttelmann et al., 2008). However, the fact that not all great apes use tools in the wild but can in captivity suggests that they all evolved from a common tool-using ancestor and that different ecological conditions fostered tool use for some species (chimpanzees and humans), whereas these abilities layed mostly dormant in others (orangutans, gorillas, and bonobos).

Some groups of chimpanzees have developed the technique of cracking nuts using stones as hammers and anvils. This is a very difficult task and often takes years to master.

asked to select one to (1) turn the light on the box (the original task) or (2) crush a cracker. The children consistently chose the same tool to turn on the light that the adult had demonstrated, even when it was a different color. In contrast, the 2- and 3-year-old children consistently used the alternate tool to crush the cracker, even though the original tool would have worked equally well.

What these results reflect is that young children do not select a tool based solely on its properties to solve a problem but on their past history with a tool. From a single demonstration by an adult, children acquired a tool category for an object and acted as if the tool was invented for that purpose. This reflects a primitive form of the design stance that older children and adults have toward tools and seems to be based on young children's belief that other people's behavior is based on intention (that is, they perform actions for a reason) (Tomasello, 1999). As a result, they quickly learn that a tool has a specific function. According to the study's authors, "young children exhibit rapid learning for artifact function, already possessing

an early foundation to some of our most remarkable capacities as tool manufacturers and users" (Casler & Kelemen, 2005, p. 479). These findings are consistent with David Geary's (2005a) proposal that tool use is part of children's intuitive notions of physics. An ability to understand how objects can be used to affect other objects and change the environment underlies tool use in humans and develops as children interact with their world (see also Smitsman & Bongers, 2002).

Sex Differences in Tool Use

Geary (2009) also predicted that, from evolutionary theory, there should be sex differences in tool use, favoring males. Male-male competition and males' role in hunting likely promoted greater throwing proficiency and use of tools, often as weapons. Although sex differences in children's tool use have not always been found (or even looked for), when they are found, they usually favor males (Barrett et al., 2007; Bates et al., 1980). For instance, in a study with 3-year-olds that used a toy-retrieval task similar to the one used by Chen and Siegler (2000, see Fig-

FIGURE 8.2 Two- and 3-year-old children who watched an experimenter insert tool (i) (below) to turn on a light were reluctant to use it for another purpose (crushing a cracker). SOURCE: Casler, K., & Kelemen, D. (2005). Young children's rapid learning about artifacts, *Developmental Science 8*, 472–480, Experiment 2.

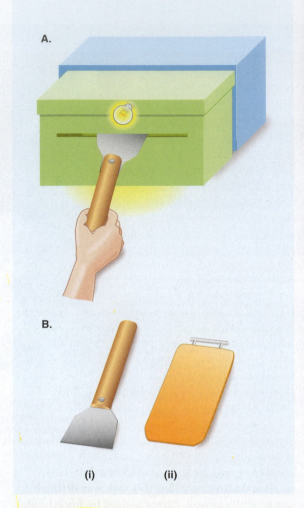

Children seem to have intuitive notions of what tools are for, based in part on how other people use them.

ure 8.1), boys selected the correct tool and retrieved the toys more often than girls, although the difference was greatly reduced after children were given a hint about how to use the tools (Gredlein & Bjorklund, 2005). Young girls were perfectly capable of using a tool to solve this simple problem; they were just less likely than boys to spontaneously use an object to achieve their goal. Thus, part of the sex difference in tool use may be motivation (boys are more motivated to use objects to solve problems) and the tendency to identify relations between objects. In support of this theory, there was a significant relationship between tool use on this task and the amount of time children spent in object-oriented play. Boys spent more time in such play (the manipulation of objects, such as banging or throwing, taking objects apart and putting them back together again, and construction), and the more time they spent in object-oriented play, the higher their tool-use scores were. Following Geary's arguments, sex differences in early behavior (here, interacting with objects) interact with inherent but still developing

intuitive physics systems, producing different patterns of behavior in boys and girls.

Reasoning

Reasoning is a special type of problem solving that usually requires one to make an *inference*. That is, when someone reasons, he or she goes beyond the information given. In reasoning, one must take the evidence presented and arrive at a new conclusion based on that evidence. The result is often new knowledge (DeLoache et al., 1998). In this section we look at the development of two types of reasoning: analogical and scientific.

Analogical Reasoning

Analogical reasoning involves using something you already know to help you understand something you do not know yet. Classic analogical reasoning problems are stated A:B :: C: ? For example, *man* is to *woman* as *boy* is to ?. The answer is *girl*. By knowing the relationship between the first two elements in the problem (a *man* is an adult male; a *woman* is an adult female), one can use that knowledge to complete the analogy for a new item (*boy*). Analogies are based on recognizing the similarity

---

reasoning A particular type of problem solving that involves making inferences.

analogical reasoning Reasoning that involves using something one already knows to help reason about something not known yet.

between items. If a child does not know the relationship between *man* and *woman*, he or she is not going to be able to solve the analogy.

Let us provide one example of how children of different ages solve problems like the "*man* is to *woman* as *boy* is to ?" one. Usha Goswami and Ann Brown (1990) showed 4-, 5-, and 9-year-old children sets of pictures of the A:B :: C: ? type (see Figure 8.3). As you can see from the figure, children had to choose from four pictures the one that best completed the analogy. For the problem shown in Figure 8.3 (*bird* is to *nest* as *dog* is to ?), the correct answer is *doghouse*. Performance increased with age (59%, 66%, and 94% correct for the 4-, 5-, and 9-year-olds, respectively), but all groups performed significantly greater than expected by chance (25%). Note that none of the four pictures are physically similar to one another. The similarity on which the analogy is based is *relational*, not perceptual.

But perhaps children were not thinking analogically at all. Maybe they simply picked the picture they thought went best with *dog*. This apparently was not the case, however. Other children were asked exactly this question: pick the one that goes best with the C term (in this case, dog). When asked to do this, children were no more likely to select the analogical choice (doghouse) than a high associate (bone). Thus, children's performance on the analogical-reasoning task cannot be attributed to responding on the basis of strictly associative or thematic relations, but rather reflects the use of true analogical reasoning.

Scientific Reasoning

One special type of reasoning is **scientific reasoning**. Piaget proposed that scientific thinking requires people to generate hypotheses and then systematically test them in experiments (Inhelder & Piaget, 1958) and does not develop until adolescence with the advent of formal operations. Although subsequent research questioned some of Piaget's ideas about the development of scientific reasoning, most agree that it is a late-developing ability (Bullock, Sodian, & Koerber, 2009; Kuhn, Amsel, & O'Loughlin, 1988).

As an example of how scientific reasoning develops, consider a study in which sixth- to ninth-grade students and adults of varying educational backgrounds were given hypothetical information about the relationship between certain foods and the likelihood of catching colds (Kuhn et al., 1988). Some foods were always associated with getting a cold (baked potatoes, for instance), some were always associated with not getting colds (cereal, for instance), and others were sometimes associated with getting colds and sometimes not. After several exposures to the various foods and their outcomes, participants were asked which foods

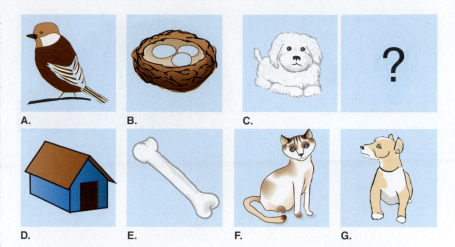

they thought were associated with colds and why. Most adolescents ignored the evidence they had been presented, at least initially, and based their decisions on prior beliefs (for example, "The juice makes a difference because my mother says orange juice is better for you"). In fact, 30% of the sixth graders never made a single spontaneous response based on the evidence they were given. Despite this, when asked how they knew one food did or did not have an effect, most participants of all ages were able to provide an evidence-based answer, although children were still less likely to do so than adults. In other words, even sixth graders are capable of reasoning from evidence, but they rarely do so spontaneously. But this task was difficult for many adults as well. Only the most highly educated adults (philosophy graduate students) consistently solved these problems using the evidence that was presented, an indication that scientific reasoning does not come easily even to adults.

Scientific reasoning is taught explicitly in school and can improve with practice. For example, when children and adolescents were repeatedly given different scientific problems to solve (for instance, determining what factors affect the speed of a car or influence school achievement), their performance improved with practice. However, improvement was greater for adolescents and adults than for preadolescents, revealing again the difficulty many children have with scientific reasoning (Kuhn et al., 1995; Schauble, 1996).

Although scientific reasoning is difficult for young children, many preadolescents are keenly interested in scientific phenomena, and parents seem to recognize this by talking to their children about scientific topics, at least in some contexts. For instance, in one study, researchers looked at interactions between parents and their preteen children while exploring interactive science exhibits

FIGURE 8.3 Example of a problem used in Goswami and Brown's study. Children must select from the set of pictures in the bottom row (pictures D through G) the one that best completes the visual analogy on the top row. (The correct answer is D.) SOURCE: Goswami, U., & Brown, A. L. (1990). Higher-order structure and relational reasoning: Contrasting analogical and thematic relations. *Cognition*, 36, 207–226.

---

scientific reasoning A type of reasoning that involves the generation of hypotheses and the systematic testing of those hypotheses.

Adolescents are capable of scientific reasoning, but it usually requires specific training.

Although young children may have difficulty with scientific reasoning, many are interested in science, and parents often promote this interest.

in museums (Crowley et al., 2001). They found that parents often talked to their children about how to select and encode relevant information. Interestingly, although the amount of talk directed to sons and daughters was comparable, parents were more likely to provide scientific explanations to boys than to girls. In a later study, parents talked more about dinosaurs to their children who knew little about dinosaurs than if their children were dinosaur experts (Palmquist & Crowley, 2007). One interpretation of this finding is that parents quickly reached the limits of their own knowledge and did not feel capable of further facilitating their children's scientific understanding.

Even when children (or adults) can reason scientifically, they seem to have particular problems when the evidence they collect contradicts their previous beliefs (Kuhn et al., 1988). Outcomes that are consistent with their prior beliefs are quickly and uncritically accepted, whereas evidence counter to their beliefs are regarded with greater skepticism (Klaczynski, 1997; Klaczynski & Narasimham, 1998). They also place more weight on results that produce good outcomes (for example, good academic performance, good health) than on results that yield negative outcomes—*a positive-outcome bias* (see DeLoache et al., 1998). Adolescents' preexisting beliefs also strongly influence their scientific reasoning.

The general conclusion of more than 50 years of research on children's scientific reasoning is reasonably straightforward. Children rarely engage in scientific reasoning, and it is only occasionally found in adolescents and adults without specific training. Scientific thinking, though certainly within the capability of older children and adults, is difficult and rarely seems to be found without explicit instruction. Perhaps we should not be surprised at this, given that science, as we know it, dates back only several hundred years. Although people are clearly capable of scientific reasoning, it apparently reflects an ability that our ancient ancestors found little need of and emerged only after literacy and the advent of modern civilization.

Basic-Level Processes: The Development of Executive Function

Before children can solve complicated problems using complex strategies, they need to develop some semblance of self-control, or self-regulation. To do this, children must be able to process information quickly and efficiently, maintaining some information in consciousness long enough to evaluate it and keeping irrelevant information out. These seemingly basic-level processes often go by the name

executive function or **executive control** (Jones, Rothbart, & Posner, 2003; Wiebe, Espy, & Charak, 2008). Executive function refers to the processes involved in regulating attention and in determining what to do with information just gathered or retrieved from long-term memory.

Executive function plays a central role in planning and behaving flexibly, particularly when dealing with novel information. It involves a related set of basic information-processing abilities, including (1) working memory, how much information one can hold in the short-term store and think about at a time; (2) how well one can inhibit responding and resist interference; (3) selective attention to relevant information; and (4) cognitive flexibility, as reflected by how easily individuals can switch between different sets of rules or different tasks (see Garon, Bryson, & Smith, 2008; Zelazo et al., 2008). In addition, each of these abilities is related to how quickly one can process information (see Concept Review 8.1, p. 322). Each of these abilities develops, and age differences in these functions determine how well children are able to regulate their behavior and thinking. For example, will be discussed in Chapter 10, various measures of executive function are related to higher cognitive abilities, including reading, mathematics, and intelligence as measured by IQ.

In this section, we examine the development of five cognitive abilities associated with executive function beginning with speed of processing (how quickly children can process information), followed by working memory, various aspects of attention, inhibition and children's abilities *not* to respond, and finally cognitive flexibility.

Speed of Processing

Age differences in **speed of processing** are central to all other aspects of cognition, from basic-level abilities, such as memory span (see later section), to higher-order cognition, such as reasoning, reading, or arithmetic. One's thinking is obviously limited by how quickly one can process information. Studies that examine speed of processing on a variety of cognitive tasks consistently reveal age-related increases: older children process information and make decisions faster than younger children (Kail & Ferrer, 2007; Miller & Vernon, 1997). For example, Figure 8.4 presents patterns of reaction times for children of different ages and young adults for five different tasks (from Kail, 1991). Some tasks were performed quickly (in milliseconds), such as the name-retrieval tasks, in which participants were shown pairs of pictures and had to determine whether they were physically identical or had the same name (for instance, different examples of a banana, one peeled and one unpeeled). Others took seconds to perform, such as mental arithmetic (for example, finding the answer

to 7 + 9 = ?). Despite differences in the nature of the tasks and how long it took to perform them, as you can see from Figure 8.4, the same basic developmental pattern was found. Other research has even shown a similar (though not identical) age trend in reaction time over the first year of life (Canfield et al., 1997; Rose et al., 2002) and between 22 and 32 months of age (Zelazo, Kearsley, & Stack, 1995).

It seems that these age differences in speed of processing are directly related to underlying differences in brain development. One factor important in influencing speed of processing is the degree to which axons are coated with *myelin*, the fatty tissue that insulates neurons and results in faster transmission of signals. As noted in Chapter 4, although most brain areas associated with sensory and motor functioning are fully myelinated by the early preschool years, myelination of the frontal cortex, which is associated with executive functioning, is not complete until the teen years and beyond (see Lenroot & Giedd, 2007).

Memory Span and Working Memory

In Chapter 2 we introduced the concept of **memory span**, the amount of information one can hold in mind at any one time. We used digit span as an example. Basically, when children are presented with randomly ordered digits, the number they can recall in exact order increases with age (Dempster, 1981; Schneider, Knopf, & Sodian, 2009). On average, 2-year-olds can remember about two numbers, 5-year-olds about 4 numbers, and 12-year-olds a little over 6 numbers, which is not so far from the average digit span of adults of 7.

Working memory span is a bit more complicated, in that it measures how many items a person can hold in immediate memory while also doing some processing, or thinking, about those items. For example, in a counting-span task, children view arrays of red circles and blue triangles and are asked to count the number of circles. Children must then recall the number of circles in that array and in each prior array. In a listening-span task, children hear a series of sentences, and they must determine if the sentence is true or false ("It snows

digit span (7 adults)

---

executive function (control) Expression used to describe the set of processes involved in regulating attention and in determining what to do with information just gathered or retrieved from long-term memory.

speed of processing How quickly any cognitive operation can be executed; hypothesized to be a measure of mental capacity and related to performance on many cognitive tasks.

memory span The number of items a person can hold in the short-term store simultaneously, assessed by testing the number of (usually) unrelated items that can be recalled in exact order at once.

working memory The capacity to store and transform information being held in the short-term system.

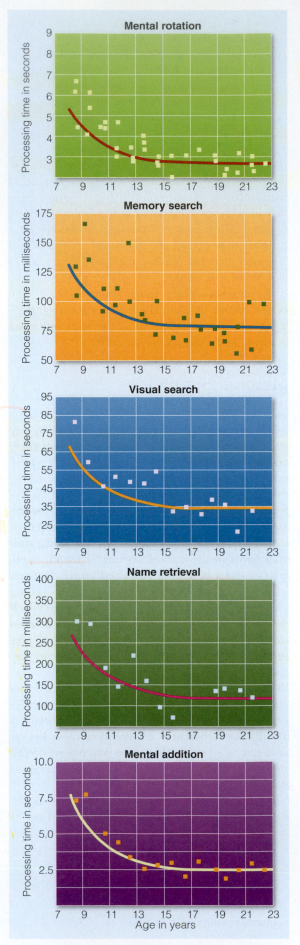

in the summer"—False; "Grass is green"—True; "Milk comes from cows"—True). They must then recall, in order, the final word in each sentence (summer, green, cows). These tests not only require that children hold information in their short-term storage, but they also require some mental effort in processing the to-be-remembered information. Similar to the findings reported for digit span, there are reliable age differences in working-memory span, although working-memory span is usually about two items less than a child's memory span (Alloway, Gathercole, & Pickering, 2006; Case, 1985; Cowan & Alloway, 2009).

There are different types of working memory (for example, memory for words, memory for visual displays), but they all show the same basic developmental trend of increases with age, approaching adult levels by the teen years (Case, 1985). Does this imply that the age differences we see in memory span and working-memory span represent absolute *capacities*—that is, the best that children at a given age can do? Or do factors affect memory span that may result in children remembering more (or less) than they typically do?

Although there does appear to be some age-related limit to how much information children of a given age can hold in memory at one time (see Cowan et al., 1999), the length of a child's memory span is influenced by a variety of factors. Take, for instance, the classic study by Michelene Chi (1978), who administered two memory-span tasks to a group of children (average age about 10 years) and graduate students at the University of Pittsburgh. One test was the standard digit-span task and the other was for chess positions on a chessboard. You may immediately think that this is not a fair comparison, because the adults were not representative of the general population, all being graduate students. However, in all fairness, the children were not typical either. They were all chess experts, winners of local tournaments or members of chess clubs.

The results of this study are shown in Figure 8.5. As you can see, the adults outperformed the children when digits had to be recalled, but the pattern was reversed when chess pieces had to be remembered (see also Schneider et al., 1993). Why the difference? Apparently, the children's greater knowledge of chess helped them encode the positions on the board better than the adults and resulted in better performance. Yet, their greater performance was limited to their area of expertise. These chess-expert children performed more like typical 10-year-olds when remembering sets of randomly presented digits.

One other advantage that having a greater knowledge base may afford children is that, because they are more familiar with the material they are being asked to remember, they may pro-

Chess-expert children have longer memory spans for positions on a chessboard than non-chess-expert adults. However, the adults have longer digit spans than the children. This finding demonstrates the role of knowledge base on memory span.

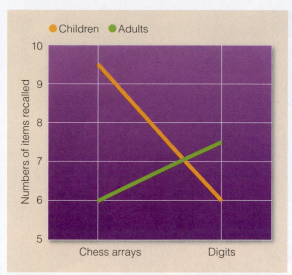

● Children ● Adults

Numbers of items recalled

Chess arrays   Digits

FIGURE 8.5 Chess-expert children had greater memory spans than adults for positions on a chessboard, but not for digits.

This research demonstrates the effect that knowledge base can have on memory span. SOURCE: Adapted from "Knowledge structures and memory development," by M. T. H. Chi. In R. Siegler, (Ed.), *Children's thinking: What develops?* Copyright © 1978 Lawrence Erlbaum Associates, Inc. Reprinted with permission.

cess that information more quickly. As it turns out, the speed with which children can identify and articulate the words they are asked to remember is related to the length of their memory span and working-memory span (Chuah & Maybery, 1999; Hulme et al., 1984). This speech rate/memory-span connection can account for the difference in digit span observed between Chinese- and English-speaking people. Beginning in preschool, Chinese-speaking children have longer memory spans than do English-speaking children (Chen & Stevenson, 1988; Geary et al., 1993). This difference is not likely the result of greater memory capacity of Chinese children or enriched educational experience, but rather of the language the children speak. The digits 1 through 9 can be articulated more rapidly in Chinese than in English, and as a result, Chinese-speaking children (and adults) have longer digit spans than English-speaking children. A similar effect has been found for bilingual Welsh children, who have longer digit spans in English, their *second* language, than in Welsh, their first language. This counterintuitive effect is attributed to the fact that number words can be articulated more rapidly in English than in Welsh (Ellis & Hennelley, 1980). The language one speaks is dependent on one's culture, and this is a subtle way in which culture

can influence thought, consistent with Vygotsky's idea that different cultures provide different *tools of intellectual adaptation* that affect how children learn to think.

Attention

In order for children to regulate, or control, their behavior and thought, they must be able to pay attention to the task at hand and selectively attend to relevant stimuli and ignore distractions. This is what we usually mean when we speak of attention. Young children's **attention span**—the amount of time a person can concentrate on a task without becoming distracted—is notoriously bad, but it improves steadily with age. For example, in one study, children between the ages of 30 and 54 months were given a series of tests of sustained visual attention, for instance, attention during play, while watching television, and during a reaction-time task in which they were asked to respond as quickly as possible when simple stimuli were presented (Ruff, Capozzoli, & Weisberg, 1998). Children's ability to sustain attention increased with age for each measure, although more slowly for some tasks (the reaction time tasks) than for others (during free play and for viewing television). Also, the correlations between the different measures of attention were low to moderate, suggesting that there was not an overall attention ability, but that individual differences in attention were tied to particular contexts.

Another important aspect of attention is the ability to focus only on chosen stimuli and not to be distracted by other noise in the environment, referred to as **selective attention**. For example, a

....

attention span The amount of time a person can concentrate on a task without becoming distracted.

selective attention Concentration on chosen stimuli without distraction by nontarget stimuli.

Because the first 10 number words can be articulated more rapidly in Chinese than in English, Chinese-speaking children have longer digit spans than English-speaking children.

9-year-old who tries to do her homework in front of the television is likely to be easily distracted. She must selectively attend to the schoolwork in her lap and filter out or ignore information coming from the TV set. Young children display relatively poor selective attention abilities, focusing their attention disproportionately on aspects of a situation that are irrelevant to the task at hand. They are easily distracted and spend much time "off task." (We are reminded of a talkative 4-year-old who switched topics in the middle of a monologue about his day at preschool, only to recognize his meandering some seconds later, saying, "Oops, I interrupted myself.") These abilities improve with age, as children are increasingly able to stay on task and select appropriate information to attend to (Lane & Pearson, 1982).

There also seems to be cultural differences in how children learn to attend to objects and events. Some have proposed that East Asians are socialized to divide their attention between objects and events in their environments, whereas Westerners are socialized to focus their attention on key features of objects (Duffy & Kitayama, 2007). This is related to hypothesized differences in holistic (Asian) versus analytic (North American) styles of reasoning that have been proposed to characterize the two cultures (Nisbett et al., 2001; Varnum et al., 2010). For example, in one study, Chinese and American children were shown pictures of three objects (for instance, a man, a woman, and a baby) and asked to group two together (Chiu, 1972). The

American children tended to group items together on the basis of category membership (for example, the man and the woman go together because they are both adults). In contrast, the Chinese children were more apt to group items together on the basis of relational-contextual criteria (for example, the woman and the baby go together "because the mother takes care of the baby").

In other work, Chinese and American adults were shown target items (for example, a tiger) on a background (for example, a jungle) and were asked to rate how much they liked each picture. While looking at the pictures, the researchers monitored their eye movements (Chua, Boland, & Nisbett, 2005). They reported that the American participants looked at the target items sooner and spent more time looking at them than did the Chinese participants. In contrast, the Chinese participants made more rapid eye movements in general, particularly to the background. This and other research (see Nisbett et al., 2001) is consistent with the position that Asians see the world in a more holistic form, being especially sensitive to relationships among objects within the current context, whereas Westerners are more apt to take an analytical perspective, focusing on individual target items. The Asian holistic (and attention-dividing) style may be better suited to East Asian societies that emphasize similarities and social cooperation, whereas the analytical (and attention-focusing) style may be better suited to North America, in which attending to one's self or specific others may provide an advantage.

In a study assessing this difference, Japanese and American adults were shown stimuli similar to those presented in Figure 8.6 (Kitayama et al., 2003). Participants were shown a box with a line drawn in it and, in a smaller box, had to reproduce either the absolute length of the line (bottom left) or the relative length of the line (bottom right). Consistent with the divided-versus-focused-attention hypothesis, the American adults were more accurate performing the absolute task, whereas the Japanese adults were more accurate performing the relative task. When does this cultural pattern develop? By 6 years of age, both Japanese and American children display the same pattern as adults in their culture do (Duffy et al., 2009; Vasilyeva, Duffy, & Huttenlocher, 2007). However, 4- and 5-year-old children in both America and Japan make more errors on the absolute task (Duffy et al., 2009). This and other research (Duffy, Huttenlocher, & Levine, 2005) suggests that both American and Japanese young children initially have an easier time dealing with relative information, but depending on cultural practices, sometime around 6 years of age, some children (in this case, Americans) become socialized to *focus* their attention, whereas others (in this case, Japanese) become socialized to *divide* their attention. A similar interpretation has been proposed for the development of analogical reasoning, with Asian preschool children performing better than Western (American) children on complex problems dealing with relationships among objects (Richland et al., 2010).

Learning How Not to Respond: Inhibition and Resistance to Interference

Thinking is usually thought of as an active process and cognitive development as a process in which children take increasing control over their own thought processes. Yet, *not* responding or *not* activating some set of cognitive operations is often as vital to sophisticated thought as activating some mental mechanism. For example, as you read this paragraph, your thoughts may drift to what you are going to do tonight after you finish your homework. If you let those thoughts intrude on your reading, you will wind up at the end of this paragraph having no idea of what you just read, although perhaps knowing that pizza and beer are in your near future. To keep these thoughts out of consciousness requires an active process of **inhibition**, which refers to the ability to prevent making some cognitive or behavioral response. Researchers have proposed that children's abilities to *inhibit* preferred or well-established responses and to keep

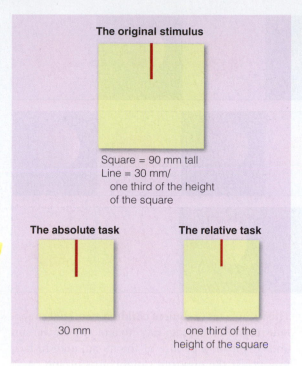

FIGURE 8.6 The frame-line test.

Children are asked to draw the line in the boxes at the bottom that is either the same absolute length as the line in the top box (absolute task) or the same relative length (relative task). Beginning at age 6, Americans perform better on the absolute task and Japanese perform better on the relative task. However, 4- and 5-year-old children in both America and Japan make more errors on the absolute task. SOURCE: Kitayama, S., Duffy, S., Kawamura, T., & Larsen, J. T. (2003). Perceiving an object and its context in different cultures: A cultural look at new look. *Psychological Science, 14*, 201–206.

intrusive thoughts out of mind plays an important role in cognitive development (Diamond & Taylor, 1996; Harnishfeger, 1995).

Many of the everyday problems that children encounter can be attributed to poor inhibition (for example, "I didn't mean to hit my brother, it just happened"). The basic idea at its simplest is that, with age, children are increasingly able to inhibit well-established and often inappropriate mental or behavioral responses and that these improved skills permit the more efficient execution of other cognitive operations.

A related concept is **resistance to interference**, which refers to "susceptibility to performance decrements under conditions of multiple distracting stimuli" (Harnishfeger, 1995, p. 188–189). Resistance to interference is seen in dual tasks, when performing one task (chewing gum or watching television) interferes with performance on a second task (walking or doing one's homework), or in selective attention, when one must focus on central information (one's homework) and ignore peripheral information (the story line of the sitcom on television).

Inhibition abilities continue to develop over early childhood and into adolescence and are assessed by a variety of simple tests (see Kochanska et al., 1996; Luria, 1961). For example, in the *day-night task*, children must say "day" each time they see a picture of the moon and "night" each time they see a picture of the sun (see Figure 8.7).

inhibition The ability to prevent oneself from making some cognitive or behavioral response.

resistance to interference The ability to ignore irrelevant information so that it does not impede task performance.

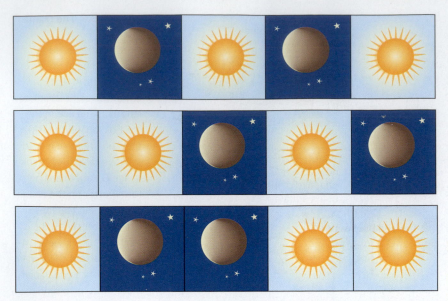

FIGURE 8.7 The day/night task is one of a host of simple tests used to assess executive function in young children.

Children must say "day" whenever they see the picture of the moon and "night" whenever they see the picture of the sun. This is exactly opposite to what children typically do, requiring them to inhibit a well-established response before giving the correct response.

This simple task requires children to inhibit prepotent responses (saying "day" to a picture of the sun and "night" to a picture of the moon) and, in fact, to say just the opposite ("night" to sun and "day" to moon), which is difficult for preschoolers. Preschoolers also have difficulty in the *tapping task,* in which they must tap once each time the examiner taps twice and tap twice each time the examiner taps once, and playing *Simon Says,* where they must perform an action only when Simon says so ("Simon says, touch your nose") (Diamond & Taylor, 1996; Sabbagh et al., 2006).

Developmental and individual differences in children's inhibitory abilities are related to several cognitive tasks. For instance, (1) children's ability to selectively forget information (for instance, "Don't remember any of the words from your last vocabulary test") is affected by their ability to keep the to-be-forgotten information out of mind (Harnishfeger & Pope, 1996; Lehman et al., 1997); (2) age differences in selective attention can be explained by young children's difficulty with ignoring task-irrelevant stimuli (see Ridderinkhof, van der Molen, & Band, 1997); and (3) young children's difficulty in inhibiting some behaviors (such as pointing to where an object is hidden) might impede their ability to deceive others in some situations (Carlson, Moses, & Hix, 1998). Moreover, as an important component in executive functioning, inhibition is related to children's ability to regulate their behavior and emotions (Eisenberg & Spinrad, 2004), understand that other people can hold false beliefs (theory of mind, Sabbagh et al., 2006), and intelligence as measured by IQ (Harnishfeger & Bjorklund, 1994), among other high-level cognitive tasks.

In Chapter 4 we noted that infants' performance on the A-not-B object permanence task (Segalowitz & Hiscock, 2002) and executive functioning

in adolescents (much of which involves inhibition, Luna et al., 2001) are closely related to the development of the frontal cortex. Other research has shown that typically developing children's performance on certain neuropsychological tests resembles that of adults with frontal lobe damage (Diamond & Taylor, 1996). In fact, neuroimaging studies report age-related relations between children's performance on inhibition tasks and brain development. More specifically, changes in areas of the prefrontal cortex, including electrical activity, volume (both neurons and presence of myelin), and connections to other brain areas have been found to be related to children's performance on inhibition tasks (see Amos & Casey, 2006).

Children sometimes have difficulty inhibiting their behavior and thoughts, and when they do more so than is typical for their age, it can result in problems in their schoolwork and social relations. Box 8.2 provides a brief look at a prominent disorder of childhood, *attention-deficit hyperactivity disorder* (ADHD), one that is sometimes characterized as reflecting underdeveloped executive functioning.

Cognitive Flexibility

Cognitive flexibility refers to the ability to shift between sets of tasks or rules (Garon et al., 2008; Zelazo et al., 2003). Many of the tasks used to assess inhibition abilities also require children to shift, or change, between a set of rules. Philip Zelazo and his colleagues have argued that the development of executive function involves the increasing ability to formulate and maintain rules, as illustrated on simplified shifting tasks, in which children must change from following one criterion to another (Zelazo et al., 2008; Zelazo et al., 2003). Such shifting is seen in the *Dimensional Card Sorting Task,* developed by Zelazo and his colleagues (Zelazo, Frye, & Rapus, 1996). In this task, preschool children are given sets of cards that vary on two dimensions. Figure 8.8 shows an example of the cards used in these studies. Children are shown two target cards, a yellow car and a green flower, for example. When playing the *color game,* they are told that all of the yellow cards go with the yellow car and all of the green cards go with the green flower. Children are then given a series of test cards (for instance, yellow flowers and green cars) and are asked to sort them by color. Most children do this easily. Then children are told they are going to play a new game, the *shape* game. (For half the children the shape game is played first, and for the other half, the color game is played first.) In the shape game, children are to place cars in the box with the yellow car and flowers in the box with the green flower. These are called *switch trials,* because the rules have been switched from sorting

cognitive flexibility The ability to shift between sets of tasks or rules.

Young children often have a difficult time not saying whatever is on their minds.

on the basis of color to shape, or vice versa. Now, most 3-year-old children fail, continuing to sort the cards according to the original dimension. Yet, when asked what the new rule is, most can easily and correctly tell the experimenter. By 4 years of age, most children perform the task correctly.

Why do children have difficulties on these tasks, and what develops so that by 4 and 5 years of age most children can follow simple rule systems relatively easily? According to Zelazo and his colleagues (1997), children gain increasing conscious control over their problem solving, as reflected by developmental differences in *reflection,* in which children can think about the contents of their own thoughts. In this case, children become conscious of the higher-order rule they are using (the cards must be sorted according to a specified dimension). With greater self-awareness, they can reflect on this rule and modify which lower-order rule (sort by color versus sort by shape) they use. In other words, children acquire rules early on and follow them in certain situations. However, coordinating rules requires greater conscious reflection, and this develops over the preschool years. As used here, reflection, and the task switching it permits, is another indication of executive function. Zelazo has also speculated that such cognitive changes in following rules are based on age-related changes in different parts of the prefrontal cortex (Bunge & Zelazo, 2006), which has been confirmed in recent research (Moriguchi & Hiraki, 2009).

The Origins of Executive Function

The various components of executive function are related to one another, yet separable. That is, people who score high on tests of working memory also score high on tests of inhibition or cognitive flexibility, but the correlations between these tasks are not

FIGURE 8.8

The Dimensional Card Sorting Task.

Children are asked to sort cards initially by one dimension (for example, color) and later by a second dimension (for example, shape). Children much younger than 4 years of age have difficulty on the switch trials and usually continue to sort by the original dimension. SOURCE: Zelazo, P. D., Frye, D., & Rapus, T. (1996). An age-related dissociation between knowing rules and using them. *Cognitive Development, 11,* 37–63.

perfect. One reason for the generally high correlations among these tasks is that they may be related to a single underlying factor that is highly heritable. This was in fact found in a recent behavioral genetics analysis based on more than 560 twins. Naomi Friedman and her colleagues (2008) reported that the heritability of executive function (combining tests of inhibition, working memory, and cognitive flexibility) is exceptionally high (99%), making it one of the most highly heritable psychological traits ever assessed. This points to differences in genetics as being primarily responsible for individual differences in executive functioning.

However, as you may recall from Chapter 3, even though a trait may be highly heritable, it does not mean that the environment cannot have a potent effect. This was shown by the results of several studies that examined executive function in children as a function of physical fitness (Buck, Hillman, & Castelli, 2008; Hillman et al., 2009), with more physically fit children showing superior executive functioning than less-fit children. For example, in one study (Hillman et al., 2009), two groups of 9-year-old children—one group described as physically fit in terms of aerobic capacity (number of laps they could do), muscle strength (doing push-ups and curl-ups), and body mass index (BMI,

BOX 8.2 **the biopsychology of childhood**

Executive Function and Attention-Deficit Hyperactivity Disorder (ADHD)

They can't sit still; they don't pay attention to the teacher; they mess around and get into trouble; they try to get others into trouble; they are rude; they get mad when they don't get their way (Henker & Whalen, 1989, p. 216).

The "they" referred to in this statement are children with **attention-deficit hyperactivity disorder (ADHD)**. Children (and adults) with ADHD display hyperactivity, impulsiveness, and difficulty sustaining attention and remaining on task (American Psychiatric Association, 1994). ADHD occurs in between 3% and 7% of children in the United States and, like many behavioral disorders, is more frequent in boys than in girls. About one-third to one-half of cases of childhood ADHD persist into adulthood (see Barkley, 1998). Although there are substantial individual differences in the severity of problems children with ADHD experience, children with ADHD are more likely than non-ADHD children to have school problems, including poor grades, being held back, suspensions, and expulsions. They are also at greater risk for delinquency, substance abuse, and troubled social relationships, both in adolescence and adulthood (see Barkley, 1997; Loe et al., 2008).

According to Russell Barkley (1997), the principal cause of ADHD is deficits in behavioral inhibition. Behavioral inhibition affects working memory (another important component of executive function), self-regulation of emotion, and internalization of speech. These abilities are critical in directing problem solving, reflecting upon one's behavior, and in what Barkley calls *reconstitution*, which involves the "creation of novel, complex goal-directed behaviors" (p. 72). Given the importance of these abilities for cognition and successful day-to-day functioning, children with deficits in behavioral inhibition would be especially disadvantaged.

Consistent with Barkley's theorizing, children with ADHD show deficits in executive function. For instance, compared to children without ADHD, children with ADHD do more poorly on comprehension tasks (Bailey et al., 2009) and working-memory tasks, and they are less proficient at imitating lengthy sequences of actions (Mariani & Barkley, 1997). They also have a poorer sense of time (Barkley et al., 1997), are less likely to use strategies on memory tasks (August, 1987), are more adversely affected by delay (Songua-Barke et al., 1992), and are more likely to be described as irritable, hostile, and excitable (see Barkley, 1990), all relative to non-ADHD children (see Barkley, 1997, for a review). These cognitive and behavioral correlates of ADHD are also associated with differences in rate of brain development. In a study contrasting 7- to 13-year-old children with and without ADHD, development of the frontal cortex, which is important in executive function, lagged about 3 years behind typical for children with ADHD, whereas development of the motor areas occurred slightly earlier (Shaw et al., 2007). This uneven pattern of brain development may account for the increased fidgeting and restlessness seen in ADHD children.

The origins of ADHD are still unclear. ADHD co-occurs with several other disorders greater than expected by chance, including bipolar disorder (Singh et al., 2006), low IQ (Kuntsi et al., 2004), and epilepsy (Dunn et al., 2003), causing some to suspect faulty genes or a disturbance in prenatal development as the cause for ADHD (Levy et al., 1997; Millberger et al., 1996). However, as we know, genes interact with environment, and one recent study reports that children with a specific allele associated with processing the neurotransmitter dopamine were more likely to develop ADHD than children not possessing the allele if their mothers smoked during pregnancy. However, these children were *least* likely to develop ADHD if their mothers did not smoke when pregnant (Pluess, Belsky & Neuman, 2009). Postnatal environment also matters, as a harsh, highly controlling style of parenting

see Chapter 4), and the other as less fit—were given a test of executive function while their brain activity was monitored. The researchers reported that physically fit children had superior executive function abilities, specifically in terms of allocating their attentional resources, reflected both by performance on the cognitive task and measures of brain functioning (EEG). Thus, although executive function may be highly heritable, it is also affected by physical fitness, which may be one good reason to keep recess and physical education in the school curriculum (see Pellegrini, 2011).

Other research has shown that executive function can be trained in young children (Diamond et al., 2007; Holmes, Gathercole, & Dunning, 2009). In one study, preschoolers were assigned to special classrooms that emphasized activities that promoted executive function, including telling oneself what one should do (self-regulatory private speech), dramatic play, and a host of activities involving memory and attention. Compared to children in control classrooms, children given the special curriculum performed significantly better on a battery of executive-function tasks (Diamond et al., 2007). Other researchers provided 4- and 6-year-olds with experience on specific tasks involving working memory, attentional control, and cognitive flexibility and reported significant improvements in subsequent measures of intelligence and executive function, relative to children in a control group (Rueda et al., 2005). The researchers also reported changes in brain functioning, such that the brain activity of trained 4-year-olds was similar to that of typical (and untrained) 6-year-olds.

Developmental improvements in speed of processing, working memory, attention, inhibition, and cognitive flexibility are all related to one another and to changes in neurological develop-

> **attention deficit hyperactivity disorder (ADHD)** An inability to sustain attention, believed to be caused by deficits in behavioral inhibition. People with ADHD display hyperactivity, impulsiveness, show great difficulty sustaining attention, and are at high risk for academic difficulties.

may also contribute to, or at least aggravate, the problem in some cases (Sroufe, 1997). However, earlier theories linking ADHD to lead poisoning, food additives, excessive consumption of sugar, and brain damage have received little support (Henker & Whalen, 1989).

Some people have questioned the statistics on the prevalence of ADHD in the United States, believing that many parents, teachers, and physicians misdiagnosis normal childhood exuberance, especially in high-activity boys, as a disorder (Panksepp, 1998; Pellegrini & Horvat, 1995). Some cases of ADHD may reflect children at the high end of a normal distribution of activity, whose propensity for activity gets them in trouble with teachers and some of their more sedentary peers. In fact, some have even suggested that the high activity of some children in ancient environments may have been advantageous. For instance, having individuals who constantly scanned the horizon for signs of predators or prey would seem to have obvious benefits, although such off-task behavior is usually maladaptive in contemporary school classrooms (Jensen et al., 1997). ADHD is a complicated disorder, and many individuals with it would fare poorly in any environment. But one must keep in mind that schools are an evolutionary novelty and that typical levels of activity and playful behavior, especially as shown by preadolescent boys, although sometimes interfering with ideal educational practices, may not, in and of themselves, be signs of pathology.

What can be done to help children with ADHD? The use of stimulant drugs such as Ritalin or Concerta helps many children. Although giving hyperactive kids stimulant drugs that increase their heart rates and respiratory levels may seem counterintuitive, they work because they affect brain chemistry (essentially activating inhibitory circuits), making children better able to focus their attention, inhibit inappropriate responses, and be less distractible and disruptive (Barkley, 1997). As a result, children with ADHD who take stimulant drugs experience improvements in school grades and peer relations (Pelham et al., 1993; Scheffler et al., 2009). Not surprisingly, there are critics of this drug approach, arguing that while the drugs may suppress the symptoms of ADHD, there are some potentially serious side effects. These include curbing appetites, disrupting sleep cycles, and reducing children's desire to play and to acquire other important skills that are not taught at school (Panksepp, 1998).

Cognitive-behavioral therapies have also resulted in academic gains for some children with ADHD. Children are taught to set academic goals and are given tokens that can be exchanged for prizes. Many children with ADHD seem to benefit most from a combination of drug and behavior therapies (Cantwell, 1996). Family therapy where parents of children with ADHD are taught to be more patient, warm, supportive, and firm with their children has also shown to produce positive results, often in combination with drug therapy (Hinshaw et al., 1997). Other research has shown that training on working-memory tasks, one aspect of executive function, results in improvements on other working-memory tasks, reasoning tasks, and even greater control of motor behavior in ADHD children (Klingberg, Forssberg, & Westerberg, 2002).

Although many children with ADHD grow out of their disorder, many carry the disability with them into adulthood and continue to have low self-esteem, experience difficulty with social relations, and display problems on some cognitive tasks requiring sustained attention (Hart et al., 1995). Although the origins of ADHD and its cure remain elusive, the difficulties of children and adults with this disorder point to the importance that effective executive function—here especially an ability to sustain attention and resist interference—can have on everyday functioning. This applies not only to cognitive tasks but also to one's social and emotional life.

ment, especially the frontal cortex. Together, these basic-level processes constitute executive function, or executive control, the ability of children to regulate one's behavior and thought. We cannot emphasize enough the importance of executive function to the development of higher-level cognition and to the regulation of one's emotions and behaviors. Moreover, some have speculated that the evolution of executive function may have been an important component in the emergence of the modern human mind (Causey & Bjorklund, 2011; Geary, 2005a; Read, 2008). Certainly, the ability to selectively attend and concentrate on the task at hand, to inhibit inappropriate behavior and thought, resist distraction, and, in general, control one's actions are critical to effective functioning in any social group, as well as constructing tools, hunting, or preparing a meal, among many other things. These abilities are better developed in humans than in other primates, in older children than in younger children, and may be a key to understanding both human cognitive evolution and development.

Strategy Development

Much thinking is done without a lot of conscious awareness of what one is doing. Even recalling a trip to Disney World, for instance, is done without much in the way of planning. On the other hand, if you were invited to give a talk to the local environmental group about your trip to the Galápagos Islands, you would likely plan ahead, decide what to talk about and what to leave out, and organize your presentation. In the latter case, you would use *strategies* to plan and present your talk.

Strategies are usually defined as deliberate, goal-directed mental operations that are aimed at solving a problem. Strategies are usually viewed as being deliberately implemented, nonobligatory (one does not have to use them to perform a task), mentally effortful, and potentially available to consciousness (Harnishfeger & Bjorklund, 1990a; Pressley & Hilden, 2006). The development of cognitive strategies is important, because strategies represent

concept review | 8.1 — Some definitions of key concepts associated with executive function

Executive function	The processes involved in regulating attention and in determining what to do with information just gathered or retrieved from long-term memory.
Speed of processing	How quickly any cognitive operation can be executed, which affects how many operations can be performed in a short period of time.
Memory span	The number of items a person can hold in the short-term store, assessed by testing the number of (usually) unrelated items that can be recalled in exact order.
Working memory	The capacity to store and transform information being held in the short-term system. *Working-memory span* is about two items less than memory span.
Attention span	The ability to concentrate or sustain attention to a particular stimulus or activity.
Inhibition	The ability to prevent from making some cognitive or behavioral response.
Resistance to interference	The ability to ignore irrelevant information so that it does not impede task performance.
Cognitive flexibility	The ability to shift between sets of tasks or rules.

one way in which children learn to take control of their own cognition—of thinking, remembering, planning, learning, and solving problems on their own, or becoming *self-directed learners.*

Children and adults use strategies to achieve specific goals that cannot be achieved "without thinking." A 2-year-old stares at the place where a favorite toy is hidden so she can find it again after a time-out; a 6-year-old counts on his fingers, holding up one finger for each item counted, to determine how many cookies he has; and a 10-year-old memorizes a simple rhyme so she can remember the number of days in each month ("Thirty days has September, April, June, and November . . ."). These are all deliberate strategies, effortful cognitive operations that are used to solve some problem. Children discover many strategies themselves while trying to come up with answers to everyday problems, while parents or teachers explicitly teach other strategies to them. The frequency and effectiveness of strategy use changes with age, as children become increasingly able to direct their own learning and problem solving.

Increases in Strategy Use, Improvements in Performance

If you look at any particular task children of different ages are asked to do, what you typically find is that older children use more effective strategies and perform better than younger children on the tasks. Younger children can often be taught to use a strategy that they do not use spontaneously, and as a result their performance will improve (Schwenck, Bjorklund, & Schneider, 2007; see Bjorklund, Dukes, & Brown, 2009). For example, simply telling young children to repeat, or rehearse, words that they are asked to remember results in children remembering more words (Ornstein, Naus, & Stone, 1977). This phenomenon has been termed a **production deficiency** (Flavell, 1970). That is, although children do not *produce* strategies spontaneously, they can be trained to use them and enhance their performance as a result.

Sometimes, children will use a strategy, either spontaneously or as a result of training, but their performance will not improve. For example, in one set of studies, 3- and 4-year-old children were shown a miniature room containing toy animals and furniture (Blumberg & Torenberg, 2005; Blumberg, Torenberg, & Randall, 2005). Children were told that one set of items was special (for example, "It's very important that the animals get fed regularly"), and the children's job was to help the experimenter take care of these special things. They were then told to remove all of the objects from the room, and later they were asked to put them back in the room where they had been placed before. A simple yet effective strategy for achieving this goal would be to remove the items according to category membership (that is, take out the special objects one after the other), something that 70% of the preschoolers did. However, using this strategy did not help them put the items back in their proper place. In other words, although children used a strategy, it did not help them achieve their goal. Using a strategy that does not improve performance is called a **utilization deficiency** (Miller, 1990; Miller & Seier, 1994) and is frequently observed in chil-

> **production deficiency** Children's tendency not to use spontaneously a strategy that they are capable of using when instructed.
>
> **utilization deficiency** Using an apparently appropriate strategy that does not improve task performance.

dren's strategy use. Utilization deficiencies are not limited to preschool children but are also seen in the behavior of older children (see Bjorklund et al., 2009; Miller, 1990).

Why should children use an effortful strategy when it does not result in any improvement? There are likely several reasons for this pattern. One explanation is that young children lack the mental resources necessary to both execute a strategy and devote to the problem at hand (Bjorklund & Harnishfeger, 1987; Miller et al., 1991). Once strategies can be executed with greater efficiency, children will begin to realize some benefit for their effort. Another reason why children use an ineffective strategy is that they may not realize that the strategy is not working for them (Ringel & Springer, 1980). In fact, young children frequently overestimate their physical and cognitive abilities, thinking they are performing better than they actually are (Shin, Bjorklund, & Beck, 2007). And finally, children may use a new strategy just for the sake of trying something new (Siegler, 1996). Although the reason adults use strategies is to enhance task performance (that's what strategies are for, after all), that may not be how children see it. Trying something new may be a goal unto itself, and the fact that it does not improve performance may be relatively unimportant to them.

One popular account of children's strategy development is Robert Siegler's (1996, 2006) **adaptive strategy choice model**. Basically, Siegler adopts the idea of natural selection from Darwin's theory of evolution and applies it to cognitive development. Stated most simply, Siegler proposes that, in cognitive development, children generate a wide variety of strategies to solve problems and, depending on the nature of the task and the goals of the child, certain strategies are selected and used frequently, whereas others that are less effective are used less often and eventually decrease in frequency (and may even go extinct). Early in development, or when a child is first learning a new task, relatively simple strategies will win most of the time. With practice and maturation, children will use other, more effortful and effective strategies more often. Thus, Siegler believes that development occurs as a series of overlapping waves, with the pattern of those waves changing over time. Figure 8.9 presents Siegler's wave approach to cognitive development. Multiple strategies are available to children at every age, but which strategies are used most frequently changes with age.

As an example, consider the variety of strategies children could use to compute simple math problems (see previous discussion in Chapter 1, p. 38). A simple strategy, called *sum,* involves counting both addends. For example, for the problem 3 + 2 = ?, a child would count "1, 2, 3 [pause] 4, **5**" to arrive at an answer. A more complicated counting

FIGURE 8.9 Siegler's strategy choice model of development. Change in strategy use is seen as a series of overlapping waves, with different strategies being used more frequently at different ages. SOURCE: Siegler, R. S. (1996). *Emerging minds: The process of change in children's thinking.* New York: Oxford University Press.

strategy is called *min* and involves starting with the larger addend and counting up from there, making the minimum number of counts. For the problem 3 + 2 = ?, a child using the min strategy would say "3" and then count up two, saying "4, **5**." A more sophisticated strategy yet is called *fact retrieval* and involves memorizing basic math facts; that is, just knowing that 2 plus 3 equals 5. Alternatively, a child could just guess.

In one study investigating multiple strategy use, kindergarten children computed moves on a board game (Chutes and Ladders) by throwing a pair of dice (Bjorklund & Rosenblum, 2002). Children used a variety of strategies to compute their moves. Moreover, they were not random but varied with the numbers on the dice. For example, children used fact retrieval for most doubles (for example, 6 + 6; 5 + 5), the min strategy when the difference between the two addends was large and the smaller number was (usually) a 1 or 2 (for example, 5 + 1; 6 + 2), and the sum strategy for all others (for example, 4 + 2; 5 + 3). Thus, not only do children use multiple and variable strategies on a task, but they are highly sensitive to factors within the testing context (here, the particular combination of numbers they were asked to add) when choosing which strategy to use.

The Development of Memory Strategies

Strategies have been extensively studied for memory development (see Bjorklund et al. 2009). Like strategy development in general, children use a variety of memory strategies, or *mnemonics,* sometimes several of them at one time. In this section we examine the development of the two most investigated types of memory strategies, *rehearsal* and *organization.*

....

adaptive strategy choice model Siegler's model to describe how strategies change over time; the view that multiple strategies exist within a child's cognitive repertoire at any one time, with these strategies competing with one another for use.

table 8.1 Typical Rehearsal Protocols for an Eighth-grade Child and a Third-grade Child

Note the use of active rehearsal by eighth graders and the more passive rehearsal style by third graders.

Word Presented	Rehearsal Sets	
	Eighth-grade Child	Third-grade Child
1. Yard	Yard, yard, yard	Yard, yard, yard, yard, yard
2. Cat	Cat, yard, cat, yard	Cat, cat, cat, cat, yard
3. Man	Man, cat, yard, man, yard, cat	Man, man, man, man, man
4. Desk	Desk, man, yard, cat, man, desk, car, yard	Desk, desk, desk, desk, desk

SOURCE: Ornstein, P. A., Naus, M. J., & Liberty, C. (1975). Rehearsal and organizational processes in children's memory. *Child Development, 46,* 818–830.

Rehearsal

When children are read a list of words to remember and they have the opportunity to practice those words, age differences are found regarding how much rehearsal they do and how many words they remember. Most 5- and 6-year-old children rehearse very little or not at all, whereas most older children rehearse more and remember more (Flavell, Beach, & Chinsky, 1966). When children are told they must say (rehearse) at least one word after each word is presented, they comply, eliminating the age differences in the amount of rehearsal. However, age differences in memory are still found, with older children (eighth graders, for example) remembering more than younger children (third graders, for example) (Ornstein, Naus, & Liberty, 1975).

The reason for this is that the younger and older children rehearse in different ways. Table 8.1 presents typical rehearsal protocols for a third- and eighth-grade child (from Ornstein et al., 1975). As you can see, the third graders usually rehearsed only one unique word at a time, two at the most. This has been called passive rehearsal. Contrast this with the eighth-grade child who usually rehearsed many different words in the same rehearsal set. This is referred to as active,

---

rehearsal A memory strategy in which target information is repeated.

passive rehearsal Style of rehearsing in which a person includes few (usually one) unique items per rehearsal set.

active (or cumulative) rehearsal Type of memory strategy in which a person repeats the most recently presented item (for example, a word) and then rehearses it with as many other different words as possible.

organization (in recall) The structure discovered or imposed upon a set of items that is used to guide memory performance.

clustering Recalling items from the same category together in a memory task.

---

or cumulative, rehearsal, and its use is associated with better memory performance (see also Guttentag, Ornstein, & Siemens, 1987). That changes in rehearsal are apparently *causing* increases in recall is demonstrated by training studies in which preteen children given instructions in cumulative rehearsal improve their memory performance (Cox et al., 1989; Ornstein et al., 1977).

Organization

Another frequently studied memory strategy is organization, which refers to the structure discovered or imposed on a set of items. For example, when trying to remember what groceries to buy at the store, you might organize the information by categories (dairy products, meats, vegetables) or meals (ingredients necessary for sweet-and-sour pork; food for Sunday's barbecue).

To study organization, children are usually asked to remember sets of categorically related items (for instance, different examples of *animals*, *fruits*, and *furniture*). One effective memory strategy is to sort the items into groups during a study phase and to recall them according to their category membership, called clustering. Like rehearsal, children's tendencies to organize information for recall, both at time of study via sorting and time of remembering via clustering, increase with age (see Bjorklund et al., 2009; Schneider, 2011). In fact, preschool and early school-age children often fail to sort items by categories at time of study or to recall them in clusters during recall (Salatas & Flavell, 1976; Schwenck, Bjorklund, & Schneider, 2009). Older children are more likely to group items by meaning and, as a result, have higher levels of recall (Best & Ornstein, 1986; Hasselhorn, 1992).

As with rehearsal, young children who do not sort or cluster items by categories spontaneously can be trained to do so, usually with corresponding improvements in memory performance (Lange & Pierce, 1992; Schwenck et al., 2007). However, like other strategies, young children trained to use an organizational strategy rarely remember as much as older children who spontaneously organize their recall, and, under most conditions, young children fail to generalize the strategy to new situations (Cox & Waters, 1986).

Like most aspects of cognition, children's tendencies to use strategies and the effectiveness of the strategies they use increase with age. However, even very young children use strategies; they just tend not to be very effective in achieving their goals. Take, for example, 18- and 24-month-old children playing a modified game of hide-and-seek (DeLoache & Brown, 1983; DeLoache, Cassidy, & Brown, 1985). An experimenter hid a toy in one of several locations in a child's home while the child watched. After being distracted for several minutes, children were permitted to retrieve the toy. Children engaged in some strategic behaviors during the delay periods, including looking or pointing at the hiding location and repeating the name of the toy.

As we have seen, the strategies children use increase in sophistication with age, as they try multiple ways to solve a problem, eventually settling on a solution they will use most of the time, depending on the context. But what accounts for the changes in strategy use we see over childhood and adolescence?

Factors That Influence Children's Strategy Use

Several factors contribute to both developmental and individual differences in children's tendencies to use and benefit from strategies. Three important ones are *mental capacity, knowledge base,* and *metacognition* (see Figure 8.10).

Mental Capacity

Concerning *mental capacity,* recall that a basic tenet of information-processing approaches is that people have limited mental resources: we can only think about or do so many things at once, and doing one effortful task interferes with doing another one (see Chapter 2). As research on the development of executive function suggests, young children have fewer mental resources available to them (as reflected by smaller working memories and slower speed of processing) than do older children. Strategies, by definition, are effortful, and their execution by young children often does not leave them with enough resources to actually benefit from their use in terms of task performance (Case, 1985; Cowan et al., 2005).

This is reflected by research showing a relationship between strategy use and working memory (Lehmann & Hasselhorn, 2007; Woody-Dorning & Miller, 2001), as well as dual-task experiments that are based on the simple idea that it is difficult to do two things at once (Guttentag, 1984; Miller et al., 1991). In one dual-task study, third- and seventh-grade children were asked to tap a finger on the space bar of a computer keyboard as fast as they could while performing a free-recall memory task (Bjorklund & Harnishfeger, 1987). In one condition, children were instructed to use a memory strategy (remember the words by categories, for example, all the animal words together, then all the furniture words, etc.). The third-grade children slowed their tapping significantly more when using the strategy than when not using it, indicating that using the strategy was effortful. However, they did *not*

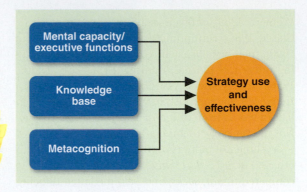

FIGURE 8.10 Three major factors influence children's strategy use: mental capacity, knowledge base, and metacognition.

The picture is more complicated than presented here. There are more factors that influence children's use and effectiveness of strategies, and these factors are not independent. For example, when children have a detailed knowledge base of a set of information, they process that information more quickly, expanding their working memory for that content.

show an increase in recall as a result of organizing the items as instructed. Seventh graders showed less interference in tapping as a result of using the strategy and, as might be expected for these older children, showed an increase in their memory performance. This and other research (see Bjorklund et al., 2009) suggests that one reason young children fail to use strategies is that they consume too much of their limited mental resources, leaving too little for performing the actual task (in this case, recalling the words).

Knowledge Base

Strategies are specific to tasks and to situations. Children use strategies to solve specific problems, perhaps school-type problems of remembering all the states and their capitals, or everyday tasks such as figuring out how much two Dairy Queen Blizzards will cost. In most cases, children already know something about the tasks they have to solve. They have stored information about the geographic location of different states, for example, or memorized their arithmetic facts. This factor, **knowledge base**—how much children know about the problems they are trying to solve—can have a significant impact on children's strategy use and task performance.

The main reason for the relationship between knowledge base and strategy use seems to be that having a detailed knowledge base results in faster processing of information within that domain (the domain of chess, baseball, or American history, for example). This in turn results in automatic rather than effortful processing, effectively expanding one's mental resources (Bjorklund, Muir-Broaddus, & Schneider, 1990; Kee, 1994). The relationship between knowledge and strategy use has been shown for a variety of domains, including mathematics (Ashcraft, 1990), reading (Daneman & Green, 1986), text comprehension (Schneider, Körkel, &

knowledge base The general background knowledge a person possesses.

Weinert, 1989), problem solving (Chi, Feltovich, & Glaser, 1981), communication (Furman & Walden, 1990), memory (Ornstein & Naus, 1985), and forming inferences (Barnes, Dennis, & Haefele-Kalvaitis, 1996), among others. As a simple example, consider a free-recall memory task in which children are given lists of words from different categories to remember. Not all category members are created equal, however; some are more typical of their categories than others, such as *shirt*, *dress*, and *coat* for clothing, compared to *hat*, *socks*, and *belt*, the latter all being common words and items, but less typical of what we think of as clothes. Children have greater category knowledge for typical than atypical category members, and as a result are more apt to use a strategy and to recall more words with the typical than the atypical set of items (Best, 1993; Schwenck et al., 2007). Also, children's world knowledge increases with age, and as it does their strategic performance on a host of tasks increases with it.

Metacognition

Finally, what a child knows about strategies and their relationship to task performance increases with age and is related to problem solving. Knowledge of one's own thinking is referred to as **metacognition**. For each type of cognition, there is a corresponding type of metacognition (for example, meta-attention, metamemory, and metalinguistics).

Children with higher levels of metacognition usually (but not always) display higher levels of cognition, and young children are generally less aware than older children of their cognitive abilities. This is especially true when it comes to using strategies. This has been found for a host of cognitive domains, including scientific reasoning (Kuhn et al., 1988), arithmetic (Carr & Jessup, 1995), attention (Miller & Weiss, 1982), and memory (DeMarie et al., 2004), among others.

Consider children's *metamemory*, their knowledge of their memory abilities. Preschool and early school-age children seem to be particularly out of touch with their memory abilities. For example, they (1) think they can remember more than they actually can (Yussen & Levy, 1975; Shin et al., 2007), (2) sometimes think they never forget (Kreutzer, Leonard, & Flavell, 1975), and (3) believe that learning pairs of unrelated words (for example, Mary/walk) would be just as easy as learning pairs of opposites (for example, boy/girl) (Kreutzer et al., 1975).

Similar patterns are found for other areas of metacognition. For instance, meta-attention, children's knowledge of how attention works, improves with age, with preschool children sometimes being unaware that paying attention is a good strategy to use when trying to remember something or make a decision. For example, in one study, 4-, 6-, and 8-year-old children were told a story about a woman who was examining a set of decorative pins so that she could select one as a gift (Flavell, Green, & Flavell, 1995). What would be on the woman's mind? Would she be focusing just on the pins, or might she have other things on her mind as well? Almost all 8-year-olds and most 6-year-olds were aware that the woman would be thinking primarily about the pins and not about other things. However, few 4-year olds had this insight. By 8 years of age, children's understanding of attentional focus was about as good as that of adults.

Although children with better metacognition often also have better cognition, the two are not always closely linked. For example, in an early study examining the relationship between metamemory and memory performance, John Cavanaugh and John Borkowski (1980) administered a battery of metamemory and memory tests to children in the first, third, and fifth grades. They reported that both metamemory knowledge and memory behavior improved with age but that, within a grade level, there was no systematic relationship between the two factors. That is, knowing a child's level of metamemory knowledge did not predict well his or her level of memory performance when age was held constant. More recent research has found stronger relationships between memory and metamemory for children over 10 years of age (Hasselhorn, 1992) and for younger children when the memory task is simple and the metamemory questions are highly related to successful task performance (Schneider & Sodian, 1988). Although the connection between metacognitive knowledge and cognitive performance is not always clear-cut, children who have greater metacognitive knowledge can monitor their task performance, use strategies more effectively, and as a result perform cognitive tasks better, which in turn will enhance their metacognitive knowledge (see Schneider & Pressley, 1997).

As with other complex aspects of cognitive development, multiple interacting factors are responsible for developmental and individual differences in children's use of strategies to solve problems, with mental capacity, knowledge base, and metacognition being only three prominent ones. The context in which children perform a task will

metacognition Knowledge about one's own thoughts and the factors that influence thinking.

determine to a large extent what strategies they will use and how effectively they use them. One overarching context effect is culture. The strategies children learn will vary among cultures (Kurtz, 1990), with differences being greatest between children in schooled versus nonschooled cultures (see Rogoff, 1990).

Culture

Memory Development

One of us (DB) has a vivid memory of an event that dates back to the first year of his life:

> My memory is of me as a sick baby. I had the croup (something like bronchitis). When I recall this memory I can feel the congestion in my chest, hear the vaporizer whir, smell the Vicks Vapo-Rub, and see the living room of my grandparents' house while looking through the bars of my crib. The memory is like a multisensory snapshot. I have no story to tell, only the recall of an instant of my life as a sickly baby. My mistake was relating this vibrant and personally poignant memory to my mother. She listened carefully and then told me that I had never had the croup; my younger brother Dick had the croup as an infant. I was about 4 years old at the time. My memory was a reconstruction—and of an event I had only *observed*, not one I had actually *experienced*. (from Bjorklund, 2005, pp. 273, 274)

Memory plays center stage in our lives, and our recollections of our past serve as the basis of our personal identity. We will even go so far as to invent or construct memories from our infancies to fill missing gaps. *Memory* refers to the contents of one's mind (one's memories). *Remembering* refers to the processes of storing new information and bringing information to consciousness. Both the contents of memory and remembering are crucial to cognition and survival. Thanks to memory, we can activate solutions for some problems we have learned to solve in the past (for example, recalling how to drive a stick-shift car after years of driving cars with automatic transmission), as well as relevant information to solve new problems (for example, remembering cities you have driven in during the past to find your way to the highway). Moreover, memory plays a central role in our personal lives, given that our recollections of our past define ourselves to ourselves and maintain critical information about social relationships.

We begin this section by examining age differences in how memories are represented in the mind, focusing on the distinction between *implicit* and *explicit memory*. We devote most of the section to the development of *autobiographical memory*,

children's ability to remember and report events that happened to them (that is, the self). We start with a look at the phenomenon of *infantile amnesia*, an inability to remember information from infancy. We then look at the development of *event memory*, a particular type of episodic memory, followed by a look at a related topic, children as eyewitnesses. Over the past couple of decades, research on this topic has informed scientists about the nature of children's memory development and the legal system about the best ways to interview children. We conclude the section with a brief look at *prospective memory*, essentially remembering to perform some act in the future.

Representation of Knowledge

One of the more widely accepted findings in memory research is the distinction between so-called implicit/procedural memory and explicit/declarative memory (Tulving, 1985, 2005). We introduced the distinction between these two types of memory in Chapter 5, when we presented evidence that the deferred imitation shown by infants and toddlers may be a preverbal form of explicit memory. Explicit, or declarative, memory is available to conscious awareness and comes in at least two forms: episodic and semantic. Episodic memory is literally memory for episodes. Information represented in episodic memory can be consciously retrieved, such as where you parked your car this morning, the gist of a conversation you had with your sister yesterday, and the trip you took to Disney World when you were 8 years old. According to Endel Tulving (1985, 2005), episodic memories are tied together by a reference to the *self*, the I or me who is involved in the various episodes.

In contrast, semantic memory refers to our knowledge of language, rules, and concepts. So, for instance, the meaning of the word *liberty*, the name of the first U.S. President, or the rules for long division are examples of semantic memory. You might remember learning the definition of *liberty* and the rules for long division in the fourth grade, or recall the first-grade class in which you learned about George Washington—all examples of episodic memory—but your actual knowledge of these words, rules, and concepts are examples of

explicit (declarative) memory Memories that are available to conscious awareness and can be directly assessed by tests of recall or recognition memory; explicit memory comes in two types, episodic and semantic memory.

episodic memory Long-term memory of events or episodes.

semantic memory Long-term memory representation of definitions and relations among language terms.

table 8.2 Characteristics of Implicit and Explicit Cognitive Systems

Implicit System	Explicit System
Unconscious	Conscious
Automatic	Controllable
Evolved early	Evolved late
Common across species	Might be unique to humans
Pragmatic, context-dependent expression (for example, social discourse)	Logical, decontextualized, abstract representations (for example, chess)
Parallel processing of multiple sources of contextual information (for example, face, body posture, vocal intonations)	Sequential processing of decontextualized abstract representations
Parallel processing results in high but effortless information-processing capacity	Sequential processing is limited to attentional and working memory resources and is therefore effortful
Unrelated to general intelligence	Correlated with general intelligence

SOURCE: From Evans, J. S. B. T. (2002). Logic and human reasoning: An assessment of the deductive paradigm. *Psychological Bulletin, 128*, p. 989.

semantic memory. Figure 8.11 and Table 8.2 show the various components of the explicit and implicit memory system and some of their characteristics.

In comparison to both episodic and semantic memory, implicit (sometimes called nondeclarative or procedural) memory refers to knowledge of procedures and feelings that are integrated but unconscious. For example, some have argued that the learning and memory observed in some types of classical and operant conditioning are unconscious and implicit, as are many familiar routines once they have become well practiced (such as tying one's shoe). Such memory is unavailable to consciousness ("memory without awareness") and can be accessed only indirectly (that is, you cannot just ask someone to remember something they know only implicitly and expect a coherent answer). For example, asking someone to describe the landscape on his ride to work each day would likely result in only a most general and cursory description, and asking someone for a description of her tennis serve would likely produce a statement only vaguely resembling the actual actions.

Developmental Differences in Implicit and Explicit Memory

In general, age differences in implicit memory are relatively small, whereas differences in explicit

memory tend to be quite substantial (Billingsley, Smith, & McAndrews, 2002; Newcombe et al., 1998; see Lloyd & Newcombe, 2009 for a review). These differences in memory performance are correlated with differences in brain development. Areas of the brain associated with implicit memory, mainly the basal ganglia and cerebellum (Gareil, 1998), develop earlier than areas of the brain associated with declarative memory, mainly the temporal lobe (Giedd et al., 1999; Lenroot & Giedd, 2006).

Let us provide one straightforward example. Four-, 5-, and 6-year-old children were shown a series of pictures and asked to identify them or to answer some questions about them (for example, "What would you use an X for?") (Hayes & Hennessy, 1996). Two days later, children were asked to identify a series of fragmented pictures, drawings of objects with many details missing, similar to those shown in Figure 8.12. For each picture, the initial presentation was substantially degraded, and gradually more detail was provided until children identified the picture. Some of the pictures were the same ones they had seen two days earlier, and some were new. Children were also asked if they remembered each picture from two days ago. Older children correctly remembered more of the pictures from two days earlier than did younger children. This is a measure of explicit memory, because it taps a specific prior experience. This type of memory typically increases with age. However, children of all ages identified the fragmented old pictures (that is, those they had seen with less detail provided) faster than the fragmented new pictures. This is a measure of implicit memory, because children's faster identification of the old pictures occurred whether they consciously remembered the picture from before or not. That is, even though children did not explicitly remember seeing many of the old pictures two days earlier, they processed those pictures faster, indicating that they did have a memory of them; the memory, however, was implicit—out of conscious awareness—and was comparable between the youngest and oldest children tested.

One developmental theory that takes the distinction between implicit and explicit representation seriously is that of Annette Karmiloff-Smith (1991, 1992). Karmiloff-Smith's theory describes how implicit representations are transformed into explicit ones. The details of her theory need not concern us here, but we would like to describe the distinction that she (and others) make between implicit and explicit representation and its development. According to Karmiloff-Smith, knowledge at the implicit level is not available to consciousness

implicit (nondeclarative or procedural) memory Memory without awareness that can be assessed only indirectly.

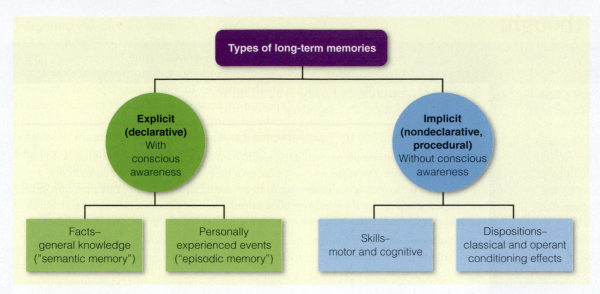

FIGURE 8.11 Classification of different types of memory.
The human memory system can be divided into two general types of memory, explicit, or declarative, which is available to consciousness, and implicit, or nondeclarative, which is not available to consciousness, which themselves can be divided further. Age differences are greater in explicit than implicit memory.

but reflects a person's intuitive understanding of the world. This, according to Karmiloff-Smith, is how all knowledge is represented for infants. Infants may learn that when they release an object it drops to the floor, to retrieve a toy hidden under a cloth, and to reproduce the sounds their mothers make, and such knowledge is highly valuable for helping them navigate their physical and social worlds. But this knowledge is out of conscious awareness, and thus there are limits to what children can do with it. Consciousness for Karmiloff-Smith permits a child to take one piece of information (reproducing a sound his mother made), reflect on it, and make some inferences (perhaps she wants me to repeat this word and associate it with that object). With consciousness, experiences can be *redescribed*, in Karmiloff-Smith's terms, permitting knowledge that was once implicit to become explicit (for example, there is a new billboard on the road to work advertising Calvin Klein underwear), or generating new insights by reflecting on what one already knows (for instance, realizing that price increases in gasoline and groceries are both related to increases in the price of oil).

The distinction between implicit and explicit memories (and between implicit and explicit cognition/learning more generally) is an important one. It may, in fact, reflect a difference in the memory systems of humans and all other animals. For the most part, nonhuman animals and human infants are limited to implicit cognition, although much of what goes on in the heads of older children and adults is also implicit in nature. In contrast, *explicit cognition* seems to be limited to *Homo sapiens* past infancy (although it may be available to some chimpanzees, see Bjorklund & Rosenberg, 2005). But the implicit/explicit memory distinction does not exhaust all ways in which knowledge is represented and develops. Psychologists have also looked at different ways in which individual experiences are represented in memory and how these memory traces change with time, experience, and development. One influential

FIGURE 8.12 Examples of fragmented pictures.
Children are initially shown the pictures with the least detail and asked to identify the object. Children are shown pictures with increasing detail until they can correctly identify it. SOURCE: Gollin, E. S. (1962). Factors affecting the visual recognition of incomplete objects: a comparative investigation of children and adults. *Perceptual Motor Skills*, 15, 583–590.

BOX 8.3
food for thought

Fuzzy-Trace Theory

How good are you really about remembering things and making simple, everyday decisions? For example, if you were considering the purchase of two identical cell phones, one on sale at Radio Shack for $159.95 and the other at Brookstone for $167.49, what information do you need to keep in mind to complete the deal? It's not as straightforward as you may think. And how does such thinking develop?

Charles Brainerd and Valerie Reyna (1993, 2002, 2005) contend that people represent, or encode, experiences on a *fuzzy-to-verbatim continuum*. At one extreme are **fuzzy traces**, or gist, which are vague, degenerated representations that maintain only the sense or pattern of recent experiences. At the other extreme are **verbatim traces**, which are elaborated, exact representations of the recently encoded information. Returning to your cell-phone purchase, to determine which is the better deal, you could remember the exact price of the two phones (verbatim information) or simply remember the gist that the phone at Radio Shack was about 10 bucks cheaper than the one at Brookstone. And when you finally buy the phone, if you are writing a check, you need to know the exact price (verbatim), whereas if you are swiping your credit card, the gist (fuzzy) amount (about $160) will do.

Note that it is easier to recall gist information than verbatim information, one important difference between the two. In addition, verbatim traces are more susceptible to interference and they deteriorate (that is, are forgotten) faster than gist traces.

Some Assumptions of Fuzzy-Trace Theory and Their Relation to Cognitive Development

1. Gist Extraction and the Fuzzy-to-verbatim Continua

Basic Assumption: People extract fuzzy, gist-like information from the stimuli and events they experience. Traces for an event exist on a fuzzy-to-verbatim continuum. At one extreme are fuzzy traces that are vague, degenerated representations that maintain only the sense or pattern of recently encoded information. At the other extreme are verbatim traces, which are elaborated, exact representations of the recently encoded information.

Age Differences: Young children's memory is specialized for encoding and processing verbatim information; with age, their ability to extract gist improves.

2. Fuzzy-processing Preference (Intuition)

Basic Assumption: People prefer to reason, think, and remember intuitively, processing fuzzy rather than verbatim traces.

Age Differences: There is a shift in the reliance on verbatim and gist traces, sometime during the elementary school years, with children becoming increasingly facile at processing gist traces. Processing of verbatim traces declines in efficiency during adolescence.

3. Output Interference

Basic Assumption: As people make responses, output interference occurs and interferes with subsequent processing.

Age Differences: Young children are more sensitive to the effects of output interference than are older children or adults.

From this perspective, people do not first encode the details of an experience, which then degrades and become fuzzy with time. Rather, any event is encoded in multiple ways, using both verbatim ($159.95 versus $167.49) and gist (cheaper at Radio Shack and about 160 bucks) traces for any particular event.

Rather than using a computer as a metaphor for the mind as information-processing theorists do, Brainerd and Reyna suggest the metaphor of *intuitionism*, in which people prefer to think, reason, and remember by processing inexact, fuzzy, gist-like memory representations rather than working logically from exact, verbatim representations. However, this preference varies with age, with younger children preferring, more so than older children, to operate with or think about more exact verbatim traces, and this has consequences for their cognition. The basic assumptions of fuzzy-trace theory and

---

memory trace theory in cognitive development is **fuzzy-trace theory**, proposed by Charles Brainerd and Valerie Reyna (1993, 2002, 2005), and this influential theory is discussed in Box 8.3.

> **fuzzy traces** Imprecise memory representations that are more easily accessed, generally require less effort to use, and are less susceptible to interference and forgetting than verbatim traces.
>
> **verbatim traces** Precise, literal memory representations that are less easily accessed, generally require more effort to use, and are more susceptible to interference and forgetting than fuzzy traces.
>
> **fuzzy-trace theory** Brainerd and Reyna's theory that proposes that information is encoded on a continuum from verbatim to fuzzy, or gistlike, traces, and that many cognitive developmental differences in aspects of cognition can be attributed to age differences in encoding and in differences in sensitivity to output interference.

The Development of Autobiographical Memory

Autobiographical memory refers to personal and long-lasting memories, which are the basis for one's personal life history (K. Nelson, 1996). Autobiographical memory develops over the preschool years. Some people, in fact, document the beginning of autobiographical memory with the offset of **infantile amnesia**, the inability to remember information from early childhood.

Infantile Amnesia

Some years ago, my (DB) wife and I wrote a column for a parenting magazine and received a let-

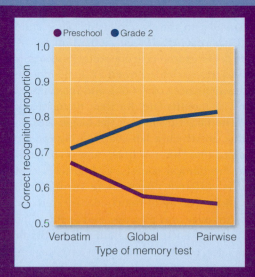

Proportion of correct recognition responses for verbatim and gist (global and pairwise) problems for preschool and second-grade children. Although both the preschool and second-graders performed comparably on the verbatim items, the older children performed better on the two test items assessing gist processing. SOURCE: Brainerd, C. J., & Gordon, L. L. (1994). Development of verbatim and gist memory for numbers. *Developmental Psychology, 30,* **163–177.**

proposed age differences are presented in the accompanying table.

Children begin life biased toward remembering and retrieving verbatim traces. They extract gist information from experiences, but, compared to older children and adults, they are biased toward the verbatim end of the continuum. Sometime during the early elementary school years, a verbatim-to-gist shift occurs, with children now showing a

gist bias. Let us demonstrate this shift in a simple experiment (Brainerd & Gordon, 1994). Preschool and second-grade children were given simple numerical problems. For example, children were told that: "Farmer Brown owns many animals. He owns 3 dogs, 5 sheep, 7 chickens, 9 horses, and 11 cows." They were then asked a series of questions, some requiring verbatim knowledge for their correct answer, such as "How many cows does Farmer Brown own, 11 or 9?" and others requiring only gist information, such as "Which of Farmer Brown's animals are the most, cows or horses?" (which they called global) and "Does Farmer Brown have more cows or more horses?" (which they called pairwise). The results of this experiment are shown in the accompanying figure. As you can see from the figure, second graders were better at remembering the numerical gist (global and pairwise questions) than those based on verbatim information, whereas the reverse was true for the preschool children. Note that the younger children did not remember more verbatim information than the older children. What differed was their pattern, with the preschool children performing better on the verbatim than the gist, with the reverse being true for the second graders.

Note that the theory does *not* propose that memory representations are transformed from verbatim to gist (or fuzzy) traces, or that young children are better at processing or remembering verbatim traces than older children are. Both verbatim and fuzzy traces exist at all ages (at least past

early infancy), and the ability to process *both* verbatim and fuzzy traces improves with age. Children simply start life with a bias toward processing verbatim relative to fuzzy traces, with this bias changing sometime in childhood.

Fuzzy-trace theory has been applied to a wide range of phenomena, including memory, reasoning, and problem solving. For example, fuzzy-trace theory has been applied to the persistence of children's false memories (see discussion on children's eyewitness memory later in this chapter). One provocative finding is that when children do recall false information, those false memories often persist, and, under some circumstances, might even be *more* resistant to forgetting than true memories (Brainerd & Mojardin, 1999; see Brainerd & Reyna, 2005). Fuzzy-trace theory accounts for this pattern by looking at the types of memory traces that are involved in true versus false memories. Correct memories are based, in part, on literal, or *verbatim,* memory traces. In contrast, because a falsely remembered event never happened, there can be no verbatim, or literal, memory trace of the event. Instead, it is based solely on *gist traces.* As noted, verbatim traces are more susceptible to forgetting than gist traces. As a result, true memories, based in part on verbatim traces, are more likely to be forgotten than false memories, which are based solely on more stable gist representations.

ter from a woman who was deeply worried that she and her husband had done something horribly wrong in raising their child. Her son was 10 years old, and he could not remember anything from his early childhood. What might they have done to cause their son to so thoroughly repress his early experiences? We assured this woman that she and her husband had done nothing to cause her son's forgetfulness, for most of us have few if any memories much before the age of 4 years (Rubin, 2000; West & Bauer, 1999).

It is not uncommon, however, to find people who can report one or two vivid memories from infancy. In fact, the story that opened the section on memory development tells of such a memory

possessed by one of the authors. But as you may recall, this memory of being a sickly baby lying in a crib was not real—it was a reconstruction of events that never happened. More common are early memories based on hearing others retelling a family story or looking at photographs or videos of events in the distant past. We know of one young man who recalled his brother falling off a porch, causing a large gash on his chin and the resulting dash to the emergency room. Problem was, the event happened several weeks before he was born. What he

autobiographical memory Personal and long-lasting memories that are the basis for one's personal life history.

infantile amnesia The inability to remember events from infancy and early childhood.

Two- to 3-year-old children who had the verbal ability to describe what went on when playing with the Magic Shrinking Machine were able to remember some of the event 6 and 12 months later. Children without sufficient verbal ability at the time of the event could not remember anything about the event later on. SOURCE: Simcock, G., & Hayne, H. (2002). Breaking the barrier? Children fail to translate their preverbal memories into language. *Psychological Science, 13,* 225–231.

development, infants represent events differently than do older children (in sensorimotor versus symbolic forms). Memories encoded in infancy using sensorimotor schemes may not be accessible (or interpretable) to the symbol-using older child or adult (Richardson & Hayne, 2007; Simcock & Hayne, 2002). For example, in one study (Simcock & Hayne, 2002), researchers showed 27- to 39-month-old children sequences of actions and interviewed them 6 and 12 months later for their memories of the event. The target event was the Magic Shrinking Machine, in which a lab coat, too big for the child, was put into "the machine," and after a few seconds of mechanical sounds, a child-sized coat emerged. Six different objects were shrunk in a similar fashion, usually to the child's amusement. Children's language was also assessed at this time using the Peabody Picture Vocabulary Test. Six or 12 months later, children were interviewed again, this time for their memories of the earlier event ("Last time I visited you, we played a really exciting game! Tell me everything you can remember about the game"). Children were also asked follow-up questions ("What were the names of the toys? How did the machine work?"). When the children were prompted to recall the earlier event, only those who had the vocabulary to describe the event *at the time of the original experience* did so. That is, children with higher verbal scores at the initial testing were able to remember aspects of the event 6 and 12 months later, whereas children of the same age but with poorer language skills were not. According to Gabrielle Simcock and Harlene Hayne (2002, p. 229), "children's verbal reports were frozen in time, reflecting their verbal skill at the time of encoding, rather than at the time of test."

As this research shows, language surely plays an important role in remembering events from our childhoods. But children's language development is not complete by age 3, and they learn to use language to organize their memories by interacting with adults. Adults provide the cues and structure for children to form narratives—stories for embedding events and later for remembering them. Only after being guided by adults can children learn to code memories and realize that language can be used to share memories with others.

Katherine Nelson (1993, p. 12) makes this point especially clear:

> The claim here is that the initial functional significance of autobiographical memory is that of sharing memory with other people, a function that language makes possible. Memories become valued in their own right—not because they predict the future and guide present action, but because they are shareable with others and thus serve a social solidarity function. I suggest that this is a universal human function, although one with variable, cul-

was recalling was a frequently told story that he had reconstructed to place himself at the scene of the action. (Which, we suppose, he was, but he was not in a position to witness the event.) What the phenomenon of infantile amnesia reflects is that infants and young children lack personal and long-lasting memories, or autobiographical memory.

Why can't we remember information from infancy and early childhood when we know from research discussed in Chapter 5 using the conjugate reinforcement and deferred-imitation procedures that the memory system is working? Recall from Chapter 5 that many 16- and 20-month-old infants can remember events they observed, as reflected by deferred imitation, for at least 12 months (Bauer et al., 2000).

Sigmund Freud (1963) had what seems today to be a bizarre proposal for infantile amnesia. According to Freud, experiences of infancy are rife with sexual overtones toward one's mother and are just generally so traumatic that they are actively repressed. We protect our adult egos, claimed Freud, by preventing these disturbing memories from rising to consciousness. However, his theory of infantile amnesia was wrong.

Modern explanations of infantile amnesia look at children's developing cognitive systems and the social environments in which they develop (see Bauer, 2007; Howe, Courage, & Rooksby, 2009). For example, recall that in Piaget's theory of cognitive turally specific rules. In this respect, it is analogous to human language itself, uniquely and universally human but culturally—and individually—variable.

Some evidence in support of Nelson's interpretation comes from research that examines the earliest memories for children in different cultures (Peterson, Wang, & Hou, 2009; Wang, 2006). For example, in a series of studies, the earliest memories of White versus Asian adults was compared, with Whites reporting earlier memories in each study by an average of about half a year. There are also cultural differences in what is remembered. For example, the childhood memories of American adults are more likely to include emotions and less likely to involve family activities than the childhood memories of Chinese adults (Wang, 2001). The reason for these differences likely lies in the parent-child interaction styles in the different cultures. This was explicitly examined in studies contrasting ways in which American and Korean mothers interact with their children and cultural differences in the recall of early memories. American mothers talked about past events more with their 3-year-old children than Korean mothers did (Mullen & Yi, 1995), consistent with the finding that American adults have earlier memories than Korean adults (Mullen, 1994).

But this cannot account for the failure to remember events from one's third or fourth years of life, so other factors are surely involved in infantile amnesia. One may be the development of *self-concept*—a sense of a personal self, clearly differentiated from others (Fivush, 1988; Howe, 2003). A child's sense of self develops gradually during the preschool years (see discussion of the development of self-concept in Chapter 7), and although young children have memories, the experiences of early childhood occurred when their sense of self was poorly developed, thus providing no anchor for such events. Unless events can be related to the self, they cannot be retrieved later.

Autobiographical memory is a complicated thing, and surely a child's ability to mentally represent experiences, his or her self-concept, and how adults in a child's life use language to communicate and tell stories all play a role in what children remember. Overall, the research evidence indicates that infantile amnesia reflects important changes occurring during early childhood—changes that permit autobiographical memory and that separate our species from all others.

Remembering Events

The offset of infantile amnesia represents the onset of autobiographical memory. What people usually remember about their lives are *events*. How do children remember the experiences, or events, of their everyday lives, and how are these memories organized? First, event memory is *constructive* in nature. Children are not remembering specific details of events, as if they are memorizing lines in a play (although children, and adults, do retain some specific, or verbatim, aspects of events, Brainerd & Reyna, 2005). Rather, they are remembering the gist of an event, transforming what was actually said and done into a memory representation. They do this based, in part, on their cognitive ability to understand the event, their prior knowledge related to the event, and the actual event.

For example, when reporting on what happened at a baseball game, children must first have the cognitive ability to understand that the important events are the ones happening on the field, not in the stands. Children who know something about baseball (the rules, the equipment, how to keep score, for example) will be able to remember and relate events more accurately than someone who knows little about the game (explaining someone stealing second base, for example). And what children remember will depend upon what actually happened. Did anyone actually try to steal second base? How many runs were scored? How children later recall those events can also be affected by the physical or social environment in which they do the remembering (for example, with fellow baseball enthusiasts or with people who care little about the game). Memory for both children and adults is not like a tape recorder but is colored by previous knowledge, expectations, and myriad other factors, all of which vary with age.

How do children, or adults for that matter, go about remembering events? One technique is to remember what happened in terms of familiar routines called scripts. Scripts are a form of schematic organization with real-world events organized according to their causal and temporal characteristics (K. Nelson, 1996; Fivush, 2008). For instance, a "trip-to-the-grocery-store" script might include getting buckled up in the back seat of the car, driving to the store, riding in the cart, getting a cookie from the "Cookie Lady," helping remove items from the cart onto the counter, returning home, and helping put away some of the groceries. Children learn what usually happens during repeated events, such as getting ready to go to school, nap time, birthday parties, and trips to a fast-food restaurant, and they remember new information in the context of these familiar routines (and they may become upset if a routine is disturbed, such as forgetting to visit the "Cookie Lady" in the grocery store).

There is substantial evidence that very young children organize events on the basis of scripts (see Bauer, 2007; Fivush, Kuebli, & Clubb, 1992).

scripts A form of schematic organization, with real-world events organized in terms of temporal and causal relations between component acts.

Young children remember specific events in terms of scripts, routine activities such as going to a fast-food restaurant.

It may seem surprising that young children's memories are so tied to recurring events. Katherine Nelson (1996, 2005) proposed one reason why this might be so. Memory, according to Nelson, has the adaptive value of helping children predict what will happen in the future. By remembering what happened in the past, children can predict what is likely to happen in the future. Thus, recurring events should be better remembered than single events. According to Nelson (1996, p. 174),

> Memory for a single, one-time occurrence of some event, if the event were not traumatic or life-threatening, would not be especially useful, given its low probability. Thus, a memory system might be optimally designed to retain information about frequent and recurrent events—and to discard information about unrepeated events—and to integrate new information about variations in recurrent events into a general knowledge system.

Memory for routine events allows infants and young children to anticipate and possibly even control events. There is no such payoff for a novel event, and thus it makes sense to forget it.

However, remembering information in terms of scripts can be a double-edged sword, in that details of an event that do not fit into a familiar script may not be remembered. For instance, in one study, 2.5-year-old children were asked questions about a recent novel experience, such as a trip to the beach, a camping trip, or a ride on an airplane (Fivush & Hammond, 1990). One might think that these young children would focus on their new experiences in recounting the event, but instead they tended to recall these special events in terms of familiar routines, as reflected by this excerpt (Fivush & Hammond, 1990, p. 231):

Interviewer: You slept outside in a tent? Wow, that sounds like a lot of fun.

Child: And then we waked up and eat dinner. First we eat dinner, then go to bed, and then wake up and eat breakfast.

Interviewer: What else did you do when you went camping? What did you do when you got up, after breakfast?

Child: Umm, in the night, and went to sleep.

It seems that everything is new to 2-year-olds, and the less they know about the world, the more they rely on familiar routines to organize their memories, even if the truly exciting new events are lost in the telling. As they get older, children will be increasingly able to embed new events into existing scripts and to modify their scripts as a result of new experiences.

Children as Eyewitnesses

One special type of event memory that has attracted the attention of psychologists and the public at large is *eyewitness memory.* Eyewitness memory is like any other type of event memory: Children view an event and at some later time are asked to remember what they experienced. However, eyewitness memory affords researchers the opportunity to investigate the development of event memory while simultaneously addressing an important issue in society.

In legal settings, whether a child is a victim or witness to a crime, how reliable is his or her testimony? How does the accuracy of children's testimony change with age? How susceptible to suggestion are children? More than a decade ago, a common bumper sticker read "Believe the Children." This was in response to a spate of legal cases in which preschool children were allegedly abused by childcare workers (see Brown, Goldstein, & Bjorklund, 2000; Bruck, Ceci, & Principe, 2006). Some argued, basically, that children this young would not lie about such events and that their accusations should be believed, despite their tender years. Others argued that young children are highly susceptible to suggestion and that children's accusations are more the product of poor interviewing techniques than actual abuse. Child development researchers responded to this socially explosive issue and began a line of research that investigated the development of children's eyewitness memory and the factors that influence its accuracy (see Brainerd & Reyna, 2005; Bruck et

Peter Cade/Getty Images

al., 2006). As a result, they learned much about the workings and development of young children's memories and also provided valuable information for the legal system.

Age Differences in Children's Eyewitness Memories

Like event memory in general, eyewitness memory tends to improve with age; older children usually remember more than younger children about what they witness (or experience) (Ornstein, Gordon, & Larus, 1992; Poole & White, 1995). In most studies, children are shown a video of some event, watch events that transpire in their school, or sometimes take part in an event (for example, playing a game with an adult). Children are usually not told ahead of time to remember anything, or even that they are in a memory study. Sometime after witnessing or experiencing the event, children are interviewed and asked to tell what happened (for example, "Tell me what happened in the video you saw," or "Tell me what happened in your classroom yesterday morning"). This is often followed by requests for more specific information (for example, "What was the boy in the video wearing?" or "What did the lady who came into your class yesterday morning do?"). Sometimes, the interviewer will suggest certain answers, some reflecting what actually happened ("Did the man play nicely with the teddy bear?") and some suggesting things that did not happen ("Did the man rip the book?") (see Brainerd & Reyna, 2005; Bruck et al., 2006).

Young children typically remember very little when they receive a general request for information ("Tell me what happened in the video you saw yesterday") but recall more information when more specific questions are asked ("Tell me what the girl was wearing"). What is interesting is that the little information that young children do recall to general prompts tends to be highly accurate and central to the event if there are no suggestions or coaching (Goodman, Aman, & Hirschman, 1987; Poole & White, 1995). For instance, in one study, 6- and 8-year-old children and adults saw a video involving a boy and a girl in a park, with the boy stealing the girl's bike (Cassel & Bjorklund, 1995). Even the youngest children tended to report when asked that the boy took the bike and that the girl did not give him permission to do so. They were much less likely than older children or adults, however, to provide descriptions of the children, the bike, or the surroundings. Thus, young children's free recall is typically low, accurate, and about central aspects of an event.

What happens when children are given more specific hints, or cues (for instance, "Tell me what the girl looked like")? As you might expect, they recall more of the details of the event. However, in addition to remembering more *correct* facts, they also tend to remember some *incorrect* "facts" as well, reducing the overall accuracy of their recall (Goodman et al., 1994; Lindberg, Keiffer, & Thomas, 2000).

How Suggestible Are Children as Witnesses?

One important and oft-investigated topic in children's eyewitness memory is the degree to which children are susceptible to suggestion. Even adults are susceptible to suggestion (Tsai, Loftus, & Polage, 2000). The question is not *whether* children are suggestible witnesses, but whether they are appreciably more suggestible than adults. Of related interest is how susceptibility to suggestion changes with age and what can be done to minimize suggestibility while maximizing accurate reporting of witnessed or experienced events.

A quick answer to the first question is that, yes, children are more susceptible to suggestion than adults. In an early review of the literature, Stephen Ceci and Maggie Bruck (1993, p. 431) concluded, "There do appear to be significant age differences in suggestibility, with preschool children being disproportionately more vulnerable to suggestion than either school-age children or adults." Most investigators looking for age differences in suggestibility have found it, although in varying degrees and sometimes only under certain circumstances (Ackil & Zaragoza, 1995; Bruck et al., 1995; Lindberg et al., 2000).

Let us provide an example from research that used several techniques to bias young children's eyewitness memory (Leichtman & Ceci, 1995). In this study, a man identified as Sam Stone visited a preschool classroom. He talked to the teacher, sat with the children during story time and commented about the story ("I know that story; it's one of my favorites!"), walked around the classroom, and finally left the room, waving good-bye to the children. Before the visit, children in the *stereotype condition* were told that Sam Stone was irresponsible and accident-prone ("That Sam Stone is always getting into accidents and breaking things!"). Children in the *suggestion* condition were interviewed several times after Sam Stone's visit and given false information (Sam ripped a book and soiled a teddy bear when he visited). Children in the *stereotype-plus-suggestion* condition received both the negative stereotype before the visit and the misinformation afterward, and children in the *control* condition received neither the stereotyped information nor the misinformation about Sam.

Ten weeks later, children were interviewed about what happened the day that Sam Stone visited their classroom. Compared to children in the

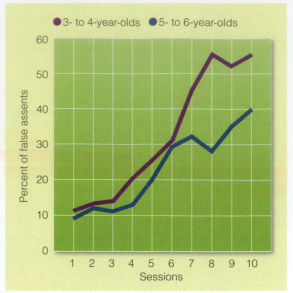

3- to 4-year-olds   5- to 6-year-olds

FIGURE 8.13 Percentage of false reports over sessions for 3- to 4-year-olds and 5- to 6-year-olds. Although few children created false memories in the early sessions, about 50% of the 3- to 4-year-olds and 40% of the 5- to 6-year-olds did by the 10th session. SOURCE: Ceci, S. J., Loftus, E. F., Leichtman, M., & Bruck, M. (1994). The role of source misattributions in the creation of false beliefs among preschoolers. *International Journal of Clinical and Experimental Hypnosis, 62,* 304–320.

© Frank Siteman/Photolibrary

Preschool children who are given suggestions, such as "Sam Stone ripped a book when he visited your classroom," are later more apt to say that Sam Stone ripped the book (when he did not) than children who are not given suggestions.

control condition, children who had been given the negative stereotypes made a modest number of false statements about Sam in the interview, and children in the suggestion condition made a substantial number of false reports. The highest levels of false reports about Sam's visit, however, came from children who received both the stereotyped information before and the misinformation after the visit; 46% of 3- and 4-year-old children and 30% of 5- and 6-year-old children said that Sam had either ripped a book or soiled a teddy bear, or both. The percentage of errors increased to 72% and 44% for the younger and older preschoolers, respectively, when they were asked specific follow-up questions concerning whether Sam had ripped a book or soiled a teddy bear.

This and related research makes it clear that young children are susceptible to suggestion and can be led to remember events differently than they actually happened. But can children ever be made to remember events that never happened at all? To what extent can children of different ages be made to believe that they have experienced major events when, in fact, these events never occurred?

This question was first investigated by Stephen Ceci and his colleagues (1994), who interviewed 3- to 6-year-old children over an 11-week period about events that might have happened to them. For example, children were asked if they ever remembered getting their finger caught in a mousetrap or taking a trip in a hot-air balloon. The percentage of false reports (that is, recalling something about the fictional event) for the younger and older children in this study over the 11-week period is shown in Figure 8.13. As you can see, few children claimed to have experienced the novel event in the first few interviews. Yet, by the end of the study, more than 50% of the 3- to 4-year-old children and nearly 40% of 5- to 6-year-olds stated that some of these events did happen to them. And once they had it in their minds that these events really happened, it was difficult to convince them otherwise, with many children continuing to believe that these events actually happened even after being told by the interviewers and their parents that the events were just made up. From these results, it seems that false memories of plausible but extraordinary events are relatively easy to put into young children's minds.

table 8.3 Some Factors That Influence Children's Eyewitness Testimony

IQ	Higher-IQ children remember more than children with lower IQs (Roebers & Schneider, 2001).
Receiving incentives	Children given incentives remember more (Roebers, Moga, & Schneider, 2001).
Stress	Moderate levels of stress seem to facilitate recall of an event relative to overly high or low levels of stress (Bahrick et al., 1998).
Emotional support	Children who have emotionally supportive mothers who discuss upcoming medical procedures with them recall less inaccurate information about the procedure than children with less sympathetic or talkative mothers (Goodman et al., 1994; 1997).
Working memory and inhibition	Better working memory and inhibitory control are associated with lower levels of suggestibility (Ruffman et al., 2001).
Theory of mind	Preschoolers who perform better on theory-of-mind tasks tend to be less suggestible than are children with poorer theory-of-mind abilities (Welch, 1999).
Source monitoring	Children who are aware of the source of information (did they see the event happen, did they hear about it from a friend, did they see it on television?) are less suggestible than children with poorer source-monitoring abilities (Mazzoni, 1998; Thierry & Spence, 2002).
Knowledge	Children with greater prior knowledge about an event are less suggestible than less-knowledgeable children (Elischberger, 2005; Ornstein & Greenhoot, 2000).

Factors Influencing Children's Eyewitness Memory: The Interview

It is not surprising that older children's eyewitness memory is typically better than that of younger children. Most aspects of explicit cognition improve with age, as children gain increasing control of their cognitive abilities. A host of factors influence children's eyewitness memory performance, some of which are listed in Table 8.3. Consider knowledge base, for example. Children who experience a stressful medical procedure recall the details of the procedure more accurately the more they know about the procedure (Ornstein et al., 2006) and recall less inaccurate information (Goodman et al., 1994).

As important as all of these factors are, perhaps the most important factor in determining the accuracy of children's eyewitness memory is how the interview is administered (Bruck et al., 2006). Interviewers must be cautious about what questions they ask children. They must balance the need to provide specific cues in order to get young children to tell them what they saw or experienced with the possibility that children will generate false memories if too many specific prompts are provided that unwittingly guide children to certain (possibly erroneous) responses. For example, it is common for young children to provide very little information to general cues, such as, "Tell me what happened when you and Bobby went to the store the other day." More specific cues may be necessary to get at critical information. For instance, "Was anyone else in the store? What did you look at? Did you talk to anyone?" Hopefully, these neutral cues will get children remembering aspects of the event that can be followed up with, "And then what happened?"

Interviewers need to be cautious before asking questions that suggest specific target behavior, for example, "Did Bobby put anything in his pocket? Did Bobby pay for everything that he took?"

Characteristics of the interviewer and the interview setting also impact what children remember. For example, children tend to remember more correct information and less incorrect information when the interviewer is warm and supportive (Quas et al., 2007). In fact, 4- to 6-year-old children who have high levels of stress show elevated levels of recall accuracy when they are questioned by an emotionally supportive interviewer but reduced levels of accuracy when questioned by a nonsupportive interviewer (Quas et al., 2004).

© HuntStock/Photolibrary

How much and how accurately children remember events is influenced by how they are interviewed and by characteristics of the interviewer.

BOX 8.4 # child development in the real world

Children's Memory and Testimony in the Real World

Most research on children's event memory, even memory of children as eyewitnesses, involves laboratory studies. Granted, some laboratories are located in children's schools, in which experimenters contrive events that simulate something that might happen in real life. Such studies are important for understanding the mechanisms involved in children's event memory and how various factors, such as background knowledge or interviewer style, affect the quantity and accuracy of what children remember. But because children's legal testimony may have significant consequences, it is important to do research in the real world, developing paradigms where researchers have some control over the situation but where children remember real events that may have legal implications.

One such research paradigm investigates children's long-term memory of events surrounding natural disasters (Ackil, Van Abbema, & Bauer, 2003; Bahrick et al., 1998). For instance, in August 1992, Hurricane Andrew struck south Florida with devastating winds, destroying many homes. Three- and 4-year-old children were interviewed between 2 and 6 months after the storm, and their recollection of events was related to the amount of destruction that occurred to each child's home (low, moderate, or high) (Bahrick et al., 1998). Not surprisingly, older children recalled more than younger children. The amount remembered varied with the severity of damage: Children whose homes were moderately damaged remembered more than children whose homes suffered low or high levels of damage. That is, a moderate degree of trauma was associated with the highest levels of recall. Children's memory for the storm remained high 6 years later, although levels of recall no longer varied with severity of stress. However, children who experienced severe stress (high level of home damage) required more prompts to recall information than did children in the low- and moderate-stress groups (Fivush et al., 2004).

Not surprisingly, mothers and their children tend to talk differently about traumatic natural events than nontraumatic ones. For instance, in a study that examined how children and their mothers discussed a tornado that struck their community versus nontraumatic events that occurred just before or just after the tornado, discussions of the tornado were longer, more detailed, and more coherent than the nontraumatic events, even 6 months after the tornado (Ackil et al., 2003).

Another way to study the effects of stress on memory has been to examine children's memories for medical procedures, some traumatic (such as trips to the emergency room) and others not (such as well-child pediatric exams). Concerning recollections of nontraumatic medical procedures, young children's memories for routine medical examinations tend to be very good (they remember most information) and accurate (they remember little incorrect information), at least when no misleading questions are asked (Baker-Ward et al., 1993; Ornstein et al., 2006). Older children remember more than younger children, and prior knowledge of the exam procedure is positively related to the amount of initial (but not delayed) recall of the events.

One particularly painful and embarrassing procedure is a voiding cystourethrogram (VCUG). Children are often restrained while a urinary catheter is inserted, and they are required to urinate during the medical procedure. Researchers have reported that children as young as 5 years of age report relatively accurate accounts of such procedures over delays longer than 1 month (Merritt, Ornstein, & Spicker, 1994; Pipe et al., 1997). Such a procedure involves many of the features of sexual abuse, making it a good model, some propose, for investigating the memories of children suspected of being victims of such abuse.

Other studies have interviewed children who are suspected or known victims of sexual abuse (Lamb & Thierry, 2005; Orbach & Lamb, 2007). In general, patterns of performance of these children in structured interviews are similar to what has been found in laboratory studies. Based on what can be confirmed from confessions of the abuser, younger children remember less information than older children, memory declines

The presence of certain objects, such as anatomically correct dolls, can also affect children's recollections. For instance, in one study, 3-year-old children were interviewed following a routine medical exam (Bruck et al., 1995). Half of the children received a genital exam by the doctor and half did not. Immediately following the examination, children were shown an anatomically correct doll and asked, "Did the doctor touch you here?", pointing to the genital area of the doll. About half of the children who received the genital exam answered correctly, whereas about half of those who did *not* receive a genital exam also said "yes." Children who said they had been touched by the doctor were then asked to "show on the doll" how the doctor had touched their genitals or buttocks. Twenty-five percent of the children who had received the genital exam responded correctly, and half of the children who did not receive the exam falsely showed anal or genital touching (see also Gordon et al., 1993). Other research indicates that interviewers who use dolls and other objects to aid recall ask fewer open-ended questions and are less likely to stay on topic than interviewers who do not use objects (Melinder et al., 2010). Results such as these call into question the use of anatomically correct dolls, at least with young children, indicating that the dolls may cause children to make accusations of abuse when no abuse occurred.

Most of the research we have presented so far has been performed under controlled conditions. However, developmental psychologists got involved in the topic of eyewitness testimony because of real-world questions about children's competencies to serve as witnesses. Some researchers have left the confines of the laboratory and investigated the over time, open-ended questions ("Tell me what happened") produce a higher ratio of correct-to-incorrect information than more specific cued questions ("Did he touch your private parts?"), and suggestive questions increase levels of inaccurate information (see Lamb & Thierry, 2005). Moreover, young children often recall more information about abuse than many laboratory studies would suggest when nonsuggestive open-ended prompts are used (Sternberg et al., 2001).

The abundance of research on children's eyewitness testimony has led to changes in how police officers, social workers, and people in the legal community interview children. As it turned out, many of the procedures traditionally used to interview children were highly suggestive, producing inaccurate information (Ceci & Bruck, 1995; Poole & Lamb, 1998). New interviewing techniques have been developed to help maximize children's accurate recall of potentially traumatic events while decreasing their recall of incorrect information (see Poole & Lamb, 1998, for reviews). For example, the National Institute of Child Health and Human Development (NICHD) protocol incorporates research findings from both laboratory and field settings (Lamb, Sternberg, & Esplin, 1998). It provides children with practice in recalling detailed accounts of events, it admonishes children to tell the truth, to say "I don't know" when they are uncertain, and to correct the interviewer when they are unsure (see Table). Although

these procedures, based on years of research into children's eyewitness testimony, do not guarantee that truth will always prevail, they increase the chances that, if abuse occurred, it will be identified, and if it did not, innocent people will not be accused of a crime.

Sequence of Phases Recommended by the NICHD Guidelines

1. Introduction of parties and their roles
2. The "truth and lie ceremony" (warning the child of the necessity to tell the truth)
3. Rapport building
4. Description of a recent salient event
5. First narrative account of the allegation
6. Narrative accounts of the last incident (if the child reports multiple incidents)
7. Cue question (for example, "You said something about a barn. Tell me about that.")
8. Paired direct-open questions about the last incident
9. Narrative account of first incident
10. Cue questions
11. Paired direct-open questions about the first incident
12. Narrative accounts of another incident that the child remembers
13. Cue questions
14. Paired direct-open questions about this incident
15. If necessary, leading questions about forensically important details not mentioned by the child
16. Invitation for any other information the child wants to mention

SOURCE: Adapted from Poole, D. A., & Lamb, M. E. (1998). *Investigative interviews of children: A guide for helping professionals.* Washington, DC: American Psychological Association, pp. 98, 99.

memories and accounts of children who are victims or suspected victims of sexual child abuse or who have undergone serious and uncomfortable medical procedures. Do the insights gained in the laboratory provide any guidance when working with children in the legal system? Are we able to develop better methods for interviewing children to enhance correct recall while minimizing false memories? Some of these issues are addressed in Box 8.4.

Interacting Factors

Research into the development of event memory in general, and eyewitness testimony in particular, has been one of the most investigated areas in cognitive development over the past two decades. Although we have learned a lot, we have also learned that there are no simple answers. A multitude of factors influence children's memories and

their susceptibility to suggestion, with these factors interacting in often complicated ways (Ghetti, 2008; Lindberg, 1991; Pipe & Salmon, 2009).

The complex and interactive nature of children's eyewitness memory is reflected in Figure 8.14 from Marc Lindberg (1991), who suggested that three major categories of factors must be considered in evaluating children's eyewitness memory and suggestibility (Lindberg, 1991; Lindberg et al., 2000). As you can see in the figure, the first important category is memory processes, consisting of different memory operations, such as the encoding, storage, and retrieval of information. Children's encoding can be affected by their expectations (for example, "That Sam Stone is always getting into accidents and breaking things!"). Once information is encoded and stored in memory, it can still be altered by subsequent experience, for

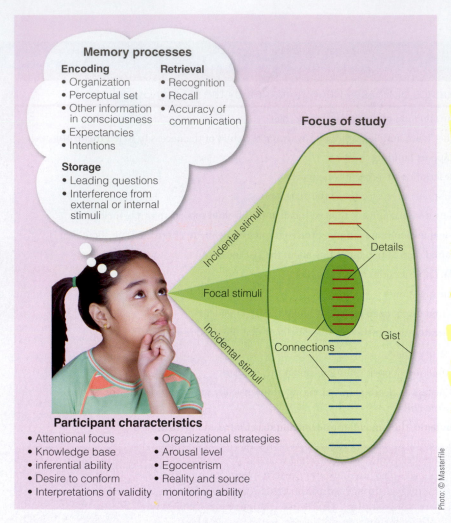

Memory processes

Encoding
- Organization
- Perceptual set
- Other information in consciousness
- Expectancies
- Intentions

Retrieval
- Recognition
- Recall
- Accuracy of communication

Storage
- Leading questions
- Interference from external or internal stimuli

Focus of study

Incidental stimuli

Focal stimuli

Incidental stimuli

Details

Gist

Connections

Photo: © Masterfile

Participant characteristics
- Attentional focus
- Knowledge base
- inferential ability
- Desire to conform
- Interpretations of validity
- Organizational strategies
- Arousal level
- Egocentrism
- Reality and source monitoring ability

FIGURE 8.14 Three major interacting classes of variables in interpreting children's eyewitness memory and suggestibility.

SOURCE: From Lindberg, M. A. (1991). An interactive approach to assessing the suggestibility and testimony of eyewitnesses. In J. Doris (Ed.), The suggestibility of children's recollections: Implications for eyewitness testimony (pp. 47–55). Washington, DC: American Psychological Association. Reprinted by permission.

instance, suggestive questions ("He ripped the book, didn't he?"). Events at time of retrieval, or recall, can also influence children's reports. For example, how is memory tested? With open-ended (free-recall) questions, cued-recall questions, or recognition? How are these questions posed?

The second category in Lindberg's taxonomy is the *focus of study*, by which he means the type of information that is being assessed. For instance, is the interviewer concerned with psychologically and legally central information (who did what to whom, critical in determining innocence or guilt in court), or is peripheral (incidental) information also important (What color shirt was the girl wearing? What type of bike was it?)?

The final category includes *participant factors.* These include the developmental abilities of children, their social, emotional, and cognitive skills, as well as their knowledge base (for example, knowing a lot versus a little about an upcoming medical procedure). Other factors can also affect children's performance, such as how stressed children were at the time of the event (or at time of retrieval), personality variables (are they anxious by nature, outgoing, withdrawn?), and their previous experiences with a situation.

As this figure shows, the factors involved in children's eyewitness memory are complex, and psychologists, police officers, and members of the legal profession can never be certain that they have a handle on every factor in any particular case. However, researchers have generally been aware of the complexity of the problem, and as a result have provided useful information, not only to educators and cognitive theorists, but also to the legal system.

Prospective Memory

Up to this point, we have been talking about the development of *retrospective memory*—remembering things that happened in the past. There is another type of memory, however, and that is **prospective memory**, which refers to remembering to do something in the future. For example, you may say to yourself that you have to stop at the store to pick up bread on the way home tonight. If you succeed in doing that, you show good prospective memory. If you arrive home and have no bread to make yourself a sandwich, you have displayed a failure of prospective memory (Einstein & McDaniel, 2005). In one of the earliest developmental studies of prospective memory, Susan Somerville and her colleagues (1983) asked children's parents to remind them to perform some task in the future, for instance, "Remind me to buy milk when we go to the store tomorrow." Some tasks were of high interest to children (for example, buying candy at the store), others were of low interest, (for example, bringing in the wash), and sometimes the delay was short (1 to 5 minutes) and other times long (morning to afternoon, or evening to the next day).

The pattern of performance was relatively similar for 2-, 3-, and 4-year-old children, and the results can be seen in Figure 8.15. Even the 2-year-olds were very good at reminding their parents when the task was one of high interest and the delay was short (5 minutes or less), succeeding 80% of the time. However, performance for all children dropped sharply for the low-interest and long-delay tasks, with none of the 2-year-olds spontaneously remembering to remind their parents about a low-interest task over a long delay. Children of all ages did a bit better when they were given a prompt ("Was there something you were supposed to remind me to do?"), improving their performance by about one-third, on average. These results suggest that motivation plays an important role in when children display prospective memory, as well as the length of time they have to wait.

---

prospective memory Remembering to do something in the future.

More recent research using controlled laboratory tasks has shown that 2-year-olds rarely perform as well as Somerville's youngest children did (Kliegel & Jäger, 2007) and that prospective memory continues to improve over the school years (Kerns, 2000; Smith, Bayen, & Martin, 2010). For example, in one study, 7- to 12-year-old children played a computer game called CyberCruiser in which they used a joystick to maneuver around obstacles. In addition, they were reminded to check occasionally to make sure they did not run out of gas and to fill up when they had less than a quarter tank of gas left. Younger children ran out of gas more often than older children did (Kerns, 2000).

Prospective memory requires a host of cognitive skills, among them a symbolic system that can represent the self in the future, which is the essence of episodic memory, and executive function (Causey & Bjorklund, 2009; MacKinlay, Kliegel, & Mäntylä, 2009). Apparently, under some limited conditions with delays of 5 minutes or less, this is something that 2-year-old children can do. However, the tendency to anticipate the future develops with age, as children's representational abilities, memories, and executive functions improve (see Atance, 2008; Kerns, 2000).

Memory is the core of cognition. Without memory there could be no learning. We remember situations that have been associated with both good and bad outcomes and the actions we took that both got us in and out of trouble. We use memory to get us through the trials and tribulations of daily life—to solve the multitude of problems that each of us faces every day. Despite some claims we often hear from laypeople, children do not remember events better than adults. Rather, event memory improves with age. Although even 2- and 3-year-old children can remember events for brief intervals, true autobiographical memory requires a sense of self and a way of relating events to other people via language. In fact, Alison Gopnik (2009) has suggested that 2- and 3-year-old children may have episodic memory but not autobiographical memory. Although they are quite capable of remembering specific past events, "they do not experience their lives as a single timeline stretching back into the past and forward into the future. They don't send themselves backward and forward along this timeline as adults do. . . . Instead, the memories are images, and thoughts pop in and out of consciousness as they are cued by present events, or by other memories, images, and thoughts" (pp. 153, 154).

Like adults, children's memory is fallible. When serving as witnesses, for example, they are susceptible to suggestion, their prior knowledge and expectations affect their likelihood of recalling events, as does how an interview is conducted. Despite their generally more suggestible nature, the accuracy of children's recollections can be predicted by knowing something about the social, cognitive, and emotional state of the child and the contexts in which the witnessed event and the interview occurred. We may never be able to guarantee the veracity of a child's memory (or that of an adult, for that matter), but developmental science has made great leaps in understanding children's memory and factors that affect its accuracy.

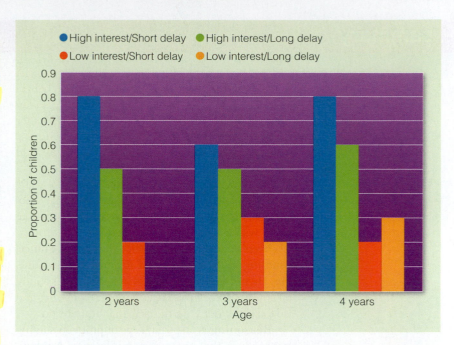

FIGURE 8.15 Proportion of children who reminded their parents to perform some task for 2-, 3-, and 4-year-old children for high- and low-interest tasks over short and long delays.
SOURCE: Adapted from Somerville, S. C., Wellman, H. M., & Cultice, J. C. (1983). Young children's deliberate reminding. *Journal of Genetic Psychology, 143,* 87–96.

With increasing age, children are better able to exert intentional control over their thoughts and behaviors. **Problem solving** involves having a goal, determining obstacles to that goal, devising strategies for overcoming the obstacles, and evaluating the results. Infants show signs of **goal-directed behavior** and problem solving in the latter part of the first year. Problem solving improves over the preschool years and is influenced by how much knowledge the problem solver has about the task to be solved or the context in which the task is embedded.

Even young children adopt the **design stance**, assuming tools are designed for an intended function. Higher levels of tool use are sometimes found for boys than for girls. Other animals construct and use tools, but not with the skill that humans do.

Reasoning is a special type of problem solving that requires that one make an inference. **Analogical reasoning** involves applying what one knows about one set of elements to relationships about different elements. Young children can solve analogical problems if they know the relationships among items. **Scientific reasoning** involves generating hypotheses about how something in the world works and then systematically testing those hypotheses and is a late-developing ability.

Executive function (or **control**) refers to the processes involved in regulating attention and in determining what to do with information just gathered or retrieved from long-term memory. It involves a related set of basic information-processing abilities, including **speed of processing**, **memory span** and **working memory**, attention, as reflected by **attention span**, **selective attention**, and **inhibition** and **resistance to interference**, and **cognitive flexibility**, each of which develops with age and is related to performance on a host of other cognitive tasks. **Attention-deficit hyperactivity disorder (ADHD)** is a common childhood disorder associated with deficient executive control.

Strategies are deliberately implemented, nonobligatory operations that are potentially available to consciousness and used to improve task performance. Children who fail to use a strategy spontaneously can often be trained to use one and improve task performance, called a **production deficiency**. Although both strategy use and task performance typically increase with age, children frequently display a **utilization deficiency**, using a strategy without experiencing any benefit from its use. Siegler's **adaptive strategy choice model** proposes that children have a variety of strategies available to them at any one time and that these strategies compete for use, with strategies changing in frequency over time.

Many factors influence children's strategy use, including *mental capacity*, as reflected by working memory; **knowledge base**, how much children know about the problems they are trying to solve; and **metacognition**, an awareness of one's cognitive abilities.

Rehearsal is an effective strategy in some memory tasks, with younger children engaging in **passive rehearsal**, usually repeating only one unique word at a time, whereas older children are more apt to engage in **active**, or **cumulative**, **rehearsal**, repeating many different words in the same rehearsal set. **Organization** is another memory strategy, with children **clustering** their recall according to category membership.

Memory can refer to the process of bringing information to consciousness (remembering) or to the contents of memory. **Implicit cognition**, or cognition without awareness, is distinguished from **explicit cognition**, or cognition with awareness. **Declarative**, or **explicit, memory** includes **episodic memory**, memory for specific events or episodes, and **semantic memory**, knowledge of language, rules, and concepts. In contrast, **implicit**, (or **nondeclarative** or **procedural**) **memory** refers to knowledge of procedures that are unconscious. Developmental differences are small or nonexistent for nondeclarative memory and substantially larger for declarative memory.

Fuzzy-trace theory assumes that memory representations exist on a continuum from **verbatim** to **fuzzy**, or gist-like, **traces**. People generally prefer to think with fuzzy rather than verbatim traces, but this develops, with young children showing more of a verbatim bias than do older children. Fuzzy-trace theory assumes that output interference causes deterioration of performance and that younger children are more susceptible to the effects of output interference than older children or adults are.

Infantile amnesia refers to the inability to recall information from infancy and early childhood. Current theories of infantile amnesia focus on the development of self-concept, developmental differences in how information is encoded, and changes in children's use of language to communicate their memories to others. The offset of infantile amnesia reflects the beginning of **autobiographical memory**, which refers to personal and long-lasting memories that are the basis for one's personal life history.

Young children's event memory is based on **scripts**, a form of schematic organization with real-world events organized by their causal and temporal characteristics. Children's early memories tend to be for routine experiences.

Much current research in event memory has focused on children as eyewitnesses. Young children's free recall of witnessed events is typically low,

accurate, and about central aspects of an event. The accuracy of children's event memory is influenced by a host of factors, including their knowledge for the event they experienced and characteristics of the interview. Young children are generally more susceptible than are older children to misleading questions (suggestions) and misinformation and can easily be caused to form false memories. Research examining children's memory for potentially traumatic events in the real world, such as uncomfortable medical procedures and sexual abuse, have confirmed many of the findings from laboratory studies and led to improved ways of interviewing child witnesses.

Prospective memory, remembering to do something in the future, is an ability that develops over the preschool years, although it continues to develop into adolescence.

Key Terms and Concepts

problem solving (p. 306)
goal-directed behavior (p. 306)
design stance (p. 308)
reasoning (p. 310)
analogical reasoning (p. 310)
scientific reasoning (p. 311)
executive function (control) (p. 313)
speed of processing (p. 313)
memory span (p. 313)
working memory (p. 313)
attention span (p. 315)
selective attention (p. 315)
inhibition (p. 317)

resistance to interference (p. 317)
cognitive flexibility (p. 318)
attention deficit hyperactivity disorder
    (ADHD) (p. 320)
production deficiency (p. 322)
utilization deficiency (p. 322)
adaptive strategy choice model (p. 323)
rehearsal (p. 324)
passive rehearsal (p. 324)
active (or cumulative) rehearsal (p. 324)
organization (in recall) (p.324)
clustering (p. 324)
knowledge base (p. 325)

metacognition (p. 326)
explicit (declarative) memory (p. 327)
episodic memory (p. 327)
semantic memory (p. 327)
implicit (nondeclarative or procedural)
    memory (p. 328)
fuzzy traces (p. 330)
fuzzy-trace theory (p. 330)
verbatim traces (p. 330)
autobiographical memory (p. 331)
infantile amnesia (p. 331)
scripts (p. 333)
prospective memory (p. 340)

Ask Yourself . . .

1. What is involved in problem solving, and how does it develop over childhood into adolescencs? What role do tools play in children's developing problem-solving skills?
2. What is meant by executive function, and what are the specific cognitive skills that comprise it?
3. How do the various components of executive function develop, and what are the consequences it has for other forms of psychological functioning?
4. What are cognitive strategies, why are they important for development, and how do they generally change over childhood?
5. What does Siegler's adaptive strategy choice model add to psychologists' understanding of strategy development?

6. How do the various memory strategies children typically use change over childhood and adolescence?
7. What three majors factors influence the memory strategies that children use?
8. What different types (and subtypes) of memory have psychologists identified? What are the developmental differences between implicit and explicit memory in children?
9. What is known about the development of autobiographical memory and the reasons for infantile amnesia? How do children remember and organize events in memory?
10. What are the major age differences found in children's eyewitness memory? How suggestible are children, and what factors affect the accuracy of their memories?

Exercises: Going Further

1. Think about some simple problems that school-age children and adolescents have to solve in their everyday lives in and out school, for example: (1) adding a set of numbers; (2) finding a pen in their backpack; (3) making lunch for themselves; (4) trying to make a new friend. Then analyze each problem in terms of the elements that are involved, the type of tools (if any) and reasoning used, and the five basic cognitive abilities implicated in executive function (speed of processing, working memory, attention, inhibition/resistance to interference, and cognitive flexibility). Eventually, describe what sort of difficulties a child with ADHD might face solving the same problems.

2. Learning to study is often a critical skill for success in school. Based on what you have read in this chapter on the development of strategies, particularly memory strategies, make a list of at least five points or recommendations you would give to children (and, if necessary, also to parents and teachers) that would help them to better remember what they learn at school.

3. You recently heard on the TV news that a former preschool teacher who had been convicted of abusing young children at the daycare center she owned was freed, after 3 years in prison, after it was discovered that the testimonies of children against her were false. Based on what you have read on children's eyewitness memory in this chapter, what do you think might have happened that resulted in this legal mistake, and how might it have been prevented?

Suggested Readings

Classic Work

Flavell, J. H. (1971). First discussants comments: What is memory development the development of? *Human Development, 14*, 272–278. This paper is the published version of John Flavell's discussion for one of the earliest symposia devoted to children's memory presented at the 1970 meeting of the Society for Research in Child Development. It is considered by many to reflect the beginning of the modern study of memory development.

Klahr, D., & Wallace, J. G. (1976). *Cognitive development: An information processing view.* Hillsdale, NJ: Erlbaum. After Piaget, information-processing approaches have been the most influential in the study of children's thinking and dominated the field over the last 30 years. In this classic book, David Klahr and John Wallace were among the first to describe the main assumptions of this approach to cognitive development.

Scholarly Work

Brainerd, C. J., & Reyna, V. F. (2005). T*he science of false memory.* Oxford, UK: Oxford University Press. This book, by the originators of fuzzy-trace theory, provides a detailed look at the research and theory pertinent to false memory creation in general, including research on children as eyewitnesses and the extent to which they remember falsely or can be misled. The book also provides an excellent account of fuzzy-trace theory. A concise summary of this work can be found in Brainerd, C. J., & Reyna, V. F. (2002). Fuzzy-trace theory and false memory. *Current Directions in Psychological Science, 11*, 164–169.

Siegler, R. S. (2000). The rebirth of learning. *Child Development, 71*, 26–35. This short paper presents some of the basic ideas of Siegler's adaptive strategy choice model, including how to use the microgenetic method to study children's learning.

Bjorklund, D. F. (2012). *Children's thinking: Cognitive development and individual differences (5th ed.).* Belmont, CA: Wadsworth. This is basically an advanced textbook on cognitive development that describes in a succinct and accessible way what is known about the various cognitive processes involved in children's thinking, including each of the topics discussed in this chapter.

Reading for Personal Interest

Thornton, S. (1998). *Children solving problems.* Cambridge, MA: Harvard University Press. This relatively old book from the Developing Child series still offers an accessible and interesting summary of some post-Piagetian research findings on cognitive development, as well as a readable account of why problem solving should be at the foundation of cognitive development research.

Lamb, M. E., Hershkowitz, I., Orbach, Y., & Esplin, P. W. (2008). *Tell me what happened: Structured investigative interviews of children victims and witnesses.* Wiley: West Sussex, England. Child forensic science is one of the fields in which cognitive development research has had a great practical impact. This book, written by leading researchers in the field, provides a recent summary of how professionals (for example, psychologists, police officers, social workers) should approach children suspected of abuse and child witnesses to obtain reliable accounts of what happened.

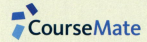

CourseMate

Cengage Learning's **Psychology CourseMate** for this text brings course concepts to life with interactive learning, study, and exam preparation tools, including quizzes and flashcards for this chapter's Key Terms and Concepts (see the summary list on page 343). The site also provides an **eBook** version of the text with highlighting and note taking capabilities, as well as an extensive library of observational videos that span early childhood through adolescence. Many videos are accompanied by questions that will help you think critically about and deepen your understanding of the chapter topics addressed, especially as they pertain to core concepts. Log on and learn more at **www.cengagebrain.com**.

9

Language Development

We begin this chapter by asking, "What is language?" We then look at nativist and social-interactionist theories of language acquisition. We next examine the various aspects of language development, including phonological, semantic, grammatical, and pragmatic development, followed by an examination of language development in atypical populations and bilingualism. We conclude the chapter with a look at the developmental relationship between language and thought.

"Me and Aunt Carol goed to the store and we seed a lady and all the onjes falled all over the floor! I dint do it, the lady did! I could of got hurt, but I dint." What can we gleam from this three-sentence statement by 3-year-old Matthew? Quite obviously, Matthew is speaking English, although the grammar is not perfect. He also has trouble pronouncing some words. "Oranges" comes out "onjes," and "didn't" comes out "dint," and his use of the past-tense verbs "goed," "seed," and "falled" makes it clear that he is not a fluent speaker of English yet. Despite these shortcomings, however, we should be impressed by the complicated ideas Matthew was able to communicate in three continuous breaths. His grasp of the language is really quite good for a little guy.

Language is a complicated phenomenon. As adults, we produce and understand language so effortlessly that it is easy to forget what a complex process it is and that children somehow become linguistic geniuses over the course of just a few years. Perhaps the first thing to realize is that language is a special form of communication, qualitatively different from the ways in which other animals send messages back and forth to one another.

What Is Language?

At its most basic level, language refers to the systematic and conventional use of sounds, signs, or written symbols for the intention of communication or self-expression (Hoff, 2009). But not all communication systems constitute language, at least as defined by human linguists. Although other animals have often-complex means of communicating (for example, the "dances" of honeybees

347

Although other animals, such as these bees, have complicated communication systems, none of these systems has the qualities of human language.

that inform other hive members of the location of flowers), these systems differ in important ways from human language. As Michael Tomasello (2006) points out, human language differs from the communication systems of other species in three important ways:

1. It is *symbolic*. The sounds of spoken language or the hand movements of sign language *represent* something independent of the actual sounds or movements.

2. It is *grammatical*. Each language has a system of rules that permits a speaker to produce and understand sentences that have never been uttered before. A language does not have a set number of sentences that all speakers memorize.

3. Although all biologically typical people acquire language, the particular language children learn to speak varies with culture.

Acquiring a language implies developing expertise in the *form* of the language (phonol-

---

phonology The actual sounds that speakers produce.

semantics The understanding of words and sentences.

grammar The linguistic rules for "tuning" words and putting words together into phrases or sentences.

pragmatics Knowledge about how language can be adjusted to fit different people and circumstances.

ogy and the structure of words and sentences), the *meaning* of language (as accomplished both through semantics and grammar), and the *use* of language (pragmatics) (Bloom, 1998; Bloom & Lahey, 1978). This means that language is made up of many components. For example, phonology can be described as the actual sounds that speakers produce; semantics refers to the underlying abstract meaning of language (the definition of those words and concepts); grammar has to do with the linguistic rules for tuning words and putting words together into phrases or sentences; and pragmatics deals with how people actually use language in a social context, or the ability to use language to get things done in the world.

Later in this chapter we examine the developmental course for each aspect of language, but first we delve into the thorny issue of *how* children acquire language, examining two major theoretical approaches to the topic.

How Children Acquire Language

Overall, we think it is quite impressive that children become experts in something as complicated as a human language within the span of five or six years. How do they do it? What are the processes by which children acquire a language, and are they similar or different from the processes they use in mastering other content such as arithmetic, navigating their neighborhoods, or learning proper social etiquette? This brings us to the realm of theory, and most of the theoretical debate surrounding language acquisition has focused on grammar. For example, children learn relatively early how to make verbs past tense, how to form questions, and how to negate a sentence, changing, for instance, the statement "You can dance" to "You can't dance," or even to "Can you dance?" This may not seem all that complicated to you, but try to describe the rules you use to make these simple conversions. They turn out to be quite complicated. Given the complexity of grammar, how are children able to master it in such a brief period of time, when their more general social and cognitive abilities seem not all that sophisticated (or at least not as sophisticated as they will become)?

At one theoretical extreme is the *empiricist position*, which holds that language is acquired the way every other complex ability is acquired, via the mechanisms of learning. This now mostly discredited position was advocated by the radical behaviorist B. F. Skinner (1957), who proposed that children learn not only words, but also grammar, via the mechanisms of operant and classical conditioning. At one level, children do learn language from experience. After all, children are not born with knowledge of one language or another but learn to speak and understand the language of their culture. Yet, most researchers today do not believe that grammar is acquired simply by conditioning. For instance, for the most part, parents do not comment on the grammatical correctness of their young children's speech but focus more on its meaning (Brown & Hanlon, 1970), which makes it difficult to explain how children could learn grammar via the principles of reinforcement. Imitation surely plays a role in language development, but not likely the role that Skinner and other behaviorists proposed. For instance, children typically do not imitate new grammatical forms, such as present progressive ("walking") or past-tense ("walked") verbs, until they are able to produce them on their own (Bloom, Hood, & Lightbown, 1974), making imitation an unlikely mechanism for acquiring grammar. Moreover, although 2- and 3-year-old children hear between 5,000 and 7,000 utterances each day, more than 20% of those utterances are typically incomplete sentence fragments, and only about 15% are in the subject-verb-object form that is standard for English (Cameron-Faulkner, Lieven, & Tomasello, 2003). Given all this, it is unlikely that children acquire language following the rules of operant conditioning.

Contemporary theoretical perspectives acknowledge that a child's language environment is important for language acquisition, but they also hold that children are especially prepared for learning language. Differences between theories focus on what children are prepared to learn. Proponents of nativist theories essentially argue that children are born with a broad theory of language that they modify in accordance with the speech they hear growing up. From this perspective, language development is a *domain-specific* skill (or perhaps a series of domain-specific skills), and the cognitive processes involved in learning a language are different from those used for other purposes. An alternative theoretical approach, the social-interactionist perspective, holds that language acquisition grows out of children's social interaction with others and is based in large part on their developing social-cognitive abilities, such as those we discussed in Chapter 7 (for instance, treating others as intentional agents, perspective taking). Although some processes may be unique to language, they are embedded within the more domain-general set of social-cognitive abilities and children's active participation in the social world. In the following sections we examine some of the evidence for each of these positions.

Nativist Theories of Language Development

Nativist theories of language development date back to ancient times. The Greek historian Herodotus related the account of King Psammetichus of Egypt, who commanded that a child be raised in total vocal isolation, never hearing a word from another human being. The King believed that the first word that such a child uttered would be from the world's oldest language. The first word this child allegedly spoke was *bekos*, the Phrygian word for bread, giving credence that Phrygian was the world's oldest language. This is only the most ancient of many stories of children being reared without language, with different accounts claiming evidence for a different oldest language (Bonvillian, Garber, & Dell, 1997). This is a nativist theory in the extreme—that the specific language humans speak is innate (although clearly modified by culture, otherwise everyone would be speaking Phrygian). Modern nativist theorists obviously do not make similar arguments. What they do propose, however, is that the structures and processes involved in acquiring language are innate and that when children are exposed to a typical language environment, they use these mechanisms to learn their mother tongue. In the words of Steven Pinker (1994), children possess a *language instinct*.

On what basis do nativists make these claims? First, the general claim is that language is a unique human ability with a strong biological basis. This argument was originally made mostly to refute the claims by learning theorists that language was the result of operant and classical conditioning. More than 40 years ago, Eric Lenneberg (1967) championed the position that language was based in biology, not in learning, arguing that at least six characteristics make it unlikely that language is learned in the way other abilities are learned. According to Lenneberg, language (1) is species specific, (2) is species uniform, (3) is difficult to prevent, (4) develops in a regular sequence, (5) has specific anatomical structures associated with its use, and (6) is sometimes affected by language disabilities that are genetically based (see Table 9.1).

This evidence makes it clear that language development has a basis in biology—that it is not simply the product of learning but a part of *Homo sapiens'* more general nature. But saying that language is based in biology, by itself, does not tell us a whole lot. We need to look at more specific theories

....

nativist theories (of language acquisition) Theories that propose that children are born with a broad theory of language that they modify in accordance with the speech they hear growing up. .

social-interactionist perspective (of language acquisition) The position that children's domain-general social-cognitive abilities and the social environment play a central role in language development.

table 9.1 Six Characteristics of Language Learning

According to Lenneberg (1967), at least six characteristics make it unlikely that language is learned in the way other abilities are learned:

1. *Language is species-specific.* Only humans possess language. Although some apes can be taught simple sign language (Savage-Rumbaugh et al., 1993), their syntactic ability is less than that of a 2-year-old child at best, and their vocabulary is limited to about 150 words (see Goméz, 2005).

2. *Language is species-uniform.* All typically developing members of *Homo sapiens* possess language.

3. *Language is difficult to prevent.* All but the most intellectually impaired children or children reared in social isolation (as the poor subject of King Psammetichus's ancient experiment) acquire language.

4. *Language develops in a regular sequence.* Children around the world acquire language in about the same way at about the same time. This is similar to the universal sequence of motor development (see Chapter 4).

5. *There are specific anatomical structures for language.* The structure of the mouth and throat are specially suited for producing speech, and specific areas of the brain are dedicated to processing language. Damage to these speech areas can result in specific types of *aphasia*, or language disability.

6. *There are language disabilities that are genetically based.* Specific language disorders run in families, suggesting that there is a genetic basis for these disorders, with some apparently being controlled by a dominant gene (Gopnik & Crago, 1991).

and research to get a better picture of how children acquire language. We do this briefly in the following sections. We first examine evidence for a *universal grammar* that all children begin life with and modify until it resembles the language spoken around them. We then look at research suggesting that there is a sensitive period for language—a time when the child is biologically prepared to learn language. Finally, Box 9.1 looks at evidence for specialization of brain function related to language, consistent with the idea that language development is governed by domain-specific neural systems.

Universal Grammar

The idea of an innate **universal grammar** is credited to the linguist Noam Chomsky (1957; for a more contemporary and accessible elaboration, see Pinker, 1994). Universal grammar refers to the basic grammatical rules that typify all languages. Children compare the structure of the language they hear to the innate grammar they were born with and make appropriate modifications. To do this task, Chomsky proposed that children are born with a specialized "mental organ," the **language acquisition device (LAD)**. Thus, they do not start out learning language cold, but they have a head start in that they possess a rudimentary theory of how the speech that surrounds them should be structured. Having an innate theory of grammar makes it easier for them to make sense of what they hear. Not all interpretations are possible; there are constraints in how words can be organized to convey meaning, and children take advantage of these constraints in figuring out the particular grammar of their mother tongue.

Children do not actually know any language at birth. They possess a set of *principles* and *parameters* that help them interpret the speech they hear. Parameters, as used here, refer to aspects of a grammar that vary across languages. For instance, all sentences in all languages have subjects. This is a universal principle; but whether or not a subject has to be explicitly stated to make a proper sentence is a parameter. In some languages, such as English, French, German, and Hindi, the subject must (usually) be stated to form a grammatical sentence (for example, "I love you" in English, "Je t'aime" in French, "Ich liebe dich" in German, "Main Tumse Prem Karta Hoon" in Hindi). In other languages, however, you can often get away without explicitly stating the subject of a sentence (for example, "Te amo" in Spanish, "Ti amo" in Italian, "Kocham cie-bie" in Polish, "Asavakit," in Greenlandic).

What children must learn from what they hear around them is whether their language requires the subject to be explicitly stated or not. Some evidence that children actually do this is that young English-speaking children often drop the subject in their simple sentences, which is not permitted in English but is in other languages (Bloom, Lightbown, & Hood, 1975). For instance, young children often say things like "Drink milk," "Want more," "Help Daddy," or "Kick ball." Adults can usually understand what children mean from this linguistic shorthand, given context. But children do not arbitrarily drop words; they seem to assume that the subject of the sentence (in all cases here, the first person singular) will be understood without being explicitly stated. (English does not always require that the subject be stated. In sentences such as "Pick me up," "Answer the phone," or "Turn left at the light," the subject "you" is implied and need not be stated.) Figure 9.1 pres-

universal grammar In nativist theories of language acquisition, the innate grammar that characterizes all human languages.

language acquisition device (LAD) In Chomsky's theory, an innate mechanism possessed by all humans at birth in order to enable them to acquire any language given a minimum linguistic input.

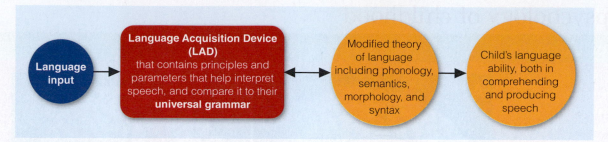

FIGURE 9.1 How some nativists view language development.
Children compare the language they hear (language input) to their innate universal grammar, via principles and parameters specified in the Language Acquisition Device. As a result, children modify their theory of language for all of the basic aspects of language (phonology, semantics, morphology, and syntax), which influences both how new language input is processed and children's language competence.

ents a simple model for how some nativists view language development.

Nativists point to the many similarities across the world's languages as support for universal grammar. For instance, all languages have extensive vocabularies divided into parts-of-speech categories that include nouns and verbs; all use prefixes and suffixes for nouns and verbs (for example, adding the "s" to make a noun plural in English); and all permit movement of grammatical categories, such as the subject-auxiliary inversion used to change declarative sentences in English into questions (for example, "I am invited" is transformed to "Am I invited?") (Hoff, 2009; Pinker, 1994). Also, children around the world acquire language at about the same rate, make the same types of grammatical mistakes, and acquire many of the same grammatical forms, further support for the presence of universal grammar and a language acquisition device.

Other evidence for universal grammar comes from research demonstrating that children will invent real languages (termed *creoles*) when exposed to the not-quite-real languages (termed *pidgins*) that adults around them speak. In fact, some have suggested that children's inventiveness when it comes to language is a principal reason why language evolved, and these ideas are examined in Box 9.2.

Is There a Sensitive Period for Acquiring Language?

Is it easier to learn a language as a child than as an adult? Is it ever too late to learn a language? If a child has not acquired a language by a certain age, is it possible that he or she will never master language? Do children learning a first language use different cognitive processes than adults do when they try to learn a second language? These questions are at the heart of the idea that there is a sensitive period for language acquisition—that children must be exposed to language early in life if they are ever to master it. A sensitive period implies that the brains of children are specially suited to learning language—any language—but with time, experience, and brain maturation, they lose their special knack for language learning, making it more difficult to learn a first or second language. This contention is consistent with a nativist perspective of language acquisition.

There are at least four sources of evidence for a sensitive period for language acquisition (Locke, 1993) (See Concept Review 9.1). First, children who experience social isolation during their childhoods rarely acquire more than a tentative mastery of language, especially grammar (Curtiss, 1977). In Chapter 1, we discussed briefly the case of Genie, a child who had been confined to her room and chained to a chair by her schizophrenic father until she was about 13 years of age. Although Genie showed substantial physical improvements as a result of educational intervention following her rescue, her level of language, particularly grammar, remained immature (Curtiss, 1977). Also discussed in Chapter 1, the occasional cases of feral, or wild, children that have been documented indicate that such children do not learn to speak with any proficiency, if at all, if they were not already speaking when they were discovered.

The second source of evidence for a sensitive period for language development comes from

---

concept review | 9.1 Evidence for a sensitive period for language acquisition

1. Children who experience prolonged social isolation rarely become proficient language users.

2. The older people are when they are first exposed to a second language, the less proficient they are in the grammar of that language, as well as in pronunciation.

3. Hearing-impaired children who are not exposed to sign language until later in life show less proficiency in American Sign Language than do hearing-impaired children who are exposed to sign language at an earlier age.

4. Recovery of language function as a result of brain damage is greater the earlier the brain damage occurs.

BOX 9.1 # the biopsychology of childhood

This Is Your Brain on Language

It has long been known that specific areas of the brain are associated with language functioning, at least in adults. Until relatively recently, most evidence of brain specialization came from studies of people with brain damage. For example, brain damage to specific areas in the left hemisphere (in right-handed people) results in specific language deficits. Damage to *Broca's area*, located in the frontal lobes, usually results in problems with speech production, whereas damage to *Wernicke's area*, located in the temporal lobe, results in problems comprehending speech, although the ability to produce speech is not usually affected (Martin, 2003). In recent decades, advances in neuroimaging technologies have provided researchers a glimpse into how the brains of intact people work while they are performing routine tasks. This research has not only confirmed the findings of the earlier brain-damage studies, but permitted scientists to examine how various aspects of language processing are reflected in brain activity and how they change over the course of development (see Sakai, 2005).

The accompanying figures present the left side of an adult brain. Figure A identifies different areas of the brain that are primarily involved in different aspects of language processing: phonology, semantics, syntax, and sentence comprehension (from Sakai, 2005). This does not mean that other areas of the brain are not also involved in language processing, for they most certainly are. Rather, these areas have been identified as being specialized for particular types of language processing. In other words, they correspond to domain-specific abilities associated with language, as hypothesized by nativist theorists.

Figure B represents what Kuniyoshi Sakai (2005) refers to as the **grammar center**, an

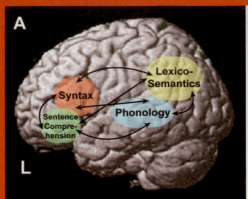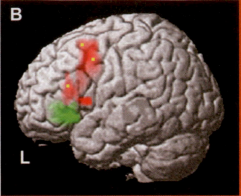

This figure shows two views of the left hemisphere. Figure A shows possible networks for various language functions. Figure B shows the grammar center and other areas involved in language, as proposed by Sakai (2005). The green area is selectively involved in comprehending sentences. The red areas are specifically involved in syntactic processing and can be regarded as the grammar center. SOURCE: From Sakai, K. L. (2005). Language acquisition and brain development. *Science, 310*, 815–919, p. 817.

area in the frontal lobe that is specifically related to processing grammatical information. This area is not only involved in processing syntax, but it also appears to be a domain-specific neural system dedicated to this task. For example, in a neuroimaging experiment, activation of the grammar center was found only when making syntactic decisions (for example, is a sentence grammatical or not?), and not on tasks involving verbal short-term memory (for example, recalling a list of words in exact orders) (Hashimoto & Sakai, 2002). This and related work caused Sakai (2005, p. 817) to conclude that "the human left frontal cortex is thus uniquely specialized in the syntactic processes of sentence comprehension, without any counterparts in other animals."

When does such hemispheric specialization begin in development? Unfortunately, there is not as much brain-imaging research on language processing in children as there is in adults. However, as you may recall from

our discussion of brain development in Chapter 4, the left hemispheres of even newborns display greater electrical activation to language than do the right hemispheres, with music and other nonlanguage sounds showing the opposite pattern (Molfese & Molfese, 1980, 1985). There is also some evidence that children's brains are especially sensitive to learning language and that different parts of the brain, in addition to those used to process language in adults' brains, are involved in language acquisition (specifically the frontal, cerebellar, and occipital regions, Redcay, Haist, & Courchesne, 2008).

Some evidence suggests that early aspects of phonology, such as babbling, are tied to areas of the brain that will later process true language. How can we know whether babbling is truly a component of later language development or merely a reflection of the exercising of the vocal apparatus, or perhaps having a function independent of true language? For instance, some

observations of people learning a second language. Although adults clearly are able to learn a second language, the later someone is exposed to a new language, the more difficult it is for him or her to acquire it, especially pronunciation and complex grammar (see Locke, 1993). Although many adults

have first-hand experience with this (despite making the effort, one of the book's authors has never been able to attain more than a toddler-level mastery of several different European languages), solid experimental evidence is harder to come by.

In one study, 46 native Chinese and Korean speakers who had immigrated to the United States between the ages of 3 and 39 years and had lived in the United States between 3 and 26 years

grammar center An area in the frontal lobe that is specifically related to processing grammatical information.

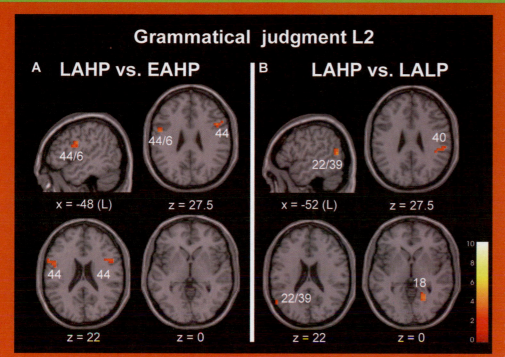

Grammatical judgment L2

A LAHP vs. EAHP

44/6
44/6
44/6
44
x = -48 (L)   z = 27.5

44   44
z = 22   z = 0

B LAHP vs. LALP

22/39
40
x = -52 (L)   z = 27.5

22/39
18
z = 22   z = 0

Bilingual speakers made grammatical judgments in their second language. For adults who were highly proficient in both languages (A), different parts of the brain were involved in making grammatical judgments for those who learned their second language late (LAHP) versus those who learned their second language early (EAHP). When considering people only who learned their second language late, different areas of the brain were involved for people with high-language proficiency (LAHP) versus low-language proficiency (LALP) in their second language (B). SOURCE: From Wartenburger, I., Heekereb, H. R., Abutalebi, J., Cappa, S. F., Villringer, A., & Perani, D. (2003). Early setting of grammatical processing in the bilingual brain. *Neuron, 37,* 159–170.

babies, who opened their mouths to the right side when babbling and to the left side when smiling, suggesting that babbling is lateralized in infants just as language is in adults, making it likely that it is indeed a precursor to true language (Holowka & Petitto, 2002).

There is also evidence that different areas of the brain are involved when a second language is learned in childhood versus in adolescence or adulthood (Kim et al., 1997; Wartenburger et al., 2003). For example, in one study, early bilinguals, who had learned both their first and second languages in childhood, showed brain activation that was essentially the same for both of their languages. This was not the case, however, for late bilinguals, who had learned their second language in adolescence or adulthood. Rather, the pattern of brain activation was different when processing their first and second languages (Wartenburger et al., 2003; see photo). These findings are consistent with the idea that children's ability to easily acquire a first or second language is related to specific brain areas that are prepared for processing language early in life, but that this neural plasticity is reduced in adolescence when other brain areas are involved in learning a second language.

There has actually never been any doubt that language is situated in the brain. There is really no other option. However, *how* language is situated in the brain and how the developing brain relates to children's changing language abilities provide vital insights into better understanding the nature of language and providing clues as to how we can intervene when children (and adults) have language impairments.

have suggested that babbling might support social relations between infants and their family members (Sachs, 1977). One way to test this is to see what side of the brain controls babbling. Researchers have shown that the side of the brain that controls babbling is the same as the side that controls later language and is different from the side that controls smiling (Holowka & Petitto, 2002).

To demonstrate this, researchers videotaped babies while babbling or smiling and noted whether their mouth openings were

greater on their left or right sides. For most adults, language is mainly located in the left hemisphere of the brain, so when they engage in linguistics tasks, their mouth openings are generally greater on the right-hand side (that are controlled by the language-dominant left hemisphere). This is in contrast to when adults are engaged in nonlinguistic tasks, when mouth openings are greater on the left-hand side (that are controlled by the right hemisphere). Similar findings were reported for a group of 5- to 12-month-old

were given a test of English grammar (Johnson & Newport, 1989). People were asked to determine whether each of 300 sentences was grammatical or not. The results of this study are shown in Figure 9.2 (on p. 356). As you can see, people who immigrated to the United States between the ages of 3 and 7 years were indistinguishable from native speakers. Grammatical proficiency decreased gradually the older people were when

they immigrated to the United States and were first exposed to English (see also Hakuta, Bialystok, & Wiley, 2003). This pattern is also true for pronunciation, with people who do not acquire a second language until their teen years usually maintaining a decided accent, even if they display a high level of grammatical competency (see Kent, 2005; Locke, 1993). These changes do not seem to reflect a sharp drop-off in an ability to learn a language,

BOX 9.2 evolution in action

Inventing Language: Children's Gift to Humankind

When did our ancestors become language users, and what survival advantages did having a language afford its early (and later) users? We do not have precise answers for these questions. The fossil record can only tell us so much, in part because most of the anatomical features associated with language are soft tissue, specific parts of the brain and throat musculature, for example, that do not fossilize. However, we can make some educated guesses about the origins of language; the inner shapes of fossilized skulls can tell us about the shape of the brains they held, and the bones surrounding the mouth and throat can give us some clues about our ancestors' ability to speak. Using these methods, some experts suggest that the first humans to use rudimentary language lived about 2 million years ago and that more complex language was used by humans about 40,000 years ago (Bickerton, 1990), perhaps much earlier (see MacWhinney, 2005).

The adaptive benefits of language seem obvious. Ancient humans who had language were better able to communicate with one another and thus better able to coordinate their actions and transmit information across generations (Pinker & Bloom, 1992). Language alone would not be enough to make this more sophisticated communication possible, for it must be accompanied by an advanced ability for social learning. Yet, having language would have provided a much more efficient means of transmitting information between people than imitation or other forms of social learning (Donald, 1991). Similarly, the emergence of language can be seen as an expression of a new mode of thinking, *symbolic thought*, which provided its bearers with advantages beyond those associated with better communication (Deacon, 1997).

Although the evolutionary origins of language must remain speculative, it seems likely that children, not adults, first invented language. For example, physician and science writer Lewis Thomas (1975) suggested that the enlarged brains of ancient humans provided the capacity to use language, but adults likely made little use of it, continuing to communicate with grunts, gestures, and individual words to express ideas. Children learned these words from their parents, but they discovered how to put them together into sentences while playing with other children. From this perspective, language was the emerging product of groups of youth who played with these new abilities in purposeless ways, leading to a useful new ability.

Children at a Nicaraguan school for the hearing-impaired created Nicaraguan Sign Language over the course of several cohorts of children.

We know that children easily *acquire* their mother tongue (see discussion of a sensitive period for language), but this seems a stretch from proposing that children *invent* language. Some support for this controversial claim comes from observations of children who invent a real language from the nonlanguage communication systems that adults around them use. Linguist Derek Bickerton (1990; Calvin & Bickerton, 2000) notes that throughout history, people of different language groups have come together, often to work, and had to communicate with one another. Gestures play a role here, but typically the language of the majority group or the language of the bosses serves as the basis for communica-

The age at which people immigrate to a new country (and learn a new language) predicts their level of grammatical proficiency better than the number of years they have lived in the country.

which one would expect for a true critical period, but they do show that learning a second language is easiest when one is young and becomes progressively more difficult with age.

Related to evidence that learning a second language is associated with the age at which people were first exposed to it are research findings for acquisition of a *first* language as a function of age of acquisition. This does not come from case studies of isolated or deprived children, but from an examination of hearing-impaired children who were not exposed to any formal language, spoken or signed, until late childhood or adolescence (Newport, 1990). Similar to the findings of people's proficiency in a second language, people's proficiency in American Sign Language—their first language—was related to the age at which they were first exposed to it and not to the number of years they had been using the language.

tion, with words from other languages sprinkled in. The result is a **pidgin**, which includes terms from a variety of languages, simple and often inconsistent word order, and little in the way of a grammatical system. A pidgin is not a true language, but it conveys necessary information within the group (the workers) and between the group and the bosses. This is the way many tourists speak when they are in a foreign country. They know a few words, may know how to make (some) nouns plural, typically use only the present tense, frequently sprinkle in words from their own language, and keep the word order simple. It is not grammatical, but it usually gets basic messages across. Based both on historical evidence and his own research of the Hawaiian language, Bickerton showed that children of pidgin speakers transform the language of their parents into a true language, termed a **creole**, often in a single generation. That is, these children do not *acquire* language in the usual sense, but *create* a language.

One may question whether the transformation of pidgins into creoles in the hands (or mouths) of youngsters is truly evidence of children inventing language. Recent research supporting the creative role of children in language comes from studies of hearing-impaired children who invented Nicaraguan Sign Language (*Idioma de Señas de Nicara-*

gua). Until the opening of a school for the hearing-impaired in the 1970s, Nicaragua had no deaf culture and no recognized sign language. At this school, hearing-impaired children lived together and learned to read Spanish, but they were not taught to sign. Children had developed idiosyncratic home signs they had used to communicate with friends and family and used these signs to communicate with other hearing-impaired children. From these interactions, a true sign language began to emerge. Over the course of three cohorts of students, children created a true sign language (that is, with syntax). Nicaraguan Sign Language was systematically modified from one cohort of children to the next, with children aged 10 years and younger generating most of the changes. In other words, sequences of children created a new sign language from the incomplete forms used by their predecessors (Senghas & Coppola, 2001; Senghas et al., 2004).

Effective communication is useful for anyone, but the adaptive value of language has typically been focused on what it does for adults, from enhancing social cooperation to wooing members of the opposite sex (Miller, 2000). Might language be especially useful (and adaptive) for children? One proposal is that language improved the communication between preschool children and their parents at a time when children

are particularly in need of assistance, specifically during the preschool years (Locke, 2009; Locke & Bogin, 2006). Recall from Chapter 4 Barry Bogin's (2001) proposal that humans invented a new stage of development—childhood—when children were no longer nursing but were still not able to prepare their own food or otherwise fend for themselves, making effective communication between parent and child especially important. The adaptive value of language became particularly important again in adolescence, being related to same-sex competition and courtship.

Although these ideas are based on a wealth of evidence on language development, how people in different cultures use language today, communication systems in other species, and fossil evidence, they must remain speculative. Nonetheless, we are confident that natural selection related to the evolution of language operated on *children*, and that something about children's brains and cognitive systems made possible the invention of language and language's many advantages.

The fourth type of evidence for a sensitive period is from recovery of language function after brain damage. We discussed some of this research briefly in Chapter 4. Basically, when the language areas of the left hemisphere are damaged early in life, there is much plasticity, with other areas of the brain taking over the language function of the destroyed areas. Although the language acquisition of young children with significant left-hemisphere damage may proceed slowly and may be somewhat impaired compared to typical children, they usually learn to speak, and their language may be indistinguishable from that of a child without brain damage to all but trained language professionals. As children age, their ability to recover from such brain damage decreases (see Huttenlocher, 2002; Stiles, 2008; Witelson, 1987).

It seems clear that learning a first or second language is easier for children than for adults, with children's flexibility in learning a language begin-

ning to decrease as they reach the school years and continuing to decrease into adolescence. In other words, children's neuronal and cognitive systems appear to be especially geared for learning both a first and second language. This does not mean that a second language cannot be learned after early childhood, but the effort required is greater, and the results, especially in pronunciation and grammar, may not be as good compared to those who learned a second language in early childhood.

We have presented only briefly some of the evidence for a nativist perspective on language learning. Much of the evidence in support of this account is quite esoteric, based on complicated

pidgins Structurally simple communication systems that arise when people who share no common language come into constant contact.

creoles Languages that develop when children transform the *pidgin* of their parents to a grammatically more complex "true" language.

FIGURE 9.2 The relationship between age at arrival in the United States and total number of correct answers on a test of English grammar. The younger people were when they moved to the United States, the better was their command of English grammar. SOURCE: "Critical period effects in second language learning: The influence of maturational state on the acquisition of English as a second language," by J. S. Johnson and E. L. Newport, 1989. *Cognitive Psychology*, *21*, 60–99. Copyright © 1989 Academic Press. Reprinted with permission.

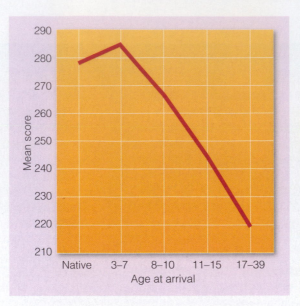

linguistic theory, and beyond the scope of this book (see Pinker, 1994). Language is species-specific and species uniform, and languages across the globe have characteristics described by theories of universal grammar. There also seems to be a sensitive period for language to develop, and this is bolstered by evidence that the brains of bilinguals who learn their second language early in life are different from those who learn their second language later in life (see discussion of this in Box 9.1). In short, there seems little doubt that children are biologically prepared to acquire language, but this does not necessarily mean that children have a language instinct or that more domain-general abilities and the social environment are not intimately involved in the process. In fact, advocates of the social-interactionist perspective of language development suggest that children's domain-general social-cognitive abilities and the social environment play a central role in language development.

The Social-Interactionist Perspective of Language Development

In reading our description of nativist approaches of language acquisition, one could get the idea that language develops independently from other cognitive and social accomplishments. After all, nativists argue that language is acquired via the operation of a set of domain-specific skills, which, by definition, are independent of other cognitive abilities. Social-interactionist theorists see things a bit differently, believing that language development is the consequence of a set of mechanisms and dispositions interacting in a dynamic manner, and that we must consider the entire web of children's developing abilities. As Michael Tomasello (2006, p. 292) stated, one of the problems in studying language is "that quite often the study of language acquisition has been cut off from the study of children's other cognitive and social skills."

So what else is going on in children's lives that is associated with, and may contribute to, language development? The simple answer is social development and children's developing social-cognitive skills. According to this view, "children's initial skills of linguistic communication are a natural outgrowth of their emerging understanding of other persons as intentional agents" (Carpenter, Nagell, & Tomasello, 1998, p. 126). Others agree, believing that there are fewer true universals in language than the nativists have claimed and that the similarities in language and language acquisition around the world are more the result of constraints of human cognition and cultural-historical factors (Evans & Levinson, 2009; Tomasello, 2008).

The Emergence of Communicative Intentions

Language is a means of communication, but infants communicate with their parents long before they learn to speak, and such prelinguistic abilities serve as the foundation for later language. As noted in Chapter 7, by the time they are 9 or 10 months old, infants engage in *shared attention*, in which two social partners share an experience. For instance, an infant may vocalize and point to a picture on a wall, directing her mother's attention to the interesting sight. Such interaction implies that infants view their social partners as *intentional agents*—people whose actions are based on what they know and what they want, and who act deliberately to achieve their goals.

What does shared attention have to do with language development? Shared-attention activities, with mothers pointing, looking at, and vocalizing about some object or event, provides a context for communication that is very different from that of any other species, and, according to some theorists, is the underlying cognitive basis for language (see Tomasello, 1999, 2005, 2006, 2008). Infants point to, look at, and vocalize about objects to their parents as well, and this enables them to direct adults' attention to objects of common interest and elicit information about those objects. For example, a child who is pointing to a particular book may switch his gaze from the book to his mother's eyes several times, causing the adult to focus on the book, too. The mother may pick up the book, hand it to the child, and say, "This is your animal book. Can you say 'book'? Do you see the pages? What's inside the book? Do you want me to read your animal book to you?"

There is a clear relationship between how soon children become involved in shared-attention activities and how soon they develop language (Camaioni & Perucchinni, 2003). For instance, in one study, researchers observed the social interaction between mothers and their infants over a period of 6 months, beginning when the babies were 9 months old (Carpenter, Akhtar, & Tomasello, 1998). They reported that mothers who engaged their infants in more shared-attention events and who used language that referred to objects that infants were holding had infants who developed better communication skills than infants of less-sharing mothers.

Gestures Pointing the Way to Language

Parents and children also often point out things to one another. Pointing can be used to indicate an item of interest to someone else (for example, pointing to a teddy bear) or to ask for something, as when an infant points to a toy ("Please give me that teddy bear"). Such pointing is one important indication of shared attention and of infants treating their communication partners as intentional agents, and some theorists have argued that infants 12 months and older use pointing to influence others' mental states (Tomasello, Carpenter, & Liszkowski, 2007).

Consistent with this position, Susan Goldin-Meadow and her colleagues have shown that pointing, and gestures more generally, serves as a prelinguistic form of communication and predicts children's subsequent language development (Goldin-Meadow, 2007; Iverson & Goldin-Meadow, 2005). For example, a child who uses the word "drink" while pointing to a juice bottle gets his or her message across loud and clear. Moreover, the age that children produce word + gesture combinations (for example, "drink" + point at juice) predicts the age that they produce their first two-word utterances (Iverson & Goldin-Meadow, 2005). Children's use of pointing and gestures is not limited to the one-word stage of language development. For instance, children say things such as "I like it" while making a drinking gesture several months before they say "I like drinking it" (Ozcaliskan & Goldin-Meadow, 2005).

Gestures seem to point the way to early language development. For example, in one study, children between 10 and 14 months of age were followed for several months as they made the transition from one-word (for example, "Drink") to two-word (for example, "Drink milk") utterances (Iverson & Goldin-Meadow, 2005). The researchers noted objects that children first identified by gesture or by speech and looked at whether those items transferred to the other modality. Figure 9.3 shows the proportion of items that were initially (1) identified in speech and stayed in speech; (2) identified in gesture and stayed in gesture; (3) identified in speech and transferred to gesture; and (4) identified in gesture and transferred to

speech. As you can see, once an object was identified in one modality, it tended to be transferred to the other modality, with this transfer being greatest from gesture to speech. This supports the *gesture-facilitation hypothesis*, which holds that the use of gestures facilitates the acquisition of spoken language. Consistent with this hypothesis, the more children use gestures at 14 months of age, the larger their vocabularies are at 54 months. Moreover, higher-SES (socioeconomic status) parents are more likely to use gestures with their infants and toddlers than are lower-SES parents, which in turn influences the gesturing and communication skills of their children, accounting in large part for the differences in vocabulary size between children from higher- and lower-SES families (Rowe & Goldin-Meadow, 2009).

There are several ways in which pointing and gestures can make the job of learning language easier (Goldin-Meadow, 2007). First, gestures could elicit from parents words and sentences children need to hear to make linguistic progress. For example, a child may point to an eating utensil and be told "spoon." Or a child may point and say "kitty" in a particular context and be told, "Yes, that's Sonny's kitty." In this latter case, a child's word + gesture becomes translated by an adult as a complete sentence. Second, using gestures has been shown to foster performance on a host of cognitive tasks, and this may also be true for learning language. For instance, encouraging school-age children to use gestures while solving math problems increases their chances of getting the problems right (Goldin-Meadow, Cook, & Mitchell, 2009; see Goldin-Meadow, 2009).

Language is not *caused* by children being able to take the perspective of another or by seeing their interaction partners as intentional agents. For example, hearing-impaired infants engage in shared

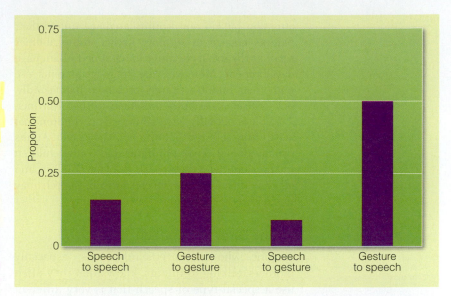

FIGURE 9.3 Proportion of objects children learned to identify by speech or gesture that either remained within the original modality (speech to speech or gesture to gesture) or transferred to the other modality (speech to gesture or gesture to speech).

Children were much more likely to acquire a new gestures and transfer it to speech than vice versa, supporting the *gesture-facilitation hypothesis*. SOURCE: From Iverson, J. M., & Goldin-Meadow, S. (2005). Gesture paves the way for language development. *Psychological Science, 16*, 368–371.

attention but do not acquire language unless their parents engage in signing. Rather, these abilities serve as the social-cognitive foundation for language development. Moreover, the language parents use with their infants is rarely presented haphazardly, but instead is carefully presented to them (Bruner, 1983). It is not only *what* adults say to children that is carefully selected, but also *how* they say it. Adults usually do not speak to infants and young children in the same way they speak to older children and other adults, and this special form of speech may make it easier for them to learn language.

Infant-Directed Speech

Anyone who has overheard adults, especially mothers, talking to infants, knows that they often use a special type of speech that is very different from the type they use when talking to adults. In everyday parlance, we call this "baby talk." ("Hey, big boy! How are you today? Huh? Are you being a good boy? Yes, you are, you're being such a good boy, aren't you? You drank all your bottle, didn't you? What a good boy!") Researchers first called this kind of speech *motherese*, because it was the type of speech that mothers used when talking to babies. However, when it was realized that not only mothers but also fathers, grandparents, 4-year-olds, and strangers in the grocery store also use this kind of language when speaking to infants and young children, it was termed **infant-directed speech**, or more generally, child-directed speech (Snow, 1972).

Infant-directed speech is characterized by high-pitched tones, exaggerated modulations, simplified forms of adult words, expansions of the child's communication sounds, and many questions and repetitions (see Hoff, 2009). Infant-directed speech is used with newborns, and adults continue to use it with children who are well into the toddler years. Curiously enough, infant-directed speech is not something adults do intentionally or with full consciousness. It is not a skill parents read about in parenting books and practice before their child is born. It is done spontaneously and is found in caregivers around the world (Fernald, 1992; Kuhl et al., 1997). In fact, for many people it is difficult *not* to speak in these exaggerated ways to young children. Even signing mothers of hearing-impaired babies make signs more slowly, repeat signs, and make more exaggerated signs to their hearing-impaired babies than when they sign to other adults (Masataka, 1996). Furthermore, hearing mothers with hearing babies also use exaggerated gestures in addi-

tion to infant-directed speech, which supports the language they use with their infants (O'Neill et al., 2005). The seeming universality of infant-directed speech caused Jerome Bruner (1983) to propose that adults have a device in their brains that responds to infants and young children by automatically altering speech to a more understandable form, and he even suggested an appropriate name, the **language acquisition support system (LASS)**, to complement Chomsky's language acquisition device (LAD). Bruner's LASS incorporates the species-typical environment that promotes language development in children, of which child-directed speech is a part.

Why do adults speak to babies this way? One reason may be that infants are more responsive to adults when they speak to them in infant-directed speech than in adult-directed speech. For instance, 4-month-old infants who have been conditioned to turn their heads to one side or the other to select which of two tapes they will listen to will also turn their heads to hear infant-directed speech rather than adult-directed speech. There is even evidence that 1-month-old babies show a preference for infant-directed speech (Cooper & Aslin, 1990, 1994). Second, babies may also be able to tell the difference between words more easily when they are spoken in infant-directed as opposed to adult-directed speech (Karzon, 1985; Moore, Spence, & Katz, 1997). For example, 1- to 4-month-old infants can tell the difference between similar three-syllable words such as *marana* and *malana* if they are spoken in the exaggerated style of infant-directed speech (for example, using a down-up-down phrasing as in "ma-LA-na"), rather than typical adult-directed speech (Karzon, 1985).

Although infant-directed speech may make some aspects of language acquisition easier for children, there may be other reasons that mothers use infant-directed speech, and the origins of such speech may have more to do with mothers trying to regulate the emotional responding of their babies than with teaching them anything about language. For instance, Anne Fernald (1992) proposed that mothers use infant-directed speech both to regulate their infants' emotions and attention and to convey their own feelings to babies. She identified four different patterns in infant-directed speech used by British, American, German, French, and Italian mothers when talking to their 12-month-old babies. These patterns were used to provide comfort to the infant, seek the infant's attention, convey approval, and express prohibition. In other words, infants from the first months of life are attentive to vocal (and likely facial) cues of their mothers, and mothers use these cues to modulate their infants' emotional expression. This type of mother-infant communication is important in developing secure attachment, and although secure attachment is not necessary for

---

infant-directed speech The specialized register of speech that adults and older children use when talking specifically to infants and young children.

language acquisition support system (LASS) According to Bruner, a series of learning and social devices that adults and older children exhibit when interacting with younger children that facilitates language acquisition.

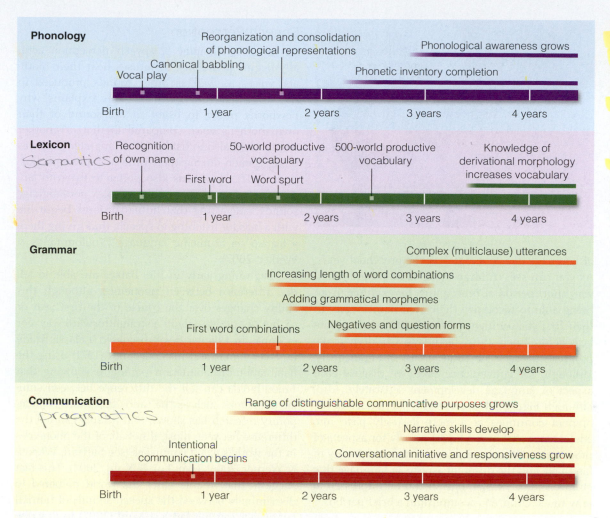

Phonology

| Reorganization and consolidation of phonological representations |
| Canonical babbling |
| Vocal play |

Phonological awareness grows
Phonetic inventory completion

Birth — 1 year — 2 years — 3 years — 4 years

Lexicon
Semantics

Recognition of own name
First word
50-world productive vocabulary
Word spurt
500-world productive vocabulary
Knowledge of derivational morphology increases vocabulary

Birth — 1 year — 2 years — 3 years — 4 years

Grammar

Complex (multiclause) utterances
Increasing length of word combinations
Adding grammatical morphemes
First word combinations
Negatives and question forms

Birth — 1 year — 2 years — 3 years — 4 years

Communication
pragmatics

Range of distinguishable communicative purposes grows
Narrative skills develop
Intentional communication begins
Conversational initiative and responsiveness grow

Birth — 1 year — 2 years — 3 years — 4 years

FIGURE 9.4 Major milestones in early language development.
"Lexicon" refers to the words that a child knows (semantics), and "communication" refers to a child's ability to use language in social situations (pragmatics). SOURCE: Hoff, E. (2009). *Language development* (4th ed.). Belmont, CA: Wadsworth, p. 7.

children to acquire language, research has shown that maltreated toddlers have significant delays in language acquisition (Cicchetti, 1989). Fernald's claim is that the evolutionary origins of language may stem in part from mothers attempting to regulate the emotions of their infants, something that infant-directed speech continues to do today (see also Trainor, Austin, & Desjardins, 2000). Consistent with Fernald's argument, evidence shows that rhesus-monkey mothers use special vocalizations with their infants that attract and engage their attention, much as human mothers do (Whitham et al., 2007).

Although infants might be biologically prepared to acquire their mother tongue, language acquisition is built on infants' social-cognitive foundation of understanding others as intentional agents. Moreover, as research on infant-directed speech makes clear, language development is embedded within the social-emotional context of the family. Parents around the world provide children with an environment that promotes communication, motivates language development, as well as provides a model for language (Hoff, 2006). Consistent with the social-interactionist perspective, language development cannot be properly understood in isolation but must be viewed in the broader context of the developing child's cognitive, social, and emotional abilities and the social environments in which he or she lives (see Locke, 1993; Tomasello, 2005).

The Course of Language Development

As mentioned in the opening paragraphs of this chapter, there are at least four aspects of language: *phonology, semantics, grammar,* and *pragmatics.* Figure 9.4 (from Hoff, 2009) presents a schematic overview of major milestones of these four aspects

© Ariel Skelley/Blend Images/Corbis

Mothers use infant-directed speech to influence their babies' mood and behavior and to communicate their own feelings to their infants.

Shortly after birth, because of what they heard in the womb, infants prefer to listen to the language their mothers speak.

© Catchlight Visual Services/Alamy

Speech Perception

As noted in Chapter 5, speech perception actually begins prenatally, as fetuses hear their mothers' voices as well as other sounds produced in the immediate environment. This explains why newborns prefer to listen to the sound of their own mother's voice compared to that of another woman and also to listen to the language that was being spoken during their time in the womb (Jusczyk, 1997). Newborns also prefer to listen to language relative to comparably complex nonlanguage sounds, suggesting that human infants begin life with a bias for listening to speech, thus giving them a leg up on acquiring language (Vouloumanos & Werker, 2007).

Beginning early in life, babies are able to tell the difference between phonemes, although this ability changes over the course of the first year or so, but not necessarily in a straightforward way. For example, in Chapter 5 we discussed a classic study by Peter Eimas and his colleagues (1971) using the habituation/dishabituation paradigm showing that 1-month-olds can tell the difference between similar phonemes such as "pa" and "ba." More contemporary research has shown that infants can tell the difference between most, if not all, of the phonemes in the world's 6,000 languages (see Saffran, Werker, & Werner, 2006; Tsao, Lui, & Kuhl, 2004). This fact suggests that infants enter the world prepared to discriminate between the speech sounds of human languages, causing Patricia Kuhl (2007) to describe young infants as "citizens of the world," in that they seem equally ready and able to acquire any of the world's languages. As also noted in Chapter 5, infants lose this ability beginning around the middle of their first year. From this time onward, they become specialists in their mother tongue, gradually losing their flexibility to differentiate among all language sounds while devoting their limited neural resources to mastering the language sounds that surround them (Kuhl et al., 2006).

Speech Production

Although there are considerable individual differences in phonological development—often attributed to the language children are acquiring—there seems to be a basic developmental path (see Concept Review 9.2, p. 362). During the first 2 months, babies produce only reflexive or vegetative sounds, such as burps, coughs and sneezes, cries, hiccups, and simple moans (Kent, 2005). Infants' vocal tract at this age is very immature. The larynx is high in the throat, the tongue fills the oral cavity, and teeth have not yet emerged, similar to the vocal structures of nonhuman primates (see Figure 9.5). Sometime between 2 and 4 months of age, some of these limitations diminish, and infants begin to make

of language development over the preschool years. As you can see, children make rapid progress in a very short period of time, going, for example, from being able to recognize their own names early in their first year of life to having a 500-word vocabulary before their third birthdays. Children make progress in each of these areas simultaneously, although, for convenience sake, we discuss each aspect of language development separately. Also, although Figure 9.4 stops at age 4, language development continues at a more leisurely pace into adolescence and beyond, particularly for aspects of pragmatics. When one thinks of the complexity of language and the different aspects of language that children must master, one should be impressed at how much children accomplish in a brief period.

Phonological Development: Sounds and Articulations

We often take for granted the physical act of speaking—making the sounds that come out as recognizable words. We become more aware of it when we try to speak a foreign language, particularly one that has very different sounds than one's native tongue (Japanese for English speakers, for example). The production of speech is an extraordinarily sophisticated phenomenon. For instance, a mature speaker can produce 7 to 8 syllables per second, each containing two or more **phonemes** (the individual sounds that make up words), or a rate of 14 to 20 phonemes per second (Kent, 2005). This feat involves advanced maturation of the brain and the speech-production systems, particularly the vocal tract, which includes the larynx, jaw, tongue, and lips. It also requires precise timing of speech rhythms and the corresponding motor control.

phonemes Individual sounds that are used to make up words.

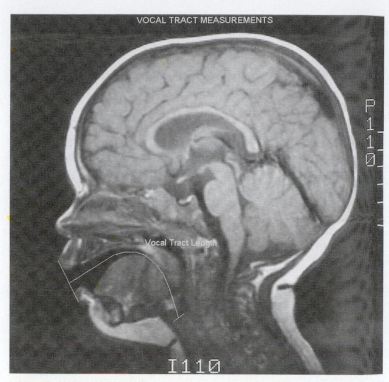

VOCAL TRACT MEASUREMENTS

Vocal Tract Length

I110

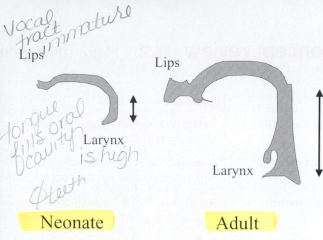

Vocal tract Immature
Lips

Tongue fills oral cavity
Larynx *is high*

∅ *teeth*

Lips

Larynx

Neonate   Adult

FIGURE 9.5 Vocal tracts of infant and adult.
Figure a is a magnetic image of a neonate's head, show-ing the length of the vocal tract. Figure b shows the difference in the length of the vocal tract between a newborn and an adult. SOURCE: From Kent, R. (2005). Speech development. In B. Hopkins (Ed.), *The Cambridge encyclopedia of child development* (pp. 257–264). New York: Cambridge University Press). Reprinted with the permission of Cambridge University Press.

a series of pleasant noises such as "ooooh," often adding the consonants of "g" or "k." These pleasing sounds are known as *cooing*, because they resemble the sounds pigeons make.

From about 4 to 6 months of age, children expe-rience a transitional period, when changes in the structure of the vocal tract let them produce more complex sounds, such as "buuuuu" and "paaaa." The sounds start to approximate those found in adult speech, and it is not surprising that this is the time when most parents report that their babies begin to "talk" for the first time (Kent, 2005; Vihman, 1996). **Babbling** begins around 6 to 10 months of age, again reflecting anatomic changes in the vocal apparatus (Ingram, 1989; Stark, 1978). This type of speech production is typically characterized by repeated sequences of consonants and vowels, such as "nanana" or "babababa." These sounds are not just produced when infants are in the presence of oth-ers, but also when they are alone. Because this type of early speech production resembles the sounds of the language being spoken around the child (for instance, English babies babble in English and Japa-nese babies babble in Japanese), it is assumed that babbling development is based, at least partially, on children reproducing sounds that they hear.

One bit of evidence for this is that hearing-impaired children do not engage in this vocal bab-bling as much as hearing children do, although they pass through the earlier stages of speech production (Oller & Eilers, 1988; Petitto, 2002). However, this does not necessarily mean that babbling mecha-nisms are impaired in hearing-impaired children. In fact, it has been found that hearing-impaired infants who are exposed to American Sign Lan-guage from early in life begin babbling with their hands around 8 months, following patterns identi-cal to those of hearing infants (Petitto, 2002; Petitto & Marentette, 1991).

From 18 months until the early school years (6 to 9 years of age), children increase their inventory of sounds, as well as their ability to produce speech. For example, an average 2-year-old can manage between 10 and 20 consonants. (Stuttering first appears between 2 and 3 years.) Young children often drop the unstressed syllables of words (*spaghetti* is pronounced as *getti*), repeat consonants (*water* is pronounced as *wawa*), and oversimplify complex consonants (*blanket* is pronounced as *bankee*). By the age of 4 to 6 years, children are able to produce almost all of the vowels and consonants of their lan-guage, except perhaps some *frictives* such as *z* and *s* (as in *z*ip, *s*on, thi*s*), the *l* (as in *l*ay), and the *r* (as in *r*ay). By 6 to 9 years of age, children can pronounce all of the sounds of their language correctly about 75% of the time (Kent, 2005). Children continue to improve in speed and efficiency of speech produc-tion into their teen years, becoming more adept at producing complex sounds and multisyllabic words at a higher speed, a consequence of better-coordi-nated speech production (Vihman, 1988). Some lan-guage combinations are more difficult than others, as reflected by some tongue twisters that give chil-dren, and many adults, difficulties (see Table 9.2).

babbling Early form of infant speech typically characterized by repeated sequences of consonants and vowels, such as "nanana" or "babababa."

Age	Milestone
0 to 2 months	**Reflexive/vegetative sounds**: Infants cry as a reaction to a distressed state and make various vegetative sounds associated with feeding and breathing, such as burps, coughs, and sneezes.
2 to 4 months	**Cooing**: Infants begin to make pleasant noises, mostly vowel sounds such as "oooh," especially during social interactions. Crying decreases and sustained laughter appears.
4 to 6 months	**Vocal play**: This is a transition between cooing and true babbling. Infants begin to utter single syllables with prolonged vowel or consonant sounds.
6 to 12 months	**Babbling**: True babbling sounds appear, such as "bababa" and "nanana." Consonant-vowel patterns are repeated, and playful variations of pitch disappear.
9 to 18 months	**Jargon**: Strings of sound are filled with a variety of intonations and rhythms to sound like meaningful speech. Infants often sound as if they are carrying on their end of a conversation, with their intonations sometimes sounding as if they reflect questions or explanations, but their "words" are only babble sounds.
19 to 24 months	Children possess between 10 and 20 consonants and can learn many new words.
25 to 36 months	Children increase the number of language sounds they can make along with increasing their vocabulary. Stuttering is often first noticed.
3 to 4 years	Almost all vowels are mastered, as well as many consonants.

SOURCE: Adapted from Kent, R. (2005). Speech development. In B. Hopkins (Ed.), *The Cambridge encyclopedia of child development* (pp. 257–264). New York: Cambridge University Press; and Stark, R. (1978). Features of infant sounds: The emergence of cooing. *Journal of Child Language, 5*, 1–12.

table 9.2 Tongue Twister Examples

Children in the early school years tend to have particular trouble with tongue twisters. Many adults find them quite difficult as well. Try saying the following out loud:

She sells sea shells by the sea shore.

Toy boat. Toy boat. Toy boat.

Friendly Frank flips fine flapjacks.

Vincent vowed vengeance very vehemently.

Which witch wished which wicked wish?

Twelve twins twirled twelve twigs.

Nine nice night nurses nursing nicely.

Crisp crusts crackle crunchily.

Give Papa a cup of proper coffee in a copper coffee cup.

Betty better butter Brad's bread.

She sifted thistles through her thistle-sifter.

Lily ladles little Letty's lentil soup.

Pick a partner and practice passing.

Just think, that sphinx has a sphincter that stinks!

Who washed Washington's white woolen underwear when Washington's washer woman went west?

word spurt Expression used to describe the rapid increase in word (mostly noun) learning observed in some children, typically occurring at about 18 months of age.

Semantic Development: Words and Meanings

The development of *semantics*, or vocabulary and meaning aspects of language, is an equally amazing phenomenon. If you do not believe this, consider the following fact: It takes almost the first 12 months of life for children to produce their first recognizable words, but by the age of 6 they will have a vocabulary of more than 10,000 words. This increases to more than 20,000 words by the time children are in the third grade, 40,000 by the fifth grade, 60,000 by 18 years, and 100,000 words by adulthood (Aitchinson, 1994; Carey, 1978; see Figure 9.6). In this section, we focus mostly on the acquisition and development of vocabulary.

Children's Growing Vocabularies

Once a child is able to produce his or her first word, it can take 3 or 4 months to increase to 10 words (Nelson, 1973), but around 18 months of age, a vocabulary explosion called the **word spurt** occurs for many children, with children adding about 30 new words per month (Benedict, 1979; Bloom, 1998). There are individual differences in when children begin their word spurt, with some children beginning shortly after their first birthdays and others not starting until age 2 or later (see Figure 9.7). However, whether the word spurt characterizes all or only some children is a matter of some controversy (Bloom, 2000; Goldfield & Reznick, 1990). Some research using different methodological procedures suggests that it might be typical for only about 20% of children, with the rest following a more linear, gradual progression of vocabulary development (Ganger & Brent, 2004).

Children's ability to learn new words based on very little input (that is, few opportunities to learn the words) has been termed **fast mapping** (Carey, 1978). To demonstrate fast mapping, 16- and 20-month-old toddlers were shown a set of objects, one of which was unfamiliar to them (for instance, a garlic press). Children were given nonsense words for the unfamiliar items (for instance, "May I have the dax?"). Some of the children learned these new words for these unfamiliar items after only a few exposures (the fast mappers). These children had larger vocabularies than the children who did not learn words for these novel items. This latter group of children was seen several months later, after they had gone through their word spurt, and now they, too, showed an ability to fast map (Mervis & Bertrand, 1994). These results indicate that the word spurt is associated with a special processing ability, reflected by fast mapping, in which children map novel words to novel objects for which they do not yet have a name.

Which words do children produce first? The earliest words tend to be common nouns that name familiar people and things (apple, daddy, dog), especially items children can manipulate or otherwise handle themselves (ball, truck). Early words also tend to be words that are relevant in social interaction (hello, bye-bye). Although nouns tend to constitute most of children's first words, verbs begin to increase in frequency following the early noun spurt (Nelson, 1973; Snedecker, Geren, & Shafto, 2007).

There are some interesting cultural differences in children's first words. Children learning English use more nouns and also so-called relational words, such as *off, up, on, down,* that must be used to complete certain verbs (for example, "pick up," "put down," "put on," "drop off") than children learning Korean and Mandarin Chinese, who use fewer nouns and exhibit more complete verb forms in their early speech (Gopnik & Choi, 1995). One of the reasons for this difference is that these expressions reflect differences in how adults in those cultures speak, and children produce more of the expressions they hear around them (Tomasello, 2006).

During the elementary school years, the pace of learning new words becomes even faster, as children learn 5 to 13 words every day (Anglin, 1993; Bloom, 1998). Unlike other aspects of language acquisition, semantic ability increases significantly as children begin the school years. This increase is largely a result of children's exposure to knowledge

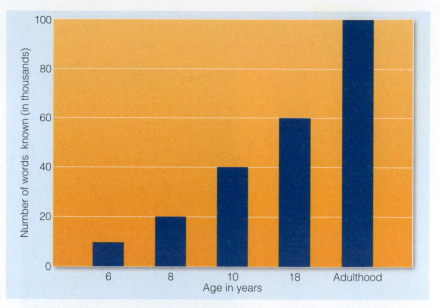

FIGURE 9.6 The rate of development of vocabulary in children and adolescents is spectacular.

Here is the estimated number of words in the vocabularies of people from 6 years old to adulthood. SOURCE: Based on Carey, S. (1978). The child as a word learner. In M. Halle, J. Bresnan, & G. A. Miller (Eds.), *Linguistic theory and psychological reality* (pp. 264–293). Cambridge, MA: MIT Press; and Aitchinson, J. (1994). *Words in the mind: An introduction to the mental lexicon* (2nd ed.). Oxford, England: Blackwell.

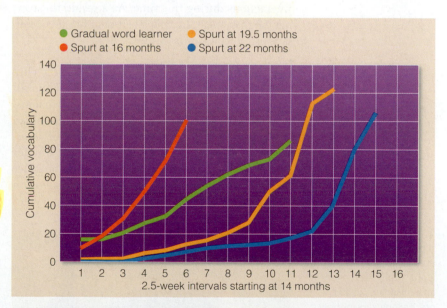

FIGURE 9.7 Different children show different times of onset of their growth spurt, although most (but not all) children show an abrupt and rapid increase in vocabulary. SOURCE: From Goldfield, B. A., & Reznick, J. S. (1990). Early lexical acquisition: Rate, content, and the vocabulary spurt. *Journal of Child Language, 17,* 171–184. Reprinted with the permission of Cambridge University Press.

underextensions Incorrectly restricting the use of a language term (for example, believing that only one's pet, Fido, deserves the label "dog").

overextensions The stretching of a familiar word beyond its correct meaning (for example, calling all four-legged mammals "doggie").

fast mapping The ability to learn new words based on very little input.

In contrast, the rate of productive vocabulary is much slower over this same time. SOURCE: From Caselli, M. C., Bates, E., Casadio, P., Fenson, J., Fenson, L., Sanders, L., & Weir, J. (1995). A cross-linguistic study of early lexical development. *Cognitive Development, 10*, 159–199. Reprinted by permission.

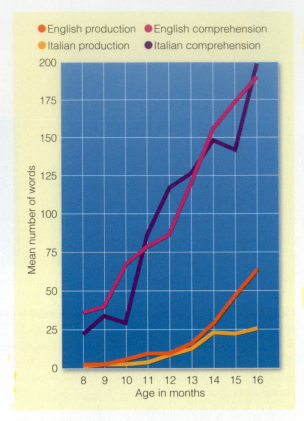

● English production ● English comprehension
● Italian production ● Italian comprehension

Mean number of words

200
175
150
125
100
75
50
25
0

8   9   10   11   12   13   14   15   16
Age in months

acquired at school as well as the increase in social interactions during this time. As a result, the average English-speaking college student has a vocabulary of 150,000 words (Miller, 1977).

Under- and overextensions. Evidence of children's developing semantic abilities is found in their use of **underextensions** and **overextensions**. An underextension is the use of a word with a broad meaning to refer to only a restricted group of items. An example would be using the word "cat" to refer to only the yellow family pet and not to the other felines in the neighborhood. An overextension is an error in the opposite direction—using a word

"Look at the rabbit!" Children seem to know that the word "rabbit" refers to the animal and not to its colors, its long ears, or how it moves across the field.

© John Short/Photolibrary

: **active, or productive, language** The language a child can actually produce, or speak.
: **passive (or receptive) language** The language that a child can understand.

with a restricted meaning, such as "Fluffy," to refer not only to the family pet but also to all cats one encounters. Although this is a common mistake young children make, it does not last for long, mainly because parents suggest more accurate terminology (MacWhinney, 2005).

Productive versus receptive language. A second important thing to note when it comes to the development of semantic abilities is that there is a difference between **active**, or **productive, language** (the words a child can actually produce) and **passive**, or **receptive, language** (the words a child can comprehend). Generally speaking, receptive language develops sooner than productive language, with children being able to recognize 10 conventional words 2 to 3 months before they can produce their first word (MacWhinney, 2005). In addition, children (as well as adults) understand far more words than they typically use themselves (Schafer & Plunkett, 1998). Figure 9.8 presents the growth curves for language production and comprehension for English- and Italian-speaking children between 8 and 16 months of age (Caselli et al., 1995). As you can see, the rate of language comprehension (receptive speech) accelerates rapidly over these months, whereas the pace of productive language is much slower.

Although the most obvious change in semantic development over the school years is children's steadily increasing vocabularies, their improving social and cognitive abilities result in children understanding multiple and nonliteral meanings of words, which is involved in literature (metaphor and idioms) and humor (Beal, 1990). We take a brief look at the role of children's increasing verbal ability in their generation and appreciation of jokes in Box 9.3.

Constraints on Word Learning

Up until now we have described some of the basics of semantic development in young children, but we must address an important question: How are children able to figure out what a particular word means from all that is associated with the utterance of that word? (See Concept Review 9.3.) For example, when a father says, "See the rabbit," how does a child know if he is referring to the animal itself, the color of the animal, the long ears, or the movement of the object across the lawn? Yet, children somehow come to understand rather quickly that the word "rabbit" refers to the animal and not to its mode of locomotion, causing some scientists to suggest that there must be *constraints* on word learning that make the task easier for children to learn the meaning of words. Perhaps children are prepared to learn the meaning of words from the beginning of life, but with some constraints that prevent them from considering *all* the possible meanings when listening to a new word.

Psychologists have proposed that constraints on word learning make it easier for children to figure out what a particular word means from all that is associated with the utterance of that word.

Constraint	Definition
Whole-object assumption	Children assume that a word refers to the whole object and not to a part of it.
Taxonomic assumption	Children initially assume that words refer to other things that are similar.
Mutual exclusivity assumption	Children assume that different words (for example, "rabbit" and "mouse") refer to different things.
Syntactic bootstrapping	The idea that the grammatical form of speech may give children important clues or guessing what a word means.

Ellen Markman (1994) proposed three specific lexical constraints, or assumptions, for word learning: (1) the whole-object assumption, in which children initially assume that a word refers to the whole object and not to a part of it. For example, when Dad says, "Look at the rabbit!" the word "rabbit" does not refer to the color, the long ears, or the hopping motion, but rather to the whole animal; (2) the taxonomic assumption, in which children initially assume that words refer to other things that are similar. For example, once children learn the word "rabbit," they assume it can be used for similar four-legged, furry animals and may mistakenly call their neighbor's cat a rabbit; and (3) the mutual exclusivity assumption, in which children assume that different words (for example, "rabbit" and "mouse") refer to different things. For instance, in one set of studies, 3-year-olds who knew the word for "cup" but not for "tongs" were asked to "Show me the dax." Eighty percent of children selected the tongs, presumably believing that "dax" refers to the novel object as opposed to being another word for "cup" (Markman & Wachtel, 1988).

Similarly, the grammatical form of speech may give children important clues for guessing what a word means. This strategy has been referred to as syntactic bootstrapping (Gleitman, 1990; Hoff & Naigles, 2002). For example, in the sentence, "Here is a dax," the use of the determiner "a" indicates that the word "dax" must be a proper noun or the name of a discrete object or thing, such as a hammer, a spoon, or a kiss. In contrast, for the sentence "I want some dax," the use of the adjective "some" indicates that the word "dax" cannot be a discrete object, but a quantity such as milk, sand, or peace and quiet (McWhinney, 2005; Smith, 1999).

The point that is most critical for our discussion here is that children are *prepared* to learn words. Whether this preparation comes in the form of lexical constraints, such as the whole-object assumption, or is a by-product of their developing social cognition, children seem *not* to experience language as random noise. Rather, their cognitive systems are ready to make sense of the connection between things they hear and things they see, making the process of word learning much easier than it would be in the absence of such constraints. We should add that the increase of children's word knowledge is not independent of environmental circumstances, including the quantity and quality of speech children are exposed to daily in contexts such as family, school, peers, and the media, and these factors vary widely from one child to another during their development (see for example, Hoff, 2003).

Grammatical Development: Learning the Rules of Language

Grammar refers to the rules that describe the structure of a language. Some of these rules refer to how words themselves are formed (morphology), whereas others refer to rules for how words are combined into sentences and how sentences are transformed into other sentences (syntax). For instance, English speakers think it is easy to turn the simple declarative sentence "The woman rides the horse" into a question ("Is the woman riding the horse?") or a negative ("The woman is not riding the horse"), or to make it past tense ("The woman

whole-object assumption A type of lexical constraint in which children assume when hearing a word that it refers to the whole object and not to some part of that object.

taxonomic assumption A type of lexical constraint in which children assume that words refer to things that are similar.

mutual exclusivity assumption A type of lexical constraint in which children believe that different words refer to different things.

syntactic bootstrapping In learning the meaning of words, the idea that the grammatical form of speech may give children important clues for guessing what a word means.

syntax The knowledge of how words are put together to form proper and understandable sentences.

BOX 9.3 **food for thought**

Humor and Semantic Development

Knock, knock.

Who's there?

Police.

Police who?

Police stop telling these awful knock-knock jokes!

Many factors influence children's sense of humor, perhaps the most important one being children's level of cognitive development. Seeing something as funny depends on a child's ability to recognize *incongruity*, or a discrepancy, between an expected or usual event and what is experienced (McGhee, 1979; Puche-Navarro, 2004). Incongruity can only be defined in terms of what children already know and their ability to see multiple interpretations of a situation or a word. As such, what is incongruous, and thus funny, to a 2-year-old (for example, calling the family cat "doggie") will be perceived as babyish and just plain stupid to an older child. Likewise, because of older children's greater knowledge base and increased abilities to process information, things they find funny (such as knock-knock jokes) will go over the heads of most preschool children.

One aspect of cognitive development that is important in children's ability to generate and understand jokes is semantic development. For example, many verbal jokes hinge around double meanings of words (see Shultz & Horibe, 1974; Shultz & Pilon,

1973). The earliest verbal jokes that children understand tend to be based on *phonological ambiguity*, in which one word sounds like another. For instance:

"Waiter, what's this?"

"That's bean soup, ma'am."

"I'm not interested in what it's been; I'm asking what it is now."

The joke centers on the different meanings of the similar-sounding words "bean" and "been." Many knock-knock jokes, including the one that opened this box, rely on this type of ambiguity for their humor. For example:

"Knock, knock."

"Who's there?"

"Freeze."

"Freeze who?"

"Freeze a jolly good fellow!"

Although 6- and 7-year-old children can appreciate the different meanings of two words that sound alike, their appreciation is limited by their attentiveness to literal (here acoustic) perceptual features.

Following close behind in appreciation are jokes based on the dual meaning of a single word, termed *lexical ambiguity*. For example:

"Order! Order in the court!"

"Ham and cheese on rye, Your Honor."

Here the humor does not derive from a confusion of two different words (like "bean"

and "been" or "police" and "please") but revolves around two different meanings of the same word. Here is one more example of lexical ambiguity:

"How do you keep a skunk from smelling?"

"Hold its nose."

Most of the verbal jokes and riddles of elementary schoolchildren are based on phonological or lexical ambiguity.

There are also more complex forms of jokes, involving ambiguities not of a single word but of the entire structure of the sentence. For example:

"I saw a man-eating shark in the aquarium."

"That's nothing. I saw a man eating herring in the restaurant."

or

"I would like to buy a pair of alligator shoes."

"Certainly. What size does your alligator wear?"

In these two cases, the jokes do not hinge on the interpretation of a single word but on how the whole sentence is interpreted. Is it a shark who eats men, or a man who is eating a shark? Are the shoes made of alligator hide, or are the shoes made to fit your pet alligator's feet? The humor is based on two different syntactical relations among words within a sentence, and appreciation of such humor is typically not attained until 11 or 12 years of age, reflecting changes in the language abilities associated with the onset of adolescence (Shultz & Horibe, 1974).

---

rode the horse") or future tense ("The woman will ride the horse"). Yet, despite the ease of converting one form of a sentence to another (present tense to past tense, for example), this knowledge is *implicit*; most people have a difficult time explaining the rules underlying these changes. (Go ahead, explain how you do it.) Moreover, it takes children time to acquire the implicit understanding of syntax that comes so easily (if not explicitly) to adults.

Morphological Development

Morphology refers to the structure of words and rules for combining the smallest units of language into words. Words are composed of **morphemes**, the

smallest unit of meaning in a language. Although a word such as "talk" is a morpheme, we can add elements to change its meaning. We can, for example, add an "ing" to make it present progressive ("talking"), add an "ed" to make it past tense ("talked"), or, treating it as a noun, add an "s" to make it plural ("talks"). These word endings ("ing," "ed," and "s") are also morphemes, providing added meaning to a word. The average number of morphemes a child uses in a sentence, or the **mean length of utterance (MLU)**, is one indication of young children's linguistic development. The sequence in which these morphological elements are acquired is the same in most English-speaking children who have been studied (Brown, 1973; de Villiers & de Villiers, 1973). The sequence of acquisition for 14 morphemes is shown in Table 9.3.

Many of the morphemes children learn are rule-based word endings, such as adding "s" to make a noun plural or "ed" to make a verb past tense.

---

morphology The knowledge of word formation.

morphemes The minimum meaningful language units.

mean length of utterance A measure of language development defined by the average number of meaningful language units (root words and endings) a child uses at any one time.

table 9.3 Mean Order of Acquisition of Morphemes

Children start using the present progressive (verb + *ing*) when their *mean length of utterance* is about 2.5 morphemes. They do not start using contractions of the verb "to be" ("the dog's big"; "I'm going") until their mean length of utterance is about 4.0 morphemes.

Morpheme	Example
1. Present progressive (verb + *ing*)	I sing*ing*; He walk*ing*
2. Preposition "in"	*in* chair; *in* car
3. Preposition "on"	*on* table; *on* head
4. Plural (noun + *s*)	apple*s*; shoe*s*
5. Past tense, irregular verbs	*went; saw; ran*
6. Possessives (noun + *'s*)	Eve*'s*; hers
7. Use of "to be" (uncontracted)	the dog *is* big; I *am* tired
8. Articles "a" and "the"	*the* man; *a* toy
9. Past tense, regular verbs (verb + *ed*)	talk*ed*; throw*ed*
10. Third person regular verbs	he run*s*; she swim*s* (adding *s* to verb)
11. Third person irregular verbs	he *does*; she *has*
12. Auxiliary verb, not contracted	I *am* going; he *is* drinking
13. The verb "to be" contracted	the dog*'s* big; I*'m* scared; they*'re* here
14. The verb "to be" contracted and used as an auxiliary	I*'m* going; she*'s* running

SOURCE: Adapted from Brown, R. (1973). *A first language: The early stages.* Cambridge, MA: Harvard University Press.

Once children learn these rules, they tend to apply them, even when they are not correct. In most languages, the majority of words follow regular rules for pluralization (adding "s") or making something past tense (adding "ed") (Pinker, 1999; Pinker & Ullman, 2002); but all languages have a few irregular words that do not follow the rules, and these are often high-frequency words, such as the verbs "to be," "to have," and "to go" in English. Children often first use the past tense of these irregular verbs correctly ("was," "had," "went"), but once they learn the rule for making a verb past tense, they seem to forget the correct version and misapply the rule to produce words such as "was-ed," "had-ed," "go-ed," and "went-ed," as well as "run-ed," "drink-ed," and "seed," and nouns such as "footes" and "mices." This misapplication of regular morphological rules is referred to as **overregularization** and is an indication that children are learning the rules of morphology. Children often continue to overregularize irregular nouns and verbs into the early school years (Marcus, 1995; Marcus et al., 1992). Overregularization has been observed in a variety of languages other than English (Slobin, 1970).

One classic technique for assessing morphological development is the "wug" test (Berko, 1958, see Figure 9.9). Children are shown a series of unfamiliar objects (for example, "This is a *wug*") or people performing unfamiliar actions (for example, "This man knows how to rick"). For the "wug" example, children are then shown two of these creatures and told, "Now there are two of them. There are two _____." If children know the regular rule for making plurals, they will say "wugs." When they see a picture of a man who knows how "to rick" and are asked what he did yesterday, children who know the rule will say that "he ricked," and if they know the rule for the present progressive, they will say that he is currently "ricking" (Marcus et al., 1992). There can be little better evidence, we believe, than this behavior to illustrate that children are learning rules for certain aspects of language production.

Syntactic Development

Syntactic development refers to how words are put together into sentences and how various sentences are transformed from one to another, like the examples we provided earlier for the sentence "The woman rides the horse." Basically, you cannot have syntax until you have sentences, which requires at least two words put together, which children do not typically do until about 18 months. However, glimpses of children's future syntactical abilities can be seen in their one-word utterances; they often get a lot of meaning out of these single words. For instance, the word "wawa" may be used to request a drink ("Could I please have a glass of water because I am very thirsty?"), to marvel at the

overregularization The tendency to extend the use of some morphological rules beyond their scope, that is, when they are not appropriate (for example, runned, foots, mices).

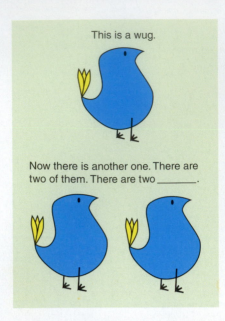

FIGURE 9.9 Example from "wug" test.

SOURCE: From Berko, J. (1958). The child's learning of English morphology. *Word, 14,* 150–177. Reprinted by permission.

table 9.4 Functions of Holophrases

Children around the world begin speaking in *holophrases,* or one-word sentences. Children can get a lot of mileage from such simple phrases. This table presents some of the functions of holophrases, or holophrastic speech, for young children.

- Request or indicate the existence of objects (for example, by naming them in a neutral tone)
- Request or describe the recurrence of objects of events (for example, "Again," "More")
- Request or describe dynamic events involving objects (for example, "Up," "Down," "Open," "Off")
- Request or describe the actions of people (for example, "Run," "Drink," "Jump")
- Comment on the location of people and things (for example, "There," "Inside")
- Ask some basic questions, with rising intonation (for example, "Where-go?" "What's-that?")
- Attribute a property to an object (for example, "New," "Pretty," "Cold")
- Mark specific social events (for example, "Bye-bye," "Hi," "Please")

SOURCE: Adapted from Tomasello, M. (2006). Acquiring linguistic constructions. In W. Damon, D. Kuhn, & R. Siegler (Eds.), *The handbook of child psychology: Cognition, perception, and language* (6th ed., pp. 255–298). New York: Wiley, p. 261.

view from the vacation cottage ("What a beautiful lake there is just beyond those trees!"), or perhaps to note that a cup of water has been dumped on a brother's head. Usually the meaning depends on intonation, gestures, and the context the child and adult are experiencing. Children from language groups all over the world use their **holophrases,** or one-word sentences (sometimes referred to as **holophrastic speech**), to accomplish at least eight different functions or purposes, which are described in Table 9.4 (Tomasello, 2006).

When children start putting two words together into sentences, they usually stick to simple constructions until their second birthdays. Children start with simple affirmative, declarative sentences, such as "I go," "Kitty bad," "Want milk," and "Daddy play." Negatives and interrogatives are more complicated and develop later. These early sentences include limited series of nouns, verbs, and adjectives but lack the morphemes that denote plurals or verb tense. They also lack determinants ("this," "that," "my," "yours"), prepositions ("in," "on," "out," "off"), and auxiliary verbs ("to be," "to have," "to do"), which serve as the glue that combines words together in sentences or that tunes the sentence to be grammatically correct and more semantically precise. Without these features, young children's language resembles old-time telegrams, in which people were charged by the word to send messages along telegraph wires ("Arrived NY. Alls well. Back Aug 3"). Because of this resemblance, it has been referred to as **telegraphic speech**. Today it might be known as TM (or text messaging) speech,

because it resembles typical text messaging ("Pick me up 8, west door, bring keys.")

Between 2 to 3 years old, the missing components of telegraphic speech are acquired—plurals, verb tenses, determinants, prepositions, and auxiliary verbs (for example, "to be," "to have") that were described earlier. These appear around the time that children are able to produce three-word sentences (Hoff, 2009). Beginning around 3 years of age, children start to use longer and more complex sentences. Children understand soon that word order is important (see Tomasello, 2006). For example, children between 2 and 3.5 years can recognize that a sentence is not worded properly when the verb used in the sentence is a familiar one; between 3.75 and 4.5 years of age, they can recognize incorrect word order even when unfamiliar verbs are used, indicating that they have acquired a better understanding of the word-order rules. For example, in one study (Akhtar, 1999), English-speaking children heard sentences with novel (that is, made up) verbs, sometimes in a familiar Subject-Verb-Object (SVO) order (for example, "Ernie meeking the car") and sometimes in sentences that used less familiar Subject-Object-Verb (SOV) order (for example, "Ernie the cow taming") or Verb-Subject-Object (VSO) order (for example, "Gopping Ernie the cow"). Children

---

holophrases (holophrastic speech) Children's use of one-word sentences.

telegraphic speech Children's economical use of words, including only high-information words that are most important in conveying meaning.

Progression of question forms in children (yes/no questions and wh- questions) presented in order of development

1. **Constructions with external question marker**

   Affirmative sentences are typically marked with intonation in *yes/no questions* ("Mommy eggnog?", "I ride train?", "Sit chair?"), and a wh- word at the beginning in *wh-questions* ("Who that?", "Where milk go?", "What cowboy doing?")

2. **Constructions with auxiliaries**

   In *yes/no questions*, auxiliaries are added at the beginning of a sentence, which usually is enough to produce a syntactically correct *yes/no question* ("Oh, did I caught it?", "Will you help me?"). However, there is no subject-auxiliary inversion in *wh-questions*, which does not generate a correct sentence ("What you did say?" "Why kitty can't stand up?")

3. **Constructions with subject-auxiliary inversion in wh- questions**

   With the introduction of subject-auxiliary inversions in *wh-questions*, they now become syntactically correct ("What did you doed?", "What does whiskey taste like?")

SOURCE: Adapted from Hoff, E. (2009). *Language development* (4th ed.). Belmont, CA: Wadsworth (p. 239).

---

as young as 2 years old had no problem with the familiar Subject-Verb-Object sentences, but about half of these young children corrected the Subject-Object-Verb or Verb-Subject-Object sentences to make them fit standard Subject-Verb-Object order (for example, "Ernie gopping the cow"). The percentage of children who corrected the unusual adult speech increased to about 90% by 4 years, reflecting children's increasing sensitivity to the familiar word order used in their mother tongue, as well as, perhaps, their comfort in correcting an adult.

In general, the production of more-complicated sentences seems to begin around the age of 2, when children are able to put four words together in their sentences (Bowerman, 1976), with most children using complex sentences by 4 years of age (Bloom, 1991; Bowerman, 1979). Examples of children's complex sentences and the order in which they are acquired are shown in Table 9.5.

One interesting change in children's language acquisition is their increasing ability to use negative and interrogative sentences. In the case of negative sentences, English-speaking children around the age of 2 typically begin using single negative words (for example, saying "no," or shaking their heads). Then they attach "no" to an affirmative sentence, such as saying "no drink milk," or "drink milk no." Later they imbed the negative word in the sentence, near the beginning, as in "I no do it," or "she no go." Finally, children are able to use negatives properly, as in "I don't want it," or "she can't have it" (Bloom, 1991).

In the case of interrogatives, linguists make a distinction between yes/no questions (such as "Rose go outside, Mommy?") and "wh"-questions (such as "Where's Daddy?" and "Why Mommy sad?"). Children produce the latter type of question sometime during their third year (Van Valin, 2002). The typical progression begins with simple modification of intonation to affirmative sentences, such as "Kitty gone?", with children raising their

table 9.5 Examples of Complex Sentences and Order of Learning

Type of Sentences	Examples
1. **Object complementation** Sentences that include direct or indirect objects	Look at me hit the ball. Marsha put it on the table.
2. **Wh-embedded clauses** Sentences with "wh" words such as "what," "why," "when," and "how"	Do you want to play when we get home? She showed me how it works.
3. **Coordination of sentences** Combining two sentences together with a conjunction, such as "and" or "but"	I tripped Justin and he fell. I like vanilla, but I like chocolate better.
4. **Subordinating conjunctions** Joining a subordinate clause to a main clause using words such as "because," "although," "if," "until," and others	I'll go to the park if Jesse goes. He ran away because he was scared.

voices at the end, as adults do, converting the previous statement into a question. This is followed by the inclusion of auxiliary verbs ("Is Kitty gone?"; "Do Mommy go?"). Finally, children begin inverting the word order of sentences to reflect adult-like language—first with yes/no questions, such as "Do you like this?" (the noun and verb are inverted from the declarative sentence "You do like this"), and then with "wh"-questions, such as "What is this?" (Radford, 1994) (see Concept Review 9.4).

The production of passive sentences ("I got hurt"; "The ball was kicked by Simone") is slower to develop than active sentences ("Simone kicked the ball"). In fact, the use of passive forms is relatively infrequent even in adult speech in English (Hoff, 2009). Passive sentences are generally avoided in English writing. For example, if you use the grammar-check program in Microsoft Word, it will identify passive sentences and recommend that you change them. English-speaking children do not produce full passive sentences until they are 4 to 5 years old (Budwig, 1990). However, in other languages that make greater use of passive sentences (Inuktitut, K'ich' Mayan, Sesotho, and Zulu), children 2 to 3 years of age produce them (see Tomasello, 2006).

Although most children have mastered the grammatical basics of their mother tongue by age 5 or 6, they continue to show mastery of the grammar of their language over the school years. For example, it is not uncommon for first- and second-grade children to overregularize words (for instance, saying "teached") or to use incorrect irregular verbs (for instance, "He don't"), which decreases throughout the school years. Children also produce longer and more complex grammatical structures, such as the full forms of passive voice and the conditional forms of sentences (for example, "If I find her number, I'll give her a call," Christie, 2002).

Development of Pragmatics: "Doing Things with Words"

In the previous sections we described how children master the basics of language, the sounds (phonology), words (semantics), and correct word forms and orders (grammar: morphology and syntax). But language is only any good if you do something with it. Being able to string words and sentences together may reflect language competence, but this is not the same as communicating effectively. Clearly, being a proficient language user requires more than the basics we have covered thus far in this chapter. What is needed is *pragmatics*, or as John Austin (1962) called it, "doing things with words." Full pragmatic competence requires that the speaker have a high level of cognitive and socioemotional competence. For example, one needs to remember previous exchanges with the person, decide how the person should be approached in the next exchange, and make inferences about their thoughts, feelings, knowledge, and beliefs. It also requires a series of specific skills linked to language use.

In this section, we first discuss *conversational skills* that focus on the development of the abilities needed to maintain successful conversations. We then examine **speech registers**, distinctive styles of speaking that are used only in specific contexts. These abilities develop systematically beginning early in infancy, but unlike other linguistic skills,

children do not typically master pragmatics until adolescence or even early adulthood.

Conversational Skills

Conversational competence refers to a set of pragmatic abilities that allow people to maintain a conversation with another person. For example, children must learn to sustain face-to-face interactions, make eye contact, initiate a verbal exchange, and take turns when speaking, all abilities that improve significantly during the preschool years (Pan & Snow, 1999). In infancy and early childhood, children's conversations with adults are asymmetric, with the adult taking the major role. Children often respond to adults' discourse with actions instead of words. For example, in response to an adult saying, "What nice new shoes you have!", a 2- or 3-year-old child may touch the shoes or sit down to take them off, whereas a slightly older child may simply (and appropriately) say "Thank you" (Allen & Shatz, 1983; Hoff-Ginsberg, 1990).

Parents promote children's conversational skills, often while teaching them good manners. For example, the bakery department at a local grocery store gives free cookies to children who ask for them. A typical encounter goes something like this:

Mother: "Ask the lady for a cookie, Ashley."

Ashley: "Can I have a cookie?"

Mother: "How do you ask?"

Ashley: "Please."

Bakery employee (handing child a cookie): "There you go, sweetie."

Mother: "What do you say, Ashley?"

Ashley: "Thank you."

Both the mother and the bakery employee know what's going on here and may exchange a few friendly words about the child or nods and smiles. Ashley is learning how to say "please" and "thank you," certainly features of good manners; but she is also learning how to make requests and how to respond when that request is granted—that is, she is learning to use language to communicate in a socially acceptable way. Parent-child conversations like these help children learn how to construct *narratives*, or stories, about past events. We discussed narratives and how parents scaffold children's storytelling (some more effectively than others) in Chapter 6.

Effective communication requires that children be able to take the perspective of another person. As noted when discussing Piaget's theory in Chapter 6, young children are often *egocentric*, failing to take the perspective of another in a social situation. With respect to communication, their egocentric worldview often results in speech that

speech register A distinct style of speaking that is used only in specific contexts (for example, when talking to children; when talking in school).

does not get the message across to a listener. This can often be seen in the phone conversations of 4-year-olds. When her grandmother asked Brittany what she was wearing today, Brittany pointed to her dress and said "This," into the phone receiver (see Warren & Tate, 1992 for other examples). Children's phone conversations increase in sophistication between 4 and 8 years of age, as they realize they must describe situations more fully when talking to someone on the phone than when talking with someone who is physically present (Cameron & Lee, 1997).

Children are not totally egocentric, however, and beginning in the preschool years will occasionally adjust or repair their speech when they make errors in communication or believe that the listener might not understand them. Such **verbal repairs** are essentially nonexistent in 1- to 3-year-olds. In contrast, 3- to 5-year-olds will sometimes modify a message to make it more understandable, with slightly older children being even more likely to correct errors in their speech (Evans, 1985; Shatz & Gelman, 1973). This is illustrated, for instance, by 4-year-old children using shorter sentences and a different tone of voice when speaking to a 2-year-old than to another 4-year-old or to an adult (Shatz & Gelman, 1973).

Let's provide an example of verbal repairs by a 7-year-old child. In telling a story about what she did over the weekend, this child realized that her message was sometimes not getting through, and she made several adjustments to her speech:

> We went to—uh me and Don went to Aunt Judy's. And . . . and uh my brother came down on Fri—Friday night, Uh there was a acc—came on the train, And there was an accident. And they thought uh . . . that uh . . . the—there was an accident with a—a van, And they thought—there was pig's blood in it. And they thought there was somebody hurt. But it was the pig. (Evans, 1985, p. 370)

Verbal repairs such as those seen in this 7-year-old's speech tend to increase over the preschool and into the early school years, reflecting children's increased tendency to monitor their speech and to be sensitive to their listeners. Verbal repairs decrease from middle childhood into adolescence as children's communication competency increases (Sabin et al., 1979).

The examples of verbal repairs just provided were in the course of a monologue. Conversations involve at least two people, and one important improvement in conversation that develops over time is how relevant the child's response is to his or her conversation partner. For example, in one study, conversations between peers were recorded for children in grades 2, 5, 9, and 12, as well as between adults (Doval & Ekerman, 1984). Older children were increasingly able to keep a conversa-

Adolescents use different styles of speech, or speech registers, when they talk to different people, such as peers, an adult in authority, and young children.

tion going by making relevant statements and taking turns speaking and keeping the conversation on topic.

Such linguistic turn-taking may have its origins in early parent-infant interaction. For example, infants and parents take turns making cooing or babbling sounds (Camaioni, 1993; Snow, 1977). Piaget referred to these interchanges as *mutual imitation*, with babies imitating adults who are imitating them. The parents are the real imitators here, but the result is bouts of turn-taking, with one partner making a sound and the other copying it, until one of them gets tired. Other examples of this preverbal turn-taking are games such as peek-a-boo (Bruner, 1983; Nelson, 1977). Not surprisingly, children whose mothers are more responsive to their vocalizations speak their first words earlier and have larger vocabularies than children whose mothers are less responsive (Bell & Ainsworth, 1972; Tamis-LeMonda, et al., 1998).

Speech Registers

One of the most distinctive pragmatic acquisitions in development is the ability to select an appropriate speech register. A speech register is a distinctive style of speaking that is used only in specific contexts. Children need to learn how to adapt the language that is appropriate to the person they are speaking with, a skill that most children do not develop until the school years (Oliver, 1995). For example, we have a different way of speaking to a close friend than to a stranger, an adult versus a child, a person in authority versus a peer. Although we might use slang and perhaps ungrammatical sentences when

---

verbal repairs Adjusting or "repairing" one's speech after making errors in communication or believing that the listener might not understand you.

table 9.6 Sample Differences between Standard English (SE) and Black English (BE)

Pronunciation and Word Forms	BE	SE
Consonant substitutions	/d/ for initial /th/	"Dey" for "They"
	/f/ or /t/ for final /th/	"toof" for "tooth"
	/v/ for medial /th/	"muvver" for "mother"
Consonant deletions	medial /r/	"doing" for "during"
	medial /l/	"hep" for "help"
	final consonants	"doe" for "door"
Syllable contractions		"spoze" for "suppose"
Stress on first syllable in (some) bisyllabic words		"Po'-lice" for "Police"
Hypercorrection		"Pickted" for "picked"
		"2 childrens" for "2 children"

Sentence Structure	BE	SE
Multiple negation	"I ain't done nothing"	"I have not done anything"
Aspect	"He be crazy"	"He's (usually) crazy"
	"He crazy"	"He's crazy (right now)"

Nonmarking or Nonmatching of Verb with Subject	BE	SE
	"She do all the work"	"She does all the work"
	"Two girl wearing hats"	"Two girls wearing hats"
Double subjects	"My daddy, he works . . ."	"My daddy works . . ."
Perfective *done*	"You done lost your mind"	"You have (already) lost your mind"

SOURCE: From Warren, A. R., & McCloskey, L. A. (1997). Language in social contexts. In J. Berko Gleason (Ed.), *The development of language,* 4th ed., Copyright © 1997. Reprinted by permission of Pearson Education, Inc.

speaking to a friend or peer ("What's up, dude?"), we are apt to use more formal language when speaking with an adult stranger ("Nice to meet you, how are you doing?"), and a different style of speech again when speaking with a small child ("And how are you doing today, huh? Are you having fun?"). In each case, we use a different language register to fit the communication purpose we intend. Sometimes these registers are different for people in different cultural groups (for example, American English versus British English, or Black English versus Standard American English).

Sometimes the speech register children use in school is different from the one they use at home or with their friends, and this can be a recipe for educational difficulties. The school language represents the standard version of the language and is typically used in the homes of middle-class families. In contrast, many African American children use a nonstandard form of English at home and in their neighborhoods, termed **Black English** (or sometimes *Ebonics,* or *African American Vernacular English [AAVE]*) (Green, 2002; Rickford, 1999).

Most Americans are familiar with Black English. Although mostly African Americans use it, not all African Americans speak it, and many non-African Americans do. Black English has some special rules of syntax and pronunciation (see Table 9.6). For example, unlike standard English, the verb "to be" is often not conjugated (for example, "I be" or "They be" as opposed to "I am" or "They are"), and sometimes it is dropped from a sentence entirely. For instance, the verb "to be" can be left out if the sentence refers to a one-time or unusual occurrence of an event, as in the sentence "He playing poker" for a person who does not usually play poker. But if the sentence refers to a recurrent event, the verb "to be" is included in the sentence. So, for example, "He be playing poker" describes a person who regularly plays poker and is playing poker at this moment (Warren & McCloskey, 1997). For the most part, Black English and standard English share common vocabulary and grammar, both are syntactically complex, and both are used to express complicated ideas and emotions (Green, 2002; Heath, 1989).

Although Black English may be syntactically sophisticated, it is not the language of the schools, nor of the mainstream American marketplace. This means that teachers, who usually speak standard

Black English (African American Vernacular English) A dialect of American English used mostly (but not exclusively) by members of the African American community, which is characterized by some special rules of pronunciation and syntax.

English, will sometimes not understand children who speak Black English, and vice versa. Children who speak Black English may therefore have difficulty following a teacher's directions and have a difficult time understanding text. As a result, they might be unfairly labeled as less bright than children who speak standard English. In support of this, the language abilities of children who speak Black English are often underestimated when they are tested using standard English (Adler, 1990; Wheldall & Joseph, 1986).

How should children whose home language is Black English be educated? Should they be taught using standard English, the dialect, or register, of the marketplace, or should they be taught using Black English, the register they know best? Research has shown that the more familiar 5- to 8-year-old African American children are with standard English, the better their reading achievement is, making the link between speech register and school success apparent (Charity, Scarborough, & Griffin, 2004). Most young speakers of Black English do learn some aspects of standard English and use it in school (DeStefano, 1972). For instance, in one study, the classroom speech of 8- to 11-year-old African American children contained more examples of standard English than did their speech out of school, indicating that elementary schoolchildren are able to switch between social (Black English) and school (standard English) registers (DeStefano, 1972). Yet, many African American adolescents *increase* their use of Black English, which is an important part of their social identity (Delpit, 1990; Delpit & Dowdy, 2002). The debate about how to educate children whose home speech register is different from the speech register used by teachers is a controversial one, involving social and political aspects, as well as linguistic and educational ones (Green, 2002).

It is important to keep in mind that Black English, or any other regional dialect, is not a linguistically inferior language relative to standard English, just as modern English is neither inferior nor superior to the Elizabethan English used by Shakespeare. Despite this, one must also be mindful that using Black English can be a detriment to children's education and the opportunity to fully partake in the American economy. But language is more than just a way to communicate. One's language also identifies its user as a member of a social group, and children and adolescents are often reluctant to give up their language style merely for the sake of doing well in school. Ideally, children would master both registers, just as children might ideally acquire a second language, and have the flexibility to switch between them as the context demands.

Although we have focused on the pragmatics of spoken language here, people today are increasingly communicating with one another via written, electronic means, and these new technologies are changing how language is used. In Box 9.4, we look at how *text messaging* is changing language.

Many African American teenagers prefer to use versions of Black English with their peers, in part as an indication of membership in a social group.

© Kris Timken/Blend Images/Corbis

Atypical Language Development

Up to this point we have described the usual course of language development, but not all children fit this pattern. Although all biologically typical children acquire language, and the sequence of language acquisition is similar for children across the globe, the typical pattern of language development can be altered by a wide range of causes. Language and communication are central to children's lives. When a child has a communication problem, such as *dyslalia*—the inability to produce some phonemes clearly—it makes social interactions problematic and also makes it difficult for a child to master reading and spelling. In this way, problems in language development can pour over into the cognitive and social realms. In this section, we will learn that research in atypical language development is fruitful in at least two senses: (1) it helps us understand and better attend to children with language problems; and (2) it provides some powerful insights concerning the role of language in cognitive development and vice versa.

BOX 9.4 child development in the real world

Do u txt? New Technologies of Communication and Language Development

You may have heard Latin described as a dead language. This is because, although it is still used in certain religious traditions and by some scholars, it is not spoken by any population of people and thus does not change. In contrast, all active languages can be described as alive in that, like living things, they change over time. The English of Chaucer is different from the English of Shakespeare, which is different from modern English. Languages change as people and cultures change, and much of the change has always come from youth. Current times are no exception, and the advent of new technologies in combination with the inventiveness of youth is resulting in a minor revolution in language. Cell phones, e-mail, text messaging, Twitter, and Internet chat rooms have become a part of our daily lives, and this includes the lives of children and adolescents. For example, a 2004 survey of schoolchildren in Northeast England revealed that 95% had a computer in their home, 83% used the Internet, 86% owned a mobile phone that they used both for "making calls" (91%) and for "text messaging" (89%) (Madell & Muncer, 2004). A 2008 survey of American adolescents found that the typical teenager made or received nearly 80 text messages per day. We will describe in Chapter 13 some of the consequences on social and cognitive development of the new technologies; here we examine some of the consequences on the use of language.

British linguist David Crystal (2001) has pointed out that the technologies of the Internet age represent not only a social revolution but also a linguistic revolution. In fact, according to Crystal, this is the largest linguistic revolution since the Middle Ages and the introduction of the printing press. With the later invention of dictionaries and grammar books in the 18th century, the English language became standardized, slowing down the rate at which it changed. These new technologies alter that. For example, Crystal (2006, p. 183) states that **Textspeak**, the sort of cryptic writing used in text messaging and e-mails, "is the latest manifestation of the human ability to be linguistically creative and to adapt language to suit the demands of diverse settings. In Textspeak, we are seeing, in a small way, language in evolution."

How are children's and adolescents' use of these new technologies affecting language? First, some forms of written language are being changed. For example, *rebus abbreviation* is one of the main features of Textspeak. A rebus represents words or names either by pictures of things that sound the same as the word or by letters or numbers. In texting, letters and numbers are used to represent syllables, words, and expressions, as in B4 ("before"); l8r ("later"), or F2T ("free to talk?"). Consonants usually have a more informational value than vowels in these expressions (for example, XLNT, "excellent"). Sometimes expressions become more sophisticated, using just the initial letters of the words of the sentence (for example, SWDYT, "So what do you think?"; LOL, "Laughing out loud"), or become really creative (for example, LSHMBB, "laughing so hard my belly is bouncing"). This does not prevent some ambiguities (for instance, Y may mean "why" or "yes"), and alternately a single expression can be written in a variety of ways, for example, "Good to see you", GTCY, GTSY, G2CY, G2SY (Crystal, 2006).

The use of these expressions has become so widespread among adolescents, and so baffling to many of their parents, that some U.S. cell-phone carries offer courses and publish pamphlets (for instance, *Txt 2 Connect with Teens: A Parent's TXT Tutorial*, published by AT&T) for parents to break the mysterious code of Textspeak (Belson, 2006). ("DO yor kds snd U msgz llk DIS 1?", queried Belson (2006) in his *The New York Times* article.) Perhaps not too surprising, some of these expressions are meant to warn the other speaker about the presence of adults and other people who could

---

How do we define a language problem? According to the American Speech-Language-Hearing Association (1993), a language problem is an impairment in the comprehension or production of spoken or written language (including other symbolic systems such as American Sign Language). These problems can be in any aspect of language, including phonology, semantics, grammar, or pragmatics. The catalog of language disorders and pathologies is beyond the scope of this book (see McCauley & Fey, 2006 and Paul, 2006 for in-depth discussions). In this section we first discuss briefly language development in some special populations of children, specifically children with sensory deficits (deafness and blindness) and children with intellectual impairment. We then look at children with specific language impairments.

Textspeak The sort of cryptic writing used in text messaging and e-mails.

Language Development in Special Populations

Hearing- and Vision-Impaired Children

Language is typically spoken, so it should not be surprising that hearing-impaired children usually do not acquire spoken language and that, without instruction in sign language, they can display significant problems in communication. However, communication also involves vision, and it would not be surprising either if being unable to see one's communication partner had some consequences on some aspects of language development.

Deafness. The most severe problems in language comprehension have traditionally been associated with deafness (see Freeman, Groenveld, & Kozak, 2005 for a detailed description). Between 1 and 2 of every 1,000 children suffers from a severe hearing loss (Carrel, 1977; Freeman, Groenveld, & Kozak, 2005). Hearing-impaired children who are

Adolescents and young adults are inventing a new language by using new technologies, such as texting with cell phones.

potentially interfere with or monitor their linguistic exchanges (G2G, "Got to go"; BRB, "Be right back"; CTN, "Can't talk now"; POS, "Parent over shoulder"; TOS, "Teacher over shoulder"; SAW, "Siblings are watching").

The new ways of using language in these technologies seem not to have changed the messages children and adolescents want to convey. It has, however, certainly created some new vocabulary, constituted by the sort of acronyms described previously (Crystal, 2006). But perhaps more than any other aspect of language, texting has affected pragmatics. Texting has become a sort of new linguistic register for children

and adolescents. Efficiency of communication needs to become adapted to the limit of the new technology (the 140 characters of a cell-phone screen), accounting in part for the extensive use of abbreviations. *Prosody*, the rhythm of language, including stress and intonation patterns, is difficult to convey in text, but Textspeak includes some electronic expressions to denote emotional states and communicate intentions. These include :-), reflecting a positive mood or indicating that one is joking; :-(, reflecting a negative mood; and the use of emoticons such as, 🙂 or 🙁 , whose meaning can be understood even by otherwise clueless parents.

Some have worried that children's and adolescents' frequent use of Textspeak and texting is having adverse effects on more formal writing. However, what little research has been done on these topics suggests that this concern is unwarranted. For example, in studies looking at the relationship between 10- and 11-year-old children's proficiency at texting and more formal assessments of spelling and writing, familiarity with textisms was not associated with poorer writing skills (Plester, Wood, & Bell, 2008).

Modes of conversation are changing, too. For instance, whereas one is greatly limited in how many conversations one can attend to at a cocktail party, that limit can almost be

ignored in a chat room, where one can listen to perhaps 30 people chatting simultaneously. The new technologies have permitted the use of the phenomenon of *framing*, in which a message can be divided by cutting and pasting it into several parts; one can then reply to any single part of the message. Crystal believes that such changes in conversational patterns are more significant, linguistically speaking, than the changes in the spelling, capitalization, and punctuation.

As the children and adolescents who are developing these new communication techniques become adults, these linguistic habits will become part of the mainstream (in fact, they already have). Will they morph into a new language? Will Textspeak not be just a technical term to describe how language is expressed in text messages but become a true language with its own syntax and vocabulary? Electronic communication in a globalized world, where there are few linguistic constraints so long as the message is understood, seems to be fertile ground for this sort of phenomenon. Given the speed with which new innovations can become part of mainstream life precisely because of these new technologies, this is a real possibility, and, as Crystal (2005) noted with respect to what the future holds, it is "quite certain we ain't seen nothin' yet."

not exposed to a natural sign language have serious problems with all aspects of language development. However, hearing-impaired children who learn to use sign language beginning early in life show approximately the same sequence, timing, and typical pattern of errors that hearing children show (Bellugi, 1988; Masataka, 2000; Maybery, 2002). For example, as we have seen, hearing-impaired infants of hearing-impaired parents "babble" with their hands when they are about 8 months old, much like hearing babies do with vocal babbling. They also produce their first words and first two-word sentences when they are approximately 12 and 18 months old, respectively, just as hearing children do. Hearing-impaired children also commit the same typical grammatical errors when learning sign language that hearing children do for spoken language, such as overregularizations (Petitto, 2002). This suggests that the human capability for language is not specific to auditory/spoken communication.

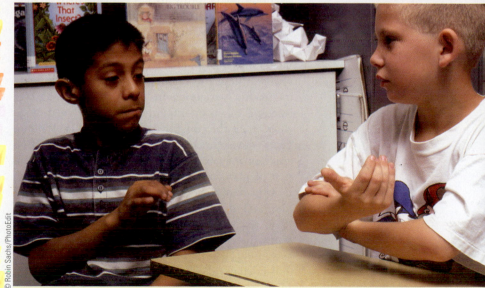

Hearing-impaired children who learn sign language early show no deficits in language development.

How deafness affects cognitive and socioemotional development has been a source of heated discussion for some time (Courtin, 2000; Oléron, 1957). Not surprisingly, severe deafness hampers the development of spoken language, which in turn can affect the development of vocabulary and reading. Despite this, deafness does not necessarily adversely affect school achievement, intelligence measured by nonverbal tests, spatial thinking, and reasoning, among other abilities (see Maybery, 2002, for a review), especially for children who learn sign language early. For example, about half of all hearing-impaired high-school children have a reading level at fourth grade or below, yet the other half read at a higher level despite their sensory disability (Chamberlain & Maybery, 2000; Maybery, 2002).

Regarding social-cognitive development, hearing-impaired children born to hearing parents (which is the case for about 90% of hearing-impaired children) show a delay in theory-of-mind development (understanding that people's actions are motivated by what they know and what they desire), regardless if they use sign language or not; in comparison, hearing-impaired children born to hearing-impaired parents exhibit the typical pattern of theory-of-mind development found in hearing children (Schick et al., 2007). This finding suggests that the interaction between hearing-impaired children and their parents affects their social-cognitive development, and social-cognitive development is delayed when there is a mismatch (hearing-impaired children with hearing parents).

Blindness. Vision-impaired children pass the same language milestones at the same time as sighted children, although the benefits of visual shared attention and pointing are not available to them (Bigelow, 2005). This is extremely important, because it has often been pointed out that, due to their loss of sight, language becomes vision-impaired children's most important tool for making sense of their environment (Bigelow, 2005). However, there are some interesting variations in the course of language learning in vision-impaired children that provide clues about the contribution of sight to typical language development. For example, vision-impaired children may have more trouble with the acquisition of phonemes that involve visible articulation movement of the lips, such as /b/ and /m/ compared to /t/ and /k/ (Mills, 1987). Perhaps not surprisingly, they frequently have more words in their vocabularies that refer to senses other than vision, such as sounds ("loud," "music"), touch ("bumpy," "soft"), and smell ("stinky," "flowers") (Bigelow, 2005). Prag-

matic competence, particularly in the case of conversations, shows slight deficits also, suggesting that vision-impaired children (and adults) are not able to fully incorporate the nonverbal cues of communication—body language and facial expressions (Gleitman & Gleitman, 1991; Pérez-Pereira & Comti-Ramsden, 1999).

Language in Children with Intellectual Impairment

Language development is often altered in children with intellectual disabilities. For example, children with *Down syndrome* not only show intellectual impairment but are also delayed to varying degrees in almost all aspects of language development. Grammatical development is especially affected. For example, it is not unusual for Down syndrome children to take up to 12 years to acquire the grammatical proficiency that most children attain in 3 years (Fowler et al., 1994). In general, linguistic abilities of children with Down syndrome lag behind their other cognitive abilities (Fowler, Gelman, & Gleitman, 1994; Hoff, 2009). This means, for example, that an 8-year-old child with Down syndrome may have the mental age of 4 years but have the language ability of a child much younger than 4. The exception is pragmatics. Children with Down syndrome are very interested in social interaction and are relatively proficient with this aspect of language (although rarely as proficient as typically developing children of the same age). For example, children with Down syndrome make more gestures than do typically developing children, are good at keeping conversations on topic, and repair their productions in the dynamic of social exchanges (Singer Harris et al., 1997; Tager-Flusberg, 1999).

Although most children with intellectual impairment, such as Down syndrome, acquire at least marginal language proficiency, there is one syndrome in which intellectual impairment is accompanied by relatively high levels of language abilities. **Williams syndrome** is a relatively rare disorder that occurs in an estimated 1 in every 7,500 to 20,000 births and is caused by the deletion of the long arm on chromosome number 7. Children with Williams syndrome display mild to moderate intellectual impairment, are distractible, tend to be overtly friendly, avoid loud sounds and physical contact, and have an affinity for music (Williams Syndrome Association, 2007, *www.williams-syndrome.org*). Although children with Williams syndrome have intellectual abilities often comparable to those of children with Down syndrome, their language abilities are typically much more advanced than their other cognitive functions (Bellugi & Wang, 1996; Bellugi et al., 2000; but see Brock, 2007, for a different viewpoint). These children typically show initial delays in language devel-

Williams syndrome A relatively rare disorder, with afflicted individuals displaying mild to moderate intellectual impairment, but having language abilities that are typically much more advanced than their other cognitive functions.

opment, but they often catch up and may in fact become quite loquacious. For example, an 8-year-old child with Williams syndrome may have a mental age of 4 but have a larger vocabulary and better pronunciation level than typical 4-year-olds (although not better than typical 8-year-olds). This is due in part to enhanced memory abilities. This finding is supported by research showing that the relationship between levels of grammatical development and working memory is higher for children with Williams syndrome than for typically developing children (Karmiloff-Smith et al., 2003; Robinson, Mervis, & Robinson, 2003). Compared with Down syndrome children, these children also display higher levels of grammatical complexity and pragmatics. With respect to pragmatics, children with William syndrome make greater use of social-evaluative devices in narratives—for example, intensifiers (*very, really*), sound effects (*ooohhh!*), and quotes (*he said*)—designed to maintain a listener's attention, continue a conversation, or take the narrator's perspective when telling a story than do typically developing children (Bellugi et al., 2007), reflecting their greater social orientation than most children.

Yet, it should be noted that children with Williams syndrome, when compared to typically developing children, do exhibit delays in language acquisition and do not fully develop language competence (Bellugi et al., 2007). For example, they rarely understand complex syntax, such as embedded sentences, and even in adolescence they have difficulties distinguishing between a joke and a lie—in other words, they make very literal interpretations of language (Mervis, 2003). Thus, these children do not show advanced language development, only levels of language development that are substantially more advanced than their level of cognitive development (but see Brock, 2007).

Evidence on the language development in children with Down and Williams syndromes also tells us something important about the relationships between language and cognition. The fact that both syndromes are associated with initial delays in language suggests that some general cognitive abilities are associated with language development. However, the fact that children with similar levels of cognitive impairment can exhibit substantial differences in linguistic proficiency indicates that language development is not simply a reflection of cognitive development. A certain level of cognitive development, whether assessed in terms of logical abilities as proposed by Piaget or basic cognitive abilities such as working memory, may be necessary for a certain level of language proficiency to develop (see Rose, Feldman, & Jankowski, 2009 for evidence of this in typically developing children). Yet, the different patterns of cognitive and language development shown by children with

Children with Williams syndrome develop language abilities greater than their level of cognitive ability would suggest. However, they are typically less proficient in language than typically developing children of the same age.

Down and Williams syndromes suggest that some aspects of language develop independently from cognition.

Specific Language Impairments

In the previous section we described patterns of language development in groups of atypical children. It should not be surprising that children with serious sensory deficits such as deafness and those with intellectual impairment also show difficulties with some aspects of language development. However, there is a relatively large group of children whose sensory abilities and intelligence are just fine. Their only identifiable problem seems to be difficulties with language. Such children are said to have **specific language impairment** (Hulme & Snowling, 2009). This category includes a wide variety of children with a large range of language-related problems (see Table 9.7). Many children with specific language impairment are late to talk, some not uttering their first words until 2 years of age. Despite an average IQ, these children have low levels of both language production and comprehension. Many have difficulty with past-tense verbs, often omitting verb endings (the "ed" that makes regular verbs past tense), and they often have difficulty using the auxiliary verb "to be," as in the

specific language impairment Children who exhibit problems that are focused in language, while other sensory and intellectual abilities are typical.

table 9.7 Characteristics of Specific Language Impairment

Diagnostic Criteria

Language is significantly below level expected from age and IQ, usually interpreted as scoring in the lowest 10% on a standardized test of expressive and/or receptive language

Nonverbal IQ and nonlinguistic aspects of development (self-help skills, social skills) fall within broadly normal limits

Language difficulties cannot be accounted for by hearing loss, physical abnormality of the speech apparatus, or environmental deprivation

Language difficulties are not caused by brain damage

Common Presenting Features

Delay in starting to talk; first words may not appear until 2 years of age or later

Immature or deviant production of speech sounds, especially in preschool children

Use of simplified grammatical structures, such as omission of past tense endings or the auxiliary "is," well beyond the age when this is usually mastered

Restricted vocabulary, in both production and comprehension

Weak verbal short-term memory, as evidenced in tasks requiring repetition of words or sentences

Difficulties in understanding complex language, especially when the speaker talks rapidly

Specific language impairment shows substantial heterogeneity, as well as age-related change, and diagnosis does not depend on presence or absence of specific language characteristics.

SOURCE: From Bishop, D. V. M. (2006). What causes specific language impairment in children? *Current Directions in Psychological Science, 15*, 217–221. Reprinted by permission.

sentence, "There [is] a pencil in the drawer." Thus, a 10-year-old child with specific language impairment may speak like a 4- or 5-year-old, stringing words together in short, ungrammatical sentences, such as "us run to store" rather than "We ran to the store" (Bishop, 2006; Joanisse, 2004). It is estimated that about 7% of American children suffer from specific language impairment, perhaps more (Tallal, 2003; Tomblin et al., 1997), with boys being more likely than girls to display language problems (Halpern, 2000; Hyde & McKinley, 1997). The frequency of specific language impairment is lower in adulthood, meaning that many children grow out of it (Bishop & Adams, 1990), either spontaneously or as a result of remediation.

It would be incorrect to refer to specific language impairment as a syndrome, because that implies a common set of symptoms. Although children diagnosed with specific language impairment share many characteristics, there are also many differences among them. As such, one would not expect to find a common cause for specific language impairment (although some recent research suggests that many children with specific language impairments have problems with speech perception, suggesting a common origin, see Joanisse, 2004; Ziegler et al., 2005). Nonetheless, behavioral genetics studies indicate that specific language impairment is highly heritable, with heritability estimates ranging from about .5 to .75. This means between 50% and 75% of the differences in specific language impairment can be accounted for by genetics (see Bishop, 2002). This is slightly higher than the heritability of IQ (between .5 and .6). However, although some genes associated with specific language impairment have been identified (Fisher, 2005), none seem to affect language directly, but rather influence some specific brain areas that affect some aspect of language processing.

Bilingualism and Second-language Learning

Bilingualism (and even multilingualism) is becoming increasingly common today, with about 50% of the children in the world being exposed to more than one language. For example, in the United States about 20% of children do not speak English as a first language, with this figure ranging up to 33% to 43% for some states, such as California, New Mexico, and Texas (U.S. Census Bureau, 2006). In Canada, where French and English are official languages, about 20% of children do not have either of them as a first language (Statistics Canada, 2007). Schoolchildren in the European Community have had second and third languages incorporated into their curricula, with English being the most common second language. In some European countries, such as Switzerland and Luxembourg, it is not unusual for people to speak three or four languages.

Costs and Benefits of Bilingualism

Are there detrimental effects of speaking two (or more) languages, or do bilingual children show developmental gains? At what age should a second

bilingualism Speaking two languages proficiently.

language be introduced for optimal learning? We may not have definitive answers for all of these questions, but research available on these issues allows us to make some preliminary conclusions.

In **simultaneous bilingualism**, children are exposed from birth to two languages. These children seem to develop two languages separately with little interference from either language. Although warnings have been given that children will not learn either language as well as they would learn one alone, this has not been shown to be the case (see De Houwer, 1995; Hakuta & García, 1989). Children who are learning two languages simultaneously do make some temporary mistakes, such as when children apply a rule from one language to their speech in another. For example, in Spanish, the adjective comes after the noun ("auto azul"), whereas in English the order is reversed ("blue car"). It would not be unusual to hear a Spanish/English-speaking child say "car blue" or "azul auto" as they are learning the two languages together. In addition, these children may have smaller vocabularies in each language during the early years of learning and a slight delay in language development compared with monolingual children, but by the age of 8 or so, there are typically no differences (Gathercole, 2002; Oller & Pearson, 2002). Bilinguals of all ages are also slower than monolinguals at retrieving individual words from their long-term memories (Bialystok, Craik, & Luk, 2008).

Becoming proficient in two languages requires more effort than learning only one language, and this should certainly not be underestimated (Pearson et al., 1997; Díaz, 1983). However, in counterbalance, the benefits of bilingualism are many. Being proficient in two languages gives children wider ranges of phonemes they are able to recognize (Bosch & Sebastián Gallés, 2001; MacWhinney, 2005). Bilingual children often develop a greater sensitivity toward the cultural values and the speakers of both of the languages they have mastered (Pérez, 2004; Snow & Yusun Kang, 2006). They show higher levels of metalinguistic awareness than monolingual children, and this has been linked to better proficiency in reading and writing and higher scores on some cognitive tasks, particularly those in which attention is an important factor or when the tasks are particularly complex or demand flexible thinking (Bialystok, 1999, 2001; 2010; Bialystok & Craik, 2010; Lambert et al., 1993). The positive influence of bilingualism on attention relies on the fact that, in order to manage two languages successfully without one interfering with the other, significant attentional control is needed. Simultaneous bilingualism seems to favor the development of executive control in children and postpones the deterioration of this mechanism in the elderly (Bialystock, 2007; Bialystok, Craik, &

In full and partial immersion programs, children are given instruction in a second language in a subject for all or a portion of the school year.

© Gabe Palmer/Corbis

Freedman, 2007; Carlson & Meltzoff, 2008). Perhaps related to their greater executive control abilities, 3-year-old bilingual children have been shown to perform better than monolingual children on theory-of-mind tasks (Kovács, 2009).

Sequential bilingualism is the situation in which children learn a second language after mastering the first. General findings are that there is a developmental lag of 3 to 5 years before children become proficient in the second language (Hakuta, 1999). However, bilingual children are a very large and diverse group, and several factors influence the acquisition of a second language, making it difficult to draw too many definite conclusions. For example, as mentioned earlier in our discussion of a sensitive period for language acquisition, the age when a child is exposed to a second language affects eventual proficiency. When the second language is begun during the first 3 to 4 years of life, aspects such as pronunciation and complex syntactic constructions are more easily acquired than if the second language is begun later (Johnson & Newport, 1989). The similarity between the two languages children are learning may also affect the degree of proficiency achieved or the ease of learning the second language. For instance, English-speaking children learning Chinese may experience more difficulty than English-speaking children learning Spanish, Chinese and English being linguistically more different than Spanish and English (Bialystok & Hakuta, 1994; Snow & Yusun Kang, 2006).

simultaneous bilingualism When children are exposed from birth to two languages.
sequential bilingualism When children learn a second language after mastering the first.
semilingualism In bilingual environments, the lack of mastery in both languages.

Another important issue concerning bilingual children is how well they have mastered the first language before the second one is introduced. Young children who arrive in a country in which the dominant language is different from their native language are often exposed to the dominant language in an academic setting. When this occurs, there is the danger of **semilingualism**—the lack of mastery of both languages. This can affect cognitive development and have negative effects on school achievement and social adaptation (Ovando & Collier, 1998; Crawford, 1997). However, when a first language is mastered by children and the second language is as highly valued as the first in social contexts, as is the case in Canada with French and English, this negative impact seems to be less or nonexistent, as children are exposed to both languages on a regular basis outside of school, within the family, and through the media (Genesse, 2003; Turnbull, Hart, & Lapkin, 2003).

The Developmental Relationship between Language and Thought

Language is a highly effective, specialized communication system; but it is not just language as a communication system that is so special. The ideas we express with language are the product of a cognitive system that is unique in the animal world. Is language merely a *symptom* of children's developing intellect—a reflection of underlying cognitive abilities—or are we thinking animals because of language? In other words, is language thought?

We may be tempted to think the latter, because for many of us thought without language is unthinkable. Most of us carry on a constant monologue in our heads and assume that without language we would be unable to think, but just a little reflection will demonstrate that this cannot be the case. We often have thoughts we have a difficult time expressing. We sometimes have a picture of something in our head or understand a problem (perhaps a math problem) intuitively but have a difficult time putting it into words. It was once thought that hearing-impaired children who were never taught sign language were intellectually impaired because they lacked language. However, what these children

lacked was a way to communicate what they knew (and a way for others to communicate with them), for, when tested in ways that overcame their communication difficulties, they displayed typical rates of cognitive development in terms of Piaget's stages (Furth, 1964). Other research shows that preverbal 12-month-old infants can use pointing to communicate about absent entities, a function that is usually handled by language (that is, talking about something that is not in one's immediate perception). Apes do not use pointing in this way (nor language), suggesting that young children's underlying cognitive abilities, not language, permits them to communicate about absent entities (Liszkowski et al., 2009). So language seems to express thought, but it is not thought itself (Pinker, 1994).

Although we do not want to equate language with thought, this does not mean that children's developing language abilities may not influence their thinking. In fact, they clearly do. Language gives us the tools to organize our thoughts, to tell stories in a coherent way, and to direct our behavior. Our discussion of language development in special populations and in bilingual children also makes it clear that, although language and thought are not one and the same, their development is related. This point was made explicit by the Soviet psychologist Lev Vygotsky (1962), who proposed that language directs much of children's intelligent behavior, with the relationship between language and thought changing with age. Vygotsky believed that language and thought are initially independent of one another. Language, or speech, is preintellectual and thought is prelinguistic. This changes over the course of development, as the two merge, with language becoming rational and thought becoming verbal.

Vygotsky focused on the phenomenon of **private speech**. Private speech is basically children talking to themselves. For instance, Piaget (1955) observed a form of private speech that he called **collective monologues** to describe children talking with one another but not necessarily to one another while playing. Consider the conversation of two preschool boys playing together: One boy says, "My *Charmander* evolves into *Charmeleon* and beats your *Balbasaur*," while the other says, "I have *Venusaur* on my DS, whose power is doubled, and can never be defeated!" These children are playing together and talking together, but their speech does not really communicate but only describes what they are doing. Piaget believed that such exchanges reflected children's egocentric view of the world and a failure to communicate and referred to it as *egocentric speech*.

Vygotsky saw things differently. He believed language played a role in influencing children's thinking and problem solving. Private speech, Vygotsky proposed, serves as a **cognitive self-guidance system**, guiding children's actions at a time when

private speech (or egocentric speech) Children's speech that is apparently produced for the self and not directed to others.

collective monologues Egocentric exchanges between two or more children with participants talking "with" one another, but not necessarily "to" one another, such that what one child says has little to do with the comments of the other.

cognitive self-guidance system In Vygotsky's theory, the use of private speech to guide problem-solving behavior.

DENNIS THE MENACE

Dennis the Menace © 1986 Hank Ketcham Enterprises North America Syndicate, Inc.

"I'M GONNA HAVE TO STOP THINKIN' OUT LOUD."

Young children often have a difficult time keeping their thoughts to themselves.

© Annie Engel/Corbis

Preschool children often talk to themselves while performing difficult tasks, such as assembling this puzzle, seemingly using language to direct their problem solving.

children cannot yet use language covertly, "in their heads." Rather, if children are going to use language to help regulate their behavior, they must make it overt: they must talk to themselves. One can easily find examples of preschool children talking to themselves while performing difficult tasks. Listen to 4-year-old Jessica, putting a puzzle together. "I gotta get all the red pieces here. Here's another one. Turn it this way. It don't fit. Okay, there's a corner piece. I gotta find one more red edge," and so on. Although some private speech simply describes what children are doing (such as the collective monologue example earlier), at other times, as in this example of Jessica, it actually directs behavior. Over the course of childhood, overt speech goes underground as covert verbal thought. Children still talk to themselves, but covertly, in their heads, using what Vygotsky called **inner speech.**

Is there any research evidence for Vygotsky's position? Studies dating back to the 1960s have found that private speech decreases over the preschool years, replaced by children whispering to themselves and reporting using inner speech to guide some of their problem solving (Winsler & Naglieri, 2003; Kohlberg, Yaeger, & Hjertholm, 1968; see Winsler, 2009 for a review). In fact, adolescents and adults still sometimes talk to themselves when facing a difficult task, but it is questionable whether such speech actually helps their performance (Duncan & Tarulli, 2009; Winsler, 2003).

Other research has shown that school-age children use private speech to help them solve a host of school-type tasks, such as addition and subtraction problems (Berk, 1986). For example, Laura Berk (1986) observed first- and third-grade children as they solved math problems every day over a 4-month period. Third-grade children were more likely than first-grade children to use private speech to guide their problem solving and used more internalized forms of speech (for example, inaudible mutterings, lip and tongue movements). First-grade children who talked to themselves while solving math problems tended to be the brighter kids, apparently realizing before their peers that there was something they could do to make their job easier. In contrast, there was no relationship between IQ and private speech for the third-grade children. This pattern reflects that brighter children begin to use private speech to guide their problem solving earlier than less-bright children and also stop sooner, as thought goes underground as inner speech.

Other research has shown that children are more apt to use private speech on difficult tasks as opposed to easy tasks and after making errors, and that their performance often improves after turning to self-instruction (Behrend, Rosengren & Perlmutter, 1989; Berk, 1992). In related research, children

inner speech In Vygotsky's theory, the covert language children use to guide their thinking and problem solving.

who are encouraged to self-explain—generate explicit explanations for problems they are solving (for example, "8 + 3 − 3 = 8, because you add 3 and take it away, so you don't really have to add and subtract all the numbers, you just know that it's 8") perform better on a variety of school-type problems than do children who are not prompted to provide such self-directed speech (Rittle-Johnson, 2006; Siegler, 2002).

Although the debate about the relationship between language and thought extends far beyond the role of private speech in children's problem solving (see Winsler, Fernyhough, & Montero, 2009), the developmental connection between the two can be informative. For example, tell-ing a young reader to "Read quietly to yourself!" may not be fruitful. Reading is considered to be a language art, and beginning readers may not be able to read solely in their heads. In fact, there is some suggestion that preschool children do not even believe that inner speech is possible. Rather, they believe that a person cannot talk to himself and think at the same time (Flavell et al., 1997). It seems unlikely that preschool children do not engage in inner speech sometimes, but it is difficult to know when the monologue that runs seemingly constantly through people's minds begins to develop, although it appears that the inner life of young children is not as (linguistically) rich as that of adults.

summary

Human language differs from the communication systems of other species in three important ways: it is *symbolic* and *grammatical*, and the particular language children learn to speak varies with culture. Children's language development can be described on several dimensions, including **phonology**, **semantics**, **grammar**, and **pragmatics**.

Empiricist theories of language acquisition have generally been discredited and replaced by **nativist** and **social-interactionist theories**. Nativist theories argue that (1) the brain is specialized for language, as evidenced by the identification of a **grammar center** in the frontal lobe; (2) children are born with a **universal grammar** that contains the basic syntactic structure of all human languages and a **language acquisition device**; and (3) there is a sensitive period for acquiring language. Some support for children's special facility for language comes from children creating **creoles** from **pidgins** after only one generation and the invention of Nicaraguan Sign Language in a series of cohorts of hearing-impaired children.

Social-interactionist theorists examine the interplay between language and cognitive and social development. Young infants are responsive to human speech and are especially responsive to **infant-directed** (or **child-directed**) **speech**.

Phonology refers to the sounds of language. Young infants can discriminate among **phonemes**, the individual sounds that make up words, and categorize language sounds much as adults do. Infants' ability to discriminate among the phonemes made in all languages declines with age, as their ability to discriminate the sounds found in their mother tongue increases. Early speech production includes **babbling**, which varies initially as a function of physical anatomy and later as a function of the language infants hear.

Semantic development refers to the development of word meaning. Children usually speak their first words around 10 months. Around 18 months of age, many children experience a **word spurt**, in which the rate of new word learning (mostly nouns) increases rapidly. This has been attributed to **fast mapping**, in which children are able to learn novel words with minimal input. Early in development, children often make **overextensions**, applying a word beyond its correct meaning (calling all four-legged animals "dog"), but they sometimes make **underextensions**, incorrectly restricting the use of a term (calling all dogs "Rex"). Children's **productive**, or **active**, **language** (what they can speak) is less than their **receptive**, or **passive**, **language** (what they can comprehend). Children's increasing semantic knowledge can be seen in their production and appreciation of verbal humor. Researchers have proposed the existence of *constraints* to make word learning easier. These include the **whole-word assumption**, the **taxonomic assumption**, and the **mutual exclusivity assumption**. The grammatical form of speech may give children important clues for guessing what a word means, referred to as **syntactic bootstrapping**.

Syntax refers to the knowledge of sentence structure, whereas **morphology** refers to the structure of words. **Morphemes** are the smallest unit of meaning in a language. The average number of morphemes used in a sentence, or the **mean length of utterance (MLU)**, is one indication of the language complexity of a preschool child. Children learn rules and **overregularize** irregular words to fit these rules (forming words such as "goed" and "mouses"). Children get a lot of meaning out of one-word utterances, called **holophrases**, or **holophrastic speech**. Early sentences are **telegraphic**, including only high-content words. Syntactic, or grammatical, development progresses quickly during the preschool years and is reflected in regular age-related changes in forming negatives, asking questions, and using the passive voice.

Pragmatics refers to knowledge about how language can be used and adjusted to fit different circumstances. Even young children are aware of some basic aspects of pragmatics, although substantial improvements are made with age. Preschool children often display poor communication skills, being less aware than older children of factors that influence the comprehension of messages. Beginning during the preschool years, children make **verbal repairs**, which indicate they are aware they are making communication errors or that the listener might not understand them. **Speech registers** refer to a distinct style of speaking that is used only in specific contexts (for example, when talking to children, when talking in school). For example, **Black English**—a dialect of American English used mostly (but not exclusively) by members of the African American community—is characterized by some special rules of pronunciation and syntax. Use of modern technologies by children and adolescents has resulted in **Textspeak**, a sort of cryptic writing used in text messaging and e-mails that is changing mainly pragmatic aspects of language.

Hearing-impaired children who learn sign language usually follow a similar pattern of language development as hearing children, suggesting that the human capability for language is not specific to spoken communications. Blind children pass the same language milestones at the same time as sighted children. Children with intellectual impairment, such as Down syndrome, typically display language development relative to or below their mental age. In contrast, children with **Williams syndrome**, who are equally intellectually impaired, often show language development more similar to their mental age. It is estimated that about 7% of American children have **specific language impairment**, with children having average IQs but difficulties in the production or comprehension of language.

Bilingualism refers to people who speak two languages. **Simultaneous bilingualism** refers to children who are exposed from birth to two languages, whereas **sequential bilingualism** refers to children who learn a second language after mastering the first. Generally, for sequential bilinguals, there is a developmental lag of 3 to 5 years before children become proficient in the second language. When children immigrate to a country in which the dominant language is different from their native language, there is the possibility of developing **semilingualism**—the lack of mastery of both languages.

Vygotsky proposed that **private speech** has a special role in guiding children's thinking and behavior. Private speech can be seen in **collective monologues**, with children speaking with one another but not necessarily to one another. Young children's private speech serves as a **cognitive self-guidance system** and is eventually replaced by covert verbal thought, or **inner speech**. Research generally provides support for Vygotsky's theory.

Key Terms and Concepts

Ask Yourself . . .

1. What is language, and how does it differ from other forms of nonhuman communication? Describe the four aspects of language (*phonology, semantics, grammar,* and *pragmatics*) discussed in this chapter.

2. How do proponents of nativist and social-interactionist theories of language differ in their views of language development? What are the main arguments to support their views? What, if anything, do these theories have in common?

3. What is the typical pattern of phonological development in English? How do children's abilities to tell the differences between different phonemes change as a result of experience with listening to their mother tongue?

4. What are the major milestones in semantic development? What mechanisms have been identified as critical for the rapid increase in vocabulary that children experience?

5. What is the typical developmental pattern for grammar (syntax and morphology) in English?

6. What is meant by pragmatics (provide examples), and how does it develop? What are the main differences between Black English, or AAVE, and standard English, and what do most linguists today believe about its linguistic status and its role in education?

7. What is a language problem according to the American Speech-Language-Hearing Association, and how do children classified as being language-impaired differ from typically developing children?

8. How does language develop in hearing- and vision-impaired children, and what does this tell us about the role of sensory input in typical language development? In the case of hearing-impaired children, what is the role of language in cognitive and socioemotional development? What about language development in children with intellectual impairment and its insights about the relationships between cognition and language?

9. What is bilingualism, and what different types are there? What are the consequences of bilingualism for language and cognitive development?

10. What position do most experts today take concerning the relationships between the development of language and thought?

Exercises: Going Further

1. Ask children of different ages (for example, 4, 8, and 12 years old) to tell you what they did last weekend, and, if possible (and always after asking permission from their parents), record what they have to say. Then, at home, compare how their linguistic productions differ regarding the four aspects of language (*phonology, semantics, grammar,* and *pragmatics*) described in the chapter.

2. As a child psychologist specializing in language development, you visit parents who are deeply concerned about their recently born hearing-impaired child. They seem particularly negative about his future cognitive and socioemotional development, as compared with "other children." They also worry about problems he will have communicating with others and even with themselves. Based on evidence described in this chapter, what would you tell them, and what recommendations, if any, would you give them?

3. You have been asked to give a talk at a school, addressed to parents and teachers, about bilingualism and its effects on intellectual development and educational achievement. The reason for the invitation is that several members of the teaching staff at the school feel a bit confused because of the contradictory information they are getting from different sources about the possible beneficial versus detrimental effects of bilingualism on children's development and academic achievement. Write 5 basic ideas summarizing the state-of-the-art thinking about this topic, including some practical recommendations.

Suggested Readings

Classic Readings

Bloom, L., & Lahey, M. (1978). *Language development and language disorders.* **New York: Wiley.** This book presents one of the first truly integrative viewpoints of what acquiring a language means. Based on the interplay of three core elements (Content, Form, and Use), Bloom and Lahey point out that the development of successful linguistic communication goes beyond the acquisition of the formal aspects of language, and that problems in the development of any of these elements can result in language disorders.

Pinker, S. (1994). *The language instinct: How the mind creates language.* **New York: Morrow.** Although it has been fewer than 20 years since its publication, this popular book has become a classic. It presents the nativist position of language acquisition perhaps more clearly and thoroughly than any other source. Whether you agree with Pinker's arguments or not, it provides an excellent look at issues dealing with the child's acquisition of language.

Vygotsky, L. S. (1934/1962). *Thought and language.* **Boston, MA: MIT Press.** This book changed the way that psychologists in general, and cognitive and developmental psychologists, in particular, view the development of language and thought, and their developmental relationships.

Scholarly Works

Hoff, E. (2009). *Language development* (4th ed.). **Belmont, CA: Wadsworth.** This textbook presents an overview of all aspects of language development, from linguistic theory to brain development.

Senghas, A., & Coppola, M. (2001). Children creating language: How Nicaraguan Sign Language acquired a spatial grammar. *Psychological Science, 12, 323–326.* This is a report of a research project looking at children's spontaneous invention of a sign language. In addition to providing fodder for debates about the nature of language development, it is an excellent demonstration of a naturalistic experiment.

Tomasello, M. (2008). *Origins of human communication.* **Cambridge, MA: MIT Press.** Michael Tomasello presents a social-constructivist approach to language as a contrast to the nativist approach advocated by people such as Noam Chomsky and Steven Pinker.

Reading for Personal Interest

Karmiloff, K., & Karmiloff-Smith, K. (2002). *Pathways to language: From fetus to adolescent.* **Cambridge, MA: Harvard University Press.** This is a comprehensive, well-grounded, and easy-to-read book about the state of the art in children's language development. The book is part of "The Developmental Child Series," addressed to a general audience.

Crystal, D. (1999). *Listen to your child: A parent's guide to children's language.* **London: Penguin.** This is a book addressed to parents to help them observe, understand, and even participate in their children's language development. David Crystal is an internationally recognized professor of linguistics who has written extensively about all aspects of the English language.

Cengage Learning's **Psychology CourseMate** for this text brings course concepts to life with interactive learning, study, and exam preparation tools, including quizzes and flashcards for this chapter's Key Terms and Concepts (see the summary list on page 383). The site also provides an **eBook** version of the text with highlighting and note taking capabilities, as well as an extensive library of observational videos that span early childhood through adolescence. Many videos are accompanied by questions that will help you think critically about and deepen your understanding of the chapter topics addressed, especially as they pertain to core concepts. Log on and learn more at **www.cengagebrain.com.**

10

© Greatstock Photographic Library/Alamy

In this chapter we investigate the concept of intelligence, first from the perspective of psychometric theory as exemplified by the IQ test. We then examine some alternative approaches to intelligence, specifically Robert Sternberg's triarchic theory and Howard Gardner's theory of multiple intelligences. We then look at the origins of individual differences in intelligence, investigating the factors that influence the establishment, maintenance, and modification of intelligence, followed by an examination of giftedness and intellectual impairment. We then turn to the acquisition of the three most important academic skills for children in modern societies: reading, writing, and arithmetic.

Jalyssa's parents always thought she was bright. She talked early, had a large vocabulary, and seemed to learn her colors, shapes, and numbers faster than her preschool classmates. When it came time to start first grade, Jalyssa's parents considered enrolling her in a private school for gifted children. But did they really know that Jalyssa was gifted? Most parents think their children are smart. Perhaps their positive impression of Jalyssa's intelligence was simply parental optimism. The school sent Jalyssa's parents to a psychologist who administered her a series of tests to assess her intelligence and the likelihood that she would do well in the school for the gifted. About a week later, Jalyssa's parents received a letter from the school inform-

ing them that their 6-year-old daughter had an IQ of 133, qualifying her for admittance.

In the previous chapters of this book, we focused on different ways in which cognition changes from infancy through adolescence. Although we occasionally discussed individual differences in children's thinking (for example, how cultural differences can affect strategy use, or how children with autism display an underdeveloped theory of mind), for the most part our attention has been on age-related differences in children's thinking. Yet, we are all aware that some children think better than others of the same age. Some kids are smarter than others. When psychologists and educators discuss relatively stable individual differences in cognitive functioning between people, they usually use the term "intelligence." Amanda gets better grades in school, follows the complicated story lines of movies and TV dramas more easily, and generally solves everyday problems more effectively than Julie, despite the two being the same age. We would typically say that Amanda is more intelligent than Julie.

For psychologists, however, intelligence is more than just a synonym for "smart." Rather, it reflects an important characteristic of individuals that can be measured and used to predict people's performance on a host of social and cognitive tasks. In fact, that is why the study of intelligence is important to child development: Children who score high on tests of intelligence tend to perform better in school, acquire important academic skills more easily, and often display better social adjustment than children who score lower on such tests. Scores on intelligence tests can alert parents, teachers, and other people concerned with a child's welfare to potential problems and their amelioration (or to potential areas of giftedness and their amplification).

In this chapter we investigate intelligence and academic achievement. However, these applied topics are not unrelated to those we examined in earlier chapters. In fact, as you will see, what underlie differences in intelligence and the acquisition of important academic skills such as reading and arithmetic are individual differences in some of the cognitive abilities that we discussed in previous chapters, including executive function, problem solving, strategy use, and metacognition, among others.

We should also say a few words about the connotation that the word "intelligence" has for most people. Although our intention is to focus on the psychological definition of the term, it also has significance from a sociological perspective. We all show different patterns of cognitive skills: Some people have better memories than others, some are more distractible, more verbal, or better with numbers than others, and most of us do not hesitate to comment on our cognitive strong and weak points. However, to say someone is of high or low intelligence means a lot more to most of us than to say someone has good or poor memory, high or low mathematical ability, or is more or less attentive. As you will see, this is partly because of how theorists and educators have defined intelligence as a set of intellectual skills that affect nearly all problems one attempts to solve. We value people of high intelligence, believing that they are more effective at a broad range of tasks, are apt to be more interesting to talk to, and are more economically successful. We likewise tend to undervalue people of low intelligence, thinking they are less skilled at performing the tasks of daily living. One often hears people saying things like, "People should have to take an IQ test before they have children" or "before they're allowed to vote." Although we cannot change peoples' connotation for the term "intelligence," we can alert students to the unconscious bias that most of us have attached to this term and emphasize that our discussion is limited to the cognitive aspects of intelligence.

Intelligence Tests and Testing

Intelligence is a lot like art: Everyone knows what it is, but it's difficult to define precisely. We like Robert Sternberg's definition of **intelligence** as "the mental activities necessary for adaptation to, as well as shaping and selecting of, any environmental context. . . . Intelligence is not just reactive to the environment but also active in forming it. It offers people an opportunity to respond flexibly to challenging situations" (1997, p. 1030). This definition suggests that intelligence is a complicated thing, involving many different processes that affect how a person functions in everyday life. This almost precludes the possibility that someone could develop a single test to assess intelligence, but this has not stopped people from trying. In fact, tests of intelligence go back more than 100 years. We are referring to the first IQ (Intelligence Quotient) test developed in France by Alfred Binet and Theodore Simon in 1905 to determine whether children could benefit from standard school instruction or if they required special education. Since then, the IQ test has gone through many changes, although the logic of test construction of modern IQ tests is similar to the first ones developed. Before discussing the construction of IQ tests, however, we need to introduce the theoretical approach behind them.

The Psychometric Approach and the IQ Test

Factors of Intelligence

IQ and other tests of intellectual abilities are the product of the testing, or **psychometric approach**. Basically, the psychometric approach holds that intelligence can be described in terms of mental **factors**, and one can infer the factors that underlie intelligence by looking at how people perform on a series of tests. For example, if people are given tests of vocabulary, reading comprehension, and verbal analogies and perform similarly on them (that is,

---

intelligence Ability to think and act in ways that are goal-directed and adaptive.

psychometric approach An approach to cognition that assumes that intelligence and other cognitive abilities can be described in terms of a series of mental factors, then, in turn, can be assessed by standardized tests.

factors In psychometric approaches to intelligence, a set of related mental skills (such as verbal or spatial skills) that underlies intellectual functioning.

people who score high on one test score high on the others, and people who score low on one test score low on the others), this is because these three tasks reflect a common factor, in this case verbal ability. Other tests can then be constructed to tap other factors (memory, reasoning, or spatial visualization, for example). The idea is that mental factors can be measured by constructing tests that assess the different facets of intelligence.

Given this approach, how many factors of intelligence are there? At one extreme is J. P. Guilford's (1988) theory that includes 180 unique intellectual factors. More influential (and older), however, is Charles Spearman's (1927) theory, proposing that intelligence can best be described in terms of a single factor (although he also proposed that there are a host of specific factors that are idiosyncratic to individuals and of little use in understanding the broader nature of intelligence). Spearman noted that people who performed well (or poorly) on individual tests that purported to assess intelligence tended to perform similarly on other tests, even if their content was seemingly unrelated. This has been confirmed by decades of research and is termed the positive manifold. If people are given a battery of different tests, all believed to tap intelligence (for example, vocabulary, general world knowledge, arithmetic, analogies), the correlations among the tests tend to be high. Spearman and others since then (Jensen, 1998) have proposed that this pattern reflects the fact that there is a single, domain-general cognitive process that underlies intelligence, termed g, or general intelligence.

Many psychometric theories over the years have suggested different numbers of factors, but most modern psychometric theorists argue for a domain-general factor of intelligence, similar to Spearman's g, with two to four second-order factors. For example, Raymond Cattell (1971) proposed that intelligence can be divided into fluid and crystallized abilities. Fluid abilities are biologically determined and reflected by tests of memory span, speed of processing, and spatial thinking. They can be thought of as domain-general cognitive processes involved in the active or effortful maintenance of information in working memory for the purpose of planning and executing goal-directed behavior (Blair, 2006). Most of the executive functions discussed in Chapter 8 would be considered measures of fluid intelligence. According to Cattell, fluid abilities are relatively unaffected by learning, culture, or experience. In contrast, crystallized abilities are best reflected by tests of verbal comprehension or social relations, skills that depend more highly on cultural context and experience.

A related psychometric theory of intelligence is called the hierarchical model of cognitive abilities (Carroll, 1993), which proposes four related sets

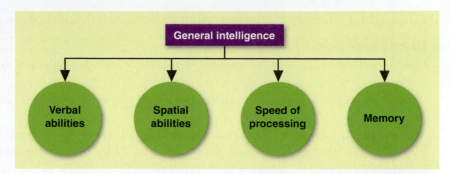

of cognitive skills (verbal, spatial thinking, speed of processing, and memory) that are all influenced by a general intellectual factor (see Figure 10.1).

As we will see when we examine some alternative approaches to intelligence, not everyone agrees with the way psychometricians define or measure intelligence. However, regardless of whether you are a fan of psychometric theory or not, it has had great influence on generations of children and society in general by way of its best-known product, the IQ test.

The IQ Test

We bet that everyone reading this book has taken an IQ test at least one time in his or her life. Many of you probably did not even know you were taking one. Although the most reliable IQ tests are administered individually and may take more than an hour to complete, paper-and-pencil versions are given routinely in school, often as subtests of achievement tests. The logic behind the construction of IQ tests is relatively simple. People are administered a series of tests believed to assess intelligence. At each age tested, test makers look for items that differentiate between people. For instance, a good 5-year-old item would be one that about half of the 5-year-olds get right and half get wrong. If too many 5-year-olds get it right or get it wrong, it does not discriminate between who is smart (the ones who get it right) and who is not (the ones who get it wrong). This, in a nutshell, is the logic of constructing IQ tests, and the test-makers

FIGURE 10.1 Hierarchical model of cognitive abilities.
Intelligence is composed of specific cognitive abilities (verbal abilities, spatial abilities, speed of processing, memory) that are intercorrelated and influenced by a higher-order general intellectual factor, g.

---

positive manifold The high correlations among scores on sets of cognitive tests that have little in common with one another in terms of content or types of strategies used.

general intelligence (g) In psychometric theory, the idea that intelligence can be expressed in terms of a single factor, called g.

fluid abilities Intellectual abilities that are biologically determined and reflected in tests of memory span and spatial thinking.

crystallized abilities Intellectual abilities that develop from cultural context and learning experience.

hierarchical model of cognitive abilities The model that proposes that intelligence is composed of specific cognitive abilities (for example, verbal, spatial, speed of processing, memory) that are intercorrelated and influenced by a higher-order general intellectual factor, g.

IQ test Tests whose main purpose is to provide an index (intelligence quotient) that quantifies intelligence level.

table 10.1 Examples of the Types of Items on Each Subtest of the WISC-IV

Verbal Comprehension Index

Similarities: Children are read two words in pairs similar to the following and are to tell how they are alike: pear-peach; inch-ounce; snow-sand.

Vocabulary: Children are read words and are to tell what each word means (for example, "What is a magazine?" "What does democracy mean?").

Comprehension: Children are asked questions assessing their knowledge of societal conventions and of appropriate behavior in a variety of situations: "What are some reasons we need soldiers?" "What are you supposed to do if you find someone's watch in school?" "Why is it important to have speed limits on roads?"

Information: Children are asked questions assessing their general world knowledge, similar to the following: "How many pennies make a dime?" "What do the lungs do?" "What is the capital of Italy?" This is an optional test, not included in the index total score.

Word Reasoning: Children are given sets of hints and must identify the object that the hints describe (for example, "This has a flat end and a long handle"; "You use it to dig holes").

Perceptual Reasoning Index

Block Design: Children are given nine cubes, colored red on two sides, white on two sides, and red and white on two sides. They are shown designs and are to reproduce them using the nine blocks. Bonus points are given for fast response times.

Picture Concepts: Children are shown pictures and must match those that belong together based on common features (for example, things to drink, toys).

Picture Completion: Children are shown black-and-white pictures and are to determine what important part of each picture is missing. This is an optional test, not included in the index total score.

Working Memory Index

Digit Span: Children are read digits at a rate of one per second and are to repeat them back in exact order. This is followed by a test in which children must repeat the numbers in the reverse order from the order the examiner spoke them.

Letter-Number Sequencing: The examiner reads children a sequence of letters and numbers (for example, 7, K, 3, P, 8, D) and asks children to recall the numbers in ascending order (3, 7, 8) and the letters in alphabetical order (D, K, P).

Arithmetic: Children are given arithmetic problems. The easiest involve counting, addition, and subtraction using physical reminders. A child might be shown a picture of nine trees and asked to cover up all but five. More complex problems are read aloud (for example, "Joyce had six dolls and lost two. How many dolls did she have left?" "Three girls had 48 cookies. They divided them equally among themselves. How many cookies did each girl get?"). This is an optional test, not included in the index total score.

Processing Speed Index

Coding: Children are shown a key associating simple geometric figures (for instance, a triangle, a square, and a circle) with other symbols (a cross, a vertical line, and so on). Children are to mark the associated symbol below a set of randomly arranged figures as quickly as possible without skipping any. Bonus points are given for fast response times.

Symbol Search: Children are shown a target symbol (for example, ≠) and beside it a series of three symbols (for example, δ∞Υ , or Υδ≠). Children must determine if the first (target) symbol is contained in the second (search) set of symbols.

Cancellation: Children are shown arrays of objects and asked to mark each object of a certain type (all the trucks, for example) as quickly as possible. This is an optional test, not included in the index total score.

---

work very hard to come up with items that differentiate between people of a given age.

IQ tests are constructed so that scores are normally distributed, with the average score at any age being 100, with a standard deviation of 15. For those students with a little statistics, the *standard deviation* is a statistical measure that assesses how scores vary around the arithmetic average, or mean. Test makers administer individual items to many children at different ages and select those items that give the test the statistical properties

they desire. Knowing one's IQ, a person can easily tell where he or she stands with respect to the general population in terms of IQ. With a mean of 100 and a standard deviation of 15, for example, a person with an IQ of 115 has a score equal to or greater than about 84% of the population. An IQ of 130 puts one at the 98th percentile. It works the same way on the opposite side of the curve: Someone with an IQ of 85 has a score equal to or greater than about 16% of the population (or equal to or less than 84% of the population).

There are several gold-standard IQ tests, among them the Wechsler scales and the Stanford-Binet. Both the Wechsler scales and the Stanford-Binet are administered individually by a highly trained

Wechsler scales Individually administered IQ tests, including the WPPSI, the WISC, and the WAIS.

Stanford-Binet An individually administered IQ test for people 2 years old to adulthood.

IQ tests like the Wechsler Scales and the Stanford-Binet are individually administered and can take more than an hour to complete.

technician, are highly standardized, and often take more than an hour to complete. To illustrate what an IQ test is like, let us briefly describe the Wechsler Scales. There are three primary Wechsler scales, developed for people of different ages: the Wechsler Preschool and Primary Scale of Intelligence (WPPSI) for children 2 to 7 years old; the WISC, for children 6 through 16 years old; and the Wechsler Adult Intelligence Scale (WAIS) for adults. The latest version of the WISC (WISC-IV, Wechsler, 2003) provides a full-scale IQ based on four separate indexes: Verbal Comprehension, Perceptual Reasoning, Working Memory, and Processing Speed. Table 10.1 lists the subtests for each index and provides brief examples of the types of items on these tests.

There are many other IQ tests, some nonverbal measures of visual reasoning (The Ravens Progressive Matrices, Raven, Raven, & Court, 2003), and many other paper-and-pencil tests that can be administered to groups of people, such as a classroom of students, with only minimal supervision. Enter "IQ test" in Google and you will find several online tests you can take in the comfort of your home. These tests do not have the reliability or validity of the individually administered Stanford-Binet or the Wechsler scales, but the logic in their construction is pretty much the same. Like the gold-standard tests, most of the easily administered tests will give you a score, with 100 being

average, that will tell you where you stand with respect to other people who have taken the test. Table 10.2 lists some of the more widely used intelligence tests for children.

The Wechsler and Stanford-Binet scales can be used with children as young as 2 years of age. Other tests have been constructed to assess intelligence in infancy and toddlerhood. Instead of an IQ score, these tests produce a DQ (developmental quotient) score that is interpreted in the same way as IQ scores. Tests such as the Bayley Scales of Infant and Toddler Development (Bayley, 1969, 2005), the Gesell Developmental Schedules (Gesell & Amatruda, 1954), and the Neonatal Behavioral Assessment Scale (Brazelton, 1973) are based on evaluations of individual differences in sensory, motor, and cognitive abilities. For example, items used to compute a developmental quotient at different age levels in the Bayley Scales include the following:

Infant/toddler tests

1 to 3 months: responds to sound of bell; vocalizes once or twice; displays social smile

5 to 7 months: smiles at mirror image; turns head after fallen spoon; vocalizes four different syllables

9 to 12 months: responds to verbal requests; stirs with spoon in imitation; attempts to scribble

14 to 17 months: says two words; shows shoes or other clothing; builds a tower of three cubes.

table 10.2 Some of the More Widely Used Intelligence Tests for Children

Infancy Intelligence Tests

(Provides a DQ = Developmental Quotient score)

- Bayley Scales of Infant and Toddler Development
- Gesell Developmental Schedules
- Neonatal Behavioral Assessment Scale

Childhood Intelligence Tests

(Provides an IQ = Intelligence Quotient score)

- Wechsler Preschool and Primary Scale of Intelligence (WPPSI)
- Wechsler Scale of Intelligence for Children (WISC)
- Stanford-Binet Scale
- The Ravens Progressive Matrices

Tests of infant intelligence, such as the Bayley Scales, produce a DQ (developmental quotient), which, like an IQ score, lets the examiner know where an infant stands with respect to other infants of the same age in terms of developmental abilities.

Cliff Moore/Photo Researchers, Inc.

These tests have been well standardized, are reliable (that is, there is high test-retest and inter-tester agreement), and describe important differences among infants (McCall, Hogarty, & Hurlburt, 1972). Whether they measure the same thing that IQ tests measure, however, is a matter of debate, an issue we will address later in this chapter.

What Does IQ Predict?

Does IQ measure anything important? Does it predict how well one will do in school or in life? Many researchers and educators think so, at least to some degree. Research has shown, for example, that IQ predicts reasonably well individual differences in academic performance, occupational status, and longevity.

First, let's examine the relationship between IQ scores and academic performance. How well do they predict academic performance? The simple answer is "pretty good." The average correlation between children's IQ scores and current and future grades is about .50 (Neisser et al., 1996; White, 2000). One interpretation of this relatively strong relationship is that the mental abilities tapped by IQ tests reflect general intelligence, or *g*, and that these intellectual skills are needed to perform well in school (Jensen, 1998).

Another way of looking at the relationship between IQ and academic performance is to examine the effects of school attendance on IQ. Stephen Ceci and Wendy Williams (1997) reviewed the relationship between schooling and IQ and reported that (1) there is a strong, positive correlation between years of education and IQ (.60 or higher); (2) there is a small but significant drop in children's IQs over summer vacation; (3) children who attend school intermittently have lower IQs than children who attend school regularly; (4) children who start school late have lower IQs than children who start school on schedule; (5) quality of schooling is related to IQ, with children attending better-quality schools having higher IQs; and (6) people who drop out of school early have lower IQs than people who stay in school. That is, although some people interpret the significant correlation between IQ and school performance as reflecting the influence of intelligence on academic achievement, others see it the other way around. The truth, we believe, lies somewhere in the middle, with the relationship between intelligence as measured by IQ and school performance being a bidirectional one.

Other evidence indicating that the relationship between school achievement and IQ may be a two-way street comes from studies that examined schooling versus age effects on IQ and academic performance. For example, in one study, researchers assessed IQ and school achievement of fourth-, fifth-, and sixth-grade Israeli children as a function of the number of years of education while controlling for age (Cahan & Cohen, 1989). They reported that children in the higher grade had higher IQ scores than children their same age in the lower grade (remember, average IQ scores do *not* get higher with age, but are standardized to have the same average at each age). Although older children did perform better than younger children overall, the effect of schooling on IQ and school performance was two to three times as large as the effect for age. Similar effects have been reported in a more recent Swedish study (Cliffordson & Gustafsson, 2008; see also Morrison, Griffith, & Alberts, 1997). In other words, when you hold age constant, children who have had more years of schooling have higher IQs, indicating a potent effect of education on intelligence.

In general, IQ scores do predict academic performance, but being schooled also affects how high one scores on an IQ test. Also, remember that although the correlation between IQ and academic performance is relatively high, it still only accounts for about 25% of the differences in school performance between children. Clearly, other factors, perhaps some in interaction with IQ, affect how well children do in school.

How does IQ do in predicting occupational status? Again, pretty well. People with higher-status (and usually higher-paying) jobs have higher IQs than people with lower-status (and usually lower-paying) jobs (Brody, 1997; Neisser et al., 1996). There are many potentially confounding factors for this relationship, the most obvious being the relationships between IQ and education and between education and occupation. Nonetheless, even when levels of education are controlled, a significant relationship between IQ and occupational status remains (Neisser et al., 1996). Also, there is a positive correlation of about .5 between IQ and job performance for people *within* a profession (among a group of lawyers or accountants, for example). People with higher IQs tend to be rated as better at their jobs than people with lower IQs, although many other factors are associated with job performance, given that 75% of the variance in job performance is left unexplained after considering the effect of IQ.

In addition to its association with academic performance and occupational status, childhood IQ is positively related with longevity (Hart et al., 2005; Deary et al., 2008) and better health (Batty et al., 2006). There are no easy explanations for these relationships. Are genes associated with high IQ also associated with longevity and health? Might these all be related to prenatal environments (healthier prenatal environments are associated with higher IQ, longevity, and health), or might the effect of IQ be related to education? Perhaps people with higher IQs are more aware of many health hazards, such as smoking and obesity, and thus choose to lead healthier lives as a result. As you will see later in this chapter, there is no simple cause for a high or low IQ, and thus the many relationships that are found between IQ and various other measures of physical, social, and cognitive functioning do not likely have a single and simple explanation.

IQ Tests and Minority Children

One criticism of IQ tests is that they discriminate against minority children. On average, the IQ

© Richard Hutchings/Corbis

IQ accounts for about 25% of individual differences in children's academic performance. However, attending school also increases IQ, making the relationship between intelligence as measured by IQ and schooling a bidirectional one.

scores of African American children are about 10 to 15 points lower than those of European American children (Herrnstein & Murray, 1994). Part of the group difference can be attributed to socioeconomic status (SES). Children from lower-SES homes score lower on IQ tests than children from middle-SES homes, and African American children are more likely than European American children to live in low-SES homes (Suzuki & Valencia, 1997). This is clearly illustrated by adoption studies in which African American children born of parents from lower-income homes were adopted by middle-class parents. In one study (Scarr & Weinberg, 1976; Weinberg et al., 1992), the average IQ of the adopted African American children was about 110, which is 20 points higher than the average IQ of comparable children being reared in the local African American community.

One possible source of differences in IQ scores between cultural minority and European American children is related to stereotype threat (Steele, 1997). People are aware of stereotypes for their particular social group, and when the stereotype is activated, people tend to confirm the negative stereotype. For example, the cultural stereotype for African Americans is that they perform poorly on IQ tests. When groups of African and European American college students were administered a test of verbal intelligence, performance of the African American students varied depending on

stereotype threat Phenomenon in which minority members perform worse on IQ or other tests after being reminded of the negative stereotype concerning their groups' performance on such tests.

whether they were told it was a test of intelligence or not. The African Americans who were told the test was assessing their intelligence scored significantly lower than those who were not told that this was an intelligence test (Steele & Aronson, 1995). This suggests that the tests may not be measuring people's intelligence, per se, but their tendency to choke under situations in which a stereotype threat was activated (but see Sackett, Hardison, & Cullen [2004], who caution that the stereotype threat does not eliminate the European/African American difference in IQ).

Another possibility for race and ethnic differences in IQ scores is that the tests are biased and based on skills and knowledge that are deemed important by the majority culture. For example, IQ differences between minority and majority children are reduced when culture-fair tests such as the nonverbal Ravens Progressive Matricies Test mentioned earlier are used (Anastasi, 1988). Minority children might not share the same values or have the same world knowledge as children from the majority culture, which can seriously hamper their performance on verbal tests. They might have different expectations concerning the type of answers the examiner is looking for. Because the test is highly standardized (that is, the test is administered the same way, regardless of who is giving or who is taking the test), an examiner cannot adjust his or her questions to assess what a child really knows. Consider this example of a 5-year-old African American child's responses to questions about similarities (from Miller-Jones, 1989, p. 362):

Tester: "How are wood and coal alike? How are they the same?"

Child: "They're hard."

Tester: "An apple and a peach?"

Child: "They taste good."

Tester: "A ship and an automobile?"

Child: "They're hard."

Tester: "Iron and silver?"

Child: "They're hard."

The child obtained zero points for his answers, but does this mean he does not know the conceptual relationship between iron and silver or between an apple and a peach? There is nothing incorrect about the child's answers, but they do not fit the test makers' conceptions, and the examiner is not allowed to ask follow-up questions, such as, "Yes, they're both hard, but how else are they alike?" This child's answers do not likely exhaust his knowledge of the relationships between these objects, but the test format precludes finding this out.

Thus, although IQ tests may be a good measure of intellectual abilities for children from the majority culture, they are not an adequate test of intelligence for children from minority homes (Miller-Jones, 1989). Furthermore, the testing situation may be less familiar to children from the minority as opposed to the majority culture, and the examiner is likely to be a member of a different ethnic and social class than the minority child, adding further to the discomfort and novelty of the testing situation.

To improve assessment of minority children with IQ and other standardized tests, psychologist Dalton Miller-Jones (1989) made several recommendations:

1. When assessing any area of intelligence, it is important to specify the cognitive processes that might be involved in the task or elicited by the stimuli.
2. Multiple tasks with different materials should be used with the same individual.
3. Tests must be appropriate for the culture from which the child comes.
4. The connection must be validated between the cognitive operations assessed by a test and the attainment of school-related concepts such as arithmetic and reading.
5. Procedures must be developed that permit an examiner to probe for the reasoning behind a child's answers.

Miller-Jones's advice is sound and applies to nonminority as well as to minority children.

Teachers also sometimes expect less of minority students, in terms of academic performance, than of children from the majority culture. Can expectations of teachers (and perhaps parents and peers) affect school performance and IQ? The answer seems to be a resounding "yes," and this is illustrated in a classic study by Robert Rosenthal and Lenore Jacobson (1968), titled *Pygmalion in the Classroom*. The title refers to a play by George Bernard Shaw in which a professor bets that in a short time he can pass off a poor, uneducated flower girl as a proper member of society. (You may know this story from the play or movie *My Fair Lady*.) The **Pygmalion effect** is a form of *self-fulfilling prophecy*, in which a person internalizes the expectations of an authority figure. In the play, the flower girl internalized the professor's perception of her. In the classroom, children internalize the intellectual expectations teachers have for them.

Rosenthal and Jacobson told elementary school teachers at the beginning of the year that some children in their class were expected to bloom intellectually. In fact, the names of the children were chosen randomly. At the end of the school year, chil-

Pygmalion effect A form of *self-fulfilling prophecy*, in which a person internalizes the expectations of an authority figure.

dren took an IQ test, and the results were compared to one that had been taken a year earlier. Children identified as bloomers gained significantly more on the IQ tests than did other children, illustrating the effect that teacher expectation can have not only on academic performance, but also on IQ scores.

Is IQ Stable over Time?

An IQ score is not intended to be a measure of intellectual *development*. Instead, it is intended to tell where a person stands with respect to same-age peers in terms of intelligence. So, for example, both the average 5-year-old and the average 10-year-old have identical IQs of 100, but one would not want to claim that the 5- and 10-year-old are equally smart. Obviously, the 10-year-old knows more and thinks differently than the 5-year-old. Yet, they are both average for their age. When we ask if intelligence as measured by IQ is *stable*, we mean "Do children maintain their same *rank order* with respect to other children at different times?" That is, will the average 5-year-old become the average 10- or 18-year-old, will the above-average pre-schooler become the high-IQ 12-year-old, and will a child with an IQ at the bottom of his kindergarten class hold the same position when he graduates from high school? If the answer is "yes" to these questions, we can say that IQ is stable over time. To the extent that children's rank order varies from time to time, the stability of IQ is reduced. For the most part, stability and rank order are measured by *cross-age correlations*. The higher the correlations between the IQ scores measured at different times, the more stable IQ is said to be.

In general, IQ tends to be highly stable over childhood into young adulthood. Table 10.3 presents the results of two longitudinal studies, examining the correlations of IQs measured at various times in childhood and IQ in young adulthood (17 or 18 years) (Bayley, 1949; Honzik, MacFarlane, & Allen, 1948). As you can see, beginning at age 6 to 7 years, the cross-age correlations are high (about .67) and only get higher the older children are when IQ is measured. Patterns such as these caused Claire Kopp and Robert McCall (1982, p. 39) to state, "following age 5, IQ is perhaps the most stable, important behavioral characteristic yet measured."

You might have noticed that the correlations between childhood and adult IQ reported in Table 10.3 are only moderate at 2 to 3 years of age and are actually negative at 1 year of age. Assessments of intelligence at 1 year were actually done using DQ tests, described earlier, which evaluate individual differences in the things infants do. There are several interpretations for these low cross-age correlations. One is that intelligence cannot be adequately measured in infancy. A second is that the nature

table 10.3 Cross-age Correlations between IQ Tests Given at Various Ages in Childhood (between 1 year and 14–15 years) and Young Adulthood IQ (that is, IQ at age 17 or 18) from Two Longitudinal Studies

Age of Initial Testing	Honzik, MacFarlane, and Allen (1948)	Bayley (1949)
1 year	—	–.14
2–3 years	.33	.40
4–5 years	.42	.52
6–7 years	.67	.68
8–9 years	.71	.80
10–11 years	.73	.87
12–13 years	.79	—
14–15 years	.76	.84

SOURCE: Honzik, M. P., MacFarlane, J. W., & Allen, L. (1948). Stability of mental test performance between 2 and 18 years. *Journal of Experimental Education, 17,* 309–324; and Bayley, N. (1949). Consistency and variability in the growth of intelligence from birth to eighteen years. *Journal of Genetic Psychology, 75,* 165–196.

of intelligence changes between infancy and childhood, and the infant tests such as the Bayley Scales do not tap the same type of intelligence as measured by later IQ tests. A third interpretation is that there is nothing wrong with the tests, intelligence just is not stable between infancy and childhood.

Aspects of intelligence seemingly do differ between infancy and childhood, accounting for the low cross-age correlations (McCall, Eichorn, & Hogarty, 1977). However, individual differences in some basic information-processing abilities of infants have been found to correlate with later IQ, suggesting that some aspects of intellectual functioning are stable over infancy and childhood. Specifically, the rate at which infants habituate to stimuli and their preference for novelty (see Chapter 5) have been found to predict IQ scores in later childhood: the faster 3- to 11-month-old infants habituate or the greater is their preference for novelty (such as looking at a new picture after being habituated to an old one), the higher their IQs during childhood tend to be (Bornstein et al., 2006; Fagan & Singer, 1983; McCall & Carriger, 1993). Average correlations between infant measures of habituation or preference for novelty and childhood IQ are about .40 or higher; this compares with correlations of about .15 or less between tests like the Bayley Scales and later IQ. (The latest version of the Bayley Scales [2005] includes items to assess some of the basic cognitive abilities believed to underlie infant intelligence. To our knowledge, there have been no studies published assessing the new Bayley Scales' ability to predict childhood IQ.).

How do we make sense of these findings? Some have suggested that habituation and preference for novelty (which is a form of recognition memory) reflect processing underlying executive

Measures of infant looking time, reflecting how efficiently babies process information, correlate significantly with childhood IQ scores.

children's speed of processing are moderately correlated with IQ (correlations between –.30 and –.50), with faster children having higher IQs than slower children (Fry & Hale, 2000; Jensen, 1998). Individual differences in working memory correlate even higher with children's fluid IQs (Hulme et al., 1984; Miller & Vernon, 1996). These patterns have caused some to claim that general intelligence, or *g*, reflects individual differences in basic-level information processing abilities, which are relatively stable over time, beginning in infancy (Fagan, 1992; Jensen, 1998).

Taken all together, what can we say about the stability of IQ? First, it is highly stable over childhood into adulthood, perhaps more so than any other important psychological characteristic. And second, it appears that individual differences in basic-level information-processing abilities, related to executive function, underlie general intelligence as measured by IQ and can be measured in infancy via habituation and preference-for-novelty tasks.

Does evidence of high stability, beginning in infancy, mean that IQ is fixed at birth or shortly thereafter and not likely to change? Not necessarily. IQ scores for some people do change substantially over childhood, with high-IQ children showing more fluctuation than average or low-IQ children (McCall, Appelbaum, & Hogarty, 1973), and, as we will see in later sections of this chapter, IQ is most apt to remain stable when a child's environment is also stable. If a child's intellectual environment changes substantially, either for the good or bad, one can expect IQ to change as well.

There is nothing magic about the IQ test (see Concept Review 10.1). It does not necessarily measure innate intelligence, nor does it necessarily

functions. Recall from our discussion of executive functions in Chapter 8 that there are age-related differences in memory span, working memory, speed of processing, the ability to inhibit thoughts and behaviors, to resist interference, and cognitive flexibility. Individual differences in these basic-level abilities are first seen in infancy and may be at the core of intelligence (Reznick, 2009; Rose et al., 2005). For instance, individual differences in

© Michael Newman/PhotoEdit

concept review | 10.1   Five critical questions and answers about IQ

1. What is IQ?	• An index/indicator of human intelligence • It is associated with many information-processing skills.
2. How is it calculated?	• It is based on a normal curve, with an average of 100 and a standard deviation of 15.
3. What does IQ predict?	• Academic performance • Occupational status • Longevity and better health
4. Is IQ stable over time?	• IQ tends to be highly stable over childhood into young adulthood. • Infancy DQ and childhood IQ are not highly correlated, although measures of habituation and preference for novelty from infancy correlate significantly with childhood IQ.
5. What are the main concerns about IQ?	• IQ discriminates against minority-group children. • Is IQ an adequate measure of human intelligence?

BOX 10.1 **big questions** *7 change in fluid intelligence*

Are People Getting Smarter? The Flynn Effect

Can a society's environment also change and have an effect on its average IQ? This is something that scientists had to consider when evidence surfaced that the average IQ of people in the developed world showed steady increases over the decades of the 20th century. This has been called the **Flynn effect**, after New Zealand psychologist James Flynn (1987, 1999, 2007), who first identified it.

There are several ways of evaluating whether average IQ scores have changed over historical time. One is to examine the scores of many people who take the same test at different times (for example, in 1960 versus in 1980). Another is to give people today versions of earlier IQ tests, standardized on samples decades before. The surprising finding is that the average scores have consistently headed upward at a rate of about five to nine points per decade. We say "surprising," because this suggests a person of average intelligence in 2010 would have the IQ of a genius in 1910, and that the above-average person living in 1920 would be classified as intellectually impaired if tested today. People today just do not seem to be that much smarter (nor should they be) than their ancestors 50 or 100 years ago. The increase appears to be larger for people on the low end of the IQ range (Teasdale & Owen, 1989), and the effect seems to be slowing down or has stopped or even reversed in recent decades (Teasdale & Owen, 2008). Moreover, the effect is not limited to the developed world but has also been observed in rural areas of Kenya (Daley et al., 2003).

The IQ change over the decades has not been equal across different items on IQ tests. Recall earlier that we made the distinction between fluid and crystallized intelligence. *Fluid intelligence* is proposed to reflect basic information-processing mechanisms as exemplified by measures of executive function, such as working memory and speed of processing. Fluid intelligence is less influenced by factors such as culture and education than *crystallized abilities*, which are assessed by tests of cultural knowledge and verbal fluency, such as vocabulary. Which type of abilities would you predict would be most affected by societal change over time? Had you asked us, we would have said crystallized abilities, based on the belief that the most substantial cultural changes over the 20th century have been in education. We would have been wrong. By far the greatest change in IQ over the 20th century occurred in fluid intelligence.

How can this pattern be explained? Some have proposed that increasing demands to the mathematics curriculum in developed nations influenced brain and cognitive development (Blair et al., 2005). Others point to improvements in nutrition and health care; more people are healthy, thus fewer people score very low on IQ tests (Daley et al., 2003; see Neisser, 1998). Another hypothesis for this pattern is that the 20th century saw a drastic change in the complexity of life, particularly the amount and nature of visual images people had to deal with (Greenfield, 1998). The 20th century saw the advent of photographs, glossy magazines, billboards, movies, television, VCRs, computers, and now video games. Children grow up inundated with visual information that must be organized and comprehended, and, the argument goes, these experiences may directly affect fluid intelligence. Flynn (2007) argues that improvements in education, greater use of technology, and more people being engaged in intellectually demanding work has led to a greater number of people dealing with abstract concepts than was the case in decades past, which, in turn, is responsible for elevated IQ scores.

The flexibility of fluid intelligence is illustrated by a study examining cognitive abilities in 8- to 14-year-old Greek and Chinese children (Demetriou et al., 2005). Although measures of general intelligence between the two groups were the same, the Chinese children outperformed the Greek children on all measures involving visual/spatial processing. The researchers attributed these substantial differences to the Chinese children's extensive practice with their logographic (pictorial symbols) writing system, in contrast to the phonetic system used by Greek children.

We take for granted the always-present visual images in our modern society. Yet, these are evolutionary novelties. Although our ancestors may have gazed at the occasional antelope painted on the cave wall, they otherwise did not deal with visual representations of things. When they saw an object or an event, it was the real thing, not a representation of something. Children, however, have the neural plasticity to learn to make sense of this plethora of visual messages, and as a result they apparently increase their IQ scores, at least the portion tapping fluid intelligence.

We should note that fluid intelligence is not the same as general intelligence (Blair, 2006), and that other aspects of intelligence as measured by IQ have not shown much in the way of change over the past 100 years. Nonetheless, the average change in IQ has been substantial. Does this make modern people geniuses and our ancestors of a century ago people with hum-drum minds? Flynn (1987) thinks not. A 50-point or greater increase in IQ since 1900 must cause one to ponder what the IQ test is actually measuring. The IQ test permits us to know where a person stands with respect to intelligence compared to other people in his or her cohort, but the fact that IQ can change so substantially over historical time emphasizes the relative nature of the measure. This does not diminish its usefulness, but it does suggest that an IQ score is not *the* measure of a permanent and stable intelligence.

reflect a constant value that will typify an individual throughout life. However, IQ does predict academic performance, occupational status, and even longevity reasonably well. Yet, the psychometric approach, with its emphasis on a single score, is not the only way to think of individual differences in intelligence. Scientists and educators have developed alternative ways of conceptualizing intelligence.

....

Flynn Effect The systematic increase in IQ scores (about 5 to 9 points per decade) observed over the 20th century.

Alternative Approaches to the Development of Intelligence

Although the psychometric approach has been extremely influential, it does not have a monopoly on studying intelligence. The testing approach to intelligence has had its critics. Some have argued that it is essentially atheoretical: Intelligence is what an IQ test says it is. This criticism is likely a bit harsh (recall the hierarchical model of cognitive abilities discussed earlier), but the very pragmatic concerns of test makers (tests are carefully constructed so that IQs are normally distributed) make it seem that theory is less important than the statistical properties of the tests. We already mentioned that IQ tests may not adequately evaluate the intelligence of minority children, and we all know of people who experience test anxiety or otherwise perform poorly on high-stakes standardized tests such as the SAT, ACT, or GRE (Graduate Record Exam).

One self-declared poor test-taker was Robert Sternberg (1985), who, when he became an experimental psychologist, decided to develop a new theory of intelligence that better reflected how people really think and solve problems. The result was the triarchic theory of intelligence, one of the most popular alternative theories of intelligence today. More recently, Sternberg refers to this as the *theory of successful intelligence,* in that it underscores "the importance of understanding intelligence not just as a predictor of academic performance . . . but also as a predictor of success in life" (Sternberg, 2004, p. 326). A competing and equally popular alternative account of intelligence is Howard Gardner's *theory of multiple intelligences.*

Sternberg's Triarchic Theory of Intelligence

Robert Sternberg's (1985, 1997) dissatisfaction with IQ tests and the psychometric approach to intelligence initially caused him to focus not on *factors* of intelligence, but on the specific cognitive abilities that underlie human thought, such as those described in Chapter 8 (for example, executive function, strategies, metacognition). However, he soon realized that describing intelligence solely in terms of information-processing mechanisms was not enough. One also had to: (1) take into account the context in which intelligence was being assessed, or the real-life problems that intelligence was being use to solve; and (2) consider how people deal with knowledge, particularly new information. To do this he proposed that three subtheories of intelligence (thus the name *triarchic* theory) were required, each focused on a different aspect of intellectual functioning. The three subtheories are called *componential, experiential,* and *contextual,* and we describe each briefly here (see Table 10.4). Rather than referring to the subtheories, Sternberg sometimes refers to the type of intelligence typified by each subtheory: *analytic* (for the componential subtheory), *creative* (for the experiential subtheory), and *practical* (for the contextual subtheory).

Componential, or Analytic, Intelligence

The core of intelligence for Sternberg is a set of information-processing mechanisms that can be used in any environmental context or culture. The componential subtheory describes the information-processing components of intelligence. This is sometimes referred to as analytic intelligence, because a person gifted in information-processing abilities is able to take apart, or analyze, problems and see solutions not seen by less-gifted individuals. Sternberg's emphasis on information-processing mechanisms as the foundation for intelligence puts him in good company. In fact, there has been an abundance of research examining both lower-level (for example, speed of processing, working memory) and higher-level (for example, strategies, metacognition) information-processes abilities and their relationship to intelligence as measured by IQ. As we noted earlier in this chapter, among both children and adults, significant relationships are found between various measures of executive function and IQ, including speed of processing (the faster one processes information, the higher IQ tends to be; Fry & Hale, 2000; Jensen, 1998) and working memory (larger working-memory spans are associated with higher IQs; Fry & Hale, 2000; Miller & Vernon, 1996).

In fact, the only psychological measures that have been found to predict school performance better than IQ are those reflecting executive function. For example, in one study, the effects of self-regulation (or self-discipline to use the authors' term) on children's academic performance accounted for more than twice as much of the differences in school grades as did IQ (Duckworth & Seligman, 2005). In other research, a measure of working memory at age 5 predicted academic performance at age 11 better than IQ, measured either at age 5 or at age 11 (Alloway & Alloway, 2010).

What causes people to get smarter with age? The simple answer from Sternberg's theory is knowledge. We saw in Chapter 8 that the more a person knows about a particular topic, the

---

triarchic theory of intelligence Sternberg's theory that describes intelligence in terms of three subtheories or types of intelligence: contextual, experiential, and componential.

componential subtheory (analytic intelligence) In Sternberg's triarchic theory, an information-processing model describing type of intelligence that includes three types of components: knowledge acquisition, performance, and metacomponents.

table 10.4 The Componential (Analytic), Experiential (Creative), and Contextual (Practical) Subtheories/Intelligence in Sternberg's Triarchic Theory of Intelligence

Some examples related to a college course on psychology are provided for each subtheory.

Componential (analytic) subtheory/intelligence: A set of information-processing mechanisms that can be used in any environmental context or culture. This type of intelligence is involved in tasks requiring the analysis of information. For example, "Compare Piaget's theory of cognitive development to Vygotsky's." It has three components:

Metacomponents: Control, monitor, and evaluate task performance and allocate attentional resources

Performance components: Components that execute strategies assembled by the metacomponents; these include encoding, mental comparison, and retrieval of information

Knowledge-acquisition components: Components involved in acquiring new knowledge and selectively acting on newly acquired information

Experiential (creative) subtheory/intelligence: Examines how people deal with novel information and the extent to which they are able to *automatize* certain processes. For example, "Design a study to test a theory of language acquisition."

Contextual (practical) subtheory/intelligence: Intelligence must be viewed in the context in which it occurs. This type of intelligence is involved in solving everyday problems. For example, "What would you do about a friend who has a substance-abuse problem?" or "What are the implications for Freud's theory of dreaming for your life?" It has three subprocesses:

Adapting: Adjusting one's behavior to obtain a good fit with one's environment

Selecting: Selecting an environment to obtain a good fit with one's abilities

Shaping: Modifying the behaviors and reactions of others so that they become more compatible to oneself

SOURCE: Adapted from Sternberg, R. J., Ferrari, M., & Clinkenbeard, P. (1996). Identification, instruction, and assessment of gifted children: A construct validation of a triarchic model. *Gifted Child Quarterly, 40,* 129–137, p. 131.

more efficiently he or she can process information within that domain, and this is explained by Sternberg's componential subtheory. Children who know a great deal about dinosaurs, for example, can incorporate new information about dinosaurs more effectively than a novice. Dinosaur experts know how to categorize a new species and know a lot of details about the extinct beasts (their diets, habitats, and offensive and defensive weapons). This in turn makes it easier for them to acquire new knowledge, further enhancing processing efficiency. New knowledge also enhances metacognition, leading to greater self-awareness about the topic ("I'm not really sure if triceratops and stegosaurus lived at the same time, come to think about it"), which, in turn, results in the increased effectiveness of metacognitive processing.

Experiential, or Creative, Intelligence

The experiential subtheory looks at how people deal with novel information. In one sense, dealing with novelty is what development is all about. Young children have been described as "universal novices": Everything is new to them. How well do children deal with new information and integrate it with what they already know? This is sometimes referred to as creative intelligence, because Sternberg believes that people gifted in the mechanisms of this subtheory are especially able to generate new ideas and solve novel problems.

The other side of the coin from processing novelty is *automatization*. By automatization, Sternberg means the ability to use relatively little mental effort to execute some task. We only automatize things we know very well. Reading is a good example. Initially, it is highly laborious, with children sounding out individual letters and in the process often missing completely the meaning of what they read. Yet, with instruction and practice, reading becomes automatic (at least partly so). When we see words in print, we cannot help but read them. Skilled reading still takes mental effort (you cannot read and pay close attention to the Red Sox game at the same time and expect to remember much from what you read), but many subprocesses of reading have become automatized, executed spontaneously and done without conscious thought. Sternberg proposed that how people respond to novelty and the ease with which they can automatize information processing are important and universal aspects of intelligence.

Contextual, or Practical, Intelligence

As we have emphasized throughout this text, development always occurs in a context, and one must understand the contexts in which children experience life (particularly social contexts) in order to understand development. Sternberg realized that this was true for intelligence as well. The contextual subtheory holds that intelligence must be

experiential subtheory (creative intelligence) In Sternberg's triarchic theory, type of intelligence concerned with how prior knowledge influences performance, specifically with the individual's ability to deal with novelty and the degree to which processing is automatized.

contextual subtheory (practical intelligence) In Sternberg's triarchic theory, type of intelligence expressed by the idea that intelligence must be viewed in terms of the context in which it occurs. People gifted in this subtheory have "street smarts."

Although the children from different cultures may experience very different environments, individual differences in intelligence can be evaluated by how well they can select environments, shape the behaviors of others, and adapt to situations, all features of Sternberg's contextual subtheory.

viewed in the context in which it occurs. Intelligence is not the same thing for a middle-class child growing up in Palm Beach, Florida, as it is for a child growing up in war-torn Afghanistan or Darfur. In other words, intelligence can only be assessed in terms of the real-world type of problems that children experience and must be evaluated within a cultural context (Sternberg, 2004). This is sometimes called practical intelligence, because people gifted in this subtheory have street smarts, making an ideal fit between themselves and whatever context they find themselves in. People with practical intelligence may also excel in social intelligence. Most real-world contexts where intelligence is useful in solving problems involve other people, and being able to deal effectively with other, sometimes contrary, members of one's own species, can be a sign of substantial practical intelligence.

One criticism of such an approach is that because children live in highly varied environments, one cannot compare two children from different cultures in terms of intelligence. Intellectual skills that are crucial for survival in one culture might not be as important in another. This is the claim of *cultural relativism,* and, if taken to the extreme, limits the usefulness of a theory of intelligence. However, within the contextual subtheory, Sternberg proposed three processes—**adaptation**, **selection**, and

adaptation (in Sternberg's theory) Adjusting one's behavior to obtain a good fit with one's environment.

selection In Sternberg's triarchic theory of intelligence, the selection of environments in which to interact.

shaping In Sternberg's triarchic theory of intelligence, the ability to modify, or shape, the behaviors of others.

theory of multiple intelligences Gardner's theory postulating eight components, or modules, of intelligence: (1) linguistic, (2) logical-mathematical, (3) musical, (4) spatial, (5) bodily-kinesthetic, (6) interpersonal, (7) intrapersonal, and (8) naturalistic.

shaping—that determine children's success in their culture, so that children can be evaluated by how well they function with respect to each process.

Adaptation refers to adjusting one's behavior to obtain a good fit with one's environment. For example, how effectively do children recognize that their attempts at joining a playgroup are not successful, and are they able to modify their behavior to become included in the games at recess and make new friends? Rather than adapting, however, children may decide they would be better off *selecting* a different environment to interact in, in this case a different group of children to play with. Although it might be nice to be part of the high-status clique at school, perhaps one would fit better with a different group of children. Maybe a child can become a leader or well-liked member of the photography club, rather than beat her head against the wall trying to impress and become one of the popular girls. Alternatively, a child may be able to *shape* the behaviors and reactions of others so that they become more compatible to him or her. For instance, a child may ingratiate himself with a group of children by learning to tell good jokes, becoming a skilled basketball player, or bringing his mother's brownies to share, and in the process change the attitude of his peers.

Children do not always have free reign to choose between adaptation, selection, and shaping. For instance, most children in schooled societies cannot select *not* to go to school. The better option for a school-phobic child is to adapt his or her behaviors to match the requirements of compulsory education, and, when possible, shape the behaviors of teachers and parents so that school becomes less of a burden. We all know children, however, who do not adapt easily to school, just as we know people who seem to make the same mistakes repeatedly, such as selecting boy- or girlfriends who never work out. We also know others who seem incapable of shaping anyone else's behavior but simply go along with whatever other people decide, sometimes for the good and sometimes not. We also all know people who excel in each of these processes.

Although Sternberg argues that the various aspects of intelligence interact, differences within an individual are likely to exist among the three forms of intelligence. That is, the three different aspects of intelligence are relatively independent, with only low to moderate correlations between assessments of analytic, creative, and practical intelligence (Sternberg, Ferrari, & Clinkenbeard, 1996). This makes the theory different from the standard psychometric approach that proposes a general intellectual factor, *g*, with performance on different tests of intelligence all correlating highly with one another.

Another perspective that assumes that there are multiple, independent types of intelligence and that challenges the psychometric approach is Howard Gardner's theory of multiple intelligences.

"YOU CAN'T BUILD A HUT, YOU DON'T KNOW HOW TO FIND EDIBLE ROOTS AND YOU KNOW NOTHING ABOUT PREDICTING THE WEATHER. IN OTHER WORDS, YOU DO TERRIBLY ON OUR I.Q. TEST."

Some theorists, such as Sternberg, believe that IQ tests are culturally biased and that one always has to consider the context in which intelligence is assessed.

Gardner's Theory of Multiple Intelligences

Howard Gardner's theory of multiple intelligences (referred to as MI by its practitioners) proposes that there are eight (maybe nine, Gardner only speculates about the spiritual/existential intelligence) unique and independent types of intelligences (see Table 10.5). Note that Gardner speaks of *intelligences*, plural, not *intelligence*, singular.

How does an intelligence get to be on Gardner's list? Certainly these are all valued human abilities that vary among individuals, but, with the exception of linguistic and logical/mathematical abilities, they are quite different from the types of intelligence tapped by IQ tests. Gardner proposed a set of eight criteria for considering an intelligence, although every criterion need not be met for a candidate to be considered (see Table 10.6). Rather, these

According to Gardner's theory, music, the visual arts, having command of one's body, and an understanding of the natural world are all forms of intelligence, along with the more conventional intelligences of verbal and quantitative skills.

table 10.5 A List of Multiple Intelligences in Gardner's Theory: Their Definition, People Who Exemplify Them, and Their Theorized Neurological Locus

Intelligence	Definition	People Who Exemplify This Intelligence	Neurological System Hypothesized to Be Associated with This Intelligence
Linguistic	Sensitive to meaning and order of words	Maya Angelou (poet) Stephen King (writer) Martin Luther King (civil rights leader and orator)	Left hemisphere, temporal and frontal lobes
Logical-mathematical	Ability to reason logically and recognize patterns and order	Bill Gates (former CEO of Microsoft) Stephen Hawking (physicist) James Watson (biologist)	Left parietal lobe; left hemisphere for verbal naming; right hemisphere for spatial organization; frontal system for planning
Musical	Sensitivity to pitch, melody, rhythm, and tone	Yo Yo Ma (cellist) Mariah Carey (singer) Wolfgang Amadeus Mozart (composer)	Right anterior temporal lobe; frontal lobes
Bodily-kinesthetic	Ability to use one's body skillfully and handle objects adroitly	David Copperfield (magician) Kobe Bryant (basketball player) Mia Hamm (soccer player)	Cerebral motor strip; thalamus; basal ganglia; cerebellum
Spatial	Ability to perceive physical environment accurately and to recreate or transform aspects of that environment	Frank Lloyd Wright (architect) Pablo Picasso (painter) Georgia O'Keefe (painter)	Right hemisphere, parietal occipital lobe
Naturalist	Ability to recognize and classify numerous species of flora and fauna	Charles Darwin (biologist) Jane Goodall (primatologist) E. O. Wilson (biologist)	Left parietal lobe (discriminating living from nonliving)
Interpersonal	Ability to understand people and relationships	Bill Clinton (politician) Ronald Reagan (politician) Madeline Albright (diplomat)	Frontal lobes
Intrapersonal	Access to one's emotional life as a means to understand oneself and others	Oprah Winfrey (talk show host) Bono (singer, philanthropist)	Frontal lobes
Spiritual/existential	Individuals who exhibit the proclivity to pose (and ponder) questions about life, death, and ultimate realities	Albert Einstein (scientist) Socrates (philosopher) Dalai Lama (Tibetan monk)	Hypothesized as specific region in the right temporal lobe

SOURCE: Adapted from Gardner, H. (1983). *Frames of mind: The theory of multiple intelligences.* New York: Basic; and Gardner, H. (1999). Are there additional intelligences? The case for naturalist, spiritual, and existential intelligences. In J. Kane (Ed.), *Education, information and transformation.* Englewood Cliffs, NJ: Prentice-Hall.

are the criteria that Gardner lists "by which each candidate intelligence can be judged" (1983, p. 66).

Gardner's has been perhaps the most widely applied theory of intelligence to education since the advent of the psychometric approach more than 100 years ago. The theory has been applied and evaluated in hundreds, if not thousands, of schools in North America and Europe, mostly in kindergarten through 12th grade (see Cuban, 2004; Hoerr, 2004), but also in college and graduate education (Díaz-LeFebvre, 2004; Shore, 2004), and in special populations, such as second-language learners (Haley, 2004) and children with ADHD (Schirduan & Case, 2004).

Table 10.7 presents some of the distinctions between a traditional classroom and one based on multiple intelligences (from Hoerr, 2004). Typically, curricula based on multiple intelligences theory give children substantial freedom to explore a range of topics, with many hands-on opportunities. Although textbooks may be used, teachers are more apt to create their own curriculum, working with their students and other teachers. Children, rather than the curriculum, are the center of a multiple-intelligences classroom, with individual differences in intellectual abilities being valued.

Gardner's theory and his approach to education are not without their critics. For example, although teachers purport to implement a multiple-intelligences curriculum, they often do not change their behavior in any substantial way, believing

Criticism ~ of Gardener's theory

table 10.6 Gardner's Criteria for an Intelligence

Gardner proposed a set of eight criteria for considering an intelligence, although every criterion need not be met for a candidate to be considered.

Criteria	Definition
Potential isolation by brain damage	Damage to specific brain areas should impair specific intelligences (for example, damage to Broca's area hinders language production).
An evolutionary history and evolutionary plausibility	There should be some evolutionary history of an intelligence, and perhaps evidence of antecedents of these abilities in other species, and a plausible evolutionary explanation of how these intelligences may have been selected.
An identifiable core operation or set of operations	Each intelligence should have associated with it one or more basic information-processing operations, specialized to deal with a particular type of input (language, music, and so on).
Susceptibility to encoding in a system	An intelligence should have its own symbol system.
A distinctive developmental progression, along with a definable set of expert end-state performances	An intelligence must develop and have an identifiable end-state—that is, a level of performance attainable by mature experts.
The existence of savants and prodigies (see Box 10.2)	An intelligence is reflected by exceptionalities and, thus, can be exhibited by savants (people with intellectual impairment but who possess an exceptional talent in a single domain) and prodigies (children with generally typical abilities in all but a small number of areas, in which they excel).
Support from experimental psychological tasks	Evidence from tasks used in cognitive psychology (for example, for reasoning, language, spatial cognition).
Support from psychometric findings	Evidence from psychometric tasks, especially those that assess linguistic and logical/mathematical abilities.

SOURCE: Adapted from Gardner, H. (1983). *Frames of mind: The theory of multiple intelligences.* New York: Basic; and Gardner, H. (1999). Are there additional intelligences? The case for naturalist, spiritual, and existential intelligences. In J. Kane (Ed.), *Education, information and transformation.* Engelwood Cliffs, NJ: Prentice-Hall.

table 10.7 Some Differences between a Traditional Classroom and One Based on Multiple Intelligences (MI)

In a Traditional Classroom	In a Multiple Intelligences (MI) Classroom
Kids with strong scholastic intelligence are smart, and the other kids aren't.	Everyone has a different profile of intelligence; we are all smart in different ways.
Teachers create a hierarchy of intellect.	Teachers use all students' intelligences to help them learn.
The classroom is curriculum centered.	The classroom is child centered.
Teachers help students acquire information and facts.	Teachers help students create meaning in a constructivist way.
The focus is on the scholastic intelligences, the 3 *R*s.	Personal Intelligences are valued: Who you are is more important than what you know.
Teachers work from texts.	Teachers create curriculum—lessons, units, themes.
Teachers assess students by paper-and-pencil, objective measures.	Teachers create assessment tools—projects, exhibitions, presentations (PEPs)—which incorporate MI.
Teachers close the door and work in isolation	Teachers work with colleagues in using MI, developing collegiality.

SOURCE: From Hoerr, T. (2004). How MI informs teaching at New City School. *Teachers College Record, 106,* 40–48.

that their instruction already incorporates many of the main principles of multiple-intelligences theory (Cuban, 2004), calling into question the extent to which a multiple-intelligence framework is being applied in many of these schools. Another criticism of multiple intelligences is that it is not a testable theory. Although some argue that the theory can both explain much of children's behavior and has generated new research questions and applications (Chen, 2004), others question its scientific merit and whether it is testable. Also, Gardner's theory includes abilities that most scientists and educators have not typically considered to be in the realm of intelligence. Musical talent has always been recognized as something special but usually distinct from intelligence. And although athletic ability and "body smarts" are certainly important human characteristics, they are not typically considered to be mental operations in the way that mathematical computation and verbal comprehension are, which have traditionally been at the center of the definition of intelligence.

BOX 10.2 **food for thought**

Savants and Prodigies

The concept of general intelligence, or *g*, holds that people's intellectual skills tend to be relatively even, or homogeneous, so that someone who is smart for one domain of knowledge is smart in most other domains as well. This is reflected by the *positive manifold*, or high correlations found when groups of people take a variety of psychometric tests. We all know people for whom this does not fit, and few people are so uniform across different tasks that these correlations are perfect. The most extreme exceptions are for people who have been described as **savants**, or prodigies. Darold Treffert (1989) has referred to savants as having "islands of genius." Most savants, or those with **savant syndrome**, show some type of intellectual disability. About half are autistic, and they are disproportionately males.

Savants have been identified for several skills, most notably in mathematics and music. The neurologist Oliver Sacks (1985), in his book *The Man Who Mistook His Wife for a Hat,* describes John and Michael, 26-year-old twin brothers who had been in institutions since the age of 7, diagnosed at various times as autistic, psychotic, or intellectually impaired. John and Michael were already well known for their extraordinary facility with the calendar, a skill possessed by many savants, being able to provide quickly the day of the week for any date in history (for example, December 9, 1786, was a Saturday). Working with these young men, Sacks discovered that they had several other remarkable abilities. Once, a box of matches fell from a table, and both cried simultaneously "111." John then said 37 three times, which Michael repeated. Upon questioning, the twins said that exactly 111 matches fell to the floor (which Sacks confirmed) and that they did not count them but "saw" them. When asked why they said 37, the two said in unison, "37, 37, 37, 111." How did they know that 111 is composed of three 37s? The twins could not provide a comprehensible answer, other than to say that they just "saw" the answer: They did no computation.

Perhaps even more extraordinary was the twins' fascination and facility with prime numbers. The twins would sometimes play a game in which they said numbers to one another and smiled. Sacks writes: "John would say a number—a six-figure number. Michael would catch the number, nod, smile and seem to savour it. Then he, in turn, would say another six-figure number, and now it was John who received, and appreciated it richly. They looked, at first, like two connoisseurs wine-tasting, sharing rare tastes, rare appreciations. I sat still, unseen by them, mesmerised, bewildered." Although it took some detective work for Sacks to figure out what the twins were doing, it turned out that the numbers that brought smiles were all, and only, prime numbers.

Musical savants are also quite common. Numerous newspaper articles and television stories have told about people with severe intellectual impairment who can play Beethoven piano sonatas after hearing them only once. For instance, Leslie Lemke was born blind with cerebral palsy and brain damage. For his first 7 years, he made no sounds or movements and showed no emotions. He

Kim Peek, one of the models for Dustin Hoffman's character in the movie *Rain Man,* began memorizing books at the age of 18 months.

did not stand unaided until age 12 and did not walk until 15. When he was 16, his mother heard music playing downstairs in the middle of the night and found Leslie playing Tchaikovsky's *First Piano Concerto.* Leslie learned to play all types of music and soon was giving concerts. His remarkable abilities have been featured on numerous television shows, including CBS's *60 Minutes.*

Perhaps the best-documented savant is Kim Peek, one of the models for Dustin Hoffman's autistic character in the classic 1988 film *Rain Main.* Kim's special skill is memory, which extends to at least 15

The theories of Sternberg, Gardner, and others (for example, Ceci, 1996) make it clear that human intelligence is not a simple matter (see Concept Review 10.2, p. 406). There are different ways to be smart, and we must look at them all if we are to get the big picture of individual differences in intellectual functioning. We must also look at variables that are not typically viewed as reflecting intelligence. For example, factors such as motivation and practice are also important in how intelligently any person functions on a particular task.

savants (savant syndrome) Individuals who show some type of genius, usually in a single area, but also display some form of mental disability in the rest.

What Are the Origins of Individual Differences in Intelligence?

One of the most vigorous debates in psychology over the last century concerned the origins of individual differences in intelligence. Are individual differences in intelligence mainly the result of experience, especially early experience, as many psychologists insisted (Hunt, 1961; Jacoby & Glauberman, 1995), or are they caused by genetics, as argued by others (Herrnstein & Murray, 1994; Jensen, 1969)? These debates continue, but we hope it

Child prodigies are usually male and found especially in the areas of mathematics and music. There is some debate concerning why there are more male than female prodigies, and socialization must be considered. Until recently, gifted women were not given the same opportunities as gifted men, even in music and art.

topics. He began memorizing books at the age of 18 months, as they were read to him, and had learned 9,000 books "by heart" by 2005 (Treffert & Christensen, 2005). In one much-cited feat, Kim read Tom Clancy's *The Hunt for Red October* in about 90 minutes. Four months later, when asked to give the name of the Russian radio operator in the book, he referred to the page describing the character and quoted several passages verbatim.

Kim was born with an enlarged head, with a damaged cerebellum and no corpus callosum, the large bundle of nerves that connects the two hemispheres. Like many savants, neuroimaging of Kim's brain revealed abnormalities of the left hemisphere. When the left hemisphere is injured, the right hemisphere may compensate, using brain tissue that would normally serve different functions. Injury to the left hemisphere may also reveal latent skills in the right hemisphere, something some have referred to as a release from the "tyranny" of the dominant left hemisphere (Treffert & Christensen, 2005). Some have suggested that savants' frequent left-hemisphere damage may explain why males show more language-related disabilities and autism than do females. Males' higher levels of testosterone may be toxic to the developing brain, and because the left hemisphere develops more slowly than the right, it is vulnerable for a longer period of time.

The **prodigy** is the other side of the coin from the savant. A prodigy is a child with generally typical abilities in all but a small number of areas (usually one). David Henry Feldman proposed that prodigies are a special form of giftedness and are characterized by "unusually strong talents in a single area such as music or mathematics, reasonably but not necessarily exceptionally high IQ, focused energy and sustained effort to achieve the highest levels of the target field, and unusual self-confidence" (1993, p. 191). Similar to savants, prodigies are more apt to be boys than girls and are most frequently

found in the areas of music. Wolfgang Amadeus Mozart was the quintessential musical prodigy. Raised in a musical family, as a preschooler he was playing instruments and composing music at a level few humans ever attain. He was touring the great capitals of Europe by age 8, but aside from his musical prowess, Wolfgang was a normal boy.

Feldman (1991) theorized that prodigies and savants represent one of two forms of intelligence that have been selected over evolutionary time. General intelligence as measured by IQ is one type of intelligence, necessary for dealing with most of the ecological and social problems people face. The other type is a highly specific talent for a relatively constrained dimension of experience. Children with these specific skills are highly motivated to practice and develop them but will likely thrive only in highly supportive environments. Feldman refers to this as "nature's gambit," with natural selection governing the production of a relatively small number of individuals with highly specific talents that is balanced with the production of a larger number of people with high levels of general intelligence, possessing skills that promote survival across a broader range of environments.

Feldman's ideas are provocative, and regardless of their eventual merit, the presence of savants and prodigies, with their patterns of intellectual skills so different from the majority of people, needs to be explained for a thorough understanding of human brain functioning, intelligence, and their development.

is clear that neither the strong nature nor nurture position is tenable today.

In this section we first briefly review the role of genes in interaction with experience in affecting children's intelligence. We then examine mainly environmental factors that influence the establishment, maintenance, and modification of intelligence in children.

Genes, Environment, and Intelligence

In previous chapters we discussed how individual differences in genes and environment interact

to produce particular patterns of development, including intellectual development. Recall from Chapter 3, for example, how the heritability of IQ (the extent to which individual difference in IQ can be attributed to genetics) among a group of adolescents varied depending on the education of their parents: It was higher for children from high-education homes (.74) than for children from low-education homes (.26) (Rowe, Jacobson, & van der Oord, 1999). Moreover, when individual genes associated with intelligence have been found, their

prodigy A child with generally typical abilities in all but a small number of areas (usually one), in which he or she displays precocious talent.

What is intelligence? Different theories have tried to characterize intelligence in different ways. These are some of the more important theories.

Domain-general views of intelligence	Domain-specific views of intelligence
Intelligence is thought of as a domain-general skill, represented by *g* (general intelligence). If one is good at one intellectual skill, for instance, one is good at others.	Intelligence is multifaceted. One can be good at one intellectual skill but not necessarily at others.
Modern *psychometric theory* generally adheres to a domain-general view of intelligence. The psychometric approach views intelligence as composed of different factors representing specific cognitive skills. However, performance on different test items is highly correlated (positive manifold), reflective of a general factor of intelligence (*g*).	*Sternberg's Triarchic Theory* Intelligence is described in terms of three subtheories, or styles of thinking • Componential/Analytical: information-processing skills • Experiential/Creative: ability to deal with novelty • Contextual/Practical: ability to select, shape, and adapt *Gardner's Theory of Multiple Intelligences* There are eight (possibly nine) independent types of intelligences: linguistic, musical, logical-mathematical, bodily-kinesthetic, spatial, naturalist, interpersonal, intrapersonal, and possibly spiritual/existential

effect is usually mediated by the environment, as in the version of one gene associated with higher IQ, but only when children were breastfed (Caspi et al., 2007), also discussed in Chapter 3. In general, many genes are involved in determining general intelligence (in interaction with the environment), but so far the quest to isolate specific genes has been elusive, likely because the effect of any single gene on general intelligence is very small in magnitude (Plomin, Kennedy, & Craig, 2006).

Establishing, Maintaining, and Modifying Intellectual Competency

It should not be surprising that a child's rearing environment can have a profound effect on his or her intelligence. In discussing experience and intelligence, it is useful to distinguish among the *establishment, maintenance,* and *modification* of intelligence. What factors contribute to the initial establishment of intellectual competence? Once established, what does it take to maintain a level of intellectual functioning? And, finally, under what conditions can intelligence be modified, either for the better or the worse?

As we have seen in the earlier chapters in this section, children get smarter as they get older in an absolute sense, and, as we saw when looking at the stability of IQ over age, most children maintain their relative rank order within a group over time. That is, children who are at the top of their class at age 7 are apt to be in a similar position at age 18.

This may cause one to believe that once intellectual competence is achieved in childhood, it is set. This is not necessarily so. Intelligence is not something that once you've got it, it's yours forever. Once a level of intellectual competence is established, it must be maintained. One important reason for the stability of IQ over time is that children's environments tend to stay relatively stable: Children in intellectually supportive environments at age 5 are apt to find themselves in similarly supportive environments at age 8, 12, and 14. Likewise, children who receive little in the way of intellectual stimulation as preschoolers are likely to find themselves in similar environments throughout their childhoods. However, when environments responsible for establishing intellectual abilities change, one can expect changes in children's intellectual performance, sometimes for the better and sometimes for the worse.

Many studies have examined aspects of children's home environments and related them to IQ and other measures of intellectual performance (Melhuish et al., 2008; NICHD Early Child Care Research Network, 2005). Here, we look at several lines of research that highlight the role experience plays in children's intellectual competence. Perhaps the clearest indication of the role of experience on intelligence comes from studies in which children were raised from shortly after birth in stultifying institutions and provided with little in the way of physical or social stimulation. We then look at *at-risk children,* whose biological states or social environments place them at risk for intellectual impairment. We conclude the section by looking at preschool compensatory education programs and their immediate and long-term effects on intelligence.

Institutionalized Children

In the early decades of the 20th century, there were numerous institutions in Europe and North America for infants and children who could not be cared for by their parents. These institutions tended to be understaffed, with children getting little in the way of social stimulation. Unfortunately, these institutions are not a thing of the past, as many children in some poorer countries today are abandoned and spend significant parts of their lives as wards of the state, sometimes receiving care that is not much better than that of institutionalized children early in the last century.

For example, with the fall of the Berlin wall in 1989 and shortly afterward the collapse of communism in Eastern Europe, one heart-wrenching discovery was institutions in Romania for infants and young children that were at least as horrendous as any that existed during the Great Depression. (The Romanian government encourged its citizens to have many children as a way to increase economic production. In fact, families with fewer than five children were punished with increased taxes. As a result, many parents could not support all of their children, and the State developed a network of institutions to handle the increase in abandoned children [Nelson et al., 2009].) UNICEF estimates that approximately 1.5 million children in Central and Eastern Europe live in public institutions, and many children in parts of Asia, South America, and Africa are abandoned, orphaned, or live in abject poverty (Nelson, 2007). We will review some of these studies in Chapter 12 on attachment and show that such children suffer severe emotional distress (Spitz, 1945). They also show signs of intellectual impairment.

With respect to cognition, children who spend their first two years in such institutions display impaired levels of basic cognitive abilities, such as visual memory, attention, and inhibitory control (Beckett et al., 2010; Pollak et al., 2010), and have lower IQs, often within the intellectually disabled range, than similar children who are adopted or placed in foster care (van IJzendoorn & Juffer, 2005; Spitz, 1945). The results of one recent study of Romanian children adopted into British homes illustrate the importance of being removed from these institutions at an early age for later IQ (Beckett et al., 2006). Figure 10.2 shows the average IQs of adopted Romanian children at ages 6 and 11 years as a function of their age of placement in United Kingdom (UK) homes. The IQs of a group of UK adopted children are also shown. As you can see, despite these children's early deprivation, those who were adopted within their first 6 months of life showed no long-term effects of their depriva-

© Bernard Bisson/Sygma/Corbis

Children living in overcrowded, understaffed institutions show significant intellectual impairment, especially if they are not removed and placed in more supportive environments before their second birthdays.

tion, having IQ scores comparable to those of the UK sample. IQs were lower for children adopted at later ages, particularly those adopted after 24 months. However, note that the 11-year IQs were higher than the 6-year IQs for these late-adopted children, suggesting a catch-up effect for the children who experienced the longest deprivation.

There are methodological problems with these studies, however. For example, children who are adopted or selected for foster care may be brighter or more maturationally advanced than children who remain institutionalized. A recent study was able to overcome this problem by randomly assigning

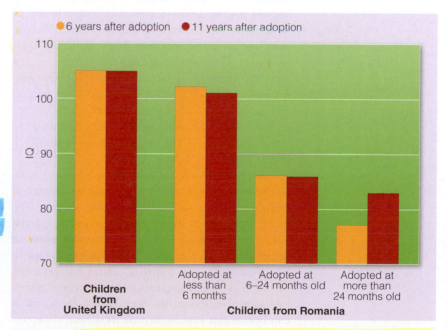

FIGURE 10.2 IQ scores for Romanian adopted children at 6 and 11 years as a function of their age of placement in adoptive homes.

Also shown are the IQs for a group of UK adopted children. The older children were before they were adopted, the lower their subsequent IQ scores tended to be.

SOURCE: Adapted from Beckett, C., Maughan, B., Rutter, M., Castle, J., Colvert, E., Groothues, C., Kreppner, J., Stevens, S., O'Connor, T. G., & Sonuga-Barke, E. J. S. (2006). Do the effects of early severe deprivation on cognition persist into early adolescence? Findings from the English and Romanian Adoptee Study. *Child Development, 77,* 696–711.

table 10.8 IQs at 54 Months for Children in the Foster Care Group by Age of Placement

Children placed in foster care before 2 years of age had significantly higher IQs than children placed in foster care after 2 years of age.

0–18 months:	85.8
18–24 months:	86.7
24–30 months:	78.1
30+ months:	71.5

SOURCE: Adapted from Nelson, C. A. III, Zeanah, C. H., Fox, N. A., Marshall, P. J., Smuke, A. T., & Guthrie, D. (2007). Cognitive recovery in socially deprived young children: The Bucharest Early Intervention Program. *Science, 318* (21 December), 1937–1940.

Romanian infants who had been abandoned at birth to either foster care or to continued institutional care. These infants were followed to 54 months of age and also compared to a group of never-institutionalized infants who were being reared by their biological families in Bucharest, Romania (Nelson et al., 2007). (To conduct such a random-assignment study raises certain ethical issues, which the authors of this study considered carefully and discussed in some detail.)

The effects of institutionalization on IQ were significant, with the Institutionalized group having an average IQ at 54 months of 73, compared to average IQs for the Foster Care group of 81 and for the Never-Institutionalized group of 109. Perhaps of greater interest were differences in IQs of children in the Foster Care group as a function of their age at placement (see Table 10.8). Children who were placed in foster care by 2 years of age had significantly higher IQs than children who were placed in foster care after age 2. In fact, as you can see from the Table, children placed in foster care after 30 months of age had IQs similar to those of children in the Institutionalized group (72 versus 73).

Research from the Romanian adoption studies reflects a reversal of the negative effects of early experience on intelligence for some of the most deprived children. Over the course of the 20th century, children who experienced extreme deprivation, often as the result of neglect or isolation caused by war, showed remarkable recovery of social and intellectual functioning when placed in supportive foster or adoptive homes (Clark & Hanisee, 1982; The St. Petersburg-USA Orphanage Research Team, 2008). When these once-deprived children receive emotional, social, and intellectual stimulation at the hands of caring foster and adoptive parents, reversals of the effects of earlier treatment can be realized. However, such reversals are more likely to occur and be of greater magnitude the earlier that children are placed in supportive homes.

Children at Risk and the Development of Intelligence

Other studies demonstrate the transaction between an infant's initial biological condition and rearing environment, with biologically at-risk infants being the most susceptible to the effects of unresponsive parenting. For example, in one study, 187 very-low-birth-weight (VLBW) infants (weighing less than 1600 grams at birth), all born at least 3 weeks prematurely and with medical problems, were followed longitudinally to 40 months of age (Landry et al., 1997). Their development was contrasted with 112 full-term infants. All infants were from lower-SES homes. About 40% of the VLBW infants were described as being at high medical risk, whereas others were described as low-risk infants. Infants were routinely given standardized language and intelligence tests, and several aspects of their mothers' behaviors were measured when the babies were 6 and 12 months of age.

Different aspects of the mothers' behaviors predicted their children's level of intellectual development. For instance, mothers who tried to maintain their children's interest in some ongoing activity had children with higher cognitive and language scores than did less-engaging mothers. Also, mothers who attempted to stop what their children were doing or saying had children with lower cognitive and language scores, causing the researchers to conclude that "children whose early experiences are frequently interrupted with requests to stop doing something are not able to assume independence in their learning at a normal rate" (Landry et al., 1997, pp. 1049–1050). This effect of restrictiveness was most pronounced, however, for VLBW children in the high-risk group. These challenged children may have interpreted their mothers' restrictive style as indicating that they are incapable of controlling their own behavior or taking initiative, which contributed to their slower intellectual development.

Similar patterns have been found in other studies: Children growing up in emotionally supportive homes and receiving cognitively rich experiences tend to have higher IQs than children growing up in homes that provide less intellectual stimulation (Brooks-Gunn, Linver, & Fauth, 2005; NICHD Early Child Care Research Network, 2002). But the adverse effects of a nonstimulating environment are often exaggerated for children with early health problems (Caughy, 1996). Early biological risk makes infants especially susceptible to the effects of poor parenting. Unfortunately, their biological impairments contribute to their problems by causing their high-stressed parents to be less responsive to them. This, in turn, results in their slower intellectual development, which fur-

BOX 10.3 # the biopsychology of childhood

The Institutionalized Brain

The negative effects of institutionalization on children's intelligence are substantial, and we should not be surprised that the brains of once-institutionalized children are different from the brains of never-institutionalized children, showing dysfunction in structure and processing in several areas (Chugani et al., 2001; Eluvathingal et al., 2006; Tottenham et al., 2010). First, consider a study by Harry Chugani and his colleagues (2001) of 10 adopted children who had formerly lived in a Romanian institution. The children ranged in age from 7 to 11 years when tested. All had been placed in an orphanage shortly after birth and remained in the institution for an average of 38 months before being adopted. The average Wechsler IQ of these children was 81, although they scored slightly higher (91) on the nonverbal Raven's Progressive Matrices IQ test. The authors used positron-emission tomography (PET) scans to compare the once-institutionalized children's brain metabolism (specifically, glucose metabolism) to that of control children and adults. The accompanying figure shows brain images reflecting areas of the brain (marked in red and yellow) where the Romanian orphan group showed lower glucose metabolism relative to age-matched children with epilepsy. Most of the areas where there were significant differences are in the prefrontal cortex and temporal lobe, both associated with higher cognitive functions. The hippocampus and amygdala, areas involved in memory and emotion, also showed differences.

Later research by this same group looked at differences in white matter (mainly myelinated axons) that transmit messages between different parts of the brain between seven Romanian orphans and a control group of children (Eluvathingal et al., 2006). They reported significant differences between the Romanian orphans and control children in a part of the brain (*uncinate fasciculus* region) that serves as a pathway between the amygdala and frontal lobes, areas involved with emotion and higher cognitive function. Other research, using electroencephalogram (EEG) event-related potentials has similarly reported less cortical activity in the brains of institutionalized (Moulson et al., 2009a; 2009b) or once-institutionalized children than in the brains of controls (Parker et al., 2005a, 2005b). Although the absolute amount of data available is still meager, the results of what studies we have paint a consistent picture, summarized succinctly by Charles Nelson (2007, p. 16): "Specifically, institutionalization appears to lead to a reduction in cortical brain activity (both metabolically and electrophysiologically) and to dysregulation of neuroendocrine systems that mediate social behavior."

What is it about the institutionalization experience that causes this change in neural structure and function? Nelson (2007) proposed that children in the most deprived of these environments do not receive the stimulation that developing brains have evolved to expect. (We discussed *experience-expectant synaptogenesis* in Chapter 4.) Young brains have evolved to expect certain species-typical experiences. These include sensory stimulation (patterned light, sound, touch), adequate nutrition, social stimulation from a caregiver, and language, among others. According to Nelson (2007, p. 16), "many forms of institutional rearing lack most elements of a mental-health-promoting environment. As a result, the young nervous system, which actively awaits and seeks out environmental input, is robbed of such input." Based on data from Romanian institutionalized children, Nelson suggests that because of inadequate experience, selective cell death, which occurs normally in all children during early development, may go awry, so that too many neurons and synapses are lost, most of which can never be replaced, which suggests a sensitive period from which these children cannot fully recover.

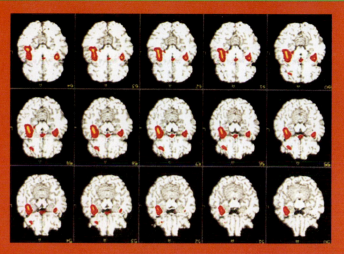

Areas in red and yellow show parts of the brain where Romanian orphan children showed significantly less glucose metabolism than control children. Most of the areas where there were significant differences are in the prefrontal cortex and temporal lobe, both associated with higher cognitive functions. **SOURCE: Chugani, H. T., Behen, M.E.; Muzik, O., Juhász, C., Nagy, F., & Chugani, D. C. (2001). Local brain functional activity following early deprivation: A study of postinstitutionalized Romanian orphans. *NeuroImage, 14*, 1290–1301.**

---

ther promotes less intellectual stimulation from their parents. The result is a transaction that is less than conducive to good intellectual functioning. Note that not all parents will respond to high-risk infants in the same way, and that if parents engage their high-risk infants, intellectual development is more likely to proceed typically.

Biological risks are only some of the factors that can adversely affect a child's intellectual development. Although far from the deprivation that institutionalized children experience, children in many homes receive little direct attention, are talked to minimally, receive harsh punishment, and live in environments that are not conducive to developing intellectual skills suited for academic learning. Few children live in perfect homes, but as the risk factors mount, so do the negative effects on intelligence. This is known as the

FIGURE 10.3 The relationship between the number of risk factors and IQ for a group of 4-year-old children.

The greater the number of risk factors, such as low family income and father absence, the lower children's IQs tended to be. SOURCE: Adapted from Sameroff, A. J., Seifer, R., Baldwin, A., & Baldwin, C. (1993). Stability of intelligence from preschool to adolescence: The influence of social risk factors. *Child Development, 64*, 80–97.

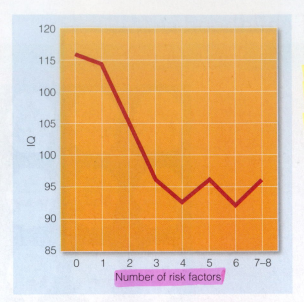

Number of risk factors

cumulative deficit effect. Multiple risks persisting over many years add up, and as a result, children who do not receive intervention display deficits in social, emotional, and cognitive functioning.

For instance, in one study, children from mostly lower-income homes were administered IQ tests at ages 4 and 13 (Sameroff et al., 1993). In addition to IQ, the researchers measured various environmental risk factors (for example, family size, father absence, maternal education, maternal stress, maternal anxiety, low income). Environmental risk factors accounted for between one-third and one-half of the variance in IQ. This relationship is clearly seen in Figure 10.3, which shows IQ scores of 4-year-old children as a function of several risk factors. Cumulated risks affect the whole child, not just intelligence. For example, in one study, cumulative-risk exposure over childhood associated with poverty (for example, substandard housing, family turmoil) was associated with dysregulated cardiovascular responses and elevated cortisol levels (a measure of stress) at age 13 (Evans & Kim, 2007).

Preschool Compensatory Education

It has long been recognized that poverty is associated with lower academic and educational attainment. Parents from poor families typically fail to provide the type of child-rearing environments associated with academic attainment, and as a result children from poverty homes start school behind their middle-class peers and usually stay behind, often losing more ground the longer they stay in

school (Ackerman & Brown, 2006; NICHD Early Child Care Research Network, 2005). Beginning in the 1960s in the United States, compensatory education programs aimed to provide preschool children at high risk for intellectual impairment and academic failure with the intellectual skills to do well in school (Klaus & Gray, 1968; Ramey, Campbell, & Finkelstein, 1984). Preschool education was not as readily available to parents as it is today, and these programs, in part, brought the importance of preschool education to the awareness of the general public. These programs were based on a variety of theoretical models, from those using behavior modification techniques as advocated by B. F. Skinner to programs based on Piagetian theory, and served as models for Head Start, the federally funded program whose goal was to provide educational opportunities to low-income children to prepare them for school. (We should note that Urie Bronfenbrenner, the originator of ecological systems theory introduced in Chapter 2, was a major force behind Head Start.)

Most compensatory education programs shared several things in common: (1) they had low student-teacher ratios, so children could receive substantial individual attention; (2) language was emphasized, including the importance of skills associated with reading (for example, letter-sound correspondence); and (3) children were taught problem-solving skills and strategies that would be useful in school, such as counting and addition strategies. Some programs focused primarily on children while in school, whereas others involved parents and home enrichment in children's early education.

Programs varied in success, but many reported IQ gains relative to control groups of 10 to 15 points or more by the time children began first grade (see Barnett, 1995). These results make it clear that the low IQs typical of poverty children are not caused solely by genes, but that children's intelligence can be modified by intellectually stimulating experience during the preschool years. The question then becomes, once intellectual competence has been established in these children, will it be maintained? Will these children, who begin first grade on par with their middle-class peers, continue to do well academically once the compensatory program has ended, or will they lose the gains from the program once they are left on their own?

The long-term effects of preschool compensatory education programs have been assessed by several researchers (see Barnett, 1995; Lazar et al., 1982). When no booster programs following the preschool programs were used, the initial gains in IQ shown by program graduates are slowly lost, and by the end of the fourth grade, levels of intellectual attainment are typically comparable between children who had participated in the programs and those who had not (Bradley, Burchinal, & Casey, 2001; Klaus & Gray, 1968). Program graduates still showed some school-related advantages, however. They were less apt to be assigned to special education classes and were less likely to be held back in a grade than control children who did not participate in the preschool programs (Lazar et al., 1982). Moreover, research has shown that children whose mothers provide stable and stimulating homes maintain higher IQs than children in less-supportive environments (Garber & Heber, 1981), pointing to the important role of parents in promoting the gains children experience in the compensatory preschool programs.

At least one exception to this pattern is the North Carolina Abecedarian Program (Campbell & Ramey, 1994; Campbell et al., 2001; 2002; Ramey et al., 2000), in which rural children identified as at risk for intellectual impairment attended an educationally oriented daycare program beginning shortly after birth and continued until they entered first grade. Children who attended the preschool program had significantly higher IQs at age 12 than did control children (94 versus 88), and they scored significantly higher on a battery of academic tests (see Figure 10.4. Many of these differences were maintained when participants were tested at age 21 (Campbell et al., 2002), although the effects were greater for women than for men. As adults, members of the experimental group continued to score higher on measures of math and reading, were more likely to attend college (36% versus 14%), were more likely to have a skilled job (47% versus 27%), were less likely to have had their first child at age 18 or younger (36% versus 45%), and were less likely to smoke (39% versus 55%) or to use marijuana (18% versus 39%) than members of the control group (Zimmerman, 2007).

Why was the Abecedarian Program more successful than other programs in fostering long-term success? We cannot say for sure, but it had many features that, in combination, may be responsible for its success: (1) it began in infancy and continued through age 5; (2) children attended all year long, not just during the school year; (3) it had a low student-to-teacher ratio that allowed the staff to individualize instruction; and (4) about half of the participants received school-age intervention (that is, a booster program) from kindergarten through the third grade. The success of programs like this demonstrates that intelligence and academic achievement are modifiable, but that once a high level of intelligence has been established, environments must be in place if it is to be maintained. Concerning Head Start, it was not set up as an experiment, making it difficult to evaluate the long-term benefits in a scientific way. However, several studies have shown that children who

In compensatory education programs, children from at-risk populations receive extensive attention from teachers, developing intellectual skills that enhance their school performance.

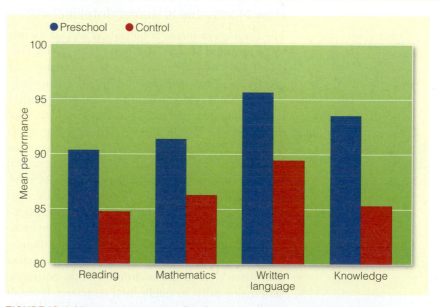

FIGURE 10.4 Mean scores on Woodcock-Johnson Psychoeducational Battery at age 12 for children who participated in the Abecedarian preschool program and control children.

As can be seen from the figure, the academic benefits of attending the programs were maintained years after the program ended. SOURCE: Adapted from data presented in Campbell, F. A., & Ramey, C. T. (1994). Effects of early intervention on intellectual and academic achievement: A follow-up study of children from low-income families. *Child Development, 65*, 684–698.

attended Head Start were more likely to complete high school (Ludwig & Miller, 2007) and, for African Americans, less likely to be charged or convicted of a crime (Graces, Thomas, & Currie, 2000). This has caused some analysts to conclude that the Head Start program, as it is currently operated, is worth the public expense from a strictly economic perspective (Ludwig & Phillips, 2008).

The long-term effects of preschool compensatory educational programs are admittedly mixed. Although some programs do show long-term benefits, we should not be surprised to learn that once the enriched environment that was responsible for establishing intellectual competence changed, children's IQs and school performance gradually declined to levels comparable to that of their peers. These children were still getting smarter with age, but the advantage that their enriched preschool environment provided them could not support the learning that was required as the curriculum became more demanding. That level of learning requires continued support, which many of these children apparently were not getting in their homes or in their schools. Not surprisingly, at-risk children who stay in compensatory education programs once they begin formal school continue to maintain an academic advantage over their peers (Becker & Gersten, 1982).

How Modifiable Is Human Intelligence?

The findings of institutionalization and compensatory education studies and those with at-risk children reflect a flexible cognitive system that can be greatly modified during childhood. Fortunately, most children in the world live in more supportive intellectual environments. Nonetheless, individual differences in the quality of child-rearing affect typically developing children's intelligence and school performance as well. The research reviewed here indicates what *can* happen to levels of intelligence during childhood and not necessarily what actually *does* happen. Children's environments do change over time, such as the transition from home to school and a corresponding shift from a family-centered to a peer-centered lifestyle. To the extent that these changes in environments do not represent major shifts in intellectual emphasis, levels of intelligence can be expected to be maintained. The more different the environments, the greater the change in level of intelligence can be expected.

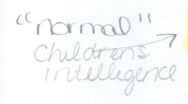

"normal"
Children's
intelligence

Intelligence at the Extremes

Intellectual Impairment

In the previous section, we discussed how social deprivation or lack of intellectual stimulation can result in intellectual impairment and how, under some circumstances, that impairment can be reversed. We never actually defined intellectual impairment and its various forms, however. It is perhaps a no-brainer to realize that intellectual impairment refers to a lower-than-average level of intelligence as measured by IQ tests. Today, most researchers and educators classify a child as being intellectually disabled if his or her IQ is 70 or below, which is two standard deviations below the average IQ of 100. In addition to a low IQ, to be classified as being intellectually disabled, a person must also show impairments in adaptive behavior, and these impairments must begin during childhood (Hodapp & Dykens, 2006).

Although there are several ways of categorizing people with intellectual impairment, one popular approach examines the likely origin of the impairment and classifies people into two groups (Hodapp & Dykens, 2006). The first is described as *organic,* and these are people whose impairment can be traced to specific biological factors, such as prenatal and birth complications (for example, anoxia, or lack of oxygen, at birth) and more than 1,000 genetic syndromes. The second group is described as *cultural familial,* and these are individuals who show no identifiable organic reason for their lower intellectual levels. The poorer mental functioning of institutionalized children and children experiencing nonstimulating homes would be attributed to cultural-familial causes. These children typically have lesser degrees of impairment than do children with organic causes.

One interesting finding about people with intellectual impairment is that their cognitive skills tend to be more similar to one another than those of higher-IQ people. Recall that the *positive manifold* refers to the fact that a high correlation exists among different types of mental tasks—people who score high on one type of task tend to score high on others, for example. These intertask correlations are even higher for people with intellectual impairment. For example, in one study, intellectually disabled adults (mean IQ = 67.5) and college students (mean IQ = 115.5) were given a battery of nine cognitive tasks and an IQ test (Detterman & Daniel, 1989). The researchers reported that correlations among the cognitive tasks were considerably higher for the low-IQ group (.60 for IQ scores and .44 for the cognitive tasks) than for the high-IQ group (.26 for IQ scores and .23 for the cognitive tasks), which means that the cognitions of low-IQ people are less varied than the cognitions of high-IQ people. One interpretation of this effect is that intellectual impairment is caused by a deficit in central (domain-general) processes (for example, working-memory resources). When sufficient central resources are available, individual differences in more specific components of intelligence can operate adequately. When there is a deficit in central resources, however, as in the case of people with intellectual impairment, individual components will not receive enough in the way of processing resources to function well, resulting in greater evenness, or homogeneity, of cognitive functioning, and thus high correlations (Detterman, 1987).

Partial confirmation for this argument comes from studies showing that children and adults with intellectual impairment have shorter working-memory spans (Henry & MacLean, 2003), perform more poorly on executive function tasks (Kittler, Krinsky-McHale, & Devenny, 2008), and process information more slowly (Saccuzzo et al., 1979) than do people without intellectual impairment. Not surprisingly, individuals with intellectual impairment also perform more poorly on higher-level cognitive tasks. For example, they are less likely to use strategies effectively on a variety of learning and memory tasks and are less likely than children without intellectual impairment to benefit from strategy training (Borkowski, Reid, & Kurtz, 1984).

The cognitive test performance of people with intellectual impairment, such as those with Down syndrome, tends to be more similar than for people with typical intelligence.

© Stockbyte/Photolibrary

Gifted Intelligence

At the other end of the IQ spectrum are children labeled as *gifted.* Usually, children with IQs two standard deviations above the mean, 130, are considered gifted. Many school districts have special programs for these high-IQ children, although children with other talents (for example, in music or painting) are sometimes also included in these programs, even if their IQs fall below the 130 mark.

Like children with intellectual impairment, gifted children also process information differently than their average peers, but in their case they are generally more, not less, effective. For example, gifted children process information more quickly (Saccuzzo, Johnson, & Guertin, 1994) and have higher levels of executive function (Arffa, 2007; Mahone et al., 2002) than do nongifted children. They are also more likely than children with average IQs to use strategies (Gaultney, Bjorklund, & Goldstein, 1996; Geary & Brown, 1991) and show greater metacognitive awareness (Alexander & Schwanenflgel, 1996; Borkowski & Peck, 1986).

One hypothesis for gifted children's greater use of strategies is that it is tied to their greater knowledge base. For example, in a study of gifted, nongifted, and mathematically disabled third- and fourth-grade children's use of mathematical strategies, David Geary and Sam Brown (1991) concluded that the gifted children's advantage was attributed to their greater knowledge of basic math facts (for example, $7 + 6 = 13$; $8 + 5 = 13$). They knew their facts better and could retrieve the answers directly without having to use a more effortful counting strategy (see discussion in the following section on children's arithmetic).

The Three Rs: Acquiring Society's Core Academic Skills

Five-year-old Nathanial had not shown any apprehension about starting kindergarten. If anything, he was looking forward to beginning school, prompted in part by the fact that he would be going to the same school as his older brother, Jeffrey. But 9-year-old Jeffrey could read, and Nathanial understood that this is something he too would have to learn how to do, and this worried him. "Mom, I just don't know how they're going to teach me how to read! How can they do it?" Three years later, after countless hours of sounding out words, his grandmother complimented him on how well he could read. Nathanial, almost conspiratorially, whispered to his grandmother, "You know, Grandma, I'm not really reading. I just look at the words and just *know* them."

Nathanial had come a long way in three years. He knew before beginning kindergarten how special and important reading was, that he would learn how to read in school, but how he would accomplish this was a mystery. After years of arduous work, Nathanial had finally broken the code, and his getting meaning from print seemed to just happen, seemingly unrelated to the effortful sounding out of individual letters that had occupied so much of his school time for the past several years. But how he did it was still a mystery.

Reading is perhaps the most important intellectual tool for people in literate societies (an example of Vygotsky's *tools of intellectual adaptation*), and it is perhaps the clearest example of

Some distinctions between biologically primary and biologically secondary abilities

Language is a good example of a biologically primary ability, whereas reading is a good example of a biologically secondary ability.

Biologically primary abilities	Biologically secondary abilities
Have undergone selection pressure and evolved to deal with problems faced by our ancestors	Do not have an evolutionary history but are built upon biologically primary abilities
Are acquired universally	Are culturally dependent, reflecting the cognitive skills that are important in a particular culture (such as reading in literate cultures)
Are acquired by children in all but the most deprived of environments	
Children are intrinsically motivated to exercise biologically primary abilities and do so spontaneously	Children are not intrinsically motivated to exercise them and must often be pressured by adults to acquire these skills
Most children attain "expert" level of proficiency	Tedious practice is sometimes necessary to master biologically secondary abilities

SOURCE: Adapted from Geary, D. C. (1995). Reflections of evolution and culture in children's cognition: Implications for mathematical development and instruction. *American Psychologist, 50*, 24–37.

what David Geary (1995, 2007a) calls **biologically secondary abilities**—cognitive skills that must be taught and are cultural inventions. Geary distinguishes these abilities from **biologically primary abilities** (see Concept Review 10.3). Biologically primary abilities have gone through selective pressure and evolved to deal with recurrent problems faced by our ancestors. Language is a good example of a biologically primary ability. Such abilities are universal, in that all biologically typical members of the species possess them, and they will develop in a species-typical fashion if children experience a species-typical environment. Children also spontaneously engage in activities that exercise biologically primary activities. For example, children will spontaneously label objects in their environment, count small quantities of objects, or use objects as tools. And although there are sometimes individual differences in the rate and eventual level of the ability achieved (for example, language disabilities), most children will attain an expert level of performance without adult instruction.

In contrast, biologically secondary abilities do not have an evolutionary history. Rather, they are based on highly specialized neurocognitive systems that are built upon biologically primary abilities that children acquire to deal with new ecological problems, unknown to our forebears, such as reading. Reading, as other skills we will examine in the next

sections, is based on the biologically primary abilities associated with language (and perhaps some other primary abilities dealing with processing visual information) and is an evolutionarily novel activity. That is, human minds did not evolve to read. Reading also requires tedious repetition and practice, and it is little wonder that many children have a difficult time learning to read. Nevertheless, most children in schooled cultures must master this skill on their way to adulthood, and success in school, and often in adult life, is related to how well one can read.

Although reading and the related skill of writing may be the essential academic skills for modern people, running close behind is a working knowledge of mathematics. Although only a minority of children in modern society master higher mathematics, such as calculus and trigonometry, nearly all master arithmetic, at least enough to balance a checkbook, make change in a store, and double a recipe. Like reading, arithmetic is based on some intuitive, biologically primary abilities but must be learned in school often through tedious drill (remember learning your multiplication tables). Such schooled abilities are, by definition, effortful mental operations and involve other basic cognitive abilities, like working memory, for their development. In this section we examine the development of three important cultural skills—reading, writing, and arithmetic—the traditional "Three Rs."

In addition to their importance to modern life, their mastery consumes many of the waking hours of elementary schoolchildren throughout the world, and for that reason alone deserves our attention. As you will see, their attainment is based on the development of some basic (and not so basic) cognitive abilities, such as those discussed in earlier chapters of this section.

biologically secondary abilities Cognitive abilities that build on biologically primary abilities but are principally cultural inventions, and often-tedious repetition and external motivation are necessary for their mastery, such as reading.

biologically primary abilities Cognitive abilities that have been selected for in evolution, are acquired universally, and children typically have high motivation to perform tasks involving them, such as language.

Learning to Read

Although nearly all children learn to read in school, children know a lot about reading before ever setting foot in a classroom. In a pre-reading, or pre-alphabetic, stage (Chall, 1979; Ehri, 1995), preschool children can identify some words on sight, such as "Coca-Cola," "McDonald's," perhaps their own names, and may know some of the letters in their name, especially the first letter (Trieman et al., 2007). Beginning with formal reading instruction in kindergarten or the first grade, children learn the sounds of letters and are able to recognize individual words on sight. (Beginning readers can get quite excited about being able to identify individual words: "I know that word. It's 'the.' And that word, too, it says 'book!'") By the third or fourth grade, most children have mastered the letter-to-sound correspondence, although reading is still typically effortful, as they continue to concentrate on what individual groups of letters mean rather than putting the words together to grasp the broader meaning of the text. Finally, beginning in the fourth or fifth grade, children's reading becomes more fluid; the connections between sounds and letters become consolidated, they can identify larger units of written language, and they recognize most written words they encounter by sight, without having to sound them out. This has been described as the transition from learning to read to reading to learn.

Not surprisingly, like many other things, children become increasingly better readers the more they read. The old adage of practice makes perfect clearly applies to reading. This results in an interesting phenomenon called the Matthew effect, in which the difference between good and poor readers increases over time (Stanovich, 1986). The name comes from the New Testament's book of Matthew, which makes the observation (basically) that the "rich get richer and the poor get poorer." ("For to everyone who has, more shall be given, and he will have an abundance; but from the one who does not have, even what he does have shall be taken away," Matthew 25:29, American Standard Version.) Good readers, because they enjoy and are relatively good at reading, read more and thus become increasingly proficient at reading, whereas poor readers, who are less skilled and enjoy it less, read less and, although they may be improving in an absolute sense, find themselves falling further behind their more skilled peers.

Although reading is very effortful initially for children, by fourth or fifth grade, most children are able to "read to learn" and may read for pleasure.

© Bobby Yip/Reuters/Corbis

examining what has been termed emergent literacy (Bialystok, 1996). Emergent literacy refers to the skills, knowledge, and attitudes that are the precursors of conventional reading and writing. Table 10.9 presents a list of eight components of emergent literacy.

Some aspects of emergent literacy are related to later reading ability (Lonigan, Burgess, & Anthony, 2000; Storch & Whitehurst, 2002). For example, understanding some of the conventions of print, such as the ability to recognize and name letters and that the letters in a word are spaced together (for example, "words" as opposed to "wo r ds") are associated with early reading skills (Levy et al., 2006; Schneider & Näslund, 1999). Aspects of linguistic awareness in the preschool years, specifically phonemic awareness—the knowledge that words consist of separable sounds—has also been found to predict later reading ability (Schneider & Näslund, 1999; Wagner et al., 1997). Not surprisingly, kindergarten and first-grade

Emergent Literacy

What type of cognitive abilities are involved in skilled reading, how do they develop, and what differentiates children who learn to read easily from those who have a difficult time breaking the code? A good place to start is with the pre-reading stage,

Matthew effect The phenomenon in which the difference between good and poor readers (or other cognitive abilities) increases over time.

emergent literacy The skills, knowledge, and attitudes that are presumed to be developmental precursors to conventional forms of reading and writing during early childhood and the environments that support these developments.

phonemic awareness The knowledge that words consist of separable sounds.

table 10.9 Some Important Emergent Literacy Skills and Knowledge

1. **Language:** Although reading is not simply a reflection of spoken language, children need to be versatile with their spoken language before they can be expected to read it.

2. **Conventions of print:** Knowledge of some of the basics of how print is organized for reading. For example, in English, children learn that reading is done left-to-right, top-to-bottom, and front-to-back.

3. **Knowledge of letters:** Most children can recite their ABCs before entering school and can identify individual letters of the alphabet.

4. **Linguistic awareness:** Children must learn to identify not only letters but also linguistic units, such as phonemes, syllables, and words.

5. **Phoneme-grapheme correspondence:** Knowledge of the sounds that correspond to letters.

6. **Emergent reading:** Many children pretend to read, taking a familiar storybook and making up a narrative.

7. **Emergent writing:** Similar to pretend reading, children often pretend to write, making squiggles on a page to "write" their name or a story.

8. **Print motivation:** Children differ in their motivation to learn to read. Children who are interested in reading and writing are more likely to notice print, ask questions about print, encourage adults to read to them, and spend more time reading once they are able.

SOURCE: Adapted from Whitehurst, G. J., & Lonigan, C. J. (1998). Child development and emergent literacy. *Child Development, 69,* 848–872.

Reading to young children is associated with improved literacy skills in the early school grades.

© Corbis Premium RF/Alamy

children who receive instruction in phonemic awareness show enhanced early-reading ability relative to children who are not given such instruction (Cunningham, 1990; Schneider et al., 1997).

Although young children may pick up some emergent literacy skills simply by living in a literate environment, parents play an important role in fostering these skills and preparing children for reading. For example, mothers and fathers who read to their children have children with better language, cognitive, and reading abilities (Oliver, Dale, & Plomin, 2005). We must be cautious in interpreting this relationship, however, for parents who read a lot to their children likely are different in many other ways than parents who read to their children less often, and these characteristics may be important in children's cognitive and reading abilities. Some of the benefits of parents reading to their young children are discussed in Box 10.4.

Cognitive Development and Reading

Several cognitive abilities are related to skilled reading and develop over the preschool and school years (Roman et al., 2009). Perhaps the most important one is **phonological recoding** (Ziegler & Goswami, 2006). We just noted that phonemic awareness—the knowledge that words consist of separable sounds—in the preschool years is a good predictor of later reading ability. The reason for this is that early reading usually means sounding out words—discovering the correspondence between letters (graphemes) and sounds (phonemes), or learning *grapheme-phoneme correspondence.* Phonological recoding is the process whereby letters and words are translated into sounds and is the basis of the **phonics** method of reading instruction used in most schools in the United States today.

As speakers (and readers) of English, you are likely aware that the correspondence between written and spoken English is highly variable and represents a difficult task for readers. For example, the playwright George Bernard Shaw commented that, following the rules of English spelling, "ghoti" should be a perfectly acceptable alternative spelling for the word "fish": "gh" as in "cough," "o" as in

phonics Reading instruction method based on learning letter-sound correspondence.
phonological recoding Reading skills used to translate written symbols into sounds and words.

"women," and "ti" as in "nation." (Go ahead, sound it out.) English has what is called a *deep orthography*, meaning the spelling system for converting letters into sounds is irregular, with there being multiple ways in which some letter combinations can be sounded out. In contrast, languages such as Spanish, Italian, or Finnish have *shallow orthographies*, with there being a close correspondence between letters and their sounds. For example, Italian uses 25 phonemes, and 33 combinations of letters are used to represent these sounds. In contrast, English uses 40 phonemes, but 1,120 different letter combinations are needed to completely represent these sounds. Thus, it may not be surprising that, although phonemic awareness and phonological decoding are important in learning to read all alphabetic languages, differences in the *transparency* of the orthographies (that is, deep versus shallow) influence how easily children learn to decode written language and become proficient readers (Ziegler & Goswami, 2006).

To illustrate the role of orthographic transparency on reading, consider the data presented in Figure 10.5. This figure presents the percentage of children in different countries who correctly read familiar real words and pseudowords (for example, *kake, joak*). Some of the children spoke and read languages with shallow orthographies (Greek, Finnish, and Italian), and others spoke and read languages with deep orthographies (French, Danish, and Scottish English). As you can see, performance was nearly perfect for children reading languages with shallow orthographies but much lower for children reading languages with deep orthographies (Seymour, Aro, & Erskine, 2003; Ziegler & Goswami, 2005). This makes learning to read languages like English so much more difficult than learning to read other European languages.

Reading Disabilities

The importance of the role of phonological decoding in learning to read is illustrated when children without reading disability are contrasted with children with reading disability, or **dyslexia**. Children are said to have a reading disability if they have great difficulty in learning to read despite an average intelligence. Stated another way, if a child's reading ability is substantially worse than his or her general intellectual ability, that child is said to have a reading disability. Perhaps the single best predictor of reading difficulty is phonological processing, including phonological recoding (Adams et al., 1998; White et al., 2006). For example, Figure 10.6 shows the number of pseudowords read by groups of children with and without reading disability at four different ages (Siegel, 1993). Pseu-

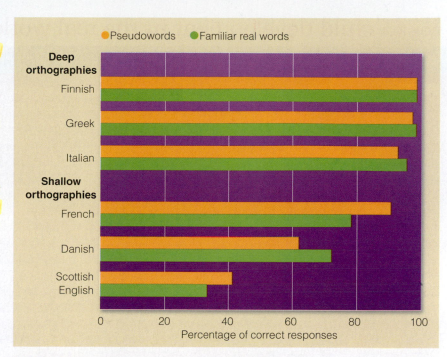

FIGURE 10.5 Percentage of correct responses of children reading familiar real words and pseudowords for languages with shallow orthographies (Finnish, Greek, and Italian) versus languages with deep orthographies (French, Danish, and Scottish English). SOURCE: Adapted from Seymour, P. H. K., Aro, M., & Erskine, J. M. (2003). Foundations of literacy acquisition in European orthographies. *British Journal of Psychology, 94,* 143–174.

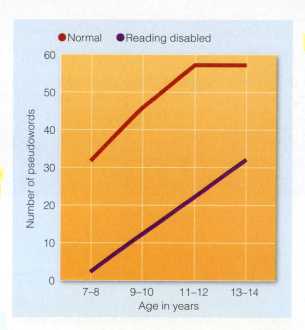

FIGURE 10.6 Accuracy of pseudoword reading as a function of age for children with and without reading disability. The number of pseudowords correctly read increased with age for both groups of children, but was higher at each age for the children without reading disability than for the children with reading disability. SOURCE: "The cognitive basis of dyslexia," by L. S. Siegel. In R. Pasnak and M. L. Howe (Eds.), *Emerging themes in cognitive development,* Vol. II: *Competencies.* Copyright © 1993 Springer-Verlag New York. Reprinted by permission

dowords like *blape* and *swup* can only be read by sounding them out. As you can see, the number of pseudowords children correctly identified increased with age for both groups, but at every age the children without reading disability read significantly more pseudowords than do children with reading disabilities. Longitudinal research suggests

....

dyslexia Difficulty in learning to read despite having an average level of intelligence and good educational opportunities.

BOX 10.4 child development in the real world

The Joys of Being Read To

The earliest contact most children have with stories is in reading picture books. This activity usually takes place when an adult (usually the mother) shows the child pictures in a book that has little written text, explaining (often in her own words) what the pictures portray. In Western cultures, this practice begins when children are about 1 year old, and, according to recent surveys, parents of preschool children report that they have available dozens of picture books and devote an average of 40 minutes per day to this activity (Rideout, Vandewater, & Wartella, 2003; Simcock & DeLoache, 2006).

When parents are participating in picture-book reading with their young children, they are actually using a scaffolding strategy, changing their dialog as the children become more proficient in language use. They are more directive when children are younger and become less so with age (DeLoache & DeMendoza, 1987). Parents establish a book-reading routine (Bruner, 1986) in which they may point out and label pictures, ask questions, provide feedback, and make categorical distinctions, such as saying, "This is a cat and this is a fish; fish live in the water." They often elaborate about the stories' plots and the details depicted in the book (Simcock & DeLoache, 2006; Symons et al., 2005).

The children's role in picture-book reading changes with age, too. Between 9 and 14 months of age, they "act upon the book," stroking the pictures, scratching at the picture with their fingers as though they are trying to pick the object up, or hitting the book to make loud sounds. At the end of this period, they become fascinated with turning pages. Around 17 months of age up until 2 years, they increasingly spend more time looking at the book than acting upon it. They point to pictures and increase their vocal exchanges, focusing more on the symbolic nature of the pictures (Bus & Van IJzendoorn, 1997; Murphy, 1978).

What does picture-book reading contribute to children's cognitive development? The contribution of picture-book reading has been studied with regard to children's language development, reading acquisition, school achievement, and theory of mind (see accompanying table with a list of main findings). One of the important findings is that parents who use highly elaborative conversational styles with their young children have children who tell richer and lengthier narratives when they reach school age than do children with parents who use less elaborative styles (McCabe & Peterson, 1991; Reese, Haden, & Fivush, 1993; Hudson, 1993). Elaborative mothers not only tell more involved stories to their children, but they are also more likely to comment on their children's responses. For example, after making a statement about some previous event (for example, "Then we sang a song"), elaborative mothers are more likely to provide comments that confirm or negate a child's statement (such as "That's right," "Yes," or "No") than less elaborative mothers are. Preschool children of elaborative mothers also remember more of the events they experience than do children of less elaborative mothers (Reese et al., 1993).

A second area of research examines the role of early picture-book reading for later reading and writing skills. It has long been thought that in Western cultures, storytelling is the "foundational pillar of literacy" (McKeough, 1998), although empirical studies have not always been consistent about this relationship (Scarborough & Dobrich, 1994). For example, in a 5-year longitudinal study carried out by Monique Sénéchal and Jo-Anne LeFevre (2002), shared, or interactive, storybook reading at home was positively related to the development of some receptive language skills, including vocabulary and listening comprehension, which, in turn, were related to children's reading level in third grade (see also Lever & Sénéchal, 2010). It turned out, however, that shared storybook reading was not related to first-grade reading, nor to the emergence of early literary skills, such as alphabet knowledge and invented spelling. In other words, there seems to be several pathways from home literacy experiences to later literacy skills,

that phonological-processing abilities remain relatively stable over childhood (Storch & Whitehurst, 2002; Wagner et al., 1997), making early intervention all the more important.

The phonological difficulties of children with reading disabilities have been found to be associated with patterns of brain activation. For example, in research with both children and adults, brain-imaging studies indicate different patterns of brain activation between nondisabled and reading-disabled children and adults, especially when the tasks require substantial phonological processing (Shaywitz, Mody, & Shaywitz, 2006; Shaywitz et al., 1998). Compared with nondisabled readers, the dyslexic readers show underactivation in some portions of the brain (mainly posterior regions) and overactivation in others (mainly anterior regions). Underactive parts of the brain include those areas typically associated with phonological processing.

Other cognitive abilities develop over the course of childhood that are related to reading ability, one particularly important skill being working memory. Skilled reading requires getting meaning from text, and that means being able to connect words and ideas from the end of a sentence to words and ideas from the beginning of a sentence. To do this skillfully, children need to be able to keep ideas in mind long enough to make those connections, and this is where working memory comes into play. Like phonological recoding skills, working memory increases with age but is greater at all ages tested for nondisabled versus disabled readers (Gathercole et al., 2006; Swanson & Jerman, 2007).

Some Potential Positive Effects of Picture-Book Reading on Development

Parents who use a more elaborative conversational style during picture-book reading have children who produce lengthier and more elaborative narratives.

Picture-book reading practices explain a portion of the individual differences in children's later literacy (for example, reading level in grade 3).

Picture-book reading practices might favor the acquisition of some devices involved in successful school achievements in some fields (for example, math).

Picture-book reading practices can enhance children's learning about the contents they read.

The use of mental descriptions and inferences by both parents and children during picture-book reading results in earlier and enhanced understanding of actions by children (theory of mind).

with picture-book reading seeming to be one of the elements that contributes indirectly to the acquisition of these later skills.

A third area in which the effects of picture-book reading are beginning to be explored is school achievements, as well as other learning outcomes. For example, in one study, 18-, 24-, and 30-month-old children were read a picture book telling the story of a child, Sandy, who was making a rattle with some toys she had found (a ball, a stick, and a jar; first putting the ball inside the jar, and then shaking the stick in the jar to make the rattle noise) (Simcock & DeLoache, 2006). Later on children were given similar objects that had been shown in the picture book and were told, "You can use these things to make a rattle. Show me how you can use these things to make a rattle." Picture books varied on the level of *iconicity* of their pictures (namely, they were composed either of color photographs, color drawings, or black-and-white line drawings). Other children were given the same set of objects but without being read the picture book. Children who were read the book imitated the target actions depicted in the picture book more than control groups of children of equivalent ages who were not read the picture book, with older children performing better than younger children. Performance was also better when the picture book was composed of more-iconic (photographs) than less-iconic (line drawings) images. The latter effect was particularly strong for the younger group of children.

A last line of research has to do with the effects of picture-book reading on theory-of-mind acquisitions. Understanding a story implies understanding not just the chronological series of events and actions described in it, but also understanding the characters' mental states and relationships, as well as the psychological causes of the actions and events involved in the story. This requires theory of mind. In this vein, mother's use of cognitive verbs (for example, "know" and "think") when reading picture books to 3- to 6-year-old children correlated with children's understanding of mental states 1 year later (Adrián, Clemente, & Villanueva, 2007). Similar results have been found in other studies (Ruffman, Slade, & Crowe, 2002; Symons et al., 2005), indicating the importance of both parents' and children's use of mental descriptions and inferences in the picture-book reading context and their facilitative effects for some theory-of-mind acquisitions.

Picture-book reading is more than just a highly enjoyable socioemotional activity for parents and children; it is also a fruitful one for children's linguistic and cognitive development. Picture-book reading has a positive impact on the way children tell stories, their subsequent reading and writing skills, and even in their development of theory of mind. The most important ingredient is not the book but the parents who are doing the reading and how they read to their children.

Sex Differences in Reading and Verbal Abilities

Boys are far more likely than girls to be identified as having reading disabilities (see Geary, 1993). This is related to a more general sex difference in reading and verbal ability, with girls and women displaying higher levels of performance than boys and men from an early age (Halpern, 1997; Hedges & Nowell, 1995). The differences are particularly large in writing. Figure 10.7 shows the results from a fourth-grade assessment of verbal abilities in 25 countries. The length of each line reflects the magnitude of the sex difference, favoring girls, in each country. In every country, females performed significantly better than males. We should note that there is even more variability within the sexes than between them. That is, although there is a substantial and consistent average difference in reading ability between boys and girls, many boys are better readers than many girls.

One possible reason for the substantial sex difference is that reading is generally regarded as a stereotypical female activity, and many boys may not be as motivated to read as girls. Consistent with this interpretation, interest level is more important for boys than for girls in reading comprehension. For example, in a study with fifth graders (Asher & Markel, 1974), sex differences favoring girls in reading ability were small and insignificant for high-interest stories but large and significant in favor of girls for low-interest stories (see also Renninger, 1992; Schiefele, Krapp, & Winteler, 1992). That is, when boys were interested in the content of the stories, they did about as well as girls; only girls performed well, however, when the stories were of low interest.

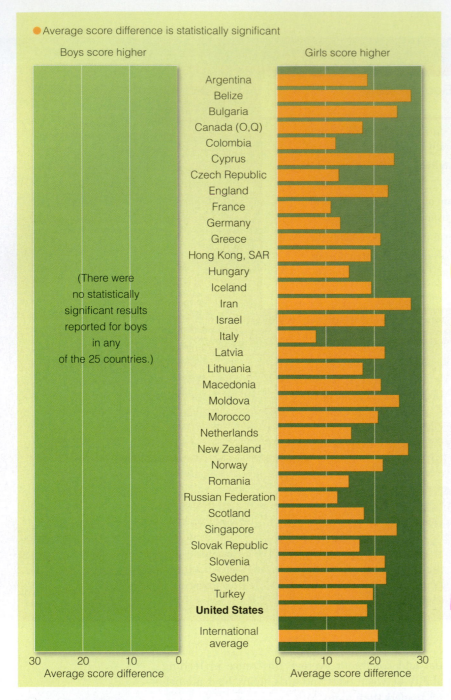

● Average score difference is statistically significant

Boys score higher   **Girls score higher**

(There were no statistically significant results reported for boys in any of the 25 countries.)

Country	Girls score higher
Argentina	
Belize	
Bulgaria	
Canada (O,Q)	
Colombia	
Cyprus	
Czech Republic	
England	
France	
Germany	
Greece	
Hong Kong, SAR	
Hungary	
Iceland	
Iran	
Israel	
Italy	
Latvia	
Lithuania	
Macedonia	
Moldova	
Morocco	
Netherlands	
New Zealand	
Norway	
Romania	
Russian Federation	
Scotland	
Singapore	
Slovak Republic	
Slovenia	
Sweden	
Turkey	
United States	
International average	

30   20   10   0
Average score difference

0   10   20   30
Average score difference

FIGURE 10.7 Sex differences in reading/verbal abilities in 25 countries. The longer the line, the greater the sex difference, favoring girls. SOURCE: From Halpern, D. F., Benbow, C. P., Geary, D. C., Gur, R. C., Hyde, J. S., & Gernsbacher, M. A. (2007). The science of sex differences in science and mathematics. *Psychological Science in the Public Interest, 8,* 1–51. Reprinted by permission.

Book publishers are aware of the importance of interest in getting boys to read and are publishing more books with topics that are more appealing to boys. The *Harry Potter* series did a lot to get boys (and girls) interested in reading, and recently publishers have come out with some boy-oriented books that are not always welcomed into the elementary school classroom. For example, a 2009 listing of popular books for boys included

- Nonfiction: *Getting to Know Your Toilet: The Disgusting Story Behind Your Home's Strangest Feature; Oh, Yuck: The Encyclopedia of Everything Nasty;* and *It's Disgusting and We Ate It! True Food Facts From Around the World and Throughout History.*

- Fiction: *Captain Underpants* (series); *Sir Fartsalot Hunts the Booger;* and *The Day My Butt Went Psycho* (trilogy). (On Amazon.com the latter book is described as "wisely rated G for Gross [Contains immature material not suitable for adults].")

Sex differences in brain structure or function may also be responsible for sex differences in reading and verbal abilities. We discussed briefly sex differences in brain development in Chapter 4. Females have proportionally more gray matter than males, and their brains are more symmetrical than males, in that the proportion of gray and white matter are more similar in the two hemispheres. Also, females are more apt than males to use language-related areas of their brains in solving complex problems (see Halpern et al., 2007). This pattern suggests that females should outperform males on verbal tasks, consistent with the findings.

How to Teach Children to Read

As we have pointed out, few children learn to read spontaneously the way they learn to talk. Most have to be instructed how to read, and although parents certainly play a role here, schools are primarily responsible for teaching children to read. Over the decades, educators have had different opinions about the best way to teach children to read, with debates often becoming quite heated. To keep it simple, there have been two basic approaches to teaching reading (see Adams et al., 1998). One is the *phonics method*, discussed briefly earlier, in which children are taught specific letter-sound relationships, often independent of any meaningful context. This usually involves a lot of repetition and drill until children know, without thinking, grapheme-phoneme correspondence. The other is the **whole-language approach**, which contends that learning is anchored on and motivated by meaning (see Adams et al., 1998). In classrooms where whole language is taught, there are labels everywhere (for example, "window," "door," "table," etc.), giving children exposure to the printed word outside of books. Thus, the whole-language approach emphasizes reading interesting and meaningful text from the very beginning. Classrooms where whole language is taught are more apt to be student rather than teacher centered, avoid drill, and integrate reading and writing across the whole curriculum.

The whole-language approach sounds much more enjoyable than the phonics approach and uses skilled reading as the model for how to teach beginning readers. Skilled reading is not done by sounding out individual words—skilled readers see words, even groups of words, and process meaning directly, only sounding out unfamiliar words. In fact, some advocates of the whole-language approach "have steadfastly, adamantly, and sometimes vitriolically denied the value and rejected the practice of skills instruction, including phonics, and this has been a point of heated contention" (Adams et al., 1998, p. 277).

Despite these claims, from the research we reviewed earlier in this chapter, it should be clear that phonological processing is essential to learning to read. Phonological skills are the single best predictor of reading ability (and disability). These skills are affected by experience, some in the home as parents read books to preschool children, and others through practice in school, accompanied by explicit instruction. If phonics is ignored, regardless of how meaningful the material that children are asked to read, children are at risk of reading disabilities. This is not to argue for a curriculum that has children reading only stories about "Dick, Jane, and their dog Spot," but it does argue for including some aspects of phonics in any reading instruction. However, it should not be surprising that some combination of phonics and meaningful reading is, on average, most effective, and that reading instruction is most effective when it is individualized to a child's learning abilities and styles (Morrison & Connor, 2009).

Learning to Write

People use the phrase "learning to write" to refer to two related phenomenon. The first is associated with "learning to read," and involves children learning how to make letters, string them together into words, and literally write information on paper for someone else to read. The other meaning refers to becoming a skilled communicator of written language, as in learning to construct proper paragraphs and eventually, one hopes, to be able to write prose that conveys information, feelings, or otherwise successfully communicates one's thoughts. Here we focus on the basics of writing, learning to physically make marks on paper that can be read by others.

Writing and Culture

Writing involves what Vygotsky (1978) called "second order symbolism," that is, becoming aware that written symbols represent oral language symbols that, in turn, represent real objects and people in the world. Not surprisingly, this is initially a difficult thing for children to understand. And because writing, like reading, is a cultural invention, how written symbols come to represent spoken words varies among cultures. For example, the English writing system, like most other Western systems,

Children in the early school years understand that written letters correspond to sounds and words, but it takes them a while to figure out the exact relationships.

is alphabetic, meaning that individual letters represent mostly individual phonemes or sounds from spoken English. However, Japanese *kana* scripts represent syllables, not phonemes, and Chinese scripts represent morphemes, the smallest unit of meaning in a language.

How one organizes written symbols on a page also varies with the writing system. For example, in modern Hebrew and Arabic writing systems, writing proceeds from right to left, instead of left to right as is done in European languages. In traditional Chinese, Japanese, and Korean writing systems (but not in modern ones), symbols are written in columns and read from top to bottom.

Learning to Put Words on Paper

Children gain a grasp of writing systems before they start school (Ferreiro & Teberosky, 1982; Tolchinsky, 2003). The printed word is everywhere in contemporary societies, and children are exposed systematically to written material, including advertisements for food and drink brands (think "McDonald's" and "Coca-Cola"), newspapers, books, and pamphlets that they see regularly in their homes. Given this exposure, it is not surprising that children as young as 4 years old can distinguish between drawings, numbers, and writing (Adams et al., 1998; Tolchinsky, 2003). For example, preschoolers produce different graphic marks when asked to draw "a house"

whole-language approach A top-down approach to teaching reading that emphasizes the readers' active construction of meaning.

than when asked to write "a house" (Tolchinsky-Landsmann & Levin, 1985); they know that letters can be linked in writing but that numbers must be separate (Tolchinsky-Landsmann & Karmiloff-Smith, 1992); and they often produce a series of curved or straight characters resembling writing when asked to write words or sentences (Ferreiro & Teberosky, 1982; Jones, 1990).

However, when preschoolers first begin to write, they do not differentiate properly the written marks from the things they actually represent. That is, they do not seem to be aware of the "alphabetic principle" (every letter represents, or corresponds to, a specific phoneme or sound) (Adams et al., 1998). Accordingly, children's first written marks depend strongly on the physical properties of the thing it represents. For example, Gustavo, a 4-year-old Spanish speaker, writes a long wavy line for the word *oso* (bear) and a short line for the word *pato* (duck), because, he says, bears are bigger than ducks; and David, another 5-year-old Spanish speaker, says that marks for writing *papá* (dad) need to be longer than marks for writing his own first and last names, because his father is bigger and older than he is (Ferreiro & Teberosky, 1982). Similar phenomena have been reported concerning the influence of the shape and color of the objects in children's first written marks. For example, preschool children will use a green crayon to write *cucumber* and a red crayon to write *tomato,* and will use more marks to write *elephant* (a large animal) than *ant* (a smaller animal) (Levin & Tolchinsky-Landsmann, 1989).

Kindergarten and first-grade children seem to understand that letters correspond to sounds, but their early attempts at writing are difficult to decipher, mainly because the young writers often cannot read and do not appreciate the convention of putting spaces between words. For example, 5-year-old Bobby wrote his first note to his mother, protesting her insistence that he wear a jacket to go outside:

Translation: "Why should I be warm enough?"
Or consider first-grade Trevor's messages:

Translation: "When I go outside I ride my bike and I play on my bike ride."

A day later, Trevor wrote:

Translation: "I like to eat pizza and I like to drink pop." (Bobby's and Trevor's handwriting samples from Adams, M. J., Treiman, R., & Pressley, M. (1998). Reading, writing, and literacy. In K. A. Renninger & I. E. Sigel (Vol. Eds.) Child psychology in practice (Vol. 4). In W. Damon (Gen. Ed.), *Handbook of child psychology.* New York: Wiley, p. 291. Reprinted by permission).

With age and experience, children learn the correct spelling of words, often by simply memorizing them. This is necessary for children learning a language such as English, where the correspondence between spelling and sound (graphemes and phonemes) is not exact. Consider, for example, a journal entry by first-grader Jillian, a classmate of Trevor's who began first grade writing much like Trevor but made more rapid progress (from Adams, M. J., Treiman, R., & Pressley, M. (1998). Reading, writing, and literacy. In K. A. Renninger & I. E. Sigel (Vol. Eds.) Child psychology in practice (Vol. 4). In W. Damon (Gen. Ed.), *Handbook of child psychology.* New York: Wiley, p. 292. Reprinted by permission.):

She misspells some words, for example, "sunfliwr" (*sunflower*), "bigr" (*bigger*), "seds" (*seeds*), and "prity" (*pretty*), and fails to use punctuation, but nonetheless she produces a script that is readable with some effort. Children learn to write as they learn to read. Children growing up in a society that uses an alphabetic script, such as English, know the difference between writing words, writing numbers, and drawing pictures, but it takes them a while to understand the connection between the letters that are written and the words they represent. As they become more familiar with what is involved in reading, they transfer that knowledge to writing, understanding, for example, the importance of grapheme-phoneme correspondence and punctuation.

But learning to write involves more than learning the letters of the alphabet, how to spell, and the rules of punctuation. Good writing involves having a goal for the written message, such as telling a good story, provoking thought, or motivating others. It requires that the writer be able to take the perspective of the reader, having an idea of the readers' backgrounds, what they are likely to know already, and what has to be explained to them. Good writing also requires that thoughts be organized in a coherent fashion and ideas conveyed clearly. Facial expressions and gestures can help a speaker get his or her message across when speaking, but these are not available to the writer. Perhaps not surprisingly, during the early elementary school years, children who are good spellers, good at telling oral stories, and good readers also tend to be good writers (Juel, 1994). Reading well, and reading more, seems to be an important predictor of children's quality of writing.

Learning Arithmetic

Three-year-old Paul was fascinated by the stairs in a neighbor's home, and, while climbing them and then scooting down them on his backside, he counted them, saying one number word for each step he traversed: "One, two, three, four, five, seven, nine, ten, elevinteen, twelveteen, fiveteen, seventeen, nineteen, *twenty*." He usually said the last number word with some authority, often stating, "There are 20 of them." Paul used some, but certainly not all, of the number words that adults in his culture use, but he obviously had some things to learn. He also likely did not understand numbers and counting the way he would in just a few years. But he was motivated to count, realizing, at some level, that this is an important thing to do.

Like reading, children's chief quantitative abilities are based on a set of biologically primary abilities, called *intuitive mathematics* (Geary, 1995), but, also like reading, they require substantial effort to master. Most children start counting using their fingers or other concrete objects but soon are able to count in their heads. This is consistent with Vygotsky's general genetic law of cultural development (see Chapter 2), which proposes that aspects of cognitive development appear first "outside" of the child (counting on one's fingers) before they appear "within" the child (counting in one's head). Sometime between 5 and 7 years of age, children acquire the ability to conserve number (see Chapter 6), realizing that the quantity of a set of items remains the same despite changes in their distribution (for example, the number of M&Ms in a row does not change when that row is stretched out). This would seem to be important for basic arithmetic. According to Piaget, without this understanding, children cannot have a true comprehension of addition, although they can be taught to memorize certain formulas (for example, $2 + 3 = 5$, but will they know what $3 + 2$ equals?).

In this section we first examine the development of early arithmetic skills, specifically addition, followed by discussions of cultural differences, disabilities, and sex differences in mathematics.

Learning to Add: The Development of Early Arithmetic Skills

Once children know how to count and have a basic idea of the conservation of number, how do they learn to add? Children's earliest attempts at addition involve counting (see Table 10.10). As we described earlier when discussing strategy development in Chapter 8, children initially use the **sum strategy**, counting all the numbers out loud (for example, for $3 + 2 = ?$, "1, 2, 3 . . . 4, **5**"). This is often followed by the **min strategy**, which involves starting with the larger addend and then counting up from there—that is, making the *minimum* number of counts. For example, given the problem $3 + 2 = ?$, a child would start with the cardinal value of the first number ("3") and continue counting from there ("4, 5").

It is easy to tell how young children are adding when they count out loud and use their fingers, but it gets more difficult when computations are done in their heads. How can you tell what strategies children are using then? One technique has been to use the amount of time it takes children to arrive at an answer and infer from the time what strategy they are using. For example, because it takes longer for children to count using the sum strategy ($3 + 2 = ?$ requires counting five items) than the min strategy ($3 + 2 = ?$ requires counting only two items), this should be reflected in children's latencies to arrive at an answer. Such *mental arithmetic* can become even faster as children progress from counting to memorizing addition facts and spitting out the answer quickly without the need for counting, a strategy called **fact retrieval**. Over the course of elementary school, children typically progress from counting out loud using the sum (and sometimes the min) strategy to mental arithmetic using laborious counting strategies to fact retrieval (see Ashcraft, 1990; Siegler, 2006). Children's math

---

sum strategy An addition strategy used by young children that involves counting together the two addends (that is, one after the other) of a problem.

min strategy An arithmetic strategy in which children faced with an addition problem start with the largest addend and count up from there.

fact retrieval The retrieval of a fact directly from long-term memory without using effortful procedures.

Young children use simple counting strategies to add, including counting on their fingers.

table 10.10 Some of the Addition Strategies Children Use for the Problem "How Much Is 3 Plus 2?"

Sum strategy: This is a counting strategy in which young children count, often on their fingers, each addend (for example, saying, "1, 2 . . . 1, 2, 3 . . .1, 2, 3, 4, **5**"; or a bit more efficiently, "1, 2, 3 . . . 4, **5**").

Min strategy: This is a more efficient counting strategy than the sum strategy, in which children count from the larger addend (in this case 3), thus making the minimum number of counts (for example, saying, "3 . . . 4, 5").

Fact retrieval: This is a noncounting strategy, in which children have memorized the answer to a problem (they just know that 2 plus 3 equals 5), and say the answer quickly without counting either out loud or covertly.

strategies become more complicated as they solve more difficult problems, increasingly including *decomposition* (Lemaire & Callies, 2009), which involves decomposing a complicated problem into a series of simpler ones. For instance, for the problem $35 + 29 = ?$, a student may decompose the problem to: $35 + 30 - 1 = 64$.

Although the reason for this change is largely a result of children being drilled to learn their addition facts (and later their multiplication tables), it is also associated with increases in cognitive efficiency. As noted in Chapter 8, children's working memory and speed of processing increase over the preschool and early school years, and these basic cognitive abilities are related to children's use of various addition strategies and to the speed and accuracy of their computation of addition problems (Berg, 2008; LeFevre et al., 2005). Children must be able to keep numerical facts in mind in order to arrive at a correct answer quickly. For example, if children are asked to add a series of numbers, such as $6 + 9 + 3 = ?$, they have to remember the sum of $6 + 9$ before adding 3. This is where working memory becomes important.

Consistent with Vygotsky's (1978) idea that cognition develops first in the social realm external to the child before becoming interiorized, recent research indicates that children's use of gestures as a strategy helps them solve math problems (Broaders et al., 2007; Goldin-Meadow, Cook, & Mitchell, 2009). In these studies, third- and fourth-grade children were given problems of the form: $3 + 5 + 7 = \underline{\quad} + 7$. To solve this, children must add together the first two numbers. For the present problem, the correct answer is 8. In one study, children who originally could not solve these problems were given instructions that included either correct gestures, partially correct gestures, or no gestures (see Figure 10.8). For correct gestures, children were taught to point with a V-hand (index and second finger) to the first two numbers in the problem ($3 + 5$ in this example), then to point with their index finger to the blank (see the top photos in Figure 10.8). For the partially correct gestures, children were taught to point with a V-hand to the second two numbers in the equation ($5 + 7$ in the example), and then to point with their index finger to the blank (see middle photos in Figure 10.8). In the no-gestures condition, children were given no instructions about gestures. All children were given a verbal lesson about how to solve these types of problems, and later given a posttest of six problems to solve.

Children who were taught to gesture correctly generally used the gestures when solving the problems and, importantly, solved significantly more problems correctly than children who were taught to use the partially correct gestures, who in turn solved more problems correctly than children who were not instructed to use gestures (see Figure 10.9). Why did the gestures help? Based on children's explanations for how they solved the problems, children who used gestures were more apt to discover the strategy of adding the first two numbers together (Goldin-Meadow et al., 2009).

Correct Gesture

Partially Correct Gesture

No Gesture

FIGURE 10.8 The three experimental conditions used in the study by Goldin-Meadow, Cook, and Mitchell (2009). Children in the Correct Gesture condition were taught to point to the first two numbers in the equation, and then point with their index finger to the blank. Children in the Partially Correct Gesture condition first pointed with a V-hand to the second two numbers in the equation, and then with their index finger to the blank. Children in the No Gesture condition received no instructions about pointing. SOURCE: From Goldin-Meadow, S., Cook, S. W., & Mitchell, Z. A. (2009). Gesturing gives children new ideas about math. *Psychological Science, 20,* 267–272.

Thus, as for strategy development in general, children's use of arithmetic strategies start simple but increase in complexity as their basic cognitive abilities improve (for example, working memory, speed of processing), and as they practice adding numbers, and perhaps learn to use their hands to help them discover new strategies. New, more efficient strategies increase in frequency but never fully replace older, simpler strategies that children will sometimes use when the newer strategies fail to produce an easy answer (Siegler, 2006).

Cultural Differences in Mathematics

As noted in Chapter 5, children have some intuitive notions of number and arithmetic, and these develop with experience. In schooled cultures, children receive formal instruction in mathematics and develop skills that are vital for life in a society with a cash economy (to say nothing of electronic bank transfers and ATM machines). But children and adults with little or no schooling also develop some basic mathematical, or quantitative, abilities,

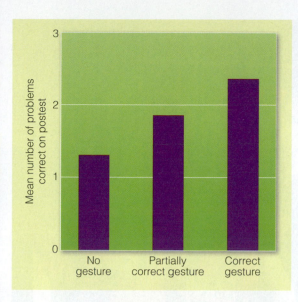

and children in different information-age cultures vary in the extent to which they master mathematics. In this section we take a brief look first at arithmetic in unschooled children and then at differences in mathematics performance between schooled children in different countries.

Arithmetic in unschooled children. Can children perform the basics of complex arithmetic without the benefit of formal schooling? This question was examined in a study that assessed arithmetic calculations by unschooled 9- and 15-year-old Brazilian street vendors (Carraher, Carraher, & Schliemann, 1985). These children, who made a living selling products on the streets, were given a series of arithmetic problems to solve. Sometimes the problems were presented the way they are in school (for example, "How much is 76 + 50?"). Children answered these school-type questions correctly only 37% of the time. Other times the problems were presented as a business transaction (for example, "If a large coconut costs 76 cruzeiros, and a small one costs 50, how much do the two cost together?"). In contrast to the school-type questions, children answered these questions correctly 98% of the time.

Why the difference? Recall our discussion of Vygotsky's sociocultural theory from Chapter 2. Cognition, Vygotsky proposed, develops in a social context to deal with the problems children face in everyday life. When children are confronted with a problem in a real-world context, where mistakes have real consequences, they learn how to solve them. The same problem, however, presented without a reason for solving it (that is, out of a real-world context), is more difficult for these unschooled children. Without the benefit of formal schooling, children and adults from a variety of professions, from street vendors and brick layers to lottery bookies, "develop at work not only fixed

FIGURE 10.9 Mean number of correct posttest problems (maximum = 6) for children in the No Gesture, Partially Correct Gesture, and Correct Gesture conditions. Children taught to use gestures correctly solved more problems than children taught to use the partially correct gestures, who in turn got more correct than children in the No Gesture condition. SOURCE: From Goldin-Meadow, S., Cook, S. W., & Mitchell, Z. A. (2009). Gesturing gives children new ideas about math. *Psychological Science, 20,* 267–272. Reprinted by Permission.

Unschooled children who sell things on the street for a living are able to make arithmetic computations better when the problem is presented as a business transaction than as a school-type problem.

procedures to solve specific problems but a conceptual and flexible understanding of the mathematical models applied to solve problems" (Schliemann, 1992, p. 2).

Academic performance by American and Asian schoolchildren. It is not a secret that children in many Japanese and Chinese schools perform better than children in most American schools at mathematics (Baker, 1992; Stevenson & Lee, 1990). In fact, American children typically fall in the middle of the pack in most international comparisons of mathematics performance, often scoring much below nations with considerably less wealth (OECD, 2004). Chinese children also tend to use a more sophisticated mix of arithmetic strategies than American children do beginning in the first grade (Geary et al., 1996; Geary, Fan, & Bow-Thomas, 1992) and even before the start of formal schooling (Geary et al., 1993).

Are Asian children just naturally smarter than American children when it comes to mathematics, or might there be some other explanations? As mentioned in Chapter 8, the names for the number words in Chinese are shorter and can be spoken more quickly than the corresponding number words in English, and this gives Chinese children longer digit spans, on average, and thus a slight advantage in processing numbers over English-speaking children (Geary et al., 1993). Recall also from Chapter 2 that the way the Chinese language uses the base-ten system to represent numbers in the teens (essentially, ten-one, ten-two, etc.) results in Chinese children being able to count to 20 before American children (Miller et al., 1995). These are examples of what Vygotsky called *tools of intellectual adaptation,* in these cases how characteristics of a culture's language can influence basic mathematical operations. The point here is that children's early arithmetic accomplishments set the stage for later achievements, and Chinese children's early advantage relative to American youngsters suggests that "Chinese children will have a consistent 3- to 4-year advantage over their American peers in the development of mathematical cognition" (Geary et al., 1992, p. 184).

Another important reason for the advantage that many Asian children have in mathematics is practice. It should not be surprising that children who practice retrieving math facts from long-term memory learn these facts more quickly and have more time to develop arithmetic strategies than do children who practice them less often (Geary et al., 1992). Research has confirmed that Chinese and Japanese schoolchildren do spend more time on mathematics, both in and out of the classroom, than American children, and that children who practice arithmetic more frequently (Chinese and Japanese children) perform better than children who practice it less often (American children) (Fuligni & Stevenson, 1995; Stevenson & Lee, 1990). This pattern of cultural difference begins in preschool (Siegler & Mu, 2008; Zhou et al., 2006). And why do Asian children spend more time practicing math than American children? The answer is not surprising—the attitudes of parents, particularly mothers. Japanese and Chinese mothers, for example, are more likely than American mothers to believe that their children's academic performance can be improved through hard work, are more involved in their children's school work, and emphasize their children's academic failures more than their successes (Ng, Pomerantz, & Lam, 2007).

Differences in math abilities between some Asian and American children have multiple causes. Some seem to be rooted in the tools of intellectual adaptation associated with how one's language represents (or even enunciates) numbers. Perhaps more importantly, differences in how much time Asian and American children spend practicing math, and how much encouragement they get for performing well in math, contributes to the cultural differences in math performance. These differences in practice and encouragement begin before children ever enter the schoolhouse door and are fostered, by and large, by the attitudes and actions of children's mothers.

© David R. Frazier Photolibrary, Inc./Alamy

Many Japanese and Chinese children perform better in math than American children, and this is related to how much time they spend on math and the efforts of their parents in fostering mathematical skills in their children.

Math Disabilities

Not all children show regular improvement in mathematical skills over the school years. As with reading, approximately 10% of school-age children display specific disabilities in mathematics (Hulme & Snowling, 2009; Mazzocco & Myers, 2003). Children with math disability tend to display two types of problems. First, beginning in kindergarten or the first grade, children with math disability tend to use less-sophisticated arithmetic strategies and show poorer knowledge of counting rules than typically developing children (Geary, 1993, Geary, Brown, & Samaranayake, 1991). Second, many children with math disability use fact retrieval less often when solving simple arithmetic problems, and when they do, they are often wrong. Also, simple practice at fact retrieval alone does not appreciably improve performance (see Geary, 1993). The source of these children's poor fact retrieval seems to be in their difficulty at keeping number names in their working memories. For instance, in one study, the digit spans for children with math disability (4.2 words) were about one word less than for nondisabled children (5.3 words) (Geary et al., 1991). Furthermore, because these children make computation errors, they arrive at many incorrect answers, and these answers can become part of their long-term memory representations of arithmetic facts. Unfortunately, they are wrong.

Sex Differences in Mathematics Ability

There has been much interest of late in sex differences in mathematical ability, in part because higher mathematics is the gateway to careers in science, a field where women are underrepresented. In this section, we examine some of the sex differences found in mathematical performance and look for the possible origins of those differences.

First, on average, girls get better school grades than boys in mathematics at all academic levels (Halpern et al., 2007). This is related in large part to girls performing better in all school subjects than boys. However, males score higher than females on standardized math tests (Halpern et al., 2007; Hedges & Nowell, 1995), although the absolute magnitude of the sex difference is small and varies in different countries (Else-Quest, Hyde, & Linn, 2010). As an example, Figure 10.10 presents the average SAT-Mathematics scores for males and females between 1967 and 2003 (from Halpern et al., 2007). As can be seen, the gap between males and females has been between 30 and 40 points for most years, with a decided male advantage. In general, females tend to perform better on familiar material, as reflected by assessments of school learning, whereas males tend to perform better applying mathematical knowledge to new contexts, as reflected by standardized tests.

However, a recent report analyzing results of standardized math tests from more than 7 million American children in grades 2 through 11 as part of No Child Left Behind assessments reported no sex differences in math scores at any grade (Hyde et al., 2008). Yet, males continued to score higher than females on the mathematics portion of the SAT by about 7%, suggesting that the small male advantage is still found, although its explanation may not be straightforward.

FIGURE 10.10 Average SAT-Mathematics scores for males and females from 1967 to 2003.

SOURCE: Halpern, D. F., Benbow, C. P., Geary, D. C., Gur, R. C., Hyde, J. S., & Gernsbacher, M. A. (2007). The science of sex differences in science and mathematics. *Psychological Science in the Public Interest, 8,* 1–51.

Although these results reflect average differences, the distribution of abilities for males and females differs greatly. Females tend to be more balanced than males, with males, as a group, showing greater variability in their mathematics performance. This means that males are more likely than females to be represented at the extremes of mathematical abilities—among the very best and the very worst performers.

What is the source of gender differences in mathematics ability? There is no simple answer to this question. As Diane Halpern and a distinguished group of scholars pointed out in an extensive look at this question, sex differences in mathematics performance are influenced by a host of interacting factors, including sociocultural forces, differences in brain structure and function, and interests and values (Halpern et al., 2007).

Children and adolescents' academic performance is influenced by the attitudes of their parents and peers. Although math is often viewed as a male subject, parents of mathematically gifted children do *not* emphasize achievement in mathematics differently for their sons and daughters (Raymond & Benbow, 1986). By adolescence, however, math and science are viewed as masculine disciplines, and girls may receive less support than boys from their peers for such activities (Stake & Nickens, 2005).

One interesting sex difference in mathematics performance concerns *stereotype threat,* in which females perform worse on a mathematics test after simply being reminded that math is typically a masculine activity (Spencer et al., 1999; see earlier discussion of stereotype threat with respect to minorities and IQ scores). This effect has been observed in children as young as 5 years old (Ambady et al., 2001) and for elementary and middle-school children (Muzzatti & Agnoli, 2007). These findings suggest that females from an early age may have the ability to perform as well as males on many mathematics tasks but are highly susceptible to the stereotype threat that identifies excellence in math as a male, and not a female, thing. One recent study suggests that first- and second-grade girls who have female teachers with high levels of math anxiety develop the stereotype that "boys are better at math than girls" and score lower on math achievement tests than boys or than girls who do not have teachers with math anxiety (Beilock et al., 2010).

Mathematically gifted adolescent males and females tend to choose different college majors and later different occupations, despite comparable mathematical ability (Benbow et al., 2000; Lubinski & Benbow, 1992). One reason for these differences may be related to values and interests. For example, when the values of mathematically gifted young adults were measured, males responded differently than females. The young men gave higher ratings than the young women to theoretical issues (for example, "knowledge for knowledge sake"), whereas the reverse was true for ratings of social issues (for example, "helping people") (Lubinski & Benbow, 1992). People with stronger theoretical values were more likely to seek training and occupations in the physical sciences, whereas people with an interest in social values were less likely to do so but pursued careers in biology, medicine, or the social sciences. This suggests that in addition to cognitive abilities, gender differences in other areas of life—possibly rooted in biology, possibly in socialization—contribute significantly to career choice. People choose a career not only because they think they will be good at it (that is, because they have the requisite intellectual abilities), but also because it fits their values and interests.

Sex differences in mathematical performance are apparently real, but they are not simple. Girls actually get better grades in math than boys at all levels, whereas boys consistently perform better than girls on standardized tests. Males are more likely to be both mathematically gifted and to be classified as math disabled than girls, a pattern of sex differences that is found in other realms as well. There seems to be no single reason for this pattern of differences. The gap between the sexes at the highest levels of achievement is declining, a result of increased academic opportunities for girls and young women. But differences in socialization practices and interests are also related to the sex differences we see in mathematics performance. And we also cannot ignore sex differences in brain development. As mentioned in our discussion of sex differences in reading ability, differences between the brains of males and females may, in part, be responsible for sex differences in some cognitive tasks. The male advantage in mathematics may be associated with their having more white matter than females (see Halpern et al., 2007, Chapter 4).

Intelligence is defined as the mental activities necessary for adaptation to, as well as shaping and selecting of, any environmental context. In the **psychometric approach,** intelligence is described in terms of **factors,** or sets of related mental abilities that underlie intelligence. The most general factor is called *g,* or **general intelligence,** which describes a domain-general mechanism that influences thinking on all tasks. The best evidence for *g* is that a person's performance on a variety of different cognitive tasks tends to be similar, termed the **positive manifold.** Others have divided intelligence into two general factors: **fluid abilities,** which are biologically determined and reflected by tests of memory span, speed of processing, and spatial thinking, and **crystallized abilities,** which are more highly dependent on experience and reflected in tests of verbal comprehension or social relations.

The **hierarchical model of cognitive abilities** proposes four related sets of cognitive skills (verbal, spatial thinking, speed of processing, and memory) that are all influenced by a general intellectual factor. The impact of the psychometric approach has been most strongly expressed in **IQ tests,** which assess intellectual abilities relative to a normative population. Frequently used IQ tests are the **Wechsler Scales** and the **Stanford-Binet,** both individually administered and highly standardized.

IQ scores predict academic performance and occupational status relatively well, although the relationship between IQ and school performance is bidirectional, with school experience affecting children's IQ level. The IQ test has been criticized for being inappropriate for minority children, who may misinterpret the testing situation and illustrate **stereotype threat,** in which minority members perform worse on IQ tests after being reminded of the negative stereotype concerning their group's performance on such tests. Teachers' expectations for their students' academic performance can also influence children's accomplishments and even their IQ scores. This is termed the **Pygmalion effect.**

IQ is highly stable over childhood and into young adulthood. Measures of preference for novelty and rate of habituation in infancy predict later IQ scores, suggesting that some basic-level cognitive abilities remain stable over infancy and into childhood and underlie general intelligence.

The **Flynn effect** refers to the systematic increase in IQ scores during the 20th century. Changes in nutrition, health, education, and a generally more complex visual environment have been hypothesized to account for this effect.

Sternberg's **triarchic theory of intelligence** consists of three subtheories, or types of intelligence: **componental (analytic), experiential (creative),** and **contextual (practical).** The componential subtheory is an information-processing account of intelligence. The experiential subtheory describes how people deal with novelty and the extent to which they can automatize cognitive functioning. The contextual subtheory states that intelligence must be evaluated in the environment in which the individual lives and includes three processes: **adaptation, selection,** and **shaping.**

Gardner's **theory of multiple intelligences** postulates eight distinct forms of intelligence: linguistic, logical-mathematical, musical, spatial, bodily-kinesthetic, interpersonal, intrapersonal, naturalistic, and a possible ninth, spiritual/existential. Gardner lists several criteria of an intelligence, including the existence of **savants** and **prodigies.**

Experience plays a role in the establishment, maintenance, and modification of intelligence. This is reflected in studies of institutionalized children, who experience deprived early environments and display intellectual impairments as a result. The longer children are institutionalized, the more difficult it is to reverse these negative effects. Both the structure (for example, white matter) and function (for example, glucose metabolism) of the brain are adversely affected by institutionalization. Children at medical risk are especially susceptible to environments in which they receive inadequate intellectual stimulation. The **cumulative deficit effect** refers to multiple risks persisting over many years, adding up and contributing to deficits in social, emotional, and cognitive functioning. Children at high risk for intellectual impairment and academic failure who receive cognitively enriched early experience through intensive **compensatory education programs** display immediate gains in IQ scores. However, once intellectual accomplishments are established, they frequently decline, although they can be maintained by subsequent booster programs.

Intellectual impairment refers to a lower-than-average level of intelligence as measured by IQ tests. When the cause of intellectual impairment is mainly based in biology (for example, anoxia at birth, genetic disorder) it is referred to as *organic,* and when there is no known biological cause for intellectual impairment, it is referred to as *cultural familial.* People who are intellectually disabled have poorer information-processing abilities than do nondisabled children. Gifted children have higher than average IQs and display enhanced information-processing abilities relative to their nongifted peers.

Reading is perhaps the most critical technological academic skill for people in schooled societies and is a good example of an ability that is primarily determined by culture (called **biologically second-ary abilities**). This is contrasted with **biologically primary abilities,** such as language, that have been selected for in evolution. **Emergent literacy** refers to the skills, knowledge, and attitudes that are presumed to be developmental precursors to conventional forms of reading and writing. The difference between good and poor readers tends to increase over time, termed the **Matthew effect,** as good readers read more often than poor readers. **Phonemic awareness** and **phonological recoding** are important skills for both beginning and later reading and the basis for the **phonics** method of reading instruction. Children with **dyslexia,** or reading disability, generally have delayed phonological processing skills and poor working memories. More boys than girls are classified as having reading disability, with females showing an overall advantage in verbal abilities relative to males.

Two broadly defined types of reading instruction have been used: phonics, which is a bottom-up system that emphasizes learning letter-sound correspondence, and the **whole-language approach,** which is a top-down system that emphasizes a reader's construction of meaning. Although reading surely involves both types of processes, research evidence makes it clear that any reading program should include some instruction in phonics.

Styles of writing vary with culture. Children in Western cultures know before starting school that writing corresponds to words and language concepts. Children's early attempts at writing ignore the *alphabetic principle*, that every letter represents or corresponds to a specific phoneme or sound. As children learn more about letter-sound correspondence, spelling, and rules of punctuation, their writing becomes more identifiable.

Early arithmetic is done out loud, often on fingers. Children's early strategies include the **sum strategy,** with children counting all numbers, and the **min strategy,** with children beginning with the larger addend and counting up from there. More sophisticated strategies include **fact retrieval,** with children retrieving addition and subtraction facts directly from long-term memory. Children actually use a variety of arithmetic strategies at any one time.

Patterns of mathematical abilities vary as a function of culture, with different values and educational practices affecting children's academic performance.

Children with math disability typically use less sophisticated strategies and show poorer knowledge of counting rules than typically developing children. They display problems with storing and retrieving math facts from long-term memory and have deficits in working memory.

Sex differences in mathematics favoring males on standardized tests have been diminishing over recent decades. Several factors have been hypothesized as responsible for sex differences, including *stereotype threat,* in which females perform worse on a mathematics test after simply being reminded that math is typically a masculine activity. The largest sex differences are found among the extremes, with proportionally more boys represented at both the top and bottom ability levels.

Key Terms and Concepts

intelligence (p. 388)

psychometric approach (p. 388)

factors (p. 388)

positive manifold (p. 389)

general intelligence (g) (p. 389)

fluid abilities (p. 389)

crystallized abilities (p. 389)

hierarchical model of
   cognitive abilities (p. 389)

IQ test (p. 389)

Wechsler scales (p. 390)

Stanford-Binet (p. 390)

stereotype threat (p. 393)

Pygmalion effect (p. 394)

Flynn effect (p. 397)

triarchic theory of intelligence (p. 398)

componential (analytic)
   subtheory/intelligence (p. 398)

experiential (creative)
   subtheory/intelligence (p. 399)

contextual (practical)
   subtheory/intelligence (p. 399)

adaptation (p. 400)

selection (p. 400)

shaping (p. 400)

theory of multiple intelligences (p. 400)

savants (savant syndrome) (p. 404)

prodigy (p. 405)

cumulative deficit effect (p. 410)

compensatory education programs (p. 410)

biologically primary abilities (p. 413)

biologically secondary abilities (p. 413)

Matthew effect (p. 415)

emergent literacy (p. 415)

phonemic awareness (p. 415)

phonics (p. 416)

phonological recoding (p. 416)

dyslexia (p. 417)

whole-language approach (p. 421)

sum strategy (p. 423)

min strategy (p. 423)

fact retrieval (p. 423)

Ask Yourself . . .

1. What is meant by the psychometric approach to intelligence? What are some of the more important theories proposed from this approach, and what do they suggest about the nature of intelligence?

2. How are IQ tests generally constructed, and how should an IQ score be interpeted? What are the more widely used IQ tests for children, and at what ages can they be used?

3. What are three outcomes that IQ tests typically predict relatively well, and what do you believe accounts for this level of predictability?

4. Why might IQ tests not be appropriate for children from minority groups, and what can be done to improve their validity in such cases?

5. What are the two important alternatives to the psychometric approach to intelligence nowadays? What shortcomings do these alternative theories see in IQ tests, and what do they propose instead?

6. What does research on institutionalized children, children at risk, and preschool compensatory programs tell us about the origins and stability of intelligence?

7. What are the cognitive features of children with intellectual impairment and children with gifted intelligence? How can the origins of these two forms of intelligence be explained?

8. How do "the three Rs" reflect David Geary's concept of *biologically secondary abilitites*? What does the sociocultural approach tell us about the relevance of these skills?

9. What are the more significant issues regarding the acquisition of reading and writing in childhood and their problems? What gender differences have often been found in reading and writing and how do you explain them?

10. What are the main findings on the acquisition of arithmetic skills, particularly addition, and how are they influenced by gender and culture?

Exercises: Going Further

1. Let's do a small field study. Interview three to five students on campus (out of psychology) on their ideas about intelligence. These can be some of the questions you ask (although you can add more and/or change some, if you want): (1) How do you define "intelligence"? (2) Why is having a high IQ considered important today, socially speaking? (3) What causes some people to be very intelligent and others not so? (4) Is intelligence stable over time? Can it be changed over time? (If the answer is "yes," ask when they think it is easier to change intelligence: during childhood or during adulthood, and why?). Then compare the results with other views of intelligence in this chapter and your own ideas about it and write your conclusions.

2. Based on evidence presented in this chapter, write a short essay titled "Intelligence at risk: On the conditions that put the development of intelligence at risk and what can be done to prevent it."

3. Design a short test to assess basic skills in reading, writing, and arithmetic in school-age children. It should not be longer than 10 to 15 items, and they should not be taken from any other existing tests on these topics. If you have a chance, give the test to some children and see what happens. Explain why you selected the final items instead of other possible ones.

Suggested Readings

Classic Works

Gould, S. J. (1981). *The mismeasure of man.* New York: Norton. This very readable book provides a history of the research, theory, and politics of intelligence assessment. In addition to pointing out skeletons in the closet associated with IQ testing, Gould provides a good critique of the history and methods of the psychometric approach. Gould doesn't shy away from controversy and shows how science and politics can never be fully separated.

Sternberg, R. J. (1985). *Beyond IQ: A triarchic theory of human intelligence.* Cambridge: Cambridge University Press. This is the long version of Sternberg's triarchic theory. It covers all the bases, beginning with an introductory chapter that provides a critique of the standard psychometric approach and why a new theory of intelligence is needed in the first place.

Gardner, H. (1983). *Frames of mind: The theory of multiple intelligences.* New York: Basic. This book laid the framework for Gardner's theory of multiple intelligences, and although Gardner and others have expanded on the theory in the nearly three decades since its publication, the basic premises have not changed.

Scholarly Works

Nelson, C. A. III, Zeanah, C. H., Fox, N. A., Marshall, P. J., Smuke, A. T., & Guthrie, D. (2007). Cognitive recovery in socially deprived young children: The Bucharest Early Intervention Program. *Science, 318* (21 December), 1937–1940. This study examines the effect of social deprivation and its reversal on IQ in a group of abandoned children who were randomly assigned to either a foster care family or to an institution. Not only are the findings of great interest, but the study raises and addresses ethical issues of doing this type of research.

Hyde, J. S., Lindberg, S. M., Linn, M. C., Ellis, A. B., & Williams, C. C. (2008). Gender similarities characterize math performance. *Science, 321,* (25 July), 494–495. This article reports the results of mathematics tests given as part of the No Child Left Behind Act, and finds that the mathematics gap between males and females has almost disappeared, at least for these tests.

Readings for Personal Interest

Wolf, M. (2007). *Proust and the squid: The story and science of the reading brain.* New York: Harper. Maryann Wolf provides a fascinating account of how our ancestors taught their brains how to read only a few thousand years ago, and in the process changed the intellectual evolution of our species.

Nelson, C. A., Furtado, E. A., Fox, N. A., & Zeanah, Jr., C. H. (2009). The deprived human brain. *American Scientist, 97* (May–June), 222–229. In this article, Charles Nelson and his colleagues describe the many effects of institutionalization, as well as children's ability to recover from such effects, as illustrated in the Bucharest Early Intervention Project.

Nisbett, R. E. (2009). *Intelligence and how to get it: Why schools and cultures count.* New York: Norton. In this highly readable book, social psychologist Richard Nisbett explores the roles of genes, family, schools, and culture on the development of intelligence. He explores many of the issues we examined in this chapter, including the effects of schooling on intelligence, why children from different cultures often seem smarter than children from other cultures, and the Flynn effect, among others.

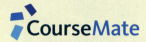

Cengage Learning's **Psychology CourseMate** for this text brings course concepts to life with interactive learning, study, and exam preparation tools, including quizzes and flashcards for this chapter's Key Terms and Concepts (see the summary list on page 431). The site also provides an **eBook** version of the text with highlighting and note taking capabilities, as well as an extensive library of observational videos that span early childhood through adolescence. Many videos are accompanied by questions that will help you think critically about and deepen your understanding of the chapter topics addressed, especially as they pertain to core concepts. Log on and learn more at **www.cengagebrain.com**.

Humans are social animals, and one can only understand human behavior and development within the social contexts in which we live. From this perspective, a significant part of becoming fully human has to do with becoming a social being. Perhaps not surprisingly the old Latin expression for "being alive" (*inter hominem esse*) means literally "being among humans," and the Latin expression for death (*inter hominem esse desinere*) means literally "stopping from being among humans." Relatedly, Vygotsky's sociocultural theory, discussed in Chapter 2, emphasizes that the origin of the most basic human behavioral systems originate and are fine-tuned in the contexts of social settings (as a consequence of a bidirectional relation between genetic and environmental factors).

In Part 3 we explore important aspects of social development. We start with emotion, temperament, and personality development. Sociality as we know it is only possible because of our ability to empathize with one another. Emotions are also a means of social communication. We not only *feel* emotions, but also *show* them, and other people pick up upon these cues and respond accordingly. Relatedly, temperament and personality reflect relatively stable aspects of how we respond to the world, most notably our social world.

Closely related to emotions is infant-parent attachment, sometime referred to as "emotional attachment," which represents a child's first important social relationship and, as research shows, underlies much of a person's psychological adjustment throughout life. Also in this chapter we look at childcare through an evolutionary lens, examining how natural selection may have prepared men and women with various relationships to children (for example, parents, grandparents, stepparents, adoptive parents) for the task of child rearing.

This is followed in Chapter 13 by an examination of the role of the family, particularly parents, in child development. Families, more than any other "institution," are responsible for socializing children. In examining the role of family in child development, we look at parenting goals, beliefs, and styles; life with siblings; and how children deal with family transitions, specifically divorce and remarriage. We also examine two other important socializing agents in children's lives: school and the media, including television, computer games, and the Internet.

Perhaps equally important as families to children are peers. Children in our culture interact with peers both in and out of school, form social hierarchies, and display both prosocial (for example, sharing, comforting) and antisocial (for example, aggression) behaviors toward their peers on a regular basis. We also examine moral development in this chapter, given that moral behavior reflects "good" and "bad" decisions as they relate to other people, and most of those other people are peers.

The final chapter in this section is devoted to the development of sexuality, gender differences, and gender identity. Attracting a mate, producing offspring, and rearing children are the *sine qua non* of evolution, making the development of sexuality and intimate relationships of central importance to child development. We examine the development of sexual behavior in childhood and adolescence, including "falling in love," and the development of sexual orientation. Although gender differences are explored throughout the book, we discuss how such differences can be understood, and conclude by looking at the development of gender identity.

Kris S. Chae/Getty Images

In this chapter we examine the development of emotions, temperament, and personality. We first look at the development of emotional expression, emotional recognition, emotional understanding, and emotional regulation, followed by a look at emotional development in adolescence and some emotional problems in childhood. We next examine the development of temperament, personality, and risk-taking. We then investigate the degree to which temperament and personality are heritable (biologically based), emerge early in development, and are stable over time.

E veryone said that Jeremy was an easy baby. He was always easy to soothe, loved to be cuddled, and slept on a regular schedule. As he grew into toddlerhood, he kept many of his traits from infancy. Jeremy was also very vigilant of his parents, cried easily if his mother or father scolded him, and was cautious in trying new things. This included new food, a topic of repeated contention between Jeremy and his parents. Mark, the family's second child, was different from his brother almost from birth. Mark experienced more extreme emotions. When he was unhappy, such as when strapped into his car seat on long trips, nothing could soothe him. His laughter was contagious and his smile could melt the coldest of hearts, but he would also laugh and smile ("smirk," his parents said) as he ran away from his parents or as he was being reprimanded for some misdeed. He seemed to know no fear, was on a first-name basis with personnel at the emergency room by the time he was 4, and, unlike his brother, he did not seem to care when his parents were upset with him and was much more likely to break the rules.

These brief descriptions of two normal brothers reflect what psychologists refer to as *personality* or, in infancy, *temperament*—relatively stable individual differences in mood and behavior. Note how our ideas of personality are tightly connected to emotions.

Personality, in many ways, reflects different ways in which people express and regulate their emotions, and our emotions are every bit as important as our intelligence in defining who we are as individuals and as a species.

We devote most of this chapter to the development of emotion in infancy, childhood, and adolescence. We follow this with a look at the closely related topics of temperament and personality and their development, as well as a topic related to personality, risk-taking.

Emotional Development

We often regard symbolic thought and language as defining features of humankind—characteristics that separate us from the rest of the animal kingdom. This may be true, but our advanced cognition would not do us much good if it were not for emotions. As evolutionary primatologist Sarah Hrdy (1999, p. 392) wrote: "What makes us humans rather than just apes is the capacity to combine intelligence with articulate empathy." Without "articulate empathy"— a sort of human glue that babies develop over time— sociability as we know it would not be possible, and we would be a very different species from the one we are today (if we existed at all). Emotions cause us to use our intelligence for some adaptive purpose; they cause us to act—to make decisions one way or another, to care about the outcomes of our behavior, and to care about other people.

You can think of emotions as being like directions on a compass, indicating a primary (but not always definitive) course of action (see Figure 11.1). For instance, the emotion of fear prepares us to flee and anger to fight; sadness and shame may cause us to withdraw or stop what we are doing. Emotions are critical for getting the things we want (food, love, safety) and avoiding the things we do not want (danger, distress, loneliness). Emotions regulate our behavior and help us communicate with others. Emotional responses often send messages to others about how we feel that we have difficulty conveying through language; this is especially important for infants and young children, who lack the linguistic competence to convey their feelings. But we cannot let emotions run our lives. Given humans' complicated social lives and the conflict that is inevitable when living in close quarters with other people, children must learn to control their emotions, and this takes time. Whereas children seem to feel and express a wide range of adult-like emotions very early in life, it takes them considerably more time to understand the significance of emotions and to control their expression.

emotion The subjective reaction that we experience in response to some environmental stimulus.

FIGURE 11.1 You can think of emotions as being like a behavioral compass, with the emotion we feel moving us in the direction of certain behaviors.

What Are Emotions? Some Important Distinctions

Most of us feel the same way about *emotion* as the ancient philosopher Agustín de Hipona felt about *time*: "I know what it is until someone asks me specifically about it." (Or the way many of us feel about art or pornography: "I may not be able to define it, but I know what it is when I see it!") Generally speaking, **emotion** is the name we give to the subjective reaction that we experience in response to some environmental stimulus, such as the happiness a child feels when he receives a gift, or the feeling of anger an adolescent experiences when she sees her boyfriend talking with another girl. It is the rapid appraisal of the personal significance of a situation that prepares a person for action (Saarni, Mumme, & Campos, 1998). The term *affect* is often used synonymously with emotion and refers to the outward expression of an emotion.

Emotions have several components. First, emotion is more than a behavioral expression. An emotional response, such as a smile, does not always mean that the person is happy; just look at the smiling faces of actors whose names are *not* called for the Oscar. Children may feel one emotion (disappointment about receiving a toy they already have as a gift) but display another (joy, to the person who gave them the toy). This reflects an ability to *regulate emotions*, something that develops over childhood. The accompanying photographs provide some examples of facial expressions of children displaying different emotions. Can you identify the emotion that goes with each face?

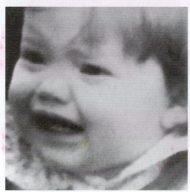
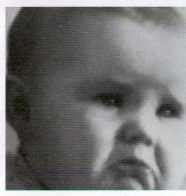

Infants and children display a wide range of facial expressions associated with specific emotions. Can you identify each emotion the children in the photographs are expressing? SOURCE: Izard, C. E., Fantauzzo, C. A., Castle, J. M., Hayness, O. M., Rayias, M. F., & Putnam, P. H. (1995). The ontogeny and significance of infant's facial expressions in the first 9 months of life: *Developmental Psychology, 31,* 997-1013.

Second, although facial expressions are perhaps the best way to read people's emotions, they are not the only way. We can recognize other people's emotions by their voice or their body language. We even do this with our pets, inferring that our dog's rapidly wagging tail when given a treat is a sign of happiness (who's to say it's not?). Third, emotions are not independent of cognitions. In fact, the same physiological arousal may represent different emotions depending on how we interpret the situation. For example, a child's increasing heart rate may reflect joy when she receives a jack-in-the-box for a gift; this same increase in heart rate may reflect fear, however, when the clown jumps out of the box and frightens her. As the American primatologist Robert Sapolsky nicely commented, "based on heart rate measures one never can know for sure if it is a murder or an orgasm that has actually taken place" (quoted in Punset, 2005).

It is also important to keep in mind that each emotion is in fact a palette of emotions. As William James pointed out more than a century ago, the number of emotions we can experience is really unlimited (Kagan, 1984; Tooby & Cosmides, 2005). We use expressions such as happy, sad, angry, and afraid to reflect subjective feelings that belong to a wide spectrum of emotions. For example, a child may feel afraid because her father had an accident; because she is facing a fierce dog; because that dog ate her homework; or because she is watching a horror movie. We would probably all agree that the kind and intensity of the fear this child would experience differs in each situation. "Fear" in this case describes not a single emotion but a family of emotions. Also, emotions are not always expressed one after another in a discrete manner but are sometimes mixed. For example, infants can express anger and fear simultaneously, and older children can experience mixed emotions such as joy and fear when, for example, they are given a beautiful bicycle that they do not yet know how to ride (Pons & Harris, 2000).

The Scientific Study of Emotions: The Functionalist Approach

The first theory and scientific study of emotions came from Charles Darwin, who in 1872 published his book *The Expression of the Emotions in Man and Animals.* In this book, Darwin focused on emotions as expressed through changes in facial muscles. He proposed that the facial expressions and emotions seen in both humans and animals were based on a common physiological system and thus reflected a *continuity of function.* In other words, the emotions of humans were based on the same underlying biological mechanisms as those of nonhuman mammals, with humans' emotions evolving from those expressed in ancestral species. According to Darwin, emotions are universal and have species-specific adaptive functions.

So, for example, "fear" would be reflected by the facial expression typically associated with the

Infants can express anger and fear simultaneously.

described six basic emotions as identified by facial expressions (surprise, anger, sadness, disgust, fear, and happiness) and insisted that each conferred some adaptive benefit to the individual person or animal expressing them (see Conrad, 2004, Fox & Stifter, 2005, and Lewis, 2004 for a more detailed discussion).

Consistent with Darwin's ideas, many researchers have argued that basic emotions, such as joy, disgust, fear, anger, and sadness, are universal and not the result of learning. We may have to learn what to fear, for example, but basic emotions are part of our human biological inheritance (see Ekman, 1995; Saarni, Campos, & Camras, 2006). This is referred to as **discrete emotion theory**, the belief that basic emotions are innate and associated with distinctive bodily and facial reactions (Izard, 1991; Tomkins, 1962). The current interest in emotion and its development extends Darwin's ideas, viewing emotions as playing an adaptive role, helping individuals to achieve specific goals related to survival. This is referred to as the **functionalist perspective**. Remember our analogy of emotions with the directions of a compass, moving our behavior in a, hopefully, adaptive direction (see Table 11.1). For example, joy helps establish and maintain social relationships; disgust helps avoid illness or contamination; fear helps avoid danger; anger tells us we are threatened and generates surplus energy to achieve a certain goal; sadness leads us to abandon an unattainable goal; and shame and guilt preserve self-esteem and/or social organization (Saarni et al., 2006). It is also worth noting that a child's emotional expressions can influence

physiological reactions experienced by animals when they felt in danger because of the recognition of a predator (widening of the eyes in anticipation of what will happen next, eyebrows drawn together, rise of the upper lip), and "surprise" would be the facial expression associated when an animal experiences something new (widening of the eyes to better see unfamiliar targets, raised eyebrows, a dropped jaw so that the lips and teeth are parted, with no tension around the mouth). Darwin

table 11.1 Possible Adaptive Goals and Action Tendencies Associated with Some Emotions

Emotion Type	Adaptive Goals/Functions	Action Tendency
Disgust	Avoiding contamination or illness	Active rejection
Joy	Establish and maintain social relationship	Active approach
Anger	Attain difficult goals; learn to overcome obstacles; communicate power/dominance	Active forward movement, especially to eliminate obstacles
Sadness	Conserve energy; learn which goals are realizable; encourage nurturance by others	Disengagement; passive withdrawal
Fear	Avoid danger; learn about events/attributes that are dangerous; maintain integrity of the self (physical and psychological integrity)	Flight; active withdrawal
Shame	Behave appropriately; learn/maintain social standards; maintain others' respect and affection; preserve self-esteem	Active or passive withdrawal; avoiding others, hiding of self
Guilt	Behave prosocially; learn/maintain social standards; communicate submission to others	Outward movement: inclination to make reparation, to inform others, and to punish oneself

Evolutionary approaches

SOURCE: Adapted from Saarni, C., Campos, J. J., Camras, L. A., & Witherington, D. (2006). Emotional development: Action, communication, and understanding. In W. Damon & R. M. Lerner (Gen. Eds.), *Handbook of Child Psychology* (6th ed.), N. Eisenberg (Vol. Ed.), Vol. 3, *Social, emotional, and personality development* (pp. 226–299). New York: Wiley, p. 229.

	Description	Development
Emotional expression	The ability to express clearly different emotions	Primary emotions, such as distress, disgust, interest, surprise, contentment, joy, anger, sadness, and fear are expressed early in the first year of life; secondary emotions, such as shame, embarrassment, coyness, shyness, empathy, guilt, jealousy, envy, pride, contempt, and gratitude, emerge in the second and third years of life.
Emotional recognition	The ability to recognize or become aware of emotions	Infants can recognize most emotional expressions of others in terms of people's faces or voices by 6 months; social referencing is seen about 12 months of age.
Emotional understanding	The ability to verbally label and comprehend the use of emotions in themselves and others	Most aspects of emotional understanding develop later than competencies in emotional expression and recognition, beginning in the preschool years and continuing into adolescence.
Emotional self-regulation	The ability to control one's emotional expression	Rudiments of emotional self-regulation are seen in shared attention and social referencing late in the first year of life, although self-regulation continues to develop throughout childhood.

the emotions and actions of others, which, in turn, will impact the child. In the following sections in this and other chapters, we will see how emotional exchanges between children and their family members, peers, and intimate partners affect social functioning and development.

The study of emotions is one of the hottest topics in psychology, including developmental psychology. Although the functionalist perspective is not the only approach of contemporary researchers who are interested in emotional development (see important work and theory by Lewis [1993], Sroufe [1996], and Trevarthen [1993]), it has revitalized research in emotional development and placed the study of emotions in an evolutionary context, as originally proposed by Darwin more than 130 years ago. Box 11.1 provides a couple of evolutionary approaches to emotions and emotional development.

The Development of Emotional Expression, Emotional Recognition, and Emotional Understanding

The following four questions are important to answer about emotional development. When and why are children able to

1. Express clearly different emotions (**emotional expression**)?
2. Recognize or become aware of emotions (**emotional recognition**)?

3. Verbally label and comprehend the use of emotions in themselves and others (**emotional understanding**)?
4. Control their emotional expression (**emotional self-regulation**)?

In this section, we look at the development of emotional expression, emotional recognition, and emotional understanding, focusing on development from infancy through childhood. We then examine the development of emotional regulation, followed by a brief discussion of emotional development in adolescence and emotional problems in children and adolescents, including dealing with stress (see Concept Review 11.1).

The Emergence of Emotional Expressions

Not all emotions are created equal. A first group of emotions, termed basic, or **primary emotions**,

discrete emotion theory The theory that basic emotions are innate and associated with distinctive bodily and facial reactions.

functionalist perspective Regarding emotional development, a theoretical perspective that views emotions as playing an adaptive role, helping individuals to achieve specific goals related to survival.

emotional expression The individual's ability to exhibit a range of emotions.

emotional recognition The ability to recognize or become aware of emotions in others.

emotional understanding The ability to verbally label and comprehend the use of emotions in oneself and others.

emotional self-regulation The ability to control one's own emotional expressions.

primary emotions Emotions that emerge during the first year of life, including distress, disgust, interest, surprise, contentment, joy, anger, sadness, and fear.

BOX 11.1 **evolution in action**

An Evolutionary Approach to Emotions and Emotional Development

Although the functional perspective takes an explicitly evolutionary approach to emotions, there is as yet no single theory about the evolutionary origins of emotions and their development (in the same way there is no single *proximal* theory of emotional development). However, there are some tenable hypotheses about the possible evolutionary origins of emotions. For example, ethologists have generally subscribed to the view that emotions evolved as "movements of expression," meaning that they mainly serve as a means of communication to other members of the species. From this perspective, emotional expressions would be part of a continuum of means of communication, the top level being human language. Consistent with this argument, there is evidence that social animals that have great need for communicating among group members, such as wolves, have a richer range of emotional expression than do nonsocial animals, such as foxes (Tembrock, 1954).

In a slow-developing species like ours, it is easy to understand how some emotional reactions, such as smiling or crying, can serve useful communicative purposes. Infants' survival depends on their caregivers' attention, and it is many months before infants have the language skills to effectively communicate their wants and needs. According to attachment theorist John Bowlby (1969), smiling plays a role in the development of infant-mother attachment (see Chapter 12). It is not by chance that adults find babies' smiles attractive. This relationship between smiles and caregiving has been honed by natural selection to increase the likelihood that mothers and infants will become attached, promoting infant survival.

With respect to crying, we saw in Chapter 3 that there are different types of cries and

The evolutionary origins of disgust are likely associated with the rejection of bad-tasting (and likely illness-inducing) foods.

© Corbis Super RF/Alamy

that caregivers can differentiate each cry's meaning within the first 3 months of life. Other research has demonstrated that mothers use the pitch and frequency of infants' cries as an indicator of infant health (Furlow, 1996; Mann, 1992). In some contexts, the vigor of an infant's cry may signal the baby's fitness and influence maternal attention. For example, Marten DeVries (1984), studying Masai mothers and infants in a pastoralist culture in Kenya, noted that only 6 of 13 babies born during a time of famine survived. Five of the six surviving infants were classified as "fussy" and cried a lot. Of the seven infants who died, six were described as "easy" babies who cried little. DeVries suggested that infants with easy temperaments were easier to ignore and thus perished in

the famine. Infants who complained through fussing and crying were more apt to be soothed and fed by their mothers.

Darwin's (1872) original hypothesis was not that emotions serve as a means of communication but that they afforded some immediate survival benefit. This is echoed by contemporary evolutionary psychologists John Tooby and Leda Cosmides (1992, 2005). Tooby and Cosmides (1992) proposed that emotions serve as a mechanism whose function is to regulate behavior depending on ecological conditions: Namely, emotions solve the problem of how to coordinate evolved cognitive mechanisms, activating some and deactivating others, depending on the environmental context. In other words, if humans evolved sets of cognitive operations for survival and reproduction (see Chapter 2), emotions would be the motivating mechanisms that decide which operations to apply depending on the situation. Adaptive cognitive mechanisms do not operate in a vacuum but are closely associated with emotional arousal.

For example, although the function of smiling and crying seems to be primarily communicative, other emotions, such as disgust or fear, provide immediate survival benefits, such as avoiding contaminated food or preventing a fall off a cliff or down a staircase. For instance, both children and adults detect threat-relevant faces—those that are angry or frightened—more readily than happy or sad faces, suggesting the existence of an evolved attention bias for threatening stimuli (LoBue, 2009). With respect to disgust, Darwin (1872, p. 253) related it to "something revolting, primarily in relation to the sense of taste, as actually perceived or vividly imagined; and secondarily to anything which causes a similar feeling, through the sense of smell, touch and even of eyesight." The evolutionary origins of disgust are likely

emerges during the first year of life, whereas a second group of emotions, termed **secondary**, or **self-conscious**, **emotions**, emerges during the second year of life or later. Primary emotions include distress, disgust, interest, surprise, contentment, joy, anger, sadness, and fear. Self-conscious emotions include shame, embarrassment, coyness, shyness, empathy, guilt, jealousy, envy, pride, contempt, gratitude, and others (Draghi-Lorenz, Reddy, & Costall, 2001; Lewis, 1993, 2000).

As mentioned earlier, according to some psychologists, primary emotions are part of humans' biological heritage and should be found universally and develop at about the same time for children in

secondary (self-conscious) emotions Emotions that emerge during the second year of life or later, including shame, embarrassment, coyness, shyness, empathy, guilt, jealousy, envy, pride, and contempt.

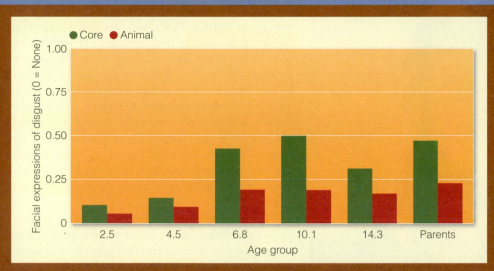

Average number of facial disgust responses for the core and animal items, by child age group. A score of 0 indicates no facial disgust response, and 1 indicates facial disgust responses to all items. As you can see, children develop disgust responses to core items first before animal items, consistent with the theory of Rozin and his colleagues (2000). SOURCE: From Stevenson, R. J., Oaten, M. J., Case, T. I., Repacholi, B. M., & Wagland, P. (2010). Children's response to adult disgust elicitors: Development and acquisition. *Developmental Psychology, 47*, 165–177. Reprinted by permission.
....

associated with the rejection of bad-tasting (and probably illness-inducing) food (Rozin & Fallon, 1980). In fact, the facial expressions accompanying disgust mimics the "propelling" of food/liquid from the mouth. The expression of these emotions in infancy likely alerts adults to a potential danger an infant might be facing (for instance, they are being fed the wrong food).

Other than nasty-tasting things, children learn what is disgusting and what is not over time, although it seems that children find it easier to acquire "disgusting" reactions to some things more than others. Paul Rozin and his colleagues (Rozin, Haidt, & McCauley, 2000) proposed that what children find disgusting should follow a developmental sequence. First to appear early in infancy should be disgusting reactions to bitter tastes (Steiner, 1979). Later in childhood, children should develop *core disgust*, negative reactions to things that could be ingested, such as some foods (for example, rotting meat) and bodily products (for example, feces and urine). This should be followed by the *animal-reminder category*, which reminds people of their animal origins and mortality. This category includes, for instance, touching a dead cat, seeing a cockroach running across the floor, seeing maggots in a garbage can, gaping wounds, and two dogs mating vigorously. Finally, children should develop disgust for *social-moral* infractions, such as stealing a bag from a disabled person, littering, or seeing a politician lying on television.

Recent research has confirmed this developmental sequence, both from parents' reports of what their children find disgusting and reactions of children to various disgusting stimuli (Stevenson et al., 2010. For example, children's reactions to several potentially disgust-inducing stimuli were evaluated, including sniffing organic fertilizer that smelled like feces; viewing a jar of maggots [actually meal worms]; and placing a favorite candy on the bottom of a new, never used, child's potty, among others. The accompanying figure shows the average number of children's facial disgust responses for the core (for example, smelling feces) and animal (for example, reactions to maggots) categories, by age. As you can see, reactions were strongest at each age for the core category, and increased with age until age 10.

An evolutionary approach to emotional development must be integrated with other contemporary approaches to the study of emotion, including neuroscience research (termed "affective neuroscience," a discipline that focuses on the study of the neural correlates of affective experience, see Fox & Stifter, 2005) and dynamic systems theory (Hoeksma, Oosterlaan, & Schipper, 2004). Dynamic systems theory views emotional systems as interconnected neurological structures that influence and are influenced by biochemicals (hormones and neurotransmitters), which themselves are bidirectionally related to events in the external environment. Such an approach, which has been adopted explicitly or implicitly by modern developmental scientists studying emotion, emphasizes the dialectical (bidirectional) interactions between biology and environment and will help improve our understanding about the evolution and development of emotions (see Camras & Witherington, 2005; Lewis, 2005).

all cultures (discrete emotion theory, see Saarni et al., 2006). In contrast, specific secondary emotions may be more subject to cultural variation (Lewis, 2000). Rather than being an integral part of humans' "animal nature," they are based in the emergence of mental representation and the development of a sense of self and others (Lewis, 1993, 2000; see Chapter 7). For example, before Josh can feel embarrassed that he failed his spelling test or guilty that he cheated on it, he must have some idea that he did something that others would disapprove of. Similarly, before Andrea can feel pride in earning her orange belt in Tae Kwon Do, she must be aware that she accomplished something difficult and that others would appreciate the effort or skill needed to perform the task. In this section we examine the development of emotional expression first for the primary emotions and then for the secondary, or self-conscious, emotions.

Infants' cries are signs of distress. By 3 months of age, babies' cries become sufficiently differentiated that a familiar adult can know if the crier is hungry, in pain, or experiencing some other form of distress.

Primary emotions. The first signal of a healthy newborn is crying. Psychoanalysts viewed neonatal crying as a symbolic indicator that the baby was "losing paradise," specifically the womb, where it had spent nine cozy months. The psychoanalysts were right about cries reflecting *distress* (although the "loss of paradise" explanation is no longer in vogue), and by 3 months of age, babies' cries become sufficiently differentiated that a familiar adult can know if the crier is hungry, in pain, or experiencing some other form of distress (Wolff, 1969).

Two other early emotional expressions that can be identified in newborns are *disgust* and *interest*. Infants make facial responses to potent-tasting liquids, such as citric acid and quinine, that have been interpreted as reflecting disgust, versus when they taste a solution of sugar water (Steiner, 1979). Young infants' facial responses to pleasant- versus unpleasant-tasting liquids are also associated with different EEG patterns (Fox & Stifter, 2005). With respect to interest, newborns and young infants visually fixate on objects or orient in the direction of someone speaking and become (seemingly) surprised when they see objects and events they had not expected (see Chapter 5 for a discussion of infant attention and cognition).

Babies also smile shortly after birth. Might these smiles be an indication of happiness or joy? Alan Sroufe (1996) seems to think so. He proposed

that **endogenous smiles**—smiles that are elicited by internal states, as opposed to something in the external environment—might be precursors of the emotion *joy*. Such smiles, however, which also occur during REM sleep, are not a reflection of "social happiness" but are signs of some positive, bodily state, such as being fed or being gently touched. In other words, smiling in newborns is best thought of as a type of reflex rather than a legitimate social response to human interactions. **Social smiling** is not seen until about 4 to 6 weeks old, and it is not frequently and unambiguously seen until about 3 months (Reilly et al., 1995). This is about the same time that *laughing* is first seen, which is interpreted universally by adults as a sign of joy.

But anyone who has dealt with young infants knows that babies also express some negative emotions. Two that become increasingly obvious when babies are about 4 to 6 months old are *anger* and *sadness*, although both have been reported in babies as young as 2 months old (see Camras, 1992), with anger being more frequent than sadness. Discrete facial expressions of anger are neatly elicited in a series of situations that produce frustration in infants, as when an interesting object or piece of food is systematically given and taken away from a baby, or when an infant's arms are restrained. In the case of sadness, a full facial configuration of this emotion seems to show up clearly only in the second half of the first year of life, mainly as a reaction to separation from a close caregiver. In fact, extreme sadness has been reported for infants separated from their mothers for extended periods (Spitz, 1945, 1965; see further discussion of this work in Chapter 12). Yet, partial facial configurations of sadness, like the "horseshoe pout" (turning down the corners of the mouth), are observed by 2 months as a reaction, for example, to a painful stimulus or the removal of an object. Nathan Fox and Cynthia Stifter (2005) pointed out how similar modern views of the function of these two emotions are to the original interpretations by Darwin (1872), who saw anger expressions basically as a result of being blocked from getting a desired goal and sadness expressions as resulting from the loss of important people.

The last important basic emotion to emerge in infancy is *fear*. As far as we know, infants are not born with any specific fears but develop them over the first year of life (Saarni et al., 2006). Fear is a response to perceived danger, and even newborns display fear in response to loss of support. When a newborn hears a loud, unexpected noise, the baby will cry and look frightened.

People seem prepared to acquire fears to particular objects and situations that would have represented danger to our ancestors. In fact, we

endogenous smile Smiles that are elicited by an infant's internal states, as opposed to something in the external environment.

social smiling Smiling in response to social events.

acquire fears to such things as spiders, snakes, and heights much more easily than we do to things that are more dangerous to modern people, such as guns, knives, and automobiles (Öhman & Mineka, 2003; Seligman, 1971). The claim is not that these fears are innate, but that we more easily learn to fear biologically relevant stimuli than biologically irrelevant ones.

Take snakes, for example. People are not the only animals afraid of snakes. Monkeys display a similar fear. Monkeys, however, require some experience with snakes before they show any fear. For instance, monkeys born in the wild react fearfully when they see a snake (even if it has been more than 20 years since seeing one), but monkeys born in the laboratory, which have never seen a snake before, do not show fear. Yet these naïve monkeys can easily develop a fear of snakes by watching videos of other monkeys reacting fearfully to the slithering serpents. These same animals, however, do not learn to act fearfully when they watch videos of other monkeys reacting fearfully to flowers or rabbits. These findings are consistent with the idea of **prepared learning**, such that infants and children (and monkeys) are prepared by natural selection to attend to and acquire some things more readily than others. Although monkeys do not have an innate fear of snakes, they have been prepared by evolution to develop such fear easily, through mechanisms of social learning (Cook & Mineka, 1989; Mineka et al., 1984).

Does a similar process occur in humans? Apparently. In a series of experiments, adults viewed a three-by-three matrix of pictures consisting either of biologically relevant stimuli (spiders or snakes) against a background of biologically irrelevant stimuli (flowers or mushrooms), or the reverse (Öhman, Flykt, & Esteves, 2001; see Figure 11.2). People had to determine as quickly as possible whether the items all came from the same category (for example, all snakes or all flowers) or from different categories (snakes and flowers). The researchers reported that the adults were faster at identifying biologically relevant stimuli (spiders and snakes) against a backdrop of biologically irrelevant stimuli (flowers) than vice versa. They interpreted this result as indicating that people attend more quickly to evolutionarily relevant stimuli (snakes and spiders) than to evolutionarily irrelevant stimuli (flowers and mushrooms). Similar findings have been reported for 3- and 5-year-old children (LoBue, 2010; LoBue & DeLoache, 2008) and 8- to 14-month-old infants (LoBue & DeLoache, 2010).

But when does such a fear develop? In a clever study, 7- to 9-month-old infants and 14- to 16-month-old toddlers watched videos of snakes and other animals (giraffes, rhinoceroses) (DeLoache & LoBue, 2009). They initially showed no greater fear

By 3 or 4 months, infants display social smiling and also begin to laugh when they are happy.

of the snakes than the other creatures, suggesting that they do not have an innate fear of snakes. The infants and toddlers then saw brief video clips of snakes and other animals associated with either a happy or fearful voice. Both the infants and toddlers looked longer at the snakes when they heard the fearful voice than when they heard the happy voice. There was no difference in looking time for the two voices when they saw videos of other animals. They interpreted these findings as indicating that infants are prepared to acquire a fear of snakes. Consistent with this interpretation, David Rakison (2005a, 2005b), using patterns of visual attention (see Chapter 5) with 10-month-old infants, concluded that babies are particularly attentive (although not necessarily fearful) of evolutionarily relevant animals (spiders and snakes) in comparison to animals that were less likely to have caused harm to ancient humans (rabbits and frogs).

What other fears do children develop, and are they for stimuli or contexts that would have been dangerous to our ancestors? Beginning around 6 months of age, infants develop a fear of heights, as reflected by their reactions on the visual cliff (see Chapter 4). As you may recall, babies before this time can recognize the visual cues associated with height (and thus potentially falling), but they do not develop fear until they have some

prepared learning The idea that animals (including humans) are "prepared" by natural selection to attend to and acquire some things more readily than others.

FIGURE 11.2 Biologically relevant and irrelevant stimuli. Adults saw a matrix of pictures consisting of biologically relevant stimuli (spiders or snakes) against a background of biologically-irrelevant stimuli (flowers or mushrooms), or the reverse. Participants in this study were faster at identifying spiders and snakes against a backdrop of flowers than vice versa (Öhman, Flykt, & Esteves, 2001).

Photos top row l to r: © amanaimages/Corbis; © amanaimages/Corbis; © Sandra Raccanello/Grand Tour/Corbis; middle row l to r: Gail Jankus/Photo Researchers, Inc.; Millard H. Sharp/Photo Researchers, Inc.; Larry Miller/Photo Researchers, Inc.; bottom row l to r: DAJ/Getty Images; © Jonathan Howell Plants/Alamy; Dennis Flaherty/Photo Researchers, Inc.

experiences dealing with heights (through crawling, for instance) (Bertenthal, Campos, & Kermoian, 1994). Also developing around 6 months of age is fear, or wariness, of strangers (see Chapter 12).

The timing and intensity of stranger distress varies from baby to baby and with the situation. For example, if an infant's mother smiles as an unfamiliar adult approaches, babies are less likely to become distressed. However, infants across diverse cultures show such distress (although not always at exactly the same time or with the same intensity, see Kagan, Keasley, & Zelazo, 1978; LaFreniere, 2005). Why might stranger distress have been adaptive for our ancestors? Although infants are dependent on adults, particularly parents, for support, fellow humans are also a potential source of danger. Consistent with this interpretation, babies show greater fear of male than female strangers, as male strangers presumably posed more danger than female strangers to infants historically (Heerwagen & Orians, 2002).

Fear of separation, or *separation distress*, also develops in the second half of the first year of life and is linked to the establishment of attachment (see Chapter 12). Infants become distressed when a parent or other attachment figure leaves

them. Again, this fear is observed in infants at about the same time universally, although there are individual and cultural differences in exactly when the fear is displayed and the extent of fear babies show, indicating that experience, in addition to neurological maturation, plays a significant role in its development (see Kagan et al., 1978; separation distress is discussed in greater detail in Chapter 12). Children routinely develop other fears during the preschool years, including fear of the dark, fear of "monsters in the closet," and fear of animals.

Fear is clearly adaptive. It helps us avoid potentially dangerous things and situations. Specific fears do not seem to be inborn but are learned. Such learning appears to emerge with the maturation of the nervous system. However, which fears are easily learned are likely governed by evolved mechanisms and may involve specific neural systems (LeDoux, 1996).

Secondary, or self-conscious, emotions. Secondary emotions are not observed in the first year of life but only become apparent later (although see Draghi-Lorenz et al., 2001 and Trevarthen, 1984 for an alternative view). According to Michael Lewis (1993), these emotions begin to develop between 15 and 18 months and are a reflection of children's emerging cognitive development, especially their ability for *self-awareness* (see Chapter 7). It is difficult to imagine children experiencing these emotions without some conscious awareness of themselves. If a child is not aware she performed a difficult task successfully, such as finishing a complicated puzzle, how can she experience pride?

Some of these emotions, such as shame and guilt, depend not only on being self-aware but also on realizing that *other* people have some expectations for one's behavior. That is, these emotions require awareness of other minds (or at least awareness of other people's expectations or their reactions to one's behavior). This has led some researchers to label these as *other-conscious emotions* (Saarni et al., 2006). These emotions have sometimes been referred to as *moral*, because they often involve an assessment of one's behavior as right or wrong in terms of a certain cultural context. For example, in Japan, being too self-centered or autonomous can trigger feelings of guilt because of the importance Japanese culture gives to interdependence.

According to Michael Lewis (1992), in the second half of the second year of life, three new secondary emotions emerge: *envy* (or *jealousy*), *nonevaluative embarrassment*, and *empathy*. Envy occurs when someone lacks a quality or possession of another person and desires it. Nonevaluative embarrassment occurs when a child has to perform some act in public, such as singing, and is similar to the discomfort adults sometimes feel when speaking in public. Such embarrassment is often associated with signs of physical discomfort or mild distress, such as blushing, which reflects the child's awareness of other people's evaluation of his or her actions. (As Mark Twain once said, "Man is the only animal that blushes. Or needs to.") Empathy refers to the ability to recognize, perceive, and feel the emotions of another. The expression of these emotions is related to maturation of the frontal cortex, as well as other brain areas, including the limbic system (Jones & Gagnon, 2007).

There is an interesting controversy concerning the emotion of jealousy and when it is first expressed in children. Jealousy is defined as fear of loss of an important relationship partner or their exclusive attention and is most readily thought of in terms of romantic relationships in adulthood. However, children and adolescents experience jealousy over peer relationships, and young children express jealousy over sibling and parent-child relationships (Volling et al., 2002). Most scientists classify jealousy as a secondary, or self-aware, emo-

tion, and thus it should not be seen until late in the second year of life. Others, however, argue that jealousy is important to survival and may have evolved to emerge early in development, perhaps in infancy (MacDonald & Leary, 2005). In support of this, several studies have shown that infants as young as 6 months old show behavioral signs of jealousy (Hart & Carrington, 2002; Hart et al., 2004). In these studies, mothers of infants spent several minutes ignoring their babies, devoting their attention instead to either a life-like doll or a book, for example. Infants showed more distress (crying) and negative emotions (angry or sad facial expressions) when mothers were interacting with the life-like doll than the book. This pattern implies that babies are not just upset because their mother is ignoring them; if that were the case, their distress would have been the same when their mother was paying attention to the book. Rather, their increased distress is because their mother is paying attention to a potential social rival. This pattern suggests that the roots of jealousy may lie more in the old part of the brain (the limbic system) and that at least facets of jealousy may be better thought of as primary emotions.

Most research and attention has been done on the development of empathy. As we mentioned earlier, **empathy** refers to the ability to recognize, perceive, and feel the emotions of another. For example, in one study, researchers examined 12- to 24-month-old children's responses to the distress of other people (Zahn-Waxler et al., 1992). They reported that empathetic responses increased with age, being particularly high for 2-year-old children, who often made facial expressions or other gestures indicative of sadness, tried to comfort distressed people, and sometimes sought information about the person's distress ("What's wrong?"). Interestingly, girls were more empathetic than boys, who were more apt to be nonresponsive to the distress of others. It is worth noting that in order for children to *express* empathy, they must be able to *recognize* emotions in others (see discussion to follow).

Some evidence suggests that monkeys and apes display empathy much as human children do. There are many anecdotes about what appears to be empathy in great apes (de Waal, 1997, 2005). One that made the news several years ago (it was captured on video: http://www.ibeatyou.com/entry/adfe0e/binti-jua) involved an 8-year-old female gorilla at the Chicago Brookfield Zoo, Binti Jua, who came to the assistance of a 3-year-old boy who fell into the primate cage. Frans de Waal

empathy The ability to recognize, perceive, and feel the emotions of another.

(1997) provides another example of a researcher at the Stuttgart Zoo who brought her new baby to show to the bonobos. Upon being shown the infant, the alpha (highest-ranking) female disappeared and returned with her own newborn. Yet, in laboratory settings, chimpanzees seem to be indifferent to the welfare of others. For instance, chimpanzees will not give food to other familiar but unrelated chimpanzees, even though there is no material cost to themselves (Silk et al., 2005; see also Jensen et al., 2006).

Children's secondary emotions expand beyond empathy and envy, usually beginning midway into their third year. Between 2.5 and 3 years of age, another five secondary emotions emerge:

- *Pride*—positive evaluation of a specific behavior or aspect of self
- *Guilt*—negative evaluation of a specific behavior or aspect of self
- *Shame*—negative global evaluation of self
- *Hubris*—positive global evaluation of self
- *Evaluative embarrassment*—a mild kind of shame when children negatively assess their own actions

Shame and pride can be seen as different sides of the same coin. For example, when children are given a simple task, such as putting a puzzle together, and they consistently fail, they express shame by averting their eyes, frowning, slumping their bodies, and making negative statements about themselves ("I'm no good at this"). In contrast, when children succeed at a difficult task, they express pride by smiling, standing up straight, looking directly at others (likely for confirmation of the good job they have done), and making positive statements ("I did it!") (Lewis, Alessandri, & Sullivan, 1992). Three- and 4-year-old children are sensitive to the difficulty of the tasks, being more likely to show shame when they fail at easy versus difficult tasks, and pride when they solve difficult versus easy tasks (Lewis et al., 1992). Children do not just hide their eyes when they feel ashamed, but shame is associated with elevated reactions to the stress hormone cortisol, especially in boys (Mills et al., 2008). Evaluative embarrassment is similar to shame but less intense and associated with the performance of specific tasks (doing poorly on a particular puzzle) and not a global assessment of one's worth.

All in all, the secondary emotions require that children be aware not only of their own feelings and thoughts, but also, to some extent, of the thoughts and feelings of others. Children's emotional reactions—to display shame or not, for example—are based not so much on what they do but on their appraisal of others' reactions to their behavior. Failing to put a puzzle together may or may not cause a child to experience a bit of shame, but that feeling can be minimized or exaggerated by how others respond to the child's actions. This requires that children be able to recognize emotions in others.

Recognizing Emotions

If emotions serve as a means of communication, it is as important to be able to recognize them as it is to express them. Babies are sensitive to others' emotions from the very beginning, at least at a rudimentary level. For example, contagious crying occurs when newborns cry in response to the cries of other newborns (although not to the cries of older infants) (Dondi, Simion, & Caltran, 1999; Martin & Clark, 1982). Perhaps even more remarkable is the demonstration by Tiffany Field and her colleagues (1982) that newborns who were shown an adult displaying happy, sad, or surprised facial expressions matched those expressions seconds later (see photos on facing page). Observers viewed videotapes of the babies, not knowing which face the newborns had looked at, and guessed correctly which face the baby had seen at rates greater than expected by chance. This is an example of *neonatal imitation* and shows the range of emotional expressions newborns are sensitive to. (We discussed neonatal imitation in greater depth in Chapter 5.)

In other contexts, 2- and 3-month-old infants alter their emotional responses, as reflected by facial expressions, when their interaction partner (particularly their mother) changes from a responsive (for example, smiling) to a neutral, or still, face (Tronick, 1989). Infants often become distressed when typical face-to-face interaction with an adult is disrupted. They seem to recognize what normal social interaction is like and become upset when their interaction partner changes the rules. Even newborns will decrease their eye contact and show signs of distress when their interaction partner becomes nonresponsive (Nagy, 2008).

It is not until they are about 6 months old, however, that infants are able to recognize most emotional expressions of others in terms of people's faces or voices. Moreover, we know that infants are more sensitive to and recognize positive emotions, such as joy, earlier than negative emotions, such as anger (Izard et al., 1995). For example, in one study, when the adult stopped responding to an infant during face-to-face interaction, she did so with a smile on her face as opposed to a neutral expression. In this context, 2-month-old babies (but not older babies) continued to smile and gaze at the adult, reflecting infants' affinity for happy faces,

---

contagious crying Crying that occurs when newborns cry in response to the cries of other newborns.

even with disruption of social interaction (Rochat, Striano, & Blatt, 2002). We are not able to know the meaning, if any, infants are attributing to these expressions, but they do pay more attention when adults "put on a happy face."

Another milestone in the development of emotional recognition is **social referencing**, which refers to "the use of another's emotional cues to clarify the interpretation of an ambiguous or uncertain event" (Thompson, 2006, p. 33). Beginning at about 12 months, children will look to other people, usually their caregivers, in order to decide how to react to a novel object, person, or event. For example, if a toddler is shown a new toy and sees his mother smiling, he will probably approach it with positive affect. If, however, his mother shows disgust or fear, he will likely display the same emotional expression and reject the toy. Several studies demonstrated that 1-year-old children's reactions to strangers, a novel toy, or their decision to cross to the deep side of a visual cliff are influenced by the emotional cues of others, usually a parent (Repacholi, 1998; Striano & Rochat, 2000). Infants can make use of a parent's facial expression, tone of voice, gestures, or combinations of these sources to determine their action in an uncertain situation (Hornik, Risenhoover, & Gunnar, 1987; Vaish & Striano, 2004). We all likely remember cases of young children who, after falling to the floor and experiencing some discomfort, look at their parents and, depending on Mom or Dad's emotional expression, begin to cry or not.

It is interesting that infants beginning around 12 months of age take the negative cues adults give them more seriously than the positive cues. This is called a *negativity bias* and is displayed by adults as well (Vaish, Grossman, & Woodward, 2008). For example, in some studies, adults made either happy, neutral, or fearful facial expressions or verbal remarks about an unfamiliar toy. Infants were later given the opportunity to interact with that toy. Infants as young as 12 months old who received negative cues subsequently played with the toy significantly less than children who were given neutral cues, whereas there was no difference in play time between those given the positive and neutral social cues (Mumme & Fernald, 2003; Mumme, Fernald, & Herrera, 1996). Infants' greater attention to negative as opposed to positive emotions is also seen in terms of brain activation (Carver & Vaccaro, 2007). Why should children show a stronger reaction to negative as opposed to positive social cues? One hypothesis is that a negativity bias evolved to help infants (and later children and adults) avoid potentially dangerous situations, making sensitivity to negative social information particularly important (Vaish

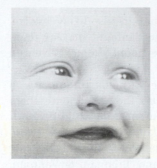

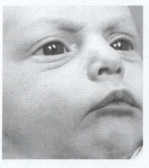
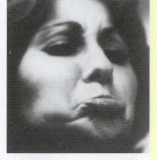

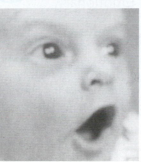
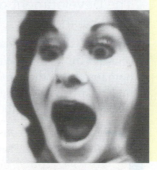

Newborn infants matched the facial expressions of an adult model, reflecting happiness, sadness, and surprise.
SOURCE: Field, T. M., Woodson, R., Greenberg, R., & Cohen, D. (1982). Discrimination and imitation of facial expression by neonates. *Science, 218,* 179–181.

Beginning in the later part of the first year, infants look to others to see how they should react.

social referencing An infant's use of another person's emotional cues to interpret an ambiguous or uncertain event.

et al., 2008). Negative cues are also likely less frequently observed for most infants, making them more salient than the more-often-experienced positive cues.

Consistent with the idea that infants attend to negative faces because they experience them less frequently is research from children with depressed mothers. Infants of depressed mothers tend to be more attentive to faces expressing positive emotions (Striano, Brennan, & Vanman, 2002). Because they frequently see the sad, angry, or neutral faces of their mothers, these negative emotional expressions do not provide much useful information, causing them to be more sensitive to happy faces. Infants, then, have some mechanism that permits them to tune out some types of facial expressions and to increase their sensitivity to others.

The Development of Emotional Understanding

The expression and recognition of emotions are central in communicating feelings. However, humans have the unique intellectual ability to understand what these emotions *mean*, both in themselves and in others. Emotional understanding further enhances people's communication ability. With understanding, we can anticipate how something we say or do will affect another person, and we can reflect upon the reasons for any emotion we are experiencing. Not surprisingly, most aspects of emotional understanding develop later than competencies in emotional expression and recognition, beginning in the preschool years and continuing into adolescence.

Based on an extensive examination of the scientific literature and results from their own research, Francisco Pons, Paul Harris, and Marc de Rosnay (2004; Pons & Harris, 2000) identified nine different components of children's emotional understanding (see Table 11.2). According to their research, emotional understanding shows steady developmental changes between the ages of 3 and 11 years and can be divided into three developmental periods.

A first period spans 3 to about 7 years. As we discussed earlier, before one can understand emotions, one must first be able to recognize them, and, during the beginning of this period, more than half of all 3-year-old children are able to recognize four out of five basic emotions on the basis of people's facial expressions (Component I in Table 11.2). Later in this period, children are able to recognize all different emotional expressions,

table 11.2 Nine Components of Children's Emotional Understanding

Component I. Recognition: *Recognizing and naming emotions based on external cues*
  Example: Naming as "happy" an appropriate facial expression as shown in photograph.

Component II. External cause: *Understanding how external causes affect emotions*
  Example: A child knows he will feel "sad" when he learns that his pet has just died.

Component III. Desire: *Understanding that emotional reactions depend on desires*
  Example: A child who likes chocolate-chip ice cream will feel "happy" about having it for dessert, whereas a child who dislikes chocolate-chip ice cream will feel sad.

Component IV. Belief: *Understanding that a belief can determine emotional reactions*
  Example: A rabbit that does not know that a fox is hidden behind nearby bushes is not "scared."

Component V. Reminder: *Understanding the relationship between memory and emotion*
  Example: A child will feel "sad" when looking at photographs of a pet that died some years ago.

Component VI. Regulation: *Understanding emotions can be cognitively managed*
  Example: A child can stop feeling "sad" about something by thinking about something else.

Component VII. Hiding: *Understanding the discrepancy between emotion (what one feels) and affect (what one shows)*
  Example: A child who feels "anger" because a peer is teasing her can show a "happy" face.

Component VIII. Mixed: *Understanding multiple or ambivalent nature of emotions*
  Example: A child can feel "happy" and "scared" if he receives a bicycle that he does not know how to ride for a gift.

Component IX. Morality: *Understanding relationships between morality and emotions*
  Example: A child can feel "sad" by lying to someone, or feel "happy" by helping.

SOURCE: Adapted from Pons, F., Harris, P. L., & de Rosnay, M. (2004). Emotion comprehension between 3 and 11 years: Developmental periods and hierarchical organization. *European Journal of Developmental Psychology, I*, 127–152.

identify their external causes, and understand the impacts of reminders on emotion (Components I, II, and V). For example, 5-year-old children understand that a girl can feel sad when she sees a dog that reminds her of one that chased away her pet rabbit (Lagattuta, Wellman, & Flavell, 1997). Even 3-year-olds display some understanding that cues that remind people of past events can evoke emotion, although this ability develops between the ages of 3 and 6 years (Lagattuta & Wellman, 2001; Stein & Levine, 1989).

During this time, children are developing an increased ability to take the perspective of others—to put oneself in another person's shoes, so to speak. This includes emotional perspectives. This involves what researchers have called *theory of mind*, the understanding that people's actions are based on what they know, think, and feel. Although theory of mind develops over childhood, major advances are seen in children being able to take the mental perspective of others around 4 years of age. We discussed theory-of-mind development in greater detail in Chapter 7.

② In a second period, beginning around 7 years of age, most children are able to understand the role of desires and belief on emotions, the fact that positive emotions can enhance thinking (Amsterlaw, Lagattuta, & Meltzoff, 2009), as well as the possibility of hiding emotions (Components III, IV and VII). For example, in one study, Pons and his colleagues (2004) told a story to 3-, 5-, 7-, 9-, and 11-year-old children about two boys, Tom and Peter, one who hated lettuce (Tom) and the other who liked lettuce very much (Peter). After making sure that the children understood and remembered this information, they were invited to lift a flap from the test booklet to reveal the contents of a box, where a head of lettuce was shown. The experimenter then asked the child if Tom, and then Peter, would feel happy, sad, just all right, or scared upon finding the lettuce. Drawings with the four emotional expressions on a child's face were available at the time of testing to help children decide. Only 20% of 3-year-olds and 55% of 5-year-olds answered these items correctly (Tom would be sad, but Peter would be happy), while 75% of 7-year-old children answered correctly.

③ In a third period of emotional understanding (around 9 to 11 years), children are able to understand the mixed nature of emotions, the possibility of regulating emotions through cognition, and the influence of morality on emotions (Components VIII, VI and IX in Table 11.2). For example, Pons and his colleagues (2004) assessed children's understanding of mixed emotions by showing them a cartoon scenario where a child, Tom, was

looking at a new bicycle. The experimenter told the children that this bicycle was given to Tom for his birthday, but that "Tom thinks he might fall off and hurt himself because he has never ridden a bicycle before." The children were then asked, "How is Tom feeling? Is he happy; sad and scared; happy and scared; or scared?" Only 20% of 7-year-olds answered this item correctly (happy and sacred), whereas 65% of 9-year-olds and 90% of 11-year-olds did so (see also Larsen, To, & Fireman, 2007). We are certain that children younger than 7 years sometimes feel mixed emotions, but apparently only older children understand this feeling.

Much of the improvement in emotional understanding in childhood can be attributed to changes in underlying cognitive abilities. Yet, such abilities do not develop in a vacuum, and specific experiences children have surely influence their emotional understanding. Emotion talk with adults helps children appreciate that different people can have different feelings about the same event (Levine, Stein, & Liwag, 1999) and provides them with a vocabulary for sharing their feelings and desires. For example, parents may identify an emotion a child is expressing, ask the reason for the feeling, and perhaps suggest a way of dealing with it. ("You look sad right now. Is something wrong? Did something happen between you and Michele?")

Along these lines, Judy Dunn and her colleagues conducted a series of studies examining emotion talk between children and family members between the ages of 18 months and 6 years (Dunn, Bretherton, & Munn, 1987; Dunn & Brown, 1994; Dunn, Brown, & Beardsall, 1991). Most of the emotion talk of young children was with their mothers as opposed to with older siblings. Mothers tended to use conversations to explain something to their children or to guide their behavior, whereas older siblings were more likely to use such conversations merely to comment on their own feelings or observations. Children in homes with high levels of distress and expression of negative emotions were less apt than children in homes with lower levels of negative emotional expression to engage in emotion talk (Dunn & Brown, 1994). This suggests that children's emotional understanding is embedded in social relationships. Mothers, in particular, seem to be important in helping children develop an understanding of emotions and perhaps the emotions of others. Moreover, some relationships (those that are more positive in tone) seem to be better for developing emotional understanding than others (those that are more negative in tone).

School-age children are better able than younger children to control their emotions and emotional expressions, pretending, for example, that a bad-tasting drink tastes good and vice versa. Girls are generally better than boys at these and other self-regulation tasks.

The Development of Emotional Self-Regulation

Up to this point we have focused on three key issues of emotional development: the emergence of primary and secondary emotions, the recognition of emotions in others, and the development of emotional understanding. The final pending issue is the development of *emotional self-regulation*. At its most basic level, emotional self-regulation can be defined as "changes associated with activation of emotions" (Cole, Martin, & Dennis, 2004, p. 320). However, this may simplify a complicated issue a bit too much. Emotions can be initiated, inhibited, intensified, prolonged, or modulated, for instance, and can be used to achieve social or individual goals (Eisenberg & Spinard, 2004).

Emotional self-regulation is important, because controlling the external expression of emotions and learning to manage our inner emotional states are critical for leading a satisfactory social life and maintaining psychological well-being. Wearing our hearts on our sleeves, expressing immediately every emotion we feel, acting on our emotional desires, or blurting out whatever thought runs through our heads can lead to nothing but trouble. This was reflected by the Jim Carrey movie some years ago, *Liar, Liar,* in which a fast-talking lawyer is cursed with having to utter the truth in all contexts. It is also easy to understand how it is important for people in some professions, such as firefighters, soldiers, air-traffic controllers, or surgeons, not to be overcome by their emotional arousal. Although emotions are like the directions of a compass, it is not always wise to follow them blindly. Getting to know when it is appropriate to follow emotions and when it is not (self-regulation) is something that develops over childhood.

One hypothesis about an early step in the evolution of human cognition posits a critical role for an increased ability to inhibit emotional expressions and control of impulsive behavior (Bjorklund & Harnishfeger, 1995; Bjorklund & Kipp, 2002). Enhancements in social complexity could not have occurred unless individuals were able to inhibit their emotional reactions and gain control of their aggressive and sexual behavior. Imagine, if you can, a meeting of elders around the campfire in which the first signs of frustration lead to fisticuffs, and sexual urges are acted upon and quickly responded to—sometimes positively and sometimes negatively. Although we do not doubt that such thoughts might have run though the elders' heads (and likely still run through the heads of contemporary city council members), the only way any governance can get done is if people demonstrate some emotional self-regulation. Once a certain level of inhibitory control had evolved, the neurological structures responsible for this increased regulation of emotional responding could then be co-opted for other purposes, both social (for example, perspective taking and cooperative behavior) and otherwise (for example, language or tool use).

Self-Regulation in Infancy and Childhood

Newborns cannot hide their emotions. By 3 months of age, infants are beginning to gain some control over their emotions, which will continue throughout the first year (Feldman, 2009). For example, they are able to soothe themselves by sucking on a pacifier or their thumbs, and they can look away or otherwise withdraw from excessive stimulation, such as a bright light (Thompson et al., 2003). This is accompanied by rapid development of the cerebral cortex between 2 and 4 months of age (Nelson, Thomas, & de Haan, 2006; see Chapter 4). Equally important during this time are infants' interactions with their caretakers. Although infants during the first several months of life show little talent at controlling their own emotions, their emotions can be regulated by external sources, usually their mothers. Mothers caress, rock, sing, and talk to babies, all in an effort to modify their infants' moods and behavior (Jahromi, Putnam, & Stifter, 2004).

Social referencing, discussed in the previous section, reflects a form of emotional self-regulation and is available late in the first year of life. Infants look to others to see the proper way to react. This requires some advanced social-cognitive skills, particularly *shared attention* (two people attending to the same object at once, Tomasello & Carpenter, 2007), which was discussed in greater detail in Chapter 7.

One paradigm that has been used with preschool and school-age children to assess expressive control of emotions involves asking children to show positive affect following a negative experience, or vice versa. For example, children may be given a foul-tasting drink and asked to pretend that it tastes good, or conversely, a pleasant-tasting drink and asked to pretend that it tastes bad. Adult judges then rate the emotional expression of the children. In a variety of studies, children as young as 3 years of age were able to pretend that a bad-tasting drink or a disappointing outcome in a game was positive, at least some of the time, although children's abilities to fool a judge generally increased with age (Feldman, Jenkins, & Popoola, 1979; Saarni, 1984). Interestingly, in most of the studies, females did better at this task than males, even in adulthood (see Bjorklund & Kipp, 1996), despite the fact that females are more emotionally expressive than males (Buck, 1982).

Factors Influencing the Development of Self-Regulation

As children's emotional understanding improves and they develop a vocabulary for emotions, they are better able to appreciate the causes and consequences of their emotions, which contribute to their increasing self-regulation abilities. Much of this improvement can be attributed to maturation of the frontal cortex (see Chapter 4), an area of the brain associated with *executive function*, processes involved in regulating attention and aspects of information processing. During this same time, children's cognitive abilities improve, including memory and representational skills (see Chapters 6, 7, and 8), and they are better able to understand the causes and consequences of their emotions and behavior related to them. Nonetheless, children generally have more difficulty regulating negative than positive emotions, and self-regulation often fails when level of arousal is high. We recall one boy who spent a portion of his birthday in his room for a time-out every year between the ages of 5 and 11 because he became overly excited and out of control during this special day.

It is not just maturational readiness that determines children's self-regulation abilities, however. It is important to note that the development of emotional self-regulation is influenced by a series of factors, one of the most relevant being culture. Children always develop self-regulation of emotions within a certain sociocultural environment that progressively lets them know, through peers, parents, schools, and media, when and how emotions should be expressed and managed.

The role of parents (and also teachers) in helping children to regulate their emotions is also crucial (Denham, 1998). We mentioned previously that mothers do a variety of things to regulate their babies' emotions. One of those things is talking to them using infant-directed speech (see Chapter 9), which may have evolved not so much as a channel to facilitate language development but to regulate infants' emotions and behaviors. Infant-directed speech usually involves high-pitched tones and exaggerated modulations (see Hoff, 2009; Chapter 9). Although there are cultural differences in the degree to which mothers and other caregivers use infant-directed speech, some aspects of it are found worldwide and might reflect a language universal (Fernald, 1992; Kuhl et al., 1997).

Throughout infancy and childhood, parents reward some emotional patterns and not others, serve as models for children to imitate, coach them to cope with emotions, and encourage them to talk about their emotional states, all helpful strategies for self-regulation (see Table 11.3). Interactions with parents serve as the context in which infants and children learn to regulate their own emotions. Ross Thompson and his colleagues (2003) suggested that, over extended periods of time, the way parents try to regulate their infants' emotions may affect their infants' style of emotional regulation. For example, parents who wait until their children express high levels of distress or are out of control before intervening are likely to have children who become distressed quickly and respond with high intensity. This, in turn, makes it difficult for a parent to soothe a child.

The picture we have painted of increasing self-regulation over childhood is a simplified one. No

table 11.3 Some Strategies for Promoting Children's Emotional Development

Help crying infants find comfort

Create an atmosphere of warmth, acceptance, and trust

Encourage children to express their feelings

Discuss emotions experienced by characters you study in literature and history

Ask children to guess what emotions people may feel in particular scenarios

Take cultural differences into account

Help children keep anxiety at a manageable level

Pay attention to your own emotions

Model appropriate ways of dealing with negative emotions

SOURCE: Adapted from McDevitt, T. M., & Ormrod, J. E. (2004). *Child development: Educating and working with children and adolescents* (2nd ed.). Upper Saddle River, NJ: Pearson, pp. 385–387.

infant-directed speech The specialized register of speech that adults and older children use when talking specifically to infants and young children.

Emotional expression	*1st year:* Primary Emotions • at birth: distress, interest, disgust • about 1–3 months: joy • about 3–6 months: anger, sadness, surprise • about 6–8 months: fear *2nd year:* Secondary (Self-conscious) Emotions • about 18–24 months: empathy, envy (jealousy) • about 30–36 months: pride, guilt, shame, hubris
Emotional recognition	*about 3 months:* sensitivity to abrupt emotional caregiver changes *about 6 months:* (implicit) recognition of all basic emotions *about 12 months:* social referencing (modeling own emotional reactions on the basis of the recognition of other people's emotional reactions)
Emotional understanding	*about 3–5 years old:* Understanding important public aspects of emotions • (explicit) recognition and naming of emotional expressions • how external causes affect others' emotions • the impact of reminders on emotions *about 7 years old:* Understanding the mentalistic nature of emotions • the role of desire and belief in emotions • the discrepancy between expressed and felt emotions *about 9–11 years old:* Understanding complexity of individual emotional behavior • the mixed nature of emotions • the relation between morality and emotions • the role of cognition in emotional regulation
Emotional self-regulation	*about 1st year:* ability to regulate some disturbing input *about 3rd year:* ability to hide real emotions *about 5–11 years:* increasing ability to self-regulate emotional states

one should be surprised to learn that there are substantial individual differences in children's emotional regulation. Some differences are associated with variations in cultural values and traditions. Others are associated with differences between the sexes. As noted earlier, girls are better than boys at certain aspects of emotional regulation, for example, inhibiting one's emotion and expressing an opposite one (Saarni, 1984). Other differences can be attributed to genetic differences and a child's particular developmental history, including interactions with parents (Fox & Stifter, 2005). Any or all of these variables may become important when facing emotional events in childhood, such as the tantrum a 2-year old throws when she doesn't get her way, linked to the regulation of anger; the overenthusiasm a 6-year-old feels in anticipation of his birthday party; or some learned fears, such as those of pets or thunderstorms, so typical during the preschool period. Many emotions and their regulation are expressed in infants' and children's interactions with their parents and are related to their attachment with their parents, which will be explored in the following chapter. A timetable for milestones in emotional development is presented in Concept Review 11.2.

Emotions in Adolescence

As we have seen, many different aspects of emotional development emerge, change, or improve over infancy and childhood. But what happens in adolescence? Perhaps the most common belief about adolescence is that this is a period of "storm and stress" (*Strum und Drang* in German, referring to "storm and urge"). The dramatic physical changes in adolescents produce a troublesome and tumultuous period in their lives, when their psychological well-being is weak and their social relations, particularly with parents and other adults, are uneasy. They feel they must rebel against and detach from their parents in order to achieve adult psychological well-being.

Although adolescence does present its challenges, most researchers today do not see it as a time of great disruption, at least not for most youngsters (Collins & Laursen, 2004). On the contrary, most adolescents in most countries studied see this period of their lives as basically a healthy, happy, and optimistic one (Larson, 2000; Stepp, 2000). This does not mean that adolescence is a paradise, though. Changes in self-image associated with changes in body proportions and function (see Chapter 4), increases in self-reflection as a by-product of their improved cognitive abilities

Although adolescence rarely runs smoothly, most teenagers in most countries see this time in their lives as basically a healthy, happy, and optimistic one.

(see Chapter 7), and difficulties adjusting to new academic and social settings have all been proposed to be stressors for adolescents that can cause problems in emotional adjustment (Petersen et al., 1993).

Although evidence is mixed, some research indicates that adolescents experience, on average, more negative emotions than children, including depression (Larson & Ham, 1993; see discussion to follow). As for positive emotions, they are more apt to experience them in interactions with their peers than with their parents (Csikszentmihalyi & Larson, 1984), which may be one reason why parents of adolescents believe their children are having a more difficult time than the adolescents report to researchers.

Researchers who specialize in studying adolescence discuss the process of **emotional autonomy** that occurs during this period. Emotional autonomy refers to increases in an adolescent's "subjective sense of his or her independence, especially in relation to parents or parental figures" (Collins & Steinberg, 2006, pp. 1035–1036). Particularly during early adolescence, this is achieved through psychologically separating from parents and often arguing or bickering with them, in an effort to establish an independent identity, much as proposed by Erik Erikson (1968; see Chapter 7). This change, however, typically spans the entire length of adolescence, rather than occurring in a sudden upheaval as proposed by the storm-and-stress theorists (Laursen & Collins, 1994; Collins & Laursen, 2004). Few adolescents detach from their par-

ents, and overt rebellion or obstinate oppositional behavior is not positively related to psychological well-being, but just the reverse (see Collins & Steinberg, 2006; Steinberg, 1990).

How easily adolescents attain emotional autonomy and demonstrate good psychosocial adjustment is related to how parents, in particular, encourage such autonomy. Parents who are emotionally warm but not intrusive are best apt to foster the development of emotional autonomy in their children (Hodges, Finnegan, & Perry, 1999). In contrast, parents who are overly controlling or hostile make the transition to adulthood and emotional autonomy more difficult, and their children are more apt to display internalizing problems, such as depression (McElhaney & Allen, 2001; see discussion below). Adolescence is also a time when sexual feelings emerge, along with desires for intimacy, topics discussed in some detail in Chapter 15.

Emotional Problems during Childhood and Adolescence

The developmental pattern of emotion we presented in the earlier sections describes what happens generally. Most children attain the various emotional milestones about the time they are expected to and grow up to exhibit high levels of

emotional autonomy In adolescence, increases in a subjective sense of independence, especially in relation to parents or parental figures.

"emotional intelligence" (Goleman, 1995)—that is, they have an ability to deal successfully with their own and other people's emotions, as well as with emotional conflicts that inevitably occur. There are individual differences. Some people are more skilled at expressing, reading, or managing emotions than others, but most people function well (or at least adequately) most of the time. But, of course, there are exceptions. Sometimes emotional development does not progress smoothly. Transient, and sometimes long-lasting, emotional problems arise.

Internalizing and Externalizing Problems

Emotional disruptions during childhood and adolescence are usually categorized as either **internalizing problems** or **externalizing problems**. Internalizing problems affect the people who experience them (they internalize their problems, or turn inward) and include anxiety disorders (phobias, post-traumatic stress disorder, obsessive-compulsive disorder), depression, and eating disorders, among others. Generally speaking, internalized forms of emotional problems are more frequent in girls than in boys (and women than in men), and this is found cross culturally (see Benenson, 2005). In contrast, externalizing problems reflect acting out, such that one's behavior adversely affects other people. **Oppositional defiant disorder** is perhaps the most frequent type of externalizing problem in childhood and is characterized by a pattern of defiant, uncooperative, and hostile behavior toward adults (particularly at home and school) that interferes with a child's daily functioning. Oppositional defiant disorder often co-occurs with attentional-deficit hyperactivity disorder (ADHD), learning disabilities, or other emotional disturbances (for example, depression, anxiety) and is typically used to describe elementary schoolchildren (Steiner & Remsing, 2007).

Oppositional defiant disorder often predicts the more serious **conduct disorder**, which is characterized by different forms of antisocial behaviors, such as physical and verbal aggression, vandalism, and theft. Conduct disorder reflects a chronic emotional pattern (in other words, it does not describe the occasional misbehaving of a child), and it affects between 2% to 6% of school-age children

internalizing problems Emotional problems that affect the people who experience them (they "internalize" their problems, or turn inward), and include anxiety disorders (phobias, posttraumatic stress disorder, obsessive-compulsive disorder), depression, and eating disorders, among others.

externalizing problems Emotional problems reflected by "acting out," such that one's behavior adversely affects other people.

oppositional defiant disorder A type of externalizing problem in childhood that is characterized by a pattern of defiant, uncooperative, and hostile behavior toward adults (particularly at home and school) that interferes with a child's daily functioning.

conduct disorder Form of externalizing problem characterized by different types of antisocial behaviors, such as physical and verbal aggression, vandalism, and theft.

(Kazdin, 1997). Externalizing problems are more frequent in boys than in girls (and men than in women) (Rutter & Garmezy, 1983). These emotional problems do not simply cause children and adolescents temporary discomfort but are sometimes associated with important societal outcomes. For example, fewer than half of children and adolescents with serious emotional problems graduate from high school (McDevitt & Ormond, 2004).

Joyce Benenson (2005) suggested that this pattern of sex differences, with females displaying more internalizing problems and males showing more externalizing problems, reflects different ways females and males approach problems, which may have been shaped in our evolutionary past. According to Benenson, aggressive behaviors characteristic of externalizing problems may increase reproductive fitness in males in terms of peer-group status and defeating opponents. In contrast, internalizing behaviors, which increase inhibitory control but also may increase anxiety and depressive symptoms, may have been especially adaptive to females for the care of offspring (see Bjorklund & Kipp, 1996), improving their reproductive fitness. For example, Benenson (2005) proposed that depressive symptoms in females might elicit help from others in caring for children.

The rate of emotional problems in children is relatively high, and by some accounts, getting higher over recent decades. Overall, according to parents' reports in 2006, about 5% of American children between 4 and 17 years of age experienced definite or severe difficulties with emotions, behavior, being able to get along with other children, or concentration (Federal Interagency Forum on Child and Family Statistics, 2008). Other researchers place the level of mental disturbance higher. For instance, rates of psychopathology reported in studies between 1963 and the mid-1990s increased with age: 8% for preschoolers; 12% for preadolescents; and 15% for adolescents (Roberts, Attkisson, & Rosenblatt, 1998). The researchers also evaluated the changes in the overall rates of psychopathology over a 40-year period, and their findings are summarized in Figure 11.3. As you can see, rates of childhood and adolescent psychopathology were relatively stable up to 1990, but nearly double after 1990. We cannot be certain whether this rapid increase is attributed to increasing stress among children and adolescents, more accurate reporting, or an increased tendency for children and adolescents (and their parents) to seek help for emotional problems, or some combination of these factors.

Childhood emotional problems foretell emotional disturbances in adulthood. For example, the median age of onset for many emotional problems is during childhood or early adolescence. (Median age refers to the age by which 50% of the cases had been identified.) For example, the median age of

Although children rarely experience depression, between 15% to 20% of adolescents experience clinical depression, and about 35% of adolescents experience depressed mood.

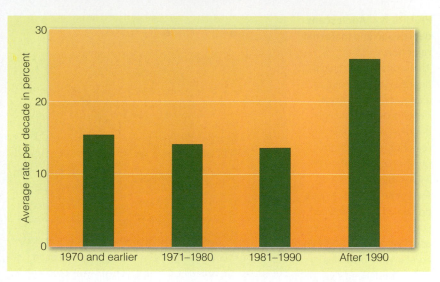

FIGURE 11.3 Average rate of psychopathology for children and adolescence over decades.

The rates were relatively constant for studies conducted in 1990 and earlier but rose sharply for studies conducted after 1990. SOURCE: Adapted from Roberts, R. E., Attkisson, C. C., & Rosenblatt, A. (1998). Prevalence of psychopathology among children and adolescents. *American Journal of Psychiatry, 155,* 715–721.

Depression [margin note]

Depression [margin note]

onset for both anxiety disorders and impulse control disorders, which include conduct disorders, is 11 years, and the median age for substance abuse is 20 years. Only **depression** has a relatively late median age of onset (30 years) (Kessler et al., 2005). Yet depression is not only an adult disease but affects many adolescents as well. Fifteen percent of people with major depression commit suicide (American Psychiatric Association, 1994). Depression is a modification in mood consisting of one or more of three components: feelings of sadness, a sense of unease (*dysphoria*), or loss of a sense of pleasure (*anhedonia*). These symptoms may be accompanied by irritability and alterations of thinking about the self, other people, or the world in general. Depression may involve several physical symptoms, including a reduction of normal metabolic and physiological processes that result in dangerous modifications of sleep patterns, eating habits, energy level, and general activity (Goodyer & Sharp, 2005).

Although depressive symptoms have been reported even in infancy (see, for example, classic research by Spitz [1965], describing depressive symptoms in infants separated from their parents because of extended hospital/institutional stays, discussed in Chapter 12), modern clinicians resist diagnosing depression in children much before the age of 6, when children are able to describe their mental state in a reliable way (Goodyer & Sharp, 2005). In general, depression is rare in children, although recent reports cite evidence of depression in preschool children persisting over a two-year period (Luby et al., 2009). For the most part, children are highly optimistic. In fact, when a child has scores on tests of optimism and pes-

simism typical for the average adult, it may be a sign of depression (Seligman, 1998). For example, only about 1% of 11-year-olds are diagnosed with clinical depression, typically characterized by a pervasive low mood, low self-esteem, and loss of interest or pleasure in usual activities. The rates of clinical depression increase substantially, however, from 15 to 18 years of age to between 15% to 20% (Hankin et al., 1998). It has also been estimated that roughly 35% of adolescents experience depressed mood, defined as a mild, reactive depression that lasts only a few months (Cicchetti et al., 1997; Petersen et al., 1993).

Several studies have found relationships between specific alleles of a gene and depression, but only under certain environmental contexts. As you may recall from Chapter 3, genes come in pairs, and sometimes there are different versions, or alleles, for a particular gene (for example, one gene for red hair and one for nonred hair—both for hair color but each allele is associated with a different outcome, or phenotype). In one study, people who had one version of a gene associated with the neurotransmitter serotonin were more likely to experience depression than people with an alternative version of this gene, but only if they experienced numerous stressful events during their childhoods. That is, rather than there being a gene *for* depression, this allele increases the likelihood of people becoming depressed when they experience stressful environments. Alternatively, people who possess other versions of the gene were less likely to experience depression given stressful life events (Caspi et al., 2003). In other research, adolescents who experienced high degrees of maternal rejection were more apt to be classified as clinically depressed than were adolescents whose mothers did not reject them, but only if they had one combination

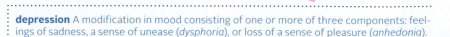

depression A modification in mood consisting of one or more of three components: feelings of sadness, a sense of unease (*dysphoria*), or loss of a sense of pleasure (*anhedonia*).

FIGURE 11.4 Adolescent depression and maternal rejection.

The incidence of clinical depression in a group of adolescents who experienced low versus high degrees of maternal rejection is a function of which combination of alleles they possessed for a gene that influences dopamine transport. As you can see, only adolescents who possessed one combination of alleles (TT) experienced significantly greater levels of clinical depression as a result of high level of maternal rejection.
SOURCE: From Haeffel, G. J., Getchell, M., Koposov, R. A., Yrigollen, C. Y., DeYoung, C. G., Klinteberg, B., Oreland, L., Ruchkin, V. V., Grigorenko, E. L. (2008). Association between polymorphisms in the dopamine transporter gene and depression: Evidence for a gene-environment interaction in a sample of juvenile detainees. *Psychological Science, 19,* 62–69. Reprinted by permission.

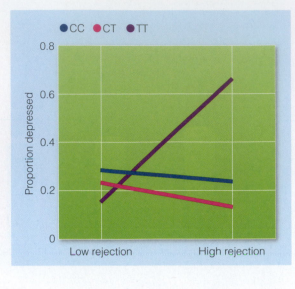

of a particular gene that influences dopamine transfer (another neurotransmitter). The relationship between being classified as depressed as a function of experiencing low or high maternal rejection is shown for the three different combinations of this gene (labeled CC, CT, and TT in Figure 11.4). As you can see from Figure 11.4, only adolescents who had the one specific combination of alleles (TT) showed elevated levels of depression in the face of maternal rejection (Haeffel et al., 2008).

The increase over the past several decades of emotional disorders in children and adolescents has been associated with advances in pharmacology, and we should not be surprised to learn that children are being medicated at all-time high levels. As of the late 1990s, about 6% of youths younger than 20 years were taking some type of mood- or behavior-altering (psychotropic) medication, including antidepressants such as Prozac and other mood-stabilizer drugs, often used to treat conduct disorders. (Children were also given stimulants such as Ritalin, mainly for the treatment of attention-deficit disorder, with and without hyperactivity. These are not disorders of emotions, but rather of attention or impulse control, and were discussed in Chapter 8.)

The rate at which these drugs were prescribed to youth tripled between 1987 and 1996 (Zito et al., 2003) and has continued to climb since then, both in the United States and in other countries. For example, in a large-scale study of seven countries (USA, Canada, Mexico, Brazil, Argentina, UK, Spain, Germany, France), changes in the rates that youth 18 and younger were prescribed psychotropic drugs between the years 2000 and 2002 were examined. The rates increased in each country, with the smallest increase being in Germany

(13%) and the largest in the UK (68%). The rate of increase in the United States was approximately 33% (Wong et al., 2004). Rates of medication for children 2 to 4 years of age are still low (about 1% in the United States), but these, too, increased three-fold over the last decade, mostly for stimulants but also for antidepressants (Zito et al., 2000).

Developmental Effects of Dealing with Stress

People face conflict that must be confronted every day, ranging from mild to life-threatening situations. Sometimes psychological or physical stress is temporary, or acute. At other times stress is constant, or chronic, such as a child living in a home where his or her parents are always fighting, or a child with a physical or mental disability that disrupts normal functioning. Although stress is inevitable in life, excessive stress, or an inability to deal with stress, can lead to emotional or adjustment problems, and this can begin in childhood.

The body deals with stress by activating a complex network of neural and biochemical responses designed to prepare the individual for challenges or threats (see Boyce & Ellis, 2005). One such response is the production of cortisol, one of several hormones and biochemicals associated with people's ability to regulate aspects of their physiology and behavior in response to stress. Cortisol influences a broad range of bodily functions, including (a) releasing energy; (b) immune activity; (c) mental activity, including attention and memory; (d) modification of neurons; (e) physical growth; and (f) reproductive hormones, including testosterone. In the short run, cortisol permits individuals to respond to changing and often unpredictable and uncontrollable events. In the long run, persistently high levels of cortisol, reflective of lack of social support or living in a constantly stressful environment, can impair cognition, delay sexual maturity, inhibit growth, damage important brain circuits, and result in poor psychological adjustment (Flinn, 2006).

One of the beauties of cortisol from the vantage point of a researcher is that it can be measured from saliva, making it easy to collect and analyze. Levels of cortisol vary over the course of the day and tend to increase as a result of physical exercise, but importantly, high or fluctuating levels of cortisol are generally associated with increased levels of psychological stress and ill health, although the relationship between these factors can be complicated.

Cortisol levels vary within children over different times of the day and among children in different living conditions. For instance, infants and toddlers in daycare showed increases in their cortisol levels during the day, whereas infants and toddlers who stayed at home showed decreases (Watamura et al., 2003). Children living in stressful environments tend to have higher cortisol levels than children living

cortisol One of several hormones and biochemicals associated with people's ability to regulate aspects of their physiology and behavior in response to stress.

in less-stressful conditions (Chen, Cohen, & Miller, 2010). For example, 20- to 60-month-old foster-care children who had experienced inadequate care early in life displayed atypical patterns of changes in cortisol over the course of the day (Dozier et al., 2006). In particular, they showed less of a decline in cortisol levels from morning to night than did nonfoster children. These findings suggest that the early care that foster children received may have interfered with their ability to regulate their neuroendocrine functioning, pointing to the importance of a child's attachment to his or her caretaker (see Chapter 12).

In other research, cortisol levels in 6- to 12-year-old children adopted 6 years earlier from Romanian orphanages were compared with early-adopted Canadian-born children (Gunnar et al., 2001). The Romanian children, who had experienced extreme deprivation early in life, had substantially higher levels of cortisol than the other children did, and levels were greater the longer the children had been in the orphanage.

Not all children react to stress in the same way. For example, although the well-known fight-or-flight response reflects how many animals, including humans, react to stressful and potentially harmful situations, it is more exaggerated in males than females. In fact, females' immediate reaction to stressful situations has been described as "tend and befriend," in which they display nurturing behavior aimed at protecting themselves and possibly their offspring and creating or maintaining social networks (Taylor et al., 2000). This difference likely evolved in part because of females' greater role in childcare, necessary for the survival of an offspring dependent on adult care for an extended period. Early experiences with stress may also interact with individual differences in children's personalities to produce different reactions to stress. These possibilities are explored in Box 11.2.

Emotions regulate our interactions with others and with the physical world, serving as a compass that orients us toward certain behaviors. We approach some people and situations with great trepidation and others with great anticipation. We feel angry when we do not get our way, happy when we do, proud when we accomplish some worthy task, and ashamed when we get caught with our hand in the cookie jar. Emotions help us to care about other people, to care what other people think or feel about us, and to direct our behavior toward some contexts and people and away from others. Emotions and our control over them develop, affecting social relationships as they do as well as responses to the many successes and failures children experience in the course of growing up.

There are also individual differences in emotional expression. Some children from early in infancy seem better able than other children to regulate their emotions and behavior; some are more volatile, responding quickly and intensely to distress, whereas others respond to negative events in a more muted fashion. Relatively stable differences in how people interpret and respond to events reflect what we typically call personality, and in infancy temperament.

The Development of Temperament

Generally speaking, temperament is the term that developmental psychologists use to refer to personality in infants and young children. The description of the two bothers, Jeremy and Mark, that opened this chapter reflects boys with different temperaments. Jerome Kagan (2003, pp. 7–8) defines temperament as "stable profiles of mood and behavior with a biological foundation that emerge early in development," whereas Mary Rothbart and John Bates (2006, p. 100) define it as "the affective, activational and attentional core of personality." Although researchers often disagree on the details about what does and does not constitute temperament, most concur that temperament (1) has a clear biological, constitutional, or inherited basis; (2) is present and observable at birth or shortly thereafter; and (3) it is relatively stable over time. As we will see, however, the degree that research evidence confirms each of these assumptions varies.

The first major longitudinal study on temperament was the New York Longitudinal Study, carried out by Alexander Thomas and Stella Chess, whose purpose was to predict children's future psychological adjustments on the basis of their temperaments measured early in life. The study began in the 1950s and continued for nearly 30 years (Thomas, Chess, & Birch, 1968; Thomas & Chess, 1977; Chess & Thomas, 1990). Parents were extensively interviewed about their infants when they were 2 and 6 months of age and several times again later in childhood. From these interviews, Thomas and Chess identified nine basic dimensions of temperament (activity level, approach/withdrawal, intensity of reactions, threshold of responsiveness, adaptability, rhythmicity, quality of mood, attention span persistence, and distractibility), and from these were able to classify infants into three broad categories of temperament: easy, difficult, and slow-to-warm-up.

temperament The term that developmental psychologists use to refer to "personality" in infants and young children.

BOX 11.2 **big questions**

Can Stress Be Good for Children? Sometimes, and for Some Children

Are children's persistent experiences with stress always maladaptive? It has long been observed that rats and mice that experience an intermediate amount of stress in infancy, such as being handled by a human, are *less* fearful as adults and respond more adaptively in novel situations than animals that do not experience stress in infancy (Denenberg et al., 1967; Meaney et al., 1991). Might the same be true for humans? In reviewing the relationship between early stress and psychological adjustment in children, the British developmental psychologist Michael Rutter (1987, p. 326) proposed that "inoculation against stress may be best provided by controlled exposure to stress in circumstances favorable to successful coping or adaptation." In other words, some stress early in life, in potentially controllable contexts, can "inoculate" children from the negative effects of stress later in life.

Perhaps more controversial is the idea that early experience with stress interacts with individual differences in aspects of children's personalities, sometimes producing adaptive long-term outcomes and sometimes producing maladaptive long-term outcomes, depending on the quality of environment children live in. Bruce Ellis, Thomas Boyce, and their colleagues (Boyce & Ellis, 2005; Ellis & Boyce, 2005; 2008; Ellis, Essex, & Boyce, 2005; Ellis, Jackson, & Boyce, 2006) proposed that individual differences in children's **biological sensitivity to context** is an important factor in determining children's long-term reactions to stress. Both genetic dispositions and early experience influence how readily young organisms respond to events in the environment (that is, how sensitive they are to context), which in turn

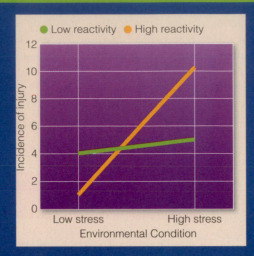

Incidence of injuries in low- and high-stress environments for rhesus monkeys classified as low- and high-reactivity. Monkeys that were highly sensitive to context had the most injuries in the high-stress environment and the fewest injuries in the low-stress environment. SOURCE: Adapted from Boyce, W. T., O'Neill-Wagner, P., Price, C. S., Haines, M., & Suomi, S. J. (1998). Crowding stress and violent injuries among behaviorally inhibited rhesus macaques. *Health Psychology,* **17, 285–289.**
....

affects their long-term reactions to stress. Some individuals who are biologically sensitive to changes in the environment may gain special benefits or experience special deficits from extreme environments, relative to less-sensitive (and more stable) individuals.

For example, research by Boyce and his colleagues (1998) measured biological reactivity to novel experiences in a troop of rhesus monkeys. Some monkeys were highly reactive to novel experiences, showing elevated cortisol levels, whereas others were less reactive. These monkeys lived in a 5-acre, wooded enclosure at the National Institute of Mental Health Primate Center.

This was a low-stress environment for the monkeys, and an examination of injuries over the course of a year indicated slightly more injuries for animals classified as low in reactivity than those classified as high in reactivity. The monkeys then experienced a highly stressful period of confinement to a 1,000-square-foot building. The rate in injuries between the high- and low-stress environments did not vary for the monkeys classified as low in biological reactivity. However, as can be seen in the Figure, rates of injuries skyrocketed for the high-reactive monkeys in the stressful environment. Whereas these monkeys had the lowest rate of injuries in the low-stress environment, they had the highest rate in the high-stress environment.

Are there similar effects with human children? In a study similar in logic to the one described with high- and low-reactive rhesus monkeys, Boyce and his colleagues (1995) measured the incidence of respiratory infections in 3- to 5-year-old children rated either low or high on the basis of cardiovascular and immunologic reactivity. The incidence of respiratory infection for low-reactive children was about the same regardless if they came from low- or high-stress homes (a little less than three infections per 3-month period) (see also Obradović et al., 2010). In contrast, high-reactive children had the lowest incidence of infections if they came from low-stress homes (slightly over two infections per 3-month period), but the highest rate if they came from high-stress homes (about 3.5 infections per 3-month period). Other work with children has shown that highly fearful and anxious children are more influenced by parental behavior (for example, maternal style of discipline) than less-anxious or aver-

biological sensitivity to context Degree to which individuals are biologically sensitive to environmental contexts.

easy babies Infants described as having regular patterns of eating, sleeping, and toileting; they easily adjust to new situations and have a generally positive mood; they are eager to approach objects and people, and react to events with low to moderate levels of intensity.

difficult babies Infants described as being unpredictable, having generally negative moods, difficulty adjusting to new situations, and react to events with high levels of intensity.

Easy babies (40% of the sample) were described as children with regular patterns of eating, sleeping, and toileting; they easily adjusted to new situations and had a generally positive mood; they were eager to approach objects and people, and they reacted to events with low to moderate levels of intensity. **Difficult babies** (10% of the sample) were described as children who behaved just the opposite of easy babies: their bodily functions were unpredictable; they had generally negative moods, difficulty adjusting to new situations,

Some monkeys fared equally well in both spacious, low-stress environments and restricted, high-stress environments, whereas others did best in low-stress and worst in high-stress environments. Might this be true of children, too? Might some children be like these monkeys—some being "orchid children," faring best in the most supportive environments and worst in the most stressful ones, and others being "dandelion children," relatively resilient to the effects of a stressful environment?

age children (Gilissen et al., 2008; Kochanska, 1993), as are infants with difficult temperaments (Stright, Gallagher, & Kelly, 2008; see Belsky, 2005; Belsky & Pluess, 2009).

Based on these and related studies, Jay Belsky (2000, 2005; Belsky et al., 2007) proposed that some children, namely those with anxious, fearful, or difficult dispositions, are more sensitive than others to individual differences in parenting. When environments are unpredictable, children who are easily able to adapt to a wide range of contexts (that is, who are highly responsive to differences in parenting behavior) will be able to adjust to novel, often less-than-optimal,

environments (for example, father absence, insensitive parenting). They will also do particularly well in enriched environments, those providing better-than-average support, resources, and opportunities. Other children, however, are more stable and less influenced by extreme environments. Parents can hedge their bets, so to speak, by producing both types of children, some who will be receptive to change and others who will thrive in the expected environment.

Ellis and Boyce (2008) note that the Swedes have the term *maskrosbarn*, or "dandelion child," to describe children who can survive and often thrive in any environment.

Like dandelions, which grow back repeatedly after being mowed down, these resilient children manage to do well in just about any environment. They also have the term *orkidebarn*, or "orchid child," to describe delicate children who flourish when given tender loving care, but who wilt if they are ignored or suffer some setbacks. Children are not all created equal, and how they are disposed to respond to stress may have a genetic basis to it that interacts with the broader environment in not-so-obvious ways.

and reacted to events with high levels of intensity. Finally, **slow-to-warm-up babies** (15% of the sample) were described as infants with a slow pattern of reaction; they had a difficult time adapting to new situations, showed a tendency to withdraw in novel situations, and were generally low in activity. In many ways, slow-to-warm-up babies were like difficult babies, although they became easier as they grew older. It is worth noting that 35% of the sample could not be classified into one of these three groups.

An important part of this study was examining what happened to these babies as they left infancy and entered childhood. Thomas and Chess noted that easy babies (now easy children) adjusted better and had fewer problems in school than did slow-to-warm-up children and especially difficult children. However, only so much could be predicted

> **slow-to-warm-up babies** Infants described as having a slow pattern of reaction; they have a difficult time adapting to new situations, show a tendency to withdraw in novel situations, and are generally low in activity.

table 11.4 Dimensions of Temperament in Infancy

Broad factors represent the three basic dimensions of temperament proposed by Rothbart and colleagues, with the orienting/regulation dimension becoming effortful control in early childhood. Narrow dimensions identify the different elements measured through different subscales, on whose basis broad dimensions were inferred.

Broad Factors	Narrow Dimensions	
Negative emotionality	Fear	Sadness
	Frustration/irritability	Falling reactivity
Surgency/extraversion	Approach	Smiling and laughter
	Vocal reactivity	Activity level
	High-intensity pleasure	Perceptual sensitivity
Orienting/regulation	Low-intensity pleasure	Cuddliness
(effortful control)	Duration of orienting	Soothability

SOURCE: Adapted from Rothbart, M. K. & Bates, J. E. (2006). Temperament. In N. Eisenberg, W. Damon, & R. M. Lerner (Eds.), *Handbook of Child Psychology: Vol. 3, Social, emotional, and personality development* (6th ed., pp. 99–166). Hoboken, New Jersey, p. 104.

by temperament. Temperament interacted with a child's immediate environment, and this interaction determined psychological adjustment. So, for example, a "difficult baby" reared by parents who were attentive and supportive could eventually be well adjusted, and, on the contrary, an "easy baby" growing up with rigid or inconsistent parents could become a poorly adjusted child. Thomas and Chess referred to this degree of compatibility between the individual's temperament and his or her social environment as "goodness-of-fit."

Following the initial publications from the New York Longitudinal Study, there was increased research exploring issues related to temperament in infants and children, which continues today, with different research teams identifying different dimensions of temperament. Some researchers focus on specific aspects of temperament and their development. For example, over the last 25 years, Jerome Kagan, Nancy Snidman, and their colleagues (Kagan, 1989, 1994, 2003; Kagan, Reznick, & Snidman, 1987; Kagan & Snidman, 2004; Kagan et al., 2007) examined the distinction between high-reactive and low-reactive infants, and inhibited and uninhibited children, based on children's reactions toward unfamiliar people, objects, and events. High-reactive children show vigorous motor activity and distress in response to unfamiliar stimuli when they are 4 months old. About 20% of children are high reactive. In their second year, these children tend to become shy, timid, and fearful in response to unfamiliar events. About one-third of high-reactive children become very fearful at that time and are called *inhibited*.

In contrast, low-reactive children show low levels of motor activity and irritability when they are 4 months old. About 40% of children are low reactive. These children tend to become sociable and fearless when they are about 2 years old, and, if minimally fearful, they are called *unin-hibited*. About one-third of the low-reactive children become uninhibited. It is worth noting that although Kagan and Snidman argue that clear signs of stable temperaments are evident shortly after birth and rooted in biology, they recognize the relevance of environment in temperament development. As Kagan points out, temperament is not destiny. Moreover, individual differences in temperament may fit better in some cultural contexts than others, as is discussed in Box 11.3.

Perhaps the most influential model of temperament today is that of Mary Rothbart and her colleagues (Rothbart, 2007; Rothbart & Bates, 1998, 2006; Rothbart & Hwang, 2005), which reduces temperament to three broad dimensions: *negative emotionality, surgency/extraversion*, and *orienting/regulation* (see Table 11.4). According to Rothbart, this three-dimensional structure of temperament, on the one hand, shows strong similarities with the structure of temperament and its individual differences found in other animals (Gosling & John, 1999), and, on the other hand, is related to three of the five personality factors described in the Five Factor Model of personality (Extraversion, Neuroticism, and Conscientiousness), which is discussed later in this chapter.

Negative emotionality is linked to anger/irritability, fearfulness, and sadness. In childhood, negative emotionality is also reflected in shyness and a resistance to control. Surgency, or extraversion, is related to positive affect and activity, and is reflected in high activity level, smiling and laughter, and high-intensity expression of pleasure. Orienting/regulation is associated with effortful control in early childhood, which is linked to the capacity to inhibit a dominant response and reorient attention to another goal. In childhood, effortful control is related to emotional self-regulation discussed earlier in this chapter. In addition to being able to regulate one's emotions, effort-

BOX 11.3 socioculturally speaking

Cultural Context and Temperament

We should likely not be surprised that temperamental characteristics measured early in life are predictive of behavior or personality later in life. It is not that early dispositions *cause* later behavior, but that these dimensions of temperament are relatively stable over time. This does not mean that temperament or personality does not develop or that the experiences of individuals over time do not affect children's personalities. In fact, although most theorists believe that temperament and personality are genetically based, most argue that they develop and are affected by context and cultural environments.

With respect to culture and temperament, Jerome Kagan (Kagan & Snidman, 2004; Kagan & Fox, 2006) points out the different developmental paths that a high-reactive trait can take for children from an individualistic society like the United States, where uncertainty, competition, and dealing with strangers is fairly common, and in an Asian society like Japan or China, where social groups are more important than individuals, and accordingly, the social structure provides a source of certainty and stability to children. Recall that Kagan defined high-reactive children as those who respond quickly to environmental change in terms of physiological measures such as heart rate and cortisol. They are sensitive to variations in the envi-

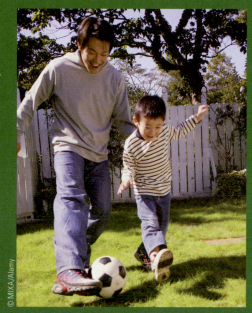

In Japan there is a style for interacting with nonintimates, called *tatemae*, and another for interacting with family and friends, called *honne*. High-reactive Japanese children, who are sensitive to contextual differences, adjust better than low-reactive children to different social environments. The opposite is true for American children, who live in a society with less social structure than the Japanese.

ronment, and this often translates into an inhibited personality type.

According to Kagan, in Japan, parents teach their children that there are two styles

of social behavior: one when dealing with nonintimates, called *tatemae*, and one when dealing with family and friends, called *honne*. High-reactive but shy Japanese children are sensitive to contextual differences, making it easy for them to determine how to behave in various situations. Low-reactive Japanese children, however, are not as sensitive to contextual differences, making it more likely that they will behave improperly—that is, mistake a *tatemae* situation for a *honne* situation. The reverse is likely to happen in the United States, Kagan claims. Here, high-reactive and shy children do not have the reliable social structure to guide their behavior that Japanese children do. Moreover, low-reactive and uninhibited children in an individualistic society, "enjoy the excitement of risk and meeting new people, and are more likely to bridle in a society where deviance is punished" (Kagan & Snidman, 2004, pp. 236, 237).

In other words, the temperamental trait is the same, but its implementation and consequences for children's development might be quite different, depending on their cultural setting. As might be expected, relationships between temperament and personality (and its development) and proximal and distal environments (for example, cultural or social differences) are bidirectional.

---

ful control is necessary for focused attention and is involved in tasks requiring *executive function*, processes involved in controlling attention and aspects of information processing (Posner, Rothbart, & Sheese, 2007; see Chapter 8).

A recent meta-analysis (a study analyzing the result of many different studies on a single topic) examining studies involving children between the ages of 3 months to 13 years reported significant gender differences in some aspects of temperament (Else-Quest et al., 2006). A large difference was found in effortful control, favoring girls, consistent with the greater incidence of externalizing disorders in boys discussed earlier in this chapter (Rutter & Garmezy, 1983). In contrast, boys displayed greater surgency than girls, consistent with their greater physical activity and involvement in rough-and-tumble play (see Chapter 14). No consistent gender differences were noted for negative affectivity.

A late temperament acquisition is effortful control, or self-regulation. Effortful control is important for the development of socialization, as well as the development of secondary emotions such as empathy or shame. The relevance of self-control for socialization is illustrated in a study that assessed 9-month-olds' abilities to delay

negative emotionality A dimension of temperament linked to anger/irritability, fearfulness, and sadness.

surgency (or extraversion) A dimension of temperament related to positive affect and activity, reflected in high activity level, smiling and laughter, and high-intensity expression of pleasure.

orienting/regulation A dimension of temperament that is associated with effortful control in early childhood, which is linked to the capacity to inhibit a dominant response and reorient attention to another goal.

effortful control In temperament theory, the ability to regulate one's emotions; effortful control is necessary for focused attention and is involved in tasks requiring *executive function*, processes involved in regulating attention and aspects of information processing.

gratification by avoiding touching a forbidden toy (Kochanska, Murray, & Harlan, 2000). Researchers then gave an extensive battery of self-control tasks to these same children at 22 and again at 33 months of age. For example, children were given a series of tasks in which they had to delay a desired response (wait until an experimenter rings a bell before getting an M&M that is in front of them under a transparent cup), walk a line slowly, or take turns with an experimenter building a tower of blocks. The researchers reported that children's self-regulation on these tasks improved between 22 and 33 months, was relatively stable within individual children over this time, and was greater for girls than for boys. They also reported that effortful control at both 22 and 33 months was related to children's regulation of their anger, suggesting an important role for self-control on social development. What is also interesting is that children's ability to delay gratification when they were 9 months old predicted their performance on the effortful-control tasks at 22 and 33 months of age.

The delay-of-gratification tasks used by Kochanska and her colleagues are variants of tasks used in a series of experiments in the 1970s by Walter Mischel (1983). In those studies, preschool children (average age = 4 years, 4 months) and an experimenter sat at a table with a bell and two treats, one of which the child could (eventually) have. In some experiments, this was one versus two marshmallows. Children were first asked which treat they would prefer, which in the case of the marshmallows was always two. Children were then told that the experimenter had to leave the room for a short while, and that "if you wait until I come back by myself then you can have this one [two marshmallows]. If you don't want to wait you can ring the bell and bring me back any time you want to. But if you ring the bell then you can't have this one [two marshmallows], but you can have that one [one marshmallow]" (Shoda, Mischel, & Peake, 1990, p. 980). The experimenter left the room and waited for the child to ring the bell or until a specified time had elapsed, usually about 15 minutes. Many of the children who participated in this study were seen again as adolescents (Eigsti et al., 2006; Shoda et al. 1990) and once again in their early thirties (Ayduck et al., 2000). The longer 4-year-olds were willing to wait before taking their treat, the better they were able to concentrate and deal with stress, and the higher were their SAT scores and school grades as teenagers. Interestingly, these simple latency measures taken at 4 years of age also predicted self-regulating abilities nearly 30 years later.

One must be cautious about making too much from a finding based on 4-year-olds' love of marshmallows and the number of seconds they will wait before getting their prize. But the fact that this simple measure was found to predict important aspects of self-control and self-regulation years later suggests that it taps a dimension that is relatively stable over time and influences significant social, emotional, and intellectual aspects of modern life.

The Development of Personality

Everyone knows what personality is. Everyone has one (even those people we say do not—they just do not have very exciting ones). But defining it precisely and differentiating it from temperament can be a bit tricky. Temperament, to most people, likely means almost the same thing as personality. What is the difference between the two, and what is the relevance of these concepts for child and adolescent development?

Like temperament, **personality** is defined as reliable behavioral traits that describe how individuals interact with their world, again emphasizing that it is biologically based, observable early in life, and stable over time. But personality is generally viewed as extending beyond temperament, including, according to Rothbart and Bates (2006, p. 100), "the content of thought, skills, habits, values, defenses, morals, beliefs, and social cognition." Similarly, Judith Harris (2005, p. 246) defined personality as "the development during childhood of chronic patterns of behavior (along with their cognitive and emotional concomitants) that differ from one individual to another. Some individuals are chronically more outgoing, or more aggressive, or more rule-abiding than others." From this perspective, temperament reflects traits that are constitutionally based and that preverbal infants can possess (as well as college students and their professors), whereas personality includes temperament but also includes higher-order cognitions and societal influences.

The concept of personality may seem to be incompatible with the concept of development. After all, personality refers to relatively stable characteristics of thinking and behaving, whereas development refers to change over time. How can something be both stable over time and changing simultaneously? One thing to keep in mind is that personality is only *relatively* stable over time and situations. As we will see, test-retest correla-

personality Reliable behavioral traits that describe how individuals interact with their world, emphasizing that it is biologically based, observable early in life, and stable over time.

tions of assessments of personality increase with age. Moreover, how a person behaves is influenced as much by the context as by any supposed personality trait (Mischel, 1973; Mischel, Shoda, & Mendoza-Denton, 2002). For example, even gregarious children tend to act in a restrained way when they are in a library, whereas inhibited children are likely to be at least somewhat outgoing at a party among friends. Furthermore, the ability to regulate one's behavior as a function of both one's feelings and the situation changes with age. Thus, personality should not be thought of as something that typifies a child in all situations and for all times, but rather as relatively stable characteristics that affect how children interpret and respond to specific situations that may very well change over time.

As an example of how characteristics of the person interact with the situation to produce behavior, consider a study that examined the behavior of children attending a six-week residential summer camp (Shoda, Mischel, & Wright, 1994). A variety of children's behavior (verbal aggression, withdrawal, friendly behavior, prosocial behavior) was observed as a function of five different psychological settings (teased, provoked, or threatened by peer; warned by adult; punished by adult; praised by adult; approached socially by peer). Would children behave similarly in different contexts (for example, show high levels of aggression when teased, warned or punished), and would they behave similarly in the same contexts at different times (for example, early in the summer versus later in the summer)? The answers to these questions were a tentative "yes," with different children showing different patterns and degrees of stability over time.

Figure 11.5 shows the level of aggression for two children at two different times (T1 and T2) for each of the five psychological settings observed (from Mischel & Shoda, 1995). Levels of aggression are presented as z scores, with higher values reflecting higher levels of aggression compared to other children and lower levels reflecting lower levels of aggression. As you can see, Child #9 displayed higher-than-average levels of aggression when warned by adults, but lower-than-average levels when teased by peers and displayed this same pattern of behavior both times. In contrast, Child #28 showed higher levels of aggression when approached socially by a peer but not when warned or punished by an adult. Again, this child's pattern of behavior was similar for the two observation periods, although not quite as stable across time as that of Child #9. Clearly, the situation dictated to a large extent how children would behave, but different children displayed different patterns of reactions to the situations, which were relatively stable over the course of the summer camp.

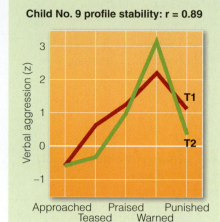
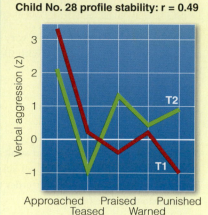

Child No. 9 profile stability: r = 0.89

Child No. 28 profile stability: r = 0.49

Although child psychologists in the 20th century often spoke of "personality development," their work was typically distinct from that of researchers who studied personality in adults. Within the past two decades, developmental psychologists began looking at children's personalities using some of the same concepts that psychologists studying adults use. The most important innovation in personality theory over the past 20 years has been the development of the **Five Factor Model** of personality (Costa & McCrae, 1988; McCrae & Costa, 1999), often referred to as *the Big Five*.

The Five Factor Model

The Five Factor Model describes human personality in terms of five core traits (see Table 11.5; see thorough discussions in Caspi, Roberts, & Shiner, 2005; Caspi & Shiner, 2006). The first factor of personality is **Extraversion**, which focuses on how gregarious, cheerful, energetic, and withdrawn (in the reverse direction) individuals are. The second factor is **Neuroticism**, which focuses on how afraid, touchy, tearful, and steady (in the reverse direction) individuals are. The third factor is **Conscientiousness**. Conscientious individuals are diligent, planful, careful, and focused, whereas those low in this trait are irresponsible, unreliable, careless, and distractible. The fourth factor is **Agreeableness**. Agreeable individuals are cooperative,

FIGURE 11.5 Consistency of aggression across contexts. Patterns of aggressive responses for two children as a function of psychological setting and time.
These two children showed different patterns of aggressive responses to different situations, indicating both the impact that context can have on behavior, but also the consistency with which individual children react to similar situations at different times. SOURCE: From Mischel, W., & Shoda, Y. (1995). A cognitive-affective system theory of personality: Reconceptualizing situations, dispositions, dynamics, and invariance in personality structure. *Psychological Review, 102*, p. 249. Reprinted by permission.

Five Factor Model A model that describes human personality in terms of five core traits: *extraversion, neuroticism, conscientiousness, agreeableness,* and *openness-to-experience.*

Extraversion Factor in the Five Factor Model that focuses on how gregarious, cheerful, energetic, and withdrawn (in the reverse direction) individuals are.

Neuroticism Factor in the Five Factor Model that focuses on how afraid, touchy, tearful, and steady (in the reverse direction) individuals are.

Conscientiousness Factor in the Five Factor Model. Conscientious individuals are diligent, planful, careful, and focused, whereas those low in this trait are irresponsible, unreliable, careless, and distractible.

Agreeableness Factor in the Five Factor Model. Agreeable individuals are cooperative, considerate, empathetic, generous, polite, and kind, whereas disagreeable individuals are aggressive, rude, spiteful, stubborn, cynical, and manipulative.

table 11.5 The Five Factor Model of Personality: Description and Some Lower-order Traits

Extraversion: Children and adults vary in their tendencies to be vigorously, actively, and surgently involved with the world around them. It encompasses at least four lower-order traits:

1. Social inhibition or shyness
2. Sociability
3. Dominance
4. Energy/activity level

Neuroticism: Just as children and adults vary in their predisposition toward positive emotions, they vary in their susceptibility to negative emotions. It encompasses at least two lower-order traits:

1. Anxious (or fearful) distress
2. Irritable distress

Conscientiousness: Children and adults vary widely in their capacities for behavioral and cognitive control. It encompasses at least six lower-order traits:

1. Self-control
2. Attention
3. Achievement motivation
4. Orderliness
5. Responsibility
6. Conventionality

Agreeableness: Agreeableness includes a variety of traits that foster congenial relationships with others. It encompasses at least three lower-order traits:

1. Antagonism
2. Prosocial tendencies
3. Cynicism/alienation

Openness-to-Experience: Openness-to-Experience is the most debated and least understood of the Big Five traits. It encompasses at least two lower-order traits:

1. Openness
2. Intellect

SOURCE: Adapted from Caspi, A., Roberts, B. W., & Shiner, R. (2005). Personality development. *Annual Review of Psychology, 56,* 453–484.

considerate, empathetic, generous, polite, and kind, whereas disagreeable individuals are aggressive, rude, spiteful, stubborn, cynical, and manipulative. The fifth factor, **Openness-to-Experience**, is the least understood and most debated factor. It focuses on how original, creative, aesthetically sensitive, knowledgeable, and curious individuals are. Personality in adults is usually measured through personality tests consisting of a series of self-descriptive adjectives that correspond to the different personality dimensions (Costa & McCrae, 1992; John, Donahue, & Kentle, 1991).

One way of thinking about how the Five Factor Model of personality influences people is to compare human behavior to the quality of a sound system. The sound (or behavior) that is produced is shaped by the volume (Extraversion), the treble versus bass scales (Neuroticism), the balance of

Openness-to-Experience Factor in the Five Factor Model that focuses on how original, creative, aesthetically sensitive, knowledgeable, and curious individuals are.

the headphones (Conscientiousness), the surround-sound effects (Agreeableness), and the different styles of music that are played—for example, classical, jazz, pop, rock, or heavy metal (Openness-to-Experience). Most Five Factor Model researchers believe that these factors are biologically grounded and cannot be easily modified. It is as if the factory settings for your stereo system were permanent, or only subject to small changes in volume, balance, and bass, for instance. Other researchers, however, believe that the settings for all of the factors are modifiable, as they are in a real stereo set, at least to a certain degree. These debates are sure to continue for some years to come, considering that the application of the Five Factor Model of personality to child development is recent. In fact, in the six editions since 1931 of the *Handbook of Child Psychology*, which is a sort of bible for researchers in the field of child and adolescent development, a chapter in personality has been included in only the two most recent editions (1998 and 2006).

Personality in Children

Although developmental research following this model is in its infancy relative to the amount of work that has been done with adults, some interesting and provocative findings have been found. Beyond temperament, personality in children has been related to children's age and gender, parental characteristics (for example, maternal depression), and sociocultural factors, such as social status (Rothbart & Hwang, 2005). It has also been related to a variety of psychological outcomes, such as school performance and social competence. In one longitudinal study, the personalities of 205 children were assessed when they were between 8 and 12 years old and again 10 and 20 years later (Shiner, 2000; Shiner et al., 2003). Most measures of childhood personality showed significant, but low, correlations with adult outcomes. For example, levels of Conscientiousness and Agreeableness when children were about 10 years old correlated with adult measures of academic attainment and rule abiding (versus antisocial behavior), ranging from .20 to .26 (that is, they accounted for between about 4% and 7% of individual differences).

Other research has reported relationships between measures of personality in childhood and internalizing and externalizing problems in adolescence. For example, low scores in childhood on both Agreeableness and Conscientiousness are moderately predictive of later juvenile delinquency (John et al., 1994; Robins et al., 1994). This can be seen in the results of a study contrasting the personality characteristics of 12- to 13-year-old delinquent and nondelinquent boys (John et al., 1994, see Figure 11.6). As you can see from the figure, the delinquent boys scored higher than their nondelinquent peers on the measure of Extraversion and much lower on the measures of Agreeableness, Conscientiousness, and Openness-to-Experience. Results from the same study showed that children diagnosed as having externalizing (acting-out) disorder scored particularly low on the personality measures of Agreeableness and Conscientiousness (see Figure 11.7).

Other research has shown that adolescents who are low on Conscientiousness are more apt to engage in health-risk behaviors, such as smoking, poor eating habits, reckless driving, and unprotected sex (see Caspi & Shiner, 2006; Hampson, 2008). For example, in an extensive review of research examining the relationship between Conscientiousness and health habits, for individuals younger than 30 years old, there were significant negative correlations ranging from .21 to .29 between Conscientiousness and a series of unhealthy habits (namely, tobacco use, alcohol abuse, drug use, risky driving, and violence). In other words, the lower a person's score on Conscientiousness, the more unhealthy habits he or she was likely to engage in (see Bogg & Roberts, 2004). Risk-taking will be examined in more detail later in this chapter.

How important is the study of personality to child and adolescent development? The answer you get to this question depends on whom you ask. As we have seen, personality measured in childhood is only moderately correlated with other measures of social and psychological functioning, such as academic performance, juvenile delinquency, and externalizing behavior, causing some to argue that the findings provide little valuable insight into development. Consider, for example, the findings of

Jim Varney/Photo Researchers, Inc.

Adolescents who score low on Conscientiousness are more apt to engage in health-risk behaviors, such as smoking, poor eating habits, reckless driving, and unprotected sex.

Howard Friedman and his colleagues (Friedman et al., 1995), who reported correlations between Conscientiousness and longevity ranging from .10 to .20. The more conscientious people were as children, the longer they tended to live. Although significant, correlations of this magnitude account for only between 1% and 4% of the individual differences in outcomes. How seriously should developmental

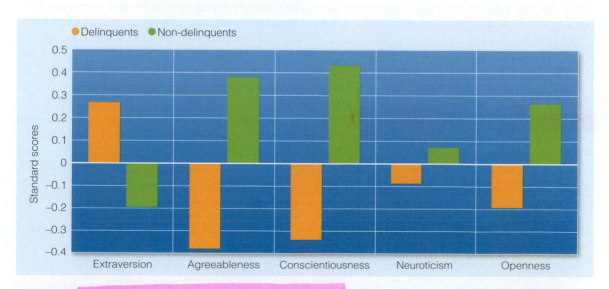

FIGURE 11.6 Relationship between personality and delinquency.
Mean differences (indicated in standard units) between delinquent and nondelinquent 12- to 13-year-old boys, on the basis of the Five Factor Model. As you can see, delinquent boys scored higher than nondelinquent boys on Extraversion and lower on Agreeableness, Conscientiousness, and Openness-to-Experience. SOURCE: From John, O. P., Caspi, A., Robins, R. W., Moffitt, T. E., & Stouthamer-Loeber, M. (1994). The "little five": Exploring the five-factor model of personality in adolescent boys. *Child Development, 65,* 160–178. Reprinted by permission.

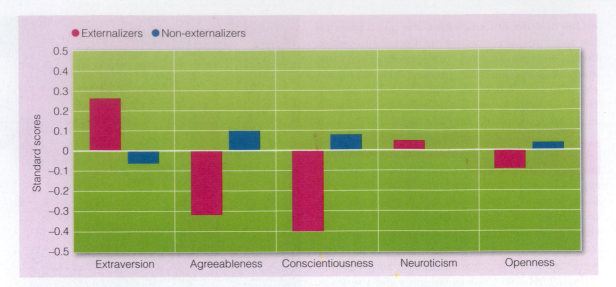

FIGURE 11.7 Relationship between personality and externalizing behavior (acting out).
Mean differences (indicated in standard units) between 12- to 13-year-old boys diagnosed as externalizers and non-externalizers on the basis of the Five Factor Model (John et al., 1994). As you can see, boys with externalizing disorder scored higher on the trait of Extraversion and lower on the traits of Agreeableness and Conscientiousness than boys without externalizing disorder. SOURCE: From John, O. P., Caspi, A., Robins, R. W., Moffitt, T. E., & Stouthamer-Loeber, M. (1994). The "little five": Exploring the five-factor model of personality in adolescent boys. *Child Development, 65,* 160–178. Reprinted by permission.

psychologists take these results given the fact that they account for so little of the differences in longevity? Yet, researchers of personality and personality development point out that, although small, these correlations are similar to those reported in most epidemiological and clinical studies (for instance, the association between the mineral density of the bones and the risk of hip fracture; Caspi & Shiner, 2006). For example, the effect of Conscientiousness on longevity found by Friedman and colleagues is larger in magnitude than the effect of chemotherapy on breast cancer survival and the 5-year survival rate following coronary bypass surgery (Bogg & Roberts, 2004). From this perspective, the findings from the developmental study of personality are of sufficient magnitude to warrant our attention (Caspi & Shiner, 2006). The debate of just how important such findings are will surely continue.

Risk-taking

By itself, **risk-taking** is neither an inherently positive nor negative characteristic, although its consequences can lead to either positive or negative outcomes for the individual or for other people (for example, a firefighter rescuing a family from a burning building, or reckless driving resulting

in the death or injury of innocent bystanders). As mentioned previously, risk-taking is associated with aspects of personality, including Conscientiousness and Openness-to-Experience in the Five Factor Model, and self-regulation more generally.

Some risk-taking is obviously a good thing. If children did not take risks, they would never leave their mothers' sides. Development involves children increasingly trying new tasks and venturing away from their safe zone into areas that are unfamiliar. In the words of Harriet Rheingold (1985), the process of development is to "render the novel familiar," and this involves taking some risks. But, in general, risk aversion is the safer and more adaptive route, with decision processes that support risk aversion generally being seen as more advanced than decision processes that support risk-taking (Reyna & Farley, 2006). Unreasonable risk-taking can result in injury, even death, although the successful risk taker can also achieve things that a more cautious child will not. In fact, risk-taking may be an effective tool in peer competition. Children who take risks and succeed are seen as leaders and may have an advantage on their more-tentative peers.

Sex Differences in Risk-taking

Boys of all ages are more apt to take risks than girls (Benenson, 2005). This difference is found in studies that examine children's self-reports, parents' reports, naturalistic observations, or emergency room records (Ginsburg & Miller, 1982; Kennedy

....
risk-taking Engaging in behaviors that can result in harm to the individual.

& Lipsitt, 1998). For example, researchers observed 430 3- to 11-year-old children at different locations at the San Antonio Zoo (Ginsburg & Miller, 1982). They watched children on the elephant ride, at the petting zoo, the burro exhibit, and along a steep embankment of a river. In each context, boys engaged in more risk-taking behaviors than girls, with overall risk-taking behaviors increasing with age.

Risk-taking has been interpreted in terms of *parental investment theory* (Trivers, 1972), which suggests that the sex that invests less in terms of parenting, which in most mammals, including humans, is males, competes more vigorously among themselves for access to the more investing sex, which in humans is females. Males, being the lesser-investing sex, compete with one another for status and to impress the girls. Taking risks and achieving success is one way boys (and men) impress other boys as well as girls (and women). Parental investment theory will be discussed in greater detail in Chapters 12 and 15.

Sex differences in risk-taking are seen at the extremes, where risky behavior results in death. One not-too-scientific way of assessing this is to examine the number of males and females who win Darwin Awards. A Darwin Award is given to individuals who perform "astounding misapplications of judgment" and thus eliminate themselves from the gene pool. Examples include things such as baking bullets in an oven, looking inside a rocket launcher, or having sex while piloting an airplane. In the fourth edition of the Darwin Awards (Northcutt, 2006), we counted 67 male recipients versus 11 female recipients, or 86% versus 14%. When honorable mentions were included—stupid risks that did not result in death—the rates changed only slightly—89% versus 11%.

Risk-taking in Adolescence

Risk-taking and risky decision-making increase into adolescence but then decrease into early adulthood (Boyer, 2006; Gardner & Steinberg, 2005). Risk-taking in adolescents has been of particular interest to psychologists (Arnett, 1992; Reyna & Farley, 2006), in part because the consequences of risky behavior in adolescents can be deadly. Sexually transmitted diseases, including HIV infection, accidents caused by reckless or drunken driving, and the use of potentially addictive drugs all increase in adolescence and can have long-term consequences on behavior and physical fitness. For instance, the rate of deaths caused by automobile accidents increases sharply for males during the late teens and continues to rise into the mid-twenties before decreasing. Females show a similar pattern, but despite the comparable number of male and female drivers, the death rate is two to three times higher for males at the same age (National Center for Health Statistics, 1999). One reason for this

Boys at all ages engage in more risky behavior than girls.

Image Source/Getty Images

age pattern is likely associated with experience driving (younger teens cannot drive and older adults have more driving experience). However, the substantially higher levels of automobile accidents for males than for females are consistent with males' overall greater levels of risky behavior relative to females.

Several researchers have noted that sensation- and novelty-seeking behaviors increase during adolescence (Spear, 2000; Steinberg, 2008, 2010; Steinberg et al., 2008). These behaviors may be evolutionarily adaptive at this time in life, as they promote the exploration of environments away from home, increasing independence, and perhaps helping to avoid inbreeding by getting exposure to potential mates outside of one's immediate group (Casey, Getz, & Galvan, 2008). Although sensation-seeking and risk-taking behaviors may be adaptive, they can also result in considerable harm. As noted, for modern adolescents, excessive drug and alcohol use, unsafe sex, and reckless driving all can have serious, sometimes deadly, consequences.

Factors Influencing Children's Risk-taking

Many factors beyond personality traits affect developmental and individual differences in risk-taking. For example, the increased risk observed in adolescence has been attributed to teenagers' difficulty with evaluating the potential costs of their actions (Arnett, 1992). This research is based primarily on the neo-Piagetian theories of David Elkind (1967; Elkind & Bowen, 1979), who proposed that adolescents experience extreme self-consciousness as they attempt to develop an adult identity. Elkind hypothesized that such egocentrism leads to what he called the **personal fable**, a belief in one's uniqueness and invulnerability. This is reflected in the often-reckless behavior of adolescents and the belief that bad things happen only to other people (for example, "I won't get pregnant," or "I can get off the tracks before the train gets here") (Arnett, 1992).

The risk-taking behavior that springs from adolescents' personal fables clearly has its drawbacks, but it might also have some adaptive value. For example, teenagers' belief in their invulnerability and their self-centeredness ensures that they will experiment with new ideas and generally behave more independently (Bjorklund & Green, 1992). Many of these experiences will be beneficial to adult functioning and might hasten entry into adult life. Many parents do not welcome such independence, for the negative consequences of much adolescent risk-taking are real, but the end result for most adolescents of their self-centeredness might be adaptive in the long run.

Another important factor in risk-taking behavior is peer pressure. In one study, children in grades 5 through 8 were asked about challenges they received from other children (Lewis & Lewis, 1984). The oldest children reported the most peer pressure to engage in risky behaviors. In fact, about half of the dares children received from other children involved placing themselves or other people in potential harm. For the seventh- and eighth-grade children, dares to boys more often involved engaging in acts of violence, whereas dares to girls were more likely to involve engaging in sexual activity.

One indication of the role of peer pressure on risky behavior is the association between risky behavior and having peers who also engage in such behavior (Jaccard, Blanton, & Dodge, 2005; Morgan & Grube, 1991). For example, in one study, researchers investigated sexual activity and binge drinking in a group of adolescents in grades 7 through 11 over a one-year period (Jaccard et al., 2005). They reported a small but significant influence of a best friend on risky behavior. Other factors, such as a youngster's relationship with his or her mother, were also related to risk-taking behavior, indicating, not surprisingly, that many factors influence adolescents' risk-taking.

As with other complex social behaviors, individual differences in risk-taking have been found to be related to specific genes, although in interaction with children's environment. For example, Gene Brody and his colleagues (2009)

demonstrated that a particular version of a gene that influences the regulation of the neurotransmitter serotonin was associated with increased risk-taking behavior (alcohol and marijuana use and sexual activity) in 11- and 12-year-old African American youth. However, children with this same "risk-prone" gene who participated in a family-based intervention program designed to promote effective parenting practices and self-regulation and coping skills showed the *lowest* level of risk-taking behavior. As we saw earlier in this chapter for depression (Caspi et al., 2003), and for antisocial behavior in Chapter 3 (Caspi et al., 2002), genes have their effects in interaction with environments, and "risk-prone" genes, in this case, can actually result in low levels of risk-taking in the right environment.

Although some people are more prone to take risks at any age, risk-taking is more than a personality trait. Males at every age are more likely to take risks than females, and the potential consequences of risk-taking increase, both the good and the bad, with age as children enter adolescence. Risk-taking is a good example of behavior that shows both change with age and stability over time. The types of risks children take change with age, but the tendency to engage in risky behavior shows some stability and correlates with personality traits. Some researchers have also pointed to age-related changes in aspects of psychobiological development, particularly changes in hormones and brain functioning, as important contributors to risk-taking in adolescence. Some of this research is examined in Box 11.4 (pp. 472–473).

The Heritability and Stability of Temperament and Personality

It is tempting to see temperament and personality, and even individual differences in risk-taking, as characteristics that are biologically based and in the genes; however, as we just saw in the research by Gene Brody and his colleagues (2009) concerning the relationship between specific genes and risk-taking, this is far too simplistic a view. Although aspects of infant temperament may relate to childhood personality, and aspects of childhood personality may relate to adult personality, the degree of prediction is far from perfect. Not all children show high degrees of stability of temperament/personality over time, and the relationship between personality characteristics and psychological functioning is typically moderate, at best.

personal fable A belief in one's uniqueness and invulnerability, which is an expression of adolescent egocentrism.

How Heritable, Early Emerging, and Stable Are Temperament and Personality?

Earlier in this chapter, we stated that temperament and personality were characterized as being biologically based and highly heritable, observed early in development, and stable over time. We believe that although most developmental psychologists would concur with this description in general, few would take an extreme position on these issues. We have seen, for instance, that one's culture and the immediate environment (one's parents, for example) influence temperament and personality and that they develop over time. In this section we take a closer look at these defining features of temperament and personality, evaluating the extent to which they are heritable, early emerging, and stable over time.

Heritability

Recall from Chapter 3 that heritability refers to the extent to which individual differences in some characteristic can be attributed to differences in genetics. If the heritability of a trait is .50, for example (which is about what it is for intelligence as measured by IQ), then 50% of differences in that trait within a population can be attributed to genetics. The other 50% are attributed to environment, gene x environment interactions, or measurement error. (Recall that the heritability statistic is not the same as a correlation, so a heritability of .60 is not the same as a correlation of .60; they are different statistics.) The heritability of a trait varies with environments. If all children grow up in exactly the same environment, heritability will be 1.0; all of the differences in a trait will be attributed to genetics, because there are no differences in environment. This is never the case for any psychological factor, or even for physical ones such as height. It is worth keeping in mind, however, that heritability is not a biological constant and can change if environmental conditions change substantially (for instance, from living in a society with substantial resources to one of extreme hardship), and it does not represent how much of any trait is inherited and how much is a result of environment. (Review discussion of heritability in Chapter 3.)

Concerning the heritability of personality, older studies, predating the advent of the Five Factor Model, reported that the correlation of identical twins was about .50, the correlation of fraternal twins was about .30 and that of nontwin siblings was about .20, and the correlation of unrelated people raised in the same household (adopted siblings, for example) was about .07 (Loehlin, 1985). These figures clearly point to a genetic influence on individual differences in personality, but not a huge one. If you recall from Chapter 3, one simple technique of computing heritability is to take the difference between the correlations of identical and nonidentical twins and multiply them by 2. In this case, the computation would be $(.50 - .30) \times 2 = .40$, meaning that about 40% of differences in personality could be attributed to genetics. More recent research examining the heritability of personality based on the Five Factor Model puts the figure at .50 (+/− .10) (Bouchard & Loehlin, 2001). This is similar to the heritability estimates obtained with the older measures and is also similar, although in most comparisons a bit lower, to the heritability found for IQ (see Chapter 3). These data suggest at least a moderate degree of genetic influence on personality, although there is plenty of room for the effects of environment.

Even though children around the world may have similar genetic disposition for a personality trait, how that trait is expressed may vary in different cultures.

BOX 11.4

the biopsychology of childhood

Hormones, Neurons, and Risk-taking in Adolescence

There are many reasons associated with increased risk-taking in adolescence, with psychobiological factors receiving considerable attention (see Boyer 2006; Casey et al., 2008; Spear, 2000). One obvious psychobiological factor that may contribute to increased risk-taking in adolescents is hormones. Sex hormones increase substantially during adolescence, and not surprisingly they are associated with greater interest in sex as well as risky sexual behavior (Halpern, Urdy, & Suchindran, 1998; Urdy, 1998). It would not be surprising then to find a relationship between testosterone level and risk-taking.

This was investigated in a sample of adolescents by Alan Booth and his colleagues (2003), who reported a relationship between testosterone levels and risk-taking behavior, but only for children who had poor parent-child relationships. Moreover, this relationship differed for boys and girls. For boys, testosterone levels were positively associated with risk-taking behaviors for children with poor parent-child relationships. There was no significant relationship between testosterone levels and risk-taking behavior for boys who had good relationships with their parents. The pattern was exactly opposite for girls: girls with *low* levels of testosterone showed greater risk-taking behavior when they had poor relationships with their parents. There were no significant relationships between testosterone levels and risk-taking for girls with good parent-child relationships. These data reflect the fact that hormonal influences on behavior interact with environmental factors, as well as a child's gender, illustrating the bidirectional nature of biologic and experiential factors over the course of development (see Chapter 2).

Others have suggested that changes in brain structure occurring during adolescence may have a greater impact than hormones on risk-taking (Casey et al., 2008; Spear, 2000). As noted in Chapter 4, major changes in brain organization occur in adolescence. Linda Spear (2000) reviewed some of these brain changes, which include the formation of new neural connections but also the relatively rapid loss of others. Most prominently affected are the frontal lobes. Frontal-lobe damage has been associated with impulsive behavior and thus risk-taking (Miller, 1992). The frontal lobes actually decrease in relative size during this time, and the organization of the frontal lobes, as reflected by neural imaging studies (Luna et al., 2001), also changes substantially.

Other maturationally paced factors are also associated with increased risk-taking in adolescence. For example, gamma-aminobutyric acid (GABA) is an excitatory neurotransmitter that decreases in prevalence in the frontal cortex during adolescence, while the neurotransmitter dopamine increases. Changes in the activation patterns of structures in the limbic system, including the amygdala, also change during the teen years. These structures are associated with emotional responding and responses to stressful situations (see Boyer, 2006; Spear, 2000). Changes in these brain structures and neurotransmitters are associated with novelty seeking and assessing the motivational value of stimuli, including potentially addicting drugs. According to Spear (2000, p. 113):

> Alterations in the incentive value attributed to stimuli could underlie many of the behavioral alterations seen in adolescence, increasing the importance of social reinforcement derived from peers and provoking the pursuit of new potentially rewarding stimuli, a quest that may

lead to increases in drug use and other risk-taking behaviors. Given the difference between adolescents and adults in functioning in these brain regions, it would be astonishing indeed if adolescents did *not* differ from adults in various aspects of their motivated behavior.

Lawrence Steinberg (2007, 2008) has posed the issue of adolescent risk-taking as reflecting a competition between two developing brain systems: the *socioemotional network*, located primarily in the limbic system, and the *cognitive-control network*, governed primarily by the frontal lobes (see Chapter 4). The socioemotional system becomes more active with the onset of puberty. In contrast, the cognitive-control system, which is related to planning, thinking ahead, and self-regulation, develops gradually over adolescence and into young adulthood. Under neutral conditions, adolescents are often able to make logical decisions as well as young adults do. However, under conditions of emotional or social arousal, or when in the presence of peers, Steinberg proposes that the socioemotional brain network becomes easily activated, overpowering the more rational cognitive-control network. Thus, adolescents are more likely to display risky behavior in the presence of peers than when performing alone, all in contrast to adults.

This last phenomenon is illustrated in a study assessing risk-taking of adolescents (13 to 16 years old), young adults (average age = 19 years), and adults (average age = 37 years) during a video driving game (Gardner & Steinberg, 2004). As can be seen in the accompanying figure, risk-taking (measured in terms of number of crashes) was comparable among the three groups when participants played the game alone. Risk was substantially greater for adolescents (and moderately greater for young adults) when

Early Emergence

Do temperamental dispositions and personality traits emerge early in development? It seems to depend on how one defines "early" and with which traits one is concerned. Some traits do seem to be present at birth or shortly thereafter, such as irritability and other variants of negative emotions. However, some of these dispositions are short lived. One of this book's author's parents relates that their oldest son was an irritable and difficult-to-soothe baby who permitted them little sleep.

This lasted for 3 months, when the baby's temperament seemed to change. Were the child's initial difficulties truly an expression of temperament, or perhaps only an undiagnosed case of colic? Based only on the description provided by his parents, one cannot know.

Moreover, temperament development is not independent of children's social environment and culture. For example, in a cross-cultural study performed in the United States and China (Ahadi, Rothbart, & Yi, 1993), American (but not Chinese)

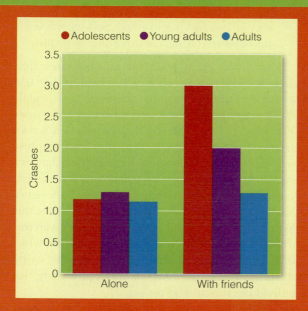

Adolescents take significantly more risks and are involved in more crashes in a video driving game when playing with friends than when playing alone. The effect is smaller for young adults and playing with friends has no effect on the driving of adults. SOURCE: Adapted from Steinberg, L., (2007). Risk taking in adolescence: New perspectives from brain and behavioral science. *Current Directions in Psychological Science,* **16, 55–59; based on data from Gardner & Steinberg, 2005.**

Death per 10 million trips for 16-, 17-, and 30- to 59-year-olds by number of passengers. SOURCE: Adapted from Chen, L-H., Baker, S.P., Braver, E.R., & Li, G. 2000. Carrying passengers as a risk factor for crashes fatal to 16- and 17-year-old drivers. *Journal of the American Medical Association,* **283, 1578–82.**

playing in the presence of friends. The presence of friends had no effect on risk-taking for adults. This pattern is consistent with actual driving statistics for vehicular deaths. Although adolescents are involved in proportionally more vehicle deaths per miles driven than are older adults, the death rate increases the more people (usually other teens) are in the vehicle (Chen et al., 2000). As can be seen from the second figure, the rate of vehicular deaths for 16- and 17-year-old drivers more than doubles when there are three or more passengers in the car relative to when teens drive alone. In contrast, there is no relationship between vehicular deaths and the number of passengers for older drivers.

It is trivial to say that children's developing brains are the cause of their risk-taking behaviors. However, species-typical patterns of brain and neurochemical (including hormonal) development appear to ready adolescents for seeking novel experiences, some of which may be viewed as risk-taking, at least from an adult's perspective. Substantial individual differences exist in how children respond to these normal changes in brain and physiological functioning. Moreover, although all typical brains may go through the same basic sequence of development, children begin life with (or develop very early) unique patterns of genetic and neuronal reactions to stress, novelty, and social stimulation in general. All of these factors interact to contribute to risk-taking behaviors in childhood and adolescence.

6- to 7-year-old children with high levels of effortful control exhibited lower levels of negative affectivity (correlation = −.28). In contrast, Chinese (but not American) children with high levels of effortful control exhibited lower levels of extraversion/surgency (correlation = −.25). This pattern may reflect cultural differences in what parents and others regard as desirable behaviors in children, with Americans emphasizing the importance of low levels of distress and Chinese frowning on high levels of outgoing behavior. In this sense, Rothbart (2007, p. 208) interestingly concludes that, "Basic biological processes of temperament appear to be shared across cultures, but outcomes vary depending on cultural values and the child's experiences."

Other aspects of temperament and personality do not emerge until later in life. For example, individual differences in effortful control are not evident until the end of the first year. Personality characteristics measured in the Five Factor Model emerge even later. For example, two of the components for the Extraversion dimension show different developmental paths. One component, "dominance," increases from adolescence through early middle age, whereas a second component, "sociability," increases in adolescence and then decreases in young adulthood through old age (Caspi et al., 2005).

Stability

Once a trait emerges, does it remain stable over time? Does an easy infant become an agreeable adult, and a fearful infant an adult who scores high on the Neuroticism scale of the Big Five? As with the issue of early emergence, it seems to depend on which trait one examines and the length of time between observations.

Avshalom Caspi and colleagues (Caspi & Shiner, 2006; Caspi, Roberts, & Shiner, 2005) identified two extreme positions with respect to the stability of personality. The traditional, or *essentialist*, position holds that stability should be high, beginning early in life, because temperament/personality is an essential and biologically based aspect of the individual and not much susceptible to environmental input. In contrast, advocates of the *radical contextualist* position insist on the importance of experiences and life transitions, suggesting that stability of these traits should be rather low.

A straightforward way of testing the validity of these two hypotheses is to assess the same people on the same traits over time. If the test-retest correlations are high (that is, if people who score high on a trait at one time score high on the same trait at another time), the trait is stable over time, consistent with the position of the essentialists. If, however, the correlations are low, suggesting that there is little stability of traits over time (that is, people do *not* maintain their rank order with respect to some personality trait at different measuring points), then the radical contextualists would declare victory.

You will probably not be surprised to learn that existing longitudinal studies based on the Five Factor Model and using test-retest correlations do not support either of these extreme views. A meta-analysis of such studies (Roberts & DelVecchio, 2000) arrived at four conclusions, which are sure to make no one from the extreme camps happy:

1. Stability estimates are moderate in magnitude, even from childhood to adulthood.
2. Stability increases with age. Test-retest correlations increased from .31 (9% of variance) across childhood to .54 (29%) during the college years, .64 (41%) at age 30, and then reached a plateau around .74 (55%) when measured between ages 50 and 70 years.
3. Stability decreases as the time interval between observations increases; that is, all else being equal, the longer the time between the two measurement points, the lower the correlation.
4. Stability does not vary markedly across the Big Five traits, either according to how personality is assessed (for example, self-reports versus observer ratings) or according to gender.

All in all, this meta-analysis indicates that there is moderate stability of personality (but not as high as with cognitive abilities), with stability increasing as people age, peaking some time after age 50. This evidence of stability, often across extended periods of time, is all the more impressive when one considers that the specific behaviors measured, and the way that personality is assessed, varies considerably with age. However, the level of stability is clearly in the moderate and not the high range. This should not be surprising given the research we have reviewed in this book showing that the experiences children have interact with their dispositions in dynamic ways, producing the individuals they are becoming.

So, is there a need to revise our original statement about the nature of temperament and personality? We think not. However, the emphasis must be made that temperament and personality are only *relatively* heritable, early emerging, and stable in comparison to other psychological characteristics, and less so than others (for example, intelligence as measured by IQ, see Chapter 3). Temperament and personality traits arise from within the child and interact within local contexts, within a specific culture, and they change over time; that is, they develop.

How Does Early Temperament and Personality Shape Later Personality?

If personality is not just a simple expression of genetically based dispositions, what then is the role of development? Avshalom Caspi and Rebecca Shiner (2006) addressed this issue and proposed six processes through which early personality and temperament might shape later personality in childhood (see Table 11.6). Caspi and Shiner's approach is similar to Sandra Scarr and Kathleen McCartney's (1983) genotype → environment theory, discussed in Chapter 3. For example, *environmental elicitation*, in which a child's temperament influences the way others treat him or her (an easy child will be treated differently than a difficult child) is similar to evocative genotype → environment effects in Scarr and McCartney's theory. Similarly, Caspi and Shiner's *environmental selection* process, in which children's temperament affects their choice of environments, is identical to

table 11.6 Processes through Which Early Temperament Shapes Personality and Later Development, Adaptation, and Psychopathology

Process	Definition	Example
Learning processes	Temperament shapes the child's experience of classical and operant condition.	Children high on Openness may find complex and novel stimuli to be reinforcing.
Environmental elicitation	Temperament shapes the response of adults and peers to the child.	Children high on Extraversion may attract peers to play with them.
Environmental construal	Temperament shapes the ways children interpret the environment and their experiences.	Children low on Agreeableness may interpret requests from adults as hostile impositions on their freedom.
Social and temporal comparisons	Temperament shapes the ways children evaluate themselves relative to others and to themselves across time.	Children high on Neuroticism may wrongly view themselves as inadequate relative to their peers.
Environmental selection	Temperament shapes children's choices about their everyday environment.	Children high on Conscientiousness may pursue challenging activities.
Environmental manipulation	Temperament shapes the ways that children alter, modify, and manipulate their environment.	Children high on Extraversion may actively persuade other children to choose them as leaders of school groups.

SOURCE: From Caspi, A., & Shiner, R. L. (2006). Personality development. In W. Damon & R. Lerner (Series Eds.) & N. Eisenberg (Vol. Ed.), *Handbook of child psychology, Vol. 3. Social, emotional, and personality development* (6th ed., pp. 300–365). New York: Wiley p. 326.

Scarr and McCartney's active genotype → environment effects. Caspi and Shiner go beyond Scarr and McCartney's earlier model, however, proposing more specific ways in which temperament and personality can affect children's experiences and thus shape their development. For instance, depending on a child's temperament, (1) some learning experiences will be more rewarding than others (*learning processes*); (2) some experiences will be interpreted differently (*environmental construal*); (3) self-evaluations will vary (*social and temporal comparisons*); and (4) the ways in which children attempt to shape their environments and people in them will also vary (*environmental manipulation*).

To some parents, their children's temperaments and personalities may seem fixed. "That's the way they are, and there's nothing I can do about it." Other parents may believe that children must be made to conform to certain expectations, regardless of whatever dispositions they bring into the world. To give some guidance to parents, Kagan and Snidman (2004, p. 33) provide the following suggestions, which we paraphrase here:

1. Acknowledge your children's temperamental biases, but do not assume that either your rearing practices or your child's willfulness are the only reasons for their behavior.
2. Acknowledge your children's malleability and capacity for change. An infant's biology does not determine what he or she will be 10 or 20 years later. Temperament is not destiny.

3. Accommodate parenting goals to children's own wishes. Rearing practices that take both parents' hopes and children's desires into account can be found if parents make the effort.

© David Young-Wolff/PhotoEdit

Characteristics of the child can evoke responses from people in his or her environment, thus shaping personality, but temperament is not destiny. How parents and others interact with children of any temperament can affect their development.

Discrete emotion theory holds that basic **emotions** are innate and associated with distinctive bodily and facial reactions, whereas the **functionalist perspective** emphasizes the universal and adaptive value of emotions. Evolutionary explanations focus either on the benefit that emotional expression has for communication between members of a species or on the survival value they provide for the individual.

Emotional expression of **primary emotions**, including interest, joy, anger, and sadness, among others, emerges during the first year, whereas **secondary**, or **self-conscious, emotions**, including shame, embarrassment, empathy, guilt, and pride, among others, require interpersonal awareness and do not emerge until the second year of life or later. The **endogenous smile** has been viewed as a precursor to joy, although **social smiling** is not unambiguously seen until about 3 months. There is evidence of **prepared learning** for some fears (of snakes, for instance), and other fears develop about the same time in most children (for example, fear of falling, of separation from caregiver, of strangers). **Emotional recognition** is seen even in newborns, reflected by **contagious crying** and neonatal imitation, although the ability to recognize emotions increases over infancy, as seen in **social referencing** and expressions of **empathy**. Children's **emotional understanding** also improves over infancy and into childhood.

Emotional self-regulation develops over infancy and through childhood. Mothers attempt to regulate their infants' emotions as reflected by their use of **infant-directed speech**. Maturation of brain areas associated with executive function play an important role in the development of emotional self-regulation.

Adolescence is no longer seen as a time of emotional "storm and stress," although adolescents experience, on average, more negative emotions than do children. Adolescents strive to achieve **emotional autonomy**, which can be fostered or hindered depending on their interactions with their parents.

The most common type of **externalizing problem** is **oppositional defiant disorder**, which predicts the more serious **conduct disorder**, both of which occur more frequently in boys, whereas **depression** is the most serious **internalizing problem**, which occurs more frequently in girls. Children who deal with chronic stress, which produces elevated levels of **cortisol**, sometimes experience health and psychological adjustment problems. However, individual differences in **biological sensitivity to context** can interact with early stress experiences and produce differential reactions to stress.

Temperament and **personality** refer to biologically based, early emerging, and stable moods and behaviors of individuals, with personality including higher-order cognitions and societal influences beyond temperament. The New York Longitudinal Study identified **easy babies**, **difficult babies**, and **slow-to-warm-up babies**, and these different temperaments predicted psychological characteristics later in childhood. Other researchers have classified temperament differently, with one taxonomy proposing the dimensions of **negative emotionality**, **surgency**, or **extraversion**, and **orienting/regulation** (including effortful control). Research has demonstrated that aspects of temperament predict later psychological characteristics, sometimes into adulthood.

The **Five Factor Model** of personality describes five core personality dimensions: **Extraversion**, **Neuroticism**, **Conscientiousness**, **Agreeableness**, and **Openness-to-Experience**. Like adults, measures of children's personality correlate moderately with many psychological outcomes. Personality development is influenced by environmental factors, such as parenting and culture, as well as how a child's genetic dispositions influence the experiences he or she has.

Risk-taking is more frequent in boys than girls at all ages. Risk-taking and risky decision making increase over childhood and into adolescence and decrease in early adulthood. Several factors influence risk-taking, including peer pressure and psychobiological development. According to Elkind, adolescents' increased self-consciousness leads to the **personal fable**, a belief in one's uniqueness and invulnerability.

Temperament and personality are moderately heritable, emerge relatively early depending on the particular trait, and are moderately stable, with stability increasing with age.

Key Terms and Concepts

emotion (p. 438)

discrete emotion theory (p. 440)

functionalist perspective (p. 440)

emotional expression (p. 441)

emotional recognition (p. 441)

emotional understanding (p. 441)

emotional self-regulation (p. 441)

primary emotions (p. 441)

secondary (self-conscious)
   emotions (p. 442)

endogenous smile (p. 444)

social smiling (p. 444)

prepared learning (p. 445)

empathy (p. 447)

contagious crying (p. 448)

social referencing (p. 449)

infant-directed speech (p. 453)

emotional autonomy (p. 455)

internalizing problems (p. 456)

externalizing problems (p. 456)

oppositional defiant disorder (p. 456)

conduct disorder (p. 456)

depression (p. 457)

cortisol (p. 458)

temperament (p. 459)

biological sensitivity to context (p. 460)

easy babies (p. 460)

difficult babies (p. 460)

slow-to-warm-up babies (p. 461)

negative emotionality (p. 463)

surgency, or extraversion (p. 463)

orienting/regulation (p. 463)

effortful control (p. 463)

personality (p. 464)

Five Factor Model (p. 465)

Extraversion (p. 465)

Neuroticism (p. 465)

Conscientiousness (p. 465)

Agreeableness (p. 465)

Openness-to-Experience (p. 466)

risk-taking (p. 468)

personal fable (p. 470)

Ask Yourself . . .

1. What do psychologists mean when they use the terms "emotion," "temperament," and "personality"?

2. Why are emotions considered so critical in human development, and how is the development of emotions related to other important aspects of child development?

3. In what important ways, if any, are the discrete emotion theory and the functionalistic perspective of emotions similar or different?

4. What four different aspects of emotion develop?

5. What are the typical developmental patterns of the four different aspects of emotions?

6. What are some of the significant emotional problems some children experience during childhood and adolescence?

7. What are the main components of temperament, and what do they reflect?

8. What are the main components of personality according to the "Five Factor Model"? What do we know about their development?

9. What do we know about the development of risk-taking in children and adolescents?

10. How heritable, early emerging, and stable are temperament and personality?

Exercises: Going Further

1. As a certified school psychologist, you are required to give a talk to a group of parents and elementary school teachers on the topic of "Understanding and Promoting Children's Emotional Development." What would be the script for your talk, and what would be the main points you would emphasize?

2. Peter is 11 years old and will be transferring from elementary to middle school. This worries his parents, who believe that adolescence in contemporary times is particularly difficult, associated with sudden and negative mood changes, as well as significant increases of risky behaviors (for instance, sex, delinquency, and substance abuse). What would you tell Peter's parents, based on what you've learned from reading this chapter?

3. Check the description of the *Five Factor Model* (pg. 465) and describe yourself in terms of the model's different dimensions. Later on, check the description of temperament traits (pg. 462) and ask your parents about your temperament when you were a child (for example, 5 years old). What would be your assessment about the development and stability of your temperament?

Suggested Readings

Classic Work

Darwin, C. (1872). *The expression of the emotions in man and animals.* **London: Murray.** You cannot get much more classic than this. Charles Darwin is of course known as the first scientist to present a coherent theory of evolution, but he was also the first to provide a serious account of emotions. The writing style of the Victorian-age Darwin is quite different from scientific writing today, and you will likely find many of the ideas presented by Darwin nearly 140 years ago surprisingly modern.

Thomas, A., Chess, S., & Birch, H. (1968). *Temperament and behavior disorders in children.* **New York: New York University Press.** Alexander Thomas and Stella Chess, with their colleague Herbert Birch, began the first longitudinal study on the consequences of infant temperament to later development. This was one of their first major publications to bring the topic of temperament in infants and children to a wider audience.

Scholarly Work

Saarni, C., Campos, J. J., Camras, L. A., & Witherington, D. (2006). Emotional development: Action, communication, and understanding. In W. Damon & R. M. Lerner (Gen. Eds.), *Handbook of Child Psychology* **(6th ed.), N. Eisenberg (Vol. Ed.), Vol. 3,** *Social, emotional, and personality development* **(pp. 226–299). New York: Wiley.** This is a thorough, up-to-date review of research on emotional development presented by scholars who have made important contributions to the field, primarily from the functionalist perspective.

Caspi, A., Roberts, B. W., & Shiner, R. I. (2005). Personality development: Stability and change. *Annual Review of Psychology,* **56, 453–484.** Avshalom Caspi and his colleagues present a relatively short (30-page) review of research and theory in personality development, including recent advances in behavioral genetics, the structure of children's personality following the Five Factor Model, and the results of longitudinal research.

Reading for Personal Interest

Damasio, A. (1994). *Descartes' error: Emotion, reason, and the human brain.* **New York: Putnam.** Leading neuroscientist Antonio Damasio presents a highly readable account of how the brain processes emotion and the intimate connection between emotion and thought. This goes to the heart of the mind-body relationship, which is at the heart of developmental psychology.

Kagan, J., & Snidman, N. (2004). *The long shadow of temperament.* **Cambridge, MA: Harvard University Press.** Jerome Kagan and Nancy Snidman present a concise and highly readable account of their 25-year longitudinal study of temperament, focusing on the dimension of inhibition. Readers will get an appreciation of the important theoretical issues, the history of the field, how this research is done, and the state of the art in temperament research.

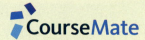

Cengage Learning's **Psychology CourseMate** for this text brings course concepts to life with interactive learning, study, and exam preparation tools, including quizzes and flashcards for this chapter's Key Terms and Concepts (see the summary list on page 477). The site also provides an **eBook** version of the text with highlighting and note taking capabilities, as well as an extensive library of observational videos that span early childhood through adolescence. Many videos are accompanied by questions that will help you think critically about and deepen your understanding of the chapter topics addressed, especially as they pertain to core concepts. Log on and learn more at **www.cengagebrain.com**.

12

© eStock Photo/Alamy

Most of this chapter examines infant-mother attachment. We focus on the theorizing of John Bowlby and Mary Ainsworth, two pioneers of modern attachment research. We then examine the development of attachment, individual differences in the quality, or security, of attachment, and the causes and consequences of individual differences in quality of attachment for psychological development and well-being. In the final section we look at the evolution of childcare, applying inclusive-fitness theory and parental investment theory to examine the care that mothers, fathers, grandparents, stepparents, and adoptive parents devote to children.

Although his parents explained to 18-month-old Stevie that his mother would be going to the hospital for a few days, he did not really understand, and after a week of being cared for by his grandparents, he was excited when his mother came home. However, the abdominal surgery his mother had prevented her from picking him up, and this made him angry with her, which he expressed by sometimes refusing to look at her and generally pouting. But at other times he crawled into bed with his mother, put his head on her shoulder, and stroked her face. One week later, when Grandma and Grandpa returned to babysit, Stevie screamed as his mom and dad left the house, despite their promise that they would be back shortly. When Mom returned home from her doctor's visit 2 hours later, Stevie's attitude quickly changed. The little boy's face burst into a huge grin, as he ran to his mother and hugged her legs. Although Stevie was not able to tell his mother in words, it seems that he was afraid that her departure and the arrival of his grandparents meant another long separation, and he was overjoyed when this was not the case.

Preverbal Stevie's distress at separation from his mother and his joy at her return are reflections of his love for his mother. More specifically, Stevie's behavior reflects his attachment to his mother. Broadly stated, the term **attachment** refers to the especially close emotional links established by a child with his or her primary caregiver(s), usually the mother, particularly visible through the sort of behaviors just described (for example, physical proximity to the caregiver(s); stress in her absence and in the presence of other less-familiar people) beginning during the second half of the first year of life. It is a biologically based motivational system that evolved to protect children from danger while motivating caregivers to provide care (Del Giudice, 2009).

Infants and children develop emotional relationships with the adults who care for them, and these relationships are of utmost importance for psychological development. In the previous chapter we discussed in some detail infants' and young children's abilities to express, recognize, understand, and regulate their emotions. Although emotions can be experienced in response to any environmental event, some of the strongest and most influential emotions are those related to other people, who often make us feel happy, sad, angry, or loved. As we noted in Chapter 11, infants experience many primary emotions within their first months of life. Developing over this same period and beyond is the closely related concept of attachment, or as it is sometimes referred to "emotional attachment." The focus of attachment research has always been on mothers, although babies become attached to fathers, grandparents, siblings, and many other people who are a regular part of their daily lives.

In this chapter, we begin with a brief history of attachment research, probably one of the more fascinating stories in modern developmental psychology. Later we provide a summary of the main concepts, ideas, and research on attachment through the progressive answering of a set of eight basic questions. In the final part of the chapter, we focus on the evolution of early parent-child care that anticipates the contents of Chapter 13 on the family.

Bowlby was influenced by the work of ethologists, who showed that early developing birds became "imprinted" to their mothers, which increased their chances for survival.

© Rosseforp/Photolibrary

Attachment

A Brief History of Attachment Research

Attachment theory was originally proposed by John Bowlby, a British psychiatrist trained in the psychoanalytical approach. Bowlby's initial ideas about attachment were influenced by three sources: (1) the mystery of the high death rates of infants staying in hospitals and orphanages; (2) ethological research conducted by Konrad Lorenz and colleagues on imprinting in birds; and (3) research with primates by Harry Harlow on "mother love," looking for the roots of an infant monkey's love for its mother.

Hospitals and Orphanages: Sources of Infant Grief and Death

One issue that attracted both the interest and efforts of physicians and other professionals during the second half of the 19th century and the first

half of the 20th century was the surprisingly high rates of mortality experienced by infants who were living in orphanages or those who had to spend a significant amount of time in hospitals because of health problems. Death rates for infants within their first year usually exceeded 50%, sometimes much higher, which was attributed to unsanitary conditions (see Blum, 2002). To reduce infection, hospitals and orphanages minimized contact between parents, staff, and infants, meaning that the lives of infants and children in these institutions were nearly devoid of social contact. This change in procedure did reduce the death rates substantially, but many infants were still dying and showing extreme emotional distress despite the more sanitary conditions.

Some physicians and psychologists made the connection between the psychological isolation infants experienced in these institutions and the elevated death rates and emotional wasting. They began conducting research to test the effects of early infant-caregiver separations and/or the lack of significant primary relationships on development (Goldfarb, 1945, 1947; Spitz, 1945, 1946). For example, René Spitz (1945, 1949) compared the psychological development of two groups of institutionalized children. Infants in one group were raised by their own mothers, whereas infants in a second group were raised from the third month of life by overworked nursery staff. Spitz examined differences in motor, social, and intellectual development, as well as mortality, between the two

attachment Close emotional relationship exhibited by a child toward a caregiver expressed by maintaining physical proximity, stress upon separation, and relief of stress upon reunion.

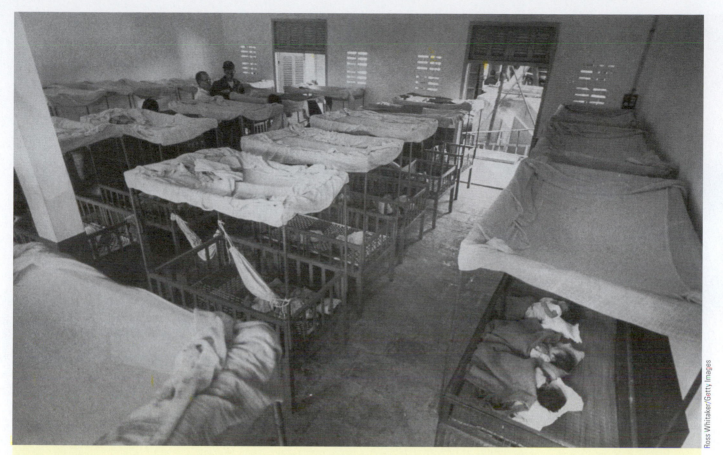

During the early part of the 20th century, infants living in orphanages and other institutions were provided with adequate medical attention but received minimal social interaction, based on the scientific beliefs at that time that social contact was unhygienic and the cause of death and disease.

groups and reported remarkable differences. The mother-raised infants developed into psychologically competent toddlers, whereas the staff-reared infants showed significant signs of impairment for all aspects of psychological development. Perhaps most striking was the difference in mortality rates: Over a 5-year period, none of 239 mother-raised infants died, whereas 37% of the staff-raised infants died over a 2-year period. Later on, Spitz (1946, 1965) identified what he called hospitalism, an almost irreversible and deathly syndrome in children who were separated from their mothers or other significant caregivers for periods longer than 5 months during their first year of life.

The findings that the lack or interruption of significant social relationships early in life could have such dramatic consequences for children's development were in the line with Bowlby's own clinical studies on juvenile thieves and their lack of significant primary relationships. Moreover, these observations made Bowlby more aware of the importance of infant-mother relationships and further increased his interest in trying to better describe their origins, mechanisms, and, if broken, their potential consequences.

Ethological Research by Lorenz and Colleagues on Imprinting in Birds

Whereas the plight of institutionalized infants made it clear to Bowlby that lack of early human contact resulted in psychopathology, evidence from the emerging field of ethology caused him to see that infant-mother attachment was important not just for humans but for many species. The work of Lorenz on imprinting in precocial (early-developing) birds particularly influenced Bowlby's thinking. Basically, Lorenz showed that, shortly after hatching, the offspring of geese, ducks, hens, and other precocial birds followed their mothers, keeping as near to them as possible, thus increasing their chances of survival. This research indicated that there was a limited time in which such imprinting could occur (a critical, or sensitive period, see Chapter 1) and that it occurred almost automatically, with little specific experience on the part of the chicks.

hospitalism The deteriorating effects on infants of long-term confinement to hospitals or similar institutions.

Human babies possess a suite of immature facial features that adults find endearing. The young of other animals possess similar features, which presumably enhance attachment between them and their mothers.

Lorenz (1943) also noticed that in many species, including humans, infants' immature features trigger caretaking behaviors. These include a head that is proportionally larger than the body, a forehead that is large in relation to the rest of the face, large eyes, rounded cheeks, a flat nose, and short limbs (see photo above of immature human features). Most adults find this combination of characteristics appealing, or cute, and are more apt to express interest in caring for younger-looking children than children who look older (Volk, Lukjanczuk, & Quinsey, 2007). Subsequent research confirmed many of Lorenz's observations and explored other child characteristics that might foster caregivers' attention and behavior (Alley, 1981, 1983). For example, people's assessments of "cuteness" also vary with their age. The preference for "babyness" is first seen between the ages of 12 and 14 years in girls and a couple of years later in boys (who enter puberty later than girls), suggesting that it may have evolved to prepare adolescents for parenthood (Fullard & Reiling, 1976). Recent research has shown that premenopausal women (ages 19 to 26 and 45 to 51) were more sensitive to infant cuteness than men and postmenopausal women (53 to 60 years), suggesting a hormonal influence on perceptions of infant cuteness, at least in women (Sprengelmeyer et al., 2009). John Bowlby found in ethology several promising hypotheses about what he later would call "attachment": (1) the main function of early infant-mother links, from an evolutionary perspective, is survival. According to Bowlby (1973, p. 276), "Protection from predators is by far the most likely function of attachment behaviour," and is seen in other species; (2) these links are especially significant early in life when human infants are particularly immature and helpless and are triggered in adults by some infantile features of babies; and (3) not all early close relationships in other species qualify as attachment: some, like those of birds, are automatic, triggered at birth (imprinting), and do not imply the development of any caregiver recognition and/or relationship, which is the case in humans. For Bowlby, only nonautomatic links, involving the development of relationships to significant adult caregivers (primarily the mother), as observed in mammals, including humans, qualified as attachment.

Why Do Infants Love Their Mothers So Much?

What is the origin of a child's love for his or her mother? There have been several different approaches to this question over the years, depending on the theoretical orientation of the person asking this question (see Table 12.1). Perhaps no one took this question more seriously, however, than Harry Harlow, an animal psychologist working with monkeys at the University of Wisconsin. Harlow's work challenged the dominant theory of

table 12.1 Why Do Infants Love Their Mothers (or Primary Caregivers) So Much?

Different theories provide different explanations to such a question. Four of the more significant ones are described here.

Theory	Description
Psychoanalytic theory	"I love you because you feed me"
Learning theory	"Rewards lead to love"
Cognitive developmental theory	"To love you I must know you"
Ethological (evolutionary) theory	"Perhaps I was born to love"

SOURCE: Adapted from Shaffer, D. R. (2009). *Social and personality development* (6th ed.). Belmont, CA: Wadsworth, pp. 157–161.

Harlow Primate Lab, University of Wisconsin–Madison

In studies by Harry Harlow and his colleagues, rhesus monkeys preferred their cloth "mothers" even though they were fed by the wire "mothers."

infant-mother attachment at that time: Sigmund Freud's claim that infants "fall in love" with their mothers because they feed them. (Curiously enough, behaviorists, who were reluctant to adopt most psychoanalytical views, would agree on this answer, but for quite different reasons; see Table 12.1.) This theory was not based on experimental research, which could not be ethically done with children. This is what Harlow tried to do through his now-classic series of studies with rhesus monkeys. (It is worth noting that most of Harlow's work with monkeys could not be ethically done today.)

In one of his most famous experiments (Harlow & Zimmerman, 1959), Harlow separated infant monkeys from their mothers shortly after birth and raised them with surrogate, or substitute, inanimate "mothers" (see photo). Some monkeys were raised in a cage with two surrogate mothers. One was a wire cylinder containing a hole in the chest area in which a bottle could be placed. The infant monkeys quickly learned to nurse from the wire mothers. The other "mother" was identical to the first but covered in cloth and did not have a bottle to feed the baby monkey. When monkeys who had been nursed by a wire mother were placed in cages where both a wire and a cloth-covered mother were available, they spent an inordinate amount of time clinging to the cloth mothers, even though the wire mothers still fed them. Furthermore, in situations where the monkeys were frightened, they would run to the cloth mother, which, much as a real mother, would serve to lessen their fear. Clearly, infant monkeys showed a preference for "contact comfort" over food. Something more complex than feeding was responsible for establishing attachment in these animals. (For a brief look at Harlow's famous experiments, go to: http://www.youtube.com/watch?v=4zeSBBbM59I&feature=related.)

Harlow suggested that food and love were two independent (though obviously related) primary needs that had to be fulfilled in order for development to proceed typically. Harlow went on to do research demonstrating that creature comfort alone is not sufficient to raise a well-adjusted monkey; social relationships, particularly with one's mother but also with peers, are vital (Harlow et al., 1966). Harlow spoke and wrote unabashedly of the nature of love and its importance in monkey and human development and that the first loving relationship a child has is with its mother. This is in stark contrast to the views of an earlier generation of psychologists. For instance, the radical behaviorist John B. Watson (1928) proposed that modern science could provide the means of rearing children better than tradition or the supposed instincts of mothers (Cairns & Cairns, 2006). Watson believed that parental love and affection were unnecessary for proper development, and, in fact, they were handicaps for raising a child to become a competent adult; too much mother love would make a child overly dependent on the approval of others and a social invalid (see Hilgard, 1987).

Harlow's research and thoughts on the nature of love (particularly mother love) and its importance in monkey and human development were compelling for Bowlby, who joined them with evidence from the effects of social separation on institutionalized infants and ethology to set the foundation of his theory.

In the next sections we summarize the basic tenets and evidence for attachment, using the list of eight core questions shown in Concept Review 12.1 as a basis for our review.

Look for answers to the following key questions in the sections of the chapter placed in parentheses. If you are able to answer to them quickly, you certainly know the basics of attachment!

1. What is attachment? (*Concept of Attachment*)
2. How does attachment develop? (*Stages of Attachment*)
3. Can attachment be established with people other than the mother? (*Fathers and Multiple Attachments*)
4. Are there individual differences in attachment? (*Types of Attachment*)
5. Are there cultural differences in attachment? (*Cultural Differences in Attachment Classification*)
6. What contributes to establishing secure attachment? (*Causes of Individual Differences in Attachment*)
7. How does attachment affect later development? (*Stability and Consequences of Secure [and Insecure] Attachment*)
8. Why does attachment affect later development? (*Internal Working Models of Attachment*)

Concept of Attachment

Imagine yourself visiting with the mother of a 3-month-old baby. One thing you may observe is that the baby will be nearly as happy in your arms as she is in the arms of her mother and will not fuss if, while you are holding her, Mom walks away. This scene would likely be very different, however, just several months later. When you visit again 5 months later, this baby, when sitting on the floor playing with a toy, will likely look up occasionally to make sure Mom is still in the vicinity, crawl toward her if she moves away, and become

Beginning in the latter half of the first year of life, infants become wary of unfamiliar adults and often seek security in their mother's (or other attachment figure's) arms.

© Michael Newman/PhotoEdit

distressed if Mom moves out of sight. Your presence will not help much and, in fact, may contribute to the infant's distress.

Why this difference? What has changed between the first and the second time you were with the baby? The answer is attachment. At 3 months of age, the baby was not yet attached to her mother, at least following Bowlby's definition, but she was by 8 months, and, accordingly, she felt uncomfortable exploring the environment and objects that surrounded her when mother was not near. She became especially stressed if mother disappeared for a while (referred to as *separation distress*) or in the presence of unfamiliar people (referred to as *fear of strangers*). This does not mean that 3-month-olds have no feelings for their mothers, and in fact, behaviors and experiences at 3 months are important precursors of later attachment behaviors (see Marvin & Britner, 1999).

In a broad sense, attachment has been described as a close emotional tie between two people that keeps them united over space and across time (Ainsworth, 1978). In a narrower sense, attachment describes the close emotional relationship that ties infants and young children to their primary caretakers, usually their mothers. Attachment is identified by a series of infant behaviors, including exploring their environment when in the presence of their attachment figure (this is what the primary caregiver is called in the field), anxiety when separated from their attachment figure, and wariness toward strangers (Cassidy & Marvin, 1992).

As mentioned earlier, Bowlby believed that an infant's attachment to its mother had substantial survival value. It is possible that infants' attachment to their mothers protected them not only from predators such as saber-toothed tigers but also from fellow humans including stepparents and co-wives (Hrdy, 1999; see discussion of *filicide* later

table 12.2 Stages of Attachments

Stage	Characteristics
Preattachment (asocial attachment) birth to 6 weeks	Babies display indiscriminate social responsiveness.
Attachment-in-the-making (indiscriminate attachment) 6 weeks to 6–8 months	Babies respond positively to nearly all normal-acting people and do not show substantial distress to strangers or to being separated from their primary caregiver.
Clear-cut attachment (specific attachment) 6–8 months to 18–24 months	Babies show a clear-cut interest in their main caregivers, usually their mothers, and react with distress when mothers leave them. They also typically display a wariness of strangers.
Reciprocal-relationship 18–24 months onward	Children are increasingly able to understand their caregivers' behaviors and needs and to show a more balanced, two-way relationship with their caregivers.

SOURCE: Adapted from Bowlby, J. (1969). *Attachment and loss: Vol. 1: Attachment.* London: Hogarth, and Schaffer, H. R. & Emerson, P. E. (1964). The development of social attachments in infancy. *Monographs of the Society for Research in Child Development, 29* (3, Serial No. 94.)

in this chapter). The evidence for this argument is admittedly circumstantial but nonetheless compelling. For instance, human, monkey, and chimpanzee infants display fear of strangers (particularly male strangers) early in infancy, especially before weaning (Heerwagen & Orians, 2002). In most female mammals, nursing inhibits ovulation. In lions, when a new male takes over the pride, he typically kills the cubs fathered by another male, which results in the cessation of nursing and the beginning of ovulation by their mothers. Although we may not like to think that fellow human beings would behave in the way unthinking male lions do, some anthropological evidence shows that such behavior may have characterized our ancestors. For example, among the hunter-gatherer Aché living in the rain forests of Paraguay, 55% of mortality in children from 0 to 5 years of age was caused by an adult human, and not always a stranger (Hill & Hurtado, 1996).

Attachment, then, can be described as a "special relationship," which is sometimes characterized as being like an "invisible thread" uniting a young child to his or her primary caregiver. The link is particularly strong between infants and their mothers, whose main functions are, evolutionary speaking, to serve as a safe haven for children in case of danger or stress and as a secure base for exploration and mastery. Accordingly, as pointed out by Ross Thompson (2006), although attachments are also established with other significant permanent caregivers, including fathers, grandparents, or stepparents, "given the functions of attachment figures in early childhood development, occasional babysitters, older peers, and teachers are unlikely to be attachment figures, and, at later stages, close friends and romantic partners

may assume attachment-like functions but are not attachment figures in the same sense" (p. 43). As Harlow and Bowlby noted, mothers are something special in the lives of young children, at least when it comes to attachment.

We should note that attachment describes only the strong emotional attraction that the babies feel *toward* their primary caregiver, usually their mother, and not the reverse. In other words, the attraction of mothers toward their children is another sort of relationship, sometimes called bonding, not attachment, and it has also been the object of research and debate (see Box 12.1). In fact, Harry and Margaret Harlow (1966) described five important relationships found in primates, including humans: attachment, bonding, peer relationships, sexual relationships, and father-offspring relationships. Therefore, as Thompson (2006) has noted, "children develop in an environment of relationships," with attachment being the first one.

Stages of Attachment

Emotional attachment is not automatically established at the moment of birth but develops gradually. From birth, parents are responsive to their infants' cries, coos, smiles, and movements, and infants respond in turn to their parents' attention. The interactions that occur during feeding or diaper changing serve as the basis for later social relationships.

Early researchers identified four stages of attachment (Bowlby, 1969; Schaffer & Emerson, 1964; see Howes, 1999 and Table 12.2). The first stage, called *preattachment*, or *asocial*, extends

Although *clear-cut attachment* is not typically seen until 8 months or so, the interactions that occur during feeding or diaper changing serve as the basis for later social relationships.

© Eric Audras/Onoky/Corbis

---

bonding The process of a mother's "falling in love" with her infant shortly after birth.

BOX 12.1 **food for thought**

Mother-Infant Bonding

Bonding developed a specific meaning for psychologists and parents in the latter decades of the 20th century. Marshall Klaus and John Kennell (1976, 1982) used the word to describe a mother "falling in love" with her infant as a result of skin-to-skin contact between the just-born baby and its mother. According to Klaus and Kennell, there is a sensitive period surrounding the birth of a baby that is essential to this bonding experience, and although women will learn to love their infants without this experience, having it can facilitate the process. Klaus and Kennell reviewed research showing that women who had close physical contact with their newborns immediately after birth, and who continued to have an extra amount of contact with their infants in the days and weeks following birth, had more positive interactions with their babies over the course of the first year than did women who had a usual amount of contact. In some cases, the effects were found to persist for months and even years (O'Connor et al., 1980).

There was immediate and substantial criticism of Klaus and Kennell's position (Goldberg, 1983; Lamb & Hwang, 1982). First, when examining other animals, the phenomenon of mother-infant bonding was best demonstrated in species such as goats and sheep that locomote shortly after birth.

Bonding, it was argued, makes some sense for such animals, because mothers must be able to recognize and keep track of their young that may wander off. Bonding makes less sense for a species such as humans, whose young are so helplessly immobile that it will be months before they can even crawl away from mother, to say nothing of run away (Lamb & Hwang, 1982).

Not only did it make no sense, but in much of the bonding research, the mother's motivation was not being taken into consideration. Women who seek out the bonding experience are likely to have different attitudes about babies and child-rearing than women who do not (Goldberg, 1983), and it may be this attitude, rather than the event, that is the principle factor in mothers' feelings and behaviors. In fact, in a study that controlled for mothers' motivation for having the bonding experience, no differences in mother-infant interactions were observed between women who had the critical skin-to-skin contact and those who did not (Svejda, Campos, & Emde, 1980). Moreover, for several generations, childbirth practices in North America and parts of Europe involved anesthetized deliveries, resulting in unconscious new mothers and groggy newborns. However, mothers still loved their babies.

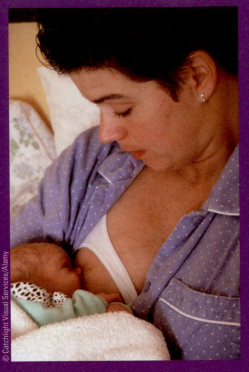

© Catchlight Visual Services/Alamy

Klaus and Kennell hypothesized that skin-to-skin contact between a mother and her newborn resulted in a mother "falling in love" with her baby.
....

More recent research on possible bonding in primates, mainly monkeys, has shown that something like bonding probably does

from approximately birth to 6 weeks and is characterized by an indiscriminate social responsiveness. Although babies show a clear interest for people's faces and voices, they do not distinguished among them, properly speaking, at least not to the extent they will in months ahead. However, infants are biased to orient to other people (see discussion later in this chapter), increasing the opportunity for developing a relationship with their caregiver.

The second stage of attachment, referred to as *attachment-in-the-making*, or *indiscriminate attachment*, extends approximately from 6 weeks to 6 to 8 months. During this phase, babies clearly enjoy human company. Infants will smile and babble at their parents or other familiar caregivers, but they will also respond positively to nearly all normal-acting people, and they do not show substantial distress at the presence of strangers or at being separated from their primary caregiver.

The third stage of attachment, *clear-cut attachment*, or *specific attachment*, begins sometime early in the second part of the first year and extends to 18 to 24 months of age (see Figure 12.1). During this time, infants show a clear-cut interest in their primary caregivers, usually their mothers, and react with distress when mothers leave them, particularly in novel situations or with an unfamiliar (or even less-familiar) person, such as a babysitter. This can sometimes be distressing to fathers, aunts, or grandparents who find that their child/niece or nephew/grandchild is not happy to be in their care. As mentioned earlier, this is called separation distress, or separation protest, or sometimes separation anxiety. Other signs that children have established an emotional attachment, discussed briefly earlier in this chapter, include using their mothers as a secure base from which to explore novel environments (usually by

Rhesus monkey mothers who have just given birth but whose infant has died will adopt (often steal) other infants and care for them as if they were their own.

Maestripieri (2001) reviewed the research literature examining *adoption* in monkeys. He reasoned that if there is a mechanism like bonding in primates, it should be seen by a willingness of mother monkeys to adopt unrelated infants shortly after giving birth themselves, especially after the death of their own baby. This was indeed the pattern. In observations at zoos and primate research centers, mother monkeys whose infants had died were observed to adopt abandoned infant monkeys, or even to kidnap infant monkeys, with most instances occurring within two weeks of giving birth. The adopted babies were usually of the same sex and similar age as their own babies had been.

Also consistent with the bonding hypothesis, Maestripieri noted that (1) when monkey mothers are separated from their own infants *during* the bonding period, they later reject the infant (and other infants) if reunited *after* the bonding period; and (2) when mothers and infants are separated *after* the bonding period, they later accept their infant (but not other infants) if reunited some significant time later. The interpretation of these findings is that mothers bond with and will later recognize their infants if they are exposed to them shortly after giving birth (usually within the first two weeks), but not if they are separated from their infants during this sensitive time.

Why should such early nurturing behavior have evolved in a species such as monkeys, whose young cannot escape their mothers? Maestripieri argues that it was not in order to recognize their young, as seems to be the case for species such as goats and sheep, but to *motivate* mothers to care for their highly dependent offspring. In most cases in the wild, mothers will become attached to their own babies. Adopting unrelated infants is not an evolutionarily wise decision, but it is likely an infrequent event in nature. On average, heightened maternal sensitivity to infants in the immediate postpartum period produced mothers who cared for their *own* babies, despite producing the occasional "error" of caring for an unrelated infant.

Maestripieri's evidence does not necessarily support Klaus and Kennell's initial proposal, and the observations are with monkeys not with humans. Nevertheless, the neuroendocrine mechanisms associated with pregnancy and birth are similar in monkeys and humans, and there is some evidence in humans that mothers' ability to recognize their infants on the basis of odor is influenced by "birth" hormones (Fleming et al., 1997). Perhaps it is time to revisit the bonding hypothesis in humans, although in a more cautious and conservative way.

---

occur in a species whose young, like humans, are relatively immobile and dependent on their mothers for an extended period. Dario 12 months) and the so-called **fear (or wariness) of strangers**.

Although babies at this time do show decided preferences for specific people and often react with stress when held by unfamiliar people, we do not want to give the impression that infants of this age react fearfully to all unfamiliar adults in most situations. Infants and toddlers are learning about a social world that includes other people, and although they may initially be wary of strangers, they can behave very comfortably with them, especially if they are reassured by a parent. (Recall our discussion of social referencing in Chapter 11.) Moreover, the extent to which infants will be fearful of strangers depends on their previous experience. Babies who have spent most of their time in the sole care of their mothers are likely to display substantial distress when handed to an unfamiliar adult, whereas babies who have a history of interacting with fathers, siblings, grandparents, and other people in general will show less, or perhaps no, distress in a similar situation.

The fourth stage, referred to as *reciprocal-relationship*, extends from 18 to 24 months on and reflects children's increasing ability to understand their caregivers' behaviors and needs, and, accordingly, to show a more balanced, two-way relationship with their caregivers. Children more readily establish new attachments beyond the earliest ones. All in all, the new cognitive and linguistic abilities children are acquiring at this time permit them

separation distress (separation protest, separation anxiety) Infants' distress response on being left by their attachment figure.

fear (or wariness) of strangers Pattern of behavior displayed by infants during second half of the first year that serves as an indication that the infant has developed an attachment for his or her caretaker.

FIGURE 12.1 The course of attachment over infancy.

SOURCE: Schaffer, H. R. & Emerson, P. E. (1964). The development of social attachments in infancy. *Monographs of the Society for Research in Child Development, 29* (3, Serial No. 94.) Reprinted by permission.

to better understand social situations, thus reducing their distress upon separation, at least in some contexts.

This final transition, beginning between 18 and 24 months of age, is associated with another well-established shift in cognitive functioning: the transition from sensorimotor to symbolic, or mental, representation (see Chapters 5 and 6). If their mother is not with them, toddlers can make reasonable guesses concerning where she might be. Note that this ability does not necessarily mean the cessation of separation distress. Dropping your 3-year-old off at nursery school may still produce complaints and tears. This is a novel situation, and the child will probably not be able to resolve the discrepancy of being separated from you and left in unfamiliar surroundings. With greater familiarity with the situation and the experience of being left with others, the distress upon separation will disappear.

Fathers and Multiple Attachments

As just noted, although mothers are usually children's primary caregivers and thus their primary attachment figures (this is why most research on attachment has focused on infant-mother relationships), children also become attached to other people. In fact, attachment figures can be either female or male, kin or nonkin, including fathers, other family members (siblings, grandparents), adoptive parents, and even teachers and daycare providers. *To whom* the child is attached is therefore not as important as having at least *someone* to be attached to. (Mothers *are* special, however, as we will make clear in our discussion of an "Evolutionary Perspective of Childcare" later in this chapter.) According to Rudolph Schaffer and Peggy Emerson (1964), by 18 months, only 13% of children in their Scottish sample were attached to only one person, and many were attached to five or more.

That young children can establish multiple attachments with different people does not necessarily mean that all of the attachment figures have the same emotional ties to them. In fact, it was initially hypothesized that a hierarchy exists among the different attachment figures, with some (for example, mothers) being more significant for the children than others (Schaffer & Emerson, 1964). Yet, modern research shows that, rather than a hierarchy, children develop different *sorts* of attachments with different figures in a way that each of them fulfills some specific socioemotional need. A good example of this is illustrated by studies that focused on the often-forgotten role of fathers in attachment (Lamb, 1975; Parke, 2002, 2008) and its differences with attachment to mothers.

Fathers traditionally have had little role in caring for infants, and even today they spend much less time interacting with infants than do mothers (Hrdy, 1999; see discussion later in chapter). However, many contemporary fathers play an increasing role in the care of their infants, and research shows that they are quite competent (see Cabrera et al., 2000; Parke, 2002) and form attachments to their babies much as mothers do (see Parke, 2008). However, mothers' and fathers' interaction styles differ. Mothers more frequently take the role of primary caregiver and are thus more apt to hold and soothe their babies, to play traditional verbal games such as peek-a-boo and pat-a-cake, and to care for their babies' needs. Fathers are more apt to play physical games with their babies involving unexpected reactions and stimulation (see Parke, 2008). Not surprisingly, babies often prefer their fathers at playtime and their mothers when they are distressed (Clarke-Stewart, 1980; Lamb, 1981).

table 12.3 Description of Strange Situation

Each episode lasts about three minutes.

Episode	Events	Attachment Behavior Observed
1	Experimenter leaves parent and baby to play	
2	Parent sits with baby	Use of parent as secure base
3	Stranger enters, talks to parent	Fear of strangers
4	Parent leaves, stranger lets baby play, offers comfort if needed	Separation distress
5	Parent returns, greets baby, offers comfort if needed, stranger leaves	Reactions to reunion
6	Parent leaves	Separation distress
7	Stranger enters, offers comfort	Fear of stranger; ability to be soothed by stranger
8	Parent returns, greets baby, offers comfort, lets baby return to play	Reactions to reunion

SOURCE: Adapted from Ainsworth, M. D. S., Blehar, M. C., Waters, E., & Wall, S. (1978). *Patterns of attachment: A psychological study of the strange situation.* Hillsdale, NJ: Erlbaum.

Moreover, it is possible for a child to be securely attached to one parent but insecurely attached to the other, with children who are securely attached to both parents showing better socioemotional adjustment than those who are securely attached to only one (Main & Weston, 1981). In other words, attachment to mothers and fathers tends to be specific to the relationship, contributing in different ways to a child's care.

Types of Attachment

The age-related pattern we presented earlier may give the impression that attachment develops the same way for children all over the world. To some extent we believe this is true, for attachment to a primary caregiver was essential for the survival of infants in our species' ancient past, continues to be critical for infants today, and is displayed, in one form or another, in most mammals. However, most research in attachment from its earliest days focused on *individual differences.* Although few infants fail to become attached to a primary caregiver, the *quality* of infant-mother attachment differs between individuals, and this has implications for later development.

As we have already pointed out, proximity to the mother or main caregiver, distress upon separation, and fear of strangers are three of the more visible signs of attachment. But how does one measure attachment scientifically, permitting the systematic assessment of different styles of attachment in children? The first and still most widely used method to measure the quality of attachment in children is a 20-minute test designed by Mary Ainsworth called the **Strange Situation** (see Table 12.3) (Ainsworth et al., 1978; Ainsworth & Wittig, 1969), which has been the workhorse of attachment research ever since its inception more than 30 years ago.

The test is built on the assumption that attachment behaviors are best elicited under conditions of mild stress. Briefly, the Strange Situation begins with a mother and her infant, between the ages of 12 and 18 months, entering a small room (although fathers and infants of other ages are sometimes tested, too). The mother interests the baby in some toys and allows the child to explore or play freely.

© KG-Photography/Corbis

Mothers and fathers interact differently with infants. Fathers are more apt to play physical games with their babies involving unexpected reactions and stimulation.

Strange Situation A technique developed by Ainsworth and her colleagues to assess quality of attachment in young children.

secure attachment Optimal type of attachment where infants display confidence when their caregivers are present, show mild distress when temporarily left alone, and quickly reestablish contact with caregivers upon their return.

table 12.4 Description of Different Styles of Attachment

Child Behavior	Secure	Insecure-Resistant	Insecure-Avoidant	Disorganized
Does infant explore when caregiver is present, providing a secure base for exploration?	Yes, actively	No, clings	Yes, but child's play is not as constructive as that of secure infants	No
Does infant respond positively to the stranger?	Yes, if caregiver is present	No, even if caregiver is present	No, often indifferent to caregiver	No, confused responses
Does infant protest when separated from caregiver?	Yes, at least mildly	Yes, extremely upset	No, seemingly unfazed	Sometimes; unpredictable
How does the infant respond to the caregiver when she returns?	Reestablish contact when the caregiver returns	Display anger and initially rejection to contact when the caregiver returns	Avoid contact with caregiver when she returns	Display inconsistent patterns of responses to caregiver on her return
Parenting Style	Sensitive, responsive	Inconsistent, often unresponsive	Rejecting-unresponsive or intrusive and overly stimulating	Frightening (for example, abusive) or frightened (for example, overwhelmed)

This is followed by a series of approximately 3-minute periods of various activities by the adults in the study. First, an unfamiliar adult enters the room, talks to the mother, and interacts with the infant. Three minutes later, the mother goes out of the room, leaving the child with the stranger. Finally, the mother returns. The behaviors that are most important for evaluating quality of attachment are those of the baby when the mother returns. Do infants run to their mothers, and are they soothed by her presence, eventually leaving her side and exploring again? Do they cling to mom for the rest of the session, or perhaps refuse to make eye contact with her, sulking in the corner? Based on babies' responses, Ainsworth and her colleagues developed three attachment classifications: secure, insecure-resistant, and insecure-avoidant (see Table 12.4). A fourth type, disorganized/disoriented (Main & Solomon, 1986) was included later. (To see a brief demonstration of the Strange Situation, go to http://www.youtube.com/watch?v=36GI_1PBQpM.)

Using the Strange Situation and based on mostly middle-class samples (see van IJzendoorn

et al., 1999), about 60% of the babies tested by Ainsworth and by others are classified as having secure attachment, at least in the United States. These infants actively explore while in the room with their mothers, and they become upset when their mothers leave them. When mother returns, a securely attached baby will often run or crawl to her, greeting her warmly. The mother is able to soothe the child to the extent that sometimes the child returns to play with the stranger.

Approximately 10% of the babies tested are classified as having insecure-resistant attachment, or ambivalent attachment. These infants appear anxious even with their mothers and tend not to explore much. They become very distressed when their mothers leave, but are ambivalent and display anger on her return. They stay near their mother after she returns but seemingly resent her earlier departure and often resist her attempts at contact. These babies are wary of the unfamiliar adult, even when the mother is present. These babies adopt a maximizing or overdependent strategy, exaggerating their signals of need in order to control their caregiver's behavior.

About 15% of the babies tested are classified as having insecure-avoidant attachment. Unlike the insecure-resistant infants, they show little distress when their mothers depart, avoid contact with the mother when she returns, and usually do not show wariness of the stranger, although they may avoid the stranger, much as they do the mother. Their attachment strategy can be described as minimizing.

The final category, disorganized/disoriented attachment, was identified by Mary Main and

insecure-resistant attachment An insecure style of attachment in which infants keep very close to their caregivers and tend not to explore much. They become distressed when their caregivers leave them temporarily but display anger and initially rejection to contact when the caregivers return.

insecure-avoidant attachment An insecure style of attachment in which infants show little distress when their caregivers depart temporarily, avoid contact with them when they return, and usually do not show wariness of the stranger.

disorganized/disoriented attachment Attachment style in which infants seek to be close to their caregivers in inconsistent ways, often showing patterns typical of secure, insecure-avoidant, and/or insecure-resistant attachment simultaneously.

Judith Solomon (1986) and includes infants who Ainsworth was not able to fit into her classification system. Initially it was thought that this category of attachment would be composed mostly of troublesome babies or infants from high-risk families, but this has not turned out to be the case. (However, the rate of this sort of attachment, as well as the two other types of insecure attachment, is more frequent among lower-income samples, families at sociodemographic risk, and clinical populations [van IJzendoorn et al., 1999].) About 15% of nonclinical middle-class children are classified as disorganized/disoriented. Unlike those in the three standard classifications, disorganized/disoriented infants show no coherent strategy for dealing with stress during separation and reunion in the Strange Situation. Disorganized/disoriented infants seek to be close to their mothers in inconsistent ways, often showing patterns typical of secure, insecure-avoidant, and/or insecure-resistant infants simultaneously (for example, strong approach to the mother followed by strong avoidance). They may sometimes look dazed and disoriented upon reunion with their mothers. They may freeze in the middle of movement, approach her backward, or wait an inordinate amount of time before deciding to approach her. They display high levels of motivational conflict, seemingly viewing their caregiver as both a source of comfort and fear.

The Strange Situation is not the only method available to measure the quality of attachment. For example, the *Cassidy-Marvin system* (Main & Cassidy, 1988; Cassidy & Marvin, 1992) assesses the quality of attachment by observing the behaviors of preschool children on reunion after one or several separations from a parent. Other measures assess attachment in a more indirect way. For instance, the **Attachment Q-Set** (Waters & Deane, 1985) uses the *Q-sort method* in which prepared statements are sorted into categories. The Attachment Q-Set consists of 90 statements, written on cards, describing children's (ages 1 to 5) behaviors (for example, "Child is strongly attracted to new activities and new toys"; "Child recognized when mother is upset. Becomes quiet or upset himself. Tries to comfort her"). The mother or a trained observer sorts cards into nine piles ranging from those in which the statements are "least like the child" to those that are "most like the child." After the statements have been sorted, the researcher compares the groupings to a profile for a securely attached child as defined by experts. The more similar the observer's groupings are with the expert's description, the more securely attached the child is.

Nor is Ainsworth's system of categorizing infants and children the only approach for describing individual differences in attachment styles. For instance, R. Chris Fraley and Susan Spieker (2003)

Infants in Ainsworth's Strange Situation become distressed when their mothers leave them. Most important for evaluating quality of attachment is how they respond when their mother returns.

examined the behavior of 1,139 15-month-old children in the Strange Situation and found that, rather than classifying children in terms of specific styles as in the Ainsworth system, individual differences in attachment were better described in terms of two continuous variables: (1) proximity seeking versus avoidance, and (2) high versus low anger/resistance. This is a promising alternative to the categorical approach of Ainsworth and her followers, but, according to some experts, more than two dimensions are necessary in order for this approach to capture the richness afforded by Ainsworth's system (Thompson, 2006).

Cultural Differences in Attachment Classification

The distributions of children in each of Ainsworth's classification categories are based mostly on data from the United States, where Ainsworth developed the Strange Situation. In fact, the numbers we provided were for mostly middle-class samples. However, most research examining attachment classification across the globe has reported remarkably similar patterns as found for the United States, strongly suggesting that the phenomenon of attachment is truly universal, with secure attachment being the norm (van IJzendoorn & Sagi-Schwartz,

---

Attachment Q-Set Method for assessing infant-caregiver attachment in which the caregiver or a trained observer sorts 90 statements describing a certain attachment relationship into preestablished categories (ranging from "most like" to "least like").

Jessica Boone/Getty Images

table 12.5 Distribution (%) of the Attachment Types (Secure, Insecure-Avoidant, and Insecure-Resistant) in Several Countries

Country	Secure	Insecure-Avoidant	Insecure-Resistant
United States (21 samples)	67	21	12
Western Europe (9 samples)	66	28	6
China	68	16	16
Indonesia	57	7	33
Japan (3 samples)	66	12	19
Israel (3 samples)	69	3	26
Uganda	57	18	25
Gusii (Africa)	61	—	—
Dogon (Africa)	69	0	8
Khayelitsha (Africa)	72	17	11

SOURCE: Adapted from van IJzendoorn, M. H., & Sagi-Schwartz, A. (2008). Cross-cultural patterns of attachment: Universal and contextual dimensions. In P. R. Shaver & J. Cassidy (Eds.), *Handbook of Attachment: Theory, research, and clinical application* (pp. 880–905). New York: Guilford, p. 899.

2008). Table 12.5 presents the percentage of infants classified as having secure, insecure-avoidant, and insecure-resistant attachments using the Strange Situation from different regions of the world (adapted from van IJzendoorn & Sagi-Schwartz, 2008). As you can see, for the most part, between about 60% and 70% of infants were classified as securely attached in samples ranging from traditional groups from Africa to the United States, China, Japan, Indonesia, Israel, and Western Europe.

However, it would be misleading to suggest that this pattern is the same in all cultural or subcultural groups. In fact, although most behavioral scientists believe that the attachment phenomenon captured by Ainsworth's classification systems is universal, this does not necessarily mean that cultural differences should not be found. According to Marinus van IJzendoorn and Abraham Sagi (1999, p. 714), "the evolutionary perspective [of attachment] leaves room for globally adaptive behavioral propensities that become realized in a specific way dependent on the cultural niche in which the child has to survive." Consistent with this perspective, some individual studies have reported substantial differences in the percentage of infants classified in the various attachment groups as a function of culture (Lamb et al., 1985; Thompson, 1998; van IJzendoorn & Sagi, 1999). For example, although about two-thirds of all Western European babies are classified as securely attached (see Table 12.5), this percentage was only 43% for a sample from northern Germany, with 46% of infants being classified as insecure-avoidant (Grossman et al., 1981, 1985). Similarly, although 55% of Israeli infants growing up on a kibbutz (a group-living community) were classified as securely attached, 37% were described as insecure-resistant (Sagi et al., 1985).

Why the difference? Do the distributions in the United States, or perhaps Japan and (most of) West-

ern Europe, where the proportions of children classified as securely attached are the highest, reflect the typical, or best-adjusted, pattern and the others reflect different levels of poor adjustment? Perhaps, but there is reason to believe that this is not the case. For example, it may be inappropriate to suggest national differences in attachment style, in that types of attachment can vary significantly *within* the same country (see van IJzendoorn & Kroonenberg, 1998, Thompson, 2006). Moreover, it seems that attachment practices in cultures different from the West may vary significantly. For example, in Bali, mothers use fake fear expressions (for example, calling out "Wild cat!" when none was around) to control their babies' exploratory behaviors (Bateson & Mead, 1942); infants respond by stopping their exploration or running to the protection of their mothers. In Tikopia, a Micronesian society, attachment to a mother's brother is promoted by systematically having "face-to-face talks" between infants and their uncles beginning early in life. Children's maternal uncles play an important role in Tikopia society, and the Tikopians believe that it was important for an infant's' attachment not be too exclusive but to extend to important relatives (Firth, 1936). According to Bretherton (1992, p. 770), this can be understood by keeping in mind that "in both cultures [Bali and Tikopia], a biological system is molded to a particular society's purposes."

Other researchers have argued that the Strange Situation is not an appropriate measure of attachment in all countries but should be adapted for specific cultures (Colin, 1996). For instance, the Strange Situation was developed to represent a moderately stressful experience for an infant. The level of stress may be much greater for Japanese infants and for Israeli kibbutz-reared infants, who rarely encounter strangers, than for American babies (Thompson, 2006). Another possibility is that attachment is expressed differently in different cultures. For example, securely attached Gusii infants from Western Kenya are greeted by handshakes from their mothers instead of hugs (Kermoian & Leiderman, 1986).

As noted in the beginning of this section, infants in most cultures are securely attached to their caregivers. However, some cultures, or specific groups within a culture, do show different patterns of attachment type, and there is currently no consensus on why they exist. Thus, there continues to be a need for more multicultural research on attachment using different procedures of assessment (van IJzendoorn & Sagi, 1999; van IJzendoorn & Sagi-Schwartz, 2008). Although attachment seems to be a universal phenomenon, a more culturally sensitive approach to the assessment of the attachment types, causes, and outcomes is called for.

Causes of Individual Differences in Attachment

Knowing that there are differences in quality of attachment that can be measured by the Strange Situation is only a beginning. Here we address the questions: "How do such differences arise?" and, particularly, "What promotes the establishment of a secure attachment?" Bowlby (1969), based on the evolutionary roots of attachment, emphasized that all children, beginning early in life, exhibit a series of *attachment behaviors* and *attachment signs*. The main purpose of attachment behaviors is to keep the mother in close proximity. These include behaviors such as following or climbing on the mother, actions that children use to stay close by the mother. In contrast, the main purpose of attachment signs is to attract the mother to the child. These include behaviors such as crying or smiling that serve as signals to parents to provide care. Ainsworth and her colleagues (1978), in contrast, emphasized *maternal sensitivity* as the main cause of individual differences in quality of attachment. These pioneers had more to say about the nature of attachment, and research evidence over the years has provided a more complete picture of the causes and consequences of attachment.

Availability of an Attachment Figure

Although it may seem obvious, the first and most important factor that affects the quality of attachment is the availability of a stable attachment figure. Many different variables can influence the quality of attachment, but, initially, nothing is as important as having someone to attach to. The relevance of this factor has been repeatedly shown by studies in which infants live in overcrowded and understaffed institutions where, although they may receive adequate nutritional and medical care, they are sorely lacking in interactions with a stable caretaker (Spitz, 1945, 1965; Bowlby, 1960). Such infants display severe social, emotional, and intellectual deficits. We briefly discussed a study by Spitz (1945) earlier in this chapter and looked at some of these studies in Chapter 10 on intelligence.

One factor that was proposed to influence the quality of attachment (especially during the early days of attachment research) was whether infants and children spend most of their time in the home with their mothers or whether they spend a significant amount of time in out-of-home care. Daycare has become a fact of life for most American families. Approximately 70% of women with preschool children in the United States work outside of the home, many full time. This figure is even greater in other countries (Melhuish, 2005). As children from all walks of life increasingly began to attend daycare beginning in the 1970s and 1980s, there was great concern that spending so much time out of the home in nonparental care would be harmful for children, particularly with respect to infant-mother attachment. The worst fears of psychologists and social-policy makers were not confirmed (Scarr, Phillips, & McCartney, 1990), but there have been lingering concerns that prolonged daycare experience can have some negative long-term effects on children (see Belsky, 1988; Lamb & Ahnert, 2006). We discuss some of these issues in Box 12.2.

Parental Sensitivity to Infants' Signals

Early research showed that mothers of securely attached infants are responsive to their babies' emotional signals, encourage them to explore, and seem to enjoy close contact with them. These women respond appropriately and reliably to the cues their babies send, and their babies are able to predict reasonably well what to expect in a wide range of situations (Ainsworth et al., 1978). Mothers of insecure-resistant infants are also interested in their babies, but they frequently misinterpret their infants' signals. They are out of sync with their babies' schedules and are often inconsistent in the enthusiasm they show toward their infants. In contrast, mothers of insecure-avoidant infants show a lack of interest in their babies—sometimes an overt resentment. They are generally unresponsive to their infants' signals (Ainsworth, 1979). These patterns do not hold up for all mothers and babies, but there is clear evidence that how mothers respond to their infants over the first year of life greatly influences the quality of attachment (see Belsky, 1999; Koren-Karie et al., 2002).

But is it really mothers' sensitivity to read and respond to their infants that is so important in determining security of attachment? It seems so, at least in part. For example, there is no evidence that individual differences in security of attachment are heritable (that is, behavioral genetic studies indicate only

BOX 12.2 child development in the real world

Daycare and Attachment

How does attending daycare affect infant-mother attachment? Do children who spend all day in daycare have different attachment relationships with their mothers? Do they develop different social, emotional, or cognitive skills than children who remain at home with their mothers?

First, daycare attendance does not dissolve the attachment relationships between infants and mothers. Early research on this topic showed that infants still preferred their mothers to their substitute caregivers (see Belsky & Steinberg, 1978; Clarke-Stewart & Fein, 1983). Differences have been found, however, in the security of infant-mother attachment between infants who attend daycare and those who are reared at home. For example, K. Allison Clarke-Stewart (1989) examined 17 published studies that evaluated the quality of attachment between children and their mothers using Ainsworth's Strange Situation. She reported that infants whose mothers worked full-time were more likely to be classified as insecurely attached (36%) than infants whose mothers did not work or who worked only part-time (29%). With a sample of 1,247 mother/infant pairs, this 7% difference was significantly greater than expected by chance. Other researchers reported similar findings (Belsky, 1988;

Michelle Del Guercio/Photo Researchers, Inc.

The effects on infant-mother attachment of attending quality daycare are small and controversial. There also seem to be some cognitive benefits for children who attend daycare, although such children are also apt to show higher levels of aggression than are children in maternal care.

Lamb, Sternberg, & Prodromidis, 1992). Nonetheless, the difference is small, and Clarke-Stewart (1989) suggested it might be because infants attending daycare may not feel as anxious about separating from their mothers in the Strange Situation as stay-at-home infants. In fact, when mothers, teachers, or observers rate quality of attachment

---

negligible genetic effect in security of attachment, Bokhorst et al., 2003; see Thompson, 2006), and infant temperament does not seem to be directly related to attachment quality (see Thompson, 1998). In an interesting study, researchers evaluated the quality of attachment of infants placed in foster care. They also assessed the children's biological and foster mothers. The attachment style of the children was better predicted by the behavior of their foster mothers than by their biological mothers (Dozier et al., 2001). That is, foster mothers who were more sensitive to infants' signals were more likely to have securely attached children regardless of the attachment style of the children's biological mothers. In other words, the behaviors of the foster mothers—specifically their sensitivity to infants' signals of physical and social needs—were primarily what governed individual differences in quality of attachment.

interactional synchrony Mother-infant harmonious interaction, where partners take turns responding to each other's leads, needs, and emotions.

Interactional Synchrony

Other factors in addition to sensitivity, such as the quality of the marital relationship, the presence of psychological problems such as depression or anxiety in mothers, and the general level of stress in the home, also contribute to attachment security (Cummings & Davies, 1994; Meins et al., 2003; van IJzendoorn & De Wolff, 1997). One important influence on attachment style is the extent to which parents and infants establish a fluid, dyadic (two-way), and coordinated relationship. Bowlby (1969) viewed attachment in terms of a "goal-corrected partnership," meaning that what actually matters is interaction, with the quality of attachment relying to a significant degree on the quality of the social interaction between mother (or the primary caregiver) and the child.

This **interactional synchrony** is often described as a sort of dance where partners take turns responding to each other's leads. This is easily seen, for example, during feeding, when the mother and the infant establish a rhythm of presenting in daily settings, no differences have been found between infants of working and non-working mothers (Belsky, 1988). Even if the attachment differences between the infants of working and nonworking mothers are real, they are not substantial and, according to Sandra Scarr and her colleagues (1990), do not constitute evidence of greater risk.

In addition to examining the effect of daycare on attachment, researchers also investigated the relationship between day-care attendance and social and intellectual development. Here the picture is mixed. Children who attend daycare have been found to display elevated levels of aggressive behavior toward peers (Belsky, 2001) and more exter-nalizing problems and conflict with adults when they are in kindergarten (NICHD Early Child Care Research Network, 2003a) rela-tive to children in maternal care. Moreover, children who regularly attend more than one childcare facility display more behavior problems and show less socially positive behavior than children who attend only a single daycare facility (Morrissey, 2009). In contrast, with respect to cognitive develop-ment, children who attend daycare often display enhanced intellectual functioning, especially for low-income children attend-ing quality daycare (NICHD Early Child Care Research Network, 2003b, 2006; Marshall, 2004; Votruba-Drzal, Coley, & Chase-Lans-dale, 2004). In fact, the most recent research based on longitudinal observations of more than 1,300 children reports that higher-quality daycare was associated with higher vocabulary scores through the end of sixth grade (Belsky et al., 2007; see also NICHD Early Child Care Research Network, 2006).

What, however, constitutes quality day-care? More than two decades ago, Sandra Scarr and her associates (1990) listed three features of daycare that are associated with the quality of a child's experience: caregiver-to-child ratio, group size, and caregiver train-ing and experience (see also Lamb & Ahnert, 2006; Marshall, 2004; Melhuish, 2005). A ratio of one caregiver to four or fewer children ensures greater physical safety and more individual attention (talking and playing). Similarly, the fewer children there are in a daycare group, the more social and intellectual stimulation children receive (de Schipper, Riksen-Walraven, & Geurts, 2006). And not surprisingly, the number of years of child-related education and work experience a daycare provider has is related to greater social and cognitive competence in children. There is nothing magic about the relationship between years of education and enhanced developmental outcomes for children. Day-care providers with more education have been found to be more responsive to children and to provide more age-appropriate activi-ties and learning opportunities to children than daycare providers with less education (see Marshall, 2004; Scarr et al., 1990).

Although many factors influence the type of experience a child has in daycare, generally speaking, quality daycare represents no risk to children. In fact, high-quality daycare has been associated with enhanced social, emo-tional, and cognitive benefits, particularly for children from disadvantageous backgrounds (Peisner-Feinberg et al., 2001; NICHD Early Child Care Research Network, 2006). One problem is that quality daycare is expensive. Unlike most European countries, the United States has no national policy on childcare and has made no commitment to provide quality childcare for all families that need it. It is too late to tell mothers to stay at home with their children. As K. Allison Clarke-Stewart (1989, pp. 271–272) wrote more than 20 years ago: "Maternal employment is a reality. The issue today, therefore, is not whether infants should be in day care but how to make their experiences there and at home supportive of their development and of their parents' peace of mind."

the breast or bottle, nursing, and pausing, coor-dinated with periods of gentle rocking (Feldman, 2007; Kaye, 1982). Such synchrony and mother's sensitivity to her infants' signals are probably more easily seen when babies are being spoon-fed. When a mother is feeding her baby strained peas, for example, is she sensitive to what her baby is doing or wants? Does she wait for her infant to open his mouth, make eye contact, and perhaps lean toward him, or is she feeding baby on her own schedule, shoveling food into the little mouth whether the infant is showing signs of readiness or not?

Positive interactional synchrony implies that mothers are sensitive to their infants' signals of physical and social need but extends beyond sim-ple sensitivity. Such synchrony (also called care-giver attunement, Harrist & Waugh, 2002) involves relatively prolonged periods of interactional exchanges with coordination of bodies and facial expressions over time. Mothers are not just behav-ing *at* their babies, putting a spoon in their mouths at irregular intervals independent of whether the baby is ready for another spoonful or not; rather, they are behaving *with* their babies, coordinating their actions, including facial expressions, contin-gent on those of their infant (Harrist & Waugh, 2002). We have all seen mothers (and fathers) with their infants in such coordinated interactions, and one can understand why it is sometimes called a dance. The importance of interactional synchrony was demonstrated in a meta-analysis examining factors that contribute to security of attachment; synchrony was found to be as important as paren-tal sensitivity in predicting quality of attachment (De Wolff & van IJzendoorn, 1997).

Maternal depression is one factor that has consistently been found to be related to quality of infant-mother interactional synchrony. Perhaps not surprisingly, depressed mothers are not as responsive to their infants as are mothers without depression, and their infants display more nega-tive and less positive emotions and generally low levels of activity (Dawson et al., 1999; Field, 1995). Infants of depressed mothers also show greater

A mother's (or father's) sensitivity to an infant's signal of physical and social need and synchrony can be observed during feeding. Are parents aware of what babies want or if they are ready for another spoonful, or do they shovel food toward an infant's mouth almost regardless of whether the baby is ready or not?

internalizing (for example, anxiety) and externalizing (for example, acting out) problems in later childhood (Gross et al., 1995; Zahn-Waxler et al., 1990). These behaviors are mirrored by differences in brain activity, especially lower levels of frontal cortex activity relative to children of nondepressed mothers (Dawson et al., 2003; Jones, Field, & Davalos, 2000).

Cognitive Factors Involved in Attachment

Cognitive developmental theory has been applied to explaining at least some aspects of the infant-mother attachment. Infants are born into a social world, and it would make sense for them to be prepared to perceive and respond to social stimuli. Research findings over the past 40 years clearly point to this conclusion (see Flavell, 2000; Kagan, 1984). Counter to beliefs prevalent throughout the first half of the 20th century, all sensory systems are functioning to some extent at birth, and infants are not born as blank slates (see Chapter 5). Rather, they prefer to look at, smell, and hear certain things. Many of these early preferences result in babies being oriented to other humans, because the things they prefer to look at, hear, and smell are associated with people.

For example, very young infants show a preference for the human face (Easterbrook et al., 1999; Maurer & Barrera, 1981) and can seemingly recognize faces hours after birth (Mondloch et al., 1999; Morton & Johnson, 1991). Also, the lenses of infants' eyes do not focus well for the first 2 months of life, with objects being most in focus only when they are a specific distance from their eyes. This distance is about 8 to 10 inches (Banks, 1980; Haynes, White, & Held, 1965), which is about the distance an infant's face is from its mother's face during nursing. Thus, if babies are going to see something with relative clarity, that something is likely to be an important social stimulus. Newborns are also able to recognize their mother's voice after birth (based on prenatal experience, DeCasper & Spence, 1986), and they prefer the odors of their mothers to those of other women within 2 weeks of age (Macfarlane, 1975). Newborns have also been shown to match the facial expressions of adults (neonatal imitation, Meltzoff & Moore, 1977; Nagy, 2006; see Chapter 5), which may maintain face-to-face interactions at a time when infants have little intentional control of their own social behavior.

A second line of cognitive research suggests that children's developing representational abilities influence their attachments. For example, Piaget proposed that infants develop a notion of *object*

permanence, the concept that objects continue to exist even after they are out of an infant's immediate perception (see Chapters 5 and 6). For instance, babies in the first half of their first year behave as if their bottle that is covered by a cloth, or falls out of their crib, no longer exists. Out of sight is out of mind, quite literally. This applies to an infant's attachment figure as well as to the bottle. Early researchers showed a connection between retrieving a covered object and attachment behavior in the middle of the first year of life (Schaffer, 1971). That is, babies who acted as if an object that was out of sight no longer existed showed fewer attachment behaviors than babies who knew that the covered object continued to exist in time and space. It is as if babies now believe that Mom is permanent, not merely an interesting reoccurring event, but an object that exists even when she in not in an infant's immediate perception. If she is not here now, she must be somewhere else.

Stability and Consequences of Secure (and Insecure) Attachment

Stability of Attachment over Time

Do attachment styles remain stable over time? If a child is classified as securely attached at 12 months, what is the likelihood that he or she will be similarly classified at 18 months? At 5 years? The research literature suggests that there is a moderate degree of stability of attachment over brief periods of time, although the degree of stability can be highly variable depending on the conditions in which children and their parents are living. For instance, in a summary of studies examining stability of attachment over periods ranging from 6 to 11 months (all using the Strange Situation on both occasions, and ranging in age of infants from 12 to 23 months), the percentage of infants who were classified the same at the two testing periods ranged between 30% and 96%, with a median value of 59% (Thompson, 2006).

Why the variation? One possibility is related to changes in ecological conditions during the testing interval. For example, in one study (Egeland & Sroufe, 1981), attachment classification for a low-income group of 12-month-old infants who were receiving excellent care was the same at 18 months in 81% of the cases. In contrast, attachment classification was much less stable (only 48%) for a group of infants who were being neglected or abused. Thus, when the environment is stable and of high quality, quality of attachment is also likely to be stable over time; when the environment is disruptive and unpredictable, as in homes where children are maltreated, changes in the quality of attachment can also be expected (see also Moss et al., 2005). In other words, highly stressful circumstances (for example, maltreatment, serious illness, divorce, parental loss) may provoke changes in parental sensitivity, which in turn will result in changes in quality of attachment (Thompson, 2006). However, changes from insensitive to more sensitive parenting can also result in changes in attachment style, in this case from insecure to secure.

The relationship between maternal responsiveness and attachment is illustrated in a study that assessed maternal responsiveness during infancy and at 12 years of age (Beckwith, Rodning, & Cohen, 1992). Mothers used the Attachment Q-Set to evaluate their children's attachment-related behavior at age 12, and the researchers assessed children's functioning on a variety of psychological measures at age 12. Not surprisingly, children who had mothers who were highly responsive both during infancy and at 12 years were functioning well. However, so were the children whose mothers were relatively unresponsive during infancy but became responsive at age 12. Both groups of children who had responsive mothers at age 12 had higher IQ scores, performed better on tests of mathematics, had more positive self-esteem, and had fewer behavioral or emotional problems than children who had consistently unresponsive mothers (both during infancy and at age 12). These findings indicate that when maternal responsiveness increases, the likelihood of a positive outcome also increases, suggesting that whatever effect quality of attachment (or maternal responsiveness) during infancy may have, it does not destine a child to any particular behavioral outcome in the future.

It is unlikely that being securely attached in infancy *causes* children to be securely attached in childhood or causes them to be more socially competent or intellectually advanced at age 12 or later on. Rather, securely attached infants receive greater support from their families in exploring the environment and feel secure and comfortable doing so. As these children grow older and their motor and cognitive skills become more advanced, they continue to receive support from their parents. That is, stability of attachment is usually correlated with continuity of parenting styles over time (Grossmann, Grossmann, & Waters, 2005; Waters, Weinfeld, & Hamilton, 2000). Children who have sensitive and responsive parents at 6, 12, and 18 months usually have sensitive and responsive parents at 3 and 5 years (Arend et al., 1979). The same parental qualities that promote secure attachment in infancy also promote the development of social and intellectual competence and of secure attachment during childhood.

Consequences of Secure (and Insecure) Attachment

Attachment has long been recognized as important for psychological development. For example, Bowlby (1969, 1973) noted that hard-core delinquent boys often shared one thing in common: They had never formed a warm attachment in infancy, making it difficult for them to form healthy social relationships later in life and giving them a dissocial perspective on the world (see also Crenshaw & Garbarino, 2007). One of the most investigated topics in attachment research is the consequence of attachment classification in infancy on a host of psychological factors later in life (see Belsky, 1999; Thompson, 2006).

Does secure attachment, as one might expect, lead to better psychological adjustment than the various types of insecure or disorganized attachment? The general answer to this question is "yes." In most cases, children who were classified as securely attached in infancy show better psychological adjustment in later childhood. In fact, the positive effects of secure attachment are so many and so rich that Teresa McDevitt and Jeanne Ormond (2004) described secure attachment as a "multivitamin" that prevents problems and fosters healthy development.

The research literature on the relationship of quality of attachment to later development is "dizzying" (Thompson, 2006) and covers almost every imaginable topic in cognitive, social, and emotional development. For example, research has shown that children with secure attachment are more independent and explore their environments more extensively and with greater autonomy than do insecurely attached children (Ainsworth et al., 1978; Hazen & Durrett, 1982). They also display richer and better organized symbolic play from 2 to 7 years old (Pipp, Easterbrooks, & Harmon, 1992; Slade, 1987), show more persistence in problem solving when they are 2 years old (Matas, Arend, & Sroufe, 1978), and have better conscience development (Kochanska et al., 2004). They have better relationships with their parents and peers than do children who are classified as insecurely attached (see McElwain et al., 2008; Schneider et al., 2001; Sroufe et al., 2005), and they display more positive personality characteristics, such as self-esteem, self-confidence, and general emotional health (Sroufe et al., 2005).

Some studies report lower levels of internalizing (for example, anxiety) and externalizing (for example, acting out) behavior problems for securely attached versus insecurely or disorganized/disoriented attached children (Fearon et al., 2010; Lewis et al., 1984; McCartney et al., 2004), although poor psychological adjustment

Young infants are attracted to the human face, which surely increases the chances that babies will form attachments to their primary caregivers.

is most apt to be found for disorganized/disoriented children (Carlson, 1998; Sroufe et al., 2005; Thompson, 2006) relative to other children. In adults, measures of attachment predict problems with depression, alcoholism, and eating disorders (Lindberg & Lindberg, 2007; Lindberg, Thomas, & Smith, 2004; Taylor & Lindberg, 2006). As mentioned previously, secure attachment is dependent upon sensitive care by children's parents, and the positive long-term effects of secure attachment are only to be found if children continue to receive sensitive care past infancy (Belsky & Pasco Fearon, 2002). As Ross Thompson (2006, p. 61) comments, "these findings suggest that later caregiving may be at least as important as early security in predicting later behavior."

Although these findings clearly show how important secure attachment is to later psychological development, this does not mean that being insecurely attached as an infant dooms a child to a life of unpopularity and behavior problems, or that securely attached children will necessarily have an easy life. For example, in their study of mental illness in 6-year-olds, Michael Lewis and his colleagues (1984) found that other life-stress and family factors were as important as quality of early attachment in predicting the emotional problems of a child: "The findings suggest that although a child's attachment relationship plays an important role in the development of psychopathology, the child is neither made invulnerable by an early secure attachment nor doomed to psychopathology by an insecure attachment" (p. 123). In other words, security of attachment is one of several factors that, in combination, contribute to individual differences in psychological development.

Are the Different Attachment Styles Differentially Adaptive?

It may seem that secure attachment and a belief that one can depend on other people is the most psychologically healthy outcome, which, as we have seen, is generally the case. However, some, including the pioneers of modern attachment theory, have argued that an insecure attachment style may provide some advantages, both immediately and in later adulthood, for some children growing up in harsh and unpredictable social environments. As Jeffry Simpson and Jay Belsky (2008, pp. 137, 138) noted, "although infants are biologically predisposed to form attachment bonds with their caregivers, the type of bonds they form ought to depend on the conditions in which they are raised, just as Bowlby (1969) and Ainsworth (1979) argued." Moreover, the specific form of attachment they form may be well

suited to their current (and perhaps, future) social environment. For example, an insecure-avoidant attachment style in boys is associated with aggressive behavior. This may be adaptive for young males as a strategy to gain status in male peer groups, particularly when other nonaggressive means for status attainment are not readily available to them (see Chapter 14). This does not mean that such boys are going to be psychologically well adjusted, only that, given the realities of their environment, adopting a trusting (secure) attachment style may actually be maladaptive if they are living in an environment in which social relationships are unpredictable and being tough is a better strategy for social and reproductive success than being cooperative. Similarly, the hypervigilant behavior of ambivalent/resistant infants may increase the amount of attention they receive from overburdened or unresponsive parents (see Chisholm et al., 2005; Del Giudice, 2009; Simpson, & Belsky, 2008). In other words, in the best of all possible worlds, children would live in an environment with responsive parents and dependable people. However, when environments are harsh and adult caregivers are undependable, children may be better served, in the long run, by having an insecure attachment style (see also Ein-Dor et al., 2010).

Stated slightly differently, quality, or style, of attachment can be thought of as adapting children to their local environment (see Chapter 2). Infants and children are sensitive to a range of ecological factors, including the attachment-related behavior of their parents, and they develop different styles of attachment depending on which fits best with their current environment, which will likely signal what their environment as an adult will be like (Belsky, 2005; Simpson & Belsky, 2008). This does not mean that insecure attachment results in competent behavior or a psychologically well-adjusted person. In fact, the opposite is usually the case (see Thompson, 2006). Rather, it adapts children to the particular conditions of their immediate family environment, which gets them through the niche of childhood.

Other researchers suggest that the influence of attachment quality in infancy extends beyond childhood and through the life span. For example, several researchers have proposed that quality of attachment in infancy and childhood, along with other aspects of children's early rearing environment, have a direct influence on subsequent mating strategies (Belsky, Steinberg, & Draper, 1991; Del Giudice, 2009; Ellis, 2004). Females are especially sensitive to quality of relationships and dependability of significant others to provide support. As we discussed in Chapter 4, when looking at factors that influence differences in pubertal

table 12.6 Attachment Styles in Adulthood

Four types of attachment styles in adulthood (secure, preoccupied, dismissing, fearful) and in infancy (shown in parentheses) can be derived by combining the positive/negative models of Internal Working Models of Self and of Others. These types of attachment have been proposed to be influential in the establishment of close relationships in adulthood, as well as in parental attitudes.

		MODEL OF SELF (Representation of Self)	
		Positive	Negative
MODEL OF OTHERS (Representation of Others)	Positive	SECURE (Secure primary attachments)	PREOCCUPIED (Insecure-resistant primary attachments)
	Negative	DISMISSING (Insecure-avoidant primary attachments)	FEARFUL (Disorganized/disoriented primary attachments)

SOURCE: Adapted by permission from Bartholomew, K., & Horowitz, L. M. (1991). Attachment styles among adults: A test of a four-category model. *Journal of Personality and Social Development, 61*, 226–244.

timing, girls who experience insecure, high-stress, undependable, and unpredictable environments mature sooner, engage in sex earlier, and invest less in the children they have than do girls who experience more secure, low-stress, dependable, and predictable environments.

Given the importance of attachment for later adjustment and humans' seemingly evolved propensity to form attachments, some have argued that parents would be best to return to a more "natural" style of rearing infants and young children. This is examined in Box 12.3.

Internal Working Models of Attachment

A central explanatory mechanism in attachment theory, originally formulated by Bowlby (1969, 1973, 1980), is the **internal working models of attachment**. Bowlby proposed these models to describe children's developing mental representations of their attachment relationships. Briefly, internal working models are sets of expectations and beliefs about the self, the world, and attachment relationships. They are constantly being revised as a result of experience (thus, they are working models).

Children's working models of their attachment figures and of themselves provide them with a set of expectations for themselves and for their mothers/caregivers under certain situations. "What will Mother do when I cry? How will she respond if I start to babble and make eye contact? Will I feel I need her assistance if that strange animal comes over and licks the milk off my face?" Mental models essentially represent a child's answer to the question: "Can I can count on my attachment figure to be available and responsive when needed?"

The possible answers are "Yes" (secure attachment), "No" (insecure-avoidant attachment), and "Maybe" (insecure-resistant attachment) (Hazan & Shaver, 1994). Attachment, when seen from this viewpoint, develops not only as a function of the quality of social interaction between a mother (or father) and child but also as a function of the changing mental models the child carries in his or her head.

In a more general sense, children's internal working models help them anticipate future social relationships and interactions. For instance, a child with an insecure-avoidant attachment to his mother may represent that people in general are not reliable and that the best way to interact with them would be to remain distant and not to show one's emotions. In contrast, a child who had established a secure attachment may represent that people are trustworthy, warm, rewarding, and open to emotional exchanges, promoting an open and positive attitude toward new people and social interactions. Children do not have a single internal working model of attachment, but multiple models, reflecting the fact that they have multiple attachment figures and that, as they get older, they also have representations of the mental models that other people have toward them.

An interesting variation of this model has been made by Kim Bartholomew and Leonard Horowitz (1991) (see Table 12.6), showing how attachment in childhood may produce, through the internal working models of attachment, four different attitudes and sets of expectations toward close emotional relationships in adulthood, as well as toward parenting, indicating how the

internal working models of attachment Mental models to describe children's developing mental representations of their attachment relationships.

BOX 12.3 # big questions

Is Natural Parenting Best?

Mothers have been caring for infants ever since there were mothers and infants. However, *how* mothers care for infants varies among cultures and has changed in Western societies over time. In traditional societies, and presumably for our hunter-gatherer ancestors, mothers and infants are often inseparable, with mothers carrying their babies on their backs or bellies wherever they go. If infants are not with their mothers, they are in close contact with other caregivers, often female relatives of the mothers. In these communities, babies typically breast-feed on demand and sleep with their parents. This is rarely the case in Western societies. Baby formula, prepared baby food, disposable diapers, baby monitors, professional childcare providers, and mothers working outside the home have changed the nature of infant care. This should not be surprising, given how different the lifestyles of people are today compared to those of our ancestors. Infants and their parents seem to have adjusted to these innovations in infant care, at least to the extent that children reared in Western nations grow up to be productive (and reproductive) members of their society.

But is this modern way of parenting good for children? Might a return to a more natural form of childcare produce healthier children? Some people think so, and there is a movement in some Western nations to do just this. Termed **natural parenting** (also referred to as *attachment parenting* or *instinctive parenting*), practionners advocate greater

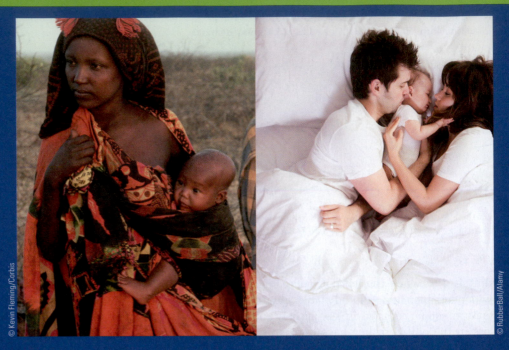

Infants in traditional societies are in near-constant contact with their mother or other caregivers, a situation that likely mirrors the experience of our ancestors. Some parents in contemporary culture advocate a return to such natural parenting, as reflected by increased physical contact, extended breast-feeding, and having infants and children sleep with their parents.

closeness between infants and parents (particularly mothers, but also fathers), increased sensitivity and responsiveness to infants' signals, and extended breast-feeding on demand (Schön, 2007). Proponents of natural parenting argue that for 99% of our species' history, infants over the first year of life, and perhaps longer, experienced constant contact and continuous care. For example, an assessment of modern hunter-gatherers showed that infants sleep with their mothers, usually continue breast-feeding until after their second birthdays or later, and are held approximately 50% of the day before they begin to crawl (Lozoff & Brittenham, 1979). Moreover, caretakers (most often mothers) tend to respond immediately and affectionately to their infants' cries. Similar patterns of infant care were found in 176 nonindustrialized societies that practice agriculture,

"intergenerational transmission of attachment patterns" may take place. Depending on children's attachment experiences, they would form a primary representation of themselves ("Model of Self" in Table 12.6) and other people ("Model of Others" in Table 12.6). If children felt they were successful in attracting adult care and comfort to fit their needs (Representation of Self = positive) and if their attachment figures exhibited sensitive care and attention toward them (Representation

of Others = positive), they would develop (in all likelihood) secure attachment. Other combinations are associated with other attachment outcomes (for example, Representation of Self = positive and Representation of Others = negative results in insecure-avoidant attachment). As can be seen in Table 12.6, crossing the dimensions of working models of self and others produces four types of attachment during childhood, as well as different types of adult attachment-like attitudes toward others, including their own children.

Contemporary research in internal working models of attachment examines how children mentally represent aspects of their socioemotional functioning and relate it to behavioral measures of attachment security (see Thompson, 2006). For

natural parenting A movement in some Western nations to return to a more "natural" form of infant care, including having greater closeness between infants and parents (particularly mothers, but also fathers), increased sensitivity and responsiveness to infants' signals, and extended breastfeeding on demand.

fishing, or herding, although fewer parents in these societies provide infants with close physical contact for more than half the day, unlike parents in hunter-gatherer communities (Lozoff & Brittenham, 1979; see also H. Keller et al., 2004).

In contrast to these more traditional communities, infants in Western countries are rarely held more than 35% of the day, with this amount decreasing considerably over the first year of life (see Schön, 2007). Cosleeping, with infants sharing their parents' bed all night, has increased in Western countries over the past several decades, but the practice still is found in fewer than 15% of families in most countries (see Schön, 2007). Breast-feeding is practiced widely in Western nations immediately after birth, with about 70% of American mothers and greater than 90% of European mothers breast-feeding their infants while still in the hospital. These figures drop to about one-third or less by 6 months of age, however, and decline even further by 12 months (Li et al., 2003; Ryan, Wenjun, & Acosta, 2002).

Although it is difficult to get definitive figures, an increasing number of Western parents are practicing aspects of natural parenting by extending how long babies are breast-fed, practicing cosleeping, and increasing the amount of contact with and sensitivity to infants (Sears & Sears, 2001; Schön, 2007). Does natural parenting have any consequences for children's development? Some characteristics of natural parenting have much in common with the practices of mothers who are sensitive and responsive to their infants' signals of physical and social needs, and so it is not surprising that most infants who experience natural parenting are securely attached to their mothers. As such, they experience the psychological and physiological benefits that such positive infant-mother relationships provide (see research reviewed in Schön, 2007, and our earlier discussion of the causes and consequences of differences in quality of attachment).

Regine Schön (2007), in an extensive review of natural parenting, concluded that natural parenting

> provides infants with an optimal environment for psychological and physiological growth during early life. It is the rearing style to which the human infant has biologically adapted over the course of evolution, with lifestyle changes in recent history being far too short in duration to have allowed any significant biological adaptation to the altered living conditions. (pp. 157–158)

The question Schön asks is how much can Western practices deviate from this pattern before infants experience negative consequences?

Human infants show substantial plasticity and an ability to adjust to a wide range of environments. If that were not the case, the "unnatural parenting" practices that characterized Western societies throughout most of the 20th century and continue today would have had dire effects on the outcomes of several generations of children. Moreover, given the wide range of physical and social environments in which humans live, if infants required "perfect parenting" to survive, the species likely would have gone extinct long ago. This is reflected in Sandra Scarr's (1992) concept of "good-enough parenting." Children have evolved, Scarr proposed, to be able to respond to a wide range of parenting styles, and everyday "good-enough" parenting is sufficient to get children through childhood to adulthood. (Scarr's ideas will be explored in greater detail in Chapter 13.) Schön (2007, p. 158), in contrast, believes "that conventional Western child-rearing approaches may have already crossed the line of optimal parenting in some areas of infant care."

We are confident that aspects of natural parenting do indeed match children's (and likely adults') evolved biases to form social relationships and thus foster positive social and emotional development. However, we would not want to characterize the practices of modern parents as "unnatural parenting" or "insensitive parenting." We are confident that infants can develop into psychologically healthy children and adults even if they sleep in their own rooms on most nights and they are not breast-fed past their first birthdays. Research has clearly shown that children's psychological development is fostered by loving parents who are sensitive to the needs of their offspring. Natural parenting can promote such development, but so can parenting practices that are closer to current cultural norms.

example, researchers have reported that securely attached 5-year-old children show greater emotional understanding and greater frequency of mother-child conversations about emotions than do children classified as insecurely attached (Ontai & Thompson, 2002; Raikes & Thompson, 2005). This suggests that secure attachment, as reflected by children's internal working models of attachment, influences emotional understanding through mother-child conversational style. Other research has similarly found associations between security of attachment measures and cognitive indices of socioemotional development, including memories of positive events, peers' behavior attributions, conscience development, and self-concept (see Thompson, 2006).

Although internal working models of attachment are best thought of as cognitive mechanisms, this does not mean that they are not influenced by more basic biological factors. The biopsychological basis of internal working models of attachment is discussed in Box 12.4.

Attachment has received much research attention over the decades, for three good reasons: (1) attachment between infants and their mothers greatly increases the chances that children will survive; (2) it is a child's first relationship, one that may serve as the basis for future relationships with other people; and (3) quality of attachment in infancy is related to behavioral, social, emotional, and cognitive adjustment later in life.

BOX 12.4 the biopsychology of childhood

The Biopsychology of the Internal Working Models of Attachment

Attachment is a complex process that involves the coordination of biological, cognitive, and behavioral systems in infants and mothers (and perhaps fathers). Daphne Bugental (2000) proposed that attachment is one of several social domains that has experienced substantial pressure from natural selection. One way in which such domains can be identified is that a set of *neurohormonal regulators* can be specified for the domain. Neurohormonal regulators refer to coordinated hormone and brain mechanisms that influence motivation and behavior. For attachment, key neurohormonal regulators include **opioids** and **oxytocin**. Naturally occurring opioids are associated with reward, or pleasure, and these chemicals are recognized by receptors in the brain (primarily the limbic system, see Chapter 4). Oxytocin has been called the "love hormone" and is produced at orgasm in both males and females, during cuddling, birth, suckling, stroking, and hugging. It reduces levels of the stress hormone cortisol and promotes relaxation and feelings of warmth and affiliation (see Carter, 1998).

In young mammals, including humans, infant distress caused by either internal states (such as hunger) or separation from the mother is associated with a reduction in opioids. This in turn activates distress vocalizations (that is, crying) in the young. When mothers hear these cries, their own levels of opioids decrease, which prompts them to provide care for their babies. When mothers comfort their infants, opioid levels increase for both, which leads to a calm and restful state. The release of oxytocin in both mother and baby during nursing, or when a mother holds and cuddles her infant, promotes positive feelings and recognition of significant social partners, which, when coupled with the increased production of rewarding opioids, sets the stage for the formation of a durable infant-mother attachment (Bugental, 2000; Chisholm et al., 2005).

Hormones have their effect on behavior by influencing brain structures, which in turn influence the production of hormones and behavior. A good place to start is the *amygdala*, an evolutionarily old structure in the limbic system that is heavily involved in determining the emotional value of a stimulus ("Is this something to fear or something to love?") (LeDoux, 1996). The *hippocampus* stores information and permits infants to match new experiences (for instance, a sensation of falling) with "old" experiences (consequences of past falls) (Chisholm et al., 2005). In the face of stress (falling, or a fear of falling), the hypothalamic-pituitary-adrenal (HPA) axis (see Chapter 4) becomes activated, generating a series of biochemicals in reaction to stress, such as cortisol, with the goal of preparing the organism for threat. Chronic stress, including ineffective and unresponsive parenting, is associated with increased cortisol levels and poor medical and psychological outcomes (Flinn, 2006).

When infants have positive and non-stressful experiences, the HPA axis regulates behavior by increasing the release of opioids and oxytocin, decreasing the production of cortisol, and promoting the recognition of the social beings associated with these good feelings. From such repeated experiences of emotional warmth, of parents who respond contingently to infants' behavior, and the neurohormonal events associated with these experiences, babies create a secure representation of their caregiver in their internal working models of attachment (Chisholm et al., 2005). In contrast, if infants' early life is dominated by unpredictability and a lack of caregiver warmth, they will have different neurohormonal experiences (increased stress hormones, decreased oxytocin and opioids), and this will result in an insecure cognitive-emotional representation of their attachment figure.

Why would parents *not* provide a supportive environment for their children, and thus one in which levels of cortisol are low and oxytocin and opioids are high? One possibility is that ecological pressures on the parents make it difficult for them to care adequately for all of their children. As a result, some offspring in a family (possibly all) experience high-stress, insecure attachment and chronically elevated levels of stress hormones (Chisholm et al., 2005). Although this seems to be maladaptive compared to the neurohormonal consequences of secure attachment, it may prepare these children for life as adults. The best predictors of future environments are current ones, and children who experience stressful environments early in life can expect similar environments in adulthood. High levels of cortisol prepare individuals to deal with difficult and threatening situations—to keep them alive and functioning despite the dangers they face. There may be negative health consequences later in life, or psychosocial maladjustment, but these later costs are compensated by more immediate benefits of having a neurohormonal system that is primed to deal with chronic conflict. This interpretation fits well with Thomas Boyce and Bruce Ellis's (2005) idea that individual differences in biological sensitivity to context interact with individual differences in children's early experience to produce different patterns of development that may prove to be adaptive for later environments (see Chapter 11, Box 11.2). With respect to experiencing stress early in life, the relative costs or benefits may also be related to individual differences at the genetic level.

A child's attachment relationship is not everything, of course. Although it may be the basis of a child's relationship with his or her parent, relationships between parents and children are complex and extend far beyond attachment, as we will see in the next chapter. Yet, given the importance of social relationships to humans, it is little wonder that this first relationship has garnered so much attention from psychologists and has been regarded by many as a cornerstone for psychological well-being.

opioids Neurohormonal regulator associated with reward, or pleasure, recognized by specific receptors in the brain.

oxytocin Neurohormonal regulator that is produced at orgasm in both males and females, during cuddling, birth, suckling, stroking, and hugging; it reduces levels of the stress hormone cortisol and promotes relaxation and feelings of warmth and affiliation.

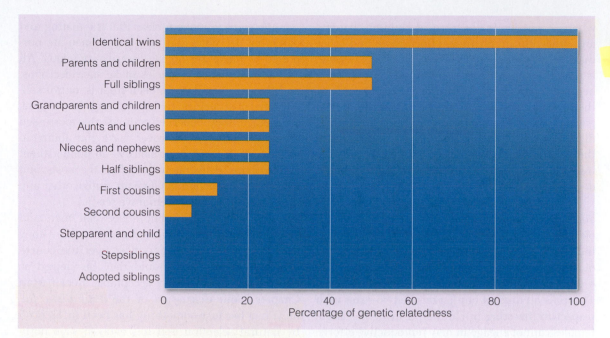

Chart: Percentage of genetic relatedness

- Identical twins: 100
- Parents and children: 50
- Full siblings: 50
- Grandparents and children: 25
- Aunts and uncles: 25
- Nieces and nephews: 25
- Half siblings: 25
- First cousins: 12.5
- Second cousins: 6.25
- Stepparent and child: 0
- Stepsiblings: 0
- Adopted siblings: 0

Percentage of genetic relatedness

An Evolutionary Perspective of Childcare

When we talk of infant-mother attachment, we implicitly assume that this psychological mechanism (or suite of mechanisms, more likely) increases the chances that a child will survive and thrive. This is to both the infant's and the parent's benefit, of course. But rearing human babies to maturity requires more than a close attachment to mothers. Humans are social animals, and this is perhaps most obvious when it comes to rearing children. It is the rare mother who is able to rear her child alone. As Hillary Clinton (1996) wrote, citing an African saying, "It takes a village to raise a child." Perhaps, but actually human *families* are the social group with the primary responsibility for rearing children. Families come in many forms (see Chapter 13), but all include genetic relatives, or kin.

The conventional Western idea of raising children is within a nuclear family—Mom, Dad, and the kids, with perhaps occasional help from Grandma or Aunt Louise. Yet, as we will see in Chapter 13, the nuclear family is not the only child-rearing arrangement that is common among humans, and in all types of families the amount of time and effort different people devote to child-rearing is unequal, with women around the globe and over historical time spending considerably more time and physical resources (milk, for instance) than men, who, in some cultures, spend virtually no time caring for their children. But neither is childcare solely the mother's responsibility. In virtually all societies, the task of child-rearing falls to families.

To understand why groups of genetic relatives may help mothers rear their children, we turn to William Hamilton's (1964) concept of inclusive fitness. Essentially, inclusive fitness refers to how many copies of one's genes make it into the next generation. Genes are passed along from parents to children but also to grandchildren. For example, a person shares 50% of his or her genes with a full sibling, 25% of genes with a half sibling, and 12.5% with first cousins (see Figure 12.2). (Recall from Chapter 3 that people actually share about 99.9% of their genes, with only 1% of genes being different among people. Siblings share 50% of those genes that differ among people, whereas first cousins share 12.5%.) The reproductive success of these blood relatives indirectly reflects one's own success. If your sister has four children, each of those nieces and nephews will share, on average, 25% of your genes. One's inclusive fitness refers not just to the number of children one has (Darwin's definition of classical fitness), but also to the copies of your genes that are represented in future generations, whether they came directly from you in the form of children and grandchildren or indirectly through a genetic relative (for example, siblings, cousins, nieces, and nephews). According to inclusive-fitness theory, the care, or investment, we provide to children should be influenced by genetic relatedness.

Biologists often talk about parents and other genetic relatives *investing* in children. Investing implies that we expect to get something back for

....

inclusive fitness In evolutionary theory, how many copies of one's genes make it into the next generation, either directly through children or indirectly through relatives who share one's genes.

what we put in. In the case of children, parents and other kin invest time, effort, food, and other material resources, and their payback, as it were, is a child who survives to adulthood to hopefully become a parent him- or herself, passing some of the investor's genes on to the next generation. As a general rule of thumb, inclusive-fitness theory predicts that, all other things being equal, the greater the genetic similarity between the child and the investor, the more care that individual should devote to the child.

Evolutionary theory also suggests that men and women (fathers and mothers) have different obligations and feelings toward their children. In humans, reproduction involves a gestation period of 9 months, plus, at least, a period of about 3 or 4 years of nurturing a highly dependent offspring. This puts an uneven burden on the two sexes with respect to investing in children. During gestation, females cannot engage in new reproductive efforts. They are already pregnant and can have only one child at a time (with the exception of multiples). After birth, as all mammals, mothers are obliged to nurse the baby. Males are not so constrained, either during gestation or after birth.

According to parental investment theory, as proposed by evolutionary biologist Robert Trivers (1972), the sexes differ in how much they invest in mating versus parenting. In most mammals, including humans, females invest more time and resources in parenting than do males. (Parental investment theory will be discussed further in Chapter 15 on the development of sexuality.) Because of these differences, men and women should have evolved different psychologies related to mating and parenting. For example, women are more generally selective in assenting to sex than are men (Oliver & Hyde, 1993), whereas men are more inclined to compete with one another for access to females and are less selective in terms of whom they have sex with. Although the males of most mammal species provide nothing in the way of childcare, human men are among the approximately 5% of male mammals that do invest in their offspring after birth. Because human children are dependent for such a long time, men can increase their inclusive fitness by investing in their offspring, and most men do, providing—if not childcare—resources to their mates and their children (Geary, 2007b). However, in both traditional and contemporary cultures, and surely in our past, women provided the bulk of the childcare.

parental investment theory Theory coming from evolutionary biology that predicts differences in behaviors between males and females as a function of how much each invests in mating versus parenting.

alloparenting Provision of care to children by individuals other than the genetic mother.

We want to make it clear that the mating and parenting decisions that men and women are purported to make are not necessarily conscious. All sexually reproducing species make such decisions, and they are based on implicit (that is, out of self-awareness) strategies that have evolved because, on average, they benefited animals that possessed them. We humans, however, have the ability to make such decisions consciously—to ponder them and perhaps deliberately calculate the costs and benefits of any action. As a result, unlike other animals, we can override them if we see fit.

Any evolved differences between men and women should not be viewed as inevitable—they can be modified by experiences over the course of development—nor should they be viewed as natural and thus socially acceptable. Recall from Chapter 2 our discussion of the *naturalistic fallacy*: Just because something has been influenced by natural selection and has evolved says nothing about its social or moral acceptability. Natural selection shaped human behavior for life in very different environments from those in which modern humans live. With our expanded brain and invention of material culture, we have evolved moral codes that in many ways were developed to combat our animal nature. Nonetheless, understanding our unconscious and animal dispositions can help us better understand contemporary behavior and sometimes to change it. This is as true of parenting as it is for any other evolutionarily significant sets of behaviors.

The Evolution of Human Childcare: Humans as Cooperative Breeders

As mentioned earlier, human mothers are not alone in caring for their infants and children. The provision of care to children by individuals other than the genetic mother is called alloparenting and has likely always played a significant role in human child-rearing (Hrdy, 1999, 2007, 2009). Other than by the father, alloparenting is usually provided by female relatives. Among traditional human groups, most care is in the form of babysitting or other types of assistance. For instance, among the Aché, a South American hunter-gatherer group, women with young children forage less than women without children. Other women, usually blood relatives, make up the difference by foraging more and sharing with the mothers (Crittenden & Marlowe, 2008; Hill & Hurtado, 1996). In many societies, preadolescent girls (often older sisters) and grandmothers babysit (see Hrdy, 1999).

Primatologist Sarah Hrdy (2007, 2009) proposed the **cooperative breeding hypothesis**, suggesting that humans evolved a system of parenting in which mothers shared the responsibility for childcare with others in the family and the larger social group. According to Hrdy, this increased social support permitted women to space their slow-developing children more closely, allowing them to care for and nourish more children than they possibly could if they were solely responsible for them. This is really more than a hypothesis, as research has shown that the chances of a child's survival increases substantially when mothers have help rearing their children, with maternal grandmothers having the greatest overall effects on children's survival (Sear & Mace, 2008). (We will have more to say about maternal grandmothers later in this chapter.)

What we want to emphasize here is that in traditional societies, and surely in our species' past, raising children was a task performed primarily by an interconnected group of mainly female relatives. Fathers played a role as well, and they are playing an ever-increasing role in information-age societies today (see Cabrera et al., 2000; Collins et al., 2000), but mothers and their female relatives have always had the principal responsibility for childcare, a pattern that continues today (Hetherington et al., 1999). Children's extended period of dependency necessitates that mothers receive help from others, usually in addition to whatever support the father provides, so that a child can reach adulthood.

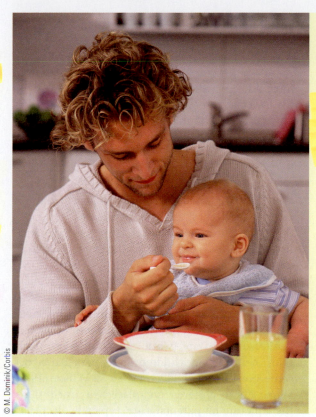

In 95% of all mammal species, fathers do not provide any form of childcare for their offspring. Human males are one of the exceptions. By providing childcare, they increase the chances that their children will survive and thrive.

Caring for and Investing in Children

We all expect mothers, fathers, and more distant relatives to provide the care, support, and the resources necessary for children to survive, and hopefully thrive. It is what parents do (or at least are supposed to do). But how much effort parents put into caring for any particular child may vary, and it may be different from the amount of care that children want from their parents. For example, parents may have several children, and although each child may want all the care and resources he or she can get, parents will want to distribute their resources among their various children (Salmon, 2005, 2007; Trivers, 1974). In fact, the efforts one puts into a particular child today may take away from efforts or resources that one can devote to future children. Strictly from the perspective of inclusive-fitness theory, it is not always in a parent's best interest to devote everything he or she can into every child.

In this section, we look at some of the factors that influence the amount of care that mothers, fathers, grandparents, stepparents, and adoptive parents make in children through the lens of evolutionary theory.

Maternal Care

Mothers' care for their children is substantial and obligatory, but some children may require more care or resources than others, and mothers may not always be able to devote the maximum amount of care that a child requires (or wants). In fact, a wise strategy for our ancestral mothers, who lived in times when resources were scarce and survival uncertain, would be to provide the most care to children who have the greatest chance of growing up and reproducing themselves. Recall that one of the principles of natural selection is that more offspring are born in a generation than will survive. The likelihood of surviving childhood for our ancestors was about 50%, meaning that about half of a woman's children would not reach adulthood (Volk & Atkinson, 2008). Given those odds, successful mothers would be those who could identify cues that signal the likelihood of a child reaching adulthood, such as good health, and then devoting the necessary

cooperative breeding hypothesis Proposal that humans evolved a system of parenting in which mothers shared the responsibility for childcare with others in the family and the larger social group.

care to those children. This means that the amount of care given to riskier children (for example, those with poor health) may have to be reduced. Although it is often difficult for contemporary people to think in this fashion ("How can a mother *not* devote all the love and care she can to her children, no matter how risky they are?"), given what we know about nurturing behavior in other species and in traditional groups of humans, and the incidence in contemporary society of children being abandoned or removed from the home to be placed in foster care, such thinking must have surely characterized our foremothers. These are not necessarily conscious thoughts, but rather implicit, and perhaps automatic, cognitions that proved adaptive to our ancestors (Bugental & Beaulieu, 2003).

What factors influence how much a woman cares for any particular child? Perhaps most obvious is a child's health. In contemporary society, children with intellectual impairment or other congenital diseases are two to ten times more likely than nonafflicted children to experience abuse sometime during childhood (Daly & Wilson, 1981). When these children are placed in institutions, the amount of parental care typically decreases substantially, with some parents rarely ever seeing their children again (Daly & Wilson, 1988a). In most cases, differential care to unhealthy children is less extreme and likely not even conscious. For example, Janet Mann (1992) observed the interactions of seven mothers and their premature, low-birth-weight, and sickly twins. At 8 months of age, all mothers displayed more positive behaviors, such as talking to, playing with, looking at, kissing, holding, and soothing, toward the healthier of the two twins.

Other factors also influence how much care a mother is likely to devote to her children. One important factor is a child's age. Until very recently, rates of infant mortality were relatively high, with death rates declining as children got older. From this perspective, mothers should devote more care and resources to older than younger children, especially when resources are scarce and investment in a younger child can result in the deterioration and possibly death of an older child. Mother's age is also an important factor. Younger women, who have many child-bearing years ahead of them, are less apt to devote considerable care to a high-risk infant than are older women, who may have fewer opportunities to have more children (Beaulieu & Bugental, 2008). The incidences of neglect and abuse are more frequently observed in younger than older mothers (Lee & George, 1999).

The amount of social support a woman has is also a cue as to how much care she should provide her children. Particularly important is support from the father of her child, as well as from

alloparents. This is less of a problem today in the developed world, where the state or other institutions (for example, churches) help single mothers and their children, but lack of social support was clearly a serious concern for our foremothers and remains a problem for many single mothers in the world today, even in the United States and other developed nations. Overall, the investment decisions a woman makes about her children will be based on the resources she has available to herself and her children, including social resources, and her judgments about how a particular child can use those investments to become a successful adult (Bugental & Beaulieu, 2003). Most of these decisions will be made out of conscious awareness.

Paternal Care

Why should fathers provide time, energy, and resources for their children? The simple answer is that a father's care is important to the survival and success of his children. This is not simply theory but based on hard facts. Data from hunter-gatherer societies (Hill & Hurtado, 1996), historical records from Western Europe (Reid, 1997), and from developing countries today (United Nations, 1985) all indicate that children's mortality rates are higher and their social status is lower when fathers are absent (see Geary, 2000, 2007b). This seems to be especially true for male offspring (Gibson, 2008). In contemporary America, the quality of a father's active involvement in the lives of his children is associated with school achievement, social skills, and emotional regulation (see Cabrera et al., 2000; Lamb, 1997).

Although women in all cultures devote more time to childcare than men (Eibl-Eibesfeldt, 1989; Whiting & Whiting, 1975), some fathers in some developed countries spend as much, or even more, time with their children than do mothers (see Parke, 2002, 2008). In modern society, good fathers not only provide financial resources but are also expected to spend considerable time with their children, including chores that once were women's work only, such as changing diapers, bathing babies, and providing night feedings. Although this may be the cultural stereotype of good fathers, the reality is that the average amount of time fathers spend with their children in the United States has not changed appreciably over the past 50 years. Whereas many fathers are spending substantially more time with their children than fathers in past generations, this is counterbalanced by fathers who have minimal or no contact with their children on a regular basis. The number of children born to single mothers, without the presence of a father in the household, has increased four-fold since 1960 (see Cabrera et al., 2000).

One factor that influences how much men contribute to their offspring is *paternity certainty*. Men can never be certain of paternity, with the *cuckoldry rate* (the rate of the domestic father not being the genetic father) hovering around 10% (see Geary, 2005c). This provides men with a moderate degree of certainty, enough to (usually) convince a man that caring for his wife's child is in his best interest, but not enough certainty to ignore hints that the child may not be his. Family members are often aware of this and frequently comment how much a new baby resembles the father, especially the mother in the presence of the father (Alvergne, Faurie, & Raymond, 2007; McLain et al., 2000). In the first study to demonstrate this, 80% of all remarks about the appearance of the baby concerned the resemblance to the father (Daly & Wilson, 1982). This phenomenon has been found in several different societies (Brédart & French, 1999; Christenfeld & Hill, 1995) and presumably serves to convince the father that the child is indeed his.

In related research, the amount of investment parents devoted to their children (measured in terms of emotional closeness, use of physical punishment, and amount of time parents spend actively interacting with their child on a daily basis) was investigated in terms of the perceived personality and physical similarity between the parent and the child. The amount of investment mothers provided their children was positively related to *personality similarity*; in contrast, the amount of investment fathers provided to their children was positively related to *physical similarity* (Heijkoop, Dubas, & van Aken, 2009). In other words, a mother's investment decisions were based on (quite likely unconsciously) on the psychological similarity between herself and her child, whereas a father's investment decisions were based on physical similarity, consistent with the idea that men are sensitive to cues of physical resemblance that indicate paternity certainty. In other studies, men rated physical resemblance of infants to themselves as more important in making hypothetical adoption decisions than did women (Volk & Quinsey, 2007).

Related to this, a recent study found that the amount of affection and attachment fathers felt toward their children was related to their ability to recognize their children on the basis of smell (Dubas, Heijkoop, & van Aken, 2009). In this study, children wore cotton T-shirts to bed for three consecutive nights and avoided scented soaps and perfumes. Parents then smelled various T-shirts and were asked if they could identify who had worn them. Fathers who could identify their children on the basis of odor were more likely to report feelings of affection and attachment and less likely to ignore their children than were fathers who could not identify the T-shirts their children wore.

The authors speculated that fathers might unconsciously use olfactory cues as signs of genetic relatedness and display more affection for and investment in those children whose odors they recognize (and thus who are likely to be theirs).

Males' care for their children may not be obligatory, but males are also biologically prepared to care for children, or at least can be induced to do so. For example, in a variety of mammal species, simple exposure to infants produces increased parental behaviors in males, accompanied by changes in levels of female hormones, such as prolactin (see Schradin & Anzenberger, 1999). Human males are not immune to these effects. For example, levels of prolactin increased in a group of men over the course of their partner's pregnancy, and levels of testosterone decreased after the birth of a baby (see Storey et al., 2000; Wynne-Edwards & Reburn, 2000).

Grandparental Care

Parents are not the only people with a genetic interest in children. Although children share 50% of their genes with each of their parents, they share 25% of their genes with each of their grandparents. As such, the attention that grandparents give to their grandchildren is not solely out of the goodness of their hearts, but, from an inclusive-fitness perspective, is in their genetic best interest.

Grandparents are in a similar situation as parents in one respect. Just as the mother always knows the baby is hers, so does the maternal grandmother know that her grandchild carries 25% of her genes. None of the other grandparents can be so certain. Although the maternal grandfather can be certain that the grandchild is his daughter's, he cannot be 100% certain that he is the genetic father of his daughter. The paternal grandparents have the same uncertainty that the father has, with cuckoldry being a possibility in two generations for the father's father. From this perspective, all other things being equal, maternal grandmothers should be willing to devote the most care, paternal grandfathers the least, and maternal grandfathers and paternal grandmothers should fall somewhere in the middle.

Several studies have examined the amount of investment grandparents provide to their grandchildren as a function of genetic relatedness and have found general support for the evolutionary model (Bishop et al., 2009; Euler & Michalski, 2007; Pashos & McBurney, 2008). Depending on the study, investment is measured in terms of time spent interacting with, emotional closeness to, resources given to, or solicitude for grandchildren. In a pioneering study, researchers interviewed German adults and asked them to rate the amount of care they received from each of their grandparents

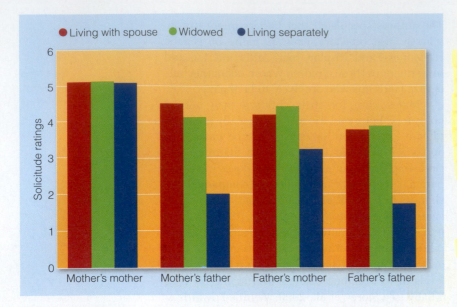

FIGURE 12.3 Solicitude ratings (expressing care and concern for the well-being of another) for four classes of grandparents toward their grandchildren.

The amount of solicitude grandparents showed their grandchildren was related to how many genes the two shared and by paternity certainty. SOURCE: Adapted from Euler, H. A., & Weitzel, B. (1996). Discriminative grandparental solicitude as reproductive strategy. *Human Nature, 7*, 39–59.

up to age 6. Figure 12.3 presents the mean solicitude ratings (expressing care and concern for the well-being of another) for the four classes of grandparents. Overall, the pattern follows predictions: maternal grandmothers had the highest solicitude ratings, paternal grandfathers the lowest, and mother's father and father's mother were in between. The patterns were basically the same whether the grandparent in question was living with a spouse, widowed, or living separately (Euler & Weitzel, 1996).

These findings are supported by a study that examined more than 150 years of German births (1720–1874) and found that children without a living maternal grandmother were more likely to die than those without a living paternal grandmother. In some age intervals, the difference in death rate was as large as 60% (Beise & Voland, 2002). Further evidence for the importance of maternal grandmothers in the success of their grandchildren comes from research in contemporary rural Ethiopia, where the help provided by maternal grandmothers was associated with lower child mortality (Gibson & Mace, 2005). Other research demonstrated that the presence of a mother's mother was associated with higher fertility and survival rates for Canadian and Finnish farm families (Lahdenperä et al., 2004).

There is at least one exception to this general pattern of greater maternal grandparent solicitude, and that is a study by Alexander Pashos (2000), who examined grandparental investment in Germany and urban and rural Greece. Pashos reported the same pattern as other researchers for

grandparents from Germany and urban Greece, but the rural Greeks displayed a different pattern. The *paternal grandparents* provided more care than the maternal grandparents in this latter group. This discrepancy was explained by the traditional family custom in rural Greece of the married couple coming to live near or with the paternal family, who have the social obligation of caring for their grandchildren, particularly for their grandsons, who are their primary heirs. This close living arrangement means that the husband's family can monitor the activities of their daughter-in-law, resulting in increased paternity certainty, so that the father's family can care for their grandchildren with increased confidence. This finding indicates the potentially strong effect of culture in modifying evolutionarily influenced patterns of care. Although the decisions of grandparents may be affected by the number of likely genes they share with their grandchildren, such decisions are, in the end, influenced as much by cultural practices.

The importance of grandparents, particularly grandmothers, may not be surprising to modern readers, but might grandmothers also have influenced human longevity? In Chapter 2 we stated that natural selection has a more potent effect on the earlier parts of the life span, before and during one's reproductive years, than it does later. After one has reproduced, natural selection is essentially powerless. One's genes are already in the next generation, and whatever good or bad qualities one has, such as genes that promote longevity or early-developing cancer, have already been passed along.

One exception to this scenario that evolutionary theorists have proposed goes by the name the grandmother hypothesis (Alexander, 1974; Hamilton, 1966). By living past one's reproductive years, women can devote their time and resources to their children and grandchildren and, as a result, increase the chances of survival of their grandchildren. This means that more of their genes will make it into future generations, and some of these genes will be associated with old age. Women who never lived long enough to become grandmothers could not provide care for their grandchildren, fewer of their grandchildren would survive, and thus fewer of their genes would be propagated.

Although it remains controversial, there is some evidence for the grandmother hypothesis. For example, among the Hazda, a group of foragers living in the African Rift Valley, postmenopausal women contribute significantly to the nutrition of their grandchildren, particularly when the mother is still nursing (Hawkes, O'Connell, & Blurton Jones, 1997; O'Connell, Hawkes, & Blurton Jones, 1999). So next time you visit your grandmother,

grandmother hypothesis Evolutionary hypothesis that by living past one's reproductive years, women can devote their time and resources to their children and grandchildren, and, as a result, increase the chances of survival of their grandchildren.

Most cultures have folktales about "wicked stepparents" such as the familiar story of Cinderella. This reflects the fact that stepparents invest less in their stepchildren than their genetic children. However, most stepparents today are not wicked but provide adequate care for their nongenetically related offspring.

you may want to thank her not only for the support she gives to you and gave to your parents when they were raising young children, but also for contributing to our species' long life spans.

Stepparent Care

In the developed world today, divorce and remarriage are common occurrences (see Chapter 13), and remarriage was also likely common, in one form or another, for our ancestors. With remarriage comes a stepparent—a genetically unrelated adult who lives with and has some responsibility toward a spouse's children. According to a strict interpretation of inclusive-fitness theory, stepparents should not provide care for their stepchildren at all. They share no genes, and thus the stepparent should not be willing to share resources or devote his or her time to a stepchild. This is not the case, however, mainly because stepchildren come with a genetic mother or father. If a man or woman wants to attract a new mate, one way to do so is to care for that person's children from a previous coupling. In fact, some people have argued that what care men provide to their stepchildren should not be viewed as investment in children, but as investment in mating opportunities; they provide for their stepchildren to gain access to their mother's companionship and affection (Anderson, Kaplan, & Lancaster, 1999a; Rowher, Herron, & Daly, 1999).

How much care do stepparents provide for their stepchildren, and is it really much different from the care provided by genetic parents? In studies ranging from the United States, South Africa, and the Caribbean, and from traditional foragers to developed countries, stepparents have been found to spend less time interacting with (Anderson et al., 1999a; Flinn, 1988; Marlowe, 1999), spend less money on education for (Anderson et al., 1999a; 1999b), and spend less money on food for (Case, Lin, & McLanahan, 2000) their stepchildren than their biological children. Many stepparents love their stepchildren and provide them with substantial resources. In fact, there is no other species in which adults so regularly shower care and resources on unrelated offspring. Despite the magnanimous gestures of support by many stepparents toward their stepchildren, many stepparents report that it is difficult to form close emotional bonds with their stepchildren. For example, in an older study conducted in the United States, only 53% of stepfathers and 25% of stepmothers claimed to have any "parental feelings" whatsoever for their stepchildren (Duberman, 1975).

One indication that stepparents do not provide the care and support that natural parents do can be seen in the incidence of child abuse. The presence of a stepparent in a family is the single best predictor of child abuse (Daly & Wilson, 1988a, 1996). In a Canadian study, Martin Daly and Margo Wilson (1985) interviewed nearly 1,000 households, some where child abuse was known to have occurred. They reported that the incidence of child abuse was 40 times greater if children lived with a stepparent versus two natural parents. This enormous difference remained even after controlling for

BOX 12.5 evolution in action

When Parents Kill Their Children

It fortunately does not happen often, and when it does it almost always makes the headlines: **filicide**, the killing of a child by a parent. Which children are apt to be victims of filicide and under what conditions are parents likely to kill their children? As we noted in Chapter 1 in discussing the history of childhood, *infanticide*, the killing of an infant, was a common practice in Europe if a child was of poor health, deformed, one of twins, illegitimate, or otherwise unwanted. Infanticide, particularly during the newborn period (termed *neonatalcide*), has been found in most traditional cultures studied. It is practiced when resources are scarce and the newborn will not likely survive or would take resources away from a mother's other children. For example, among the Eipo of West New Guinea, mothers give birth alone outside and, based on the apparent health of the infant, decide whether to bring the baby to the village or to abandon it in the bush wrapped in leaves and branches (Schiefenhövel 1988). These decisions are also made based on the resources available to support a new baby, as the village can only support a limited number of people.

A child's age is also a factor in filicides in the developed world. The accompanying figure presents data based on child homicides committed by natural parents and nonrelatives in Canada between 1974 and 1983 (Daly & Wilson, 1988a). As you can see, the likelihood of a nonrelative killing a child is relatively low and stays low until the teen years. In contrast, the likelihood that a child will be killed by a natural parent is high during the first year of life and drops off sharply thereafter. For the most part, if a parent kills a child, the father is the probable perpetrator. The exception is during infancy, when genetic mothers are the most likely culprits (Harris et al., 2007). This is especially true for the youngest homicide victims, newborns. When a newborn is killed or abandoned to die, it is usually the mother who does so (Overpeck et al., 1998).

It is not just the child's age that is a predictor of child homicide, but also the mother's age (Day & Wilson, 1988a; Overpeck et al., 1998). For example, based on homicide rates in Canada between 1974 and 1983, teenage mothers were more than four times as likely to kill their babies as were women in their twenties, a pattern that has also been found in traditional groups (Bugos & McCarthy, 1984). Why are younger mothers more apt to kill their children? One reason may be

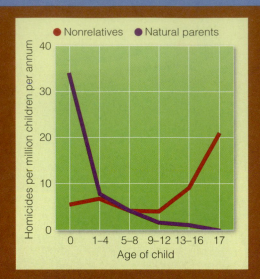

Risk of homicide by a natural parent in relationship to the child's age: Canada 1974–1983. SOURCE: Adapted from Daly, M., & Wilson, M. (1988). *Homicide.* **New York: Aldine.**

the greater emotional immaturity typically shown by teenage mothers. Many such young women also lack social support, making it difficult for them to raise a child. Recall also that younger women have many childbearing years ahead of them, making the death of an infant less of a loss in terms of potential fertility relative to older women.

---

factors such as socioeconomic status, family size, and mother's age.

Consistent with inclusive-fitness theory, stepparents devote fewer resources, spend less time interacting with, and feel less emotionally attached to their stepchildren than do biological parents. They are also more likely than biological parents to abuse or kill their stepchildren, a topic we examine more closely in Box 12.5. Yet, most stepparents provide adequate, or even substantial, care to their genetically unrelated wards. Perhaps rather than lamenting the phenomenon of "the wicked stepparent," which is found in folktales in all cultures (including the familiar Cinderella), we should be impressed with how flexible human behavior can be and with the vast majority of stepparents who provide loving care to their stepchildren. Nonetheless, differences in care do exist, and these differences, under some ecological conditions, can have severe consequences.

Adoptive Parents and Children

Stepparents are not the only people who willingly raise children who are unrelated to them. Humans across the globe adopt children and raise them as their own. In many societies, current and in the past, the adopted children are often relatives—the children of a deceased sibling, for instance (Silk, 1987). In contemporary Western societies, however, people adopt genetically unrelated children, often going to great expense and trouble to do so. From an inclusive-fitness point of view, this makes little sense; adoptive parents, who share no genes with their adopted offspring, should be as attentive to and investing in their adoptive children as stepparents and less investing than genetic parents. As you may expect, however, this is not what actually happens. In fact, research has shown that, compared to children being raised by two genetic parents, adopted children actually receive *more* investment. For example, adopted children are more likely to have computers in the home, attend religious ser-

filicide The killing of a child by a parent.

Risk of being killed by a stepparent versus a natural parent in relationship to child's age: Canada, 1974–1983. SOURCE: Adapted from Daly, M., & Wilson, M. (1988). Evolutionary social psychology and family homicide. *Science, 242*, 519–524.
....

In recent years, researchers have begun to pay particular attention to filicides by non-biological parents (that is, stepparents). As we noted in the text, the presence of a step-parent in a family, especially a stepfather, is a potent predictor of child abuse. Might this also be so for child homicide? In pioneering work, Martin Daly and Margo Wilson (1988a) examined the incidence of child homicide in natural (genetic) and stepfamilies. They reported that the difference between natural and stepfamilies in child homicide was even greater than for cases of child abuse. In one study assessing 408 filicides in Canada, the risk of being killed by a stepparent was far greater than by a natural parent, especially during the first two years of life (Daly & Wilson, 1988b; see accompanying figure). A similar study conducted in the United States reported that children younger than 2 years of age were 100 times as likely to be killed by a stepparent than by a natural parent (Daly & Wilson, 1988a; see also Harris et al., 2007).

The increased risk of death in stepfamilies has even been reported for unintentional deaths (for example, drowning). In an Australian study examining fatal injuries of children 5 years of age and younger between 2000 and 2003, stepchildren were reported to be at an increased risk for unintentional fatal injury of any type relative to children in intact families or children in single-parent families (Tooley et al., 2006). It should not be surprising, however, to find that this relationship varies with culture. For example, the greater risk of filicide by a stepparent relative to a genetic parent is substantially less in Sweden, where there is state-sponsored social support, resulting in virtually no economic costs to unrelated stepfathers (Temrin, Nordlund, & Sterner, 2004).

vices, and eat dinner with their families than children living with their biological parents (see Hamilton, Cheng, & Powell, 2007). In families with at least one genetic and one adoptive child, parents are more likely to provide their adoptive children with preschool education, private tutoring, summer school, rent, and personal loans (Gibson, 2009).

How can this pattern be explained? First, adoptive parents are not typical of the general population. Couples who choose to rear unrelated children are different from stepparents, who agree to care for unrelated children in exchange for the affection and companionship of a spouse. Adoptive parents in the United States undergo an extensive screening process, making it likely that those selected to be adoptive parents would make the commitment to invest considerable love, attention, and resources to an adopted child. There may also be both a biological and social imperative for childless couples to have children. For example, people who are childless in American society are sometimes seen as selfish and materialistic, making adoption a way (perhaps unconsciously) for infertile couples not only to satisfy a biological yearning to have children but also to conform to social norms (Callan, 1985).

Although parents may invest somewhat more in their adoptive children than their biological offspring, the psychological outcomes of adoptive children are often less positive than those of biological children. Compared to biological children, adoptive children are more apt to have addiction problems, eating disorders, learning disabilities, and personality disorders, as well as lower school achievement (Brand & Brincich, 1999; Miller et al., 2000). In fact, the greater investment of time and money parents provide to adopted children may, in some cases, be a matter of the squeaky wheel getting greased. For example, one reason why adopted children are more apt to have private tutors or attend summer school may be because of their lower academic achievement (Gibson, 2009).

Why do adopted children have more problems than biological children? Perhaps some of these children's problems stem from difficulty dealing with the knowledge that they were given up by their birthparents. However, just as adoptive parents are not representative of the general population, neither are birthparents who put up their children for adoption, many of whom do so because they feel they are unable to raise a child as a result of their substance abuse, mental health, or domestic problems (Neil, 2000). To the extent that adjustment problems are heritable (see Chapter 3), many adopted children's genetic dispositions, possibly in interaction with problems dealing with being given away by their birthparents, may put them at a greater risk for psychological problems than biological children. However, the majority of adopted children, just as the majority of children reared by their biological parents, display no serious adjustment problems (Brand & Brincich, 1999), making adoption a positive alternative both for childless couples and children whose birthparents are unable or unwilling to care for them.

Evolutionary theory provides some general guidelines that suggest who should invest in children (genetic relatives, with investment varying as a function of degree of relatedness) and factors that affect the degree of care and solicitude a person should provide for children (for example, health of the child, scarcity of resources, paternity certainty). These same factors influence parental investment made by other animals, by people from diverse cultures, and during different historical epochs. Although human parents may have the same deep concerns as other animal parents, they also have a social structure and a cognitive system that allows them to think beyond a gene's-eye view of life to provide for children who, in centuries past, would have received reduced care. Taking an inclusive-fitness perspective can help us understand and predict the behavior of parents, but we are more than our genes, and evolutionary theory should be seen only as the foundation for comprehending human parenting, not as the whole edifice.

summary

Attachment refers to a close emotional relationship between a child and his or her caregiver. Bowlby's theorizing was influenced (1) by high death rates and psychological deterioration of infants housed in orphanages (**hospitalism**) due, presumably, to lack of social interaction; (2) ethological theory; and (3) the research on "mother love" by Harry Harlow.

Attachment is not instantaneous at birth, although research into **bonding** suggests that monkey and perhaps human mothers are biologically primed shortly after birth to form an emotional bond with their babies.

Stages of attachment have been proposed. During the clear-cut attachment, or specific attachment, stage, beginning between 6 and 8 months, most infants develop **separation distress** (or **separation protest**) and a **fear (or wariness) of strangers**.

Based on the **Strange Situation**, four attachment classifications have been described: (1) **secure**, (2) **insecure-resistant**, (3) **insecure-avoidant**, and (4) **disorganized/disoriented**. Secure attachment results when mothers are responsive to their babies' emotional signals, encourage them to explore, enjoy close contact with their infants, and develop **interactional synchrony** with their infants. Securely attached infants are more independent and as children have a better self-concept, more positive social relationships, greater cognitive skills, and less psychopathology relative to insecure and, especially, disorganized children. Distributions of infants according to Ainsworth's classification vary among cultures. Alternative methods have been developed to measure attachment, including the **Attachment Q-Set**, which uses the *Q-sort method* in which prepared statements are sorted into categories.

Some have argued for the practice of **natural parenting**, fostering greater closeness between infants and parents, increased sensitivity and responsiveness to infants' signals, and extended breastfeeding on demand.

The development of children's attachment has been described in terms of their **internal working models of attachment**. A set of neurohormonal regulators has been specified for attachment, including **opioids**, associated with reward, and **oxytocin**, which promotes relaxation and feelings of warmth and affiliation.

Inclusive fitness refers to how many copies of one's genes make it into the next generation, which is hypothesized to influence the amount of care or investment people provide to children. **Parental investment theory** postulates that there is a trade-off between how much individuals invest in mating versus parenting, with mammal females, including humans, having obligatory investment in infants that males do not.

The demands of a slow-developing child required that mothers receive help from others in child-rearing (**alloparenting**). The **cooperative breeding hypothesis** suggests that humans evolved a system of parenting in which mothers shared the responsibility for childcare with others.

The amount of care mothers devote to their children is related to a variety of factors, including the child's health and age, mother's age, and amount of social support available. Paternal care is related to child survival, health, and success, especially in high-stress environments. Grandparents, particularly maternal grandmothers, are important alloparents. Grandparental care is related to paternity certainty. The **grandmother hypothesis** proposes that the care that grandmothers provide for their grandchildren may have been selected in evolution, contributing to human longevity.

Stepparents, on average, provide less care for children than do genetic parents, and although most stepparents provide support for their stepchildren, there is a higher incidence of child abuse and **filicide** (the killing of a child) by stepparents than genetic parents. Unlike stepparents, adoptive parents provide *more* care for their adoptive children than for their biological children.

Key Terms and Concepts

attachment (p. 481)

hospitalism (p. 483)

bonding (p. 487)

separation distress (separation protest, separation anxiety) (p. 488)

fear (or wariness) of strangers (p. 489)

Strange Situation (p. 491)

secure attachment (p. 491)

insecure-resistant attachment (p. 492)

insecure-avoidant attachment (p. 492)

disorganized/disoriented attachment (p. 492)

Attachment Q-Set (p. 493)

interactional synchrony (p. 496)

internal working models of attachment (p. 501)

natural parenting (p. 502)

opioids (p. 504)

oxytocin (p. 504)

inclusive fitness (p. 505)

parental investment theory (p. 506)

alloparenting (p. 506)

cooperative breeding hypothesis (p. 507)

grandmother hypothesis (p. 510)

filicide (p. 512)

Ask Yourself . . .

1. What is attachment, why is it supposed to be important for human development, and how can one identify attachment based on overt behaviors of infants and mothers?

2. How does attachment develop, and what are the stages?

3. Can infants establish attachments with people other than their mothers? With whom, under which circumstances, and with what differences?

4. What are the major individual differences in attachment, and how can these different attachment types be measured?

5. Are there cultural differences in attachment? How are these cultural differences explained/understood?

6. What factors contribute to the establishment of secure attachment and why?

7. How does attachment affect later behaviors and psychological characteristics?

8. Why does attachment affect later development? What are internal models of attachment, and how do psychologists believe they work?

9. Why does Sarah Hrdy think that human beings are "cooperative breeders," and what have been some of the consequences for child rearing or, perhaps, human evolution, of cooperative breeding?

10. Based on the evolutionary theory of childcare (basically inclusive fitness theory and parental investment theory), what factors influence maternal care, paternal care, grandparental care, stepparental care, and adoptive-parents care?

Exercises: Going Further

1. Is attachment destiny? What do you think? A classmate of yours argues that, although textbooks says that establishing attachment is critical for children's psychological development, especially during the first year of life, she knows parents who took their children to daycare beginning at 1 month of age, and they seemed to grow up all right. Also, she seriously doubts that being insecurely attached in childhood makes children more prone to become a delinquent or be psychologically maladjusted as adolescents or adults. How would you respond to her?

2. If you ever plan to become a parent, what things about relating to children, if any, would you try to keep in mind in order to increase the likelihood of developing a secure attachment relationship with your sons and daughters?

3. According to what you have read on evolutionary theory of childcare in this chapter, make a list of the facts that would potentially increase the probability of child abuse, neglect, or filicide. Then explain why.

Suggested Readings

Classic Work

Bowlby, J. (1969). *Attachment and loss: Vol. 1: Attachment.* **London: Hogarth.** This is the first of a series of three books by John Bowlby, the grandfather of attachment research. It presents his ethological theory and his own earlier research that brought him to the field of attachment.

Daly, M., & Wilson, M. (1988). *Homicide.* **New York: Aldine.** As the authors of one of the founding documents of evolutionary psychology, Martin Daly and Margo Wilson review evidence documenting, among many other things, some of the factors associated with the most drastic form of parental disinvestment, filicide.

Scholarly Work

Sroufe, A., Egeland, B., Carlson, E., & Collins, W. (2005). *Minnesota Longitudinal study of risk and adaptation from birth to maturity: The development of the person.* **New York: Guilford.** This book by Alan Sroufe and his colleagues at the University of Minnesota summarizes the results from their longitudinal research, examining attachment and other aspects of psychological functioning in a large sample of people, including some who were at high risk for psychological problems. This research team has published important research on attachment and related topics for more than 30 years, and this book represents the culmination of their efforts.

Hrdy, S. B. (2009). *Mothers and others: The evolutionary origins of mutual understanding.* **Cambridge, MA: Belnap Press.** It is difficult to know where to place this highly readable and informative book. On the one hand, it is a scholarly work, presenting between two covers a nearly exhaustive look at the role of mothers—human and otherwise—and others—fathers and especially grandmothers—on child-rearing from an evolutionary perspective. Yet, it is so clearly written with an abundance of interesting and informative examples, that we also considered listing it under "Reading for Personal Interest." Hrdy argues that humans' tendency to cooperate arose as a need to care for highly dependent children and that such cooperative breeding set the stage for the advent of the modern human mind.

Reading for Personal Interest

Karen, R. (1998). *Becoming attached: First relationships and how they shape our capacity to love.* **New York: Oxford University Press.** Psychologist and science writer Robert Karen presents a history of attachment theory and addresses questions that parents frequently ask about attachment. This 500-page book is accessible to the general reader, while maintaining a high level of scholarship.

Sears, W., & Sears, M. (2001). *The attachment parenting book: A Commonsense guide to understanding and nurturing your baby.* **New York: Little, Brown and Company.** This book describes attachment parenting and outlines the steps that will create lasting bonds between parents and their children.

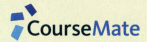
CourseMate

Cengage Learning's **Psychology CourseMate** for this text brings course concepts to life with interactive learning, study, and exam preparation tools, including quizzes and flashcards for this chapter's Key Terms and Concepts (see the summary list on page 515). The site also provides an **eBook** version of the text with highlighting and note taking capabilities, as well as an extensive library of observational videos that span early childhood through adolescence. Many videos are accompanied by questions that will help you think critically about and deepen your understanding of the chapter topics addressed, especially as they pertain to core concepts. Log on and learn more at **www.cengagebrain.com**.

13

In this chapter we look at contexts in which children acquire the knowledge, values, and behaviors of their culture. The bulk of the chapter deals with the family, as this has always been the principal institution for socializing children. We next examine parenting goals, beliefs, and styles, and how parents' behaviors influence their children's development, while also considering the effect of culture, neighborhoods, and children themselves on parenting behavior and child outcomes. The role of siblings in child development is briefly examined, followed by an assessment of how children cope with family transitions, specifically divorce and remarriage. Two other important contexts for socialization are then examined: the school and media, the latter including television, the Internet, and other contemporary forms of electronic communication that have changed how children come to acquire the knowledge and values of their culture.

A successful financial consultant, a woman in her early thirties, was reflecting on her life as a career woman and a mother. "I love my job and I love my daughter even more, but I probably could have timed things better. I started my career early and had children late, so right when I'm the busiest with work, I have a young child to care for. But I'm not complaining. I have a wonderful support system. My ex-husband is very involved with caring for Emma, although he has his own work, too, and I'm blessed having both my mother and my mother-in-law nearby. My mother, especially, makes things work. I don't know what I'd do without her. Emma goes to preschool three mornings a week, and my mom picks her up and takes care of her the rest of those days. My mother-in-law—actually my ex-mother-in-law—babysits with her on Tuesdays, and on Thursdays I've arranged my schedule so I work at home in the morning to take care of Emma myself. I admit that sometimes I plop her in front of the TV so I can get some work done. Then I drop her off at my sister's in the afternoon. I've had to take her to an occasional "emergency" client meeting, but everyone seems to understand. It's great. Emma has lots of different people to interact with all week, so she doesn't get bored, but no one spends more total time with her than I do, which is important to me."

Rearing children can be an arduous task. It is not for the faint of heart. Although we talk of parents rearing children, the job is actually done by a host of people and institutions. The family is our species' primary vehicle for rearing children. We take families for granted. Everyone has one. Some may be more supportive than others; some have relatives crawling out of the woodwork, whereas others are self-contained; some may be nuclear, whereas others are blended, broken, dysfunctional, or unconventional. Families consist of individuals, the two most important from the perspective of the child being the mother and the father, but siblings, grandparents, aunts, and uncles, and often stepparents, are also involved. This is not a coincidence, for as we saw in the previous chapter, humans, like a handful of other species, rear offspring cooperatively, with fathers and other, mainly female, members of the social group providing assistance to the mother. We also saw in Chapter 12 that a mother's investment in her children is obligatory: Until the recent invention of baby formula, she was the only one who could feed the infant. Fathers, however, also have an interest in the care and welfare of their children, as do grandparents, siblings, and stepparents, all to varying degrees.

Families serve many functions for children and adolescents, not the least of which is ensuring that children get the necessary nutritional, medical, and physical support they need to survive. Families are also the initial, and for many years the primary, source of emotional support for children, as well as the institution that first introduces them to the norms, rules, values, and beliefs of one's culture—in other words, that *socializes* children.

Families are not solely responsible for socializing children, however. In modern societies, other institutions also take some responsibility, the most important of which is schools (see Meece & Eccles, 2010). Another important source of socialization in contemporary cultures is *media*, forms of communication such as television, computers, and cell phones that have transformed how youth acquire culturally and developmentally important information. The bulk of this chapter is devoted to the family as part of a dynamic system that includes the child, but also the community and larger society. In the latter part of the chapter we examine the role of formal schooling and media as a socializing agents for children and adolescents.

monogamy Family structure in which one man and one woman rear their genetic children.

polyandry Family structure in which one woman has multiple husbands.

polygyny Family structure in which one man has multiple wives.

biparental families Family structure in which both mother and father provide some support.

The Family

Families come in many forms, some with children and some without, some with fathers and some without, and some with grandparents, aunts, uncles, and cousins, and some without. From the perspective of child development, however, the family is the social group that is principally responsible for the care and rearing of children. Families are typically composed of genetically related people (or kin), although children frequently live with stepparents and step- or half-siblings.

In Western culture, marriage and thus family structure is based on **monogamy**, in which one man and one woman rear their genetic children. Yet, **polygyny**, the practice of one man having several wives, is also quite common across the globe (particularly in traditional societies), and likely was typical for our ancestors. However, even in societies in which polygyny is allowed, it is only occasionally practiced. That is because a man must have substantial resources to support several wives and their children, and as a result only the wealthiest men in a society typically have more than one wife at a time. (Serial monogamy, in which people have several spouses in succession but only one at a time, is practiced in many societies, including the United States and Europe, where divorce and remarriage are common.

Much less common is one woman having several husbands, a practice known as **polyandry**. When it does occur, typically two brothers will share a wife. Because brothers share 50% of their genes, any child their wife has will be related to them, either sharing 50% of a man's genes (if he is the father) or 25% of his genes (if his brother is the father). This situation usually occurs when resources are scarce and one man cannot support a wife and family alone. When one of the brothers acquires enough resources to support a wife on his own, he often does so, leaving the polyandrous family (Schmitt, 2005). Polyandry as a mating strategy is also common in some hunter-gatherer South American groups, in which people believe that a child possesses some part of every man with whom a woman has had sex during the 10-month period before birth (termed by anthropologists as *partible paternity*). A pregnant woman may have a husband, but she often initiates affairs with other, often high-status, men. As a result, these men may protect or even provide resources to "their" child, resulting in a higher survival rate than for children without "multiple fathers" (see Beckerman & Valentine, 2002).

In a classical anthropological study about marriage customs among 856 societies around the world, researchers reported that about 55% of cultures were primarily monogamous (with just occasional polygamous marriages) and about 44% were polygamous, including both polygyny (multiple wives) and polyandry (multiple husbands) (Bourguignon & Greenbaum, 1973). However, as we mentioned, even among societies where polygamy is accepted, most marriages are monogamous.

Within any particular family structure there are many ways in which children can be cared for. Allison Clarke-Stewart (1984) listed several arrangements that are common in contemporary culture: children can be cared for at home by their mother, or if their mother works they can be cared for at home by their father, another family member, or a nanny; they can be cared for out of the home by other family members (going to Grandma's or to Auntie Sarah's every day) or a babysitter; or they can be in a daycare center. They can be cared for out of the home part time (just mornings, or three days a week) or full time. Moreover, within Western culture, the family structure has changed considerably over the past 50 years or so (see Table 13.1), providing even more variability in childcare practices than was the case for earlier generations. Thus, although family is clearly central to a child's development, across the globe, across historical time, and among different people within a culture, there is great variability in children's experiences within a family, and thus different influences on children's developmental outcomes.

Although there are substantial differences in how families are constituted both across cultures and within a single culture, humans, as a species, form **biparental families** (both mother and father

© Images of Africa Photobank/Alamy

Although polygyny, one man having several wives, is practiced in many traditional cultures, only the most wealthy men in a society can afford to support more than one wife and their children.

provide some support) and *extended families*, with several genetically related adults typically helping to tend the young (Emlen, 1995). This arrangement is critical for rearing children. As noted previously in this book, children take a long time to attain maturity and are dependent on adults for their care and survival years after most other animals have become parents themselves. As any modern parent knows, it is expensive to raise a child, and it likely always has been. Our ancient ancestors may not have had to worry about the expense of a college education,

table 13.1 Family Changes

Families have changed over the past 50 years or so in the developed world. These changes present new challenges for parents and new contexts for children in which to develop. The following is a list of some of the differences in modern families within Western culture.

Relative to 50 Years Ago:

There is greater isolation from extended families as young adults move away from home to find work.

There are more single-parent families, as divorce rates increase and out-of-wedlock births become less of a social stigma.

There are more reconstructed or blended families as divorce frequently leads to remarriage.

Women with young children are more apt to work out of the home, many full time.

Women are postponing childbirth until later ages.

Families are smaller; couples are having fewer children.

Many husbands/fathers are taking an increasingly active role in housework and child-rearing. At the same time, many other fathers are abandoning their children and provide little or no support to them.

There is a greater range of alternatives for childcare, including all-day centers and educational preschools.

There are more intercultural/interethnic couples rearing children.

There are more single-gender families (gay and lesbian parents).

SOURCE: Adapted from Valentine, G., & Holloway, S. L. (2002). Cyberkids? Exploring children's identities and social networks in on-line and off-line worlds. *Annals of the Association of American Geographers, 82,* 302–319.)

table 13.2 Estimated Annual and Total Costs for Raising a Child

For two-parent families living in a city or suburb in the Northeast United States in 2006 dollars for three income levels. Totals represent raising a child from birth to age 18.

Annual household income under $38,000		Annual household income between $38,000 and $64,000		Annual household income over $64,000	
Expense	Annual Cost	Expense	Annual Cost	Expense	Annual Cost
Housing	$3,437	Housing	$4,460	Housing	$6,677
Food	$1,705	Food	$2,007	Food	$2,428
Transportation	$972	Transportation	$1,433	Transportation	$1,982
Clothing	$507	Clothing	$597	Clothing	$757
Healthcare	$625	Healthcare	$832	Healthcare	$965
Childcare/education	$313	Childcare/education	$1,113	Childcare/education	$1,737
Miscellaneous	$765	Miscellaneous	$1,152	Miscellaneous	$1,867
College (public)	$12,796	College (public)	$12,796	College (public)	$12,796
Total cost for 18 years is	**$206,416**	**Total cost for 18 years is**	**$259,876**	**Total cost for 18 years is**	**$348,418**

SOURCE: From Babycenter, www.babycenter.com/cost-of-raising-child-calculator.

but the cost in time, energy, and resources to keep a child alive and fit until he or she could be self-sufficient has likely always been dear, and the job is likely more than a single adult can be expected to handle. Table 13.2 provides an idea of the cost of raising a child in the United States today up to age 18, dollar-wise, based on children living in a two-parent family, for three different income levels.

The Dynamic Nature of Families

Regardless of the society in which one lives, families do not exist in isolation but are part of a larger, intertwined community and must be viewed as *dynamic systems* (Cox & Paley, 2003; Lerner et al., 2002). As discussed in Chapters 1 and 2, there are bidirectional effects between all levels of organization, and this includes between children, their parents, and others in the community. Children affect and shape their parents as much as parents affect children. With families, however, relationships are not only bidirectional but multidirectional. Recall Urie Bronfenbrenner's (1979) ecological systems theory presented in Chapter 2. Children's development is influenced by the microsystem, which includes the family. The impact of the family on a child is affected by the quality of the marital relationship, relationships among siblings, and parents' satisfaction with work, among many other things. The family, and thus the child, is also embedded within a larger community. What type of experiences are children likely to have in their neighborhoods or in their schools? What type of educational, recreational, religious, and economic opportunities will children have?

Figure 13.1 presents a *developmental contextual view* of development (from Lerner, 1991), which is conceptually similar to both Bronfenbrenner's ecological systems theory discussed in Chapter 2 and developmental systems theory (Gottlieb, Wahlsten, & Lickliter, 2006) discussed in Chapter 1. Lerner's model, however, shows the complex web of interactions that influences a child's development, all changing over time. Notice that there is no unit marked "family" in this figure; rather, characteristics of the child and parents interact with other subnetworks, including the "marriage network," "work network," "social network," and "school network." Each of these networks changes over time. Some changes influence an entire society, which can have a profound impact on families (Parke, 2004). For example, many changes over the latter part of the 20th century had an initially gradual but eventually profound effect on families: for example, (1) birth control became readily available, resulting in decreased fertility rates and "sexual liberation"; (2) women entered the workforce in greater numbers; (3) parenthood was delayed for many people; (4) divorce rates increased, resulting in an increase in the number of single-parent families; and (5) television and other forms of mass media (for example, the Internet) became commonplace.

The psychologies and biologies of children and adults are contained within a complex system of interacting units. As Figure 13.1 illustrates, it may be difficult or impossible to consider all of the many factors that affect children as family members at one time, and much of the research that we report in this chapter looks, by necessity, at only a small slice of the many interactions that influence development. Nonetheless, we ask the reader to be mindful that children and families exist in a complex web of interactions that we must consider in order to appreciate how families and their members affect how children develop.

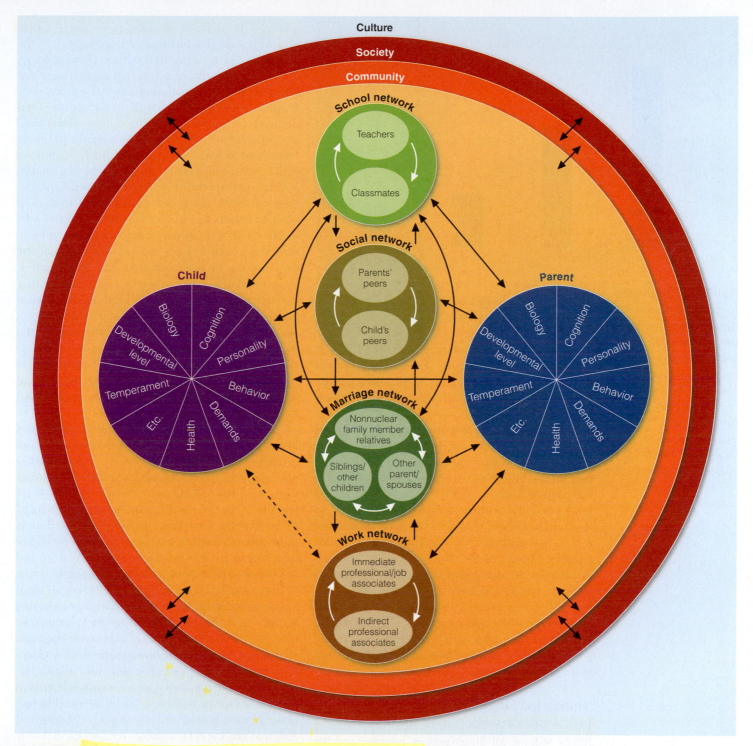

FIGURE 13.1 **A developmental contextual model of person-context interaction.**
Children's lives can be seen as a web of interactions, involving characteristics of the child, parents, the family, and the greater community, all changing over time. SOURCE: "Changing organism-context relations as the basic process of development: A developmental contextual perspective," by R. M. Lerner, 1991, *Developmental Psychology, 27,* 27–32. Copyright © 1991 American Psychological Association. Reprinted with permission.

Alternative Family Arrangements

Although there have been many variations, in the United States and Europe the traditional family has involved a mother, father, and children living in the same household. Although this is still the norm in the Western world, within the past several decades, alternative families have become increasingly common. First, divorce has increased sharply since the middle of the 20th century, with many children who once lived in two-parent families living in single-parent families, at least for awhile. With the increase in divorce has come an increase in remarriage, producing stepfamilies. We discussed the investment that stepparents make in

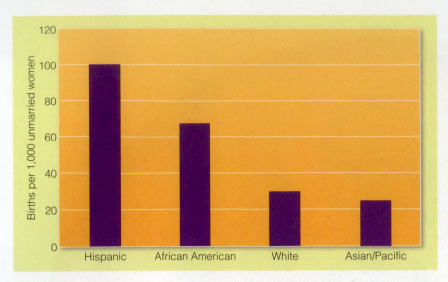

FIGURE 13.2 Birthrates for unmarried women by race and ethnicity, United States, 2005.

SOURCE: Adapted from Martin, J. A., Hamilton, B. E., Sutton, P. D., Ventura, S. J., Menacker, F., Kirmeyer, S., & Munson, M. L. (2007). Births: Final data for 2005. *National Vital Statistics Reports*, 56 (Number 6). Washington, DC: U.S. Department of Health and Human Services.

their stepchildren in Chapter 12, and we will discuss children's adjustment to divorce and remarriage in some detail later in this chapter.

The increase in single-parent families is not all a result of divorce, however. The societal taboo of out-of-wedlock births has essentially disappeared. In 2005, 36.9% of all births in the United States were to unwed mothers, an increase from 18.4% only 25 years earlier (Martin et al., 2007). But this large cohort is not homogeneous. Although many such births were the result of unplanned pregnancies, many others were planned, often by older and economically well-off women who intended to raise a child without a father's influence. And speaking of fathers, changes in societal values have meant that mothers are not automatically given primary custody of the child in divorce, resulting in more single-parent families headed by men. In addition, gay and lesbian couples are openly raising children as a family, another result of societal change within the past 25 years. In this section, we briefly examine some of these alternative family arrangements and how they impact child-rearing and child development.

Unmarried Single-Parent Families

Most single-parent families are headed by women. About half of all single-parent mothers are the result of divorce, but an increasing number of women are having children without being married and raising children without the assistance of the child's father (or a stepfather). The birthrate for unmarried women varies substantially by race and ethnicity (see Figure 13.2), with Hispanic women having the highest rate, followed by African American, White, and Asian/Pacific Islander women.

There is great variability in this group of single mothers. For example, adolescents are, on

single mothers by choice Usually older, well-educated, and economically stable women who choose to rear children without a partner.

average, the most disadvantaged of single mothers. Although the birthrate for teenagers in the United States is at an all-time low (Martin et al., 2007), the majority of adolescent mothers are not married, and most teen mothers come from poor families with low educational backgrounds. Teen mothers are more apt to drop out of school than are other teens, and for those who do graduate from high school, they are less likely to pursue higher education (Weinraub, Horvath, & Gringlas, 2002). Coupled with their economic hardships, the immaturity of many teen mothers and their own need to establish an adult identity often results in less-than-optimal parenting behaviors. Adolescent single mothers are likely to have unrealistic expectations of their children and to provide a more restrictive and less intellectually stimulating environment than other adult mothers do (Brooks-Gunn & Furstenberg, 1986). Whether these effects are a result of the age of the mothers or of the lower levels of income and education of these young women is debatable, but the bottom line is that teenage mothers are often deficient in parenting skills, and their children grow up in poor and disruptive neighborhoods.

A very different group of single mothers has been called **single mothers by choice**. These are usually older women (middle to upper thirties) who are better educated and economically stable. (See the Single Mothers by Choice organization's website: http://www.singlemothersbychoice.com.) This situation was illustrated in the 2008 movie *Baby Mama*, starring Tina Fey as a top executive who had little time for romantic relationships but felt the need to become a mother. Her solution was to hire a surrogate mother (Amy Poehler), an alternative afforded by the new technologies of assisted fertility (see Chapter 3). Although most women in this group consciously decide to become pregnant or to adopt a child, some become pregnant accidentally but are excited to raise the child alone. The motivation for many of these women is "the ticking of their biological clock" (Bock, 2000), although some women choose this alternative as a result of feminist ideology (Eiduson & Weisner, 1978). Many single-by-choice mothers adopt special-needs children, which brings its own complications, and like other single mothers, they face the difficulties of finding daycare, balancing work and family life, and receiving emotional support for themselves and their children. In fact, these concerns are similar for any working mother, not just single mothers.

How do single mothers, whether by choice or otherwise, and their children fare? Marsha Weinraub and her colleagues (Gringlas & Weinraub, 1995; Weinraub & Wolf, 1983, 1987; see Weinraub et al., 2002 for a review) examined a group they

Minority teenagers are more likely to be single mothers. These teenagers tend to be less educated and economically disadvantaged, making raising a child alone all the more difficult.

Some—mainly older, better-educated, and financially stable—women are choosing to have or adopt children and raise them without a partner. These women refer to themselves as *single mothers by choice*.

called *solo mothers*—adult women rearing children from birth without a partner. They reported that, compared to two-parent families, solo mothers worked longer hours, had greater financial difficulties, reported more stressful life events, and received less emotional support for their parenting efforts. Stressful life events affected the children of solo mothers more so than children from two-parent homes. Stressed solo mothers were less nurturing, communicated with their children less effectively, and generally showed poorer parenting skills than stressed mothers in two-parent families, and their preadolescent children displayed increased behavior problems as a result.

Single fathers face many of the same problems as single mothers. Although there are far fewer single-father families than single-mother families, they have been increasing in the United States and other European countries in recent decades. According to the U.S. Census Bureau (2006), in 2005 there were 12.9 million single-parent families. Most of them (10.4 million, 81%) were single-mother families, but a sizeable minority (2.5 million, 19%) were single-father families. Most single-parent fathers gained their status because of divorce, and they are usually better off financially and better educated than single-parent mothers, particularly those mothers who never married (Amato, 2000). Fathers who seek custody as a result of divorce were often highly involved in childcare *before* the divorce and open to the possibility of single parenthood (Greif, 1985). These men, who may not be typical of the adult male population, encounter the same problems as single-parent mothers, but they seem to do as good a job of dealing with their children as women in similar situations (Amato, 2000).

Compared to single mothers, single fathers are less apt to be criticized by others for their parenting behavior and are more likely to be seen as "noble." However, some single fathers report that they are viewed with suspicion as potential child predators. Other parents may be reluctant to have their children play or have sleepovers at male-headed households (Anderson, 2003). Single fathers frequently use their extended family and girlfriends for social support, and the noncustodial parent is more likely to remain involved with the children than when mothers have custody (Anderson, 2003).

All in all, single parenthood is a difficult task, regardless if the parent is the mother or the father. In their review of the research on solo parents, Weinraub and her colleagues (2002, p. 129)

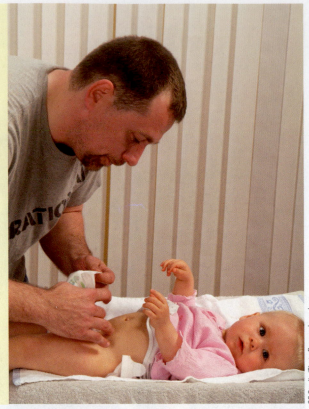

Although most single parents are mothers, about 19% of single-parent households in the United States are headed by men. Most such men gained custody of their children after divorce and were involved in childcare before the divorce.

CC Studio/Photo Researchers, Inc.

cases, gay or lesbian couples serve as foster parents, or a lesbian will become pregnant, often via artificial insemination, and raise the child with her partner (Gates et al., 2007). Although there are fewer children being raised in gay and lesbian households than in either single-mother or single-father households, the number of children living with a gay or lesbian parent is substantial. Table 13.3 presents some statistics about gay and lesbian parents in the United States (from Gates et al., 2007).

Same-sex couples raising adopted children are older, more educated, and have more economic resources than other adoptive parents, and they are at least as emotionally healthy as heterosexual divorced women (see Gates et al., 2007; Patterson, 2002). The legal system in many states has been concerned that children growing up with an openly homosexual parent or living with two same-sex adults will be adversely affected. These concerns are especially apparent when making decisions about custody in divorce or in adoption.

One issue that has concerned the court system is whether children's sexual identity will be adversely affected by being raised by same-sex parents. The research evidence has been consistent. Children with gay or lesbian parents do not typically experience gender confusion, and they are as likely to identify themselves as heterosexual as adults as children growing up with heterosexual parents are (Golombok & Tasker, 1996; Patterson, 2002). There are, nonetheless, perhaps not surprisingly, some differences between children growing up with homosexual parents and those growing up with heterosexual parents. For example, compared to children from heterosexual families, children with gay or lesbian parents express more liberal attitudes toward sexuality, have more sexual partners from puberty to young adulthood, are likely to have more homosexual or bisexual friends, are less gender stereotyped concerning issues such as clothing, activities, and occupational preferences, and as young adults they are more likely to have

concluded "that reduced social supports and increased stresses may be more common for solo parents, even when there are no separation, divorce, and custody difficulties and even when the mothers are mature, well educated, and from secure financial circumstances." In other words, raising children is a difficult task, and lack of support from a spouse can make the task even more demanding.

Gay and Lesbian Parents

Although gay marriage is still not legal in most states, gay and lesbian couples are increasingly living together openly, and many of these couples have children. Most of the children in these families are from a previous heterosexual partnership that ended in divorce, or they are adopted. In other

table 13.3 Some Statistics about Gay and Lesbian Parents in the United States

More than one in three lesbians have given birth and one in six gay men have fathered or adopted a child.

More than 50% of gay men and 41% of lesbians want to have a child.

An estimated 2 million gay and lesbian people are interested in adopting.

An estimated 65,500 adopted children are living with a lesbian or gay parent.

Gay and lesbian parents are raising 4% of all adopted children in the United States.

An estimated 14,100 foster children are living with lesbian or gay parents.

Gay and lesbian parents are raising 3% of foster children in the United States.

A national ban on gay and lesbian foster care could cost from $87 million to $130 million.

Costs to individual states could range from $100,000 to $27 million.

SOURCE: Adapted from Gates, G. J., Badgett, M. V. L., Macomber, J. E., & Chambers, K. (2007). *Adoption and Foster Care by Gay and Lesbian Parents in the United States.* Washington, DC: The Urban Institute.

Gay and lesbian couples are increasingly serving as parents of biological, adopted, or foster children. The psychological outcome for children raised by homosexual parents is as good as that of children raised by heterosexual parents.

experimented with same-sex relationships (Golombok & Tasker, 1996; Stacey & Biblarz, 2001). Also, general levels of psychological adjustment are as good for children reared by gay or lesbian parents as for children reared by heterosexual parents (Golombok et al., 2003; Patterson, 2006; Wainright & Patterson, 2008). In short, gay and lesbian parents seem as capable as heterosexual parents of raising psychologically healthy children.

Parenting Goals, Beliefs, and Styles

At its most basic, "parenting" refers to how parents raise their children, with some forms of parenting presumably being better than others. Of course, before one identifies one style of parenting as better than another, it is important to know what the parents' *goals* are for their children (Darling & Steinberg, 1993). Although all parents want what is best for their children, what is best surely varies among parents of different cultures (or subcultures) and also as a function of other factors for people within the same culture, such as socioeconomic status (SES), which is usually measured in terms of income, number of years of education, or occupational status. Parents may also have different *beliefs* about parenting and child development, such as how competent or independent children should be at different ages and what a parent's role should be in influencing development (Sigel & McGillicuddy-DeLisi, 2002). And finally, parents have different *styles* of interacting with their chil-

dren (Baumrind, 1967). In this section we investigate parenting goals, beliefs, and styles and their impact on children's development.

Parenting Goals and Beliefs

The basic goals of parenting are universal. Parents want to keep their children safe, instill in them the important values of their culture, and provide an environment for them that will promote their development in their local community and the attainment of a productive adulthood (García Coll & Patcher, 2002). What those specific values are and how they are achieved varies among cultures, within cultures, and within parents over time. (For instance, we know of some parents whose goals for their children became less lofty as their offspring reached adolescence, going from "being popular, playing on varsity sports teams, and acceptance to an Ivy League college" to "staying alive, not becoming pregnant, and not getting convicted of a felony.")

Consistent differences have been observed between lower- and higher-SES parents in some specific *goals* they expect their children to achieve. For example, lower-SES mothers rate obedience, respect, and quiet behavior as more important than higher-SES mothers (Harwood, Miller, & Lucca Irizarry, 1995). In general, lower-SES parents are more likely to value conformity to social rules for their children, whereas higher-SES parents are more likely to value independence and self-directedness (Hoff, Laursen, & Tardiff, 2002; Tudge et al., 2000).

What do parents know, or *believe*, about development? What do they expect of their infants and children at different ages? As it turns out, like

table 13.4 Parenting Styles

Parenting styles can be classified according to warmth (high versus low) that parents display and the amount of control (high versus low) they try to impose on their children's behavior.

Control	Warmth	
	High (warm, responsive)	Low (rejecting, unresponsive)
High (demanding, restrictive)	Authoritative	Authoritarian
Low (undemanding, permissive)	Permissive	Uninvolved

SOURCE: Adapted from Maccoby, E., & Martin, J. A. (1983). Socialization in the context of the family: Parent-child interaction. In P. H. Mussen (Series Ed.) and E. M. Hetherington (Vol. Ed.), *Handbook of child psychology* (4th ed., Vol 4, pp. 1–102). New York: Wiley.

parental goals, *parental beliefs* also differ between higher- and lower-SES parents (Hoff et al., 2002). Mothers from higher-SES backgrounds expect their children to attain important social and cognitive milestones, such as feeling emotion, talking, and thinking, earlier compared to mothers from lower-SES backgrounds. In contrast, lower-SES mothers believe that their children will achieve certain biosocial milestones, such as using the toilet, sleeping through the night, and no longer using a pacifier, earlier than higher-SES mothers (Mansbach & Greenbaum, 1999; von der Lippe, 1999). Parents of different social classes emphasize the abilities they value most—cognitive abilities in higher-SES parents and biosocial abilities in lower-SES parents.

Parenting Styles

Parenting style refers to the general way parents interact with their children. Psychologists typically describe parenting style in terms of two dimensions: (1) the degree of *warmth* a parent shows toward a child, and (2) the degree of *control* a parent attempts to exert over a child's behavior. Parental warmth is reflected by being loving and attentive to children and their needs and by active involvement in children's lives. Control refers to parents' attempts to promote more mature behavior in their children and can be done by a variety of methods. Parenting style can be divided into four general types, as a function of where a parent falls (high versus low) on these two dimensions (see Table 13.4).

Most modern research in parenting styles can trace its roots to the work of Diana Baumrind (1967, 1971, 1972, 1991), who found that most parents can be

① warmth°
② control°

described as using one of three general styles: **authoritative** (high warmth, high control), **authoritarian** (low warmth, high control), or **permissive** (high warmth, low control). Eleanor Maccoby and John Martin (1983) completed the matrix, adding **uninvolved** (or **neglectful**) **parenting** (low warmth, low control).

Authoritative parents set clear standards and enforce their rules with warmth and explanations. They are accepting of children, often listening to their children's justifications for their behavior or reasons for their requests, and they sometimes make exceptions accordingly. They value conformity along with self-reliance and take into consideration children's uniqueness when setting and enforcing rules. When disciplining children, they often explain their reasoning, using such opportunities for teaching. Their goal is for children to achieve self-regulation—to be in charge of their own actions—rather than following arbitrary rules. Box 13.1 (p. 530) presents some tools for changing children's behavior based on developing a self-disciplined child.

Authoritarian parents expect absolute obedience. They establish the rules and expect their children to obey them without question. They frequently enforce the rules by coercive control, including physical punishment and withdrawal of affection. Although both authoritative and authoritarian parents score high on the control dimension, they do so in different ways. Authoritarian parents do less explaining during discipline and, rather than promoting self-regulation and autonomy, they make decisions for the child and rarely listen to their children's point of view.

Permissive parents, in contrast, generally exert little control over their children, although they maintain warm relations with them. In these families, children pretty much do what they want, receiving little guidance or direction from their parents. Children are permitted, sometimes encouraged, to make many decisions, often before they have the maturity to do so. It is important to note here that most permissive parents are not neglectful or just too lazy to exert control. Rather, most believe that the best way to raise and educate children is to give them as much freedom as possible, and the parents behave accordingly.

parenting style The general way parents interact with their children.

authoritative parenting style Style of parenting in which parents set clear standards and enforce the rules with warmth and explanations.

authoritarian parenting style A style of parenting in which parents expect absolute obedience and frequently enforce rules with physical punishment and withdrawal of love.

permissive parenting style A style of parenting in which parents are warm and friendly but exert little control over their children's behaviors.

uninvolved (or neglectful) parenting style Parenting style in which parents are disengaged from their children. They are emotionally cold and indifferent and demand little from their children.

Uninvolved parents are disengaged from their children. They are emotionally cold and indifferent and demand little from their children. However, contrary to permissive parents, their lack of control over their children is not based on attitudes or beliefs about how best to raise a child. Rather, they are more concerned with themselves (parent-centered) than with their children (child-centered). This is why they are sometimes referred to as *neglectful parents,* because their actions are associated with potentially harmful environments for children.

It should not be surprising that these general parenting styles are associated with different characteristics in children (see Concept Review 13.1). As you might expect, on average, children of authoritative parents fare best in middle-class culture. These children are more independent and socially responsible than the children of authoritarian, permissive, or uninvolved parents. They tend to be self-reliant, self-controlled, and curious. They get along well with other children, have high self-esteem, perform well academically, and, as adolescents, display self-reliance, coping skills, and have relatively few drug and behavior problems (Collins & Steinberg, 2006; Mayseless, Scharf, & Sholt, 2003; Pettit, Dodge, & Brown, 1988).

Children of authoritarian parents tend to be withdrawn, irritable, and indifferent to new experiences (Baumrind, 1967). These children often have low self-esteem, can perform poorly in school, and are more apt to be rejected by their school peers (Coopersmith, 1967; Lamborn et al., 1991; Pettit et al., 1988). When physical punishment is used to enforce the rules, they are apt to be highly aggressive and bully others (Olweus, 1980; Sternberg et al., 2006). Children who experience harsh parenting also display an increase in externalizing behavior, such as conduct disorder (Gershoff, 2002). Recent research

has shown that this connection is especially strong for children who display a physiological sensitivity to stress as measured by skin conductance level reactivity (Erath, El-Sheikh, & Cummings, 2009). Eight- and 9-year-old children with lower skin conductivity reactions, which is a reflection of fearfulness, and who experienced harsh punishment, had higher levels of externalizing behavior than children who experienced harsh punishment but had higher levels of skin conductance reactivity. This pattern reflects a transaction between a child's biological responsivity to stress and parenting style.

Permissive parents, at first glance, may seem to be the ideal, from a child's point of view. After all, children are seldom criticized or reprimanded, and if the parents are warm and loving, who could ask for anything more? But freedom that exceeds what is appropriate for a child's developmental level can be confusing and frightening. Without proper guidance from parents, young children cannot learn to regulate their own behavior. Self-control and self-discipline are not attained if parents fail to set rules or enforce them. Research shows that children of permissive parents tend to be impulsive and aggressive, often acting out of control. In one study, a generally permissive style of parenting during the preschool years predicted later drug use in adolescent girls (Block, Block, & Keyes, 1988). In general, adolescents with permissive parents get into more trouble at school and have a higher rate of drug use than do adolescents with authoritative parents (Lamborn et al., 1991).

Perhaps the most notable characteristic of children of uninvolved parents is a disruption in attachment relationships as infants and toddlers and in peer relationships as children (Thompson, 1998). As adolescents, these children frequently display a wide range of problem behaviors, including drug use,

concept review | 13.1 Parent and child characteristics for authoritative, authoritarian, permissive, and uninvolved parenting styles

Type	Parent behavior	Child characteristics
Authoritative	Make reasonable, age-appropriate demands; promotes self-regulation; warm; receptive; rational; verbal give-and-take; value discipline, self-reliance, and uniqueness	Independent; socially responsible; self-controlled, explorative; self-reliant
Authoritarian	Exert strict control; critical evaluation of child's behavior and attitudes; little verbal give-and-take; cold; emotionally rejecting; does not promote autonomy	Withdrawn; discontented; distrustful of others
Permissive	Noncontrolling; nondemanding; little punishment or exercising of power; use of reasoning; warm and accepting	Lacking in self-reliance and self-control
Uninvolved	Emotionally cold; indifferent; noncontrolling; parent-centered rather than child-centered	Disruptions of attachment and peer relationships; behavioral problems

BOX 13.1 child development in the real world

Tools for Changing Behavior

What specific techniques do parents use to control children's behavior? If you look on the self-help shelves of most bookstores, you will find a section on child-rearing, some dealing specifically with "how to discipline your child." Most parenting books advocate an *authoritative style* of parenting—a combination of parental warmth and control. In this box we present a partial list of "tools for changing children's behavior," adapted from Chapter 2 of Barbara and David Bjorklund's (1990) book, *Parents' Book of Discipline*. The theme of the book was how to raise a "self-disciplined child," and the focus was on preschool children. But the general techniques and ideas presented here are similar to those found in other parenting books and provide some specific examples of how parents can deal with the inevitable problems children present.

Childproofing

Childproofing is usually thought of in terms of keeping children safe, not as a tool for discipline. Are there things lying around the house that, although not dangerous, are likely to attract young children and invite damage? Think of situations that a preschooler might get into around the house and try to structure your home to avoid disastrous ones.

Communication

We communicate to children through words, gestures, and context, and most of the time children seem to understand adults' intentions, but not always. Use words that children understand, and realize that they sometimes don't interpret words in the same way as adults do.

Young children are often very literal. For example, when a parent says to a 3-year-old, "Wash your hands," the child is likely to return with clean hands but covered with dirt from the wrists up. Other examples are "pick up your toys" (no mention of putting them away) or "give your brother some cereal"

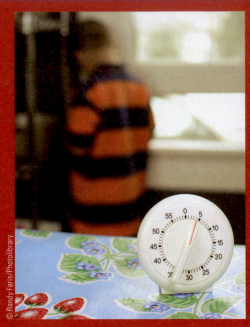

When children misbehave, giving them a time-out for a specific, and usually short, period of time can help parents gain control of the situation (and help children to gain control of their own behavior). Sometimes a timer can be used so children have an idea of the duration of their time-out.

....

(no mention of putting it in a bowl or adding milk). Preschoolers who make these mistakes aren't being wise guys; they are just learning the language.

Rewards for Nonproblem Behavior

"Catch 'em doing good." One popular and time-tested technique of controlling children's behavior is granting rewards when they do something good. These rewards increase the chance that the child will repeat those behaviors. Star charts, gifts for good behavior, hugs, praise, increased privileges, money, and trips to fun places are all examples of rewards.

Remedies for Problem Behaviors
Removing the Child

Even after a house is childproofed, young children can get into things they shouldn't.

Perhaps the best way to handle problems that childproofing can't solve is simply to remove the child from the offending situation. The first thing parents should do when a toddler gets into things he or she should not is to say "no" firmly (yelling is not necessary), pick the child up, remove him or her from the immediate environment, and place the child somewhere out of sight from the scene of the potential crime.

Natural Consequences

If the behavior you expect from your child is important, there are usually some natural consequences. Repeatedly telling a 3-year-old to put his jar of soap bubbles on the table or else he'll knock it over can get old. When the child knocks the jar over and his bubble-blowing game comes to an end, the lesson for a child should be clear. When children must bear the consequences of their own actions, it teaches them lessons that lectures rarely can.

Taking away Privileges (and Toys)

After a warning, parents can intervene and take away some pleasant object.

Time-outs and Isolation

After a warning (or two), parents can suspend the ongoing activity for a given length of time in hopes it will result in better behavior when it resumes. For example, two children playing with blocks who have been warned to stop arguing can have the blocks taken away for 3 minutes (a portable timer is nice for this) while they think about playing nicely. Sometimes sending a child to his or her room is a wonderful device, again, for a specified amount of time.

Spanking

Spanking is very controversial (see discussion of spanking later in this chapter). Parents usually spank when they have lost control of the situation and their children, and they often feel guilty about it later. When parents are able to anticipate discipline problems and take action early to prevent them, they find that they remain in control and spanking decreases.

---

sexual promiscuity, antisocial behavior, and internalizing problems, such as depression and social withdrawal (Baumrind, 1991; Lamborn et al., 1991). We should note that any given parent could display a variety of behaviors when interacting with his or her children, most reflecting one parenting style (authoritative, for example), but others reflecting other styles (authoritarian, for example). That is, few if any mothers and fathers will be the "absolute authoritarian" or the "perfect permissive" parent. Few people are that consistent. Moreover, a person's primary parenting style may vary over time with the same child or be different for different children. People change, sometimes as a result of experience rearing children, and thus they sometimes treat later-born children differently than the way they treated earlier-born children. In addition, characteristics of children can evoke different reactions from parents, and we have seen more than one parent who controls a "difficult child" with an iron fist but is putty in the hands of a child with a very different temperament. There may also be differences between the parenting styles of mothers and fathers. Thus, although the standard textbook picture one gets is of children exposed to a single household parenting style, the more common scenario is for children to experience a variety of parental reactions to their behaviors, with perhaps one style characterizing most of a child's experience.

Factors That Influence Parenting Style

The picture of parenting styles and their effects on children just presented is, by necessity, a simplistic one. Just as children's development is influenced by a host of interacting factors, so are parents' behaviors with respect to how they treat their children. Why are some parents authoritative, others authoritarian, and still others permissive or uninvolved? Jay Belsky (1984) proposed a dynamic model in which several different factors interact to determine parenting style. The parent's personality—as shaped by his or her own developmental history—determines parenting style to a large extent. But personality and parenting style are also affected by other factors, including the marital relationship, work, and social support. Each of these factors can affect parenting indirectly by influencing the parent's personality; these factors can also have a more direct effect on specific parenting practices. Last but not least are the characteristics of the child. Different children bring out different responses in parents, making the child an important component in how he or she is treated. We investigate some of the factors that influence parenting style and their effects on children in the following paragraphs.

Parents' Emotional Adjustment

Considerable evidence supports the dynamic view of parenting as presented by Belsky and others (Lerner et al., 2002). Psychologically mature and healthy people are more likely than less-well-adjusted people to show effective parenting skills. For example, mothers suffering from depression are often ineffective parents. They frequently use disruptive, hostile, and rejecting child-rearing prac-

tices and tend to view their children more negatively and be more punitive in their interactions with their children (see Downey & Coyne, 1990). The children of depressive parents (particularly mothers) are often insecurely attached, have difficult temperaments as infants, react negatively to stress, are more likely to display poor school performance, and have fewer interpersonal skills when interacting with peers than are children of nondepressed mothers (see Zahn-Waxler, Duggal, & Gruber, 2002).

Parents' Marriage

Belsky (1984) proposed that marriage is the principal support system for parents. There is ample evidence linking marital problems with use of physical punishment, infrequent use of reasoning as a discipline style, and generally negative outcomes for children (see Cummings & Davies, 1994; Davies et al., 2006). One effect of marital conflict on children is indirect. Parents may be consumed with their marital difficulties and devote less effort to effective parenting practices. They may fail to set appropriate limits and respond angrily when children misbehave. Children, in turn, express anger toward their parents and engage in heightened levels of noncompliance behaviors, perhaps in an attempt to gain their parents' attention (Katz & Gottman, 1997).

Children are sometimes directly involved in parental conflict, witnessing their mother and father arguing and fighting, and what parents fight about has an influence on how children react to marital conflicts they witness. For example, in a longitudinal study examining the effects of marital conflict on changes in children's behavior, parental conflict predicted changes in externalizing behaviors (aggression, delinquency) 2 years later. Interestingly, parental arguments *about the children* had the largest impact on children (Jenkins et al., 2005). Perhaps such disagreements were more salient to children than parental arguments not related directly to them, or perhaps children felt responsible for their parents' disagreements. The cause of this effect is not certain, but the fact that all marital discord does not adversely affect children's behavior is worthy of note. Although both boys and girls experience the negative effects of parental conflict, the consequences of marital discord tend to be greater for boys than for girls. This is primarily because parents are generally more protective of their daughters than of their sons and are more likely to quarrel in the presence of their sons than their daughters (Hetherington & Stanley-Hagan, 2002).

Other research has shown that husbands and wives who generally agree about parenting styles have more congenial homes that are conducive to

Children are more affected by parents' arguing when they argue about the children. Boys are more apt to be affected by parents' arguments, because parents are more likely to argue in front of boys than girls.

good parenting and have children who are intellectually and socially competent (Block, Block, & Morrison, 1981; Vaughn, Block, & Block, 1988). One study suggests that it may not be agreement per se that is so important; rather, husbands and wives who agree on child-rearing tend to have more positive parenting skills (often both authoritative) than do husbands and wives who disagree (Deal, Halverson, & Wampler, 1989).

Some of the best outcomes occur not only when mothers and fathers agree with one another in terms of style of parenting, but when they engage in **co-parenting**, consciously coordinating their child-rearing practices. Susan McHale and her colleagues (2002) describe effective co-parenting as occurring when "the significant adult figures collaborate to provide a family context that communicates to children solidarity and support between parenting figures, a consistent and predictable set of rules and standards (regardless of whether the child lives in a single household or multiple ones), and a safe and secure home base" (p. 76). When both parents practice warm, authoritative-type parenting, the result can be a high degree of family harmony. You may think that all parents at least attempt such co-parenting practices, but sometimes parents disagree with one another, and the result can often be disharmony, which can adversely affect children's social and emotional development

co-parenting The practice whereby parents consciously coordinate their child-rearing practices.

(McHale & Rasmussen, 1998). Mothers, as the primary caretaker in most families, often play the role of gatekeeper, determining a father's access to his children and the decisions he is allowed to make regarding them (Beitel & Parke, 1998). When fathers are left out of the decision-making process, or made to believe they are incompetent when it comes to dealing with children, they often withdraw from their children. Although successful co-parenting does not mean that both parents provide an equal amount of caregiving to their child, it does mean that both parents have a say about child-rearing and that both are actively involved in their child's life.

Social Support

Parents do not raise children alone but typically rely on others, often kin, to help with child-rearing (see Chapter 12), and the availability of such social support can have a significant impact on parent-child relationships. Having an extended family or a network of friends provides the parent (particularly the mother) with a source of emotional support and important knowledge about child-rearing that serves, in many cases, to influence specific parenting behaviors (Cochran & Niego, 2002; Weinraub, Horvath, & Gringlas, 2002). This can be especially important for single mothers. In one study, friendships and community support influenced mothers' perceptions of and reactions to daily child-rearing hassles to a greater extent than did support from husbands (Crnic & Greenberg, 1990). In other research, women who had support in childcare, mainly in the form of babysitting or talking about child-rearing, were less dominating, more sensitive to the needs of their children, and emotionally warmer than women without such support (see Cochran & Niego, 2002).

Economic Stability and Socioeconomic Status (SES)

Clearly, poverty, loss of a job, or other significant life stressors influences the quality of parent-child interactions. In a review of the effects of economic hardship on parenting in African American families, Vonnie McLoyd (1990, p. 322) noted

> mothers who are poor, as compared to their advantaged counterparts, are more likely to use power-assertive techniques in disciplinary encounters and are generally less supportive of their children. They value obedience more, are less likely to use reasoning, and are more likely to use physical punishment as a means of disciplining and controlling the child.

Also, children, mostly from poverty families, who live in hectic, unstructured, and unpredictable homes, experience increased feelings of helplessness and psychological distress relative to those living in more structured homes (Evans et al., 2005).

Although such effects are associated with long-term poverty, evidence suggests that parents become more irritable, hostile, and depressed as a result of economic loss or other specific contextual factors (for example, changing residences, changes in mother's relationship) and, as a consequence, react toward their children in punitive and erratic ways (Ackerman, Brown, & Izard, 2004; Conger et al., 1984). One study of adolescents in a Midwestern farming community that was experiencing hard times found a connection between economic hardship, parents' behavior, and adolescents' functioning (Lempers et al., 1989). As a result of economic hardship, parents became less nurturant and less consistent toward their children. These changes resulted in feelings of depression and loneliness in many adolescents that were associated, in turn, with delinquency and drug use.

At the less extremes of economic hardship, parenting style has been found to vary with SES. Higher-SES parents are more apt than lower-SES parents to use authoritative parenting techniques (high control, high warmth) (Hoff et al., 2002). This pattern has been found in different ethnic groups within the United States (Bluestone & Tamis-LeMonda, 1999; Dornbusch et al., 1987) and in non-Western cultures as well (Chen, Dong, & Zhou, 1997; von der Lippe, 1999). Compared to higher-SES parents, lower-SES parents have been found to talk to their children less; be more controlling, disapproving, and restrictive; and to use more punitive disciplinary techniques (see Hoff et al., 2002). For example, lower-SES parents are more likely to use spanking (hitting the child on the buttocks or extremities without leaving a bruise or inflicting physical harm) as a disciplinary technique than are higher-SES parents (Gershof, 2002; Kazdin & Benjet, 2003). Although spanking is effective in altering a child's immediate behavior, it is associated with poorer mental health and increased antisocial behavior in both children and adults and poorer quality of parent-child relationship (Gershof, 2002). We should note that although spanking is officially outlawed in many countries, including Austria, Croatia, Cyprus, Denmark, Finland, Germany, Israel, Italy, Latvia, Norway, and Sweden (Gershof, 2002), it is used in varying degrees of frequency and intensity by the majority of American parents (65% in a 2007 ABC News poll). Although most psychologists advocate against spanking, some suggest that the negative consequences of spanking are the result of only the most severe forms of physical punishment and that the across-the-board sanction against spanking is not warranted by the data (Baumrind et al., 2002).

Before claiming that spanking is the *cause* of poor mental health and behavioral problems, it is important to note that it is also associated with a host of other parenting behaviors, some of which are also associated with SES. For instance, parents who spank their children, compared to parents who do not, hug and play with their children less, have higher rates of substance abuse and mental illness, and experience higher levels of stress and marital discord (Kazdin & Benjet, 2003). Spanking, then, may simply be a symptom of an authoritarian parenting style, which is associated with SES level.

It should be obvious that living in poverty is not good for anyone, child or adult, and that parents living in poverty are more apt to use parenting techniques that are not conducive to good psychological outcomes for their children. However, poverty is not destiny. Many parents living under harsh conditions do an excellent job of caring for their children, despite their economic situation, and many well-to-do parents provide less-than-optimal conditions for their children. Box 13.2 provides some of the perils of affluence that befall many children from higher-income homes in the United States today.

Child Maltreatment

Although many factors influence how parents treat their children and thus children's development, most parents treat their children within a broadly defined acceptable level. However, some parents cross the line and engage in child maltreatment, which is one of the causes of serious emotional problems in childhood and adolescence. **Child maltreatment** is defined as intentional abuse or neglect of anyone younger than 18 years of age that endangers their well-being. In 2006 the rate of substantiated cases of child maltreatment was 12.1 per 1,000 children between the ages of 0 and 17 in the United States (Federal Interagency Forum on Child and Family Statistics, 2008). Dante Cicchetti and Sheree Toth (2006, p. 504) identified four categories of child maltreatment:

1. *Physical abuse*: The infliction of bodily injury on a child other than by accident
2. *Sexual abuse*: Sexual or attempted sexual contact between a caregiver or other responsible adult with a child for the caregiver's gratification or financial benefit
3. *Neglect*: The failure to provide minimum care and appropriate supervision
4. *Emotional maltreatment*: Persistent and extreme thwarting of a child's basic emotional needs

At the extreme of physical abuse is *filicide*, the killing of a child by a parent or stepparent. Although filicide is rare, it is not unheard of. For

---

child maltreatment The intentional abuse or neglect of anyone under 18 years of age that endangers their well-being.

BOX 13.2 **food for thought**

The Perils of Affluence

There is a good reason why researchers and social-policy makers have focused on the effects of poverty on child development. The connections between poverty and a host of behavioral, intellectual, economic, and social factors are well established. Children growing up in poverty do more poorly in school, are more likely to be involved in the juvenile-justice system, display poorer mental health, have a greater incidence of substance abuse, and fare more poorly in the job market than children growing up in more-affluent homes. These effects are not inevitable, but, on average, the effects of poverty on development are significant (Magnuson & Duncan, 2002).

But affluent children in contemporary society do not necessarily have it easy, or at least they, too, have their problems. In the United States in particular, there is great diversity in economic resources, and many children grow up in homes with affluence that only the most wealthy families experienced just several generations ago. Children from these homes experience different pressures.

Beginning often in the preschool years, the lives of many middle- and upper-middle-class children are highly structured. Parents enroll children in a variety of after-school and weekend activities, from T-ball and ballet to tae kwon do and violin lessons. They arrange playdates for their children. Many of these children are engaged in organized sports, but, unlike generations past, all decisions related to the game are made by adults, often with parents cheering (sometimes screaming) from the sidelines. (The exception to this seems to be basketball, with as few as two children needed to make a game by anyone who can throw a ball to the 10-foot basket, which usually excludes children much below the age of 10 or so. Lower baskets are available for younger children.) Parents keep their children busy in the belief that these activities will provide their children with skills necessary to compete in school, college, and in the adult world in general (see Bjorklund, 2007a). They have been called *helicopter parents*, because they hover over their children, ensuring their children's safety and that they get the experiences they need to succeed.

© Bill Aron/PhotoEdit

Middle- and high-school children from affluent homes are more likely to use alcohol and cigarettes than are children from more mainstream homes and children living in poverty. Many such adolescents experience *achievement pressure,* **viewing their achievement failures, such as doing poorly in school, as personal failures, which they believe is emphasized by their parents.**

Suniya Luthar and her colleagues (Luthar, 2003; Luthar & Latendresse, 2005; Luthar & Sexton, 2004) have examined the lives of middle- and high-school children from affluent homes, with family median incomes often exceeding $100,000, and compared them with inner-city children, with family incomes around $30,000. Perhaps somewhat surprisingly, children from the affluent homes had a higher incidence of alcohol use, cigarette smoking, and marijuana and hard-drug use than the national norm *and* their inner-city counterparts. These children also reported higher levels of anxiety and somewhat higher levels of depression than the inner-city youth, with these effects getting larger, or first appearing, as children moved from middle school to high school.

Why should such privileged youth display problems more typically associated with children living in low-income environments? Luthar and her colleagues speculated that these children experienced substantial *achievement pressure;* they viewed achievement failures (for instance, doing poorly in school) as personal failures. Similarly, many of these children perceived their parents as overemphasizing their accomplishments at the expense of emphasizing their character. They were what they did, as opposed to who they were. Luthar identified a second factor she called *isolation from adults.* This isolation was both literal and emotional. Adolescents who felt distant from their parents, either in time spent with them or in emotional closeness, showed more distress and greater substance abuse than did less-isolated teens.

The surprising finding in this work is that adolescents at the socioeconomic extremes are more similar in many ways than they are different. Lack of interest in school, poor academic performance, substance abuse, and delinquency were found in both groups, all greater than typically observed in the general population of adolescents. According to Luthar and Latendresse (2005, p. 52): "The American dream spawns widespread beliefs that Ivy League educations and subsequently lucrative careers are critical for children's long-term happiness. In the sometimes single-minded pursuit of these goals, let us not lose sight of the possible costs to mental health and well-being of all concerned."

example, in the United States between 1976 and 1994, there were 3,925 cases in which a child 5 years of age or younger was murdered by a genetic parent or a stepparent (Weekes-Shackelford & Shackelford, 2004). Moreover, about 10% of cases of sudden infant death syndrome (SIDS) and other unexplained infant deaths are believed to be a result of filicide, making it a more prevalent cause of infant mortality than the official statistics may imply (Koenen & Thompson, 2008). (We discussed filicide in greater depth in Chapter 12.) More common is *physical abuse* that does not result in death, with *neglect* being the most frequent type of child maltreatment. *Emotional maltreatment* involves a parent persistently rejecting, ignoring, belittling, and criticizing a child and often co-occurs with physical abuse. We discuss sexual abuse in Chapter 15.

Child maltreatment produces what Cicchetti and Toth (2006, p. 504) describe as "a clear deviation from the average expectable environment," meaning that children in such homes experience species-atypical environments that are not conducive to supporting normal psychological development.

There are many causes for child maltreatment. Parents of maltreated children tend to have poor impulse control, low self-esteem, problems with substance abuse, and often lack social support (Emery & Laumann-Billings, 1998). Some characteristics of the children themselves are associated with abuse. For example, child abuse has been found to occur at a higher frequency for sickly than for healthy infants and children, with the illness occurring before the abuse (Sherrod et al., 1984). Similarly, children born prematurely are more likely than full-term children to be abused sometime during childhood (Martin et al., 1974). The reason may lie in the characteristics of unhealthy babies. Abusive mothers have been reported to be more likely than nonabusive mothers to find the cries of infants aversive (Frodi & Lamb, 1980). The cries of most premature or sickly babies truly are aversive; abusive parents presumably react even more negatively to them, and these feelings persist even after the sickly cries have disappeared. Sickly children, or children who have an especially difficult temperament, may be singled out by stressed parents because their behavior is so irritating to them, making them the whipping boys (or girls) for dysfunctional families.

Children can be maltreated in contexts other than the family as well, such as at school, or for many children in the world, in a state-run institution or orphanage. We discussed such maltreatment and its effects on attachment briefly in Chapter 12 and looked at the effects of such institutionalization on intelligence in Chapter 10.

Not surprisingly, maltreated children fare less well than nonmaltreated children on a host of psy-

© Ted Foxx/Alamy

Parents with poor impulse control, low self-esteem, and lack of social support are more apt than other parents to abuse their children. Child maltreatment can have significant long-term negative effects on children's psychosocial development.

chosocial measures. As one would expect, maltreated children have less secure and warm relationships with their parents, lower self-esteem, and display less empathy than nonmaltreated children (Cicchetti & Toth, 2006; Main & George, 1985). Children who are treated harshly by their parents are more aggressive (Cullerton-Sen et al., 2008), often being bullies (see Chapter 14), generally have more conflicts with their peers, perform poorly in school, and have fewer friends (Eckenrode, Laird, & Doris, 1993; Salzinger et al., 2001; Trickett & Kuczynski, 1986).

Some of the most serious effects of child maltreatment, however, are seen in adolescence. As noted in Chapter 11, some emotional problems, such as depression, are more apt to be identified in adolescence than during childhood, and maltreated children are more likely than nonmaltreated children to display a host of emotional problems. These include both internalizing behaviors, such as depression and anxiety, and externalizing behaviors, such as conduct disorder. Maltreated children are also more likely than nonmaltreated children to display eating disorders, sexual dysfunction, and hyperactivity during adolescence (Cicchetti & Toth, 2006; Keiley et al., 2001).

There should likely be little surprise that child maltreatment results in less-than-optimal psychological outcomes. Although parents differ widely in how they treat their children (in their parenting style), children throughout history could expect reasonably supportive and protective parents. Children are frequently kept close to their mothers for extended periods of time and given substantial

Chinese parents score high on the authoritarian scale, because they exert a high level of control over their children's activities and rarely ask their children's opinions. However, given differences in values between Chinese and American cultures, such parenting practices may actually reflect a loving and caring approach to child-rearing that is well suited to their culture.

freedoms and respect in traditional cultures (Harkness & Super, 1995; Konner, 2010). Even in less-developed communities today, such as the Mayans of Guatemala, toddlers in particular are given privileged status and are permitted to get what they want and not expected to follow rules for sharing, unlike American toddlers (Mosier & Rogoff, 2003). In part, modern societies' attitudes toward children may result in adults expecting more from children than they once did, or that adults in more traditional cultures do. For some subset of parents (for example, those with poor impulse control, lack of social support, and substance abuse), children's actions may not match their expectations, and this may contribute to child maltreatment.

Cultural and Ethnic Differences

How a society raises its children is a function of what type of adult it wants to produce. It may seem obvious that a self-reliant, independent, exploring, and trusting person would be the most competent adult, and this is very likely true for middle-class American society. But is it also true for Japanese, German, and Iraqi children? Is it true for American children growing up in areas of urban poverty or on Native American reservations? Maybe not. Certainly there is great variability in what constitutes an effective adult in different cultures (and subcultures) around the world. When evaluating the best way to rear children, one must keep in mind the skills and attitudes that will serve them best, both in

their immediate environments and when they reach adulthood.

As one example, consider the parenting style of many Chinese parents. When using Baumrind's scales to evaluate them, they tend to score high on the authoritarian dimension (Chao, 1994). But does authoritarian mean the same thing in China as it does in the United States? One reason that Chinese parents come across as highly authoritarian is that, unlike Western parents, they rarely seek their children's opinions, consider their wishes, or offer them alternatives. Rather, they exert a high level of control over their children's activities, particularly those related to their education, and insist on maintaining social order. Yet, there are differences in cultural values that make any direct comparison between Asian and Western parenting styles inappropriate. For example, the Western ideal of independence and autonomy is foreign to many Asian cultures, where the emphasis is on maintaining group cohesion, both in the family and in the society at large. As such, the seemingly restrictive and authoritarian behavior of Chinese parents actually reflects a loving and caring approach to child-rearing that is well suited to their culture, if not to middle-class Western ideals (see Chao & Tseng, 2002).

For another example closer to home, one of Baumrind's (1972) early studies indicated that the negative effects of authoritarian parenting observed for European American children were not found for African American children (at least girls). Subsequent research indicated, in fact, some positive consequences of restrictive parenting for African American children in high-risk and dangerous neighborhoods (Dearing, 2004; Lamborn, Dornbusch, & Steinberg, 1996). For example, Eric Dearing (2004) assessed aspects of parenting behavior (restrictive/controlling versus supportive) and child outcomes (academic performance, depression) in samples of African American, European American, and Latino American children in the Boston, Massachusetts area. Families varied in socioeconomic status and the quality of the neighborhoods in which they lived. Dearing found that restrictive parenting, which emphasized parental authority, control, and close monitoring of children, was especially detrimental for European American children in high-risk neighborhoods. In contrast, this same type of restrictive parenting was associated with more positive academic outcomes for African American children in similar environments, although the benefits of such restrictive parenting diminished as children grew older. At the same time, supportive parenting had a particularly strong, positive effect for African American youth in impoverished neighborhoods with respect to depression. The effects for the Latino American children were similar for those of the African American children, only less pronounced.

These findings, and others like them (Baldwin, Baldwin, & Cole, 1990), suggest that authoritarian parenting may play a protective role for some children in high-risk environments, at least during certain times in development (see Teti & Candelaria, 2002). These results indicate that the effects of different parenting practices vary with ethnicity, neighborhood quality, and age of the child. In other words, there are no (or very few) truly universal effects of parenting styles on children's behavior; rather, the influences of parenting style on children vary as a function of a variety of interacting factors (Bornstein, 2006; Collins et al., 2000). Thus, one cannot give a simple recipe for what it is to be a "good" parent, because good depends on culture, community standards, and children's temperament, among other factors. As mentioned earlier, parents' goals differ depending on culture and socioeconomic level, and parents' specific goals will affect parenting style. Parents around the globe want their children to become effective, independent adults, but what this means can differ in different communities. Some parents admittedly do a better job than others in achieving this goal, but there is no one-size-fits-all package for good parenting.

We should not be surprised that different styles of parenting have different consequences for child development in different environments. Both children and adults have been prepared by natural selection to be sensitive to one another and to the contexts in which they live. Although we can imagine no environment in which uninvolved parenting is adaptive, it is easier to appreciate how an authoritarian parenting style may result in adaptive behavior in some environments for some children some of the time. For a species as cognitively flexible as *Homo sapiens*, natural selection would not have restricted parent-child relationships to a narrow range of alternatives. Rather, because of our ancestors' behavioral plasticity, they were able to evaluate environmental conditions and adjust their parenting behaviors to produce adaptive offspring. The "decisions" our ancestors made, and the decisions parents make today, are sometimes conscious and deliberate. At other times, however, they are implicit and out of conscious awareness.

Families and Neighborhoods

As we know from developmental contextual models (Bronfenbrenner & Morris, 2006; Lerner, 2006), families are embedded within a broader community. The neighborhoods families live in affect children both directly and indirectly. Direct influences include the peers children interact with, the schools they attend, and the opportunities for nonfamily activities they provide (organized soccer, pickup basketball games, drug sales on the corner). Indirect influences include how neighborhoods affect parents. Do parents have many friends or family members in the immediate area who can be expected to keep an eye on children when they are away from home? Is the crime rate in the neighborhood high, causing parents to restrict children's out-of-house activities? What types of role models are available for parenting behavior? Do other parents use corporal punishment to control children?

One issue that has received substantial research attention is the effects of living in impoverished and high-risk neighborhoods on children's development (Magnuson & Duncan, 2002; Odgers et al., 2009). In 2003, 17% of American children 17 years and younger lived below the poverty line, defined as an income of $18,810 for a family of four. Of single-mother households with children, 42% were below the poverty line. These figures were higher for younger (0 to 5 years) than for older (6 to 17 years) children and for African American than for European American households (Federal Interagency Forum on Child and Family Statistics, 2005). We have already seen that lower-SES parents are more apt than higher-SES parents to use authoritarian parenting styles, including physical punishment, (Hoff et al., 2002), but residence in an impoverished neighborhood seems to exacerbate any effects associated with low SES. For example, in one study, African American children from single-parent families showed elevated levels of aggression if they lived in economically disadvantaged neighborhoods, compared to similar children living in more advantaged neighborhoods (Kupersmidt et al., 1995).

The results of many studies assessing child and adolescent outcomes as a result of the quality of the neighborhood (usually evaluated in terms of income level and crime rate) have found that living in impoverished neighborhoods is associated with poorer academic performance, lower IQ scores, and higher incidence of mental health problems, juvenile delinquency, and risky sexual behavior (Leventhal & Brooks-Gunn, 2000, 2003), and effects are especially strong if children spend many hours each day unsupervised (Lord & Mahoney, 2007). These effects are not independent of families, however. Parenting styles interact with quality of neighborhoods and peer deviance to influence children's behavior, including delinquency (Chung & Steinberg, 2006; Kohen et al., 2008).

But are the neighborhoods contributing to these outcomes, or is it simply the fact that poor

BOX 13.3

the biopsychology of childhood

Stress, Family Life, and Cortisol Levels

Wayonne's dirt bomb struck the bright yellow dress hanging on the clothesline, making an impressive star-shaped smudge. His older cousin Jenny turned angrily from sweeping the house yard to chase him with her broom. Granny Deedee's yell halted their squabble. Jenny's face morphed from stifled argument to guilt, head bowed. She later confided to me that she felt upset because granny did not understand; her frustration was compounded by the rule that she must accept granny's authority without disagreement. . . . Jenny's cortisol level, measured from her saliva that I collected from all children in the community several times a day, rose from 1.4 to 4.2 µg/dl. The next day her secretory immunoglobulin-A levels dropped from 6.04 to 3.6 mg/dl. Four days later she had common cold symptoms: runny nose, headache, and low-grade fever. (Flinn, 2006, p. 140)

© Mark V. Flinn

Like children all over the world, many of the everyday stresses that children in the small rural community of Bwa Mawego on the Caribbean island of Dominica experience have to do with family conflict or change.

This account of a child's stressful encounter with family members, changes in biochemicals indicative of stress, and her subsequent illness was reported by Mark Flinn as part of his longitudinal study of family life and its effects on health and well-being in the small rural community of Bwa Mawego on the Caribbean island of Dominica. Flinn has been studying children on this island in a naturalistic setting since 1988, and, as of 2006, had collected 30,122 cortisol samples from 282 children and their families (Flinn, 2006; Flinn, Ward, & Noone, 2005). We saw in Chapter 11 that persistently high levels of cortisol are often associated with negative psychological and health outcomes. Flinn and his colleagues have been particularly interested in the relationship between children's psychological and medical health and family-related stress, as measured by easily obtained cortisol samples.

For example, Flinn and his colleagues report that high-stress events, resulting in a 100% to 200% increase in cortisol levels, are most usually associated with family conflict or change. Specific family interactions, such as the one between Jenny and Granny

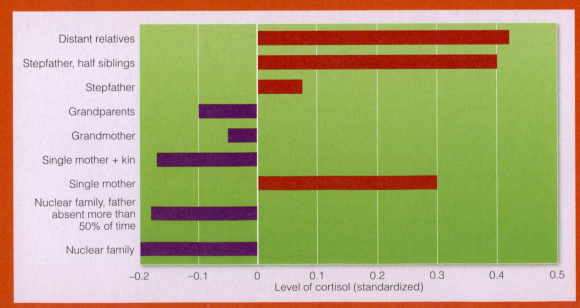

Figure legend (x-axis categories from top to bottom): Distant relatives; Stepfather, half siblings; Stepfather; Grandparents; Grandmother; Single mother + kin; Single mother; Nuclear family, father absent more than 50% of time; Nuclear family. X-axis: Level of cortisol (standardized), −0.2, −0.1, 0, 0.1, 0.2, 0.3, 0.4, 0.5

Figure A   Average levels of the stress hormone cortisol (standardized) for children living in different households from Bwa Mawego. Negative values reflect lower cortisol levels than average, whereas positive values reflect higher cortisol levels than average. Children living with their mothers and other family members have lower levels of cortisol than children living with a stepfather or distance relatives. Adapted from Flinn, M. V., & England, B. G. (2003). Childhood stress: endocrine and immune responses to psychosocial events. In J. M. Wilce (Ed.), SOURCE: *Social & cultural lives of immune systems* (pp. 107–147). London: Routledge Press.

Deedee, can result in temporary elevations in cortisol levels followed by mild illness. Other stressful family interactions may be more prolonged, such as a disagreement between a husband and wife resulting in the husband leaving and returning a week later. Still others may reflect chronic stress, such as living with stepparents or distant relatives rather than with one's biological family.

For example, the accompanying figure (A) shows the average cortisol levels for children from Bwa Mawego with different living arrangements (Flinn & England, 2003). These are *standardized* levels, with the average of the sample set at zero. Negative values reflect lower cortisol levels than average, whereas positive values reflect higher cortisol levels than average. Notice that children living (a) in nuclear families (with mom and dad and perhaps siblings), (b) in nuclear families with the father absent greater than 50% of the time, (c) with single mothers living with kin, or with their (d) grandmother or (e) grandparents, have lower-than-average levels of cortisol, whereas children living with (f) a stepfather, (g) stepfather with half siblings, or (h) distant relatives, all had higher-than-average levels of cortisol.

The effects of chronic stress on cortisol levels and subsequent health can be seen by examining children who experienced family trauma at different times in their lives. Flinn (2006) defined "family trauma" as including parental divorce, parental death, or child abuse. He then examined average cortisol levels and subsequent ill health when children were 10 years old as a function of their age when they first experienced the trauma. The accompanying figure (B) shows the average levels of cortisol for (a) control children (those not experiencing family trauma), children who experienced the trauma (b) while still in utero, (c) between birth and 3 years, and (d) between 3 and 6 years of age. As you can see, children who experienced family trauma, even as fetuses, had significantly higher levels of cortisol (again expressed as standard scores) than did children in the control condition. But what about children's health? Figure C shows the proportion of days children in each of these groups were sick. Again, children in each of the family trauma groups reported more days sick than children in the control groups who experienced no such trauma.

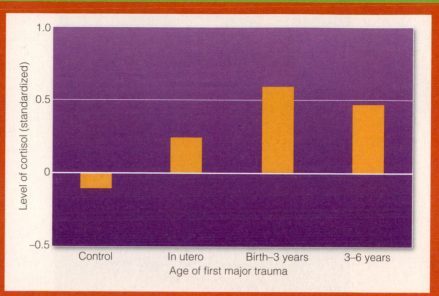

Figure B Average cortisol levels (standardized) for 10-year-old children who had no early family trauma (control) compared with children who had first experienced family trauma in utero, birth to 3 years, and 3 to 6 years. SOURCE: Adapted from Flinn, M. V. (2006). Evolution and ontogeny of stress response to social challenges in the human child. *Developmental Review, 26,* 138–174.

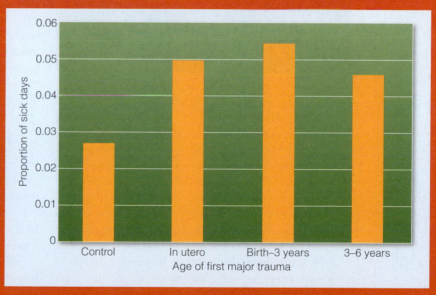

Figure C Average number of sick days for 10-year-old children who had no early family trauma (control) compared with children who had first experienced family trauma in utero, birth to 3 years, and 3 to 6 years. SOURCE: Adapted from Flinn, M. V. (2006). Evolution and ontogeny of stress response to social challenges in the human child. *Developmental Review, 26,* 138–174.

Stress, particularly when dealing with family members, is unavoidable, in part because of the unpredictable nature of social relationships and the near-constant interaction family members have with one another. Humans' hormone and neurological systems have evolved to deal with stress in adaptive ways, beginning in childhood. Flinn (2006, p. 161) writes, "Childhood appears necessary and useful for acquiring the informa-

tion and practice to build and refine mental algorithms critical for negotiating the social relationships and the web of ever-changing relationships that are key to the success of our species." However, success at navigating immediate social environments may produce biochemical responses that are associated with negative long-term consequences.

Research has shown that African American children living in impoverished neighborhoods, compared to children of comparable SES living in better neighborhoods, have poorer academic performance, lower IQ scores, and higher incidence of mental health problems, juvenile delinquency, and risky sexual behavior.

Mario Tama/Getty Images

people live in poor neighborhoods, and such people, for whatever reasons, engage in parenting styles associated with negative child outcomes? In other words, neighborhood effects are not easily separated from family effects. Families have some choice as to where they live (although some families have considerably more choice than others). Moreover, it is difficult to separate the effects of family SES from the economic conditions of a neighborhood. Experimental studies with random assignment of families to neighborhoods is necessary to separate the effects of family from the effects of neighborhood on child outcomes, and it would seem that such studies would be difficult, if not impossible, to do. Researchers cannot assign some people to a poverty group and another to an affluent group and assess the consequences on child development, but several government-sponsored programs have provided improved housing and thus better neighborhoods for impoverished people and compared child outcomes with children whose families did not move (Rubinowitz & Rosenbaum, 2000; Leventhal & Brooks-Gunn, 2003).

One such project is the Moving to Opportunity Program, in which approximately 4,600 families in five cities in the United States were randomly given vouchers allowing them to move out of high-crime/ high-poverty public housing and into private housing in low-poverty neighborhoods (Bembry & Norris, 2005; Leventhal & Brooks-Gunn, 2003, 2004). Initial results demonstrated that children and adolescents who moved to more advantaged neighborhoods had higher levels of academic achievement and better mental health than their peers who remained in high-poverty neighborhoods (Katz, Kling, & Liebman, 2001; Leventhal & Brooks-Gunn, 2003, 2004). A five-year follow-up of program participants 14 to 20 years old in New York City, however, failed to find maintenance of the academic benefits reported earlier (Leventhal, Fauth, & Brooks-Gunn, 2005). This finding is counter to previous research with other relocation programs (Rubinowitz & Rosenbaum, 2000). Tama Leventhal and her colleagues (Leventhal, Fauth, & Brooks-Gunn, 2005) suggested several reasons for the negative findings, perhaps the most important being that, although children were living in more affluent neighborhoods, they were not attending better schools. Rather, they attended New York City public schools with a similar ethnic and socioeconomic mixture as children who did not relocate, presumably being less apt to attend charter or private schools than the more affluent children in their neighborhoods. Previous research had shown that school composition might have a greater impact on adolescents' academic performance than the quality of the neighborhood (Chase-Lansdale & Gordon, 1996; Teitler & Weiss, 2000). We will investigate the role of schools on the socialization of children later in this chapter.

Children's Influence on Parents and Parenting

Individual differences in children's personality, temperament, physical abilities, or intelligence can affect how others respond to them, and this includes parents. An easygoing infant will be treated differently than an irritable one; a high-energy child will have different experiences in the home than a more sedate child; and a headstrong, noncompliant child will evoke different reactions than an obedient child from his or her parents. As we saw in previous chapters, many of these infant and child characteristics have a strong genetic component and are not easily modified by experience. This does not mean, however, that children's behavior is determined by genes; rather, constitutional differences in children influence their behavior, which in turn affects how parents perceive and respond to them. These are "evocative genotype → environment effects" in Scarr and McCartney's (1983) model (see Chapter 3). Parents' behavior in turn influences children's behavior, and the cycle continues. In other words, a bidirectional relationship exists between children and their parents.

How Important Are Parents for Healthy Psychological Development?

As we have seen in this chapter, many factors influence children's development within families. These include the presence of social support, parenting goals, beliefs, and style, the neighborhoods in which children grow up, child maltreatment, and characteristics of the children themselves. Moreover, these factors are all highly interactive, making it necessary to view the family as part of a dynamic system. But at the center of the family, as far as children are concerned, are the parents. How important are parents for healthy psychological development? At one level, they are essential. As noted in Chapter 12, children without parents fare less well than children with parents, but that is not the level at which psychologists and the public at large evaluate the effects of parenting on child development. Given the host of other interacting influences, how much do individual differences in parenting behavior affect how a child develops?

The traditional answer to this question has always been that such differences matter a lot. Why would psychologists devote so much time and effort to the topic if individual differences in how parents treat their children did not have some consequences for how they grow up? Sandra Scarr (1992, 1993) disagreed and provided an alternative account as an extension of her genotype → environment theory discussed in Chapter 3 (Scarr & McCartney, 1983). Scarr (1992, p. 15) proposed that "ordinary differences between families have little effect on children's development, unless the family is outside of a typical developmental range. Good enough, ordinary parents probably have the same effects on their children's development as culturally defined super-parents." According to Scarr, active genotype → environment effects cause children to seek environments consistent with their temperaments. Experiences in these environments shape children's personalities and intellects, but their genotype drives those experiences, and these active genotype → environment effects increase with age as parents' direct (nongenetic) influences wane.

Scarr's proposal is that children in all parts of the world and throughout history (and prehistory) have developed to become productive (and reproductive) members of their societies despite substantial differences in child-rearing practices. The bottom line is that high-quality parenting is not necessary for survival; rather, the species evolved so that children could tolerate great flexibility in child-rearing practices and still grow up to be typi-

If a culture restricts children's opportunities (for example, preventing girls from attending school as in some extreme Islamic societies), active genotype → environment effects in Scarr's model cannot be realized, and they will not develop to their full potential.

cal. **Good-enough parents** are indeed good enough to raise successful offspring, with "successful" defined as being able to reproduce.

Most of us, however, are not satisfied that children grow up simply to reproduce themselves; we want them to become well-adjusted and socially successful members of their cultures. Scarr is surely correct in her assertion that children do not require "super parenting" in order to survive, but this is not the level at which most psychologists are concerned, and her theory was severely criticized (Baumrind, 1993; Jackson, 1993). Even if one grants that active genotype → environment effects direct children to particular types of experiences, children must have opportunities to seek their niche. If children's opportunities are restricted because of cultural strictures (girls are not educated) or local limitations (neighborhood jobs are few), they will not be able to reach their full potential.

Scarr (1993) admitted that in some environments good-enough parents may not be adequate. If children are not able to take advantage of the opportunities that the majority culture offers, their social, intellectual, and economic development will surely suffer. The difference between Scarr and her critics is primarily one of emphasis. In the best Darwinian tradition, Scarr's principal concern is how children become functioning members of their species. In contrast, her critics emphasize individual differences among children within a culture.

good-enough parents The controversial proposal by Scarr that individual differences in parenting have little consequence for children's development and that "good enough" parents are adequate for proper development.

It is unquestionable that parents play an important role in children's lives. Yet, children have evolved to be able to tolerate a wide range of parental behaviors and grow up to be normal. Normal, however, covers a broad range of outcomes, especially when considering adaptation to modern economic and social life and not just procreation. It is at this level that individual differences in parenting contribute importantly to psychological development. And children's psychological development is influenced by a host of factors beyond the actions of their parents, making it impossible to predict any child's outcome based solely on his or her parents' behavior. Parents can neither take all the credit nor need they take all the blame for their children's lot in life. In fact, the evolutionary primatologist Sarah Hrdy (1999) notes that, unlike in most Western societies, in most traditional societies, parents take little credit or blame for how their children turn out. Development is not something that is viewed as highly influenced by a parent's actions; this makes a child's outcome something that is not the consequence of particularly good (or bad) parenting.

Living with Siblings

Most people in the world grow up with brothers and sisters, and they likely always did. For instance, 80% of people in the United States and the United Kingdom have siblings (Dunn, 2005). (An interesting exception is contemporary China, with its **One-Child Policy**, which is examined in Box 13.4.) Siblings, on average, share 50% of their genes with one another, and from an inclusive-fitness perspective (see Chapter 12), they should display substantial cooperation.

Judy Dunn (2002) states that three characteristics typify sibling relationships: (1) emotions are often extreme and freely expressed between siblings; (2) there is substantial intimacy between and personal knowledge of siblings; and (3) there are substantial individual differences in the nature of sibling relationships across childhood and adolescents. With respect to emotional intensity, about one-fifth of all interactions among preschool siblings can be described as intense and negative, a far higher percentage than is found among friends. However, many interactions among these same siblings are also intensely positive, making sibling relationships ones in which strong mixed emotions are common (Dunn, Creps, & Brown, 1996). Concerning intimacy, siblings spend more time interacting with one another

than with their parents (McHale & Crouter, 1996), and as a result know each other very well. This intimate knowledge can be used to comfort a sibling in time of stress, but is often used to tease a sibling in a way that a less-knowledgeable peer cannot. And finally, although most siblings share intimate knowledge of one another and display intense emotions, there is a wide range of ways in which these relationships develop. Some siblings express mainly positive emotions toward one another, overt hostility reflects other sibling relationships, whereas others are ambivalent toward one another.

Siblings learn a lot from each other, sometimes directly, with the older sibling playing the role of teacher, and sometimes indirectly during play or while one is caring for the other (Brody, 2004; Zukow-Goldring, 2002). Typically, younger siblings benefit from an older sibling's teaching. Younger siblings pay attention to what older siblings do; they mimic their actions, ask them for suggestions, and comply with their instructions (Abramovitch et al., 1986; Azmita & Hesser, 1993; Dunn & Kendrick, 1982). Older siblings may model competent social or problem-solving behavior, use language in a way that adults do not, demonstrate how to perform household chores, or express nurturing, all of which can result in more advanced development or competent behavior by the younger sibling (Dunn & Kendrick, 1982; Ellis & Rogoff, 1982). And both younger and older siblings

Daniel Pangbourne/Getty Images

Older siblings often play the role of teacher to a younger sibling. The interactions between siblings can sometimes be intense, both positively and negatively.

One-Child Policy Official policy in China that limits the number of children to one per family.

Siblings have intimate knowledge of one another, which can be used to comfort or torment one another.

learn to cooperate, share, help, and empathize by interacting with and watching one another (Lewis, 2005).

Yet, with the exception of monozygotic twins, siblings are not genetically identical and thus have their own unique self-interests. These self-interests are likely to come into conflict as siblings compete for a fair share of their parents' limited resources (Michalski & Euler, 2007). Parents have only so much time and money to go around, and giving to one child may result in a loss to another—or at least seem that way to a child. Many families have a child who keeps close inventory of who gets what and believes that he or she is not getting his or her fair share. The lament of many an adult to his or her siblings, "Mom always did like you best," is spoken only half in jest. In fact, often despite claims to the contrary, it is quite common for parents to be closer or more supportive of one child over others (see Suitor et al., 2008).

Conflict and Cooperation among Siblings

Siblings can be the closest of friends and the worst of enemies, sometimes within the span of a few hours (Furman & Buhrmester, 1985; Garcia et al., 2000). The conflict begins as soon as the second child in a family is born. Each first-born is an only child for some period of time, and the birth of a sibling changes that status to that of older sibling. Most people are aware of the phenomenon of regression, where a child acts immature for his or her age, such as whining, having toileting accidents, or wanting to be fed or clothed by a parent. This often occurs when Mom and Dad bring home a new baby. The older child's immature behavior is an attempt to garner more attention from the parents, which has been lost with the addition of the new baby.

Researchers have examined changes in the security of attachment between first-born children and their mothers as a result of the birth of a second child. For example, in one study, children

displayed more signs of insecure attachment 1 to 2 months after a sibling was born relative to a few months before the birth (Teti et al., 1996). The decline in attachment security was especially sharp for children 2 years of age and older. The authors speculated that by 2 years, children have the cognitive ability to feel threatened by the addition to the family, something that younger toddlers and infants do not. In other research, preschool girls who had a positive relationship with their mothers before the birth of a sibling had particularly strong negative reactions to their new brother or sister, which persisted for at least 14 months after the birth (Dunn & Kendrick, 1981).

As children grow up, they become increasingly independent and interact more with peers and less often with siblings. Nonetheless, parents

The birth of a sibling can cause conflict for an older child, who may show signs of regression and seek his or her parents' attention.

BOX 13.4 socioculturally speaking

China's One-Child Policy

Perhaps you are an only child of two parents who were themselves only children. If you are, you would have no siblings, no aunts or uncles, and no cousins. Although this is not an unheard-of situation, it is relatively rare throughout the world, except in China. In 1979, China enacted its *One-Child Policy*, limiting the number of children to one per family, enforced through heavy fines and pressure from employers and government officials.

Other nations have reduced their fertility and in the process increased their economic standing in the world, but they have done so gradually, over decades or even centuries. China did it in a single generation. Moreover, Chinese culture has a tradition of large families. Before the One-Child Policy, the fertility rate was 5.8 births per woman in China; within 2 years of enactment of the law, the birthrate had dropped to 2.3 births per woman. Although one child per family may be the rule of the land, rural families still, on average, have more than one child, reflecting both tradition and the needs of farming families, but in urban areas, nearly all children are singletons.

The intention of the policy was to reduce China's exploding population and to permit parents to invest heavily in fewer children, allowing children (and China) to attain higher educational and economic achievement. To this extent, the policy has been a huge success, but there have been unintended consequences.

Vanessa Fong (2004) spent 27 months living among urban Chinese families between 1997 and 2002, studying how this One-Child Policy had affected individuals, families, and the culture of China. Parents make great sacrifices for their singleton children.

Many urban parents, according to Fong, live in third-world conditions but provide first-world environments and opportunities for their only child. As a result of being the recipient of heavy parental investment, these children develop a sense of entitlement and a self-centeredness that disturbs their parents and grandparents, who are the primary contributors of children's spoiled attitudes. Fong reports that Chinese adults have developed a vocabulary to describe singletons. These include terms such as *little suns*, because the parents' lives revolve around them, and *little emperors*, "conjuring up the comical image of a small child lording it over worshipful adults" (Fong, 2004, p. 29).

Are China's singleton children truly spoiled and psychologically maladjusted compared to children growing up in multi-child families? Fong cites research documenting small but significant differences in the personalities, attitudes, and social behaviors of singleton Chinese children relative to nonsingletons. Compared to nonsingletons, singleton Chinese children have been found to be uncooperative, disrespectful of elders and of others' property, unable to care for themselves, obstinate, unable to delay gratification, bossy, moody, and to have short tempers (Tao & Chiu, 1985; Tao et al., 1995; see Fong, 2004). Fong, however, sees little difference in the behaviors and attitudes of China's singleton teenagers and those of children in developed countries. Today's Chinese children may be spoiled and feel entitled relative to their parents when they were teenagers, but, according to Fong, they are similar to American or European children, brought up in small families, receiving substantial investment in time and resources from their parents.

How do Chinese adolescents feel about being only children? Of course, these children have little with which to contrast their experience in a nation of singletons, but multiple-child families are not unheard of in China, and children can imagine what life would be like with brothers or sisters. When Fong (2004, p. 2) asked a group of high-school seniors if they would like to have a sibling if they could, she got a variety of answers:

- "No, I wouldn't want to share my things."
- "An older sister would be nice, but a younger brother would be horrible. He would be favored, get all the good food, and leave none for me."
- "It's better for parents to have only one child. With lots of children, they won't care about any of them."
- "Many families favor one child over others, so I'm glad I don't have siblings. My family's poor, so they wouldn't be able to support two children."
- "I'd like an older brother, because he could teach me about life, and help me out. In times of failure, an older brother's encouragement would be even more effective than a parent's."
- "I'd like an older brother, because he could help me support our parents when they're old."

These varied responses obviously reflect the particular personalities and experiences of each respondent, but they also reveal children's awareness of the importance of parents to the lives of children and how siblings can be both competitors of and comrades with children, being their greatest source of support in some contexts ("an older brother's encouragement would be even more effective than a parent's") and

encourage children to interact and watch out for one another, and this persists long after children leave home. In fact, research indicates that sibling relationships remain important throughout the lifespan, often increasing in middle and late adulthood (Bedford, Volling, & Avioli, 2000). Parents' emphasis on sibling solidarity makes good sense from the perspective of inclusive fitness, although it is admittedly difficult to separate the extent to which this emphasis is a result of genetic similarity (we are naturally disposed to cooperate with our siblings) or culture (society emphasizes the importance of cooperating with siblings). Recent research has demonstrated that full siblings are more likely to invest in one another (for example, lend or give money) than are half siblings, even if they grow up in the same house and presumably had comparable pressure to cooperate (Pollet, 2007).

One study that tried to tease apart the cultural from the inclusive-fitness contributions to family their greatest nemesis in others ("a younger brother would . . . get all the good food, and leave none for me").

The transition from large to small families (and from agrarian and communist economies to urban and capitalist ones) has been abrupt, and Chinese families have retained many traditional values that may conflict with their rearing children to be first-world citizens. For example, Chinese families have always favored boys over girls. Although more boys than girls are born throughout the world (in the United States, about 104 boys are born for every 100 girls, see Chapter 3), the discrepancy is particularly great in China, where, according to 2000 census figures, 116.9 boys were born for every 100 girls. The discrepancy is likely due to selective abortion of female fetuses. Although prenatal screening is illegal in China, portable ultrasound machines have made their way to the provinces, and many parents, based on the sex of their fetus, decide whether to abort or not (Chu, 2001).

In addition, foreign adoptions of Chinese children have been on the rise (though the practice decreased in 2002 with the SARS outbreak), and most of these adoptees are girls (Connelly, 2004). This imbalance in the birth of boys and girls results in an imbalance in the numbers of men and women in adulthood. According to some estimates, by the second decade of the 21st century, 40 million Chinese men will not be able to marry and have a family, because there will not be enough Chinese women to go around. This imbalance is also resulting in women balking at arranged marriages and being pickier in their choice of a mate, leaving many less-successful men without marriage opportunities (Wiseman, 2002).

baobao ou/Getty Images

The One-Child Policy in China has resulted in many children being indulged by their parents and seen as "little emperors."

In most of the world, most children have siblings, or if they do not they often have cousins. Being an only child, however, is not an unusual occurrence, especially in recent years, where family size in the West has decreased relative to earlier decades. In developed countries, there is little difference in the personalities or intelligence of only children compared to children from multi-child families, but family size can have a stupendous impact on child-rearing and to the greater society when nearly all families are limited to one child only, as has happened in contemporary China. Some of the outcomes were expected, and in fact planned: Parents will invest substantially more in a single child, preparing him or her for success in a competitive society. Others were unexpected, such as the continued preference for boys over girls, and the resulting sex imbalance, which will likely have substantial, but yet unknown, consequences on society and family life for subsequent generations.

solidarity was performed by William Jankowiak and Monique Diderich (2000), who examined relationships among adult siblings in a polygamous, Mormon community in the southwestern United States. (Polygamy is not legal in the United States and is not sanctioned by the Mormon Church. However, there are several renegade religious communities located mainly in the Western United States that practice polygamy.) In these communities, the father is the official head of the family and all of his children are equal, regardless of whom their mother is. This relationship is emphasized in the home, the church, and the school. No distinction is made between full and half siblings, and cooperation among half siblings within the polygamous family is emphasized. It was thus somewhat surprising that, when asked to respond to a series of questions related to sibling solidarity, consistent differences were found between full and half siblings.

In polygamous families in the American Southwest, where all of a father's children are viewed as equal, siblings express more solidarity toward their full than their half siblings, something that is promoted by the mothers.

Stephan Gladieu/Getty Images

gave preferential treatment to their own children over those of the other wives. For example, they would take their children into their bedrooms to watch television or read, and children generally congregated with their own mothers and full siblings. Thus, it appears that the mothers' behavior in polygamous families promotes greater solidarity among full siblings.

Living Together, Growing Apart

We mentioned in Chapter 3 that siblings become *less* alike the older they get (McCartney et al., 1990). This somewhat counterintuitive finding that the longer people live together, the less alike in terms of personality they become was explained in terms of Scarr and McCartney's (1983) *genotype → environment theory*. As children get older, they are less under the control of their parents and have more freedom to choose environments in which they feel comfortable (active genotype → environment effects). Because siblings are not genetically identical, their different genotypes influence them to select different types of environments (for example, more sedentary activities for an introverted child, more social activities for an extroverted child), and experiences in these environments influence their developing personalities.

In addition to active genotype → environment effects causing siblings to become increasingly different as they age, experiences within the family, in particular experiences with the parents, can affect the personality development of siblings, as well as the relationship between siblings. Sibling relationships tend to be more harmonious when the children within a family are treated similarly. When parents show favoritism toward one child versus another, relationships between siblings tend to be more trou-

Figure 13.3 shows the percentage of full and half siblings who were nominated for different measures of solidarity, from feelings of closeness and whom one would invite to attend a wedding reception or birthday party, to whom is the parent of one's favorite baby, whom one would give money to, or ask to babysit. In every case, people nominated full siblings more than half siblings, despite growing up in the same house with both their full and half sibs and the official social dogma that stresses equality among a man's children. As inclusive-fitness theory predicts, genetic relatedness counts, although the mechanisms behind this effect likely lie with the children's mothers. Despite the community standard, mothers frequently

FIGURE 13.3 Percentage of full and half siblings nominated for different measures of solidarity in a polygamous society. Despite official community standards to show equal solidarity to all of a father's children, as adults, people in this polygamous community consistently rated being closer to their full siblings than to their half siblings. SOURCE: Based on data from Jankowiak, W., & Diderich, M. (2000). Sibling solidarity in a polygamous community in the USA: Unpacking inclusive fitness. *Evolution and Human Behavior, 21,* 125–139.

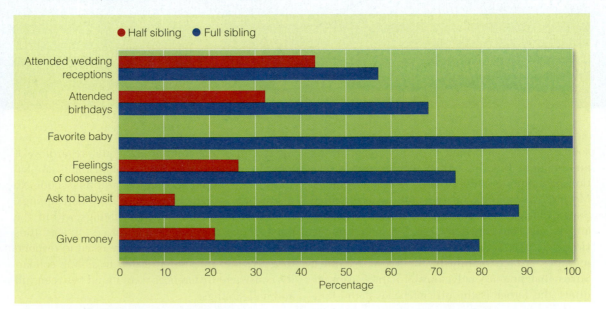

bling, and this is especially apt to happen when families experience stress (see Dunn, 2005). In general, experiences *within* a family may differ widely between siblings, and these differences contribute to the often-diverging personalities of siblings over time. One may think that two children living in the same family would share common experiences and thus be similarly affected by their family. However, families are experienced differently by different children, causing them to move in different developmental trajectories toward adulthood (Dunn & Plomin, 1990).

Does Birth Order Really Matter?

The birth order of a child in a family surely has a profound influence on that child's development, including his or her personality, and has been a much-investigated topic of research dating back to the early part of the 20th century and continuing today (Adler, 1927; Ernst & Angst, 1983; Sulloway, 1996). However, birth order is complicated by so many other factors that it has been difficult for researchers to reach any definitive conclusions about its role in development. For example, in addition to birth order, there are the issues of spacing between children, family size, the sex of one's siblings (and one's own sex), economic level of the family, and a host of other ecological factors that substantially complicate the picture. As we saw previously, the birth of a sibling can have predictable negative effects on a child (Teti et al., 1996), but whether such effects have long-term influences on children remains debatable.

When birth-order effects are found, they are often small and require large samples in order for differences to be statistically significant. Nonetheless, some reliable findings have been reported. For example, IQ tends to vary with birth order, with earlier-born children having higher IQs than later-born children, although the absolute magnitude of IQ differences is small (Galbraith, 1982; Zajonc & Marcus, 1975). Earlier-born children tend to attain more years of education (see Figure 13.4) and have jobs with higher occupational status than later-born children (Herrera et al., 2003).

Most people have a story about the importance of birth order on their own lives (the authors of this book certainly do, both first-borns). Each new child added to a family changes the family dynamics and influences people's experiences within the family. From this perspective, birth order is clearly psychologically important. However, although some effects of birth order are reliably obtained, at least when large numbers of people are sampled, most effects are unique to the individual and his or her family. Birth order is important, but the way it is important varies substantially among different families.

Coping with Family Transitions: Children and Divorce

Families differ from culture to culture, but the ideal American and European family, at least in most of the 20th century, was the nuclear family: husband, wife, and minor children. Life today, however, is not as simple as it used to be. The incidence of divorce increased dramatically over the past 50 years (although it has slowed down in recent years), and it is estimated that in the United States 40% of children born to married parents will experience divorce over the course of childhood, a rate that is similar to that of many Western European countries. This increased divorce rate is a result of societal changes over the past half century. For example, the availability of reliable and safe birth control ("the pill") helped foster the sexual revolution, and the stigma of divorce, single-parent families, and having babies out of wedlock have all but disappeared in some parts of society. The increased personal freedom afforded to both women and men associated with changing societal roles made no-fault divorce an option that was not available to previous generations.

About 90% of the children of divorce live with their mothers in single-parent homes for some time. About 65% of divorced mothers and 75% of divorced fathers remarry (Cherlin & Furstenberg, 1994), meaning that many of these children will eventually become part of a stepfamily. The incidence of divorce is higher, however, for once-divorced people, making it possible that these children will

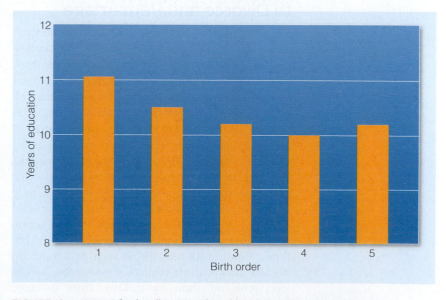

FIGURE 13.4 Years of schooling completed by birth order and family size.
SOURCE: Adapted from Herrera, N. C., Zajonc, R. B., Wieczorkowska, G., & Chicomski, B. (2003). Beliefs about birth rank and their reflection in reality. *Journal of Social and Personality Psychology, 85*, 142–150.

Girls from divorced homes are more likely than girls from non-divorced homes to be sexually active and become pregnant as teenagers.

© Chris Rout/Alamy

(Hetherington, Stanley-Hagan, & Anderson, 1989; Wallerstein, Corbin, & Lewis, 1988). They may grieve for the absent parent and defy the custodial parent's rules and requests. Within the two-year period following divorce, most parents and children show signs of good adjustment, particularly when compared to the period immediately following the divorce (Hetherington et al., 1985; Wallerstein et al., 1988), although, overall, children in divorced and remarried families continue to show poorer social adjustment and lower school performance than children in nondivorced families (Avenevoli, Sessa, & Steinberg, 1999; Chase-Lansdale, Cherlin, & Kiernam, 1995).

Sex differences in children's reactions to divorce have been mixed. Earlier studies reported that boys show more problems with divorce than girls (Amato, 2001; Hetherington et al., 1985), although other studies find the reverse (Allison & Furstenberg, 1989) or no sex differences (Sun & Li, 2002). However, boys and girls may show *different* reactions to divorce. For example, in a longitudinal study (Hetherington et al., 1985), boys from divorced homes showed more antisocial, acting-out, coercive, and noncompliant behaviors at home and at school than did boys from nondivorced homes 2 and 6 years following divorce. These boys also had difficulty with peer relationships and school achievement. In the same study, adolescent girls from divorced homes frequently displayed increased conflict with their mothers, lowered self-esteem, and higher rates of sexual behavior than did girls from nondivorced homes. The risk of becoming a teenage mother triples for girls from divorced homes. Mavis Hetherington (1998) reported that such girls were more likely than girls from nondivorced families to get married at a young age and be pregnant before marriage.

There is some suggestion that the poorer adjustment to divorce early on, especially for boys, may be a reaction not to divorce per se, but to marital conflict in general. In one study, the personalities of many children, some of whose parents subsequently divorced, were evaluated (Block, Block, & Gjerde, 1986). The researchers reported that many of the behavior and personality problems others have found in boys from divorced homes (for example, aggression and poor impulse control) were found in boys years *before* their parents divorced, presumably as a consequence of marital and family conflict.

Girls typically display poorer adjustment to remarriage than boys. Because most children of divorce live with their mothers, the mother's remarriage is usually investigated rather than the father's. In a longitudinal study, girls showed increased behavior problems after their mother's remarriage, whereas boys' behavior problems decreased (Hetherington et al., 1985; see also Hetherington

go through yet another transition sometime before they reach adulthood. What are the effects of these transitions on children? And what factors lead to children's positive or negative adjustment?

Children's Adjustment to Divorce and Remarriage

The patterns of psychological adjustment are similar for children of divorce in single-parent families and for children in stepfamilies. On average, these children display more behavior problems, more psychological distress, and lower academic achievement than do children from nondivorced families, at least initially (Lansford, 2009; Hetherington & Stanley-Hagan, 2002). There are many reasons for children's reactions. Divorced mothers, particularly, often feel depressed and stressed by the economic hardships that divorce typically brings, and as a result they sometimes engage in less-than-optimal parenting practices (Hetherington & Stanley-Hagan, 2002). However, children who remain in highly conflicted families (that is, whose warring parents do not get divorced) often display even more behavioral problems than do children from divorced homes (Jekielek, 1998; Morrison & Coirio, 1999).

Children's initial reactions to divorce may include anger, resentment, anxiety, depression, regression, sleep disturbances, and even guilt

table 13.5 Some Marital Behaviors Observed in Adult Children of Divorce

Although many of these behaviors also describe people in relationships who did not experience divorce as children, they seem to be especially frequent in this group.

- Gets angry easily
- Has feelings that are easily hurt
- Is jealous
- Is domineering
- Is critical and will not talk to the other (spouse)
- Has had a sexual relationship with someone else
- Has irritating habits
- Is not home enough
- Spends money foolishly
- Maladjustment in modesty (too self-critical)
- Submissiveness (docile, dependent, and passive behaviors)
- Distrustful
- Inability to self-evaluate
- Uncooperativeness
- Hostile passive behavior
- Keeps opinions to self

SOURCE: Adapted from Wolfinger, N. H. (2001). Transmission of divorce: Do people replicate the patterns of marital instability they grew up with? *Journal of Family Issues, 21*, 1061–1086.

& Clingempeel, 1992). Many girls in single-parent homes have considerable freedom and responsibility and develop a close, adultlike relationship with their mothers; thus, they see remarriage as a threat to both their independence and their relationship with their mothers. These feelings, it seems, are only slightly influenced by the stepfather. Research indicates that a daughter's rejection of her stepfather is not related to how hard he tries to get along. A boy, in contrast, may have less to lose with a new stepfather and much to gain, in that the stepfather may get the boy's mother "off his back" (Hetherington, 1989).

The effects of divorce extend beyond childhood and adolescence, however, and into adulthood. Children from divorced homes are more likely to become divorced when they marry (Wolfinger, 2000). One possible reason for the increased divorce rate among children of divorce is that they develop poor interpersonal skills. For example, Nicholas Wolfinger (2000) summarized marital behavior characteristics of children of divorce, and some of these are listed in Table 13.5. Although these behaviors are not unique to people who went through divorce as children, they seem to be more frequent in this group, possibly accounting for their higher divorce rate (see Amato, 1996; Silvestri, 1992).

What Factors Lead to Good or Poor Adjustment in Divorced and Remarried Families?

What factors influence how well a child will react to family changes brought about by divorce? Concerning remarriage, adjustment seems to be most difficult for children entering adolescence. Remarriage in early childhood often results in increased security for children (particularly boys), and older adolescents and young adults may perceive some relief from the economic, emotional, and social responsibilities they feel toward their divorced mothers (Hetherington & Stanley-Hagan, 2002). Younger adolescents seem not to benefit from a mother's remarriage as much as both younger and older children do, in part because of the stress young teens experience dealing with their own pubertal transition (Hetherington, 1993).

As in intact homes, the amount of stress, presence or absence of social support, and personality characteristics of both parents and children interact to produce adaptive or maladaptive behavior patterns (Hetherington, 1989; Hetherington & Stanley-Hagan, 2002). For example, in the studies by E. Mavis Hetherington and her colleagues, children with difficult temperaments showed increased behavior problems with increases in stress. The relationship was not as straightforward for children with easy temperaments, however. For these children, an intermediate amount of stress led to the best adjustment; having some practice solving moderately stressful problems in a supportive environment gave them more patience, more persistence, and more flexibility with problem-solving tasks and in social relations (Hetherington, 1989). This finding is consistent with the theorizing of Michael Rutter (1987, p. 326), who proposed that children who have experience controlling stressful situations become inoculated against stress and are able to deal with difficult situations more effectively than are noninoculated children (see discussion of children and stress in Chapter 11 and Box 11.2). Rutter's idea of "inoculation against stress" holds true for children in all types of families—married or divorced. Research findings indicate, however, that the value of these early experiences in dealing with stress depends on a child's temperament.

Perhaps the single most important factor in determining a child's long-term response to divorce and remarriage is quality of parenting. As with intact families, children adjust best when their parents practice authoritative rather than authoritarian or permissive parenting. In a longitudinal study by Hetherington and her colleagues (1989; Hetherington & Clingempeel, 1992), authoritative parenting, characterized by warmth and firm but responsive

Divorce is difficult for both parents and children, but parents can help children through the process by practicing authoritative parenting and communicating effectively with both their former spouse and their children.

© Dean Mitchell/Alamy

control, was associated with positive social adjustment and low rates of behavior problems. The one exception to this pattern was for stepfathers in the first 2 years following remarriage: apparently, *any* attempt by the stepfather to take control of family discipline was met with hostility by the children, especially when remarriage occurred when the children were in early adolescence (between 9 and 15 years). After 2 years, however, authoritative parenting by the stepfather was associated with fewer behavior problems and greater acceptance by their stepsons but not their stepdaughters. The best strategy for stepfathers in gaining the acceptance of their stepchildren appears to be to establish a positive relationship with the child before taking an active role in discipline and decision-making. According to Hetherington and her colleagues (1985, p. 529), "the most successful stepfathers appear to be those who offer emotional support to the mother and support her in her disciplinary role, rather than those who try to take over the role of disciplinarian or who remain uninvolved."

How Can Parents Help Children Deal with Divorce?

Divorce is almost never easy, either for the parents or the children, and there can be long-term negative consequence of divorce for children. How can parents help their children deal with divorce? Many books have been written on the subject, and most communities have support groups for single mothers and

divorced fathers, so divorcing parents have plenty of sources to seek advice. We would like to summarize briefly some of the advice given by experts on the topic (Hetherington & Kelly, 2002; Teyber, 2001):

- *Many children blame themselves for their parents' divorce.* Young children's thinking is self-centered (egocentric, to use Piaget's term), and they incorrectly believe that they are responsible for important events surrounding them, including their parents' conflict. This may come as a surprise to many parents, who should take the time to explain to their children that they are in no way responsible for the marital breakup.
- *Many children harbor the idea that their parents will reunite, that divorce is not permanent.* Parents should make it clear to children that the split is permanent and that it is an adult decision (that is, the children do not have a say in the divorce). Along with explaining the permanence of divorce, parents should explain to children what divorce will mean for them, how their lives will change (for example, they will be visiting Daddy on the weekends), and how it will not change (for example, Mommy and Daddy will always love them, and the children will be living in the same house and going to the same school).
- *Children are adversely affected by witnessing their parents fighting.* Parents should buffer their children from parental hostilities as much as possible. To do this may require parents working on their own communication skills (that is, how they communicate with one another, not just with their children) and consciously deciding to treat the former spouse with respect and dignity.
- *Children need both of their parents.* Children adjust best when both parents remain involved with the children. This is even true after one or both parents remarry, although the nature of the relationship with the noncustodial parent may change.
- *Children adjust best during divorce when the other parts of their lives remain relatively stable.* If possible, parents should maintain family routines, keep children in the same schools, use the same babysitter, and, in general, stick to regular daily schedules.
- *Practice authoritative parenting.* Divorce understandably causes stress in parents, and stress can lead to poor parenting decisions. Parents may be on edge and easily lose their tempers, resulting in harsher parenting techniques than one typically uses, or the difficulties surrounding the divorce and adjusting to a new lifestyle may cause parents to be less attentive to children, resulting in a permissive parenting style. This is not the time for parents to slack off on their parenting skills. In fact, because

table 13.6 Guidelines for Parents in Blended Families

1. *Appreciate the importance of children's relationship with their natural parent.* Children will see the stepparent as less of a competitor if adults can affirm and overtly support the children's relationship with both of their natural parents.

2. *Love isn't necessary.* Partners in a remarriage should drop the expectation that stepchildren and stepparents love each other. This expectation puts an unrealistic burden on both children and stepparents. Furthermore, when older children are involved, stepparents should move into the parenting role slowly, if at all. An older friend is a more workable role than parent in many cases.

3. *Remember that children have no choice.* It is important to remember that parents choose to remarry, whereas children simply become part of a stepfamily. . . . Although parents want to talk with children about the new marriage and reassure them about the concerns they may have, the responsibility for the decision to marry should be left to the parent, not shared with the children.

4. *Establish a coalition.* The remarried couple needs to establish their own marital coalition. This . . . means that the couple needs to be able to put other demands on hold, find time to be alone, and prevent children and others from repeatedly coming between them and disrupting their relationship or their ability to communicate. Establishing a successful marital coalition also means that each feels secure that the other is looking out for him or her and will be available and responsive if called upon.

SOURCE: Adapted from Teyber, E. (2001). *Helping children cope with divorce.* San Francisco; Jossey-Bass, pp. 253, 254.

of the difficulties that divorce has for children, the warm, structured environment afforded by an authoritative parenting style is especially important for children's adjustment.

As mentioned earlier, many divorced parents remarry, meaning that children often find themselves as part of a stepfamily, sometimes referred to as a *blended family.* Edward Teyber (2001), in his book *Helping Children Cope with Divorce,* produced a short list of guidelines for parents in blended families, which we reproduce in part in Table 13.6.

What, then, can we say about the effects of divorce on children? These transitions are stressful and result in behavior and psychological problems for children. Children show substantial resiliency to divorce and remarriage, however, with most adjusting within 2 years. Yet, many children carry the scars of a disrupted family life for years. Rather than seeing divorce and remarriage as predictors of inevitable adjustment problems, E. Mavis Hetherington and Margaret Stanley-Hagan (2002) view family transitions as placing children at risk. Whether children's long-term adjustment will be positive or negative depends on a web of interacting factors. According to Hetherington (1989, p. 13), "depending on the characteristics of the child, particularly the age and gender of the child, the available resources, subsequent life experiences, and especially interpersonal relationships, children in the long run may be survivors, losers, or winners of their parents' divorce or remarriage." There is no single factor that determines how children will react to divorce. Like development in general, a child's psychological adjustment is influenced by multidirectional interactions among a host of factors, with some being associated with positive outcomes and others associated with negative outcomes. Parents, however, are not helpless in the matter, and how they deal with their children before, during, and after the divorce can greatly influence children's eventual adjustment.

Other Contexts for Socialization

Children today acquire important cultural values and technological skills much as our ancestral fore-children did—by watching, working, and playing with adults and other children. But modern life has supplemented these natural techniques with new institutions and technological tools that were unknown to our ancestors. The most important institution for socialization outside of the family is the school. Formal schooling is relatively new to our species. It dates back to the beginning of writing, about 6,000 years ago, but it has only been within the last century that a majority of people on the planet attended school. One reason for the need of formal schooling was the invention of new technologies that could not easily be acquired "on the job." Different cultures developed ways of conveying information that required considerable time to learn. Reading is a prime example. With the advent of reading, writing, and mathematics, there was an explosion of information that required more schooling to master.

Over the last century, however, new methods of communication have developed that have changed how children get and use important information. These are collectively referred to as **media**, and

media Historically recent forms of communication (information transmission), such as television, the press, computers, and cell phones, that have transformed how youth acquire culturally and developmentally important information.

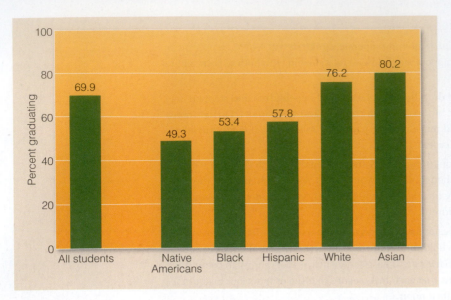

FIGURE 13.5 USA

National graduation rates by race/ethnicity, 2003–2004.

As you can see, whereas about 70% of adolescents graduate from high school, there is great discrepancy of graduation rates as a function of race and ethnicity. SOURCE: From Swanson, C. B. (2008). *Cities in crisis: A special analytic report of high school graduation.* Bethesda, MD: EPE Research Center, Figure 1. Reprinted by permission.

include television, radio, computers, cell phones, the Internet, and the host of ever-expanding ways children and adults use for telecommunicating. In this section we examine briefly how schooling and media have changed and are changing the ways in which children learn to be effective members of their society. We examine more specific influences of formal schooling (such as learning to read, children's acquisition of arithmetic competency) and the media (the effect of video on aggressive behavior, video games as play) in other chapters.

Peers also play an important role in children's development, and much of children's interactions with their peers is done in school and, recently, through the new electronic media. We will discuss aspects of children's peer interaction, specifically cooperating and competing with one another, in Chapter 14. In this chapter we focus on the more general socialization effect of schools and media on children.

Formal Schooling

School has become such a routine aspect of modern life that few people ever stop to consider how unusual it is. Learning is important to many other animals, and certainly was always important to our ancestors. But no other species educates its young by removing them from their families for several hours each day, segregating them by age when possible, and leaving them in the control of unrelated and unfamiliar adults whose job it is to impart critical cultural knowledge to their young wards. Such an arrangement was unknown to our ancestors, was practiced only by the elite until recent times, and is still unheard of for traditional groups of people today.

The length of formal schooling a society requires of its children is associated with how much core cultural knowledge needs to be acquired for

people to become successful adults. These include technological skills such as reading, writing, basic mathematics, and the ability to use the Internet, but also the major values and accomplishments of one's culture, including its history, form of government, and its economic practices. In years past, 4 or perhaps 8 years of schooling were enough to be able to master the intricacies of a family farm or small business. In today's information-age societies, 12 years of education seems to be the bare minimum for economic success. As a friend once related to his goddaughter upon her graduation from high school, "No one, and I mean no one, graduates from high school with any marketable skills. High school grads are just warm, energetic bodies, waiting to be trained in something." Additional formal education, including technical training (to become a dental hygienist or air-conditioning repair person, usually 2 years beyond high school), a college education (usually 4 years beyond high school), or professional training (a law degree, MBA, or medical degree, 2 or more years beyond college) are expected for most people in developed countries.

Despite the importance of education beyond high school, approximately 30% of American adolescents never graduate from high school. Based on graduation rates for the years 2003–2004 (Swanson, 2008), overall, girls (73.6%) are more apt to graduate than boys (66%), and graduation rates are higher for teenagers living in small towns (70.6%) and rural (73.2%) and suburban (74.9%) areas than for teenagers living in urban districts (60.4%). The largest discrepancies in graduation rates are in terms of race/ethnicity. As you can see from Figure 13.5, White and Asian adolescents graduate at substantially higher rates than Native American, Black, and Hispanic adolescents, the graduation rates for the latter groups hovering around 50%. Also, having a high-school degree is clearly associated with economic success. For example, based on 1999 data, people older than 25 years of age who did not earn a high-school diploma or GED (graduate equivalent degree) earned an average annual income of $15,334. In contrast, people with a high-school diploma or GED had annual incomes 91% greater, averaging $29,294 (Greene, 2002).

Recall in Chapter 1 we discussed the invention of childhood. Neil Postman (1982) speculated that serious changes in the way adults viewed and treated children came about with the invention of moveable print in the 1400s and the subsequent importance of literacy. Before this time, most people could learn what they needed to know to make a living via hands-on experience. Learning was done in context, with the skills one needed being modeled or taught by an expert, often one's parent. That changed when the written word became commonplace. From this time, according to Postman, what differentiated adults from children was literacy, and becoming an adult required often-arduous instruction in learning to read. What also changed was the amount of knowledge that could be (or needed to be) learned. Literacy spawned other new technologies, discoveries, and ways of doing business, and as a result, the successful adult needed to know more than the skills that could be acquired in a standard hands-on apprenticeship. Thus, public schools for the common child came into existence, and with them a powerful new institution of socialization.

In the United States and Europe, public schools became increasingly popular in the 1800s, although the children of the elite were still frequently educated either at home or by private institutions. (Many middle- and upper-class families believed that the purpose of public schools was to "civilize the lower classes" [Williams, 1989, p. 72].) By the late 19th century and the heyday of the Industrial Revolution, most American parents recognized that they could not educate and socialize their children alone and increasingly accepted the role of formal schooling for the economic betterment of their children (Epstein & Sanders, 2002). Universal education approached reality in the early 20th century, although in 1900 fewer than 10% of all American children graduated from high school (Nichols & Good, 2000). By the 1980s, greater than 70% of children in the United States would graduate from high school, a figure that remains essentially unchanged today (Federal Interagency Forum on Child and Family Statistics, 2005; Swanson, 2008).

The purpose of schools is not only to teach the three Rs, but also to instill the values and beliefs of one's community. During colonial times in the United States, public schools were fully integrated within the community and governed by the same people who ran the church and town (Epstein & Sanders, 2002). Over the course of the 20th century, in part because of the changing nature of the family (see Table 13.1, p. 521), schools were expected to take on ever-increasing responsibilities. These have included the preservation of democracy, easing the assimilation of immigrants, raising health standards, eliminating poverty, promoting racial and ethnic integration, and enhancing the moral character of youth, among many others (Lapsley & Narvaez, 2006; Williams, 1989).

In addition, schools serve a social function. Children of similar ages congregate together and develop friendships and social skills. In some sense, it is difficult to separate the social influences of the school from the social influences of the community. Children's peers play an important role in their development and socialization, and most children living in a community (or neighborhood) attend the same school. Of course, parents are the ones who determine which neighborhoods children will live in, and thus which schools they will attend, so the impact of the family is felt even here.

Schools in many ways are extensions of families. Some parents take an active role in their children's schooling, visiting the school frequently, consulting with teachers and administrators, and helping with homework. Other parents view school and home as separate entities and expect the school to do its job while they do theirs. Not surprisingly, parental involvement in schools is related to parental education (more highly educated parents are more likely to become involved in their children's school) and to school success, in the predicted direction (Epstein & Sanders, 2002; Hill & Taylor, 2004). Schools, much like parents, can also be rated in terms of their disciplinary style, some being authoritarian, others authoritative, and others permissive. E. Mavis Hetherington and John Kelly (2002) noted that children from divorced homes with permissive or authoritarian parents are less apt to become psychologically maladjusted if they attend a school with an authoritative (warmth with control) style of discipline. In other words, how schools "parent" their students can interact with the parenting experiences children have at home.

Schools are a fact of modern life. Nations are deeply concerned about the quality of their educational systems, mostly to ensure that their children are well prepared for the jobs that will be available when they grow up. Schools provide an educated workforce for a community, and educational practices will vary depending on a nation's economy. Schools also provide direct instruction in cultural practices (for example, respect for authority, norms of social behavior) and local and national values. For instance, most schools in the United States promote patriotism, respect for one's government, and good sportsmanship. Locally, schools may promote preservation of the Everglades if you live in south Florida, or seeing the father/husband as the primary source of family status if you live in a polygamous community in the Southwest. Schools also socialize by being the place where children meet and interact with other children, and, as we will see in Chapter 14, one's peers are an important source for learning the way to behave in many situations.

Media

The invention of moveable type and the subsequent advent of (near) universal education resulted in a radical change in childhood, which was accompanied by equally radical changes in the economic and social lives of people in the developed world. With increased education (for women as well as for men) came improved living standards, population shifts from farms to cities, and smaller families with greater investment in the fewer children that parents had. These changes, however, occurred relatively gradually, over the course of several centuries.

A new revolution has been upon the world for the past half-century or so and has changed how children are socialized. Although radio, movies, and phonographs were available in the first half of the 20th century, the 1950s saw the mass availability of television. By the end of the 1950s, 90% of American homes had at least one television. By the turn of the 21st century, most homes with children had several TVs, with many children having a television set in their rooms (Comstock & Scharrer, 2006). The latter part of the 20th century saw the invention of VCRs, DVDs, CD players, handheld video games, personal computers, cell phones, MP3 players, and the Internet with its myriad opportunities. Many college students reading this book will never remember a time without e-mail, picture phones, webcams, iPods®, text messaging, Twittering, televisions without remotes, homes without a computer or an Internet connection, YouTube, MySpace, Facebook, or similar Internet meeting places. We hesitate to appear too trendy by listing the latest in multimedia gadgets or Internet activities, because new media and Internet uses are developing constantly, making any list made today obsolete by the time of publication.

Most college students today, and certainly nearly all who will follow them, are *digital natives*, people who grew up with digital media and take them for granted. Members of their parents' and grandparents' generation have learned to use the new media, but it rarely comes easily to them. Using the new media is like using a second language to people such as the authors of this book, whereas it is like using a first language to most people younger than 30 today. It should not be surprising that such a near-universal change in how people gather information and communicate has

had (and will continue to have) a significant impact on child development.

Media Exposure and Involvement

Television is in nearly every home in America and Europe, making it an equal-opportunity medium, being available to children of all socioeconomic and ethnic backgrounds. This cannot be said for the newer media, particularly computers. In a 2001 survey of computer and Internet availability in the United States, the majority of White (77%) and Asian (76%) households had computers, in comparison to only 41% for both Black and Latino families (DeBell & Chapman, 2003; see also Calvert et al., 2005). However, a 2007 survey of American teens 12 to 17 years old reported that 97% played video games of some sort, making such games, like television, an equal-opportunity medium (Lenhart et al., 2008). This phenomenon is not limited to the United States. In a five-country survey of Brazil, Germany, Japan, the United Kingdom, and the United States of the media habits of Millennials (people between the ages of 14 and 25), 75% stated that they view the computer as more of an entertainment device than their TV (Deloitte, 2009).

Children use media in their daily lives. The Kaiser Family Foundation surveyed the media usage of more than 3,000 children and adolescents between 2 and 18 years of age in 1999 (Roberts et al., 1999) and again in 2004 for 8- to 18-year-old children only (Roberts et al., 2005). In the 1999 survey, they reported that the typical home had three TV sets, three tape players, three radios, two VCRs, two CD players, one video-game console, and one computer. The left-hand column of Table 13.7 presents the average time per day (hours and minutes) that 8- to 18-year-olds spent with various types of media in the 2004

table 13.7 Average Time per Day (Hours and Minutes) of 8- to 18-Year-Olds' Media Exposure and Media Use, and Involvement in Selective Nonmedia Activities

Medium	Hours/Minutes per Day	Activity	Hours/Minutes per Day
TV	3:04	Hanging out with parents	2:17
Videos/DVDs/movies	1:11	Hanging out with friends	2:16
Print media/reading	0:43	Exercising, sports, etc.	1:25
Audio media	1:44	Pursuing hobbies, clubs, etc.	1:00
Computers	1:02	Talking on telephone	0:53
Video games	0:49	Doing homework	0:50
Working at a job	0:35	Doing chores	0:32
Total exposure	**8:33**	**Total exposure**	**8:49**
Total use*	**6:21**		

* Adjusted for time youth spend using two or more media simultaneously

SOURCE: Adapted from Roberts, D. F., Foehr, U. G., & Rideout, V. (2005). *Generation M: Media in the lives of 8–18 year olds.* Palo Alto, CA: Henry J. Kaiser Family Foundation.

survey. These rates were similar to those reported in 1999 with two exceptions. Children in the 2004 survey stated they spent more time with computers (1 hour 2 minutes) and playing video games (49 minutes) per day than was reported in 1999 (27 and 26 minutes, respectively). One striking thing to note is that the *exposure* to all media is more than 8.5 hours per day. This constitutes half or more of children's waking day. However *total use* is only 6 hours and 21 minutes. This difference reflects multitasking, children using two media simultaneously, such as listening to the radio and surfing the Web.

The right-hand column of Table 13.7 presents the amount of time 8- to 18-year-old children and adolescents reported spending in nonmedia activities on a typical day. As you can see, overall, they spent slightly more time on nonmedia than media activities, but there was substantial overlap between these two categories. For instance, children often used media while hanging out with parents or friends (for example, playing video games, watching television, listening to music). It is interesting to note that although TV watching was the most frequent single activity, hanging out with parents or friends were also high in frequency (each over 2 hours per day), as was physical activity (nearly 1.25 hours per day). So children and adolescents' involvement with media seems not to be *replacing* other more traditional forms of social interaction or activity, but it does appear to be modifying it.

Even very young children are heavily involved in media. Although the American Academy of Pediatrics (1999) recommends that children younger than 2 years of age not be exposed to "electronic screens," their advice falls mainly on deaf ears. Based on data collected in 2003 as part of the Kaiser Family Foundation study (see Rideout, Vandewater, & Watella, 2003), the percentage of children who watched television (including videotapes and DVDs) was 52%, 60%, 71%, and 79% for children younger than 12 months, 1, 2, and 3 years of age, respectively (Anderson & Pempek, 2005). For those who watched television and videotapes, the average amount of time watching per day was 2 hours and 24 minutes for children younger than 1 year of age; 2 hours and 53 minutes for 1-year-olds; 3 hours and 14 minutes for 2-year-olds; and 2 hours and 58 minutes for 3-year-olds. Figures were similar when measured 2 years later (Kaiser Family Foundation, 2006). In 2006, *BabyFirstTV* became the first television network geared solely for babies (and their parents, of course).

Based on a 2005 survey (Kaiser Family Foundation, 2006), parents of young children are about evenly split on whether they believe TV for infants and toddlers has an overall positive effect—mainly facilitating learning (38%)—or an overall negative effect (31%). (We examined the effects on cognition

Children and adolescents spend more than 6 hours per day with media of various types, and more than 8 hours if you count multitasking. Although some of children's media use is done alone, others use media in interactions with parents or peers.

Although the American Academy of Pediatrics recommends against children younger than 2 years of age watching television, and many parents have mixed feelings about it, many children younger than 3 years of age watch, on average, more than 2 hours of media (television or DVDs/videos) each day.

of such baby videos in Chapter 5.) Nonetheless, most parents of young children cannot imagine life without TV. Television, and increasingly other forms of media, are part of the fabric of family life. Parents use media to make their lives more manageable: it keeps children occupied so parents can get some work done; it calms children down; reduces family squabbles; and children who have a television set in their rooms (one-third of children between birth and 6 years) permit parents to watch shows they want to see while still keeping children happy.

table 13.8 Pathological Video Game Use

Youngsters 8 to 18 years of age were considered pathological video-game users if they exhibited 6 or more of the 11 criteria listed here. Boys (12%) were more apt to be classified as pathological video-game users than girls (3%).

1. Over time, have you been spending much more time thinking about playing video games, learning about video-game playing, or planning the next opportunity to play?

2. Do you need to spend more and more time and/or money on video games in order to feel the same amount of excitement?

3. Have you tried to play video games less often or for shorter periods of time, but are unsuccessful?

4. Do you become restless or irritable when attempting to cut down or stop playing video games?

5. Have you played video games as a way of escaping from problems or bad feelings?

6. Have you ever lied to family or friends about how much you play video games?

7. Have you ever stolen a video game from a store or a friend, or have you ever stolen money in order to buy a video game?

8. Do you sometimes skip household chores in order to spend more time playing video games?

9. Do you sometimes skip doing homework in order to spend more time playing video games?

10. Have you ever done poorly on a school assignment or test because you spent too much time playing video games?

11. Have you ever needed friends or family to give you extra money because you spent too much money on video-game equipment, software, or game/Internet fees?

SOURCE: Gentile, D. (2009). Pathological video-game use among youth ages 8 to 18. *Psychological Science, 20,* 594–602.

Preschool children also use computers and play video games. In the 2005 survey, 70% of children 4 to 6 years of age had used a computer, as had 31% of children 3 years of age and younger. On average, 27% of 4- to 6-year-olds used a computer on a typical day, spending a little more than 1 hour at the keyboard. Thirty-seven percent of 4- to 6-year-olds could turn the computer on by themselves and load a CD-ROM. Concerning video games, 25% of 4- to 6-year-olds played several times a week, and 50% had played video games at least occasionally, with boys (56%) playing more than girls (36%) (Rideout et al., 2003).

Media's influence on children's behavior. How has this rapidly changing media influenced children and their socialization? Most of the research has been done on television, because this is the oldest and still the most frequently used of the newer media. We saw in Chapter 4 that children who spend a lot of time watching television or are otherwise involved in media use are more sedentary (Norman et al., 2005), which is associated with the increasing obesity problem among children seen in the United States. We will discuss in Chapter 14 research indicating that watching violent video is associated with increased levels of aggression in children. The potentially negative influence of viewing aggressive video on children's behavior has been a concern to researchers and policy makers since the 1960s (see Comstock & Scharrer, 2006). Analyses of more than 40 years of research indicate that children who watch more violence in the media display higher levels of aggression and violent behavior both immediately and in the future, although this effect is more prominent for some children than for others (Anderson et al., 2003, 2010; Huesmann et al., 2003).

The effects of media viewing on aspects of young children's cognitive development have recently been investigated (see Courage & Howe, 2010). For example, one study reported that, for children younger than 3, the amount of violent and, to a somewhat lesser extent, nonviolent entertainment television they watched was associated with attentional problems 5 years later. For instance, each hour per day that children younger than 3 watched television doubled their risk for subsequent attentional problems. In contrast, there was no effect of watching educational television on later attentional problems in young children (Zimmerman & Christakis, 2007). Other studies, however, found smaller or no effects on attention of video viewing by preschool children (see Courage & Setliff, 2009; Foster & Watkins, 2010).

A recent survey of children's video-game use reported that about 8% of video-game players can be described as pathological, with consequences for their physical and cognitive/academic functioning (Gentile, 2009). More than 1,000 youngsters 8 to 18 years old answered surveys about their video-game use. Children were considered pathological video-game users if they exhibited 6 or more of the 11 criteria listed in Table 13.8. More boys (12%) than girls (3%) fit this description. Children classified as pathological video-game users received lower grades

table 13.9 Number of Studies Reporting Negative and Positive Association between Media and Health Outcomes

	Obesity	Tobacco Use	Drugs Use	Alcohol Use	Low Academic Achievement	Sexual Activity	ADHD
Media associated with *negative* health outcomes	63	21	6	8	20	13	10
Media associated with *positive* health outcomes	1	1	0	1	5	1	0

SOURCE: Adapted from Nunez-Smith, M., Wolf, E., Huang, H. M., Chen, P. G., Lee, L., Emanuel, E. J., & Gross, C. P. (2008). *Media and child and adolescent health: A systematic review*. Common Sense Media.

in school, had more difficulty paying attention in class, and reported greater wrist and finger pain, compared to nonpathological gamers. Pathological gamers were also more likely than nonpathological gamers to be diagnosed with attention deficit disorder, to feel addicted to video games, and to have been in a fight within the past year. A recent meta-analysis reported that exposure to violent video games is causally related to increases in aggressive behavior and thought and to decreases in empathy and prosocial behavior (Anderson et al., 2010).

A recent meta-analysis of 173 studies dating back to the 1980s explored the relationship between children's media use and a variety of health outcomes (Nunez-Smith et al., 2008). The authors reported that most studies found reliable negative associations between the number of hours children used the various forms of media and obesity, tobacco, alcohol, and drug use, academic achievement, a possible link to ADHD and initiation of sexual behavior. The breakdown of the number of studies that reported negative and positive associations between media use and each of these health-related areas is presented in Table 13.9.

The relationship between media exposure and sexual attitudes and behavior has been of substantial interest to parents, psychologists, and social policy makers, among others. The media play a substantial role in children's **sexual socialization**, "the process by which knowledge, attitudes, and values about sexuality are acquired" (Ward, 2003, p. 348). Although children and adolescents typically report that they get most of their information about sex from their peers, the media is usually close behind, and sometimes listed ahead of peers (Kaiser Family Foundation & Children Now, 1997; see Ward, 2003). And there is plenty of opportunity for acquiring sexual information via the media. In an extensive literature review, L. Monique Ward (2003) noted several factors that contribute to the influence of the media on sexual socialization. Sexual content is pervasive in the media, and children and adolescents spend more than 6 hours per day interacting

Greg Ceo/Getty Images

Although explicit sexual acts are rarely shown on television, kissing, flirting, and much talk of sex is, and youth who view more sexual content in the media are more apt to be sexually active.

with media. One conservative estimate puts the number of sexual references, jokes, and innuendoes children will encounter from media each year at nearly 15,000 (Strasburger & Donnerstein, 1999). Unlike parents, school, or religious institutions, which have strong interests in socializing youth to mainstream values and beliefs, media outlets are out to make a profit and are more likely to provide content reflective of what adolescents want (and sex sells). Moreover, adolescents have greater control in the messages they receive from the media than they do from other agents of socialization, such as parents or school (Arnett, 1995), making it a valuable and valued source of information for teenagers.

Ward (2003) examined how television presents sexual situations. She reported that most sexual content is not visual, but verbal. Kissing, flirting, hugging, and erotic touching are also frequent, but explicit sexual behavior is rare. Most sexual action occurs between nonmarried people, with little

sexual socialization The process by which knowledge, attitudes, and values about sexuality are acquired.

discussion of sexual planning (use of contraception) or the potential consequences of sex (pregnancy, sexually transmitted diseases). Women's bodies are more apt to be sexualized than men's. Although less studied, similar patterns were observed for music videos and R-rated movies. In fact, the incidence of female nudity was four times greater than for male nudity in movies (Greenberg et al., 1993). Finally, the frequency of sexual references in the media has increased substantially since the 1970s. For prime-time TV programming, the incidence of sexual references increased by a factor of 10 from the 1970s to the 1990s (see Ward, 2003). Magazines, including those for general readership such as *Newsweek* and *People*, and those geared to teenage girls such as *Seventeen* and *YM*, frequently deal with sexual issues, often more explicitly than television.

There is little doubt that sexual reference is prevalent in the media. Jane Brown (2002) stated that sexual content in the mainstream media has an impact on sexual socialization in at least three ways: (1) by keeping sexual behavior on public and personal agendas; (2) by presenting relatively consistent sexual and relationship norms; and (3) by rarely including sexually responsible models. But does such exposure affect children's and adolescents' attitudes and behavior? What empirical research has been done points to a connection between media exposure to sex and sexual attitudes. In general, youth who view genre with sexually oriented messages, such as soap operas and music videos, express more liberal and stereotypical attitudes about sex, and this effect is especially strong in females (Strouse & Buerkel-Rothfuss, 1987; Ward, 2002). Concerning sexual behavior, young women who frequently view music videos report a greater number of sex partners than do young women who watch music videos less often (Strouse & Buerkel-Rothfuss, 1987; Strouse, Buerkel-Rothfuss, & Long, 1995). In a national survey of nearly 1,800 adolescents, the television-viewing habits and sexual experiences of 12- to 17-year-olds were assessed twice, one year apart (Collins et al., 2004). The researchers reported that the more sexual content adolescents viewed at the initial observation, the more likely they were to report having initiated both advanced noncoital sexual activities and intercourse 1 year later. Adolescents in the 90th percentile of sexual-TV viewing were approximately twice as likely as adolescents in the 10th percentile to initiate intercourse within the year. It made no difference whether TV sexual exposure included only talk of sex or depicted sex.

Socializing on the Net

Newer than television, and some would say even more revolutionary, is the personal computer and the Internet. The Internet has revolutionized modern culture in ways unanticipated by its first users. Its value as a source of communication and information is obvious. (I doubt that we would be writing this book if it were not for the easy access to a world of knowledge about children, adolescents, and development that the Internet puts at our fingertips, and our ability to communicate rapidly and cheaply between Spain and the United States.) This is not the place for a discussion of how the personal computer has changed modern life. We would like to focus, however, on how the Internet has become an important agent in socialization for children and adolescents.

Teenagers throughout the developed world are heavy users of the Internet. Boys tend to play more computer and video games than girls (Subrahmanyam et al., 2001; Willoughby, 2008), but there appear to be no gender differences in overall Internet use (Gross, 2004). Adolescents spend most of their time online communicating with people they interact with offline (Gross, 2004; Ito et al., 2008). Although early research found that heavy Internet users showed evidence of depression and social isolation, later research contradicted this (see Barch & McKenna, 2004). In a study of seventh- and tenth-grade American children, no relationship was noted between Internet use and psychological well-being (Gross, 2004). However, frequent use of instant messaging has been found to be associated with compulsive Internet use and depression 6 months later, although it was also associated with lower levels of loneliness (van den Eijnden et al., 2008). In general, although early studies tended to emphasize the negative effects on social behavior of adolescents' Internet use, more recent studies find mainly positive effects (see Valkenburg & Peter, 2009).

A perhaps unforeseen use of the Internet is as a forum for socialization. Children and adolescents not only play games on the Net, but they also conduct research for school projects, write e-mails to one another, and meet new people and try out new identities online. The Internet has features that make it qualitatively different from more traditional venues of socialization. It is (or can be) anonymous. People cannot see or hear the message sender, and this may encourage users to disguise or exaggerate certain characteristics. Although teenagers spend more online time communicating with friends than in anonymous chat rooms—online sites in which groups of people can exchange messages without their identity being known (Gross, 2004)—a majority of computer-using adolescents visit chat rooms, at least occasionally (see Subrahmanyam, Greenfield, & Tynes, 2004; Valkenburg et al., 2005).

One use of Internet chat rooms for many teens is to try out new identities. A major accomplishment of adolescence is developing a sense of identity (Erikson, 1968, see Chapter 7). Identity can be defined as "the aspect of the self that is accessible and salient in a particular context and that interacts with the environment" (Finkenhauer et al., 2002, p. 2). People may have only one self, but they have many different identities that vary across contexts such as family, school, and peers (Harter, 1999). In the quest of developing social and sexual senses of identity, teenagers can conduct **identity experiments** (Valkenburg et al., 2005), pretending online to be someone they are not.

In one study, 600 Dutch adolescents, ranging in age from 9 to 18 years, were queried about their Internet use and whether they ever pretended to be someone they were not online (Valkenburg et al., 2005). Eighty-two percent of the youth said they participated in chat rooms or used instant messaging, and of these 50% stated that they engaged, at least occasionally, in identity experiments. Pretending to be someone they were not decreased with age: 72% for 9- to 12-year-olds; 53% for 13- to 14-year-olds; and 28% for 15- to 18-year-olds. This finding is consistent with research and theory suggesting that younger adolescents especially are in the process of developing a sense of identity (Erikson, 1968; Harter, 1999, see Chapter 7), and they seem to be using chat rooms to experiment with new ones.

Boys and girls were equally likely to experiment with their identity, although they did so differently. Girls were more apt to pretend to be older and more beautiful, whereas boys were more likely to pretend to be macho. The emphasis on beauty for girls and manliness for boys fits gender stereotypes (and predictions from evolutionary psychology), which tend to be heightened for adolescents. This is consistent with research that looked at personal homepages of males and females. Females tended to present themselves as nice and attractive, whereas males tended to emphasize their status and competence (Döring, 2002).

The researchers examined the reasons adolescents gave for pretending to be someone else on line and discerned three factors: *social compensation*, *social facilitation*, and *self-exploration* (see Table 13.10). Younger adolescents were more likely than older adolescents to engage in identity experiments in order to make friends (social facilitation), and girls were more likely than boys to give self-exploration and social compensation reasons for pretending they were someone they were not. Children who were introverted were more likely than extroverts to provide social compensation reasons for pretending to be someone else. (See Table 13.11 for some interviews with adolescents on reasons they gave for pretending to be someone else online.)

Although many adolescents engage in identity experiments online, most of their interactions seem to reflect relatively honest presentations of a developing self and an opportunity to discuss often sensitive and embarrassing issues, particularly related to romantic relationships and sex, in an anonymous social context (Subrahmanyam et al., 2004). Teenagers are exploring the same topics online that they are exploring offline. The Internet does not so much create new contexts for adolescents as it provides a qualitatively different venue for dealing with issues that adolescents have always been concerned with. According to Kaveri Subrahmanyam and her colleagues (2004, p. 663), "the medium is not doing something to adolescents; they, instead, are doing something with the medium."

An example of consumers (mostly youth and young adults) doing something with the Internet medium can be seen on MySpace.com, created in 2004 and, by 2006, registering 160,000 new members per day (Pace, 2006). As of 2006, it estimated that it had 106 million accounts worldwide. According to the MySpace.com website, it is "an online service that allows . . . members to set up unique personal profiles that can be linked together through networks of friends. MySpace members can view each others' profiles, communicate with old friends and meet new friends on the service, share photos, post journals and comments, and describe their interests." Facebook is even more popular, with more than 500 million members worldwide. A 2006 survey by the Pew Internet & American Life Project reported that 55% of American teenagers between 12 and 17 years use online social network sites such as MySpace and Facebook (Lenhart & Madden, 2007).

table 13.10 Adolescents' Motives for Engaging in Internet-based Identity Experiments

Social Compensation
To feel less shy
Because I dare to say more
Because I can talk more easily
To talk more easily about certain topics

Social Facilitation
To make new friends
To get to know people more easily
To get a date or relationship

Self-exploration
To explore how others react to me
To try out how it is to be someone else
Because I think up how I will look

SOURCE: Adapted from Valkenburg, P. M., Schouten, A. P.; Jochen, P. (2005) Adolescents' identity experiments on the Internet. *New Media & Society, 17,* 383–402.

identity experiments Practice whereby adolescents pretend to be someone they are not online.

table 13.11 Some Excerpts from Interviews with Adolescents on Their Reasons for Engaging in Identity Experiments Online

Gail Valentine and Sarah Holloway interviewed British students, 11 to 16 years of age, about their online activities. Excerpts from several of these interviews are presented here.

Helen: . . . often when you meet new people you're really sort of, you're nervous and you, you know, you really don't know what to say. But you can, when, when you're on the 'net you don't have to say, oh, you can be somebody who you're not really and you can be all outgoing and everything because you're not really seeing them. . . . You're never gonna see the face unless you decide to meet them or something and then you probably feel you know 'em cos you've been talking to them for days and days.

Rachel: Yeah. But like whatever you say, they don't, they can't really judge you on it 'cos they don't really know you, so it's really good. (p. 309)

Steve: I think it's quite fun because you can meet new friends and all that.

Interviewer: Have you met new people at all on that [chat rooms]?

Steve: Yeah, I've met quite a few. Met a few girls as well.

Interviewer: You say you were talking to a couple of girls you know there. Is it easier to talk to girls on the chat line?

Steve: Yeah.

Interviewer: Have you got many friends [online] who are girls?

Steve: Yeah, because one girl, if a girl comes up to you and they think you're ugly they just carry on walking, so if you speak to them on the Internet they don't know what you look like, so they just carry on talking to you, which makes it easier. (p. 309)

Interviewer: Do you, when you do that [go to the Teen Chat Room], do you, er, how do you kind of represent yourself on screen? You just give yourself a nickname or something like that, is that how it works?

Andy: Well, you just give yourself a name, just make something up and then just describe yourself or whatever.

Interviewer: And so you can just pretend to be somebody else?

Andy: Yeah.

Interviewer: Do, have you done that, have you pretended to be?

Andy: Yeah.

Interviewer: What have you done?

Andy: I posed to be a bouncer. [laughs]

Interviewer: A bouncer? . . . Why was that?

Andy: Oh, I don't know. It was just that I was in this room, the Teen Chat one, and there was this, there's girls on it, so, so I pretended to be a bouncer of 22. (p. 310)

SOURCE: Adapted from Valentine, G., & Holloway, S. L. (2002). Cyberkids? Exploring children's identities and social networks in on-line and off-line worlds. *Annals of the Association of American Geographers, 82,* 302–319.

MySpace and Facebook members create their own homepage/website that includes a personal profile, photos, e-mail service with instant messaging, and may include a blog. "Friends" are people whom the Facebook user has permitted access to his or her "space," although people can browse Facebook sites and send messages to the page owner requesting to be put on the "friends" list. Friends can make comments on the website, which all other friends can see, much like a chat room. MySpace and Facebook are free, although like many chat rooms, advertisements are constantly popping up.

Internet chat rooms, including venues such as Facebook.com and others like it (Friendster.com, MySpace.com), provide adolescents and emerging adults with opportunities for communicating with friends, meeting new friends, and exploring aspects of their developing identities that were not available to earlier generations. Youth on these websites are almost always interacting with people they know, extending their offline relationships online. Coupled with cell-phone technology that permits instant messaging and Twittering (a micro-blogging service in which people can send short text messages to people on their Twitter list), young people can be constantly in touch with one another, hanging out and extending friendships in the virtual world (Ito et al., 2008).

However, with the many advantages come some dangers. Adolescents can become victims of cyber-predators. The anonymity of cyber-communication not only permits youth to try out new identities, but it also lets others conceal their identities, which can lead to unwanted cybersexual solicitation. Parents may not be able to prevent children from some unwanted exposure to pornography or sexual predators, but the negative effects of Internet use can be minimized and the benefits maximized if parents set rules and guidelines for Internet use, monitor their children's computer use, and establish a warm and communicative relationship with their children (Greenfield, 2004).

Social websites are also interacting with other video technology to cause unanticipated problems. For example, teenagers are using their cell phones to send naked pictures of themselves to their boyfriends or girlfriends (a practice called "sexting"), and some of these photos are finding their way on the Web. Officials who investigate child pornography are increasingly finding that photographs of naked teens are often self-portraits, meant only for a small private audience. A 2008 survey found that 22% of teenage girls (11% of girls between 13 and 16 years old) reported having electronically sent, or posted online, nude or semi-nude images of themselves (The National Campaign to Prevent Unplanned Teen Pregnancy, 2008), and in 2008 and 2009, teenagers from several states faced child pornography charges for sexting nude pictures of themselves to their friends.

A recent survey of 190 MySpace websites of 18- to 20-year-olds reported that 4% mentioned sexual activity and 85% mentioned substance use on their profiles (Moreno et al., 2009). In the past, the poor decisions that adolescents frequently make stayed local; with today's technology, such decisions can result in criminal charges and follow a person for years to come (Associated Press, June 5, 2008). However, teens can be sensitive to adult comments and modify their web pages accordingly. For example, in the study reported by Megan Moreno and her colleagues (2009) in which mention of sex or substance abuse was noted on 18- to 20-year-olds' MySpace pages, 42% of them later removed such references or set their profiles to "private" when they were sent an e-mail from the lead author of the study, "Dr. Meg," that said in part, "You seemed to be quite open about sexual issues or other behaviors such as drinking or smoking. Are you sure this is a good idea? . . . You might want to consider revising your page to better protect your privacy."

Another unanticipated side effect of venues like MySpace and Facebook is that employers can check out potential employees' websites to see if they say anything about themselves that may make them a less-than-optimal employee. Video clips of young adults doing Jell-O shots and dancing on tables, intended to be shared only with friends, may make a greater impression on an employer than a carefully choreographed interview could.

The Good, the Bad, and the Ugly

In most academic discussions of children's exposure to television and other media, the emphasis is usually on the negative—why TV is bad for kids or how television viewing or video-game playing is changing the nature of childhood. There is good reason for this, as television is a relatively new vehicle for socialization ("new" in that it has a history of barely 60 years, although most readers of this book, as well as its authors, do not remember a time before television), and the Internet is even newer. However, not all change is bad. Although we can be concerned about what children are *not* doing when they are watching TV, playing video games, or surfing the Web (not running around outside, not socializing with family or friends), we should not forget that television and other digital media provide many positive and enriching experiences for children. Beginning in the preschool years, programs such as *Sesame Street* educate children, narrowing the knowledge gap between children of means and those without.

© Barbara Bjorklund

Teenagers do a lot of socializing on the Web, using online services such as MySpace and Facebook to stay in touch with friends and to meet new people.

Television provides children knowledge of the wider world, usually in the context of entertainment. It gives children from rural communities ideas of what life is like in the big cities and vice versa. It also helps children to understand and tell stories. In fact, as television shows have developed over the decades, the plots have become more complex, requiring greater cognitive sophistication to follow them. Young children may not be able to keep up with the story line of *Grey's Anatomy* or *Law and Order*, but both children's shows and those for adults have become more sophisticated with time, reflecting corresponding changes in the mental abilities of the viewing audience (Johnson, 2005). With respect to video games, they seem to afford a type of *discovery learning* that is disappearing from children's schools. Moreover, video-game playing is not always a solitary experience but often involves competition and collaboration with a peer. That is, playing video games can be a social experience as well as a private one.

We mean neither to praise the rise of new communication technologies as the savior of humankind nor to lament their advent as the destruction of a once-idyllic childhood. Television, video games, the Internet, and a host of other new technologies have become an important part of life for contemporary children, adolescents, and adults, and we should learn as much about the effects of these evolutionarily novel forms of socialization on children's development as we can so that we, as parents and as a society, can make the most of them. Moreover, whatever the potential influence of television and other media on children's development is, parents need not be helpless bystanders (Comstock & Scharrer, 2006). Parents can limit and monitor their children's TV viewing habits and Internet use and can explain complicated scenarios in television stories, as well as the purpose of commercials. They can get information about the content of video games and websites and decide which are appropriate for their children and which are not. Parents who leave their children to select their own diet of television, video games, and websites, believing they are powerless to combat the influence of the media, are mistaken and are missing an opportunity to affect important aspects of their children's socialization.

summary

Families are humans' principal vehicle for rearing children. There are different forms of marriage, and thus family structure, including **monogamy** (one man, one woman), **polygyny** (one man, many women), and **polyandry** (one woman, many men). Humans form **biparental families** (both mother and father provide some support) and *extended families*, with several genetically related adults typically helping to tend the young. The effect of families on children and socialization must also be viewed from a *developmental contextual* perspective.

Increases in the divorce rate and changes in societal values have resulted in an increase in single-parent families. Most single-parent families are headed by women. Adolescents are, on average, the most disadvantaged of single mothers, whereas **single mothers by choice** tend to be older and economically more advantaged. Single-parent mothers tend to work longer hours, have greater financial difficulties, report more stressful life events, and receive less emotional support for their parenting efforts than mothers in two-parent families. An increasing number of men are serving as single parents, with almost all of these men gaining their status through divorce. Many children are also being raised by gay or lesbian parents, and such children tend to grow up normally, without sexual confusion.

Parents' goals and beliefs differ as a function of culture and SES. There are four basic **parenting** styles, defined along the dimensions of warmth and control: **authoritative** (high warmth, high control), **authoritarian** (low warmth, high control), **permissive** (high warmth, low control) and **uninvolved** (or **neglectful**) (low warmth, low control). Children of authoritative parents are more independent, curious, responsible, and socially competent than are children of authoritarian, permissive, or uninvolved parents.

Multiple factors influence parenting style, including parents' emotional adjustment, marital satisfaction, social support, economic stability, SES, cultural and ethnic differences, and the interaction of families with neighborhoods. Some of the best outcomes occur when parents engage in **co-parenting**, consciously coordinating their parenting actions as a team. Individual differences in children's personality, temperament, physical abilities, or intelligence also influence how their parents respond to them. Children experience stress in families, which is reflected by levels of cortisol, which is related to health. **Child maltreatment** is associated with a host of negative psychological outcomes. Sandra Scarr proposed that because of the substantial influence of active genotype $\rightarrow$ environment effects, **good-enough parents** are sufficient to raise a child.

Siblings both cooperate and compete with one another. Most sibling relationship involve extreme and freely expressed emotions and substantial intimacy. However, there is also great variation in the nature of sibling relationships across childhood and adolescence. The birth of a new sibling often results in conflict, which can last for a considerable time after the birth. Older siblings (especially girls) often help care for and nurture younger siblings. The **One-Child Policy** in China has resulted in some societal consequences of reducing family size.

Almost all children show some negative reactions immediately after their parents divorce, including anger, resentment, depression, and even guilt. Most children show good adjustment within 2 years following the divorce, but many do not. Girls are more adversely affected than boys by their mother's remarriage. Many of the same factors that influence a child's psychological adjustment in intact families, particularly quality of parenting, also affect how well children adjust to divorce and remarriage.

School is the most important institution of socialization outside of the family. The need for schooling was brought about by the increasing importance of literacy to adult functioning. Children acquire not only technological knowledge such as reading at school but also the norms and values of their culture.

Since the middle of the 20th century, **media**, in the form of television, computers, and other forms of mass communication/entertainment, have revolutionized the way children are socialized. Children from the early preschool years on are exposed to many hours of media each day. There is evidence that certain types of media exposure are related to levels of aggression and **sexual socialization**. Adolescents use the Internet frequently and often try out new identities, or conduct **identity experiments**, while online.

Key Terms and Concepts

monogamy (p. 520)
polygyny (p. 520)
polyandry (p. 520)
biparental families (p. 521)
single mothers by choice (p. 524)
parenting style (p. 528)

authoritative parenting style (p. 528)
authoritarian parenting style (p. 528)
permissive parenting style (p. 528)
uninvolved (or neglectful) parenting style (p. 528)
co-parenting (p. 532)

child maltreatment (p. 533)
good-enough parents (p. 541)
One-Child Policy (p. 542)
media (p. 551)
sexual socialization (p. 557)
identity experiments (p. 559)

Ask Yourself . . .

1. Why are families so important to child development, and what are the typical traits of human families? What are some of the ways that contemporary families are organized that differ from generations past, and what are the consequences of these differences for child development?

2. How are families viewed from a developmental systems perspective? Why is it important to take such a view of families?

3. What is meant by parenting, and, according to your textbook, what are three important ways that parenting practices differ?

4. What are the main parenting styles that have been identified? How do differences in parenting styles relate to children's psychological development?

5. What are the main types of child maltreatment and their consequences for children?

6. How might parenting be influenced by poverty, cultural/ethnic differences, and the neighborhoods in which families live?

7. To what extent are parents important for healthy psychological development, according both to traditional views and to Sandra Scarr's good-enough parents perspective?

8. What are sibling relationships like during child development? What impact does having siblings have on children's development?

9. Why do boys often react differently to divorce and remarriage than girls? What factors promote a good (versus a poor) psychological adjustment to divorce and remarriage?

10. How does formal schooling and the media affect children's and adolescents' psychological development, particularly their socialization?

Exercises: Going Further

1. As a developmental psychologist, you have been hired to participate in a "school for parents," with the purpose of talking about the keys of good parenting. You have been thinking of preparing a *Tips for Good Parenting* handout that summarizes the main points you plan to address. What would be your 10 key points?

2. One of your friends is a family lawyer who often deals with divorce. On the basis of her experience, she tells you that there is a point where she quickly detects when a divorce process will go smoothly or not. Then she asks you, "Do you know under which conditions a divorce will have more (versus less) damaging effects for children's later psychological development?" What would you tell your friend based on the research evidence you are familiar with?

3. Terry is a 75-year-old grandfather who has been living with his son's family since his wife passed away. He is worried about some of his grandsons' behaviors. To his taste, he commented to his son, they spend too much time watching TV or connected to the Internet. He feels this cannot be good for them, because, he argues, they do not play as much as children used to and do not socialize as much with other children. What would you tell Terry about his concerns?

Suggested Readings

Classic Work

Belsky, J. (1984). **The determinants of parenting: A process model.** *Child Development, 55,* 83–96. Jay Belsky has been a leading researcher in the area of parenting for more than 30 years. This paper presents one of the early dynamic models of parenting, which continues to be useful today as a framework for understanding the many interactive influences parents have on children's development.

Baumrind, D. (1971). **Current patterns of parental authority.** *Developmental Psychology Monographs, 4,* (1, Pt. 2). Although Diana Baumrind was not the first researcher to investigate parenting styles, her work beginning in the 1960s established a new paradigm for understanding and investigating parenting influences, and this monograph was important in bringing her research to the attention of developmental psychologists.

Scholarly Work

Collins, W. A., Maccoby, E. E., Steinberg, L., Hetherington, E. M., & Bornstein, M. H. (2000). **Contemporary research on parenting: The case for nature and nurture.** *American Psychologist, 55,* 218–232. This review article, co-authored by some of the most influential researchers in the area of parenting, presents a concise, integrated review of contemporary research and issues on parenting.

Bornstein, M. H. (Ed.). (2005). *Handbook of parenting* (2nd ed.). Mahwah, NJ: Erlbaum. This five-volume handbook, edited by leading parenting researcher Marc Bornstein, provides as thorough an examination of topics on parenting as one is apt to find, ranging from parenting in primates to the effects of media on child development and just about everything in between.

Reading for Personal Interest

Hetherington, E.M., & Kelly, J. (2002). *For better or worse: Divorce reconsidered.* New York: Norton. This book by E. Mavis Hetherington, the leading researcher on the effects of divorce on children, and science writer John Kelly provides a view of what has become a common occurrence in modern society, in what Hetherington calls the "postnuclear family experience." Hetherington points out that while divorce can be damaging in the short run, it can provide positive opportunities for change, both for parents and children.

Roberts, D. F., Foehr, U. G., & Rideout, V. (2005). *Generation M: Media in the lives of 8–18 year olds.* Palo Alto, CA: Henry J. Kaiser Family Foundation. Although the full report may be a bit more detail than most people want, the executive summary, complete with graphs, provides a concise and readable report of this representative study of media use of more than 2,000 American youngsters (available at *www.kff.org/entmedia/7250.cfm*).

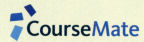

Cengage Learning's **Psychology CourseMate** for this text brings course concepts to life with interactive learning, study, and exam preparation tools, including quizzes and flashcards for this chapter's Key Terms and Concepts (see the summary list on page 563). The site also provides an **eBook** version of the text with highlighting and note taking capabilities, as well as an extensive library of observational videos that span early childhood through adolescence. Many videos are accompanied by questions that will help you think critically about and deepen your understanding of the chapter topics addressed, especially as they pertain to core concepts. Log on and learn more at **www.cengagebrain.com**.

Competing and Cooperating with Peers

Peers play an important role in a child's socialization. In this chapter we examine the development of peer interactions and relationships. We look at popularity, giving special attention to rejected, or low-status, children. We then examine the formation and function of children's peer groups and prosocial behaviors, including comforting, sharing, and helping, followed by a look at the antisocial behavior of aggression. We conclude the chapter with an examination of the development of moral reasoning and moral behaviors.

Derek got out of work early one Friday afternoon and decided to pick up his 4- and 9-year-old sons from their after-school daycare program. Four-year-old Shawn yelled "Daddy!" when he saw his father and jumped into his arms, ready to head home. Nine-year-old Bobby, in contrast, did not want to go. He wanted to stay and play with his friends. He and four or five other boys had some outdoor games to play, a racetrack to build out of blocks, and possibly even a chess game. Bobby loved his father and brother, but at the moment, he would rather spend time with his friends.

As we have mentioned repeatedly throughout this book, humans are a social species, and this extends beyond the family to same-age members of the social group, beginning relatively early in life.

There is strength in numbers, and social species often use their social affiliations to ward off predators or to capture prey themselves. Such cooperation can extend to sharing resources, assisting one another in the many tasks of daily living, and helping to raise offspring. In fact, the major accomplishments of any human society are not achieved by individuals working alone, but by people working cooperatively. Different people contribute their efforts and ideas to achieve a single goal (building a house, for instance), coordinating their actions in accordance with their abilities to attain an outcome that would be impossible to achieve by one person working alone.

But social life brings its own set of problems. It is not always in one's best interest to cooperate. Sometimes one is better off going it alone and at other times competing overtly with fellow group members. In fact,

As children get older, they are increasingly influenced by their peers, as the relative influence of their parents wanes.

there is as much, if not more, competition for resources *within* members of a species as there is *among* species. Competition is also common among members of a social group. For most species, including humans for most of our time on this planet, resources were scarce; those individuals who garnered more or higher-quality resources (food, shelter, clothing, mates) were, on average, more successful in a Darwinian sense than those who garnered less. We should not be surprised, then, that competition for resources, status, and whatever benefits a society has to offer are as much a part of *Homo sapiens*' social nature as is cooperation.

Children obviously learn much of their social protocols and skills from their parents and other adults, but they perhaps learn even more valuable lessons from interacting with their peers. Peer relationships are among equals, unlike children's relationships with adults (especially parents and teachers), where there is always a power differential. There are also differences in power, or status, among children in a peer group (see our discussion of dominance hierarchies later in this chapter), but the fact that peers are all members of a common cohort and share common experiences means that children can get important and unique experiences out of peer relationships (Hartup, 1983).

Beginning in the preschool years and continuing through adolescence, peers become increasingly important agents of socialization. Children's parents can influence the quality of playmates available to

their offspring, in part by selecting the neighborhood in which the family lives and the school their children attend (see Chapter 13), but parents' influence wanes (although never disappears) as the influence of children's peers' waxes. Judith Harris (1995, 1998) provided a somewhat controversial (some would say extreme) hypothesis based on the increasing influence of peers on children's lives. In her **group socialization theory**, she argued that children's personalities are shaped chiefly by their interactions with their peers and not through interactions with their parents. According to Harris, children seek not to be like their parents so much as they seek to be like their peers.

Recall our discussion of Sandra Scarr and Kathleen McCartney's (1983) genotype → environment theory in Chapter 3. As children get older, their genetically based psychological and behavioral dispositions (their genotypes) increasingly influence the types of experiences they seek. When children are young, what they will experience is largely determined by their parents. As they get older and become more independent, children increasingly choose where they go, what they do, and with whom they do it. These self-selected experiences affect children's developing personalities and intellects. As a result, children become less like their siblings, both in terms of personality characteristics and IQ, the older they get (McCartney, Harris, & Bernieri, 1990; Turkheimer & Walden, 2000).

Harris proposed that such a trend makes good evolutionary sense, in that, as adults, children will operate outside of the home and cooperate and compete with agemates of their social group. Becoming too well adapted to the home and too agreeable to the demands of one's parents is not (usually) conducive to one's inclusive fitness, given that success as an adult will depend on how well one gets along with peers (including potential mates) more so than family members. We do not want to give the impression that parents' influence on their children disappear—far from it. Rather, our intent is to demonstrate the increasing influence of peers, in addition to parents and other forces, on children's psychological development.

Harris couched her theory in terms of evolutionary adaptations that humans share with other social primates. These include (1) group affiliation and in-group favoritism; (2) fear of, and/or hostility toward, strangers; (3) within-group status seeking; and (4) the seeking and establishment of close dyadic relationships (see Table 14.1). These evolutionary adaptations are thought of as predispositions that are operating early in life but nonetheless develop over childhood. Although humans may share these adaptations with other social primates, our species' social relationships are far more complex than those of other animals. In fact, among primates, the size of the neocortex is highly correlated with the size and complexity of the social group (correlation between size of neocortex and group size = .76; see Dunbar, 1992, 2001), sug-

group socialization theory Judith Harris's theory that children's personalities are shaped chiefly by their interactions with their peers and not through interactions with their parents.

David R. Frazier/Photo Researchers, Inc.

table 14.1 Four Evolutionary Adaptations That Affect Social Living

These social biases influence children's interactions with other people and are supported to various degrees by experience.

1. Group affiliation and in-group favoritism
2. Fear of, and/or hostility toward, strangers
3. Within-group status seeking
4. Seeking and establishment of close dyadic relationships

SOURCE: Adapted from Harris, J. R. (1995). Where is the child's environment? A group socialization theory of development. *Psychological Review, 102,* 458–489.

Interactions refer to any social activity two or more individuals engage in and include what the individuals are doing and how they are doing it. The boys here are wrestling, but the interaction would be described as either play or fighting depending on the children's intent.

gesting to some that human intelligence has its origins in dealing with other members of our species (see Box 7.1 in Chapter 7 for a discussion on the evolution of self-awareness).

In this chapter, we examine several aspects of children's lives with their peers. How can we best conceptualize children's peer interactions with respect to the universal features of social cooperation and competition? The ethologist Robert Hinde (1976, 1983) proposed that social behaviors be described in terms of *interactions*, *relationships*, and *structure*, the latter referring to behavior in social groups (see also Rubin, Borkowski, & Laursen, 2009).

Following Hinde's classification, in the first section we examine children's peer interactions and relationships. When and how do children relate to one another? We then examine the dynamics of peer groups. Next we look at positive, or prosocial, behaviors, including comforting, sharing, and helping. This is followed by an examination of the so-called antisocial behavior of aggression. Although most adults usually view child aggression negatively, it can be effective for children in gaining resources and manipulating social relationships, both useful in competing with other children. We conclude the chapter with a look at the development of moral reasoning and moral behavior, specifically lying, cheating, and distributing resources fairly (or unfairly).

The Development of Peer Interactions and Relationships

Interactions

Interactions refer to any social activity two or more individuals engage in and include what the individuals are doing (for example, wrestling) and how they are doing it (for example, playfully or with hostility). Among children, interactions may be conversations, eye contact and smiles, play-

ing chase games, sharing or comforting, hitting, pushing, playing dolls, or trading Pokémon cards, among a host of other possible activities children partake in. The sophistication of the interaction depends on the developmental level of the children involved, as well as the context, including how familiar the children are with one another.

Infancy and Toddlerhood

Infants younger than 1 year of age rarely have the opportunity to interact with one another. Until their locomotive skills develop enough so they can move to or from another child, their peer relationships are limited to situations in which an adult places one infant close to another. Such opportunities do arise in daycare centers and research laboratories (Eckerman, Whatley, & Kutz, 1975); when they do, some form of interaction tends to occur. For example, 3- and 4-month-old infants will reach out and touch one another, and 6-month-olds will smile and vocalize to each other (Dufee & Lee, 1973). As babies begin to crawl, they will mutually explore each other's eyes, ears, and mouths, often smiling or vocalizing as they do. But infant-infant interaction is infrequent, even when the opportunities are there (Becker, 1977; Eckerman et al., 1975). In a daycare setting, for example, infants are seven

interactions Any social activity in which two or more individuals engage and that includes what the individuals are doing (for example, wrestling) and how they are doing it (for example, playfully or aggressively).

Infants rarely interact with one another, but when they do have an opportunity, they will often smile and explore one another's faces.

Toddlers also often experience conflict, particularly over possession of toys.

times more likely to interact with an adult than with another infant (Finkelstein et al., 1978).

Life changes dramatically for children once they learn to walk. They can now get to places and into things they could not even dream of before. Although many toddlers around the world spend the majority of their time with adults rather than other children, toddlers in some countries attend daycare, increasing their opportunity for peer interaction. The fact that toddlers are in a group, however, does not mean that they will interact. In fact, when toddlers are observed together, they spend the majority of their time in solitary activities (Bronson, 1981; Mueller & Brenner, 1977). The amount of social contact among toddlers is greater for children who are well acquainted with one another, but even in these situations, children this age spend about half their time playing alone (Rubenstein & Howes, 1976).

When toddlers do interact, what do they do? One interesting observation is that during the second year of life, toddlers increasingly copy the behaviors of other toddlers, and some have argued that such mutual imitation is the basis for more cooperative exchanges, particularly those involved in pretense, or make-believe play (Howes, 1992). For older toddlers (between 18 and 24 months), some of their time together is spent with toys or other objects (Eckerman et al., 1975; see Hay, Caplan, & Nash, 2009). As should be clear to anyone who has worked in a daycare center or babysat with two or more toddlers, much of toddlers' inter-

action with toys is less than positive. In fact, there is much conflict, often over possession of toys. For example, Kenneth Rubin and his colleagues (1998) reported that more than 70% of 2-year-old children were involved in at least one conflict with another child during a 50-minute observation (see also Hay, Castle, & Davies, 2000; Hay & Ross, 1982).

Childhood and Adolescence

During the preschool years, loosely defined as ages 2 to 5, the amount of social contact between children increases considerably (Coplan & Arbeau, 2009; Parten, 1932). For example, in a longitudinal study that observed children at four-month intervals from 16 to 32 months, researchers counted the total number of acts a child performed that were imitated or coordinated with those of a peer (Eckerman, Davis, & Didow, 1989). They found that the number of coordinated acts (mutual actions children engage in when having a conversation or playing a game, for example) and imitations increased with age (see Figure 14.1). This increase was gradual between 16 and 24 months, and then rose sharply at 28 months. Sharing and expressions of sympathy also increase over the preschool and school years (see Eisenberg & Fabes, 1998), although even many 5-year-olds find the concept of sharing a difficult one to grasp (see discussion of sharing later in this chapter).

As children enter adolescence, they become increasingly independent of their parents and spend more time with peers. In fact, by some estimates, adolescents spend more than twice as much time

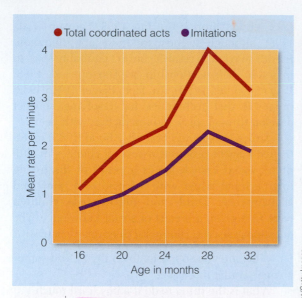

FIGURE 14.1 Toddlers' coordination of actions with peers and imitation of other children increase with age. The average (mean) number of both coordinated actions and imitations increased from 16 to 28 months, and then declined slightly at 32 months of age. SOURCE: Adapted from Eckerman, Davis, & Didow (1989). *Child Development, 60,* 440–453. Reproduced with permission of Blackwell Publishing Ltd.

Adrian Weinbrecht/Getty Images

An important form of peer interaction involves gossiping, sharing information about other people in the group. Adolescents who gossip excessively, however, can sometimes get a bad reputation.

interacting with peers as they do with their parents (Csikszentmihalyi & Larson, 1984). Before adolescence, most of children's interaction is done in same-sex groups. This begins to change in adolescence, as teenagers spend more time in mixed-sex groups.

One form of interaction that increases substantially during adolescence is gossip (Kuttler, Parker, & La Greca, 2002). Adolescents' concern about their acceptance in their peer group increases in middle childhood, and gossip helps to foster friendships, group solidarity, and social reputations. Gossiping about others identifies people who are not in the social group or who are not conforming to the group's standards (that is, social cheaters), while bolstering one's own position in the group. Gossiping may have a cost, however. Children or adolescents who gossip excessively may be judged as spreading false claims out of jealousy (Kuttler et al., 2002).

Tattling, in which children report negative peer behavior to an authority figure, may be a developmental precursor of gossiping. In one of the few systematic studies of children's tattling, preschoolers tattled an average of about 1.25 times per day and were generally truthful in their negative reports about others (Ingram & Bering, 2010). Gordon Ingram and Jesse Bering reported that tattling was used mostly by dominant children and that tattling was positively correlated with indirect (as opposed to direct and physical) aggression. They suggested that tattling serves as a form of *cheater detection*. Children use tattling to prevent other children from breaking social contracts (see Box 7.1 in Chapter 7). As such, they view tattling as being an adaptive (and evolved) behavior for young children, and a precursor to gossiping, which also keeps other members in the peer group in line (that is, conforming to group standards).

[handwritten margin note: tattling is precursor to gossiping]

Relationships

Relationships are interactions between two individuals occurring over time. According to Hinde (1979), a relationship involves a series of interactions such that "the behavior of each takes some account of the behavior of the other" and "each interaction is affected by interactions in the past and may affect interactions in the future" (p. 14). Relationships require not only enhanced social and cognitive skills in which one individual takes into account the behaviors of another, but also familiarity. People in relationships know one another and have some expectations of interacting with each other in the future. One particular type of relationship that is especially important to children is **friendship**. Friendship is defined as a *reciprocal* relationship, in that two children each nominate one another as a friend and have positive feelings toward one another (Rubin, Bukowski, & Parker, 2006).

Researchers have often described the development of friendship in terms of stages (Bigelow,

relationships Frequent interactions between two individuals occurring over time.

friendships A reciprocal relationship between peers, in that two children each nominate one another as a friend and have positive feelings toward one another.

1977; Damon, 1977; Selman, 1980); see Concept Review 14.1. During the preschool years, Stage 1, friends are other children who participate in shared activities. In other words, friendship for young children is defined primarily in terms of physical proximity. In Stage 2, beginning around 5 to 7 years, friends are viewed as children who are nice, fun to be with, and who share things. A friend will let a child borrow a pencil, take a turn on the swing, or help clean up a mess. Such friendships, however, are temporary and are both easily formed and easily terminated. Even at this age, however, having friends is important to children. For example, in a study of Finnish children, first graders without friends were apt to display adjustment problems and were more apt to be described as "isolated" one year later (Laursen et al., 2007).

In Stage 3, between the ages of about 6 and 12 years, children view friendship as following agreed-upon rules, such as reciprocity, loyalty, and commitment. A friend is not just a playmate—someone a child happens to be playing with—but someone who has shared interests and special personality characteristics. Friends at this stage tend to resemble each other both in behavior and attitudes (Hartup, 1996; Rubin et al., 2006); for instance, children who are both active are more likely to be friends than are an active and a sedentary child. Beginning around 11 or 12 years of age in Stage 4, friendship involves empathy, understanding, and self-disclosure: friends share unconditional positive regard and intimate communication. Children become more knowledgeable about their friends and see their friendships as being more exclusive and individualized (Berndt, 2002).

Although friends are, by definition, people who like one another, this does not mean that everything always runs smoothly. In fact, conflict occurs about as often between friends as between nonfriends (Dunn & Cutting, 1999; Laursen et al., 1996), although friends are more apt than nonfriends to want to resolve conflict equitably so as to maintain their relationship (see Hartup et al., 1988; Laursen et al., 2001). In fact, Piaget (1965/1932) proposed that techniques for resolving conflict develop through play and interaction with peers.

Janice Nelson and Frances Aboud (1985) investigated Piaget's proposal, assessing changes in children's social knowledge as a result of discussing interpersonal issues with a friend or a nonfriend acquaintance. Third- and fourth-grade children were first given a pretest of social knowledge. The questions raised social/moral dilemmas, such as:

- "What are you supposed to do if you find someone's wallet in a store?"
- "What is the thing to do if a boy (girl) much smaller than you starts to fight with you?"

Children were then paired with either a friend or a nonfriend acquaintance from their school class and asked to discuss one of the questions from the pretest. Following this activity, each child was asked individually for a solution to the problem he or she had been discussing.

Friends were more critical of each other during their discussions than were nonfriends, but they were also more likely to provide detailed reasons for their own point of view. Pairs of friends changed the most in terms of social knowledge as a result of their discussions. When friends disagreed, their ultimate solutions to the dilemmas were more mature than when nonfriends disagreed. In other words, healthy social conflict between friends resulted in greater growth in social knowledge than did conflict between nonfriends (see also Killian & Nucci, 1995; Laursen & Pursell, 2009).

There are differences in the typical friendships of boys and girls. For instance, girls' friendships are

concept review | 14.1 Stages of children's friendships

Although different researchers describe children's friendships somewhat differently and have proposed different numbers of stages of friendship, the following list of stages captures the changing nature of children's friendships from the preschool years to adolescence.

Stage 1 (preschool years)	Friends are children who participate in shared activities. Friends are defined primarily in terms of physical proximity.
Stage 2 (5 to 7 years)	Friends are nice to be with and share activities and things. Friendships are both easily made and easily terminated.
Stage 3 (6 to 12 years)	Friendship follows agreed-upon rules, such as reciprocity, loyalty, and commitment. Friends have shared interests and attitudes.
Stage 4 (11 or 12 years and older)	Friendship involves empathy, understanding, and self-disclosure: friends share unconditional positive regard and intimate communication.

Social status is important, especially in high school.

characterized by greater intimacy and self-disclosure than those of boys (Rubin et al., 2004; Zarbatany, McDougall, & Hymel, 2000). Boys' friendships are apt to be marked by physical activities that do not involve the exchange of as much personal information as girls' friendships. However, boys tend to express their intimacy through shared activity more so than girls (McNelles & Connolly, 1999). Girls' friendships are also more likely to occur in isolation or in small social groups, whereas boys' friendships are more likely to involve a larger social network (Baumeister & Sommer, 1997; see further discussion below).

Peer Groups

In reading the previous sections, it would be easy to get the idea that children interact in groups of two or three, usually with other children who can be regarded as friends. They do, but childhood peer interactions often occur in groups, including both close friends and mere acquaintances. The time children spend in cohesive peer groups increases with age. Preschoolers congregate in sandboxes or on jungle gyms, but their groups are usually only loosely organized; tomorrow's group may be very different from today's, and the only purpose or goal they share is to play. During the school years, however, children begin to see themselves as members of a true **peer group**. According to David Shaffer (2009), a peer group is a confederation that (1) interacts on a regular basis; (2) defines a sense of belonging; (3) shares implicit or explicit norms for the behavior of group members; and (4) develops a hierarchical organization, or **dominance hierarchy**. One form of peer group is called a clique. **Cliques** are defined as small, relatively stable social groups that children join voluntarily. Cliques are differentiated from **crowds**, which are usually composed of several different cliques and are only loosely organized around a shared activity or reputation (Brown, 2004). Some crowds found in many American high schools include the "jocks," "nerds" (or "geeks"), "brains," "populars" (or "preppies"), "Goths," and "druggies," among others.

Within peer groups, social status becomes important. Social status is something most of us associate with adulthood. People differ in the perceived importance of their jobs, the neighborhoods in which they live, the amount of money they make, and the status symbols they possess. But adults do not hold a monopoly on social status. Within any group of children, there are some who are more popular or have greater social impact than others.

Popularity and Social Status

Popularity means likeability—the extent to which a child is sought out by others. *Social status* refers to social standing—the extent to which a child is considered a valued member of a group. Popularity and social status are typically assessed using *sociometric techniques*, in which children are asked to nominate children with whom they would like to associate (positive nominations) and with whom they would *not* like to associate (negative nominations) (Cillessen, 2009; Jiang & Cillessen, 2005). For example, children may be asked to list the three children in their class they most like or would most like to interact with, as well as the three children they like the least and least want to interact with. Based on peer nominations, children are usually assigned to one of five categories: popular, rejected, neglected, controversial, or average (see Concept Review 14.2).

Popular children are those who have many positive nominations and few negative ones. That is, they are well-liked children who have considerable social impact (that is, they are mentioned frequently). **Rejected children** are also mentioned

---

peer groups Peer organizations where members interact on a regular basis, define a sense of belonging, share implicit or explicit norms for the behavior of their members, and develop a hierarchical organization.

dominance hierarchy The relatively stable organization of a group in which some members are seen as leaders and others as followers.

cliques Small, relatively stable social groups that children join voluntarily.

crowds Large groups of adolescents who share activities or have similar stereotype reputations (such as "jocks" or "druggies").

popularity Likeability; the extent to which a child is sought out by others.

popular children Children who are mentioned frequently and positively by their peers in a sociometric assessment.

rejected children Children who are mentioned frequently and negatively by their peers in a sociometric assessment.

Popular	Children receive many positive nominations and few negative ones. They are liked by a large number of their peer group.
Rejected	Children received many negative nominations and few positive ones. They are disliked by many of their peer group.
Neglected	Children receive few nominations, and the ones they do get are usually negative. These children are neither especially liked nor disliked, but are often ignored or go unnoticed.
Controversial	These children are mentioned frequently but receive comparable numbers of positive and negative nominations. That is, about as many children in the peer group like these children as dislike them.
Average-status	As the name indicates, these children receive an average number of both positive and negative nominations. About one-third of children in a typical classroom are classified as average.

High school students are often members of identifiable crowds, which are loosely organized around a shared activity or reputation, such as the "band geeks" and "skateboarders" seen here.

frequently, but most nominations are negative. **Neglected children** are mentioned infrequently, and when they are mentioned, the nominations are usually negative. **Controversial children** are mentioned frequently, but they get nearly as many negative nominations as they do positive ones (you either love them or hate them). Combined, these four classifications constitute about two-thirds of children

neglected children Children who are not often nominated or referred to (either positively or negatively) by other children in a sociometric assessment.

controversial children Children who are mentioned frequently in a sociometric assessment but get nearly as many negative nominations as they do positive ones.

average-status children Children who receive a moderate number of both positive and negative nominations in a sociometric assessment.

in a typical elementary school class. The remaining one-third of children receive a moderate number of both positive and negative nominations and are called **average-status children** (Coie, Dodge, & Coppotelli, 1982; Rubin et al., 2006). When measured this way, popularity essentially boils down to *social preference*—with whom do children like and not like to interact (Bukowski et al., 2000).

An alternative to sociometric measures of popularity is *perceived popularity*, in which children list others in their group who possess various psychological characteristics (for example, leadership, winning disputes, positive self-concept, social poise) and physical features (for example, erect posture, athletic, attractive, maintains eye contact) thought to reflect popularity and high status (Parkhurst & Hopmeyer, 1998; Weisfeld, Bloch, & Ivers, 1984). Although there is moderate overlap in classification when children are rated in terms of both sociometric and perceived popularity, the overlap is not perfect, and the two measures seem to be assessing somewhat different constructs (Parkhurst & Hopmeyer, 1998). Specifically, perceived popularity is more related to social dominance (see discussion to follow) than is sociometric popularity.

Characteristics of Popular and Unpopular Children

Why are some children popular and others rejected? What are the consequences of a child's social standing for later life, and to what extent can children change their status? Early research examined some physical characteristics of children as they relate to popularity. For example, attractive children are more likely to be popular than less attractive children, whereas children with unusual names and children with physical, behavioral, or mental handicaps are apt to be less popular (see Hartup, 1983). Of greater significance to a child's social standing, however, are behavioral or psychological characteristics.

If we look at the general characteristics of popular and unpopular school-age children (or high- and low-status children), a coherent pattern emerges (Asher & McDonald, 2009; Rubin et al., 2006). Popular children are described as being considerate and helpful. They follow the rules, particularly rules for social interaction. For school-age children, academic and athletic competence is highly valued, but social competence is increasingly viewed as an important component of popularity. In contrast, rejected or low-status children tend to be aggressive (especially boys), disruptive, hyperactive, and they do not follow the rules. Between one-third and one-half of rejected children display elevated levels of aggression compared to about 10% of nonrejected children (Bierman, Smoot, & Aumiller, 1993; Coie & Koeppl, 1990). Rejected girls are often socially withdrawn. Also, rejected children often lack academic as well as social skills. John Coie and his colleagues (1990) suggested that social rejection comes *before* social withdrawal. First, children are rebuffed in their attempts to join a group; as a result, they become withdrawn, making few overtures to other children.

In comparison to rejected children, there are few systematic differences in behavior of neglected children, probably because of the relatively unstable nature of this status, even over brief periods. That is, because children who are rated as neglected at one time frequently change their status (some becoming rejected, some average), and there is little in common that characterizes these children (Rubin et al., 2006). Finally, controversial children, who receive many positive and negative nominations, tend to show characteristics of both popular and rejected children (Coie & Dodge, 1988; Rubin et al., 2006).

What specific social skills do unpopular children lack that their higher-status and more popular peers possess? Kenneth Dodge and his colleagues suggested that low-status children process social information ineffectively (Dodge & Feldman, 1990; Dodge et al., 1986; Dodge et al., 2003). Specifically, Dodge proposed that low-status children misinterpret the social intentions of others and are lacking in three areas of social competence: (a) searching for possible social responses, (b) evaluating a social situation, and (c) enacting a social behavior. Other researchers have noted the importance of *responsiveness* (responding to a peer's social gestures) and *relevance* (making contextually appropriate responses) in children's interactions (Asher, 1983; Putallaz & Gottman, 1981). For example, in one study, preschoolers, when interacting with children they did not know, were less responsive and more likely to make irrelevant comments (for example, commenting on what they had for lunch while the rest of the group is talking about playing a game) than were liked

© Radius Images/Alamy

Many children experience loneliness, with loneliness being especially high in rejected children.

children. When interacting with a peer they knew, disliked children were not only less responsive and relevant but also communicated less effectively with the other child (Black & Hazen, 1990).

It seems clear that rejected or unpopular children lack many of the social skills of their better-liked peers. But do unpopular children appropriately perceive their own situation, or are they so out of touch with the reality of the peer group that they do not understand the rejection and isolation imposed on them by their peers?

Steven Asher and his colleagues investigated children's perceptions of their social situations and reported that unpopular children do feel the sting of peer rejection (Asher, Hymel, & Renshaw, 1984; Asher et al., 1990). Asher and his colleagues gave children a set of statements and asked them to select one that described them. Some of the following statements were used by Asher and his colleagues (1984):

- It's easy for me to make new friends at school.
- I have nobody to talk to.
- I'm good at working with other children.
- It's hard for me to make friends.
- I have lots of friends.
- I feel alone.
- I can't find a friend when I need one.
- It's hard to get other kids to like me.
- I don't have anyone to play with.
- I get along with other kids.
- I feel left out of things.
- There's nobody I can go to when I need help.
- I don't get along with other children.
- I'm lonely.
- I am well-liked by the kids in my class.
- I don't have any friends.

SOURCE: Adapted with permission from Asher, S. R., Hymel, S., & Renshaw, P. D. (1984). Loneliness in children. *Child Development, 55*, 1456–1464, Table 1.

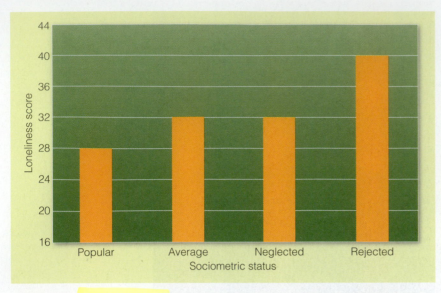

FIGURE 14.2 Loneliness scores for popular, average, neglected, and rejected third- through sixth-grade children.
Rejected children surely feel the sting of their rejection. SOURCE: Adapted from Asher, S. R., Hymel, S., & Renshaw, P. D. (1984). Loneliness in children. *Child Development, 55*, 1456–1464.

Greater than 10% of the third- through sixth-grade children who took the test reported feelings of loneliness and social dissatisfaction. These feelings were related to social status: rejected children reported considerably more loneliness and social dissatisfaction than did their more popular peers. This relationship is shown in Figure 14.2 for third-

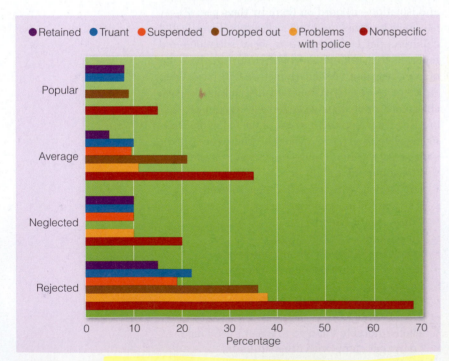

FIGURE 14.3 The relationship between children's sociometric status in fifth grade and academic and behavior problems through high school.
Children who were classified as rejected in elementary school are particularly likely to have school and behavioral problems in high school. SOURCE: Adapted from Kupersmidt, J. B., & Coie, J. D. (1990). Preadolescent peer status and aggression as predictors of externalizing problems in adolescence. *Child Development, 61*, 1350–1362.

through sixth-grade children. This pattern of data is robust: it has been found for other samples of school-age children, for preschoolers, and for middle-school children (Asher et al., 1990).

What, if any, are the long-term consequences of childhood social status? In one study, researchers assessed the social status of children in the fifth grade and followed these children for seven years until the completion of high school (Kupersmidt & Coie, 1990). They reported that children who had been classified as rejected in the fifth grade experienced more behavior problems in high school than other children. Figure 14.3 shows the pattern. Rejected children are more likely than other children to drop out of school, get in trouble with the police, and experience other behavior problems. Other research has confirmed this pattern, with children who are rejected in elementary school—particularly aggressive-rejected children—later displaying more externalizing problems than average children (Dodge et al., 2003; Ladd, 2006).

Social status alone, however, does not determine children's social functioning. For example, a recent study of young adolescents found that 13-year-olds who felt positively about their own social standing, even if they were not popular, showed good social functioning one year later. However, low-popularity children who did not see themselves as fitting in fared particularly poorly one year later (McElhaney, Antonishak, & Allen, 2008).

Origins of Ineffective Social Skills

What are the origins of the poor social skills of unpopular children? Are some children simply born with personalities that destine them to be popular and well-liked, and others with personalities that destine them to be unpopular? Or do parents contribute significantly to children's eventual social status?

Several studies have examined the relationship between parents' social behavior and their children's social standing, and all report differences in how the parents of low- versus high-status children interact with their offspring in social situations (Putallaz & Heflin, 1990). For example, Martha Putallaz (1987) looked at the social interaction of first-grade children and their mothers, comparing it to the children's social status and their interactions with unfamiliar children. In general, mothers who expressed warmth, showed a concern for feelings and open communication, and exerted a moderate degree of control but were not demanding, were more apt to have socially competent and high-status children than were mothers who did not display these characteristics. In other research, quality of attachment and the parent-child relationship have been found to predict quality of children's friendship relationships, with securely attached children having higher-quality friendships than insecurely attached children (Hodges, Finnegan, & Perry, 1999; Schneider et al., 2001).

Although parental behavior obviously has an impact on children's social behavior, certain characteristics of the children also contribute to their social behavior and, most importantly, interact with how others (including their parents) perceive and treat them. We saw in Chapter 11 that individual differences in children's personalities and temperaments influence how people view them. For example, Kenneth Rubin and his colleagues (1990) suggested that infants who are fussy, unpredictable, overactive, and difficult to soothe (difficult babies) may be viewed as aversive, especially by parents who have few sources of social support and who are experiencing considerable stress as a result of low income or marital problems. These children may then be treated with less nurturance and responsiveness than easier infants would be. This pattern of negative parent-infant interaction can persist into childhood, with children displaying hostile and aggressive behavior toward their peers as a result of the social interaction modeled by their parents. Behavior and reputations tend to remain stable in childhood: Other children expect hostility and aggression from these children, leading to rejection and making it difficult for the children to break out of the established pattern.

What can parents do to increase the likelihood that their children will be popular, or at least not rejected and lonely? There are no guarantees, but establishing warm, reciprocal relationships with their children is a start. This is the basis of secure parent-child attachment, which sets the stage for future interactions with others outside of the family. Securely attached children expect social interactions to be positive, and they are thus inclined to seek interaction with other children. They have also developed a reciprocal relationship with a warm and sensitive caregiver that helps them understand the necessary give-and-take of any successful social relationship. Securely attached children also tend to be emotionally positive, enthusiastic, and confident, characteristics that other children find attractive (Elicker, Englund, & Sroufe, 1992). Parents can also promote more sophisticated social behavior in their children by actually teaching them how to enter social groups and reminding them of how other children like to be treated. Finally, parents can model competent social behavior in their interactions with others. Parents who display anger at the first sign of conflict, who interrupt others when they are speaking, and who respond to children (and others) in inappropriate or non-contingent ways, are modeling the *wrong* way to interact socially. One way that parents can promote socially sophisticated behavior in their children is to engage in it themselves.

"Us" versus "Them"

Being in a group provides children with some semblance of social identity. Children come to value positively other people in their group and value outsiders or members of other groups less positively. This leads to feelings of in-group favoritism and out-group discrimination. The earliest form of this is for sex, which is perhaps the largest group to which people are members, but it soon extends to other categories, including ethnicity, nationality, religion, or the school one attends.

Sex Segregation

Beginning in the preschool years, children tend to segregate themselves into same-sex groups, with this tendency increasing during the school years (Maccoby & Jacklin, 1987). Beginning about 5 to 6 years of age, boys prefer to interact in larger groups than do girls. As we mentioned earlier in our discussion of peer relationships, girls tend to prefer to interact in smaller, more stable and intimate groups, often just in pairs (Benenson, 2005; Fabes, Hanish, & Martin, 2003). This is true not only in Western cultures but also in traditional cultures, when there are sufficient numbers of boys and girls in a community to warrant separate groups (Edwards & Whiting, 1988).

Although parents and teachers seem to foster same-sex interaction (Lewis et al., 1975), there are also differences in play styles between boys and girls that further make each gender more comfortable interacting with children from their own sex.

© M. A. Battiliana/Alamy

Children's temperament can affect how parents and peers treat them, with difficult children often finding it difficult to establish friendships with other children.

Beginning around 5 or 6 years of age, children tend to play in sex-segregated groups. Boys' groups tend to be larger and less intimate than girls' groups.

For example, boys engage in more vigorous rough-and-tumble play than girls and focus their interactions on movable toys, whereas girls are more apt to engage in dramatic play and more sedentary activities (see Box 14.1).

However, differences in the preferred activities of boys and girls do not account for the sex differences in preferred group size. For example, when boys and girls are given the same material to be used in free play, boys tend to organize themselves in large playgroups, whereas girls tend to play in pairs (Benenson, Apostoleris, & Parnass, 1997).

Children's sex-segregated playgroups reflect an early indication of children's in-group favoritism and out-group discrimination (Patterson & Bigler, 2006; Powlishta, 1995). For instance, in one study, 8- to 10-year-old children watched videos and rated unfamiliar boys and girls on a variety of dimensions (masculinity, femininity, liking). Much like the in-group favoritism observed for adults, children evaluated same-sex children more positively than opposite-sex children (Powlishta, 1995; see also Egan & Perry, 2001).

Children develop valuable social skills within these same-sex groups. This is illustrated by what happens when children's primary friendships are with children of the opposite sex. For example, in one study, third- and fourth-grade children who had primarily opposite-sex friends were less-well-adjusted socially than children with only (or primarily) same-sex friends, although they were better adjusted than children without friends (Kovacs et al., 1996).

In-group Favoritism and Out-group Discrimination

Sex is not the only basis on which children make in-group/out-group distinctions. For example, in the United States, White children show a pro-White/anti-Black bias by 6 years of age and perhaps younger (Aboud, 2003; Bigler & Liben, 1993). Such in-group favoritism and out-group discrimination in most U.S. children usually begins to decline by 7 years of age and disappears by age 12 (see Aboud, 1988; Apfelbaum et al., 2008). Similarly, preschool and first-grade children tend to view peers who play with out-group members less positively than peers who play only with other in-group children, although these effects tends to disappear by 9 years of age (Castelli, De Amicis, & Sherman, 2007).

Some have proposed that the early out-group discrimination is not so much hostility against the out-group (members of a different gender or race) as it is strong attachment and favoritism for the in-group (Brewer, 1999; Pfeifer et al., 2007). This was supported in research that measured 4- to 7-year-old White Canadian children's attitudes about their own race and those of Black children (Aboud, 2003). In two studies, one in which children attended a mostly-White school and another in which children attended a school with greater racial diversity, favoritism toward one's own race developed earlier and was stronger than out-group discrimination against children of a different race. Young children seem not so much to harbor hostility toward out-group members (in this case Black children), but rather, out-group members suffer from comparisons with the in-group.

in-group favoritism Showing a decided preference for the attitudes and behaviors exhibited by members of one's social group.

out-group discrimination Showing a negative attitude toward members of social groups different from one's own.

One technique that has been used successfully in discerning implicit (that is, unconscious) in-group and out-group biases in adults is the *Implicit Association Test* (Greenwald, McGhee, & Schwartz, 1998). This test uses the speed with which people make decisions about words or concepts (for example, "good" and "bad") when they are associated with different social groups (for example, White versus Black faces). Participants perform several reaction-time tasks, responding as quickly as they can. In the critical series of tests, participants see a Black (or White) face and a set of positive (for example, *joy, happy, love*) or negative (for example, *hate, sad, enemy*) words. For instance, in one block of trials, participants must hit one key when they see a Black face and a positive word and another key when they see a White face and a negative word. Then the relationships are switched, and they must hit one key when they see a Black face and a negative word and a different key when they see a White face and a positive word. Adults typically have faster reaction times when White faces are paired with positive words and Black faces are paired with negative words, revealing an implicit bias for White and against Black faces. We are reluctant to refer to such a pattern as reflecting prejudice, for the pattern is also found for African American participants, suggesting that African Americans have internalized White American values and norms. Furthermore, most people's explicit (that is, conscious) attitudes are not prejudicial. However, such patterns do reveal that adults have come to unconsciously associate positive values with White faces and negative values with Black faces. (To try this out yourself, go to www.implicit.harvard.edu.)

Andrew Scott Baron and Mahzarin Banaji (2006) developed a child-friendly Implicit Association Test and assessed implicit and explicit racial attitudes for 6- and 10-year-old White children and adults. The children responded just like the adults did, showing fast reaction times to White faces paired with positive attributes and to Black faces paired with negative attributes, indicating a positive same-race bias. Although implicit bias did not vary with age, explicit, or conscious, bias did; 6-year olds were the most negatively biased against Blacks, with adults showing no explicit race bias. Similar same-race biases reported for White American children have been found in Japanese children (Dunham, Baron, & Banaji, 2006), suggesting that the same-race bias is universal and emerges early in development (see Dunham, Baron, & Banaji, 2008 for a review).

The tendency to self-segregate into same-sex (and often same-race) groups appears early in childhood, and children quickly develop positive biases for their own group and later acquire negative biases for members of out-groups. That such biases appear so early and are seemingly universal suggests that the process of group identification develops spontaneously as a result of day-to-day social interaction. The fact that in contemporary America explicit (if not implicit) negative attitudes toward out-group members decrease with age and are virtually nonexistent in most samples of college students indicates the potent effect that socialization can have on what is seemingly an evolved tendency to view one's own group favorably and members of out-groups with some caution and perhaps disdain.

The emergence of in-group favoritism and out-group discrimination is nicely illustrated in classic studies by Muzafer Sherif and his colleagues (1961). In the Robbers Cave experiment, 22 unacquainted fifth-grade boys attending summer camp were divided into two groups. Over the course of several weeks, each group participated in enjoyable activities such as crafts, building hideouts, and playing organized games. This was done separately in each group, with one group of boys not being aware initially of the other group. Group cohesiveness was emphasized, in part by organizing activities that required cooperation. For example, one evening the staff failed to cook dinner, and the boys had to divide responsibilities and prepare the meal themselves. Over time, clear positions of status emerged, with some boys becoming recognized leaders and others followers. Both groups even adopted names: Rattlers and Eagles.

Once group cohesion had been established, the two groups were brought together, and a series of friendly competitions was arranged (for example, baseball, tug-of-war). Although the boys did not know it, the camp counselors arranged the games so that each group won and lost equally. When a group lost a competition, conflict arose,

Children also segregate themselves into groups by race and show a same-race bias. In the United States, this bias tends to decrease over childhood, and most adults profess no race bias. However, tests of implicit bias indicate that a same-race bias exists for people of all ages tested, at least for White participants.

© Bill Aron/PhotoEdit

BOX 14.1 **evolution in action**

Social Play: The Evolved Work of Children

To say that "children play" seems trivial. As the pioneering Italian educator Maria Montessori said, "Play is the child's work." Play is usually defined as a "purposeless" activity that children engage in spontaneously and enjoy. It has also been said that nothing important is produced during play and children engage in it for its own sake. Most psychological scientists would not agree. Although it may have no obvious immediate purpose, it nonetheless is an important activity that has some function, either immediate or delayed, for the players (Pellegrini, 2011). Moreover, something as "expensive" as play (it takes up about 10% of children's and animals' time, Fagen, 1981) should have some benefit to the individual, otherwise it would have been eliminated by natural selection.

Play is actually quite complicated, and there are a variety of types of play. Play can be solitary or social, involve a high degree of pretense (make-believe) or none at all, and be active or sedentary. We have examined play in several chapters in this book, notably in Chapter 6 when we talked about pretend, or fantasy, play and its role in cognitive development. Here we want to say a little bit about *social play*, especially sex differences in play style, the possible consequences play may have for children's development, and the possible benefit of play from an evolutionary perspective.

First, most social animals play, but not equally. For example, social play, but not nonsocial play, is related to the size of the amygdala and hypothalamus in nonhuman primates, even after controlling for the size of other brain structures (Lewis & Barton, 2006). This relationship (the larger the amygdala and hypothalamus the more social play) may be related to these structures' abilities to process social/emotional content (recognizing facial expressions, for instance), which are developed through social play (Lewis & Barton, 2006). Social play, then, may be especially adaptive for social primates, and the most social primate with the most complicated social play is *Homo sapiens*.

As mentioned in the text, boys' play tends to be much more vigorous than that of girls. During the preschool years, both boys and girls engage in locomotor play, which involves a lot of running and perhaps some rough-housing. However, *rough-and-tumble*

Boys more so than girls engage in rough-and-tumble play, which involves vigorous behaviors such as running, wrestling, kicking, and tumbling.

altrendo images/Getty Images

play becomes more vigorous and rougher as children get older and is something that boys do more than girls. Rough-and-tumble play refers to vigorous behaviors such as wrestling, kicking, and tumbling that could easily be mistaken for fighting except for the playful context (Pellegrini & Smith, 1998). Also, when children fight they tend to disperse after the conclusion of the bout; they tend to stay together and continue to play after rough-and-tumble play. The sex difference in rough-and-tumble play is not limited to Western societies but is found in all human cultures and many species of mammals (see Pellegrini, 2011; Pellegrini & Smith, 1998). Fathers spend more time than mothers engaging in rough-and-tumble play and do so more with their sons than their daughters (see Pellegrini & Smith, 1998). Recent research has shown a relationship between levels of prenatal testosterone and male-typical play activity during childhood, including rough-and-tumble play. For both boys and girls, higher levels of prenatal testosterone measured from amniotic fluid were positively correlated with higher levels of male-typical play activities during childhood (Auyeung et al., 2009).

What might be the benefits of rough-and-tumble play for boys? Some have suggested that most of the benefits are deferred to later in life (Geary, 2009; Smith, 1982). This would have been especially true for our ancestors in terms of practice for hunting and fighting skills, including coalitional warfare, important in traditional environments. Boys also use rough-and-tumble play to establish leadership in their immediate social group. A boy's position in the social hierarchy (see discussion later in this chapter) is more often based on physical skill than that of girls (Hawley, 1999), and the high incidence of rough-and-tumble play among boys may enhance their ability to read the social signals of other boys (Pellegrini & Smith, 1998), which is important at all stages of life. Recall also that in traditional environments, and certainly in the environments in which our ancestors lived, the children one played with were most likely the same people you would be cooperating and competing with as an adult. This was probably particularly true for boys, who, in most cases, were more apt to remain with their birth group, compared to girls, who were more likely to migrate to other groups to find mates (Owens & King, 1999). Rough-and-tumble play can also provide children with some immediate nonsocial benefits. For example, vigorous exercise play strengthens children's bones and muscles (Bruner, 1972).

Some have suggested that girls actively avoid contact with boys because of their roughness, accounting for the sex-segregated

Both boys and girls engage in symbolic social play, although the themes of their play tend to be different. Girls' play often emphasizes relationships (for example, playing house or school), whereas boys' play is more often focused on aggression, power, and dominance.

playgroups that typify childhood (Haskett, 1971). Play-style compatibility is only part of the story, however. Anthony Pellegrini and his colleagues (2007) followed a group of pre-school children across the school year. They noted that sex segregation began early in the year, with both high-activity and low-activity boys tending to play in mostly-boy groups. The same was true for low-activity girls, who played mostly with other low-activity girls. However, high-activity girls were more likely to play in sex-integrated groups, probably because their activity level was more compat-ible with that of boys. Over the course of the school year, however, these high-activity girls tended to restrict their play to other high-activity girls. Whether boys avoided the girls or vice versa is not known, but compatibility of play style seemed less important in choos-ing whom to play with than the sex of the playmate. This was true for boys at the begin-ning of the school year and for girls toward the end, although girls tended to play with other girls on the basis of their activity level.

Beginning in the preschool years, both boys and girls engage in *symbolic, fantasy,* or *make-believe play*, much of it social (see Chapter 6). However, the content of such play tends to differ between the sexes. For instance, beginning around 6 years of age, the themes of girls' make-believe play often emphasizes relationships, for example, play-ing house or school ("You be the baby and I'll be the mommy"). Such play is often focused on parenting (Geary, 2009). Again, this is not restricted to Western societies but is found in both developed and traditional cul-tures (Eibl-Eibesfeldt, 1989; Geary, 2009). What function might such play afford girls? Developing social skills and relationships with other girls can provide both immediate and deferred benefits, but the specific content of girls' play may prepare them to carry out the traditional roles that women played over our species' evolutionary history (and continue to play in most cultures today).

Boys engage in fantasy play too, but the content of their fantasy tends to be very dif-ferent than that of girls and is more often focused on aggression, power, and domi-nance, and is often part of rough-and-tumble play. When boys play with dolls ("action fig-ures" they will tell you) they more likely are in the role of superhero or combatant rather than caretakers. Thus, the patterns of fantasy play shown by boys and girls can be viewed as preparations for the roles (for example, par-enting, male-male competition) they will have as adults, or would have had in ancient envi-ronments (see Pellegrini & Bjorklund, 2004).

One interesting finding is that sex dif-ferences in play style extend beyond the

playground to the virtual world. For example, when preteen children play online multiuser games in which two or more players interact with avatars (characters that represent them in the game), boys tend to engage in more play, such as chase games or hide-and-seek, whereas girls tend to talk more. When pairs include one boy and one girl, the interactions run less smoothly, with boys encouraging girls to play more and girls encouraging boys to talk more (Calvert et al., 2003). Even when chil-dren adopt an avatar of the opposite sex, their play style is still characteristic of their biologi-cal sex, suggesting that this type of "gender bending" is not a reflection of a cross-sex behavioral disposition (Calvert et al., 2009).

Play is serious business for children, and social play may be the most serious. Social play is often the primary vehicle by which children develop friendships and peer rela-tionships in general, which are so important to a child's social and emotional develop-ment. However, it appears that boys and girls are biased to engage in different types of play, and that these biases may have pre-pared our juvenile ancestors for life in a tra-ditional group. Although social roles are more flexible today than they were in the past, play remains important as children's means for developing social skills and possibly physical skills that will be useful when they grow up.

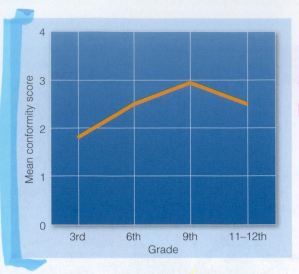

often including threats of physical attack against one another or a change in leadership. As competition continued, however, within-group conflict decreased and group solidarity increased, often expressed by hostility toward the other group. The groups would abuse each other verbally ("You're not Eagles, you're pigeons!"); they engaged in raids on the other campsite and theft or destruction of property; and counselors had to intervene to stop true violence (rock throwing). Thus, competition between groups led, after a brief period of disharmony, to greater within-group cohesion and overt hostility toward the other group.

The researchers attempted to reduce the hostility between the groups, initially by bringing the groups together for some noncompetitive activities, such as meals and movies. These attempts were disastrous; if anything, they increased hostility between the groups. The counselors then devised a series of events that required the cooperation of members of both groups. For instance, the water supply "broke down" one hot day, and boys from both groups had to search for the source of the trouble. They had to inspect a mile of pipe and finally found a clogged valve at the tank. They celebrated together when the problem had been fixed. On another occasion, a truck engine failed, requiring the boys to act cooperatively to get the truck started. They first tried pushing the truck, but to no avail. One boy then had the idea of tying their tug-of-war rope to the truck and having a "tug of war against the truck." All the boys from both groups pulled on the rope, and, with the counselor inside, the truck finally started, with boys from both groups yelling, "Yeah! We won the tug-of-war against the truck!" These and other situations that provided a common goal reduced hostility and fostered friendship between former "enemies." How do you take two initially hostile groups and create in them feelings of in-group belongingness? The answer is to promote cooperation toward a common goal.

The findings from Sherif's study illustrate at least three of the four evolutionary adaptations proposed in Harris's (1995) group selection theory: social affiliation and within-group favoritism, status-seeking behaviors and establishment of social hierarchies, and between-group hostilities.

It is worth mentioning here that some have speculated that in-group favoritism/out-group discrimination may have its origins in infancy (Spelke & Kinzler, 2007). Infants as young as 3 months of age show a preference for looking at faces from their own race (Kelly et al., 2005; Bar-Haim et al., 2006; see discussion in Chapter 5). Elizabeth Spelke and Katherine Kinzler (2007) proposed that identifying with members of one's social group would have been of great importance to our ancestors, and that natural selection biased infants to use cues such as race or language to produce a preference for group members. Thus, the more explicit "us versus them" bias that we see in childhood likely has its origins in infancy.

Conformity to Peer Pressure

Conformity refers to adjusting one's behavior to that of group norms. Conformity has developed a bad reputation, especially among parents whose children claim that "everyone else" is allowed to do whatever the parents have just forbidden. However, conformity to group norms is necessary for any society to function.

It is during the school years when the peer group, or cliques, becomes especially important for children that conformity to peer pressure truly begins, generally peaking in early adolescence (Berndt, 1979; Gavin & Furman, 1989). For example, in one study, children ranging from third to twelfth grades were presented with situations in which peers urged them to engage in antisocial, neutral, or prosocial behaviors (Berndt, 1979). Figure 14.4 shows the age trend for conformity for antisocial acts. As can be seen, ninth-graders were the most susceptible to peer pressure, with both younger and older children being less influenced by their peers. Despite the beliefs of many parents of adolescents, children of all ages are *less* likely to conform to peer pressure for antisocial behavior than for more positive behavior (Berndt, 1979; Brown, Clasen, & Eicher, 1986), and teenagers perceive less peer pressure for misconduct (for example, drug/alcohol use, unsafe sex practices, delinquent behavior) than for positive group behaviors, such as socializing with friends (Brown et al., 1986).

However, as should not be surprising to anyone, teenagers are not immune to peer pressure for behaviors deemed inappropriate by adults. For example, in one study, groups of 16- and 17-year-old male high-school students participated in a chat room and thought they were interacting with other adolescents. In actuality, the "other adolescents" were confederates of the experimenter. The adolescents tended to approve of aggressive and health-risk behaviors, including vandalism, substance abuse, verbal teasing, and physical aggression, that were suggested by their chat-room partners. Conformity was especially strong when such behaviors were endorsed by children who were presumed to be high-status peers (Cohen & Prinstein, 2006).

Dominance Hierarchies

It is usually within peer groups that children (or adults for that matter) compete with one another for status and resources, as well as cooperate with one another to achieve specific goals. In this section we discuss the formation and functioning of children's dominance hierarchies. We examine prosocial and antisocial behaviors (mainly aggression), which often occur within peer groups, in later sections.

Dominance hierarchies—pecking orders of social influence—get their name from social birds. Birds high in the social order literally peck the heads of birds lower in the social order. By knowing who pecks whom, one can determine an individual's position in the social group, or the pecking order. Other nonpecking social animals, including many primates, also form social, or dominance, hierarchies, with individuals high in the social order (with the top animal often referred to as the alpha male or alpha female) physically dominating individuals beneath them. Although you may think that such groups would constantly be fighting with one another, this is not the case. Once a hierarchy is formed, individuals know their place and aggression is reduced, with a simple look by a more dominant individual being enough to keep a lower-ranking individual in his or her place.

Humans, perhaps the most social of all animals, also establish dominance hierarchies, although a bit differently from other species. Dominance hierarchies can be seen even among preschoolers (Hawley, 2003; Vaughn & Santos, 2009) and can best be thought of in terms of leadership. Dominant individuals are leaders of their groups, whom others look up to and who make decisions that other children tend to follow. Leaders use a variety of strategies, both cooperative and aggressive, to establish and maintain their high status (Hawley, 1999; Pellegrini et al., 2007). Dominance hierarchies reduce antagonism within the group, distribute scarce resources, and focus division of labor (Hawley, 1999; Savin-Williams, 1979). For example, in the initial phases of group formation, children (especially boys) use aggression selectively in their competition with peers over resources. Once dominance hierarchies are established, rates of aggression decline and leaders use prosocial and cooperative strategies more often (Hawley, 2003; Pellegrini & Bartini, 2000).

However, even for older children, physical dominance remains important among some groups of youngsters, particularly boys. In a study of 12- to 14-year-old boys and girls at summer camp, boys were more apt than girls to assert themselves physically and to argue with cabin-mates (Savin-Williams, 1979). But dominance hierarchies within a cabin, for both boys and girls, were shaped by factors other than physical assertiveness, including pubertal maturation, athletic ability, and group leadership.

It is interesting to note that rates of aggression are *positively* correlated with popularity for preschool children (Hawley, 2003; Pellegrini et al., 2007), and sometimes for older children as well (Cillessen & Mayeux, 2007; Hawley, Card, & Little, 2008; Rose, Swanson, & Waller, 2004). Although aggression is typically viewed negatively, children who use it effectively, for example when coming to the aid of friends, can gain some benefits with respect to popularity and social status (see Hawley, 2008; Hawley, Little, & Rodkin, 2007).

In his discussion of aggression among non-human primates, Franz de Waal (1982, 1989) proposed that, in some situations, aggression leads to affiliation when combatants reconcile after fights. Dominant members of a group maintain their high status, because other (subordinate) members remain in the group and continue to support them. If chimpanzees, monkeys, or children are free to leave the group, leaders would be wise to reconcile after aggressive bouts to help cement the social order and enable the group to continue their interaction. It does not make any sense for a leader to be so aggressive that he frightens his subordinates away and then has no one to lead. For example, in studies from various countries looking at reconciliation after conflicts in preschool and school-age children, most report, perhaps counterintuitively, that the *aggressors* initiate affiliative behaviors more often than the victims (Butovskaya, 2007; Fujisawa, Kutsukake, & Hasegawa, 2005). Most invitations to reconcile are accepted. For instance, in one study, approximately two-thirds of all post-conflict affiliative behaviors resulted in reconciliation, with children continuing to play together. The rates of successful bids to reconcile were the same regardless of whether they were made by the aggressor or the victim (Ljungberg et al., 2005). This mixture of aggression, reconciliation, and cooperation probably comes together in the formation and maintenance of dominance hierarchies.

Reconciliation has been less studied than aggression, but it surely plays an important role in group cohesion. Reconciliation has been reported in a vast array of cultures for children between preschool age and adolescence, with researchers reporting that the type of affiliative behavior used to reconcile differs among cultures. For example, Japanese preschool children are more likely to explicitly apologize (Fujisawa et al., 2005), whereas Swedish preschoolers are more apt to make an "invitation to play" (Ljungberg et al., 2005). Girls are also more skilled than boys at negotiating peaceful reconciliation (Butovskaya, Timentschik, & Burkova, 2007). Reconciliation attempts are more apt to be made between friends, or at least between children who associated with one another frequently before the conflict, pointing to the role of reconciliation in maintaining group cohesion and harmony (Verbeek & de Waal, 2001).

Reconciling also plays a positive role in reducing stress, especially for victims (Butovskaya, 2008; Fujisawa et al., 2005). For example, Japanese researchers found that preschool victims of aggression showed declines in a behavioral index of stress (the frequency of self-directed behaviors, such as touching one's face or clothing, thumb-sucking) following reconciliation (Fujisawa et al., 2005). Similarly, 7- to 15-year-old Russian children who did not reconcile after a conflict displayed elevated levels of cortisol relative to children who did reconcile (Butovskaya, 2008). Reconciliation thus seems to be beneficial to individuals (both leaders/aggressors and victims) and the group.

One does not need scientific research to know that children's peers play an important role in their lives and their development. Children tell us this, and anyone who has made it to adulthood has personally experienced the benefits of friendship and likely also experienced the sting of peer rejection. Although children have many one-on-one relationships with friends, much interaction occurs within social groups. Beginning in the preschool years, these groups tend to be segregated by sex. Leaders emerge and children find their place or their role within a group. Groups develop rules and expectations for their members, and with increasing age, children tend to conform to those social norms. Peer groups are embedded within a community and are affected by the values and norms of the community. Thus parents, teachers, and other people with whom children interact on a regular basis continue to have an influence on their behavior and development. Nonetheless, peer groups constitute an important force in the socialization for children in cultures all over the world.

The Development of Prosocial Behaviors

Although much of children's interactions with one another can be defined as fun and games, a substantial amount of interaction involves cooperating or competing with one another. Some cooperation and competition is done in a playful spirit during games, but other interaction is more serious in nature. Positive behaviors typically used to foster social relations have been termed **prosocial behaviors**. Children engage in these behaviors voluntarily with the goal to benefit other people (Eisenberg, Fabes, & Spinard, 2006; Grusec, Davidov, & Lundell, 2003). Other behaviors, more apt to be used in competition, can be called, for want of a better term, **antisocial behaviors**. We will examine one much-studied antisocial behavior, aggression, in the next major section of this chapter and other antisocial behaviors in the section on moral development at the end of this chapter. Table 14.2 lists some examples of prosocial and antisocial behaviors.

Perhaps somewhat ironically, it is relatively easy to understand how antisocial behaviors, reflecting the darker side of human nature, could have been selected for over the course of evolution. Cheating a peer—getting more from a deal than is fair—would be to the advantage of the successful cheater, for example. Evolutionary theory has had a more difficult time explaining the prevalence of prosocial behaviors. In particular, **altruism**—doing something for another at some cost to one's self—should provide more costs than benefits to an individual. Altruism and related cooperative behaviors that people and other social animals engage in can be explained by William Hamilton's (1964) *inclusive fitness theory*, which we introduced in Chapter 12. Recall that according to the theory, people's social behaviors will vary according to the degree of genetic relatedness among interactants. Individuals will be more cooperative to those who are closely related to them relative to more distant kin and nonkin (Dunbar & Spoor, 1995). This is because by helping people who share genes with you, you are, in a sense, fostering their development and thus the continuance of genes you have in common.

How, though, does cooperating with family members explain prosocial behavior with nonkin? It is assumed that ancient human environments contained a high percentage of kin (Hinde, 1980). Thus, in most groups, people not only shared genes with fellow members, but they also shared a social history. Because of the familiarity that people had with others in the group and the high likelihood of future interactions, cooperation among fellow group members became a good strategy for social

table 14.2 Some Examples of Prosocial and Antisocial Behaviors

Prosocial Behaviors or Strategies
Comforting
Sharing
Helping

Antisocial Behaviors or Strategies
Lying and cheating
Distributing resources unfairly
Physical and indirect aggression

table 14.3 Hoffman's Levels of Empathy Development

Martin Hoffman suggested that children's ability to express empathy affected their prosocial behavior. He proposed four levels in the development of empathy:

1. **Global empathy (birth to 1 year):** Infants experience distress merely by witnessing distress in others. They cannot distinguish the distress others experience from the distress they feel.

2. **Egocentric empathy (1 to 2 years):** Toddlers realize that others experience distress independent of their own feelings. However, they do not understand the internal state of others and assume it is the same as their own.

3. **Veridical empathic distress (2 to 10 years):** Over this time, children become increasingly aware of how others feel and that other people's perspectives and feelings may be different from their own. As children's perspective-taking skills improve over childhood, so too does their ability to express empathy.

4. **Empathy for another's life conditions (11 years and older):** Children can express empathy for a person's larger life experience, and begin to feel empathic for groups of people, not just individuals.

success (at least in some contexts with some individuals). This is captured by the concept of **reciprocal altruism** (Trivers, 1971). Individuals will cooperate with those with whom they will interact in the future. Costs associated with cooperative and altruistic behaviors will be minimized by others reciprocating the good turn. Similarly, acts of aggression or deceptions will also be reciprocated. The golden rule, "Do unto others as you would have others do unto you," is found, in some version, in most of the world's religions and makes good inclusive-fitness sense, especially if you are likely to be interacting in the future with the people you are doing good to. Research has consistently shown that human adults behave altruistically both in natural settings and experiments, and some have proposed that the need to cooperate and compete with fellow humans provided the selective pressure necessary for altruism to evolve in our ancestors (Bowles, 2006; Tomasello, 2009).

In this section we discuss the development of three specific types of prosocial behaviors: comforting, helping, and sharing, as well as factors that promote their development. We then have a separate section on the related topic of moral development. We first, however, examine what many believe is the foundation of prosocial behavior: empathy.

Behavior, Empathy, and the Development of Social Cognition

What factors must be present for children to behave in a prosocial way—that is, to behave in a way that helps others—possibly even to their own detriment? Martin Hoffman (1981, 2000) postulated that feelings of *empathy*, or empathic arousal, are necessary before prosocial behavior is possible (see Chapters 11). Empathy can be seen as a special case of perspective taking and thus social cognition (see Chapter 7). As noted in Chapter 11, empathy is more than perspective taking but also an emotion in which a person vicariously experiences the feelings, thoughts, or attitudes of another. Children first learn to recognize that distress in someone else is the cause of their own ill feelings and then learn to feel better by doing something to relieve the other person's discomfort.

Hoffman postulated four levels in the development of empathy (see Table 14.3). The first level, from birth to about 1 year, he called *global empathy*: infants experience distress merely by witnessing distress in others. They cannot distinguish the distress others experience from the distress they feel. For example, a 1-year-old will put her thumb in her mouth, whimper, and bury her head in her mother's lap upon seeing another child fall and cry. She responds to the other child's distress as if the event had happened to her. This reaction decreases substantially during the second year (Thompson, 1987). Evidence of global empathy is seen in a study that demonstrated empathic crying in newborns (Sagi & Hoffman, 1976). Infants younger than 3 days old were exposed to the cries of another baby, an artificial simulation of an infant's cry, or nothing. Babies who heard the real infant crying began to cry themselves and to show other signs of distress such as grimacing and kicking (see also Martin & Clark, 1982). Hoffman proposed that such responding reflects a specific empathy in newborns to the cries of human infants. Other equally loud sounds, even simulated cries, do not have the same effect.

At the second level, *egocentric empathy* (or quasi-egocentric empathy), toddlers 1 to 2 years old realize that others experience distress independent of their own feelings. However, they do not understand the internal state of others and assume it is the same as their own. Thus, for example, a child will give his crying mother a teddy bear because it comforts him when he is sad. The term

reciprocal altruism The idea that individuals will cooperate with those who cooperate with them and with whom they will interact in the future.

egocentric as used here does not refer to a personality characteristic, but rather comes from Piaget's theory of cognitive development (see Chapters 2 and 6) and refers to young children having a difficult time taking the psychological perspective of others. Egocentric empathy is not empathy based on selfishness but empathy based on a cognitive limitation.

Level 3, *veridical empathic distress*, is empathy for another person's feelings. Beginning sometime during the second year, children become increasingly aware of how others feel and that other people's perspectives and feelings may be different from their own. As children's perspective-taking abilities improve over childhood, so too does their ability to express empathy (see discussion of perspective taking in Chapter 7). Finally, around age 11, children achieve Level 4, *empathy for another's life conditions*. Children can now express empathy for a person's larger life experience, not just specific situations, and begin to feel empathy for groups of people (minorities, victims of child abuse, children in developing countries), not just individuals.

This discussion of empathy suggests that children's ability to take the perspectives of others is at the root of sharing, cooperating, helping, and prosocial behavior in general. Children develop the ability to recognize and identify with the feelings of others. According to Hoffman, perceiving distress in others causes discomfort to a child, which is relieved by comforting others. As social perspective-taking abilities improve, so too does empathy and the likelihood of engaging in positive social behaviors. For example, young children who are able to recognize themselves in a mirror (see discussion of mirror self-recognition in Chapter 7) tend to be more empathic and to show greater levels of prosocial behavior than do same-age children who do not recognize their mirror images (Johnson, 1982). Prosocial behavior, then, can be seen as a product of children's developing social cognition and the need to affiliate and cooperate with others. Being able to empathize with others does not necessarily mean that children (or adults) will behave prosocially, however. The ability to take the perspective and appreciate the feelings of another can also be used to manipulate and possibly take advantage of others. How empathic abilities are used depends on the individual's motivation.

Comforting

Researchers have shown that infants as young as 1 year of age will comfort another person who is distressed, usually by patting, hugging, or offering some valued object (Zahn-Waxler & Radke-Yarrow,

1982). Attempts to comfort a distressed person become more elaborate over the second and third years, including expressing concern, providing suggestions, and giving gifts (Zahn-Waxler, Radke-Yarrow, & King, 1979). The following excerpt from a mother's observations is an example of comforting by a 22-month-old:

Today there was a little 4-year-old girl here, Susan. Todd (96 weeks) and Susan were in the bedroom playing and all of a sudden Susan started to cry and ran to her mother. Todd slowly followed after and watched. I said, "What happened?" and she said, "He hit me." I said, "Well, tell him not to hit you," and I said, "Todd!" He didn't seem particularly upset; he was watching her cry. I said, "Did you hit Susan? Why would you hit Susan? You don't want to hurt people." Then they went back in the bedroom and there was a second run-in and she came out. That's when I said sternly, "No, Todd, you mustn't hit people." He just watched her sniffle as she was being stroked by her mom, and her mom was saying, "He's just a little boy and boys do that sometimes." On the table right by us were some fallen petals from a flower and he picked up one little petal and smiled and handed it to her and said, "Here." She kind of reached and took it and then he searched for other petals and gave them to her; so he was trying to either make up or give her something to stop the crying (Zahn-Waxler et al., 1979, p. 322).

Sharing

Sharing can be observed in small amounts among toddlers. For example, 12-month-olds will point out objects to other people, sharing the sights they see with someone else (Rheingold, Hay, & West, 1976). But sharing sights and sharing toys are different things, and spontaneous sharing of valuable possessions is something that toddlers and 2-year-olds do not do often or easily. Yet, infants as young as 8 months of age will occasionally share objects, and this increases over the next year or so (Hay, 1994; Hay & Rheingold, 1983). Sharing is more common among 3- and 4-year-olds, but many children, well into the early school years, find sharing toys a difficult concept to put into practice (Yarrow & Waxler, 1976). In fact, in a study that looked at conflict between pairs of 21-month-olds, 84% of all disputes concerned struggles over toys (Hay & Ross, 1982).

Other research indicates that toddlers who have had others share with them are more likely to share their own toys when given the opportunity. In one study, pairs of children (ages 29 to 36 months), accompanied by their mothers, were separated by a see-through gate (Levitt et al., 1985). Only one child in each pair was given toys to play with. If the child with the toys did not share with

Sean Justice/Getty Images

Young children are more apt to share with another child if that child had shared with them previously, demonstrating the concept of reciprocity.

the other child within 4 minutes, the child's mother encouraged her child to share. After another minute, all of the toys were removed. Following this, another set of toys was introduced, but this time they were given to the child who initially had no toys. The researchers reported that none of the children shared spontaneously, confirming our earlier description of toddlers as nonsharers. This was true even though many of the "toy-deprived" children stood at the gate watching the other child, who was "keenly aware of the other child's presence and actions, even though they often turned their backs to the other child" (p. 123). When asked by their mothers to share, 13 of 20 children did so. What is more interesting here is that children who received toys in the second phase of the experiment were more likely to share if they had been shared with first. In fact, in 9 out of 10 cases, when the first child did not share, the second child did not either. Thus, these young children displayed the principle of reciprocity: "I'll share with you if you shared with me." Yet even children who were shared with earlier only shared after being requested to do so by their mothers.

Sharing is more common in older children. For example, in one study, children ranging in age from 5 to 14 years were given the opportunity to share some candy with other children in their school (Green & Schneider, 1974). The children had earned five candy bars by assisting the experimenter on a project to "help poor children." Among 5- and 6-year-olds, 60% shared at least one candy bar; the percentage of children sharing increased to 92% for 7- and 8-year-olds and 100% for 9- and 10-year-olds and 13- and 14-year-olds. Also, the average number of candy bars shared (maximum = 5) increased with age (5/6-year-olds = 1.36; 7/8-year-olds = 1.84; 9/10-year-olds = 2.88; 13/14-year-olds = 4.24). Thus, at least when requested by an adult, children's willingness to share with unspecified peers increases steadily over the school years.

Recently, child development researchers have used games developed by economists to assess children's willingness to share. In the *Dictator Game*, one player is given some resource—usually money when the game is played by adults, often stickers or candy when played by children. The player is then told that he or she can share some of the resource with another child, usually an unnamed child from the same classroom. In these situations, preschool children typically share fewer resources than older children, although even 4-year-old children will share some (usually very few) resources with a peer, indicating some rudimentary notion of altruism in young children (Benenson, Pascoe, & Radmore, 2007; Blake & Rand, 2010). Some research reports that girls are more likely to make fair (that is, 50/50) splits than boys, who are more apt to keep more of the resources for themselves (Gummerum et al., 2008).

Helping

Anyone who has spent much time with preschoolers knows that they often want to help—assist-

HELPING

ing a parent, for example, in cooking dinner, mowing the lawn, or repairing a leaky faucet. Such help often increases the work for the adult performing the task, but young children seem earnest in their attempts to assist. Harriet Rheingold (1982) asked the parents of 18- to 30-month-old children and other adults to perform some common household chores and recorded the children's reactions. Rheingold reported that children spontaneously and promptly assisted the adults in most of the tasks they performed, regardless of whether the adult was the child's parent or an unfamiliar person.

Spontaneous helping increases over the school years. In one study, children between the ages of 5 and 14 years of age were asked to help an adult put together books for poor children (Green & Schneider, 1974). In the process of working, the adult "accidentally" knocked over some pencils as he walked across the room. The adult made no comment about the pencils, other than to say "uh" and shrug when they fell. The percentage of children who spontaneously picked up the pencils increased with age; about half of the 5- and 6-year-olds picked up the pencils, but virtually all of those older than 9 did so.

In other contexts, very young children will offer help to an adult in need. For example, in one study, 18-month-old children and, to a lesser extent, enculturated (human-reared) chimpanzees, spontaneously offered help to an adult, for example by picking up a marker from the table (Warneken & Tomasello, 2006). However, children (and chimpanzees) would do this only if the adult was trying to achieve a specific goal (for example, he accidentally dropped the marker), but not when the adult did not need help (for example, he deliberately threw the marker on the table). Thus, by 18 months of age, children will provide assistance to someone else and can determine, at some level, situations in which help is needed and when it is not (see also Over & Carpenter, 2009).

Most research on children's prosocial behavior falls into the categories of comforting, sharing, and helping, although this obviously does not exhaust all of the options. Some other potentially prosocial behaviors, such as treating other children fairly, will be discussed in the section on moral development, focusing on young children's typically *unfair* distribution of resources.

One interesting study that we think falls under the heading of prosocial behavior is Genyue Fu and Kang Lee's (2007) assessment of the development of *flattery*. In their study, preschool children were asked to evaluate drawings made by an adult. Sometimes the adult who drew the picture was present, and sometimes the

adult was not present. The presence of the artist made no difference for 3-year-old children; they called it like they saw it, rating the drawings the same whether the person who drew the picture was present or not. In contrast, 5- and 6-year-old children inflated their ratings in the presence of the person who made the drawings compared to when the artist was absent. Four-year-old children showed a mixture of these behaviors. Thus, flattery, or perhaps social tact (or "social grooming" as the authors refer to it), appears to develop during the preschool years, as children acquire sensitivity for other people's feelings, at least with respect to evaluations of their artistic work.

Factors Related to Individual Differences in Children's Prosocial Behaviors

Although prosocial behavior is observed universally, significant individual differences in the incidence of prosocial behavior have also been reported (see Eisenberg et al., 2006). For example, a small but consistent sex difference favoring girls has been found in children's prosocial behaviors (see Eisenberg & Fabes, 1998; Eisenberg et al., 2006). In this section, we examine some of the factors related to individual differences in prosocial behavior.

Biological Bases

As we have emphasized throughout this book, all behavior is mediated by the interaction of biological and environmental factors, and it is impossible to state how much of any specific behavior can be attributed to biology and how much to environment. Nonetheless, behavioral genetic techniques allow one to get an idea of the degree to which individual differences in a trait are heritable, at least under certain cultural conditions.

With respect to prosocial behavior, studies with adults have shown that between 40% and 70% of differences in nurturing, empathy, and altruism are associated with genetic differences (Hastings et al., 2005; Rushton et al., 1986). Genetic contributions to individual differences in prosocial behavior when measured in childhood are typically smaller, although still significant. In one study following 9,424 sets of twins between the ages of 2 and 7 years, the amount of shared environmental effect (as reflected by living in the same home) on prosocial behavior (based on parent and teacher ratings) decreased from .47 at 2 years of age to .03 at 7 years of age, while genetic effects increased from .32 to .61 (Knafo & Plomin, 2006). This is consistent with other research demonstrating a decreasing effect of parents on children's intellect, personality, and social behavior with age (see Harris, 1995). Although such research suggests a strong genetic component to prosocial behavior, approximately half of the individual differences are attributed to nongenetic factors (some report greater than 50%, Deater-Deckard et al., 2001), implying an important role for the environment.

What, however, is being inherited? One possibility is that the tendency to engage in prosocial behavior is related to temperament, aspects of which have been found to be at least moderately heritable (see Chapter 11). For example, children who can regulate their emotions and are low in impulsivity are more likely to be emotionally positive and to be prosocial (see Eisenberg & Fabes, 1998; Eisenberg et al., 2000; Eisenberg, Wentzel, & Harris, 1998).

Influences of Parents and Peers

The extent to which children act in prosocial ways is related to how their parents act. Children who view their parents as warm and loving are more generous, supportive, comforting, and cooperative than other children (Hoffman, 1975). In general, parents who display an authoritative parenting style that emphasizes firm control but sensitivity to children's needs (see Chapter 13) have been found to be more prosocial both at home and at school (Krevans & Gibbs, 1996; Robinson et al., 1994). In a study with preschoolers, prosocial children were apt to have mothers who focused on their children's misdeeds ("Look what you did!") and who made it clear that they expected proper behavior ("Don't you see you hurt Amy? Don't ever pull hair!"). Effective mothers did not calmly reason with their preschool children but were adamant about their feelings. These same mothers also modeled empathic behavior, comforting their own children when they were hurt (Zahn-Waxler et al., 1979).

Apparently, however, explicitly rewarding children to share leads to *less*, not more, sharing later on. In studies with 20-month-old toddlers (Warneken & Tomasello, 2008) and with 6- to 12-year-old children (Fabes et al., 1989), those who were rewarded for sharing (for example, permitted to play with a special toy, as in Warneken & Tomasello, 2008) subsequently shared less when given the opportunity relative to children who received only praise or no reward. Why should receiving an explicit reward for sharing actually reduce later sharing? One hypothesis has been called the *overjustification effect* (Deci, 1971; Lepper, Greene, & Nisbett, 1973), in which receiving extrinsic rewards induces an extrinsic motivational orientation (that is, people expect to get something for their actions), reducing intrinsic motivation for the same activity. For instance, when children who enjoyed drawing were given explicit rewards for their artwork, they were less motivated to draw later on than children who were not given explicit rewards (Lepper et al., 1973).

It should not be surprising that children's behavior is associated with the company they keep. With respect to prosocial behavior, it is more often seen among friends than among peers who are not friends (Brendt, 1985). Friends also display similar levels of prosocial behavior (Barry & Wentzel, 2006; Wenzel, Barry, & Caldwell, 2004).

Antisocial Behavior: The Development of Aggression

The term "antisocial behavior" is likely a misnomer. These behaviors are clearly social. They could more accurately be called "anti-positive social behaviors," but that's a mouth full and not likely to catch on. Antisocial behaviors refer to behaviors that are geared toward injuring others, either directly through aggression or indirectly through lying and cheating. Children who engage in such behaviors often gain something in the process, sometimes immediately. They may get a toy that another child had possession of, more than their fair share of some resource such as food, toys, or time on a swing, or just avoid getting punished for some misdeed. In this section we look at the development of aggression. We examine the topics of lying, cheating, and the unfair distribution of resources later in the chapter in the section on moral development.

Aggression has been a favorite topic of psychologists throughout the 20th century and continues today. Aggression is typically defined simply as behavior intended to harm another person. Usually, the target of aggression also perceives that he or she has been hurt (Underwood, 2002). Freud and the early behaviorists viewed aggression as a "drive" that children must learn to control or direct into socially appropriate channels. Psychologists often distinguish between instrumental and hostile aggression. Instrumental aggression is behavior aimed at acquiring some concrete goal or object, such as a toy preschoolers fight over. In contrast, hostile aggression refers to more personally oriented actions in which a child's intent is to hurt another child, either physically or emotionally, by ridiculing or name calling, for example.

We mentioned previously that scientists have had an easier time explaining the adaptive value of

---

aggression Behavior intended to harm another person.

instrumental aggression Type of aggression used as a mean to attain a certain goal (for example, a toy), not as a goal itself.

hostile aggression Personally oriented aggression in which a child's intent is to hurt another child (not as a mean for attaining a goal).

FIGURE 14.5 Proportion of physical, verbal, and indirect aggression as percentage of total aggression scores.
Peer-estimated data for girls (n = 1025) and boys (n = 1069) for three age groups from Finland, Israel, Italy, and Poland. SOURCE: From Österman, K., Bjorkqvist, K., Lagerspetz, Kirsti M.J.; Kaukiainen, A., Landau, S. F., Fraczek, A., Caprara, G. V. (1998). Cross-cultural evidence of female indirect aggression. *Aggressive Behavior, 24,* 1–8. Reprinted by permission.

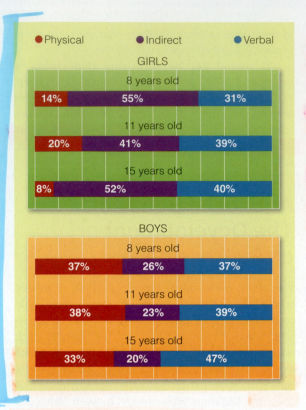

● Physical   ● Indirect   ● Verbal

GIRLS

8 years old
14% | 55% | 31%

11 years old
20% | 41% | 39%

15 years old
8% | 52% | 40%

BOYS

8 years old
37% | 26% | 37%

11 years old
38% | 23% | 39%

15 years old
33% | 20% | 47%

aggression than of prosocial behaviors. For instance, some researchers view aggression as a behavioral technique for obtaining resources, and thus as a normal and functional part of life (Campbell, 2005; Pellegrini & Archer, 2005), which can sometimes be adaptive to individuals and their friends, reflecting the "bright side to bad behavior" (Hawley, 2008; Hawley et al., 2007). Individuals can gain an advantage by aggressing against others, especially if the risk to one's self is low. Although we may typically think of aggression negatively, individuals who use it successfully will be at an advantage (in a Darwinian sense) relative to individuals who do not use aggression, or who use it unsuccessfully. Individuals who fight back against an aggressor would also be at an advantage relative to individuals who "roll over" and become hapless victims of aggression. In fact, we saw in our discussion of social dominance that high-status children often use aggression in combination with prosocial behaviors (Hawley, 1999, 2008). When most psychologists look at aggression, however, they rarely see it as a positive approach to a problem. Rather, aggression is seen as generally maladaptive (see Smith, 2007), especially now in our history when the tools of violence are no longer fists, sticks, and stones but assault rifles, nerve gas, and nuclear missiles.

Aggression is universal, found in varying degrees in all human cultures and within the behavioral repertoire of every healthy individual. Yet aggression is not an inevitable response to any particular stimulus; social pressures determine, to a substantial degree, the conditions under which an aggressive response is appropriate or not. Thus, the question of whether aggression is innate or learned is not a useful one. As human beings, we are all capable of acting aggressively, but as members of a culture, we are all subject to societal pressures that influence when, how, and to what extent we will behave aggressively.

The Development of Aggression

Aggression is not limited to any one age group. Moreover, the nature of aggression tends to change with age, making it difficult to compare levels of aggression between younger and older children. Nor is aggression limited to one sex. Boys are, however, on average, more aggressive than girls at every age, beginning in toddlerhood (Baillargeon et al., 2007; Dodge, Coie, & Lynam, 2006).

Aggression comes in various forms. Perhaps the most obvious is *physical aggression*, including hitting, pushing, punching, and kicking. *Verbal aggression* includes yelling or name-calling. **Indirect aggression** (also referred to as *social* or *relational aggression*) has been defined as "a noxious behavior in which the target person is attacked not physically or directly through verbal intimidation but in a more circuitous way, through social manipulation" (Kaukiainen et al., 1999, p. 83). Indirect aggression can involve shunning other children and spreading rumors, among other strategies aimed at impairing peer relationships (see Crick & Grotpeter, 1995).

Sex differences are often found in aggressive expression, with boys typically showing higher levels of physical aggression than girls, and girls displaying higher levels of relational, or indirect, aggression than boys. This is illustrated in the results of a survey of 8-, 11-, and 15-year-old children from Finland, Italy, and Poland (see Figure 14.5). As can be seen, girls at all ages engaged in greater levels of indirect aggression than boys, with boys engaging in more physical aggression than girls (Österman et al., 1998). However, note that about 25% of the aggression displayed by boys at each age was indirect, and between 8% and 20% of girls' aggression was physical, meaning that neither type of aggression is the sole purview of one sex or the other. In fact, many studies report that boys engage in just as much relational aggression as girls, with the main sex difference being that boys engage in substantially more physical aggression than girls (see Card et al., 2008).

indirect aggression Type of aggression in which the target person is attacked not physically or directly through verbal intimidation but in a more circuitous way, through social manipulation.

Although boys engage in more physical aggression than girls at all ages, girls engage in substantial levels of indirect, or relational, aggression, ridiculing or harming the reputation of other girls.

Although males are generally considered to be more aggressive than females, female indirect aggression has been getting increased attention lately, both by psychological researchers and the society at large. This is reflected by several movies depicting relational aggression in teenage girls. This excerpt from the 2004 movie *Mean Girls* sums up much of the plot of the movie and reflects adolescent indirect aggression at its best (or worst):

Janis: [to the female student body] Okay, yeah. I've got an apology. So, I have this friend who is a new student this year. And I convinced her that it would be fun to mess up Regina George's life. So I had her pretend to be friends with Regina, and then she would come to my house after and we would just laugh about all the dumb stuff Regina said. And we gave her these candy bar things that would make her gain weight, and then we turned her best friends against her. And then . . . Oh yeah, Cady— you know my friend Cady? She made out with her boyfriend, and we convinced him to break up with her. Oh, God, and we gave her foot cream instead of face wash. (http://www.imdb.com/title/tt0377092 /quotes)

Although it may seem counterintuitive, overall levels of aggression tend to *decrease* over childhood for both boys and girls (see Dodge et al., 2006). We say counterintuitive because most people see the aggression of older children, often expressed in bullying (see Box 14.2), as more problematic and hurtful to others than the aggression displayed by younger children. Although this may be the case, preschoolers in particular use aggression to deal with other children, although such aggression rarely has the negative consequences that the aggression used by older and stronger children does.

How early is peer aggression displayed? Physical aggression has been observed between infants 1 year of age and younger (Hay, Nash, & Pedersen, 1983). When talking about infants, aggression involves pushing, hitting, or forcefully taking something away from another child. This may bring tears to the eyes of the victim, but it rarely involves the more serious physical harm that is seen in the aggressive interactions of older children. Levels of aggression are higher at 24 and 36 months (Alink et al., 2006) and generally decrease from about 2 to 5 years (Cummings, Iannotti, & Zahn-Waxler, 1989). The earliest peer aggression usually occurs in disputes over objects, particularly toys. In fact, a fair amount of the interaction between toddlers is conflictual (up to 50%), though not aggressive, per se (Dodge et al., 2006).

The general decline in levels of aggression over the preschool years is seen in a longitudinal study by Mark Cummings and his colleagues (1989). They observed pairs of 2-year-old children playing at home and recorded the incidence of (a) bodily aggression (hitting, kicking, pushing, or biting the other child), (b) object-related aggression (attempting to take away an object the other child had), (c) initiations of aggression (starting an aggressive bout), and (d) average duration of an aggressive

BOX 14.2 child development in the real world

Bullying

During late childhood and early adolescence, aggression is frequently expressed by **bullying** (Espelage, Holt, & Poteat, 2010; Rigby, 2002; Salmivalli & Peets, 2009). Bullying involves persistent and repeated cases of aggression committed by a more powerful individual over a less powerful one (Olweus, 1993). Bullying can be physical, involving shoving, tripping, and hitting, or it can be indirect, or relational, involving hurting feelings or exclusion from a social group, sometimes referred to as *emotional violence*.

Bullies constitute about 10% of the elementary school population in most industrialized countries (Boulton & Underwood, 1992, in the UK; Olweus, 1993, in Scandinavia; Pellegrini & Bartini, 2000, in the U.S.). Bullying usually decreases over the elementary school years and often increases again in early adolescence as children move from primary to middle school; it tends to drop again in later adolescence (Berger, 2007; Pellegrini & Bartini, 2000).

Nearly all children are bullied at one time or another, but a sizeable minority of children have been classified as *victims*—the persistent targets of bullies. Although the rates vary from study to study, approximately 10% of children identify themselves as repeated targets of bullies (or are identified by teachers or other children as victims). This means not only that children get picked on occasionally, but they are likely to be targets of bullies over the course of at least several months, sometimes years (see Rigby, 2002). Girls and boys are equally likely to be targets of bullies (Veenstra et al., 2007), although the type of harassment each receives tends to differ. Boys are usually bullied by other boys and are more apt to be physically attacked. Girls are more apt to be bullied by other girls in the form of indirect, or relational, aggression. For example, when girls bully other girls, they are less likely to hit or kick them but more likely to call them names or exclude them from social activities. Girls do get hit occasionally, usually by other girls, but sometimes by boys who bully both same- and opposite-sex children (see Rigby, 2002).

Percentage of Students between the Ages of 8 and 11 Years Indicating That If They Bullied Someone It Would Be for Specified Reasons		
Reason	Boys	Girls
Because they annoyed me	68.2	60.7
To get even	64.0	46.0
For fun	16.0	10.0
Because others were doing it	14.0	13.3
Because they were wimps	11.3	7.0
To show how tough one is	11.3	7.0
To get things or money from them	6.1	4.2

*N*s range from 1535 to 1770.

SOURCE: Rigby, F. (2002). Bullying in childhood. In P. K. Smith & C. H. Hart (Eds.) *Blackwell handbook of childhood social development* (pp. 549–568). Blackwell: Oxford, UK.

Who are the victims and what effect does being bullied have on them? Not all children are equally likely to be bullied. Children whose attachment style to their mothers is described as anxious/resistant are more likely to be victims than children whose attachment style is described as avoidant (who tend to be bullies) or as secure (who tend to be neither victims or bullies) (Ireland & Power, 2004). Victims tend to be physically weak children who have few friends (Hodges & Perry, 1999; Pellegrini & Bartini, 2000). Indeed, the lack of friends makes victims especially vulnerable to bullying. Somewhat ironically, some victimized children are highly aggressive themselves. Such children often use aggression ineffectively; they have been referred to as **provocative victims**, because their aggressive behavior irritates other children and provokes victimization from others (Hodges, Malone, & Perry, 1997; Olweus, 1995).

Bullying in school can make a child's life miserable and have serious consequences for children's psychological well-being. For instance, compared to nonvictimized children, targets of bullies are more likely to have low self-esteem, sleeping problems, headaches, bed wetting, antisocial behavior, experience loneliness, and show signs of stress and depression (Boulton & Smith, 1994; Ladd, Kochenderfer, & Coleman, 1997;

see Rigby, 2002). Some of these effects are observed as early as 5 to 7 years of age (Snyder et al., 2003). At the extreme, persistent bullying can lead to suicide or homicide. As the popular press had noted, Columbine killers Eric Harris and Dylan Klebold were repeated victims of bullies.

Why do children bully? What excuses do children who bully give for their behavior? Ken Rigby (2002) reports the results of a survey from more than 1,500 8- and 11-year-old children from Australia who were asked about their reasons for bullying another child. These data are shown in the above table. As you can see, most children, both boys and girls, said that if they bullied someone it would be because the victim annoyed them. This is consistent with the findings that victims tend to be weaker children with few or no friends. Their lack of friendship may reflect relatively poor social skills, thus making them annoying in the eyes of the bully. But we want to be careful here and not blame the victim. Bullies may be looking for reasons to pick on easy marks who are not likely to fight back and who have few friends to come to their assistance. (A sizeable percentage also stated that they would bully other children "because they were wimps," an indication that they are taking into consideration the probability that their victims will not fight back.) Getting even with a

---

bullying The persistent and repeated cases of aggression committed by a more powerful individual over a less powerful one. This phenomenon is common in schools around the world.

child for a past offense was also selected by a high percentage of boys (especially) and girls, with bullying "for fun" receiving 16% and 10% nominations for boys and girls, respectively.

How can parents deal with bullying in schools? James Garbarino and Ellen deLara, in their 2003 book, *And Words Can Hurt Forever: How to Protect Adolescents from Bullying, Harassment, and Emotional Violence*, provide some suggestions for how parents who have children being bullied in school can help them cope, and these are summarized in the accompanying table. Schools are not helpless in combating bullying, and should not, for example, act as if bullying is an inevitable part of childhood. Successful programs have been implemented to reduce bullying. Such programs include a warm, positive involvement from adults both in school and at home, monitoring of students' activities in and out of school, and firm limits on unacceptable behavior. Also, when rules are broken, nonhostile, nonphysical punishments are used (Olweus, 1995).

Although bullying has been most thoroughly studied in school settings, a new venue for bullying has recently been identified: the Internet. **Cyber bullying** refers to verbal harassment that occurs online. It can take the form of threatening e-mails, instant messages, or text messages to cell phones. Cyber bullying also includes "borrowing" someone's screen name and pretending to be that person while online and forwarding private messages, pictures, or videos to others. For example, a 14-year-old Florida girl gave her MySpace password to a friend who, after a falling out occurred between the girls, changed the website (and the password), making sexually explicit statements on the website and seeking many new friends, which resulted in unwanted attention and humiliation for the girl. Police eventually closed the website, and legal charges are pending (*Palm Beach Post*, June 8, 2008).

According to I-Safe America, Inc., www.isafe.org/imgs/pdf/education/CyberBullying.pdf), 42% of fourth- to eighth-grade stu-

dents surveyed claimed to have experienced cyber bullying, while 53% admitted to having said mean or hurtful things to others online. Interestingly, children who are cyber bullies are more likely to be bullies in school, and similarly, children who are victims of cyber bullying are often victims of bullying at school (Raskauskas & Stoltz, 2007). Children can more easily escape cyber bullying than in-person bullying. They do not have to turn on the computer or read disturbing and threatening messages. But today's teens and preteens are well connected (see Chapter 13), making it almost as difficult for some children to avoid cyber bulling as it is to avoid bullying on the playground or in the school hallways.

Dealing with Bullying Is Difficult for Children and Parents

James Garbarino and Ellen deLara provide the following advice to parents concerning how to deal with bullies in the schools:

1. *Accept the fact that there is at least some degree of bullying, harassment, and emotional violence in your teenager's school.*

2. *Come together with your parenting partner.* This includes a spouse, stepparent, domestic partner, and anyone else who is willing to be your partner for the sake of your child's well-being.

3. *Sit down and talk to your child.* Learn how the school works. If you have a chance, talk to your child's friends as well.

4. *Form a community team with other parents and youth.* Get involved with the PTA or PTO, have discussions with other parents and involve your faith community.

5. *Make sure your team is really a team.* A team functions as a cooperative group. Not everyone sees the world in the same way, and many people minimize the psychological significance of bullying.

6. *With your team in place, talk to your school administrators.* You may start with a teacher you know, but also talk with the principal, assistant principal, and superintendent. Learn how the school views bullying and emotional violence.

7. *Find out about programs the school has to deal with school violence.* How successful have they been?

8. *Know the law.* All schools are subject to the Safe and Drug Free Schools initiative, mandating that American schools do everything in their power to provide a safe environment.

9. *Exercise your right to contact your school board president and members of the board.* Elected school board members should be happy to hear your concerns about the safety and climate of the school, and be persistent, remembering that systems are resistant to change.

10. *Regroup with your team to share information to see where the specific problems are for your child and in the school itself.*

11. *Formulate plans for change.* Make plans for dealing with the problem at the individual level (for example, talking to your child about new ways to deal with problems at school) and at the organizational level (for example, talking to school officials about creating a safer school environment).

SOURCE: Adapted from Garbarino, J., & deLara , E. (2003). *And words can hurt forever: How to protect adolescents from bullying, harassment, and emotional violence.* Free Press: New York, pp. 13–15.

provocative victims Victims of bullies who are highly aggressive themselves.

cyber bullying Verbal harassment that occurs online and is common for children who spend time on the Internet.

table 14.4 Average Number of Aggressive Incidents per Hour and Average Duration of Aggressive Bouts at Ages 2 and 5

Aggressive Measure	Age 2	Age 5
Bodily aggression	3.00	1.74
Object-related aggression	6.02	4.92
Initiation of aggression	6.98	3.78
Duration (in seconds)	14.11	7.60

SOURCE: Adapted from "Aggression between peers in early childhood: Individual continuity and developmental change," by E. M. Cummings, R. J. Iannotti, and C. Zahn-Waxler, *Child Development* (1989), *60*, 887–895. Copyright: The Society for Research in Child Development, Inc. Reprinted by permission.

episode. They watched the same children 3 years later, at age 5, in a similar situation. Table 14.4 summarizes the findings of this study. Five-year-old children were less likely to initiate or engage in aggression, and aggressive bouts were of shorter duration, compared to these same children at age 2. The incidence of physical aggression continues to decline over childhood into adolescence (Cairns et al., 1989; NICHD Early Child Care Research Network, 2004).

Although physical aggression is substantially lower in adolescence than in childhood, the consequences of adolescent aggression can be especially serious. The disagreements and quarrels of young children often lead to tears; they do not usually lead to bodily injury, which is a more common occurrence in adolescence. For example, arrests for violent crimes and assaults increase sharply between the ages of 10 and 19 years (Cairns & Cairns, 1986).

There is evidence that individual differences in aggression are relatively stable; that is, children who rate high on aggression compared to their peers at one age are likely to retain their high rank when aggression is measured at a later age. For example, Cummings and his associates (1989) reported substantial stability for aggression between ages 2 and 5, especially for boys. Other researchers (Cairns et al., 1989) reported relatively high stability of teacher ratings of aggression for both boys and girls between the fourth and ninth grades, and another study found that children described as highly aggressive at 13 and 15 years of age were more likely to be involved in criminal and antisocial activities at age 24 (Olweus, 1987). In general, serious aggression is more likely to be displayed by adults and adolescents who were highly aggressive as children (see Broidy et al., 2003).

When looking at the most serious form of aggression, the rates of both being a victim or perpetrator of homicide are highest during adolescence and young adulthood, with levels of homicide being substantially greater for males than for females. (Of course, one does not need to be aggressive to be a victim of homicide, but highly aggressive individuals seem to put themselves in situations that increase their chances of being murdered.) This phenomenon has been found in all cultures and time periods studied (Daly & Wilson, 1988). Figure 14.6 presents the homicide victimization rate by age for Whites and African Americans in the United States between 1995 and 1997, separately for males and females (National Center for Health Statistics, United States, 1999). As can be seen, males are more likely than females to be the victims of homicide, with rates peaking between 15 and 24 years of age and decreasing thereafter. Also, the rates for African Americans are substantially higher than for Whites. The likelihood of *committing* a homicide follows a nearly identical pattern (see Daly & Wilson, 1988).

How can this **young-male syndrome** be explained? We discussed in Chapter 12 Robert Triver's (1972) parental investment theory, which proposed that males, who in humans are the less-investing sex, compete among themselves for access to females. The rates of homicide are highest during the ages when males are most likely to be in the mating market. Deaths among adolescent males and young men sometimes occur over fights for resources, insults to one's reputation, or arguments over females. Despite the societal penalties and presumed stupidity of much of this behavior in contemporary culture, human males have inherited a psychology that was adapted to different conditions in which risky competition, on average, resulted in increased inclusive fitness (see discussion of adolescent risk behavior in Chapter 11).

Using aggression to obtain resources, to enhance one's status, and to impress females is apt to be greatest when resources are limited, life expectancy is low, and competition is thus heightened. Under such conditions, males can be expected to engage in heightened levels of violence against other males. The age pattern for African American males shown in Figure 14.6 is similar to that of Whites, but the absolute rate is higher, associated with reduced access to educational and economic opportunities for many inner-city African Americans in comparison to Whites. Such behaviors are not programmed or inevitable, but they are shaped by experience and are more likely to be expressed in some social environments than others.

Factors That Influence Aggression

The acceptability of aggression varies considerably among cultures. Some groups reward aggressive behavior and encourage children to "stand up for themselves"; others view aggression as a serious transgression, with children being encouraged to cooperate and handle their differences in nonaggressive ways (Eibl-Eibesfeldt, 1989). Childhood aggression is generally frowned upon by most parents in modern societies, in part because it is not viewed as adaptive. Society, in the form of police and the legal system, has gradually taken over the responsibilities of protection that once belonged to individuals and families. Most parents thus expect children to suppress their aggressive impulses, because, in a culture of law and order, official agencies are supposed to act on their behalf (Besag, 1989). Some children and adults live in subcultures where law and order do not prevail, making aggression, at least in the short run, an adaptive response to some situations.

Aggression, as any social behavior, is influenced by many factors, including genetics, hormones, temperament, family, peers, and in the developed world at least, the visual media, especially television.

Genetics

Genes are involved in all behavior, including aggression. Behavioral genetic studies examine the degree to which people who share genes show similar patterns of aggression (see Chapter 3). If monozygotic twins are more similar in their levels or types of aggression than regular siblings, and siblings are more alike than unrelated people, then one can assume that the genes people share play a role in regulating aggression. As we will see, a genetic explanation does not mean that environment is not also important.

Antisocial behavior, including aggression, has been investigated in more than 100 behavioral genetic studies from a wide range of countries and using a variety of measures (see Dodge et al., 2006; Rhee & Wildman, 2002). Summarizing the results from 42 samples of twins and 10 samples of adopted siblings, Soo Hyun Rhee and Irwin Wildman (2002) reported that approximately 41% of individual differences in levels of aggression could be accounted for by genetic effects, 16% by shared environmental influences (basically, children growing up in the same home), and 43% by nonshared environmental influences (experiences unique to each individual). Perhaps not surprisingly, these findings indicate that aggression and antisocial behavior cannot be simply explained; levels of aggression show both moderate genetic and environmental effects.

Even when we know that specific genes influence aggressive or antisocial behavior, one must always consider the role of the environment in the expression of that behavior. Recall from Chapter 3 the work of Avshalom Caspi and his colleagues (2002), who examined antisocial behavior in a group of boys as a function of the quality of their home environment and their level of the enzyme monoamine oxidase A (*MAOA*). *MAOA* has been definitively linked to aggression in animals and antisocial behavior in humans and is associated with genes on the X chromosome. Caspi et al. reported the expected relationship between levels of *MAOA* and antisocial behavior, but only for boys who were reared in abusive homes. There was no relationship between *MAOA* levels and antisocial behavior for boys raised in supportive homes (see also Foley et al., 2004). In other words, knowing that specific genes underlie behavior is not enough to predict outcomes. Genes are expressed in environments, and different environments can result in very different behavioral patterns.

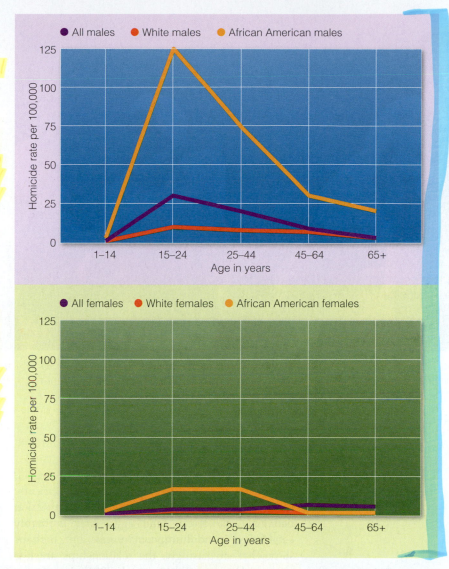

FIGURE 14.6 Homicide victimization rates per 100,000 resident population by age and sex in the United States, 1995–1997, presented separately for White and African Americans.

SOURCE: Adapted from data from National Center for Health Statistics, 1999, pp. 189–191.

Temperament can have an indirect effect on children's aggression. Highly active children can tire their mothers, who engage in more permissive parenting, which in turn leads to elevated levels of aggression in the children.

© Catchlight Visual Services/Alamy

in life (Rothbart & Hwang, 2005). In other research, fearlessness and stimulation seeking at age 3 predicted aggression at age 11 (Raine et al., 1998), and ratings of impulsivity in kindergarten boys correlated with delinquency at age 13 (Tremblay et al., 1994). Similarly, children, especially boys, with poor self-regulation abilities, including difficulties with inhibiting inappropriate behaviors, have been found to display greater levels of antisocial behaviors (Lynam & Henry, 2001).

Dan Olweus (1980) assessed the effects of early temperament (general activity level, intensity of temperament from calm to hot-tempered), along with environmental factors (mother's negativism, mother's permissiveness, mother's and father's use of punitive discipline methods) on peer ratings of aggressiveness in sixth- and ninth-grade Swedish boys. He found that the best predictors of children's aggression were mothers' negativism and permissiveness, although children's temperaments also had a significant, though slightly smaller, direct effect on aggression; of greater significance, however, was the *indirect* effect that early temperament had on aggression. According to Olweus, an impetuous and active boy may tire his mother, causing her to become more permissive, which then leads to increased aggression in the child. Similarly, the punitive and hostile responses of many parents of aggressive children may stem, in part, from the antisocial behavior of their children, particularly in parents who lack coping skills (Patterson, 1986). This is exactly the type of relationship one would expect to find following the developmental contextual models described in Chapter 2. Characteristics of the children interact with characteristics of the parents to produce a pattern of development that cannot be explained by looking solely at the child or at the environment, but only by looking at their ongoing transaction (see Sameroff, 2009).

Hormonal Influences

It would likely not surprise anyone that aggression has been linked to sex hormones, specifically the male hormone testosterone. The connection between testosterone and aggression is firmly established in nonhuman mammals, but, perhaps somewhat surprisingly, the relationships are less clear in humans (Dodge et al. 2006). In a meta-analysis, researchers reported moderate but significant correlations between testosterone levels and aggression in both males and females (Book, Starzyk, & Quinsey, 2001). What is interesting from our perspective is that the magnitude of the correlations was greater for younger participants: .21 for people 13 to 20 years old, .18 for people 21 to 35 years old, and .10 for people older than 35. In addition to hormones, individual differences in the neurotransmitter serotonin have also been implicated in childhood aggression and antisocial behavior (van Goozen et al., 2007).

serotonin

Temperamental Influences

Do the temperaments of some children predispose them to be aggressive? Are some children naturally more aggressive than others? We discussed temperament in Chapter 11 and noted that some personality dispositions are present early in life, remain relatively stable, and are associated with different behavioral outcomes. For example, children who are more extraverted as infants are apt to show more anger/frustration and aggression later

Family Influences

The family is a potent influence on a child's aggressive behavior. Many aggressive children come from homes where parents practice aggression themselves (McCord, 1979; Patterson, 1986). For example, children with physically abusive parents are more aggressive than children with nonabusive parents, both at home and in school (Dodge et al, 2008; Trickett & Kuczynski, 1986). In one study, parents from abusive and nonabusive families recorded incidents of their children's misbehavior and their responses to those incidents (Trickett & Kuczynski, 1986). Children from abusive homes committed more aggressive acts than did children from nonabusive homes, and their parents' responses generally took the form of physical punishment, regardless of the nature of the misbehavior. Parents from nonabusive families were more likely to use reasoning and simple commands to handle their children's misbehavior. The effects of parental maltreatment on aggression differ somewhat for boys and girls, with maltreated boys showing elevated levels of physical aggression, whereas maltreated girls display heightened levels of relational aggression (Cullerton-Sen et al., 2008).

Parents of aggressive children often do not set clear limits for their children's behavior and are ineffective at stopping their children's aggression when it occurs (Olweus, 1980; Patterson & Stouthamer-Loeber, 1984). These parents may nag, threaten, and scold, but they rarely follow through on their ultimatums (Patterson, 1986). Paradoxically, such permissiveness often results in children who are out of control and parents who resort to physical punishment. As David Perry and his colleagues stated (1990, p. 139): "Parents who are ineffective at nipping deviant behavior in the bud sometimes find themselves becoming more and more exasperated as their child's deviant behavior escalates. They may suddenly explode with anger and assault the child."

Gerald Patterson proposed a theory of aggressive development centered around family interaction style (Patterson, 1980, 1986). Patterson sees the parents of aggressive children as having many deficiencies in parenting skills, including feelings of hostility toward their children, permissive and inconsistent discipline, and a failure to monitor the behavior and whereabouts of their children. Patterson proposed that much aggression in children is an attempt to "turn off" the threats and aversive stimulation coming from parents or siblings. Not all of the aversive stimulation is serious. Some of the bothersome irritants include parents' lack of attention, expressions of disapproval, or teasing. All children experience such irritations growing up in families, but when the home atmosphere lacks warmth and security, these minor irritants can be the source of major disruptions. Aggression in these contexts sometimes works, with aggressive children getting their way, thus reinforcing the use of aggression as a way to solve problems.

What can parents do to reduce levels of aggression in their children? To some extent, the answer is to get control over their own lives. Parents who are overly stressed, especially when having to deal with a rambunctious child, tend to let their children get out of hand and then sometimes snap, resorting to harsh physical punishment, which only exacerbates the situation. Although children with different temperaments will respond differently to parents' attempts to control their behavior, the best advice continues to be to practice a warm, authoritative parenting style, where rules are clear and enforced, and communication with the child is open.

Peer Influences

Most aggression in childhood is directed at other children. As noted earlier, children often use aggression or the threat of aggression to establish dominance hierarchies. Once a dominance hierarchy is established, there is less aggression among members of the group. When a conflict does occur, children use body and facial gestures as signs of dominance or submission; these gestures serve as signals to let others know what would likely happen if the conflict came to blows, thus settling the conflict without the need for actual fighting (Strayer & Strayer, 1976; Zivin, 1977).

Aggressive children at all ages are usually not as popular as their less-aggressive peers (Kupersmidt, & Dodge, 2004; Perry, Perry, & Rasmussen, 1986). As mentioned earlier, many rejected children are also highly aggressive (Coie & Koeppl, 1990); however, not all aggressive children are rejected. In one study, aggressive fourth- and seventh-graders were found to be less popular overall than their less-aggressive peers, but they were no more apt to be rejected than nonaggressive children (Cairns et al., 1988). Aggressive children were involved in social networks and were often listed by their peers as "best friends." The catch is that aggressive children tend to be friends with other aggressive children, who maintain and possibly increase their aggressiveness (Patterson, 1986). However, we also noted earlier that many popular children are rated by their teachers or peers as aggressive. Such children use aggression to help or defend friends. They often reconcile after aggressive bouts, and aggression is just one tactic in their social toolbox. They are also likely to use prosocial/cooperative behaviors in their interactions with peers (Hawley, 2003, 2007). Aggression, then, should be seen as one set of behaviors used in combination with other behaviors to achieve social goals and in forming and maintaining social relationships.

Social Information Processing and Aggression

Aggression is rarely a reflexive act. Rather, like most aspects of social interaction, children must evaluate a situation and decide how to behave. Kenneth Dodge and his colleagues (Crick & Dodge, 1994; Dodge, 1986; Dodge et al., 1986) formulated *social information-processing theory* to explain the development of social behavior, including aggression. (We discussed some of Dodge's ideas with respect to low-status children earlier in this chapter.) Just as children must encode, categorize, evaluate, and retrieve information to solve intellectual problems, so too must they go through the various stages of information processing to solve social problems. The more skillfully social information is processed,

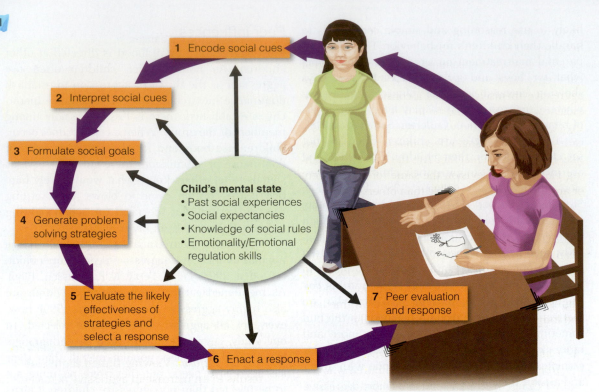

FIGURE 14.7 Dodge's social information processing model.

SOURCE: Adapted from Dodge, K. A., Pettit, G. S., McClaskey, C. L., & Brown, M. M. (1986). Social competence in children. *Monographs of the Society for Research in Child Development, 51* (Serial No. 213).

1 Encode social cues

2 Interpret social cues

3 Formulate social goals

4 Generate problem-solving strategies

Child's mental state
- Past social experiences
- Social expectancies
- Knowledge of social rules
- Emotionality/Emotional regulation skills

5 Evaluate the likely effectiveness of strategies and select a response

7 Peer evaluation and response

6 Enact a response

the more socially competent a child will be. Dodge's social information-processing model is graphically presented in Figure 14.7.

Many aggressive children show distinct patterns of social information processing (see Crick & Dodge, 1996; Dodge et al., 2006). For instance, highly aggressive children are more attentive to potentially aggressive cues (Gouze, 1987)—phase 1 in the model presented in Figure 14.7—and less likely to recall relevant social cues from a videotape than are less-aggressive children (Dodge et al., 1995). Highly aggressive children are also more likely to interpret an ambiguous situation (for example, a peer spills water on you) as having an aggressive, rather than accidental, intent (Graham & Hudley, 1994) than are less-aggressive children, which is phase 2 in the model. This **hostile attributional bias** results in children responding aggressively to perceived threats and insults. This causes parents, teachers, and peers to dislike them, reinforcing aggressive children's view that they are unpopular and that others treat them badly, exaggerating the cycle of aggressive behavior in such children.

Aggressive children also tend to have different goals than nonaggressive children (phase 3 in the model). For instance, aggressive behavior has been linked to present-oriented (as opposed to future-oriented) goals and to performance-competitive (as opposed to social-relational) goals (see Dodge et al., 2006). Aggressive children tend to generate

more atypical and socially inappropriate responses than less-aggressive children do (phase 4, see Coie & Dodge, 1998) and have a difficult time inhibiting their aggressive responses (Perry, Perry, & Rasmussen, 1986). Aggressive children perceive aggressive responses as socially appropriate and normative (phase 5; Guerra, Huesmann, & Hanish, 1995), believe that they can engage in aggression relatively easily (Perry et al., 1986), and increasingly value the rewards that aggression brings (Menon et al., 2007).

How children think about social situations will influence how they behave in social situations. Although we have focused on aggression here, individual and developmental differences in social information processing are important components in any type of social behavior, prosocial and antisocial. Examinations of how children think about social situations, including the goals they wish to achieve and the strategies they have available to achieve those goals, can help us understand and possibly change the social behavior of children.

The Influence of Visual Media

We discussed the influence of visual media on children's lives in Chapter 13, focusing on new means of communication among children and teens, sexual socialization, and conducting identity experiments. However, the media topic most investigated by social scientists is violence. Since the 1960s, researchers, social policy makers, and the public at large have been concerned about the possible relationship between violence in the visual media

hostile attributional bias The tendency for highly aggressive children to interpret an ambiguous situation as having an aggressive, rather than accidental, intent.

(mainly television) and aggression (Comstock & Scharrer, 2007).

The research questions are basic ones. Will children who watch violence on TV become more aggressive themselves? Does a constant diet of TV violence desensitize children to real pain and suffering? Or might viewing violence on television have a cathartic, or cleansing, effect, making children *less* likely to aggress in real life? Are the effects of watching violence on television the same for all children, or are some more susceptible than others?

In analyzing more than 40 years of research—including correlational, experimental, laboratory, field, and longitudinal studies—the results are relatively straightforward. Craig Anderson and his colleagues (2003, p. 81) concluded that exposure to violence in the media "increases the likelihood of aggressive and violent behavior in both immediate and long-term contexts." More specifically:

1. *Children can and do learn aggressive behavior from watching it on television.* Children who watch aggressive TV tend to be *more* aggressive (not less) immediately afterward than children who do not watch such programming. For example, in early laboratory studies in which preschoolers watched as people displayed novel aggressive behaviors (for instance, kicking and punching an adult-size inflated plastic clown), children imitated the behaviors when given an opportunity (Bandura, Ross, & Ross, 1963; Bandura & Walters, 1963).

2. *Children who watch more aggressive television at home are, on average, more aggressive than children who watch less aggressive television at home* (Hearold, 1986). Moreover, the amount of aggressive television children watch predicts their level of aggression as adults (Huesmann, 1986; Huesmann et al., 2003; Lefkowitz et al., 1972). For example, in one study, the amount of aggressive television boys watched in the third grade predicted the amount of aggressive behavior they displayed at age 19 (Lefkowitz et al., 1972). Even more dramatic is the follow-up to this study done when the participants were age 30 (Huesmann, 1986). As can be seen in Figure 14.8, the amount of aggressive television boys watched at 8 years of age clearly predicted criminal behavior at 30, with children who watched more hours of aggressive television being involved in more serious crimes. These findings led L. Rowell Huesmann (1986, pp. 129–130) to conclude "if a child's observation of media violence promotes learning of aggressive habits, it can have harmful lifelong consequences. Consistent with this theory, early television habits are in fact correlated with criminality."

3. *The effects of aggressive television on children are not uniform.* Viewing filmed aggression results in an increase in aggressive behavior only for some children, primarily those who are more aggressive than average to begin with. In an early study by Lynette Friedrich and Aletha Stein (1973), preschool children who were shown aggressive TV shows (such as "Batman" and "Superman") became more aggressive in the classroom. But the increase in aggression was found only for those children who were rated high in aggression before watching the shows; viewing aggressive TV shows had no noticeable effect on children who were initially rated low in aggression. Similar findings were reported for groups of male adolescent delinquents living in minimum-security institutions (Parke et al., 1977). Boys who viewed aggressive films showed more general and verbal aggression than did those who viewed neutral films, but, again, the effects were most pronounced for those boys who were initially high in aggression.

Other research has shown that 5- to 7-year-old boys are more apt than girls to increase their aggressive behaviors after watching an aggressive cartoon program (Boyatzis et al., 1995), and more recent research has shown that preschool boys (but not girls) who watched violent made-for-children television programs displayed more antisocial behavior 5 years later than children whose television diet consisted of less-violent programs (Christakis & Zimmerman, 2007).

What can we conclude, then, about the effect of television violence on children's behavior? First, most researchers would agree there is a causal relationship: viewing aggressive film produces aggressive behavior in children. However, most would

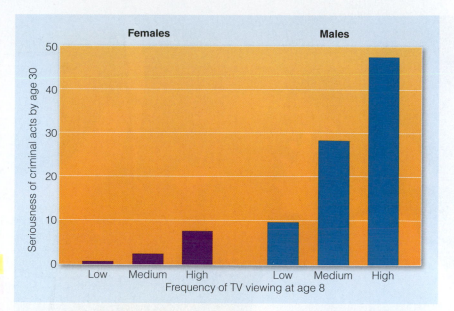

Females **Males**

Seriousness of criminal acts by age 30

Frequency of TV viewing at age 8

Low Medium High Low Medium High

FIGURE 14.8 Relationship between frequency of TV viewing at age 8 and seriousness of criminal convictions at age 30.

The more television that children watch, the more likely they are to commit serious crimes as adults. This effect is especially strong in males. SOURCE: From "Psychological processes promoting the relation between exposure to media violence and aggressive behavior by the viewer," by L. R. Huesmann. (1986) *Journal of Social Issues*, *42*, 125–139. Copyright: 1986 by Plenum Publishing Corporation. Reprinted by permission.

Many children play video games with violent content. Although fewer studies have been done on the effect of playing such games on aggression, what research has been done finds a positive relationship.

also agree that this effect is limited: aggressive television has its greatest influence on children who are highly aggressive to begin with. And even those who believe that aggressive television is generally harmful to children will acknowledge that television is only *one* of the many causes of aggression.

Much has changed since the early days of research on the relationships of children's viewing violence and their subsequent aggressive behavior. For one thing, there is more visual media than just television. Although children still spend more time watching television than interacting with other forms of visual media (Roberts et al., 2005), they also watch movies, videotapes, DVDs, and play video games, some with violent content (see a discussion of the role of this expanding media on children's behavior in Chapter 13). In fact, although many video games, particularly for younger children, have little or no violent content, many others contain military, fantasy, or crime-related scenarios in which killing one's opponents, often quite brutally, is the goal of the game. Research on the relationship between playing violent video games and children's aggression is relatively new, but two meta-analyses reported significant correlations between these variables (Anderson & Bushman, 2001; Sherry, 2001). The effects are small to moderate in magnitude and reflect only short-term relationships. Unlike the research on violent television and aggressive behavior, little is known about the long-term effects of playing violent video games and aggressive behavior.

A Social-Cognitive Framework for Relating to Others: The Case of Moral Development

Closely related to the development of prosocial and antisocial behavior is the development of morality. Morality and its development have long been the concerns of philosophers, politicians, religious leaders, and people involved with the socialization of children, dating back at least to the ancient Greeks. More recently, morality and moral development have attracted the attention of behavioral scientists (see Turiel, 2006). *Morality* is related to sets of beliefs or values and to how people behave in relation to those beliefs, specifically as these beliefs relate to our relationships and interactions with other people and social rules and conventions.

The very idea of morality only makes sense if people have intentions. Were actions taken on purpose, or was someone just a victim of circumstances? Did someone know what he or she was doing? Are they responsible for their actions? We do not hold infants, who lack a developed sense of self, morally responsible for their behavior. They do not have the knowledge that what they did was wrong, nor the ability to put themselves in someone else's shoes to appreciate how spilling chocolate milk on a new white carpet may make their mother feel. Similarly, we do not hold the male lion morally responsible for killing the cubs of a female lion, because the purpose of this action is to hasten her estrus cycle so she can bear *his* offspring. This is what animals have evolved to do, and without self- and other-awareness and theory of mind (see Chapter 7), they cannot be held morally accountable.

Not so for humans, but determining what is moral and what is not is hardly a trivial matter. Specific beliefs and behaviors vary among cultures, religions, and historical epochs. For instance, in some cultures it was once acceptable to stone a woman to death for the sin of adultery (men rarely suffered a similar fate for the same offense), something that is abhorrent to people in most cultures today. Even within modern societies there is great debate over what constitutes moral behavior. For example, the European Union has eliminated capital punishment, and most Europeans see the practice as a throwback to more primitive times. Americans, in contrast, are more likely to view the death penalty as morally appropriate.

Because values change with historical time and vary among cultures, it is impossible to identify a universal set of moral values or behaviors and chart their development. These problems have been bypassed somewhat by studying children's moral reasoning—how children at different ages respond to moral dilemmas. The particular answer a person gives to any moral dilemma is not important; rather, the sophistication of how people reason about the decisions they make is what defines the developmental stage of moral development. Jean Piaget (1965/1932) was the first to investigate moral reasoning in detail; his work was extended by Lawrence Kohlberg (1969, 1984) and more recently by a large group of developmental psychologists (see Damon, 1988; Turiel, 2006).

Piaget's Theory of Moral Reasoning

Consider the following two stories from Piaget (1965, p. 122):

> A little boy who is called John is in the room. He is called to dinner. He goes into the dining room. But behind the door there is a chair, and on the chair there was a tray with fifteen cups on it. John couldn't have known that there was all this behind the door. He goes in, the door knocks against the tray, bang go the fifteen cups and they all get broken.

> Once there was a little boy whose name was Henry. One day when his mother was out he tried to get some jam out of the cupboard. He climbed up into a chair and stretched out his arm. But the jam was too high up and he couldn't reach it and have any. But while he was trying to get it he knocked over a cup. The cup fell down and broke.

Piaget gave these and other stories to children of different ages and asked them who was naughtier—John who broke 15 cups by accident, or Henry, who broke one cup while sneaking some jam from the cupboard. Not surprisingly, children about 10 years of age and older said that Henry was naughtier. After all, the only reason the cup broke was that he was doing something he was not supposed to be doing. John, in contrast, was a victim of circumstance. He was doing exactly what his mother told him, and he could not have known that the tray of cups was behind the door. But ask a younger child and the answer is often very different. John is naughtier than Henry because he broke 15 cups and Henry broke only one. Yes, they admit, John did not know the cups were behind the door, and yes, Henry was doing something that he was not supposed to be doing, but these young children cannot ignore the magnitude of the crimes. Fifteen cups are smashed to smithereens because of John's actions. Intention means little to the young child; the greater the damage, the naughtier the behavior.

Based on this research, Piaget proposed three basic stages of moral reasoning: (1) the premoral stage (approximate ages, 2 to 5 years), (2) the stage of moral realism (approximate ages, 6 to 10 years), and (3) the stage of moral relativism (approximate ages, 10 to 12 years and beyond).

During the **premoral stage**, children are generally unaware of rules as being cooperative agreements. When playing games, they make up their own rules and think that the point of the game is to play and not necessarily to win. For example, when 5-year-old Madison watched older children in the family play Monopoly®, she thought the aim of the game was to move the pieces around the board and give money and hotels to everyone. Although she could count the spots on the dice and move accordingly, she did not know the rest of the rules and did not seem to care when the others tried to teach them to her.

The stage of **moral realism** begins about age 5 or 6. Children now understand that families and societies must live by rules. To these children, the rules—whether for games of marbles (a favorite topic for Piaget, if not for today's children), traffic laws, or classroom behavior—are absolute, passed on by some high authority figure (for instance, God, the police, one's parents), and *all* violations of them are wrong. Piaget referred to this as **heteronomous morality** (or **moral absolutism**) ("heteronomous" refers to being under the rule of another). Speeding, for example, is wrong in all circumstances, even on a trip to the emergency room. As in the stories of John and Henry, motivation is not considered. Although these children seem to grasp the idea of doing something "on purpose" versus "by accident," they do not consider intentionality when evaluating right or wrong. Children in this stage also believe in **immanent justice**: good deeds will be rewarded and misdeeds will be punished. Thus, if something bad happens to a person, that person presumably deserved it. (Many adults in both traditional and technological cultures hold on to this belief.)

---

moral reasoning How people at different ages respond to moral dilemmas.

premoral stage In Piaget's theory of moral development, the stage at which children are unaware of rules as cooperative agreements.

moral realism In Piaget's theory of moral development, children's rigid understanding of moral principles that are seen in terms of an "objective" assessment of a behavior's consequence (for example, number of cups broken), regardless of any other contextual and personal considerations (for example, if cups were broken accidentally or intentionally).

heteronomous morality (*moral absolutism*) In Piaget's theory of moral development, the stage in which children, typically 5- to 10-year-olds, think that what is moral is what adults and other authorities say is moral. Moral rules are seen in a rigid way, as unchangeable, and not as a result of a social agreement or consensus.

immanent justice The belief that good deeds will be rewarded and misdeeds will be punished.

In the stage of **moral relativism**, or **autonomous morality**, beginning about age 10 or 11, children come to realize that social rules are arbitrary agreements among people that can be modified through social discussion. The Monopoly® rules can be changed if everyone agrees to play by house rules. Social laws can be challenged and even modified or overthrown. For children in this stage, rule breakers are judged not only by their behavior but also by their motivations. The person who is racing down the road to get his daughter to the emergency room is no longer considered a wrongdoer.

According to Piaget, morality develops through interactions with peers more so than through interactions with adults. Concepts of sharing, reciprocity, cooperation, and fair play are more apt to develop in interactions among equals. When children interact with peers, they are more likely to take their perspectives than when they interact with adults. They are also more likely to see themselves as responsible partners in social exchanges. Consistent with Piaget's approach, William Damon (1988) proposed that important aspects of morality are learned through play with peers. Children learn that not all social rules must be dictated by an authority figure, but some can be established through interactions among friends, realizing that social rules can be created via cooperation among equals.

Piaget's theory was influential in directing research on children's moral reasoning, and much subsequent research confirmed his ideas. However, as with other aspects of Piaget's theory, young children are often more competent than Piaget believed them to be. For example, research has shown that children in Piaget's moral realism stage, and even in his premoral stage, often do consider intentions when judging actions (Leslie, Knobe, & Cohen, 2006; Nobes & Pawson, 2009). And young children do not always view adults—even their parents—as absolute authority figures (Tisak, 1986). Yet, Piaget was the first to describe children's moral reasoning in terms of stages, and this approach was adopted by Lawrence Kohlberg, whose theory of moral development dominated research in the field for 30 years.

Kohlberg's Theory of Moral Development

Kohlberg (1969, 1984) continued Piaget's method of presenting children with moral dilemmas, such as the following:

> In Europe, a woman was near death from cancer. One drug might save her, a form of radium that a druggist in the same town recently discovered. The druggist was charging $2,000, ten times what the drug cost him to make. The sick woman's husband, Heinz, went to everyone he knew to borrow the money, but he could get together only about half of what it cost. He told the druggist that his wife was dying and asked him to sell the drug cheaper or let him pay later. But the druggist said no. The husband got desperate and broke into the man's store to steal the drug for his wife. Should the husband have done this? (Kohlberg, 1969, p. 379).

Kohlberg was not concerned with whether children viewed the action as right or wrong; rather, he was interested in how they reasoned about the action and the thinking behind their reasoning. Kohlberg developed a theory that sees moral reasoning as progressing through three levels, each containing two stages. It is not a stage theory in the strictest sense, because, although people progress from lower to higher stages as a function of cognitive development, once they attain the ability to reason at a higher level they do not always function at that level. Kohlberg's stages of moral development are summarized in Table 14.5.

Children at the level of **preconventional morality** conform to rules in order to gain rewards and avoid punishment. Moral reasoning is internalized as "good" actions are those that are rewarded, and "bad" actions are those that are punished. In stage 1, beginning usually during the preschool years, *getting caught* doing a misdeed is wrong—not the deed itself. Children at this stage think much like the moral realists of Piaget's theory: The

Similar to children in Piaget's stage of moral realism, children in Kohlberg's Stage 1 of preconventional morality believe that good actions are those that are rewarded, and bad actions are those that are punished. Stealing cookies isn't necessarily bad, but getting caught is.

Smith Collection/Getty Images

table 14.5 Kohlberg's Stages of Moral Development

Level/Stage	Description
Level 1 **Preconventional morality**	Obey rules to get rewards and avoid punishment; no internalized rules or standards, only consequences of one's actions
Stage 1 Orientation toward punishment and unquestioning deference to superior power	Obey rules to avoid punishment; morality defined only by physical consequences
Stage 2 Naive hedonism	Do good deeds for the reward they bring, immediate or future; fairness, reciprocity, sharing strictly pragmatic
Level 2 **Conventional morality**	Defer to rules imposed by legitimate authority (parental, religious, legal)
Stage 3 Good-boy/good-girl orientation	Behave to help or please others, win their approval; intention is important; golden rule
Stage 4 Orientation toward authority, fixed rules, and maintenance of the social order	Do one's duty, respect authority, maintain the existing social order; law-and-order stage
Level 3 **Postconventional morality**	Follow personal, internalized moral principles
Stage 5 Social-contract orientation	Rules and laws must be democratic, based on generally agreed-upon rights, open to challenge and change, morality underlying U.S. Constitution
Stage 6 Morality of individual principles and conscience	Ethical principles are self-chosen, abstract, universal

amount of punishment a person receives should be proportional to the amount of harm done; motivation or intention is not important, only the magnitude of the crime. In the case of Heinz and the drug, a stage 1 child is likely to say that Heinz should not steal the drug, because he would be breaking the law and would get caught. The drug is very expensive, making its theft a serious crime. During stage 2, children act in ways that will satisfy their needs; what is good is what brings good things to them. This is the morality of the marketplace: "You scratch my back and I'll scratch yours." Good deeds will likely pay off in the future, and this prospect of rewards justifies following rules or helping other people. During this stage, children take the intention of the actor into consideration when judging how right or wrong an action is. Looking again at the story of Heinz, a stage 2 child may say that he should not have stolen the drug because the druggist just wants to make money like everybody else.

At the second level, **conventional morality**, children (or adults) try to conform to rules imposed by some legitimate authority, such as parents, school officials, or the legal system. In stage 3, following a parent's wishes or the teacher's rules wins the child approval from these authorities. However, the others are mainly one's friends and relations.

A stage 3 person strives to be viewed as nice, seeking approval from significant people in his or her life (including peers). Stage 3 morality is expressed by the golden rule, found in one form or another in nearly all of the world's religions: do unto others as you would have them do unto you. A stage 3 reason for Heinz's stealing the drug might be that a loving husband cannot be blamed for trying to save his wife; in fact, he might be blamed if he did not try to save her.

In stage 4, people conform to rules and conventions to maintain social order. Social rules, such as "Thou shalt not steal," or "Buckle up—It's the law," are seen as dictated by legitimate authorities and worth preserving. Children consider the perspective of the generalized other; they care about what other people, particularly people in authority, might think. A stage 4 antitheft argument would hold that one must follow the law, regardless of circumstances.

moral relativism (*autonomous morality*) In Piaget's theory of moral development, children's realization that social rules are arbitrary agreements among people that can be modified through social discussion.

preconventional morality In Kohlberg's theory, the first level of moral development, in which children conform to rules to gain rewards and avoid punishment.

conventional morality The second level in Kohlberg's theory of moral development, in which people try to conform to rules imposed by some legitimate authority, such as parents, school officials, or the legal system.

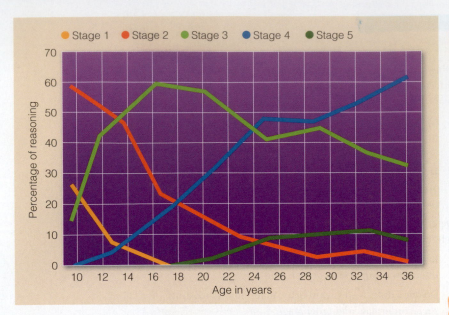

FIGURE 14.9 Changes in moral reasoning between 10 and 36 years of age by male participants.

Levels of moral reasoning progress from mostly preconventional at age 10 (Stage 2) to conventional (Stages 3 and 4) in adolescence and adulthood. Very few people provide moral reasoning at the postconventional levels (Stages 5 and 6) at any age. SOURCE: From Colby, A., Kohlberg, L., Gibbs, J., & Liberman, M. (1983). A longitudinal study of moral judgment. *Monographs of the Society for Research in Child Development, 48* (Nos. 1–2, Serial No. 200). Reprinted by permission.

It is only at the third level, **postconventional morality**, that individuals develop a set of principles that go beyond any external authority figure. This level is never seen before adolescence and is rarely used in adulthood. Postconventional morality reflects the internalization of a personal set of moral values. In stage 5, rules must be arrived at through a democratic process, and laws that are restrictive to members of society can be questioned and changed. This stage of moral reasoning is reflected in the United States Constitution. A stage 5 reason for Heinz's stealing the drug would be based on the recognition that this is a special condition; although it is against the law to steal, most people would recognize the uniqueness of the situation and believe that Heinz is justified in stealing the drug.

In stage 6, an individual defines right and wrong on the basis of self-chosen moral principles that are abstract and can be applied universally (for example, universal justice, individual rights). However, this stage is almost never realized by people in any society, and Kohlberg came to think of it as a hypothetical construct—an ideal level of moral reasoning one can aspire to, rather than one that people actually use. A stage 6 reason for stealing the drug would be that human life is above any law.

Kohlberg's theory is a considerable extension over Piaget's. Piaget's final stage, moral relativism, is achieved by most children around 10 to 12 years of age, implying that an adult's moral reasoning is no more sophisticated than that of a 12-year-old. Kohlberg's theory addresses in more detail the moral reasoning of adolescents and adults. According to Kohlberg, most adolescent moral reasoning is at stage 3, and reasoning at stages 5 and 6 is virtually nonexistent until early adulthood, if at all (Colby et al., 1983). Figure 14.9 presents the results of a 20-year longitudinal study of the stages of moral reasoning by age (Colby et al., 1983). As you can see, at age 10 preconventional reasoning (stage 2) prevails, with conventional reasoning (stages 3 and 4) increasing steadily over adolescence and into adulthood. Postconventional moral reasoning (stages 5 and 6) never exceeds greater than 10% of participants' justifications at any age.

Cultural and Sex Differences in Moral Reasoning

As noted, stage 6 moral reasoning is more of an ideal than a reality. Also, stage 5 is typically reached only by educated people in developed societies, and as you can see from Figure 14.9, not many of them. In fact, there is a substantial relationship between adults' levels of moral reasoning and years of formal education (Colby et al., 1983; Rest & Thoma, 1985). People from small, traditional communities rarely achieve moral reasoning beyond stage 3 (Kohlberg, 1969). This suggests that the social and political values of Western civilization play a significant role in determining one's adult level of moral reasoning, at least as defined by Kohlberg. Kohlberg proposed that the thinking skills of people from societies with little formal schooling are limited to concrete operational abilities (in Piaget's theory, see Chapters 2 and 6), and that postconventional reasoning depends on formal operations that are achieved through formal education in adolescence for people growing up in developed societies. Other interpretations are possible, however. For example, the small, tight-knit social groups typical of traditional societies function on the basis of interpersonal relationships, making stage 3 reasoning (loyalty to friends, following the golden rule) a highly adaptive form of morality in those societies. People in traditional societies are not less moral than people in developed societies, but the structure of their culture does not require the more abstract cognitive abilities associated with societies in the developed world. Nonetheless, Kohlberg insisted that basic moral values and their development were universal, and more contemporary research has generally supported this belief (Gibbs et al., 2007; Snarey, 1985).

Some early studies reported sex differences in moral reasoning, with males typically peaking at stage 4 and females at stage 3 (Haan, Langer, & Kohlberg, 1976; Holstein, 1976). In response to these findings, Carol Gilligan (1977, 1982) suggested that women are reared to be attentive to interpersonal

postconventional morality In Kohlberg's theory, the third level of moral development, in which individuals develop a set of principles that go beyond any authority figure.

relationships and to care for other people, whereas men are brought up to consider moral dilemmas as unavoidable conflicts that social rules and institutions are designed to resolve. Gilligan argued that moral reasoning follows different criteria for women and men: a morality of caring versus a morality of abstract justice.

Gilligan's theory highlights the male bias in Kohlberg's approach (that is, that females were not as moral as males). However, subsequent research found little evidence of sex differences in moral reasoning (Walker, 1986, 1991). In a review of 80 studies of moral development, only 22 reported sex differences, with about half of them showing higher levels in males and half in females (Walker, 1991). A more recent meta-analysis (Jaffee & Hyde, 2000) reported that females were somewhat more likely than males to display a care orientation and males slightly more likely than females to display a justice orientation in their moral judgments, consistent with Gilligan's theory. However, the absolute differences between the sexes were small and did not offer strong support of women's predominant use of a care orientation and men of a justice orientation in their moral reasoning.

Despite the lack of strong research support for Gilligan's positions, her work redefined what constitutes an adequate description of moral development. According to Mary Brabeck (1983, p. 289), "When Gilligan's and Kohlberg's theories are taken together, the moral person is seen as one whose moral choices reflect reasoned and deliberate judgments that ensure justice be accorded each person, while maintaining a passionate concern for the well-being and care of each individual."

The Development of Moral Behavior

Piaget's and Kohlberg's theories emphasize how children learn to think about moral issues—about the development of moral reasoning. However, we know only too well that people who are quite capable of high levels of moral reasoning do not always behave morally. This is readily seen in the behavior of high-profile politicians whose transgressions—be they inappropriate sexual dalliances, misleading the public, or padding their own pockets with taxpayers' money—make front-page news. Children are no different. In this section we examine the relationship between moral reasoning and moral (and immoral) behavior, as well as the development of several moral behaviors: lying, cheating, and judgments about distributing resources fairly (or unfairly).

© Jim West/Alamy

Some studies show a relationship between moral reasoning and moral behavior. However, not all studies find these relationships, and when they do, the associations are usually small.

The Relationship between Moral Reasoning and Moral Behavior

In a review of 75 studies, Augusto Blasi (1980) reported that 76% of the studies found a significant relationship between moral reasoning and behavior. In one interesting seminaturalistic study, researchers evaluated the moral reasoning of college students who joined a campus free-speech and human-rights demonstration during the 1960s (Haan, Smith, & Block, 1968). They found that protesters showed generally higher levels of moral reasoning on Kohlberg's scale than did nonprotesting students.

At first look, these findings would seem to indicate a strong relationship between moral reasoning and moral behavior, but that is not always the case. For example, in most of the studies reviewed by Blasi, the significant relationships between moral reasoning and behavior were only moderate. And the college protesters in the study by Haan et al. did not all display postconventional (stages 5 and 6) moral reasoning; some, in fact, were clearly preconventional (stages 1 and 2), expressing rebellious motivations for protesting rather than the higher moral principles of postconventional students. More recent research continues to show the often inconsistent relationship between moral reasoning and moral behavior, with some studies finding relationships (see

Gibbs, 2006) and others not (see Krebs & Denton, 2005). Thus, it seems that moral reasoning does influence moral behavior, but the relationship is not clear-cut. Many factors determine the moral stance a person will take in any situation, and moral reasoning ability is only one of them.

Lying and Cheating

In a classic study by Hugh Hartshorne and Mark May (1928–1930), more than 10,000 children, ages 8 to 16 years, were observed in situations where they were tempted to lie, cheat, and steal. The most remarkable finding of this study was that there seemed to be no general trait for honesty, lying, and/or cheating. Children who were honest in one situation would lie or cheat in another. In other words, moral behavior was situationally specific: Whether children would lie, cheat, or steal depended on the situation and not on the individual's overall level of moral character. In a more recent survey of more than 29,000 high-school students, 30% admitted stealing something from a store within the last year, 42% admitted lying to save money, and 23% said they stole something from a parent or relative. Yet, 97% of these same students said that it was important to be a person of good character, and 77% said, "When it comes to doing what is right, I am better than most people I know" (Josephson Institute, 2008).

Most research on honesty in the past decade or so has focused on lying in preschoolers and young school-age children. In a typical situation, children are shown an attractive toy and asked not to touch it while the experimenter is out of the room. Under such conditions, most young children cannot resist the temptation and touch the toy (Polak & Harris, 1999; Talwar, Gordon, & Lee, 2007). This should not be surprising, for as we saw in Chapter 11 in our discussion of self-regulated behavior, the basic cognitive abilities underlying self-regulation are slow to develop (see also a discussion of executive function in Chapter 8). Perhaps more pertinent to our discussion of antisocial behavior is what do children do when asked about a possible transgression, or what do they do when confronted with a misdeed. What most young children do in such situations is lie, although usually not very effectively. In one study using this "don't-touch-the-toy" paradigm, most 3- to 7-year-old children touched the toy and were later asked about it. Do children become more honest with age? Apparently not in these situations. Whereas about half of the 3-year-olds later lied about their actions, almost all of the 4- to 7-year-old children lied (Talwar & Lee, 2002). Although most preschoolers will tell lies to avoid being caught misbehaving, they judge lying to be wrong and truth-telling to be the "right thing to do" (see Lee, 2000).

Children can seemingly tell the difference between truth and lies as young as 3 years of age.

For example, in one study, 3-, 4-, and 5-year-old children were told a story in which a bear prepares a snack for his friend. While the bear is not looking, a cockroach walks across the snack. The bear's friend then enters and asks the bear if the snack is okay to eat. The bear says yes. Children are then asked whether this was a mistake or did the bear tell a lie (Siegal & Peterson, 1998). Overall, 76% of children accurately identified that the bear made a mistake and did not tell a lie. In a "lie" condition, in which the bear saw the cockroach walk across the snack, 77% of children correctly identified the action of the bear as a lie. There were no significant differences in the accuracy of children's judgments as a function of age, indicating that by age 3, children can differentiate between a mistake and a lie.

Can children detect when someone is lying, or do they know how people supposedly behave when they lie? Research from a variety of cultures has demonstrated what is called the *Deceiver Stereotype*, in which liars are believed to have lags in their speech, to fidget, smile inappropriately, and break eye contact and look downward (The Global Deception Research Team, 2006). However, as it turns out, people are not very good at judging when someone is lying, in part because most people know these stereotypes, and they consciously avoid these behaviors when telling a lie. (And when they do engage in these behaviors, they are not necessarily lying.) When do children learn the Deceiver Stereotype? In one study, both 6- and 9-year-old children believed that people who avert their eyes while speaking are more likely to be telling a lie than people not averting their eyes, with this effect being stronger in the 9-year-olds and in girls relative to boys of both ages (Einav & Hood, 2008).

Other research suggests that this ability develops a little later. For instance, in another study, 7- to 15-year-old children were asked to answer some questions truthfully and others untruthfully, and they were also asked what they knew about where people usually look when they are telling the truth and when they are lying. Eleven-, 13-, and 15-year-old children knew the Deceiver Stereotype and said that people maintain eye gaze when they are telling the truth and avert their gaze downward when they lie. As a result, when instructed to provide a convincing lie, they maintained eye gaze. In contrast, 7- and 9-year-old children believed that people look up when telling the truth, and as a result they averted their eye gaze upward when lying (McCarthy & Lee, 2009). Although the research findings are somewhat contradictory, it seems that children do not understand the Deceiver Stereotype with respect to eye gaze and behave accordingly until late childhood or early adolescence.

Telling effective lies is not easy. First of all, it requires a certain level of self-regulation, or executive function (see Chapter 11 for discussion of self-regulation with respect to emotional control and Chapter 8 for discussion of the development of executive function). For example, children must be able to inhibit saying the first thing that comes into their minds, which may be the truth ("I did it. I broke the lamp") and generate an alternative answer ("The cat did it"). Second, successful lying requires deliberately creating a false belief in another person. This involves what has been called theory of mind, which we discussed in some detail in Chapter 7. With respect to lying, children must understand that other people can have knowledge that is different from their own ("Mom doesn't know how the lamp got broken") and that the decisions people make are based on what they know and what they want. Theory of mind requires children to take the perspective of another and then to modify their behavior based on what the other person wants and knows ("Julie wants to play with the toy but doesn't know where it is") and on their own wants and knowledge ("I want to play with the toy, I know where it is, and I'm not telling her"). Both executive function and theory of mind develop over the preschool years into the early school years and correspond to a time when children improve their ability at telling lies (Talwar & Lee, 2002; 2008). Children begin telling lies around 3 years of age, but their limited self-regulation and perspective-taking abilities makes them ineffective liars. Their ability to tell effective lies ("I didn't peek behind the screen, and I don't know what the 'special toy' looks like—really") increases with age and is related to their improved executive function and theory-of-mind skills (Talwar & Lee, 2008).

Although even preschool children can tell the difference between the truth and lies and believe that lying is generally wrong, judging the morality of lies can sometimes be tricky. When truthful information would hurt someone's feelings, children often believe that lying is acceptable (Bussey, 1999). And what if a lie helps many people, even if it has some negative consequences for an individual? How one judges these types of lies seems to depend on the culture in which one grows up. For instance, Genyue Fu and his colleagues (2007) presented 7-, 9-, and 11-year-old Chinese and Canadian children situations in which the protagonist in a story told a lie that helped or hurt either themselves, a friend, or a group, such as a school class or a basketball team. Children were asked what they would do (tell the truth or a lie) or to evaluate the person in the story who told the truth or lied.

Chinese children, who come from a society where group solidarity is emphasized, were more likely to lie to benefit the group and evaluated lying that benefited the group less negatively than lying that benefited the individual. Canadian children, who come from a more individualistic society, responded

Chinese children, who grow up in a collectivist culture, are more likely to view lying that benefits the group as appropriate (or at least not as inappropriate) than lying that benefits themselves or a friend. Western children, growing up in individualistic cultures, respond just the opposite.

oppositely. They were more likely to lie to benefit themselves or a friend and evaluated such lying less negatively than lying that benefited the group. In other research, 7-, 9-, and 11-year-old Chinese children were more likely to say that lying was okay (or at least not as bad) if it was for the good of the group (their school class) than for the good of the individual, with this effect increasing with age (Fu et al., 2008).

The likely source of these cultural differences can be found in Chinese and Canadian schools. Beginning in elementary school, Chinese children become members of various formal groups, are evaluated in terms of their contribution to group success, and must collaborate with other children in their group to achieve both personal and collective goals. Canadian children, much like their counterparts in the United States, experience substantially less systematic and long-term groupings in school. Loyalty to a school class is not emphasized, and children are more likely to be encouraged to assert their rights and to present themselves in a positive and forthright way. One consequence of these differing school and cultural values is how children evaluate lying.

All people lie, sometimes to protect others' feelings (so-called white lies) but often to protect themselves. Honesty is valued in all cultures, and children learn early that lying is wrong, although this tends not to stop them from lying when the situation calls

Preschoolers and young schoolage children have a sense of fairness when it comes to distributing some commodity, at least when they have the smaller share. They're apt to think an unequal distribution is fair if they have the larger portion.

uted, are quite self-serving in their decision-making. They typically want as much as they can get, almost regardless of what other children get or how much they deserve (Damon, 1994; Lane & Coon, 1972). For example, in one study, pairs of 3- to 5-year-old children were given either two or four stickers and asked a series of questions. Did they realize how many stickers they versus the other child had? Was this distribution fair? If not, what should be done about it? Even the youngest children recognized the unfairness of the distribution when *they* had received the smaller amount. In contrast, children of all ages were generally pleased when they had the larger number of stickers and judged the distribution as fair (LoBue et al., 2010).

By 5 years of age, children are more apt make equal distributions of resources, although children do not make decisions about the distribution of rewards based on the relative contributions of different members for several years (Huntsman, 1984). In an interesting study of how children distribute rewards as a function of the effort children put into a project, Mordecai Nisan (1984) had first- and fifth-grade children from an Israeli kibbutz and from a city perform a task (for example, coloring in stars). They were told that an unseen child in the next room was doing a similar task. In one condition, children were told that they and their counterpart were working "as a group." After coloring in a certain number of stars, the experimenter stopped the child and went to the next room to collect the paper of the other child. The target child colored either more stars than the hypothetical child in the next room (15 versus 5) or fewer stars (5 versus 15). The experimenter told the child that he or she would get 20 pieces of gum to distribute between the two of them, one piece of gum for each star colored, and that the child should distribute the gum as he or she saw fit.

What is interesting was that the kibbutz children were more apt to distribute the rewards equally (10 to each child), whereas children from the city were more likely to distribute the rewards on the basis of the amount of effort children expended on the task (that is, equitably). This is consistent with the emphasis on group solidarity in an Israeli kibbutz, indicating a significant role of socialization in judgments of fairness. Also interesting are differences in how the older city and kibbutz children judged the effort that the unseen child in the next room was putting into the task. City children inferred amount of effort as a function of output (for example, how many stars were colored), whereas kibbutz children were more likely to assume that the children in the next room were working as hard as they themselves were, even if they produced less.

We can summarize research findings on children's sense of fairness quickly. Even children 3 and

for it. Lying is also a consummate social-cognitive skill. Effective lies require executive function skills and theory of mind—knowing what other people know and how they think. These skills develop over childhood, as does children's sense of honesty.

How can parents promote truth-telling in their children? Basically, by doing the same things they do to promote other forms of prosocial behavior and conscience development. Children should be told the value of truth-telling using authoritative-style parenting practices. Parents should also model truth-telling. Children who are told that it is wrong to lie but watch their parent, for example, return a garment he or she wore once to a big party and tell the sales clerk that it was never worn, or it just doesn't fit, are getting mixed messages, and they are more likely to follow what their parents do rather than what they say.

Distributing Resources Fairly (or Unfairly)

Social animals need some way of determining whether resources are being distributed fairly. Are some people getting more than they deserve and others getting less? What, exactly, is a *fair* distribution of resources? From a strictly selfish perspective, the more one gets the better. Fairness implies that people get what they deserve, even if that means that the individual gets less than he or she could have gotten.

When do children develop a concept of fairness? Most research suggests that children much younger than 5 have little sense of fairness. Most 4-year-olds, when presented either with hypothetical or real situations in which some valued resource (for example, cookies or stickers) is to be distrib-

4 years of age seem to have some sense of fairness, at least when they are getting the lesser of a deal. This sense of fairness is intuitive (Haidt, 2001) and can rarely be verbalized. When given opportunities to distribute resources, younger children generally keep more for themselves than do older children, although many children have some sense of equal sharing by the age of 5. With age and experience, children are increasingly likely to see fairness in terms of equitable distributions (that is, rewards according to effort expended), and such attitudes are likely a reflection of socialization, as they vary depending on a child's rearing environment. Young children's fair distribution of resources, such as candy, is also related to theory of mind. In one study, preschool children who passed false-belief tasks, indicative of belief-desire reasoning, were more apt to make fair distributions of candies between themselves and a peer than were children who failed such tasks (Takagishi et al., 2010).

Is fairness limited to humans? There is at least one study in the primate literature suggesting that monkeys may have some appreciation of when they are not being treated fairly. Sarah Brosnan and Franz de Waal (2003) had pairs of female capuchin monkeys exchange small rocks for food rewards. Monkeys happily exchanged rocks for slices of cucumbers until they observed another monkey receiving more desirable grapes for their efforts. Under these conditions, some monkeys stopped performing the task, and others continued to trade rocks for cucumber but refused to eat the slices. Basically, much like young children, the monkeys responded negatively when they thought another monkey was getting a better deal. We cannot state that the motivation behind the monkeys' behavior was one of social injustice—perhaps they were simply unhappy receiving a cucumber when they knew a delicious grape was available—but these findings suggest that the roots of evaluating fairness in some social contexts lie deep in our evolutionary history.

Developing a Conscience

Moral reasoning reflects how a person *thinks* about moral dilemmas; in contrast, moral behavior, such as helping or comforting, reflects a person's actions. However, as we have seen, moral thought is not always expressed as moral behavior, and the motivations for moral behavior may not always be what they seem. Many people conceptualize morality as the internalization of values, specifically a sense of right or wrong, or what is more commonly called **conscience**. For Freud, conscience was reflected by the superego, or the ethical component of personality. One's conscience regulates one's behavior to be consistent with internalized values, rules, and norms.

Grazyna Kochanska (1993, 1994) has conceptualized conscience development in terms of self-regulation. According to Kochanska (1993, p. 325–326), conscience develops as a result of "the gradual developmental shift from external to internal regulation that results in the child's ability to conform to societal standards of conduct and to restrain antisocial or destructive impulses, even in the absence of surveillance." From this perspective, the development of conscience represents a special case of the development of self-regulations, discussed previously in Chapter 11.

Conscience is more than the development of self-regulation but also entails the internalization of societal norms and values and an emotional discomfort when one violates such values. Feelings of guilt can result when one behaves in a way that goes against accepted societal values, even though no one else was aware of the infraction. Having a conscience implies that one will (likely) maintain social rules even though no immediate external authority enforces such rules.

Kochanska and her colleagues propose that conscience develops as a result of bidirectional relationships between mothers and their children. Children's temperaments, for example, influence the likelihood that they will transgress against social (in this case, maternal) rules: Impulsive children find it more difficult to control their behavior and as a result find it more difficult to internalize social values than do less-impulsive children. Different styles of parental socialization may thus work differently with different children (Kochanska, 1997). For example, whereas explaining the importance of some social rules and reasoning with children may be an effective means of developing conscience in most children, this approach may be less effective with impulsive youngsters.

Kochanska and her colleagues (2004) reported that maternal parenting style is an important predictor of children's conscience development. For example, children who were classified as securely attached in the Strange Situation at 14 months (see Chapter 12) and who had mothers who were responsive to their children and used gentle discipline were more likely to internalize their mothers' values and generally accept their parents' attempts at socialization at 56 months than children with less-supportive mothers. Kochanska et al. (2004, pp. 1237, 1238) state, "An adaptive parenting style—warm, sensitive, and avoiding power assertion—remains a necessary factor for an effective promotion of self-regulated conduct and other aspects of moral internalization."

For many people, morality is strictly a function of culture. However, as we have seen throughout

© Bob Daemmrich/PhotoEdit

Parenting style is important in the development of conscience, although children with different temperaments may respond differently to parents' attempts to instill values. For instance, impulsive children may find it more difficult than less-impulsive children to internalize social values.

conscience The internalization of values, specifically a sense of right or wrong.

BOX 14.3 **big questions**

Did Humans Evolve to Be Moral?

Marc Hauser (2006) proposed that human's moral sense is akin to language: People have an innate *moral grammar*, similar to the universal grammar that linguist Noam Chomsky proposed for language (see Chapter 9). All biologically typical children acquire language, although the specific language they learn to speak is strictly a function of their environment. Similarly, Hauser claims that all biologically typical children will acquire an understanding of right and wrong, although the particular moral code they acquire will depend on the society in which they grow up. Hauser's proposal is that humans possess a moral sense of judging right and wrong that is unique in the animal world (although glimpses of some aspects of human-type morality can be found in primates), and, moreover, such thinking is not merely a reflection of humans' general intellectual abilities but is specific to the moral arena.

On what basis does Hauser make these claims? Hauser proposes that people's sense of morality is based on the evolution and subsequent development of social cognition. Hauser recognizes the importance of empathy and other emotions in moral judgments. For example, late in the second year of life, children display envy and embarrassment, and often by 2 years of age they experience guilt, shame, and pride (see Chapter 11). These secondary, or social, emotions have also been described as moral emotions, in that children are evaluating their own behavior in terms of some internal or external standard (see Bloom, 2004).

In addition, however, Hauser proposes that humans judge the *intention* of an action: Did Alison purposefully not say 'hi' to me, or did she just not see me? Is Jamal sincerely sorry for what he did, or is he just pretending to be? As children's abilities to read intentions, to empathize, and to take the perspective of others increase (along with the ability to regulate their emotions), children's moral compass becomes more like that of people in their community.

Hauser is not saying that children are born knowing right from wrong. What children enter the world with, claims Hauser, is a set of moral guidelines (a moral grammar) that, in interaction with their developing social-cognitive abilities and social environment, results in their acquiring (or at least being able to recognize) right from wrong as defined in their culture. According to Hauser (2006, p. 165), "we are born with abstract rules or principles, with nurture entering the picture to set the parameters and guide us toward the acquisition of particular moral systems."

The social-cognitive roots of morality can be seen developing in the first year of life. For example, beginning about 9 months of age, infants begin to display *shared attention*, which refers to two people both attending to the same thing or event and sharing that experience (see an in-depth discussion of shared attention in Chapter 7). They apparently realize, at some level, that another person can have a different perspective from their own (Tomasello, 1999). Shortly after their first birthdays, babies are able to judge the *intentions* of another. For example, when 18-month-olds watch an adult perform some actions on objects, they will later imitate failed attempts (for example, the adult's hand slips and fails to remove the end of a dumbbell), but not seemingly accidental actions, indicating that they were aware of what the model *intended* to do (Meltzoff, 1995). Evaluations of the appropriateness (morality) of behavior, judgments of fairness, and judgments of right and wrong all seem to require the combination of intentionality, empathy, and perspective taking, all characteristics of human social cognition and each developing over infancy and childhood.

Jonathan Haidt (2001) similarly uses an analogy to language acquisition to describe moral development and proposed that a culture can emphasize three general forms of moral intuitions: (1) the *ethic of autonomy*, focusing on individual rights and freedoms; (2) the *ethic of community*, focusing on family, tribe, nation, and other groups of people; and (3) the *ethic of divinity*, focusing on spirituality (see Shweder et al., 1997). Similar to Hauser, Haidt proposes that children are prepared by evolution to develop moral intuitions in all three areas, but the degree to which they do is a function of their cultural experiences during childhood. Just as children are rarely taught how to speak, but acquire language from implicit exposure to others around them, so too are children rarely taught the specifics of right or wrong. Rather, from day-to-day experiences with parents, other adults, and peers, children come to adopt the values of their community and will later find it difficult to appreciate the competing values of other cultural groups.

Both Hauser and Haidt interpret the research findings as reflecting an innate moral grammar, with children developing moral codes much as they develop language. We see the evidence as consistent with the position that morality and moral development are by-products of human social cognition. We agree that morality and moral reasoning are not simply based on more general mechanisms of reasoning, as Piaget and Kohlberg seemed to have argued. However, neither do we believe that they can be separated from more general social-cognitive abilities. Moral feelings, behavior, and reasoning can be viewed as forms of social cognition. As *Homo sapiens* evolved social-cognitive skills for empathy, cooperation, and competition beyond that of their great ape cousins, it became almost inevitable that they would make evaluations of fairness, judge the intentions of others, and establish rules for proper social discourse. From this perspective, human morality is an outgrowth of human social cognition.

---

this text, nothing is solely a function of culture (or biology, or parents, or any single "cause"). In fact, several theorists have argued that morality has a biological and evolved basis (Bloom, 2004; Hinde, 1999; Krebs, 2008). Most such theories are based on considerations of humans' propensity for empathy and the other moral emotions (for example, embarrassment, envy, pride, shame), reciprocal altruism, and the necessity of competing and cooperating with other people over extended periods. In Box 14.3 we discuss briefly Marc Hauser's evolutionary theory of morality, as presented in his 2006 book *Moral Minds*, primarily because of his consideration of moral development.

According to **group socialization theory**, peers are the primary agents in children's socialization. Humans possess four evolutionary adaptations toward social life: (1) group affiliation and in-group favoritism; (2) fear of, and/or hostility toward, strangers; (3) within-group status seeking; and (4) the seeking and establishment of close dyadic relationships.

Interactions are social behaviors between individuals; **relationships** involve interactions that are affected by past and future interactions. The quality of peer relationships increases substantially during the early school years as children's cognitive abilities improve. Children's ideas of **friendship** change over time. Friendship in adolescence emphasizes greater self-disclosure and intimacy than in childhood, especially for girls.

During the school years, **peer groups** become increasingly important, and **dominance hierarchies** are established. **Cliques** are defined as small and relatively stable social groups that children join voluntarily, whereas **crowds** are larger groups of adolescents who share activities or have similar stereotype reputations (such as "jocks" or "druggies"). Based on peer ratings of **popularity** and social impact, children can be classified into one of five groups: **popular children, rejected children, neglected children, controversial children**, and **average-status children**. High-status children are socially more competent than low-status children, who have poor social information-processing abilities. Children's temperaments and parental characteristics are both related to social status. Research has demonstrated long-term effects of peer rejection.

The preference for same-sex playmates increases in school-age children, and gender serves as one basis for children's **in-group favoritism** and **out-group discrimination**. Children are more apt to conform to group pressure for positive group behavior than for misconduct. Dominance hierarchies reduce antagonisms within a group and focus division of labor.

Prosocial behaviors, such as comforting, sharing, and helping, increase with age. **Altruism** involves doing something for another at some cost to one's self. **Reciprocal altruism** explains how prosocial behaviors could have evolved by proposing that individuals will cooperate with those with whom they will interact in the future. Individual differences in prosocial behavior are related to differences in temperament, the extent to which parents foster prosocial behavior, and culture.

Antisocial behaviors refer to behaviors that are geared toward injuring others, either directly through aggression or indirectly through lying and cheating. **Aggression** is quite common among preschoolers but decreases from the early school

years into adolescence. **Instrumental aggression** is behavior aimed at acquiring some concrete goal or object, whereas **hostile aggression** refers to more personally oriented actions in which a child's intent is to hurt another child. The nature of aggressive behavior changes with age. There are various forms of aggression, including physical aggression, verbal aggression, and **indirect** (or relational) **aggression**. Boys generally engage in more physical aggression and girls generally engage in more indirect aggression. **Bullying** involves persistent and repeated cases of aggression committed by a more powerful individual over a less powerful one and is common in schools around the world. Some victims of bullies are highly aggressive themselves and have been called **provocative victims**. **Cyber bullying** refers to verbal harassment that occurs online and is common for children who spend time on the Internet. Adolescent and young-adult males sometimes engage in violent behavior, especially when living under conditions of economic hardship, referred to as the **young-male syndrome**. Aggression in children is influenced by genetics, hormones, a child's temperament, parenting style, peers, and deficits in social information processing. Aggressive children display a **hostile attributional bias**, in which they attribute hostile intentions to the actions of others. Watching violence on television has been found to increase aggression, primarily for children who were highly aggressive to begin with.

Morality and moral development have been investigated primarily through assessments of **moral reasoning**. Piaget proposed three stages of moral reasoning: (1) **premoral** (2 to 5 years); (2) **moral realism** (6 to 10 years), during which children believe in **heteronomous morality** (or **moral absolutism**), and **immanent justice**; and (3) **moral relativism**, or **autonomous morality** (10 years and older).

Kohlberg expanded on Piaget's theory, postulating three levels of moral reasoning—**preconventional**, **conventional**, and **postconventional**—with two stages at each level. The reasoning of most adolescents is at the conventional level, and people in nontechnological societies rarely reason in post-conventional ways. Gilligan proposed that moral reasoning differs between the sexes, although research suggests that sex differences in moral reasoning are inconsistent and small. Moral behavior is often contextually determined and is not highly correlated with levels of moral reasoning. Children can distinguish truth from lies early, and they believe that lying is generally wrong. Children's sense of fairness develops with age, with preschool children being more self-serving in their judgments than older children.

Children's development of **conscience** is influenced by characteristics of the child, including self-regulation, temperament, and parenting style. Some have proposed that humans have an innate moral grammar, similar to the universal grammar proposed for language.

Key Terms and Concepts

group socialization theory (p. 568)
interactions (p. 569)
relationships (p. 571)
friendships (p. 571)
peer groups (p. 573)
dominance hierarchies (p. 573)
cliques (p. 573)
crowds (p. 573)
popularity (p. 573)
popular children (p. 573)
rejected children (p. 573)
neglected children (p. 574)
controversial children (p. 574)
average-status children (p. 574)

in-group favoritism (p. 578)
out-group discrimination (p. 578)
prosocial behaviors (p. 584)
antisocial behaviors (p. 584)
altruism (p. 584)
reciprocal altruism (p. 585)
aggression (p. 589)
instrumental aggression (p. 589)
hostile aggression (p. 589)
indirect aggression (p. 590)
bullying (p. 593)
provocative victims (p. 593)
cyber bullying (p. 593)
young-male syndrome (p. 594)

hostile attributional bias (p. 598)
moral reasoning (p. 601)
premoral stage (p. 601)
moral realism (p. 601)
heteronomous morality (or moral
   absolutism) (p. 601)
immanent justice (p. 601)
moral relativism (p. 603)
autonomous morality (p. 603)
preconventional morality (p. 603)
conventional morality (p. 603)
postconventional morality (p. 604)
conscience (p. 609)

Ask Yourself . . .

1. What are the main tenets of Judith Harris's group socialization theory? How does her theory fit with an evolutionary perspective of social development?
2. What is the difference between peer interactions and relationships, and how does each develop during childhood and adolescence?
3. What function, if any, do dominance hierarchies serve in children's peer groups?
4. How can children's status within a peer group be measured? What are the different status categories children might belong to?
5. What are the main psychological differences between popular and unpopular, or rejected, children? What factors seem to contribute to children being popular or unpopular with their peers?

6. How is in-group favoritism and out-group discrimination expressed in children? How can cooperation and solidarity between children from different groups be promoted?
7. What are three prosocial behaviors that have been frequently studied in children, and how do they develop? How can they be promoted?
8. Are boys really more aggressive than girls? How is aggression expressed in boys and girls, and what factors contribute to aggressive behavior over childhood and adolescence?
9. How does moral reasoning develop, according to Piaget and Kohlberg? How does moral reasoning relate to moral behavior?
10. What is meant by conscience, and how can parents promote the development of conscience in their children?

Exercises: Going Further

1. Here you have the results of a sociogram. Children were asked to indicate, first, two children in their class they would like a lot to sit next to and, later, two children they would never like to sit next to. What would be the probable social status (popular, neglected, rejected, controversial, or average status) of each of these children, according to the table below, and what would that mean in practical terms?

Name	Acceptance Points	Rejection Points	Possible Status
John	13	0	
Mary	9	6	
Betty	0	0	
Peter	1	9	
Kimberly	5	2	
Marcus	2	2	
Jason	5	6	
Julie	1	1	
Lewis	0	7	
Frank	4	1	

2. Some directors of after-school programs are concerned about recent increases in bullying among children at their centers. They do not understand why some children can be so aggressive and mean, whereas others are not. What would you tell them, based on current evidence on the development of antisocial and prosocial behaviors, and what recommendations, if any, would you give them?

3. This is a question asked by a parent to a school psychologist at the annual parents' meeting: "When can we expect children to be responsible for their own behavior, and why? Are there differences among different types of behaviors, or are they all the same?" What would be your reply?

Suggested Readings

Classic Readings

Hinde, R. A. (1976). Interactions, relationships, and social structure. *Man,* *11,* 1–17. In this brief article, ethologist Robert Hinde presented his formulations for thinking about social relations in humans as well as other social species. Hinde's organization has been accepted by most contemporary researchers of children's peer relationships.

Kohlberg, L. (1969). Stage and sequence: The cognitive-developmental approach to socialization. In D. A. Goslin (Ed.), *Handbook of socialization theory and research.* **Chicago: Rand McNally**. Kohlberg introduced his theory of moral development in this chapter, including his methodology of presenting people with moral dilemmas and classifying their responses according to stages of moral development. Most research on moral development over the past 40 years has been based, directly or indirectly, on this seminal work.

Bandura, A., Ross, D., & Ross, S. A. (1963). Vicarious reinforcement and imitative learning. *Journal of Abnormal and Social Psychology, 67,* 601–607. This is the famous "bobo doll" study, in which children watched adults beat up an inflatable doll and then joyfully imitated the adults' specific aggressive behaviors. This study began a line of research examining the social learning of aggressive actions.

Scholarly Readings

Rubin, K. H., Bukowski, W. M., & Laursen, B. (Eds.) (2009). *Handbook of peer interactions, relationships, and groups.* **New York: Guilford**. This edited volume includes 33 chapters, written by the foremost leaders in the field. The chapters contain up-to-date reviews on nearly every issue investigated by developmental psychologists related to peer interactions and relationships over the last four decades.

Gibbs, J. C., Basinger, K. S., Grime, R. L., & Snarey, J. R. (2007). Moral judgment development across cultures: Revisiting Kohlberg's universality claim. *Developmental Review, 27,* 443–500. This article presents an updated review of moral judgment across different cultures and finds evidence for "common moral values, basic moral stage development, and related social perspective-taking across cultural groups."

Dodge, K. A., Coie, J. D., & Lynam, D. (2006). Aggression and antisocial behavior in youth. In W. Damon & R. M. Lerner (Gen. Eds.), *Handbook of Child Psychology* (6th ed.), N. Eisenberg (Vol. Ed.), Vol. 3, *Social, emotional, and personality development,* (pp. 719–788). New York: Wiley. Kenneth Dodge and his colleagues review the vast literature on the development of aggression and antisocial behavior and examine the many factors associated with aggression.

Tomasello, M. (2009). *Why we cooperate.* **Cambridge, MA: MIT Press**. In this short book, Michael Tomasello provides a concise and highly readable review of his group's research with both children and great apes, examining the evolution and development of cooperative behavior.

Readings for Personal Interest

Cohen, C. (2000). *Raise your child's Social IQ: Stepping stones to people skills for kids.* **Washington, DC: Advantage Books**. This book, by a director of social-skills training groups, provides parents with ways in which they can enhance their children's social skills, including hints to help children join a group, choose friends, notice what people around you are feeling, and how to handle anger.

Garbarino, J., & deLara, E. (2003). *And words can hurt forever: How to protect adolescents from bullying, harassment, and emotional violence.* **Free Press: New York**. This book describes the roles of the bully and victim in schools and provides parents, teachers, and children ways to deal with bullying.

Hauser, M. D. (2006). *Moral minds: How nature designed our universal sense of right and wrong.* **New York: HarperCollins**. In this book, Marc Hauser presents his theory about how humans' sense of right and wrong evolved and how it develops in children. Although controversial, it integrates work from human psychology, primatology, and philosophy to get a glimpse at our moral minds.

Underwood, M, (2003). *Social aggression among girls.* **Guilford: New York**. This easy-to-read book provides a systematic look at how girls from the preschool years through adolescence express anger and act aggressively.

CourseMate

Cengage Learning's **Psychology CourseMate** for this text brings course concepts to life with interactive learning, study, and exam preparation tools, including quizzes and flashcards for this chapter's Key Terms and Concepts (see the summary list on page 612). The site also provides an **eBook** version of the text with highlighting and note taking capabilities, as well as an extensive library of observational videos that span early childhood through adolescence. Many videos are accompanied by questions that will help you think critically about and deepen your understanding of the chapter topics addressed, especially as they pertain to core concepts. Log on and learn more at **www.cengagebrain.com**.

15

The Development of Sexuality and Gender Identity

The development of sexuality and gender identity are the focus of this chapter. We first look at some evolutionary issues, such as why sexual reproduction evolved in the first place, different reproductive strategies, and how sex differences in parental investment may have influenced the psychologies of men and women. We then examine the development of sexual behaviors, from the preschool years through adolescence, including a look at "falling in love." We next discuss the origins of sexual orientation, concluding that both biological and environmental factors in interaction must be considered. A brief discussion of gender differences follows, and we conclude the chapter looking at the development of gender identity and gender knowledge.

Sixth-grader Josh sat with his mother, holding the book about "the birds and the bees" she had given him. "So, do you have any questions?" his mother asked. Josh hesitated and said he thought he understood it pretty well, although it was really still a bit mysterious to him, but he was not about to talk to his mother about it. This book wasn't his first exposure to sex. He and his friends had been talking about it for some months now. They covered the topic in Health class, although that was mainly about boys' bodies and nothing about girls' bodies, and certainly nothing about how boys and girls, you know, "do it," or even what "it" was. One of his friends had an encyclopedia with a large section for the entry "coitus" including illustrations, which he and his friends pored over. Now every time he saw a couple with a child, he was reminded that the couple had to have had sex to make a baby. He looked at girls a bit differently too, and wondered if they were as curious and mystified as he was about it all.

Josh was at the beginning of his sex education. It would be a few more years before he kissed a girl, and even longer before he experienced coitus, but he knew he liked girls, had an idea of the basic male and female anatomy, and was nervously looking forward to learning more. Like Josh, boys and girls today become aware of their sexual nature as they approach puberty, and it is a topic, one way or another, that will greatly affect them for the rest of their lives.

Living beings are born, grow up, reproduce, and die. Once an organism is born, it must develop to adulthood and reproduce before death. Otherwise, the cycle of life for a particular individual (and for an individual's genes) comes to an end. It may seem all too obvious, but this means that surviving to adulthood and reproducing are the cornerstones of evolution and thus life itself. This is true not only for biology (literally, "the study of life") but also for psychology (literally "the study of the mind"). People must not only be *biologically* well adapted to survive and reproduce, but also *psychologically* well adapted. For most animals, reproduction is a social phenomenon, with male and female joining together to create a new individual. In humans, as well as other mammals, successful reproduction involves more than the joining of egg and sperm, but protracted gestation within the female and an extended period of dependency when the infant requires substantial care from its parents or other caretakers. This makes sex, and the behaviors, attitudes, and cognitions associated with it, of vital importance to human beings. And because we believe that everything develops, it makes the development of sexuality and the associated concept of gender identity of great interest and significance.

Sexuality refers to an individual's erotic thoughts and activities, whereas **gender identity** refers to a person's sense of self as a male or a female. According to John Money (1986), gender identity consists of three factors: (1) *morphological gender*, the body one has; (2) *personal gender*, the concept of oneself as a male or female; and (3) *sexual (or erotic) orientation*, which gender one is sexually attracted to. While few people question the fact that all typical adult humans have erotic thoughts and most engage in erotic behavior, little is known about how these important components of our gender identity develop. We are not naïve enough to think that such a complex set of thoughts and behaviors appears fully developed on one's wedding night (or to be more liberal, on one's 18th birthday), but much of the course of the development of sexuality over childhood and adolescence remains unclear.

We begin this chapter by looking at sex from an evolutionary perspective. We then examine the development of sexuality, beginning in infancy and continuing through adolescence and young adulthood. What is the normal, or typical, pattern of sexual development? Is it appropriate to think of prepubescent children as sexual beings? We next look specifically at factors that influence one's sexual orientation, focusing on the origins of homosexuality. We then briefly examine gender differences and how such dif-

ferences can be explained. (Most gender differences have been discussed in the chapters in which the specific content is examined.) The final section looks at the development of gender identity, especially the cognitive factors that affect how children come to see themselves as men and women.

Sex, Evolution, and Gender Differences

Reproduction is the essence of survival. Although species reproduce in many different ways, they can be divided into two basic categories: sexual and asexual. At its most basic, sexual reproduction involves the joining of the nuclei of two specific cells called gametes (ovum and sperm in humans), usually from two different members of the species. There are some animals called *hermaphrodites* in which an individual produces both the male and female gametes, but these animals will not concern us here. We will be sticking to sex between two unique individuals, male and female, in this chapter. In contrast, asexual reproduction involves the generation of new life from a single cell, often simply by cellular divisions (mitosis), where the nuclear genes replicate themselves, separate, and divide into two daughter cells. Where there was one, there are now two genetically identical individuals. Sexual reproduction then is usually biparental, whereas asexual reproduction is monoparental (Nason, 1965).

Reproductive Strategies and Mating Systems

There are other important distinctions in how different animals reproduce than just the sexual/asexual one. As discussed in Chapter 13, one important distinction is family structure. Some species practice *monogamy*, meaning that once two members have had sex, they stay together for an extended period, often until the offspring can fend for themselves. Other species practice *polygamy*, with one individual (either the male or female) having several sexual partners. In humans, the most common form of polygamy is *polygyny*, with one man having several wives.

Another distinction relates to the number of offspring produced and the amount of resources or nurturing that one invests in them. Two extreme strategies are typically described. One, termed *r* strategies, is common among insects and consists of producing many offspring with minimal investment or nurturing. Mother mosquitoes, for example, lay hundreds of eggs at a time and then fly off to die. As Darwin noted, most members of a species die before ever reaching adulthood, and species fol-

sexuality An individual's erotic thoughts and activities.

gender identity The ability of children to identify themselves as either boys or girls.

***r* strategies** A reproductive strategy in which many offspring are produced with minimal investment or nurturing.

Buss, D.M. (2008). Evolutionary psychology: The new science of the mind (3rd ed.). Pearson: Boston, p. 151. Ronald Hess/Elsevier Science

Men find women with low waist-to-hip ratios (far left) more attractive relative to women with higher waist-to-hip ratios (far right). Lower waist-to-hip ratios have been found to be associated with greater health and fertility.

lowing an *r* strategy hedge their bets by producing many offspring, expecting that some fraction of them will live. In contrast, most birds and mammals follow **K strategies**, in which fewer offspring are produced, but each requires more investment in terms of resources or nurturing. The evolutionary bet here is that producing fewer higher-quality and better-adapted offspring will result in a high-enough survival rate to continue the species (see Figueredo et al., 2006). Most *K*-strategy species produce offspring that are slow to develop. For example, all mammals have a period of infancy in which they get their nutrition directly from their mothers. Humans are an extreme example of a *K*-strategy species (along with chimpanzees, elephants, dolphins, and some others), although even for humans different ecological conditions can result in variations in terms of how many offspring a woman has and how much investment her children get (see discussion later in this chapter).

As mentioned in Chapter 13, humans are a marginally monogamous/marginally polygamous sexually reproducing species, following a *K* strategy (few offspring, substantial investment), but this is only the tip of the iceberg. Natural selection influenced the ways males and females think and behave, enhancing the chances that they will have sex and children, and that their children will in turn have children. According to evolutionary psychology, the modern human mind was shaped during the Pleistocene, the last 2 millions years or so (see Chapter 2). Life in the Pleistocene was tougher than it is today, in the sense that Stone Age technology was not as advanced as today's. Resources were limited, and the likelihood of dying before reaching adulthood was far greater than it is today, by some estimates about 50% (Volk & Atkinson, 2008). In such contexts, good decisions matter, perhaps meaning the difference between life and death, and this was no less true in the case of mating: good mating choices increased the probabilities of a high reproductive fitness, whereas bad choices decreased such probabilities. This produces some new provoking questions: Which were the good and the bad mating choices? And were these choices different for males and females? One particularly bad mating decision would be having sex with one's sibling; the topic of incest avoidance is discussed in Box 15.1.

Parental Investment Theory

We introduced **parental investment theory** (Trivers, 1972) in Chapter 12. Basically, this theory holds that there is a tradeoff between investing time and resources in parenting and mating and that the sex that invests more in parenting (which in humans and most mammals is females) will be the choosier sex when it comes to selecting a mating partner, whereas the sex that invests less in parenting (which in humans and most mammals is males) will be more competitive among themselves for access to the more-investing sex. In humans, the burden of caring for an infant requires that mothers receive help from others, referred to as *alloparenting* and discussed in Chapter 12. Fathers frequently serve as alloparents, but their investment is not obligatory. In practical terms, this means that, with respect to children, females are the more-investing sex, and as such making a bad mating decision (that is, choosing a bad mate) is likely to be more costly for them than for males.

Following this logic, the desirable features that enhance reproductive fitness would be different for men and women. For women, healthy and competitive males, who are able to provide resources and

K strategies A reproductive strategy in which few offspring are produced but each requires substantial investment in terms of resources or nurturing.

parental investment theory Theory coming from evolutionary biology that predicts differences in behaviors between males and females as a function of how much each invests in mating versus parenting.

BOX 15.1 **evolution in action**

The Case of Incest Avoidance

Why don't we fall in love with our siblings? We may love our siblings like brothers or sisters, but we feel neither lust nor romantic attraction to them. In fact, the very thought of such things fills us with disgust. Why should this be?

One of the advantages of sexual reproduction over asexual reproduction is genetic variability. When two animals that are closely related breed, there is an increased chance that the offspring will inherit genes associated with unfavorable outcomes—recessive alleles that, when they occur in pairs, result in death or disease. Species have developed techniques of **incest avoidance** to prevent such inbreeding depression. For example, in some animals, one sex typically leaves the natal group upon maturity, decreasing the chance that it will mate with a close relative. In most monkeys, the males emigrate. In baboons, chimpanzees, and prehistoric humans (see Owens & King, 1999), the females usually leave the home base in search of a mate. Alternatively, there may be characteristics of close relatives that make them unappealing as a potential mate, and this seems to be the case with humans.

Society certainly makes it clear for humans that having sex with a sibling (or parents having sex with their children) in unacceptable. All cultures have incest taboos. Sigmund Freud (1952) believed that these societally imposed taboos were

© Ted Spiegel/Corbis

Boys and girls raised together on Israeli _kibbutzim_ rarely engaged in sexual intercourse as adolescents and adults, and never married.

necessary, because children have an inherent desire for sexual relations with their opposite-sex parent (the Oedipus and Electra complexes), and these desires extend to opposite-sex siblings. In contrast, evolutionary theorists propose that, like other animals, humans have mechanisms that inhibit the likelihood of inbreeding. The first such theorist to propose that people inherently avoid sexual relations with close kin was the Finnish anthropologist Edward Westermarck (1891). Westermarck observed that people who cohabitate with one another from early in childhood rarely ever marry, regardless of their genetic relationship. Siblings naturally grow up together, and this

early familiarity results in a lack of sexual attraction when they become adolescents and adults.

Evidence in support of the **Westermarck effect** and against Freud's hypothesis comes from several sources. The first is from the work of Arthur Wolf (1995), who studied the tradition of _minor marriages_ in Taiwan during the late 19th and early 20th centuries. As in many cultures, families sometimes arranged the marriages of their young children years before reaching adulthood. In Taiwan, the tradition was that the bride-to-be would move into the home of the boy's family, and the future bride and groom would be reared together as brother and sister. This arrangement permits the boy's family to keep tabs on his future wife, increasing paternity certainty when they are ready to marry. Wolf noted that when the girl moved in with the boy's family before she was 30 months of age, she often later objected to marrying her adopted brother. When these minor marriages did happen, the divorce rate was three times greater, produced 40% fewer children, and the wives admitted to having more extramarital affairs, all relative to major marriages.

Another source of evidence for the Westermarck effect comes from studies of people reared together from early childhood in Israeli cooperative communities (_kibbutzim_). Joseph Shepher (1983) observed that such children, although frequently engag-

protection to them and their offspring, but are also willing to engage in some childcare, would be the good choices. Men, in contrast, should be more concerned with the fertility and health of females: Are they capable of getting pregnant, and are they healthy enough to care for a young child? Following mainstream evolutionary psychological theory (see Buss, 2005; Schmitt, 2005), natural selection shaped the human mind so that females are attracted to male traits associated with the ability and willingness to provide resources, such as high status and physical prowess (see Table 15.1, p. 620). In contrast, men's psychology has been shaped by natural selec-

tion to be attracted to women who show signs of youth (associated with fertility) and health, such as clear skin, symmetrical features, white teeth, absence of sores and lesions, and a small waist-to-hip ratio, as well as signs of sexual loyalty.

Women and men differ on the ideal age of a mate. Women (including teenage girls) prefer a mate several years older than they are, which corresponds to actual marriage practices (Kenrick & Keefe, 1992). Men in all cultures tend to prefer younger women, with the age discrepancy in an ideal mate actually increasing as men age. That is, older men prefer women who are increasingly younger than they are. This likely reflects men's ability to recognize reproductive value, the number of children a woman can have in her lifetime. Although this cannot be directly measured, age is perhaps the best single indication of reproductive

incest avoidance Avoiding having sex with a close relative.

Westermarck effect The phenomenon that people who cohabitate with one another from early in childhood rarely ever find one another sexually attractive, regardless of their genetic relationship.

ing in heterosexual play during childhood, rarely engaged in sexual intercourse as adolescents and adults, and there were no marriages between 2,769 couples from 211 *kibbutzim*.

These studies suggest that genetically unrelated people who spend much of their early lives together do not find one another sexually attractive as adults. But what about siblings? Are the same mechanisms in play for them as well? This question was addressed by Irene Bevc and Irwin Silverman (1993, 2000), who interviewed people about the incidence of post-childhood sex with siblings. Because the incidence of such activities is low, they recruited volunteers by placing ads in major newspapers in Toronto to answer survey questions about sexual relations between brothers and sisters (Bevc & Silverman, 2000). They classified sexual activity as either "mature," which included completed or attempted genital, anal, or oral intercourse, or "immature," which included fondling, exhibitionism, and touching. From this sample, they found 54 cases of people who had admitted having intercourse with a sibling. Similar to the results of an earlier survey of college students (Bevc & Silverman, 1993), they reported that siblings who had been separated during early childhood were more likely than nonseparated pairs to have engaged in genital intercourse. There was no effect of separation, however, for imma-

ture sexual behaviors. Bevc and Silverman (2000) suggested that early cohabitation results in reduced incidence of reproductive sexual behavior (that is, intercourse), but not necessarily in a reduction of nonreproductive sexual behaviors (such as fondling and exhibitionism). They also hypothesized, consistent with Wolf (1995), that the sensitive period for the incest-inhibition effect is before the age of 3.

Consistent with these findings, anecdotal evidence shows that siblings who were separated early in childhood often have uncomfortable feelings of sexual attraction for one another when they meet as adults. One survey of post-adoption counselors in London indicated that about 50% of clients who had been reunited with siblings as adults experienced "strong, sexual feelings" (Greenberg & Littlewood, 1995).

What is the mechanism for the effect of early cohabitation and subsequent incest avoidance? To avoid inbreeding, people have to be able to (1) detect kin, and (2) regulate sexual motivation based on the likelihood that another person of the opposite sex is a close relative. Several mechanisms have been suggested (see Tal & Lieberman, 2007). One possibility is knowledge that one's mother cared for other children (knowledge an older sibling would have of a younger sibling) and, relatedly, the length of time two children resided together, both of which have been found to be associated

with feelings of incest disgust (Lieberman, Tooby, & Cosmides, 2007). Another likely candidate is olfactory (smell) cues. In fact, there is evidence that people can identify their genetic relatives based on smell and find the odor of some kin more aversive than others.

In a series of studies, Glenn Weisfeld and his colleagues (2003) had family members wear T-shirts on two consecutive nights and avoid using perfumes or scented soaps. People were then given the T-shirts and asked to identify on the basis of smell who had worn each shirt. Immediate family members exhibited particular patterns of aversions to each other's odors. Fathers showed aversions to their daughters' odors (but not to their sons'), whereas mothers did not display any aversions; opposite-sex (but not same-sex) sibling pairs showed aversions to each other's odors; and daughters displayed aversions to their fathers' odors. The only cases in which aversion was mutual was the brother-sister and father-daughter pairs, which represent the greatest danger of incest. These patterns of aversion were found whether or not the person smelling the T-shirt could recognize who had worn the shirt. The findings by Weisfeld and his colleagues make a strong argument that the Westermarck effect is governed, at least in part, by the nose.

value. Thus, from an inclusive-fitness perspective, an ideal mate for a man is not someone who is just a few years younger than he is, but one who has high reproductive value.

There is one exception to this trend of men preferring younger women, and that is adolescent males. Douglas Kenrick and his colleagues (1996) asked teenage boys and girls to describe the type of person they would find most attractive: "I'd like you to think for a second about what type of person you would find attractive. Imagine you were going on a date with someone. Assume that the person would be interested in you, and that you were available to go on a date, and that things like parental permission and money aren't important" (p. 1505). Each participant was then asked questions about the minimum, maximum, and ideal age of an ideal date. Teenage girls displayed

the same pattern that adult women show, preferring slightly older males as dates, with this difference increasing with age. That is, whereas 12- to 15-year-old girls said an ideal date would be one or two years older than they are, older teens (16 to 18 years) expressed interest in dates five or more years older than themselves. Teenage boys actually showed a somewhat similar pattern, which is different from that shown by adult men. Their ideal date was someone who was several years older than themselves, not several years younger as is the case for men worldwide.

Why this difference? This discrepancy actually is consistent with the hypothesis that these adolescent males are basing their judgments in terms of physical cues of reproductive value, just as their older male counterparts are. Women in their late teens and early twenties are more fertile

table 15.1 Natural Selection May Have Biased Women's Choices in a Mate

Below are listed some hypothesized preferences for women when looking for a long-term mate.

Adaptive Problem	Evolved Mate Preference
Selecting a mate who is able to invest	• Good financial prospects • Social status • Older age • Ambition/industriousness • Size, strength, athletic ability
Selecting a mate who is willing to invest	• Dependability and stability • Love and commitment cues • Positive interactions with children
Selecting a mate who is able to physically protect self and children	• Size (height) • Strength • Bravery • Athletic ability
Selecting a mate who will show good parenting skills	• Dependability • Emotional stability • Kindness • Positive interactions with children
Selecting a mate who is compatible	• Similar values • Similar ages • Similar personalities
Selecting a mate who is healthy	• Physical attractiveness • Symmetry • Healthy

SOURCE: Adapted from Buss, D. M. (2008). *Evolutionary psychology: The new science of the mind* (3rd ed). Boston: Pearson, p. 109.

than girls in their early teens, and thus are selected by teenage boys as being most desirable. In reality, these older women would not be interested in these teenage boys, given women's consistent preference for older, not younger, men. Nonetheless, when teenage boys are thinking of an ideal date, it is for the same type of women that older men prefer as mates, those who display signs of health and fertility.

This description of the evolution of male and female psychologies and their mating choices may produce some misconceptions. A first misconception is thinking that males and females are intentionally and coldly conscious when making mating decisions. Evolutionary psychologists and biologists often talk of mating strategies, but as we mentioned in Chapter 2, these are not intentional tactics to achieve specific goals. Recall that evolutionary psychologists propose that humans and other animals evolved sets of information-processing mechanisms adapted to deal with recurrent problems our ancestors faced. These are unconscious cognitions that have been shaped by natural selection over thousands, or even millions, of years that were associated with reproductive success. Such strategies are used not only by humans but also by other animals. Unlike other animals, however, humans have the potential to make some of these strategies conscious, but men and women's mating psychologies largely operate under the radar of self-awareness.

A second misconception is thinking that, given that the sexes have evolved different psychologies, these sex differences are natural and should be promoted in society today. This is the *naturalistic fallacy* discussed in Chapter 2. Humans, more so than any other animal, are not victims of our genes or evolutionary past. Understanding human nature does not justify behaviors that we in modern culture find troublesome, nor does it imply that such outcomes are inevitable.

A third misconception is believing that the only purpose of sex is reproduction. Certainly today with readily available contraception, sex and reproduction can be separated to an extent that was impossible for our ancestors. Moreover, sex is also a social behavior—and likely always has been for members of our species—bonding two people together and perhaps being important in the establishment of the human family (Crook, 1980). There is precedent in the animal world for this. Bonobos often engage in sex when they discover a fruiting tree. Seemingly, the sexual activity relaxes group members and reduces aggression associated with competition over food. Similarly, homosexual activity, although clearly nonreproduc-

Women are attracted to physical features in men as signs of health, but also find men attractive who have resources and who are likely to be good caretakers for children.

tive, can have an important social value and also is observed in many species of animals in the wild (Bagemihil, 1999).

At this point, readers may be asking themselves, "What does all this have to do with the development of sexuality and gender identity in children and adolescents?" Actually, quite a lot. Sexuality, reproduction, and gender identity are central to human life and surely experienced selection pressures over the course of human evolution. Not too long ago, there were heated debates among psychologists about the role that biology played in gender development, with many arguing that nearly all aspects of gender other than those associated with getting pregnant and giving birth were a result of how children were reared. These psychologists believed that biology (and certainly evolution) played no important role (see Maccoby & Jacklin, 1974), but times have changed. Today, most experts in the field of gender development agree with Diane Ruble, Carol Martin, and Sheri Berenbaum (2006, p. 889) that "Evolutionary and comparative approaches put human gender development into context."

The Development of Sexual Behavior in Childhood and Adolescence

Conducting research on childhood sexuality has not been easy in most Western countries in general, and particularly in the United States, primarily because of a deep-rooted cultural reluctance to view children as sexual beings. Instead, children are approached from a romantic, idealized perspective that considers them as "sexually innocent" (Fisher, 2005; Kaeser, DiSalvo, & Moglia, 2000). More is known about children's sexual behavior in hunter-gatherer societies, where attitudes toward sexual behavior in childhood are more relaxed. In such cultures, children have first-hand knowledge of sex, usually sleeping in the same room (and sometimes in the same bed) as their parents. They frequently engage in sex play during childhood, often mimicking sexual intercourse and sometimes mocking it. Adults in these cultures expect such play behavior, and, although they may not encourage it, believe it to be a normal part of growing up (see Konner, 2010).

In contrast, adults in contemporary Western societies often have difficulty distinguishing between natural, healthy, childhood sexual development and potentially problematic sexual behaviors. The difficulty in telling the differences between "good and bad touching," for example, has resulted in a total hands-off policy for some people who deal with children, to the extent that some teachers and childcare workers are prohibited from hugging a child in distress in order to avoid any misunderstanding (Johnson, 1999; Barrett, 2000). For example, teachers in some of Florida's public schools cannot accompany kindergarten children to the bathroom if they soil their pants over concern about "bad touching." These attitudes have resulted in inadequate research on the topic of childhood sexuality. For instance, childhood sexuality has been considered by most research-funding institutions as too controversial and politically incorrect; researchers have had to deal with difficulties obtaining representative samples

table 15.2 A Classification of Children's Sex-Related Behaviors

Communicative Behaviors
- Verbal: for example, "Talks about sexual acts"
- Nonverbal: for example, "Shy about undressing"

Exhibition and Voyeur Behaviors
- Exhibitionism: for example, "Shows sex (private) parts to adults"
- Voyeurism: for example, "Tries to look at people when they are nude or undressing"

Modeling Behaviors
- Sexually implicit: for example, "Playing doctor games"
- Sexually explicit: for example, "Imitates sexual behavior with dolls or stuffed animals"

Self-touching Behaviors
- For example, "Touches sex (private) parts at home"
- For example, "Masturbates with hand"

Touching-others Behaviors
- Direct: for example, "Touches other people's sex (private) parts"
- Indirect: for example, "Hugs adults he or she does not know well"

SOURCE: Adapted from the Child Sexual Behavior Inventory, Friedrich, W. N., Grambsch, P., Broughton, D., Kuiper, J., & Beilke, R. (1991). Normative sexual behavior in children. *Pediatrics, 88*, 456–464, and Kaeser, F., DiSalvo, C., & Moglia, R. (2000). Sexual behaviors of young children that occur in schools. *Journal of Sex Education and Therapy, 25*, 277–285.

of children for their studies, as well as the pressures of potential legal suits (Fisher, 2005; Kaeser et al., 2000). The consequence of this global negative view of childhood sexuality has resulted in an extraordinarily poor record of research on ordinary, typical sexual development in children. There were notable exceptions, including the pioneering work done by Alfred Kinsey and his colleagues at the Kinsey Institute for Sexual Research at the University of Indiana in Bloomington (1948, 1953; Ramsey, 1943a) and a handful of mostly European researchers (Gunderson, Melas, & Skar, 1981; Langfeldt, 1981), but generally, childhood sexuality was off the research radar.

The study of childhood sexuality can be seen as the final frontier in sex research. We have volumes written about adult sexuality, but the bulk of scientific inquiry into childhood sexuality is limited to how sexual pathology develops and the effects of sexual child abuse on its victims. We find ourselves in the curious situation of knowing more about the development of sexual deviance than the development of sexual normalcy (Finkelhor, 1979; Fischer, 2005).

Despite the taboos, scientists realized the importance of understanding sexual development, both for its own sake and in order to understand adult sexuality, and new research endeavors were undertaken beginning about 20 years ago, starting with the publication of several large-sample surveys on normative sexual development (Fried-

rich et al., 1991; Friedrich et al., 1998; Schoentjes & Deboutte, 1999), and a small increase of research on typical sexual behavior in children, some even during the preschool period (Friedrich & Trane, 2002). There have been basically three lines of research on children's sexual behaviors (Heiman et al., 1998). One line focuses on surveys completed by parents or, less often, caretakers such as school teachers, about their observations of children's sexual activities (Friedrich et al., 1998; Schoentjes & Deboutte, 1999). A second line of research, referred to as *retrospective studies*, is based on the memories of adults about their early childhood sexual experiences (Haugaard, 1996; Lamb & Coakley, 1993). A third research line focuses on the study of children who are under treatment because of their sexual behaviors (Gil & Johnson, 1993; Johnson, 1993). Understandably, given the continued sensitivity of the topic of childhood sexuality for many adults in modern society, including those who fund research, there are few direct observational studies of children's sexual behaviors, as well as studies that interview children themselves about their sexuality (Shoenjtes & Deboutte, 1999).

A Classification of Sexual Behaviors in Children

But what exactly are sexual behaviors in the context of childhood? Table 15.2 presents a classification of such behaviors, based on items in the Child Sexual Behavior Inventory designed by William Friedrich and his colleagues (Friedrich et al., 1991; 1992; 2001), and a classification of sexual behaviors by Frederick Kaeser and his colleagues (2000). The inventory consists of sets of 44 items describing specific sexually related behaviors (for example, "Uses words that describe sex acts"). Kaeser et al. (2000) classified children's sexual behaviors into five broad categories: Communicative behaviors, Exhibition and voyeur behaviors, Modeling behaviors, Self-touching behaviors, and Touching-others behaviors.

The first types of sexual behaviors listed in Table 15.2 are *communicative behaviors*. These include sexual language addressed to other children and/or to adults (for example, "Talks about sex acts"; "Talks in a flirtatious manner"), as well as writings and/or drawings of a sexual nature, and modesty behaviors (for example, "Shy about undressing").

A second category is *exhibition and voyeur behaviors*. These include body exposure (for example, "Shows sex [private] parts to children"; "Shows sex [private] parts to adults") and interest in other people's sexual nature ("Tries to look at people when they are nude or undressing"; "Tries to view pictures of nude or partially dressed people").

A third category is *modeling behaviors,* which involves modeling adult behavior that may or may not be sexually explicit and can be practiced alone or with other children. (Examples of modeling behaviors that are explicitly sexual are "Imitates the act of sexual intercourse"; "Makes sexual sounds [sighing, moaning, heavy breathing, etc.]"; "Imitates sexual behavior with dolls or stuffed animals.") Modeling behaviors that are not sexually explicit include several types of sex-role play, such as playing doctor, and gender-identity oriented behaviors (for example, "Pretends to be the opposite sex when playing"; "Dresses like the opposite sex").

A fourth category is *self-touching behaviors.* These include touching one's own erotic areas and masturbation (for example, "Rubs body against people or furniture"; "Masturbates with hand").

The fifth category of sexual behaviors that can be observed in children is *touching-others behaviors.* These behaviors can be addressed to adults or to other children and can either be explicitly sexual in nature (for example "Touches or tries to touch their mother's or other women's breasts"; "When kissing tries to put tongue in other person's mouth") or not (for example, "Hugs adults he or she does not know well"; "Stands too close to people").

We should be cautious in interpreting these behaviors as sexual. They obviously are not aimed at reproduction, and most young children, at least, would have no knowledge of adult sexual behavior and its purpose. It may be better to describe these as presexual or sex-related behaviors, in that they reflect children's emerging interest in special parts of their own bodies and those of other people (parts of the bodies that are usually covered when in public and that differentiate males and females) and children's knowledge of social conventions. For example, "modesty behaviors" may be an indication of children's lack of awareness of cultural values about displaying one's body in public, as may some self-touching behaviors. Young children who touch women's breasts (especially only their own mothers') may be curious about breast-feeding or curious about these obvious morphological differences, not because they are seeking sexual arousal. Even exhibition and voyeur behavior such as "showing sex parts to adults" may simply reflect a burgeoning awareness of genital sex differences, as reflected by one 6-year-old boy who ran naked from his bedroom, stopped in front of his father's girlfriend, and said, "Now you know what a penis looks like, Georgia." Nonetheless, these behaviors are sex-related in that they are associated with the genitals or other sexualized parts of the body (for example, women's breasts) and societal conventions about displaying them. Our intention is not to ascribe sexual motivations to children comparable to that experienced by adults, but to see these behaviors as precursors to the more mature sexual behaviors in adolescence and adulthood.

The Emergence of Sexual Behavior

The pioneering sex researcher Alfred Kinsey was one of the first scientists who reported, based on empirical data, the existence of childhood sexuality. In a series of his classic studies on male and female sexual behavior (Kinsey, Pomeroy, & Martin, 1948; Kinsey et al., 1953), he found that 48% of women and 57% of men reported having experienced some sort of sexual experience before adolescence, with genital exhibition being the most frequent, followed by "incidental touching" of genitals. More recent retrospective studies report even higher levels of childhood sexual experiences. For example, 85% of a sample of female college undergraduates claimed having participated in at least one childhood sexual game (about 30% involving genital fondling), with 76% experiencing it with playmates (Lamb & Coakley, 1993). The median age of this sexual experience was about 7.5 years, with 44% of cases involving cross-gender play and 56% same-gender play. Similarly, 59% of male and female college students remembered at least one episode (but most reported two or three) of sexual experience with other children before the age of 13, involving mostly activities such as exposing oneself, looking at others' genitals, or fondling of nongenital areas (Haugaard, 1996). In other words, retrospective studies consistently show the existence of sexual experiences in children before adolescence (Heiman et al., 1998).

These retrospective studies provide only the most general outline for childhood sexual experiences. What types of sexual experiences do children have? At what age do they begin, and how do they develop? In a general sense, sexual responsivity is present from birth. For example, male infants have erections, and vaginal lubrication has been observed in female infants within 24 hours after birth (Johnson, 1999; Masters, Johnson, & Kolodny, 1985). In fact, ultrasound pictures of 7-month-old male fetuses show that penile erections occur before birth (Calderone, 1983). Fondling of genitals has also been reported in infants (Meizner, 1987). Masturbation similar to the rhythmic manipulation found among adults appears at about 2.5 to 3 years of age (Martinson, 1994; DeLamater & Friedrich, 2002).

It is important to keep in mind that infants have a natural tendency toward self-exploration and self-stimulation of body parts and functions. Children become progressively interested in sexual issues, first concerning their own body and later other people's bodies (Gil, 1993; Schuhrke, 2000), and this progression continues during the preschool

FIGURE 15.1 Mean of Child Sexual Behavior Inventory (CSBI) items for boys and girls from 2 to 12 years old in a normative sample of the Dutch community in Belgium.

Adults rated the incidence of each of 44 sex-related behaviors in children. Sex-related behaviors were highest in children 5 years of age and younger and declined steadily to the preteen years. (*Note:* A similar profile was reported for a U.S. sample, Friedrich et al., 1991, 1998.) SOURCE: From Schoentjes, E. & Deboutte, D. (1999). Child sexual behavior inventory: A Dutch-speaking normative sample. *Pediatrics, 104* (4), 885–893. Copyright © 1999 by the American Academy of Pediatrics. Reprinted by permission.

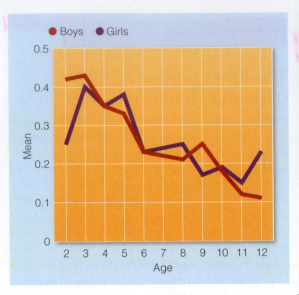

● Boys ● Girls

Ariel Skelley/Getty Images

period. Parents' responses to these emerging sexual behaviors seem to be important for subsequent sexual development. Some parents react in a caring, healthy way, establishing the basis for positive sexual development, whereas others feel threatened and react harshly, punishing children's typical sexual behavior, promoting guilty and inhibited sexual development (Thanasiu, 2004).

Sexual behaviors actually decrease from 2 to 12 years, as children gain increasing control over their own behavior and become increasingly aware of cultural norms about modesty.

Sex-related Behavior in Childhood

Sexual behavior in childhood develops. The available research shows some significant and consistent age differences regarding the level and type of sex-related activity that children exhibit (Heiman et al., 1998), which is influenced by a host of factors, including family attitudes and behaviors, context (for example, home versus daycare center), and culture. The most significant finding regarding the level of sex-related activity is that overt sex-related behaviors decrease between the preschool years and age 12. Figure 15.1 presents the average scores on the Child Sexual Behavior Inventory for boys and girls between 2 and 12 years of age from a large Dutch Belgium sample (Schoentjes & Deboutte, 1999). Adults in contact with children were asked to rate the frequency of each of 44 items (plus three more items added by researchers) for children over the last 6 months, according to one of four levels: 0 = never; 1 = less than once a month; 2 = 1 to 3 times a month; 3 = at least once a week. As can be seen, sex-related behaviors were highest in children 5 years of age and younger and declined steadily to the preteen years. A similar developmental pattern using this same inventory was reported for U.S. children (Friedrich et al., 1991, 1998). The data of any children suspected of sexual abuse were omitted from these analyses, so these numbers reflect normative patterns (See Box 15.2, p. 627).

Why the steady decrease in sex-related behavior over childhood? Could this reflect Freud's latency period, when children become essentially asexual? Most contemporary researchers think not, but rather they believe that children are becoming more conscious of cultural norms and are also increasingly able to regulate their behavior in response to social pressures (Reynolds, Herbenick, & Bancroft, 2003; Friedrich & Trane, 2002). Remember that the survey data are based on observations by adults of children's behavior, not behaviors children themselves report engaging in. For instance, parents frequently convey to children, either implicitly or explicitly, that some behaviors belong to the private realm instead of the public one—that there are times and places for satisfying one's sexual curiosity (Friedrich & Trane, 2002; Hornor, 2004). This combination of increased awareness and self-regulation may explain the increase in modesty seen during the elementary school age, particularly from 6 to 9 years old (DeLamater & Friedrich, 2002). It also suggests the very real possibility that sex-related activity in childhood is underestimated when based on adult reports (Heiman et al., 1998).

Developmental differences in the types of sex-related behaviors exhibited by children have also been reported. Tables 15.3 and 15.4 present the percentage of children displaying selected sex-related behaviors obtained from the Child Sexual Behavior Inventory, separately for preschool (Table 15.3) and school-age (Table 15.4) children. These data are

table 15.3 Percentage of Preschool Children Displaying Selected Sex-Related Behaviors

Percentages presented separately for boys and girls for the U.S. sample when significant differences between boys and girls were found.

	Dutch Sample	American Sample
Communicative Behaviors		
Walking around house without clothes	58%	57% (boys = 48%; girls = 65%)
Walking around house in underclothes	63%	65% (boys = 55%; girls = 75%)
Getting undressed in front of others	63%	56% (boys = 50%; girls = 62%)
Asking questions about sexuality	34%	item not available
Talking flirtatiously	16%	12% (boys = 9%; girls = 16%)
Exhibition and Voyeur Behavior		
Sitting with crotch or underwear exposed	50%	47% (boys = 35%; girls = 59%)
Showing sex parts to adults	21%	22% (boys = 26%; girls = 18%)
Showing sex parts to other children	13%	12% (boys = 16%; girls = 8%)
Trying to look at people undressing	37%	34%
Modeling Behaviors		
Playing doctor-type games	53%	item not available
Playing with opposite-sex toys	59%	67%
Pretending to be other sex while playing	14%	19%
Self-touching Behaviors		
Touching sex parts at home	78%	59%
Touching sex parts in public	30%	27% (boys = 36%; girls = 19%)
Scratching anal and/or crotch areas	53%	63%
Masturbates with hand	9%	19%
Touching-others Behaviors		
Touching breasts	63%	46%
Kissing nonfamily adults	57%	47% (boys = 41%; girls = 52%)
Kissing nonfamily children	63%	48% (boys = 41%; girls = 55%)
Touching other people's sex parts	22%	7%

SOURCE: Schoentjes, E. & Deboutte, D. (1999). Child sexual behavior inventory: A Dutch-speaking normative sample. *Pediatrics, 104* (4), 885–893; and Friedrich, W. N., Grambsch, P., Broughton, D., Kuiper, J., & Beilke, R. (1991). Normative sexual behavior in children. *Pediatrics, 88,* 456–464.

from two large, normative samples: William Friedrich et al.'s (1991) study conducted in the United States and Eric Schoentjes and Dirk Deboutte's (1999) study conducted in the Dutch-speaking community in Belgium. In both studies, children between the ages of 2 and 12 years were observed. Data concerning sex differences were available for the U.S. sample, and percentages of boys and girls are presented separately in the tables when significant differences between them were found.

Preschool Children

Data for preschool children (2 to 6 years for the U.S. sample, 2 to 5 years for the Dutch sample) are presented in Table 15.3. With respect to communicative behaviors, children displayed a relative absence of modesty regarding nudity in the presence of familiar people, particularly girls, and moderate rates of asking questions about sexuality and talking flirtatiously, again especially girls. Rates of exhibition and voyeur behaviors were generally in the low to moderate range, although boys were reported to show their genitals to others more so than girls. Many children played doctor-type games or engaged in opposite-sex activities, both sexually nonexplicit behaviors. Rates of self-touching were high, especially in the home, as were rates of touching others, including touching breasts and kissing unfamiliar adults and children.

As noted by other authors, these behaviors reflect a strong but natural and healthy interest of preschoolers for aspects of their own and other people's sex-related behavior (Davies, Glaser, & Kossoff, 2000; DeLamater & Friedrich, 2002;

table 15.4 Percentage of School-age Children Displaying Selected Sex-Related Behaviors

Percentages presented separately for boys and girls for the U.S. sample when significant differences between boys and girls were found.

	Dutch Sample	American Sample
Communicative Behaviors		
Walking around house without clothes	26%	17% (boys = 21%; girls = 12%)
Walking around house in underclothes	40%	30% (boys = 44%; girls = 16%)
Getting undressed in front of others	35%	22%
Asking questions about sexuality	65%	item not available
Shy about undressing in front of others	31%	51%
Using words that describe sex acts	26%	16%
Talking about sex acts	24%	10%
Exhibition and Voyeur Behavior		
Trying to look at nude pictures of people	25%	23% (boys = 27%; girls = 18%)
Trying to look at people when they are nude	24%	22% (boys = 28%; girls = 15%)
Sitting with crotch or underwear exposed	26%	23% (boys = 16%; girls = 30%)
Showing sex parts to adults	5%	9%
Showing sex parts to other children	5%	3%
Modeling Behaviors		
Playing doctor-type games	27%	item not available
Playing with opposite-sex toys	30%	37%
Pretending to be other sex while playing	3%	6%
Self-touching Behaviors		
Touching sex parts at home	44%	27% (boys = 36%; girls = 18%)
Touching sex parts in public	13%	10%
Scratching anal and/or crotch areas	29%	38%
Masturbates with hand	6%	10%
Touching-others Behaviors		
Touching breasts	23%	11%
Kissing nonfamily adults	34%	23% (boys = 19%; girls = 26%)
Kissing nonfamily children	32%	16% (boys = 10%; girls = 21%)

SOURCE: Schoentjes, E. & Deboutte, D. (1999). Child sexual behavior inventory: A Dutch-speaking normative sample. *Pediatrics, 104* (4), 885–893; and Friedrich, W. N., Grambsch, P., Broughton, D., Kuiper, J., & Beilke, R. (1991). Normative sexual behavior in children. *Pediatrics, 88,* 456–464.

Thanasiu, 2004). Young children develop an understanding of themselves and their world through play and their direct action on their surroundings (see Piaget, 1983). This is no less the case for sexuality. In fact, sexual play in typically developing children is exploratory, light-hearted, and spontaneous; it happens occasionally, under mutual agreement among participants. Children involved in this play are usually close in age, and sexual play does not involve high levels of fear, anger, or anxiety (although it can sometimes produce embarrassment to the children who practice it). It is also sensitive to adult supervision and control; for example, it decreases if caregivers tell children to stop (Johnson, 1999; Silovsky & Bonner, 2004). Moreover, in an 18-year longitudinal study by UCLA researchers, it was found that sex-play experiences are unrelated to long-term psychological adjustment (Okami, Olmstead, & Abramson, 1997).

School-age Children

Data for school-age children (7 to 12 years for the U.S. sample, 6 to 12 years for the Dutch sample) are presented in Table 15.4. As mentioned previously, based on parents' reports, school-age children showed a significant decrease in most of the high-frequency sex-related behaviors exhibited by preschoolers (for example, being seen naked by others, self-touching, and touching others). Despite the decreases—often declining by greater than 50% relative to the rates shown by preschoolers—these behaviors did not disappear. In fact, some behaviors not witnessed at appreciable levels for preschoolers were at moderately high rates during

BOX 15.2 child development in the real world

Child Sexual Abuse and the Boundaries of Typical Sexual Behavior

As we have emphasized throughout this chapter, the development of sexuality in children is a natural and healthy phenomenon. However, sexuality, like many other aspects of life, can be a double-edged sword, as exemplified by child sexual exploitation (through prostitution and pornography), adolescent pregnancy, and child sexual abuse.

Sexual abuse is considered one of the four categories of child maltreatment (jointly with physical abuse, neglect, and emotional maltreatment, see Chapter 13), and it is defined as "sexual contact or attempted sexual contact between a caregiver or other responsible adult and a child for purposes of the caregiver's gratification or financial benefit" (Cicchetti & Toth, 2006, p. 504). Child sexual abuse can involve different forms of sexual activity, such as fondling, genital touching, vaginal/anal intercourse, oral-genital contact, genital-genital contact, or exposure to pornography (Hornor, 2004).

Although cases of sexual abuse substantiated by Child Protective Services in the United States dropped 40% from 1992 to 2000, there are still an estimated minimum of 89,500 cases per year in the United States (Finkelhor & Jones, 2004), with a substantial number of cases involving children younger than 7 years of age (nearly 38% in 1998 statistics by the National Center on Child Abuse and Neglect; Bruck, Ceci, & Principe, 2006). In 2002, the rate of child sexual abuse was estimated at 1.2 cases per 1,000 children (see Bruck et al., 2006). Moreover, different from other forms of child abuse (for example, physical abuse), where external signs of maltreatment are easier to identify, sexual abuse can often go undetected. Research on issues related to child sexual abuse has increased in recent decades, with much of it focusing on developing interview techniques for suspected child victims and for psychotherapy procedures with abused children (see Goodman, Emery, & Haugaard, 1998; Bruck et al., 2006; Cicchetti & Toth, 2006).

How is one to determine if a child has been sexually abused or not? Findings are not conclusive, but researchers have identified correlates of child sexual abuse that can be used to alert parents, teachers, or other caretakers of potential (but not certain) problems. Marsha Heiman and her colleagues (1998) summarized some of those basic data as follows: First, sexually abused children exhibit higher amounts of sexual behaviors of every type than do non–sexually abused children. This can be confusing, given that typical (that is, nonabused) preschoolers often exhibit more sexual behaviors than typical school-age children. Second, children who have experienced sexual abuse display different types of sexual behaviors than nonabused children, particularly those that resemble adult sexuality. It is important to note, however, that children may exhibit one or more of these behaviors and still not have been sexually abused. Third, we know that the dynamic quality of sexual behavior is sometimes altered in children who have been sexually abused, with children exhibiting, for example, more compulsive, coercive, and/or dominant sex play. We must be careful, however, in interpreting children's behavior as evidence of abuse, as even experts are often unable to differentiate abused from nonabused children based on their behaviors alone (see Bruck et al., 2006).

Children who are victims of sexual abuse often display a variety of nonspecific behavioral changes, including sudden changes in personality, secondary enuresis/ecopresis, nightmares/sleep difficulties, lying, stealing, fire setting, temper tantrums, truancy, running away, destructiveness, aggression, sudden avoidance of certain people and/or places, regressive behavior, poor peer relationships, sudden decline in school performance, posttraumatic stress disorder, depression, poor self-esteem, and/or substance abuse (Hornor, 2004; Kendall-Tackett, Williams & Finkelhor, 1993). However, it is important to note that many nonabused children may also display some of these behaviors, making the behaviors unreliable signs of sexual abuse. Moreover, about one-third of sexually abused children show no symptoms, although it is not clear why (Kendall-Tackett et al., 1993).

Once sexual abuse is discovered, how do children respond? In a review of 45 studies, 50% to 66% of sexually abused children showed a reduction of negative symptoms 12 to 18 months after disclosure. However, 10% to 24% displayed an increase in symptomatolgy, and 6% to 19% experienced continued sexual abuse (Kendall-Tackett et al., 1993). Some symptoms, such as fear and somatic signs, were more likely to diminish, whereas other symptoms, such as aggressiveness and sexual preoccupation, were less likely to decrease and sometimes increased after disclosure. Some factors, such as the duration and the frequency of the abuse, the severity of the abuse, the use or not of force, the closeness of the relationship with the perpetrator, and the degree of maternal support, seem to impact the severity of children's symptoms and the likelihood of a successful recovery (Kendall-Tackett et al., 1993). Sexual child abuse apparently has some long-term consequences for women's mating strategies as well. For instance, one study reports that women who experienced sexual abuse as children have their first menstrual period, sexual relationship, and first childbirth earlier than nonabused women (Vigil, Geary, & Byrd-Craven, 2005).

Early detection and therapy for child abuse are important, particularly during the preschool years, when children are less able to get help, especially if the abuse occurs within the family. Accordingly, teachers are often the first to detect that something unusual is happening to a child. Also, early detection shortens the suffering of children and increases the chances of a more successful therapeutic intervention (see Cicchetti & Toth, 2006).

the school years, such as using words that describe sex acts, talking about sex acts, and an interest in looking at nude people, especially for boys.

As mentioned previously, it is unlikely that the decrease in sexual behaviors observed by parents and teachers reflects a reduced interest in things sexual in children during the elementary school years. For example, although the rate of masturbation observed by parents ranged between 5% and 10% for the U.S. and Dutch samples for 7- to

Some common sex-related behaviors in typical children from 2 to 12, as reported by parents

Ages 2–6	• Uninhibited about their own nudity (that is, low sense of modesty) • Curious about sexual and genital parts • Highly involved in sex play (for example, playing house; doctors; moms/dads) • Touch their private parts, even in public • May experience pleasure from touching their genitals • Touch women's breasts and kisses to nonfamiliar adults and children
Ages 7–12	• Shyness and modesty sense about their own nudity • Use language to express sexual knowledge and asking questions about it • Interested in sexual contents and issues (for example, looking at nude pictures; sex play) • Touches their private parts at home • May experience pleasure from touching their genitals • Significant decrease of touching others behaviors (for example, breast or kissing nonfamiliar)

SOURCE: Schoentjes, E. & Deboutte, D. (1999). Child sexual behavior inventory: A Dutch-speaking normative sample. *Pediatrics, 104* (4), 885–893; Friedrich, W. N., Fisher, J., Broughton, D., Houston, M., & Shafran, C. R. (1998). Normative sexual behavior in children: A contemporary sample. *Pediatrics, 101* (4), 1–8; and Friedrich, W. N., Grambsch, P., Broughton, D., Kuiper, J., & Beilke, R. (1991). Normative sexual behavior in children. *Pediatrics, 88*, 456–464.

In the United States and parts of Europe, it is common for preteens to have heterosexual parties and to engage in group dating.

Nicki Pardo/Getty Images

12-year-old children, about 40% of women and 38% of men recall having masturbated before puberty when asked retrospectively (Bancroft, Herbenick, & Reynolds, 2003; see also Langfeldt, 1981 and Ramsey, 1943). Relatedly, adolescents report having experienced their first sexual attraction at 10 to 12 years, with their first sexual fantasies occurring some months to one year later, and group dating and heterosexual parties happening at the end of this period (DeLamater & Friedrich, 2002).

Although school-age children are certainly not preoccupied with sex, it seems unlikely that Freud's idea of sexual latency during this time is accurate. Certainly, as it is often said, "more research is required." (See Concept Review 15.1.)

Sexual Behavior in Adolescence

As we saw in Chapter 4, during puberty a series of important physical changes take place. Some of the more distinctive are the development of primary and secondary sexual characteristics. *Primary sexual characteristics* are those directly involved in the formation of the male and female reproductive systems (for example, testicle maturation and penis growth in males, and ovary maturation and uterus growth in females). *Secondary sexual characteristics* are those not directly involved in the reproductive system (for example, voice change in males and breast growth in females).

Puberty has several effects on sexuality. Perhaps the most significant consequence of pubertal change is an increase of sexual activation and interest. One of the effects of sex hormones is the lowering of thresholds for activation of brain pathways dealing with erotic content. These brain pathways were formed prenatally, and now, years later, are being "turned on" by adult hormones (Money, 1988). Another effect is strictly social. For example, children who have well-developed secondary sexual characteristics will be perceived by others as being closer to adulthood. They are apt to be given more freedom and privileges than their younger-appearing peers and to have older friends who participate in adultlike activities. Because our self-perception is based partially on how others perceive us, it is obvious that a physically mature young person will also begin to think of him- or herself as being psychologically and socially mature (Brooks-Gunn, 1989; see Chapter 4).

In this section, we look at the development of physical and emotional intimate relationships in adolescence, examining the development of sexual behaviors across this period of life. We follow this by a brief section looking at what is involved in falling in love.

table 15.5 Sexual Behaviors in U.S. Youth in Grades 9 to 12

Sexual Intercourse at least once	47%
Sexual Intercourse before age 13	7%
Currently Sexually Active (that is, had sexual intercourse during 3 months before the survey)	34%
Condom Use	63%
Birth Control Pill Use	17%
Four or more sex partners	14%
Pregnancy	4%
AIDs or HIV Infection Education	88%

SOURCE: Center for Disease Control. (2005). *Assisted Reproductive Technology (ART) Report.* http://www.cdc.gov/art/ART2005/index.htm. Downloaded January 9, 2008.

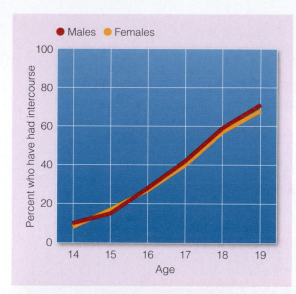

● Males ● Females

FIGURE 15.2 The percentage of U.S. male and female teenagers who have had sexual intercourse by age. Rates are nearly identical for boys and girls. SOURCE: Guttmacher Institute. (2006). *Facts on American teens' sexual and reproductive health.* New York: Alan Guttmacher Institute. Reprinted by permission.

Establishing Physical and Emotional Intimacy during Adolescence

As mentioned earlier, sexual attraction begins, on average, at 10 years of age, with variations depending on gender, culture, and sexual orientation (Herdt & McClintock, 2000); first sexual fantasies typically occur some months to one year later (DeLamater & Friedrich, 2002). There seems to be a typical sequence in sexual development for most American youth: erotic fantasies, followed by the beginning of masturbation, making out and petting, and sexual intercourse of different kinds. Erotic fantasies are actually the most common sexual experience during adolescence (Collins & Steinberg, 2006; Feldman, Turner, & Araujo, 1999).

Masturbation is practiced almost universally by teenage boys and by many teenage girls and is often accompanied by sexual fantasies. One study showed that more than 90% of adolescents who masturbate reported that they also fantasized during masturbation (Sorenson, 1973). Fantasies enhance the pleasure of masturbation. According to William Masters, Virginia Johnson, and Robert Kolodny (1985), masturbation with fantasies serves several useful purposes during adolescence. It is a safe substitute for intercourse and also provides a chance to rehearse mentally for later sexual situations and to practice using sexual imagery for future relationships. Regardless of how typical and useful masturbation is during adolescence, more than 50% of the teenagers interviewed in one study reported guilt and other negative feelings about it "sometimes" or "often" (Sorenson, 1973).

Many adolescents move on to sexual behavior with a partner. Figure 15.2 presents the percentage of American teenagers reporting having had sexual intercourse, broken down by age (14 to 19 years). As can be seen, the rates are similar for both males and females at all ages, are very low during the early teen years, and increase to about 70% by

© Bubbles Photolibrary/Alamy

The percentage of American adolescents who have had sexual intercourse increases over the teen years, with about 70% reporting having had sex by age 19.

age 19 (Guttmacher Institute, 2006). Data collected by the National Center for Chronic Disease Prevention and Health Promotion in 2003 for students in grades 9 to 12 reveal some interesting information about sexual practices in American youth (Grunbaum et al., 2004; see Table 15.5). As can be seen from the table, 46% of high-school students

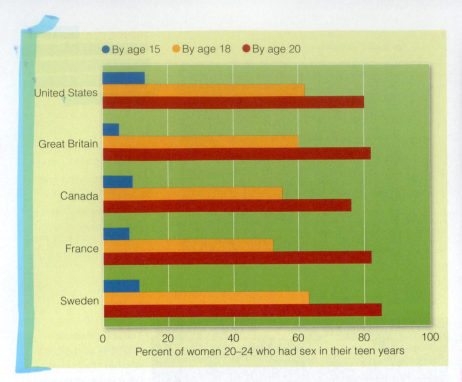

By age 15   By age 18   By age 20

United States

Great Britain

Canada

France

Sweden

0   20   40   60   80   100
Percent of women 20–24 who had sex in their teen years

FIGURE 15.3

Differences in levels of teenage sexual activity in five developed countries.

SOURCE: Adapted from Guttmacher Institute (2002). *Teenagers sexual and reproductive health: Developed countries.* New York: Alan Guttmacher Institute.

A recent study reported that 26% of girls between the ages of 14 and 19 in the United States are infected with at least one of the most common STDs.

reported having had sexual intercourse at least once during their lifetimes. Moreover, about 7% of high-school students reported having had their first sexual intercourse before the age of 13; 14% reported having had four or more sex partners in their lives; and 34% reported being currently sexually active. These values tended to vary with ethnicity, being higher in African American and Hispanic youth than White youth, with males reporting higher rates of sexual activity than females. One must be cautious in interpreting results such as these, however, in that adolescents may under-report or over-report their level of sexual activity based on what they think the interviewer wants to hear and the image they want to portray.

More American adolescents become sexually active before the age of 15 than adolescents in most other developed countries, such as Canada, France, Great Britain, and Sweden, and they have more sexual partners in a year than teens from these other nations (Guttmacher Institute, 2002, see Figure 15.3). Rates of teenage pregnancies are also higher for American youth than in most Western European countries (Darroch et al., 2001). Moreover, the rates of sexually transmitted diseases (STDs) are exceptionally high in American adolescents and young adults. For example, of all the new cases of STDs reported in the United States in the year 2000, nearly half of them (9.1 million) were contracted by people between the ages of 15 and 24 years (Weinstock, Berman, & Cates, 2004). The skyrocketing rate of STDs in American teenagers was brought to light by a 2008 study by the Centers for Disease Control (Forhan et al., 2008): The researchers estimated that 26% of girls between the ages of 14 and 19 in the United States—about 3.2 million

teenage girls—are infected with at least one of the most common STDs. The rate of infection for sexually active teens was about 40%.

Earlier-than-average involvement in adult sexual experiences is related to psychosocial adjustment problems in adolescence, potentially affecting academic achievement, relationships with parents, and may be a contributing factor to drug or alcohol abuse (Jessor et al., 1983). Precocious sexual activity may also increase the risk of pregnancy, health risks, and sexual exploitation (Collins & Steinberg, 2006).

Many factors influence adolescents' sexual behavior, including relationships with parents and peers (Collins & Steinberg, 2006; Zimmer-Gembeck & Helfand, 2008), and socioeconomic status. For example, teenage girls growing up in poor neighborhoods and who have a history of conduct disorder report becoming sexually active earlier than girls growing up in more-advantaged neighborhoods (Dupéré et al., 2008). Not surprisingly, many adolescents report feeling pressure from partners or friends to become involved in sexual activities or to engage in some sexual practices, for example, using or not using condoms (Henry et al., 2007). Curiosity, feelings of being grown up, and not wanting to be different from friends are some reasons for initiating intercourse in adolescent girls younger than 15 (Rosenthal et al., 2001).

As noted earlier, culture is a major factor in adolescents' sexual behavior. Why are rates of teenage sex, births, and STDs lower in countries that seemingly have more permissive attitudes about sex, such as France and Sweden, than in the United States? Perhaps it is, in part, the consistency of the message that children receive. The American culture presents an ambiguous message to its children about sexuality. On the one hand, television, movies, popular music, magazines, and pop culture in general promote sexuality. As a result, children know more about sex earlier than in past generations. In fact, when 10- to 15-year-old adolescents were asked about their sources of information about sex and intimacy, mass media (movies, TV, magazines, and music) was most frequently mentioned, ahead of parents, peers, and sex education programs (Kaiser Family Foundation, 1997). Even parents who want to limit their children's exposure to sex find it difficult, given the content of many TV programs, as well as television advertisements (for example, for undergarments from *Victoria's Secret* and drugs for erectile dysfunction).

On the other hand, America has not lost touch with its puritanical beginnings. Federal guidelines from the George W. Bush Administration advocated abstinence-only sex education, fearing that teaching children about safe sex is giving them implicit permission to have sex (Landry, Kaeser, & Richards, 1999). Similar concerns have arisen over access to birth control and inoculation of girls against human papillomavirus (HPV) before they become sexually active. These conflicting messages come through clearly (if ambiguously) to American adolescents, and the result seems to be greater sexual activity and the associated consequences than in Western countries with more permissive (and consistent) attitudes.

Moreover, abstinence-only sex education seems not to be effective in preventing teenagers from having sex and the consequences that adolescent sexual activity can bring. In a review of 13 absti-

nence-only sex education programs involving nearly 16,000 American youth, none reported decreases in having unprotected sex, number of sex partners, or reduction in STDs compared to controls (Underhill, Montgomery, Operario, 2007). In fact, there is evidence that some abstinence-only sex education programs are associated with *increased* rates of becoming a parent, at least for teenage boys (DiCenso et al., 2002), and that "virginity-pledgers" are less apt to use birth control or condoms than "nonpledgers" (Rosenbaum, 2009). In contrast, teenagers who participate in curriculum-based sex and STD/HIV education programs have been shown to delay the initiation of sexual activity, have sex less often or with fewer partners, and are more apt to practice safe sex than are teenagers not attending such programs (Kirby & Laris, 2009).

Some American organizations, such as Advocates for Youth (Feijoo, 2001), suggest taking a cue from some Western European countries with respect to teenage sexuality. These organizations argue that adolescents have the right to proper sexual education and sexual-health services and deserve respect from society concerning these issues. They propose that a responsible society should provide adolescents with the tools for enjoying healthy and safe sexuality (Feijoo, 2001). Some of their suggestions are summarized in Table 15.6.

Falling in Love and Romantic Relationships

Adolescents do not expend all of their passions on sex. Adolescence is also characterized by falling in love. Few scientists study falling in love, but those who do find that it typically happens first in adolescence, can happen over and over again, and lasts anywhere from a few hours to two years, when it can be replaced by the more mellow state of being in love (Fisher, 2004). Falling in love seems to involve more environmental factors than puberty

table 15.6 Ten Recommendations to Improve Adolescent Sexual Health in the United States

1. Value and respect adolescents and expect and promote teens to act responsibly
2. Use research as the basis for public health policy (not politics or religion)
3. Promote a national will to reduce unintended pregnancy and sexual infections
4. Government support for long-term and consistent public education campaigns
5. Facilitate the access of youth to free or low-cost contraception
6. Integrate sexual education across subjects of school curricula at all grade levels
7. Favor a higher family involvement in sexual education process and institutions
8. See intimate sexual relationships as a positive component of emotional maturation
9. Favor a sexual behavior ethics based on responsibility, respect, tolerance, and equity
10. Take into consideration cultural and values diversity concerning immigrant population

SOURCE: Adapted from Feijoo, A. N. (2001). *Adolescent sexual health in Europe and the US: Why the difference?* (2nd ed.). Washington, DC: Advocates for Youth.

Some adolescents are deeply in love, find it difficult to be apart, and want to share everything.

does, because children with precocious puberty do not fall in love until they reach their teenage years, even though they have masturbation fantasies and nocturnal emissions at ages consistent with their physical development. Some people in their thirties and forties may have developed typically, even had children, but never have fallen in love (Money & Tucker, 1975).

"Falling in love" sounds more like a topic for poets and novelists than scientists, and artists surely have examined it extensively. What do we mean when we say someone falls in love? Most people have experienced the feeling, and in fact, it seems to be universal for the species. In a survey of 166 societies, there was evidence of romantic love in 147 of them. Moreover, there was no evidence that romantic love did not exist in the remaining 19; the societies had just not been studied thoroughly enough to confirm its presence (Jankowiak & Fisher, 1992).

When people fall in love they focus their attention on their beloved, usually on his or her positive qualities. People in love are unable to feel romantic love toward anyone but their beloved. The love-possessed often feel extreme emotions, including exhilaration, euphoria, a pounding heart, or increased energy. This is sometimes accompanied by a loss of appetite, anxiety, or sleeplessness (see Fisher, 2000, 2004). What causes these feelings and what are they good for? It is obvious that sex is good for reproduction, but what's love got to do with it? Is love merely a by-product of sex, providing no adaptive benefit itself? At one level we know it is not that simple. People can fall in love without having sex, and they can also have sex without falling in love. But it would also be foolish to believe that romantic love and sex are totally independent. As we will see, the biology of sex and of falling in love have some things in common, and the combination of sex and love may not only produce happy people, but also increase the chance that babies will grow up and fall in love themselves.

Lust, Attraction, and Attachment

Anthropologist Helen Fisher (2000, 2004) has proposed that falling in love involves three primary emotion systems (lust, attraction, and attachment)

that evolved to support mating, reproduction, and parenting. The first, *lust,* is equivalent to the sex drive or to Freud's concept of the libido. Lust is driven in both men and women primarily by the sex hormone androgen (testosterone being a potent example of an androgen hormone). At puberty, when levels of sex hormones increase markedly, adolescents become sexually excited by members of the opposite sex (or by the same sex for homosexual youth). However, lust is not love, nor does it promote long-term attachment. For example, when male sparrows were injected with testosterone, thereby increasing lust, they abandoned their mates to pursue other females (Wingfield, 1994). In our own species, men with high levels of testosterone are less likely to marry and have less-stable marriages when they do (Booth & Dabs, 1993).

Fisher defined *attraction* as synonymous with romantic love. Some of the characteristics of attraction that we mentioned briefly can be seen in other animals and are associated with activation in specific areas of the brain and the presence of specific neurochemicals. For example, romantic love is associated with an increase in the neurotransmitter dopamine, high levels of which are related to heightened attention, motivation, goal-directed behaviors, euphoria, and increased mental activity, among other characteristics associated with romantic love (see Fisher, 2000). Romantic love is also associated with increased levels of norepinephrine in the central nervous system, which is itself associated with increased memory for new stimuli and events. The love-possessed focus their attention on their loved one and remember often trivial details related to them. Fisher speculated that the inability of those in love to keep thoughts of their beloved out of their mind is similar to obsessive-compulsive disorder and associated with low levels of the neurotransmitter serotonin.

What purpose does romantic love serve? First, it seems obvious that the near-exclusive focus of lovers on one another promotes an exclusive sexual relationship. Although attraction is not the result of sex, most people in love feel a strong sexual desire for their beloved, accompanied by sexual exclusivity and heightened feelings of jealousy if they think their partner may be interested in another person. Sex and pregnancy can and do occur without love, but the attraction lovers feel toward one another may dissuade one from having sex with other people, thus increasing paternity certainty for men and the likelihood of receiving the support of her mate should a pregnancy result for women.

Researchers have noted that neurotransmitter levels associated with being in love typically return to normal levels between 6 and 18 months after initially falling in love (see Fisher, 2000). This time frame is certainly long enough for pregnancy to occur, but if such passionate love wanes, what is to keep a man and a woman together following the birth of a baby? Human children are particularly slow to grow up, and mothers require the support of others, their mates especially, in rearing a child. It is the third emotional system, attachment, that facilitates the longer-term relationships necessary to rear children.

Among developmental psychologists, attachment usually refers to the relationship between children and their mothers or other caretakers (see Chapter 12). Attachment in Fisher's theory, however, refers to male-female bonding. Men and women who are attached express feelings of closeness, security, anxiety when separated from one's partner for an extended length of time, and mild euphoria when with one's partner (Liebowitz, 1983). Such attachment feelings are associated with the hormones vasopressin and oxytocin. These same hormones are released during sexual intercourse and are also associated with infant-mother attachment (see Chapter 12).

Fisher (2000) speculated that human pair bonding evolved as females required increasing protection and resources to care for their long-dependent offspring. Similarly, it became in men's inclusive-fitness interest to support their mates and their mates' offspring. Most men would not have access to the resources necessary to support multiple wives and their children. Furthermore, the survival of their dependent and slow-developing offspring would be greatly benefited by paternal support (Geary, 2005c; see Chapter 12). As a result, it became in both men's and women's best genetic interest to work together to rear their offspring, and the attachment system, Fisher proposed, evolved to serve this need. (As an aside, Fisher is the chief scientific consultant for the online dating service *Chemstry.com*, where she applies her evolutionary-based theory in constructing personality questionnaires to match potential partners.)

Falling in love is not unique to adolescents. People of all ages display basically the same behavioral and physiological reactions when falling in love, regardless if one is 16 or 60 (Fisher, 2004). However, falling in love, perhaps several times, is almost a rite of passage for adolescents. Much of teenagers' time is spent thinking about or being involved in romantic relationships. In Western cultures, romantic relationships are part of dating—of having boyfriends and girlfriends—and we examine briefly adolescent romantic relationships in the following section.

Adolescent Romantic Relations

During the elementary school years, most peer interaction is done in same-sex groups (Maccoby, 1988, see Chapter 14). Whereas preadolescents spend less than an hour per week interacting with members of the opposite sex, this changes in adolescence. For example, a sample of 12th-grade American students reported spending an average of 5 to 10 hours per week interacting with members of the opposite sex, and another 5 to 8 hours per week thinking about members of the opposite sex (Richards et al., 1998). It is from these groups that initial romantic relationships develop, first typically beginning with boy-girl group dating and eventually resulting in dyadic romantic relationships (Connolly et al., 2004). Thus, the likelihood of establishing a romantic relationship in early adolescence is related to the size of the mixed-sex peer group to which one belongs (Connolly, Furman, & Konarski, 2000).

We should be careful not to confuse adolescent romantic relationships with romantic love. Not all dating couples are in love, of course. In fact, having a boyfriend or girlfriend may be seen as a status symbol among one's peers. There may be pressure from peers to establish a romantic relationship, and an adolescent may see having a boy- or girlfriend as a sign of normalcy and belonging (Collins & Steinberg, 2006). Nonetheless, romantic love and sexual relationships can and often do result from adolescent dating.

Do romantic relationships in adolescents foster good development? That depends on several factors. Romantic relationships are seen as part of typical development, and as such signal to adolescents that they are developing normally. Such relationships can contribute to the development of identity (see Chapter 7), sexuality, relationships with close peers, and even scholastic achievement and career planning (Furman, 2002). However, there is also a downside to romantic relationships. Early involvement in romantic relationships and having a large number of sexual partners are associated with adjustment problems in adolescence (Zimmer-Gembeck, Siebenbruner, & Collins, 2001). Adolescents who have had romantic partners are also more apt to experience depression, likely as the result of the breakups that are the almost inevitable product of teenage romances (Davila, 2008; Monroe et al., 1999). And romantic relationships can lead to

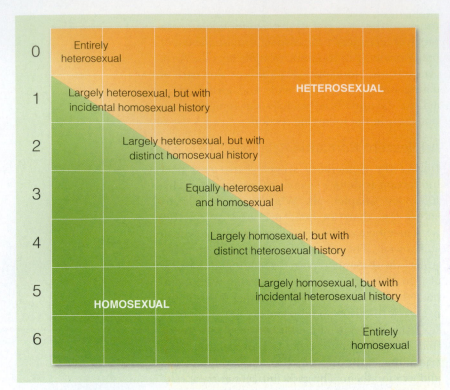

0	Entirely heterosexual	
1	Largely heterosexual, but with incidental homosexual history	**HETEROSEXUAL**
2	Largely heterosexual, but with distinct homosexual history	
3	Equally heterosexual and homosexual	
4	Largely homosexual, but with distinct heterosexual history	
5	**HOMOSEXUAL** Largely homosexual, but with incidental heterosexual history	
6		Entirely homosexual

FIGURE 15.4 **The continuum of sexuality.**
It has been suggested that sexual orientation is not a dichotomy between heterosexuality and homosexuality, but rather a continuum, meaning that people can vary in the degree of their heterosexual or homosexual behavior. In this figure, 0 corresponds to exclusively heterosexual and 6 corresponds to exclusively homosexual. The light and shaded areas for ratings 1 through 5 reflect degree of heterosexual (light areas) and homosexual (shaded areas) orientation. SOURCE: From Kinsey, A. C., Pomeroy, W. B., Martin, C. E., & Gebhard, P. H. (1953). *Sexual behavior in the human female.* Philadelphia: Saunders. Reprinted by permission.

having sex, which can result in pregnancy and sexually transmitted diseases (Furman, 2002).

Adolescent romantic relationships have only recently received research attention (see Furman & Collins, 2009). This may seem a bit strange, given the amount of time adolescents spend seeking, thinking about, and being involved in such relationships. What work has been done has been limited almost exclusively to Western cultures. Although falling in love and sexual attraction are universal, teenage romantic relationships and dating are only one of a variety of ways that boys and girls and men and women become involved. Further research clearly needs to explore falling in love and romantic relationships in a larger range of cultures and contexts and for homosexual and bisexual relationships as well as heterosexual ones.

The Development of Sexual Orientation

Ritch Savin-Williams (2006, p. 41) defines sexual orientation as "the preponderance of erotic arousals, feelings, fantasies, and behaviors we have for males, females, or both." However, sexuality is complicated, and it is also not as easy to classify sexual orientation as most of us believe. We usually think of sexual orientation in terms of a dichotomy, with two distinct categories being heterosexual and homosexual; or we think of a trichotomy: heterosexual, homosexual, and bisexual (Brown, 1987). In actuality, sexual orientation is best viewed as a continuum, with het-

erosexuality at one end, homosexuality at the other, and various degrees of bisexuality in between (Diamond, 2008; Ellis, Burke, & Ames, 1987). Figure 15.4 presents this continuum graphically (from Kinsey et al., 1953). This figure in no way reflects the percentages of people who are homosexual, heterosexual, and bisexual, but only how sexual orientation can be viewed on a continuum.

Sexual orientation has at least three components: *sexual/romantic attraction* or arousal (to which sex do people feel most attracted?), *sexual behavior* (with which sex do people have voluntary sexual acts, which may or may not involve intercourse and orgasm?), and *sexual identity* (how do people describe themselves: heterosexual, gay, lesbian, or bisexual?). Perhaps surprisingly, these three components of sexual orientation are not always highly correlated. For example, depending on which component one uses, rates of homosexuality can vary greatly. Table 15.7 presents a summary of rates of homosexuality in four countries, based separately on each of the three components of sexual orientation: attraction, behavior, and identity (from Savin-Williams, 2006). As you can see, depending on which measure is used, the rates vary between 1% and 21%. If we describe homosexuality in terms of exclusive attraction to members of the same sex, the estimate is between 3% and 7% (Epstein, 2006).

As Table 15.7 indicates, although a minority of people identify themselves as homosexual, a greater proportion experience same-sex attraction or engage in homosexual behavior at some time during their lives. For example, in the classic studies of Kinsey and his colleagues (1948, 1953), 37% of men and 13% of women reported having engaged in homosexual behavior at sometime in their lives, most usually during adolescence. The results of more contemporary research indicate that between 5% and 10% of adolescent males and 6% of adolescent females have had same-sex sexual experiences, mostly with peers (Bancroft et al., 2003; Turner et al, 1998), with many such experiences being only dalliances as a by-product of curiosity (DeLamater & Friedrich, 2002). Thus, contrary to what many people believe, sexual orientation is a complex, multicomponent concept whose full scientific understanding is still far from being complete. In the remainder of this section, we use the terms *heterosexual* and *homosexual* to refer to people's primary sexual orientation.

Heterosexuality is the norm in most societies, as it must be in order to procreate the species. However, it is important to point out that homosexuality is not a pathology, but rather a typical variation within our species and other species. Homosexuality has been found in all cultures throughout history and is condoned by the majority of human

table 15.7 Rates of Homosexuality in Four Countries Depending on the Criteria Used: Sexual/Romantic Attraction, Sexual Behavior, or Sexual Identity

As you can see, the frequency of homosexuality depends on which criterion you use.

Country	Attraction		Behavior		Identity	
	Male	Female	Male	Female	Male	Female
United States:						
Youth	6%	3%	11%	5%	8%	3%
Young adults	13%	5%	4%	3%	4%	3%
Adults	8%	8%	4%	9%	1%	2%
Australia: Adults	17%	15%	8%	16%	4%	7%
Turkey: Young adults	7%	6%	4%	5%	2%	2%
Norway: Adolescents	21%	9%	7%	6%	5%	5%

SOURCE: Savin-Williams, R. C. (2006). Who's gay? Does it matter? *Current Directions in Psychological Science, 15*, 40–44. Reprinted by permission.

societies (Crompton, 2003; Ford & Beach, 1951). In fact, in some societies, a prolonged period of homosexuality before marriage and the commencement of heterosexual relations is typical (Crompton, 2003; Money, 1988). For example, various tribes in the Pacific islands of Melanesia have institutionalized bisexuality, requiring that males between the ages of 9 and 19 leave their families and reside in a single house in the village where males congregate. Until the age of 19, which is the prescribed age of marriage, they all participate in homosexual activities. After marriage, homosexual activities cease or are infrequent (Money, 1988). Even in societies where homosexuality is discouraged or even severely punished, its incidence is substantial. Homosexual behavior is not unique to humans but has been observed in 470 different animal species (Bagemihil, 1999), including our close genetic relatives, chimpanzees and bonobos (Dixson, 1998).

What Causes Sexual Orientation?

From an evolutionary perspective, heterosexuality should be the norm, given that it is necessary to reproduce the species. This makes homosexuality a bit of a conundrum for evolutionary theorists. How could sexual behavior that does not promote reproduction evolve? There are hypotheses about this, but there are no definitive answers (Konner, 2010). For example, many homosexuals reproduce, just not at the same rate as heterosexuals (Muscarella, 2000). Thus, it is not that homosexuality leads to a genetic dead end, but simply that homosexuals, on average, have fewer offspring than heterosexuals.

Environmental Explanations of Sexual Orientation

Environmental accounts hold that children learn their sexual orientation in childhood, and although society may not approve of or reinforce a homosexual orientation, perhaps a child's parents unwittingly do. Although environmental explanations are widely believed, research has generally failed to find strong support for them. The most influential theorist of this type was Sigmund Freud (1953). Freud believed that homosexuality was caused by problems in a child's psychosexual development. Children who have distant relationships with their same-sex parent are less apt to identify with them and do not develop gender-typical behaviors (McConaghy & Silove, 1992; Bailey et al., 1995). A related hypothesis is that a domineering mother and/or weak father results in a homosexual orientation in boys.

Other environmental explanations have tied sexual orientation to the acquisition of sex roles. Children whose mannerisms and interests resemble those of the opposite sex may be responded to by others with reciprocal mannerisms, causing sex-role confusion (East, 1946). For example, the boy who plays with dolls and acts effeminately will be perceived in the way girls are generally perceived and treated accordingly. Based on social reinforcement, children may come to see themselves as others see them, making a homosexual orientation part of their self-description (Kagan, 1964; Plummer, 1981).

There has been little support for these early environmental explanations of sexual orientation. Perhaps the most compelling data against the environmental explanation comes from detailed interviews of more than 1,300 men and women, including both homosexuals and heterosexuals, by Alan Bell, Martin Weinberg, and Sue Keifer Hammersmith (1981) from the Kinsey Institute. For example, Bell et al. examined the hypothesis that male homosexuality is associated with strong mothers and weak fathers. They concluded that there was no evidence of a connection between male homosexuality and strong mothers and that a boy's relationship with his mother and his future

Some beliefs

Little Support!

Although there is no evidence that playing with dolls, for example, causes boys to be homosexual, extreme effeminate behavior in boys, including preferences for girls' play activities, is a good (but not perfect) predictor of adult homosexuality.

sexual orientation was hardly worth mentioning. Bell and his colleagues stated that, in most cases, there was nothing that parents did to make their children homosexuals. This is further supported by research discussed in Chapter 13 showing that children raised by lesbian or gay parents grow up to be as psychologically well-adjusted, and just as likely to have a heterosexual orientation, as children raised by heterosexual parents (see Golombok & Tasker, 1996; Patterson, 2002).

Another popular theory holds that young boys are seduced into homosexuality by older males. The Kinsey Institute group found no support for this theory either (Bell et al., 1981). Homosexual men generally recalled their first homosexual experiences as being with males close to their own age. In fact, the childhood sexual experiences reported by homosexual and heterosexual men in the Kinsey study were strikingly similar. Both reported early sex play with both boys and girls. However, the experience in itself is not as important as the feelings that accompany it. Significantly more homosexuals than heterosexuals reported feelings of homosexual arousal during late childhood and adolescence, often before any type of sexual experience had occurred.

Evidence that effeminate boys often "turn off" their fathers was reported in a longitudinal study by Daniel Green (1987). He followed 44 extremely effeminate boys from preadolescence to adulthood and compared them to a matched set of noneffeminate boys. Green reported that the "sissy" boys had poorer relationships with their fathers and that the fathers were apt to express displeasure with their effeminate sons. Green believed that the effeminate behavior was the cause of the fathers' displeasure rather than being the result of the fathers' attitudes. Early effeminate behavior has been found to be a predictor of later homosexuality (Green, 1987; Zucker & Bradley, 1995). For example, of the 44 effeminate boys in Green's study, 33 grew up to be homosexual or bisexual. However, as should be obvious, not all homosexual men are effeminate and not all effeminate men are homosexual. For example, 11 of the boys in Green's study grew up to be heterosexuals, and 18% of the homosexual men in the Bell et al. (1981) study described themselves as being "very masculine" as boys. Moreover, most of the homosexual men in the Bell et al. study did not profess enjoying girls' games and activities as children, nor described themselves as being feminine.

Yet, many homosexual men and women display signs of gender nonconformity (that is, engage in opposite-sex behavior) in childhood (Drummond et al., 2008). This was nicely demonstrated in a study that looked at childhood home videos of homosexual and heterosexual men and women. Observers who did not know the adult sexual orientation of the children they viewed in the videos rated the pre-homosexual children as engaging in more gender nonconformist behaviors than pre-heterosexual children. This effect was found for both men and women (Rieger et al., 2008).

Genetic/Hormonal Explanations of Sexual Orientation

Genetic or hormonal explanations of sexual orientation have an equally impressive history as the environmental explanations. Early proponents of nonspecific inborn causes of sexual orientation were offered by Richard von Kraft-Ebbing (1965/1886) and Havelock Ellis (1915). Since that time, much has been learned about the biology of sexuality and gender development.

Evidence from behavioral genetic studies indicates a higher concordance rate of homosexuality among identical twins than among nonidentical twins. In research with men, given that one sibling was a homosexual, the probability that the second one was also gay was about 52% for identical (monozygotic) twins, 22% for nonidentical (dizygotic) twins, and 11% for adopted brothers (Bailey & Pillard, 1991). In research examining female homosexuality, given that one twin was a lesbian (not bisexual), the probability that the second one was also a lesbian was about 38% for identical (monozygotic) twins, 15% for nonidentical (dizygotic) twins, and 3% for adopted sisters (Bailey et al., 1993). Robert Epstein (2006) noted that the heritability of sexual orientation is moderate, about the same as that of handedness (between

.25 and .50 in males, and a bit lower in females), and substantially lower than that of height (.84) or head circumference (.90). This suggests that there is more to sexual orientation than can be attributed to genes alone, although genes may play an indirect role as well as a direct one.

In Chapter 3, we discussed the chromosomal and hormonal basis of gender differentiation. To reiterate briefly, prenatal hormones determine whether male or female genitals are constructed and also influence the developing brain and subsequent sex-related behavior. In nonhuman mammals, variations in prenatal hormone exposure affect adult sexual orientation (Money & Ehrhardt, 1972). For example, in species that produce litters such as mice and rats, a female fetus may be surrounded in the uterus by either other female or by male fetuses. Male fetuses produce androgens, some of which seep out of the amniotic sac and can be absorbed by fetuses around them. Female rats that are in close proximity to multiple male fetuses in the uterus (and thus exposed to higher-than-typical levels of androgen), versus those that are not, display more male-typical behaviors as adults, sometimes including mounting other females (see Clark & Galef, 1995). Given the many similarities in the reproductive biologies of mammals, including humans, it is tempting to conclude that our sexual orientation must be affected by the same biological factors that affect rats, sheep, and monkeys.

Other research indicates that the likelihood of being homosexual for a man is related to the number of older brothers he has. Anthony Bogaert (2006) examined four samples of homosexual and heterosexual men and found that the number of older biological brothers a man had was the best predictor of homosexual adult status. Having sisters or older step- or half-brothers did not predict one's sexual orientation, nor did maternal age or other family-related variables. Bogaert concluded that these data point to a strong role for prenatal effects in the origins of male homosexuality, suggesting that there is a "maternal memory" for male gestations or births. One hypothesis for this effect is that having a male fetus alters a woman's immune system. Male fetuses are interpreted as foreign to a woman's body, and as a result she develops some male antibodies, which in turn affect subsequent male fetuses.

Exposure to excessive male hormones has been associated with an increased incidence of homosexuality and gender-atypical play patterns in girls. **Congenital adrenal hyperplasia** (CAH) results when a female fetus is exposed to excessive levels of androgen produced by the fetus's (or the mother's) adrenal glands (comparable to what is typically produced in males). These androgenized females are more masculine in their play activities and attitudes as girls and have more masculine mannerisms

(Berenbaum & Hines, 1992; Servin et al., 2003), even though, as children, their parents give them more positive feedback for playing with girls' toys than parents of unaffected girls (Pasterski et al., 2005). Although there are limited data on the sexual orientation of CAH girls, as adults, these women report less sexual experience and a higher frequency of homosexual and bisexual fantasies than unaffected women (Zucker et al., 1996), and although most of them are exclusively heterosexual, there is a higher incidence of bisexuality or homosexuality than in other women (see Ruble et al., 2006).

There is some additional evidence that sexual orientation is related to prenatal experiences. For example, research indicates an increase in male homosexuality as a function of extreme stress experienced by mothers during pregnancy. In several studies, mothers of homosexual men recalled more stressful episodes during their pregnancies than did mothers of heterosexual men (Ellis et al., 1988). There was no relationship between homosexuality and maternal stress for females. Results of animal research have similarly reported feminization of male rats as a result of prenatal stress, with the effects on female rats being generally minimal (Beckhardt & Ward, 1982; Politch & Herrenkohl, 1984).

Issues related to being homosexual and "coming out" are examined in Box 15.3. p. 639.

A Biosocial Perspective of Sexual Orientation and Gender Identity

Even if genetics and prenatal hormones should prove to be the primary cause of sexual orientation, this does not mean that learning cannot have an influence. Patterns of sexual practices vary widely around the world, indicating a flexibility of sexual behavior in humans not found in other mammals (Money, 1988; Money & Ehrhardt, 1972). John Money (1986, 1988; Money & Ehrhardt, 1972) developed a **biosocial theory of gender identity and sexual orientation**, proposing that prenatal and adolescent hormones, in addition to experiences during childhood, determine one's sexual identity. Money (1986, 1988) compared the development of gender identity and sexual orientation to the development of language. Biology dictates that children will learn language in all but a silent environment, but the language they learn will depend on what speech they are exposed to. Furthermore, if

---

congenital adrenal hyperplasia (CAH) A condition in which a fetus is exposed to excessive levels of androgen; in females this can result in greater male-stereotyped behaviors.

biosocial theory of gender identity and sexual orientation The theory that prenatal and adolescent hormones, in addition to experiences during childhood, determine one's sexual identity.

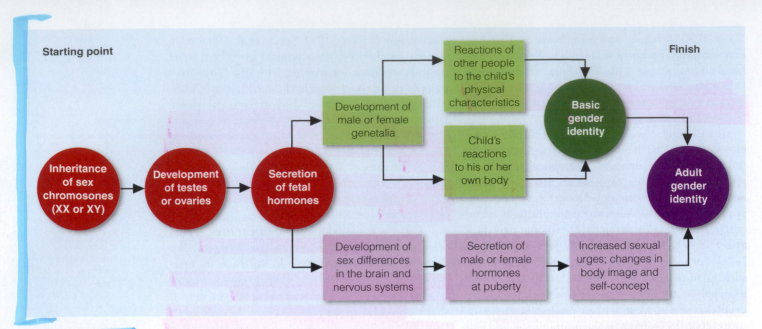

Starting point | **Finish**

Inheritance of sex chromosones (XX or XY) → Development of testes or ovaries → Secretion of fetal hormones

Development of male or female genetalia → Reactions of other people to the child's physical characteristics / Child's reactions to his or her own body → Basic gender identity → Adult gender identity

Development of sex differences in the brain and nervous systems → Secretion of male or female hormones at puberty → Increased sexual urges; changes in body image and self-concept

FIGURE 15.5 Critical events in Money and Ehrhardt's (1972) biosocial theory of gender identity.

According to this theory, gender identity is the result of the interaction of biologic (genes, hormones) and environmental factors, as well as children's reactions to their bodies and other people's reactions. SOURCE: Adapted from Money, J., & Ehrhardt, A. A. (1972). *Man and woman, boy and girl.* Baltimore: Johns Hopkins University Press.

language is to be learned proficiently, exposure to it must occur early in life (Johnson & Newport, 1989; Lenneberg, 1967; see Chapter 9). Something similar may occur for the development of sexual orientation. For example, one of the effects of sex hormones during puberty is the lowering of thresholds for activation of brain pathways dealing with erotic content. These brain pathways were formed prenatally, and now, years later, are being "turned on" by adult hormones (Money, 1988; Money & Tucker, 1975).

It is important to state that one's erotic orientation (for example, being heterosexual) is not determined at puberty, only the activation of that content. In boys, sex hormones influence directly their nocturnal emissions (wet dreams) and sexual thoughts. In girls, pubertal hormones pique their sexual interest, but actual sexual behavior is more dependent on social influence than it is for boys (Money & Tucker, 1975). According to Money and Tucker (1975), these preferences are unavoidable, unchangeable, and probably have been set for life (Money & Tucker, 1975). Other researchers examining gender identity or sex differences have proposed similar biosocial theories (Casey, 1996; Halpern, 2004), some of which will be discussed later in this chapter. Money and Ehrhardt's biosocial model for gender identity is presented in Figure 15.5.

Because both prenatal and postnatal experiences (including exposure to hormones) affect sexual orientation, does this imply that people can choose their sexual orientation? Obviously, if nonbiological factors do have an influence on sexual orientation, at least in part of the continuum of sexual orientation (see Figure 15.4), something other than biology, as traditionally understood, affects one's sexual orientation. But this is a far cry from considering sexual orientation an *intentional* and

individual choice. We fully agree with John Money (1988, p. 11) on this issue:

A heterosexual man or women does not become heterosexual by preference. There is no option, no plan. Becoming heterosexual is something that happens—an example of the way things are, like being tall or short, left-handed or right-handed, colorblind or color seeing. Being homosexual is no more a preference than being heterosexual. No one, boy or girl, man or woman, prefers to be homosexual instead of heterosexual. Likewise, no one prefers to be bisexual instead of monosexual. One is or is not bisexual, homosexual, or heterosexual.

Consistent with Money's argument, the great bulk of data available on the stability of sexual orientation indicates that changes are rare, for both men and women (Rosario et al., 2006).

Understanding Gender Differences

A small group of elementary schoolchildren was asked who their friends were, boys or girls, and why they liked them (Bjorklund & Bjorklund, 1992, p. 364). Here are a few examples of what some girls and boys had to say:

Lynsey (age 7) Girls like to talk about things girls like, and boys like to talk about things boys like. Some girls are interested in what boys like, and some boys like to talk about things girls like. Girls can share different ideas than boys, and boys will share different ideas than girls.

Rhodine (age 10) Girls are nice. They're not as rough as boys. They share things. They help you. Boys are rough. I didn't like to play with boys when I was little, but I think I'll like them better when I'm older. Maybe they'll be nicer.

BOX 15.3 **food for thought**

Coming Out: The Progression of Sexual Identity in Gays, Lesbians, and Bisexuals

Recognizing privately and sometimes publicly (coming out) that one is a member of a sexual-minority group is usually a gradual and often (unfortunately) difficult process (see accompanying table). Many children become aware of same-sex attraction when they are approximately 8 to 10 years old (Savin-Williams, 1998a), years before most children display mature sexual feelings or behaviors. For example, when the AIDS epidemic hit in the 1980s, one 8-year-old boy, already being aware of his homosexual orientation, made the connection between homosexuality, AIDS, and death (missing the part about sexual contact), and believed that he was destined for an early demise. This first stage is extremely variable, however, with some children not developing this awareness until adolescence. For women, it is not uncommon that their first awareness of being a lesbian or bisexual does not occur until after years of maintaining heterosexual relationships and even motherhood (D'Augelli & Patterson, 2001; Rotheran-Borus & Langabeer, 2001).

This first recognition phase may be followed by a test and exploration stage, where children feel ambivalent about their distinctive feelings and continue to explore their sexual orientation. This stage often takes place when children are approximately between 10 and 13 years old.

The third milestone is identity acceptance, a period that typically extends from 13 to 17 years and is characterized by an explicit, though private, recognition of one's sexual identity ("I am gay," "I am a lesbian"), and sometimes with the first experiences of homosexual sex. Although the average age at which children identify themselves as a sexual minority is about 15 (Savin-Williams & Cohen, 2004), this, again, is extremely variable. Moreover, boys typically do not label themselves as gay or bisexual until after they have had sex with another boy; girls, in contrast, are more likely to have already labeled themselves as lesbian or bisexual before engaging in homosexual acts (Savin-Williams & Diamond, 2000).

A final point in this process is identity integration. At this stage, some **sexual-**

Carolyn A. McKeone/Photo Researchers, Inc.

The process of coming out for sexual-minority youth can be long and difficult, but many people with a homosexual orientation are aware of their orientation before adolescence, whereas others, particularly females, may not be aware of it until after maintaining heterosexual relationships for a number of years.

minority youth begin to feel proud of belonging to a sexual-minority community and initiate disclosure to others. On average, this takes place when they are between 17 and 19 years old, with the first disclosures being made to peers and/or siblings. Parents are often told one to two years later, if at all (Savin-Williams & Diamond, 2000; Savin-Williams, 1998b). When sexual-minority youth tell their parents, they usually tell their mothers rather than their fathers (Savin-Williams & Ream, 2003). Going public with one's sexual-minority orientation can often lead to anger, disappointment from one's parents, loss of some heterosexual friends, and verbal and physical aggression by peers, at least initially (Savin-Williams & Ream, 2003; D'Augelli, 1998).

Social acceptance of a sexual-minority orientation is even more difficult in some ethnic groups (more in Latin and Asian American groups than in European American groups) and in some conservative religious groups (D'Augelli, 2004). Accordingly, it is no wonder that some youth choose to hide their sexual identity from family and peers. In fact, psychological maladjustment and its consequences (for example, school problems, substance abuse) among youth who have openly expressed their sexual identity is much higher than in their het-

erosexual peers, particularly concerning suicide attempts (see Rotheram-Borus & Langabeer, 2001; D'Augelli, 2004; Savin-Williams, 2006).

Given the societal expectation of heterosexuality, recognizing and accepting one's identity as a sexual-minority youth tends to be a long and sometimes complex process. Not all sexual-minority youth in modern culture follow the stages described (and even not at the same pace when they do follow them), and not all sexual-minority youth accept their own sexuality when they become aware of it. Moreover, not all young people who accept it make it public (for different reasons, not necessarily social fears). However, when youth truly accept their own sexuality and count on the support of family and friends (which does not always happen), there is good psychological adjustment (D'Augelli, 2004) despite personal victimization, social discrimination, and cultural stigmatization that continues to exist in certain segments of some societies (including the United States) (Savin-Williams, 2006). Quite often, having friends with the same sexual-minority identity is helpful for developing a healthy sense of sexual and gender identity and psychological adjustment (Savin-Williams, 1998a).

A Coming-Out Path Process in Gays and Lesbians

First recognition	8–10 years old
Test and exploration	10–13 years old
Identity acceptance	13–17 years old
Identity integration	17–19 years old

SOURCE: Adapted from Savin-Williams, R. C. (1998a) *And then I became gay: Young men's stories.* New York: Routledge; and Savin-Williams, R. C., & Diamond, L. M. (2000). Sexual identity trajectories among sexual-minority youths: Gender comparisons. *Archives of Sexual Behavior, 29,* 419–440.

sexual-minority youth Youth whose sexual orientation is not heterosexual.

Scott (age 6) I like to play with boys best. Boys normally want to play Nintendo. We'll ride bikes, jump ramps, and ride through piles of dirt. And we do karate fights together. All girls do is sit around and do nothing. They boss you around, especially when it comes to sisters.

Harris (age 10) Boys—they're more active. They're not afraid to climb stuff and go into the woods and forests and do dangerous things. Sometimes boys are mean. Girls are always nice. But girls will scratch you if they get mad at you. I used to think they would bite.

Although these children's brief descriptions of friendship may reflect a bit of schoolyard sexism, they reflect the fact that boys and girls of this age interact with other children who are like them (see Chapter 14). And gender is perhaps the most obvious factor for school-age children in determining who is like them.

A chapter on sexuality and gender development would not be complete without some mention of gender differences. Men and women, boys and girls differ in more ways than their reproductive organs. There has been much scientific interest in sex differences and the origins of those differences. In many cases, differences between males and females have no import or interest. Looking for differences between the sexes just because you can has little justification. However, given the significance of sex in reproducing the species, it should not be surprising that differences between males and females exist, possibly related to the best interest of getting men's and women's genes into the next generation and rearing their children to adulthood.

One persistent question researchers have asked is about the origins of sex differences. Are differences between males and females attributed mainly to their unique biologies, starting with the genes and including hormone exposure? Or do sex differences arise mostly because of differences in societal, parental, and peer pressures and expectations? Perhaps some are primarily the former and others primarily the latter. This has led to the distinction in academic psychology between *sex differences*, those differences that can be attributed mainly to biology, and *gender differences*, those differences that can be attributed mainly to cognitive and sociocultural factors. This distinction may be well-meaning, but we believe that it perpetuates a false nature-nurture dichotomy: the belief that the contributions of biology and culture (or genes and environment, or biology and learning) can be neatly separated and packaged. We use the terms sex and gender differences interchangeably in this and other chapters (cf., Halpern, 2004).

We wish to emphasize here that behaviors, cognitions, and attitudes develop in a web of interactions beginning with genes and extending through culture, and that changes in any aspect of such a developmental system can have a substantial impact on the outcome of a given child (see Chapter 2). This is no less true when behaviors, cognitions, and attitudes develop differently between males and females. Thus, the finding of a sex difference for a particular characteristic does not imply that males and females are genetically destined to be different. Rather, the finding of a reliable sex difference implies only that the two sexes develop different patterns under certain conditions. Identifying the origin of a difference requires careful examination and will surely involve factors that have traditionally been thought of as biological in nature, as well as those traditionally thought of as environmental.

Sex differences are particularly interesting from an evolutionary perspective, because, following parental investment theory discussed earlier in this chapter and in Chapter 12, males and females evolved different psychologies to reflect their somewhat different self-interests with respect to mating and parenting. Such differences, however, are sensitive to early environments and develop as a result of a host of interacting factors. Rather than providing an exhaustive inspection of sex differences here, most psychological differences between boys and girls and their supposed causes and consequences have been discussed in other chapters throughout this book (for example, sex differences in play style in Chapter 14). Here we provide some cautions in interpreting sex differences, highlight some of the most frequently found sex differences (see Concept Review 15.2, p. 642), and outline a model for understanding sex differences in cognitive abilities that can be applied in general form to understanding most psychological sex differences.

Things to Keep in Mind When Evaluating Sex Differences

There are several important things to keep in mind when examining sex differences and their development. First, the magnitude of the differences is often small, with substantial overlap in the distributions (Hyde, 2005; Ruble et al., 2006). Moreover, there is great variability in the population for nearly every trait analyzed. This means, for example, that for an ability with an average female advantage, such as reading literacy, there will be many boys who perform better than many girls. In fact, Janet Shibley Hyde (2005, 2007) proposed that most psychological sex differences are so small in magnitude, vary with age, and depend on context that we should talk more of gender similarities and less of gender differences. We do not, however, want to minimize the possible significance of sex differences or propose that because they are small they are not real. They may vary with context and not always be found, but, particularly when there are good theoretical reasons to expect sex differences in some situations, they can provide valuable insights into human development and behavior.

Second, when substantial sex differences are found, boys and girls typically show different patterns of behaviors rather than one being superior to the other. For example, with respect to mental disorders, boys are more likely than girls to display psychiatric disorders during childhood, including speech and language problems, autism, attention deficit disorder, and oppositional and conduct disorders. Girls, however, show higher rates of mental disorders than boys in adolescence, including separation anxiety disorder, depression, generalized anxiety disorder, and some specific phobias (see Hartung & Widiger, 1998). In general, and independent of age, boys are more apt to display externalizing behaviors (for example, conduct disorders), whereas girls are more likely to display internalizing behaviors (for example, depression, see Chapter 11).

Along these same lines, it is good to keep in mind that "different" means just that, and not necessarily better or worse. In fact, from an evolutionary perspective, there is often no best solution for solving a specific problem. Adaptive solutions will vary as a function of ecological conditions, and what may be well suited to one environment may not be so well suited to another. This seems to be the case for many sex differences. For example, trying to go from one's home to that of a new friend involves the use of navigational skills. Males tend to perform such tasks through the calculation of distances and directions (for example, using maps). Females, in contrast, tend to use landmarks in their navigation (for example, the location of a coffee shop or a certain bookstore), which is associated with their greater proficiency at recalling locations (see Benenson, 2005). Additional fMRI (functional magnetic resonance imaging) research shows that this differential pattern may have a correspondence in the brain. For example, it has been found that for solving an identical navigation task, men use the left hippocampus (involved in the processing of geometric cues) and women use the right parietal and prefrontal regions (involved in the processing of landmarks) (Grön et al., 2000). This clearly reflects a sex difference, but one type of solution is not necessarily better or worse than the other.

It is also worth noting that for most characteristics, males are more variable than females. There are often more males represented at both the highest and lowest ranges of a trait. This finding has usually been interpreted as reflecting the fact that males are more influenced than females by environmental factors (see Halpern et al., 2007).

Patterns of Sex Differences

Some of the largest sex differences are found in mortality rates, with boys having higher mortality rates than girls at all ages, beginning prenatally and continuing into adulthood (see Chapter 3). This pattern is found cross-culturally. In fact, when infant mortality rates in a country are greater for females than for males, selective female infanticide must be considered as a plausible reason (Benenson, 2005).

Perhaps the largest and most reliable behavioral sex differences are in throwing velocity and distance, with boys, beginning early in life, showing a consistent advantage relative to girls (Blakemore et al., 2008; Thomas & French, 1985; see Chapter 4). Risk-taking also shows relatively large sex differences, with boys exhibiting higher rates of risk-taking than girls beginning in early childhood and peaking in adolescence (see Benenson, 2005; Chapter 14). Unlike throwing distance or death, there is no single, undisputable measure of risk-taking. Examples of behaviors described by researchers as risk-taking include "ignoring adult prohibitions, climbing in dangerous places or

Girls generally do better in school than boys, getting higher grades in all subjects. Despite this, boys typically get higher scores on standardized math tests than girls.

Physical and mental health	*Morbidity and mortality rates* (females have lower mortality rates than males) *Mental disorders* (males are more apt to display externalizing problems, females internalizing problems) *School adaptation* (girls adapt better than boys) *Aggressive behaviors* (boys are more physically aggressive than girls)
Physical development	*Activity level* (boys are more active than girls) *Motor-skills and muscle strength* (boys can throw farther than girls; girls have better fine motor coordination and flexibility than boys) *Growth rate and neurological development* (girls exhibit earlier neurological development than boys)
Cognitive development	*Spatial abilities* (boys are better at mental rotation and spatial perception than girls) *Mathematical abilities* (girls get better grades than boys in math classes; boys perform better on standardized math tests than girls) *Linguistic abilities* (girls develop language sooner, have higher reading literacy and verbal fluency than boys; boys are more apt to have language and reading disabilities than girls)
Socioemotional development	*Emotional patterns* (females are more socially oriented and sensitive and emotionally expressive than males) *Risk-taking behaviors* (boys exhibit more risk-taking behaviors than girls) *Interest areas and activities* (boys show a higher interest in mechanical, inanimate objects and how they work than girls; girls show a higher interest in people and human relationships than boys. *Play style and social organization* (boys' play is characterized by rough-and-tumble play and an interest in attaining dominance, whereas girls are more cooperative and enabling of others)

SOURCE: Adapted from Benenson, J. F. (2005). Sex differences. In B. Hopkins (Ed.), *The Cambridge encyclopedia of child development* (pp. 366–373). New York: Cambridge University Press; and Ruble, D. N., Martin, C. L., & Berenbaum, S. A. (2006). Gender development. In W. Damon & R. M. Lerner (Series Eds.) & N. Eisenberg (Vol. Ed.), *Handbook of child psychology, vol. 3. Social, emotional, and personality development* (6th ed., pp. 858–932). Hoboken, NJ: John Wiley & Sons.

bicycling recklessly, physically aggressing against or directly verbally denigrating others, taking intellectual risks that could increase payoffs but reduce odds of success, and, when older, gambling, driving at high speeds, and engaging in sexual behaviors that facilitate contraction of diseases" (Benenson, 2005, p. 367).

Within the social realm, some sex differences are consistently reported. For example, boys are more physically aggressive than girls beginning in the preschool years (see Chapter 14). This is reflected in boys' greater preference for rough-and-tumble play relative to the more sedentary play style preferred by many (but not all) girls (see Pellegrini & Smith, 1998; Chapter 14). Boys and girls also differ in the content of their fantasy play. Girls' fantasy play frequently emphasizes relationships (for example, playing house, school), glamour, romance, and vulnerability (for example, princess fantasies), whereas boys' fantasy play more likely emphasizes dominance, involving action heroes, aggression, themes of danger, and protection against vulnerability (for example, supermen fantasies) (see Benenson, 2005; Ruble et al., 2006;

Chapter 14). Beginning in the preschool years, females are more socially expressive and responsive than males, as measured by indicators such as social gazing, expression of emotions, and general facial expressiveness (Hall et al., 2000; see Ruble et al., 2006; Chapter 11).

Sex differences tend to be smaller and less consistently found for some aspects of cognition and academic achievement (see Chapter 10). For example, most (but not all) studies report that the rate of language acquisition is faster for girls than for boys (Bornstein & Haynes, 1998; Galsworthy et al., 2000), and advantages in favor of females have been found in a long list of language/verbal abilities (overall verbal skills, vocabulary, reading comprehension, essay writing, and speech production), excepting for analogies, where males outperformed females (see Ruble et al., 2006; Chapter 9). Boys, in contrast, usually show better spatial abilities than girls. Girls get better grades in school and perform better on tests based on material learned in school than boys (including mathematics); in contrast, boys do better than girls on standardized tests of mathematics and science (Halpern, 2000, 2004; Chapter 10).

A Model for Understanding the Development of Psychological Sex Differences

Diane Halpern (2000, 2004) developed a model designed to explain sex differences in cognitive abilities, which, in general form, we believe is a good way to view the development of many psychological sex differences. Halpern argues that to understand sex differences on academic tasks, one must go beyond describing the nature of the task (for example, verbal, quantitative, visuospatial) and examine how information is acquired, stored, selected, retrieved, and used, each of which can vary depending on a variety of personal and contextual factors. Whereas girls may score higher on math tests than boys in school, for example, the reverse tends to be true on standardized tests, at least in some situations. There are no true or absolute sex differences here, merely differences in levels of performance in specified conditions.

Halpern argues that we cannot specify how much of average differences between males and females on any task are a result of nature or nurture. Rather, the relationship between nature and nurture is a dynamic one, interacting and varying over time. What children learn alters their brains. This in turn affects their ability to acquire and perform specific skills, which leads children to select new experiences, which will change the structure of their brains. According to Halpern (2004, p. 138):

> Differences in the interests of females and males both derive from differences in the areas in which they have achieved success and lead to further differential success in these areas because of differential knowledge and experience. Learning is both a biological and an environmental variable, and biology and environment are as inseparable as conjoined twins who share a common heart.

The Development of Gender Identity and Cognition

Most researchers view gender identity primarily as a cognitive phenomenon, with children acquiring knowledge about themselves and other people and integrating this knowledge into a coherent framework (Martin & Ruble, 2004; Ruble et al., 2006). Variants of Albert Bandura's social cognitive/social learning theory (Bandura, 1989; Perry & Bussey, 1984; see Chapter 2) have been influential in explaining how children acquire the knowledge and behaviors of their same-sex gender, as well as explaining some patterns of sex differences. In fact, it seems obvious to us that children learn what it means to be a man or a woman in society primarily by observing how others behave. More recent theories apply ideas from cognitive development to explain when and how such information is acquired.

As Diane Ruble and her colleagues (2006) have pointed out, gender operates at the *macrosystem level* (see Bronfenbrenner's theory in Chapter 2). It permeates every aspect of a child's social environment and every aspect of adult life (from culture and values, to work, school, leisure time, friendship, and family relationships). Gender is implicitly or explicitly everywhere. In a very general sense, we know that in most cultures women are gender typified in terms of being more expressive than men, more passive, cooperative, prosocial, dependent, and socially oriented. Men, in contrast, are gender typified in terms of being more instrumental than women, more active, competitive, aggressive, independent, and object-oriented. Although there are substantial individual differences in these traits, these stereotypes are familiar to most people within a culture (even if they do not believe them to be true) and serve as part of the broader social environment in which children develop their own sense of gender identity.

Children's gender identity is related to their overall psychological adjustment. For example, Susan Egan and David Perry (2001) defined gender identity as involving four dimensions:

1. Knowledge of membership in a gender category (that is, being male or female)
2. Felt compatibility with one's gender group (that is, *gender typicality*)
3. Felt pressure for gender conformity
4. Attitudes toward gender groups

In a series of studies, Egan, Perry, and their colleagues reported considerable variability in terms of gender typicality, felt pressure, and attitudes toward gender groups in fourth- through eighth-grade children. Moreover, individual differences in these various measures of gender identity predicted psychological adjustment. Especially affected were children who scored low on gender typicality (that is, who did not see themselves as typical of other children of the same sex) and high on felt pressure (that is, who perceived substantial pressure to conform to gender stereotypes). These children were more likely to display internalizing problems than were other children (Carver, Yunger, & Perry, 2003; Egan & Perry, 2001; Yunger, Carver, & Perry, 2004). These findings argue for the importance of the cognitive organization of children's gender identity in influencing their psychological adjustment and behavior.

Until about 6 or 7 years of age, children believe that wearing the clothes of the opposite sex or engaging in opposite-sex activities changes the individual, at least temporarily, into a member of that sex.

Gender cognition organizes and interprets information in the world, influencing children's behavior, motivation, and interests. It also influences some cognitive processes (for example, memory and reasoning) for gender-related information (Martin et al., 2002). Moreover, children are tremendously active in the search and construction of gender rules and regularities, as they are in general for all the other aspects of the social and nonsocial world (Piaget, 1983; Ruble et al., 2006). In the following sections we discuss two cognitive theories that focus on the development of gender knowledge in children: **gender development theory** and **gender schema theory**.

Gender Development Theory

Two-year-old Jorge's grandmother was changing his diapers, when he looked down, put his thumb and index finger around his penis, and said with great satisfaction, "Penis at Grandma's house. Penis at Mommy's house!" Jorge had seemed to realize that an often-covered part of his anatomy remained constant regardless of where he had his diapers changed.

gender development theory The theory that the development of gender identity follows a similar course as described by Piaget's theory of cognitive development.

gender schema theory The theory that gender development is based on children's developing understanding of *gender schemas*.

gender constancy The concept that gender remains the same despite changes in physical appearance, time, and behavior; includes gender identity, gender stability, and gender consistency.

Given the view that gender identity can best be explained as (primarily) a cognitive phenomenon, it is not surprising that early accounts of the development of gender identity followed the ideas of the Swiss psychologist Jean Piaget (see Chapters 2 and 6). Piaget (1983) argued that children progress through relatively discrete stages in their ability to understand the world. In particular, it was not until children were 5 to 7 years of age that they understood that superficial changes to a substance (for example, rolling a ball of clay into a sausage) did not change the amount of stuff in that substance. Piaget referred to this understanding as *conservation*, a belief in the quantitative constancy of matter.

Lawrence Kohlberg (1966) applied Piagetian ideas to develop the concept of **gender constancy**. Gender constancy refers to the idea that children realize that gender remains stable independent of changes in physical appearance. Following the tenets of Piaget's theory, children would not develop gender constancy until they enter the concrete operational stage, about 7 years of age. This is because it is not until this age that children are able to conserve matter—to realize, for example, that the amount of lemonade one has to drink is the same regardless of the shape of the glass it is in. Following theory, they should also not have a solid understanding that one's gender remains unchanged despite changes in appearance or activity.

We provided an example of a young child's belief that the clothes one wears temporarily changes one's gender in Chapter 6 when discussing preoperational children's thinking. As you may recall, a 3-year-old boy, wanting to ride to preschool in his grandfather's stick-shift Chevy, requested that his grandmother wear his grandfather's hat. This, he believed, would temporarily turn his grandmother into a man and give her the ability to drive a stick-shift car, which, when wearing her "grandmother clothes," she could not do.

Gender constancy shows a developmental progression between about 2 and 7 years of age (Ruble et al., 2007; Slaby & Frey, 1975). In an early investigation, Ronald Slaby and Karin Frey (1975) interviewed children between the ages of 2 and 5.5 years about their beliefs in the constancy of gender. Slaby and Frey identified three substages of gender constancy: gender identity, gender stability, and gender consistency. *Gender identity* in this context refers to the ability to identify oneself as male or female and to accurately identify the gender of others. Children typically can answer correctly questions about gender identity by about 2.5 years of age. *Gender stability* refers to the knowledge that gender remains stable over time. Thus, little girls at some point come to believe that they will become mothers when they grow up, and little boys believe that they will become fathers. The questions were asked to make it clear that the children were expressing not just a preference but a necessity; for example, they asked boys, "Could you ever be a mommy when you grow up?" Most children passed gender stability questions by about 4 or 5 years of age. *Gender consistency* refers to the knowledge that gender remains the same despite changes in behavior or dress. The researchers tested this knowledge with questions such as: "If you wore boys' clothes, would you be a girl or a boy?" and "If you played girls' games, would you be a boy or a girl?" These questions might seem trivial to an adult, but answers by preschool children can be quite revealing (for example, "I can't wear girls' clothes, 'cause then I'd be a girl!"). Gender consistency was the last ability to develop, with most children answering these questions correctly by 6 or 7 years of age.

Other researchers have replicated the basic pattern of gender constancy development (that is, identity → stability → consistency), and it has been observed both in Western (Eaton & Von Bargen, 1981; Ruble, Balaban, & Cooper, 1981) and non-Western (Munroe, Shimmin, & Munroe, 1984) cultures. Children tend to pass gender constancy questions earlier when they are related to themselves ("If *you* wore girls' clothing, would you be a girl or a boy?"), rather than when they are asked about other children. Preschool children in the United States are also more likely to answer questions correctly when they are asked about children of their own sex rather than opposite-sex children (Eaton & Von Bargen, 1981). These and related findings (Szkrybalo & Ruble, 1999) indicate that beliefs about the constancy of gender are not fully established until middle childhood. However, they also indicate that even preschoolers sometimes believe that gender is constant over time and situations. The range of situations in which they believe this, however, is limited and expands with age.

Does gender constancy have any consequences for how children behave or think? Research dating back to Slaby and Frey's (1975) pioneering study has shown that children who score high on tests of gender constancy (for example, pass questions of gender stability and/or gender consistency) are more attentive to same-sex models and more likely to play with toys that they watched same-sex children play with, than children who score low on tests of gender constancy (Luecke-Aleksa et al., 1995; Ruble et al., 1981). These effects are sometimes greater for boys than for girls.

However, effects of individual differences in gender constancy on gender-related behavior are not always found (see Ruble et al., 2006), making

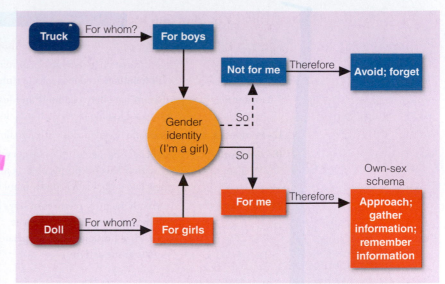

← Last to develop

it clear that there is much more to gender than just knowing it is constant over time and situations. In recent years, researchers have emphasized the role of knowledge of gender stereotypes as an important factor, with **gender schemas** playing a central role as the organizing mechanism underlying children's gender knowledge.

Gender Schema Theory

Schemas are mental/cognitive structures that consist of a set of expectations and associations that guide how information in a particular domain is processed and remembered. A *gender schema* influences how children process information related to gender and serves as a way for them to organize information about sex. According to Diane Ruble and her colleagues (2006, p. 908) "gender schemas are interrelated networks of mental associations representing information about the sexes. Schemas are not passive copies of the environment, but instead they are active constructions, prone to errors and distortions." Contrary to cognitive development theory, schemas would be operative once children are able to identify themselves as males or females. It is not necessary for gender constancy to develop before children begin to take gender seriously. Figure 15.6 presents a model of how children might interpret gender-relevant information (from Martin & Halverson, 1987). Based on their observations of others, children develop some idea of sex stereotypes (dolls are for girls; trucks are for boys). Once children have identified themselves as one gender or the other, they label objects and activities that are "for their gender" as being "for them"

FIGURE 15.6 A model of how gender knowledge may be processed beginning in early childhood in agreement with a gender schema theory approach. Once children identify themselves as boys or girls, they label objects, behaviors, and attitudes as for one gender or the other, and incorporate the gender-appropriate ones and avoid the gender-inappropriate ones. SOURCE: Martin, C. L., & Halverson, C. F. (1987). The roles of cognition in sex role acquisition. In D. B. Carter (Ed.), *Current conceptions of sex roles and sex typing: Theory and research*. New York: Praeger. Reproduced with permission of ABC-CLIO, LLC.

gender schema A mentalistic structure consisting of a set of expectations and associations that guide processing with respect to gender.

table 15.8 Timeline for Early Gender Development

Age	Gender-based Knowledge and Perception
6–8 months	Discriminate between voices of males and females Will habituate (reduce looking time) to one category of faces (male or female)
9–11 months	Discriminate between male and female faces Associate female faces with female voices
12–14 months	Associate female faces with female voices and male faces with male voices
18–20 months	Associate sex-stereotypic objects with appropriate gender (that is, associate male faces with male-stereotypic objects and female faces with female-stereotypic objects) Associate verbal labels (lady, man) with appropriate faces
24–26 months	Correctly identify pictures of boys and girls Imitate gender-related sequences Generalize imitation to appropriate gender (for example, using a male doll to imitate a masculine activity)

SOURCE: Adapted from Martin, C. L., Ruble, D. N., & Szkrybalo, J. (2002). Cognitive theories of early gender development. *Psychological Bulletin, 128*, 903–933.

and therefore incorporate those objects, behaviors, or attitudes into their own-sex schemas. Objects or activities they interpret as being "for the other gender" are labeled as "not for me" and are avoided, not attended to, or forgotten.

Gender schema theory has contributed to a more dynamic view of gender-knowledge development and to the recognition that even infants and toddlers have developing gender knowledge. Table 15.8 presents some milestones in children's gender knowledge between 6 and 26 months of age (Martin, Ruble, & Szkrybalo, 2002). As can be seen from the table, children as young as 6 to 8 months old can discriminate between voices of males and females, and they respond to gender cues (for example, associate female faces with female voices and male faces with male voices) by about 12 to 14 months.

Although even infants make distinctions between males and females, they do not seem to have any knowledge of gender stereotypes. This knowledge, however, develops early during the preschool years. Most studies assessing children's knowledge of gender stereotypes use concrete objects (for example, hammer, doll) or specific activities (for example, playing football, jumping rope) as stimuli (see Ruble et al., 2006). Children are typically shown some objects or pictures of some activities and asked if they are usually for girls, boys, or both. Not surprisingly, older children generally show greater gender-stereotype knowledge than do younger children (see Ruble et al., 2006; Signorella, Bigler, & Liben, 1993, for reviews). Girls are also more likely to say that a toy or activity is appropriate for both sexes, reflecting greater flexibility regarding sex stereotypes in girls than in boys (see Ruble et al., 2006).

Carol Martin and Diane Ruble (2004) proposed that gender stereotyping can be described as involving three phases (see Figure 15.7, see also Trautner et al., 2005). The first reflects children learning about gender-related characteristics during the toddler and preschool years. This is followed by a period of consolidation, in which gender-related activities are viewed in a rigid manner, so that children view cross-gender play and activities negatively. Boys and men behave in one way, and girls and women behave in another. Such rigidity of gender stereotypes peaks between 5 and 7 years of age. (The 4-year-old daughter of one of the authors displayed such rigidity when commenting on her father's choice of a shirt: "Daddy," she said. "You can't wear that pink shirt. Pink is only for girls.") Children's gender stereotypes become less rigid over the elementary school years until adolescence, when it increases again.

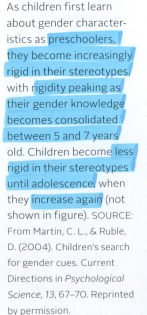

FIGURE 15.7 A model of phase changes in the rigidity of children's gender stereotypes as a function of age. As children first learn about gender characteristics as preschoolers, they become increasingly rigid in their stereotypes, with rigidity peaking as their gender knowledge becomes consolidated between 5 and 7 years old. Children become less rigid in their stereotypes until adolescence, when they increase again (not shown in figure). SOURCE: From Martin, C. L., & Ruble, D. (2004). Children's search for gender cues. Current Directions in *Psychological Science, 13*, 67–70. Reprinted by permission.

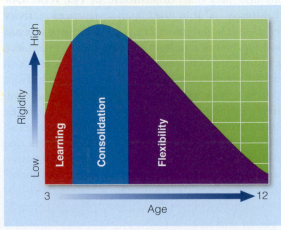

Perhaps not surprisingly, both periods of gender rigidity seem to correspond with milestones in subsequent gender identity development: the acquisition of gender constancy around 5 to 7 years of age and, in adolescence, awareness of sexual orientation (see earlier discussion). Sex-typed behaviors are relatively stable, with children who show the most highly sex-typed behavior during the preschool years (between 2.5 and 5 years) being the most sex-typed at age 8 (Golombok et al., 2008).

One purpose of gender schemas is to organize information to make it more memorable. Information that is consistent with one's gender stereotypes should be more readily remembered than inconsistent information (Bauer, 1993; Liben & Signorella, 1993). Several studies have confirmed this hypothesis, finding that both boys and girls seem to remember and understand same-sex stereotypes better than opposite-sex stereotypes (Liben & Signorella, 1993; Martin, Wood, & Little, 1990), and that these effects are more extreme in boys than in girls (Boston & Levy, 1991). Consistent with these observations, boys show sex-stereotyped toy preferences earlier than girls (Bauer, 1993; O'Brien & Huston, 1985) and avoid opposite-sex toys more than girls (Fagot, Leinbach, & Hagan, 1986).

Let us provide an example of sex differences in knowledge of gender stereotypes in a group of very young children. Patricia Bauer (1993) showed groups of 25-month-old toddlers a series of six activities: two stereotypically masculine activities (for example, building a house), two stereotypically feminine activities (for example, putting a diaper on a baby), and two neutral activities (for example, having a birthday party). The toddlers were encouraged to imitate each activity, both immediately and after a two-week delay. Girls displayed comparable levels of imitation for the three types of activities. Boys, in comparison, showed higher levels of imitation for the masculine and neutral activities than for the feminine activities. These findings suggest that, at least for boys, gender schemas are operating as early as 2 years of age, with boys avoiding traditionally feminine activities.

One interpretation of these findings is that young boys are more strongly sex-stereotyped than young girls (Bauer, 1993). However, other research suggests that young children's preference for same-sex toys is independent of their knowledge of gender stereotypes. For example, boys and girls generally display a preference for sex-typed toys regardless of their level of gender knowledge (Fagot et al., 1986), with this effect being particularly strong in boys (Perry, White, & Perry, 1984). These results, coupled with the findings that

© Davis Barber/PhotoEdit

Boys show gender stereotypes earlier than girls, and are more apt to select "boy" toys and avoid "girl" toys.

girls who are exposed to high levels of androgen before birth show toy preferences similar to those of boys, suggest that early toy preference is influenced more by biological than by cognitive factors.

Shari Berenbaum's studies of CAH girls suggest that exposure to prenatal androgen has a defeminizing effect on toy preferences (Berenbaum & Hines, 1992). This does not mean, however, that androgen has a direct effect on toy preference. We seriously doubt that there is a part of the brain that causes us to find toy guns attractive and baby dolls unattractive, or vice versa. One possibility is that androgen influences activity level, temperament, or motor skills, which leads to a preference for more stereotypically masculine toys and activities (Halverson & Waldrop, 1973; O'Brien & Huston, 1985).

These findings in no way imply that children's gender-related behavior is biologically fixed. Children around the world are exposed to a wide variety of culturally appropriate male and female models, and the social setting, more than anything else, determines what behaviors children will adopt for their own (see Box 15.4). But it should not be surprising that biology can predispose male and female children toward certain

BOX 15.4 socioculturally speaking

Rites of Passage: The Navajo Kinaaldá Ceremony for Girls

Rite of passage is a term used by anthropologists to describe those ceremonies or rituals held by some human groups with the purpose of publicly formalizing a life transition, such as birth, coming-of-age, marriage, and death. Events such as baptism of newborns, marriages, confirmation, bar mitzvahs, funerals, and high-school graduations are some examples of rites of passage in our modern Western societies.

Some of the more important rites of passage occur at puberty, marking the change from childhood to adulthood. In fact, formal **puberty rites** have been found in about half of all societies studied (Schlegel & Barry, 1991). Quite often, those rites are directly related to gender-typing; that is, the socialization of young people into their socially accepted male or female adult roles, which, in traditional societies, are different between men and women (Schleger & Barry, 1980; Weisfeld & Janisee, 2005).

According to the French anthropologist Arnold Van Gennep (1960/1908), rites of passage include at least three phases: (1) separation of individuals from their previous social status (for example, childhood if talking about puberty rites); (2) transition to a new status (which often includes a short period of training by elder members of the society); and (3) a welcoming to the new social roles (that is, recognition of adult duties and rights, often gender-typed, within the social group). Although puberty rites are practiced in contemporary Western culture, as reflected by confirmation in Christian churches or Bar (or Bat) Mitzvah in Jewish families, they do not reflect the true coming-of-age transition that they do in traditional societies.

As an example of puberty rites, we describe the Kinaaldá ceremony of initiation for girls among the Navajo. This American Indian tribe lives on a reservation (the Navajo Nation) located in the Four Corners region of the United States, a 24-square-mile area distributed among New Mexico, Arizona, Colorado, and Utah. Based on the 2000 U.S. Census, 269,202 individuals identify themselves as Navajo, and two-thirds of them live in the Navajo Nation.

The Kinaaldá is a four-day ceremony beginning between the first and the second menstrual cycle of Navajo girls. Kinaaldá is essentially a celebration of entry into womanhood through an identification of the girls with *Changing Woman*, a holy figure among the Navajo, representing the ideals of the Navajo woman. Changing Woman represents the ultimate mother; she is associated with the Earth, represents the universal cycle of life, and is always good, giving, and nurturing (Markstrom & Iborra, 2003). Importantly, the Navajo do not provide a sexist interpretation of the ceremony. Contrary to the European society, there are few power differences between men and women among the Navajo, and they value equally the masculine and the feminine aspects of the personality. Accordingly, the ceremony is seen as an affirmation of the feminine side of women. As is typically the case with rites of passage, the ceremony is multipurposed (see accompanying table).

According to the description provided by Carol Markstrom and Alejandro Iborra (2003), girls are first dressed with distinctive clothes and jewelry, their hair is tied back, and some food restrictions are imposed. They are secluded for up to four days from the group and put under the supervision of the Ideal Woman, a mentor selected by the family who is believed to be able to guide the girl toward the Changing Woman. During the first three days, the girl is submitted to different activities, including face painting, running, and grinding corn for the preparation of the corn cake. In the Navajo tradition, running is thought to make girls strong and prepare them for adversities in life and is also believed to predict the quality and longevity of life. It seems to be taken seriously by girls, with some running five miles a day. The corn that girls grind is a symbol of fertility. They spend the night singing in a *hogan* (a traditional Navajo house, made of wooden logs and mud), preparing for the final-day preparations, including washing their hair,

Purposes of the Kinaaldá Ceremony for the Girl

- To celebrate her change in status from child to adult
- To ensure her reproductive capability
- To instruct her on the proper roles of the Navajo women in the established social order
- To test and build her endurance and strength
- To give her good posture and physical beauty
- To focus her personality development
- To make her generous and giving
- To give her strength for later difficulties in life
- To influence her future endeavors
- To ensure harmony in her future and to protect her from misfortune
- To impress on her an identity that is embedded in Changing Woman

SOURCE: From Markstrom, C.A., & Iborra, A. (2003). Adolescent identity formation and rites of passage: The Navajo Kinaaldá ceremony for girls. *Journal of Research on Adolescence, 13*, 399–425, p. 408. Reprinted by permission.

adorning special jewelry, face painting, and the final run.

During the last day of Kinaaldá, the girl (now a woman) is given a new name, signaling her new identity, social status, and expected social role. She also makes the ritual of blessing others. Often people offer personal objects, such as car keys, house keys, or wallets to be blessed. In the Navajo tradition, the first menstrual period is a time of joy for girls, and their early menses are believed to have powers for blessing and healing others. Finally, the girl serves the corn cakes she prepared earlier to others. In the four days following Kinaaldá, the new identity affirmation takes place, with the new woman resting and reflecting on the meaning and relevance of the experience.

puberty rites Rituals practiced in many cultures to mark a child's transition from childhood to young adulthood.

general types of behavior (boys more to manipulation of objects and large-muscle activity, perhaps, and females to social relationships). And it is interesting that boys tend to be more strongly sex-typed (that is, approach and attend to male and avoid female activities/models) than girls. Might this also reflect a biological influence? Biology is not destiny, and, as has been made clear throughout this book, there are no pure biological or environmental effects on development. But acknowledging that some aspects of gender behavior are influenced by biological dispositions in interaction with a child's social environment can help us better understand the developmental process of gender identification.

Gender identity and knowledge about gender stereotypes develop over childhood. The roots of gender identity are firmly planted in prenatal hormone exposure, but gender identity is far more than biology. Whatever biologically influenced biases children have toward male or female activities, they are modified by the culture they grow up in. But more to the point, children are not passive recipients of gender-related information but actively seek out such information in their endeavor to figure out what it means in their culture to be a man or a woman.

Children are little scientists when it comes to understanding gender, generating theories about sex differences and then testing them. Many of those theories are wrong. For example, a 6-year-old boy noticing that an infant girl had brown hair, just like his, asked if that meant "she will be a boy when she gets older." A 4-year-old eating at an Italian restaurant with his parents and another couple noticed that his father and the other gentleman had ordered pizza, whereas his mother had ordered lasagna. In the car on the way home, the child announced that he had figured it out: "Men eat pizza and women don't."

Children continually acquire knowledge about what differentiates males and females in their culture, and with this knowledge they continually revise their theories about sex differences (see discussion of "theory theories" of cognitive development in Chapter 6). Their early theories are simplistic, based on the grossest of characteristics (clothing, for example) and often not even tangentially related to cultural sex stereotypes. However, much like the scientist delving into a new field of inquiry, they discard old theories, try new ones, and eventually acquire the meaning of gender that is implicitly agreed upon by members of their society.

summary

Sexuality refers to an individual's erotic thoughts and activities; gender identity refers to a person's sense of self as a male or a female.

Humans follow a *K strategy* of reproduction, having few offspring and investing heavily in them, in contrast to a reproductive strategy in which many offspring are produced and little investment is provided (*r strategy*).

Parental investment theory postulates that there is a trade-off between how much individuals invest in mating versus parenting. Females are the more-investing sex, and this has resulted in males and females developing different psychologies in pursuit of their inclusive-fitness interests. Incest avoidance is enhanced when children spend their early years together (the Westermarck effect) and is influenced through olfaction.

Childhood sexuality has been an understudied topic. Many preschool and school-age children engage in sex-related behaviors with other children, with the incidence of such behaviors decreasing over childhood. Children who have been sexu-

ally abused often engage in more adult-like sexual behaviors than do nonabused children. The incidence of sexual behaviors in children is influenced by culture, context, and family factors. Masturbation usually increases during adolescence, accompanied by erotic fantasies. Most teenagers engage in heterosexual sex play (petting), with many having intercourse.

The teen years are also associated with falling in love, which appears to be a universal phenomenon and associated with a host of neurochemical changes in the brain. During adolescence, interactions with members of the opposite sex increase and often lead to dating. Establishing romantic relationships is seen as a normal part of adolescence and viewed by most teenagers as normative development.

Research on the origins of sexual orientation has typically focused on homosexuality. Although environmental explanations for homosexuality continue to be popular, recent evidence points to the importance of genetic and hormonal factors.

For example, **congenital adrenal hyperplasia (CAH)** results when a female fetus is exposed to excessive levels of androgen, and this results in greater male-stereotyped behaviors.

According to the **biosocial theory of gender identity and sexual orientation**, prenatal and adolescent hormones, in addition to experiences during childhood, determine one's sexual identity.

Gender differences have been extensively studied. Many gender differences reflect small differences between the sexes that vary with age and context. Much like differences in sexual orientation, gender differences can best be understood by considering how biological and environmental factors interact over the course of development.

Gender development theory interprets the development of gender identity in terms of Piaget's stages of cognitive development. Children's knowledge of **gender constancy** develops over the preschool years, with *gender identity* preceding *gender stability*, which precedes *gender consistency*. **Gender schema theory** proposes that children develop **gender schemas**, mentalistic structures consisting of a set of associations and expectations related to gender. These schemas influence how children process information related to gender and are related to their knowledge of sex stereotypes and gender-related behavior. As children's knowledge of gender expands, their schemas change, resulting in a more sophisticated use of gender in classifying people and behavior. Many cultures have **puberty rites** to mark a child's transition from childhood to young adulthood.

Key Terms and Concepts

sexuality (p. 616)
gender identity (p. 616)
r strategies (p. 616)
K strategies (p. 617)
parental investment theory (p. 617)
incest avoidance (p. 618)

Westermarck effect (p. 618)
congenital adrenal hyperplasia (CAH) (p. 637)
biosocial theory of gender identity and sexual orientation (p. 637)
sexual-minority youth (p. 639)

gender development theory (p. 644)
gender schema theory (p. 644)
gender constancy (p. 644)
gender schema (p. 645)
puberty rites (p. 648)

Ask Yourself . . .

1. What are the principal characteristics of human mating and reproductive systems?
2. How might the different amounts of time and effort that men and women devote to child-rearing influence important aspects of their psychological (particularly sexual) development?
3. What is the state-of-art scientific knowledge about sexual development in children and adolescents compared to other areas of development, and what are the reasons for the difference?
4. All societies have taboos about incest, but most nonhuman animals also have evolved ways of avoiding incest without the need of taboos. Other than societal taboos, what factors seem to contribute to the development of incest avoidance in humans?
5. Are children sexual beings? What is the typical developmental pattern of sex-related behaviors in childhood?

6. When does sexual attraction usually begin? What are the main features of adolescent sexual experiences in the United States, and what factors influence them?
7. What are the main components of falling in love and romantic relationships, and how do they take place in adolescence?
8. What is sexual orientation according to Savin-Williams? What factors contribute to a person's sexual orientation?
9. What are some of the most frequently reported sex differences, and how should these differences be interpreted?
10. What is usually meant by gender identity? What are some explanations for how, when, and why gender identity is acquired?

Exercises: Going Further

1. Two parents attend your child psychologist consultation with the following issue: They are both concerned about some sex-related behaviors observed lately in their 4-year-old daughter, Joanna. According to their report, Joanna seems very interested in watching them and her brother Mike get undressed. She also seems to like to walk naked in front of them. Mike, who is 9 years old, never did such things, they say. What additional questions would you ask them to determine if Joanna's behavior is typical for her age or not, and what would you tell them about their young daughter's sex-related behaviors?

2. Alan, age 17, has recently come out and told his parents he is gay. His parents tell you how surprised they were at the beginning, although they also tell you they had no significant problems in accepting it. However, you also know that they sometimes comment to close friends about their concerns that they may have done something wrong to make their son decide to become gay, and if there were still time to do something to change Alan's sexual orientation. What would you tell them?

3. Ask three college students about traits they think men and women differ on in the physical, cognitive, and socioemotional domains. Then ask them why or how they think these differences came about. Compare the students' answers with evidence presented in this chapter and write your conclusions.

Suggested Readings

Classic Works

Kinsey, A. C., Pomerantz, W. B., & Martin, C. E. (1948). *Sexual behavior in the human male.* **Bloomington, IN: Indiana University Press.** This book, along with the 1953 book, *Sexual behavior in the human female*, revolutionized research into sexuality by documenting adults' sexual behaviors and their recollections of sexual feelings and activities in childhood and adolescence.

Money, J., & Ehrhardt, A. (1972). *Man & Woman: Boy & Girl.* **Baltimore, MD: John Hopkins University Press.** John Money was a pioneer in research on children's sexuality, and this book, written with his colleague Anke Ehrhardt, presents an extensive review of the basic biology of sex differentiation, as well as biologic and environmental factors that influence sexual orientation and psychological sex differences.

Maccoby, E. E., & Jacklin, C. N. (1974). *The psychology of sex differences.* **Stanford, CA: Stanford University Press.** When it was first published, this book presented a thorough review of psychological sex differences, focusing primarily on children. It remained the bible for researchers in the field for many years to come.

Scholarly Works

Geary, D. C. (2009). *Male, female: The evolution of human sex differences* **(2nd ed.). Washington, DC: American Psychological Association.** David Geary provides a comprehensive review of psychological sex differences from the perspective of evolutionary theory. As a developmental, as well as an evolutionary, psychologist, Geary focuses much of his book on sex differences in childhood.

Ruble, D. N., Martin, C. L., & Berenbaum, S. (2006). Gender development. In W. Damon & R. M. Lerner (Gen. Eds.), *Handbook of Child Psychology* **(6th ed.), N. Eisenberg (Vol. Ed.), Vol. 3,** *Social, emotional, and personality development* **(pp. 858–932). New York: Wiley.** This is a comprehensive review of gender development and gender differences written by three of the leading experts on these topics.

Readings for Personal Interest

Johnson, T. C. (1999). *Understanding your child's sexual behavior: What's natural and healthy.* **New Harbinger Publications.** In this book, Toni Cavanaugh Johnson describes healthy, typical childhood sexual behaviors and compares them with behaviors that may indicate that children need help.

Savin-Williams, R. C. (2001). *Mom, Dad, I'm Gay: How Families Negotiate Coming Out.* **Washington, DC: American Psychological Association.** Based on interviews with more than 150 teenagers, Ritch Savin-Williams describes the process of coming out for sexual-minority youth and provides suggestions for how to make the process a successful one.

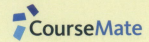

Cengage Learning's **Psychology CourseMate** for this text brings course concepts to life with interactive learning, study, and exam preparation tools, including quizzes and flashcards for this chapter's Key Terms and Concepts (see the summary list on page 651). The site also provides an **eBook** version of the text with highlighting and note taking capabilities, as well as an extensive library of observational videos that span early childhood through adolescence. Many videos are accompanied by questions that will help you think critically about and deepen your understanding of the chapter topics addressed, especially as they pertain to core concepts. Log on and learn more at **www.cengagebrain.com**.

Glossary

A-not-B task Object permanence task, in which the infant has to retrieve a hidden object at one location (B), after having retrieved it several times previously from another one (A). (Chapter 5)

accommodation (in Piaget's theory) The process of changing a mental structure to incorporate new information; contrast with *assimilation*. (Chapter 6)

accommodation (of the lens) The process of adjusting the lens of the eye to focus on objects at different distances. (Chapter 5)

active (or cumulative) rehearsal Type of memory strategy in which a person repeats the most recently presented item (for example, a word) and then rehearses it with as many other different words as possible; contrast with *passive rehearsal*. (Chapter 8)

active, or productive, language The language a child can actually produce, or speak; contrast with *receptive language*. (Chapter 9)

adaptation (in Piaget's theory) The process of adjusting one's cognitive structures to meet environmental demands; includes the complementary processes of *assimilation* and *accommodation*. See also *organization*. (Chapter 6)

adaptation (in Sternberg's theory) Adjusting one's behavior to obtain a good fit with one's environment. (Chapter 10)

adaptations In evolutionary theory, universal and reliably developing inherited features that arose as a result of natural selection and helped to solve some problem in the environment of evolutionary adaptedness. (Chapter 2)

adaptive strategy choice model Siegler's model to describe how strategies change over time; the view that multiple strategies exist within a child's cognitive repertoire at any one time, with these strategies competing with one another for use. (Chapter 8)

adrenarche The onset of androgen production by the adrenal glands. (Chapter 4)

African American Vernacular English See *Black English*.

aggression Behavior intended to harm another person. (Chapter 14)

Agreeableness Factor in the Five Factor Model. Agreeable individuals are cooperative, considerate, empathetic, generous, polite, and kind, whereas disagreeable individuals are aggressive, rude, spiteful, stubborn, cynical, and manipulative. (Chapter 11)

alleles Different versions of the same gene. (Chapter 3)

alloparenting Provision of care to children by individuals other than the genetic mother. (Chapter 12)

altruism Doing something for another at some cost to one's self. (Chapter 14)

analogical reasoning Reasoning that involves using something one already knows to help reason about something not known yet. (Chapter 8)

analytic subtheory/intelligence See *componential subtheory/intelligence*.

androgen A class of hormones, including testosterone, that are found at higher levels in males than females and that influence physical growth and sexual development. (Chapter 4)

animism Attributing human properties, like hopes, feelings, and thoughts, to inanimate things. (Chapter 6)

anorexia nervosa An eating disorder characterized by excessive dieting and weight loss that affects adolescents and young adults, especially girls; contrast with *bulimia*. (Chapter 4)

antisocial behaviors Behaviors that favor one's own interests at the expense of others' interests (such as lying, stealing, and hitting someone); contrast with *prosocial behaviors*. (Chapter 14)

Apgar scale A test that evaluates a baby's biological fitness at birth. (Chapter 3)

apoptosis See *selective cell death*.

applied behavioral analysis Extension of B. F. Skinner's behaviorism to practical settings. (Chapter 2)

apprenticeship in thinking Routine transactions between children and adults, with novice children improving their skills and understanding through participation with more skilled partners in culturally organized activities. (Chapter 2)

assimilation In Piaget's theory, the process of incorporating information into already existing cognitive structures; contrast with *accommodation*. (Chapter 6)

assisted reproductive techniques (ART) Technologies, most including *in vitro fertilization*, that facilitate couples to become parents. (Chapter 3)

attachment Close emotional relationship exhibited by a child toward a caregiver expressed by maintaining physical proximity, stress upon separation, and relief of stress upon reunion. (Chapter 12)

Attachment Q-Set Method for assessing infant-caregiver attachment in which the caregiver or a trained observer sorts 90 statements describing a certain attachment relationship into preestablished categories (ranging from "most like" to "least like"). (Chapter 12)

attention deficit hyperactivity disorder (ADHD) An inability to sustain attention, believed to be caused by deficits in behavioral inhibition. People with ADHD display hyperactivity, impulsiveness, show great difficulty sustaining attention, and are at high risk for academic difficulties. (Chapter 8)

attention span The amount of time a person can concentrate on a task without becoming distracted. (Chapter 8)

authoritarian parenting style A style of parenting in which parents expect absolute obedience and frequently enforce rules with physical punishment and withdrawal of love; contrast with *authoritative, permissive,* and *uninvolved parenting styles*. (Chapter 13)

authoritative parenting style Style of parenting in which parents set clear standards and enforce the rules with warmth and explanations; contrast with *authoritarian, permissive,* and *uninvolved parenting styles*. (Chapter 13)

autism A developmental disorder characterized by severe social and communication disabilities. (Chapter 7)

autobiographical memory Personal and long-lasting memories that are the basis for one's personal life history. (Chapter 8)

autosomes Chromosome pairs 1 through 22. (Chapter 3)

average-status children Children who receive a moderate number of both positive and negative nominations in a sociometric assessment. (Chapter 14)

axon The long fiber of a neuron that carries messages from that cell to another. (Chapter 4)

babbling Early form of infant speech typically characterized by repeated sequences of consonants and vowels, such as "nanana" or "babababa." (Chapter 9)

behavioral genetics Discipline that focuses on the study of genetic effects on behavior. (Chapter 3)

behaviorism Theory popular in the United States throughout the middle of the 20th century, holding that behavior and development are shaped by environmental influences. (Chapter 2)

belief-desire reasoning The process whereby we explain and predict what people do based on what we understand their desires and beliefs to be. (Chapter 7)

bicultural identity The ability of people to integrate their ethnic identity with that of the majority culture in which they are living. (Chapter 7)

bilingualism Speaking two languages proficiently. (Chapter 9)

binocular convergence The ability of *both* eyes to focus together on the same object, which is necessary for depth perception. (Chapter 5)

binocular vision See *stereoscopic vision*.

biological sensitivity to context Degree to which individuals are biologically sensitive to environmental contexts. (Chapter 11)

biologically primary abilities Cognitive abilities that have been selected for in evolution, are acquired universally, and children typically have high motivation to perform tasks involving them, such as language; contrast with *biologically secondary abilities*. (Chapter 10)

biologically secondary abilities Cognitive abilities that build on biologically primary abilities but are principally cultural inventions, and often-tedious repetition and external motivation are necessary for their mastery, such as reading; contrast with *biologically primary abilities*. (Chapter 10)

biosocial theory of gender identity and sexual orientation The theory that prenatal and adolescent hormones, in addition to experiences during childhood, determine one's sexual identity. (Chapter 15)

biparental families Family structure in which both mother and father provide some support. (Chapter 13)

Black English (African American Vernacular English) A dialect of American English used mostly (but not exclusively) by members of the African American community, which is characterized by some special rules of pronunciation and syntax. (Chapter 9)

blastocyst Early stage in prenatal development, in which the zygote begins dividing and forms into a hollow sphere. (Chapter 3)

BMI See *body mass index*.

body mass index (BMI) A measure of weight in relation to height. (Chapter 4)

bonding The process of a mother's "falling in love" with her infant shortly after birth. (Chapter 12)

brain stem The evolutionarily oldest part of the brain that contains cells that control relatively primitive responses associated with defense and attack behavior, feeding, freezing, sexual behavior, and facial expressions. (Chapter 4)

bulimia Eating disorder in which people will sometimes eat excessively and then force themselves to vomit to avoid weight gain; contrast with *anorexia nervosa*. (Chapter 4)

bullying The persistent and repeated cases of aggression committed by a more powerful individual over a less powerful one. This phenomenon is common in schools around the world. (Chapter 14)

case study Detailed description of a single individual made by an expert observer. (Chapter 1)

categorization The process of treating different objects as member of the same category. (Chapter 5)

category prototype The central tendency, "best example," of a cognitive category. (Chapter 5)

cephalocaudal development The head-to-foot sequence of physical growth. (Chapters 3 and 4)

cerebral cortex (neocortex) The outer layer of the brain that gives humans their highly developed intelligence. (Chapter 4)

cerebral lateralization (cerebral dominance) Functional specialization of the two hemispheres of the brain. (Chapter 4)

Cesarean section (C-section) Delivery of a baby through a surgical incision in the abdomen. (Chapter 3)

child maltreatment The intentional abuse or neglect of anyone under 18 years of age that endangers their well-being. (Chapter 13)

Child Study Movement Social movement begun in the United States around 1900 that proposed the systematic application of science principles to the study of children. (Chapter 1)

chromosomes The rod-shaped strands of DNA found in the nucleus of cells that contain genetic information. (Chapter 3)

chronosystem In Bronfenbrenner's ecological systems theory, the system that reflects the fact that the child and the other systems change with time. (Chapter 2)

class inclusion In Piaget's theory, the knowledge that a subordinate class (for example, dogs) must always be smaller than the superordinate class in which it is contained (for example, animals). (Chapter 6)

clinical interviews Interviews, used extensively by Piaget, in which the examiner probes a child's knowledge about a given topic. (Chapter 1)

cliques Small, relatively stable social groups that children join voluntarily; contrast with *crowds*. (Chapter 14)

clustering Recalling items from the same category together in a memory task. (Chapter 8)

co-parenting The practice whereby parents consciously coordinate their child-rearing practices. (Chapter 13)

cognitive flexibility The ability to shift between sets of tasks or rules. (Chapter 8)

cognitive self-guidance system In Vygotsky's theory, the use of private speech to guide problem-solving behavior. (Chapter 9)

cohort effects The psychological effects associated with being a member of a group born at a particular time (for example, a generation) and place; the fact that people who are living in a culture at the same time are influenced by the same historical events. (Chapter 1)

collective monologues Egocentric exchanges between two or more children with participants talking "with" one another, but not necessarily "to" one another, such that what one child says has little to do with the comments of the other. (Chapter 9)

compensatory education programs Programs designed to provide preschool children from low-income homes with the intellectual skills necessary to perform well in primary school. (Chapter 10)

componential subtheory (analytic intelligence) In Sternberg's triarchic theory, an information-processing model describing type of intelligence that includes three types of components knowledge acquisition, performance, and metacomponents. (Chapter 10)

concordance rates The probability that one member of a pair of individuals (for example, identical or fraternal twins) will display a trait possessed by the other member. (Chapter 3)

concrete operational period The third major stage of cognitive development in Piaget's theory, in which children can decenter their perception, are less egocentric, and can think logically about concrete objects. (Chapters 2 and 6)

conduct disorder Form of externalizing problem characterized by different types of antisocial behaviors, such as physical and verbal aggression, vandalism, and theft. (Chapter 11)

congenital adrenal hyperplasia (CAH) A condition in which a fetus is exposed to excessive levels of androgen; in females this can result in greater male-stereotyped behaviors. (Chapter 15)

conjugate reinforcement procedure Conditioning procedures used in memory research with infants, in which children's behaviors, for example, kicking, control aspects of a visual display. (Chapter 5)

conscience The internalization of values, specifically a sense of right or wrong. (Chapter 14)

Conscientiousness Factor in the Five Factor Model. Conscientious individuals are diligent, planful, careful, and focused, whereas those low in this trait are irresponsible, unreliable, careless, and distractible. (Chapter 11)

conservation In Piaget's theory, the knowledge that the quantity of a substance remains the same despite changes in its form. (Chapter 6)

contagious crying Crying that occurs when newborns cry in response to the cries of other newborns. (Chapter 11)

contextual subtheory (practical intelligence) In Sternberg's triarchic theory, type of intelligence expressed by the idea that intelligence must be viewed in terms of the context in which it occurs. People gifted in this subtheory have "street smarts." (Chapter 10)

controversial children Children who are mentioned frequently in a sociometric assessment but get nearly as many negative nominations as they do positive ones. (Chapter 14)

conventional morality The second level in Kohlberg's theory of moral development, in which people try to conform to rules imposed by some legitimate authority, such as parents, school officials, or the legal system. (Chapter 14)

cooperative breeding hypothesis Proposal that humans evolved a system of parenting in which mothers shared the responsibility for child care with others in the family and the larger social group. (Chapter 12)

core knowledge Expression used by some infant researchers to refer to the set of knowledge that young infants possess in certain domains, including objects, people and social relations, numbers and quantities, and geometry. (Chapter 5)

correlational studies Type of study that examines two or more factors to determine if changes in one are associated with changes in another. (Chapter 1)

cortisol One of several hormones and biochemicals associated with people's ability to regulate aspects of their physiology and behavior in response to stress. (Chapter 11)

creative subtheory/intelligence *See* experiential subtheory/intelligence.

creoles Languages that develop when children transform the *pidgin* of their parents to a grammatically more complex "true" language. See *pidgins*. (Chapter 9)

critical period See *sensitive period*.

cross-sectional studies Type of developmental studies that compares different individuals of different ages at the same point in time; compare with *longitudinal studies*. (Chapter 1)

cross-sequential approach Type of developmental studies that combines aspects of cross-sectional and longitudinal designs; groups of participants at different ages are tested, and then followed longitudinally. (Chapter 1)

crossing over A process of genetic exchange that occurs during meiosis, when two corresponding chromosomes exchange pieces of DNA. (Chapter 3)

crowds Large groups of adolescents who share activities or have similar stereotype reputations (such as "jocks" or "druggies"); contrast with *cliques*. (Chapter 14)

crystallized abilities Intellectual abilities that develop from cultural context and learning experience; contrast with *fluid abilities*. (Chapter 10)

C-section See *Cesarean section*.

cumulative deficit effect The phenomenon by which multiple risks persisting over many years add up, resulting in children who display deficits in social, emotional, and cognitive functioning. (Chapter 10)

cumulative rehearsal See *active rehearsal*.

cyber bullying Verbal harassment that occurs online and is common for children who spend time on the Internet. (Chapter 14)

decentration In Piaget's theory, the ability of concrete operational children to consider multiple aspects of a stimulus or situation at once; contrast with *perceptual centration*. (Chapter 6)

deferred adaptations Aspects of childhood that serve as preparations for adulthood and were selected over the course of evolution; contrast with *ontogenetic adaptations*. (Chapter 2)

deferred imitation Imitation of a modeled act some time after viewing the behavior. Deferred imitation is a reflection of memory. (Chapter 5)

dendrites The numerous fibers of a neuron that receive messages from other neurons. (Chapter 4)

dentate gyrus Part of the hippocampus that continues to develop after birth and plays an important role in memory. (Chapter 5)

dependent variables The "outcome" variable, or behavior, that is being studied. (Chapter 1)

depression A modification in mood consisting of one or more of three components: feelings of sadness, a sense of unease (*dysphoria*), or loss of a sense of pleasure (*anhedonia*). (Chapter 11)

depth perception The ability to discriminate visual patterns denoting depth; see also *bifoveal fixation, visual cliff*. (Chapter 5)

design stance The assumption that tools are designed for an intended function. (Chapter 8)

development Predictable changes that occur in structure or function over the life span. (Chapter 1)

developmental contextual approaches Perspective that views development as the result of bidirectional interaction between all levels of biological and experiential variables. (Chapters 1 and 2)

developmental function The form that development takes over time. (Chapter 1)

developmental psychology The scientific discipline that examines changes in psychological characteristics occurring over a lifetime (as well as the physical changes associated with them). (Chapter 1)

developmental systems theory The perspective that development is not simply "produced" by genes, nor constructed by the environment, but emerges from the continuous, bidirectional interaction between all levels of biological and environmental factors. (Chapters 1 and 2)

differentiation (of neurons) The final stage of neuronal development, in which neurons gain in size, produce more dendrites, extend their axons farther away from the cell body, and form new synaptic connections. (Chapter 4)

difficult babies Infants described as being unpredictable, having generally negative moods, difficulty adjusting to new situations, and react to events with high levels of intensity. (Chapter 11)

discontinuity versus continuity of development The scientific debate over whether developmental change is gradual (continuous) or relatively abrupt (discontinuous). (Chapter 1)

discrete emotion theory The theory that basic emotions are innate and associated with distinctive bodily and facial reactions. (Chapter 11)

dishabituation The tendency to show renewed interest in a stimulus when some features of it have been changed; contrast with *habituation*. (Chapter 5)

disorganized/disoriented attachment Attachment style in which infants seek to be close to their caregivers in inconsistent ways, often showing patterns typical of secure, avoidant, and/or resistant attachment simultaneously; compare to *secure, insecure-avoidant*, and *insecure-resistant attachment*. (Chapter 12)

DNA Deoxyribonucleic acid, the self-replicating molecule of which chromosomes are made. (Chapter 3)

domain-general mechanisms General, underlying cognitive abilities that influence performance over a wide range of situations (or domains); contrast with *domain-specific mechanisms*. (Chapter 2)

domain-specific mechanisms Cognitive abilities specific to one cognitive domain under control of a specific mind/brain function; contrast with *domain-general mechanisms*. (Chapter 2)

dominance hierarchy The relatively stable organization of a group in which some members are seen as leaders and others as followers. (Chapter 14)

Down syndrome Chromosome abnormality, in which an individual has an extra 21st chromosome; also known as *trisomy 21*. (Chapter 3)

dynamic system A set of elements that undergoes change over time as a result of interactions among the elements. Dynamic systems theories propose that developmental differences emerge as a result of the self-organization of lower-level elements. (Chapter 2)

dyslexia Difficulty in learning to read despite having an average level of intelligence and good educational opportunities. (Chapter 10)

easy babies Infants described as having regular patterns of eating, sleeping, and toileting; they easily adjust to new situations and have a generally positive mood; they are eager to approach objects and people, and react to events with low to moderate levels of intensity. (Chapter 11)

ecological systems theory Bronfenbrenner's theory that views development as occurring within embedded spheres: *microsystem, mesosystem, exosystem macrosystem*, and the *chronosystem*. (Chapter 2)

effortful control In temperament theory, the ability to regulate one's emotions; effortful control is necessary for focused attention and is involved in tasks requiring *executive function*, processes involved in regulating attention and aspects of information processing. (Chapter 11)

egocentric speech See *private speech*.

egocentrism In Piaget's theory, the tendency to interpret objects and events from one's own perspective. (Chapter 6)

embryonic phase The prenatal period from approximately 2 to 8 weeks after conception, during which organs are formed and begin to function. (Chapter 3)

emergent literacy The skills, knowledge, and attitudes that are presumed to be developmental precursors to conventional forms of reading and writing during early childhood and the environments that support these developments. (Chapter 10)

emotion The subjective reaction that we experience in response to some environmental stimulus. (Chapter 11)

emotional autonomy In adolescence, increases in a subjective sense of independence, especially in relation to parents or parental figures. (Chapter 11)

emotional expression The individual's ability to exhibit a range of emotions. (Chapter 11)

emotional recognition The ability to recognize or become aware of emotions in others. (Chapter 11)

emotional self-regulation The ability to control one's own emotional expressions. (Chapter 11)

emotional understanding The ability to verbally label and comprehend the use of emotions in oneself and others. (Chapter 11)

empathy The ability to recognize, perceive, and feel the emotions of another. (Chapter 11)

empiricism Philosophical perspective that nature provides only species-general learning mechanisms, with cognition arising as a result of experience; contrast with *nativism*.. (Chapter 1)

emulation A form of social learning that refers to understanding the goal of a model and engaging in similar behavior to achieve that goal, without necessarily reproducing the exact actions of the model. (Chapter 7)

encephalization quotient A measurement to evaluate the expected brain weight/body weight ratio for animals. (Chapter 4)

endocrine system A system of glands that produces hormones, many of which are responsible for directing growth. (Chapter 4)

endogenous smile Smiles that are elicited by an infant's internal states, as opposed to something in the external environment; contrast with *social smiling*. (Chapter 11)

environment of evolutionary adaptedness Ancestral environments during which human nature was shaped. (Chapter 2)

epigenesis The emergence of new structures and functions during the course of development. (Chapter 1)

episodic memory Long-term memory of events or episodes; contrast with *semantic memory*; see also *autobiographical memory*. (Chapter 8)

equilibration In Piaget's theory, the process by which balance is restored to the cognitive structures. (Chapter 6)

estrogen Hormone produced primarily by the ovaries that regulates female sexual development during puberty. (Chapter 4)

evolutionary developmental psychology The application of the principles of modern evolutionary biology to explain human development. (Chapter 2)

evolutionary psychology The application of the principles of modern evolutionary biology to explain human behavior. (Chapter 2)

evolved cognitive mechanisms Information-processing mechanisms shaped by natural selection during the *environments of evolutionary adaptedness* to deal with specific and recurrent problems faced by our ancestors, such as getting food, avoiding predators, and finding and keeping a mate. (Chapter 2)

executive function (control) Expression used to describe the set of processes involved in regulating attention and in determining what to do with information just gathered or retrieved from long-term memory. (Chapter 8)

exosystem In Bronfenbrenner's ecological systems theory, all of the social systems in which children are *not* regularly part of, but which nonetheless influence their lives. (Chapter 2)

experience-dependent synaptogenesis Processes whereby synapses between neurons are formed and maintained as a result of the unique experiences of an individual; contrast with *experience-expectant synaptogenesis*. (Chapter 4)

experience-expectant synaptogenesis Processes whereby synapses between neurons are formed and maintained when an organism has species-typical experiences; as a result, functions (such as vision) will develop for all members of a species given a species-typical environment; contrast with *experience-dependent synaptogenesis*. (Chapter 4)

experiential subtheory (creative intelligence) In Sternberg's triarchic theory, type of intelligence concerned with how prior knowledge influences performance, specifically with the individual's ability to deal with novelty and the degree to which processing is automatized. (Chapter 10)

experimental studies Type of studies in which a researcher manipulates one or more factors, then observes how these manipulations change the behavior under investigation. (Chapter 1)

explicit (declarative) memory Memories that are available to conscious awareness and can be directly assessed by tests of recall or recognition memory; explicit memory comes in two types, *episodic* and *semantic memory*; contrast with *implicit memory*. (Chapter 8)

externality effect The tendency of young infants (1-month-olds) to direct their attention primarily to the outside of a figure and to spend little time inspecting internal features. (Chapter 5)

externalizing problems Emotional problems reflected by "acting out," such that one's behavior adversely affects other people. (Chapter 11)

Extraversion Factor in the Five Factor Model that focuses on how gregarious, cheerful, energetic, and withdrawn (in the reverse direction) individuals are. (Chapter 11)

eye-hand coordination Moving the hands in coordination with incoming visual information. (Chapter 4)

fact retrieval The retrieval of a fact directly from long-term memory without using effortful procedures. (Chapter 10)

factors In psychometric approaches to intelligence, a set of related mental skills (such as verbal or spatial skills) that underlies intellectual functioning. (Chapter 10)

fallopian tube The tubes through which mature ova travel from the ovaries to the uterus, and where conception takes place. (Chapter 3)

false-belief tasks A type of task, used in theory-of-mind studies, in which the child must infer that another person holds a belief that is false. (Chapter 7)

fantasy play See *symbolic play*.

fast mapping The ability to learn new words based on very little input. (Chapter 9)

fear (or wariness) of strangers Pattern of behavior displayed by infants during second half of the first year that serves as an indication that the infant has developed an attachment for his or her caretaker. (Chapter 12)

Fetal Alcohol Syndrome (FAS) Syndrome characterized by a set of symptoms that occur in children as a result of alcohol consumption by the mother during pregnancy, including physical abnormalities and intellectual deficits. (Chapter 3)

fetal phase The prenatal period from approximately 8 weeks after conception to birth. (Chapter 3)

filicide The killing of a child by a parent. (Chapter 12)

finalism Young children's tendency to attribute human causes to natural events. (Chapter 7)

fine motor behaviors Motor behaviors having to do with control of the hands. (Chapter 4)

Five Factor Model A model that describes human personality in terms of five core traits: *extraversion, neuroticism, conscientiousness, agreeableness*, and *openness-to-experience*. (Chapter 11)

fluid abilities Intellectual abilities that are biologically determined and reflected in tests of memory span and spatial thinking; contrast with *crystallized abilities*. (Chapter 10)

Flynn Effect The systematic increase in IQ scores (about 5 to 9 points per decade) observed over the 20th century. (Chapter 10)

formal operational period In Piaget's theory, the final stage of cognitive development, in which children are able to apply abstract logical rules. (Chapters 2 and 6)

friendships A reciprocal relationship between peers, in that two children each nominate one another as a friend and have positive feelings toward one another. (Chapter 14)

frontal lobe Part of the brain that is implicated in human "thinking," including the planning of voluntary behaviors. (Chapter 4)

function In developmental psychology, action related to a structure, such as movement of a muscle, nerve firing, or the activation of a mental representation; contrast with *structure*; see *bidirectionality of structure and function*. (Chapter 1)

functionalist perspective Regarding emotional development, a theoretical perspective that views emotions as playing an adaptive role, helping individuals to achieve specific goals related to survival. (Chapter 11)

fuzzy traces Imprecise memory representations that are more easily accessed, generally require less effort to use, and are less susceptible to interference and forgetting than *verbatim traces*. (Chapter 8)

fuzzy-trace theory Brainerd and Reyna's theory that proposes that information is encoded on a continuum from verbatim to fuzzy, or gistlike, traces, and that many cognitive developmental differences in aspects of cognition can be attributed to age differences in encoding and in differences in sensitivity to output interference. (Chapter 8)

g See *general intelligence*.

gender constancy The concept that gender remains the same despite changes in physical appearance, time, and behavior; includes *gender identity, gender stability*, and *gender consistency*. (Chapter 15)

gender development theory The theory that the development of gender identity follows a similar course as described by Piaget's theory of cognitive development. (Chapter 15)

gender identity The ability of children to identify themselves as either boys or girls. (Chapter 15)

gender schema theory The theory that gender development is based on children's developing understanding of *gender schemas*. (Chapter 15)

gender schema A mentalistic structure consisting of a set of expectations and associations that guide processing with respect to gender. (Chapter 15)

gene The basic unit of heredity; segment of DNA that codes for a particular protein. (Chapter 3)

general genetic law of cultural development In Vygotsky's theory, the idea that cognition occurs on two planes: first the social, between individuals, and later the psychological, as it is internalized by the child. (Chapter 2)

general intelligence (*g*) In psychometric theory, the idea that intelligence can be expressed in terms of a single factor, called *g*. (Chapter 10)

genetic determinism The idea that one's genes determine one's behavior. (Chapter 1)

genotype → environment theory Scarr and McCartney's theory that one's genotype (genetic constitution) influences which environments one encounters and the type of experiences one has, or that genes drive experience (Chapter 3)

genotype An individual's entire genetic endowment; compare with *phenotype*. (Chapter 3)

germinal phase Earliest phase of prenatal development, beginning when the ovum is penetrated by a sperm in the fallopian tube and starts its journey, as a *zygote*, down to the uterus. (Chapter 3)

goal-directed behavior Means-end, that is intentional, problem solving, first seen in the latter part of the first year. (Chapters 6 and 8)

good-enough parents The controversial proposal by Scarr that individual differences in parenting have little consequence for children's development and that "good enough" parents are adequate for proper development. (Chapter 13)

grammar The linguistic rules for "tuning" words and putting words together into phrases or sentences. (Chapter 9)

grammar center An area in the frontal lobe that is specifically related to processing grammatical information. (Chapter 9)

grandmother hypothesis Evolutionary hypothesis that by living past one's reproductive years, women can devote their time and resources to their children and grandchildren, and, as a result, increase the chances of survival of their grandchildren. (Chapter 12)

gross motor behaviors Motor behaviors associated with large muscles, such as arms and legs. (Chapter 4)

group socialization theory Judith Harris's theory that children's personalities are shaped chiefly by their interactions with their peers and not through interactions with their parents. (Chapter 14)

growth curves Graphic representation of the growth rate of an organism. (Chapter 4)

growth spurt Rapid change in growth of body occurring during puberty, which typically begins earlier in girls than boys. (Chapter 4)

guided participation The process and system of involvement of individuals with others as they communicate and engage in shared activities; contrast with *zone of proximal development*; see also *sociocultural perspective*. (Chapter 2)

habituation Decrease in the response to a stimulus that has been presented repeatedly; contrast with *dishabituation*. (Chapter 5)

heritability The extent to which differences in any trait within a population can be attributed to inheritance. (Chapter 3)

heteronomous morality *(moral absolutism)* In Piaget's theory of moral development, the stage in which children, typically 5- to 10-year-olds, think that what is moral is what adults and other authorities say is moral. Moral rules are seen in a rigid way, as unchangeable, and not as a result of a social agreement or consensus. (Chapter 14)

hierarchical model of cognitive abilities The model that proposes that intelligence is composed of specific cognitive abilities (for example, verbal, spatial, speed of processing, memory) that are intercorrelated and influenced by a higher-order general intellectual factor, *g*. (Chapter 10)

holophrases (holophrastic speech) Children's use of one-word sentences. (Chapter 9)

hominids Group of animals in the line that led to *Homo sapiens*. (Chapter 2)

horizontal décalage In Piaget's theory, the progressive acquisition of a certain skill within the same intellectual stage. (Chapter 6)

hormones Chemical substances produced by the endocrine glands and sent through the bloodstream transporting instructions from one part of the body to another. (Chapter 4)

hospitalism The deteriorating effects on infants of long-term confinement to hospitals or similar institutions. (Chapter 12)

hostile aggression Personally oriented aggression in which a child's intent is to hurt another child (not as a mean for attaining a goal); compare to *instrumental aggression*. (Chapter 14)

hostile attributional bias The tendency for highly aggressive children to interpret an ambiguous situation as having an aggressive, rather than accidental, intent. (Chapter 14)

human genome A description of all of a human's genetic material. (Chapter 3)

human growth hormone Pituitary hormone that stimulates duplication of most body cells, affecting growth. (Chapter 4)

hypothalamus Part of the brain that controls most body systems by regulating the production of hormones in response to both internal and environmental events. (Chapter 4)

hypothetico-deductive reasoning In Piaget's theory, a formal operational ability to think by generating and testing hypothesis. See *scientific reasoning*. (Chapter 6)

identity experiments Practice whereby adolescents pretend to be someone they are not online. (Chapter 13)

identity status approach Marcia's extension of Erikson's theory of adolescent identity that pays special attention to occupational and ideological (for example, politics, religion) aspects of identity. (Chapter 7)

identity The process of forming a coherent identity. A self-portrait of the different pieces of the self integrated in a coherent mode/way (including, for example, physical, sexual, ideological, intellectual, relational, vocational, and cultural/ethnic aspects). (Chapter 7)

idiographic approach Approach to psychology that is concerned with individual differences among people, as opposed to concern with features that all people have in common; compare to *normative approach*. (Chapter 1)

imaginary audience Expression of adolescent egocentrism, with adolescents feeling that they are constantly "on stage," or playing to an imaginary audience. (Chapter 6)

imaginary friends Make-believe friends. (Chapter 6)

imitative learning A form of social learning that requires that the observer take the perspective of the model, understand the model's goal, and reproduce important portions of the model's behavior. (Chapter 7)

immanent justice The belief that good deeds will be rewarded and misdeeds will be punished. (Chapter 14)

implicit (nondeclarative or procedural) memory Memory without awareness that can be assessed only indirectly; contrast with *explicit memory*. (Chapter 8)

in vitro fertilization (IVF) Fertilization of the egg by the sperm outside of the woman's body. (Chapter 3)

in-group favoritism Showing a decided preference for the attitudes and behaviors exhibited by members of one's social group; contrast with *out-group discrimination*. (Chapter 14)

incest avoidance Avoiding having sex with a close relative. (Chapter 15)

inclusive fitness In evolutionary theory, how many copies of one's genes make it into the next generation, either directly through children or indirectly through relatives who share one's genes. (Chapter 12)

independent variables In experimental studies, the factors, or variables, that are modified to see their effect on the dependent, or outcome, variables. (Chapter 1)

indirect aggression Type of agression in which the target person is attacked not physically or directly through verbal intimidation but in a more circuitous way, through social manipulation. (Chapter 14)

inductive reasoning The type of thinking that goes from specific observations to broad generalizations, characteristic of formal operational thought. (Chapter 6)

infant-directed speech The specialized register of speech that adults and older children use when talking specifically to infants and young children. (Chapters 9 and 11)

infantile amnesia The inability to remember events from infancy and early childhood. (Chapter 8)

inhibition The ability to prevent oneself from making some cognitive or behavioral response. (Chapter 8)

inner speech In Vygotsky's theory, the covert language children use to guide their thinking and problem solving. (Chapter 9)

insecure-avoidant attachment An insecure style of attachment in which infants show little distress when their caregivers depart temporarily, avoid contact with them when they return, and usually do not show wariness of the stranger; compare to *secure, insecure-resistant,* and *disorganized/ disoriented attachment.* (Chapter 12)

insecure-resistant attachment An insecure style of attachment in which infants keep very close to their caregivers and tend not to explore much. They become distressed when their caregivers leave them temporarily but display anger and initially rejection to contact when the caregivers return; compare to *secure, insecure-avoidant,* and *disorganized/disoriented attachment.* (Chapter 12)

instructed learning See *teaching.*

instrumental aggression Type of aggression used as a mean to attain a certain goal (for example, a toy), not as a goal itself; compare with *hostile aggression.* Chapter 14)

instrumental conditioning See operant conditioning.

intellectual realism In Piaget's theory, children drawing based on what they know about objects rather than what they see; contrast with *visual realism.* (Chapter 6)

intelligence Ability to think and act in ways that are goal-directed and adaptive. (Chapter 10)

intentional agents Individuals who cause things to happen and whose behavior is designed to achieve some goal. (Chapter 7)

interactional synchrony Mother-infant harmonious interaction, where partners take turns responding to each other's leads, needs, and emotions. (Chapter 12)

interactions Any social activity in which two or more individuals engage and that includes what the individuals are doing (for example, wrestling) and how they are doing it (for example, playfully or aggressively). (Chapter 14)

intermodal perception The ability to associate and interconnect information provided by different senses about a certain experience. (Chapter 5)

internal working models of attachment Mental models to describe children's developing mental representations of their attachment relationships. (Chapter 12)

internalizing problems Emotional problems that affect the people who experience them (they "internalize" their problems, or turn inward), and include anxiety disorders (phobias, posttraumatic stress disorder, obsessive-compulsive disorder), depression, and eating disorders, among others; contrast with *externalizing problems.* (Chapter 11)

invisible displacements An object permanence task in which an object is hidden first in one container and then under another container out of the sight of the observer. Infants typically pass this task around 18 months. (Chapter 5)

IQ test Tests whose main purpose is to provide an index (intelligence quotient) that quantifies intelligence level. (Chapter 10)

joint attention See *shared attention.*

K strategies A reproductive strategy in which few offspring are produced but each requires substantial investment in terms of resources or nurturing; contrast with *r strategies.* (Chapter 15)

kangaroo care A practice that has been found to improve premature infants' development, consisting of putting them between the mother's breasts to facilitate nursing and to keep the baby warm. (Chapter 3)

kinetic cues Information about depth of objects associated with the movement of objects we are watching. (Chapter 5)

knowledge base The general background knowledge a person possesses. (Chapter 8)

Kwashiorkor Nutritional condition in which children receive just enough calories to survive, usually from starches, but do not receive adequate amounts of proteins. These children develop extended bellies, lose their hair, and become listless and irritable. (Chapter 4)

language acquisition device (LAD) In Chomsky's theory, an innate mechanism possessed by all humans at birth in order to enable them to acquire any language given a minimum linguistic input; contrast with *language acquisition support system (LASS).* (Chapter 9)

language acquisition support system (LASS) According to Bruner, a series of learning and social devices that adults and older children exhibit when interacting with younger children that facilitates language acquisition; contrast with *language acquisition device (LAD).* (Chapter 9)

law of independent assortment Mendel's law stating that different traits are inherited independently, so that the inheritance of one trait does not affect inheritance of another. See also *law of segregation.* (Chapter 3)

law of segregation Mendel's law stating that for each inherited trait there are two elements of heredity that segregate clearly during reproduction so that an offspring receives either one element or another, never some blend of both. See also *law of independent assortment.* (Chapter 3)

limbic system Part of the inner brain that mediates learning, memory, and emotion. (Chapter 4)

longitudinal studies Type of developmental studies that assesses developmental change by following a person or group of people over an extended period of time; compare with *cross-sectional studies.* (Chapter 1)

macrosystem In Bronfenbrenner's ecological systems theory, all the values, attitudes, laws, ideology, and so forth of the culture in which children and adolescents live. (Chapter 2)

marasmus A nutritional condition, in which the body wastes away when infants receive a diet low in all essential nutrients, often because their mothers are too malnourished to provide adequate breast milk. (Chapter 4)

Matthew effect The phenomenon in which the difference between good and poor readers (or other cognitive abilities) increases over time. (Chapter 10)

mean length of utterance A measure of language development defined by the average number of meaningful language units (root words and endings) a child uses at any one time. (Chapter 9)

mechanistic theories Theories of development that liken people to machines, such as the mind-as-a-computer model of information-processing approaches. (Chapter 2)

media Historically recent forms of communication (information transmission), such as television, the press, computers, and cell phones, that have transformed how youth acquire culturally and developmentally important information. (Chapter 13)

meiosis The type of cell division that occurs when sperm and ova are being formed, resulting in half the number of chromosomes in each gamete compared to body cells. (Chapter 3)

memory span The number of items a person can hold in the short-term store simultaneously, assessed by testing the number of (usually) unrelated items that can be recalled in exact order at once. (Chapter 8)

menarche A woman's first menstrual period. (Chapter 4)

mesosystem In Bronfenbrenner's ecological systems theory, all the possible *microsystems* in interaction. (Chapter 2)

metacognition Knowledge about one's own thoughts and the factors that influence thinking. (Chapter 8)

microgenetic studies Studies assessing some target behaviors of participants repeatedly over relatively short intervals of time, usually days or weeks. (Chapter 1)

microsystem In Bronfenbrenner's ecological systems theory, all of the different social systems in which a child is an active participant (for example, a child's family, school, and peer group). (Chapter 2)

migration (of neurons) The movement of neurons in the brain to their permanent positions in the brain, most of which is completed during the prenatal period. (Chapter 4)

mimicry A form of social learning that involves the duplication of a behavior without any understanding of the goal of that behavior. (Chapter 7)

min strategy An arithmetic strategy in which children faced with an addition problem start with the largest addend and count up from there; compare to *sum strategy*. (Chapter 10)

mindblindness Expression used to describe the difficulty that people with autism typically show in "reading" other people's minds. (Chapter 7)

mirror neuron A neuron, found in both monkeys and humans, that fires both when an individual acts and when an individual observes the same action performed by another. (Chapter 7)

monocular (pictorial) cues Cues used to understand visual perspective; such cues permit the perception of three dimensions from a two-dimensional target, as in a picture or a painting. (Chapter 5)

monogamy Family structure in which one man and one woman rear their genetic children. (Chapters 13 and 15)

monogenic inheritance Traits that are influenced by only a single pair of genes. (Chapter 3)

moral absolutism See *heteronomous morality*.

moral realism In Piaget's theory of moral development, children's rigid understanding of moral principles that are seen in terms of an "objective" assessment of a behavior's consequence (for example, number of cups broken), regardless of any other contextual and personal considerations (for example, if cups were broken accidentally or intentionally). (Chapter 14)

moral reasoning How people at different ages respond to moral dilemmas. (Chapter 14)

moral relativism *(autonomous morality)* In Piaget's theory of moral development, children's realization that social rules are arbitrary agreements among people that can be modified through social discussion. (Chapter 14)

morphemes The minimum meaningful language units. (Chapter 9)

morphology The knowledge of word formation. (Chapter 9)

multiple classification The ability to classify items in terms of more than one dimension simultaneously, such as shape and color. (Chapter 6)

mutations Irregularities in the DNA duplication process that result in an altered genetic message. (Chapter 3)

mutual exclusivity assumption A type of lexical constraint in which children believe that different words refer to different things. (Chapter 9)

myelin (myelination) A sheet of fatty substance that develops progressively around the neurons to promote faster transmission of electrical signals through the nervous system. (Chapter 4)

nativism Philosophical perspective that human intellectual abilities are innate; contrast with *empiricism*. (Chapter 1)

nativist theories (of language acquisition) Theories that propose that children are born with a broad theory of language that they modify in accordance with the speech they hear growing up; contrast with *social-interactionist perspective*. (Chapter 9)

natural (prepared) childbirth Method of labor and childbirth that does not involve anesthetics, in which a woman and her partner/coach receive education in areas such as relaxation and breathing. (Chapter 3)

natural parenting A movement in some Western nations to return to a more "natural" form of infant care, including having greater closeness between infants and parents (particularly mothers, but also fathers), increased sensitivity and responsiveness to infants' signals, and extended breastfeeding on demand. (Chapter 12)

natural selection Primary mechanism for species evolution described by Darwin, in which some members of a species are more fit than others and thus more likely to survive and reproduce. (Chapter 2)

naturalistic fallacy The erroneous idea that something is good because it is natural. (Chapter 2)

naturalistic studies Studies in which the researcher observes individuals in their own environments, intervening as little as possible. (Chapter 1)

nature/nurture Debate concerning the degree to which biology ("nature") and experience ("nurture") influence the development of any psychological characteristic and its development. (Chapter 1)

negative emotionality A dimension of temperament linked to anger/irritability, fearfulness, and sadness. (Chapter 11)

neglected children Children who are not often nominated or referred to (either positively or negatively) by other children in a sociometric assessment. (Chapter 14)

neglectful parenting style See *uninvolved parenting style*.

neocortex See *cerebral cortex*.

neonatal imitation The ability of newborns to reproduce some specific behaviors, such as certain facial expressions, that they have seen in others. (Chapter 5)

neonate An infant from birth through the first month of life. (Chapter 3)

neoteny Retention of the infantile characteristics of an evolutionary ancestor. (Chapter 4)

neuralation The first stage of neuronal development, in which the neural tube develops, which is the source of the central nervous system. (Chapter 4)

neuroconstructivism Theoretical perspective in which brain development is viewed as a dynamic process, the result of interactions among genes, neurons, behavior, cognition, and environment. (Chapter 4)

neuroimaging techniques Technologies that permit imaging of brain activities, including high-density event-related potentials, positron emission tomography (PET), and functional magnetic resonance imaging (fMRI). (Chapter 4)

neuron Nervous system cell through which electrical and chemical signals are transmitted. (Chapter 4)

Neuroticism Factor in the Five Factor Model that focuses on how afraid, touchy, tearful, and steady (in the reverse direction) individuals are. (Chapter 11)

neurotransmitters Chemicals that move across synapses and are "read" at the dendrites of adjacent cells, which convert the message back to an electrical signal and pass it on to its cell body. (Chapter 4)

nonshared environment An environment that is unique to an individual, not shared by a sibling, for instance; compare to *shared environment*. (Chapter 3)

norm of reaction All of the possible phenotypes that could result from a single genotype, given all of the possible environments an organism could be exposed to. (Chapter 3)

normative approach Approach in psychology concerned with features that all people have in common; compare to *idiographic approach*. (Chapter 1)

numerosity The ability to determine quickly the number of items in a set without counting. (Chapter 5)

obesity A body weight that is 20% or more higher than normal for the person's height, age, sex, and stature. (Chapter 4)

object constancy The knowledge that an object remains the same despite changes in how it is viewed (for example, from a different perspective, or distance). (Chapter 5)

object continuity The knowledge that objects are cohesive entities and move continuously through space. (Chapter 5)

object permanence The knowledge that objects have an existence in time and space independent of one's own perception or action on those objects. (Chapter 5)

observational studies Studies in which researchers identify a type of behavior they are interested in and observe children in specific situations for the incidence of those behaviors. They can be naturalistic or structured and typically do not involve an experimental manipulation of variables; contrast with *experimental studies*. (Chapter 1)

One-Child Policy Official policy in China that limits the number of children to one per family. (Chapter 13)

ontogenetic adaptations Behaviors that play a specific role in survival for an individual at one time only and then disappear when they are no longer needed; contrast with *deferred adaptations*. (Chapter 2)

ontogeny Development of the individual over his or her lifetime. (Chapter 1)

Openness-to-Experience Factor in the Five Factor Model that focuses on how original, creative, aesthetically sensitive, knowledgeable, and curious individuals are. (Chapter 11)

operant (instrumental) conditioning Learning procedure where behavior is shaped through rewards and punishment. (Chapter 2)

operations In Piaget's theory, types of cognitive schemes that are mental (that is, require symbols), derive from action, exist in organized systems, and follow a set of logical rules, most importantly that of reversibility. (Chapter 6)

opioids Neurohormonal regulator associated with reward, or pleasure, recognized by specific receptors in the brain. (Chapter 12)

oppositional defiant disorder A type of externalizing problem in childhood that is characterized by a pattern of defiant, uncooperative, and hostile behavior toward adults (particularly at home and school) that interferes with a child's daily functioning. (Chapter 11)

ordinality A basic understanding of *more than* and *less than* relationships. (Chapter 5)

organismic theories Developmental theories that take a holistic (organism-like) view of development, seeing people as whole beings who cannot be understood by decomposing them into their constituent parts. (Chapter 2)

organization (in Piaget's theory) The cognitive mechanism that keeps the different mental schemes integrated with one another in a hierarchical nature. See also *adaptation*. (Chapter 6)

organization (in recall) The structure discovered or imposed upon a set of items that is used to guide memory performance. (Chapter 8)

orienting/regulation A dimension of temperament that is associated with effortful control in early childhood, which is linked to the capacity to inhibit a dominant response and reorient attention to another goal. (Chapter 11)

out-group discrimination Showing a negative attitude toward members of social groups different from one's own; contrast with *in-group favoritism*. (Chapter 14)

overextensions The stretching of a familiar word beyond its correct meaning (for example, calling all four-legged mammals "doggie"); contrast with *underextensions*. (Chapter 9)

overregularization The tendency to extend the use of some morphological rules beyond their scope, that is, when they are not appropriate (for example, runned, foots, mices). (Chapter 9)

oxytocin Neurohormonal regulator that is produced at orgasm in both males and females, during cuddling, birth, suckling, stroking, and hugging; it reduces levels of the stress hormone cortisol and promotes relaxation and feelings of warmth and affiliation. (Chapter 12)

parental investment theory Theory coming from evolutionary biology that predicts differences in behaviors between males and females as a function of how much each invests in mating versus parenting. (Chapters 12 and 15)

parenting style The general way parents interact with their children. (Chapter 13)

parsimony Preference for the simplest scientific explanation for a phenomenon. (Chapter 1)

passive (or receptive) language The language that a child can understand; contrast with *active language*. (Chapter 9)

passive rehearsal Style of rehearsing in which a person includes few (usually one) unique items per rehearsal set; contrast with *active rehearsal*. (Chapter 8)

peer groups Peer organizations where members interact on a regular basis, define a sense of belonging, share implicit or explicit norms for the behavior of their members, and develop a hierarchical organization. (Chapter 14)

perceptual centration In Piaget's theory, the tendency of preoperational children to attend to one aspect of a situation to the exclusion of others; contrast with *decentration*. (Chapter 6)

permissive parenting style A style of parenting in which parents are warm and friendly but exert little control over their children's behaviors; contrast with *authoritarian, authoritative,* and *uninvolved parenting styles*. (Chapter 13)

personal fable A belief in one's uniqueness and invulnerability, which is an expression of adolescent egocentrism. (Chapters 6 and 11)

personality Reliable behavioral traits that describe how individuals interact with their world, emphasizing that it is biologically based, observable early in life, and stable over time. (Chapter 11)

perspective taking The ability to take the point of view of others. (Chapter 7)

phenotype The actual expression of a genetic trait; compare with *genotype*. (Chapter 3)

phonemes Individual sounds that are used to make up words. (Chapters 5 and 9)

phonemic awareness The knowledge that words consist of separable sounds; contrast with *phonological recoding*. (Chapter 10)

phonics Reading instruction method based on learning letter-sound correspondence; see also *phonological recoding*. (Chapter 10)

phonological recoding Reading skills used to translate written symbols into sounds and words; contrast with *phonemic awareness*. (Chapter 10)

phonology The actual sounds that speakers produce. (Chapter 9)

phylogeny Evolution of the species. (Chapter 1)

pictorial cues See *monocular cues*.

pidgins Structurally simple communication systems that arise when people who share no common language come into constant contact; contrast with *creoles*. (Chapter 9)

pituitary gland The master gland that produces hormones that influence growth. (Chapter 4)

placenta The organ along the uterine wall of a pregnant woman that serves as the transport system between mother and fetus. (Chapter 3)

plasticity The extent to which behavior or brain functioning can be changed. (Chapters 1 and 4)

polyandry Family structure in which one woman has multiple husbands. (Chapters 13 and 15)

polygenic inheritance Inherited traits that are determined by multiple genes. (Chapter 3)

polygyny Family structure in which one man has multiple wives. (Chapters 13 and 15)

popular children Children who are mentioned frequently and positively by their peers in a sociometric assessment. (Chapter 14)

popularity Likeability; the extent to which a child is sought out by others. (Chapter 14)

positive manifold The high correlations among scores on sets of cognitive tests that have little in common with one another in terms of content or types of strategies used. (Chapter 10)

postconventional morality In Kohlberg's theory, the third level of moral development, in which individuals develop a set of principles that go beyond any authority figure. (Chapter 14)

postpartum depression A mother's strong feelings of sadness or resentment shortly after giving birth. (Chapter 3)

practical subtheory/intelligence See *contextual subtheory/intelligence*.

pragmatics Knowledge about how language can be adjusted to fit different people and circumstances. (Chapter 9)

preconventional morality In Kohlberg's theory, the first level of moral development, in which children conform to rules to gain rewards and avoid punishment. (Chapter 14)

preformationism The idea that development is just the expression of previously fully formed structures. (Chapter 1)

premoral stage In Piaget's theory of moral development, the stage at which children are unaware of rules as cooperative agreements. (Chapter 14)

prenatal period The 38 weeks the embryo/fetus spends developing inside the mother's reproductive system, beginning at conception and ending at birth. (Chapter 3)

preoperational period In Piaget's theory, the second major stage of cognitive development (approximately ages 2 to 7), characterized by prelogical, intuitive thought. (Chapters 2 and 6)

prepared childbirth See *natural childbirth*.

prepared learning The idea that animals (including humans) are "prepared" by natural selection to attend to and acquire some things more readily than others. (Chapter 11)

primary emotions Emotions that emerge during the first year of life, including distress, disgust, interest, surprise, contentment, joy, anger, sadness, and fear. (Chapter 11)

primary sexual characteristics Characteristics associated directly with reproduction, such as maturation of the gonads and anatomy of the genitals; contrast with *secondary sexual characteristics*. (Chapter 4)

private speech (or egocentric speech) Children's speech that is apparently produced for the self and not directed to others. (Chapter 9)

problem solving Process in which someone has a specific goal in mind that cannot be attained immediately because of the presence of one or more obstacles; problem solving involves a goal, obstacles to that goal, strategies for overcoming the obstacles, and an evaluation of the results. (Chapter 8)

procedural memory See *nondeclarative memory*.

prodigy A child with generally typical abilities in all but a small number of areas (usually one), in which he or she displays precocious talent; contrast with *savant*. (Chapter 10)

production deficiency Children's tendency not to use spontaneously a strategy that they are capable of using when instructed; contrast with *utilization deficiency*. (Chapter 8)

progesterone A hormone produced by the ovaries that promotes sexual development. (Chapter 4)

proliferation The process of nerve-cell division by mitosis. (Chapter 4)

promiscuous teleology Children's tendency to reason about events and objects in terms of purpose. (Chapter 7)

prosocial behaviors Behaviors that benefit other people. (Chapter 14)

prospective memory Remembering to do something in the future. (Chapter 8)

provocative victims Victims of bullies who are highly aggressive themselves. (Chapter 14)

proximodistal development Pattern of development in which body grows from the center to the periphery. (Chapter 4)

psychometric approach An approach to cognition that assumes that intelligence and other cognitive abilities can be described in terms of a series of mental factors, then, in turn, can be assessed by standardized tests. (Chapter 10)

psychosocial moratorium A sort of time-out period when, where possible, young people have a chance to explore who they are and what they want to be, in both the near and distant future. (Chapter 7)

puberty Period in life in which children attain adult size and physical characteristics, including sexual maturity. (Chapter 4)

puberty rites Rituals practiced in many cultures to mark a child's transition from childhood to young adulthood. (Chapter 15)

Pygmalion effect A form of *self-fulfilling prophecy*, in which a person internalizes the expectations of an authority figure. (Chapter 10)

quasi-experimental studies Studies in which assignment of participants to conditions is not made at random (for example, males vs. females). (Chapter 1)

questionnaires A form of self-reports, in which participants respond to a series of questions designed to get at some specific aspect of people's behavior, thinking, or feelings. (Chapter 1)

r strategies A reproductive strategy in which many offspring are produced with minimal investment or nurturing; contrast with *K strategies*. (Chapter 15)

reasoning A particular type of problem solving that involves making inferences. (Chapter 8)

receptive language See *passive language*.

reciprocal altruism The idea that individuals will cooperate with those who cooperate with them and with whom they will interact in the future. (Chapter 14)

reciprocal determinism In Bandura's theory, the belief that children have as much of an effect on their environment as their environment has on them. (Chapter 2)

reflective abstraction In Piaget's theory, the ability to reflect upon knowledge one already possesses, and without the need of additional information from the external environment, to arrive at new knowledge; characteristic of adolescent thought. (Chapter 6)

rehearsal A memory strategy in which target information is repeated; see also *active rehearsal* and *passive rehearsal*. (Chapter 8)

rejected children Children who are mentioned frequently and negatively by their peers in a sociometric assessment. (Chapter 14)

relationships Frequent interactions between two individuals occurring over time; compare to *interactions*. (Chapter 14)

reliability The trustworthiness of a research finding; includes interobserver reliability and *replicability*. (Chapter 1)

resistance to interference The ability to ignore irrelevant information so that it does not impede task performance. (Chapter 8)

reversibility In Piaget's theory, the knowledge that an operation can be reversed, characteristic of the concrete operational period. (Chapter 6)

Rh factor incompatibility Mismatch between the mother's and the fetus's Rh type (a blood protein). Namely if Rh of the fetus is positive, and Rh of its mother is negative, complications can occur because of the production of antibodies in the mother that can attack red blood cells in the fetus. (Chapter 3)

risk-taking Engaging in behaviors that can result in harm to the individual. (Chapter 11)

savants (savant syndrome) Individuals who show some type of genius, usually in a single area, but also display some form of mental disability in the rest; contrast with *prodigy*. (Chapter 10)

scheme An abstract representation of an object or event. (Chapter 6)

scientific reasoning A type of reasoning that involves the generation of hypotheses and the systematic testing of those hypotheses. (Chapter 8)

scripts A form of schematic organization, with real-world events organized in terms of temporal and causal relations between component acts. (Chapter 8)

second language/second culture learners People whose first language and first culture are not those of their adopted country. (Chapter 9)

secondary (self-conscious) emotions Emotions that emerge during the second year of life or later, including shame, embarrassment, coyness, shyness, empathy, guilt, jealousy, envy, pride, and contempt. (Chapter 11)

secondary sexual characteristics Physical characteristics developed in puberty that signal sexual maturity but are not directly related to changes in reproductive organs (for example, pubic and underarm hair, breasts in girls, changes in the voice and shape of the face in boys); contrast with *primary sexual characteristics*. (Chapter 4)

secure attachment Optimal type of attachment where infants display confidence when their caregivers are present, show mild distress when temporarily left alone, and quickly reestablish contact with caregivers upon their return; compare to *insecure-avoidant, insecure-resistant,* and *disorganized/disoriented attachment*. (Chapter 12)

selection In Sternberg's triarchic theory of intelligence, the selection of environments in which to interact. (Chapter 10)

selective attention Concentration on chosen stimuli without distraction by nontarget stimuli. (Chapter 8)

selective cell death (apoptosis) Early developmental process in which neurons that are not activated by sensory and motor experience die. (Chapter 4)

self-concept The way a person defines himself or herself. (Chapter 7)

self-efficacy The extent to which a person views him- or herself as an effective individual. (Chapter 7)

self-esteem The judgments people make of their general self-worth and the feelings associated with those judgments. (Chapter 7)

semantic memory Long-term memory representation of definitions and relations among language terms; contrast with *episodic memory*. (Chapter 8)

semantics The understanding of words and sentences. (Chapter 9)

semilingualism In bilingual environments, the lack of mastery in both languages. (Chapter 9)

sensitive period The time in development (usually early in life) when a certain skill or ability can be most easily acquired. (Chapter 1)

sensorimotor period In Piaget's theory, the first major stage of cognitive development (birth to approximately 2 years), in which children understand their world through sensory and motor experiences. (Chapters 2 and 6)

separation distress (separation protest, separation anxiety) Infants' distress response on being left by their attachment figure. (Chapter 12)

sequential bilingualism When children learn a second language after mastering the first. (Chapter 9)

seriation The ability to order objects according to the quantitative dimension of a certain trait. (Chapter 6)

sex chromosomes In humans, the 23rd chromosome pair that determines gender. (Chapter 3)

sex-linked inheritance Recessive traits that are inherited by way of a single gene on the sex chromosomes, usually the X chromosome; also called X-linked inheritance. (Chapter 3)

sexual socialization The process by which knowledge, attitudes, and values about sexuality are acquired. (Chapter 13)

sexual-minority youth Youth whose sexual orientation is not heterosexual. (Chapter 15)

sexuality An individual's erotic thoughts and activities. (Chapter 15)

shaping In Sternberg's triarchic theory of intelligence, the ability to modify, or shape, the behaviors of others. (Chapter 10)

shared attention (joint attention) Two people both attending to the same thing or event and sharing that experience. (Chapter 7)

shared environment An environment shared by different family members (for example, two siblings); contrast with *nonshared environment.* (Chapter 3)

sickle-cell anemia A disease associated with two recessive genes that causes malformations of the red blood cells; however, carriers of a single recessive gene have heightened resistance to malaria. (Chapter 3)

SIDS See *Sudden Infant Death Syndrome.*

simultaneous bilingualism When children are exposed from birth to two languages. (Chapter 9)

single mothers by choice Usually older, well-educated, and economically stable women who choose to rear children without a partner. (Chapter 13)

slow-to-warm-up babies Infants described as having a slow pattern of reaction; they have a difficult time adapting to new situations, show a tendency to withdraw in novel situations, and are generally low in activity. (Chapter 11)

social cognition Thinking about the self, other people, and social relationships. (Chapter 7)

social learning/social cognitive theory Bandura's theory of how individuals operate cognitively on their social experiences and how these cognitive operations influence behavior and development. (Chapter 2)

social referencing An infant's use of another person's emotional cues to interpret an ambiguous or uncertain event. (Chapter 11)

social smiling Smiling in response to social events; contrast with *endogenous smiles.* (Chapter 11)

social-interactionist perspective (of language acquisition) The position that children's domain-general social-cognitive abilities and the social environment play a central role in language development; contrast with *nativist theories.* (Chapter 9)

sociocultural theory A perspective of cognitive development that emphasizes that individual development is socially mediated, and historically and culturally conditioned. (Chapter 2)

sociodramatic play Play in which children take on different roles and follow a story line as if they were in a theatrical performance. (Chapter 6)

sociohistorical context The values, tools, and institutions found in one's society. (Chapter 2)

source monitoring The awareness of the origins of one's memories, knowledge, or beliefs. (Chapter 6)

specific language impairment Children who exhibit problems that are focused in language, while other sensory and intellectual abilities are typical. (Chapter 9)

speech register A distinct style of speaking that is used only in specific contexts (for example, when talking to children; when talking in school). (Chapter 9)

speed of processing How quickly any cognitive operation can be executed; hypothesized to be a measure of mental capacity and related to performance on many cognitive tasks. (Chapter 8)

spermarche A male's first ejaculation. (Chapter 4)

stability In developmental psychology, the degree to which a person maintains over time the same rank order in comparison with peers for a particular characteristic. (Chapter 1)

standardized tests Special types of questionnaires that are administered following consistent, standardized instructions. (Chapter 1)

Stanford-Binet An individually administered IQ test for people 2 years old to adulthood. (Chapter 10)

stereoscopic (or binocular) vision The ability to integrate the images provided by each eye into a single, richer one. (Chapter 5)

stereotype threat Phenomenon in which minority members perform worse on IQ or other tests after being reminded of the negative stereotype concerning their groups' performance on such tests. (Chapter 10)

Strange Situation A technique developed by Ainsworth and her colleagues to assess quality of attachment in young children. (Chapter 12)

structure In developmental psychology, a substrate of the organism that develops, such as muscle, nervous tissue, or mental knowledge; contrast with *function*; see *bidirectionality of structure and function.* (Chapter 1)

structured interviews Interviews in which participants are asked a set of standardized questions under conditions in which the researcher can control extraneous factors that may influence a child's behavior. (Chapter 1)

Sudden Infant Death Syndrome (SIDS) The death of a seemingly healthy infant during sleep for no apparent reason during the first year of life. (Chapter 3)

sum strategy An addition strategy used by young children that involves counting together the two addends (that is, one after the other) of a problem; compare to *min strategy.* (Chapter 10)

surgency (or extraversion) A dimension of temperament related to positive affect and activity, reflected in high activity level, smiling and laughter, and high-intensity expression of pleasure. (Chapter 11)

symbolic (fantasy) play Pretending; it involves an 'if-then' orientation to objects, actions, and peers. (Chapter 6)

synapses The tiny spaces between the dendrite of one neuron and the axon of another through which chemical messages are passed; the structures through which neurons communicate. (Chapter 4)

synaptogenesis The process of synapse formation. (Chapter 4)

syntactic bootstrapping In learning the meaning of words, the idea that the grammatical form of speech may give children important clues for guessing what a word means. (Chapter 9)

syntax The knowledge of how words are put together to form proper and understandable sentences. (Chapter 9)

taxonomic assumption A type of lexical constraint in which children assume that words refer to things that are similar. (Chapter 9)

teaching (instructed learning) A form of social learning in which a more accomplished person intentionally conveys his or her knowledge and/or skills to a less accomplished person. (Chapter 7)

telegraphic speech Children's economical use of words, including only high-information words that are most important in conveying meaning. (Chapter 9)

temperament The term that developmental psychologists use to refer to "personality" in infants and young children. (Chapter 11)

teratogens External agents, such as drugs and radiation, that can have harmful effects on a developing embryo or fetus. (Chapter 3)

testosterone A form of androgen or male hormone, produced primarily by the testes, that promotes sexual maturation. (Chapter 4)

Textspeak The sort of cryptic writing used in text messaging and e-mails. (Chapter 9)

theory of mind A person's concepts of mental activity; used to refer to how children conceptualize mental activity and how they attribute intention to and predict the behavior of others; see also *belief-desire reasoning.* (Chapter 7)

theory of multiple intelligences Gardner's theory postulating eight components, or modules, of intelligence: (1) linguistic, (2) logical-mathematical, (3) musical, (4) spatial, (5) bodily-kinesthetic, (6) interpersonal, (7) intrapersonal, and (8) naturalistic. (Chapter 10)

theory theories Approach to cognitive development that combine neonativism and constructivism, proposing that cognitive development progresses by children generating, testing, and changing their naïve theories about the physical and social world. (Chapter 6)

thyroxine A hormone produced by the thyroid gland that influences growth and prenatal brain development. (Chapter 4)

tools of intellectual adaptation Vygotsky's term for tools a culture provides for thinking and problem solving. (Chapter 2)

triarchic theory of intelligence Sternberg's theory that describes intelligence in terms of three subtheories or types of intelligence: contextual, experiential, and componential. (Chapter 10)

Turner syndrome A chromosomal disorder in females in which one X chromosome is missing, resulting in a total complement of only 45 chromosomes. (Chapter 3)

underextensions Incorrectly restricting the use of a language term (for example, believing that only one's pet, Fido, deserves the label "dog"); contrast with *overextensions.* (Chapter 9)

uninvolved (or neglectful) parenting style Parenting style in which parents are disengaged from their children. They are emotionally cold and indifferent and demand little from their children; contrast *with authoritarian, authoritative,* and *permissive parenting styles.* (Chapter 13)

universal grammar In nativist theories of language acquisition, the innate grammar that characterizes all human languages. (Chapter 9)

utilization deficiency Using an apparently appropriate strategy that does not improve task performance; contrast with *production deficiency.* (Chapter 8)

validity The extent to which a measurement accurately assesses what it purports to measure. (Chapter 1)

verbal repairs Adjusting or "repairing" one's speech after making errors in communication or believing that the listener might not understand you. (Chapter 9)

verbatim traces Precise, literal memory representations that are less easily accessed, generally require more effort to use, and are more susceptible to interference and forgetting than fuzzy traces. (Chapter 8)

vicarious reinforcement In Bandura's social cognitive theory, learning from observing others' behaviors and their consequences, without the need to receive specific reinforcement for one's behavior. (Chapter 2)

violation-of-expectation method Based on habituation/dishabituation procedures, techniques in which increases in infants' looking time at impossible events are interpreted as reflecting a violation of what they expected to see. (Chapter 5)

visual acuity The ability to see something sharply and clearly. (Chapter 5)

visual preference paradigm In research with infants, observing the amount of time infants spend looking at different visual stimuli to determine which one they prefer (that is, look at more often); such preferences indicate an ability to discriminate between stimuli. (Chapter 5)

visual realism In children's drawing, children's tendency to draw what they actually see; contrast with *intellectual realism.* (Chapter 6)

visual self-recognition The ability to recognize oneself in a mirror; a form of self-recognition. (Chapter 7)

visual tracking The ability to follow a moving object with one's eyes. (Chapter 5)

wariness of strangers See *fear of strangers.*

Wechsler scales Individually administered IQ tests, including the WPPSI, the WISC, and the WAIS. (Chapter 10)

Westermarck effect The phenomenon that people who cohabitate with one another from early in childhood rarely ever find one another sexually attractive, regardless of their genetic relationship. (Chapter 15)

whole-language approach A top-down approach to teaching reading that emphasizes the readers' active construction of meaning. (Chapter 10)

whole-object assumption A type of lexical constraint in which children assume when hearing a word that it refers to the whole object and not to some part of that object. (Chapter 9)

Williams syndrome A relatively rare disorder, with afflicted individuals displaying mild to moderate intellectual impairment, but having language abilities that are typically much more advanced than their other cognitive functions. (Chapter 9)

word spurt Expression used to describe the rapid increase in word (mostly noun) learning observed in some children, typically occurring at about 18 months of age. (Chapter 9)

working memory The capacity to store and transform information being held in the short-term system. (Chapter 8)

young-male syndrome High levels of aggressive and violent behavior committed by adolescent and young-adult males. (Chapter 14)

zone of proximal development In Vygotsky's theory, the difference between a child's actual level of ability and the level of ability that he or she can achieve when working under the guidance of a more qualified instructor (adult or older child). see *sociocultural theory.* (Chapter 2)

zygote The single-celled organism formed from the union of egg and sperm at the earliest phase of prenatal development. (Chapter 3)

References

Aboud, F. E. (1988). *Children and prejudice.* Cambridge, MA: Blackwell.

Aboud, F. E. (2003). The formation of in-group favoritism and out-group prejudice in young children: Are they distinct? *Developmental Psychology, 39,* 48–60.

Abramovitch, R., Corter, C., Pepler, D. J., & Stanhope, L. (1986). Sibling and peer interaction: A final follow-up and a comparison. *Child Development, 57,* 217–229.

Abrams, D., Rutland, A., & Cameron, L. (2003). The development of subjective group dynamics: Children's judgments of normative and deviant in-group and out-group individuals. *Child Development, 74,* 1840–1856.

Abravanel, E., & Sigafoos, A. D. (1984). Explaining the presence of imitation during early infancy. *Child Development, 55,* 381–392.

Ackerman, B. P., & Brown, E. D. (2006). Income poverty, poverty co-factors, and the adjustment of children in school. In R.V. Kail (Ed.), *Advances in child development and behavior* (Vol. 34, pp. 91–129). Oxford, UK: Elsevier.

Ackerman, B. P., Brown, E. D., & Izard, C. E. (2004). The relations between contextual risk, earned income, and the school adjustment of children from economically disadvantaged families. *Developmental Psychology, 40,* 204–216.

Ackil, J. K., Van Abbema, D. L., & Bauer, P. J. (2003). After the storm: Enduring differences in mother-child recollections of traumatic and nontraumatic events. *Journal of Experimental Child Psychology, 84,* 286–309.

Ackil, J. K., & Zaragoza, M. S. (1995). Developmental differences in eyewitness suggestibility and memory for source. *Journal of Experimental Child Psychology, 60,* 57–83.

Adams, M. J., Treiman, R., & Pressley, M. (1998). Reading, writing, and literacy. In W. Damon (Gen. Ed.), *Handbook of child psychology* (5th ed.). In K. A. Renninger & I. E. Sigel (Vol. Eds.), Vol. 4: *Child psychology in practice.* New York: Wiley.

Adams, R. (2003, December 9). Baby's first pictures. *The Washington Post,* pp. F1, F5.

Adelson, E., & Fraiberg, S. (1974). Gross motor development in infants blind from birth. *Child Development, 45,* 114–126.

Adey, P. S., & Shayer, M. (1992). Accelerating the development of formal thinking in middle and high school students: II. Postproject effects on science achievement. *Journal of Research in Science Teaching, 29,* 81–92.

Adler, A. (1927). *Understanding human nature.* Garden City, NY: Garden City Publishing.

Adler, S. (1990). Multicultural clients: Implications for the SLP. *Language, Speech, and Hearing in the Schools, 21,* 135–139.

Adolph, K. E. (1997). Learning in the development of locomotion. *Monographs of the Society of Child Development, 62* (Serial No. 251).

Adolph, K. E. (2008). Learning to move. *Current Directions in Psychological Science, 17,* 213–218.

Adolph, K. E., & Avolio, A. M. (2000). Infants adapt locomotion to changing body dimensions. *Journal of Experimental Psychology: Human Perception and Performance, 26,* 1148–1166.

Adolph, K. E., & Berger, S. A. (2006). Motor development. In W. Damon & R. Lerner (Gen. Eds.), *Handbook of child psychology* (6th ed.). In D. Kuhn & R. S. Siegler (Vol. Eds.), Vol. 2: *Cognition, perception, and language* (pp. 161–213). New York: Wiley.

Adolph, K. E., Vereijken, B., & Denny, M. A. (1998). Learning to crawl. *Child Development, 69,* 1299–1312.

Adrián, J. E., Clemente, R. A., & Villanueva, L. (2007). Mothers' use of cognitive state verbs in picture-book reading and the development of children's understanding of mind: A longitudinal study. *Child Development, 78,* 1052–1067.

Aguiar, A., & Baillargeon, R. (1998). Eight-and-a-half-month-old infants' reasoning about containment events. *Child Development, 69,* 636–653.

Ahadi, S. A., Rothbart, M. K., & Ye, R. (1993). Children's temperament in the U.S. and China: Similarities and differences. *European Journal of Personality, 7,* 359–378.

Ainsworth, M. D. S., (1979). Infant-mother attachment. *American Psychologist, 34,* 932–937.

Ainsworth, M. D. S., Blehar, M. C., Waters, E., & Wall, S. (1978). *Patterns of attachment: A psychological study of the strange situation.* Hillsdale, NJ: Erlbaum.

Ainsworth, M. D. S., & Wittig, B. A. (1969). Attachment and exploratory behavior in one-year-olds in a strange situation. In B. M. Foss (Ed.), *Determinants of infant behaviour* (Vol. 4, pp. 111–136). London: Methuen.

Aitchinson, J. (1994). *Words in the mind: An introduction to the mental lexicon* (2nd ed.). Oxford, UK: Blackwell.

Akhtar, N. (1999). Acquiring basic word order: Evidence for data-driven learning of syntactic structure. *Journal of Child Language, 26,* 339–356.

Alberto, P. A., & Troutman, A. C. (2005). *Applied behavior analysis for teachers* (7th ed.). Englewood Cliffs, NJ: Prentice-Hall.

Alexander, J. M., & Schwanenflugel, P. J. (1996). Development of metacognitive concepts about thinking in gifted and nongifted children: Recent research. *Learning and Individual Differences, 8,* 305–325.

Alexander, R. D. (1974). The evolution of social behavior. *Annual Review of Ecology and Systematics, 5,* 325–384.

Alexander, R. D. (1989). Evolution of the human psyche. In P. Mellers & C. Stringer (Eds.), *The human revolution: Behavioural and biological perspectives on the origins of modern humans* (pp. 455–513). Princeton, NJ: Princeton University Press.

Alink, L. R. A., Mesman, J., van Zeijl, J., Stolk, M. N., Juffer, F., Koot, H. M., Bakermans-Kranenburg, M. J., & van IJzendoorn, M. H. (2006). The early childhood aggression curve: Development of physical aggression in 10- to 50-month-old children. *Child Development, 77,* 954–966.

Allen, R., & Shatz, M. (1983). 'What says meow?': The role of context and linguistic experience in very young children's responses to *what-* questions. *Journal of Child Language, 10,* 321–335.

Alley, T. R. (1981). Head shape and the perception of cuteness. *Developmental Psychology, 17,* 650–654.

Alley, T. R. (1983). Growth-produced changes in body shape and size as determinants of perceived age and adult caregiving. *Child Development, 54,* 241–248.

Allison, P. D., & Furstenberg, F. F., Jr. (1989). How marital dissolution affects children: Variation by age and sex. *Developmental Psychology, 25,* 540–549.

Allman, J. M. (1999). *Evolving brains*. New York: Scientific American Library.

Alloway, T. P., & Alloway, R. G. (2010). Investigating the predictive roles of working memory and IQ in academic attainment. *Journal of Experimental Child Psychology, 106,* 20–29.

Alloway, T. P., Gathercole, S. E., & Pickering, S. J. (2006). Verbal and visuospatial short-term and working memory in children: Are they separable? *Child Development, 77,* 1698–1716.

Als, H. (1995). The preterm infant: A model for the study of fetal brain expectation. In J-P. Lecanuet, W. Fifer, N. Krasnegor, & W. Smotherman, (Eds.), *Fetal development: A psychobiological perspective.* Hillsdale, NJ: Erlbaum.

Alvergne, A., Faurie, C., & Raymond, M. (2007). Differential facial resemblance of young children to their parents: Who do children look like more? *Evolution and Human Behavior, 28,* 135–144.

Amato, P. R. (1996). Explaining the intergenerational transmission of divorce. *Journal of Marriage & the Family, 58,* 628–640.

Amato, P. R. (2000). Diversity within single-parent families. In D. H. Demo, K. R. Allen, & M. A. Fine (Eds.), *Handbook of family diversity* (pp. 149–172). New York: Oxford University Press.

Amato, P. R. (2001). Children of divorce in the 1990s: An update of the Amato and Keith (1991) meta-analysis. *Journal of Family Psychology, 15,* 355–370.

Ambady, N., Shih, M., Kim, A., & Pittinsky, T. L. (2001). Stereotype susceptibility in children: Effects of identity activation on quantitative performance. *Psychological Science, 12,* 385–390.

American Academy of Pediatrics. (1999). Media education. *Pediatrics, 104,* 257–270.

American Academy of Pediatrics, Committee on Injury and Poison Prevention. (2001). Injuries associated with infant walkers. *Pediatrics, 108,* 790–792.

American Academy of Pediatrics, Task Force on Sudden Infant Death Syndrome. (2005). The changing concept of sudden infant death syndrome. *Pediatrics, 116,* 1245–1255.

American Academy of Pediatrics, Work Group on Breastfeeding. (1997). Breastfeeding and the use of human milk. *Pediatrics, 100,* 1035–1039.

American Psychiatric Association. (1994). *Diagnostic and statistical manual of mental disorders* (4th ed.). Washington, DC: American Psychiatric Association.

American Speech-Language-Hearing Association. (1993). *Definitions of communication disorders and variations* [Relevant Paper]. Available from www.asha.org/policy.

Amos, D., & Casey, B. J. (2006). Beyond what develops when: Neuroimaging may inform how cognition changes with development. *Current Directions in Psychological Science, 15,* 24–29.

Amsterlaw, J., Lagattuta, K. H., & Meltzoff, A. N. (2009). Young children's reasoning about the effects of emotional and physiological states on academic performance. *Child Development, 80,* 115–133.

Anastasi, A. (1988). *Psychological testing* (6th ed.). New York: Macmillian.

Anderson, C. (2003). The diversity, strengths, and challenges of single-parent households. In F. Walsh (Ed.), *Normal family processes: Growing diversity and complexity* (3rd ed., pp. 121–152). New York: Guilford.

Anderson, C. A., Berkowitz, L., Donnerstein, E., Huesmann, L. R., Johnson, J. D., Linz, D., Malamuth, N. M., & Wartella, E. (2003). The influence of media violence on youth. *Psychological Science in the Public Interest, 4,* Number 3.

Anderson, C. A., & Bushman, B. J. (2001). Effects of violent video games on aggressive behavior, aggressive cognition, aggressive affects, physiological arousal, and prosocial behavior: A meta-analytic review of the scientific literature. *Psychological Science, 12,* 353–359.

Anderson, C. A, & Pempek, T. A. (2005). Television in the very young. *American Behavioral Scientists, 48,* 505–522.

Anderson, C. A., Shinuya, A., Ihori, N., Swing, E. L., Bushman, B. J., Sakamoto, A. K., Rothstein, H. R., & Saleen, M. (2010). Violent video game effects on aggression, empathy, and prosocial behavior in Eastern and Western countries: A meta-analytic review. *Psychological Bulletin, 136,* 151–173.

Anderson, K. G., Kaplan, H., & Lancaster J. (1999). Paternal care by genetic fathers and stepfathers I: Reports from Albuquerque men. *Evolution and Human Behavior, 20,* 405–431.

Anderson, K. G., Kaplan, H., Lam, D., & Lancaster J. (1999). Paternal care by genetic fathers and stepfathers II: Reports by Xhosa high school students. *Evolution and Human Behavior, 20,* 433–451.

Anderson, S. E., & Whitaker, R. C. (2009). Prevalence of obesity among U.S. preschool children in different racial and ethnic groups. *Archives of Pediatric and Adolescence Medicine, 163,* 344–348.

Anglin, J. M. (1993). Vocabulary development: A morphological analysis. *Monographs of the Society for Research in Child Development, 58* (Serial No. 238).

Annett, M. (1970). The growth of manual preference and speech. *British Journal of Psychology, 61,* 545–558.

Annett, M. (1985). *Left, right, hand, and brain: The right shift theory.* London: Erlbaum.

Apfelbaum, E. P., Pauker, K., Ambaby, N., Norton, M. I., & Sommers, S. R. (2008). Learning (not) to talk about race: When older children underperform in social categorization. *Developmental Psychology, 44,* 1513–1518.

Apgar, V. (1953). A proposal for a new method of evaluation in the newborn infant. *Current Research in Anesthesia and Analgesia, 32,* 260–267.

Arend, R., Gove, F., & Sroufe, L. A. (1979). Continuity of individual adaptation from infancy to kindergarten: A predictive study of ego-resiliency and curiosity in preschoolers. *Child Development, 50,* 950–959.

Arffa, S. (2007). The relationship of intelligence to executive function and non-executive function measures in a sample of average, above average, and gifted youth. *Archives of Clinical Neuropsychology, 22,* 969–978.

Ariès, P. (1962). *Centuries of childhood: A social history of family life.* New York: Knopf.

Arnett, J. (1992). Reckless behavior in adolescence: A developmental perspective. *Developmental Review, 12,* 339–373.

Arnett, J. (1995). Adolescents' use of media for self-socialization. *Journal of Youth and Adolescence, 24,* 519–534.

Arnett, J. J. (2004). *Emerging adulthood: The winding road from late teens through the twenties.* New York: Oxford University Press.

Arterberry, M., Yonas, A., & Bensen, A. S. (1989). Self-produced locomotion and the development of responsiveness to linear perspective and texture gradients. *Developmental Psychology, 25,* 976–982.

Ashcraft, M. H. (1990). Strategic processing in children's mental arithmetic: A review and proposal. In D. F. Bjorklund (Ed.), *Children's strategies: Contemporary views of cognitive development.* Hillsdale, NJ: Erlbaum.

Asher, S. R. (1983). Social competence and peer status: Recent advances and future directions. *Child Development, 54,* 1427–1434.

Asher, S. R., Hymel, S., & Renshaw, P. D. (1984). Loneliness in children. *Child Development, 55,* 1456–1464.

Asher, S. R., & Markel, R. A. (1974). Sex differences in comprehension of high- and low-interest reading material. *Journal of Educational Psychology, 66,* 680–687.

Asher, S. R., & McDonald, K. L. (2009). The behavioral basis of acceptance, rejection, and perceived popularity. In K. H. Rubin, W. M. Bukowski, & B. Laursen (Eds.), *Handbook of peer interactions, relationships, and groups* (pp. 232–248). New York: Guilford.

Asher, S. R., Parkhurst, J. T., Hymel, S., & Williams, G. A. (1990). Peer rejection and loneliness in childhood. In S. R. Asher and J. D. Coie (Eds.), *Peer rejection in childhood.* Cambridge, UK: Cambridge University Press.

Asher, S. R., & Renshaw, P. D. (1981). Children without friends: Social knowledge and social skill training. In S. R. Asher & J. M. Gutterman (Eds.), *The development of children's friendships.* New York: Cambridge University Press.

Aslin, R. N. (1977). Development of binocular fixation in human infants. *Journal of Experimental Child Psychology, 23,* 133–156.

Aslin, R. N. (2007). What's in a look? *Developmental Science, 10*, 48–53.

Aslin, R. N., Jusczyk, P. W., & Pisoni, D. B. (1998). Speech and auditory processing during infancy. In W. Damon (Gen. Ed.), *Handbook of child psychology* (5th ed.). In D. Kuhn & R. S. Siegler (Vol. Eds.), Vol. 2: *Cognitive, language, and perceptual development*. New York: Wiley.

Associated Press. (June 8, 2008). Naked truth: Photos can haunt teens later. In *The Palm Beach Post*.

Astuti, R. (2001). Are we all natural dualists? A cognitive developmental approach (The 2000 Malinowski Memorial Lecture). *Journal of the Royal Anthropological Institute, 7*, 429–447.

Astuti, R., Solomon, G. E. A., & Carey, S. (2004). Constraints on conceptual development: A case study of the acquisition of folkbiological and folksociological knowledge in Madagascar. *Monographs of the Society for Research in Child Development, 69* (Serial No. 277).

Atance, C. M. (2008). Future thinking in young children. *Current Directions in Psychological Science, 17*, 295–298.

Atran, S. (1994) Core domains versus scientific theories. In L. Hirschfeld & S. Gelman (Eds.), *Mapping the mind: Domain-specificity in cognition and culture*. New York: Cambridge University Press.

Atran, S. (1998) Folkbiology and the anthropology of science: Cognitive universals and cultural particulars. *Behavioral and Brain Sciences, 21*, 547–609.

Atran, S. (2002). *In gods we trust: The evolutionary landscape of religion*. New York: Oxford University Press.

Atran, S., Medin, D., & Ross, N. (2004.). Evolution and devolution of knowledge: A tale of two biologies. *Journal of the Royal Anthropological Society, 10*, 395–420.

August, G. J. (1987). Production deficiencies in free recall: A comparison of hyperactive, learning-disabled, and normal children. *Journal of Abnormal Child Psychology, 15*, 429–440.

Austad, S. N. (1997). *Why we age: What science is discovering about the body's journey through life*. New York: Wiley.

Austin, J. L. (1962). *How to do things with words*. Cambridge, MA: Harvard University Press.

Australian Institute of Family Studies. (2008). *Growing up in Australia:* The Longitudinal Study of Australian Children: 2007–08 Annual Report. Melbourne: Australian Institute of Family Studies.

Auyeung, B., Baron-Cohen, S., Ashwin, E., Knickmeyer, R., Taylor, K., Hackett, G., & Hines, M. (2009). Fetal testosterone predicts sexually differentiated childhood behaviors in girls and boys. *Psychological Science, 20*, 144–148.

Avenevoli, S., Sessa, F. M., & Steinberg, L. (1999). Family structure, parenting practices, and adolescent adjustment: An ecological examination. In E. M. Hetherington (Ed.), *Coping with divorce, single parenting and remarriage: A risk and resiliency perspective* (pp. 65–90). Mahwah, NJ: Erlbaum.

Avis & J., & Harris, P. L. (1991). Belief-desire reasoning among Baka children: Evidence for a universal conception of mind. *Child Development, 62*, 460–467.

Ayduk, O., Mendoza-Denton, R., Mischel, W., Downey, G., Peake, P. K., & Rodriguez, M. (2000). Regulating the interpersonal self: Strategic self-regulation for coping with rejection sensitivity. *Journal of Personality and Social Psychology, 79*, 776–792.

Aylward, G. P. (1997). *Infant and early childhood neuropsychology*. New York: Plenum Press.

Azmita, M., & Hesser, J. (1993). Why siblings are important agents of cognitive development: A comparison of siblings and peers. *Child Development, 64*, 430–444.

Baer, D. M., Wolf, M. M., & Risley, R. R. (1968). Some current dimensions of applied behavioral analysis. *Journal of Applied Behavioral Analysis, 1*, 91–97.

Bagemihil, B. (1999). *Biological exuberance: Animal homosexuality and natural diversity*. New York: St. Martin's Press.

Bahrick, L. E. (1995). Intermodal origins of self-perception. In P. Rochat (Ed.), *The self in infancy: Theory and research*. New York: Elsevier Science.

Bahrick, L. E., Lickliter, R., & Flom, R. (2004). Intersensory redundancy guides the development of selective attention, perception, and cognition in infancy. *Current Directions in Psychological Science, 13*, 99–102.

Bahrick, L. E., Parker, J. F., Fivush, R., & Levitt, M. (1998). The effects of stress on young children's memory for a natural disaster. *Journal of Experimental Psychology: Applied, 4*, 308–331.

Bahrick, L. E., & Pickens, J. N. (1995). Infant memory for object motion across a period of three months: Implications for a four-phase attention function. *Journal of Experimental Child Psychology, 59*, 343–371.

Bai, D. L., & Bertenthal, B. I. (1992). Locomotor status and the development of spatial skills. *Child Development, 63*, 215–226.

Bailey, J. M., Bobrow, D., Wolfe, M., & Mikach, S. (1995). Sexual orientation of adult sons and gay fathers. *Developmental Psychology, 31*, 124–129.

Bailey, J. M., & Pillard, R. C. (1991). A genetic study of male sexual orientation. *Archives of General Psychiatry, 48*, 1089–1096.

Bailey, J. M., Pillard, R. C., Neale, M. C., & Agyes, Y. (1993). Heritable factors influence sexual orientation in women. *Archives of General Psychiatry, 50*, 217–223.

Bailey, U. L., Lorch, E. P., Milich, R., & Charnigo, R. (2009). Developmental changes in attention and comprehension among children with attention deficit hyperactivity disorder. *Child Development, 80*, 1842–1855.

Baillargeon, R. (1987). Object permanence in 3 1/2- and 4 1/2-month-old infants. *Developmental Psychology, 23*, 655–664.

Baillargeon, R. (2004). Infants' reasoning about hidden objects: Evidence for event-general and event-specific expectations. *Developmental Science, 7*, 391–424.

Baillargeon, R. (2008). Innate ideas revisited: For a principle of persistence in infants' physical reasoning. *Perspectives on Psychological Science, 3*, 2–13.

Baillargeon, R., & De Vos, J. (1991). Object permanence in young infants: Further evidence. *Child Development, 62*, 1227–1246.

Baillargeon, R., Kotovsky, L., & Needham, A. (1995). The acquisition of physical knowledge in infancy. In G. Lewis, D. Premack, & D. Sperber (Eds.), *Casual understandings in cognition and culture*. Oxford, UK: Oxford University Press.

Baillargeon, R. H., Zoccolillo, M., Keenan, K., Côté, P., Wu, H-X., Boivin, M., & Tremblay, R. E. (2007). Gender differences in physical aggression: A prospective population-based survey of children before and after 2 years of age. *Developmental Psychology, 43*, 13–26.

Baird, A. A., Kagan, J., Gaudette, T., Walz, K. A., Hershlag, N., & Boas, D. A. (2002). Frontal lobe activation during object permanence: Data from near-infrared spectroscopy. *NeuroImage, 16*, 120–126.

Baker-Ward, L., Gordon, B. N., Ornstein, P. A., Larus, D. M., & Clubb, P. A. (1993). Young children's long-term retention of a pediatric visit. *Child Development, 64*, 1519–1533.

Baker, D. P. (1992). Compared to Japan the U.S. is a low achiever—really. *Educational Research, 22*, 18–20.

Baker, R. R., & Bellis, M. A. (2007). Human sperm competition: Ejaculate adjustment by males and the function of masturbation. In T. K. Shackelford & N. Pound (Eds.), *Sperm competition in humans: Classic and contemporary readings*. New York: Springer.

Baldwin, A. L., Baldwin, C., & Cole, R. E. (1990). Stress-resistant families and stress-resistant children. In J. Rolf, A. S. Masten, D. Cicchetti, K. H. Nuechterlein, & S. Weintraub (Eds.), *Risk and protective factors in the development of psychopathology* (pp. 257–280). New York: Cambridge University Press.

Ball, W., & Tronick, E. (1971). Infant responses to impending collision: Optical and real. *Science, 171*, 818–820.

Balter, M. (2001). Scientists spar over claims of earliest human ancestor. *Science, 291* (23 February), 1460–1461.

Bancroft, J., Herbenick, D., & Reynolds, M. (2003). Masturbation as a marker of sexual development: Two studies 50 years apart. In J. Bancroft (Ed.), *Sexual development*. Bloomington, IN: Indiana University Press.

Bandura, A. (1977). *Social learning theory*. Englewood Cliffs, NJ: Prentice-Hall.

Bandura, A. (1986). *Social foundations of thought and action: A social cognitive theory*. Englewood Cliffs, NJ: Prentice-Hall.

Bandura, A. (1989). Social cognitive theory. In R. Vasta (Ed.), *Annals of child development: Six theories of child development* (Vol. 6). Greenwich, CT: JAI Press.

Bandura, A. (1994). Self-efficacy. In V. S. Ramachaudran (Ed.), *Encyclopedia of human behavior* (Vol. 4, pp. 71–81). New York: Academic Press.

Bandura, A. (1997). *Self-efficacy: The exercise of control*. New York: Freeman.

Bandura, A. (2006). Toward a psychology of human agency. *Perspectives on Psychological Science, 1*, 164–180.

Bandura, A., Ross, D., & Ross, S. A. (1963). Vicarious reinforcement and imitative learning. *Journal of Abnormal and Social Psychology, 67*, 601–607.

Bandura, A., & Walters, R. H. (1963). *Social learning and personality development*. New York: Holt, Rinehart & Winston.

Banks, M. S. (1980). The development of visual accommodation during early infancy. *Child Development, 51*, 646–666.

Banks, M., & Salapatek, P. (1983). Infant visual perception. In P. H. Mussen (Ed.), *Manual of child psychology* (4th ed.). In M. M. Haith & J. J. Campos (Vol. Eds.), Vol. 2: *Infancy and developmental psychobiology* (pp. 435–571). New York: Wiley.

Banks, W. C. (1976). White preference in Blacks: A paradigm in search of a phenomenon. *Psychological Bulletin, 83*, 179–186.

Banks-Wallace, J. (2002). Talk that talk: Storytelling and analysis rooted in African American oral tradition. *Qualitative Health Research, 12*, 410–426.

Bar-Haim, Y., Ziv, T., Lamy, D., & Hodes, R. (2006). Nature and nurture in own-race face processing. *Psychological Science, 17*, 159–163.

Barch, J. A., & McKenna, K. Y. A. (2004). The internet and social life. *Annual Review of Psychology, 55*, 573–590.

Bard, K. (2007). Neonatal imitation in chimpanzees (*Pan troglodytes*). *Animal Cognition, 10*, 233–242.

Bardi, L., Simion, F., & Regolin, L. (April 2009). *Sensitivity to biological motion in newborn babies: Role of configural information*. Poster presented at meeting of the Society for Research in Child Development, Denver, CO.

Barker, R. G. (1965). Explorations in ecological psychology. *American Psychologist, 20*, 1–14.

Barkley, R. A. (1990). Attention deficit disorders: History, definition, and diagnosis. In M. Lewis & S. M. Lewis (Eds.), *Handbook of developmental psychopathology: Perspectives in developmental psychology*. New York: Plenum.

Barkley, R. A. (1997). Behavioral inhibition, sustained attention, and executive functions. Constructing a unifying theory of ADHD. *Psychological Bulletin, 121*, 65–94.

Barkley, R. A. (1998). *Attention deficit hyperactivity disorder: A handbook for diagnosis and treatment*. New York: Guilford.

Barkley, R. A., Koplowitz, S., Anderson, T., & McMurray, M. B. (1997). Sense of time in children with ADHD: Effects of duration, distraction, and stimulant medication. *Journal of the International Neuropsychological Society, 3*, 359–369.

Barkow, J. H., Cosmides, L., & Tooby, J. (Eds.). (1992). *The adapted mind: Evolutionary psychology and the generation of culture*. New York: Oxford University Press.

Barnes, M. A., Dennis, M., & Haefele-Kalvaitis, J. (1996). The effects of knowledge availability and knowledge accessibility on coherence and elaborative inferencing in children six to fifteen years of age. *Journal of Experimental Child Psychology, 61*, 216–241.

Barnett, W. S. (1995). Long-term effects of early childhood programs on cognitive and school outcomes. *The Future of Children, 5* (No. 3, Winter).

Baron, A. S., & Banaji, M. R. (2006). The development of implicit attitudes. *Psychological Science, 17*, 53–58.

Baron-Cohen, S. (1995). *Mindblindness: An essay on autism and theory of mind*. Cambridge, MA: MIT Press.

Baron-Cohen, S. (2005). The Empathizing System: A revision of the 1994 model of the Mindreading System. In B. J. Ellis & D. F. Bjorklund (Eds.), *Origins of the social mind: Evolutionary psychology and child development* (pp. 468–492). New York: Guilford.

Baron-Cohen, S., Leslie, A. M., & Frith, U. (1985). Does the autistic child have a 'theory of mind'? *Cognition, 21*, 37–46.

Barrett, A. (2000). Review of T. C. Johnson (1999). Understanding your child's sexual behavior: What's natural and healthy (book). *Canadian Journal of Human Sexuality, 9*, 141–143.

Barrett, H. C. (2005). Cognitive development and the understanding of animal behavior. In B. J. Ellis & D. F. Bjorklund (Eds.), *Origins of the social mind: Evolutionary psychology and child development* (pp. 438–467). New York: Guilford.

Barrett, H. C., & Behne, T. (2005). Children's understanding of death as the cessation of agency: A test using sleep versus death. *Cognition, 96*, 93–108.

Barrett, T. M., Davis, E. F., & Needham, A. (2007). Learning about tools in infancy. *Developmental Psychology, 43*, 352–368.

Barry, C. M., & Wentzel, K. R. (2006). Friend influence on prosocial behavior: The role of motivational factors and friendship characteristics. *Developmental Psychology, 42*, 153–163.

Bartholomew, K., & Horowitz, L. M. (1991). Attachment styles among adults: A test of a four-category model. *Journal of Personality and Social Development, 61*, 226–244.

Barton, R. A., & Harvey, P. H. (2000). Mosaic evolution of brain structure in mammals. *Nature, 405*, 1055–1058.

Bates, E., Carlson-Luden, V., & Bretherton, I. (1980). Perceptual aspects of tool use in infancy. *Infant Behavior and Development, 3*, 127–140.

Bates, J. E., Viken, R. J., Alexander, D. B., Beyers, J., & Stockton, L. (2002). Sleep and adjustment in preschool children: Sleep diary reports by mothers relate to behavior reports by teachers. *Child Development, 73*, 62–74.

Bateson, G., & Mead, M. (1942). *Balinese character: A photographic analysis*. New York: New York Academy of Sciences.

Bateson, P. (2002). The corpse of a wearisome debate. *Science, 297*, 2212–2213.

Bathurst, K., & Gottfried, A. W. (1987). Untestable subjects in child development. *Child Development, 58*, 1135–1144.

Batki, A., Baron-Cohen, S., Wheelwright, S., Connellan, J., & Ahluwalia, J. (2000). Is there an innate gaze module? Evidence from human neonates. *Infant Behavior & Development, 23*, 223–229.

Batty, G. D., Der, G., Macintyre, S., Deary, I. J. (2006). Does IQ explain socioeconomic inequalities in health? Evidence from a population based cohort study in the west of Scotland. *British Medical Journal, 332*, 580–584.

Bauer, P. J. (1993). Memory for gender-consistent and gender-inconsistent event sequences by twenty-five-month-old children. *Child Development, 64*, 285–297.

Bauer, P. J. (2002). Long-term recall memory: Behavioral and neuro-developmental changes in the first 2 years of life. *Current Directions in Psychological Science, 11*, 137–141.

Bauer, P. J. (2007). *Remembering the times of our lives: Memory in infancy and beyond*. Mahwah, NJ: Erlbaum.

Bauer, P. J., Wenner, J. A., Dropik, P. L., & Wewerka, S. S. (2000). Parameters of remembering and forgetting in the transition from infancy to early childhood. *Monographs of the Society for Research in Child Development, 65* (Serial No. 263).

Bauer, P. J., Wiebe, S. A., Waters, J. M., & Bangston, S. K. (2001). Reexposure breeds recall: Effects of experience on 9-month-olds' ordered recall. *Journal of Experimental Child Psychology, 80*, 174–200.

Baumeister, R. F., & Sommer, K. L. (1997). What do men want? Gender differences and two spheres of belongingness—Comment on Cross and Madson, 1997. *Psychological Bulletin, 122*, 38–44.

Baumrind, D. (1967). Child care practices anteceding three patterns of preschool behavior. *Genetic Psychology Monographs, 75,* 43–88.

Baumrind, D. (1971). Current patterns of parental authority. *Developmental Psychology Monographs, 4* (1, Pt. 2).

Baumrind, D. (1972). An exploratory study of socialization effects on black children: Some black-white comparisons. *Child Development, 43,* 261–267.

Baumrind, D. (1991). The influence of parenting style on adolescent competence and substance use. *Journal of Early Adolescence, 11,* 56–95.

Baumrind, D. (1993). The average expectable environment is not good enough: A response to Scarr. *Child Development, 64,* 1299–1317.

Baumrind, D., Larzelere, R. E., & Cowan, P. A. (2002). Ordinary physical punishment: Is it harmful? Comments on Gershoff (2002). *Psychological Bulletin, 128,* 580–589.

Bayley, N. (1949). Consistency and variability in the growth of intelligence from birth to eighteen years. *Journal of Genetic Psychology, 75,* 165–196.

Bayley, N. (1969). *The Bayley Scales of Infant Development.* New York: Psychological Corporation.

Bayley, N. (2005). *Bayley Scales of Infant and Toddler Development® (3rd ed., Bayley-III®).* San Antonio, TX: Harcourt Assessment.

Beal, C. R. (1990). The development of text evaluation and revision skills. *Child Development, 61,* 247–258.

Beaulieu, D. A., & Bugental, D. (2008). Contingent parental investment: An evolutionary framework for understanding early interaction between mothers and children. *Evolution and Human Behavior, 29,* 249–255.

Becker, J. M. T. (1977). A learning analysis of the development of peer-oriented behavior in nine-month-old infants. *Developmental Psychology, 13,* 481–491.

Becker, W. C., & Gersten, R. (1982). A follow-up of Follow Through: The later effects of the direct instruction model for children in fifth and sixth grades. *American Educational Research Journal, 19,* 75–92.

Beckett, C., Castle, J., Rutter, M., & Sonuga-Barke, E. J. (2010). Institutional deprivation, specific cognitive functions, and scholastic achievement: English and Romanian adoptees (ERA) study findings (pp. 125–142). In M. Rutter, E. J. Sonuga-Barke, C. Ceckett, J. Castle, J. Kreppner, R. Kumsta, W. Scholtz, S. Stevens, & C. A. Bell (Eds.) Deprivation-specific psychological patterns: Effects of institutional deprivation. *Monographs of the Society for Research in Child Development, 75* (Serial No. 295).

Beckerman, S., & Valentine, P. (Eds.). (2002). *Partible paternity: The theory and practice of multiple fatherhood in South America.* Gainsville, FL: University of Florida Press.

Beckett, C., Maughan, B., Rutter, M., Castle, J., Colvert, E., Groothues, C., Kreppner, J., Stevens, S., O-Connor, T. G., & Sonuga-Barke, E. J. S. (2006). Do the effects of early severe deprivation on cognition persist into early adolescence? Findings from the English and Romanian Adoptee Study. *Child Development, 77,* 696–711.

Beckhardt, S., & Ward, I. L. (1982). Reproductive functioning in the prenatally stressed female rat. *Developmental Psychobiology, 16,* 111–118.

Beckwith, L. Rodning, C., & Cohen, S. (1992). Preterm children at early adolescence and continuity and discontinuity in maternal responsiveness from infancy. *Child Development, 63,* 1198–1208.

Bedford, V. H., Volling, B. L., & Avioli, P. S. (2000). Positive consequences of sibling conflict in childhood and adulthood. *International Journal of Aging & Human Development, 51,* 53–56.

Behrend, D. A., Rosengren, K., & Perlmutter, M. (1989). A new look at children's private speech: The effects of age, task difficulty, and parent presence. *International Journal of Behavioral Development, 12,* 305–320.

Beilin, H. (1992). Piaget's enduring contribution to developmental psychology. *Developmental Psychology, 28,* 191–204.

Beilock, S. L., Gunderson, E. A., Ramirez, G., & Levine, S. C. (2010). Female teachers' math anxiety impacts girls math achievement. *Proceedings of the National Academy of Sciences (USA), 107,* 1860–1863.

Beise, J., & Voland, E. (2002). A multilevel event history analysis of the effects of grandmothers on child mortality in a historical German population (Krummhorn, Ostfriesland, 1720–1987). *Demographic Research, 7,* 469–498.

Beitel, A. H., & Parke, R. D. (1998). Parental involvement in infancy: The role of maternal and paternal attitudes. *Journal of Family Psychology, 12,* 268–288.

Bell, A. P., Weinberg, M. S., & Hammersmith, S. K. (1981). *Sexual preference: Its development in men and women.* Bloomington: Indiana University Press.

Bell, M. A., & Fox, N. A. (1992). The relations between frontal brain electrical activity and cognitive development during infancy. *Child Development, 63,* 1142–1163.

Bell, M. A., Wolfe, C. D., & Adkins, D. R. (2007). Frontal lobe development during infancy and childhood: Contributions of brain electrical activity temperament, and language to individual differences in working memory and inhibition control. In D. Coch, K. W. Fischer, & G. Dawson (Eds.), *Human behavior, learning, and the developing brain: Typical development* (pp. 247–276). New York: Guilford.

Bell, S., & Ainsworth, M. (1972). Infant crying and maternal responsiveness. *Child Development, 43,* 1171–1190.

Bellinger, D., Leviton, A., Waternaux, C., Needleman, H., & Rabinowitz, M. (1987). Longitudinal analysis of prenatal and postnatal lead exposure and early cognitive development. *New England Journal of Medicine, 316,* 1037–1043.

Bellugi, U. (1988). The acquisition of a spatial language. In F. Kessel (Ed.), *The development of language and language researchers. Essays in honor of Roger Brown.* Hillsdale, NJ: Erlbaum.

Bellugi, U., Järvinen-Pasley, A., Doyle, T. F., Reilly, J., Reiss, A. L., & Korenberg, J. R. (2007). Affect, social behavior, and the brain in Williams syndrome. *Current Directions in Psychological Science, 16,* 99–104.

Bellugi, U., Lichtenberger, L., Jones, W., Lai, Z., & St. George, M. (2000). The neurocognitive profile of Williams syndrome: A complex pattern of strengths and weaknesses. *Journal of Cognitive Neuroscience, 12,* 7–29.

Bellugi, U., & Wang, P. P. (1998). Williams syndrome: From cognition to brain to gene. In G. Edelman & B. H. Smith (Eds.), *Encyclopedia of neuroscience.* Amsterdam, The Netherlands: Elsevier Press.

Belsky, J. (1984). The determinants of parenting: A process model. *Child Development, 55,* 83–96.

Belsky, J. (1988). The "effects" of infant day care reconsidered. *Early Childhood Research Quarterly, 3,* 235–272.

Belsky, J. (1999). Modern evolutionary theory and patterns of attachment. In J. Cassidy & P. R. Shaver (Eds.), *Handbook of attachment: Theory, research, and clinical applications* (1st ed., pp. 141–161). New York: Guildford.

Belsky, J. (2000). Conditional and alternative reproductive strategies: Individual differences in susceptibility to rearing experience. In J. Rodgers & D. Rowe (Eds.), *Genetic influences on fertility and sexuality* (pp. 127–146). Boston, MA: Kluwer.

Belsky, J. (2001). Emanuel Miller Lecture: Developmental risks (still) associated with early child care. *Journal of Child Psychology and Psychiatry, 42,* 845–859.

Belsky, J. (2005). Differential susceptibility to rearing influence. In B. J. Ellis & D. F. Bjorklund (Eds.), *The origins of the social mind: Evolutionary psychology and child development* (pp. 139–163). New York: Guilford.

Belsky, J., Bakermans-Kranenburg, M. J., & van IJzendoorn, M. H. (2007). For better *and* worse: Differential susceptibility to environmental influences. *Current Directions in Psychological Science, 16,* 300–304.

Belsky, J., & Pasco Fearon, R. M. (2002). Infant-mother attachment security, contextual risk, and early development: A moderational analysis. *Development and Psychopathology, 14,* 293–310.

Belsky, J., & Pluess, M. (2009). Beyond disthesis-stress: Differential susceptibility to environmental influences. *Psychological Bulletin, 135,* 885–908.

Belsky, J., & Steinberg, L. D. (1978). The effects of day care: A critical review. *Child Development, 49,* 929–949.

Belsky, J., Steinberg, L., & Draper, P. (1991). Childhood experience, interpersonal development, and reproductive strategy: An evolutionary theory of socialization. *Child Development, 62*, 647–670.

Belsky, J., Steinberg, L., Houts, R. M., Friedman, S. L., Dehart, G., Cauffman, E., Roisman, G. I., Halpern-Felsher, B. L., & Susman, E. (2007). Family rearing antecedents of pubertal timing. *Child Development, 78*, 1302–1321.

Belsky, J., Steinberg, L., Houts, R. M., Halpern-Felsher, B. L., & the NICHD Early Child Care Research Network. (2010). The development of reproductive strategy in females: Early maternal harshness → earlier menarche → increased sexual risk taking. *Developmental Psychology, 46*, 120–128.

Belson, K. (2006). A parent's guide to teenspeak by text message. *The New York Times*, November 26, Ideas & Trends, *http://travel.nytimes.com/2006/11/26/weekinreview/26belson.html*. (Downloaded June 2, 2010).

Bembry, J. X., & Norris, D. F. (2005). An exploratory study of neighborhood choices among Moving to Opportunity participants in Baltimore, Maryland: The influence of housing search assistance. *Journal of Sociology & Social Welfare, 32*, 93–107.

Benbow, C. P., Lubinski, D., Shea, D. L., & Eftekhari-Sanjani, H. (2000). Sex differences in mathematical reasoning ability at age 13: Their status 20 years later. *Psychological Science, 11*, 474–480.

Benedict, H. (1979). Early lexical development: Comprehension and production. *Journal of Child Language, 6*, 183–200.

Benenson, J. F. (2005). Sex differences. In B. Hopkins (Ed.), *The Cambridge encyclopedia of child development* (pp. 366–373). New York: Cambridge University Press.

Benenson, J. F., Apostoleris, N. H., & Parnass, J. (1997). Age and sex differences in dyadic and group interaction. *Developmental Psychology, 33*, 538–543.

Benenson, J. F., Pascoe, J., & Radmore, N. (2007). Children's altruistic behavior in the dictator game. *Evolution and Human Behavior, 28*, 168–173.

Berch, D. B., & Bender, B. C. (Eds.). (1990). *Sex chromosome abnormalities and human behavior*. Boulder, CO: Waterview Press.

Berenbaum, S. A., & Hines, M. (1992). Early androgens are related to childhood sex-typed toy preferences. *Psychological Science, 3*, 203–206.

Berg, D. H. (2008). Working memory and arithmetic calculation in children: The contributory roles of processing speed, short-term memory, and reading. *Journal of Experimental Child Psychology, 99*, 288–308.

Berger, K. S. (2007). Update on bullying at school: Science forgotten? *Developmental Review, 27*, 90–126.

Bering, J. M., & Bjorklund, D. F. (2004). The natural emergence of afterlife reasoning as a developmental regularity. *Developmental Psychology, 40*, 217–233.

Bering, J. M., & Bjorklund, D. F. (2007). The serpent's gift: Evolutionary psychology and consciousness. In P. D. Zelazo, M. Moscovitch, & E. Thompson (Eds.). *Cambridge Handbook of Consciousness*. New York: Cambridge University Press.

Bering, J. M., Hernández Blasi, C., & Bjorklund, D. F. (2005). The development of "afterlife" beliefs in religiously and secularly schooled children. *British Journal of Developmental Psychology, 23*, 587–607.

Bering, J. M., & Parker, B. D. (2006). Children's attributions of intentions to an invisible agent. *Developmental Psychology, 42*, 253–262.

Berk, L. E. (1986). Relationship of elementary school children's private speech to behavioral accompaniment to task, attention, and task performance. *Developmental Psychology, 22*, 671–680.

Berk, L. E. (1992). Children's private speech: An overview of theory and the status of research. In R. M. Diaz & L. E. Berk (Eds.), *Private speech: From social interaction to self-regulation*. Hillsdale, NJ: Erlbaum.

Berk, L. E. (2005). Why parenting matters. In S. Olfman (Ed.), *Childhood lost: How American culture is failing our kids* (pp. 19–53). Westport, CT: Praeger.

Berko, J. (1958). The child's learning of English morphology. *Word, 14*, 150–177.

Bernal, M. E., Knight, G. P., Ocampo, K. A., Garza, C. A., & Cota, M. K. (1993). Development of Mexican American identity. In M. E. Bernal & G. P. Knight (Eds.), *Ethnic identity: Formation and transmission among Hispanics and other minorities* (pp. 31–46). Albany, NY: State University of New York Press.

Berndt, T. J. (1979). Developmental changes in conformity to peers and parents. *Developmental Psychology, 15*, 608–616.

Berndt, T. J. (1985). Prosocial behavior between friends in middle childhood and early adolescence. *Journal of Early Adolescence, 5*, 307–317.

Berndt, T. J. (2002). Friendship quality and social development. *Current Directions in Psychological Sciences, 11*, 7–10.

Bernstein, A. C. (1978). *Flight of the stork*. New York: Delacorte Press.

Bernstein, A. C., & Cowan, P. A. (1975). Children's concepts of how people get babies. *Child Development, 46*, 77–91.

Bertenthal, B. I. (1996). Origins and early development of perception, action, and representation. *Annual Review of Psychology, 47*, 431–435.

Bertenthal, B. I., & Campos, J. J. (1987). New directions in the study of early experience. *Child Development, 58*, 560–567.

Bertenthal, B. I., Campos, J., & Barrett, L. (1984). Self-produced locomotion: An organizer of emotional, cognitive, and social development in infancy. In R. Emde & R. Harmon (Eds.), *Continuities and discontinuities in development*. New York: Plenum.

Bertenthal, B. I., Campos, J. J., & Haith, M. M. (1980). Development of visual organization: The perception of subjective contours. *Child Development, 51*, 1072–1080.

Bertenthal, B. I., Campos, J. J., & Kermoian, R. (1994). An epigenetic perspective on the development of self-produced locomotion and its consequences. *Current Directions in Psychological Science, 3*, 140–145.

Bertenthal, B. I., Proffitt, D. R., & Cutting, J. E. (1984). Infant sensitivity to figural coherence in biomechanical motions. *Journal of Experimental Child Psychology, 37*, 213–230.

Bertenthal, B. I., Proffitt, D. R., & Kramer, S. J. (1987). Perception of biomechanical motions by infants: Implementation of various processing constraints. *Journal of Experimental Psychology: Human Perception & Performance, 13*, 577–585.

Berzonsky, M. D., & Adams, G. R. (1999). The identity status paradigm: Still useful after thirty-five years. *Developmental Review, 19*, 557–590.

Besag, V. E. (1989). *Bullies and victims in schools*. Philadelphia: Open University Press.

Best, D. L. (1993). Inducing children to generate mnemonic organizational strategies: An examination of long-term retention and materials. *Developmental Psychology, 29*, 324–336.

Best, D. L., & Ornstein, P. A. (1986). Children's generation and communication of mnemonic organizational strategies. *Developmental Psychology, 22*, 845–853.

Bevc, I., & Silverman, I. (1993). Early proximity and intimacy between siblings and incestuous behavior: A test of the Westermark theory. *Ethology and Sociobiology, 14*, 171–181.

Bevc, I., & Silverman, I. (2000). Early separation and sibling incest: A test of the revised Westermark theory. *Evolution and Human Behavior, 21*, 151–161.

Bhatt, R. S., Bertin, E., Hayden, A., & Reed, A. (2005). Face processing in infancy: Developmental changes in the use of different kinds of relational information. *Child Development, 76*, 169–181.

Bialystok, E. (1996). Preparing to read: The foundations of literacy. In H. W. Reese (Ed.), *Advances in child development and behavior* (Vol. 26). San Diego: Academic.

Bialystok, E. (1999). Cognitive complexity and attentional control in the bilingual mind. *Child Development, 70*, 636–644.

Bialystok, E. (2001). *Bilingualism in development: Language, literacy, and cognition*. New York: Cambridge University Press.

Bialystok, E. (2007). Language acquisition and bilingualism: Consequences for a multilingual society. *Applied Psycholinguistics, 28*, 393–397.

Bialystok, E. (2010). Global-local and trial-making by monolingual and bilingual children: Beyond inhibition. *Developmental Psychology, 46*, 93–105.

Bialystok, E., Craik, F. I. M., & Freedman, M. (2007). Bilingualism as a protection against the onset of symptoms of dementia. *Neuropsychologia, 45*, 459–464.

Bialystok, E., Craik, F., & Luk, G. (2008). Cognitive control and lexical access in younger and older individuals. *Journal of Experimental Psychology: Learning, Memory, and Cognition, 34*, 859–873.

Bialystok, E., & Hakuta, K. (1994). *In other words*. New York: Basic Books.

Bickerton, D. (1990). *Language and species*. Chicago: University of Chicago Press.

Bierman, K. L., Smoot, D. L., & Aumiller, K. (1993). Characteristics of aggressive-rejected, aggressive (nonrejected), and rejected (nonaggressive) boys. *Child Development, 64*, 139–151.

Bigelow, A. (2005). Blindness. In B. Hopkins (Ed.), *The Cambridge encyclopedia of child development* (pp. 409–413). New York: Cambridge University Press.

Bigelow, B. J. (1977). Children's friendship expectations: A cognitive-developmental study. *Child Development, 48*, 246–253.

Bigler, R. S., & Liben, L. S. (1993). A cognitive-developmental approach to racial stereotyping and reconstructive memory in Euro-American children. *Child Development, 64*, 1507–1519.

Bijou, S. W., & Baer, D. M. (1961). *Child development* (Vol. 1). New York: Appleton-Century-Crofts.

Billingsley, R. L., Smith, M. L., & McAndrews, M. P. (2002). Developmental patterns on priming and familiarity in explicit recollection. *Journal of Experimental Child Psychology, 82*, 251–277.

Biringen, Z., Emde, R. N., Campos, J. J., & Applebaum, M. I. (1995). Affective reorganization in the infant, the mother and the dyad: The role of upright locomotion and its timing. *Child Development, 66*, 499–514.

Bishop, D. I., Meyer, B. C., Schmidt, T. M., and Gray, B. R. (2009). Differential investment behavior between grandparents and grandchildren: The role of paternity uncertainty. *Evolutionary Psychology, 7*, 66–77.

Bishop, D. V. M. (2002). The role of genes in the etiology of specific language impairment. *Journal of Communication Disorders, 35*, 311–328.

Bishop, D. V. M. (2006). What causes specific language impairment in children? *Current Directions in Psychological Science, 15*, 217–221.

Bishop, D. V. M., & Adams, C. (1990). A prospective study of the relationship between specific language impairment, phonological disorders and reading retardation. *Journal of Child Psychology and Psychiatry, 31*, 1027–1050.

Bjorklund, B. R., & Bee, H. L. (2008). *The journey of adulthood*. Upper Saddle River, NJ: Prentice-Hall.

Bjorklund, B. R., & Bjorklund, D. F. (1990). *Parents' book of discipline*. New York: Ballantine.

Bjorklund, D. F. (1987). A note on neonatal imitation. *Developmental Review, 7*, 86–92.

Bjorklund, D. F. (1997). The role of immaturity in human development. *Psychological Bulletin, 122*, 153–169.

Bjorklund, D. F. (2005). *Children's thinking: Cognitive development and individual differences* (4th ed.). Pacific Grove, CA: Wadsworth.

Bjorklund, D. F. (2007). *Why youth is not wasted on the young: Immaturity in human development*. Oxford, UK: Blackwell.

Bjorklund, D. F., & Bering, J. M. (2003). Big brains, slow development, and social complexity: The developmental and evolutionary origins of social cognition. In M. Brüne, H. Ribbert, & W. Schiefenhövel (Eds.). *The social brain: Evolutionary aspects of development and pathology* (pp. 133–151). New York: Wiley.

Bjorklund, D. F., & Bjorklund, B. R. (1992). *Looking at children: An introduction to child development*. Pacific Grove, CA: Brooks/Cole.

Bjorklund, D. F., Cormier, C., & Rosenberg, J. S. (2005). The evolution of theory of mind: Big brains, social complexity, and inhibition. In W. Schneider, R. Schumann-Hengsteler, & B. Sodian (Eds.), *Young children's cognitive development: Interrelationships among executive functioning, working memory, verbal ability and theory of mind* (pp. 147–174). Mahwah, NJ: Erlbaum.

Bjorklund, D. F., Dukes, C., & Brown, R. D. (2009). The development of memory strategies. In M. L. Courage & N. Cowan (Eds.), *The development of memory in infancy and childhood* (pp. 145–175). New York: Psychology Press.

Bjorklund, D. F., & Ellis, B. J. (2005). Evolutionary psychology and child development: An emerging synthesis. In B. J. Ellis & D. F. Bjorklund (Eds.), *Origins of the social mind: Evolutionary psychology and child development* (pp. 3–18). New York: Guilford.

Bjorklund, D. F., Ellis, B. J., & Rosenberg, J. S. (2007). Evolved probabilistic cognitive mechanisms. In R. V. Kail (Ed.), *Advances in child development and behavior* (Vol. 35, pp. 1–39). Oxford, UK: Elsevier.

Bjorklund, D. F., Gaultney, J. F., & Green, B. L. (1993). "I watch, therefore I can do:" The development of meta-imitation over the preschool years and the advantage of optimism in one's imitative skills (pp. 79–102). In R. Pasnak & M. L. Howe (Eds.), *Emerging themes in cognitive development* (Vol. 1). New York: Springer-Verlag.

Bjorklund, D. F., & Green, B. L. (1992). The adaptive nature of cognitive immaturity. *American Psychologist, 47*, 46–54.

Bjorklund, D. F., & Harnishfeger, K. K. (1987). Developmental differences in the mental effort requirements for the use of an organizational strategy in free recall. *Journal of Experimental Child Psychology, 44*, 109–125.

Bjorklund, D. F., & Harnishfeger, K. K. (1995). The role of inhibition mechanisms in the evolution of human cognition and behavior. In F. N. Dempster & C. J. Brainerd (Eds.), *New perspectives on interference and inhibition in cognition* (pp. 141–173). New York: Academic Press.

Bjorklund, D. F., & Hernández Blasi, C. (2005). Evolutionary developmental psychology. In D. Buss (Ed.), *The handbook of evolutionary psychology* (pp. 828–850). Hoboken, NJ: Wiley.

Bjorklund, D. F., Hubertz, M. J., & Reubens, A. C. (2004). Young children's arithmetic strategies in social context: How parents contribute to children's strategy development while playing games. *International Journal of Behavioral Development, 28*, 347–357.

Bjorklund, D. F., & Kipp, K. (1996). Parental investment theory and gender differences in the evolution of inhibition mechanisms. *Psychological Bulletin, 120*, 163–188.

Bjorklund, D. F., & Kipp, K. (2002). Social cognition, inhibition, and theory of mind: The evolution of human intelligence. In R. J. Sternberg & J. C. Kaufman (Eds.), *The evolution of intelligence* (pp. 27–53). Mahwah, NJ: Erlbaum.

Bjorklund, D. F., Muir-Broaddus, J. E., & Schneider, W. (1990). The role of knowledge in the development of strategies. In D. F. Bjorklund (Ed.), *Children's strategies: Contemporary views of cognitive development*. Hillsdale, NJ: Erlbaum.

Bjorklund, D. F., & Pellegrini, A. D. (2000). Child development and evolutionary psychology. *Child Development, 71*, 1687–1798.

Bjorklund, D. F., & Pellegrini, A. D. (2002). *The origins of human nature: Evolutionary developmental psychology*. Washington, DC: American Psychological Association.

Bjorklund, D. F., Periss, V., & Causey, K. (2009). The benefits of youth. *European Journal of Developmental Psychology, 6*, 120–137.

Bjorklund, D. F., & Rosenberg, J. S. (2005). The role of developmental plasticity in the evolution of human cognition. In B. J. Ellis & D. F. Bjorklund (Eds.), *Origins of the social mind: Evolutionary psychology and child development* (pp. 45–75). New York: Guilford.

Bjorklund, D. F., & Rosenblum, K. E. (2002). Context effects in children's selection and use of simple arithmetic strategies. *Journal of Cognition and Development, 3*, 225–242.

Black, B., & Hazen, N, L. (1990). Social status and patterns of communication in acquainted and unacquainted preschool children. *Developmental Psychology, 26*, 379–387.

Black, J. E., Jones, T. A., Nelson, C. A., & Greenough, W. T. (1998). Neuronal plasticity and the developing brain. In N. E. Alessi, J. T. Coyle, S. I. Harrison, & S. Eth (Eds.), *Handbook of child and adolescent psychiatry. Vol. 6: Basic psychiatric science and treatment*. New York: Wiley.

Blair, C. (2006). How similar are fluid cognition and general intelligence? A developmental neuroscience perspective on fluid cognition as an aspect of human cognitive ability. *Behavioral and Brain Sciences, 29,* 109–160.

Blair, C., Gamson, D., Thorne, S., & Baker, D. (2005). Rising mean IQ: Cognitive demand of mathematics education for young children, population exposure to formal schooling, and the neurobiology of the prefrontal cortex. *Intelligence, 33,* 93–106.

Blake, P. R., & Rand, D. G. (2010). Currency value moderates equity preference among young children. *Evolution and Human Behavior, 31,* 210–218.

Blakemore, J. E. O., Berenbaum, S. A., & Liben, L. S. (2008). *Gender development.* New York: Psychology Press.

Blanck, H. M., Marcus, M., Tolbert, P. E., Rubin, C., Henderson, A. K., Hertzberg, V. S., Zhang, R. H., & Cameron, L. (2000). Age at menarche and Tanner stage in girls exposed *in utero* and postnatally to polybrominated biphenyl. *Epidemiology, 11,* 641–647.

Blasi, A. (1980). Bridging moral cognition and moral action: A critical review of the literature. *Psychological Bulletin, 88,* 593–637.

Block, J. H., Block, J., & Morrison, A. (1981). Parental agreement-disagreement on child-rearing orientations and gender-related personality correlates in children. *Child Development, 52,* 965–974.

Block, J., Block, J. H., & Gjerde, P. F. (1986). The personality of children prior to divorce: A prospective study. *Child Development, 57,* 827–840.

Block, J., Block, J. H., & Keyes, S. (1988). Longitudinally foretelling drug usage in adolescence: Early childhood personality and environmental precursors. *Child Development, 59,* 336–355.

Bloom, L. (1991). *Language development from two to three.* New York: Cambridge University Press.

Bloom, L. (1998). Language acquisition in developmental contexts. In W. Damon (Gen. Ed.), *Handbook of child psychology* (5th ed.). In D. Kuhn & R. S. Siegler (Vol. Eds.), Vol. 2: *Cognitive, language, and perceptual development.* New York: Wiley.

Bloom, L., Hood, L., & Lightbown, P. (1974). Imitation in language development: If, when and why. *Cognitive Psychology, 6,* 380–420.

Bloom, L., & Lahey, M. (1978). *Language development and language disorders.* New York: Wiley.

Bloom, L., Lightbown, P., & Hood, L. (1975). Structure and variation in child language. *Monographs of the Society for Research in Child Development, 40* (Serial No. 160).

Bloom, P. (2000). *How children learn the meanings of words.* Cambridge, MA: MIT Press.

Bloom, P. (2004). *Descartes' baby: How the science of child development explains what makes us human.* New York: Basic Books.

Bloom, P., & Markson, L., (1998). Capacities underlying word learning. *Trends in Cognitive Science, 2,* 67–73.

Bloome, D., Champion, T., Katz, L., Morton, M. B., & Muldrow, R. (2001). Spoken and written narrative development: African American preschoolers as storytellers and storymakers. In J. L. Harris, A. G. Kamhi, & K. E. Pollock (Eds.), *Literacy in African American communities* (pp. 45–76). Mahwah, NJ: Erlbaum.

Bluestone, C., & Tamis-LeMonda, C. S. (1999). Correlates of parenting styles in predominately working- and middle-class African American mothers. *Journal of Marriage and the Family, 61,* 881–893.

Blum, D. (2002). *Love at Goon Park: Harry Harlow and the science of affection.* Norwood, MA: Perseus Publishing.

Blumberg, F. C., & Torenberg, M. (2005). The effects of spatial configuration on preschoolers' attention strategies, selective attention, and incidental learning. *Infant and Child Development, 14,* 243–258.

Blumberg, F. C., & Torenberg, M., & Randall, J. D. (2005). The relationship between preschoolers' selective attention and memory for location strategies. *Cognitive Development, 20,* 242–255.

Bock, J. D. (2000). Doing the right thing? Single mothers by choice and the struggle for legitimacy. *Gender and Society, 14,* 62–86.

Bock, J., & Johnson, S. E. (2004). Play and subsistence ecology among the Okavango Delta Peoples of Botswana. *Human Nature, 15,* 63–81.

Boesch-Achermann, H., & Boesch, C. (1993). Tool use in wild chimpanzees: New light from dark forests. *Current Directions in Psychological Science, 2,* 18–21.

Boesch, C., & Tomasello, M. (1998). Chimpanzee and human culture. *Current Anthropology, 39,* 591–604.

Bogaert, A. F. (2006). Biological versus nonbiological older brothers and men's sexual orientation. *Proceedings of the National Academy of Sciences (USA), 103,* 10771–10774.

Bogg, T., & Roberts, B. W. (2004). Conscientiousness and health behaviors: A meta-analysis. *Psychological Bulletin, 130,* 887–919.

Bogin, B. (1999). *Patterns of human growth* (2nd ed.). Cambridge, UK: Cambridge University Press.

Bogin, B. (2001). *The growth of humanity.* New York: Wiley.

Bogin, B. (2003). The human pattern of growth and development in paleontological perspective. In J. L. Thompson, G. E. Krovitz, & A. J. Nelson (Eds.), *Patterns of growth and development in the genus* Homo (pp. 15–44). Cambridge, UK: Cambridge University Press.

Bogin, B., Smit, P., Orden, A. B., Varela, S. S., & Loucky, J. (2002). Rapid change in height and body proportions of Maya American children. *American Journal of Human Biology, 14,* 753–761.

Boismeyer, J. D. (1977). Visual stimulation and wake-sleep behavior in human neonates. *Developmental Psychobiology, 10,* 219–227.

Bokhorst, C., Bakermans-Kranenburg, M., Pasco Fearon, R., van IJzendoorn, M., Fonagy, M, P., & Schuengel, C. (2003). The importance of shared environment in mother-infant attachment security: A behavioral genetic study. *Child Development, 74,* 1769–1782.

Bonner, J. T. (1988). *The evolution of complexity by means of natural selection.* Princeton, NJ: Princeton University Press.

Bonvillian, J. D., Garber, A, M., & Dell, S. B. (1997). Language origin accounts: Was the gesture in the beginning? *First Language, 17,* 219–239.

Book, A. S., Starzyk, K. B., & Quinsey, V. L. (2001). The relationship between testosterone and aggression: A meta-analysis. *Aggression and Violent Behavior, 6,* 579–599.

Booth, A., & Dabs, J. M. (1993). Testosterone and men's marriages. *Social Forces, 72,* 463–477.

Booth, A., Johnson, D. R., Granger, D. A., Crouter, A. C., & McHale, S. (2003). Testosterone and child and adolescent adjustment: The moderating role of parent-child relationships. *Developmental Psychology, 39,* 85–98.

Borke, H. (1975). Piaget's mountains revisited: Changes in the egocentric landscape. *Developmental Psychology, 11,* 240–243.

Borkowski, J. G., & Peck, V. A. (1986). Causes and consequences of metamemory in gifted children. In R. J. Sternberg and J. C. Davidson (Eds.), *Conceptions of giftedness.* Cambridge, UK: Cambridge University Press.

Borkowski, J. G., Reid, M. K., & Kurtz, B. E. (1984). Metacognition and retardation: Pragmatic, theoretical, and applied perspectives. In P. H. Brooks, R. Sperber, & C. McCauley (Eds.), *Learning and cognition in the mentally retarded.* Hillsdale, NJ: Erlbaum.

Bornstein, M. H. (2006). Parenting science and practice. In W. Damon & R. M. Lerner (Gen. Eds.), *Handbook of child psychology* (6th ed.). In K. A. Renninger & I. E. Sigel (Vol. Eds.), Vol. 4: *Child psychology in practice* (pp. 893–949). New York: Wiley.

Bornstein, M. H., Ferdinandsen, K., & Gross, C. G. (1981). Perception of symmetry in infancy. *Developmental Psychology, 17,* 82–86.

Bornstein, M. H., Hahn, C-S., Bell, C., Haynes, O. M., Slater, A., Golding, J., Wolke, D., & the ALSPAC Study Team. (2006). Stability on cognition across childhood. *Psychological Science, 17,* 151–158.

Bornstein, M. H., & Haynes, O. M. (1998). Vocabulary competence in early childhood: Measurement, latent construct, and predictive validity. *Child Development, 69,* 654–671.

Bornstein, M., Haynes, O. M., Pascual, L., Painter, K. M., & Galperin, C. (1999). Play in two societies. *Child Development, 70,* 317–331.

Bosch, L., & Sebastián-Gallés, N. (2001). Evidence of early language discrimination abilities in infants from bilingual environments. *Infancy, 2,* 29–49.

Boston, M. B., & Levy, G. D. (1991). Changes and differences in preschoolers' understanding of gender scripts. *Cognitive Development, 6,* 417–432.

Botting, N., Powls, A., Cooke, R. W. I., & Marlow, N. (1997). Attention deficit hyperactivity disorders and other psychiatric outcomes in very low birthweight children at 12 years. *Journal of Child Psychology and Psychiatry, 38,* 931–941.

Botting, N., Powls, A., Cooke, R. W. I., & Marlow, N. (1998). Cognitive and educational outcome of very-low-birthweight children in early adolescence. *Developmental Medicine and Child Neurology, 40,* 652–660.

Bouchard, T. J., Jr., & Loehlin, J. C. (2001). Genes, personality and evolution. *Behavior Genetics, 31,* 243–273.

Bouchard, T. J., Jr., Lykken, D. T., McGue, M., Segal, N. L., & Tellegen, A. (1990). Sources of human psychological differences: The Minnesota study of twins reared apart. *Science, 250,* 223–228.

Boulton, M., & Smith, P. K. (1990). Affective bias in children's perceptions of dominance. *Child Development, 61,* 221–229.

Boulton, M. J., & Underwood, K. (1992). Bully/victim problems among middle school children. *British Journal of Educational Psychology, 62,* 73–87.

Boulton, M. J., & Smith, P. K. (1994). Bully/victim problems among middle school children *British Journal of Educational Psychology, 62,* 73–87.

Bourguignon, E., & Greenbaum, L. S. (1973). *Diversity and homogeneity in world societies.* New Haven, CT: HRAF Press.

Bowerman, M. (1976). Semantic factors in the acquisition of rules for word use and sentence construction. In D. M. Morehead & A. E. Morehead (Eds.), *Normal and deficient child language.* Baltimore, MD: University Park Press.

Bowerman, M. (1979). The acquisition of complex sentences. In P. Fletcher & M. Garman (Eds.), *Language acquisition* (pp. 285–306). Cambridge, UK: Cambridge University Press.

Bowlby, J. (1960). Grief and mourning in infancy and early childhood. *The Psychoanalytic Study of the Child, VX,* 3–39.

Bowlby, J. (1969). *Attachment and loss.* Vol. 1: *Attachment.* London: Hogarth.

Bowlby, J. (1973). *Attachment and loss.* Vol. 2: *Separation: Anxiety and anger.* London: Hogarth Press and Institute of Psycho-Analysis.

Bowlby, J. (1980). *Attachment and loss.* Vol. 3: *Loss: Sadness and depression.* London: Hogarth Press and Institute of Psycho-Analysis.

Bowles, S. (2006). Group competition, reproductive leveling, and the evolution of altruism. *Science, 314* (8 December), 1569–1572.

Boyatzis, C. J., Matillo, G., & Nesbitt, K. M. (1995). Effects of the Mighty Morphin Power Rangers on children's aggression with peers. *Child Study Journal, 25,* 45–55.

Boyce, W. T., Chesney, M., Alkon–Leonard, A., Tschann, J., Adams, S., Chesterman, B., Cohen, F., Kaiser, P., Folkman, S., & Wara, D. (1995). Psychobiologic reactivity to stress and childhood respiratory illnesses: Results of two prospective studies. *Psychosomatic Medicine, 57,* 411–422.

Boyce, W. T., & Ellis, B. J. (2005). Biological sensitivity to context: I. An evolutionary-developmental theory of the origins and functions of stress reactivity. *Development & Psychopathology, 17,* 271–301.

Boyce, W. T., O'Neill–Wagner, P., Price, C. S., Haines, M., & Suomi, S. J. (1998). Crowding stress and violent injuries among behaviorally inhibited rhesus macaques. *Health Psychology, 17,* 285–289.

Boyer, P. (2001). *Religion explained: The evolutionary origins of religious thought.* New York: Basic Books.

Boyer, T. W. (2006). The development of risk-taking: A multi-perspective review. *Developmental Review, 26,* 291–345.

Boyes, M. C., & Chandler, M. (1992). Cognitive development, epistemic doubt, and identity formation in adolescents. *Journal of Youth and Adolescence, 21,* 277–304.

Brabeck, M. (1983). Moral judgment: Theory and research on differences between males and females. *Developmental Review, 3,* 274–291.

Bradley, R. H., Burchinal, M. R., & Casey, P. H. (2001). Early intervention: The moderating role of the home environment. *Applied Developmental Science, 5,* 2–8.

Brainerd, C. J. (1978). *Piaget's theory of intelligence.* Englewood Cliffs, NJ: Prentice-Hall.

Brainerd, C. J., & Allen, T. W. (1971). Training and generalization of density conservation: Effects of feedback and consecutive similar stimuli. *Child Development, 42,* 693–704.

Brainerd, C. J., & Gordon, L. L. (1994). Development of verbatim and gist memory for numbers. *Developmental Psychology, 30,* 163–177.

Brainerd, C. J., & Mojardin, A. H. (1999). Children's and adults' spontaneous false memories for sentences: Long-term persistence and mere-testing effects. *Child Development, 69,* 1361–1377.

Brainerd, C. J., & Reyna, V. F. (1993). Domains of fuzzy trace theory. In M. L. Howe & R. Pasnak (Eds.), *Emerging themes in cognitive development.* Vol. 1: *Foundations.* New York: Springer-Verlag.

Brainerd, C. J., & Reyna, V. F. (2002). Fuzzy-trace theory and false memory. *Current Directions in Psychological Science, 11,* 164–169.

Brainerd, C. J., & Reyna, V. F. (2005). *The science of false memory.* Oxford, UK: Oxford University Press.

Brand, A. E., & Brinich, P. M. (1999). Behavior problems and mental health contacts in adopted, foster, and nonadopted children. *Journal of Child Psychology and Psychiatry, 40,* 1221–1229.

Bräuer J., Call J., & Tomasello, M. (2005). All great ape species follow gaze to distant locations and around barriers. *Journal of Comparative Psychology, 119,* 145–154.

Brazelton, T. B. (1973). *Neonatal Behavioral Assessment Scale.* Clinics in Developmental Medicine, No. 50. Philadelphia, PA: Lippincott.

Brazelton, T. B., & Nugent, J. K. (1995). *Neonatal Behavioral Assessment Scale.* London: Mac Keith Press.

Brédart, S., & French, R. M. (1999). Do babies resemble their fathers more than their mothers? A failure to replicate Christenfeld and Hill (1995). *Evolution and Human Behavior, 20,* 129–135.

Bremner, A. J., & Mareschal, D. (2004). Reasoning . . . what reasoning? *Developmental Science, 7,* 419–421.

Bretherton, I. (1992). The origins of attachment theory: John Bowlby and Mary Ainsworth. *Developmental Psychology, 28,* 759–775.

Brewer, M. B. (1999). The psychology of prejudice: In-group love or out-group hate? *Journal of Social Issues, 55,* 429–444.

Bril, B., & Sabatier, C. (1986). The cultural context of motor development: Postural manipulations in the daily life of Bambara babies (Mali). *International Journal of Behavioral Development, 9,* 439–453.

British Medical Association. (2005). *Preventing childhood obesity.* London: British Medical Association.

Britton, J. R., Britton, H., & Gronwaldt, V. (2006). Breastfeeding, sensitivity, and attachment. *Pediatrics, 118,* e1436–e1443.

Broaders, S., Cook, S. W., Mitchell, Z., & Goldin-Meadow, S. (2007). Making children gesture brings out implicit knowledge and leads to learning. *Journal of Experimental Psychology: General, 136,* 539–550.

Brock, J. (2007). Language abilities in Williams syndrome: A critical review. *Development and Psychopathology, 19,* 97–127

Brockington, I. (1996). *Motherhood and mental health.* Oxford, UK: Oxford University Press.

Brody, G. H. (2004). Siblings' direct and indirect contributions to child development. *Current Directions in Psychological Science, 132,* 124–126.

Brody, G. H., Beach, S. R. H., Philbert, R. A., Chen, Y-f., & McBride Murry, V. (2009). Prevention effects moderate the association of 5-HTTLPR and youth risk behavior initiation: Gene x environment hypothesis tested via a randomized prevention design. *Child Development, 80,* 645–661.

Brody, N. (1997). Intelligence, schooling, and society. *American Psychologist, 52,* 1046–1050.

Broidy, L. M., et al. (2003). Developmental trajectories of childhood disruptive behavior and adolescent delinquency: A six-site, cross-national study. *Developmental Psychology, 39,* 222–245.

Bronfenbrenner, U. (1977). Toward an experimental ecology of human development. *American Psychologist, 32,* 513–531.

Bronfenbrenner, U. (1979a). Contexts of child rearing problems and prospects. *American Psychologist, 34*, 844–850.

Bronfenbrenner, U. (1979b). *The ecology of human development.* Cambridge, MA: Harvard University Press.

Bronfenbrenner, U. (1989). Ecological systems theory. In R. Vasta (Ed.), *Annals of child development, 6*, 187–249.

Bronfenbrenner, U. (2000). Ecological theory. In A. Kazdin (Ed.), *Encyclopedia of psychology.* Washington, DC: American Psychological Association and Oxford University Press.

Bronfenbrenner, U., & Ceci, S. J. (1994). Nature-nurture reconceptualized in developmental perspective: A bioecological model. *Psychological Review, 101*, 568–586.

Bronfenbrenner, U., & Morris, P. A. (2006). The bioecological model of human development. In W. Damon & R. M. Lerner (Gen. Eds.), *Handbook of child psychology* (6th ed.). In R. M. Lerner (Vol. Ed.), Vol. 1: *Theoretical models of human development* (pp. 793–828). New York: Wiley.

Bronson, W. C. (1981). *Toddlers' behaviors with agemates: Issues of interaction, cognition, and affect.* Norwood, NJ: Ablex.

Brooks-Gunn, J., & Furstenberg, F. F., Jr. (1986). Antecedents and consequences of parenting: The case of adolescent motherhood. In A. Fogel and G. Melson (Eds.), *Origins of nurturance: Developmental, biological, and cultural perspectives on caregiving* (pp. 233–258). Hillsdale, NJ: Erlbaum.

Brooks-Gunn, J., & Furstenberg, F. F., Jr. (1989). Adolescent sexual behavior. *American Psychologist, 44*, 249–257.

Brooks-Gunn, J., & Lewis, M. (1984). The development of early self-recognition. *Developmental Review, 4*, 215–239.

Brooks-Gunn, J., Linver, M. R., & Fauth, R. C. (2005). *Children's competence and socioeconomic status in the family and neighborhood.* New York: Guilford.

Brooks-Gunn, J., & Warren, M. P. (1985). Measuring physical status and timing in early adolescence: A developmental perspective. *Journal of Youth and Adolescence, 14*, 163–189.

Brosnan, S. F., & de Waal, F. (2003). Monkeys reject unequal pay. *Nature, 425*, 297–299.

Brown, B. (2004). Adolescent's relationships with peers. In R. Lerner & L. Steinberg (Eds.), *Handbook of adolescent psychology.* New York: Wiley.

Brown, B. B., Clasen, D. R., & Eicher, S. A. (1986). Perceptions of peer pressure, peer conformity dispositions, and self-reported behavior among adolescents. *Developmental Psychology, 22*, 521–530.

Brown, J. D. (2002) Mass media influences on sexuality. *Journal of Sex Research, 39*, 42–45.

Brown, J. V., Bakeman, R., Coles, C. D., Platzman, K. A., & Lynch, M. E. (2004). Prenatal cocaine exposure: A comparison of 2-year-old children in parental and nonparental care. *Child Development, 75*, 1282–1295.

Brown, R. (1973). *A first language: The early stages.* Cambridge, MA: Harvard University Press.

Brown, R. (1987). *Social psychology.* New York: Free Press.

Brown, R. D., Goldstein, E., & Bjorklund, D. F. (2000). The history and zeitgeist of the repressed/false-memory debate: Scientific and sociological perspectives on suggestibility and childhood-memory. In D. F. Bjorklund (Ed.), *False-memory creation in children and adults: Theory, research, and implications* (pp. 1–30). Mahwah, NJ: Erlbaum.

Brown, R., & Hanlon, C. (1970). Derivational complexity and the order of acquisition in child speech. In R. Brown (Ed.), *Psycholinguistics.* New York: Free Press.

Bruce, V., Doyle, T., Dench, N., & Burton, M. (1991). Remembering facial configurations. *Cognition, 38*, 109–144.

Bruck, M., Ceci, S. K., Francoeur, E., & Barr, R. (1995). "I hardly cried when I got my shot!" Influencing children's reports about a visit to their pediatrician. *Child Development, 66*, 193–208.

Bruck, M., Ceci, S. J., & Principe, G. F. (2006). The child and the law. In W. Damon & R. M. Lerner (Gen. Eds.), *Handbook of child psychology* (6th ed.). In K. A. Renninger & I. E. Sigel (Vol. Eds.), Vol. 4: *Child psychology in practice* (pp. 776–816). New York: Wiley.

Bruner, J. (1986). *Actual minds, possible worlds.* Cambridge, MA: Harvard University Press.

Bruner, J. (1990). *Acts of meaning.* Cambridge, MA: Harvard University Press.

Bruner, J. S. (1972). The nature and uses of immaturity. *American Psychologist, 27*, 687–708.

Bruner, J. S. (1983). *Child's talk: Learning to use language.* New York: Norton.

Buccino, Vogt, G. S., Ritzl, A., Fink, G. R., Zilles, K., Freund, H-J., & Rizzolatti, G. (2004). Neural circuits underlying imitation learning of hand actions: An event-related fMRI study, *Neuron, 42*, 323–334.

Buck, R. (1982). Spontaneous and symbolic nonverbal behavior and the ontogeny of communication. In R. S. Feldman (Ed.), *Development of nonverbal behavior in children* (pp. 29–62). New York: Springer-Verlag.

Buck, S. M., Hillman, C. H., & Castelli, D. M. (2008). Aerobic fitness influences Stroop task performance in preadolescent children. *Medicine & Science in Sports & Exercise, 40*, 166–172.

Buckhalt, J. A., El-Sheikh, M., Keller, P. S., & Kelly, R. J. (2009). Concurrent and longitudinal relations between children's sleep and cognitive functioning: The moderating role of parent education. *Child Development, 80*, 875–892.

Budwig, N. (1990). The linguistic marking of nonprototypical agency: An exploration into children's use of passives. *Linguistics, 28*, 1221–1252.

Bugental, D. B. (2000). Acquisition of the algorithms of social life: A domain-based approach. *Psychological Bulletin. 26*, 187–209.

Bugental, D. B., & Beaulieu, D. A. (2003). A bio-social-cognitive approach to understanding and promoting the outcomes of children with medical and physical disorders. In R. V. Kail (Ed.), *Advances in child development and behavior* (Vol. 31, 329–361). New York: Elsevier.

Bugental, D. B., & Grusec, J. E. (2006). Socialization processes. In W. Damon & R. M. Lerner (Gen. Eds.), *Handbook of Child Psychology* (6th ed.). In N. Eisenberg (Vol. Ed.), Vol. 3: *Social, emotional, and personality development* (pp. 366–428). New York: Wiley.

Bugos, P. E., & McCarthy, L. M. (1984). Ayoreo infanticide: A case study. In G. Hausfater & S. B. Hrdy (Eds.), *Infanticide: Comparative and evolutionary perspectives* (pp. 503–520). New York: Aldine de Gruyter.

Bukowski, W. M., Sippola. L., Hoza, B., & Newcomb, A. F. (2000). Pages from a sociometric notebook: An analysis of nomination and rating scale measures of acceptance, rejection and social preference. In A. H. N. Cillesen & W. M. Bukowski (Eds.), Recent advances in the measurement of acceptance and rejection in peer system (pp. 11–26), *New Directions for Child and Adolescent Development, 88*. San Francisco: Jossey-Bass.

Bull, J. J. (1980). Sex determination in reptiles. *Quarterly Review of Biology, 55*, 3–21.

Buller, D. J. (2005). *Adapting minds: Evolutionary psychology and the persistent quest for human nature.* Boston: MIT Press.

Bullock, M., Sodian, B., & Koerber, S. (2009). Doing experiments and understanding science: Development of scientific reasoning from childhood to adulthood. In W. Schneider, & M. Bullock (Eds.), *Human development from early childhood to early adulthood: Findings from a 20 year longitudinal study* (pp. 173–197). New York: Psychology Press.

Bullough, V. L. (1981). Age at menarche: A misunderstanding. *Science, 213*, 356–366.

Bunge, S. A., & Zelazo, P. D. (2006). A brain-based account of the development of rule use in childhood. *Current Directions in Psychological Science, 15*, 118–121.

Bureau, M. A., Shapcott, D., Berthiaumes, Y., Monette, J., Blouin, D., Blanchard, P., & Begin, R. (1983). Maternal cigarette smoking and fetal oxygen transport: A study of P50, 2, 3–diphosphoglycerate, total hemoglobin, hematocrit, and type F hemoglobin in fetal blood. *Pediatrics, 72*, 22–26.

Bus, A. G., & van IJzendoorn, M. H. (1997). Affective dimension of mother-infant picturebook reading. *Journal of School Psychology, 35*, 47–60.

Bushnell, I. W. R., Sai, F., & Mullin, J. T. (1989). Neonatal recognition of the mother's face. *British Journal of Developmental Psychology, 7,* 3–15.

Buss, D. M. (1995). Evolutionary psychology: A new paradigm for psychological science. *Psychological Inquiry, 6,* 1–30.

Buss, D. M. (Ed.) (2005). *The handbook of evolutionary psychology.* Hoboken, NJ: Wiley.

Buss, D. M. (2008). *Evolutionary psychology: The new science of the mind* (3rd ed.). Pearson: Boston.

Buss, D. M. (2009). The great struggles of life: Darwin and the emergence of evolutionary psychology. *American Psychologist, 64,* 140–148.

Buss, D. M., Haselton, M. G., Shackelford, T. K., Bleske, A. L., & Wakefield, J. C. (1998). Adaptations, exaptations, and spandrels. *American Psychologist, 53,* 533–548.

Bussey, K. (1999). Children's categorization and evaluation of different types of lies and truths, *Child Development, 70,* 1338–1347.

Butovskaya, M. L. (2001). Aggression, friendship, and aggression in primary school children. In M. Martinez (Ed.), *Prevention and control of aggression and the impact on its victims.* New York: Plenum Publishers.

Butovskaya, M. L. (2007). Reconciliation after conflicts: Ethological analysis of post-conflict interactions in Kalmyk children. In J. M. Ramirez & D. S. Richardson (Eds.), *Cross-cultural approaches to aggression and reconciliation* (pp. 267–190). Huntington, NY: Nova Science Publishers.

Butovskaya, M. L. (2008). Reconciliation, dominance, and cortisol level in children and adolescents (7- to 15-year-old boys). *Behaviour, 145,* 1557–1576.

Butovskaya, M. L., Timentschik, V. M., & Burkova, V. N. (2007). Aggression, conflict resolution, popularity, and attitude to school in Russian adolescents. *Aggressive Behavior, 33,* 170–183.

Buttelmann, D., Carpenter, M., Call, J., & Tomasello, M. (2008). Rational tool use and tool choice in human infants and great apes. *Child Development, 79,* 609–626.

Byrne, R. (1995). *The thinking ape: Evolutionary origins of intelligence.* New York: Oxford University Press.

Byrne, R. W. (2005). Social cognition: Imitation, imitation, imitation. *Current Biology, 15,* R489–R500.

Byrne, R., & Whiten, A. (Eds.) (1988). *Machiavellian intelligence: Social expertise and the evolution of intellect in monkeys, apes, and humans.* Oxford: Clarendon.

Cabrera, N. J., Tamis-LeMonda, C. S., Bradley, R. H., Hofferth, S., & Lamb, M. E. (2000). Fatherhood in the twenty-first century. *Child Development, 71,* 127–136.

Cahan, S., & Cohen, N. (1989). Age versus schooling effects on intelligence development. *Child Development, 60,* 1239–1249.

Cairns, R. B. (1998). The making of developmental psychology. In W. Damon (Gen. Ed.), *Handbook of child psychology* (5th ed.). In R. Learner (Vol. Ed.), Vol. 1: *Theories of theoretical models of human development.* New York: Wiley.

Cairns, R. B., & Cairns, B. D. (1986). The developmental-interactional view of social behavior: Four issues of adolescent aggression. In D. Olweus, J. Block, & M. Radke-Yarrow (Eds.), *Development of antisocial and prosocial behavior: Research, theories, and issues.* New York: Academic Press.

Cairns, R. B., & Cairns, B. D. (2006). The making of developmental psychology. In W. Damon & R. M. Lerner (Gen. Eds.), *Handbook of child psychology* (6th ed.). In R. M. Lerner (Vol. Ed.), Vol. 1: *Theoretical models of human development* (pp. 89–165). New York: Wiley.

Cairns R. B., Cairns, B. D., Neckerman, H. J., Ferguson, L. L., & Gariépy, J. (1989). Growth and aggression: Childhood to early adolescence. *Developmental Psychology, 25,* 320–330.

Cairns R. B., Cairns, B. D., Neckerman, H. J., Gest, S. D., & Gariépy, J. J. (1988). Social networks and aggressive behavior: Peer support or peer rejection? *Developmental Psychology, 24,* 815–823.

Calderone, M. (1983). Fetal erection and its message to us. *SIECUS Report, 11* (5/6), 9–10.

Caldwell, B. M., & Bradley, R. H. (1978). *Home observation for measurement of the environment.* Little Rock: University of Arkansas at Little Rock.

Callan, V. (1985). Perceptions of parents, the voluntarily and involuntarily childless: A multidimensional scaling analysis, *Journal of Marriage and the Family, 4,* 1045–1050.

Calvert, S. L., Mahler, B. A., Zehnder, S. M., Jenkins, A., & Lee, M. (2003). Sex differences in preadolescent children's online interactions. Symbolic modes of self-presentation and self-expression. *Journal of Applied Developmental Psychology, 24,* 627–644.

Calvert, S. L., Rideout, V. J., Woolard, J. L., Barr, R. F., & Strouse, G. A. (2005). Age, ethnicity, and socioeconomic patterns in early computer use: A national survey. *American Behavioral Scientist, 48,* 590–607.

Calvert, S. L., Strouse, G. A., Strong, B. L., Huffaker, D. A., & Lai, S. (2009). Preadolescent girls' and boys' virtual MUD play. *Journal of Applied Developmental Psychology, 24,* 627–644.

Calvin, W. H., & Bickerton, D. (2000) *Lingua ex Machina: Reconciling Darwin and Chomsky with the human brain.* Cambridge, MA: MIT Press.

Camaioni, L. (1993). The development of intentional communication. In N. Jacqueline & C. Luigia (Eds.), *New perspectives in early communicative development* (pp. 82–97). London: Routledge.

Camaioni, L., & Perucchini, P. (2003). *Profiles in declarative/imperative pointing and early word production.* Paper presented at the European Conference for Developmental Psychology, Milan, Italy.

Cameron, C. A., & Lee, K. (1997). Bridging the gap between home and school with voice-mail technology. *Journal of Educational Research, 90,* 182–190.

Cameron-Faulkner, T., Lieven, T., & Tomasello, M. (2003). A construction-based analysis of child-directed speech. *Cognitive Science, 27,* 843–873.

Campbell, A. (2005). Aggression. In D. Buss (Ed.), *The handbook of evolutionary psychology* (pp. 628–652). Hoboken, NJ: Wiley.

Campbell, F. A., Pungello, E. P., Miller-Johnson, S., Burchinal, M., & Ramey, C. T. (2001). The development of cognitive and academic abilities: Growth curves from an early childhood educational experiment. *Developmental Psychology, 37,* 231–242.

Campbell, F. A., & Ramey, C. T. (1994). Effects of early intervention on intellectual and academic achievement: A follow-up study of children from low-income families. *Child Development, 65,* 684–698.

Campbell, F. A., Ramey, C. T., Pungello, E., Sparling, J., & Miller-Johnson, S. (2002). Early childhood education: Young adult outcomes from the Abecedarian project. *Applied Developmental Science, 6,* 42–57.

Campos, J. J., Anderson, D. I., Barbu-Roth, M. A., Hubbard, E. M., Hertenstein, M. J., & Witherington, D. (2000). Travel broadens the mind. *Infancy, 1,* 149–220.

Campos, J., Langer, A., & Krowitz, A. (1970). Cardiac responses on the visual cliff in pre-motor human infants. *Science, 170,* 195–196.

Camras, L. A. (1992). Expressive development and basic emotions. *Cognition and Emotion, 6,* 267–283.

Camras, L. A., & Witherington, D. C. (2005). Dynamic systems approaches to emotional development. *Developmental Review, 25,* 328–350.

Canfield, R. L., Smith, E. G., Brezsnyak, M. P., & Snow, K. L. (1997). Information processing through the first year of life. *Monographs of the Society for Research in Child Development, 62* (Serial No. 250).

Cantwell, D. (1996). Attention deficit disorder: A review of the past 10 years. *Journal of the American Academy of Child and Adolescent Psychiatry, 35,* 978–987.

Capon, N., & Kuhn, D. (1979). Logical reasoning in the supermarket: Adult females' use of a proportional reasoning strategy in an everyday context. *Developmental Psychology, 15,* 450–452.

Card, N. A., Stucky, B. D., Sawalani, C. M., & Little, T. D. (2008). Direct and indirect aggression during childhood and adolescence: A meta-analytic review of gender differences, intercorrelations, and relations to maladjustment. *Child Development, 79,* 1185–1229.

Cardno, A. G., & Gottesman, I. I. (2000). Twin studies of schizophrenia: From bow-and-arrow concordances to star wars Mx and functional genomics. *American Journal of Medical Genetics, 97,* 12–17.

Carey, S. (1978). The child as a word learner. In M. Halle, J. Bresnan, & G. A. Miller (Eds.), *Linguistic theory and psychological reality* (pp. 264–293). Cambridge, MA: MIT Press.

Carey, S. (1985). Are children fundamentally different kinds of thinkers and learners than adults? In S. F. Chapman, J. W. Segal, & R. Glaser (Eds.), *Thinking and learning skills* (Vol. 2). Hillsdale, NJ: Erlbaum.

Carey, S. (1999). Sources of conceptual change. In E. K. Scholnick, K. Nelson, S. A. Gelman, & P. Miller (Eds.), *Conceptual development: Piaget's legacy* (pp. 293–326). Hillsdale, NJ: Erlbaum.

Carlson, E. (1998). A prospective longitudinal study of attachment disorganization/disorientation. *Child Development, 69*, 1107–1128.

Carlson, E. A., Sroufe, L. A., & Egeland, B. (2004). The construction of experience: A longitudinal study of representation and behavior. *Child Development, 75*, 66–83.

Carlson, S. M., & Meltzoff, A. N. (2008). Bilingual experience and executive functioning in young children. *Developmental Science, 11*, 282–298.

Carlson, S. M., Moses, L. J., & Hix, H. R. (1998). The role of inhibitory processes in young children's difficulties with deception and false belief. *Child Development, 69*, 672–691.

Carmichael, L. (1970). The onset and early development of behavior. In P. H. Mussen (Ed.), *Carmichael's handbook of child psychology* (3rd ed.), Vol. 1. New York: Wiley.

Carnethon, M. R., Gulati, M., & Greenland, P. (2005). Prevalence and cardiovascular disease correlates of low cardiorespiratory fitness in adolescents and adults. *Journal of the American Medical Association, 294*, 2981–1988.

Caron, A. J. (2009). Comprehension of the representational mind in infancy. *Developmental Review, 29*, 69–95.

Carpendale, J. I. M., & Lewis, C. (2004). Constructing an understanding of mind: The development of children's social understanding within social interaction. *Behavioral and Brain Sciences, 27*, 79–151.

Carpenter, M., Akhtar, N., & Tomasello, M. (1998). Fourteen- through 18-month-old infants differentially imitate intentional and accidental actions. *Infant Behavior & Development, 21*, 315–330.

Carpenter, M., Nagell, K., & Tomasello, M. (1998). Social cognition, joint attention, and communicative competence from 9 to 15 months of age. *Monographs of the Society for Research in Child Development, 63* (Serial No. 255).

Carr, M., & Jessup, D. L. (1995). Cognitive and metacognitive predictors of mathematics strategy use. *Learning and Individual Differences, 7*, 235–247.

Carraher, T. N., Carraher, D., & Schliemann, A. D. (1985). Mathematics in the streets and in the schools. *British Journal of Developmental Psychology, 3*, 21–29.

Carrel, R. E. (1977). Epidemiology of hearing loss. In S. E. Gerber (Ed.), *Audiometry in infancy* (pp. 3–16.) New York: Grune and Stratton.

Carroll, J. B. (1993). *Human cognitive abilities.* New York: Cambridge University Press.

Carter, C. S. (1998). Neuroendocrine perspectives on social attachment and love. *Psychoneuroendocrinology, 23*, 779–818.

Carter, R. (1999). *Mapping the mind.* Berkeley: University of California Press.

Carver, L. J., & Bauer, P. J. (1999). When the event is more than the sum of its parts: Individual differences in 9-month-olds long-term ordered recall. *Memory, 2*, 147–174.

Carver, L. J., & Vaccaro, B. G. (2007). 12-month-old infants allocate increased neural resources to stimuli associated with negative adult emotion. *Developmental Psychology, 43*, 54–69.

Carver, P. R., Yunger, J. L., & Perry, D. G. (2003). Gender identity and adjustment in middle childhood. *Sex Roles, 49*, 95–109.

Case, A., Lin, I-F., & McLanahan, S. (2000). How hungry is the selfish gene? *Economic Journal, 110*, 781–804.

Case, R. (1985). *Intellectual development: Birth to adulthood.* New York: Academic Press.

Case, R. (1991). Stages in the development of the young child's first sense of self. *Developmental Review, 11*, 210–230.

Case, R. (1992). *The mind's staircase: Exploring the conceptual underpinnings of children's thought and knowledge.* Hillsdale, NJ: Erlbaum.

Caselli, M. C., Bates, E., Casadio, P., Fenson, J., Fenson, L., Sanders, L., & Weir, J. (1995). A cross-linguistic study of early lexical development. *Cognitive Development, 10*, 159–199.

Casey, B. J., Getz, S., & Galvan, A. (2008). The adolescent brain. *Developmental Review, 28*, 62–77.

Casey, M. B. (1996). Understanding individual differences in spatial ability within females: A nature/nurture interactionist framework. *Developmental Review, 16*, 241–260.

Casler, K ., & Kelemen, D. (2005).Young children's rapid learning about artifacts. *Developmental Science, 8*, 472–480.

Casler, K., & Keleman, D. (2008). Developmental continuity in tele-functional explanation: Reasoning about nature among Romanian Romani adults. *Journal of Cognition and Development, 9*, 340–362.

Caspi, A., Lyman, D., Moffitt, T., & Silva, P. (1993). Unraveling girls' delinquency: Biological, dispositional, and contextual contributions, to adolescent misbehavior. *Developmental Psychology, 29*, 19–30.

Caspi, A., McClay, J., Moffitt, T. E., Mill, J., Martin, J., Craig, I. W., Taylor, A., & Poulton, R. (2002). Role of genotype in the cycle of violence in maltreated children. *Science, 297* (2 August), 851–854.

Caspi, A., Roberts, B. W., & Shiner, R. (2005). Personality development. *Annual Review of Psychology, 56*, 453–484.

Caspi, A., & Shiner, R. L. (2006). Personality development. In W. Damon & R. Lerner (Gen. Eds.), *Handbook of child psychology* (6th ed.). In N. Eisenberg (Vol. Ed.), Vol. 3: *Social, emotional, and personality development* (pp. 300–365). New York: Wiley.

Caspi, A., Sugden, K., Moffitt, T. E., Taylor, A., Craig, I. W., & Harrington, H., et al. (2003). Influence of life stress on depression: Moderation by a polymorphism in the 5-HTT gene. *Science, 301,* 386–389.

Caspi, A., Williams, B., Kim-Cohen, J., Craig, I. W., Milne, B. J., Poulton, R., Schalkwyk, L. C., Taylor, A., Werts, H., & Moffitt, T. E. (2007). Moderation of breastfeeding effects on the IQ by genetic variation in fatty acid metabolism. *Proceeding of the National Academy of Science (USA), 104*, 18860–18865.

Cassel, W. S., & Bjorklund, D. F. (1995). Developmental patterns of eyewitness memory and suggestibility: An ecologically based short-term longitudinal study. *Law & Human Behavior, 19*, 507–532.

Cassidy, J., & Marvin, R. S. (1992). *Attachment organization in preschool children: Coding guidelines* (4th ed.). Unpublished manuscript, MacArthur Working Group on Attachment, Seattle, WA.

Cassidy, J., & Shaver, P. R. (Eds.), *Handbook of attachment: Theory, research, and clinical applications.* New York: Guildford.

Castelli, L., De Amicis, L., & Sherman, S. J. (2007). The loyal member effect: On the preference for ingroup members who engage in exclusive relations with the ingroup. *Developmental Psychology, 43*, 1347–1359.

Cattell, R. B. (1971). *Abilities: Their structure, growth and action.* Boston: Houghton Mifflin.

Caughy, M. O. (1996). Health and environmental effects on the academic readiness of school-age children. *Developmental Psychology, 32*, 515–522.

Causey, K., & Bjorklund, D. F. (2011). The evolution of cognition. In V. Swami & A. Clow (Eds.), *Evolutionary psychology: A critical reader.* London: British Psychological Society.

Cavanagh, S. E. (2004). The sexual debut of girls in early adolescence: The intersection of race, pubertal timing, and friendship group characteristics. *Journal of Research in Adolescence, 14*, 285–312.

Cavanaugh, J. C., & Borkowski, J. G. (1980). Searching for metamemory-memory connections: A developmental study. *Developmental Psychology, 16*, 441–453.

Ceci, S. J. (1996). *On intelligence: A bio-ecological treatise on intellectual development* (2nd ed.). Cambridge, MA: Harvard University Press.

Ceci, S. J., & Bruck, M. (1993). Suggestibility of the child witness: A historical review and synthesis. *Psychological Bulletin, 113*, 403–439.

Ceci, S. J., & Bruck, M. (1995). *Jeopardy in the courtroom: A scientific analysis of children's testimony.* Washington, DC: American Psychological Association.

Ceci, S. J., Loftus, E. F., Leichtman, M., & Bruck, M. (1994). The role of source misattributions in the creation of false beliefs among preschoolers. *International Journal of Clinical and Experimental Hypnosis, 62*, 304–320.

Ceci, S. J., & Williams, W. M. (1997). Schooling, intelligence, and income. *American Psychologist, 52*, 1051–1058.

Centers for Disease Control and Prevention. (2009). Autism Information Center. Accessed at: http://www.cdc.gov/ncbddd/autism/faq_prevalence.htm#whatisprevalence (Downloaded February 1, 2009).

Chall, J. S. (1979). The great debate: Ten years later, with a modest proposal for reading stages. In L. B. Resnick & P. A. Weaver (Eds.), *Theory and practice of early reading.* Hillsdale, NJ: Erlbaum.

Chamberlain, C., & Mayberry, R. I. (2000). Theorizing about the relationship between ASL and reading. In C. Chamberlain, J. Morford, & R. I. Mayberry (Eds.), *Language acquisition by eye* (pp. 221–260). Mahwah, NJ: Erlbaum.

Champion, T. B. (1998). "Tell me somethin´ good": A description of narrative structures among African American children. *Linguistics and Education, 9*, 251–286.

Chao, R. K. (1994). Beyond parental control and authoritarian parenting style: Understanding Chinese parenting through the cultural notion of training. *Child Development, 65*, 1111–1119.

Chao, R. K., & Tseng, V. (2002). Asian-American parents. In M. Bornstein (Ed.), *Handbook of parenting, Vol. 4: Social conditions and applied parenting* (2nd ed., pp. 59–93). Mahwah, NJ: Erlbaum.

Charity, A. H., Scarborough, H. S., & Griffin, D. M. (2004). Familiarity with school English in African American children and its relation to early reading achievement. *Child Development, 75*, 1340–1356.

Charlesworth, R. (1996). *Understanding child development* (4th ed.). Albany, NY: Delmar.

Charpak, N., Ruiz-Pelaz, J., & Figueroa, Z. (2005). Influence of feeding patterns and other factors on early somatic growth of healthy, preterm infants in home-based kangaroo mother care: A cohort study. *Journal of Pediatric Gastroenterology & Nutrition, 41*, 430–437.

Charpak, N., Ruiz, J., Zupan, J., Cattaneo, A., Figueroa, Z., Tessier, R., Cristo, M., Anderson, G., Ludington, S., Mendoza, S., Mokhachane, M., & Worku, B. (2005). Kangaroo mother care: 25 years after. *Acta Paediatrica, 94*, 514–522.

Chase-Lansdale, P. L., & Gordon, R. A. (1996). Economic hardship and the development of five- and six-year olds: Neighborhood and regional perspectives. *Child Development, 67*, 3338–3378.

Chase-Lansdale, P. L., Cherlin, A. J., & Kiernam, K. K. (1995). The long-term effects of parental divorce on the mental health of young adults: A developmental perspective. *Child Development, 66*, 1614–1634.

Chen, C., & Stevenson, H. W. (1988). Cross-linguistic differences in digit span of preschool children. *Journal of Experimental Child Psychology, 46*, 150–158.

Chen, E., Cohen, S., & Miller, G. E. (2010). How low socioeconomic status affects 2-year hormonal trajectories in children. *Psychological Science, 21*, 31–37.

Chen, J-Q. (2004). Theory of Multiple Intelligences: Is it a scientific theory? *Teachers College Record, 106*, 17–23.

Chen, L-H., Baker, S. P., Braver, E. R., & Li, G. (2000). Carrying passengers as a risk factor for crashes fatal to 16- and 17-year-old drivers. *Journal of the American Medical Association, 283*, 1578–1582.

Chen, X., Dong, Q., & Zhou, H. (1997). Authoritative and authoritarian parenting practices and social and school performance in Chinese children. *International Journal of Behavioral Development, 21*, 855–873.

Chen, Z., & Siegler, R. S. (2000). Across the great divide: Bridging the gap between understanding of toddlers' and older children's thinking. *Monographs of the Society for Research in Child Development, 65* (Serial No. 261).

Cherlin, A. J., & Furstenberg, F. F. (1994). Stepfamilies in the United States. *Review of Sociology, 20*, 359–381.

Chess, S., & Thomas, A. (1990). New York Longitudinal Study: The young adult periods. *Canadian Journal of Psychiatry, 35*, 557–561.

Chi, M. T. H. (1978). Knowledge structure and memory development. In R. Siegler (Ed.), *Children's thinking: What develops?* Hillsdale, NJ: Erlbaum.

Chi, M. T. H., Feltovich, P. J., & Glaser, R. (1981). Categorization and representation of physics problems by experts and novices. *Cognitive Science, 5*, 121–152.

Chiriboga, C. A., Burst, J. C. M., Bateman, D., & Hauser, W. A. (1999). Dose-response effect of fetal cocaine exposure on newborn neurologic function. *Pediatrics, 103*, 79–85.

Chisholm, J. S. (1963). *Navajo infancy: An ethological study of child development.* New York: Aldine.

Chisholm, J. S., Burbank, V. K., Coall, D. A., & Gemmiti, F. (2005). Early stress: Perspectives from developmental evolutionary ecology (pp. 76–107). In B. J. Ellis & D. F. Bjorklund (Eds.), *Origins of the social mind: Evolutionary psychology and child development.* New York: Guilford.

Chiu, L. H. (1972). A cross-cultural comparison of cognitive styles in Chinese and American children. *International Journal of Psychology, 7*, 235–242.

Chomsky, N. (1957). *Syntactic structures.* The Hague, The Netherlands: Mouton.

Christakis, D. A., & Zimmerman, F. J. (2007). Violent television viewing during preschool is associated with antisocial behavior during school age. *Pediatrics, 120*, 993–999.

Christenfeld, N., & Hill, E. (1995). Whose baby are you? *Nature, 378*, 669.

Christie, F. (2002). *Classroom discourse analysis: A functional perspective.* London: Continuum.

Chu, J. (2001). Prenatal sex determination and sex-selective abortion in rural central China. *Population and Development Review, 27*, 259–282.

Chua, H. F., Boland, J. E., & Nisbett, R. E. (2005). Cultural variation in eye movements during scene perception. *Proceeding of the National Academy of Sciences USA, 102*, 12629–12633.

Chuah, Y. M. L., & Maybery, M. T. (1999). Verbal and spatial short-term memory: Common sources of developmental change? *Journal of Experimental Child Psychology, 73*, 7–44.

Chugani, H. T., Behen, M. E., Muzik, O., Juhász, C., Nagy, F., & Chugani, D. C. (2001). Local brain functional activity following early deprivation: A study of postinstitutionalized Romanian orphans. *NeuroImage, 117*, 1290–1301.

Chugani, H. T., Phelps, M. E., & Mazziotta, J. C. (1987). Positron emission tomography study of human brain functional development. *Annals of Neurology, 22*, 487–497.

Chung, H. L., & Steinberg, L. (2006). Relations between neighborhood factors, parenting behaviors, peer deviance, and delinquency among serious juvenile offenders. *Developmental Psychology, 42*, 319–331.

CIA World Factbook. (2007). Washington, DC.

Cicchetti, D. (1989). How research on child maltreatment has informed the study of child development: Perspectives from developmental psychopathology. In D. Cicchetti & V. Carlson (Eds.), *Child maltreatment: Theory and research on causes and consequences of child abuse and neglect.* New York: Cambridge University Press.

Cicchetti, D., & Rogosch, F. A. (2001). Diverse patterns of neuroendocrine activity in maltreated children. *Development and Psychopathology, 13*, 677–693.

Cicchetti, D., Rogosch, F. A., & Toth, S. L. (1997). Ontogenesis, depressotypic organization, and the depressive spectrum. In S. S. Luthar, J. A. Burack, D. Cicchetti, & J. R. Weisz (Eds.), *Developmental psychopathology: Perspectives on adjustment, risk, psychopathology: Perspectives on adjustment, risk, and disorder* (pp. 273–313). Cambridge, UK: Cambridge University Press.

Cicchetti, D., & Toth, S. L. (2006). Developmental psychopathology and preventative intervention. In W. Damon & R. M. Lerner (Gen. Eds.), *Handbook of child psychology* (6th ed.). In K. A. Renninger & I. E. Sigel (Vol. Eds.), Vol. 4: *Child psychology in practice* (pp. 497–547). New York: Wiley.

Cillessen, A. H. N. (2009). Sociometric methods. In K. H. Rubin, W. M. Bukowski, & B. Laursen (Eds.), *Handbook of peer interactions, relationships, and groups* (pp. 82–99). New York: Guilford.

Cillessen, A. H. N., & Mayeux, L. (2007). Variations in the association between aggression and social status: Theoretical and empirical perspectives. In P. H. Hawley, T. D. Little, & P. C. Rodkin (Eds.), *Aggression and adaptation: The bright side to bad behavior* (pp. 135–156). Mahwah, NJ: Erlbaum.

Clark, E. A., & Hanisee, J. (1982). Intellectual and adaptive performance of Asian children in adoptive American settings. *Developmental Psychology, 18*, 595–599.

Clark, J. E. (2005). Locomotion. In B. Hopkins (Ed.), *The Cambridge encyclopedia of child development* (pp. 336–339). New York: Cambridge University Press.

Clark, M. M., & Galef, B. G., Jr. (1995). Parental influence on reproductive life history strategies. *Trends in Ecology and Evolution, 10*, 151–153.

Clarke-Stewart, K. E. (1980). The father's contribution to children's cognitive and social development in early childhood. In F. A. Pedersen (Ed.), *The father-infant relationship: Observational studies in a family setting.* New York: Praeger.

Clarke-Stewart, K. (1984). Day care: A new context for research and development. In A. Collins (Ed.), *Minnesota Symposium on Child Psychology.* Hillsdale, NJ: Erlbaum.

Clarke-Stewart, K. A. (1989). Infant day care: Maligned or malignant? *American Psychologist, 44*, 266–273.

Clarke-Stewart, K. A., & Fein, G. G. (1983). Early childhood programs. In P. H. Mussen (Gen. Ed.), *Handbook of child psychology* (4th ed.). In M. M. Haith & J. J. Campos (Vol. Eds.), Vol. 2: *Infancy and developmental psychobiology.* New York: Wiley.

Clearfield, M. W., Osborne, C. N., & Mullen, M. (2008). Learning by looking: Infants' social looking behavior across the transition from crawling to walking. *Journal of Experimental Child Psychology, 100*, 297–307.

Clearfield, M. W., & Westfahl, S. M-C. (2006). Familiarization in infants' perception of addition problems. *Journal of Cognition and Development, 7*, 27–43.

Clements, W. A., & Perner, J. (1994). Implicit understanding of belief. *Cognitive Development, 9*, 377–395.

Clements, W. A., Rustin, C. L., & McCallum, S. (2000). Promoting the transition from implicit to explicit understanding: A training study of false belief. *Developmental Science, 3*, 81–92.

Cleveland, E. S., & Reese, E. (2005). Maternal structure and autonomy support in conversations about the past: Contributions to children's autobiographical memory. *Developmental Psychology, 41*, 376–388.

Cliffordson, C., & Gustafsson, J-E. (2008). Effects of age and schooling on intellectual performance: Estimates obtained from analysis of continuous variation in age and length of schooling. *Intelligence, 36*, 143–152.

Clifton, R. K., Rochat, P., Litovsky, R. Y., & Perris, E. E. (1991). Object representation guides infants' reaching in the dark. *Journal of Experimental Psychology: Human Perception and Performance, 17*, 323–329.

Clinton, H. R. (1996). *It takes a village.* New York: Simon & Shuster.

Coalition to Stop the Use of Child Soldiers. (2004). *Child soldiers: Global report 2004.* London: Coalition to Stop the Use of Child Soldiers.

Coch, D., Fischer, K. W., & Dawson, G. (Eds.) (2007). *Human behavior, learning, and the developing brain: Typical development.* New York: Guilford.

Cochran, M., & Niego, S. (2002). Parenting and social networks. In W. Damon & R. M. Lerner (Gen. Eds.), *Handbook of child psychology* (6th ed.). In K. A. Renninger & I. E. Sigel (Vol. Eds.), Vol. 4: *Child psychology in practice* (pp. 817–863). New York: Wiley.

Cohen, G. L., & Prinstein, M. J. (2006). Peer contagion of aggression and health risk behaviors among adolescent males: An experimental investigation of effects on public conduct and private attitudes. *Child Development, 77*, 967–983.

Cohen, L. B., & Cashon, C. H. (2006). Infant Cognition. In W. Damon & R. M. Lerner (Gen. Eds.), *Handbook of child psychology* (6th ed.). In D. Kuhn & R. S. Siegler (Vol. Eds.), Vol. 2: *Cognition, Perception, and Language* (pp. 214–251). New York: Wiley.

Coie, J. D., & Dodge, K. A. (1988). Multiple sources of data on social behavior and social status in the school: A cross-age comparison. *Child Development, 59*, 815–829.

Coie, J. D., Dodge, K. A., & Kupersmidt, J. B. (1990). Peer group behavior and social status. In S. R. Asher & J. D. Coie (Eds.), *Peer rejection in childhood.* Cambridge, UK: Cambridge University Press.

Coie, J. D., Dodge, K. A., & Coppotelli, H. (1982). Dimensions and types of social status: A cross-age perspective. *Developmental Psychology, 18*, 557–570.

Coie, J. D., & Koeppl, G. K. (1990). Adapting intervention to the problems of aggressive and disruptive rejected children. In S. R. Asher & J. D. Coie (Eds.), *Peer rejection in childhood.* Cambridge, UK: Cambridge University Press.

Colby, A., Kohlberg, L., Gibbs, J., & Lieberman, M. (1983). A longitudinal study of moral judgment. *Monographs of the Society for Research in Child Development, 48* (Serial No. 200).

Cole, M. (1990). Cognitive development and formal schooling: The evidence from cross-cultural research. In L. C. Moll (Ed.), *Vygotsky and education.* New York: Cambridge University Press.

Cole, M. (2006). Culture and cognitive development in phylogenetic, historical, and ontogenetic perspectives. In W. Damon & R. M. Lerner (Gen. Eds.), *Handbook of child psychology* (6th ed.). In D. Kuhn & R. S. Siegler (Vol. Eds.), Vol. 2: *Cognition, perception, and language,* (pp. 636–683). New York: Wiley.

Cole, P. M., Martin, S. E., & Dennis, T. A. (2004). Emotion regulation as scientific construct: Methodological challenges and directions for child development research. *Child Development, 75*, 317–333.

Colin, V. L. (1996). *Human attachment.* New York: McGraw-Hill.

Collie, R., & Hayne, R. (1999). Deferred imitation by 6- and 9-month-old infants: More evidence for declarative memory. *Developmental Psychobiology, 35*, 83–90.

Collins, R. L., Elliott, M. N., Berry, S. H., Kanouse, D. E., Kunkel, D., Hunter, S. B., & Miu, A. (2004). Watching sex on television predicts adolescent initiation of sexual behavior. *Pediatrics, 114*, e280–e289.

Collins, W. A., & Laursen, B. (2004). Parent-adolescent relationships and influences. In R. Lerner & L. Steinberg (Eds.), *Handbook of adolescent psychology* (2nd ed, pp. 331–361). New York: Wiley.

Collins, W. A., Maccoby, E. E., Steinberg, L., Hetherington, E. M., & Bornstein, M. H. (2000). Contemporary research on parenting: The case for nature and nurture. *American Psychologist, 55*, 218–232.

Collins, W. A., & Steinberg, L. (2006). Adolescent development in interpersonal context. In W. Damon & R. M. Lerner (Gen. Eds.), *Handbook of child psychology* (6th ed.). In N. Eisenberg (Vol. Ed.), Vol. 3: *Social, emotional, and personality development* (pp. 1003–1067). New York: Wiley.

Commons, M. L., & Richards, F. A. (1984). A general model of stage theory—and—Applying the general stage model. In M. L. Commons, F. A. Richards, & C. Armon (Eds.), *Beyond formal operations,* Vol. 1: *Late adolescent and adult cognitive development* (pp. 120–140, 141–157). New York: Praeger.

Commons, M. L., & Richards, F. A. (2003). Four postformal stages. In J. Demick & C. Andreoletti (Eds.), *Handbook of adult development* (pp. 199–219). New York: Kluwer Academic/Plenum.

Comstock, G., & Scharrer, E. (2006). Media and popular culture. In W. Damon & R. M. Lerner (Gen. Eds.), *Handbook of child psychology* (6th ed.). In K. A. Renninger & I. E. Sigel (Vol. Eds.), Vol. 4: *Child psychology in practice* (pp. 817–863). New York: Wiley.

Comstock, G., & Scharrer, E. (2007). *Media and the American child.* New York: Academic Press.

Conger, R. D., McCarty, J. A., Yang, R. K., Lahey, R. B., & Kroop, J. P. (1984). Perception of child, child-rearing values, and economic distress as mediating links between environmental stressors and observed maternal behavior. *Child Development, 55*, 2234–2247.

Connelly, B. (2004). The problem behind Chinese adoptions. *The American Enterprise, 15*, 42+.

Connolly, J., Craig, W., Goldberg, A., & Pepler, D. (2004). Mixed-gender groups, dating, and romantic relationships. *Journal of Research on Adolescence, 14*, 185–207.

Connolly, L., Furman, W., & Konarski, R. (2000). The role of peers in the emergence of heterosexual romantic relationships in adolescence. *Child Development, 71,* 1395–1408.

Conrad, R. (2004). "As if she defied the world in her joyousness": Rereading Darwin on emotion and emotional development. *Human Development, 47,* 40–65.

Cook, M., & Mineka, S. (1989). Observational conditioning of fear to fear-relevant versus fear-irrelevant stimuli in rhesus monkeys. *Journal of Abnormal Psychology, 98,* 448–459.

Cooley, C. H. (1902). *Human nature and the social order.* New York: Scribner's.

Cooper, R. P., & Aslin, R. N. (1990). Preference for infant-directed speech in the first month after birth. *Child Development, 61,* 1584–1595.

Cooper, R. P., & Aslin, R. N. (1994). Developmental differences in infant attention to the spectral properties of infant-directed speech. *Child Development, 65,* 1663–1677.

Coopersmith, S. (1967). *The antecedents of self-esteem.* New York: W. H. Freeman.

Coplan, R. J., & Arbeau, K. A. (2009). Peer interaction and play in early childhood. In K. H. Rubin, W. M. Bukowski, & B. Laursen (Eds.), *Handbook of peer interactions, relationships, and groups* (pp. 143–161). New York: Guilford.

Corballis, M. C. (1990). *The lopsided ape: The evolution of the generative mind.* New York: Oxford University Press.

Cosmides, L., & Tooby, J. (1992). Cognitive adaptations for social exchange. In J. H. Barkow, L. Cosmides, & J. Tooby (Eds.), *The adapted mind: Evolutionary psychology and the generation of culture* (pp. 163–228). New York: Oxford University Press.

Costa, P. T., & McCrae, R. R. (1988). Personality in adulthood: A 6-year longitudinal study of self-reports and spouse ratings on the NEO personality inventory. *Journal of Personality and Social Psychology, 54,* 853–863.

Costa, P. T., & McCrae, R. R. (1992). *NEO PI-R. Professional manual.* Odessa, FL: Psychological Assessment Resources, Inc.

Courage, M. L., & Howe, M. L. (2001). Long-term retention in 3.5-month-olds: Familiarization time and individual differences in attentional style. *Journal of Experimental Child Psychology, 79,* 271–293.

Courage, M. L., & Howe, M. L. (2010). To watch or not to watch: Infants and toddlers in a brave new electronic world. *Developmental Review, 30,* 101–115.

Courage, M. L., Murphy, A. N., Goulding, S., & Setliff, A. E. (2010). When television is on: The impact of infant-directed video on 6- and 18-month-olds' toy play and on parent-infant interaction. *Infant Behavior and Development, 33,* 176–188.

Courage, M. L., & Setliff, A. E. (2009). Debating the impact of television and video material on very young children: Attention, learning, and the developing brain. *Child Development Perspectives, 3,* 72–78.

Courtin, C. (2000). The impact of sign language on the cognitive development in deaf children: The case of theories of mind. *Journal of Deaf Studies and Deaf Education, 5,* 266–276.

Cowan, N., & Alloway, T. (2009). Development of working memory in childhood. In M. L. Courage & N. Cowan (Eds.), *The development of memory in infancy and childhood* (pp. 304–342). New York: Psychology Press.

Cowan, N., Elliott, E. M., Saults, J. S., Morey, C. C., Mattox, S., Hismjatulli, & Conway, A. R. A. (2005). On the capacity of attention: Its estimation and its role in working memory and cognitive aptitudes. *Cognitive Psychology, 51,* 42–100.

Cowan, N., Nugent, L. D., Elliott, E. M., Ponomarev, I., & Saults, J. S. (1999). The role of attention in the development of short-term memory: Age differences in the verbal span of apprehension. *Child Development, 70,* 1082–1097.

Cox, B., C., Ornstein, P. A., Naus, M. J., Maxfield, D., & Zimler, J. (1989). Children's concurrent use of rehearsal and organizational strategies. *Developmental Psychology, 25,* 619–627.

Cox, D., & Waters, H. S. (1986). Sex differences in the use of organization strategies: A developmental analysis. *Journal of Experimental Child Psychology, 41,* 18–37.

Cox, M. J., & Paley, B. (2003). Understanding families as systems. *Current Directions in Psychological Science, 12,* 193–196.

Cox, M. V. (2005). *The pictorial world of the child.* New York: Cambridge University Press.

Cox, M. V., & Parkin, C. E. (1986). Young children's human figure drawing: Cross-sectional and longitudinal studies. *Educational Psychology, 6,* 353–368.

Coyle, T. R. (2001). Factor analysis of variability measures in eight independent samples of children and adults. *Journal of Experimental Child Psychology, 78,* 330–358.

Crabtree, J. W., & Riesen, A. H. (1979). Effects of the duration of dark rearing on visually guided behavior in the kitten. *Developmental Psychobiology, 12,* 291–303.

Crawford, J. (1997). The campaign against proposition 227: A post mortem. *Bilingual Research Journal, 21,* 1–23.

Crawford, L. (April 21, 2008). Helicopter moms vs. free-range kids. *Newsweek.* Accessed at *http://freerangekids.wordpress.com/2008/04/06/why-i-let-my-9-year-old-ride-the-subway-alone/.* (Downloaded June 2, 2010).

Crenshaw, D., & Garbarino, J. (2007). The hidden dimensions: Profound sorrow and buried potential in violent youth. *Journal of Humanistic Psychology, 47,* 160–174.

Crick, N. R., & Dodge, K. A. (1994). A review and reformulation of social information-processing mechanisms in children's social adjustment. *Psychological Bulletin, 115,* 74–101.

Crick, N. R., & Dodge, K. A. (1996). Social-information-processing mechanisms in reactive and proactive aggression. *Child Development, 67,* 993–1002.

Crick, N. R., & Grotpeter, J. K. (1995). Relational aggression, gender, and social psychological adjustment. *Child Development, 66,* 710–722.

Crittenden, A. N., & Marlowe, F. W. (2008). Allomaternal care among the Hadza of Tanzania. *Human Nature, 19,* 249–262.

Crnic, K. A., & Greenberg, M. T. (1990). Minor parenting stress in young children. *Child Development, 61,* 1628–1637.

Croll, J., Newmark-Sztainer, D., Story, M., & Ireland, M. (2002). Prevalence and risk and protective factors related to disordered eating behaviors among adolescents: Relationship to gender and ethnicity. *Journal of Adolescent Health, 31,* 166–175.

Crompton, L. (2003). *Homosexuality and civilization.* Cambridge, MA: Harvard University Press.

Crook, J. M. (1980). *The evolution of human consciousness.* Oxford, UK: Clarendon Press.

Crowley, K., Callanan, M. A., Tennenbaum, H. R., & Allen, E. (2001). Parents explain more often to boys than to girls during shared scientific thinking. *Psychological Science, 12,* 258–261.

Crystal, D. (2001). *Language and the Internet.* Cambridge, UK: Cambridge University Press.

Crystal, D. (2005). *The scope of Internet linguistics.* Paper given online to the American Association for the Advancement of Science (AAAS) meeting, Washington, DC. [http://www.davidcrystal.com/DC_articles/Internet2.pdf]

Crystal, D. (2006). TXT NY1? In S. Tresman & A. Cooke (eds.), *The dyslexia handbook* (pp. 179–183). Reading: British Dyslexia Association.

Csikszentmihalyi, M., & Larson, R. (1984). *Being adolescent.* New York: Basic Books.

Cuban, L. (2004). Assessing the 20-year impact of Multiple Intelligences on schooling. *Teachers College Record, 106,* 140–146.

Cullerton-Sen, C., Cassidy, A. R., Murray-Close, D., Cicchetti, D., Crick, N. R., & Rogosch, F. A. (2008). Childhood maltreatment and the development of relational and physical aggression: The importance of a gender-informed approach. *Child Development, 79,* 1736–1751.

Cummings, E. M., & Davies, P. T. (1994). Maternal depression and child development. *Journal of Child Psychology and Psychiatry and Allied Disciplines, 35,* 73–112.

Cummings, E. M., Iannotti, R. J., & Zahn-Waxler, C. (1989). Aggression between peers in early childhood: Individual continuity and developmental change. *Child Development, 60,* 887–895.

Cummins, D. D. (1998). Social norms and other minds: The evolutionary roots of higher cognition. In D. D. Cummins & C. Allen (Eds.), *The evolution of mind.* New York: Oxford University Press.

Cunningham, A. E. (1990). Explicit versus implicit instruction in phonemic awareness. *Journal of Experimental Child Psychology, 50,* 429–444.

Curtiss, S. (1977). *Genie: A psycholinguistic study of a modern day "wild child."* New York: Academic.

D'Augelli, A. R. (1998). Review of growing up in a lesbian family: Effects on child development. *Journal of Marriage and the Family, 60,* 265–266.

D'Augelli, A. R., & Patterson, C. J. (Eds.). (2001). *Lesbian, gay, and bisexual identities and youths: Psychological perspectives.* New York: Oxford University Press.

Daley, T. C., Whaley, S. E., Sigman, M. D., Espinosa, M. P., & Neumann, C. (2003). IQ on the rise: The Flynn Effect in rural Kenyan children. *Psychological Science, 14,* 215–210.

Dalton, K. M., Nacewicz, B. M., Johnstone, T., Schaefer, H. S., Gernsbacher, M. A., Goldsmith, H. H., Alexander, A. L., & Davidson, R. J. (2005). Gaze fixation and the neural circuitry of face processing in autism. *Nature Neuroscience, 8,* 519–526.

Daly, M., & Wilson, M. (1981). Abuse and neglect of children in evolutionary perspective. In R. D. Alexander & D. W. Tinkle (Eds.), *Natural selection and social behavior* (pp. 405–416). New York: Chiron.

Daly, M., & Wilson, M. (1982). Whom are newborn babies said to resemble? *Ethology and Sociobiology, 3,* 69–78.

Daly, M., & Wilson, M. (1985). Child abuse and other risks of not living with both parents. *Ethology and Sociobiology, 6,* 197–210.

Daly, M., & Wilson, M. (1988a). *Homicide.* New York: Aldine.

Daly, M., & Wilson, M. (1988b). Evolutionary social psychology and family homicide. *Science, 242,* 519–524.

Daly, M., & Wilson, M. (1996). Violence against children. *Current Directions in Psychological Science, 5,* 77–81.

Damon, W. (1977). *The social world of the child.* San Francisco: Jossey-Bass.

Damon, W. (Ed.) (1978). *Social cognition.* San Francisco: Jossey-Bass.

Damon, W. (Ed.). (1983). *Social and personality development: Essays on the growth of the child.* New York: W. W. Norton.

Damon, W. (1988). *The moral child: Nurturing children's natural moral growth.* New York: Free Press.

Damon, W. (1994). *Moral child: Nurturing children's natural moral growth.* New York: Simon & Schuster.

Daneman, M., & Green, I. (1986). Individual differences in comprehending and producing words in context. *Journal of Memory and Language, 25,* 1–18.

Darling, N., & Steinberg, L. (1993). Parenting style as context: An integrative model. *Psychological Bulletin, 113,* 487–496.

Darroch, J. E., Singh, S., Frost, J. J., and the Study Team. (2001). Differences in teenage pregnancy rates among five developed countries: The roles of sexual activity and contraceptive use. *Family Planning Perspectives, 33,* 244–250.

Darwin, C. (1859). *On the origin of species.* New York: Modern Library.

Darwin, C. (1871). *The descent of man, and selection in relation to sex.* London: John Murray.

Darwin, C. (1872). *The expression of emotions in man and animals.* Chicago, IL: University of Chicago Press.

Dasen, P. R. (Ed.). (1977). *Piagetian psychology: Cross-cultural contributions.* New York: Gardner.

Davies, P. T., Moon, R. Y., Sachs, H. C., & Ottolini, M. C. (1998). Effects of sleep position on infant motor development. *Pediatrics, 102,* 1135–1140.

Davies, P. T., Sturge-Apple, M. L., Winter, M. A., Cummings, E. M., & Farrell, D. (2006). Child adaptational development in contexts of intraparental conflict over time. *Child Development, 77,* 218–233.

Davies, S. L., Glaser, D., & Kossoff, R. (2000). Children's sexual play and behavior in pre-school settings: Staffs' perceptions, reports, and responses. *Child Abuse and Neglect, 17,* 59–66.

Davila, J. (2008). Depressive symptoms and adolescent romance: Theory, research, and implications. *Child Development Perspectives, 2,* 26–31.

Davis, D. L., Gottlieb, M. B., & Stampnitzky, J. R. (1998). Reduced ratio of male to female births in several industrial countries: A sentinel health indicator? *Journal of the American Medical Association, 279,* 1018–1020.

Davis-Unger, A. C., & Carlson, S. M. (2008). Development of teaching skills and relations to theory of mind in preschoolers. *Journal of Cognition and Development, 9,* 26–45.

Dawson G., Ashman S. B., Panagiotides, H., Hessl D., Self J., Yamada E., & Embry L. (2003). Preschool outcomes of children of depressed mothers: Role of maternal behavior, contextual risk, and children's brain activity. *Child Development, 74,* 1158–1175.

Dawson, G., Frey, K., Self, J., Panagiotides, H., Hessel, D., Yamada, E., et al. (1999). Frontal brain activity in infants of depressed and nondepressed mothers: Relation to variations in infant behavior. *Development and Psychopathology, 11,* 589–605.

Dawson, G., Toth, K., Abbott, R., Osterling, J., Munson, J., Estes, A., & Liaw, J. (2004). Early social attention impairments in autism: Social orienting, joint attention, and attention to distress. *Developmental Psychology, 40,* 271–283.

Dawson, M. (2004) The misbehavior of behaviorists: Ethical challenges to the Autism-ABA industry. Accessed at: http://www.sentex.net/~nexus23/naa_aba.html (Downloaded May 21, 2008).

de Beer, G. (1958). *Embryos and ancestors* (3rd Ed). Oxford: Clarendon Press.

de Haan, M. (2001). The neuropsychology of face processing during infancy and childhood. In C. A. Nelson & M. Luciana (Eds.), *Handbook of developmental cognitive neuroscience* (pp. 381–398). Cambridge, MA: MIT Press.

de Haan, M., & Johnson, M. (Eds.) (2003). *The cognitive neuroscience of development.* Hove, East Sussex, UK: Psychology Press.

de Haan, M., Bauer, P. J., Georgieff, M. K., & Nelson, C. A. (2000). Explicit memory in low-risk infants aged 19 months born between 27 and 42 weeks gestation. *Developmental Medicine and Child Neurology, 42,* 304–312.

de Haan, M., Oliver, A., & Johnson, M. H. (1998). Electro physiological correlates of face processing by adults and 6-month-old infants. *Journal of Cognitive Neural Science* (Annual Meeting Supplement), 36.

De Houwer, A. (1995). Bilingual language acquisition. In P. Fletcher & B. MacWhinney (Eds.), *The handbook of child language* (pp. 219–250). Oxford, UK: Blackwell.

De Lisi, R., & Staudt, J. (1980). Individual differences in college students' performance on formal operations tasks. *Journal of Applied Developmental Psychology, 1,* 163–174.

de Mause, L. (1974). The evolution of childhood. In L. de Mause (Ed.), *The history of childhood.* New York: Psychohistory Press.

De Schipper, E. J., Riksen-Walraven, J. M. A., & Geurts, S. A. E. (2006). Effects of child-caregiver ratio on the interactions between caregivers and children in child care centers: An experimental study. *Child Development, 77,* 861–874.

de Villiers, J. G., & de Villiers, P. A. (1973). A crosssectional study of the acquisition of grammatical morphemes in child speech. *Journal of Psycholinguistic Research, 2,* 267–278.

De Vries, R. (1969). Constancy of generic identity in the years three to six. *Monographs of the Society for Research in Child Development, 34* (Serial No. 127).

de Waal, F. B. M. (1982). *Chimpanzee politics: Power and sex among apes.* London: Jonathan Cape.

de Waal, F. B. M. (1989). *Peace making among primates.* Cambridge, MA: Harvard University Press.

de Waal, F. B. M. (1997). *Bonobo the forgotten ape.* Berkeley and Los Angeles: University of California Press.

de Waal, F. (2005). *Our inner ape: A leading primatologist explains why we are who we are.* New York: Penguin.

de Weerd, A. W., & van den Bossche, R. A. (2003). The development of sleep during the first months of life. *Sleep Medicine Review, 7,* 179–191.

De Wolff, M. S., & van IJzendoorn, M. H. (1997). Sensitivity and attachment: A meta-analysis on parental antecedents of infant attachment. *Child Development, 68,* 571–591.

Deacon, T. W. (1997). *The symbolic species: The co-evolution of language and the brain.* New York: Norton.

Deák, G., O., Ray, S. D., & Brenneman, K. (2003). Children's perseverative appearance-reality errors are related to emerging language skills. *Child Development, 74,* 944–964.

Deal, J. E., Halverson, C. F., & Wampler, K. S. (1989). Parental, marital, family, and child characteristics. *Child Development, 60*, 1025–1034.

Deardoff, J., Fonzales, N. A., Christopher, F. S., Roosa, M. W., & Millsap, R. E. (2005). Early puberty and adolescent pregnancy: The influence of alcohol use. *Pediatrics, 116*, 1451–1456.

Dearing, E. (2004). The developmental implications of restrictive and supportive parenting across neighborhoods and ethnicities: Exceptions to the rule. *Applied Developmental Psychology, 25*, 555–575.

Deary, I. J., Batty, G. D., Pattie, A., & Gale, C. R. (2008). More intelligence, more dependable children live longer: A 55-year longitudinal study of a representative sample of the Scottish nation. *Psychological Science, 19*, 874–880.

Deater-Deckard, K., Dunn, J., O'Connor, T. G., Davies, L., Golding, J., & the ALSPAC Study Team. (2001). Using the stepfamily genetic design to examine gene-environment processes in child and family functioning. *Marriage and Family Review, 33*, 131–156.

DeBell, M., & Chapman, C. (2003). *Computer and Internet use by children and adolescents in 2001* (National Center for Education Statistics). Washington, DC: U.S. Department of Education.

DeCasper, A. J., & Fifer, W. P. (1980). Of human bonding: Newborns prefer their mother's voice. *Science, 208*, 1174–1176.

DeCasper, A. J., & Spence, M. J. (1986). Prenatal maternal speech influences newborns' perception of speech sounds. *Infant Behavior and Development, 9*, 133–150.

Deci, E. L. (1971). Effects of externally mediated rewards on intrinsic motivation. *Journal of Personality and Social Psychology, 18*, 105–115.

Del Giudice, M. (2009). Sex, attachment, and the development of reproductive strategies. *Behavioral and Brain Sciences, 32*, 1–21.

Del Giudice, M., Angeleri, R., & Manera, V. (2009). The juvenile transition: A developmental switch point in human life history. *Developmental Review, 29*, 1–31.

DeLamater, J., & Friedrich, R. (2002). Human sexual development. *Journal of Sex Research, 39*, 10–14.

Delevati, N. M., & Bergamasco, N. H. P. (1999). Pain in the neonate: An analysis of facial movements and crying in response to nociceptive stimuli. *Infant Behavior & Development, 22*, 137–143.

DeLoache, J. S. (1987). Rapid change in the symbolic functioning of very young children. *Science, 238*, 1556–1557.

DeLoache, J. S. (1991). Symbolic functioning in very young children: Understanding of pictures and models. *Child Development, 62*, 736–752.

DeLoache, J. S. (1995). Early understanding and use of symbols: The model model. *Current Directions in Psychological Science, 4*, 109–113.

DeLoache, J. S. (2000). Dual representation and young children's use of scale models. *Child Development, 71*, 329–338.

DeLoache, J. S., & Brown, A. L. (1983). Very young children's memory for the location of objects in a large scale environment. *Child Development, 54*, 888–897.

DeLoache, J. S., Cassidy, D. J., & Brown, A. L. (1985). Precursors of mnemonic strategies in very young children's memory for the location of hidden objects. *Child Development, 56*, 125–137.

DeLoache, J. S. & DeMendoza, O. A. P. (1987). Joint picturebook reading of mothers and one-year-old children. *British Journal of Developmental Psychology, 5*, 111–123.

DeLoache, J. S., & LoBue, V. (2009). The narrow fellow in the grass: Human infants associate snakes and fear. *Developmental Science, 12*, 201–207.

DeLoache, J. S., & Marzolf, D. P. (1992). When a picture is not worth a thousand words: Young children's understanding of pictures and models. *Cognitive Development, 7*, 317–329.

DeLoache, J. S., Miller, K. F., & Pierroutsakos, S. L. (1998). Reasoning and problem solving. In W. Damon (Gen. Ed.), *Handbook of child psychology* (6th ed.). In D. Kuhn & R. S. Siegler (Vol. Eds.), Vol. 2: *Cognitive, language, and perceptual development*. New York: Wiley.

DeLoache, J. S., Pierroutsakos, S. L., & Uttal, D. H. (2003). The origins of pictorial competence. *Current Directions in Psychological Science, 12*, 114–118.

Deloitte's State of the Media Democracy Survey (3rd ed.): Rethink what you know. (2009). Accessed at: http://www.deloitte.com/dtt/article/0,1002,sid%253D108581%2526cid%253D235500,00.html (Downloaded January 18, 2009).

Delpit, L. D. (1990). Language diversity and learning. In S. Hynds & D. L. Rubin (Eds.), *Perspectives on talk and learning*. Urbana, IL: National Council of Teachers of English.

Delpit, L. D., & Dowdy, J. K. (2002). *The skin that we speak: Thoughts on language and culture in the classroom*. New York: New Press.

Delpit, L. D. (1990). Language diversity and learning. In S. Hynds & D. L. Rubin (Eds.), *Perspectives on talk and learning*. Urbana, IL: National Council of Teachers of English.

Delval, J. (1994). *El desarrollo humano* [Human development]. Madrid: Siglo XIX.

DeMarie, D., Miller, P. H., Ferron, J., & Cunningham, W. R. (2004). Path analysis tests for theoretical models of children's memory performance. *Journal of Cognition and Development, 5*, 461–492.

Demetriou, A., Xiang Kui, Z., Spanoudis, G., Christou, C., Kyriakides, L., & Platsidou, M. (2005). The architecture, dynamics, and development of mental processing: Greek, Chinese, or Universal? *Intelligence, 33*, 109–141.

Dempster, F. N. (1981). Memory span: Sources of individual and developmental differences. *Psychological Bulletin, 89*, 63–100.

Denenberg V. H., Brumaghim, J. T., Haltmeyer, G. C., & Zarrow, M. X. (1967). Increased adrenocortical activity in the neonatal rat following handling. *Endocrinology, 81*, 1047–1052.

Denham, S. (1998). *Emotional development in young children*. New York: Guilford.

Dennett, D. (1990). The interpretation of texts, people, and other artifacts. *Philosophy and Phenomenological Quarterly, 1* (supplement), 177–194.

Dennis, W. (1973). *Children of the Crèche*. New York: Appleton-Century-Crofts.

Desai, D. V., & Dhanani, H. (2004). Sickle cell disease: History and origin. *The Internet Journal of Hematology, 1* (2).

DeStefano, J. (1972). Social variation in language: Implications for teaching reading to Black ghetto children. In J. A. Figurel (Ed.), *Better reading in urban schools*. Newark, DE: International Reading Association.

Detterman, D. K. (1987). What does reaction time tell us about intelligence? In P. E. Vernon (Ed.), *Speed of information processing and intelligence*. Norwood, NJ: Ablex.

Detterman, D. K., & Daniel, M. H. (1989). Correlations of mental tests with each other and with cognitive variables are highest for low IQ groups. *Intelligence, 13*, 340–359.

DeVries, M. W. (1984). Temperament and infant mortality among the Masai of East Africa. *American Journal of Psychiatry, 141*, 1189–1194.

Diamond, A. (1985). Development of the ability to use recall to guide action as indicated by infants' performance on AB. *Child Development, 56*, 868–883.

Diamond, A. (1991). Frontal lobe involvement in cognitive changes during the first year of life. In K. R. Gibson & A. C. Petersen (Eds.), *Brain maturation and cognitive development: Comparative and cross-cultural perspectives*. New York: Aldine de Gruyter.

Diamond, A., Barnett, W. S., Thomas, J., & Munro, S. (2007). Preschool program improves cognitive control. *Science, 318*, 1387–1388.

Diamond, A., & Taylor, C. (1996). Development of an aspect of executive control: Development of the abilities to remember what I said and to "Do as I say, not as I do." *Developmental Psychobiology, 29*, 315–324.

Diamond, J. (1989). The cruel logic of our genes. *Discover, 10*, 72–78.

Diamond, J. (1997). *Guns, germs, and steel: The fates of human societies*. New York: W. W. Norton.

Diamond, L. M. (2008). Female bisexuality from adolescence to adulthood: Results from a 10-year longitudinal study. *Developmental Psychology, 44*, 5–14.

Díaz-Lefebvre, R. (2004). Multiple intelligences, learning for understanding, and creative assessment: Some pieces to the puzzle of learning. *Teachers College Record, 106*, 49–57.

Diaz, R. M. (1983). Thought and two languages: The impact of bilingualism on cognitive development. *Review of Research in Education, 10*, 23–54.

DiCenso, A., Guyatt, G. H., Willan, A., & Griffith L. (2002). Interventions to reduce unintended pregnancies among adolescents: Systematic review of randomised controlled trials. *British Medical Journal, 324,* 1426–1430.

Dick, D. M., Rose, R., Viken, R. J., & Kaprio, J. (2000). Pubertal timing and substance use: Associations between and within families across late adolescence. *Developmental Psychology, 36,* 180–189.

Dick-Read, G. (1959). *Childbirth without fear: The principle and practices of natural childbirth.* New York: Harper & Brothers. (Original work published in 1944).

Diener, M. (2000). Gift from the gods: A Balinese guide to early child rearing. In J. DeLoache & A. Gotlieb (Eds.), *A world of babies: Imagined childcare guides for seven societies.* Cambridge, UK: Cambridge University Press.

Dieter, J. N., Field, T., Hernandez-Reif, M., Emory, E. K., & Redzepi, M. (2003). Stable preterm infants gain more weight and sleep less after five days of massage therapy. *Journal of Pediatric Psychology, 28,* 403–411.

Dietrich, K. N., Berger, O. G., Succop, P. A., Hammond, P. B., & Bornschein, R. L. (1993). The developmental consequences of low to moderate prenatal and postnatal lead exposure: Intellectual attainment in the Cincinnati Lead Study cohort following school entry. *Neurotoxicology and Teratology, 13,* 37–44.

DiPietro, J. A. (2004). The role of prenatal maternal stress in child development. *Current Directions in Psychological Science, 13,* 71–74.

Dirix, C. E. H., Nijhuis, J. G., Jongsma, H. W., & Hornstra, C. (2009). Aspects of fetal learning and memory. *Child Development, 80,* 1251–1258.

Dixson, A. F. (1998). *Primate sexuality.* New York: Oxford University Press.

Dobzhansky, T. (1955). *Evolution, genetics, and man.* New York: Wiley.

Dodge, K. A. (1986). A social information processing model of social competence in children. In M. Perlmutter (Ed.), *Minnesota symposium on child psychology* (Vol. 18). Hillsdale, NJ: Erlbaum.

Dodge, K. A., Coie, J. D., & Lynam, D. (2006). Aggression and antisocial behavior in youth. In W. Damon & R. M. Lerner (Gen. Eds.), *Handbook of child psychology* (6th ed.). In N. Eisenberg (Vol. Ed.), Vol. 3: *Social, emotional, and personality development* (pp. 719–788). New York: Wiley.

Dodge, K. A., & Feldman, E. (1990). Issues in social cognition and sociometric status. In S. R. Asher and J. D. Coie (Eds.), *Peer rejection in childhood.* Cambridge, UK: Cambridge University Press.

Dodge, K. A., Greenberg, M. T., Malone, P. S., & Conduct Problems Prevention Research Group. (2008). Testing an idealized cascade model of the development of serious violence in adolescence. *Child Development, 79,* 1907–1927.

Dodge, K. A., Lansford, J. E., Burks, V. S., Bates, J. E., Pettit, G. S., Fontaine, R., et al. (2003). Peer rejection and social information-processing factors in the development of aggressive behavior problems in children. *Child Development, 74,* 374–393.

Dodge, K. A., Pettit, G. S., Bates, J. E., & Valente, E. (1995). Social information-processing patterns partially mediate the effect of early physical abuse on later conduct problems. *Journal of Abnormal Psychology, 104,* 632–643.

Dodge, K. A., Pettit, G. S., McClaskey, C. L., & Brown, M. M. (1986). Social competence in children. *Monographs of the Society for Research in Child Development, 51* (Serial No. 213).

Dohnt, H., & Tiggerman, M. (2006). The contribution of peer and media influences to the development of body satisfaction and self-esteem in young girls: A prospective study. *Developmental Psychology, 42,* 929–936.

Doman, G. (1984). *How to multiply your baby's intelligence.* Garden City, NY: Doubleday.

Donald, M. (1991). *Origins of the modern mind.* Cambridge, MA: Harvard University Press.

Dondi, M., Simion, F., & Caltran, G. (1999). Can newborns discriminate between their own cry and the cry of another newborn infant? *Developmental Psychology, 35,* 418–426.

Döring, N. (2002). Personal home pages on the web: A review of research. *Journal of Computer Mediated Communication, 7, No. 3.* Accessed at http://jcmc.indiana.edu/vol7/issue3/doering .html (Downloaded June 10, 2010).

Dornbusch, S. M., Ritter, P. L., Liederman, P. H., Roberts, D. F., & Fraleigh, M. J. (1987). The relation of parenting style to adolescent school performance. *Child Development, 58,* 1244–1257.

Doval, B., & Eckerman, C. O. (1984). Developmental trends in the quality of conversation achieved by small groups of acquainted peers. *Monographs of the Society for Research in Child Development, 49* (Serial No. 206).

Downey, G., & Coyne, J. C. (1990). Children of depressed parents: An integrative review. *Psychological Bulletin, 108,* 50–76.

Dozier, M., Peloso, E., Gordon, M. K., Manni, M., Gunnar, M. R., Stovall-McClough, K. C., & Levine, S. (2006). Foster children's diurnal production of cortisol: An exploratory study. *Child Maltreatment, 11,* 189–197.

Dozier, M., Stovall, K., Albus, K., & Bates, B. (2001). Attachment for infants in foster care: The role of caregiver state of mind. *Child Development, 72,* 1467–1477.

Drachman, D. B., & Coulombre, A. J. (1962). Experimental clubfoot and arthrogryposis multiplex congenita. *Lancet, 2,* 523–526.

Draghi-Lorenz, R., Reddy, V., & Costall, A. (2001). Rethinking the development of "non basic" emotions: A critical review of existing theories. *Developmental Review, 21,* 263–304.

Draper, P., & Harpending, H. (1987). A sociobiological perspective on human reproductive strategies. In K. B. MacDonald (Ed.). *Sociobiological perspectives on human development* (pp. 340–372). New York: Springer Verlag.

Drummond, K. D., Bradley, S. J., Peterson-Badali, M., & Zucker, K. J. (2008). A follow-up study of girls with gender identity disorder. *Developmental Psychology, 44,* 34–45.

Dubas, J. S., Heijkoop, M., & van Aken, M. A. G. (2009). A preliminary investigation of parent-progeny olfactory recognition and parental investment. *Human Nature, 20,* 80–92.

Duberman, L. (1975). *The reconstituted family: A study of remarried couples and their children.* Chicago: Nelson-Hall.

DuBois, D. L., Holloway, B. E., Valentine, J. C., & Harris, C. (2002). Effectiveness of mentoring programs for youth: A meta-analytic review. *American Journal of Community Psychology, 30,* 157–197.

Duckworth, A. L., & Seligman, M. E. P. (2005). Self-discipline outdoes IQ in predicting academic performance of adolescence. *Psychological Science, 16,* 939–944.

Dufee, J. T., & Lee, L. C. (1973, August). *Infant-infant interaction in a daycare setting.* Paper presented at the meeting of the American Psychological Association, Montreal, Canada.

Duffy, S., Huttenlocher, J., & Levine, S. (2005). It's all relative: How young children encode extent. *Journal of Cognition and Development, 6,* 51–63.

Duffy, S., & Kitayama, S. (2007). Mnemonic context effect in two cultures: Attention to memory representations? *Cognitive Science, 31,* 1–12.

Duffy, S., Toriyama, R., Itakura, S., & Kitayama, S. (2009). Development of cultural strategies of attention in North American and Japanese children. *Journal of Experimental Child Psychology, 102,* 351–359.

Dunbar, R. I. M. (1992). Neocortex size as a constraint on group size in primates. *Journal of Human Evolution, 20,* 469–493.

Dunbar, R. I. M. (2001). Brains on two legs: Group size and the evolution of intelligence. In F. B. M. de Waal (Ed.), *Tree of origins: What primate behavior can tell us about human social evolution* (pp. 173–191). Cambridge, MA: Harvard University Press.

Dunbar, R. I. M. (2010). Brain and behaviour in primate evolution. In P. M. Kappler & J. B. Silk (Eds.), *Mind the gap: Tracing the origins of human universals* (pp. 315–330). New York: Springer.

Dunbar, R. I. M., & Spoor, M. (1995). Social networks, support cliques, and kinship. *Human Nature, 6,* 273–290.

Duncan, P., Ritter, P., Dornbusch, S., Gross, R., & Carlsmith, J. (1985). The effects of pubertal timing on body image, school behavior, and deviance. *Journal of Youth and Adolescence, 14,* 227–236.

Duncan, R., & Tarulli, D. (2009). On the persistence of private speech: Empirical and theoretical considerations. In A. Winsler, C. Fernyhough, & I. Montero, (Eds.), *Private speech, executive functioning, and the development of verbal self-regulation* (pp. 176–187). Cambridge, UK: Cambridge University Press.

Dunham, Y., Baron, A. S., & Banaji, M. R. (2006). From American city to Japanese village: A cross-cultural; investigation of implicit race attitudes. *Child Development, 77,* 1268–1281.

Dunham, Y., Baron, A. S., & Banaji, M. R. (2008). The development of implicit intergroup cognition. *Trends in Cognitive Science, 12,* 248–253.

Dunn, D. W., Austin J. K., Harezlak, J., & Ambrosius, W. T. (2003). ADHD and epilepsy in childhood. *Developmental Medicine and Child Neurology, 45,* 50–54.

Dunn, J. (2002). Sibling relationships. In P. K. Smith & C. H. Hart (Eds.), *Blackwell handbook of childhood social development* (pp. 223–237). Oxford, UK: Blackwell.

Dunn, J. (2005). Siblings and peers. In B. Hopkins (Ed.), *The Cambridge encyclopedia of child development* (pp. 374–377). New York: Cambridge University Press.

Dunn, J., Bretherton, I., & Munn, P. (1987). Conversations about feeling states between mothers and their young children. *Developmental Psychology, 23,* 132–139.

Dunn, J. Brown, J., & Beardsall, L. (1991). Family talk about feeling states and children's later understanding of other's emotions. *Developmental Psychology, 27,* 448–455.

Dunn, J., & Brown, J. (1994). Affect expression in the family, children's understanding of emotions, and their interactions with others. *Merrill-Palmer Quarterly, 40,* 123–137.

Dunn, J., Creps, C., & Brown, J. (1996). Children's family relationships between two and five: Developmental changes and individual differences. *Social Development, 5,* 230–250.

Dunn, J., & Cutting, A. (1999). Understanding others and individual differences in friendship interactions in young children. *Social Development, 8,* 201–219.

Dunn, J., & Kendrick, C. (1981). Interaction between young siblings: Association with the interaction between mother and firstborn child. *Developmental Psychology, 17,* 336–343.

Dunn, J., & Kendrick, C. (1982). *Siblings: Love, envy, and understanding.* Cambridge, MA: Harvard University Press.

Dunn, J., & Plomin, R. (1990). *Separate lives: Why siblings are so different.* New York: Basic Books.

Dupéré. V., Lacourse, E., Willms, J. D., Leventhal, T., & Tremblay, R. E. (2008). Neighborhood poverty and early transition to sexual activity in young adolescents: A developmental ecological approach. *Child Development, 79,* 1463–1476.

East, W. N. (1946). Sexual offenders. *Journal of Nervous and Mental Disease, 103,* 626–666.

Easterbrook, M. A., Kisilevsky, B. S., Hains, S. M. J., & Muir, D. W. (1999). Faceness or complexity: Evidence from newborn visual tracking of facelike stimuli. *Infant Behavior & Development, 22,* 17–35.

Eaton, W. O., & Von Bargen, D. (1981). Asynchronous development of gender understanding in preschool children. *Child Development, 52,* 1020–1027.

Eckenrode, J., Laird, M., & Doris, J. (1993). School performance and disciplinary problems among abused and neglected children. *Developmental Psychology, 29,* 53–62.

Eckerman, C. O., Davis, C. C., & Didow, S. M. (1989). Toddlers' emerging ways of achieving social coordinations with a peer. *Child Development, 60,* 440–453.

Eckerman, C. O., Whatley, J. L., & Kutz, S. L. (1975). Growth of social play with peers during the second year of life. *Developmental Psychology, 11,* 42–49.

Edwards C. P., & Whiting, B. B. (1988). *Children of different worlds.* Cambridge, MA: Harvard University Press.

Egan, S. K., & Perry, D. G. (2001). Gender identity: A multidimensional analysis with implications for psychosocial adjustment. *Developmental Psychology, 37,* 451–463.

Egeland, B., & Sroufe, L.A. (1981). Attachment and early maltreatment. *Child Development, 52,* 44–52.

Ehri, L. C. (1995). Phases of development in learning to read words by sight. *Journal of Research in Reading, 18,* 116–125.

Eibl-Eibesfeldt, I. (1970). *Ethology: The biology of behavior.* New York: Holt, Rhinehart & Winston.

Eibl-Eibesfeldt, I. (1989). *Human ethology.* New York: Aldine de Gruyter.

Eiduson, B. T., & Weisner, T. S. (1978). Alternative family styles: Effects on young children. In J. H. Stevens, Jr., & M. Matthews (Eds.), *Mother/father/child relationships* (pp. 197–221). Washington, DC: National Association for the Education of Young Children.

Eigsti, I-M., Zayas, V., Mischel, W., Shoda, Y., Ayduk, O., Dadlani, M. B., Davidson, M. C., Aber, J. L., & Casey, B. J. (2006). Predicting cognitive control from preschool to late adolescence and young adulthood. *Psychological Science, 17,* 478–484.

Eilers, R. W., Gavin, W. J., & Wilson, W. R. (1979). Linguistic experience and phonemic perception in infancy: A cross-linguistic study. *Child Development, 50,* 14–18.

Eimas, P. D., & Quinn, P. C. (1994). Studies on the formation of perceptually based basic-level categories in young infants. *Child Development, 65,* 903–917.

Eimas, P. D., Siqueland, E. R., Jusczyk, P., & Vigorito, J. (1971). Speech perception in infants. *Science, 71,* 303–306.

Einav, S., & Hood, B. (2008). Tell-tale eyes: Children's attribution of gaze aversion as a lying cue. *Developmental Psychology, 44,* 1655–1667.

Ein-Dor, T., Mikulincer, M., Doron, G., & Shaver, P. S. (2010). The attachment paradox: How can so many of us (the insecure ones) have no adaptive advantages? *Perspectives on Psychological Science, 5,* 123–141.

Einstein, G. O., & McDaniel, M. A. (2005). Prospective memory: Multiple retrieval processes. *Current Directions in Psychological Science, 14,* 286–290.

Eisenberg, A. (1985). Learning to describe past experiences in conversation. *Discourse Processes, 8,* 177–204.

Eisenberg, M. E., Olson, R. E., Newmark-Sztainer, D., Story, M., & Bearinger, L. H. (2004). Correlations between family meals and psychosocial well-being among adolescent girls. *Archives of Pediatric Adolescent Medicine, 158,* 792–796.

Eisenberg, N., & Fabes, R. A. (1998). Prosocial development. In W. Damon (Gen. Ed.), *Handbook of child psychology* (5th ed.). In N. Eisenberg (Vol. Ed.), Vol. 3: *Social emotional and personality development* (701–778). New York: Wiley.

Eisenberg, N., Fabes, R. A., Guthrie, I. K., & Reiser, M. (2000). Dispositional emotionality and regulation: Their role in predicting quality of social functioning. *Journal of Personality and Social Psychology, 78,* 136–157.

Eisenberg, N., Fabes, R. A., & Spinrad, T. L. (2006). Prosocial development. In W. Damon & R. M. Lerner (Gen. Eds.), *Handbook of child psychology* (6th ed.). In N. Eisenberg (Vol. Ed.), Vol. 3: *Social, emotional, and personality development* (pp. 646–718). New York: Wiley.

Eisenberg, N., & Spinrad, T. L. (2004). Emotion-related regulation: Sharpening the definition. *Child Development, 75,* 334–339.

Eisenberg, N., Wentzel, M., & Harris, J. D. (1998). The role of emotionality and regulation in empathy-related responding. *School Psychology Review, 27,* 506–521.

Ekman, P. (1995). Strong evidence for universals in facial expressions: A reply to Russell´s mistaken critique. *Psychological Bulletin, 115,* 268–287.

El-Sheikh, M., Buckhalt, J. A., Mize, J., & Acebo, C. (2006). Marital conflict and disruption of children's sleep. *Child Development, 77,* 31–43.

Elicker, J., Englund, M., & Sroufe, L. A. (1992). Predicting peer competence and peer relationships in childhood from early parent-child relationships. In R. D. Parke & G. W. Ladd (Eds.), *Family-peer relationships: Models of linkage* (pp. 77–106). Hillsdale, NJ: Erlbaum.

Elischberger, H. B. (2005). The effects of prior knowledge on children's memory and suggestibility. *Journal of Experimental Child Psychology, 92,* 247–275.

Elkind, D. (1967). Egocentrism in adolescence. *Child Development, 38,* 1025–1033.

Elkind, D. (1998). *Reinventing childhood: Raising and educating children in a changing world.* Rosemont, NJ: Modern Learning Press.

Elkind, D., & Bowen, R. (1979). Imaginary audience behavior in children and adolescents. *Developmental Psychology, 15,* 38–44.

Ellis, B. J. (2004). Timing of pubertal maturation in girls: An integrated life history approach. *Psychological Bulletin, 130,* 920–958.

Ellis, B. J., Bates, J. E., Dodge, K. A., Fergusson, D. M., Horwood, L. J., Pettit, G. S., & Woodward, L. (2003). Does father absence place daughters at special risk for early sexual activity and teenage pregnancy? *Child Development, 74,* 801–821.

Ellis, B. J., & Boyce, W. T. (2008). Biological sensitivity to context. *Current Directions in Psychological Science, 17,* 183–187.

Ellis, B. J., & Essex, M. J. (2007). Family environments, adrenarche, and sexual maturation: A longitudinal test of a life history model. *Child Development, 78,* 1799–1817.

Ellis, B. J., Essex, M. J., & Boyce, W. T. (2005). Biological sensitivity to context: II. Empirical explorations of an evolutionary–developmental theory *Development and Psychopathology, 17,* 303–328.

Ellis, B. J., & Graber, J. (2000). Psychosocial antecedents of variation in girls' pubertal timing: Maternal depression, stepfather presence, and marital and family stress. *Child Development, 71,* 485–501.

Ellis, B. J., Jackson, J. J., & Boyce, W. T. (2006). The stress response systems: Universality and adaptive individual differences. *Developmental Review, 26,* 175–212.

Ellis, B. J., McFadyen-Ketchum, S., Dodge, K. A., Pettit, G. S., & Bates, J. E. (1999). Quality of early family relationships and individual differences in the timing of pubertal maturation in girls: A longitudinal test of an evolutionary model. *Journal of Personality and Social Psychology, 77,* 387–401.

Ellis, H. (1915). *Studies in the psychology of sex.* Vol. 2: *Sexual inversion.* Philadelphia: Davis.

Ellis, L., Ames, A., Pekham, W., & Burke, D. (1988). Sexual orientation of human offspring may be altered by severe maternal stress during pregnancy. *The Journal of Sex Research, 25,* 152–157.

Ellis, L., Burke, D. M., & Ames, A. (1987). Sexual orientation measures as a continuous variable. *Archives of Sexual Behavior, 16,* 523–529.

Ellis, N. C., & Hennelley, R. A. (1980). A bilingual word-length effect: Implications for intelligence testing and the relative ease of mental calculation in Welsh and English. *British Journal of Psychology, 71,* 43–52.

Ellis, S., & Rogoff, B. (1982). The strategies and efficacy of child versus adult teachers. *Child Development, 43,* 730–735.

Elman, J. L., Bates, E. A., Johnson, M. H., Karmiloff-Smith, A., Parisi, D., & Plunket, K. (1996). *Rethinking innateness: A connectionist perspective on development.* Cambridge, MA: MIT Press.

Else-Quest, N. M., Hyde, J. S., Goldsmith, H. H., & Van Hulle, C. A. (2006). Gender differences in temperament: A meta-analysis. *Psychological Bulletin, 132,* 33–72.

Else-Quest, N. M., Hyde, J. S., & Linn, M. C. (2010). Cross-national patterns of gender differences in mathematics: A meta-analysis. *Psychological Bulletin, 136,* 103–127.

Eluvathingal, T. J., Chugani, H. T., Behen, M. E., Juhász, C., Muzik, O., Maqbool, M., Chugani, D. C., & Makki, M. (2006). Abnormal brain connectivity in children after early severe socioemotional deprivation: A diffusion tensor imaging study. *Pediatrics, 117,* 2093–2100.

Embry, D. D. (2002). The Good Behavior Game: A best practice candidate as a universal behavioral vaccine. *Clinical Child and Family Psychology Review, 5,* 273–297.

Emery, R. E., & Laumann-Billings, L. (1998). An overview of the nature, causes, and consequences of abusive family relationships. *American Family Psychology, 13,* 568–579.

Emlen, S. T. (1995). An evolutionary theory of the family. *Proceedings of the National Academy of Science (USA), 92,* 8092–8099.

Epstein, J. L., & Sanders, M. G. (2002). Family, school, and community partnerships. In M. H. Bornstein (Ed.), *Handbook of parenting* (2nd ed.), Vol. 5: *Practical issues in parenting* (pp. 407–437). Mahwah, NJ: Erlbaum.

Epstein, R. (2006). Do gays have a choice? *Scientific American Mind, 17,* 50–57.

Erath, S. A., El-Sheikh, M., & Cummings, E. M. (2009). Harsh parenting and child externalizing behavior: Skin conductance level reactivity as a moderator. *Child Development, 80,* 578–592.

Erikson, E. H. (1950). *Childhood and society.* New York: Norton.

Erikson, E. H. (1968). *Identity: Youth and crisis.* New York: Norton.

Eriksson, P. E., Perfilieva, E., Bjork-Eriksson, T., Albom, A. M., Nordborg, C., Peterson, D. A., & Gage, F. H. (1998). Neurogenesis in the adult human hippocampus. *Nature Medicine, 4,* 1313–1317.

Ernst, C., & Angst, J. (1983). *Birth order: Its influence on personality.* Berlin: Springer-Verlag.

Espelage, D. L., Holt, M. K., & Poteat, V. P. (2010). Individual and contextual influences on bullying: Perpetration and victimization. In, J. L. Meece & J. S. Eccles (Eds.), *Handbook of research on schools, schooling, and human development* (pp. 146–159). New York: Routledge.

Estivill, E., & De Béjar, S. (1996). *Duérmete niño* [Sleep my child]. Barcelona, Spain: Plaza y Janés.

Etienne, A. S. (1976/1977). L'etude comparative de la permanence de l'objet chez l'animal [Comparative study of object permanence in animals]. *Bulletin de Psychologie, 30,* 187–197.

Euler, H. A., & Weitzel, B. (1996). Discriminative grandparental solicitude as reproductive strategy. *Human Nature, 7,* 39–59.

Euler, H. A., & Michalski, R. L. (2007). Grandparental and extended kin relationships. In C. S. Salmon and T. K. Shackelford (Eds.), *Family relationships: An evolutionary perspective* (pp. 39–68). New York: Oxford University Press.

Evans, G. W., Gonnella, C., Marcynyszyn, L. A., Gentile, L., & Salpekar, N. (2005). The role of chaos in poverty and children's socioemotional adjustment. *Psychological Science, 16,* 560–565.

Evans, G. W., & Kim, P. (2007). Childhood poverty and health: Cumulative risk exposure and stress dysregulation. *Psychological Science, 18,* 953–957.

Evans, M. A. (1985). Self-initiated speech repairs: A reflection of communicative monitoring in young children. *Developmental Psychology, 21,* 365–371.

Evans, M. E. (2001). Cognitive and contextual factors in the emergence of diverse belief systems: Creation versus evolution. *Cognitive Psychology, 42,* 217–266.

Evans, N., & Levinson, S. (2009). The myth of language universals: Language diversity and its importance for cognitive science. *Behavioral and Brain Science, 32,* 429–492.

Fabes, R. A., Fultz, J., Eisenberg, N., May-Plumlee, T., & Christopher, F. S. (1989). Effects of rewards on children's prosocial motivation: A socialization study. *Developmental Psychology, 25,* 509–515.

Fabes, R. A., Hanish, L. D., & Martin, C. L. (2003). Children at play: The role of peers in understanding the effects of child care. *Child Development, 74,* 1039–1043.

Fagan, J. F., III. (1974). Infant recognition memory: The effects of length of familiarization and type of discrimination task. *Child Development, 45,* 351–356.

Fagan, J. F., III. (1992). Intelligence: A theoretical viewpoint. *Current Directions in Psychological Science, 1,* 82–86.

Fagan, J., Prigot, J., Carroll, M., Pioli, L., Stein, A., & Franco, A. (1997). Auditory context and memory retrieval in young infants. *Developmental Psychology, 68,* 1057–1066.

Fagan, J. F., III, & Singer, J. T. (1983). Infant recognition memory as a measure of intelligence. In L. P. Lipsitt & C. K. Rovee-Collier (Eds.), *Advances in infancy research* (Vol. 2). Norwood, NJ: Ablex.

Fagen, R. (1981). *Animal play behavior.* New York: Oxford University Press.

Fagot, B. I., Leinbach, M. D., & Hagan, R. (1986). Gender labeling and the adoption of sex-typed behaviors. *Developmental Psychology, 22,* 440–443.

Fantz, R. L. (1958). Pattern vision in young infants. *Psychological Record, 8,* 43–47.

Fantz, R. L. (1961). The origin of form perception. *Scientific American, 204,* 66–72.

Farah, M. J., Levinson, K. L., & Klein, K. L. (1995). Face perception and within-category discrimination in prosopagnosia. *Neuropsychologia, 33,* 661–674.

Farroni, T., Mansfield, E. M. Lai, C., & Johnson M. H., (2003). Motion and mutual gaze in directing infants' spatial attention. *Journal Experimental Child Psychology, 85,* 199–212.

Farroni, T., Csibra, G., Simion, F., & Johnson, M. H. (2002). Eye contact detection in humans from birth. *Proceedings of the National Academy of Science (USA), 99,* 9602–9605.

Farroni, T., Johnson, M. H., & Csibra, G. (2004). Mechanisms of eye gaze perception during Infancy. *Journal of Cognitive Neuroscience, 16,* 1320–1326.

Farroni, T., Menon, E., & Johnson, M. H. (2006). Factors influencing newborns' preferences for faces with eye contact. *Journal of Experimental Child Psychology, 96,* 298–308.

Fearon, R. P., Bakermans-Kranenburg, M. J., Lapsley, A-M., & Roisman, G. I. (2010). The significance of insecure attachment and disorganization in the development of children's externalizing behavior: A meta-analytic study. *Child Development, 81,* 435–456.

Federal Interagency Forum on Child and Family Statistics. (2005). *America's Children, Key National Indicators of Well-Being.* Washington, DC: U.S. Government.

Federal Interagency Forum on Child and Family Statistic (2008). *America's children in brief: Key national indicators of well being.* Washington, DC: U.S. Government.

Feigenson, L., Carey, S., & Hauser, M. (2002). The representations underlying infants' choice of more: Object files versus analog magnitudes. *Psychological Science, 13,* 150–156.

Feijoo, A. N. (2001). *Adolescent sexual health in Europe and the US: Why the difference?* (2nd ed.). Washington, DC: Advocates for Youth.

Fein, G. (1981). Pretend play: An integrative review. *Child Development, 52,* 1095–1118.

Feinberg, I. (1982/83). Schizophrenia: Caused by a fault in programmed synaptic elimination during adolescence? *Journal of Psychiatric Research, 4,* 319–334.

Feiring, C., & Taska, L. S. (1996). Family self-concept: Ideas on its meaning. In B. Bracken (Ed.), *Handbook of self-concept* (pp. 317–373). New York: Wiley.

Feldman, D. H. (1991). *Nature's gambit: Child prodigies and the development of human potential.* New York: Teachers College Press.

Feldman, D. H. (with L. T. Goldsmith). (1993). Child prodigies: A distinctive form of giftedness. *Gifted Child Quarterly, 37,* 188–193.

Feldman, R. (2007). Parent-infant synchrony. *Current Directions in Psychological Science, 16,* 340–345.

Feldman, R. (2009). The development of regulatory functions from birth to 5 years: Insights from premature infants. *Child Development, 80,* 544–561.

Feldman, R., & Eidelman, A. I. (2003). Direct and indirect effects of breast milk on the neurobehavioral and cognitive development of premature infants. *Developmental Psychobiology, 43,* 109–119.

Feldman, R. S., Jenkins, L., & Popoola, O. (1979). Detection of deception in adults and children via facial expressions. *Child Development, 50,* 350–355.

Feldman, R. Weller, A., Zagoory-Sharon, O., & Levine, A. (2007). Evidence for a neuroendocrinological foundation of human affiliation: Plasma oxytocin levels across pregnancy and the postpartum period predict mother-infant bonding. *Psychological Science, 18,* 965–970.

Feldman, R., & Eidelman, A. I. (2004). Parent–infant synchrony and the social–emotional development of triplets. *Developmental Psychology, 40,* 1133–1147.

Feldman, S. S., Turner, R. A., & Araujo, K. (1999). Interpersonal context as an influence on sexual timetables of youths: Gender and ethnic effects. *Journal of Research on Adolescence, 9,* 25–52.

Fennell, E. B., Satz, P., & Morris, R. (1983). The development of handedness and dichotic ear listening asymmetries in relation to school achievement: A longitudinal study. *Journal of Experimental Child Psychology, 35,* 248–262.

Fenzel, L. M. (1994). A prospective analysis of the influence of parents' behaviors and values on the adjustment of African-American middle school students. *Research in Middle Level Education, 17,* 1–11.

Fergusson, D. M., Horwood, L. J., & Lynskey, M. (1994). The childhood of multiple-problem adolescents: A 15-year longitudinal study. *Journal of Child Psychology and Psychiatry, 35,* 1123–1140.

Fernald, A. (1992). Human maternal vocalizations to infants as biologically relevant signals: An evolutionary perspective. In J. H. Barkow, L. Cosmides, & J. Tooby (Eds.), *The adaptive mind: Evolutionary psychology and the generation of culture* (pp. 391–428). New York: Oxford University Press.

Fernandez, O., Sabharwal, M., Smiley, T., Pastuszak, A., Koren, G., & Einarson, T. (1998). Moderate to heavy caffeine consumption during pregnancy and relationship to spontaneous abortion and abnormal fetal growth: A metaanalysis. *Reproductive Toxicology, 12,* 435–444.

Ferrari, P. F., Visalberghi, E., Paukner, A., Fogassi, L., Ruggiero, A., et al. (2006). Neonatal imitation in rhesus macaques. *PLoS Biology, 4* (9), e302.

Ferreiro, E., & Teberosky, A. (1982). *Literacy before schooling.* Portsmouth, NH: Heinemann.

Field, T. (1995). Infants of depressed mothers. *Infant Behavior and Development, 18,* 1–13.

Field, T., Diego, M., Dieter, J., Hernandez-Reif, M., Schanberg, S., Kuhn, C., Yando. R., & Bendell, D. (2004). Prenatal depression effects on the fetus and the newborn. *Infant Behavior & Development, 27,* 216–229.

Field, T. M., Healy, B., Goldstein, S., Perry, S., Bendell, D., Schanberg, S., Zimmerman, E. A., & Kuhn, C. (1988). Infants of depressed mothers show "depressed" behavior even with nondepressed adults. *Child Development, 59,* 1569–1579.

Field, T. M., Woodson, R., Greenberg, R., & Cohen, D. (1982). Discrimination and imitation of facial expression by neonates. *Science, 218,* 179–181.

Fifer, W. P. (2005). Normal and abnormal prenatal development. In B. Hopkins (Ed.), *The Cambridge encyclopedia of child development* (pp. 173–192). New York: Cambridge University Press.

Figueredo, A. J., Vásquez, G., Brumbach, B. H., Schneider, S. M. R., Sefcek, J. A., Tal, I. R., Hill, D., Wenner, C. J., & Jacobs, W. J. (2006). Consilience and life history theory: From genes to brain to reproductive strategy. *Developmental Review, 26,* 243–275.

Finkelhor, D. (1979). *Sexually victimized children.* New York: Free Press.

Finkelhor, D., & Jones, L. M. (2004). Explanations for the decline in child sexual abuse cases (*Juvenile Justice Bulletin* No. NC199298). Washington, DC: Office of Juvenile Justice and Delinquency Prevention.

Finkelstein, N. W., & Ramey, C. T. (1977). Learning to control the environment in infancy. *Child Development, 48,* 806–819.

Finkelstein, N. W., Dent, C., Gallagher, K., & Ramey, C. T. (1978). Social behavior of infants and toddlers in a daycare environment. *Developmental Psychology, 14,* 257–262.

Finkenhauer, C., Engels, R. C. M. E., Meeus, W., & Oosterwegel, A. (2002). Self and identity in early adolescence: The pains and gains of knowing who and what you are. In T. M. Brinthaupt & R. P. Lipka (Eds.), *Understanding early adolescent self and identity: Applications and interventions* (pp. 25–56). Albany, NY: SUNY Press.

Firth, R. (1936). *We, the Tikopia.* London: Allen & Unwin.

Fischer, K. W. (1980). A theory of cognitive development: The control and construction of hierarchies of skills. *Psychological Review, 87,* 477–531.

Fischer, N. L. (2005). The more things change . . . The Kinsey Institute on child sexuality [Review of the book *Sexual development in childhood* edited by J. Bancroft]. *Journal of Sex Research, 42,* 271–273.

Fisher, H. (2000). Lust, attraction, attachment: Biology and evolution of the three primary emotion systems for mating, reproduction, and parenting. *Journal of Sex Education and Therapy, 25,* 96–104.

Fisher, H. (2004). *Why we love: The nature and chemistry of romantic love.* New York: Holt.

Fisher, S. E. (2005). Dissection of molecular mechanisms underlying speech and language disorders. *Applied Psycholinguistics, 26,* 111–128.

Fitzpatrick, L. A. (2004). Sex-differences in skeletal development. In V. M. Miller, & M. Hay (Eds.), *Advances in molecular and cell biology: Principles of sex-based differences.* New York: Elsevier.

Fivush, R. (1988). The functions of event memory: Some comments on Nelson and Barsalou. In U. Neisser & E. Winograd (Eds.), *Remembering reconsidered: Ecological and traditional approaches to the study of memory*. New York: Cambridge University Press.

Fivush, R. (2008). Remembering and reminiscing: How individual lives are constructed in family narratives. *Memory Studies, 1*, 49–58.

Fivush, R., Haden, C. A., & Reese, E. (2006). Elaborating on elaborations: Role of maternal reminiscing style in cognitive and socioemotional development. *Child Development, 77*, 1568–1588.

Fivush, R., & Hamond, N. R. (1990). Autobiographical memory across the preschool years: Toward reconceptualizing childhood amnesia. In R. Fivush & J. A. Hudson (Eds.), *Knowing and remembering in young children*. Cambridge, UK: Cambridge University Press.

Fivush, R., Kuebli, J., & Clubb, P. A. (1992). The structure of events and event representations: A developmental analysis. *Child Development, 63*, 188–201.

Fivush, R., McDermott Sales, J., Goldberg, A., Bahrick, L., & Parker, J. (2004). Weathering the storm: Children's long-term recall of Hurricane Andrew. *Memory, 12*, 104–118.

Flavell, J. H. (1963). *The developmental psychology of Jean Piaget*. Princeton, NJ: D. Van Nostrand.

Flavell, J. H. (1970). Developmental studies of mediated memory. In H. W. Reese & L. P. (Eds.), *Advances in child development and child behavior* (Vol. 5). New York: Academic Press.

Flavell, J. H. (1978). Developmental stage: Explanans or explanandum? *Behavioral and Brain Sciences, 2*, 187.

Flavell, J. H., Beach, D. R., & Chinsky, J. H. (1966). Spontaneous verbal rehearsal in a memory task as a function of age. *Child Development, 37*, 283–299.

Flavell, J. H., Everett, B. A., Croft, K., & Flavell, E. (1981). Young children's knowledge about visual perception: Further evidence for level 1–level 2 distinction. *Developmental Psychology, 17*, 99–107.

Flavell, J. H., Green, F. L., & Flavell, E. R. (1986). Development of knowledge about the appearance-reality distinction. *Monographs of the Society for Research in Child Development*, (Serial No. 212).

Flavell, J. H., Green, F. L., & Flavell, E. R. (1995). The development of children's knowledge about attentional focus. *Developmental Psychology, 31*, 706–712.

Flavell, J. H., Green, F. L., & Flavell, E. R. (2000). Development of children's awareness of their own thoughts. *Journal of Cognition and Development, 1*, 97–122.

Flavell, J. H., Green, F. L., Flavell, E. R., & Grossman, J. B. (1997). The development of children's knowledge about inner speech. *Developmental Psychology, 68*, 39–47.

Flavell, J. H., Miller, P. H., & Miller, S. A. (2002). *Cognitive development* (4th ed.). Upper Saddle River, NJ: Prentice-Hall.

Flaxman, S. M., & Sherman, P. W. (2000). Morning sickness: A mechanism for protecting mother and embryo. *Quarterly Review of Biology, 75*, 113–148.

Fleming, A. S., Ruble, D., Krieger, H., & Wong, P. Y. (1997). Hormonal and experiential correlates of maternal responsiveness during pregnancy and the puerperium in human mothers. *Hormones and Behavior, 31*, 145–158.

Fleming, A. S., Steiner, M., & Corter, C. (1997). Cortisol, hedonics, and maternal responsiveness in human mothers. *Hormones and Behavior, 32*, 85–98.

Flinn, M. V. (1988). Step and genetic parent/offspring relationships in a Caribbean village. *Ethology and Sociobiology, 9*, 335–369.

Flinn, M. V. (2006). Evolution and ontogeny of stress response to social challenges in the human child. *Developmental Review, 26*, 138–174.

Flinn, M. V., & England, B. G. (2003). Childhood stress: Endocrine and immune responses to psychosocial events. In J. M. Wilce (Ed.), *Social & cultural lives of immune systems* (pp. 107–147). London: Routledge Press.

Flinn, M. V., Geary, D. C., & Ward, C. V. (2005). Ecological dominance, social competition, and coalitionary arms races: Why humans evolved extraordinary intelligence. *Evolution and Human Behavior, 26*, 10–46.

Flinn, M. V., Ward, C. V., & Noone, R. J. (2005). Hormones and the family. In D. M. Buss (Ed.), *The handbook of evolutionary psychology* (pp. 552–580). New York: Wiley.

Flynn, E., O'Malley, C., & Wood, D. (2004). A longitudinal, microgenetic study of the emergence of false belief understanding and inhibition skills. *Developmental Science, 7*, 103–115.

Flynn, J. R. (1987). Massive IQ gains in 14 nations: What IQ tests really measure. *Psychological Bulletin, 101*, 171–191.

Flynn, J. R. (1999), Searching for justice: The discovery of IQ gains over time. *American Psychologist, 54*, 5–20.

Flynn, J. R. (2007). *What is intelligence? Beyond the Flynn Effect*. New York: Cambridge University Press.

Fogel, A. (1997). *Infancy: Infant, family, and society* (3rd ed.). St. Paul, MN: West Publishing Company.

Foley, D. L., Eaves, L. J., Wormley, B., Silberg, J., Maes, H., Kuhn, J., et al., (2004). Childhood adversity, monoamine oxidase A genotype, and risk for conduct disorder. *Archives of General Psychiatry, 61*, 738–744.

Foley, M. A., & Ratner, H. H. (1998). Distinguishing between memories for thoughts and deeds: The role of prospective processing in children's source monitoring. *British Journal of Developmental Psychology, 16*, 465–484.

Foley, M. A., Ratner, H. H., & Passalacqua, C. (1993). Appropriating the actions of another: Implications for children's memory and learning. *Cognitive Development, 8*, 373–401.

Fomon, S. J., & Nelson, S. E. (2002). Body composition of the male and female reference infants. *Annual Review of Nutrition, 22*, 1–17.

Fong, V. L. (2004). *Only hope: Coming of age under China's One-Child Policy*. Stanford, CA: Stanford University Press.

Ford, C. S., & Beach, F. A. (1951). *Patterns of sexual behavior*. New York: Harper & Row.

Forhan, S. E., Gottlieb, S. L., Sternberg, M. R., Xu, F., Deblina Datta, S., Berman, S., &. Markowitz, L. E. (March 2008). *Prevalence of sexually transmitted infections and bacterial vaginosis among female adolescents in the United States: Data from the National Health and Nutrition Examination Survey (NHANES) 2003–2004.* Paper presented at meeting of National STD Prevention Conference, Chicago, Illinois.

Foster, E. M., & Watkins, S. (2010). The value of reanalysis: TV viewing and attention problems. *Child Development, 81*, 368–375.

Fowler, A., Gelman, R., & Gleitman, L. (1994). The course of language learning in children with Down syndrome. In H. Tager-Flusberg (Ed.), *Constraints on language acquisition: Studies of atypical populations*. Hillsdale, NJ: Lawrence Erlbaum Associates.

Fox, N., & Stifter, C. A. (2005). Emotional development. In B. Hopkins (Ed.), *The Cambridge encyclopedia of child development* (pp. 234–241). Cambridge, UK: Cambridge University Press.

Fox, S. E., Levitt, P., & Nelson, C. A., III (2010). How timing and quality of early experience influence the development of brain architecture. *Child Development, 81*, 28–40.

Fraley, R. C., & Spieker, S. J. (2003). Are infant attachment patterns continuously or categorically distributed? A taxometric analysis of Strange Situation behavior. *Developmental Psychology, 39*, 387–404.

Francks, C. et al. (2007). LRRTM1 on chromosome 2p12 is a maternally suppressed gene that is associated paternally with handedness and schizophrenia. *Molecular Psychiatry, 2*, 786–792.

Frankenburg, W. K., & Dodds, J. B. (1967). The Denver developmental screening test. *Journal of Pediatrics, 71*, 181–191.

Frankenburg, W. K., Fandal, A. W., Sciarillo, W., & Burgess, D. (1981). The newly abbreviated and revised Denver Developmental Screening Test. *Journal of Pediatrics, 99*, 995–999.

Fredriksen, K., Rhodes, J., Reddy, R., & Way, N. (2004). Sleepless in Chicago: Tracking the effects of adolescent sleep loss during the middle school years. *Child Development, 75*, 84–95.

Freeman, N. H., & Janikoun, R. (1972). Intellectual realism in children's drawings of a familiar object with distinctive features, *Child Development, 43*, 1116–1121.

Freeman, R. D., Groenveld, M., & Kozak, F. K. (2005). Hearing disorders. In B. Hopkins (Ed.), *The Cambridge encyclopedia of child development* (pp. 437–441). New York: Cambridge University Press.

French, S. A., Story, M., & Jeffrey, R. W. (2001). Environmental influences on eating and physical activity. *Annual Review of Public Health, 22,* 309–335.

Freud, S. (1952). *Totem and taboo.* (James Strachey, trans.). New York: Norton.

Freud, S. (1963). Three essays on the theory of sexuality. In J. Strachey (Ed. and Trans.), *The standard edition of the complete psychological works of Sigmund Freud* (Vol. 7). London: Hogarth.

Fried, P. A., & Smith, A. M. (2001). A literature review of the consequences of prenatal marijuana exposure: An emerging theme of a deficiency in executive function. *Neurotoxicology and Teratology, 23,* 1–11.

Friedman, H. S., Tucker, J., Schwartz, J. E., Martin, L. R., Tomlinson-Keasey, C., Wingard, D., & Criqui, M. (1995). Childhood conscientiousness and longevity: Health behaviors and cause of death. *Journal of Personality and Social Psychology, 68,* 696–703.

Friedman, N. P., Miyake, A., Young, S. E., DeFries, J. C., Corley, R. P., & Hewitt, J. K. (2008). Individual differences in executive functions are almost entirely genetic in origin. *Journal of Experimental Psychology: General, 137,* 201–225.

Friedman, S. (1972). Habituation and recovery of visual response in the alert human newborn. *Journal of Experimental Child Psychology, 13,* 339–349.

Friedrich, L. K., & Stein, A. H. (1973). Aggressive and prosocial television programs and the natural behavior of preschool children. *Monographs of the Society for Research in Child Development, 38* (Serial No. 151).

Friedrich, W. N., & Trane, S. T. (2002) Sexual behavior in children across multiple settings. *Child Abuse & Neglect, 26,* 243–245.

Friedrich, W. N., & Grambsch, P. (1992). Child sexual behavior inventory: Normative and clinical comparisons. *Psychological Assessment, 4,* 303–311.

Friedrich, W. N., Fisher, J., Broughton, D., Houston, M., & Shafran, C. R. (1998). Normative sexual behavior in children: A contemporary sample. *Pediatrics, 101,* 1–8.

Friedrich, W. N., Fisher, J., Dittner, C., Acton, R., Berliner, L., Butler, I. et al. (2001). Child behavior inventory: Normative, psychiatric, and sexual abuse comparisons. *Child Maltreatment, 6,* 37–49.

Friedrich, W. N., Grambsch, P., Broughton, D., Kuiper, J., & Beilke, R. (1991). Normative sexual behavior in children. *Pediatrics, 88,* 456–464.

Frith, C. D., & Frith, U. (1999). Interacting minds: A biological basis. *Science, 286* (5539), 2470–2473.

Frodi, A. M., & Lamb, M. E. (1980). Child abusers' responses to infant smiles and cries. *Child Development, 51,* 238–241.

Fry, A., & Hale, S. (2000). Relationships among processing speed, working memory and fluid intelligence in children. *Biological Psychology, 54,* 1–34.

Fu, G., & Lee, K. (2007). Social grooming in the kindergarten: The emergence of flattery behavior. *Developmental Science, 10,* 255–265.

Fu, G., Evans, A. D., Wang, L., & Lee, K. (2008). Lying in the name of the collective good: A developmental study. *Developmental Science, 11,* 495–503.

Fujisawa, K. K., Kutsukake, N., & Hasegawa, T. (2005). Reconciliation pattern after aggression among Japanese preschool children. *Aggressive Behavior, 31,* 138–152.

Fuligni, A. J., & Stevenson, H. W. (1995). Time use and mathematics achievement among American, Chinese, and Japanese high school students. *Child Development, 66,* 830–842.

Fullard, W., & Reiling, A. M. (1976). An investigation of Lorenz's "babyness." *Child Development, 47,* 1191–1193.

Furlow, F. B. (1996). Human neonatal cry quality as an honest sign of fitness. *Evolution and Human Behavior, 18,* 175–193.

Furman, L. N., & Walden, T. A. (1990). Effects of script knowledge on preschool children's communicative interactions. *Developmental Psychology, 26,* 227–233.

Furman, W. (2002). The emerging field of adolescent romantic relationships. *Current Directions in Psychological Sciences, 11,* 177–180.

Furman, W., & Buhrmester, D. (1985). Children's perception of the personal relationships in their social networks, *Developmental Psychology, 21,* 1016–1024.

Furman, W., & Collins, W. A. (2009). Adolescent romantic relationships and experiences. In K. H. Rubin, W. M. Bukowski, & B. Laursen (Eds.) *Handbook of peer interactions, relationships, and groups* (pp. 341–360). New York: Guilford.

Furth, H. G. (1964) Research with the deaf: Implications for language and cognition. *Psychological Bulletin, 62,* 251–267.

Gagne, S. S. (2001). Toxoplasmosis. *Primary Care Update in Obstetrics and Gynecology, 8,* 122–126.

Galbraith, R. C. (1982). Sibling spacing and intellectual development: A closer look at the confluence model. *Developmental Psychology, 18,* 151–173.

Galik, K., Senut, B., Pickford, M., Gommery, D., Treil, J., Kuperavage, A. J., & Eckhardt, R. B. (2004). External and internal morphology of the BAR 1002'00 *Orrorin tugenensis* femur. *Science, 305* (3 Sept.), 1450–1454.

Gallay, M., Baudouin, J-Y., Durand, K., Lemoine, C., & Lécuyer, R. (2006). Qualitative difference in the exploration of upright and upside-down faces in four-month-old infants: An eye-movement study. *Child Development, 77,* 984–996.

Gallup, G. G., Jr. (1979). Self-recognition in chimpanzees and man: A developmental and comparative perspective. In M. Lewis & L. A. Rosenblum (Eds.), *Genesis of behavior.* Vol. 2: *The child and its family.* New York: Plenum.

Galsworthy, M. J., Dionne, G., Dale, P. S., & Plomin, R. (2000). Sex differences in early verbal and non-verbal cognitive development. *Developmental Science, 3,* 206–215.

Ganger, J., & Brent, M. R. (2004). Reexamining the vocabulary spurt. *Developmental Psychology, 40,* 621–632.

Gangestad, S. W., & Thornhill, R. (1997). Human sexual selection and developmental stability. In J. A. Simpson & D. T. Kenrick (Eds.), *Evolutionary social psychology* (pp. 169–195). Mahwah, NJ: Erlbaum.

Garbarino, J., & deLara , E. (2003). *And words can hurt forever: How to protect adolescents from bullying, harassment, and emotional violence.* New York: Free Press.

Garber, H. L., & Heber, R. (1981). The efficacy of early intervention with family rehabilitation. In E. M. Hetherington & R. D. Parke (Eds.), *Contemporary readings in child psychology* (2nd ed.). New York: McGraw-Hill.

García Coll, C., Patcher, L. M. (2002). Ethnic and minority parenting. In M. Bornstein (Ed.), *Handbook of parenting: Social conditioning and applied parenting* (pp 1–20), Mahwah, NJ.

Garcia, M. M., Shaw, D. S., Winslow, E. B., & Yaggi, K. E. (2000). Destructive sibling conflict and the development of conduct problems in young boys. *Developmental Psychology, 36,* 44–53.

Garciaguirre, J. S., Adolph, K. E., & Shrout, P. E. (2007). Baby carriage: Infants walking with loads. *Child Development, 78,* 664–680.

Gardiner, A. K., Gray, S. K., & Bjorklund, D. F. (April, 2009). *Two- and three-year-olds judge tool functionality more accurately after tool-use observation than haptic experience.* Poster presented at the biannual meeting of the Society for Research in Child Development, Denver, Colorado.

Gardiner, A., Greif, M., & Bjorklund, D. F. (2011). Guided by intention: Preschoolers' imitation reflects inferences of causation. *Journal of Cognition and Development.*

Gardner, H. (1980). *Artful scribbles: The significance of children´s drawings.* New York: Basic Books.

Gardner, H. (1983). *Frames of mind: The theory of multiple intelligences.* New York: Basic.

Gardner, H. (1999). Are there additional intelligences? The case for naturalist, spiritual, and existential intelligences. In J. Kane (Ed.), *Education, information and transformation.* Engelwood Cliffs, NJ: Prentice-Hall.

Gardner, M., & Steinberg, L. (2004). Peer influence on risk taking, risk preference, and risky decision making in adolescence and adulthood: An experimental study. *Developmental Psychology, 41,* 625–635.

Gardner, M., & Steinberg, L. (2005). Peer influence on risk taking, risk preference, and risky decision making in adolescence and adulthood: An experimental study. *Developmental Psychology, 41,* 625–635.

Gareil, J. D. (1998). Cognitive neuroscience of human memory. *Annual Review of Psychology, 49,* 87–115.

Garnham, W. A., & Ruffman, T. (2001). Doesn't see, doesn't know: Is anticipatory looking really related to understanding belief? *Developmental Science, 4,* 94–100.

Garon, N., Bryson, S. E., & Smith, I. M. (2008). Executive function in preschoolers: A review using an integrative framework. *Psychological Bulletin, 134,* 31–60.

Gates, G. J., Badgett, M. V. L., Macomber, J. E., & Chambers, K. (2007). *Adoption and foster care by gay and lesbian parents in the United States.* Washington, DC: Urban Institute.

Gathercole, S. E., Alloway, T. P., Willis, C., & Adams, A-M. (2006). Working memory in children with reading disabilities. *Journal of Experimental Child Psychology, 93,* 265–281.

Gathercole, V. C. M. (2002). Grammatical gender in bilingual and monolingual children: A Spanish morphosyntactic distinction. In D. Kimbrough Oller & R. E. Eilers (Eds.), *Language and literacy in bilingual children.* (pp. 207–219). Cleveland, OH: Multilingual Matters Limited.

Gaultney, J. F., Bjorklund, D. F., & Goldstein, D. (1996). To be young, gifted, and strategic: Advantages for memory performance. *Journal of Experimental Child Psychology, 61,* 43–66.

Gauvain, M. (2001). *The social context of cognitive development.* New York: Guilford.

Gauvain, M. (2009). Social and cultural transactions in cognitive development: A cross-generational view. In Sameroff, A. (Ed.), *The transactional model of development: How children and contexts shape each other* (pp. 163–182). Washington, DC: American Psychological Association.

Gauvain, M. (2011). Sociocultural contexts of development In P. D. Zelazo (Ed.), *Oxford handbook of developmental psychology.* Oxford, UK: Oxford University Press.

Gava, L., Valenza, E., Turati, C., & de Schonen, S. (2008). Effect of partial occlusion on newborns' face preference and recognition. *Developmental Science, 11,* 563–574.

Gavin, L. A., & Furman, W. (1989). Age differences in adolescents' perceptions of their peer groups. *Developmental Psychology, 25,* 827–834.

Ge, X., Brody, G. H., Conger, R. D., Simons, R. L., & Murry, V. (2002). Contextual amplification of pubertal transition effects on deviant peer affiliation and externalizing behavior among African American children. *Developmental Psychology, 38,* 42–54.

Geary, D. C. (1993). Mathematical disabilities: Cognitive, neuropsychological, and genetic components. *Psychological Bulletin, 114,* 345–362.

Geary, D. C. (1995). Reflections of evolution and culture in children's cognition: Implications for mathematical development and instruction. *American Psychologist, 50,* 24–37.

Geary, D. C. (2005a). *The origin of mind: Evolution of brain, cognition, and general intelligence.* Washington, DC: American Psychological Association.

Geary, D. C. (2005b). Evolution and cognitive development. In R. L. Burgess & K. MacDonald (Eds.), *Evolutionary perspectives on human development* (pp. 99–133). Thousand Oaks, CA: Sage.

Geary, D. C. (2005c). Evolution of paternal investment. In D. M. Buss (Ed.), *The handbook of evolutionary psychology* (pp. 483–505). New York: Wiley.

Geary, D. C. (2007a). Educating the evolved mind: Conceptual foundations for an evolutionary educational psychology. In J. S. Carlson & J. R. Levin (Eds.), *Educating the evolved mind: Conceptual foundations for an evolutionary educational psychology* (pp. 1–99). Charlotte, NC: Information Age Publishing.

Geary, D. C. (2007b). Evolution of fatherhood. In C. Solomon & T. K. Shackelford (Eds.), *Family relationships: Evolutionary perspectives.* New York: Oxford University Press.

Geary, D. C. (2009). *Male, female: The evolution of human sex differences* (2nd ed.). Washington, DC: American Psychological Association.

Geary, D. C., & Bjorklund, D. F. (2000). Evolutionary developmental psychology. *Child Development, 71,* 57–65.

Geary, D. C., Bow-Thomas, C. C., Fan, L., & Siegler, R. S. (1993). Even before formal instructions. Chinese children outperform American children in mental arithmetic. *Cognitive Development, 8,* 517–529.

Geary, D. C., Bow-Thomas, C. C., Liu, F., & Siegler, R. S. (1996). Development of arithmetic competencies in Chinese and American children: Influence of age, language, and schooling. *Child Development, 67,* 2022–2044.

Geary, D. C., & Brown, S. C. (1991). Cognitive addition: Strategy choice and speed-of-processing differences in gifted, normal and mathematically disabled children. *Developmental Psychology, 27,* 398–406.

Geary, D. C., Brown, S. C., & Samaranayake, V. A. (1991). Cognitive addition: A short longitudinal study of strategy choice and speed of processing differences in normal and mathematically disabled children. *Developmental Psychology, 27,* 787–797.

Geary, D. C., Fan, L., & Bow-Thomas, C. C. (1992). Numerical cognition: Loci of ability differences comparing children from China and the United States. *Psychological Science, 3,* 180–185.

Gelman, R. (1969). Conservation acquisition: A problem of learning to attend to relevant attributes. *Journal of Experimental Child Psychology, 7,* 167–187.

Gelman, R., & Williams, E. M. (1998). Enabling constraints for cognitive development and learning: Domain-specificity and epigenesis. In W. Damon (Gen. Ed.), *Handbook of child psychology* (5th ed.). In D. Kuhn & R. S. Siegler (Vol. Eds.), Vol. 2: *Cognition, perception, and language* (pp. 575–630). New York: Wiley.

Genereux, R., & McKeough, A. (2007). Developing narrative interpretation: Structural and content analyses. *British Journal of Educational Psychology, 77,* 849–872.

Genesee, F. (2003). Rethinking bilingual acquisition. In J. M. deWaele (Ed.), *Bilingualism: Challenges and directions for future research* (pp. 158–182). Clevedon, UK: Multilingual Matters.

Gentile, D. (2009). Pathological video-game use among youth ages 8 to 18. *Psychological Science, 20,* 594–602.

German, T., & Johnson, S. (2002). Function and the origins of the design stance. *Journal of Cognition and Development, 3,* 279–300.

Gershoff, E. T. (2002). Parental corporal punishment and associated child behaviors and experiences: A meta-analytic and theoretical review. *Psychological Bulletin, 128,* 539–579.

Gesell, A. (1933). Maturation and the patterns of behavior. In C. Murchison (Ed.), *Handbook of child psychology* (2nd ed., rev., pp. 209–235). Worcester, MA: Clark University Press.

Gesell, A., & Amatruda, C. (1954). *Developmental diagnosis.* New York: Paul B. Holber.

Ghetti, S. (2008). Rejection of false events in childhood: A metamemory account. *Current Directions in Psychological Science, 17,* 16–20.

Ghim, H. R. (1990). Evidence for perceptual organization in infants: Perception of subjective contours by young infants. *Infant Behavior and Development, 13,* 221–248.

Gibbons, A. (2008). The birth of childhood. *Science, 322* (14 November), 1040–1043.

Gibbs, J. C. (2006). Should Kohlberg's cognitive developmental approach to morality be replaced with a more pragmatic approach? Comment on Krebs and Denton (2005). *Psychological Review, 113,* 666–671.

Gibbs, J. C., Basinger, K. S., Grime, R. L., & Snarey, J. R. (2007). Moral judgment development across cultures: Revisiting Kohlberg's universality claim. *Developmental Review, 27,* 443–500.

Gibson, E. J., & Walker, A. S. (1984). Development of knowledge of visual-tactual affordances of substance. *Child Development, 55,* 453–460.

Gibson, K. (2009). Differential parental investment in families with both adopted and genetic children. *Evolution and Human Behavior, 30,* 184–189.

Gibson, M. A. (2008). Does investment in the sexes differ when fathers are absent? Sex-biased infant survival and child growth in rural Ethiopia. *Human Nature, 19,* 263–276.

Gibson, M. A., & Mace, R. (2005). Helpful grandmothers in rural Ethiopia: A study of the effect of kin on child survival and growth. *Evolution and Human Behavior, 26,* 469–482.

Giedd, J. N., Bluenthal, J., Jeffries, N. O., Castellanos, F. X., Liu, H., Zijdenbos, A., Pauàs, A., Evans, A. C., & Rapoport, J. L. (1999). Brain development during childhood and adolescence: A longitudinal MRI study. *Nature Neuroscience, 2,* 861–863.

Gil, E. (1993). Age-appropriate sex play versus problematic sexual behaviors. In E. Gil & T. C. Johnson (Eds.), *Sexualized children: Assessment and treatment of sexualized children and children who molest.* New York: Launch Press.

Gil, E., & Johnson, T. C. (Eds.). (1993). *Sexualized children: Assessment and treatment of sexualized children and children who molest.* Rockville, MD: Launch Press.

Gilbert-Barness, E. (2000). Maternal caffeine and its effect on the fetus. *American Journal of Medical Genetics, 93,* 253.

Gilissen, R., Bakermans-Kranenburg, M. J., van IJzendoorn, M. H., & Van der Veer, R. (2008). Parent-child relationship, temperament, and physiological reactions to fear-inducing film clips: Further evidence for differential susceptibility. *Journal of Experimental Child Psychology, 99,* 182–195.

Gilligan, C. (1977). In a different voice: Women's conceptions of self and morality. *Harvard Educational Review, 47,* 481–517.

Gilligan, C. (1982). *In a different voice: Psychological theory and women's development.* Cambridge, MA: Harvard University Press.

Gilsanz, V., & Ratib, O. (2005). *Hand bone age: A digital atlas of skeletal maturity.* New York: Springer.

Ginsburg, H. (1997). *Entering the child's mind: The clinical interview in psychological research and practice.* New York: Cambridge University Press.

Ginsburg, H. J., & Miller, S. M. (1982). Sex differences in children's risk-taking behavior. *Child Development, 53,* 426–428.

Giusti, R. M., Iwamoto, K., & Hatch, E. E. (1995). Diethylstilbestrol revisited: A review of the long-term health effects. *Annals of Internal Medicine, 122,* 778–788.

Gleitman, L. R. (1990). The structural sources of verb meanings. *Language Acquisition, 1,* 3–55.

Gleitman, L. R., & Gleitman, H. (1991). *Language.* In H. Gleitman (Ed.), *Psychology* (pp. 333–390). New York: Norton.

Gliga, T., & Csibra, G. (2007). Seeing the face through the eyes: A developmental perspective on face expertise. *Progress in Brain Research, 164,* 323–339.

Gliga, T., & Dehaene-Lambertz, G. (2007). Development of a view-invariant representation of the human head. *Cognition, 102,* 261–288.

Gluckman, P., & Hanson, M. (2005). *The fetal matrix: Evolution, development, and disease.* Cambridge, UK: Cambridge University Press.

Goldberg, M. H. (2003). The third-molar "problem." *Journal of the American Dental Association, 134,* 1037.

Goldberg, R. F., & Thompson-Schill, S. L. (2009). Developmental "roots" in mature biological knowledge. *Psychological Science, 20,* 480–487.

Goldberg, S. (1983). Parent-infant bonding: Another look. *Child Development, 54,* 1355–1382.

Goldfarb, W. (1945). Effects of psychological deprivation in infancy and subsequent stimulation. *American Journal of Psychiatry, 102,* 18–33.

Goldfarb, W. (1947). Variations in adolescent adjustment of institutionally reared children. *American Journal of Orthopsychiatry, 17,* 449–457.

Goldfield, B. A., & Reznick, J. S. (1990). Early lexical acquisition: Rate, content, and the vocabulary spurt. *Journal of Child Language, 17,* 171–184.

Goldin-Meadow, S. (2007). Pointing sets the stage for learning language—and creating language. *Child Development, 78,* 741–745.

Goldin-Meadow, S. (2009). How gesture promotes learning throughout childhood. *Child Development Perspectives, 3,* 106–111.

Goldin-Meadow, S., Cook, S. W., & Mitchell, Z. A. (2009). Gesturing gives children new ideas about math. *Psychological Science, 20,* 267–272.

Goldman, R., & Goldman, J. (1982). *Children's sexual thinking: A comparative study of children aged 5 to 15 years in Australia, North America, Britain, and Sweden.* London: Routledge & Kegan Paul.

Goleman, D. P. (1995). *Emotional intelligence: Why it can matter more than IQ for character, health and lifelong achievement.* Bantam Books: New York.

Golomb, C. (2002). *Child art in context: A cultural and comparative perspective.* Washington, DC: American Psychological Association Press.

Golomb, C. (2004). *The child's creation of a pictorial world* (2nd ed.). Mahwah, NJ: Erlbaum.

Golombok, S., & Tasker, F. (1996). Do parents influence the sexual orientation of their children? Findings from a longitudinal study of lesbian families. *Developmental Psychology, 32,* 3–11.

Golombok, S., Murray, C., Jadva, V., MacCallum, F., & Lycett, E. (2004). Families created through surrogacy arrangements: Parent-child relationships in the 1st year of life. *Developmental Psychology, 40,* 400–411.

Golombok, S., Perry, B., Burston, A., Murray, C., Mooney-Somers, J., Stevens, M., & Golding, J. (2003). Children with lesbian parents: A community study. *Developmental Psychology, 39,* 20–33.

Golombok, S., Rust, J., Zervoulis, K., Croudace, T., Golding, J., & Hines, M. (2008). Developmental trajectories of sex-types behavior in boys and girls: A longitudinal general population study of children aged 2.5–8 years. *Child Development, 79,* 1583–1593.

Gómez, J. C. (2004). *Apes, monkeys, children, and the growth of mind.* Cambridge, MA: Harvard University Press.

Gómez, J. C., & Martín-Andrade, B. (2005). Fantasy play in apes. In P. K. Smith & A. Pellegrini (Eds); The *nature of play: great apes and humans;* (pp. 139–172). New York: Guilford.

Goodall J. (1986). *The chimpanzees of Gombe.* Cambridge, MA: Belknap Press.

Goodenough, F. L. (1926). *The measurement of intelligence through drawing.* Yonkers-on-the-Hudson, NY: Holt.

Goodman, G. S., Aman, C. J., & Hirschman, J. (1987). Child sexual and physical abuse: Children's testimony. In C. J. Ceci, M. P. Toglia, & D. F. Ross (Eds.), *Children's eyewitness memory.* New York: Springer-Verlag.

Goodman, G. S., Quas, J. A., Batterman-Faunce, J. M., Riddlesberger, M. M., & Kuhn, J. (1994). Predictors of accurate and inaccurate memories of traumatic events experienced in childhood. *Consciousness and Cognition, 3,* 269–294.

Goodman, G. S., Quas, J. A., Batterman-Faunce, J. M., Riddlesberger, M. M., & Kuhn, J. (1997). Children's reactions to and memory for a stressful event: Influences of age, anatomical dolls, knowledge, and parental attachment. *Applied Developmental Science, 1,* 54–75.

Goodman, G., Emery, R., & Haugaard, J. J. (1998). Developmental psychology and the law: Divorce, child maltreatment, foster care, and adoption. In I. Sigel & A. Renninger (Eds.) *Handbook of child psychology* (5th ed.), Vol. 4: *Child psychology in practice* (pp. 775–876). New York: Wiley.

Goodman, J. F. (1992). *When slow is fast enough: Educating the delayed preschool child.* New York: Guilford.

Goodrich, F. W., Jr. (1950). *Natural childbirth.* New York: Prentice-Hall.

Goodyer, I. M., & Sharp, C. (2005). Child depression. In B. Hopkins (Ed.), *The Cambridge encyclopedia of child development* (pp. 420–423). Cambridge, UK: Cambridge University Press.

Gopnik, A. (1996). The post-Piaget era. *Psychological Science, 7,* 221–225.

Gopnik, A. (2009). *The philosophical baby: What children's minds tell us about truth, love, and the meaning of life.* New York: Farrar, Straus & Giroux.

Gopnik, A., & Choi, S. (1995.) Names, relational words, and cognitive development in English and Korean speakers: Nouns are not always learned before verbs. In M. Tomasello & W. E. Merriman (Eds.), *Beyond names for things: Young children's acquisition of verbs* (pp. 63–80). Hillsdale, NJ: Erlbaum.

Gopnik, A., & Meltzoff, A. N. (1997). *Words, thoughts, and theories.* Cambridge, MA: MIT Press.

Gopnik, M., & Crago, M. D. (1991). Familial aggregation of a developmental language disorder. *Cognition, 39,* 1–50.

Gordon, B. N., Ornstein, P. A., Nida, R. E., Follmer, A., Crenshaw, M. C., & Albert, G. F. (1993). Does the use of dolls facilitate children's memory of visits to the doctor? *Applied Cognitive Psychology, 7,* 459–474.

Gordon, C. M., Goodman, E., Emans, S. J., et al. (2002). Physiologic regulators of bone turnover in young women with anorexia nervosa. *Journal of Pediatrics, 141,* 64–70.

Gordon, P. (2004). Numerical cognition without words: Evidence from Amazonia. *Science, 306* (15 October), 496–499.

Gosling, S. D., & John, O. P. (1999). Personality dimensions in non-human animals: A cross-species review. *Current Directions in Psychological Science, 8,* 69–75.

Gosso, Y., Otta, E., de Lima Salum e Morais, M., Leite Ribeiro, F. J., & Raad Bussab, V. S. (2005). Play in hunter-gatherer society. In A. D. Pellegrini & P. K. Smith (Eds.), *Play in humans and great apes* (pp. 213–253). Mahwah, NJ: Erlbaum.

Goswami, U., & Brown, A. L. (1990). Higher-order structure and relational reasoning: Contrasting analogical and thematic relations. *Cognition, 36,* 207–226.

Gottlieb, G. (1991). Experiential canalization of behavioral development: Results. *Developmental Psychology, 27,* 35–39.

Gottlieb, G. (1992). *Individual development & evolution: The genesis of novel behavior.* New York: Oxford University Press.

Gottlieb, G. (1997). *Synthesizing nature-nurture: Prenatal roots of instinctive behavior.* Mahwah, NJ: Erlbaum.

Gottlieb, G. (2000). Environmental and behavioral influences on gene activity. *Current Directions in Psychological Science, 9,* 93–102.

Gottlieb, G. (2007). Probabilistic epigenesis. *Developmental Science, 10,* 1–11.

Gottlieb, G., Wahlsten, D., & Lickliter, R. (2006). The significance of biology for human development: A developmental psychobiological systems view. In W. Damon & R. M. Lerner (Gen. Eds.), *Handbook of child psychology* (6th ed.). In R. M. Lerner (Vol. Ed.), Vol. 1: *Theoretical models of human development* (pp. 210–257). New York: Wiley.

Gould, S. J. (1977). *Ontogeny and phylogeny.* Cambridge, MA: Harvard University Press.

Gouze, K. R. (1987). Attention and social problem-solving as correlates of aggression in preschool males. *Journal of Abnormal Child Psychology, 15,* 181–197.

Graber, J. A., Brooks-Gunn, J., & Warren, M. P. (1995). The antecedents of menarcheal age: Heredity, family environment and stressful life events. *Child Development, 66,* 346–359.

Graber, J., Brooks-Gunn, J., & Warren, M. (1994). Prediction of eating problems: An 8-year study of adolescent girls. *Developmental Psychology, 30,* 823–834.

Graber, J., Lewinsohn, P., Seeley, J., & Brooks-Gunn, J. (1997). Is psychopathology associated with the timing of pubertal development? *Journal of the American Academy of Child and Adolescent Psychiatry, 36,* 1768–1776.

Graces, E., Thomas, D., & Currie, J. (2002). Longer term effects of Head Start. *American Economic Review, 92,* 999–1012.

Graham, S., & Hudley, C. (1994). Attributions of aggressive and nonaggressive African-American early adolescent boys: A study of construct accessibility. *Developmental Psychology, 30,* 365–373.

Grant, B. R., & Grant, P. R. (1989). Natural selection in a population of Darwin's finches. *American Naturalist, 133,* 377–393.

Grant, B. R., & Grant, P. R. (1993). Evolution of Darwin's finches caused by rare climate event. *Proceedings of the Royal Society of London B, 251,* 111–117.

Grant, P. R., & Grant, B. R. (2002). Unpredictable evolution in a 30-year study of Darwin's finches. *Science, 296* (April 26), 707–711.

Grant, P. R., & Grant, B. R. (2006). Evolution of character displacement in Darwin's finches. *Science, 313* (14 July), 224–226.

Gray-Little, B., & Hafdahl, A. R. (2000). Factors influencing racial comparisons of self-esteem: A quantitative review. *Psychological Bulletin, 126,* 26–54.

Gredlein, J. M., & Bjorklund, D. F. (2005). Sex differences in young children's use of tools in a problem-solving task: The role of object-oriented play. *Human Nature, 16,* 211–232.

Green, D. (1987). *The "sissy boy syndrome" and the development of homosexuality.* New Haven, CT: Yale University Press.

Green, F. P., & Schneider, F. W. (1974). Age differences in the behavior of boys on three measures of altruism. *Child Development, 45,* 248–251.

Green, L. J. (2002). *African American English: A linguistic introduction.* Cambridge, UK: Cambridge University Press.

Greenberg, B., Siemicki, M., Dorfman, S., Heeter, C., Stanley, C., Soderman, A., & Lisangan, R. (1993). Sex content in R-rated films viewed by adolescents. In B. S. Greenberg, J. D. Brown, & N. L. Buerkel-Rirhfuss (Eds.), *Media, sex, and the adolescent* (pp. 29–44). Cresskill, NJ: Hampton Press.

Greenberg, M., & Littlewood, R. (1995). Post-adoption incest and phenotypic matching: Experience, personal meanings and biosocial implications. *British Journal of Medical Psychology, 68,* 29–44.

Greenberger, E., O'Neil, R., & Nagel, S. K. (1994). Linking workplace and homeplace: Relations between the nature of adults' work and their parenting behavior. *Developmental Psychology, 30,* 990–1002.

Greene, E. (1996). Effect of light quality and larval diet on morph induction in the polymorphic caterpillar Nemoria arizonaria (*Lepidoptera: Geometridae*). *Biological Journal of the Linnean Society, 58,* 277–285.

Greene, J. P. (2002). High school graduation rates in the United States (Revised, 2002). Manhattan Institute for Policy Research. http://www.manhattan-institute.org/html/cr_baeo.htm#03. Downloaded, November 29, 2008.

Greenfield, P. M. (1998). The cultural evolution of IQ. In U. Neisser (Ed.), *The rising cure: Long-term gains in IQ and related measures* (pp. 81–123). Washington, DC: American Psychological Association.

Greenfield, P. M. (2004). Inadvertent exposure to pornography on the Internet: Implications of peer-to-peer file-sharing networks for child development and families. *Journal of Applied Developmental Psychology, 25,* 741–750.

Greenfield, P. M. (2009). Linking social change and developmental change: Shifting pathways of human development. *Developmental Psychology, 45,* 401–418.

Greenfield, P. M., & Childs, C. P. (1991). Developmental continuity in biocultural context. In R. Cohen, & A. W. Siegel (Eds.), *Context and development.* Hillsdale, NJ: Erlbaum.

Greenhoot, A. F., & Semb, P. A. (2008). Do illustrations enhance preschoolers' memories for stories? Age-related change in the picture facilitation effect. *Journal of Experimental Child Psychology, 99,* 271–287.

Greenough, W. T., Black, J. E., & Wallace, C. S. (1987). Experience and brain development. *Child Development, 58,* 539–559.

Greenwald, A. G., McGhee, D. E., & Schwartz, J. K. L. (1998). Measuring individual differences in implicit cognition: The implicit association test. *Journal of Personality and Social Psychology, 74,* 1464–1480.

Gregg, N. M. (1942). Congenital cataract following German measles in mother. *Transactions of the Ophthalmological Society of Australia, 3,* 35–46.

Greif, G. L. (1985). *Single fathers.* Lexington, MA: Heath.

Greif, M. L., Kemler Nelson, D., Keil, F., & Gutierrez, F. (2006). What do children want to know about animals and artifacts? *Psychological Science, 17,* 455–459.

Gringlas, M., & Weinraub, M. (1995). The more things change: Single parenting revisited. *Journal of Family Issues, 16,* 29–52.

Grön, G., Wunderlich, A. P., Spitzer, M., Tomczak, R., & Riepe, M. W. (2000). Brain activation during human navigation: Gender-different neural networks as substrate of performance. *Nature Neuroscience, 3,* 404–408.

Gross, D., Conrad, B., Fogg, L., Willis, L., & Garvey, C. (1995). A longitudinal study of maternal depression and preschool children's mental health. *Nursing Research, 44,* 96–101.

Gross, E. F. (2004). Adolescent Internet use: What we expect, what teens report. *Journal of Applied Developmental Psychology, 25,* 633–649.

Grossmann, K. E., Grossmann, K., & Waters, E. (2005). (Eds.) *Attachment from infancy to adulthood: The major longitudinal studies.* New York: Guilford.

Grossmann, K. E., Grossmann, K., Huber, F., & Wartner, U. (1981). German children's behavior towards their mothers at 12 months and their fathers at 18 months in Ainsworth's strange situation. *International Journal of Behavioral Development, 4,* 157–181.

Grotevant, H. D., & Cooper, C. R. (1998). Individuality and connectedness in adolescent development: Review and prospects for research on identity, relationships, and context (pp. 3–37). In E. Skoe & A. von der Lippe (Eds.), *Personality development in adolescence: A cross national and life span perspective.* Routledge & Kegan Paul, London.

Grunau, R. E., Oberlander, T. F., Whitfield, M. F., Fitzgerald, C., Morison, S. J., & Saul, J. P. (2001). Pain reactivity in former extremely low birth weight infants at corrected age 8 months compared with term born controls. *Infant Behavior & Development, 24,* 41–55.

Grunbaum, J. A., et al. (2004). Youth risk behavior surveillance, United States, 2003. *Morbidity & Mortality Weekly Report Surveillance Summaries, 53* (SS-2), 1–95.

Grusec, J. E., Davidov, M., & Lundell, L. (2003). Prosocial and helping behavior. In P. K. Smith & C. H. Hart (Eds.), *Blackwell handbook of childhood social development,* Oxford, UK: Blackwell.

Guay, F., Marsh, H. W., & Boivin, M. (2003). Academic self-concept and academic achievement: A developmental perspective on their causal ordering. *Journal of Educational Psychology, 95,* 124–136.

Guerra, N. G., Huesmann, L. R., & Hanish, L. (1995). The role of normative beliefs in children's social behavior. In N. Eisenberg (Ed.), *Review of personality and social psychology. Social development* (Vol. 15, pp. 140–158). Thousand Oaks, CA: Sage.

Guilford, J. P. (1988). Some changes in the structure-of-the-intellect model. *Educational and Psychological Measurement, 48,* 1–4.

Gummerum, M., Keller, M., Takezawa, M., & Mata, J. (2008). To give or not to give: Children's and adolescents' sharing and moral negotiations in economic decision situations. *Child Development, 79,* 562–576.

Gundersen, B. H., Melas, P. S., & Skar, J. E. (1981). Sexual behavior of preschool children: Teachers' observations. In L. L. Constantine & F. M. Martinson (Eds.), *Children and sex: New findings, new perspectives.* Boston: Little, Brown.

Gunnar, M. R., Morison, S. J., Chisholm, K., & Schuder, M. (2001). Salivary cortisol levels in children adopted from Romanian orphanages. *Development and Psychopathology, 13,* 611–628.

Guo, G., Roettger, M. E., & Cai, T. (2008). The integration of genetic propensities into social-control models of delinquency and violence among male youths. *American Sociological Review, 73,* 543–556.

Gur, R. C., Turetsky, B. I., Matsui, M., Yan, M., Bilker, W., Hughett, P., & Gur, R. E. (1999). Sex differences in brain gray and white matter in healthy young adults: Correlations with cognitive performance. *The Journal of Neuroscience, 19,* 4065–4072.

Gur, R. E., & Gur, R. C. (1990). Gender differences in regional cerebral blood flow. *Schizophrenia Bulletin, 16,* 247–254.

Gustafson, G., Wood, R., & Green, J., (2000). Can we hear the causes of infants' crying? In R. Barr, B. Hopkins, & J. Green, (Eds.). *Crying as a sign, a signal, and a symptom* (pp. 8–22). London: MacKeith Press.

Guthrie, R. D. (2005). *The nature of paleolithic art.* Chicago: University of Chicago Press.

Guthrie, S. (1993). *Faces in the clouds.* Oxford, UK: Oxford University Press.

Guttentag, R. E. (1984). The mental effort requirement of cumulative rehearsal: A developmental study. *Journal of Experimental Child Psychology, 37,* 92–106.

Guttentag, R. E., Ornstein, P. A., & Seimens, L. (1987). Children's spontaneous rehearsal: Transitions in strategy acquisition. *Cognitive Development, 2,* 307–326.

Guttmacher Institute. (2002). *Teenagers sexual and reproductive health: Developed countries.* New York: Alan Guttmacher Institute.

Guttmacher Institute. (2006). *Facts on American teens' sexual and reproductive health.* New York: Alan Guttmacher Institute.

Haan, N. L., Langer, J., & Kohlberg, L. (1976). Family patterns of moral reasoning. *Child Development, 47,* 1204–1206.

Haan, N. L., Smith, M. B., & Block, J. (1968). Moral reasoning of young adults: Political-social behavior, family background, and personality correlates. *Journal of Personality and Social Psychology, 10,* 183–201.

Hadders-Algra, M. (2002). Two distinct forms of minor neurological dysfunction: Perspectives emerging from a review of data of the Groningen Perinatal Project. *Developmental Medicine and Child Neurology, 44,* 561–571.

Hadders-Algra, M. (2005). Prematurity and low birthweight. In B. Hopkins (Ed.), *The Cambridge encyclopedia of child development* (pp. 442–447). New York: Cambridge University Press.

Haden, C. A., Ornstein, P. A., Eckerman, C. O., & Didow, S. M. (2001). Mother-child conversational interactions as event unfold: Linkages to subsequent remembering. *Child Development, 72,* 1016–1031.

Haeffel, G. J., Getchell, M.,. Koposov, R. A., Yrigollen, C. Y., DeYoung, C. G., Klinteberg, B., Oreland, L., Ruchkin, V. V., & Grigorenko, E. L. (2008). Association between polymorphisms in the dopamine transporter gene and depression: Evidence for a gene-environment interaction in a sample of juvenile detainees. *Psychological Science, 19,* 62–69.

Haidt, J. (2001). The emotional dog and its rational tail: A social intuitionist approach to moral judgment. *Psychological Review, 108,* 814–834.

Haier, R. J., Jung R. E., Yeo, R. A., Head, K., & Alkire, M. T. (2005). The neuroanatomy of general intelligence: Sex matters. *Neuroimage, 25,* 320–327.

Haig, D. (1993). Genetic conflicts in human pregnancy. *Quarterly Review of Biology, 68,* 495–532.

Haight, W. L., & Miller, P. J. (1993). *Pretending at home: Early development in a sociocultural context.* Albany: State University of New York Press.

Haith, M. M. (1993). Preparing for the 21st century: Some goals and challenges for studies of infant sensory and perceptual development. *Developmental Review, 13,* 354–371.

Haith, M. M. (1966). The response of the human newborn to visual movement. *Journal of Experimental Child Psychology, 3,* 235–243.

Hakuta, K. (1999). The debate on bilingual education. *Developmental and Behavioral Pediatrics, 20,* 36–37.

Hakuta, K., Bialystok, E., & Wiley, E. (2003). Critical evidence: A test of the critical period hypothesis for second-language acquisition. *Psychological Science, 14,* 31–38.

Hakuta, K., & Garcia, E. E. (1989). Bilingualism and education. *American Psychologist, 44,* 374–379.

Haley, M. H. (2004). Learner-centered instruction and the theory of multiple intelligences with second language learners. *Teachers College Record, 106,* 163–180.

Hall, B. K. (2005). *Bone and cartilage: Developmental skeletal biology.* New York: Academic Press.

Hall, J. A., Carter, J. D., & Horgan, T. G. (2000). Gender differences in nonverbal communication of emotion. In A. H. Fischer (Ed.), *Gender and emotion* (pp. 97–117). Cambridge, UK: Cambridge University Press.

Halpern, C. T., King, R. B., Oslak, S. G., & Udry, J. R. (2005). Body mass index, dieting, romance, and sexual activity in adolescent girls: Relationships over time. *Journal of Research on Adolescence, 15,* 535–559.

Halpern, C. T., Urdy, J., & Suchindran, C. (1998). Monthly measures of salivary testosterone predict sexual activity in adolescent males. *Archives of Sexual Behavior, 27,* 445–465.

Halpern, D. F. (1997). Sex differences in intelligence. *American Psychologist, 52,* 1091–1102.

Halpern, D. F. (2000). *Sex differences in cognitive abilities* (3rd ed.). Mahwah, NJ: Erlbaum.

Halpern, D. F. (2004). A cognitive-process taxonomy for sex differences in cognitive abilities. *Current Directions in Psychological Science, 13*, 135–139.

Halpern, D. F., Benbow, C. P., Geary, D. C., Gur, R. C., Hyde, J. S., & Gernsbacher, M. A. (2007). The science of sex differences in science and mathematics. *Psychological Science in the Public Interest, 8*, 1–51.

Halverson, C. F., & Waldrop, M. F. (1973). The relations of mechanically recorded activity level to varieties of preschool play behavior. *Child Development, 44*, 678–681.

Hamilton, L., Cheng, S., & Powell, B. (2007). Adoptive parents, adaptive parents: Evaluating the importance of biological ties for parental investment. *American Sociological Review, 72*, 95–116.

Hamilton, W. D. (1964). The genetical theory of social behavior. *Journal of Theoretical Biology, 7*, 1–52.

Hamilton, W. D. (1966). The moulding of senescence by natural selection. *Journal of Theoretical Biology, 12*, 12–45.

Hamlin, J. K., Hallinan, E. V., & Woodward, A. L. (2008). Do as I do: 7-month-old infants selectively reproduce others' goals. *Developmental Science, 11*, 487–494.

Hammes, B., & Laitman, C. J. (2003). Diethylstilbestrol (DES) update: Recommendations for the identification and management of DES-exposed individuals. *Journal of Midwifery and Women's Health, 48*, 19–29.

Hampson, S. E. (2008). Mechanisms by which childhood personality traits influence adult well-being. *Current Directions in Psychological Science, 17*, 264–268.

Han, J. J., Leitchman, M. D., & Wang, Q. (1998). Autobiographical memory in Korean, Chinese, and American children. *Developmental Psychology, 34*, 701–713.

Hankin, B. L., Abramson, L. Y., Moffitt, T. E., Silva, P. A., McGree, R., & Angell, K. E. (1998). Development of depression from preadolescence to young adulthood: Emerging gender differences in a 10-year-longitudinal study. *Journal of Abnormal Psychology, 107*, 128–140.

Hansen, M. et al. (2005). The impact of school daily schedule on adolescent sleep. *Pediatrics, 115*, 1555–1561.

Hare, B., Call, J., Agentta, B., & Tomasello, M. (2000). Chimpanzees know what conspecifics do and do not see. *Animal Behaviour, 59*, 771–785.

Hare, B., Call, J., & Tomasello, M. (2001). Do chimpanzees know what conspecifics know? *Animal Behaviour, 61*, 139–151.

Harkness, S., & Super, C. (1995). Culture and parenting. In M. Bornstein (Ed.), *Handbook of parenting* (Vol. 2, pp. 211–234). Hillsdale, NJ: Erlbaum.

Harlow, H. F., Harlow, M. K., Dodsworth, R. O., & Arling, G. L. (1966). Maternal behavior of rhesus monkeys deprived of mothering and peer associations as infants. *Proceedings of the American Philosophical Society, 110*, 88–98.

Harlow, H. F., & Zimmerman, R. (1959). Affectional responses in the infant monkey. *Science, 130*, 421–432.

Harnishfeger, K. K. (1995). The development of cognitive inhibition: Theories, definitions, and research evidence. In F. Dempster & C. Brainerd (Eds.), *New perspectives on interference and inhibition in cognition*. New York: Academic Press.

Harnishfeger, K. K., & Bjorklund, D. F. (1990). Children's strategies: A brief history. In D. F. Bjorklund (Ed.), *Children's strategies: Contemporary views of cognitive development*. Hillsdale, NJ: Erlbaum.

Harnishfeger, K. K., & Bjorklund, D. F. (1994). Individual differences in inhibition: Implications for children's cognitive development. *Learning and Individual Differences, 6*, 331–355

Harnishfeger, K. K., & Pope, R. S. (1996). Intending to forget: The development of cognitive inhibition in directed forgetting. *Journal of Experimental Child Psychology, 62*, 292–315.

Harris, D. B. (1971). The case method in art education. In G. Kensler (Ed.), *A report on a preconference education research training program for descriptive research in art education* (pp. 29–49). Reston, VA: National Art Education Association.

Harris, G. T., Hilton, N. Z., Rice, M. E., & Eke, A. W. (2007). Children killed by genetic parents versus stepparents. *Evolution and Human Behavior, 28*, 85–95.

Harris, J. R. (1995). Where is the child's environment? A group socialization theory of development. *Psychological Review, 102*, 458–489.

Harris, J. R. (1998). *The nurture assumption: Why children turn out the way they do*. New York: Free Press.

Harris, J. R. (2005). Social behavior and personality development: The role of experiences with siblings and with peers. In B. J. Ellis & D. F. Bjorklund (Eds.), *Origins of the social mind: Evolutionary psychology and child development* (pp. 245–270). New York: Guilford.

Harris, L. J. (2005). Handedness. In B. Hopkins (Ed.), *The Cambridge encyclopedia of child development* (pp. 321–326). New York: Cambridge University Press.

Harris, L. J., & Carlson, D. F. (1993). Hand preference for visually-guided reaching in human infants and adults. In J. Ward (Ed.), *Current behavioral evidence of primate asymmetries* (pp. 285–305). New York: Springer-Verlag.

Harris, P. (2006). Social cognition. In W. Damon & R. M. Lerner (Gen. Eds.), *Handbook of child psychology* (6th ed.). In D. Kuhn & R. S. Siegler (Vol. Eds.), Vol. 2: *Cognition, perception, and language* (pp. 811–858). New York: Wiley.

Harris, P. L., Brown, E., Marriott, C., Whittall, S., & Harmer, S. (1991). Monsters, ghosts and witches: Testing the limits of fantasy-reality distinction in young children. *British Journal of Developmental Psychology, 9*, 105–123.

Harris, P. L., de Rosnay, M., & Pons, F. (2005). Language and children's understanding of mental states. *Current Directions in Psychological Science, 14*, 69–73.

Harrist, A. W., & Waugh, R. M. (2002). Dyadic synchrony: Its structure and function in children's development. *Developmental Review, 22*, 555–592.

Hart C. L., Taylor, M. D., Smith, G. D., Whalley, L. J., Starr, J. M., Hole, D. J., Wilson, V., & Deary, I. J. (2005). Childhood IQ and all-cause mortality before and after age 65: Prospective observational study linking the Scottish Mental Survey 1932 and the Midspan studies. *British Journal of Health Psychology, 10*, 153–165.

Hart, E. L., Lahey, B. B., Loeber, R., Applegate, B., & Frick, P. J. (1995). Developmental change in attention-deficit hyperactivity disorder in boys: A four-year longitudinal study. *Developmental Psychology, 23*, 195–205.

Hart, S., & Carrington, H. (2002). Jealousy in 6-month-old infants. *Infancy, 3*, 395–402.

Hart, S. L., Carrington, H. A., Tronick, E. Z., & Carroll, S. R. (2004). When infants lose exclusive maternal attention: Is it jealousy? *Infancy, 6*, 57–78.

Harter, S. (1985). *Manual for the self-perception profile for children*. Denver, CO: University of Denver.

Harter, S. (1996). Historical roots of contemporary issues involving self-concept. In B. A. Bracken (Ed.), *Handbook of self-concept: Developmental, social, and clinical considerations*. New York: Wiley.

Harter, S. (1999). *The construction of the self: A developmental perspective*. New York: Guilford.

Harter, S. (2004). The developmental emergence of self-esteem: Individual differences in change and stability. In D. Mroczek & T. Little (Eds.), *The handbook of personality* (pp. 44–59). New York: Erlbaum.

Harter, S. (2006). The self. In W. Damon (Gen. Ed.), *Handbook of child psychology* (5th ed.). In N. Eisenberg (Vol. Ed.), Vol. 3: *Social, emotional and personality development* (pp. 505–570). New York: Wiley.

Harter, S., Bresnick, S., Bouchey, W. A., & Whitesell, N. R. (1997). The development of multiple role-related selves during adolescence. *Development and Psychopathology, 9*, 835–854.

Harter, S., & McCarley, K. (2004, April). *Is there a dark side to high self-esteem leading to adolescence violence?* Poster presented at the American Psychological Association Convention, Honolulu, Hawaii.

Harter, S., & Pike, R. (1984). The pictorial scale of perceived competence and social acceptance for young children. *Child Development, 55,* 1969–1982.

Harter, S., Waters, P., & Whitesell, N. R. (1998). Relational self-worth: Differences in perceived worth as a person across interpersonal contexts among adolescents. *Child Development, 69,* 756–766.

Hartshorne, H., & May, M. S. (1928–1930). *Studies in the nature of character: Vol. 1, Studies in deceit; Vol. 2, Studies in self-control; Vol. 3, Studies in the organization of character.* New York: Macmillan.

Hartung, C. M., & Widiger, T. A. (1998). Gender differences in the diagnosis of mental disorders: Conclusions and controversies of the *DSM-IV. Psychological Bulletin, 18,* 461–471.

Hartup, W. W. (1983). Peer relations. In P. H. Mussen (Gen. Ed.), *Handbook of child psychology* (4th ed.). In E. M. Hetherington (Vol. Ed.), Vol. 4: *Socialization, personality, and social development.* New York: Wiley.

Hartup, W. W. (1996). The company they keep: Friendships and their developmental significance. *Child Development, 67,* 1–13.

Hartup, W. W., Laursen, B., Stewart, M. I., & Eastenson, A. (1988). Conflict and the friendship relations of young children. *Child Development, 59,* 1590–1600.

Harwood, R. L., Miller, J. G., & Lucca Irizarry, N. (1995). *Culture and attachment: Perceptions of the child in context.* New York: Guilford.

Hasher, L., & Zacks, R. T. (1979). Automatic and effortful processes in memory. *Journal of Experimental Psychology: General, 108,* 356–388.

Hashimoto, R., & Sakai, K. L. (2002). Specialization in the left prefrontal cortex for sentence comprehension. *Neuron, 35,* 589–597.

Haskett, G. J. (1971). Modification of peer preferences of first-grade children. *Developmental Psychology, 4,* 429–433.

Hasselhorn, M. (1992). Task dependency and the role of category typicality and metamemory in the development of an organizational strategy. *Child Development, 63,* 202–214.

Hastings, P. D., Zahn-Waxler, C., & McShane, K. E. (2005). We are, by nature, moral creatures: Biological bases of concern for others. In M. Killen & J. Smetana (Eds.), *Handbook of moral development.* Mahwah, NJ: Erlbaum.

Hatano G., & Inagaki, K. (1992). Desituating cognition through the construction of conceptual knowledge. In P. Light & G. Butterworth (Eds.), *Context and cognition: Ways of knowing and learning* (pp. 115–133). New York: Harvester.

Hatch E. E., Palmer, J. R., Titus-Ernstoff, L., Noller, K. L. , Kaufman, R. H., et al. (1998). Cancer risk in women exposed to diethylstilbestrol in utero. *Journal of the American Medical Association, 280,* 630–634.

Haugaard, J. J. (1996). Sexual behaviors between children: Professionals' opinions and undergraduates' recollections. *Families in Society, 77,* 81–89.

Hauser, M. D. (2000). *Wild minds: What animals really think.* New York: Holt.

Hauser, M. D. (2006). *Moral minds: How nature designed our universal sense of right and wrong.* New York: HarperCollins.

Hauser, M. D., & McDermott, J. (2003). The evolution of the music faculty: A comparative perspective. *Nature Neuroscience, 6,* 663–668.

Hawkes, K., O'Connell, J. F., & Blurton Jones, N. G. (1997). Hadza women's time allocation, offspring provisioning, and the evolution of post-menopausal lifespans. *Current Anthropology, 38,* 551–578.

Hawley, P. H. (1999). The ontogenesis of social dominance: A strategy-based evolutionary perspective. *Developmental Review, 19,* 97–132.

Hawley, P. H. (2003). Strategies of control, aggression and morality in preschoolers: An evolutionary perspective. *Journal of Experimental Child Psychology, 85,* 213–235.

Hawley, P. H. (2007). Social dominance in childhood and adolescence: Why social competence and aggression may go hand in hand. In P. H. Hawley, T. D. Little, & P. C. Rodkin. (Eds.), *Aggression and adaptation: The bright side to bad behavior* (pp. 1–30). Mahwah, NJ: Erlbaum.

Hawley, P. H. (2008). Competition and social and personality development: Some consequences of taking Darwin seriously. *Anuario de Psicologia, 39,* 193–208.

Hawley, P. H., Card, N. A., & Little, T. D. (2008). The myth of the alpha male: A new look at dominance-related beliefs and behaviors among adolescent males and females. *International Journal of Behavioral Development, 32,* 76–88.

Hawley, P. H., Little, T. D., & Rodkin, P. C. (Eds.) (2007). *Aggression and adaptation: The bright side to bad behavior.* Mahwah, NJ: Erlbaum.

Hay, D. F. (1994). Prosocial development. *Journal of Child Psychology and Psychiatry, 35,* 29–71.

Hay, D. F., Caplan, M., & Nash, A. (2009). The beginnings of peer relations. In K. H. Rubin, W. M. Bukowski, & B. Laursen (Eds.), *Handbook of peer interactions, relationships, and groups* (pp. 121–142). New York: Guilford.

Hay, D. F., Castle, J., & Davies, L. (2000). Toddlers' use of force against familiar peers: A precursor to serious aggression? *Child Development, 71,* 457–467.

Hay, D. F., Nash, A., & Pedersen, J. (1983). Interaction between 6-month-old peers. *Child Development, 54,* 557–562.

Hay, D. F., & Rheingold, H. L. (1983). The early appearance of some valued behaviors. In D. L. Bridgeman (Ed.), *The nature of prosocial development: Interdisciplinary theories and strategies* (pp. 73–94). New York: Academic Press.

Hay, D. F., & Ross, H. S. (1982). The social nature of early conflict. *Child Development, 53,* 105–113.

Hayes, B. K., & Hennessy, R. (1996). The nature and development of nonverbal implicit memory. *Journal of Experimental Child Psychology, 63,* 22–43.

Haynes, H., White, B. L., & Held, R. (1965). Visual accommodation in human infants. *Science, 148,* 528–530.

Hazen, C., & Shaver, P. R. (1994). Attachment as an organizational framework for research on close relationships. *Psychological Inquiry, 5,* 1–22.

Hazen, N. L., & Durrett, M. E. (1982). Relationship of security of attachment and cognitive mapping abilities in 2-year-olds. *Developmental Psychology, 18,* 751–759.

Hearold, S. (1986). A synthesis of 1043 effects of television on social behavior. In G. Comstock (Ed.), *Public communication and behavior* (Vol. 1). New York: Academic Press.

Heath, S. B. (1989). Oral and literate traditions among Black Americans living in poverty. *American Psychologist, 44,* 367–373.

Hebb, D. O. (1974). What psychology is about. *American Psychologist, 29,* 71–79.

Hedges, L. V., & Nowell, A. (1995). Sex differences in mental test scores, variability, and numbers of highscoring individuals. *Science, 269* (July 7), 41–45.

Hedley, A. A., Ogden, C. L., Johnson, C. L. (2004). Prevalence of overweight and obesity among US children, adolescents, and adults, 1999–2002. *Journal of the American Medical Association, 291,* 2847–2850.

Heerwagen, J. H., & Orians, G. H. (2002). The ecological world of children. In P. H. Kahn, Jr., & S. R. Kellert (Eds.), *Children and nature: Psychological, sociological, and evolutionary investigations* (pp. 29–64). Cambridge, MA: MIT Press.

Heijkoop, M., Dubas, J. S., & van Aken, M. A. G. (2009). Parent-child resemblance and kin investment: Physical resemblance or personality similarity? *European Journal of Developmental Psychology, 6,* 64–69.

Heiman, M. L., Leiblum, S., Esquilin, S. C., & Pallitto, L. M. (1998). A comparative survey of beliefs about "normal" childhood sexual behaviors. *Child Abuse & Neglect, 22* (4), 289–304.

Heimann, M. (1989). Neonatal imitation gaze aversion and mother-infant interaction. *Infant Behavior & Development, 12,* 495–505.

Hendler, M., & Weisberg, P. (1992). Conservation acquisition, maintenance, and generalization by mentally retarded children using equality-rule training. *Journal of Experimental Child Psychology, 54,* 258–276.

Hendrick, V., & Altshuler, T. M. (1999). Biological determinants of postpartum depression. In L. J. Miller (Ed.), *Postpartum mood disorders* (pp. 62–82). Washington, DC: American Psychiatric Press.

Henker, B., & Whalen, C. K. (1989). Hyperactivity and attention deficits. *American Psychologist, 44,* 216–223.

Henley, D. V., Lipson, N., Korach, K. S., & Bloch, C. A. (2007). Prepubertal gynecomastia linked to lavender and tea tree oils. *New England Journal of Medicine, 365*, 479–485.

Henry, D. B., Schoeny, M. E., Deptula, D. P., & Slavick, J. T. (2007). Peer selection and socialization effects on adolescent intercourse without a condom and attitudes about the costs of sex. *Child Development, 78*, 925–838.

Henry, L. A., & MacLean, M. (2003). Relationships between working memory, expressive vocabulary and arithmetic reasoning in children with and without intellectual disabilities. *Educational and Child Psychology, 20*, 51–63.

Hepper, P. G., McCartney, G. R., & Shannon, E. A. (1998). Lateralized behaviour in first trimester human fetuses. *Neuropsychologia, 36*, 531–534.

Herbert, J., Gross, J., & Hayne, H. (2007). Crawling is associated with more flexible memory retrieval by 9-month-old infants. *Developmental Science, 10*, 183–189.

Herdt, G., & McClintock, M. (2000). The magical age of 10. *Achieves of Sexual Behavior, 29*, 587–606.

Herman-Giddens, M. E., SloraDagger, E. J., Wasserman, R. C., Bourdony, C. J., Bhapkar, M. V., Koch, G. G., &. Hasemeier, C. M. (1997). Secondary sexual characteristics and menses in young girls seen in office practice: A study from the Pediatric Research in Office Settings Network. *Pediatrics, 99*, 505–512.

Hernández Blasi, C. (2000). Dossier documental: Neurociencia cognitiva evolutiva: Mentes, cerebros y desarrollo (Documental dossier: Cognitive development neuroscience: Minds, brains and development). *Infancia y Aprendizaje, 91*, 111–127.

Hernández Blasi, C., Bering, J. M., & Bjorklund, D. F. (2003). Psicología Evolucionista del Desarrollo: Contemplando la ontogénesis humana desde los ojos del evolucionismo (Evolutionary developmental psychology: Viewing human ontogeny through the eyes of evolutionary theory.) *Infancia y Aprendizaje, 26*, 267–285.

Hernández Blasi, C., & Bjorklund, D. F. (2003). Evolutionary developmental psychology: A new tool for better understanding human ontogeny. *Human Development, 46*, 259–281.

Herrera, N. C., Zajonc, R. B., Wieczorkowska, G., & Chicomski, B. (2003). Beliefs about birth rank and their reflection in reality. *Journal of Social and Personality Psychology, 85*, 142–150.

Herrmann, E., Call, J., Hernández-Lloreda, M. V., Hare, B., & Tomasello, M. (2007). Humans have evolved specialized skills of social cognition: The cultural intelligence hypothesis. *Science, 317*, 1360–1366.

Herrnstein, R. J., & Murray, C. (1994). *The bell curve: Intelligence and class structure in American life*. New York: Simon & Schuster.

Hetherington, E. M. (1989). Coping with family transitions: Winners, losers, and survivors. *Child Development, 60*, 1–14.

Hetherington, E. M. (1993). An overview of the Virginia longitudinal study of divorce and remarriage with a focus on early adolescence. *Journal of Family Psychology, 7*, 1–18.

Hetherington, E. M. (1998). Social capital and the development of youth from nondivorced, divorced, and remarried families. In A. Collins (Ed.), *Relationships as developmental contexts: The 29th Minnesota symposium on child psychology*. Hillsdale, NJ: Erlbaum.

Hetherington, E. M., & Clingempeel, W. G. (1992). Coping with marital transitions: A family systems perspective. *Monographs of the Society for Research in Child Development* (Serial No. 227).

Hetherington, E. M., Cox, M., & Cox, R. (1985). Long-term effects of divorce and remarriage on the adjustment of children. *Journal of the American Academy of Child Psychiatry, 24*, 518–530.

Hetherington, E. M., Henderson, S. H., & Reiss, D. (1999). Adolescent siblings in stepfamilies: Family functioning and adolescent adjustment. *Monographs of the Society for Research in Child Development, 64* (Serial No. 259).

Hetherington, E. M., & Kelly, J. (2002). *For better or worse*. New York: Norton.

Hetherington, E. M., & Stanley-Hagan, M. (2002). Parenting in divorced and remarried families. In M. H. Bornstein (Ed.), *Handbook of parenting* (2nd ed.), Vol. 3: *Being and becoming a parent* (pp. 287–315). Mahwah, NJ: Erlbaum.

Hetherington, E. M., Stanley-Hagan, M., & Anderson, E. R. (1989). Marital transitions: A child's perspective. *American Psychologist, 44*, 303–312.

Hickling, A. K., & Gelman, S. A. (1994). How does your garden grow? Early conceptualization of seeds and their place in the plant growth cycle. *Child Development, 66*, 856–876.

Hilgard, E. R. (1987). *Psychology in America: A historical survey*. San Diego: Harcourt Brace Jovanovich.

Hill, J. O., & Peters, J. C. (1998). Environmental contributions to the obesity epidemic. *Science, 280*, 1371–1374.

Hill, K., & Hurtado, A. M. (1996). *Ache life history: The ecology and demography of a foraging people*. New York: Aldine de Gruyter.

Hill, N. E., & Taylor, L. C. (2004). Parental school involvement and children's academic achievement. *Current Directions in Psychological Science, 13*, 161–164.

Hillman, C. H., Buck, S. M., Themanson, J. R., Pontifex, M. B., & Castelli, D. M. (2009). Aerobic fitness and cognitive development: Even-related brain potential and task performance indices of executive control in preadolescent children. *Developmental Psychology, 45*, 114–129.

Hinde, R. A. (1976). Interactions, relationships, and social structure. *Man, 11*, 1–17.

Hinde, R. A. (1979). *Toward understanding relationships*. Ontario/London: Academic Press.

Hinde, R. A. (1980). *Ethology*. London: Fontana.

Hinde, R. (1983). Ethology and child development. In J. J. Campos and M. H. Haith (Eds.). *Handbook of child psychology: Infancy and developmental psychobiology* (Vol. II, pp. 27–94). New York: Wiley.

Hinde, R. A. (1999). Causes of social development from the perspective of an integrated developmental science. In G. Butterworth & P. Bryant (Eds.), *Causes of development* (pp. 161–185). London: Harvester Wheatsheaf.

Hinshaw, S. P., Zupan, B. A., Simmel, C., Nigg, J. T., & Melnick, S. (1997). Peer status in boys with attention-deficit hyperactivity disorder: Predictions from overt and covert antisocial behavior, social isolation, and authoritative parenting beliefs. *Child Development, 68*, 880–896.

Hobson, R. P., Chidambi, G., Lee, A., & Meyer, J. (2006). Foundations for self-awareness: An exploration through autism. *Monographs of the Society for Research in Child Development, 71* (Serial No. 284).

Hodapp, R. M., & Dykens, E. M. (2006). Mental retardation. In W. Damon & R. M. Lerner (Gen. Eds.), *Handbook of child psychology* (6th ed.). In K. A. Renninger & I. E. Sigel (Vol. Eds.), Vol. 4: *Child psychology in practice* (pp. 453–496). New York: Wiley.

Hodges, E. V. E., Finnegan, R. A., & Perry, D. G. (1999). Skewed autonomy-relatedness in preadolescents' conceptions of their relationships with mother, father, and best friend. *Developmental Psychology, 35*, 737–748.

Hodges, E. V. E., Malone, M. J., & Perry, D. G. (1997). Individual risk and social risk as interacting determinants of victimization in the peer group. *Developmental Psychology, 33*, 1032–1039.

Hodges, E. V. E., & Perry, D. G. (1999). Personal and interpersonal antecedents of victimization by peers. *Journal of Personality and Social Psychology, 76*, 677–685.

Hoek, H. W., & van Hoeken, D. (2003). Review of the prevalence and incidence of eating disorders. *International Journal of Eating Disorders, 34*, 383–396.

Hoeksma, J. B., Oosterlaan, J., & Schipper, E. M. (2004). Emotion regulation and the dynamics of feeling: A conceptual and methodological framework. *Child Development, 74*, 354–360.

Hoekstra, R. E., Ferra, T. B., Couser, R. J., Payne, N. R., & Connett, J. E. (2004). Survival and long-term neurodevelopmental outcome of extremely premature infants born at 23–26 weeks' gestational age at a tertiary center. *Pediatrics, 113*, e1–e6.

Hoerr, T. (2004). How MI informs teaching at New City School. *Teachers College Record, 106*, 40–48.

Hoff, E. (2003). The specificity of environmental influence: Socioeconomic status affects early vocabulary development via maternal speech. *Child Development, 74*, 1368–1378.

Hoff, E. (2006). How social contexts support and shape language development. *Developmental Review, 26*, 55–88.

Hoff, E. (2009). *Language development* (4th ed.). Belmont, CA: Wadsworth..

Hoff, E., Laursen, B., & Tardiff, T. (2002). Socioeconomic status and parenting. In M. H. Bornstein (Ed.), *Handbook of parenting* (2nd ed.), *Vol. 2: Biology and ecology of parenting* (pp. 231–252). Mahwah, NJ: Erlbaum.

Hoff, E., & Naigles, L. (2002). How children use input to acquire a lexicon. *Child Development, 73*, 418–433.

Hoff-Ginsberg, E. (1990). Maternal speech and the child's development of syntax: A further look. *Journal of Child Language, 17*, 85–99.

Hoffer, M. A. (1981). *The roots of behavior.* San Francisco: W. H. Freeman.

Hofferth, S. L. (1990). Trends in adolescent sexual activity, contraception, and pregnancy in the United States. In J. Bancroft & J. Reinisch (Eds.), *Adolescence and puberty.* New York: Oxford University Press.

Hoffman, M. L. (1975). Altruistic behavior and the parent-child relationship. *Journal of Personality and Social Psychology, 31*, 937–943.

Hoffman, M. L. (1981). Is altruism part of human nature? *Journal of Personality and Social Psychology, 40*, 121–137.

Hoffman, M. L. (2000). *Empathy and moral development: Implications for caring and justice.* New York: Cambridge University Press.

Hogrefe, G.-J., Wimmer, H., & Perner, J. (1986). Ignorance versus false belief: A developmental lag in attribution of epistemic states. *Child Development, 57*, 567–582.

Holmboe, K., Pasco Fearon, R. M., Csibra, G., Tucker, L., & Johnson, M. H. (2008). "Freeze-Frame": A new infant inhibition task and its relation to frontal cortex tasks in infancy and early childhood. *Journal of Experimental Child Psychology, 100*, 89–114.

Holmes, J., Gathercole, S. E., & Dunning, D. L. (2009). Adaptive training leads to sustained enhancement of poor working memory in children. *Developmental Science, 12*, F9–F15.

Holowka, S., & Petitto, L. A. (2002). Left hemisphere cerebral specialization for babies while babbling. *Science, 297* (30 August), 1515.

Holstein, C. (1976). Irreversible, stepwise sequence in the development of moral judgment: A longitudinal study of males and females. *Child Development, 47*, 51–61.

Honzik, M. P., MacFarlane, J. W., & Allen, L. (1948). Stability of mental test performance between 2 and 18 years. *Journal of Experimental Education, 17*, 309–324.

Hood, B. M. (2004). Is looking good enough or does it beggar belief? *Developmental Science, 7*, 415–417.

Hopkins, B. (1993). On the developmental origins of human handedness. In Annual Report 1992–1993, no. 16, *Research and Clinical Center for Child Development*, Hokkaido University, Sapporo, Japan.

Horner, V., & Whiten, A. (2005). Causal knowledge and imitation/emulation switching in chimpanzees (*Pan troglodytes*) and children (*Homo sapiens*). *Animal Cognition, 8*, 164–181.

Hornik, R., Risenhoover, N., & Gunnar, M. (1987). The effects of maternal positive, neutral, and negative affect communication on infant responses to new toys. *Child Development, 58*, 937–944.

Hornor, G. (2004). Sexual behavior in children: Normal or not? *Journal of Pediatric Health Care, 18*, 57–64.

Howe, M. L. (2003). Memories from the cradle. *Current Directions in Psychological Science, 12*, 62–65.

Howe, M. L., Courage, M. L., & Rooksby, M. (2009). The genesis and development of autobiographical memory. In M. L. Courage & N. Cowan (Eds.), *The development of memory in infancy and childhood* (pp. 178–196). New York: Psychology Press.

Howes, C. (1992). *The collaborative construction of pretend.* Albany: State University of New York Press.

Howes, C. (1999). Attachment relationships in the context of multiple caregivers. In J. Cassidy & P. Shaver (Eds.) *Handbook of attachment* (1st ed., pp. 671–687). New York: Guilford.

Hrdy, S. B. (1999). *Mother nature: A history of mothers, infants, and natural selection.* New York: Pantheon Books.

Hrdy, S. B. (2007). Evolutionary context of human development: The cooperative breeding model. In C. Solomon & T. K. Shackelford (Eds.), *Family relationships: Evolutionary perspectives.* New York: Oxford University Press.

Hrdy, S. B. (2009). *Mothers and others: The evolutionary origins of mutual understanding.* Cambridge, MA: Belknap Press.

Hubbs-Tait, L., Nation, J. R., Krebs, N. F., & Bellinger, D. C. (2005). Neurotoxicants, micronutrients, and social environments: Individual and combined effects on children's development. *Psychological Science in the Public Interest, 6*, 57–121.

Hudson, J. A. (1993). Reminiscing with mothers and others: Autobiographical memory in young two-year-olds. *Journal of Narrative & Life History, 3*, 1–32.

Huesmann, L. R., Moise-Titus, J., Podolski, C-L., & Eron, L. D. (2003). Longitudinal relations between children's exposure to TV violence and their aggressive and violent behavior in young adulthood: 1977–1992. *Developmental Psychology, 39*, 201–221.

Huesmann, R. L. (1986). Psychological processes promoting the relation between exposure to media violence and aggressive behavior by the viewer. *Journal of Social Issues, 42*, 125–139.

Hughes, C., & Ensor, R. (2007). Executive function and theory of mind: Predictive relations from ages 2 to 4. *Developmental Psychology, 43*, 1447–1459.

Huizink, A. C., Mulder, E. J., & Buitelaar, J. K. (2004). Prenatal stress and risk for psychopathology: Specific effects or induction of general susceptibility? *Psychological Bulletin, 130*, 115–142.

Hulme, C., & Snowling, M. J. (2009). *Developmental disorders of language learning and cognition.* Chichester, UK: Wiley.

Hulme, C., Thomson, N., Muir, C., & Lawrence, A. (1984). Speech rate and the development of spoken words: The role of rehearsal and item identification processes. *Journal of Experimental Child Psychology, 38*, 241–253.

Humphrey, D. E., & Humphrey, G. K. (1988). Sex differences in lateralized preference for grasping and reaching in infants. In M. A. Goodale (Ed.), *Vision and action: The control of grasping* (pp. 80–97). Norwood, NJ: Ablex.

Humphrey, N. K. (1976). The social function of intellect. In P. P. G. Bateson & R. A. Hinde (Eds.), *Growing points in ethology* (pp. 303–317). Cambridge, UK: Cambridge University Press.

Hunt, J. McV. (1961). *Intelligence and experience.* New York: Ronald Press.

Huntsman, R. W. (1984). Children's concepts of fair sharing. *Journal of Moral Education, 13*, 31–39.

Huttenlocher, P. (2002). *Neural plasticity: The effects of environment on the development of the cerebral cortex.* Cambridge, MA: Harvard University Press.

Huttenlocher, P. (1979). Synaptic density in human frontal cortex: Developmental changes and effects of aging. *Brain Research, 163*, 195–205.

Huttenlocher, P., & Dabholkar, A. S. (1997). Regional differences in synaptogenesis in human cerebral cortex. *Journal of Comparative Neurology, 387*, 167–178.

Hyde, J. S. (2005). Gender similarity hypothesis. *American Psychologist, 60*, 581–592.

Hyde, J. S. (2007). New directions in the study of gender similarities and differences. *Current Directions in Psychological Science, 15*, 259–263.

Hyde, J. S., Lindberg, S. M., Linn, M. C., Ellis, A. B., & Williams, C. C. (2008). Gender similarities characterize math performance. *Science, 321* (25 July), 494–495.

Hyde, J. S., & McKinley, N. M. (1997). Gender differences in cognition: Results from meta-analyses. In P. J. Caplan, M. Crawford, J. S. Hyde, & J. R. E. Richardson (Eds.), *Gender differences in human cognition.* (p. 30–51). New York: Oxford University Press.

Inagaki, K. (1990). The effects of raising animals on children's biological knowledge. *British Journal of Developmental Psychology, 8*, 119–129.

Inagaki, K., & Hatano, G. (1991). Constrained person analogy in young children's biological inference. *Cognitive Development, 6*, 219–231.

Inagaki, K., & Hatano, G. (1993). Young children's understanding of the mind-body distinction. *Child Development, 64*, 1534–1549.

Inagaki, K., & Hatano, G. (2002). *Young children's naive thinking about the biological world.* New York: Psychology Press.

Inagaki, K., & Hatano, G. (2006). Young children's conception of the biological world. *Current Directions in Psychological Science, 15*, 177–181.

Ingram, D. (1989). *First language acquisition: Method, description, and explanation.* London: Cambridge University Press.

Ingram, G., & Bering, J. M. (in press). Children's tattling: A developmental precursor to gossip? *Child Development* 2010; *81*, 945–957.

Inhelder, B., & Piaget, J. (1958). *The growth of logical thinking from childhood to adolescence.* New York: Basic.

Institute of Medicine of the National Academies (2004). *Infant formula: Evaluating the safety of new ingredients.* Washington, DC: National Academy Press.

Institute of Medicine of the National Academies. (2005). *Preventing childhood obesity: Health in the balance.* Washington, DC: Author.

International Human Genome Sequencing Consortium. (2001). Initial sequencing and analysis of the human genome. *Nature, 409* (15 February), 860–921.

International Task Force on Obesity. (2004). *Obesity in children and young people: A crisis in public health.* Accessed at: www.iotf.org.

Ireland, J. L., & Power, C. L. (2004). Attachment, emotional loneliness, and bullying behaviour: A study of adult and young offenders. *Aggressive Behavior, 30*, 298–312.

Ishikawa, S. S., & Raine, A. (2002). Behaviorial genetics and crime. In J. Glicksohn (Ed.), *The neurobiology of criminal behavior* (pp. 81–111). Springer: New York.

Israel, A. C., & Ivanova, M. Y. (2002). Global and dimensional self-esteem in preadolescent and early adolescent children who are overweight: Age and gender differences. *International Journal of Eating Disorders, 31*, 424–429.

Itard, J. M. G. (1962). *The wild boy of Aveyron* (G. Humphrey & M. Humphrey, trans.). New York: Appleton-Century-Crofts.

Ito, M., Horst, H., Bittanti, M., Boyd, D., Herr-Stephenson, B., Lange, P. G., Pascoe, C. J., & Robinson, L. (2008). *Living and learning with new media: Summary of findings from the Digital Youth Project.* Chicago: The John D. and Catherine T. MacArthur Foundation.

Iverson, J. M., & Goldin-Meadow, S. (2005). Gesture paves the way for language development. *Psychological Science, 16*, 368–371.

Izard, C. E. (1991). *The psychology of emotions.* New York: Plenum Press.

Izard, C. E., Fantauzzo, C. A., Castle, J. M., Hayness, O. M., Rayias, M. F., & Putnam, P. H. (1995). The ontogeny and significance of infant's facial expressions in the first 9 months of life. *Developmental Psychology, 31*, 997–1013.

Jaccard, J., Blanton, H., & Dodge, T. (2005). Peer influences on risk behavior: An analysis of the effects of a close friend. *Developmental Psychology, 41*, 135–147.

Jackson, J. F. (1993). Human behavioral genetics: Scarr's theory, and her views on intervention: A critical review and commentary on their implications for African American children. *Child Development, 64*, 1318–1332.

Jacobi, C., Hayward, C., de Zwaan, M., Kraemer, H. C., & Agras, W. S. (2004). Coming to terms with risk factors for eating disorders: Application of risk terminology and suggestions for a general taxonomy. *Psychological Bulletin, 130*, 19–65.

Jacobson, J. L., & Jacobson, S. W. (2002). Effects of prenatal alcohol exposure on child development. *Alcohol Research & Health, 26*, 282–286.

Jacobson, S. W. (1979). Matching behavior in the young infant. *Child Development, 50*, 425–430.

Jacoby, R., & Glauberman, N. (Eds.). (1995). *The bell curve debate.* New York: Random House.

Jaffee, S., & Hyde, J. S. (2000). Gender differences in moral orientation: A meta-analysis. *Psychological Bulletin, 126*, 703–726.

Jahromi, L. B., Putnam, S. P., & Stifter, C. A. (2004). Maternal regulation of infant reactivity from 2 to 6 months. *Developmental Psychology, 40*, 477–487.

James, M., Draycott, T., Fox, R., & Read, M. (1999). *Obstetrics and gynecology.* London: Harcourt International.

Jankowiak, W., & Fisher, E. (1992). Romantic love: A cross-cultural perspective. *Ethnology, 31*, 149–156.

Jankowiak, W., & Diderich, M. (2000). Sibling solidarity in a polygamous community in the USA: Unpacking inclusive fitness. *Evolution and Human Behavior, 21*, 125–139.

Jekielek, S. M. (1998). Parental conflict, marital disruption and children's emotional well-being. *Social Forces, 76*, 905–936.

Jenkins, J. M., & Astington, J. W. (1996). Cognitive factors and family structure associated with theory of mind development in young children. *Developmental Psychology, 32*, 70–78.

Jenkins, J., Simpson, A., Dunn, J., Rasbash, J., & O'Connor, T. G. (2005). Mutual influence of marital conflict and children's behavior problems: Shared and nonshared family risks. *Child Development, 76*, 24–39.

Jensen, A. R. (1969). How much can we boost I.Q. and scholastic achievement? *Harvard Educational Review, 33*, 1–123.

Jensen, A. R. (1998). *The g factor: The science of mental ability.* Westport, CT: Praeger.

Jensen, K., Hare, B., Call, J. & Tomasello, M. (2006). What's in it for me? Self-regard precludes altruism and spite in chimpanzees. *Proceedings of the Royal Society of London, 273*, 1013–1021.

Jensen, P. S., Mrazek, D., Knapp, P. K., Steinberg, L., Pfeffer, C., Schwalter, J., & Shapiro, T. (1997). Evolution and revolution in Child Psychiatry: ADHD as a disorder of adaptation. *Journal of the American Academy of Child & Adolescent Psychiatry, 36*, 1672–1681.

Jerison, H. J. (1973). *Evolution of the brain and intelligence.* New York: Academic Press.

Jessor, R., Costa, F., Jessor, L., & Donovan, J. E. (1983). Time of first intercourse: A prospective study. *Journal of Personality and Social Psychology, 44*, 608–620.

Jiang, X. L., & Cillessen, A. H. N. (2005). Stability of continuous measures of sociometric status: A meta-analysis. *Developmental Review, 25*, 1–25.

Joanisse, M. F. (2004). Specific language impairment in children: Phonology, semantics, and the English past tense. *Current Directions in Psychological Science, 13*, 156–160.

Joffe, T. H. (1997). Social pressures have selected for an extended juvenile period in primates. *Journal of Human Evolution, 32*, 593–605.

Johanson, D., & Edgar, B. (1996) *From Lucy to language.* New York: Simon & Schuster.

John, O. P., Caspi, A., Robins, R. W., Moffitt, T. E., & Stouthamer-Loeber, M. (1994). The "little five": Exploring the five-factor model of personality in adolescent boys. *Child Development, 65*, 160–178.

John, O. P., Donahue, E. M. & Kentle, L. K. (1991). *The big five inventory.* Berkeley, CA: Institute of Personality and Social Research, University of Berkeley.

Johnson, D. B. (1982). Altruistic behavior and the development of the self in infants. *Merrill-Palmer Quarterly, 28*, 379–388.

Johnson, J. S., & Newport, E. L. (1989). Critical period effects in second language learning: The influence of maturational state on the acquisition of English as a second language. *Cognitive Psychology, 21*, 60–99.

Johnson, M. H. (1997). *Developmental cognitive neuroscience.* Oxford, UK: Blackwell.

Johnson, M. H. (1998). The neural basis of cognitive development. In W. Damon (Gen. Ed.), *Handbook of child psychology* (5th ed.). In D. Kuhn & R. S. Siegler (Vol. Eds.), Vol. 2: *Cognition, perception, and language.* New York: Wiley.

Johnson, M. H. (2000). Functional brain development in infants: Elements of an interactive specialization framework. *Child Development, 71*, 75–81.

Johnson, M. H. (2005). Cognitive neuroscience. In B. Hopkins (Ed.), *The Cambridge encyclopedia of child development* (pp. 478–481). Cambridge, UK: Cambridge University Press.

Johnson, M. H. (2007). The social brain in infancy: A developmental cognitive neuroscience approach. In D. Coch, K. W. Fischer, & G. Dawson (Eds.), *Human behavior, learning, and the developing brain: Typical development* (pp. 115–137). New York: Guilford.

Johnson, M. H., & de Haan, M. (2001). Developing cortical specialization for visual-cognitive function: The case of face recognition. In J. L. McClelland, & R. S. Siegler, (Eds.), *Mechanisms of cognitive development: Behavioral and neural perspectives.* Mahwah, NJ: Erlbaum.

Johnson, M. H., Dziurawiec, S., Ellis, H. D., & Morton, J. (1991). Newborns' preferential tracking of faces and its subsequent decline. *Cognition, 40*, 1–19.

Johnson, S. P., Hannon, E. E., & Amos, D. (2005). Perceptual development. In B. Hopkins (Ed.), *Cambridge encyclopedia of child development* (pp. 210–216). Cambridge, UK: Cambridge University Press.

Johnson, T. C. (1993). Assessment of sexual behavior problems in preschool-aged and latency-aged children. In A. Yates (Ed.), *Child and adolescent psychiatric clinics of North America. Vol. 2: Sexual and gender disorders* (pp. 431–450). Philadelphia, PA: Saunders.

Johnson, T. C. (1999). *Understanding your child's sexual behavior: What's natural and healthy.* Oakland, CA: New Harbinger Publications.

Jones, L. B., Rothbart, M. K., & Posner, M. I. (2003). Development of executive attention in preschool children. *Developmental Science, 6,* 498–504.

Jones, M. (1990). Children's writing. In R. Grieve & M. Hughes (Eds.), *Understanding children: Essays in honors of Margaret Donaldson* (pp. 94–120). Oxford, UK: Blackwell.

Jones, M. C. (1965). Psychological correlates of somatic development. *Child Development, 36,* 899–911.

Jones, M. C., & Bayley, N. (1950). Physical maturing among boys as related to behavior. *Journal of Educational Psychology, 41,* 129–148.

Jones, N. A., & Gagnon, C. M. (2007). The neurophysiology of empathy. In T. Farrow & T. Woodruff (Eds.), *Empathy in mental illness.* New York: Cambridge University Press.

Jones, N. A., Field, T., & Davalos, M. (1998). Massage therapy attenuates right frontal EEG asymmetry in one-month-old infants of depressed mothers. *Infant Behavior and Development, 21,* 527–530.

Jones, N. A., Field, T. M., & Davalos, M. (2000). Right frontal EEG asymmetry and lack of empathy in preschool children of depressed mothers. *Child Psychiatry and Human Development, 30,* 189–204.

Jones, N. A., & Gagnon, C. (2007). The neurophysiology of empathy. In T. Farrow & P. Woodruff (Eds.), *Empathy in mental illness* (pp. 217–241). Cambridge, UK: Cambridge University Press.

Jones, N. A. & Mize, K. D. (2007). Touch interventions positively affect development. In L. L'Abate (Ed.), *Low-cost approaches to promote physical and mental health.* New York: Springer.

Joseph, R. M., & Tanaka, J. (2003). Holistic and part-based face recognition in children with autism. *Journal of Child Psychology and Psychiatry, 44,* 529–542.

Josephson Institute's 2008 Report Card on the Ethics of American Youth. (November 30, 2008). *http://charactercounts.org/programs/reportcard/index.html.* (Downloaded December 1, 2008).

Juel, C. (1994). *Learning to read and write in one elementary school.* New York: Springer-Verlag.

Jusczyk, P. W. (1997). *The discovery of spoken language.* Cambridge, MA: MIT Press.

Kaeser, F., DiSalvo, C., & Moglia, R. (2000). Sexual behaviors of young children that occur in schools. *Journal of Sex Education and Therapy, 25,* 277–285.

Kagan, J. (1964). Acquisition and significance of sex typing and sex role identity. In M. L. Hoffman & L. W. Hoffman (Eds.), *Review of child development research* (Vol. 1, pp. 137–168). New York: Russell Sage.

Kagan, J. (1971). *Change and continuity in infancy.* New York: Wiley.

Kagan, J. (1976). New views on cognitive development. *Journal of Youth and Adolescence, 5,* 113–129.

Kagan, J. (1984). *The nature of the child.* New York: Basic Books.

Kagan, J. (1989). Temperamental contributions to social behavior. *American Psychologist, 44,* 668–674.

Kagan, J. (1994). *Galen's prophecy: Temperament in human nature.* Cambridge, MA: Harvard University Press.

Kagan, J. (2003). Biology, context, and developmental inquiry. *Annual Reviews Psychology, 54,* 1–23.

Kagan, J., & Fox, N. (2006). Biology, culture and temperamental biases. In W. Damon & R. Lerner (Gen. Eds.), *Handbook of child psychology* (6th ed.). In N. Eisenberg (Vol. Ed.), Vol. 3 (pp. 167–225). New York: Wiley.

Kagan, J., Keasley, R. B., & Zelazo, P. R. (1978). *Infancy: Its place in human development.* Cambridge, MA: Harvard University Press.

Kagan J., Reznick, J. S., & Snidman N. (1987). The physiology and psychology of behavioral inhibition in children. *Child Development, 58,* 1459–1473.

Kagan, J., & Snidman, N. (2004). *The long shadow of temperament.* Cambridge, MA: Belknap Press.

Kagan, J., Snidman, N., Kahn, V., & Towsley, S. (2007). The preservation of two infant temperaments into adolescence. *Monographs of the Society for Research in Child Development, 72* (Serial No. 287).

Kail, R. (1991). Development of processing speed in childhood and adolescence. In H. W. Reese (Ed.), *Advances in child development and behavior* (Vol. 23). San Diego: Academic Press.

Kail, R. V., & Ferrer, E. (2008). Processing speed in childhood and adolescence: Longitudinal models for examining developmental change. *Child Development, 78,* 1760–1770.

Kaiser Family Foundation (2006). *Generation M: Media in the Lives of 8–18 Year-Olds.* Menlo Park, CA: Kaiser Family Foundation.

Kaiser Family Foundation & Children Now. (1997). *Talking with kids about tough issues: A national survey.* Palo Alto, CA: Henry J. Kaiser Family Foundation.

Kaplan, H., & Dove, H. (1987). Infant development among the Ache of Eastern Paraguay. *Developmental Psychology, 23,* 190–198.

Kaplan, H., Hill, K., Lancaster, J., & Hurtado, A. M. (2000). A theory of human life history evolution: Diet, intelligence, and longevity. *Evolutionary Anthropology, 9,* 156–185.

Karmiloff-Smith, A. (1990). Constraints on representational change: Evidence from children's drawings. *Cognition, 34,* 57–83.

Karmiloff-Smith, A. (1991). Beyond modularity: Innate constraints and developmental change. In S. Carey & R. Gelman (Eds.), *The epigenesis of mind: Essays on biology and cognition.* Hillsdale, NJ: Erlbaum.

Karmiloff-Smith, A. (1992). *Beyond modularity: A developmental perspective on cognitive science.* Cambridge, MA: MIT Press.

Karmiloff-Smith, A. (2009). Nativism versus neuroconstructivism: Rethinking the study of developmental disorders. *Developmental Psychology, 45,* 56–63.

Karzon, R. G. (1985). Discrimination of polysyllabic sequences by one- to four-month-old infants. *Journal of Experimental Child Psychology, 39,* 326–342.

Katz, L. F., & Gottman, J. M. (1996). Spillover effects of marital conflict: In search of parenting and coparenting mechanisms. In J. P. McHale & P. A. Cowan (Eds.), *Understanding how family-level dynamics affect children's development: Studies of two-parent families* (pp. 57–76). San Francisco: Jossey-Bass.

Katz, L. F., Kling, J. R., & Liebman, J. B. (2001). Moving to Opportunity in Boston: Early results of a randomized mobility experiment. *Quarterly Journal of Economics, 116,* 607–654.

Katz, M. B. (1986). *In the shadow of the poor house: A social history of welfare in America.* New York: Basic Books.

Kaukiainen, A., Björkqvist, K., Lagerspertz, K., Österman, K., Salmivalli, C., Rothberg, S., & Ahlbo, A. (1999). The relationship between social intelligence, empathy, and three types of aggression. *Aggressive Behavior, 25,* 81–89.

Kaye, K. (1982). *The mental and social life of babies: How parents create persons.* Chicago: University of Chicago Press.

Kazdin, A. E. (1997). Conduct disorders across the life span. In S. S. Luthar, J. A. Burack, D. Cicchetti, & J. R. Weisz (Eds.), *Developmental psychopathology: Perspectives on adjustment, risk, psychopathology: Perspectives on adjustment, risk, and disorder* (pp. 248–272). Cambridge, UK: Cambridge University Press.

Kazdin, A. E., & Benjet, C. (2003). Spanking children: Evidence and issues. *Current Directions in Psychological Science, 12,* 99–103.

Kee, D. W. (1994). Developmental differences in associative memory: Strategy use, mental effort, and knowledge-access interactions. In H. W. Reese (Ed.), *Advances in child development and behavior* (Vol. 25). New York: Academic Press.

Keen, R. (2003). Representation of objects and events: Why do infants look so smart and toddlers look so dumb? *Current Directions in Psychological Science, 12,* 79–83.

Keil, F.C. (2007). Biology and beyond: Domain specificity in a broader developmental context. *Human Development, 50,* 31–38.

Keiley, M., Howe, T. R., Dodge, K. A., Bates, J. E., & Pettit, G. S. (2001). The timing of child physical maltreatment: A cross-domain growth analysis of impact on adolescent externalizing and internalizing problems. *Development and Psychopathology, 28,* 161–179.

Kelemen, D. (2004). Are children "intuitive theists"? Reasoning about purpose and design in nature. *Psychological Science 15,* 295–301.

Keller, A., Ford, L. H., Jr., & Meachum, J. A. (1978). Dimensions of self-concept in preschool children. *Developmental Psychology, 14,* 483–489.

Keller, H., Lohaus, A., Kuensemueller, P., Abels, M., Yovsi, R., Voelker, S., Jensen, H., Papaligoura, Z., Rosabal-Coto, M., Kulks, D., & Mohite, P. (2004). The bio-culture of parenting: Evidence from five cultural communities. *Parenting: Science and Practice, 4,* 25–50.

Kellman, P. J., & Arterberry, M. E. (2006). Perceptual development. In W. Damon (Gen. Ed.), *The handbook of child psychology* (6th ed.). In D. Kuhn & R. Siegler (Vol. Eds.), *Cognition, perception, and language* (pp. 109–160). New York: Wiley.

Kelly, D. J., Liu, S., Lee, K., Quinn, P. C., Pascalis, O., Slater, A. M., & Ge, L. (2009). Development of the other-race effect in infancy: Evidence toward universality? *Journal of Experimental Child Psychology, 104,* 105–114.

Kelly, D. J., Quinn, P. C., Slater, A. M., Lee, K., Ge, L., & Pascalis, O. (2007). The other-race effect develops during infancy. *Psychological Science, 18,* 1084–1089.

Kelly, D. J., Quinn, P. C., Slater, A. M., Lee, K., Gibson, A., Smith, M., et al. (2005). Three-month-olds, but not newborns, prefer own-race faces. *Developmental Science, 8,* F31–F36.

Kelly, Y., Sacker A., Gray R., Kelly J., Wolke D., & Quigley, M. A. (2009). Light drinking in pregnancy, a risk for behavioural problems and cognitive deficits at 3 years of age? *International Journal of Epidemiology, 38,* 129–140. *http://ije.oxfordjournals.org/cgi/reprint/dyn230v1.*

Kendall-Tackett, K. A., Williams, L. M., & D. Finkelhor, D. (1993). The impact of sexual abuse on children: A review and synthesis of recent empirical studies. *Psychological Bulletin, 113,* 164–180.

Kennedy, C. M., & Lipsitt, L. P. (1998). Risk-taking in preschool children. *Journal of Pediatric Nursing, 13,* 77–84.

Kenrick, D. T., & Keefe, R. C. (1992). Age preferences in mates reflect sex difference s in reproductive strategies. *Behavioral and Brain Sciences, 15,* 75–133.

Kenrick, D. T., Keefe, R. C., Gabrielidis, C., & Cornelius, J. S. (1996). Adolescents' age preferences for dating partners: Support for an evolutionary model of life-history strategies. *Child Development, 67,* 1499–1511.

Kent, R. (2005). Speech development. In B. Hopkins (Ed.), *The Cambridge encyclopedia of child development* (pp. 257–264). New York: Cambridge University Press.

Kermoian, R., & Campos, J. J. (1988). Locomotor experience: A facilitator of spatial cognitive development. *Child Development, 59,* 908–917.

Kermoian, R., & Leiderman, P. H. (1986). Infant attachment to mother and child caretaker in an East African community. *International Journal of Behavioral Development, 9,* 455–469.

Kerns, K. A. (2000). The CyberCruiser: An investigation of development of prospective memory in children. *Journal of the International Neuropsychological Society, 6,* 62–70.

Kessel, B. (1995). Reproductive cycles in women: Quality of life impact. In B. P. Sachs, R. Beard, E. Papiernik, & C. Russell (Eds.), *Reproductive health care for women and babies* (pp. 18–39). New York: Oxford University Press.

Kessen, W. (1965). *The child.* New York: Wiley.

Kessler, R. C., Chiu, W. T., Demler, O., et al. (2005). Prevalence, severity, and comorbidity of 12-month DSM IV disorders in the National Comorbidity Survey Replication. *Archives of General Psychiatry, 62,* 617–627.

Killian, K. (1994). Fearing fat: A literature review of family systems understandings ad treatments of anorexia and bulimia. *Family Relations, 43,* 311–318.

Killian, M., & Nucci, L. P. (1995). Morality, autonomy, and social conflict. In M. Killen & D. hart (Eds.), *Morality in everyday life: Developmental perspectives* (pp. 52–86). Cambridge, UK: Cambridge University Press.

Kim-Cohen, J., Moffitt, T. E., Caspi, A., & Taylor, A. (2004). Genetic and environmental processes in young children's resilience and vulnerability to socioeconomic deprivation. *Child Development, 75,* 651–668.

Kim, K., Smith, P. K., & Palermiti, A. (1997). Conflict in childhood and mating development. *Evolution and Human Behavior, 18,* 110–142.

Kim, K. H. S., Relkin, N. R., Lee, K-M., & Hirsch, J. (1997). Distinct cortical areas associated with native and second languages. *Nature, 388* (12 July), 171–174.

Kimura, D. (1999). *Sex and cognition.* Cambridge, MA: MIT Press.

King, G. (2004). *Woman, child for sale: The new slave trade in the 21st century.* New York: Chamberlain Brothers.

Kinsey, A. C., Pomeroy, W. N., & Martin, C. E. (1948). *Sexual behavior in the human male.* Philadelphia: Saunders.

Kinsey, A. C., Pomeroy, W. B., Martin, C. E., & Gebhard, P. H. (1953). *Sexual behavior in the human female.* Philadelphia: Saunders.

Kirby, D., & Laris, B. A. (2009). Effective curriculum-based sex and STD/HIV education programs for adolescents. *Child Development Perspectives, 3,* 21–29.

Kirschner, S., & Tomasello, M. (2009). Joint drumming: Social context facilitates synchronization in preschool children. *Journal of Experimental Child Psychology, 102,* 299–314.

Kisilevsky, B. S., Hains, S. M. J., Lee, K., Xie, X., Huang, H., Ye, H. H., Zhang, K., & Wang, Z. (2003). Effects of experience on fetal voice recognition. *Psychological Science, 14,* 22–224.

Kitayama, S., Duffy, S., Kawamura, T., & Larsen, J. T. (2003). Perceiving an object and its context in different cultures: A cultural look at new look. *Psychological Science, 14,* 201–206.

Kittler, P. M., Krinsky-McHale, S. J., &. Devenny, D. A. (2008). Dual-task processing as a measure of executive function: A comparison between adults with Williams and Down Syndromes. *American Journal on Mental Retardation, 113,* 117–132.

Klaczynski, P. A. (1997). Bias in adolescents' everyday reasoning and its relationship with intellectual ability, personal theories, and self-serving motivation. *Developmental Psychology, 33,* 273–283.

Klaczynski, P. (2008). There's something about obesity: Culture, contagion, rationality, and children's responses to drinks "created" by obese children. *Journal of Experimental Child Psychology, 99,* 58–74.

Klaczynski, P., & Daniel, D. B. (2008). Thin idealization, body esteem, causal attributions, and ethnic variations in the development of obesity stereotypes. *Journal of Applied Developmental Psychology, 30,* 537–551.

Klaczynski, P. A., & Narasimham, G. (1998). Development of scientific reasoning biases: Cognitive versus ego-protective explanations. *Developmental Psychology, 34,* 175–187.

Klaus, M. H., & Kennell, J. H. (1976). *Maternal–infant bonding.* St. Louis, MO: Mosby.

Klaus, M. H., & Kennell, J. H. (1982). *Parent–infant bonding.* St. Louis, MO: Mosby.

Klaus, M. H., Kennell, J., Berkowitz, G., & Klaus, P. (1992). Maternal assistance and support in labor: father, nurse, midwife, or doula? *Clinical Consultations in Obstetrics and Gynecology, 4,* 211–217.

Klaus, M. H., Kennell, J. H., & Klaus, P. H. (1995). *Bonding: Building the foundations of secure attachment and independence.* Reading, MA: Addison-Wesley.

Klaus, R. A., & Gray S. (1968). The early training project for disadvantaged children: A report after five years. *Monographs of the Society for Research in Child Development, 33* (Serial No. 120).

Klein, H. (1991) Couvade syndrome: Male counterpart to pregnancy. *International Journal of Psychiatry in Medicine, 21,* 57–69.

Kliegel, M., & Jäger, T. (2007). The effects of age and cue-action reminders on event-based prospective memory performance in preschoolers. *Cognitive Development, 22,* 33–46.

Klin, A., Jones, W., Schultz, R., Volkmar, F., & Cohen, D. (2002). Visual fixation patterns during viewing of naturalistic social situations as predictors of social competence in individuals with autism. *Archive of General Psychiatry, 59,* 809–816.

Klin, A., Lin, D. J., Gorrindo, P., Ramsay, G., & Jones, W. (2009). Two-year-olds with autism orient to non-social contingencies rather than biological motion. *Nature, 459* (14 May), 257–262.

Kling, K. C., Hyde, J. S., Showers, C. J., & Buswell, B. N. (1999). Gender differences in self-esteem: A meta-analysis. *Psychological Review, 125,* 470–500.

Klingberg, T., Forssberg, H., & Westerberg, H. (2002). Training of working memory in children with ADHD. *Journal of Clinical and Experimental Neuropsychology, 24,* 781–791.

Knafo, A., & Plomin, R. (2006). Prosocial behavior from early to middle childhood: Genetic and environmental influences on stability and change. *Developmental Psychology, 42,* 771–786.

Kochanska, G. (1993). Toward a synthesis of parental socialization and child temperament in early development of conscience. *Child Development, 64,* 325–347.

Kochanska, G. (1994). Beyond cognition: Expanding the search for the early roots of internalization and conscience. *Developmental Psychology, 30,* 20–22.

Kochanska, G. (1997). Multiple pathways to conscience for children with different temperaments: From childhood to age 5. *Developmental Psychology, 33,* 228–240.

Kochanska, G., Aksan, N., Knaack, A., & Rines, H. M. (2004). Maternal parenting and children's conscience: Early security as moderator. *Child Development, 75,* 1229–1242.

Kochanska, G., Murray, K. T., & Harlan, E. (2000). Effortful control in early childhood: Continuity and change, antecedents, and implications for social development. *Developmental Psychology, 36,* 220–232.

Kochanska, G., Murray, K. T., Jacques, T. Y., Koenig, A. L., & Vandegeest, K. A. (1996). Inhibitory control in young children and its role in emerging internalization. *Child Development, 67,* 490–507.

Koenen, M. A., & Thompson, Jr., J. W. (2008). Historical review and prevention of child death by parent. *Infant Mental Health Journal, 29,* 61–75.

Kohen, D. E., Leventhal, T., Dahinten, V. S., & McIntosh, C. N. (2008). Neighborhood disadvantage: Pathway effects of young children. *Child Development, 79,* 156–169.

Kohlberg, L. (1966). A cognitive-developmental analysis of children's sex-role concepts and attitudes. In E. E. Maccoby (Ed.), *The development of sex differences.* Stanford, CA: Stanford University Press.

Kohlberg, L. (1969). Stage and sequence: The cognitive-developmental approach to socialization. In D. A. Goslin (Ed.), *Handbook of socialization theory and research.* Chicago: Rand McNally.

Kohlberg, L. (1984). *Essays on moral development,* Vol. 2: *The psychology of moral development.* San Francisco: Harper & Row.

Kohlberg, L., Yaeger, J., & Hjertholm, E. (1968). Private speech: Four studies and a review of theories. *Child Development, 39,* 691–736.

Kolb, B. (1989). Brain development, plasticity and behaviour. In M. Johnson (1993) (Ed.), *Brain development and cognition* (pp. 338–357). Oxford, UK: Blackwell.

Kolb, B., Gibb, R., & Robinson, T. E. (2003). Brain plasticity and behavior. *Current Directions in Psychological Sciences, 12,* 1–5.

Kolb, B., & Whishaw, I. Q. (1981). Neonatal frontal lesions in the rat: Sparing of learned but not species-typical behavior in the presence of reduced brain weight and critical thickness. *Journal of Comparative and Physiological Psychology, 95,* 235–276.

Koluchova, J. (1976). Severe deprivation in twins: A case study. In A. M. Clarke and A. D. B. Clarke (Eds.), *Early experience: Myth and evidence.* London: Open Books.

Komlos, J., & Lauderdale, B. E. (2007). Underperformance in affluence: The remarkable relative decline in American heights in the second half of the 20th century. *Social Science Quarterly, 88,* 283–304.

Konner, M. (2010). *The evolution of childhood: Relationships, emotions, mind.* Cambridge, MA: Belknap Press.

Konopka, G. (1976). *Young girls: A portrait of adolescence.* New York: Harrington Park Press.

Kopp, C. B., & McCall, R. B. (1982). Predicting later mental performance for normal, at-risk, and handicapped infants. In P. B. Baltes & O. G. Brim (Eds.), *Life-span development and behavior* (Vol. 4). New York: Academic.

Kopp, C. B., Sigman, M., & Parmelee, A. H. (1974). Longitudinal study of sensorimotor development. *Developmental Psychology, 10,* 687–695.

Koren-Karie, N., Oppenheim, D., Dolev, S., Sher, E., & Etzion-Carasso, A. (2002). Mothers' insightfulness regarding their infants' internal experience: Relations with maternal sensitivity and infant attachment. *Developmental Psychology, 38,* 534–542.

Korner, A. F., & Thoman, E. B. (1970). Visual alertness in neonates as evoked by maternal care. *Journal of Experimental Child Psychology, 10,* 67–78.

Korner, A. F., & Thoman, E. B. (1972). The relative efficacy of contact and vestibular-proprioceptive stimulation in soothing neonates. *Child Development, 43,* 433–454.

Kotovsky, L., & Baillargeon, R. (1994). Calibration-based reasoning about collision events in 11-month-old infants. *Cognition, 51,* 107–129.

Kotovsky, L., & Baillargeon, R. (2000). Reasoning about collisions involving inert objects in 7.5-month-old infants. *Developmental Science, 3,* 344–359.

Kovács, A. M. (2009). Early bilingualism enhances mechanisms of false-belief reasoning. *Developmental Science, 12,* 48–54.

Kovacs, D. M., Parker, J. G., & Hoffman, L. W. (1996). Behavioral, affective, and social correlates of involvement in cross-sex friendship in elementary school. *Child Development, 67,* 2269–2286.

Krachun, C., Carpenter, M., Call, J., & Tomasello, M. (2009). A competitive nonverbal false belief task for children and apes. *Developmental Science, 12,* 521–535.

Kraft-Ebbing, R. (1965). *Psychopathia sexualis* (Franklin S. Klaf, Trans.). New York: Stein & Day. (Original work published 1886).

Kratochwill, T. R., & Goldman, J. A. (1973). Developmental changes in children's judgments of age. *Developmental Psychology, 9,* 358–362.

Krautter, T. H., & Lock, J. (2004). Treatment of adolescent anorexia nervosa using manualized family-based treatment. *Clinical Case Studies, 3,* 107–123.

Krebs, D. L. (2008). Morality: An evolutionary account. *Perspectives on Psychological Development, 3,* 149–172.

Krebs, D. L., & Denton, K. (2005). Toward a more pragmatic approach to morality: A critical evaluation of Kohlberg's model. *Psychological Review, 112,* 629–649.

Kreutzer, M. A., Leonard, C., & Flavell, J. H. (1975). An interview study of children's knowledge about memory. *Monographs of the Society for Research in Child Development, 40* (Serial No. 159).

Krevans, J., & Gibbs, J. C. (1996). Parents' use of inductive discipline: Relations to children's empathy and prosocial behavior. *Child Development, 67,* 3263–3277.

Krishnamoorthy, J., Hart, C., & Jelalian, E. (2006). The epidemic of childhood obesity: Review of research and implications for public policy. *Social Policy Report, Society for Research in Child Development, 19* (11).

Kroger, J. (2005). Identity statuses. In C. B. Fisher & R. M. Lerner (Eds.), *Encyclopedia of applied developmental science* (Vol. 1, pp. 567–568). Thousand Oaks, CA: Sage.

Kroupina, M. G., Bauer, P. J., Gunnar, M. R., & Johnson, D. E. (2010). Institutional care as a risk for declarative memory development. In P. J. Bauer (Ed.), Varieties of early experience: Implications for the development of declarative memory in infancy. *Advances in Child Development and Behavior, 38.* London, UK: Elsevier.

Krumhansl, C. L., & Jusczyk, P. W. (1990). Infants' perception of phrase structure in music. *Psychological Science, 1,* 70–73.

Kuhl, P. (October 2007). *Language and the infant brain: How children learn.* Plenary talk presented at meeting of the Cognitive Development Society, Santa Fe, New Mexico.

Kuhl, P. K., & Meltzoff, A. N. (1982). The bimodal perception of speech in infancy. *Science, 218,* 1138–1141.

Kuhl, P. K., Andruski, J. E., Christovich, I. A., Christovich, L. A., Kozhevnikova, E. V., Ryskina, V. L., Stolyarova, E. I., Sundberg, U., & Lacerda, F. (1997). Cross-language analysis of phonetic units in language addressed to infants. *Science, 277* (1 August), 684–686.

Kuhl, P. K., Stevens, E., Hayashi, A., Deguchi, T., Kiritani, S., & Iverson, P. (2006). Infants show a facilitation effect for native language phonetic perception between 6 and 12 months. *Developmental Science, 9,* F13–F21.

Kuhlmeier, V. (2005). Symbolic insight and inhibitory control: Two problems facing young children an symbolic retrieval tasks. *Journal of Cognition and Development, 6,* 365–380.

Kuhn, D. (2006). Do cognitive changes accompany developments in the adolescent brain? Perspectives of *Psychological Science, 1,* 59–67.

Kuhn, D., Amsel, E., & O'Loughlin, M. (1988). *The development of scientific thinking skills.* San Diego: Academic.

Kuhn, D., Garcia-Mila, M., Zohar, A., & Andersen, C. (1995). Strategies of knowledge acquisition. *Monographs of the Society for Research in Child Development, 60* (Serial No. 245).

Kuntsi, J., Eley, T. C., Taylor, A., Hughes, C., Asherson, P., Caspi, A., & Moffitt T. E. (2004). Co-occurrence of ADHD and low IQ has genetic origins. *American Journal of Medical Genetics Part B (Neuropsychiatric Genetics), 124,* 41–47.

Kupersmidt, J. B., & Coie, J. D. (1990). Preadolescent peer status and aggression as predictors of externalizing problems in adolescence. *Child Development, 61,* 1350–1362.

Kupersmidt, J. B., & Dodge, K. A. (Eds.). (2004). *Children's peer relations: From development to intervention.* Washington, DC: American Psychological Association.

Kupersmidt, J. B., Griesler, P. C., DeRosier, M. E., Patterson, C., & Davis, P. W. (1995). Childhood aggression and peer relations in the context of family and neighborhood factors. *Child Development, 66,* 360–375.

Kuttler, A. F., Parker, J. G., & La Greca , A. M. (2002). Developmental and gender differences in preadolescents' judgments of the veracity of gossip. *Merrill Palmer Quarterly, 48,* 105–132.

Ladd, G. W. (2006). Peer rejection, aggressive or withdrawn behavior, and psychological maladjustment from ages 5 to 12: An examination of four predictive models. *Child Development, 77,* 922–846.

Ladd, G. W., Kochenderfer, B. J., & Coleman, C. C. (1997). Classroom peer acceptance, friendship, and victimization: Distinct relational systems that contribute uniquely to children's school adjustment? *Child Development, 68,* 1181–1197.

LaFreniere, P. (2005). Human emotions as multipurpose adaptation. In R. L. Burgess & K. MacDonald (Eds.), *Evolutionary perspectives on human development* (pp. 189–205). Thousand Oaks, CA: Sage.

LaFromboise, T., Coleman H. L., & Gerton J. (1993). Psychological impact of biculturalism: Evidence and theory. *Psychological Bulletin, 114,* 395–412.

Lagattuta, K. H., & Wellman, H. M. (2001). Thinking about the past: Early knowledge about links between prior experience, thinking, and emotion. *Child Development, 72,* 82–102.

Lagattuta, K. H., Wellman, H. M., & Flavell, J. H. (1997). Preschoolers understanding of the link between thinking and feeling: Cognitive cuing and emotional change. *Child Development, 68,* 1081–1104.

Lahdenperä, M., Lummaa, V., Helle, S., Tremblay, M., & Russell, A. F. (2004). Fitness benefits of prolonged post-reproductive lifespan in women. *Nature, 428,* 178–181.

Lai, C-Q (2006). How much of human height is genetic and how much is due to nutrition? *Scientific American,* Accessed at: http://www.scientificamerican.com/article.cfm?id=how-much-of-human-height (Downloaded June 2, 2010).

Lamb, M. E. (1981). The development of father-infant relationships. In M. E. Lamb (Ed.), *The role of the father in child development.* New York: Wiley.

Lamb, M. E. (Ed.). (1997). *The role of the father in child development* (3rd ed.). New York: Wiley.

Lamb, M. E., & Ahnert, L. (2006). Nonparental child care: Context, concepts, correlates, and consequences. In W. Damon & R. M. Lerner (Gen. Eds.), *Handbook of child psychology* (6th ed.). In K. A. Renninger & I. E. Sigel (Vol. Eds.), Vol. 4: *Child psychology in practice* (pp. 950–1016). New York: Wiley.

Lamb, M. E., & Hwang, C. P. (1982). Maternal attachment and mother-neonate bonding: A critical review. In M. E. Lamb & A. L. Brown (Eds.), *Advances in developmental psychology* (pp. 1–39). Hillsdale, NJ: Erlbaum.

Lamb, M. E., Sternberg, K. J., & Esplin, P. W. (1998). Conducting investigative interviews of alleged sexual abuse victims. *Child Abuse & Neglect, 22,* 813–823.

Lamb, M. E., Sternberg, K. J., & Prodromidis, M. (1992). Nonmaternal care and the security of infant-mother attachment: A reanalysis of the data. *Infant Behavior and Development, 15,* 71–83.

Lamb, M. E., & Thierry, K. L. (2005). Understanding children's testimony regarding their alleged abuse: Contributions of field and laboratory analog research. In D. M. Teti (Ed.), *Handbook of research methods in developmental psychology.* Malden, MA: Blackwell.

Lamb, M. E., Thompson, R. A., Gardner, W., & Charnov, E. (1985). *Infant-mother attachment: The origins and developmental significance of individual differences in strange situation behavior.* Hillsdale, NJ: Erlbaum.

Lamb, S., & Coakley, M. (1993). "Normal" childhood sexual play in games: Differentiating play from abuse. *Child Abuse & Neglect, 17,* 515–526.

Lamb, S., & Zakhireh, B. (1997). Toddlers' attention to the distress of peers in a day care setting. *Early Education and Development, 8,* 105–118.

Lambert, W. E., Genesee, F., Holobow, N. E., & Chartrand, L. (1993). Bilingual education for majority English-speaking children. *European Journal of Psychology of Education, 8,* 3–22.

Lamborn, S. D., Dornbusch, S. M., & Steinberg, L. (1996). Ethnicity and community contexts as moderators of the relations between family decision making and adolescent adjustment. *Child Development, 67,* 283–301.

Lamborn, S. D., Mounts, N., Steinberg, L., & Dornbusch, S. M. (1991). Patterns of competence and adjustment from authoritative, authoritarian, indulgent, and neglectful families. *Child Development, 62,* 1049–1065.

Lancy, D. F. (1996). *Playing on the mother-ground.* New York: Guilford.

Landry, D. J., Kaeser, L., & Richards, C. L. (1999). Abstinence promotion and the provision of information about contraception in public school district sexuality education policies. *Family Planning Perspective, 31,* 280–286.

Landry, S. H., Smith, K. E., Miller-Loncar, C. L., & Swank, P. R. (1997). Predicting cognitive-language and social growth curves from early maternal behaviors in children at varying degrees of biological risk. *Developmental Psychology, 33,* 1040–1053.

Lane, D. M., & Pearson, D. A. (1982). The development of selective attention. *Merrill-Palmer Quarterly, 28,* 317–337.

Lane, I. M., & Coon, R. C. (1972). Reward allocation in preschool children. *Child Development, 43,* 1382–1389.

Lange, G., & Pierce, S. H. (1992). Memory-strategy learning and maintenance in preschool children. *Developmental Psychology, 28,* 453–462.

Langfeldt, T. (1981). Childhood masturbation: Individual and social organization. In L. L. Constantine & F. M. Martinson (Eds.), *Children and sex: New findings, new perspectives.* Boston: Little, Brown.

Langlois, J. H., Ritter, J. M., Roggman, L. A., & Vaughn, L. S. (1991). Facial diversity and infant preferences for attractive faces. *Developmental Psychology, 27,* 79–84.

Langlois, J. H., Roggman, L. A., Casey, R. J., Ritter, J. M., Rieser-Danner, L. A., & Jenkins, V. Y. (1987). Infant preferences for attractive faces: Rudiments of a stereotype? *Developmental Psychology, 23,* 363–369.

Lansford, J. E. (2009). Parental divorce and children's adjustment. *Perspectives on Psychological Science, 4,* 140–152.

Lapsley, D. K., & Narvaez, D. (2006). Character education. In W. Damon & R. M. Lerner (Gen. Eds.), *Handbook of child psychology* (6th ed.). In K. A. Renninger & I. E. Sigel (Vol. Eds.), Vol. 4: *Child psychology in practice* (pp. 248–296). New York: Wiley.

Largo, R. H., Caflish, J. A., Hug, F., Muggli, K., Molnar, A. A., Molinari, L. et al. (2001a). Neuromotor development from 5 to 18 years, Pt. 1: Timed performance. *Developmental Medicine and Child Neurology, 43,* 436–443.

Largo, R. H., Caflish, J. A., Hug, F., Muggli, K., Molnar, A. A., Molinari, L. et al. (2001b). Neuromotor development from 5 to 18 years, Pt. 2: Associated movements. *Developmental Medicine and Child Neurology, 43,* 444–453.

Larsen, J. T., To, Y. M., & Fireman, G. (2007). Children's understanding and experience of mixed emotions. *Psychological Science, 18,* 186–191.

Larson, R. W. (2000). Toward a psychology of positive youth development. *American Psychologist, 55,* 170–183.

Larson, R., & Ham, M. (1993). Stress and "storm and stress" in early adolescence: The relationship of negative events with dysphoric affect. *Developmental Psychology, 29,* 130–140.

Latner, J. D., & Stunkard, A. J. (2003). Getting worse: The stigmatization of obese children. *Obesity Research, 11,* 452–456.

Laursen, B., Bukowski, W. M., Aunola, K., & Nurmi, J-E. (2007). Friendship moderates prospective associations between social isolation and adjustment problems in young children. *Child Development, 78,* 1395–1404.

Laursen, B., & Collins, W. (1994). Interpersonal conflict during adolescence. *Psychological Bulletin, 115,* 197–209.

Laursen, B., Finkelstein, B. D., & Betts, N. T. (2001). A developmental meta-analysis of peer conflict resolutions. *Developmental Review, 21,* 423–449.

Laursen, B., Hartup, W. W., & Koplas, A. L. (1996). Toward understanding peer conflict. *Merrill-Palmer Quarterly, 42,* 281–297.

Laursen, B., & Pursell, G. (2009). Conflict in peer relationships. In K. H. Rubin, W. M. Bukowski, & B. Laursen (Eds.), *Handbook of peer interactions, relationships, and groups* (pp. 232–248). New York: Guilford.

Lazar, I., Darlington, R., Murray, H., Royce, J., & Snipper, A. (1982). Lasting effects of early education: A report from the Consortium for Longitudinal Studies. *Monographs of the Society for Research in Child Development, 47* (Serial No. 195).

Le Grand, R., Mondloch, C. J., Maurer, D., & Brent, H. P. (2001). Early visual experience and face processing. *Nature, 410,* 890.

Leavens, D. A., Hopkins, W. D., & Bard, K. A. (2005). Understanding the point of chimpanzee pointing. Epigenesis and ecological validity. *Current Directions in Psychological Science, 14,* 185–189.

LeDoux, J. E. (1996). *The emotional brain: The mysterious underpinnings of emotional life.* New York: Simon & Schuster.

Lee, B. J., & George, R. M. (1999). Poverty, early childbearing and child maltreatment: A multinomial analysis. *Children & Youth Services Review, 21,* 755–780.

Lee, K. (2000). Lying as doing deceptive things with words: A speech act theoretical perspective. In J. W. Astington (Ed.), *Mind in the making* (pp. 177–196). Oxford, UK: Blackwell.

Lee, K. A., McEnany, G., & Weekes, D. (1999). Gender differences in sleep patterns for early adolescents. *Journal of Adolescent Health, 24,* 16–20.

Lee, S. J., Ralston, H. J. P., Drey, E. A., Partridge, J. C., & Rosen, M. A. (2005). Fetal pain: A systematic multidisciplinary review of the evidence. *Journal of the American Medical Association, 294,* 947–954.

LeFevre, J., DeStefano, D., Coleman, B., & Shanahan, T. (2005). Mathematical cognition and working memory. In J. I. D. Campbell (Ed.), *Handbook of mathematical cognition* (pp. 361–378). New York: Psychology Press.

Lefkowitz, M. M., Eron, L. D., Walder, L. O., & Huesmann, L. R. (1972). Television violence and child aggression: A follow-up study. In G. A. Comstock & E. A. Rubinstein (Eds.), *Television and social behavior,* Vol. 3: *Television and adolescent aggressiveness.* Washington, DC: U.S. Government Printing Office.

Legerstee, M. (1991). The role of person and object in eliciting early imitation. *Journal of Experimental Child Psychology, 51,* 423–433.

Lehman, E. B., McKinley-Pace, M. J., Wilson, J. A., Savsky, M. D., & Woodson, M. E. (1997). Direct and indirect measures of intentional forgetting in children and adults: Evidence for retrieval inhibition and reinstatement. *Journal of Experimental Child Psychology, 64,* 295–316.

Lehmann, M., & Hasselhorn, M. (2007). Variable memory strategy use in children's adaptive intratask learning behavior: Developmental changes and working memory influences in free recall. *Child Development, 78,* 1068–1082.

Leichtman, M. D., & Ceci, S. J. (1995). The effect of stereotypes and suggestion on preschoolers reports. *Developmental Psychology, 31,* 568–578.

Lemaire, P., & Callies, S. (2009). Children's strategies in complex arithmetic. *Journal of Experimental Child Psychology, 103,* 49–65.

Lempers, J. D., Clark-Lempers, D. S., & Simon, R. L. (1989). Economic hardship, parenting and distress in adolescence. *Child Development, 60,* 25–39.

Lenhart, A., Kahne, J., Middaugh, E., Macgill, A. R., Evans, C., & Vitak, J. (September 2008). Teens, video games and civics: Teens' gaming experiences are diverse and include significant social interaction and civic engagement. Pew Internet and American Life Project. Accessed at: www.pewinternet.org/PPF/r/263/report_display.asp (Downloaded September 18, 2008).

Lenhart. A., & Madden, M. (January, 2007). Social networking websites and teens: An overview. Pew Internet & American Life Project. Accessed at: http://www.pewinternet.org/ (Downloaded January 11, 2007).

Lenneberg, E. H. (1967). *Biological foundations of language.* New York: Wiley.

Lenroot, R. K., & Giedd, J. N. (2007). The structural development of the human brain as measures longitudinally with magnetic resonance imaging. In D. Coch, K. W. Fischer, & G. Dawson (Eds.), *Human behavior, learning, and the developing brain: Typical development* (pp. 50–73). New York: Guilford.

Lenroot, R. K., & Giedd, J. N. (2006). Brain development in children and adolescents: Insights from anatomical magnetic resonance imaging. *Neuroscience and Biobehavioral Reviews, 30,* 718–729.

Lepper, M. R., Greene, D., & Nisbett, R. E. (1973). Undermining children's intrinsic interest with extrinsic rewards: A test of the overjustification hypothesis. *Journal of Personality and Social Psychology, 28,* 129–137.

Lerner, R. M. (1991). Changing organism-context relations as the basic process of development: A developmental contextual perspective. *Developmental Psychology, 27,* 27–32.

Lerner, R. M. (2006). Developmental science, developmental systems, and contemporary theories of human development. In W. Damon & R. M. Lerner (Gen. Eds.), *Handbook of child psychology* (6th ed.). In R. M. Lerner (Vol. Ed.), Vol. 1: *Theoretical models of human development* (pp. 1–17). New York: Wiley.

Lerner, R. M., Rothbaum, F., Boulos, S., & Castellino, D. R. (2002). Developmental systems perspective on parenting. In M. H. Bornstein (Ed.), *Handbook of parenting* (2nd ed.), Vol. 2: *Biology and ecology of parenting* (pp. 315–344). Mahwah, NJ: Erlbaum.

Leslie, A. M., Knobe, J., & Cohen, A. (2006). Acting intentionally and the side-effect effect. *Psychological Science, 17,* 421–427.

Leventhal, T., & Brooks-Gunn, J. (2000). The neighborhood they live in: The effects of neighborhood residence upon child and adolescent outcomes. *Psychological Bulletin, 126,* 309–337.

Leventhal, T., & Brooks-Gunn, J. (2003). Moving to Opportunity: An experimental study of neighborhood effects on mental health. *American Journal of Public Health, 93,* 1576–1582.

Leventhal, T., & Brooks-Gunn, J. (2004). A randomized study of neighborhood effects on low-income children's educational outcomes. *Developmental Psychology, 40,* 488–507.

Leventhal, T., Fauth, R. C., & Brooks-Gunn, J. (2005). Neighborhood poverty and public policy: A 5-year follow-up of children's educational outcomes in the New York City Moving to Opportunity demonstration. *Developmental Psychology, 41,* 933–952.

Lever, R. J., & Sénéchal, M. (2010). Discussing stories: On how a dialogic reading intervention improves kindergarteners' oral narrative construction. *Journal of Experimental Child Psychology*.

Levin, I., & L. Tolchinsky-Landsmann, L. (1989). Becoming literate: Referential and phonetic strategies in early reading and writing. *International Journal of Behavioral Development, 12*, 369–384.

Levine, L. J., Stein, N. L., & Liwag, M. D. (1999). Remembering children's emotions: Sources of concordance and discordance between parents and children. *Developmental Psychology, 35*, 790–801.

Levine, M. (2006). *The price of privilege: How parental pressure and material advantages are creating a generation of disconnected and unhappy kids.* New York: Harper Paperbacks.

Levitt, M. J., Weber, R. A., Clark, M. C., & McDonnell, P. (1985). Reciprocity of exchange in toddler sharing behavior. *Developmental Psychology, 21*, 122–123.

Levy, B. A., Gong, Z., Hessels, S., Evans, M. A., & Jared, D. (2006). Understanding print: Early reading development and the contributions of home literacy experiences. *Journal of Experimental Child Psychology, 93*, 63–93.

Levy, F., Hay, D. A., McStephen, M., Wood, C., & Waldman, I. (1997). Attention-deficit hyperactivity disorder: A category or a continuum? Genetic analysis of a large-scale twin study. *Journal of the American Academy of Child and Adolescent Psychiatry, 36*, 737–744.

Lewin, K. (1952). *Field theory in social science; selected theoretical papers by Kurt Lewin.* London: Tavistock.

Lewis, C. (2005). Parenting and the family. In B. Hopkins (Ed.), *The Cambridge encyclopedia of child development* (pp. 340–343). Cambridge, UK: Cambridge University Press.

Lewis, C. E., & Lewis, M. A. (1984). Peer pressure and risk-taking behaviors in children. *American Journal of Public Health, 74*, 580–584.

Lewis, K., P., & Barton, R. A. (2006). Amygdala size and hypothalamus size predict social play frequencies in nonhuman primates: A comparative analysis using independent contrasts. *Journal of Comparative Psychology, 120*, 31–37.

Lewis, M. (1991). Ways of knowing: Objective self-awareness of consciousness? *Developmental Review, 11*, 231–243.

Lewis, M. (1993). The emergence of human emotions. In M. Lewis & J. M. Haviland (Eds.), *Handbook of emotions* (pp. 223–235). New York: Guilford.

Lewis, M. (2000). Self-conscious emotions: Embarrassment, pride, shame, and guilt. In M. Lewis & J. Haviland (Eds.), *Handbook of emotions* (2nd ed., pp. 623–636). New York: Guilford.

Lewis, M. (2004). Emotional development: Past, present and future. *Human Development, 47*, 66–70.

Lewis, M. (2005). The child and its family: The social network model. *Human Development, 48*, 8–27.

Lewis, M., & Brooks-Gunn, J. (1979). *Social cognition and the acquisition of self.* New York: Plenum.

Lewis, M., & Carmody, D. P. (2008). Self-representation and brain development, *Developmental Psychology, 44*, 1329–1334.

Lewis, M., & Ramsay, D. (2004). Development of self-recognition, personal pronoun use, and pretend play during the 2nd year. *Child Development, 75*, 1821–1831.

Lewis, M., Alessandri, S. M., & Sullivan, M. W. (1992). Differences in shame and pride as a function of children's gender and task difficulty. *Child Development, 63*, 630–638.

Lewis, M., Sullivan, M. W., Stanger, C., & Weiss, M. (1989). Self development and self-conscious emotions. *Child Development, 60*, 146–156.

Lewis, M., Young, G., Brooks, J., & Michalson, L. (1975). The beginning of friendship. In M. Lewis & L. A. Rosenblum (Eds.), *Friendship and peer relations.* New York: Wiley.

Lewis, M. D. (2000). The promise of dynamic systems approaches for an integrated account of human development. *Child Development, 71*, 36–43.

Lewis, M. D. (2005). Bridging emotion theory and neurobiology through dynamic systems modeling. *Behavioral and Brain Sciences, 28*, 169–245.

Lewkowicz, D. J. (2000). The development of intersensory temporal perception: An epigenetic systems/limitations view. *Psychological Bulletin, 126*, 281–308.

Lewkowicz, D. J. & Ghazanfar, A. A. (2006). The decline of cross-species intersensory perception in human infants. *Proceedings of the National Academy of Sciences (USA), 103*, 6771–6774.

Lewkowicz, D. J., & Ghazanfar, A. A. (2009). The emergence of multisensory systems through perceptual narrowing. *Trends in Cognitive Sciences.* Accessed at: 10.1016/j.tics.2009.08.004.

Lewkowicz, D. J., Leo, I., & Simion, F. (2010). Intersensory perception at birth: Newborns match non-human primate faces & voices. *Infancy, 15*, 46–60.

Li, R., Zhao, Z., Mokdad, A., Barjer, L., & Grunner-Strawn, L. (2003). Prevalence of breastfeeding in the United States: The 2001 National Immunization Survey. *Pediatrics, 111*, 1198–1201.

Liben, L. S., & Signorella, M. L. (1993). Gender-schematic processing in children: The role of initial interpretations of stimuli. *Developmental Psychology, 29*, 141–149.

Lickliter, R. (1990). Premature visual stimulation accelerates intersensory functioning in bobwhite quail neonates. *Developmental Psychobiology, 23*, 15–27.

Lickliter, R. (2000). The role of sensory stimulation in perinatal development: Insights from comparative research for care of the high-risk infant. *Developmental and Behavioral Pediatrics, 21*, 437–447.

Lickliter, R., & Berry, T. D. (1990). The phylogeny fallacy: Developmental psychology's misapplication of evolutionary theory. *Developmental Review, 10*, 348–364.

Lieberman, D., Tooby, J., & Cosmides, L. (2007). The architecture of human nature. *Nature, 445*, 727–731.

Liebowitz, M. R. (1983). *The chemistry of love.* Boston, MA: Little, Brown.

Lillard, A. (1998). Ethnopsychologies: Cultural variations in theories of mind. *Psychological Bulletin, 123*, 3–32.

Lillard, A. S. (2001). Pretend play as Twin Earth: A social-cognitive analysis. *Developmental Review, 21*, 495–531.

Lindberg, M. A. (1991). An interactive approach to assessing the suggestibility and testimony of eyewitnesses. In J. Doris (Ed.), *The suggestibility of children's recollections: Implications for eyewitness testimony* (pp. 47–55). Washington, DC: American Psychological Association.

Lindberg, M. A., Keiffer, J., & Thomas, S. W. (2000). Eyewitness testimony for physical abuse as a function of personal experience, development, and focus of study. *Journal of Applied Developmental Psychology, 21*, 555–591.

Lindberg, M. A., & Lindberg, C. Y. (2007, March). *The roles of attachment patterns in the development of alcoholism.* Paper presented at the Society for Research in Child Development, Boston, MA.

Lindberg, M. A., Thomas, M., & Smith, L. (2004, May). *Empirical support for an attachment hypothesis of eating disorders.* Paper presented at American Psychiatric Association, New York, New York.

Lipko, A. R., Dunlosky, J., & Merriman, W. E. (2009). Persistent overconfidence despite practice: The roles of task experience in preschooler's recall predications. *Journal of Experimental Child Psychology, 103*, 152–166.

Lipsitt, L. P. (2003). Crib death: A biobehavioral phenomenon? *Current Directions in Psychological Science, 12*, 1164–1170.

Liszkowski, U., Carpenter, M., & Tomasello, M. (2007). Pointing out new news, old news, and absent referents at 12 months of age. *Developmental Science, 10*, F1–F7.

Liszkowski, U., Schäfer, M., Carpenter, M., & Tomasello M. (2009). Prelinguistic infants, not chimpanzees, communicate about absent entities. *Psychological Science, 20*, 654–660.

Liu, D., Wellman, H. M., Tardif, T., & Sabbagh, M. A. (2008). Theory of mind development in Chinese children: A meta-analysis of false-belief understanding across cultures and languages. *Developmental Psychology, 44*, 523–531.

Livesley, W., & Bromley, D. (1973). *Person perception in childhood and adolescence.* New York: Wiley.

Ljungberg, T., Horowitz, L., Jansson, L., Westlund, K., & Clarke, C. (2005). Communicative factors, conflict progression, and use of reconciliatory strategies in pre-school boys—A series of random events or a sequential process? *Aggressive Behavior, 31*, 303–323.

Lloyd, M. E., & Newcombe, N. S. (2009). Implicit memory in childhood: Reassessing developmental invariance. In M. L. Courage & N. Cowan (Eds.), *The development of memory in infancy and childhood* (pp. 92–113). New York: Psychology Press.

LoBue, V. (2009). More than just another face in the crowd: Superior detection of threatening facial expressions in children and adults. *Developmental Science, 12*, 305–313.

LoBue, V. (2010). And along came a spider: An attentional bias for the detection of spiders in young children and adults. *Journal of Experimental Child Psychology, 107*, 59–66.

LoBue, V., & DeLoache, J. (2008). Detecting the snake in the grass: Attention to fear-relevant stimuli by adults and young children. *Psychological Science, 19*, 284–289.

LoBue, V., & DeLoache, J. S. (2010). Superior detection of threat-relevant stimuli in infancy. *Developmental Science, 13*, 221–228.

LoBue V., Nishida, T., Chiong, C., Deloache, J., & Haidt, J. (2010). When getting something good is bad: Even 3 year olds react to inequality. *Social Development*. Accessed at: doi: 10.1111/j.1467-9507.2009.00560.x

Locke, J. L. (1993). *The child's path to spoken language*. Cambridge, MA: Harvard University Press.

Locke, J. L. (2009). Evolutionary developmental linguistics: Naturalization of the faculty of language. *Language Sciences, 31*, 33–59.

Locke, J. L., & Bogin, B. (2006). Language and life history: A new perspective on the development and evolution of human language. *Behavioral and Brain Sciences, 29*, 259–280.

Lockl, K., & Schneider, W. (2007). Knowledge about the mind: Links between theory of mind and later metamemory. *Child Development, 78*, 148–167.

Lockman, J. J. (2000). A perception-action perspective on tool use development. *Child Development, 71*, 137–144.

Loe, I. M., Balestrino, M. D., Phelps, R. A., Kurs-Lasky, M., Chaves-Gnecco, D., Paradise, J. L., & Feldman, H. M. (2008). Early histories of school-aged children with attention-deficit/hyperactivity disorder. *Child Development, 79*, 1853–1868.

Loehlin, J. C. (1985). Fitting heredity-environment models jointly to twin and adoption data from the California Psychological Inventory. *Behavior Genetics, 15*, 199–221.

Logan, B. (1991). Infant outcomes of a prenatal stimulation pilot study. *Pre and Perinatal Psychology Journal, 6*, 7–31.

Lonigan, C. J., Burgess, S. R., & Anthony, J. L. (2000). Development of emergent literacy and early reading skills in preschool children: Evidence from a latent-variable longitudinal study. *Developmental Psychology, 36*, 596–613.

Looft, W. R., & Bartz, W. H. (1969). Animism revived. *Psychological Bulletin, 71*, 1–19.

Lopez, D. F., Little, T. D., Oettingen, & Baltes, P. B. (1998). Self-regulation and school performance: Is there optimal level of action-control? *Journal of Experimental Child Psychology, 70*, 54–74.

Lord, H., & Mahoney, J. L. (2007). Neighborhood crime and self-care: Risks for aggression and lower academic performance. *Developmental Psychology, 43*, 1321–1333.

Lorenz, K. Z. (1943). Die angeboren Formen moglicher Erfahrung [The innate forms of possible experience]. *Zeitschrift fur Tierpsychologie, 5*, 233–409.

Lourenço, O., & Machado, A. (1996). In defense of Piaget's theory: A reply to 10 common criticisms. *Psychological Review, 103*, 143–164.

Louv, R. (2005). *Last child left in the woods: Saving our children from nature-deficit disorder*. Chapel Hill, NC: Algonquin Books.

Lovaas, O. I. (1987). Behavioral treatment and normal educational and intellectual functioning in young autistic children. *Journal of Consulting and Clinical Psychology, 55*, 3–9.

Lovaas, O. I. (2003). *Teaching individuals with developmental delays: Basic intervention techniques*. Austin, TX: Pro-Ed.

Low, J. (2010). Preschoolers' implicit and explicit false-belief understanding: Relations with complex syntactical mastery. *Child Development, 81*, 597–615.

Lozano, M., Mosquera, M., Bermúdez de Castro, J. M., Arsuaga, J. L., & Carbonell, E. (2009). Right handedness of *Homo heidelbergensis* from Sima de los Huesos (Atapuerca, Spain) 500,000 years ago. *Evolution & Human Behavior, 30*, 369–376.

Lozoff, B., & Brittenham, G. (1979). Infant care: Cache or carry. *The Journal of Pediatrics, 95*, 478–483.

Lubinski, D., & Benbow, C. P. (1992). Gender differences in abilities and preferences among the gifted: Implications for the math-science pipeline. *Current Directions in Psychological Science, 1*, 61–66.

Luby, J. L., Si, X., Belden, A. C, Tandon, M., & Spitznagel, E. (2009). Preschool depression: Homotypic continuity and course over 24 months. *Archives of General Psychiatry, 66*, 897–905.

Ludwig, J., & Miller, D. L. (2007). Does Head Start improve children's life chances? Evidence from a regression discontinuity design. *Quarterly Journal of Economics, 122*, 159–208.

Ludwig, J., & Phillips, D. A. (2008). Long-term effects of Head Start on low-income children. *Annals of the New York Academy of Science, 113*, 257–286.

Luecke-Aleska, D., Anderson, D. R., Collins, P. A., & Schmitt, K. L. (1995). Gender constancy and television viewing. *Developmental Psychology, 31*, 773–780.

Lumeng, J. C., Appugliese, D., Cabral, H. J., Bradley, R. H., & Zuckerman, B. (2006). Neighborhood safety and overweight status in children. *Archives of Pediatric & Adolescence Medicine, 160*, 25–31.

Lumey, L. H. (1992). Decreased birthweight in infants after maternal in utero exposure of the Dutch famine of 1944–1945. *Paediatric & Perinatal Epidemiology, 6*, 240–253.

Lumley, J. (2003). Defining the problem: The epidemiology of preterm birth. *British Journal of Obstetrics and Gynecology, 110*, suppl. 20, 3–7.

Luna, B., Thulborn, K. R., Monoz, D. P., Merriam, E. P., Garver, K. E., Minshew, N. J., Keshavan, M. S., Genovese, C. R., Eddy, W. F., & Sweeney, J. A. (2001). Maturation of widely distributed brain function subserves cognitive development. *NeuroImage, 13*, 786–793.

Luria, A. R. (1961). *The role of speech in the regulation of normal and abnormal behavior*. New York: Liveright.

Luria, A. R. (1976). *Cognitive development: Its cultural and social foundations*. Cambridge, MA: Harvard University Press.

Luria, A. R. (1979). *The making of a mind: A personal account of Soviet Psychology*. Cambridge, MA: Harvard University Press.

Luthar, S. S. (2003). The culture of affluence: Psychological costs of material wealth. *Child Development, 74*, 1581–1593.

Luthar, S. S., & Latendresse, S. J. (2005). Children of the affluent: Challenges to well-being. *Current Directions in Psychological Science, 14*, 49–53.

Luthar, S. S., & Sexton, C. (2004). The high price of affluence. In R. V. Kail (Ed.), *Advances in Child Development, 32* (pp. 126–162). San Diego, CA: Academic Press.

Lynam, D. R., & Henry, B. (2001). The role of neuropsychological deficits in conduct disorders. In J. Hill & B. Maughan (Eds.), *Conduct disorders in childhood and adolescence* (pp. 235–263). New York: Cambridge University Press.

Lynch, M. P., Eilers, R. E., Oller, K., & Urbano, R. C. (1990). Innateness, experience, and music perception. *Psychological Science, 1*, 272–276.

Lyons, D. E., Young, A. G., & Keil, F. C. (2007). The hidden structure of overimitation. *Proceedings of the National Academy of Sciences (USA), 104*, 19751–19756.

Maccoby, E. E. (1988). Gender as a social category. *Developmental Psychology, 24*, 755–756.

Maccoby E. E., & Jacklin, C. N. (1987). Gender segregation in childhood. In H. W. Rose (Ed.), *Advances in child development and behavior* (Vol. 20, pp. 239–287). New York: Academic Press.

Maccoby, E. E., & Jacklin, C. N. (1974). *The psychology of sex differences*. Stanford, CA: Stanford University Press.

Maccoby, E., & Martin, J. A. (1983). Socialization in the context of the family: Parent-child interaction. In P. H. Mussen (Series Ed.) and E. M. Hetherington (Vol. Ed.), *Handbook of child psychology* (4th ed., Vol. 4, pp. 1–102). New York: Wiley.

MacDonald, G., & Leary, M. R. (2005). Why does social exclusion hurt? The relationship between social and physical pain. *Psychological Bulletin, 131*, 202–223.

MacDonald, K. (1985). Early experience, relative plasticity, and social development. *Developmental Review, 5,* 99–121.

MacDonald, K., & Hershberger, S. L. (2005). Theoretical issues in the study of evolution and development. In R. L. Burgess & K. MacDonald (Eds.), *Evolutionary perspectives on human development* (2nd ed.). Thousand Oaks, CA: Sage.

MacFarlane, A. (1975). Olfaction in the development of social preferences in the humane neonate. *CIBA Foundation Symposium 33: Parent-infant interaction.* Amsterdam, The Netherlands: Elsevier.

MacKinlay, R., Kliegel, M, & Mäntylä, T. (2009). Predictors of time-based prospective memory in children. *Journal of Experimental Child Psychology, 102,* 251–264.

MacLean, P. D. (1990). *The triune brain in evolution: Role in paleocerebral functions.* New York: Plenum.

MacWhinney. B. (2005). Language evolution and human development. In B. J. Ellis & D. F. Bjorklund (Eds.), *Origins of the social mind: Evolutionary psychology and child development* (pp. 383–410). New York: Guilford.

Madell, D., & Muncer, S. (2004). Back from the beach but hanging on the telephone? English adolescents' attitudes and experiences of mobile phones and the Internet. *CyberPsychology and Behavior, 7,* 359–367.

Maestripieri, D. (2001). Is there mother-infant bonding in primates? *Developmental Review, 21,* 93–120.

Maestripieri, D., & Pelka, S. (2002). Sex differences in interest in infants across the lifespan: A biological adaptation for parenting? *Human Nature, 13,* 327–344.

Maestripieri, D., & Roney, J. R. (2006). Evolutionary developmental psychology: Contributions from comparative research with nonhuman primates. *Developmental Review, 26,* 120–137.

Maestripieri, D., Roney, J. R., DeBias, N., Durante, K. M., & Spaepen, G. M. (2004). Father absence, menarche and interest in infants among adolescent girls. *Developmental Science, 7,* 560–566.

Magnuson, K. A., & Duncan, G. J. (2002). Parents in poverty. In M. H. Bornstein (Ed.), *Handbook of parenting* (2nd ed.), Vol. 4: *Social conditions and applied parenting* (pp. 95–122). Mahwah, NJ: Erlbaum.

Mahone, E. M., Hagelthorn, K. M., Cutting, L. E., Schuerholz, L. J., Pelletier, S. F., Rawlins, C., Singer, H. S., &. Denckla, M. B. (2002). Effects of IQ on executive function measures in children with ADHD. *Child Neuropsychology, 8,* 52–65.

Main, M., & Cassidy, J. (1988). Categories of response to reunion with the parent at age 6: Predictable from infant attachment classification and stable over a 1-month period. *Developmental Psychology, 24,* 415–426.

Main, M., & George, C. (1985). Responses of abused and disadvantaged toddlers to distress in agemates: A study in the day care setting. *Developmental Psychology, 21,* 407–412.

Main, M., & Solomon, J. (1986). Discovery of a disorganized/disoriented attachment pattern. In T. B. Brazelton & M. N. Youngman (Eds.), *Affective development in infancy.* Norwood, NJ: Ablex.

Main, M., & Weston, D. R. (1981). The quality of the toddler's relationship to mother and to father: Related to conflict and the readiness to establish new relationships. *Child Development, 52,* 932–940.

Makin, J. W., & Porter, R. H. (1989). Attractiveness of lactating females' breast odors to neonates. *Child Development, 60,* 803–810.

Malina, R. M. (2005). Milestones of motor development and indicators of biological maturity. In B. Hopkins (Ed.), *The Cambridge encyclopedia of child development* (pp. 528–534). New York: Cambridge University Press.

Mann, J. (1992). Nurture or negligence: Maternal psychology and behavioral preference among preterm twins. In J. Barkow, L. Cosmides, & J. Tooby (Eds.), *The adapted mind: Evolutionary psychology and the generation of culture* (pp. 367–390). New York: Oxford University Press.

Mansbach, I. K., & Greenbaum, C. W. (1999). Developmental maturity expectations of Israeli fathers and mothers: Effects of education, ethnic origin, and religiosity. *International Journal of Behavioral Development, 23,* 771–797.

March of Dimes. (2006). *Birth defects: 8 million annually worldwide.* Accessed at: http://www .marchofdimes.com/aboutus/15796_18678.asp. (Downloaded January 29, 2009).

Marcia, J. E. (1980). Identity in adolescence. In J. Adelson (Ed.), *Handbook of adolescent psychology.* New York: Wiley.

Marcia, J. E. (1994). Ego identity and object relations. In J. M. Masling & R. F. Bornstein (Eds.), *Empirical perspectives on object relations theory.* Washington, DC: American Psychological Association.

Marcus, G. F. (1995). Children's overregularization of English plurals: A quantitative analysis. *Journal of Child Language, 22,* 447–460.

Marcus, G. F., Pinker, S., Ullman, M., Hollander, M., Rosen, T. J., & Xu, F. (1992). Overregularization in language acquisition. *Monographs of the Society for Research in Child Development, 57* (Serial No. 228).

Mariani, M. A., & Barkley, R. A. (1997). Neuropsychological and academic functioning in preschool boys with attention deficit hyperactivity disorder. *Developmental Neuropsychology, 13,* 111–129.

Markman, E. M. (1994). Constraints on word meaning in early language acquisition. In L. Gleitman & B. Landau (Eds.), *The acquisition of the lexicon.* Cambridge, MA: MIT Press.

Markman, E. M., & Wachtel, G. A. (1988). Children's use of mutual exclusivity to constrain the meaning of words. *Cognitive Psychology, 20,* 121–157.

Marks, A. K., Szalacha, L. A., Lamarre, M., Boyd, M. J., & Coll, C. G. (2007). Emerging ethnic identity and interethnic group social preferences in middle childhood: Findings from the Children of Immigrants Development in Context (CIDC) study. *International Journal of Behavioral Development, 31,* 501–513.

Markstrom, C. A., & Iborra, A. (2003). Adolescent identity formation and rites of passage: The Navajo Kinaalda ceremony for girls. *Journal of Research on Adolescence, 13,* 399–425.

Marlier, L., Schaal, B., & Soussignan, R. (1998). Neonatal responsiveness to the odor of amniotic and lacteal fluids: A test of perinatal chemosensory continuity. *Child Development, 69,* 611–623.

Marlowe, F. (1999). Showoffs or providers? The parenting effort of Hazda men. *Evolution and Human Behavior, 20,* 391–404.

Marshall, N. L. (2004). The quality of early child care and children's development. *Current Directions in Psychological Science, 13,* 165–168.

Marshall, P. J. (2009). Relating psychology and neuroscience. *Perspectives on Psychological Science, 4,* 113–125.

Martin, C. L., & Halverson, C. F. (1987). The roles of cognition in sex role acquisition. In D. B. Carter (Ed.), *Current conceptions of sex roles and sex typing: Theory and research.* New York: Praeger.

Martin, C. L., & Ruble, D. (2004). Children's search for gender cues. *Current Directions in Psychological Science, 13,* 67–70.

Martin, C. L., Ruble, D. N., & Szkrybalo, J. (2002). Cognitive theories of early gender development. *Psychological Bulletin, 128,* 903–933.

Martin, C. L., Wood, C. H., & Little, J. K. (1990). The development of gender stereotype components. *Child Development, 61,* 1891–1904.

Martin, G. B., & Clark, R. D., III. (1982). Distress crying in neonates: Species and peer specificity. *Developmental Psychology, 38,* 3–9.

Martin, H., Breezley, P., Conway, E., & Kempe, H. (1974). The development of abused children: A review of the literature. *Advances in Pediatrics, 21,* 119–134.

Martin, J. A., Hamilton, B. E., Sutton, P. D., Ventura, S. J., Menacker, F., Kirmeyer, S., & Munson, M. L. (2007). Births: Final data for 2005. *National Vital Statistics Reports, 56* (Number 6). Washington, DC: U. S. Department of Health and Human Services.

Martin, R. C. (2003). Language processing: Functional organization and neuroanatomical basis. *Annual Review of Psychology, 54,* 55–89.

Martini, M. (1994). Peer interactions in Polynesia: A view from Marquesas. In J. L. Roopnarine, J. E. Johnson, & F. H. Hooper (Eds.), *Children's play in diverse cultures* (pp. 73–103). Albany, NY: State University of New York Press.

Martinson, F. M. (1994). *The sexual life of children.* Westport, CT: Bergin & Garvey.

Marvin, R., & Britner, P. (1999). Normative development: The ontogeny of attachment. In Cassodu & P. Shaver (Eds.), *Handbook of Attachment* (1st ed., pp. 671–687). New York: Guilford.

Masataka, N. (1996). Perception of motherese in a signed language by 6-month-old deaf infants. *Developmental Psychology, 32*, 874–879.

Masataka, N. (1999). Preferences for infant-directed singing in 2-day old hearing infants of deaf parents. *Developmental Psychology, 35*, 1001–1005.

Masataka, N. (2000). The role of modality and input in the earliest stage of language acquisition: Studies of Japanese Sign Language. In C. Chamberlain, J. P. Morford, & R. I. Mayberry (Eds.), *Language acquisition by eye*. Mahwah NJ: Erlbaum.

Masataka, N. (2007). Music, evolution and language. *Developmental Science, 10*, 35–39.

Masoni, S., Maio A., Trimarchi, G., de Punzio C., & Fioretti, P. (1994). The couvade syndrome. *Journal of Psychosomatic Obstetrics & Gynecology, 15*, 125–131.

Masten, A. S., & Coatsworth, J. D. (1998). The development of competence in favorable and unfavorable environments. *American Psychologist, 53*, 205–220.

Masters, W. A., Johnson, V. A., & Kolodny, R. (1985). *Human sexuality* (2nd ed.). Boston: Little, Brown.

Matas, L., Arend, R. A., & Sroufe, L. A. (1978). Continuity and adaptation in the second year: The relationship between quality of attachment and later competence. *Child Development, 49*, 547–556.

Mathews, F., Johnson, P. J., & Neil, A. (2008). You are what your mother eats: Evidence for maternal preconception diet influencing foetal sex in humans. *Proceedings of the Royal Society B, 275*, 1661–1668.

Matsuzawa, T., & Yamakoshi, G. (1996). Comparison of chimpanzee material culture between Bossou and Nimba, West Africa. In A. Russon, K. Bard, & S. T. Parker (Eds.), *Reaching into the thought: The minds of the great apes* (pp. 211–232). Cambridge, UK: Cambridge University Press.

Matthews, J. (1999). *The art of childhood and adolescence: The construction of meaning*. London: Falmer Press.

Maurer, D., & Barrera, M. (1981). Infants' perception of natural and distorted arrangements of a schematic face. *Child Development, 52*, 196–202.

Maurer, D., Le Grand, R., & Mondloch, C. J. (2002). The many faces of configural processing. *Trends in Cognitive Sciences, 6*, 255–260.

Maurer, D., Lewis, T. L., Brent, H. P., & Levin, A. V. (1999). Rapid improvement in the acuity of infants after visual input. *Science, 286*, 108–110.

Maurer, D., Mondloch C. J., & Lewis, T. L. (2007). Effects of early visual deprivation on perceptual and cognitive development. *Progress in Brain Research, 164*, 87–104.

Maurer, D., Stager, C., & Mondloch, C. (1999). Cross-modal transfer of shape is difficult to demonstrate in 1-month-olds. *Child Development, 70*, 1047–1057.

Mayberry, R. I. (2002). Cognitive development in deaf children: The interface of language and perception in neuropsychology. In Segalowitz, S. I., & Rapin, I. (Eds.), *Handbook of neuropsychology* (2nd ed). New York: Elsevier Science.

Mayseless, O., Scharf, M., & Sholt, M. (2003). From authoritative parenting practices to an authoritarian context: Exploring the person-environment fit. *Journal of Research on Adolescence, 13*, 427–456.

Mazzocco, M. M. M., & Myers, G. F. (2003). Complexities in identifying and defining mathematics learning disability in the primary school-age years. *Annals of Dyslexia, 53*, 218–253.

Mazzoni, G. (1998). Memory suggestibility and metacognition in child eyewitness testimony: The roles of source monitoring and self-efficacy. *European Journal of Psychology of Education, 13*, 43–60.

McCabe, A., & Peterson, C. (Eds.). (1991). *Developing narrative structure*. Hillsdale, NJ: Erlbaum.

McCabe, M. P., & Ricciardelli, L. A. (2004). A longitudinal study of pubertal timing and extreme body change behaviors among adolescent boys and girls. *Adolescence, 3*, 145–166.

McCall, R. B. (1977). Challenges to a science of developmental psychology. *Child Development, 48*, 333–344.

McCall, R. B., Appelbaum, M. I., & Hogarty, P. S. (1973). Developmental changes in mental performance. *Monographs of the Society for Research in Child Development, 38* (Serial No. 150).

McCall, R. B., & Carriger, M. S. (1993). A meta-analysis of infant habituation and recognition memory performance as predictors of later IQ. *Child Development, 64*, 57–79.

McCall, R. B., Eichorn, D. H., & Hogarty, P. S. (1977). Transitions in early mental development. *Monographs of the Society for Research in Child Development, 42* (Serial No. 171).

McCall, R. B., Hogarty, P. S., & Hurlburt, N. (1972). Transitions in infant sensori-motor development and the prediction of childhood IQ. *American Psychologist, 27*, 728–748.

McCall, R. B., Kennedy, C. B., & Appelbaum, M. I. (1977). Magnitude of discrepancy and the distribution of attention in infants. *Child Development, 48*, 772–785.

McCarthy, A., & Lee, K. (2009). Children's knowledge of deceptive gaze cues and its relation to their actual lying behavior. *Journal of Experimental Child Psychology, 103*, 117–134.

McCartney, G. R., & Hepper, P. G. (1999) Development of lateralized behaviour in the human fetus from 12 to 27 weeks' gestation. *Developmental Medicine and Child Neurology, 41*, 83–86.

McCartney, K., Owen, M., Booth, C., Clarke-Stewart, A., & Vandell, D. (2004). Testing a maternal attachment model of behavior problems in early childhood. *Journal of Child Psychology and Psychiatry, 45*, 765–778.

McCartney, K., Harris, M. J., & Bernieri, F. (1990). Growing up and growing apart: A development metaanalysis of twin studies. *Psychological Bulletin, 107*, 226–237.

McCauley, R., & Fey, M. E. (Eds.) (2006). *Treatment of language disorders in children*. Baltimore: Brookes Publishing.

McConaghy, N., & Silove, D. (1992). Do sex-linked behaviors in children influence relationships with their parents? *Archives of Sexual Behavior, 21*, 469–479.

McCord, J. (1979). Some child-rearing antecedents of criminal behavior in adult men. *Journal of Personality and Social Psychology, 37*, 1477–1486.

McCrae, R. R., & Costa, P. T. (1999). A five-factor theory of personality. In L. A. Pervin & O. P. John (Eds.), *Handbook of personality theory and research* (pp. 139–153). New York: Guilford.

McDevitt, T. M., & Ormond, J. E. (2004). *Child development: Educating and working with children and adolescents* (2nd ed.). Upper Saddle River, NJ: Pearson.

McDonough, L., Mandler, J. M., McKee, R. D., & Squire, L. R. (1995). The deferred imitation task as a nonverbal measure of declarative memory. *Proceedings of the National Academy of Sciences (USA), 92*, 7580–7584.

McDougall, I., Brown, F. H., & Fleagle, J. G. (2005). Stratigraphic placement and age of modern humans from Kibish, Ethiopia. *Nature, 433* (17 Feb), 733–736.

McEachin, J. J., Smith, T., & Lovaas, O. I. (1993). Long-term outcome for children with autism that received early intensive behavioral treatment. *American Journal on Mental Retardation, 97*, 359–372.

McElhaney, K. B., & Allen, J. P. (2001). Autonomy and adolescent social functioning: The moderating effect of risk. *Child Development, 72*, 220–231.

McElhaney, K. B., Antonishak, J., & Allen, J. P. (2008). "They like me, they like me not": Popularity and adolescents' perception of acceptance predicting social functioning over time. *Child Development, 79*, 720–731.

McElwain, N. L., Booth-LaForce, C., Lansford, J. E., Wu, X., & Dyer, W. J. (2008). A process model of attachment—Friend linkages: Hostile attribution bias, language ability, and mother-child affective mutuality as intervening mechanisms. *Child Development, 79*, 1891–1906.

McGhee, P. E. (1979). *Humor: Its origins and development*. San Francisco: W. H. Freeman.

McGown, C., Gregory, A., & Weinstein, R. S. (2010). Expectations, stereotypes, and self-fulfilling prophecies in classroom and school life. In J. L. Meece & J. S. Eccles (Eds.), *Handbook of research on schools, schooling, and human development* (pp. 256–274). New York: Routledge.

McGraw, M. B. (1943). *Neuromuscular maturation of the human infant*. New York: Hafner.

McGrew, W. C. (1992). *Chimpanzee material culture: Implication for human evolution*. Cambridge, UK: Cambridge University Press.

McGrew, W. C., & Tutin, C. E. G. (1973). Chimpanzee tool use in dental grooming. *Nature, 241*, 477–478.

McGuigan, N., & Whiten, A. (2009). Emulation and "over-emulation" in the social learning of causally opaque versus causally transparent tool use by 23-and 30-month-old children. *Journal of Experimental Child Psychology, 104*, 367–381.

McGuigan, N., Whiten, A., Flynn, E. F., & Horner, V. (2007). Imitation of casually necessary versus unnecessary tool use by 3- and 5-year-old children. *Cognitive Development, 22*, 356–364.

McHale, J., & Rasmussen, J. (1998). Coparental and family group-level dynamics during infancy: Early family precursors of child and family functioning during preschool. *Development and Psychopathology, 10*, 39–58.

McHale, J., Khazan, I., Erera, P., Rotman, T., DeCourcey, W., & Mcconnell, M. (2002). Coparenting in diverse family systems. In M. H. Bornstein (Ed.), *Handbook of parenting* (2nd ed.), Vol. 3: *Being and becoming a parent* (pp. 75–107). Mahwah, NJ: Erlbaum.

McHale, S. M., & Crouter, A. C. (1996). The family context of children's sibling relationships. In G. Brody (Ed.), *Sibling relationships: The causes and consequences* (pp. 173–195). Norwood, NJ: Ablex.

McKenna, J. J. (2005). Sudden infant death syndrome. In B. Hopkins (Ed.), *The Cambridge encyclopedia of child development* (pp. 453–457). New York: Cambridge University Press.

McKenna, J. J., & McDade, T. (2005). Why babies should never sleep alone: A review of the co-sleeping controversy in relation to SIDS, bedsharing and breast feeding. *Pediatric Respiratory Review, 6*, 134–152.

McKeough, A. (1998). Storytelling: A foundational pillar of literacy. Accessed at: http://www.nald.ca/library/research/stortell/Storytelling.pdf (Downloaded February 3, 2009).

McKeough, A., Genereux, R., & Jeary J. (2006). Structure, content, and language usage: How do exceptional and average storywriters differ? *High Ability Studies, 17*, 203–222.

McLain, D. K., Setters, D., Moulton, M. P., & Pratt, A. E. (2000). Ascription of resemblance of newborns by parents and nonrelatives. *Evolution and Human Behavior, 21*, 11–23.

McLoyd, V. C. (1990). The impact of economic hardship on black families and children: Psychological distress, parenting, and socioemotional development. *Child Development, 61*, 311–346.

McManus, I. C., & Bryden, M. P. (1993). Handedness on Tristan da Cunha: The genetic consequences of social isolation. *International Journal of Psychology, 28*, 831–843.

McNeill, W. H. (1995). *Keeping together in time: Dance and drill in human history*. Cambridge, MA: Harvard University Press.

McNelles, L., & Connolly, J. (1999). Intimacy between adolescent friends: Age and gender differences in intimate affect and intimate behaviors. *Journal of Research on Adolescence, 9*, 143–159.

Mead, M., & Newton, N. (1967). Cultural patterning of perinatal behavior. In S. A. Richardson & A. F. Guttmacher (Eds.), *Childbearing: Its social and psychological aspects* (pp. 142–244). Baltimore, MD: Williams & Wilkins.

Meaney, M. J., Mitchell, J. B., Aitken, D. H., Bhatnagar, S., Bodnoff, S. R., Iny, L. J., & Sarrieau, A. (1991). The effects of neonatal handling on the development of the adrenocortical response to stress: Implications for neuropathology and cognitive deficits in later life. *Psychoneuroendocrinology, 16*, 85–103.

Medin, D. L., & Atran, S. (1999). *Folkbiology*. Cambridge, MA: MIT Press.

Meece, J. L. & J. S. Eccles, J. S. (Eds.) (2010). *Handbook of research on schools, schooling, and human development*. New York: Routledge.

Meeus, W., Iedema, J., Helsen, M., & Volleberg, W. (1999). Patterns of adolescent identify development: Review of literature and longitudinal analysis. *Developmental Review, 19*, 419–461.

Mehler, J., Jusczyk, P., Lambertz, G., Halsted, N., Bertoncini, J., & Amiel-Tison, C. (1988). A precursor of language acquisition in young infants. *Cognition, 29*, 143–178.

Meilman, P. W. (1979). Cross-sectional age changes in ego identity status during adolescence. *Developmental Psychology, 15*, 230–231.

Meins, E., Fernyhough, C., Wainwright, R., Clark-Carter, D., Gupta, M. D., Fradley, R. et al. (2003). Pathways to understanding mind: Construct validity and predictive validity of maternal mind-mindedness. *Child Development, 74*, 1194–1211.

Meizner, I. (1987). Sonographic observation of in utero fetal "masturbation." *Journal of Ultrasound in Medicine, 6*, 11.

Melhuish, E. C. (2005). Daycare. In B. Hopkins (Ed.), *The Cambridge encyclopedia of child development* (pp. 309–312). Cambridge, UK: Cambridge University Press.

Melhuish, E. C., Sylva, K., Sammons, P., Siraj-Blatchford, I., Taggart, B., Phan, M. B., & Malin, A. (2008). Preschool influences on mathematics achievement. *Science, 321* (29 August), 1161–1162.

Melinder, A. M., Alexander, K. W., Cho, Y., Goodman, G. S., Thoresen, C., Lonnum, C. K., & Magnussen, S. (2010). Children's eyewitness memory: A comparison of two interviewing strategies. *Journal of Experimental Child Psychology, 105*, 156–177.

Melis, A. P., Call, J., & Tomasello, M. (2006). Chimpanzees conceal visual and auditory information from others. *Journal of Comparative Psychology, 120*, 154–162.

Meltzoff, A. N. (1990). Towards a developmental cognitive science: The implications of cross-modal matching and imitation for the development of memory in infancy. In A. Diamond (Ed.), The development and neural bases of higher cognitive functions, *Annals of the New York Academy of Sciences, 698*, 1–31.

Meltzoff, A. N. (1995). Understanding the intentions of others: Re-enactment of intended acts by 18-month-old children. *Developmental Psychology, 31*, 838–850.

Meltzoff, A. N., & Borton, R. W. (1979). Intermodal matching by human neonates. *Nature, 282*, 403–404.

Meltzoff, A. N., & Moore, M. K. (1977). Imitation of facial and manual gestures by human neonates. *Science, 198*, 75–78.

Meltzoff, A. N., & Moore, M. K. (1985). Cognitive foundations and social functions of imitation and intermodal representation in infancy. In J. Mehler & R. Fox (Eds.), *Neonate cognition: Beyond the booming buzzing confusion*. Hillsdale, NJ: Erlbaum.

Mendelson, M. J., & Haith, M. M. (1976). The relation between audition and vision in the human newborn.

Mendle, J., Turkheimer, E., & Emery, R. E. (2007). Detrimental psychological outcomes associated with early pubertal timing in adolescent girls. *Developmental Review, 27*, 151–171.

Menon, M., Tobin, D. D., Corby, B. C., Menon, M., Hodges, E. V. E., & Perry, D. G. (2007). The developmental costs of high self-esteem for antisocial children. *Child Development, 78*, 1627–1639.

Menzel, E. W., Jr. (1974). A group of young chimpanzees in a 1-acre field: Leadership and communication. In A. M. Schrier & F. Stollnitz (Eds.), *Behavior of nonhuman primates* (Vol. 5, pp. 83–153). New York: Academic Press.

Mereu, G., Fà, M., Ferraro, L., Casiano, R., Antonelli, T., Tattoli, M., Ghiglieri, V., Tanganelli, S., Gessa, G. L., & Cuomo, V. (2003). Prenatal exposure to a cannabinoid agonist produces memory deficits linked to dysfunction in hippocampal long-term potentiation and glutamate release. *Proceedings of the National Academy of Sciences (USA), 100*, 4915–4920.

Merola, J. L., & Liederman, J. (1985). Developmental changes in hemispheric independence. *Child Development, 56*, 1184–1194.

Merritt, K. A., Ornstein, P. A., & Spicker, B. (1994). Children's memory for a salient medical procedure: Implications for testimony. *Pediatrics, 94*, 12–23.

Mervis, C. B. (2003). Williams syndrome: 15 years of psychological research. *Developmental Neuropsychology, 23,* 1–12.

Mervis, C. B., & Bertrand, J. (1994). Acquisition of the novel name-nameless category (N3C) principle. *Child Development, 65,* 1646–1662.

Mervis, C. B., & Rosch, E. (1981). Categorization of natural objects. *Annual Review of Psychology, 32,* 89–115.

Michael, A., & Eccles, J. (2003). When coming of age means coming undone. Links between puberty and psychosocial adjustment in European American and African American girls. In C. Haywood (Ed.), *Gender differences at puberty.* Cambridge, UK: Cambridge University Press.

Michalski, R. L., & Euler, H. A. (2007). Sibling relationships. In C. A. Salmon & T. K. Shackelford (Eds.), *Family relationships: An evolutionary perspective* (pp. 185–204). New York: Oxford University Press.

Millberger, S., Biederman, J., Faraone, S. V., Chen, L., & Jones, J. (1996). Is maternal smoking during pregnancy a risk factor for attention deficit hyperactivity disorder in children? *American Journal of Psychiatry, 153,* 1138–1142.

Miller, B. C., Fan, X., Christensen, M., Grotevant, H. D., & van Dulmen, M. (2000). Comparisons of adopted and nonadopted adolescents in a large, nationally representative sample. *Child Development, 71,* 1458–1473.

Miller, G. (2000). *The mating mind: How sexual choice shaped the evolution of human nature.* New York: Anchor.

Miller, G. A. (1977). *Spontaneous apprentices: Children and language.* New York: Seabury.

Miller, K. F., Smith, C. M., Zhu, J., & Zhang, H. (1995). Preschool origins of cross-national differences in mathematical competence. *Psychological Science, 6,* 56–60.

Miller, L. A. (1992). Impulsivity, risk-taking, and the ability to synthesize fragmented information after frontal lobectomy. *Neuropsychologia, 30,* 69–79.

Miller, L. T., & Vernon, P. A. (1996). Intelligence, reaction time, and working memory in 4- to 6-year-old children. *Intelligence, 22,* 155–190.

Miller, L. T., & Vernon, P. A. (1997). Developmental changes in speed of information processing in young children. *Developmental Psychology, 33,* 549–554.

Miller, P. H. (1990). The development of strategies of selective attention. In D. F. Bjorklund (Ed.), *Children's strategies: Contemporary views of cognitive development.* Hillsdale, NJ: Erlbaum.

Miller, P. H., & Coyle, T. R. (1999). Developmental changes: Lessons from microgenesis. In E. K. Scholnick, K. Nelson, S. A. Gelman, & P. H. Miller (Eds.), *Conceptual development: Piaget's legacy* (pp. 209–239). Mahwah, NJ: Erlbaum.

Miller, P. H., & Seier, W. L. (1994). Strategy utilization deficiencies in children: When, where, and why. In H. W. Reese (Ed.), *Advances in child development and behavior* (Vol. 25). New York: Academic.

Miller, P. H., Seier, W. L., Probert, J. S., & Aloise, P. A. (1991). Age differences in the capacity demands of a strategy among spontaneously strategic children. *Journal of Experimental Child Psychology, 52,* 149–165.

Miller, P. H., & Weiss, M. G. (1982). Children's and adults knowledge about what variables affect selective attention. *Child Development, 53,* 543–549.

Miller-Jones, D. (1989). Culture and testing. *American Psychologist, 44,* 360–366.

Milligan, K., Astington, J. W., & Dack, L. A. (2007). Language and theory of mind: Meta-analysis of the relationship between language ability and false-belief understanding. *Child Development, 78,* 622–646.

Mills, A. (1987). The development of phonology in the blind child. In B. Dodd & R. Campbell (Eds.), *Hearing by eye: The psychology of lipreading* (pp. 145–162). London: Erlbaum.

Mills, R. S. L., Imm, G. P., Walling, B. R., & Weiler, H. A. (2008). Cortisol reactivity and regulation associated with shame responding in early childhood. *Child Development, 44,* 1369–1380.

Milner, B. (1964). Some effects of frontal lobectomy in man. In J. M. Warren & K. Akert (Eds.), *The frontal granular cortex and behavior.* New York: McGraw-Hill.

Mineka, S., Davidson, M., Cook, M., & Keir, R. (1984). Observational conditioning of snake fear in rhesus monkeys. *Journal of Abnormal Psychology, 93,* 355–372.

Mischel, W. (1973). Toward a cognitive social learning reconceptualization of personality. *Psychological Review, 80,* 252–283.

Mischel, W. (1983). Delay of gratification as process and as person variable in development. In D. Magnusson & V. P. Allen (Eds.), *Human development: An interactional perspective* (pp. 149–165). New York: Academic Press.

Mischel, W., & Shoda, Y. (1995). A cognitive-affective system theory of personality: Reconceptualizing situations, dispositions, dynamics, and invariance in personality structure. *Psychological Review, 102,* 246–268.

Mischel, W., Shoda, Y., & Mendoza-Denton, R. (2002). Situation-behavior profiles as a locus of consistency in personality. *Current Directions in Psychological Science, 11,* 50–54.

Moffitt, T. E., Caspi, J., Belsky, J., & Silva, P. A. (1992). Childhood experience and the onset of menarche: A test of a sociobiological hypothesis. *Child Development, 63,* 47–58.

Moffitt, T. W., Caspi, A., & Rutter, M. (2006). Measured gene-environment interactions in Psychology: Concepts, research strategies, and implications for research, intervention, and public understanding of genetics. *Perspective on Psychological Science, 1,* 5–27.

Molfese, D. L., & Molfese, V. J. (1980). Cortical responses of preterm infants to phonetic and nonphonetic speech stimuli. *Developmental Psychology, 16,* 574–581.

Molfese, D. L., & Molfese, V.J. (1985). Electrophysiological indices of auditory discrimination in newborn infants: The bases for predicting later language development? *Infant Behavior and Development, 8,* 197–211.

Mondloch, C. J., Dobson, K. S., Parsons, J., & Mauer, D. (2004). Why 8-year-olds cannot tell the difference between Steve Martin and Paul Newman: Factors contributing to the slow development of sensitivity to the spacing of facial features. *Journal of Experimental Child Psychology, 89,* 159–181.

Mondloch, C. J., Lewis, T. L., Budreau, D. R., Maurer, D., Dannemiller, J. L., Stephens, B. R., & Kleiner-Gathercoal, K. A. (1999). Face perception during early infancy. *Psychological Science, 10,* 419–422.

Money, J. (1986). *Lovemaps: Clinical concepts of sexual/erotic health and pathology, paraphilias, and gender transposition in childhood, adolescence, and maturity.* New York: Irvington.

Money, J. (1988). *Gay, straight, and in-between: The sexology of erotic orientation.* New York: Oxford University Press.

Money, J., & Ehrhardt, A. A. (1972). *Man and woman, boy and girl.* Baltimore, MD: Johns Hopkins University Press.

Money, J., & Tucker, P. (1975). *Sexual signatures: On being a man or a woman.* Boston: Little, Brown.

Monk, C. S., Webb, S. J., & Nelson, C. A. (2001). Prenatal neurobiological development: Molecular mechanisms and anatomical change. *Developmental Neuropsychology, 19,* 211–236.

Monroe, S. M., Rohde, P., Seeley, J. R., & Lewinsohn, P. M. (1999). Life events and depression in adolescence: Relationship loss as a prospective risk factor for first onset of major depressive disorder. *Journal of Abnormal Psychology, 108,* 606–614.

Montemayor, R., & Eisen, M. (1977). The development of self-conceptions from childhood to adolescence. *Developmental Psychology, 13,* 314–319.

Montepare, J. M., & McArthur, L. B. (1986). The influence of facial characteristics on children's age perceptions. *Journal of Experimental Child Psychology, 42,* 303–314.

Montgomery, S. M., Bartley, M. J., & Wilkinson, R. G. (1997). Family conflict and slow growth. *Archives of Diseases of Childhood, 77,* 326–330.

Moore, D. S. (2001). *The dependent gene: The fallacy of "nature vs. nurture."* New York: Freeman Books.

Moore, D. S., & Cocas, L. A. (2006). Perception precedes computation: Can familiarity preferences explain apparent calculation by human babies? *Developmental Psychology, 42,* 666–678.

Moore, D. S., Spence, M. J., & Katz, G. S. (1997). Six-month-olds' categorization of natural infant-directed utterances. *Developmental Psychology, 33,* 980–989.

Moore, K. L., & Persaud, T. V. N. (2003). *The developing human: Clinically oriented embryology* (7th ed.). Saunders: Philadelphia.

Moreno, M. A., VanderStoep, A., Parks, M. R., Zimmerman, F. J., Kurth, A., & Christakis, D. A. (2009). Reducing at-risk adolescents' display of risk behavior on a social networking web site. *Archives of Pediatrics & Adolescent Medicine, 163*, 35–41.

Morgan, M., & Grube, J. W. (1991). Closeness and peer group influence. *British Journal of Social Psychology, 30*, 159–169.

Moriguchi, Y., & Hiraki, K. (2009). Neural origin of cognitive shifting in young children. *Proceeding of the National Academy of Sciences (USA), 106*, 6017–6021.

Morris, J. S., Frith, C. D., Perrett, D. I., Rowland, D., Young, A. W., & Calder, A. J. (1996). A differential neural response in the human amygdala to fearful and happy facial expressions. *Nature, 383*, 812–815.

Morrison, D. R., & Coiro, M. J. (1999). Parental conflict and marital disruption: Do children benefit when high-conflict marriages are dissolved? *Journal of Marriage and the Family, 61*, 626–637.

Morrison, F. J., & Connor, C. M. (2009). The transition to school: Child-instruction transactions in learning to read. In A. Sameroff (Ed.), *The transactional model of development: How children and contexts shape each other* (pp. 183–201). Washington, DC: American Psychological Association.

Morrison, F. J., Griffith, E. M., & Alberts, D. M. (1997). Nature-nurture in the classroom: Entrance age, school readiness, and learning in children. *Developmental Psychology, 33*, 254–262.

Morrissey, T. W. (2009). Multiple child-care arrangements and young children's behavioral outcomes. *Child Development, 80*, 59–76.

Morrongiello, B. A., Fenwich, K. D., Hillier, L., & Chance, G. (1994). Sound localization in newborn human infants. *Developmental Psychobiology, 27*, 519–538.

Morrow, E. M., Yoo, S-Y., Flavell, S. W., Kim, T-K. et al. (2008). Identifying autism loci and genes by tracing recent shared ancestry. *Science, 321* (11 July), 218–223.

Morss, J. R. (1990). *The biologising of childhood: Developmental psychology and the Darwinian myth.* Hillsdale, NJ: Erlbaum.

Mortensen, E. L., Michaelsen, K. F., Sanders S. A., & Reinisch, J. M. (2002). The association between duration of breastfeeding and adult intelligence. *Journal of the American Medical Association, 287*, 2365–2371.

Morton, J., & Johnson, M. H. (1991). Conspec and Conlearn: A two-process theory of infant face recognition. *Psychological Review, 98*, 164–181.

Mosier, C. E., & Rogoff, B. (2003). Privileged treatment of toddlers: Cultural aspects of individual choice and responsibility. *Developmental Psychology, 39*, 1047–1060.

Moss, E., Cyr, C., Bureau, J-F., Tarabulsy, G. M., & Dubois Comtois, K. (2005). Stability of attachment during the preschool period. *Developmental Psychology, 41*, 773–783.

Moulson, M. C., Fox, N. A., Zeanah, C. H., & Nelson, C. A. (2009). Early adverse experiences and the neurobiology of facial processing. *Developmental Psychology, 45*, 17–30.

Moulson, M. C., Westerlund, A., Fox, N. A., Zeanah, C. H., & Nelson, C. A. (2009). The effects of early experience on face recognition: An event-related potential study of institutionalized children in Romania. *Child Development, 80*, 1039–1056.

Mueller, E., & Brenner, J. (1977). The origins of social skills and interaction among playgroup toddlers. *Child Development, 48*, 854–861.

Muise, A. M., Stein, D. G., & Arbess, G. (2003). Eating disorders in adolescent boys: A review of the adolescent and young adult literature. *Journal of Adolescent Health, 33*, 427–435.

Mulder, E. J., Robles de Medina, P. G., Huizink, A. C., van den Bergh, B. R., Buitelaar, J. K., & Visser, G. H. (2002). Prenatal maternal stress: Effects on pregnancy and the (unborn) child. *Early Human Development, 73*, 1–14.

Mullen, M. K. (1994). Earliest recollections of childhood: A demographic analysis. *Cognition, 52*, 55–79.

Mullen, M. K., & Yi, S. (1995). The cultural context of talk about the past: Implications for the development of autobiographical memory. *Cognitive Development, 10*, 407–419.

Müller, G. B. (2003). Embryonic motility: Environmental influences and evolutionary innovation. *Evolution & Development, 5*, 56–60.

Mumme, D. L., & Fernald, A. (2003). The infant as onlooker: Learning from emotional reactions observed in a television scenario. *Child Development, 74*, 221–237.

Mumme, D. L., Fernald, A., & Herrera, C. (1996). Infants' responses to facial and vocal emotional signals in a social referencing paradigm. *Child Development, 67*, 3219–3237.

Munro, G., & Adams, G. R. (1977). Ego-identity formation in college students and working youth. *Developmental Psychology, 13*, 523–524.

Munroe, R. H., Shimmin, H. S., & Munroe, R. L. (1984). Gender understanding and sex role preference in four cultures. *Developmental Psychology, 20*, 673–682.

Murphy, C. M. (1978). Pointing in the context of a shared activity. *Child Development, 49*, 371–380.

Muscarella, F. (2000). The evolution of homoerotic behavior in humans. *Journal of Homosexuality, 40*, 51–77.

Musher-Eizenman, D. R., Holub, S. C., Miller, A. B., Goldstein, S. E., & Edwards-Leeper, L. (2004). Body size stigmatization in preschool children: The role of control attributions. *Journal of Pediatric Psychology, 29*, 613–620.

Must, A., & Strauss, R. S. (1999). Risks and consequences of childhood and adolescent obesity. *International Journal of Eating Disorders, 23*, S2–S11.

Mustanski, B. S., Viken, R. J., Kaprio, J., Pulkkinen, L., & Rose, R. J. (2004). Genetic and environmental influences on pubertal development: Longitudinal data from Finnish twins at ages 11 and 14. *Developmental Psychology, 40*, 1188–1198.

Muzzatti, B., & Agnoli, F. (2007). Gender and mathematics: Attitudes and stereotype threat susceptibility in Italian children. *Developmental Psychology, 43*, 747–459.

Myowa-Yamakoshi, M., Tomonaga, M., Tanaka, M., & Matsuzawa, T. (2004). Imitation in neonatal chimpanzees (*Pan troglodytes*). *Developmental Science, 7*, 437–442.

Nagell, K., Olguin, K., & Tomasello, M. (1993). Processes of social learning in the tool use of chimpanzees (*Pan troglodytes*) and human children (*Homo sapiens*). *Journal of Comparative Psychology, 107*, 174–186.

Nagy, E. (2006). From imitation to conversation: The first dialogues with human neonates, *Infant and Child Development, 15*, 223–232.

Nagy, E. (2008). Innate intersubjectivity: Newborns' sensitivity to communication disturbance. *Developmental Psychology, 44*, 1779–1784.

Nanez, J. E., & Yonas, A. (1994). Effects of luminance and texture motion on infant defensive reactions to optical collision. *Infant Behavior and Development, 17*, 165–174.

Nason, A. (1965). *Textbook of modern biology.* New York: Wiley.

National Academy of Sciences. (2000). *Sleep needs, patterns and difficulties of adolescents: Summary of a workshop.* Accessed at: www.nap.edu/openbook/030907177/html/3.html.

National Center for Health Statistics. (1999). *Health, United States.* Hyattsville, MD.

National Institute of Child Health and Development. (2005). *Autism overview: What we know.* Rockville, MD: Author.

National Institute of Drug Abuse. (2006). What are the effects of maternal cocaine use? www.nida.nih.gov/ResearchReports/Cocaine/cocaine4.htm#maternal.

National Sleep Foundation. (2007). *Children's sleep habits.* www.sleepfoundation.org.

Neil, E. (2000). The reasons why young children are placed for adoption: Findings from a recently placed sample and a discussion of implications for subsequent identity development. *Child & Family Social Work, 5*, 303–316.

Neiss, M. B., Sedikides, C., & Stevenson, J. (2002). Self-esteem: A behavioural genetic perspective. *European Journal of Personality, 16*, 1–17.

Neisser, U. (Ed.). (1998). *The rising curve: Long-term gains in IQ and related measures.* Washington, DC: American Psychological Association.

Neisser, U., Boodoo, G., Bouchard, T. J., Boykin, A. W., Brody, N., Ceci, S. J., Halpern, D. F., Loehlin, J. C., Perloff, R., Sternberg, R. J., & Urbina, S. (1996). Intelligence: Knowns and unknowns. *American Psychologist, 51*, 77–101.

Nelson, C. A. (2001). Neural plasticity and human development: The role of experience in sculpting memory systems. *Developmental Science, 3*, 115–130.

Nelson, C. A. (2007). A neurobiological perspective on early human deprivation. *Child Development Perspectives, 1*, 13–18.

Nelson, C. A., Furtado, E. A., Fox, N. A., & Zeanah, Jr., C. H. (2009). The deprived human brain. *American Scientist, 97* (May-June), 222–229.

Nelson, C. A., Thomas, K. M., & de Haan, M. (2006). Neural bases of cognitive development. In W. Damon & R. M. Lerner (Gen. Eds.), *Handbook of child psychology* (6th ed.). In D. Kuhn & R. S. Siegler (Vol. Eds.), Vol. 2: *Cognition, perception, and language* (pp. 3–57). New York: Wiley.

Nelson, C. A. III, Zeanah, C. H., Fox, N. A., Marshall, P. J., Smuke, A. T., & Guthrie, D. (2007). Cognitive recovery in socially deprived young children: The Bucharest Early Intervention Program. *Science, 318* (21 December), 1937–1940.

Nelson, J., & Aboud, F. E. (1985). The resolution of social conflict between friends. *Child Development, 56*, 1009–1017.

Nelson, K. (1973). Structure and strategy in learning to talk. *Monographs of the Society for Research in Child Development, 38* (Serial No. 149).

Nelson, K. (1977). Aspects of language acquisition and form use from age 2 to age 20. *Journal of the American Academy of Child Psychiatry, 16*, 121–132.

Nelson, K. (1993). The psychological and social origins of autobiographical memory. *Psychological Science, 4*, 7–14.

Nelson, K. (1996). *Language in cognitive development: The emergence of the mediated mind.* New York: Cambridge University Press.

Nelson, K. (2005). Evolution and development of human memory systems. In B. J. Ellis & D. F. Bjorklund (Eds.), *Origins of the social mind: Evolutionary psychology and child development* (pp. 354–382). New York: Guilford.

Nelson, K., & Gruendel, J. (1981). Generalized event representations: Basic building blocks of cognitive development. In M. Lamb & A. Brown (Eds.), *Advances in developmental psychology* (Vol. 1). Hillsdale, NJ: Erlbaum.

Nestle, M., & Jacobson, M. F. (2000). Halting the obesity epidemic: A public health policy approach. *Public Health Reports, 115*, 12–24.

Neumark-Sztainer, D., Falkner, N., Story, M., Perry, C., Hannan, P. J., & Mulet, S. (2002). Weight-teasing among adolescents: Correlations with weight status and disordered eating behaviors. *International Journal of Obesity, 26*, 125–131.

Neumark-Sztainer, D., Story, M., Dixon, L., & Murray, D. (1998). Adolescents engaging in unhealthy weight control behaviors: Are they at risk for other health-compromising behaviors? *American Journal of Public Health, 88*, 952–955.

Neville, H. (2007). Experience shapes human brain development and function. Invited Address at the Biennial Meeting of the Society for Research in Child Development, Boston, Massachusetts.

Newcombe, N. S. (2002). The nativist-empiricist controversy in the context of recent research on spatial and quantitative development. *Psychological Science, 13*, 395–401.

Newcombe, N. S., & Huttenlocher, J. (1992). Children's early ability to solve perspective-taking problems. *Developmental Psychology, 28*, 635–643.

Newcombe, N., Huttenlocher, J., & Learmonth, A. (1999). Infants' coding of location in continuous space. *Infant Behavior & Development, 22*, 483–510.

Newcombe, N., Huttenlocher, J., Drummey, A. B., & Wiley, J. (1998). The development of spatial location coding: Use of external frames of reference and dead reckoning. *Cognitive Development, 13*, 185–200.

Newport, E. L. (1990). Maturational constraints on language learning. *Cognitive Science, 14*, 11–28.

Newport, E. L. (1991).Contrasting concepts of the critical period for language. In S. Carey & R. Gelman (Eds.), *Epigenesis of mind: Essays in biology and knowledge.* Hillsdale, NJ: Erlbaum.

Ng, F. F-Y., Pomerantz, E. M., & Lam, S-F. (2007). European American and Chinese parents' responses to children's success and failure: Implications for children's responses. *Developmental Psychology, 43*, 1239–1255.

NICHD Early Child Care Research Network. (2002). Child-care structure → process → outcome: Direct and indirect effects of child-care quality on young children's development. *Psychological Science, 13*, 199–206.

NICHD Early Child Care Research Network. (2003). Does quality child care affect child outcomes at age 4 1/2? *Developmental Psychology, 39*, 451–469.

NICHD Early Child Care Research Network. (2004). Trajectories of physical aggression from toddlerhood to middle childhood: Predictors, correlates, and outcomes. *Monographs of the Society for Research in Child Development, 69* (Serial No. 278).

NICHD Early Child Care Research Network. (2005a). Predicting individual differences in attention, memory, and planning in first graders from experiences at home, child care, and school. *Developmental Psychology, 41*, 99–114.

NICHD Early Child Care Research Network. (2005b). Duration and developmental timing of poverty and children's cognitive and social development from birth through third grade. *Child Development, 76*, 795–810.

NICHD Early Child Care Research Network. (2006a). Infant-mother attachment classification: Risk and protection in relation to changing maternal caregiving quality. *Developmental Psychology, 42*, 38–58.

NICHD Early Child Care Research Network. (2006b). Child-care effect size for the NICHD Study of Early Child Care and Youth Development. *American Psychologists, 61*, 99–116.

Nichols, S. L., & Good, T. L. (2000). Education and society, 1900–2000: Selected snapshots of then and now. In T. L. Good (Ed.), *American education: Yesterday, today, and tomorrow* (pp. 1–52). Chicago, IL: Chicago University Press.

Nicolopoulou, A., & Richner, E. S. (2007). From actors to agents to persons: The development of character representation in young children's narratives. *Child Development, 78*, 412–429.

Nicolopoulou, A., Scales, B., & Weintraub, J. (1994). Gender differences and symbolic imagination in the stories of four year olds. In A. H. Dyson & C. Genishi (Eds.), *The need for story: Cultural diversity in classroom and community* (pp. 102–123). Urbana, IL: National Council of Teachers of English.

Nielsen, M., Simcock, G., & Jenkins, L. (2008). The effect of social engagement on 24-month-olds' imitation from live and televised models. *Developmental Science, 11*, 722–731.

Nielsen, M., Suddendorf, T., & Slaughter, V. (2006). Mirror self-recognition beyond the face. *Child Development, 77*, 176–185.

Nisan, M. (1984). Distributive justice and social norms. *Child Development, 55*, 1020–1029.

Nisbett, R. E., Peng, K., Choi, I., & Norenzayan, A. (2001). Culture and systems of thought: Holistic vs. analytic cognition. *Psychological Review, 108*, 291–310.

Nobes, G., & Pawson, C. (2009). The influence of negligence, intention, and outcome on children's moral judgments. *Journal of Experimental Child Psychology, 104*, 382–397

Nolte, D. L. (1998). *Children learn what they live.* New York: Workman.

Nord, M., Andrews, M., & Carlson, S. (2004). *Household food security in the United States, 2003.* U.S. Department of Agriculture, Economic Research Service, Food Assistance and Nutrition Report 42.

Norman, G. J., Schmid, B. A., Sallis, J. F., Calfas, K. J., & Patrick, K. (2005). Psychosocial and environmental correlates of adolescent sedentary behaviors. *Pediatrics, 116*, 908–916.

Northcutt, W. (2006). *The Darwin Awards: Intelligent design.* New York: Dutton.

Northoff, G., & Panksepp, J. (2008). The trans-species concept of self and the subcortical-cortical midline system. *Trends in Cognitive Science, 12*, 259–264.

Norton, S. J., Gorga, M. P., Widen, J. E., Folsom, R. C., Sininger, Y., Cone-Wesson, B., Vohr, B. R., Mascher, K., & Fletcher, K. (2000). Identification of neonatal hearing impairment: Evaluation of transient evoked otoacoustic emission, distortion product otoacoustic emission, and auditory brain stem response test performance. *Ear and Hearing, 21*, 508–528.

Nunez-Smith, M., Wolf, E., Huang, H. M., Chen, P. G., Lee, L., Emanuel, E. J., & Gross, C. P. (2008). *Media and child and adolescent health: A systematic review.* San Francisco: Common Sense Media.

Nyiti, R. M. (1982). The validity of "cultural differences explanation" in the rate of Piagetian cognitive development. In D. A. Wagner & H. W. Stevenson (Eds.), *Cultural perspectives on child development*. San Francisco: W. H. Freeman.

O'Brien, M., & Huston, A. C. (1985). Development of sex-typed play behavior in toddlers. *Developmental Psychology, 21*, 866–871.

O'Connell, J. F., Hawkes, K., & Blurton Jones, N. G. (1999). Grandmothering and the evolution of *Homo erectus*. *Journal of Human Evolution, 36*, 461–485.

O'Connor, S., Vietze, P. M., Sherrod, K. B., Sandler, H. M., & Altemeier, W. A. (1980). Reduced incidence of parenting inadequacy following rooming-in. *Pediatrics, 66*, 176–183.

O'Neill, D. K., & Shultis, R. (2007). The emergence of the ability to track a character's mental perspective in narrative. *Developmental Psychology, 43*, 1032–1037.

O'Neill, M., Bard, K. A., Linnell, M., & Fluck, M. (2005). Maternal gestures with 20-month-old infants in two contexts. *Developmental Science, 8*, 352–359.

O'Railly, R., and Müller, F. (2001). *Human embryology and teratology* (2nd ed.). New York: Wiley-Liss.

Oakes, L. M. (2009). The "Humpty Dumpty Problems" in the study of early cognitive development. *Perspectives on Psychological Science, 4*, 352–358.

Oberman, L. M., Hubbard, E. M., McCleery, J. P., Altschuler, E. L., & Pineda, J. A., & Ramachandran, V. S. (2005). EEG evidence for mirror neuron dysfunction in autism spectrum disorder. *Cognitive Brain Research, 24*, 190–198.

Obradović, J., Bush, N. R., Stamperdahl, J., Adler, N. E., & Boyce, W. T. (2010). Biological sensitivity to context: The interactive effects of stress reactivity and family adversity on socioemotional behavior and school readiness. *Child Development, 81*, 270–289.

Odgers, C. L., Moffitt, T. E., Tqach, L. M., Sampson, R. J., Taylor, A., Matthews, C. L., & Caspi, A. (2009). The protective effects of neighborhood collective efficacy on British children growing up in deprivation: A developmental analysis. *Developmental Psychology, 45*, 942–957.

OECD. (2004). *Learning for tomorrow's world: First results from PISA 2003*. Paris: Organization for Economic Co-operation and Development.

Ogbu, J. (2003). *Black American students in an affluent suburb: Study of academic disengagement*. Mahwah, NJ: Erlbaum.

Öhman, A., Flykt, A., & Esteves, F. (2001). Emotion drives attention: Detecting the snake in the grass. *Journal of Experimental Psychology: General, 130*, 466–478.

Öhman, A., & Mineka, S. (2003). The malicious serpent: Snakes as a prototypical stimulus for an evolved module of fear. *Current Directions in Psychological Science, 12*, 5–9.

Ohring, M. B., Graber, J. A., & Brooks-Gunn, J. (2002). Girls' recurrent and concurrent body dissatisfaction: Correlates and consequences over 8 years. *International Journal of Eating Disorders, 31*, 404–415.

Okami, P., Olmstead, R., & Abramson, P. R. (1997). Sexual experiences in early childhood: 18-year longitudinal data from the UCLA Family Lifestyles Project. *Journal of Sex Research, 34*, 339–347.

Olds, D. L., Henderson, C. R., & Tatelbaum, R. (1994). Intellectual impairment in children of women who smoke cigarettes during pregnancy. *Pediatrics, 93*, 221–227.

Oléron, P. (1957). *Recherches sur le développement mental des sourds-muets. Contribution à l´étude du problème "langage et pensée"* [*Investigations of deaf children's mental development. Contribution to the study of the "language and thought" problem*]. Paris: CNRS.

Olivares, J., Lázquez, M., Fleta, J., Moreno, L. A., Pérez-González, J. M., & Bueno, M. (2005). Cardiac findings in adolescents with anorexia nervosa at diagnosis and after weight restoration. *European Journal of Pediatrics, 164*, 383–386.

Oliver, B. R., Dale, P. S., & Plomin, R. (2005). Predicting literacy at age 7 from preliteracy at age 4: A longitudinal genetic analysis. *Psychological Science, 16*, 861–865.

Oliver, E. I. (1995). The writing quality of seventh, ninth, and eleventh graders, and college freshmen: Does theoretical specification in writing prompts make a difference? *Research in the Teaching of English, 29*, 422–450.

Oliver, M. B., & Hyde, J. S. (1993). Gender differences in sexuality: A meta-analysis. *Psychological Bulletin, 114*, 29–36.

Oller, D. K., & Eilers, R. (1988). The role of audition in babbling. *Child Development, 59*, 441–449.

Oller, D. K., & Pearson, B. Z. (2002). Assessing the effects of bilingualism: A background. In D. K. Oller & R. E. Eilers (Eds.), *Language and literacy in bilingual children* (pp. 3–21). Clevedon, UK: Multilingual.

Olson, K. R., & Dweck, C. S. (2009). Social cognitive development: A new look. *Child Development Perspectives, 3*, 60–65.

Olson, S. (2002). *Mapping human history: Genes, race, and our common origins*. Boston: Houghton Mifflin.

Olson, K. R., & Dweck, C. S. (2008). A blueprint for social cognitive development. *Perspectives on Psychological Science, 3*, 193–202.

Olweus, D. (1980). Familial and temperamental determinants of aggressive behavior in adolescent boys: A causal analysis. *Developmental Psychology, 16*, 644–660.

Olweus, D. (1987, Fall). Schoolyard bullying: Grounds for intervention. *School Safety*, 4–11.

Olweus, D. (1993). *Bullying at school*. Cambridge, MA: Blackwell.

Olweus, D. (1995). Bullying or peer abuse at school: Facts and interventions. *Current Directions in Psychological Science, 4*, 196–200.

Onishi, K. H., & Baillargeon, R. (2005). Do 15-month-old infants understand false belief? *Science, 308* (8 April), 255–258.

Ontai, L. L., & Thompson, R. A. (2002). Patterns of attachment and maternal discourse effects on children's emotion understanding from 3 to 5 years of age. *Social Development, 11*, 433–450.

Oppenheim, R. W. (1981). Ontogenetic adaptations and retrogressive processes in the development of the nervous system and behavior. In K. J. Connolly & H. F. R. Prechtl (Eds.), *Maturation and development: Biological and psychological perspectives* (pp. 73–108). Philadelphia, PA: International Medical Publications.

Orbach, Y., & Lamb, M. E. (2007). Young children's references to temporal attributed of allegedly experienced events in the course of forensic interviews. *Child Development, 78*, 1100–1120.

Orme, N. (2001). *Medieval children*. New Haven, CT: Yale University Press.

Ornstein, M., Ohlsson, A., Edmonds, J., & Asztalos, E. (1991). Neonatal follow-up of very low birthweight/extremely low birthweight infants to school age: A critical overview. *Acta Paediatrica, 80*, 741–748.

Ornstein, P. A., Baker-Ward, L., Gordon, B. N., Pelphrey, K. A., Tyler, C. S., & Gramzow, E. (2006). The influence of prior knowledge and repeated questioning on children's long-term retention of the details of a pediatric examination, *Developmental Psychology, 42*, 332–344.

Ornstein, P. A., Gordon, B. N., & Larus, D. M. (1992). Children's memory for a personally experienced event: Implications for testimony. *Applied Developmental Psychology, 6*, 49–60.

Ornstein, P. A., & Greenhoot, A. F. (2000). Remembering the distant past: Implications of research on children's memory for the recovered memory debate. In D. F. Bjorklund (Ed.), *False-memory creation in children and adults: Theory, research, and implications*. Mahwah, NJ: Erlbaum.

Ornstein, P. A., & Naus, M. J. (1985). Effects of the knowledge base on children's memory strategies. *Advances in Child Development and Behavior, 19*, 113–148.

Ornstein, P. A., Naus, M. J., & Liberty, C. (1975). Rehearsal and organizational processes in children's memory. *Child Development, 46*, 818–830.

Ornstein, P. A., Naus, M. J., & Stone, B. P. (1977). Rehearsal training and developmental differences in memory. *Developmental Psychology, 13*, 15–24.

Österman, K., Björkqvist, K., & Lagerspetz, K. M. J. et al. (1998). Cross-cultural evidence of female indirect aggression. *Aggressive Behavior, 24*, 1–8.

Ostrov, J. M., & Bishop, C. M. (2008). Preschoolers' aggression and parent-child conflict: A multiinformant and multimethod study. *Journal of Experimental Child Psychology, 99*, 309–322.

Ostrovsky, Y., Andalman, A., & Sinha, P. (2006). Vision following extended congenital blindness. *Psychological Science, 12*, 1009–1014.

Ovando, C. J., & Collier, V. P. (1998). *Bilingual and ESL classrooms: Teaching in multicultural contexts.* Boston: McGraw-Hill.

Over, H., & Carpenter, M. (2009). Eighteen-month-old infants show increased helping following priming with affiliation. *Psychological Science, 20,* 1189–1193.

Overpeck, M. D., Brenner, R. A., Trumble, A. C., Trifiletti, L. B., & Berendes, H. W. (1998). Risk factors for infant homicide in the United States. *New England Journal of Medicine, 339,* 1211–1216.

Owens, K., & King, M-C. (1999). Genomic views of human history. *Science, 286* (15 October), 451–453.

Oyama, S. (2000). *The ontogeny of information: Developmental systems and evolution* (2nd ed.). Durham, NC: Duke University Press.

Ozcaliskan, S., & Goldin-Meadow, S. (2005). Gesture is at the cutting edge of early language development. *Cognition, 96,* B101–B113.

Pace, N. (2006, January 3). Q&A: MySpace founders Chris DeWolfe and Tom Anderson. *Forbes.* Accessed at: http://www.forbes.com/2006/01/04/myspace-dewolfe-anderson-cx_np_0104myspace.html. (Downloaded Jun2 3, 2010).

Palm Beach Post (June 8, 2008). Bullies tap into Web to ambush. Local News, p. 1.

Palmquist, S., & Crowley, K. (2007). From teachers to testers: How parents talk to novice and expert children in a natural history museum. *Science Education, 91,* 783–804.

Pan, B. A., & Snow, C. E. (1999). The development of conversation and discourse. In M. Barrett (Ed.), *The development of language* (pp. 229–250). London: UCL Press.

Panksepp, J. (1998). Attention deficit hyperactivity disorders, psychostimulants, and intolerance of childhood playfulness: A tragedy in the making? *Current Directions in Psychological Science, 7,* 91–98.

Papousek, H. (1977). The development of learning ability in infancy (Entwicklung der Lernfähigkeit im Säuglingsalter). In G. Nissen (Ed.), *Intelligence, learning, and learning disabilities (Intelligenz, Lernen und Lernstörungen).* Berlin: Springer-Verlag.

Parer, J. T. (1998). Effects of fetal asphyxia on brain cell structure and function: Limits of tolerance. *Comparative Biochemistry and Physiology, 199A,* 711–716.

Park, J. H., Schaller, M., & Crandall, C. S. (2007). Pathogen-avoidance mechanisms and the stigmatization of obese people. *Evolution and Human Behavior, 28,* 410–414.

Parke, R. D. (2002). Fathers and families. In M. H. Bornstein (Ed.), *Handbook of parenting,* Vol. 3: *Being and becoming a parent* (2nd ed., pp. 27–73). Mahwah, NJ: Erlbaum.

Parke, R. D. (2004). Fathers, families, and the future: A plethora of plausible predictions. *Merrill-Palmer Quarterly, 50,* 456–470.

Parke, R. D. (2008). Gender differences and similarities in parental behavior. *Who is called a "parent" and why? An interdisciplinary investigation of core questions at the heart of today's family debates.* Paper presented at workshop held at the University of Virginia, Charlottesville, October 16–18, 2008.

Parke, R. D., Berkowitz, L., Leyens, J. P., West, S. G., & Sebastian, R. J. (1977). Some effects of violent and non-violent movies on the behavior of juvenile delinquents. In L. Berkowitz (Ed.), *Advances in experimental social psychology* (Vol. 10). New York: Academic Press.

Parker, J. F. (1995). Age differences in source monitoring of performed and imagined actions on immediate and delayed tests. *Journal of Experimental Child Psychology, 60,* 84–101.

Parker, S. T., & McKinney, M. L. (1999). *Origins of intelligence: The evolution of cognitive development in monkeys, apes, and humans.* Baltimore, MD: The Johns Hopkins University Press.

Parker, S. W., Nelson, C. A., & The Bucharest Early Intervention Core Group. (2005a). An event-related potential study of the impact of institutional rearing on face recognition. *Development and Psychopathology, 17,* 621–639.

Parker, S. W., Nelson, C. A., & The Bucharest Early Intervention Core Group. (2005b). The impact of early institutional rearing on the ability to discriminate facial expressions of emotion: An event-related potential study. *Child Development, 76,* 54–72.

Parkhurst, J. T., & Hopmeyer, A. (1998). Sociometric popularity and peer-perceived popularity: Two distinct dimensions of peer status. *The Journal of Early Adolescence, 18,* 125–144.

Parten, M. (1932). Social participation among preschool children. *Journal of Abnormal and Social Psychology, 27,* 243–269.

Pascalis, O., de Haan, M., & Nelson, C. A. (2002). Is face processing species-specific during the first year of life? *Science, 296* (17 May), 1321–1323.

Pascalis, O., & Kelly, D. J. (2009). The origins of face processing in humans. *Perspectives on Psychological Science, 4,* 200–209.

Pascual-Leone, J. (1970). A mathematical model for the transition rule in Piaget's developmental stages. *Acta Psychologia, 32,* 301–345.

Pascual-Leone, J. (2000). Is the French connection neo-Piagetian? Not nearly enough! *Child Development, 71,* 843–845.

Pashos, A. (2000). Does paternal uncertainty explain discriminative grandparental solicitude? A cross-cultural study in Greece and Germany. *Evolution and Human Behavior, 21,* 97–109.

Pashos, A., & McBurney, D. H. (2008). Kin relationship and caregiving biases of grandparents, aunts, and uncles: A two-generational questionnaire study. *Human Nature, 19,* 311–330.

Pasterski, V. L., Geffner, M. E., Brain, C., Hindmarch, P., Brooks, C., & Hines, M. (2005). Prenatal hormones and postnatal socialization by parents as determinates of male-typical toy play in girls with congenital adrenal hyperplasia. *Child Development, 76,* 264–278.

Patterson, C. J. (2002). Lesbian and gay parenthood. In M. H. Bornstein (Ed.), *Handbook of parenting* (2nd ed.), Vol. 3: *Being and becoming a parent* (pp. 317–338). Mahwah, NJ: Erlbaum.

Patterson, C. J. (2006). Children of lesbian and gay parents. *Current Directions in Psychological Science, 15,* 241–244.

Patterson, G. R. (1980). Mothers: The unacknowledged victims. *Monographs of the Society for Research in Child Development, 45* (Serial No. 186).

Patterson, G. R. (1986). Performance models for antisocial boys. *American Psychologist, 41,* 432–444.

Patterson, G. R., & Stouthamer-Loeber, M. (1984). The correlation of family management practices and delinquency. *Child Development, 55,* 1299–1307.

Patterson, M. L., & Werker, J. F. (2003). Two month-old infants match phonetic information in lips and voice. *Developmental Science, 6,* 191–196.

Patterson, M. M., & Bigler, R. S. (2006). Preschool children's attention to environmental messages about groups: Social categorization and the origins of intergroup bias. *Child Development, 77,* 847–860.

Paukner, A., Anderson, J. R., Borelle, E., Visalberghi, E., & Ferrari, P. F. (2005). Macaques (*Macaca nemestrina*) recognize when they are being imitated. *Biology Letters, 1,* 219–222.

Paul, R. (2006). *Language disorders from infancy through adolescence: Assessment and intervention* (3rd ed). Philadelphia, PA: Mosby.

Pawluck, D. E., & Gorey, K. M. (1998). Secular trends in the incidence of anorexia nervosa: Integrative review of population-based studies. *International Journal of Eating Disorders, 23,* 347–352.

Pearson, B. Z., Fernández, S. C., Lewedag, V., & Oller, D. K. (1997). The relation of input factors to lexical learning by bilingual infants (ages 10 to 30 months). *Applied Psycholinguistics, 18,* 41–58.

Peisner-Feinberg, E. S., Burchinal, M. R., Clifford, R. M., Culkin, M. L., Howes, C., Sharon Kagan, L., & Yazejian, N. (2001). The relation of preschool child-care quality to children's cognitive and social developmental trajectories through second grade. *Child Development, 72,* 1534–1553.

Pelham, W. E., Jr., Carlson, C., Sams, S. E., Vallano, G., Dixon, M. J., & Hoza, B. (1993). Separate and combined effects of methylphenidate and behavior modification on boys with attention deficit-hyperactivity disorder in the classroom. *Journal of Consulting and Clinical Psychology, 61,* 506–515.

Pellegrini, A. D. (2011). Play. In P. Zelazo (Ed.), *Oxford handbook of developmental psychology.* New York: Oxford University Press.

Pellegrini, A. D., & Archer, J. (2005). Sex differences in competitive and aggressive behavior: A view from sexual selection theory. In B. J. Ellis and D. F. Bjorklund (Eds.), *Origins of the social mind: Evolutionary psychology and child development* (pp. 219–244). New York: Guilford.

Pellegrini, A. D., & Bartini, M. (2000). A longitudinal study of bullying, victimization, and peer affiliation during the transition from primary to middle school. *American Educational Research Journal, 37*, 699–726.

Pellegrini, A. D., & Bjorklund, D. F. (2004). The ontogeny and phylogeny of children's object and fantasy play. *Human Nature, 15*, 23–43.

Pellegrini, A. D., & Horvat, M. (1995). A developmental contextual critique of Attention Deficit Hyperactivity Disorder. *Educational Researcher, 24*, 13–20.

Pellegrini, A. D., & Long, J. D. (2003). A sexual selection theory longitudinal analysis of sexual segregation and integration in early adolescence. *Journal of Experimental Child Psychology, 85*, 257–278.

Pellegrini, A. D., Long, J. D., Roseth, C., Bohn, K., & Van Ryzin, M. (2007). A short-term longitudinal study of preschool children's sex segregation: The role of physical activity, sex, and time. *Journal of Comparative Psychology, 121*, 282–289.

Pellegrini, A. D., & Smith, P. K. (1998). Physical activity play: The nature and function of neglected aspect of play. *Child Development, 69*, 577–598.

Pelphrey, K. A., & Carter, E. J. (2008). Brain mechanisms for social perception: Lessons from autism and typical development. *Annals of the New York Academy of Sciences, 1145*, 283–299.

Pennisi, E. (2005). Why do humans have so few genes? *Science, 309* (July), 80.

Perera, F. P., Li, Z., Whyatt, R., Hoepner, L., Wang, S., Camann, D., & Rauh, V. (2009). Prenatal airborne polycyclic aromatic hydrocarbon exposure and child IQ at age 5 years. *Pediatrics, 124*, e195–e202.

Pérez, B. (2004). *Becoming biliterate: A study of two-way bilingual immersion education.* Mahwah, NJ: Erlbaum.

Pérez-Pereira, M., & Conti-Ramsden, G. (1999). *Language development and social interaction in blind children.* Hove, England: Psychology Press.

Perner, J. (1991). *Understanding the representational mind.* Cambridge, MA: MIT Press.

Perner, J., Ruffman, T., & Leekam, S. R. (1994). Theory of mind is contagious: You catch it from your sibs. *Child Development, 67*, 1228–1238.

Perry, D. G., & Bussey, K. (1984). Social development. Upper Saddle River, NJ: Prentice-Hall.

Perry, D. G., Perry, L. C., & Boldizar, J. P. (1990). Learning of aggression. In M. Lewis & S. Miller (Eds.), *Handbook of developmental psychopathology.* New York: Plenum.

Perry, D. G., Perry, L. C., & Rasmussen, P. (1986). Cognitive learning mediators of aggression. *Child Development, 57*, 700–711.

Perry, D. G., White, A. J., & Perry, L. C. (1984). Does early sex typing result from children's attempts to match their behavior to sex role stereotypes? *Child Development, 55*, 2114–2121.

Petersen, A. C., Compas, B. E., Brooks-Gunn, J., Stemmler, M., Ey, S., & Grant, K. E. (1993). Depression in adolescence. *American Psychologist, 48*, 155–168.

Peterson, C. C., Wellman, H. M., & Liu, D. (2005). Steps in theory-of-mind development for children with deafness or autism. *Child Development, 76*, 502–517.

Peterson, C., & McCabe, A. (1983). *Developmental psycholinguistics: Three ways of looking at a child's narrative.* New York: Plenum.

Peterson, C., Wang, Q., & Hou, Y. (2009). "When I was little": Childhood recollections in Chinese and European Canadian grade school children. *Child Development, 80*, 506–518.

Peterson, C. E., & McCabe, A. (2004). Echoing our parents: Parental influences on children's narration. In M. W. Pratt & B. E. Fiese (Eds.), *Family stories and the life course: Across time and generations* (pp. 27–54). Mahwah, NJ: Erlbaum.

Petitto, L. A. (2000). On the biological foundations of human language. In K. Emmorey and H. Lane (Eds.), *The signs of language revisited: An anthology in honor of Ursula Bellugi and Edward Klima.* Mahwah, NJ: Erlbaum.

Petitto, L. A., & Marentette, P. F. (1991). Babbling in the manual mode: Evidence for the ontogeny of language. *Science, 251*, 1483–1496.

Pettit, G. S., Dodge, K. A., & Brown, M. M. (1988). Early family experience, social problem solving patterns, and children's social competence. *Child Development, 59*, 107–120.

Pfeifer, J. H., Rubble, D. N., Bachman, M. A., Alvarez, J. M., Cameron, J. A., & Fuligni, A. J. (2007). Social identities and intergroup bias in immigrant and nonimmigrant children. *Developmental Psychology, 43*, 496–507.

Phinney, J. S., Horenczyk, G., Liebkind, K., & Vedder, P. (2001). Ethnic identity, immigration, and well-being: An interactional perspective, *Journal of Social Issues, 57*, 493–510.

Phinney, J. S., Romero, I., Nava, M., & Huang, D. (2001). The role of language, parents, and peers in ethnic identity among adolescents in immigrant families. *Journal of Youth and Adolescence, 30*, 135–153.

Piaget, J. (1929). *The child's conception of the world.* Lanham, MD: Rowman & Littlefield.

Piaget, J. (1930). *The child's conception of physical causality.* London: Routledge & Kegan Paul.

Piaget, J. (1952). *The origins of intelligence in children.* New York: Norton.

Piaget, J. (1954). *The construction of reality in the child.* New York: Basic.

Piaget, J. (1955). *The language and thought of the child.* New York: World.

Piaget, J. (1962). *Play, dreams, and imitation in childhood.* New York: Norton.

Piaget, J. (1965/1932). *The moral judgment of the child.* New York: Free Press.

Piaget, J. (1969). *The child's conception of the world.* Totowa, NJ: Littlefield & Adams.

Piaget, J. (1972). *Play and development.* Maria W. Piers (Ed.). New York: Norton.

Piaget, J. (1983). Piaget's theory. In P. H. Mussen (Gen. Ed.), *Handbook of child psychology* (4th ed.). In J. H. Flavell & E. M. Markman (Vol. Eds.), Vol. 3: *Cognitive development.* New York: Wiley.

Piaget, J., & Inhelder, B. (1956). *The child's conception of space.* London: Routledge.

Piaget, J., & Inhelder, B. (1969). *The psychology of the child.* New York: Basic.

Pierce, B. A. (1990). *Family genetic sourcebook.* New York: Wiley.

Pinker, S. (1994). *The language instinct: How the mind creates language.* New York: Morrow.

Pinker, S. (1997). *How the mind works.* New York: Norton.

Pinker, S. (1999). *Words and rules: The ingredients of language.* New York: HarperCollins.

Pinker, S., & Bloom, P. (1992). Natural language and natural selection. In J. H. Barkow, L. Cosmides, & J. Tooby (Eds.), *The adapted mind: Evolutionary psychology and the generation of culture* (pp. 451–494). New York: Oxford University Press.

Pinker, S., & Ullman, M. (2002). The past and future of the past tense. *Trends in Cognitive Science, 6*, 456–463.

Pipe, M. E., Goodman, G. S., Quas, J., Bidrose, S., Ablin, D., & Craw, S. (1997). Remembering early experiences during childhood: Are traumatic events special? In D. J. Read & D. S. Lindsay (Eds.), *Recollections of trauma: Scientific evidence and clinical practice* (pp. 417–423). New York: Plenum Press.

Pipe, M-E., & Salmon, K. (2009). Memory development and the forensic context. In M. L. Courage & N. Cowan (Eds.), *The development of memory in infancy and childhood* (pp. 242–282). New York: Psychology Press.

Pipp, S. L., Easterbrooks, M. A., & Harmon, R. J. (1992). The relation between attachment and knowledge of self and mother in one- to three-year-old infants. *Child Development, 63*, 738–750.

Pitman, C. A., & Shumaker, R. W. (2009). Does early care affect joint attention in great apes (*Pan troglodytes, pan paniscus, Pongo abelii, Pongo pygmaeus, Gorilla gorilla*)? *Journal of Comparative Psychology, 123*, 334–341.

Plester, B., Wood, C., & Bell, V. (2008). Txt msg n school literacy: Does texting and knowledge of text abbreviations adversely affect children's literacy attainment? *Literacy, 42*, 137–144.

Plomin R., & Daniels, D. (1987). Why are children in the same family so different from each other? *Behavioral and Brain Sciences, 10*, 1–16.

Plomin, R., DeFries, J. C., McClearn, G. E., & McGuffin, P. (2008). *Behavioral genetics* (5th ed.). New York: Worth.

Plomin, R., DeFries, J. C., & Loehlin, J. C. (1977). Genotype-environment interaction and correlation in the analysis of human behavior. *Psychological Bulletin, 84*, 309–322.

Plomin, R., Kennedy, J. K. J., & Craig, I. W. (2006). The quest for quantitative trait loci associated with intelligence. *Intelligence, 34*, 513–526.

Plomin, R., & Schalkwyk, L. C. (2007). Microarrays. *Developmental Science, 10*, 19–23.

Plotkin, H. (2001). Some elements of a science of culture. In E. Whitehouse (Ed.), *The debated mind: Evolutionary psychology versus ethnography* (pp. 91–109). New York: Berg.

Plotnik, J. M., de Waal, F. B. M., & Reiss, D. (2006). Self-recognition in an Asian elephant. *Proceedings of the National Academy of Sciences (USA), 103*, 17053–17057.

Pluess, M., Belsky, J., & Neuman, R. J. (2009). Prenatal smoking and ADHD: DRD4-7R as a plasticity gene. *Biological Psychiatry*. Published online June 5, 2009. Accessed at: doi:10.1016/j.biopsych.2009.04.019.

Plumert, J. M. (1995). Relation between children's overestimation of their physical abilities and accident proneness. *Developmental Psychology, 31*, 866–876.

Plumert, J. M., Kearney, J. K., & Cremer, J. F. (2007). Children's road crossing: A window into perceptual-motor development. *Current Directions in Psychological Science, 16*, 255–258.

Plumert, J. M., & Nichols-Whitehead, P. (1996). Parental scaffolding of young children's spatial communication. *Developmental Psychology, 32*, 523–532.

Plumert, J. M., & Schwebel, D. C. (1997). Social and temperamental influences on children's overestimation of their physical abilities: Links to accidental injuries. *Journal of Experimental Child Psychology, 67*, 317–337.

Plummer, K. (1981). Pedophilia: Constructing a sociological baseline. In M. Cook & K. Howells (Eds.), *Adult sexual interest in children*. New York: Academic Press.

Poirier, F. E., & Smith, E. O. (1974). Socializing functions of primate play. *American Zoologist, 14*, 275–287.

Polak, A., & Harris, P. L. (1999). Deception by young children following noncompliance. *Developmental Psychology, 35*, 561–568.

Politch, J. A., & Herrenkohl, L. R. (1984). Effects of prenatal stress on reproduction in male and female mice. *Physiology and Behavior, 32*, 95–99.

Pollak, S. D., Nelson, C. A., Schlaak, M. F., Roeber, B. J., Wewerka, S. S., Wiik, K. L., Frenn, K. A., Loman, M. M., & Gunnar, M. R. (2010). Neurodevelopmental effects of early deprivation in postinstitutionalized children. *Child Development, 81*, 224–236.

Pollet, T. V. (2007). Genetic relatedness and sibling relationship characteristics in a modern society. *Evolution and Human Behavior, 28*, 176–185.

Pons, F., & Harris, P. (2000). *Test of Emotion Comprehension—TEC*. Oxford, UK: Oxford University Press.

Pons, F., Harris, P. L., & de Rosnay, M. (2004). Emotion comprehension between 3 and 11 years: Developmental periods and hierarchical organization. *European Journal of Developmental Psychology, 1*, 127–152.

Pons, P., Lewkowicz, D. J., Soto-Faraco, S., & Sebastián-Gallés, N. (2009). Narrowing of intersensory speech perception in infancy. *Proceedings of the National Academy of Science (USA) 106*, 10598–10602.

Poole, D. A., & Lamb, M. E. (1998). *Investigative interviews of children: A guide for helping professionals*. Washington, DC: American Psychological Association.

Poole, D., & White, L. (1995). Tell me again and again: Stability and change in the repeated testimonies of children and adults. In. M. S. Zaragoza, J. R. Graham, C. N. Gordon, R. Hirschman, & Y. S. Ben Porath (Eds.), *Memory and testimony in the child witness*. Newbury Park, CA: Sage.

Porter, R, H., & Winberg, J. (1999). Unique salience of maternal breast odors for newborn infants. *Neuroscience and Biobehavioral Reviews, 23*, 439–449.

Posner, M. I., Rothbart, M. K., & Sheese, B. E. (2007). Attention genes. *Developmental Science, 10*, 24–29.

Postman, N. (1982). *The disappearance of childhood*. New York: Vintage Books.

Poulin-Dubois, D. Serbin, L., Derbyshire, A. (1998). Toddlers' intermodal and verbal knowledge about gender. *Merrill-Palmer Quarterly, 44*, 338–354.

Poulin-Dubois, D., Serbin, L. A., Kenyon, B., & Derbyshire, A. (1994). Infants' intermodal knowledge about gender. *Developmental Psychology, 30*, 436–442.

Povinelli, D. J., & Eddy, T. J. (1996). What young chimpanzees know about seeing. *Monograph of the Society for Research in Child Development, 61* (Serial No. 247).

Povinelli, D. J., Landau, K. R., & Perilloux, H. K. (1996). Self-recognition in young children using delayed versus live feedback: Evidence of a developmental asynchrony. *Child Development, 67*, 1540–1554.

Povinelli, D. J., Nelson, K. E., & Boysen, S. T. (1992). Comprehension of role reversal in chimpanzees: Evidence of empathy. *Animal Behaviour, 43*, 633–640.

Povinelli, D. J., & Simon, B. B. (1998). Young children's understanding of briefly versus extremely delayed images of the self: Emergence of the autobiographical stance. *Developmental Psychology, 34*, 188–194.

Powlishta, K. K. (1995). Intergroup processes in childhood: Social categorization and sex role development. *Developmental Psychology, 31*, 781–788.

Prechtl, H. F. R., & O'Brien, M. J. (1982). Behavioural states of the full term newborn: Emergence of a new concept. In P. Stratton (Ed.), *Psychobiology of the newborn* (pp. 53–73). New York: Wiley.

Prehn-Kristensen, A., Göder, R., Breßmann, I., Chirobeja, S., Ferstl, R., & Baving, L. (2009). Sleep in children enhances preferentially emotional declarative but not procedural memories. *Journal of Experimental Child Psychology, 104*, 132–139.

Preissler, M. A., & Bloom, P. (2007). Two-year-olds appreciate the dual nature of pictures. *Psychological Science, 18*, 1–2.

Premack, D., & Woodruff, G. (1978). Does the chimpanzee have a theory of mind? *Behavioral and Brain Sciences, 1*, 515–526.

Pressley, M., & Hilden, K. R. (2006). Cognitive strategies. In W. Damon & R. M. Lerner (Gen. Eds.), *Handbook of child psychology* (6th ed.). In D. Kuhn & R. S. Siegler (Vol. Eds.), Vol. 2: *Cognition, perception, and language* (pp. 511–556). New York: Wiley.

Principe, G. F., & Smith, E. (2008). Seeing things unseen: Fantasy beliefs and false reports. *Journal of Cognition and Development, 9*, 89–111.

Prior, H., Schwarz, A., & Güntürkün, O. (2008). Mirror-induced behavior in the magpie (*Pica pica*): Evidence of self-recognition. *PLoS Biology 6*, e202. Accessed at: doi:10.1371/journal.pbio.0060202.

Profet, M. (1992). Pregnancy sickness as adaptation: A deterrent to maternal ingestion of teratogens. In J. H. Barkow, L. Cosmides, & J. Tooby (Eds.), *The adaptive mind: Evolutionary psychology and the generation of culture* (pp. 327–365). New York: Oxford University Press.

Provine, R. R., & Westerman, J. A. (1979). Cross the midline: Limits of early eye-hand behavior. *Child Development, 50*, 437–441.

Puche-Navarro, R. (2004). Graphic jokes and children's mind: An unusual way to approach children's representational activity. *Scandinavian Journal of Psychology, 45*, 343–355.

Puhl, R. M., & Latner, J. D. (2007). Stigma, obesity, and the health of the nation's children. *Psychological Bulletin, 133*, 557–580.

Punset, E. (2005). *El viaje a la felicidad: Las nuevas claves científicas* [The journey to happiness: The new scientific cues]. Barcelona, Spain: Destino.

Putallaz, M. (1987). Maternal behavior and children's sociometric status. *Child Development, 58*, 324–340.

Putallaz, M., & Gottman, J. M. (1981). An interactional model of children's entry into peer groups. *Child Development, 52*, 402–408.

Putallaz, M., & Heflin, A. H. (1990). Parent-child interaction. In S. R. Asher & J. D. Coie (Eds.), *Peer rejection in childhood*. Cambridge, UK: Cambridge University Press.

Quas, J. A., Bauer, A., & Boyce, W. T. (2004). Physiological reactivity, social support, and memory in early childhood. *Child Development, 75*, 797–814.

Quas, J. A., Malloy, L. C., Melinder, A., Goodman, G. S., & D'Mello, M. (2007). Developmental differences in the effects of repeated interviews and interviewer bias on young children's event memory and false reports. *Developmental Psychology, 43*, 823–837.

Quinlan, R. J. (2003). Father absence, parental care, and female reproductive development. *Evolution and Human Behavior, 24*, 376–390.

Quinn, P. C., Kelly, D. J., Lee, K., Pascalis, O., & Slater, A. M. (2008). Preference for attractive faces in human infants extends beyond conspecifics. *Developmental Science, 11*, 76–83.

Quinn, P. C., Yahr, J., Kuhn, A., Slater, A. M., & Pascalis, O. (2002). Representation of the gender of human faces by infants: A preference for female. *Perception, 31*, 1109–1121.

Radford, A. (1994). The syntax of questions in child English. *Journal of Child Language, 21*, 211–236.

Raff, R. A. (1996). *The shape of life: Genes, development and the evolution of animal form.* Chicago: University of Chicago Press.

Raikes, H. A., & Thompson, R.A. (2005). Efficacy and social support as predictors of parenting stress among families in poverty. *Infant Mental Health Journal, 26*, 177–190.

Raine, A., Reynolds, C., Venables, P. H., Mednick, S. A., & Farrington, D. P. (1998). Fearlessness, stimulation-seeking, and large body size at age 3 years as early predispositions to childhood aggression at age 11 years. *Archives of General Psychiatry, 55*, 745–751.

Rakison, D. (2005a). Infant perception and cognition: An evolutionary perspective on early learning. In B. J. Ellis & D. F. Bjorklund (Eds.), *Origins of the social mind: Evolutionary psychology and child development* (pp. 317–353). New York: Guilford.

Rakison, D. (April, 2005b). *Mechanisms for predator detection and response in infancy.* Paper presented at a meeting of the Society for Research in Child Development, Atlanta, Georgia.

Rakison, D., & Poulin-Dubois, D. (2001). Developmental origin of the animate-inanimate distinction. *Psychological Bulletin, 127*, 209–228.

Ramachandran, V. S. (2000). Mirror neurons and imitation learning as the driving force behind "the great leap forward" in human evolution. The Third Culture. Accessed at: www.edge.org/3rd_culture/ramachandran/ramachandran_index.html.

Ramachandran, V. S., & Oberman, L. M. (2006). Broken mirrors: A theory of autism. *Scientific American, 295* (Number 5), 62–69.

Raman, L., & Gelman, S. A. (2008). Do children endorse psychosocial factors in the transmission of illness and disgust? *Developmental Psychology, 44*, 801–813.

Ramey, C. T., Campbell, F. A., Burchinal, M., Skinner, M. L., Gardner, D. M., & Ramey, S. L. (2000). Persistent effects of early childhood education on high-risk children and their mothers. *Applied Developmental Science, 4*, 2–14.

Ramey, C. T., Campbell, F. A., & Finkelstein, N. W. (1984). Course and structure of intellectual development in children at risk for developmental retardation. In P. H. Brooks, R. Sperber, & C. McCauley (Eds.), *Learning and cognition in the mentally retarded.* Hillsdale, NJ: Erlbaum.

Ramsey, G. V. (1943). The sexual development of boys. *The American Journal of Psychology, 56*, 217–233.

Ramsey-Rennels, J. L., & Langlois, J. H. (2006). Infants' differential processing of female and male faces. *Current Directions in Psychological Science, 15*, 59–62.

Ramsey, J. L., Langlois, J., Nathan C., & Mart, N. C. (2005). Infant categorization of faces: Ladies first. *Developmental Review, 25*, 212–246.

Raskauskas, J., & Stoltz, A. D. (2007). Involvement in traditional and electronic bullying among adolescents. *Developmental Psychology, 43*, 564–575.

Raven, J., Raven, J. C., & Court, J. H. (2003). *Manual for Raven's Progressive Matrices and Vocabulary Scales. Section 1: General Overview.* San Antonio, TX: Harcourt Assessment.

Raymond, C. L., & Benbow, C. P. (1986). Gender differences in mathematics: A function of parental support and student sex typing? *Development Psychology, 22*, 808–819.

Read, D. W. (2008). Working memory: A cognitive limit to non-human primate recursive thinking prior to hominid evolution. *Evolutionary Psychology, 6*, 676–714.

Redcay, E., Haist, F., & Courchesne, E. (2008). Functional neuroimaging of speech perception during a pivotal period in language acquisition. *Developmental Science, 11*, 237–252.

Reed, R. K. (2005). *Birthing fathers: The transformation of men in American rites of birth.* New Brunswick, NJ: Rutgers University Press.

Reese, E., Haden, C., & Fivush, R. (1993). Mother-child conversations about the past: Relationships of style and memory over time. *Cognitive Development, 8*, 403–430.

Reese, H. W., & Overton, W. F. (1970). Models of development and theories of development. In L. R. Goulet & P. B. Baltes (Eds.), *Life-span development psychology: Research and theory* (pp. 115–145). New York: Academic Press.

Regalski, J. M., & Gaulin, S. J. C. (1993). Whom are Mexican infants said to resemble? Monitoring and fostering confidence in the Yucatan. *Ethology and Sociobiology, 14*, 97–113.

Reid, A. (1997). Locality of class? Spatial and social differentials in infant and child mortality in England and Wales, 1895–1911. In C. A. Corsini & P. P. Viazzo (Eds.), *The decline of infant and child mortality: The European experience: 1750–1990* (pp. 129–154). The Hague, The Netherlands: Martinus Nijhoff.

Reilly, J. S., Harrison, D., & Klima, E. S. (1995). Emotional talk and talk about emotions. *Genetic Counseling, 6*, 158–159.

Reis, H. T., & Collins, W. A. (2004). Relationships, human behavior, and psychological science. *Current Directions in Psychological Science, 14*, 233–237.

Reiss, D., & Marino, L. (2001). Mirror self-recognition in the bottlenose dolphin: A case of cognitive convergence. *Proceedings of the National Academy of Sciences (USA), 98*, 5937–5942.

Renninger, K. A. (1992). Individual interest and development: Implications for theory and practice. In K. A. Renninger, S. Hidi, & A. Krapp (Eds.), *The role of interest in learning and development.* Hillsdale, NJ: Erlbaum.

Repacholi, B. (1998). Infants' use of attentional cues to identify the referent of another person's emotional expression. *Developmental Psychology, 34*, 1017–1025.

Repacholi, B. M., & Gopnik, A. (1997). Early reasoning about desires: Evidence from 14- and 18-month-olds. *Developmental Psychology, 33*, 12–21.

Rest, J. R., & Thoma, S. J. (1985). Relation of moral judgment development to formal education. *Developmental Psychology, 21*, 709–714.

Reuhl, K. R., & Chang, L. W. (1979). Effects of methylmercury on the development of the nervous system: A review. *Neurotoxicology, 1*, 121–155.

Reuven, B., Sekal, R., & Stavy, R., (2010). Persistence of the intuitive conception of living things in adolescence. *Journal of Science Education and Technology, 19*, 20–26.

Reyna, V. F., & Farley, F. (2006). Risk and rationality in adolescent decision making. *Psychological Science in the Public Interest, 7*, 1–44.

Reynolds, M. A., Herbenick, D. L., & Bancroft, J. (2003). The nature of childhood sexual experiences: Two studies 50 years apart. In J. Bancroft (Ed.), *Sexual development in childhood* (pp. 134–155). Indiana: Indiana University Press.

Reynolds, M. A., Schieve, L. A., Martin, J. A., Jeng, G., & Macaluso, M. (2003). Multiple births conceived using Assisted Reproductive Technology, United States, 1997–2000. *Pediatrics, 111*, 1159–1162.

Reznick, J. S. (2009). Working memory in infants and toddlers. In M. L. Courage & N. Cowan (Eds.), *The development of memory in infancy and childhood* (pp. 343–365). New York: Psychology Press.

Reznick, J. S., Fueser, J. J., & Bosquet, M. (1998). Self-corrected reaching in a three-location delayed response search task. *Psychological Science, 9*, 66–70.

Rhee, S. H., & Wildman, I. D. (2002). Genetic and environmental influences on antisocial behavior: A meta-analysis of twin and adoption studies. *Psychological Bulletin, 128*, 490–529.

Rheingold, H. L. (1982). Little children's participation in the work of adults: A nascent prosocial behavior. *Child Development, 53*, 114–125.

Rheingold, H. L. (1985). Development as the acquisition of familiarity. *Annual Review of Psychology, 36*, 1–17.

Rheingold, H. L., Hay, D. F., & West, M. J. (1976). Sharing in the second year of life. *Child Development, 47*, 1148–1158.

Rice, C. et al. (2009). Prevalence of autism spectrum disorders—Autism and Developmental Disabilities Monitoring Network, United States, 2006. *Morbidity and Mortality Weekly Report* (December 18), *58*, 1–20.

Richards, M. H., Crowe, P. A., Larson, R., & Swarr, A. (1998). Developmental patterns and gender differences in the experience of peer companionship during adolescence. *Child Development, 69*, 154–163.

Richardson, R., & Hayne, H. (2007). You can't take it with you: The translation of memory across development. *Current Directions in Psychological Science, 16*, 223–227.

Richerson, P. J., & Boyd, R. (2005). *Not by genes alone: How culture transformed human evolution.* Chicago: University Chicago Press.

Richert, R., Robb, M. B., Fender, J. G., & Wartella, E. (2010). Word learning from baby videos. *Archives of Pediatric and Adolescent Medicine, 164* (No. 5). Published online, March 1. www.archpediatrics.com Richert, R., Robb, M. B., Fender, J. G., & Wartella, E. (2010). Word learning from baby videos. *Archives of Pediatric and Adolescent Medicine, 164* (No. 5). Published online, March 1. www.archpediatrics.com.

Richland, L. E., Chan, T-K., Morrison, R. G., & Au, T. (2010). Young children's analogical reasoning across cultures: Similarities and differences. *Journal of Experimental Child Psychology, 105*, 146–153.

Richmond, J., & Nelson, C. A. (2007). Accounting for changes in declarative memory: A cognitive neuroscience perspective. *Developmental Review, 27*, 349–373.

Richner, E. S., & Nicolopoulou, A. (2001). The narrative construction of differing conceptions of the person in the development of young children's social understanding. *Early Education and Development, 12*, 393–432.

Rickford, J. R. (1999). *African American vernacular English.* Malden, MA: Blackwell.

Ridderinkhof, K. R., van der Molen, M., & Band, G. P. H. (1997). Sources of interference from irrelevant information: A developmental study. *Journal of Experimental Child Psychology, 65*, 315–341.

Rideout, V., Vandewater, E. A., & Wartella, E. A. (2003). *Zero to six: Electronic media in the lives of infants, toddlers, and preschoolers.* Menlo Park, CA: Kaiser Family Foundation.

Riegel, F. K. (1976). The dialectics of human development. *American Psychologist, 31*, 689–700.

Rieger, G., Linsenmeier, J. A. W., Gygax, L., & Bailey, J. M. (2008). Sexual orientation and childhood gender nonconformity: Evidence from home videos. *Developmental Psychology, 44*, 46–58.

Rigby, K. (2002). Bullying in childhood. In P. K. Smith & C. H. Hart (Eds.), *Blackwell handbook of childhood social development* (pp. 549–568). Oxford, UK: Blackwell.

Richland, L. E., Chan, T-K., Morrison, R. G., & Au, T. (2010). Young children's analogical reasoning across cultures: Similarities and differences. *Journal of Experimental Child Psychology, 105*, 146–153.

Rilling, J. K., & Insel, T. R. (1999). The primate neocortex in comparative perspective using magnetic resonance imaging. *Journal of Human Evolution, 37*, 191–223.

Ringel, B. A., & Springer, C. J. (1980). On knowing how well one is remembering: The persistence of strategy use during transfer. *Journal of Experimental Child Psychology, 29*, 322–333.

Rittle-Johnson, B. (2006). Promoting transfer: Effects of self-explanation and direct instruction. *Child Development, 77*, 1–29.

Rittle-Johnson, B., & Siegler, R. S. (1999). Learning to spell: Variability, choice, and change in children's strategy use. *Child Development, 70*, 332–348.

Rizzolatti, G., & Craighero, L. (2004). The mirror neuron system. *Annual Review of Neuroscience, 27*, 169–192.

Rizzolatti, G., Fadiga, L., Fogassi, L., Gallese, V. (1996). Premotor cortex and the recognition of motor actions. *Cognitive Brain Research, 3*, 131–141.

Rizzolatti, G., Fogassi, L., & Gallese, V. (2006). Mirrors in the mind. *Scientific American, 295*, 54–61.

Roberts, B. W., & DelVecchio, W. F. (2000). The rank-order consistency of personality from childhood to old age: A quantitative review of longitudinal studies. *Psychological Bulletin, 126*, 3–25.

Roberts, D. F., Foehr, U. G., & Rideout, V. (2005). *Generation M: Media in the lives of 8–18 year olds.* Palo Alto, CA: Henry J. Kaiser Family Foundation.

Roberts, D. F., Foehr, U. G., Rideout, V., & Vrodie, M. (1999). *Kids and media @ the new millennium.* Menlo Park, CA: Kaiser Family Foundation.

Roberts, K., & Horowitz, F. D. (1986). Basic level categorization in seven- and nine-month-old infants. *Journal of Child Language, 13*, 191–208.

Roberts, R. E., Attkisson, C. C., & Rosenblatt, A. (1998). Prevalence of psychopathology among children and adolescents. *American Journal of Psychiatry, 155*, 715–725.

Robin, D. J., Berthier, N. E., & Clifton, R. K. (1996). Infants' predictive reaching for moving objects in the dark. *Developmental Psychology, 32*, 824–835.

Robins, R. W., John, O. P., & Caspi, A. (1994). Major dimensions of personality in early adolescence: The Big Five and beyond. In C. F. Halverson, J. A. Kohnstamm, & R. P. Martin (Eds.), *The developing structure of temperament and personality from infancy to adulthood* (pp. 267–291). Hillsdale, NJ: Erlbaum.

Robinson, B. F., Mervis, C. B., & Robinson, B. W. (2003). The roles of verbal short-term memory and working memory in the acquisition of grammar by children with Williams syndrome. *Developmental Neuropsychology, 23*, 13–32.

Robinson, J. L., Zahn-Waxler, C., & Emde, R. N. (1994). Patterns of development in early emphatic behavior: Environmental and child constitutional influences. *Social Development, 3*, 125–145.

Rochat, P. (2009). *Other minds: Social origins of self-consciousness.* New York: Cambridge University Press.

Rochat, P., Striano, T., & Blatt, L. (2002). Differential effects of happy, neutral, and sad still-faces on 2-, 4- and 6-month-old infants. *Infant and Child Development, 11*, 289–303.

Rodríguez, C. (2007). Object use, communication and signs. The triadic basis of early cognitive development. In J. Valsiner, & A. Rosa (Eds.), *The Cambridge handbook of socio-cultural psychology* (pp. 257–276). New York: Cambridge University Press.

Roebers, C. M., Moga, N., & Schneider, W. (2001). The role of accuracy motivation on children's and adults' event recall. *Journal of Experimental Child Psychology, 78*, 313–329.

Roebers, C. M., & Schneider, W. (2001). Individual differences in children's eyewitness recall: The influence of intelligence and shyness. *Applied Developmental Science, 5*, 9–20.

Roffwarg, H. P., Muzio, J. N., & Dement, W. C. (1966). Ontogenetic development of the human sleep-dream cycle. *Science, 152*, 604–619.

Rogoff, B. (1990). *Apprenticeship in thinking: Cognitive development in social context.* New York: Oxford University Press.

Rogoff, B. (1998). Cognition as a collaborative process. In W. Damon (Gen. Ed.), *Handbook of child psychology* (5th ed.). In D. Kuhn & R. S. Siegler (Vol. Eds.), Vol. 2: *Cognition language, and perceptual development* (pp. 679–744). New York: Wiley.

Rogoff, B. (2003). *The cultural nature of human development.* New York: Oxford University Press.

Rogoff, B., Paradise, R., Arauz, R., Correa-Chávez, M., & Angelillo, C. (2003). Firsthand learning through intent participation. *Annual Review of Psychology, 54*, 175–203.

Roman, A. A., Kirby, J. R., Parrila, P. K., Wade-Woolley, L., & Deacon, S. H. (2009). Toward a comprehensive view of the skills involved in word reading in grades 4, 6, and 8. *Journal of Experimental Child Psychology, 102*, 96–113.

Rosario, M., Schrimshaw, E. W., Hunter, J., & Braun, L. (2006). Sexual identity development among lesbian, gay, and bisexual youths: Consistency and change over time. *Journal of Sex Research, 43*, 46–58.

Rosch, E. (1975). Cognitive representations of semantic categories. *Journal of Experimental Psychology: General, 7*, 192–233.

Rose, A. J., Swanson, L. P., & Waller, E. M. (2004). Overt and relational aggression and perceived popularity: Developmental differences in concurrent and prospective relations. *Developmental Psychology, 40*, 378–387.

Rose, S. A., Feldman, J. F., & Jankowski, J. J. (2009). A cognitive approach to the development of early language. *Child Development, 80*, 134–150.

Rose, S. A., Feldman, J. F., Jankowski, J. J., & Van Rossem, R. V. (2005). Pathways from prematurity and infant abilities to later cognition. *Child Development, 76*, 1172–1184.

Rose, S. A., Feldman, J. F., Jankowski, J. J., & Caro, D. M. (2002). A longitudinal study of visual expectation and reaction time in the first year of life. *Child Development, 73*, 47–61.

Rose, S. A., Gottfried, A. W., & Bridger, W. H. (1981). Cross-modal transfer in 6-month-old infants. *Developmental Psychology, 17*, 661–669.

Rosenbaum, J. E. (2009). Patient teenagers? A comparison of the sexual behavior of virginity pledgers and matched nonpledgers. *Pediatrics, 123*, e110–e120.

Rosenberg, K. R., & Trevathan W. (2001). The evolution of human birth. *Scientific American, 285*, 72–77.

Rosenberg, M. (1986). Self-concept from middle childhood through adolescence. In J. Suls & A. Greenwald (Eds.), *Psychological perspectives on the self* (Vol. 3). Hillsdale, NJ: Erlbaum.

Rosenblum, G. D., & Lewis, M. (1999). The relations among body image, physical attractiveness, and body mass in adolescents. *Child Development, 70*, 50–64.

Rosenthal, R., & Jacobson, L. (1968). *Pygmalion in the classroom: Teacher expectation and pupils' intellectual development*. New York: Rinehart and Winston.

Rosenthal, S. L., Von Ranson, K. M., Cotton, S., Biro, F. M., Mills, L., &, Succop, P. A. (2001). Sexual initiation: Predictors and developmental trends. *Sexually Transmitted Diseases, 28*, 527–532.

Roth, G., & Dicke, U. (2005). Evolution of the brain and intelligence. *Trends in Cognitive Sciences, 9*, 249–257.

Rothbart, M. K. (2007). Temperament, development, and personality. *Current Directions in Psychological Science, 16*, 207–212.

Rothbart, M. K., & Bates, J. E. (2006). Temperament. In W. Damon (Gen. Ed.), *Handbook of child psychology* (6th ed.). In N. Eisenberg & R. M. Lerner (Vol. Eds.), Vol. 3: *Social, emotional, and personality development* (pp. 99–166). Hoboken, NJ: Wiley.

Rothbart, M. K., & Hwang, J. (2005). Temperament. In B. Hopkins (Ed.), *The Cambridge encyclopedia of child development* (pp. 387–390). New York: Cambridge University Press.

Rotheram-Borus, M. J., & Langabeer, K. A. (2001). Development trajectories of gay, lesbian, and bisexual youths. In A. R. D'Augelli, & C. Petterson (Eds.), *Lesbian, gay and bisexual identities among youth: Psychological perspectives* (pp. 97–128). New York: Oxford University Press.

Rovee-Collier, C. (1999). The development of infant memory. *Current Directions in Psychological Science, 8*, 80–85.

Rovee-Collier, C., & Gerhardstein, P. (1997). The development of infant memory. In N. Cowan (Ed.), *The development of memory in childhood*. Hove, East Sussex, UK: Psychology Press.

Rowe, D. C., Jacobson, K. C., & van der Oord, E. J. C. G. (1999). Genetic and environmental influences on vocabulary IQ: Parental education level as a moderator. *Child Development, 70*, 1151–1162.

Rowe, M. L., & Goldin-Meadow, S. (2009). Differences in early gesture explain SES disparities in child vocabulary size at school entry. *Science, 323* (13 February), 951–953.

Rowher, S., Herron, J. C., & Daly, M. (1999). Stepparental behavior as mating effort in birds and other animals. *Evolution and Human Behavior, 20*, 367–390.

Rozin, P., & Fallon, A. E. (1980). Psychological categorization of foods and non-foods: A preliminary taxonomy of food rejections. *Appetite, 1*, 193–201.

Rozin, P., Haidt, J., & McCauley, C. R. (2000). Disgust. In M. Lewis & J. M. Haviland-Jones (Eds.), *Handbook of emotions*. New York: Guilford.

Rubenstein, A. J., Kalakanis, L., & Langlois, J. H. (1999). Infant preferences for attractive faces: A cognitive explanation. *Developmental Psychology, 35*, 848–855.

Rubenstein, J., & Howes, C. (1976). The effects of peers on toddler interaction with mothers and toys. *Child Development, 47*, 597–605.

Rubin, D. C. (2000). The distribution of early childhood memories. *Memory, 8*, 265–269.

Rubin, K. H., Bukowski, W. M., & Laursen, B. (Eds.). (2009). *Handbook of peer interactions, relationships, and groups*. New York: Guilford.

Rubin, K. H., Bukowski, W., Parker, J. G. (1998). Peer interactions, relationships, and groups. In W. Damon (Gen. Ed.), *Handbook of child psychology* (5th ed.). In N. Eisenberg (Vol. Ed.), Vol. 3: *Social, emotional, and personality development* (pp. 619–700). New York: Wiley.

Rubin, K. H., Bukowski, W. M., & Parker, J. G. (2006). Peer interactions, relationships, and groups. In W. Damon & R. M. Lerner (Gen. Eds.), *Handbook of child psychology* (6th ed.). In N. Eisenberg (Vol. Ed.), Vol. 3: *Social, emotional, and personality development* (pp. 571–645). New York: Wiley.

Rubin, K. H., Dwyer, K. M., Booth, C. L., Kim, A. H., Burgess, K. B., & Ross-Kasnor, L. (2004). Attachment, friendship, and psychosocial functioning in early adolescence. *Journal of Early Adolescence, 24*, 326–356.

Rubin, K. H., Fein, G., & Vandenberg, B. (1983). Play. In E. M. Hetherington (Ed.), *Handbook of child psychology*, Vol. IV: *Socialization, personality and social development* (pp. 693–774). New York: Wiley.

Rubin, K. H., LeMare, L. J., & Lollis, S. (1990). Social withdrawal in childhood: Developmental pathways to peer rejection. In S. R. Asher & J. D. Coie (Eds.), *Peer rejection in childhood*. Cambridge, UK: Cambridge University Press.

Rubinowitz, L. S., & Rosenbaum, J. E. (2000). *Crossing the class and color lines: From public housing to white suburbia*. Chicago: Chicago University Press.

Ruble, D. N., Balaban, T., & Cooper, J. (1981). Gender constancy and the effects of sex-typed televised toy commercials. *Child Development, 52*, 667–673.

Ruble, D. N., Martin, C. L., & Berenbaum, S. A. (2006). Gender development. In W. Damon & R. M. Lerner (Gen. Eds.), *Handbook of child psychology* (6th ed.). In N. Eisenberg (Vol. Ed.), Vol. 3: *Social, emotional, and personality development* (pp. 858–932). Hoboken, NJ: Wiley.

Ruble, D. N., Taylor, L. J., Cyphers, L., Greulich, F. K., Lurye, L. E., & Shrout, P. E. (2007). The role of gender constancy in early gender development. *Child Development, 78*, 1121–1136.

Ruda, M. A., Ling, Q-D., Hohmann, A. G., Bo Peng, Y., & Tachibana, T. (2000). Altered nociceptive neuronal circuits after neonatal peripheral inflammation. *Science, 289* (28 July), 628–630.

Rueda, M. R., Rothbart, M. K., McCandliss, B. D., Saccomanno, L., & Posner, M. I. (2005). Training, maturation, and genetic influences on the development of executive attention. *Proceedings of the National Academy of Science (USA), 102*, 14931–14936.

Ruff, H. A., Capozzoli, M., & Weisberg, R. (1998). Age, individuality, and context as factors in sustained visual attention during the preschool years. *Developmental Psychology, 34*, 454–464.

Ruffman, T., Perner, J., Naito, M., Parkin, L., & Clements, W. A. (1998). Older (but not younger) siblings facilitate false belief understanding. *Developmental Psychology, 34*, 161–174.

Ruffman, T., Rustin, C., Garnham, W., & Parkin, A. (2001). Source monitoring and false memories in children: Relation to certainty and executive functioning. *Journal of Experimental child Psychology, 80*, 95–111.

Ruffman, T., Slade, L., & Crowe, E. (2002). The relation between children's and mothers' mental-state language and theory-of-mind understanding. *Child Development, 73*, 734–751.

Ruffman, T., Slade, L., Devitt, K., & Crowe, E. (2006). What mothers say and what they do: The relation between parenting, theory of mind, language and conflict/cooperation. *British Journal of Developmental Psychology, 24*, 105–124.

Rugani, R., Fontanari, L., Simoni, E., Regolin, L., & Giorgio Vallortigara, G. (2009). Arithmetic in newborn chicks. *Proceedings of the Royal Society B, 276*, 2451–2460.

Rushton, J. P., Fulker, D. W., Neale, M. C., Nias, D. K. B., & Eysenck, H. J. (1986). Altruism and aggression: The heritability of individual differences. *Journal of Personality and Social Psychology, 31*, 459–466.

Rutter, M. (1987). Psychosocial resilience and protective mechanisms. *American Journal of Orthopsychiatry, 57,* 316–331.

Rutter, M. (2006). *Genes and behavior: Nature-nurture interplay explained.* Malden, MA: Blackwell.

Rutter, M. (2007). Gene-environment interdependence. *Developmental Science, 10,* 12–18.

Rutter, M., & the English and Romanian Adoptees Study Team (1998). Developmental catch-up and deficit following adoptions after severe global and early deprivation. *Journal of Child Psychology and Psychiatry, 39,* 465–476.

Rutter, M., & Garmezy, N. (1983). Developmental psychopathology. In P. H. Mussen (Series Ed.) & E. M. Hetherington (Vol. Ed.), *Handbook of child psychology* (4th ed.)., Vol. 4: *Socialization, personality, and social development* (pp. 775–911). New York: Wiley.

Ryan, A. S., Wenjun, Z., & Acosta, A. (2002). Breastfeeding continues to increase into the new millennium. *Pediatrics, 110,* 1103–1109.

Saarni, C. (1984). An observational study of children's attempts to monitor their expressive behavior. *Child Development, 55,* 1504–1513.

Saarni, C., Campos, J. J., Camras, L. A., & Witherington, D. (2006). Emotional development: Action, communication, and understanding. In W. Damon & R. M. Lerner (Gen. Eds.), *Handbook of child psychology* (6th ed.). In N. Eisenberg (Vol. Ed.), Vol. 3: *Social, emotional, and personality development* (pp. 226–299). New York: Wiley.

Saarni, C., Mumme, D., & Campos, J. (1998). Emotional development: Action, communication, and understanding. In W. Damon (Gen. Ed.), *Handbook of child psychology* (5th ed.). In N. Eisenberg (Vol. Ed.), Vol. 3: *Social, emotional and personality development* (pp. 237–309). New York: Wiley.

Sabbagh, M. A., Xu, F., Carlson, S. M., Moses, L. J., & Lee, K. (2006). The development of executive functioning and theory of mind. *Psychological Science, 17,* 74–81.

Sabin, E. J., Clemmer, E. J., O'Connell, D. C., & Kowal, S. (1979). A pausological approach to speech development. In A. W. Siegman & S. Feldstein (Eds.), *Of speech and time: Temporal speech patterns in interpersonal contexts.* Hillsdale, NJ: Erlbaum.

Saccuzzo, D. P., Johnson, N. E., & Guertin, T. L. (1994). Information processing in gifted versus nongifted African American, Latino, Filipino, and white children: Speeded versus nonspeeded paradigms. *Intelligence, 19,* 219–243.

Saccuzzo, D. P., Kerr, M., Marcus, A., & Brown, R. (1979). Input capability and speed of processing in mental retardation. *Journal of Abnormal Psychology, 88,* 341–345.

Sachs, J. (1977). The adaptive significance of linguistic input to prelinguistic infants. In C. E. Snow & C. A. Ferguson (Eds.), *Talking to children: Language input and acquisition.* Cambridge, UK: Cambridge University Press.

Sackett, P. R., Hardison, C. M., & Cullen, M. J. (2004). On interpreting stereotype threat as accounting for African American–White differences on cognitive tests. *American Psychologist, 59,* 7–13.

Sacks, O. (1985). *The man who mistook his wife for a hat.* New York: Touchstone Books.

Saffran, J., Werker, J., & Werner, L. A. (2006). The infant's auditory world: Hearing, speech and the beginnings of language. In W. Damon & D. Kuhn (Gen. Eds.), *The handbook of child psychology* (6th ed.). In R. Siegler (Vol. Ed.), *Cognition, perception, and language.* New York: Wiley.

Saffran, J. R., & Griepentrog, G. J. (2001). Absolute pitch in infant auditory learning: Evidence for developmental reorganization. *Developmental Psychology, 37,* 74–85.

Sagi, A., & Hoffman, M. L. (1976). Empathic distress in the newborn. *Developmental Psychology, 12,* 175–176.

Sagi, A., Lamb, M. E., Lewkowicz, K. S., Shoham, R., Dvir, R., & Estes, D. (1985). Security of infant-mother, father, metapelet attachments among kibbutz-reared Israeli children. *Monographs for the Society for Research in Child Development, 50* (1–2), 257–275.

Sakai, K. L. (2005). Language acquisition and brain development. *Science, 310,* 815–819.

Salapatek, P. (1975). Pattern perception in early infancy. In L. B. Cohen & P. Salapatek (Eds.), *Infant perception: From sensation to cognition* (Vol. 1). New York: Academic.

Salatas, H., & Flavell, J. H. (1976). Behavioral and metamnemonic indicators of strategic behaviors under remember instructions in first grade. *Child Development, 47,* 81–89.

Sallows, G. O., & Graupner, T. D. (2005). Intensive behavioral treatment for children with autism: Four-year outcome and predictors. *American Journal on Mental Retardation, 110,* 417–438.

Salmivalli, C., & Peets, K. (2009). Bullies, victims, and bully-victim relationships in middle childhood and early adolescence. In K. H. Rubin, W. M. Bukowski, & B. Laursen (Eds.), *Handbook of peer interactions, relationships, and groups* (pp. 322–340). New York: Guilford.

Salmon, C. A. (2005). Parental investment and parent-offspring conflict. In D. M. Buss (Ed.), *The handbook of evolutionary psychology* (pp. 506–527). New York: Wiley.

Salmon, C. A. (2007). Parent-offspring conflict. In C. Salmon & T. S. Shackelford (Eds.), *Family relationships: An evolutionary perspective* (pp. 145–161). Oxford, UK: Oxford University Press.

Salmon, K., Champion, F., Pipe, M., Mewton, L., & McDonald, S. (2008). The child in time: The influence of parent-child discussion about a future experience on how it is remembered. *Memory, 16,* 485–499.

Salzinger, S., Feldman, R. S., Ng-Mak, D. S., Mojica, E., & Stockhammer, T. F. (2001). The effect of physical abuse on children's social and affective status: A model of cognitive and behavioral processes explaining the association. *Development and Psychopathology, 13,* 805–825.

Samarapungavan, A., Vosniadou, S., & Brewer, W. F. (1998). Mental models of the earth, sun and the moon: Indian children's cosmologies. *Cognitive Development, 11,* 491–521.

Sameroff, A. (2010). A unified theory of development: A dialectic integration of nature and nurture. *Child Development, 81,* 6–22.

Sameroff, A. (Ed.). (2009). *The transactional model of development: How children and contexts shape each other.* Washington, DC: American Psychological Association.

Sameroff, A. J., Seifer, R., Baldwin, A., & Baldwin, C. (1993). Stability of intelligence from preschool to adolescence: The influence of social risk factors. *Child Development, 64,* 80–97.

Sandelowski, M. (1984). *Pain, pleasure, and American children: From Twilight Sleep to the Read Method, 1914–1916.* Westport, CT: Greenwood Press.

Sandman, C. A., Washwa, P., Hetrick, W., Porto, M., & Peeke, H. V. S. (1997). Human fetal heart rate dishabituation between thirty and thirty-two weeks gestation. *Developmental Psychology, 68,* 1031–1040.

Sanson, A., Nicholson, J., Ungerer, J., Zubrick, S., Wilson, K., Ainley, J., Berthelsen, D., Bittman, M., Broom, D., Harrison, L., Rodgers, B., Sawyer, M., Silburn, S., Strazdins, L., Vimpani, G., & Wake, M. (2002). *Longitudinal study of Australian children.* Melbourne: Australian Institute of Family Studies.

Savage-Rumbaugh, E. S., Murphy, J., Sevcik, R. A., Brakke, K. E., Williams, S. L., & Rumbaugh, D. M. (1993). Language comprehension in ape and child. *Monographs of the Society for Research in Child Development, 58* (Serial No. 233).

Savin-Williams, R. C. (1979). Dominance hierarchies in groups of early adolescents. *Child Development, 50,* 923–935.

Savin-Williams, R. C. (1998a). *And then I became gay: Young men's stories.* New York: Routledge.

Savin-Williams, R. C. (1998b). The disclosure to families of same-sex attractions by lesbian, gay, and bisexual youths. *Journal of Research on Adolescence, 8,* 49–68.

Savin-Williams, R. C. (2006). Who's gay? Does it matter? *Current Directions in Psychological Science, 15,* 40–44.

Savin-Williams, R. C., & Cohen, K. M. (2004). Homoerotic development during childhood and adolescence. *Child and Adolescent Psychiatric Clinics of North America, 13,* 529–549.

Savin-Williams, R. C., & Diamond, L. M. (2000). Sexual identity trajectories among sexual-minority youths: Gender comparisons. *Archives of Sexual Behavior, 29,* 419–440.

Savin-Williams, R. C., & Ream, G. L. (2003). Sex variations in the disclosure to parents of same-sex attractions. *Journal of Family Psychology, 17*, 429–438.

Scammon, R. E. (1930). The measurement of the body in childhood. In J. A. Harris, C. M. Jackson, D. G. Paterson, & R. E. Scammon (Eds.), *The measurement of man.* Minneapolis: University of Minnesota Press.

Scarborough, H. S., & Dobrich, W. (1994). On the efficacy of reading to preschoolers. *Developmental Review, 14*, 245–302.

Scarr, S. (1976). An evolutionary perspective on infant intelligence: Species, patterns, and individual variations. In M. Lewis (Ed.), *The origins of infant intelligence.* New York: Plenum.

Scarr, S. (1992). Developmental theories for the 1990s: Development and individual differences. *Child Development, 63*, 1–19.

Scarr, S. (1993). Biological and cultural diversity: The legacy of Darwin for development. *Child Development, 64*, 1333–1353.

Scarr, S., & McCartney, K. (1983). How people make their own environments: A theory of genotype → environment effects. *Child Development, 54*, 424–435.

Scarr, S., Phillips, D., & McCartney, K. (1990). Facts, fantasies and the future of child care in the United States. *Psychological Science, 1*, 26–35.

Scarr, S., & Weinberg, R. A. (1976). IQ test performance of black children adopted by white families. *American Psychologist, 31*, 726–739.

Schaal, B., Marlier, L., & Soussignan, R. (2000). Human foetuses learn odours from their pregnant mother's diet. *Chemical Senses, 25*, 729–737.

Schafer, G., & Plunkett, K. (1998). Rapid word learning by fifteen-month-olds under tightly controlled conditions. *Child Development, 69*, 309–320.

Schaffer, H. R. (1971). *The growth of sociability.* Baltimore, MD: Penguin.

Schaffer, H. R. (2000). The early experience assumption: Past, present, and future. *International Journal of Behavioural Development, 24*, 5–14.

Schaffer, H. R., & Emerson, P. E. (1964). The development of social attachments in infancy. *Monographs of the Society for Research in Child Development, 29* (Serial No. 94).

Schauble, L. (1996). The development of scientific reasoning in knowledge-rich context. *Developmental Psychology, 32*, 102–119.

Scheffler, R. M., Brown, T. T., Fulton, D. D., Hinshaw, S. P., Levine, P., & Stone, S. (2009). Positive association between attention-deficit/hyperactivity disorder medication use and academic achievement during elementary school. *Pediatrics, 123*, 1273–1279.

Schellenberg, E. G., & Trehub, S. E. (1999). Culture-general and culture-specific factors in the discrimination of melodies. *Journal of Experimental Child Psychology, 74*, 107–127.

Schick, B., de Villiers, P., & de Villiers, J., & Hoffmeister, R. (2007). Language and theory of mind: A study of deaf children. *Child Development, 78*, 376–396.

Schiefele, U., Krapp, A., & Winteler, A. (1992). Interest as a predictor of academic achievement: A meta-analysis of research. In K. A. Renninger, S. Hidi, & A. Krapp (Eds.), *The role of interest in learning and development.* Hillsdale, NJ: Erlbaum.

Insert:Schiefenhövel, W. (1988). Geburtsverhalten und reproduktiver Strategien der Eipo. Ergebnisse humanethologischer und ethnomedizinischer Untersuchungen im zentralen Bergland von Irian Jaya (West-Neuguinea), Indonesien. [Fertility behavior and reproductive strategies of Eipo. Human-ethnomedical studies and results in the central highlands of Irian Jaya (West New Guinea), Indonesia]. Schriftenreihe: *Mensch, Kultur und Umwelt im zentralen Bergland von Westneuguinea* (16). Berlin: Reimer.

Schirduan, V., & Case, K. S. (2004). Mindful curriculum leadership for students with attention deficit hyperactivity disorder: Leading in elementary schools by using Multiple Intelligences Theory (SUMIT). *Teachers College Record, 106*, 87–95.

Schissel, M. J. (1970). *Dentistry and its victims.* New York: St. Martin's Press.

Schlagmüller, M., & Schneider, W. (2002). The development of organizational strategies in children: Evidence from a microgenetic longitudinal study. *Journal of Experimental Child Psychology, 81*, 298–319.

Schlegel, A., & Barry, H. (1991). *Adolescence: An anthropological inquiry.* New York: Free Press.

Schlegel, A., & Barry, H., III (1980). The evolutionary significance of adolescent initiation ceremonies, *American Ethnologist, 7*, 696–715.

Schliemann, A. D. (1992). Mathematical concepts in and out of school in Brazil: From developmental psychology to better teaching. *Newsletter of the International Society for the Study of Behavioural Development* (Serial No. 22, No. 2), 1–3.

Schlottmann, A., & Ray, E. (2010). Goal attribution to schematic animals: Do 6-month-olds perceive biological motion as animate? *Developmental Science, 13*, 1–10.

Schmidt, M. E., Pempek, T. A., Kirkorian, H. L., Lund, A. F., & Anderson, D. R. (2008). The effects of background television on the toy play behavior of very young children. *Child Development, 79*, 1137–1151.

Schmitt, D. P. (2005). Fundamentals of human mating strategies. In D. M. Buss (Ed.), *The handbook of evolutionary psychology* (pp. 258–291). New York: Wiley.

Schneider, B. H., Atkinson, L., & Tardif, C. (2001). Child-parent attachment and children's peer relations: A quantitative review. *Developmental Psychology, 37*, 86–100.

Schneider, W. (2010). Memory development in childhood. In U. Goswami (Ed.), *Blackwell handbook of childhood cognitive development* (2nd ed.). London: Blackwell.

Schneider, W., & Bullock, M. (Eds.). (2009). *Human development from early childhood to early adulthood: Findings from a 20-year longitudinal study.* New York: Psychology Press.

Schneider, W., Gruber, H., Gold, A., & Opwis, K. (1993). Chess expertise and memory for chess positions in children and adults. *Journal of Experimental Child Psychology, 56*, 328–349.

Schneider, W., Knopf, M., & Sodian, B. (2009). Verbal memory development from early childhood to adulthood. In W. Schneider, & M. Bullock (Eds.), *Human development from early childhood to early adulthood: Findings from a 20-year longitudinal study* (pp. 63–90). New York: Psychology Press.

Schneider, W., Körkel, J., & Weinert, F. E. (1989). Domain-specific knowledge and memory performance: A comparison of high- and low-aptitude children. *Journal of Educational Psychology, 81*, 306–312.

Schneider, W., Küspert, P., Roth, E., & Visé, M. (1997). Short- and long-term effects of training phonological awareness in kindergarten: Evidence from two German studies. *Journal of Experimental Child Psychology, 66*, 311–340.

Schneider, W., & Näslund, J. C. (1999). The impact of early phonological processing skills on reading and spelling in school: Evidence from the Munich Longitudinal Study. In F. E. Weinert & W. Schneider (Eds.), *The Munich Longitudinal Study on the Genesis of Individual Competencies (LOGIC).* Cambridge, UK: Cambridge University Press.

Schneider, W., & Pressley, M. (1997). *Memory development between 2 and 20* (2nd ed.). Mahwah, NJ: Erlbaum.

Schneider, W., & Sodian, B. (1988). Metamemory-memory behavior relationships in young children: Evidence from a memory-for-location task. *Journal of Experimental Child Psychology, 45*, 209–233.

Schoentjes, E., & Deboutte, D. (1999). Child sexual behavior inventory: A Dutch-speaking normative sample. *Pediatrics, 104*, 885–893.

Schön, R. A. (2007). Natural parenting—Back to basics in infant care. *Evolutionary Psychology, 5*, 102–183.

Schradin, C., & Anzenberger, G. (1999). Prolactin, the hormone of paternity. *News in Physiological Sciences, 14*, 223–231.

Schuhrke, B. (2000). Young children's curiosity about other people's genitals. *Journal of Psychology & Human Sexuality, 12*, 27–48.

Schwenck, C., Bjorklund, D. F., & Schneider, W. (2007). Factors influencing the incidence of utilization deficiencies and other patterns of recall/strategy-use relations in a strategic memory task. *Child Development, 78*, 1771–1787.

Schwenck, C., Bjorklund, D. F., & Schneider, W. (2009). Developmental and individual differences in young children's use and maintenance of a selective memory strategy. *Developmental Psychology, 45*, 1034–1050.

Scott, L. S., Pascalis, O., & Nelson, C. A. (2007) A domain general theory of the development of perceptual discrimination. *Current Directions in Psychological Science, 16*, 197–201.

Sear, R., & Mace, R. (2008). Who keeps children alive? A review of the effects of kin on child survival. *Evolution and Human Behavior, 29*, 1–18.

Sears, W., & Sears, M. (2001). *The attachment parenting book: A commonsense guide to understanding and nurturing your baby*. New York: Little, Brown.

Seefeldt, V., & Haubenstricker, J. (1982). Patterns, phases, or stages: An analytical model for the study of developmental movement. In J. A. S. Kelso & J. E. Clark (Eds.), *The development of movement control and coordination*. New York: Wiley.

Segalowitz, S. J., & Hiscock, M. (2002). The neuropsychology of normal development: Developmental neuroscience and a new constructivism. In S. J. Segalowitz & I. Rapin (Eds.), *Handbook of neuropsychology* (2nd ed.), Vol. 8, *Part I: Child neuropsychology*. Amsterdam, The Netherlands: Elsevier.

Seligman, M. E. (1971). Phobias and preparedness. *Behavior Therapy, 2*, 307–320.

Seligman, M. E. P. (1998). *Learned optimism: How to change your mind and your life* (2nd ed.). New York: Free Press.

Selman, R. L. (1980). *The growth of interpersonal understanding*. New York: Academic Press.

Sénéchal, M., & LeFevre, J. (2002). Parental involvement in the development of children's reading skill: A five-year longitudinal study. *Child Development, 73*, 445–460.

Senghas, A., & Coppola, M. (2001). Children creating language: How Nicaraguan Sign Language acquired a spatial grammar. *Psychological Science, 12*, 323–326.

Senghas, A., Kita, S., & Ozyürek, A. (2004). Children creating core properties of language: Evidence from an emerging sign language in Nicaragua. *Science, 305* (17 September), 1179–1782.

Seress, L. (2001). Morphological changes of the human hippocampal formation from midgestation to early childhood. In C. A. Nelson & M. Luciana (Eds.), *Handbook of developmental cognitive neuroscience* (pp. 45–58). Cambridge, MA: MIT Press.

Servin, A., Nordenström, A., Larsson, A., & Bohlin, G. (2003). Prenatal androgens and gender-typed behavior: A study of girls with mild and severe forms of congenital adrenal hyperplasia. *Developmental Psychology, 39*, 440–450.

Seymour, P. H. K., Aro, M., & Erskine, J. M. (2003). Foundations of literacy acquisition in European orthographies. *British Journal of Psychology, 94*, 143–174.

Shackelford, T. K., & Larsen, R. J. (1997). Facial asymmetry as an indicator of psychological, emotional, and physiological distress. *Journal of Personality and Social Psychology, 72*, 456–466.

Shaffer, D. R. (2009). *Social and personality development*. (6th ed.) Belmont, CA: Wadsworth.

Shapiro, L. R., & Hudson, J. A. (1991). Tell me a make-believe story: Coherence and cohesion in young children's picture-elicited narratives. *Developmental Psychology, 27*, 960–974.

Shatz, M., & Gelman, R. (1973). The development of communication skills. *Monographs of the Society for Research in Child Development, 38* (Serial No. 152).

Shaw, P., Eckstrand, K., Sharp, W., Blumenthal, J., Lerch, J. P., Greenstein, D., Clasen, L., Evans A., Giedd, J., & Rapoport, J. L. (2007). Attention-deficit/hyperactivity disorder is characterized by a delay in cortical maturation. *Proceedings of the National Academy of Science (USA), 104*, 19649–19654.

Shaw, P., Greenstein, D., Lerch, J., Clasen, L., Lenroot, R., Gogtay, N., Evans, A., Rapoport, J., & Giedd, J. (2006). Intellectual ability and cortical development in children and adolescents. *Nature, 440* (30 March), 676–679.

Shaywitz, S. E., Mody, M., & Shaywitz, B. A. (2006). Neural mechanisms in dyslexia. *Current Directions on Psychological Science, 15*, 278–281.

Shaywitz, S. E., Shaywitz, B. A., Pugh, K. R., Fulbright, R. K., Constable, R. T., Mencl, W. E., Shankweiler, D. P., Liberman, A. M., Skudlarski, P., Fletcher, J. M., Katz, L., Marchione, K. E., Lacadie, C., Gatenby, C., & Gore, J. C. (1998). Functional disruption in the organization of the brain for reading in dyslexia. *Proceedings of the National Academy of Science (USA), 95*, 2636–2641.

Shepher, J. (1983). *Incest: A biosocial view*. New York: Academic Press.

Sher, G., Davis, V. M., & Stoess, J. (2005). *In vitro fertilization: The A.R.T.* of making babies*. New York: Checkmark Books.

Sherif, M. H., Harvey, O. J., White, B. J., Hood, W. R., & Sherif C. W. (1961). *Inter-group conflict and cooperation: The Robbers Cave experiment*. Norman: University of Oklahoma Press.

Sherrod, K. B., O'Connor, S., Vietze, P. M., & Altemeier, W. A. (1984). Child health and maltreatment. *Child Development, 55*, 1174–1183.

Sherry, J. L. (2001). The effects of violent video games on aggression: A meta-analysis. *Human Communication Research, 27*, 409–431.

Shin, H-E., Bjorklund, D. F., & Beck, E. F. (2007). The adaptive nature of children's overestimation in a strategic memory task. *Cognitive Development, 22*, 197–212.

Shiner, R. L. (2000). Linking childhood personality with adaptation: Evidence for continuity and change across time into late adolescence. *Journal of Personality and Social Psychology, 78*, 310–325.

Shiner, R. L., Masten, A. S., & Roberts, J. M. (2003). Childhood personality foreshadows adult personality and life outcomes two decades later. *Journal of Personality, 71*, 1145–1170.

Shipman, P. (1994). *The evolution of racism: Human differences and the use and abuse of science*. New York: Simon & Schuster.

Shoda, Y., Mischel, W., & Peake, P. K. (1990). Predicting adolescent cognitive and social competence from preschool delay of gratification: Identifying diagnostic conditions. *Developmental Psychology, 26*, 978–986.

Shoda, Y., Mischel, W., & Wright, J. C. (1994). Intra-individual stability in the organization and patterning of behavior: Incorporating psychological situations into idiographic analyses of personality. *Journal of Personality and Social Psychology, 65*, 1023–1035.

Shonkoff, J. P., & Phillips, D. A. (2000). *From neurons to neighborhoods: The science of early childhood development*. Washington, DC: National Academy Press.

Shore, J. R. (2004). Teacher education and Multiple Intelligences: A case study of multiple intelligences and teacher efficacy in two teacher preparation courses. *Teachers College Record, 106*, 112–139.

Shorter, E. (1982). *History of women's bodies*. New York: Basic Books.

Shultz, T. R., & Horibe, F. (1974). Development of the appreciation of verbal jokes. *Developmental Psychology, 10*, 13–20.

Shultz, T. R., & Pilon, R. (1973). Development of the ability to detect linguistic ambiguity. *Child Development, 44*, 728–733.

Shuwairi, S. M. (2009). Preference for impossible figures in 4-month-old infants. *Journal of Experimental Child Psychology, 104*, 115–123.

Shuwairi, S. M., Albert, M. K., & Johnson, S. P. (2007). Discrimination of possible and impossible objects in infancy. *Psychological Science, 18*, 303–307.

Shweder, R. A., Much, N. C., Mahapatra, M., & Park, L. (1997). The big three of morality (autonomy, community, divinity) and the big three explanations of suffering. In A. Brandt & P. Rozin (Eds.), *Morality and health*. New York: Routledge and Kegan Paul.

Siegal, M. (2008). *Marvelous minds: The discovery of what children know*. Oxford, UK: Oxford University Press.

Siegal, M., Butterworth, G., & Newcombe P. A. (2004). Culture and children's cosmology. *Developmental Science, 7*, 308–324.

Siegal, M., & Peterson, C. C. (1998). Preschoolers' understanding of lies and innocent and negligent mistakes. *Developmental Psychology, 34*, 332–341.

Siegal, M., & Share, D. L. (1990). Contamination sensitivity in young children. *Developmental Psychology, 26*, 455–458.

Siegel, L. S. (1993). The cognitive basis of dyslexia. In R. Pasnak & M. L. Howe (Eds.), *Emerging themes in cognitive development*, Vol. 2: *Competencies*. New York: Springer-Verlag.

Siegler, R. S. (1996). *Emerging minds: The process of change in children's thinking*. New York: Oxford University Press.

Siegler, R. S. (2000). The rebirth of children's learning. *Child Development, 71*, 26–35.

Siegler, R. S. (2002). Microgenetic studies of self-explanation. In N. Garnott & J. Parziale (Eds.), *Microdevelopment: A process-oriented perspective for studying development and learning* (pp. 31–58). Cambridge, UK: Cambridge University Press.

Siegler, R. S. (2006). Microgenetic analyses of learning. In W. Damon & R. M. Lerner (Gen. Eds.), *Handbook of child psychology* (6th ed.). In D. Kuhn & R. S. Siegler (Vol. Eds.), Vol. 2: *Cognition, perception, and language* (pp. 464–510). New York: Wiley.

Siegler, R. S., & Alibali, M. W. (2004). *Children's thinking* (4th ed.). Upper Saddle River, NJ: Prentice Hall.

Siegler, R. S., & Jenkins, E. (1989). *How children discover new strategies*. Hillsdale, NJ: Erlbaum.

Siegler, R. S., & Mu., Y. (2008). Chinese children excel on novel mathematics problems even before elementary school. *Psychological Science, 19*, 759–763.

Sigel, I., & McGillicuddy-DeLisi, A. V. (2002). Parent beliefs are cognitions: The dynamic belief systems model. In M. H. Bornstein (Ed.), *Handbook of parenting* (2nd ed.), Vol. 3: *Being and becoming a parent* (pp. 485–508). Mahwah, NJ: Erlbaum.

Signorella, M. L., Bigler, R. S., & Liben, L. S. (1993). Developmental differences in children's gender schemata about others: A meta-analytic review. *Developmental Review, 13*, 147–183.

Silbereisen, R., Petersen, A., Albrecht, H., & Kracke, B. (1989). Maturational timing and the development of problem behavior: Longitudinal studies in adolescence. *Journal of Early Adolescence, 9*, 247–268.

Silk, J. B. (1987). Adoption and fosterage in human societies: Adaptations or enigmas? *Cultural Anthropology, 2*, 39–49.

Silk, J. B., Brosnan, S. F., Vonk, J., Henrich, J., Povinelli, D. J., Richardson, A. S., Lambet, S. P., Mascaro, J., & Schapiro, S. J. (2005). Chimpanzees are indifferent to the welfare of unrelated group members. *Nature, 347*, 1357–1359.

Silovsky, J. F., & Bonner, B. L. (2004). Sexual development and sexual behavior problems in children ages 2–12. *National Centre on Sexual Behavior of Youth (NCSBY) Fact Sheet*, Number 4, 4 pgs.

Silvestri, S. (1992). Marital instability in men from intact and divorced families: Interpersonal behavior, cognitions, and intimacy. *Journal of Divorce and Remarriage, 18*, 79–108.

Simcock, G., & DeLoache, J. (2006). Get the picture? The effects of iconicity on toddlers' re-enactment from picture books. *Developmental Psychology, 42*, 1352–1357.

Simcock, G., & Hayne, H. (2002). Breaking the barrier? Children fail to translate their preverbal memories into language. *Psychological Science, 13*, 225–231.

Simon, T. J., Hespos, S. J., & Rochat, P. (1995). Do infants understand simple arithmetic? A replication of Wynn (1992). *Cognitive Development, 10*, 253–269.

Simpson, J. A., & Belsky, J. (2008). Attachment theory within a modern evolutionary framework chapter. In P. R. Shaver & J. Cassidy (Eds.), *Handbook of attachment: Theory, research, and clinical application* (2nd ed., pp. 131–157). New York: Guilford.

Simpson, J. L., & Elias, S. (2003). *Genetics in obstetrics and gynecology* (3rd ed.). Philadelphia: Saunders.

Singer Harris, N. G., Bellugi, U., Bates, E., Jones, W., & Rossen, M. (1997). Contrasting profiles of language development in children with Williams and Down syndromes. *Developmental Neuropsychology, 13*, 345–370.

Singer, M. I., & Miller, D. B. (1999). Contributors to violent behavior among elementary and middle school children. *Pediatrics, 104*, 878–884.

Singh, M. K., DelBello, M. P., Kowatch, R. A., & Strakowski, S. M. (2006). Co-occurrence of bipolar and attention-deficit hyperactivity disorders in children. *Bipolar Disorders, 8*, 710–720.

Skeels, H. M. (1966). Adult status of children with contrasting early life experiences. *Monographs of the Society for Research in Child Development, 31* (Serial No. 105).

Skeels, H. M., & Dye, H. B. (1939). A study of the effects of differential stimulation on mentally retarded children. *Program of the American Association of Mental Deficiency, 44*, 114–136.

Skinner, B. F. (1938). *The behavior of organisms: An experimental analysis*. Cambridge, Massachusetts: B. F. Skinner Foundation.

Skinner, B. F. (1953). *Science and human behavior*. New York: Macmillan.

Skinner, B. F. (1957). *Verbal behavior*. New York: Appleton-Century-Crofts.

Skinner, B. F. (1971). *Beyond freedom and dignity*. New York: Hackett.

Skoczenski, A. M., & Norcia, A. M. (2002). Late maturation of visual hyperacuity. *Psychological Science, 13*, 537–541.

Skouteris, H., Spataro, J., & Lazarids, M. (2006). Young children's use of a delayed video representation to solve a retrieval problem pertaining to self. *Developmental Science, 9*, 505–517.

Skuse, D. H. (1993). Extreme deprivation in early childhood. In D. Bishop & K. Mogford (Eds.), *Language development in exceptional circumstances*. Hove, UK: Psychology Press.

Slaby, R. G., & Frey, K. S. (1975). Development of gender constancy and selective attention to same-sex models. *Child Development, 46*, 849–856.

Slade, A. (1987). Quality of attachment and early symbolic play. *Developmental Psychology, 23*, 78–85.

Slater, A. (1995). Visual perception and memory at birth. In C. Rovee-Collier & L. P. Lipsitt (Eds.), *Advances in infancy research* (Vol. 9). Norwood, NJ: Ablex.

Slater, A. M., Mattock, A., Brown, E., & Bremner, G. J. (1991). Form perception at birth: Cohen and Younger (1984) revisited. *Journal of Experimental Child Psychology, 51*, 395–406.

Slater, A. M., Von der Schulenburg, C., Brown, E., Badenoch, M., Butterworth, G., & Parsons, S. (1998). Newborn infants prefer attractive faces. *Infant Behavior and Development, 21*, 345–354.

Slaughter, V., Jaakkola, K., & Carey, S. (1999). Constructing a coherent theory. Children's biological understanding of life and death. In M. Siegel & C. Peterson (Eds.) *Children's understanding of biology and health* (pp. 71–98). Cambridge, UK: Cambridge University Press.

Slobin, D. I. (1970). Universals of grammatical development in children. In G. B. Flores, J. Arcais, & W. J. M. Levelt (Eds.), *Advances in psycholinguistics*. Amsterdam, The Netherlands: North-Holland.

Smith, E. P., Walker, K., Fields, L., Brookins, C. C., & Seay, R. C. (1999). Ethnic identity and its relationship to self-esteem, perceived efficacy, and prosocial attitudes in early adolescence. *Journal of Adolescence, 22*, 867–880.

Smith, K. E., & Buyalos, R. P. (1996). The profound impact of patient age on pregnancy outcome after early detection of fetal cardiac activity. *Fertility and Sterility, 56*, 35–45.

Smith, L. B. (1999). Do infants possess innate knowledge structures? The con side. *Developmental Science, 2*, 133–144.

Smith, P. K. (1982). Does play matter? Functional and evolutionary aspects of animal and human play. *Behavioral and Brain Sciences, 5*, 139–184.

Smith, P. K. (2005). Social and pretend play in children. In A. D. Pellegrini & P. K. Smith (Eds.), *Play in humans and great apes* (pp. 173–209). Mahwah, NJ: Erlbaum.

Smith, P. K. (2007). Why has aggression been thought of as maladaptive? In P. H. Hawley, T. D. Little, & P. C. Rodkin, (Eds.), *Aggression and adaptation: The bright side to bad behavior* (pp. 65–84). Mahwah, NJ: Erlbaum.

Smith, R. E., Bayen, U. J., & Martin, C. (2010). The cognitive processes underlying event-based prospective memory in school age children and young adults: A formal model-based study. *Developmental Psychology, 46*, 230–244.

Smitsman, A. W., & Bongers, R. M. (2002). Tool use and tool making: A developmental action perspective. In J. Valsiner and K. J. Connolly (Ed.), *Handbook of developmental psychology* (pp. 172–193). London: Sage.

Snarey, J. (1985). Cross-cultural universality of social-moral development: A critical review of Kohlbergian research. *Psychological Bulletin, 97*, 202–232.

Snedecker, J., Geren, J., & Shafto, C. L. (2007). Starting over: International adoption as a natural experiment in language development. *Psychological Science, 18,* 79–87.

Snell, E. K., Adam, E. K., & Duncan, G. J. (2007). Sleep and body mass index and overweight status of children and adolescents. *Child Development, 78,* 309–323.

Snow, C. (1972). Mother's speech to children learning language. *Child Development, 43,* 549–565.

Snow, C. E., (1977). Mothers' speech research: From input to interaction. In C. E. Snow & C. A. Ferguson (Eds.), *Talking to children: Language input and acquisition.* Cambridge: Cambridge University Press.

Snow, C. E., & Yusun Kang, J. (2006). Becoming bilingual, biliterate, and bicultural. In K. A. Renninger & I. E. Sigel (Vol. Eds.) *Child psychology in practice* (Vol. 4). In W. Damon (Gen. Ed.), *Handbook of child psychology.* New York: Wiley.

Snyder, J., Brooker, M., Patrick, M. R., Synder, A., Schrepferman, L., & Stoolmiller, M. (2003). Observed peer victimization during elementary school: Continuity, growth, and relation to risk for child antisocial and depressive behavior. *Child Development, 74,* 1881–1898.

Sokol, R. J., Delaney-Black, V., & Nordstrom, B. (2003). Fetal alcohol spectrum disorder. *Journal of the American Medical Association, 290,* 2996–2999.

Soley, G., & Hannon, E. E. (2010). Infants prefer the musical meter of their own culture: A cross-cultural comparison. *Developmental Psychology, 46,* 286–292.

Solomon, G. E. A., Johnson, S. C, Zaitchik, D., & Carey, S. (1996). Like father, like son: Young children's understanding of how and why offspring resemble their parents. *Child Development, 67,* 151–171.

Somel, M., Franz, H., Yan, Z., Lorec, A., Guo, S., Giger, T., Kelso, J., Nickel, B., Dannemann, M., Bahn, S., Webster, M. J., Weickert, C., Lachmann, M., Pääbo, S., & Khaitovich, P. (2009). Transcriptional neoteny in the human brain. *Proceedings of the National Academy of Sciences (USA), 106,* 5743–5748.

Somerville, C. J. (1982). *The rise and fall of childhood.* Beverly Hills, CA: Sage.

Somerville, S. C., Wellman, H. M., & Cultice, J. C. (1983). Young children's deliberate reminding. *Journal of Genetic Psychology, 143,* 87–96.

Song, H., & Baillargeon, R. (2008). Infants' reasoning about others' false perceptions. *Developmental Psychology, 44,* 1789–1795.

Sonuga-Barke, E. J. S., Taylor, E., Sembi, S., & Smith, J. (1992). Hyperactivity and delay aversion—I. The effect of delay on choice. *Journal of Child Psychology and Psychiatry, 33,* 399–409.

Sood, B., Delaney-Black, V., Covington, C., Nordstrom, B., Ager, J., Templin, T., Janisse, J., Martier, S., & Sokol, R. J. (2001). Prenatal alcohol exposure and childhood behaviour at age 6 to 7 years: I. Dose-response effect. *Pediatrics, 108,* E34.

Sorenson, R. C. (1973). *Adolescent sexuality in contemporary America.* New York: World.

Southgate, V., Johnson. M. H., Osborne, T., & Csibra, G. (2009). Predictive motor activation during action observation in human infants. *Biology Letters, 5,* 769–772.

Sowell, E. R., Thompson, P. M., Holmes, C. J., Jernigan, T. L., & Toga, A. W. (1999). *In vivo* evidence for post-adolescent brain maturation in frontal and striatal regions. *Nature Neuroscience, 1,* 859–861.

Spear, L. P. (2000). Neurobehavioral changes in adolescence. *Current Directions in Psychological Science, 9,* 111–114.

Spear, L. P. (2007). Brain development and adolescent behavior. In D. Coch, K. W. Fischer, & G. Dawson (Eds.), *Human behavior, learning, and the developing brain: Typical development* (pp. 362–396). New York: Guilford.

Spearman, C. (1927). *The abilities of man.* New York: Macmillan.

Spelke, E. S. (1991). Physical knowledge in infancy: Reflections on Piaget's theory. In S. Carey & R. Gelman (Eds.), *Epigenesis of mind: Essays in biology and knowledge.* Hillsdale, NJ: Erlbaum.

Spelke, E. S. (2000). Core knowledge. *American Psychologist, 55,* 1233–1243.

Spelke, E. S., & Cortelyou, A. (1981). Perceptual aspects of social knowing: Looking and listening in infancy. In M. E. Lamb & L. R. Sherrod (Eds.), *Infant social cognition: Empirical and theoretical considerations.* Hillsdale, NJ: Erlbaum.

Spelke, E. S., & Kinzler, K. D. (2007). Core knowledge. *Developmental Science, 10,* 89–96.

Spencer, J. P., Blumberg, M. S., McMurray, B., Robinson, S. R., Samuelson, L. K., & Tomblin, J. B. (2009). Short arms and talking legs: Why we should no longer abide the nativist-empiricist debate. *Child Development Perspectives, 3,* 79–87.

Spencer, S. J., Steele, C. M., & Quinn, D. M. (1999). Stereotype threat and women's math performance. *Journal of Experimental Social Psychology, 35,* 4–28.

Spitz, R. (1945). Hospitalism: An inquiry into the genesis of psychiatric conditions in early childhood. *Psychoanalytic Study of the Child, 1,* 53–74.

Spitz, R. (1947). *Grief: A peril in infancy* [Film]. Educational Media Collection (http://www.css.washington.edu/emc/title/1216).

Spitz, R. (1949). The role of ecological factors in emotional development in infancy. *Child Development, 20,* 145–155.

Spitz, R. (1965). *The first year of life.* New York: International Universities Press.

Spreen, O., Risser, A., & Edgell, D. (1995). *Developmental neuropsychiatry.* New York: Oxford University Press.

Sprengelmeyer, R., Perrett, D. I., Fagan, E. C., Cornwell, R. E., Lobmaier, J. S., Sprengelmeyer, A., Aasheim, H. B. M., Black, I. M., Cameron, L. M., Crow, S., Milne, N., Rhodes, E. C., & Young, A. W. (2009). The cutest little baby face: A hormonal link to sensitivity to cuteness in infant faces. *Psychological Science, 20,* 149–154.

Springer, C., & Andrews, P. (2005) *The complete world of human evolution.* New York: Thames & Hudson.

Springer, K. (1999). How a naïve theory of biology is acquired. In M. Siegal & C. C. Peterson (Eds.), *Children's understanding of biology and health* (pp. 45–70). Cambridge, UK: Cambridge University Press.

Sroufe, A. (1996). *Emotional development.* Cambridge, UK: Cambridge University Press.

Sroufe, A., Egeland, B., Carlson, E., & Collins, W. (2005). *Minnesota longitudinal study of risk and adaptation from birth to maturity: The development of the person.* New York: Guilford.

Sroufe, L. A. (1997). Psychopathology as an outcome of development. *Child Development, 56,* 1–14.

St. James-Roberts, I. (2005). Prolonged infant crying and colic. In B. Hopkins (Ed.), *The Cambridge encyclopedia of child development* (pp. 448–452). New York: Cambridge University Press.

Stacey, J., & Biblarz, T. J. (2001). (How) does the sexual orientation of parents matter? *American Sociological Review, 66,* 159–183.

Stadler, M. A., & Ward, G. C. (2005). Supporting the narrative development of young children. *Early Childhood Education Journal, 33,* 73.

Stake, J. E., & Nickens, S. D. (2005). Adolescent girls' and boys' science peer relationship and perceptions of the possible self as scientist. *Sex Roles, 52,* 1–12.

Stanovich, K. E. (1986). Matthew effects in reading: Some consequences of individual differences in the acquisition of literacy. *Reading Research Quarterly, 21,* 360–406.

Stark, R. (1978). Features of infant sounds: The emergence of cooing. *Journal of Child Language, 5,* 1–12.

Starkey, P., Spelke, E. S., & Gelman, R. (1990). Numerical abstraction by human infants. *Cognition, 36,* 97–127.

Statistics Canada. (2007). *The evolving linguistic portrait, 2006 census.* (Catalogue no. 97-555-XIE).

Steele, C. M. (1997). A threat in the air: How stereotypes shape intellectual identity and performance. *American Psychologist, 52,* 613–629.

Steele, C. M., & Aronson, J. (1995). Stereotype threat and the intellectual test performance of African Americans. *Journal of Social and Personality Psychology, 69,* 797–811.

Steenari, M., Vuontela, A., Paavonen, E. J., Carlson, S., Fjallberg, M., & Aronen, E. T. (2003). Working memory and sleep in 6- to 13-year-old schoolchildren. *Journal of the American Academy of Child and Adolescent Psychiatry, 42,* 85–92.

Stein, J. H., & Reiser, L. W. (1994). A study of white, middle-class adolescent boys' responses to "semenarche" (the first ejaculation). *Journal of Youth and Adolescence, 23,* 373–384.

Stein, N. L., & Glenn, C. (1979). An analysis of story comprehension in elementary school children. In R. D. Freedle (Ed.). *Advances in discourse processes. Vol. 2. New directions in discourse processes* (pp. 53–119). Norwood, NJ: Ablex.

Stein, N. L., & Levine, L. (1989). The causal organization of emotional knowledge: A developmental study. *Cognition and Emotion, 3,* 343–378.

Stein, Z., Susser, M., Saenger, G., & Marolla, F. (1975). *Famine and human development: The Dutch hunger winter of 1944–1945.* New York: Oxford University Press.

Steinberg, L. (1990). Autonomy, conflict, and harmony in the family relationship. In S. S. Feldman & G. R. Elliott (Eds.), *At the threshold: The developing adolescent* (pp. 255–276). Cambridge, MA: Harvard University Press.

Steinberg, L. (2007). Risk taking in adolescence: New perspectives from brain and behavioral science. *Current Directions in Psychological Science, 16,* 5559.

Steinberg, L. (2008). A social neuroscience perspective on adolescent risk-taking. *Developmental Review, 28,* 78–106.

Steinberg, L. (2010). A dual systems model of adolescent risk-taking. *Developmental Psychobiology, 52,* 216–224.

Steiner, H., & Remsing, L. (2007). Work group on quality issues: Practice parameter for the assessment and treatment of children and adolescents with oppositional defiant disorder. *Journal of the American Academy of Child and Adolescence Psychiatry, 46,* 126–141.

Steiner, J. E. (1979). Human facial expressions in response to taste and smell stimulation. In H. W. Reese & L. P. Lipsitt (Eds.), *Advances in child development and behavior* (Vol. 13, pp. 257–295). New York: Academic.

Steingraber, S. (2007). *The falling age of puberty in U.S. girls: What we know, what we need to know.* Breast Cancer Fund. Accessed at: www.breastcancerfund.org. (Downloaded November 11, 2008).

Stephen, E. H., & Chandra, A. (2006). Declining estimates of infertility in the United States: 1982–2000. *Fertility and Sterility, 86,* 516–523.

Stepp, L. S. (2000). *Our last best shot: Guiding our children through early adolescence.* New York: Riverside Books.

Sternberg, K. J., Baradaran, L. P., Abbott, C. B., Lamb, M. E., & Guterman, E. (2006). Type of violence, age, and gender differences in the effects of family violence on children's behavior problems: A mega-analysis. *Developmental Review, 26,* 89–112.

Sternberg, K. J., Lamb, M. E., Orbach, Y., Esplin, P. W., & Mitchell, S. (2001). Use of a structured investigative protocol enhances young children's responses to free recall prompts in the course of forensic interviews. *Journal of Applied Psychology, 86,* 997–1005.

Sternberg, R. J. (1985). *Beyond IQ: A triarchic theory of human intelligence.* Cambridge, UK: Cambridge University Press.

Sternberg, R. J. (1997). The concept of intelligence and its role in lifelong learning and success. *American Psychologist, 52,* 1030–1037.

Sternberg, R. J. (2004). Culture and intelligence. *American Psychologist, 59,* 325–338.

Sternberg, R. J., Ferrari, M., & Clinkenbeard, P. (1996). Identification, instruction, and assessment of gifted children: A construct validation of a triarchic model. *Gifted Child Quarterly, 40,* 129–137.

Stevenson, H. W., & Lee, S. Y. (1990). Context of achievement. *Monographs of the Society for Research in Child Development, 55* (Serial No. 221).

Stevenson, R. J., Oaten, M. J., Case, T. I., Repacholi, B. M., & Wagland, P. (2010). Children's response to adult disgust elicitors: Development and acquisition. *Developmental Psychology, 46,* 165–177.

Steward, A. L., Rifkin, L., Amess, P. N., Kirkbride, V., Townsend, J. P., Miller, D. H., Lewis, S. W., Kingsley, D. P. E., Moseley, I. F., Foster, O., & Murray, R. M. (1999). Brain structure and neurocognitive and behavioural function in adolescents who were born very preterm. *Lancet, 353,* 1653–1657.

Stice, E., Presnell, K., & Bearman, S. K. (2001). Relation of early menarche to depression, eating disorders, substance abuse, and comorbid psychopathology among adolescent girls. *Developmental Psychology, 37,* 608–619.

Stickgold, R., Hobson, R. J. A., Fosse, R., & Fosse, M. (2001). Sleep, learning, and dreams: Off-line memory reprocessing. *Science, 294* (2 November), 1052–1057.

Stice, E., Shaw, H., & Marti, C. N. (2006). A meta-analytic review of obesity prevention programs for children and adolescents: The skinny on interventions that work. *Psychological Bulletin, 132,* 667–691.

Stiles, J. (2008). *The fundamentals of brain development.* Cambridge, MA: Harvard University Press.

Stiles, J., Reilly, J., Paul, B., & Moses, P. (2005). Cognitive development following early rain injury: Evidence for neural adaptation. *Trends in Cognitive Sciences, 9,* 136–143.

Stipek, D. (1984). Young children's performance expectations: Logical analysis or wishful thinking? In J. G. Nicholls (Ed.), *Advances in motivation and achievement,* Vol. 3: *The development of achievement motivation.* Greenwich, CT: JAI.

Stipek, D., & Daniels, D. (1988). Declining perceptions of competence: A consequence of changes in the child or the educational environment? *Journal of Educational Psychology, 80,* 352–356.

Stoffman, N., Schwarta, B., Austin, S. B., Grace, E., & Gordon, C. M. (2005). Influence of bone density results on adolescents with anorexia nervosa. *International Journal of Eating Disorders, 37,* 250–255.

Stone, C. A., & Day, M. C. (1978). Levels of availability of a formal operational strategy. *Child Development, 49,* 1054–1065.

Stone, L. J., Smith, H. T., & Murphy, L. B. (Eds.). (1973). *The competent infant: Research and commentary.* New York: Basic Books.

Storch, S. A., & Whitehurst, G. J. (2002). Oral language and code-related precursors to reading: Evidence from a longitudinal structural model. *Developmental Psychology, 38,* 934–947.

Stores G. (1999). Children's sleep disorders: Modern approaches, developmental effects, and children at special risk. *Developmental Medicine & Child Neurology, 41,* 568–573.

Storey, A. E., Walsh, C. J., Quinton, R. L., & Wynne-Edwards, K. E. (2000). Hormonal correlates of paternal responsiveness in new and expectant fathers. *Evolution and Human Behavior, 21,* 79–95.

Strasburger, V. C., & Donnerstein, E. (1999). Children, adolescents, and the media: Issues and solutions. *Pediatrics, 103,* 129–139.

Strauss, M. S., & Curtis, L. E. (1981). Infant perception of numerosity. *Child Development, 52,* 1146–1152.

Strauss, R. S., & Pollack, H. A. (2003). Social marginalization of overweight children. *Archives of Pediatric and Adolescent Medicine, 157,* 746–752.

Strayer, F. F., & Strayer, J. (1976). An ethological analysis of social agonism and dominance relations among preschool children. *Child Development, 47,* 980–989.

Streri, A., Lhote, M., & Dutilleul, S. (2000). Haptic perception in newborns. *Developmental Science, 3,* 319–327.

Streri, A., & Spelke, E. S. (1989). Effects of motion and figural goodness on haptic object perception in infancy. *Child Development, 60,* 1111–1125.

Striano, T., Brennan, P. A., & Vanman, E.J. (2002). Maternal depressive symptoms and 6-month-old infants' sensitivity to facial expressions. *Infancy, 3,* 115–126.

Striano, T., & Rochat, P. (2000). Emergence of selective social referencing in infancy. *Infancy, 1,* 253–508.

Stright, A. D., Gallagher, K. C., & Kelly, K. (2008). Infant temperament moderates relations between maternal parenting in early childhood and children's adjustment in first grade. *Child Development, 79*, 186–200.

Strouse, J. S., & Buerkel-Rethfuss, N. (1987). Self-reported media exposure and sexual attitudes and behaviors of college students. *Journal of Sex Education and Therapy, 13*, 43–51.

Strouse, J. S., Buerkel-Rethfuss, N., & Long, E. C. (1995). Gender and family as moderators of the relationship between music video exposure and adolescent sexual permissiveness. *Adolescence, 30*, 505–521.

Subrahmanyam, K., Greenfield, P. M., & Tynes, B. (2004). Constructing sexuality and identity in an online teen chat room. *Applied Developmental Psychology, 25*, 651–666.

Subrahmanyam, K., Greenfield, P. M., Kraut, R. E., & Gross, E. (2001). The impact of computer use on children's development. *Journal of Applied Developmental Psychology, 22*, 7–30.

Suddendorf, T. (2003). Early representational insight: Twenty-four-month-olds can use a photo to find an object in the world. *Child Development, 74*, 896–904.

Suddendorf, T., & Whiten, A. (2001). Mental evolution and development: Evidence for secondary representation in children, great apes, and other animals. *Psychological Bulletin, 127*, 629–650.

Suitor, J. J., Sechrist, J., Plikuhn, M., Pardo, S. T., & Pillemer, K. (2008). Within-family differences in parent-child relations across the life course. *Current Directions in Psychological Science, 17*, 334–338.

Sullivan, M. W., Rovee-Collier, C. K., & Tynes, D. M. (1979). A conditioning analysis of infant long-term memory. *Child Development, 50*, 152–162.

Sulloway, F. J. (1996). *Born to rebel: Birth order, family dynamics, and creative lives.* New York: Pantheon.

Sun, Y., & Li, Y. (2002). Children's well-being during parents' marital disruption process: A pooled time-series analysis. *Journal of Marriage and Family, 64*, 472–488.

Sundet, J. M., Eriksen, W., & Tambs, K. (2008). Intelligence correlations between brothers decrease with increasing age differences: Evidence for shared environmental effects in young adults. *Psychological Science, 19*, 843–847.

Suomi, S., & Harlow, H. (1972). Social rehabilitation of isolate-reared monkeys. *Developmental Psychology, 6*, 487–496.

Super, C. (1976). Environmental effects on motor development: The case of "African infant precocity." *Developmental Medicine and Child Neurology, 18*, 561–567.

Sur, M., & Leamey, C. A. (2001). Development and plasticity areas and networks. *Nature Reviews Neuroscience, 2*, 251–262.

Surbey, M. K. (1990). Family composition, stress, and the timing of human menarche. In T. E. Ziegler & F. B. Bercovitvch (Eds.), *Socioendocrinology of primate reproduction* (pp. 11–32). New York: Wiley-Liss.

Surbey, M. K. (1998). Parent and offspring strategies in the transition at adolescence. *Human Nature, 9*, 67–94.

Susser, M., & Stein, Z. (1994). Timing in prenatal nutrition: A reprise of the Dutch Famine Study. *Nutrition Review, 52*, 84–94.

Sussman, A. L. (2001). Reality monitoring of performed and imagined interactive events: Developmental and contextual effects. *Journal of Experimental Child Psychology, 79*, 115–138.

Sutcliffe, J. S. (2008). Insights into pathogenesis of autism. *Science, 321* (11 July), 208–209.

Suzuki, L. A., & Valencia, R. R. (1997). Race-ethnicity and measured intelligence: Educational implications. *American Psychologist, 52*, 1103–1114.

Svejda, M., Campos, J. J., & Emde, R. N. (1980). Mother-infant "bonding": Failure to generalize. *Child Development, 51*, 775–779.

Swamy, G. K., Ostbye, T., & Skjaerven, R. (2008). Association of preterm birth with long-term survival, reproduction, and next-generation preterm birth. *Journal of the American Medical Association, 299*, 1429–1436.

Swanson, C. B. (2008). *Cities in crisis: A special analytic report of high school graduation.* Bethesda, MD: EPE Research Center.

Swanson, H. L., & Jerman, O. (2007). The influence of working-memory on reading growth in subgroups of children with reading disabilities. *Journal of Experimental Child Psychology, 96*, 249–283.

Symons, D. K., Peterson, C. C., Slaughter, V., Roche, J., & Doyle, E. (2005). Theory of mind and mental state discourse during book reading and story-telling tasks. *British Journal of Developmental Psychology, 23*, 81–102.

Symons, L. A., Hains, S. M. J., & Muir, D. W. (1998). Look at me: Five-month-old infants' sensitivity to very small deviations in eye-gaze during social interactions. *Infant Behavior and Development, 21*, 531–536.

Szkrybalo, J., & Ruble, D. N. (1999). "God made me a girl": Sex-category constancy judgments and explanations revisited. *Developmental Psychology, 35*, 393–402.

Tager-Flusberg, H. (Ed.) (1999). *Neurodevelopmental disorders.* Cambridge, MA: MIT Press.

Takagishi, H., Kameshima, S., Schug, J., Koizumi, M., & Yamagishi, T. (2010). Theory of mind enhances preference for fairness. *Journal of Experimental Child Psychology, 105*, 130–137.

Tal, I., & Lieberman, D. (2007). Kin selection and the development of sexual aversions: Toward an integration of theories on family sexual abuse. In C. Salmon & T. S. Shackelford (Eds.), *Family relationships: An evolutionary perspective.* Oxford, UK: Oxford University Press.

Tallal, P. (2003). Language learning disabilities: Integrating research approaches. *Current Directions in Psychological Science, 12*, 206–212.

Talwar, V., Gordon, H. M., & Lee, K. (2007). Lying in the elementary school years: Verbal deception and its relation to second-order belief understanding. *Developmental Psychology, 43*, 804–810.

Talwar, V., & Lee, K. (2002). Development of lying to conceal a transgression: Children's control of expressive behaviour during verbal deception. *International Journal of Behavioral Development, 26*, 436–444.

Talwar, V., & Lee, K. (2008). Social and cognitive correlates of children's lying behavior. *Child Development, 79*, 866–881.

Tamis-LeMonda, C. S., Bornstein, M. H., Kahana-Kalman, R., Baumwell, L., & Cyphers, L. (1998). Predicting variation in the timing of language milestones in the second year: An events-history approach. *Journal of Child Language, 25*, 675–700.

Tanner, J. M. (1978). *Foetus into man: Physical growth from conception to maturity.* Cambridge, MA: Harvard University Press.

Tanner, J. M. (1981). *A history of the study of human growth.* Cambridge, UK: Cambridge University Press.

Tanner, J. M. (1990). *Foetus into man: Physical growth from conception to maturity (Revised and enlarged edition).* Cambridge, MA: Harvard University Press.

Tao, K-T., & Chiu, J-H. (1985). One-child-per-family policy: A psychological perspective. In W. S. Teng & D. Y. U. Wu (Eds.), *Chinese culture and mental health* (pp. 153–165). Orlando, FL: Academic Press.

Tao, K.-T., Qiu, J.-H., Li, B.-L., Tseng, W.-S., Hsu, J., & McLaughlin, D. G. (1995). One-child-per-couple family planning and child behaviour development: Six-year follow-up study in Nanjing. In T.-Y. Lin, W.-S. Tseng, & Y.-K. Yeh (Eds.), *Chinese societies and mental health* (pp. 341–374). New York: Oxford University Press.

Tardif, T., & Wellman, H. M. (2000). Acquisition of mental state language in Mandarin- and Cantonese-speaking children. *Developmental Psychology, 36*, 25–43.

Task Force on Obesity. (2004). *Obesity in children and young people, a crisis in public health.* www.iotf.org.

Tattersall, I. (1998). *Becoming human: Evolution and human intelligence.* San Diego, CA: Harcourt Brace.

Taylor, J., & Lindberg, D. R. (2006, April). *Analyzing depression from a developmental systems perspective.* Paper presented at a meeting of the Conference on Human Development, Louisville, Kentucky.

Taylor, M. (1999). *Imaginary companions and the children who create them.* New York: Oxford University Press.

Taylor, M. J., Batty, M., & Itier, R. J. (2004). The faces of development: A review of early face processing over childhood. *Journal of Cognitive Neuroscience, 16*, 1426–1442.

Taylor, M., Carlson, S. M., Maring, B. L., Gerow, L., & Charley, C. M. (2004). The characteristics and correlates of fantasy in school-age children: Imaginary companions, impersonation, and social understanding. *Developmental Psychology, 40*, 1173–1187.

Taylor, S. E., Klein, L. C., Lewis, B. P., Gruenenwald, T. L., Gurung, R. A., & Updegraff, J. A. (2000). Biobehavioral responses to stress in females: Tend-and-befriend, not fight-or-flight. *Psychological Review, 107*, 411–429.

Teasdale, T. W., & Owen, D. R. (1989). Continuing secular increases in intelligence and a stable prevalence of high intelligence levels. *Intelligence, 13*, 255–262.

Teasdale, T. W., & Owen, D. R. (2008). Secular declines in cognitive test scores: A reversal of the Flynn effect. *Intelligence, 36*, 121–126.

Teitler, J. O., & Weiss, C. C. (2000). Effects of neighborhood and school environments on transitions to first sexual intercourse. *Sociology of Education, 73*, 112–132.

Tembrock, G. (1954). Rotfuchs und Wolf. *Z. Säugetierkde, 19*, 152–159.

Temrin, H., Nordlund, J., & Sterner, S. (2004). Are stepchildren overrepresented as victims of lethal parental violence in Sweden? *Proceedings of the Royal Society, London B, Biology Letters, 271*, S124–S126.

Teti, D. M., & Candelaria, M. A. (2002). Parenting competence. In M. H. Bornstein (Ed.), *Handbook of parenting* (2nd ed.), Vol. 4: *Social conditions and applied parenting* (pp. 149–180). Mahwah, NJ: Erlbaum.

Teti, D. M., Sakin, J. W., Kucera, E., Corns, K. M., & Eiden, R. D. (1996). And baby makes four: Predictors of attachment security among preschool-age firstborns during the transition to siblinghood. *Child Development, 67*, 579–596.

Teyber, E. (2001). *Helping children cope with divorce.* San Francisco: Jossey-Bass.

Thanasiu, P. L. (2004). Childhood sexuality: Discerning healthy from abnormal sexual behaviors. *Journal of Mental Health Counseling, 26*, 309–319.

The Global Deception Research Team. (2006). A world of lies. *Journal of Cross-Cultural Psychology, 37*, 60–74.

The National Institute of Mental Health. (2007). Depression: The invisible disease. Accessed at: http://www.nimh.nih.gov/publicat/invisible.cfm (Downloaded May 17, 2007).

The St. Petersburg-USA Orphanage Research Team. (2008). The effects of early social-emotional and relationship experience on the development of young orphanage children. *Monographs of the Society for Research in Child Development, 73* (Serial No. 291).

Thelen, E. (1979). Rhythmical sterotypies in normal human infants. *Animal Behavior, 27*, 699–715.

Thelen, E. (1981). Rhythmical behavior in infancy: An ethological perspective. *Developmental Psychology, 17*, 237–257.

Thelen, E. (1995). Motor development: A new synthesis. *American Psychologist, 50*, 79–95.

Thelen, E., & Fisher, D. M. (1982). Newborn stepping: An explanation for a "disappearing reflex." *Developmental Psychology, 18*, 760–770.

Thelen, E., Fisher, D. M., & Ridley-Johnson, R. (1984). The relationship between physical growth and a newborn reflex. *Infant Behavior and Development, 7*, 479–493.

Thelen, E., & Smith, L. B. (1994). *A dynamic systems approach to the development of cognition and action.* Cambridge, MA: MIT Press.

Thelen, E., & Smith, L. B. (2006). Dynamic systems theories. In W. Damon & R. M. Lerner (Gen. Eds.), *Handbook of child psychology* (6th ed.). In R. M. Lerner (Vol. Ed.), Vol. 1: *Theoretical models of human development* (pp. 258–312). New York: Wiley.

Thierry, K. L., & Spence, M. J. (2002). Source-monitoring training facilitates preschoolers' eyewitness memory performance. *Developmental Psychology, 38*, 428–437.

Thomas, A., & Chess, S. (1977). *Temperament and development.* New York: Brunner/Mazel.

Thomas, A., Chess, S., & Birch, H. (1968). *Temperament and behavior disorders in children.* New York: New York University Press.

Thomas, J. R., & French, K. E. (1985). Gender differences across age in motor performance: A meta-analysis. *Psychological Bulletin, 98*, 260–282.

Thomas, L. (1975). *Lives of a cell: Notes of a biology watcher.* New York: Penguin.

Thomas, S. C., & Johnson, M. H. (2008). New advances in understanding sensitive periods in brain development. *Current Directions in Psychology Science, 17*, 1–5.

Thompson, R. A. (1987). Development of children's inferences of the emotions of others. *Developmental Psychology, 23*, 124–131.

Thompson, R. A. (1998). Early sociopersonality development. In W. Damon (Gen. Ed.), *Handbook of child psychology* (6th ed.). In N. Eisenberg (Vol. Ed.), Vol. 3: *Social, emotional and personality development* (pp. 23–104). New York: Wiley.

Thompson, R. A. (2006). The development of the person: Social understanding, relationships, conscience, self. In W. Damon & R. M. Lerner (Gen. Eds.), *Handbook of child psychology* (6th ed.). In N. Eisenberg (Vol. Ed.), Vol. 3: *Social, emotional, and personality development* (pp. 24–98). New York: Wiley.

Thompson, R., Easterbrooks, M. A., & Padilla-Walker, L. (2003). Social and emotional development in infancy. In R. Lerner, M. A. Easterbrooks, & J. Mistry (Eds.), *Handbook of psychology*, Vol. 6: *Developmental psychology* (pp. 91–112). New York: Wiley.

Tinbergen, N. (1963). On the aims and methods of ethology. *Zeitschrift fur Tierpsychologie, 20*, 410–433.

Tisak, M. S. (1986). Children's conceptions of parental authority. *Child Development, 57*, 166–176.

Tither, J. M., & Ellis, B. J. (2008). Impact of fathers on daughters' age at menarche: A genetically and environmentally controlled sibling study. *Developmental Psychology, 44*, 1409–1420.

Tolchinsky, L. (2003). *The cradle of culture and what children know about writing and numbers before being taught.* Mahwah, NJ: Erlbaum.

Tolchinsky-Landsmann, L., & Karmiloff-Smith, A. (1992). Children's understanding of notations as domains of knowledge versus referential-communicative tools. *Cognitive Development, 7*, 287–300.

Tolchinsky-Landsmann, L., & Levin, I. (1985). Writing in preschoolers: An age-related analysis. *Applied Psycholinguistics, 6*, 319–339.

Tomasello, M. (1999). *The cultural origins of human cognition.* Cambridge, MA: Harvard University Press.

Tomasello, M. (2000). Culture and cognitive development. *Current Directions in Psychological Science, 9*, 37–40.

Tomasello, M. (2005). *Constructing a language: A usage-based theory of language acquisition.* Cambridge, MA: Harvard University Press.

Tomasello, M. (2006). Acquiring linguistic constructions. In W. Damon (Gen. Ed.), *The handbook of child psychology* (6th ed.). In D. Kuhn & R. Siegler (Vol. Eds.), *Cognition, perception, and language* (pp. 255–298). New York: Wiley.

Tomasello, M. (2008). *Origins of human communication.* Cambridge, MA: MIT Press.

Tomasello, M. (2009). *Why we cooperate.* Cambridge, MA: MIT Press.

Tomasello, M., & Call, J. (1997). *Primate cognition.* New York: Oxford University Press.

Tomasello, M., Call, J., & Hare, B. (2005). Chimpanzees understand psychological states—the question is which ones and to what extent. *Trends in Cognitive Science, 7*, 153–156.

Tomasello, M., & Carpenter, M. (2005). The emergence of social cognition in three young chimpanzees. *Monographs of the Society for Research in Child Development, 70* (Serial No. 279).

Tomasello, M., & Carpenter, M. (2007). Shared intentionality. *Developmental Science, 10*, 121–125.

Tomasello, M., Carpenter, M., & Liszkowski, U. (2007). A new look at infant pointing. *Child Development, 78*, 705–722.

Tomasello, M., Carpenter, M., Call, J., Behne, T., & Moll, H. (2005). Understanding and sharing intentions: The origins of cultural cognition. *Behavioral and Brain Sciences, 28*, 675–692.

Tomasello, M., & Farrar, J. J. (1986). Joint attention and early language. *Child Development, 57*, 1454–1463.

Tomasello, M., & Herrmann, E. (2010). Ape and human cognition: What's the difference? *Current Directions in Psychological Science, 19*, 3–8.

Tomasello, M., Kruger, A. C., & Ratner, H. H. (1993). Cultural learning. *Behavioral and Brain Sciences, 16*, 495–511.

Tomasello, M., & Moll, H. (2010). The gap is social: Human shared intentionality and culture. In P. M. Kappler & J. B. Silk (Eds.), *Mind the gap: Tracing the origins of human universals* (pp. 331–350). New York: Springer.

Tomblin, J. B., Records, N. L., Buckwalter, P., Zhang, X., Smith, E., & O'Brien, M. (1997). Prevalence of specific language impairment in kindergarten children. *Journal of Speech and Hearing Research, 40*, 1245–1260.

Tomkins, S. S. (1962). Affect, imagery, consciousness, Vol. 1: *The positive emotions.* New York: Springer.

Tondel, G. M., & Candy, T. R. (2008). Accommodation and vergence latencies in human infants. *Vision Research, 48*, 564–576.

Tooby, J., & Cosmides, L. (1992). The psychological foundations of culture. In L. Cosmides, J. Tooby, & J. H. Barkow (Eds.), *The adapted mind* (pp. 19–136). New York: Oxford University Press.

Tooby, J., & Cosmides, L. (2005). Conceptual foundations of evolutionary psychology. In D. M. Buss (Ed.), *The handbook of evolutionary psychology* (pp. 5–67). Hoboken, NJ: Wiley.

Tooley, G. A., Karakis, M., Stokes, M., & Ozanne-Smith, J. (2006). Generalising the Cinderella effect to unintentional childhood fatalities. *Evolution and Human Behavior, 27*, 224–230.

Toth, S. L., Cicchetti, D., Macfie, J., Maughan, A., & VanMeehan, K. (2000). Narrative representations of caregivers and self in maltreated children. *Attachment and Human Development, 2*, 271–305.

Tottenham, N., Hare, T. A., Quinn, B. T., et al. (2010). Prolonged institutional rearing is associated with atypically large amygdala volume and difficulties in emotional regulation. *Developmental Science, 13*, 46–61.

Trainor, L. J. (1996). Infant preferences for infant-directed versus noninfant-directed playsongs and lullabies. *Infant Behavior and Development, 19*, 83–92.

Trainor, L. J., Austin, C. M., & Desjardins, R. N. (2000). Is infant-directed speech prosody a result of the vocal expression of emotion? *Psychological Science, 11*, 188–195.

Trainor, L. J., & Heinmiller, B. M. (1998). The development of evaluative responses to music: Infants prefer to listen to consonance over dissonance. *Infant Behavior and Development, 21*, 77–88.

Trautner, H. M., Ruble, D. N., Cyphers, L., Kirsten, B., Behrendt, R., & Hartmann, P. (2005). Rigidity and flexibility of gender stereotypes in children: Developmental or differential? *Infant and Child Development, 14*, 365–380.

Treffert, D. A. (1989). *Extraordinary people: Understanding "idiot savants."* New York: Harper & Row.

Treffert, D. A., & Christensen, D. D. (2005). Inside the mind of a savant. *Scientific American, 293* (6). Accessed at: http://www.scientificamerican.com/article.cfm?id=inside-the-mind-of-a-sava. (Downloaded June 3, 2010).

Trehub, S. E. (2003). The developmental origins of musicality. *Nature Neuroscience, 6*, 669–673.

Trehub, S. E., & Nakata, T. (2001–2002). Emotion and music in infancy. *Musicae Scientiae* (special issue), 37–61.

Trehub, S. E., & Schellenberg, E. G. (1995). Music: Its relevance to infants. *Annals of Child Development, 11*, 1–24.

Trehub, S. E., Trainor, L. J., & Unyk, A. M. (1993). Music and speech processing in the first year of life. In H. W. Reese (Ed.), *Advances in child development and behavior* (Vol. 24). San Diego: Academic.

Tremblay, R. E., Pohl, R. O., Vitaro, R., & Dobkin, P. L. (1994). Predicting early onset of male antisocial behavior from preschool behavior. *Archives of General Psychiatry, 51*, 732–739.

Trevarthen, C. (1984). Emotions in infancy. In K. R. Scherer & P. Ekman (Eds.), *Approaches to emotions* (pp. 129–157). London: Erlbaum.

Trevarthen, C. (1993). The functions of emotions in early infancy communication and development. In L. Camaioni, & J. Nadel (Eds.), *New perspectives in early communicative development* (pp. 48–81). London: Routledge.

Trevathan, W. R. (2005). The birth process. In B. Hopkins (Ed.), *The Cambridge encyclopedia of child development* (pp. 183–187). New York: Cambridge University Press.

Trickett, P. K., & Kuczynski, L. (1986). Children's misbehavior and parental discipline strategies in abusive and nonabusive families. *Developmental Psychology, 22*, 115–123.

Trieman, R., Cohen, J., Mulqueeny, K., Kessler, B., & Schechtman, S. (2007). Young children's knowledge about printed names. *Child Development, 78*, 1458–1471.

Trionfi, G., & Reese, E. (2009). A good story: Children with imaginary companions create richer narratives. *Child Development, 80*, 1301–1313.

Trivers, R. L. (1971). The evolution of reciprocal altruism. *Quarterly Review of Biology, 46*, 35–57.

Trivers, R. (1972). Parental investment and sexual selection. In B. Campbell (Ed.), *Sexual selection and the descent of man* (pp. 136–179). New York: Aldine de Gruyter.

Trivers, R. L. (1974). Parent-offspring conflict. *American Zoologist, 14*, 249–264.

Tronick, E. Z. (1989). Emotions and emotional communication in infants. *American Psychologist, 44*, 112–119.

Tronick, E. Z., Messinger, D. S., Weinberg, M. K., et al. (2005). Cocaine exposure is associated with subtle compromises of infants' and mothers' social-emotional behavior and dyadic features of their interaction in the face-to-face still-face paradigm. *Developmental Psychology, 41*, 711–722.

Tronick, E. Z., Thomas, R. B., & Daltabuit, M. (1994). The Quechua manta pouch: A caretaking practice for buffering the Peruvian infant against the multiple stressors of high altitude. *Child Development, 65*, 1005–1013.

Troseth, G. L. (2003). TV guide: Two-year-old children learn to use video as a source of information. *Developmental Psychology, 39*, 140–150.

Trzesniewski, K. H., Donnellan, M. B., & Robins, R. W. (2003). Stability of self-esteem across the lifespan. *Journal of Personality and Social Psychology, 84*, 205–220.

Trzesniewski, K. H., Donnellan, M. B., & Robins, R. W. (2008). Do today's young people really think they are so extraordinary? An examination of secular trends in narcissism and self-enhancement. *Psychological Science, 19*, 181–188.

Tsai, A., Loftus, E., & Polage, D. (2000). Current directions in false-memory research. In D. F. Bjorklund (Ed.), *False-memory creation in children and adults: Theory, research, and implications* (pp. 31–44). Mahwah, NJ: Erlbaum.

Tsao, F.-M., Lui, H.-M., & Kuhl, P. K. (2004). Speech perception in infancy predicts language development in the second year of life: A longitudinal study. *Child Development, 75*, 1067–1084.

Tudge, J. R. H., Hogan, D. M., Snezhkova, I. A., Kulakova, N. N., & Eta, K. E. (2000). Parents' child-rearing values and beliefs in the United States and Russia: The impact of culture and social class. *Infant and Child Development, 9*, 105–121.

Tulkin, S. R., & Konner, M. J. (1973). Alternative conceptions of intellectual functioning. *Human Development, 16*, 33–52.

Tulving, E. (1985). Memory and consciousness. *Canadian Psychology, 26*, 1–12.

Tulving, E. (2005). Episodic memory and autonoesis: Uniquely human? In H. S. Terrace & J. Metcalfe (Eds.), *The missing link in cognition: Origins of self-reflective consciousness* (pp. 3–56). New York: Oxford University Press.

Turati, C. (2004). Why faces are not special to newborns: An alternative account of the face preference. *Current Directions in Psychological Science, 13*, 5–8.

Turati, C., Macchi Cassia, V., Simion, F., & Leo, I. (2006). Newborns' face recognition: Role of the inner and outer facial features. *Child Development, 77*, 297–311.

Turiel, E. (2006). The development of morality. In W. Damon & R. M. Lerner (Gen. Eds.), *Handbook of child psychology* (6th ed.). In N. Eisenberg (Vol. Ed.), Vol. 3: *Social, emotional, and personality development* (pp. 789–857). New York: Wiley.

Turkewitz, G., & Kenny, P. (1982). Limitations on input as a basis for neural organization and perceptual development: A preliminary theoretical statement. *Developmental Psychobiology, 15*, 357–368.

Turkheimer, E., & Waldron, M. (2000). Nonshared environment: A theoretical, methodological, and quantitative review. *Psychological Bulletin, 126*, 78–108.

Turkheimer, E., Haley, A., Waldron, M., D'Onofrio, B., & Gottesman, I. I. (2003). Sociometric status modifies heritability of IQ in young children. *Psychological Science, 14*, 623–628.

Turnbull, M., Hart, D., & Lapkin, S. (2003). Grade 6 French immersion students' performance on large-scale literacy and mathematics: Exploring two hypotheses. *Alberta Journal of Educational Research, 49*, 6–23.

Turner, C. F., Ku, L., Rogers, S. M., Lindberg, L. D., Pleck, J. H., & Sonenstein, F. L. (1998). Adolescent sexual behavior, drug use, and violence: Increased reporting with computer survey technology. *Science, 280*, 867–873.

Twenge, J. M. (2006). *Generation Me: Why today's young Americans are more confident, assertive, entitled—and more miserable than ever before.* New York: Free Press.

Twenge, J. M., & Campbell, W. K. (2001). Age and birth cohort differences in self-esteem: A cross-temporal meta-analysis. *Personality and Social Psychology Review, 5*, 321–344.

Twenge, J. M., & Crocker, J. (2002). Race and self-esteem: Meta-analyses comparing Whites, Blacks, Hispanics, Asians, and American Indians and comment on Gray-Little and Hafdahl (2000). *Psychological Bulletin, 128*, 371–408.

U.S. Census Bureau. (2006). *Language spoken at home.* Accessed at: http://factfinder.census.gov/servlet/STTable?_bm=y&-geo_id=01000US&-qr_name=ACS_2006_EST_G00_S1601&-ds_name=ACS_2006_EST_G00_ (Downloaded February 3, 2009).

U.S. Department of Health and Human Services. (2006). Accessed at: http://www.surgeongeneral.gov/news/speeches/06272006a.html (Downloaded January 24, 2008).

U.S. Census Bureau. (2006). *Families and Living Arrangements: 2006.* Accessed at: http://www.census.gov/population/www/socdemo/hh-fam.html (Downloaded December 1, 2008).

Ulijaszek, F. J., Johnson, F. E., & Preece, M. A. (1998). *Human growth and development.* Cambridge, UK: Cambridge University Press.

Ulijaszek, S. J., Johnston, F. E., & Preece, M. A. (Eds.). (1998). *The Cambridge encyclopedia of human growth and development.* Cambridge, UK: Cambridge University Press.

Umiltà, M. A., Kohler, E., Gallese, V., Fogassi, L., Fadiga, L. et al. (2001). "I know what you are doing": A neurophysiological study. *Neuron, 32*, 91–101.

Underhill, K., Montgomery, P., & Operario, D. (2007). Sexual abstinence only programmes to prevent HIV infection in high income countries: Systematic review. *British Medical Journal, 335*, 245 (4 August, online edition).

Underwood, M. (2002). Sticks and stones and social exclusion: Aggression among boys and girls. In P. K. Smith & C. H. Hart (Eds.), *Blackwell handbook of childhood social development* (pp. 533–548). Oxford, UK: Blackwell.

Ungerer, J. A., Zelazo, P. R., Kearsley, R. B., & O'Leary, K. (1981). Developmental changes in the representation of objects in symbolic play from 18 to 34 months of age. *Child Development, 52*, 186–195.

United Nations. (2006). AIDS Epidemic Update: December 2006. Accessed at: http://www.unaids.org/en/KnowledgeCentre/HIVData/EpiUpdate/EpiUpdArchive/2006/Default.asp (Downloaded January 29, 2009).

United Nations. (1985). *Socio-economic differentials in child mortality in developing countries.* New York: Author.

Uzgiris, I. C. (1983). Organization of sensorimotor intelligence. In M. Lewis (Ed.), *Origins of intelligence: Infancy and early childhood* (2nd ed.). New York: Plenum.

Uzgiris, I. C., & Hunt, J. McV. (1975). *Assessment in infancy: Ordinal scales of psychological development.* Urbana: University of Illinois Press.

Vaish, A., & Striano, T. (2004). Is visual reference necessary? Contribution of facial versus vocal cues in 12-month-olds' social referencing behavior. *Developmental Science, 7*, 261–269.

Vaish, A., Grossman, T., & Woodward, A. (2008). Not all emotions are created equal: The negativity bias in social-emotional development. *Psychological Bulletin, 134*, 383–403.

Valentine, G., & Holloway, S. L. (2002). Cyberkids? Exploring children's identities and social networks in on-line and off-line worlds. *Annals of the Association of American Geographers, 82*, 302–319.

Valentine, J. C., DuBois, D. L., & Cooper, H. (2004). The relation between self-beliefs and academic achievement: A systematic review. *Educational Psychologist, 39*, 111–133.

Valkenburg, P. M., & Peter, J. (2009). Social consequences of the internet for adolescents: A decade of research. *Current Directions in Psychological Science, 18*, 1–5.

Valkenburg, P. M., Schouten, A. P., & Jochen, P. (2005). Adolescents' identify experiments on the internet. *New Media & Society, 17*, 383–402.

Van den Eijnden, R. J. J. M., Meerkerk, G.-J., Vermulst, A. D., Spijkerman, R., & Engels, R. C. M. E. (2008). Online communication, compulsive Internet use, and psychosocial well-being among adolescents: A longitudinal study. *Developmental Psychology, 44*, 655–665.

Van Gelder, R. S., Dijkman, M. M. T. T., Hopkins, B., van Geijn, G. P., & Homeau-Long, D. C. (1989). Fetal head orientation preference at the gestational ages of 16 and 24 weeks. *Journal of Clinical and Experimental Neuropsychology, 11*, 364.

Van Gennep, A. (1960). *The rites of passage* (M. Vizedom & G. Caffe, Trans.). Chicago: University of Chicago Press (Original work published 1908).

Van Goozen, S. H. M., Fairchild, G., Snoek, H., & Harold, G. T. (2007). The evidence for a neurobiological model of childhood antisocial behavior. *Psychological Bulletin, 133*, 149–182.

van IJzendoorn, M. H., & De Wolff, M. S. (1997). In search of the absent father: Meta-analyses of infant-father attachment: A rejoinder to our discussants. *Child Development, 68*, 604–609.

van IJzendoorn, M. H., & Juffer, F. (2005). Adoption is a successful natural intervention enhancing adopted children's IQ and school performance. *Current Directions in Psychological Science, 14*, 326–330.

van IJzendoorn, M. H., & Kroonenberg, P. M. (1988). Cross-cultural patterns of attachment: A meta-analysis of the Strange Situation. *Child Development, 59*, 147–156.

van IJzendoorn, M. H., & Sagi, A. (1999). Cross-cultural patterns of attachment: Universal and contextual dimensions. In J. Cassidy & P. R. Shaver (Eds.), *Handbook of attachment: Theory, research, and clinical applications* (1st ed., pp. 713–734). New York: Guilford.

van IJzendoorn, M. H., & Sagi-Schwartz, A. (2008). Cross-cultural patterns of attachment: Universal and contextual dimensions. In P. R. Shaver & J. Cassidy (Eds.), *Handbook of Attachment: Theory, research, and clinical application* (2nd ed., pp. 880–905). New York: Guilford.

van IJzendoorn, M. H., Schuengel, C., & Bakermans-Kranenburg, M. J. (1999). Disorganized attachment in early childhood: Meta-analysis of precursors, concomitants, and sequelae. *Development and Psychopathology, 11*, 225–249.

van Lier, P. A. C., Vitaro, F., Wanner, B., Vuijk, P., & Crijnen, A. M. (2005). Gender differences in developmental links among antisocial behavior, friends' antisocial behavior, and peer rejection in childhood: Results from two cultures. *Child Development, 76*, 841–855.

van Loosbroek, E., & Smitsman, A. W. (1990). Visual perception of numerosity in infancy. *Developmental Psychology, 26*, 916–922.

van Shaik, C. P., Fox, E., & Sitompul, A. (1996). Manufacture and use of tools in wild Sumatran orangutans. *Naturwissenschaften, 83*, 186–188.

Vance, M. L., Mauras, N., & Wood, A. (1999). Growth hormone therapy in children and adults. *New England Journal of Medicine, 341*, 1206–1216.

Van Valin, R. D. (2002). The development of subject-auxiliary inversion in English wh-questions: An alternative analysis. *Journal of Child Language, 29*, 161–175.

Varnum, M. E., Grossmann, I., Kitayama, S., & Nisbett, R. E. (2010). The origin of cultural differences in cognition: The social orientation hypothesis. *Current Directions in Psychological Science, 19*, 9–13.

Vasilyeva, M., Duffy, S., & Huttenlocher, J. (2007). Developmental changes in the use of absolute and relative information: The case of spatial extent. *Journal of Cognition and Development, 8,* 455–471.

Vaughn, B. E., Block, J. H., & Block, J. (1988). Parental agreement on child rearing during early childhood and the psychological characteristics of adolescents. *Child Development, 59,* 1020–1033.

Vaughn, B. E., & Santos, A. J. (2009). Structural descriptions of social transactions among young children: Affiliation and dominance in preschool groups. In K. H. Rubin, W. M. Bukowski, & B. Laursen (Eds.), *Handbook of peer interactions, relationships, and groups* (pp. 195–214). New York: Guilford.

Veenstra, R., Lindenberg, S., Zijlstra, B. J. H., De Winter, A. F., Verhulst, F. C., & Ormel, H. (2007). The dyadic nature of bullying and victimization: Testing a dual-perspective theory. *Child Development, 78,* 1843–1854.

Verbeek, P., & de Waal, F. B. M. (2001). Peacemaking among preschool children. *Peace and Conflict: Journal of Peace Psychology, 7,* 5–28.

Vereijken, B. (2005). Motor development. In B. Hopkins (Ed.), *The Cambridge encyclopedia of child development* (pp. 217–226). New York: Cambridge University Press.

Vigil, J. M., Geary, D. C., & Byrd-Craven, J. (2005). A life history assessment of early childhood sexual abuse in women. *Developmental Psychology, 41,* 553–561.

Vihman, M. M. (1988). Later phonological development. In J. Bernthal & N. Bambson (Eds.), *Articulation and phonological disorders* (2nd ed., pp. 110–144). New York: Prentice-Hall.

Vihman, M. M. (1996). *Phonological development: The origins of language in the child.* Oxford: Basil Blackwell.

Vinter, A. (1986). The role of movement in eliciting early imitations. *Child Development, 57,* 66–71.

Visalberghi, E., & Limongelli, L. (1996). Acting and understanding: Tool use revisited through the minds of capuchin monkeys. In A. Russon, K. Bard, & S. T. Parker (Eds.), *Reaching into thought: The minds of the great apes* (pp. 57–79). Cambridge, UK: Cambridge University Press.

Visintine, A. M., Nahmias, A. J., & Josey, W. E. (1978). Genital herpes. *Perinatal Care, 2,* 32–41.

Volbert, R. (2000). Sexual knowledge of preschool children. *Journal of Psychology and Human Sexuality, 12,* 22–48.

Volk, T., & Atkinson, J. (2008). Is child death the crucible of human evolution? *Journal of Social, Cultural, and Evolutionary Psychology, 2,* 247–260.

Volk, A. A., Lukjanczuk, J. L., & Quinsey, V. L. (2007). Perceptions of child facial cues as a function of child age. *Evolutionary Psychology,* www.epjournal.net, 5, 801–814.

Volk, A. A., & Quinsey, V. L. (2007). Parental investment and resemblance: Replications, Refinements, and revisions. *Evolutionary Psychology,* www.epjournal.net, 5, 1–14.

Volkow, N. (April 2007). *Drug addiction: A brain developmental disorder 2—Adolescence-typical alcohol sensitivities and intake.* Invited address presented at meeting of the Society for Research in Child Development, Boston, Massachusetts.

Volling, B. L., McElwain, N. L., & Miller, A. L. (2002). Emotion regulation in context: The jealousy complex between young siblings and its relations with child and family characteristics. *Child Development, 73,* 581–600.

Volpe, E. P. (1971). *Human heredity and birth defects.* Indianapolis: Bobbs-Merrill.

Von der Lippe, A. L. (1999). The impact of maternal schooling and occupation on child-rearing attitudes and behaviours in low income neighborhoods in Cairo, Egypt. *International Journal of Behavioral Development, 23,* 703–729.

von Hofsten, C. (2005). Prehension. In B. Hopkins (Ed.), *The Cambridge encyclopedia of child development* (pp. 348–351). New York: Cambridge University Press.

von Kraft-Ebbing, R. (1965/1886). *Psychopathia sexualis* (Franklin S. Klaf, Trans.). New York: Stein & Day. (Original work published 1886.)

Vorhees, C. V., & Mollnow, E. (1987). Behavioral teratogenesis: Long-term influences on behavior from early exposure to environmental agents. In J. D. Osofsky (Ed.), *Handbook of infant development* (2nd ed., pp. 913–971). New York: Wiley.

Vosniadou, S., & Brewer, W. F. (1992). Mental models of the earth: A study of conceptual change in childhood. *Cognitive Psychology, 24,* 535–585.

Votruba-Drzal, E., Coley, R. L., & Chase-Lansdale, P. L. (2004). Child care and low-income children's development: Direct and moderated effects. *Child Development, 75,* 296–312.

Vouloumanos, A., & Werker, J. F. (2007). Listening to language at birth: Evidence for a bias for speech in neonates. *Developmental Science, 10,* 159–171.

Vygotsky, L. S. (1962). *Thought and language.* Cambridge, MA: MIT Press.

Vygotsky, L. S. (1978). *Mind in Society: The development of higher psychological processes.* Cambridge, MA: Harvard University Press.

Vygotsky, L. S. (1981). The instrumental method in psychology. In J. V. Wertsch (Ed.), *The concept of activity in Soviet psychology* (pp. 134–143). Armonk, NY: Sharpe.

Wagner, R. K., Torgesen, J. K., Rashotte, C. A., Hecht, S. A., Barker, T. A., Burgess, S. R., Donahue, J., & Garon, T. (1997). Changing relations between phonological processing abilities and word-level reading as children develop from beginning to skilled readers: A 5-year longitudinal study. *Developmental Psychology, 33,* 468–479.

Wainright, J. L., & Patterson, C. J. (2008). Peer relations among adolescents with female same-sex parents. *Developmental Psychology, 44,* 117–126.

Wakschlag, L. S., Leventhal, B. L., Pine, D. S., Pickett, K. E., & Carter, A. S. (2006). Elucidating early mechanisms of developmental psychopathology: The case of prenatal smoking and disruptive behavior. *Child Development, 77,* 893–906.

Walhstrom, K. (2003). Later high-school start times still working. *The Education Digest, 68,* 49–53.

Walk, R. D., & Gibson, E. J. (1961). A comparative and analytical study of visual depth perception. *Psychological Monographs, 75* (No. 519).

Walker-Andrews, A. S. (1997). Infants' perception of expressive behaviors: Differentiation of multimodal information. *Psychological Bulletin, 121,* 437–456.

Walker, L. J. (1986). Sex differences in the development of moral reasoning: A rejoinder to Baumrind. *Child Development, 57,* 522–526.

Walker, L. J. (1991). Sex differences in moral reasoning. In W. M. Kurtines & J. L. Gewirtz (Eds.), *Handbook of moral behavior and development,* Vol. 2: *Research* (pp. 333–364). Hillsdale, NJ: Erlbaum.

Wallerstein, J. S., Corbin, S. B., & Lewis, J. M. (1988). Children of divorce: A ten-year study. In E. M. Hetherington & J. Arastem (Eds.), *Impact of divorce, single-parenting and stepparenting on children.* Hillsdale, NJ: Erlbaum.

Walton, G. E., Bower, N. J. A., & Bower, T. G. R. (1992). Recognition of familiar faces by newborns. *Infant Behavior and Development, 15,* 265–269.

Wang, S., Kaufman, L., & Baillargeon, R. (2003). Should all stationary objects move when hit? Developments in infants' causal and statistical expectations about collision events. *Infant Behavior & Development, 26,* 529–567.

Wang, Q. (2001). Culture effects on adults' earliest childhood recollection and self-description: Implications for the relation between memory and the self. *Journal of Personality and Social Psychology, 81,* 220–233.

Wang, Q. (2006), Earliest recollections of self and others in European American and Taiwanese young adults. *Psychological Science, 17,* 708–714.

Wang, Q., Leichtman, M. D., & Davies, K. I. (2000). Sharing memories and telling stories: American and Chinese mothers and their 3-year-olds. *Memory, 8,* 159–177.

Ward, L. M. (2003). Understanding the role of entertainment media in the sexual socialization of American youth: A review of empirical research. *Developmental Review, 23,* 347–388.

Warneken, F., & Tomasello, M. (2006). Altruistic helping in human infants and young chimpanzees. *Science, 311,* 1301–1303.

Warneken, F., & Tomasello, M. (2008). Extrinsic rewards undermine altruistic tendencies in 20-month-olds. *Developmental Psychology, 44,* 1785–1788.

Warren, A. R., & McCloskey, L. A. (1997). Language in social contexts. In J. Berko Gleason (Ed.), *The development of language* (4th ed.). Boston, MA: Allyn & Bacon.

Warren, A. R., & Tate, C. S. (1992). Egocentrism in children's telephone conversations: Recent evidence regarding Piaget's position. In R. Diaz & L. Berk (Eds.), *From social interaction to self-regulation.* Hillsdale, NJ: Erlbaum.

Warren, M. P., & Brooks-Gunn, J. (1989). Delayed menarche in athletes: The role of low energy intake and eating disorders and their relation to bone density. In C. Laron & A. D. Rogol (Eds.), *Hormones and sport* (Vol. 55, pp. 41–54). Serono Symposia Publications, Raven Press.

Wartella, E., Richert, R. A., & Robb, M. B. (2010). Babies, television and videos: How did we get here? *Developmental Review, 30,* 116–127.

Wartenburger, I., Heekereb, H. R., Abutalebi, J., Cappa, S. F., Villringer, A., & Perani, D. (2003). Early setting of grammatical processing in the bilingual brain. *Neuron, 37,* 159–170.

Wason, P., & Johnson-Laird, P. (1972). *Psychology of reasoning: Structure and content.* Cambridge, MA: Harvard University Press.

Watamura, S. E., Donzella, B., Alwin, J., & Gunnar, M. R. (2003). Morning-to-afternoon increases in cortisol concentrations for infants and toddlers at child care: Age differences and behavioral correlates. *Child Development, 74,* 1006–1020.

Waterman, A. S. (1982). Identity development from adolescence to adulthood: An extension of theory and a review of research. *Developmental Psychology, 18,* 341–358.

Waterman, A. S. (1999). Identity, the identity statuses, and identity status development: A contemporary statement. *Developmental Review, 19,* 591–621.

Waters, E., & Deane, K. E. (1985). Defining and assessing individual differences in attachment relationships: Q-methodology and the organization of behavior in infancy and early childhood. In I. Bretherton & E. Waters (Eds.), Growing points of attachment theory and research, *Monographs of the Society for Research in Child Development, 50* (Serial No. 209), 41–65.

Waters, E., Weinfield, N. S., & Hamilton, C. E. (2000). The stability of attachment security from infancy to adolescence to early adulthood: General discussion. *Child Development, 71,* 703–706.

Wechsler, D. (2003). *Wechsler Intelligence Scale for Children* (4th ed., WISC-IV). Toronto, Ontario: The Psychological Corporation.

Weekes-Shackelford, V. A., & Shackelford, T. K. (2004). Methods of filicide: Stepparents and genetic parents kill differently. *Violence and Victims, 19,* 75–81.

Weese-Mayer, D. E., Ackerman, M. J., Marazita, M. L., & Berry-Kravis, E. M. (2007). Sudden Infant Death Syndrome: Review of implicated genetic factors. *American Journal of Medical Genetics (Part A), 143A,* 771–788.

Weikum, W. M., Vouloumanos, A., Navarra, J., Soto-Faraco, S., Sebastián-Gallés, N., &. Werker, J. F. (2007). Visual language discrimination in infancy. *Science* (25 May 2007), *316,* 1159.

Weinberg, R. A., Scarr, S., & Waldman, I. D. (1992). The Minnesota Transracial Adoption Study: A follow-up of IQ test performance at adolescence. *Intelligence, 16,* 117–135.

Weinert, F. E., & Schneider, W. (Eds.) (1999). *Individual development from three to twelve: Findings from the Munich Longitudinal Study.* Cambridge, UK: Cambridge University Press.

Weinraub, M., & Wolf, B. (1983). Effects of stress and social supports on mother-child interactions in single and two-parent families. *Child Development, 54,* 1297–1311.

Weinraub, M., & Wolf, B. (1987). Stressful life events, social supports, and parent-child interactions: Similarities and differences in single-parent and two-parent families. In Z. Boukydis (Ed.), *Research on support for parents and infants in the postnatal period* (pp. 114–135). Norwood, NJ: Ablex.

Weinraub, M., Horvath, D. L., & Gringlas, M. B. (2002). Single parenthood. In M. H. Bornstein (Ed.), *Handbook of parenting* (2nd ed.), Vol. 3: *Being and becoming a parent* (pp. 109–140). Mahwah, NJ: Erlbaum.

Weinstock, H., Berman, S., & Cates, Jr., W. (2004). Sexually transmitted diseases among American youth: Incidence and prevalence estimates, 2000. *Perspectives on Sexual and Reproductive Health, 36,* 6–10.

Weisfeld, G., Bloch, S. A., & Ivers, J. W. (1984). Possible determinants of social dominance among adolescent girls. *Journal of Genetic Psychology, 144,* 115–129.

Weisfeld, G. E., Czilli, T., Phillips, K. A., Gal, J. A., & Lichtman, C. M. (2003). Possible olfaction-based mechanisms in human kin recognition and inbreeding avoidance. *Journal of Experimental Child Psychology, 85,* 279–295.

Weisfeld, G. E., & Janisee, H. C. (2005). Some functional aspects of human adolescence. In B. J. Ellis & D. F. Bjorklund (Eds.), *Origins of the social mind: Evolutionary psychology and child development* (pp. 189–218). New York: Guilford.

Welch, M. K. (1999). Preschoolers' understanding of mind: Implications for suggestibility. *Cognitive Development, 14,* 101–131.

Welch-Ross, M. K. (1995). An integrative model of the development of autobiographical memory. *Developmental Review, 15,* 338–365.

Wellman, H. M. (1990). *The child's theory of mind.* Cambridge, MA: MIT Press.

Wellman, H. M., Cross, D., & Watson, J. (2001). Meta-analysis of theory-of-mind development: The truth about false belief. *Child Development, 72,* 655–684.

Wellman, H. M., Fang, F., Liu, D., Zhu, L., & Liu, G. (2006). Scaling theory-of-mind understanding in Chinese children. *Psychological Science, 17,* 1075–1081.

Wenner, J. A., Burch, M. M., Lynch, J. S., & Baer, P. J. (2008). Becoming a teller of tales: Associations between children's fictional narratives and parent-child reminiscence narratives. *Journal of Experimental Child Psychology, 101,* 1–19.

Wentzel, K. R., Barry, C. M., & Caldwell, K. (2004). Friendships in middle school: Influences on motivation and school adjustment. *Journal of Educational Psychology, 96,* 195–203.

Wertsch, J. V., & Tulviste, P. (1992). L. S. Vygotsky and contemporary developmental psychology. *Developmental Psychology, 28,* 548–557.

West, T. A., & Bauer, P. J. (1999). Assumptions of infantile amnesia: Are there differences between early and later memories? *Memory, 7,* 257–278.

Westermark, E. A. (1891). *The history of human marriage.* New York: Macmillan.

Wetherby, A., Woods, J., Allen, L., Cleary, J., Dickinson, H., & Lord, C. (2004). Early indicators of autism spectrum disorders in the second year of life. *Journal of Autism and Developmental Disorders, 34,* 473–493.

Wheldall, K., & Joseph, R. (1986). Young black children's sentence comprehension skills: A comparison of performance in standard English and Jamaican Creole. *First Language, 6,* 149–154.

White, S. H. (2000). Conceptual foundations of IQ testing. *Psychology, Public Policy, and Law, 6,* 33–43.

White, S., Milne, E., Rosen, S., Hansen, P., Swettenham, J., Frith, U., & Ramus, F. (2006). The role of sensorimotor impairments in dyslexia: A multiple case study of dyslexic children. *Developmental Science, 9,* 237–269.

Whitehurst, G. J., & Lonigan, C. J. (1998). Child development and emergent literacy. *Child Development, 69,* 848–872.

Whiten, A. (2010). Ape behavior and the origins of human culture. In P. M. Kappler & J. B. Silk (Eds.), *Mind the gap: Tracing the origins of human universals* (pp. 429–450). New York: Springer.

Whiten, A., Custance, D. M., Gómez, J. C., Teixidor, P., & Bard, K. A. (1996). Imitative learning of artificial fruit processing in children (*Homo sapiens*) and chimpanzees (*Pan troglodytes*). *Journal of Comparative Psychology, 110,* 3–14.

Whiten, A., Goodall, J., McGrew, W. C., Nishida, T., Reynolds, V., Sugiyama, Y. et al. (1999). Cultures in chimpanzees. *Nature, 399,* 682–685.

Whitham, J. C., Gerald, M. S., Santiago, C., & Maestripieri, D. (2007). Intended receivers and functional significance of grunt and girney vocalizations in free-ranging female rhesus macaques. *Ethology, 113,* 862–874.

Whiting, B. B. (1974). Folk wisdom and child rearing. *Merrill-Palmer Quarterly, 20,* 9–19.

Whiting, B. B., & Whiting, J. W. (1975). *Children of six cultures: A psycho-cultural analysis.* Cambridge, MA: Harvard University Press.

Wichström, L. (2001). The impact of pubertal timing on adolescents' alcohol use. *Journal of Research on Adolescence, 11,* 131–150.

Widaman, K. F. (2009). Phenylketonuria in children and mothers. *Current Directions in Psychological Science, 18,* 48–52.

Wiebe, S. A., Espy, K. A., & Charak, D. (2008). Using confirmatory factor analysis to understand executive control in preschool children: I. Latent structure. *Developmental Psychology, 44,* 575–587.

Wilcock, A., Kobayashi, L., & Murray, I. (1997). Twenty-five years of obstetric patient satisfaction in North America: A review of the literature. *Journal of Pediatric and Neonatal Nursing, 10,* 36–47.

Willatts, P. (1990). Development of problem-solving strategies in infancy. In D. F. Bjorklund (Ed.), *Children's strategies: Contemporary views of cognitive development*. Hillsdale, NJ: Erlbaum.

Williams Syndrome Association. (2007). www.williams-syndrome.org.

Williams, H. G. (1983). *Perceptual and motor development*. Englewood Cliffs, NJ: Prentice-Hall.

Williams, J. H., Whiten, A., Suddendorf, T., and Perrett, D. I. (2001). Imitation, mirror neurons and autism. *Neuroscience & Biobehavioral Review, 25*, 287–295.

Williams, M. R. (1989). *Neighborhood organizing for urban school reform*. New York: Teachers College Press.

Willis, B. M., & Levy, B. S. (2002). Child prostitution: Global health burden, research needs, and interventions. *The Lancet, 359*, 1417–1421.

Willoughby, T. (2008). A short-term longitudinal study of Internet and computer game use by adolescent boys and girls: Prevalence, frequency of use, and psychosocial factors. *Developmental Psychology, 44*, 195–204.

Wilson, B. (1997). Types of child art and alternative developmental accounts: Interpreting the interpreters. *Human Development, 40*, 155–168.

Wilson, B., & Wilson, M. (1981). The case of the disappearing two-eyed profile: Or how little children influence the drawings of little children. *Review of Research in Visual Arts Education, 15*, 1–18.

Wilson, B., & Wilson, M. (1987). Pictorial composition and narrative structure: Themes and the creation of meaning in the drawings of Egyptian and Japanese children. *Visual Arts Research, 13*, 10–21.

Wilson, D. S. (2007). *Evolution for everyone: How Darwin's theory can change the way we think about our lives*. New York: Delta.

Wilson, E. O. (1984). *Biophilia*. Cambridge, MA: Harvard University Press.

Wimmer, H., & Perner, J. (1983). Beliefs about beliefs: Representation and constraining function of wrong beliefs in young children's understanding of deception. *Cognition, 13*, 103–128.

Wimmer, M., & Howe, M. (2010). Are children's memory illusions created differently than adults'? Evidence from levels-of-processing and divided attention paradigms. *Journal of Experimental Child Psychology*.

Wingfield, J. C. (1994). Hormone-behavior interactions and mating systems in male and female birds. In R. V. Sort and E. Balaban (Eds.), *The difference between the sexes*. New York: Cambridge University Press.

Winner, E. (2006). Development in the arts: Music and drawing. In W. Damon (Ed.), *Handbook of child psychology* (6th ed.). In R. Siegler & D. Kuhn (Vol. Eds.), Vol. 2: *Cognitive language and perceptual development* (pp. 859–904). New York: Wiley.

Winner, E., Blank, P., Massey, C., & Gardner, H. (1983). Children's sensitivity to aesthetic properties of line drawings. In D. Rogers & J. A. Sloboda (Eds.), *The acquisition of symbolic skills*. London: Plenum Press.

Winsler, A. (2003). Overt and covert verbal problem-solving strategies: Developmental trends in use, awareness, and relations with task performance in children age 5 to 17. *Child Development, 74*, 659–678.

Winsler, A. (2009). Still talking to ourselves after all these years: A review of current research on private speech. In A. Winsler, C. Fernyhough, & I. Montero (Eds.). (2009). *Private speech, executive functioning, and the development of verbal self-regulation* (pp. 3–41). Cambridge, UK: Cambridge University Press.

Winsler, A., Fernyhough, C., Montero, I. (Eds.). (2009). *Private speech, executive functioning, and the development of verbal self-regulation*. Cambridge, UK: Cambridge University Press.

Winsler, A., & Naglieri, J. (2003). Overt and covert verbal problem-solving strategies: Developmental trends in use, awareness, and the relations with task performance in children aged 5 to 17. *Child Development, 74*, 659–678.

Wiseman, P. (June 19, 2002). China thrown off balance as boys outnumber girls. USA Today. Accessed at: http://www.usatoday.com/news/world/2002/06/19/china-usat.htm. (Downloaded June 3, 2010).

Witelson, S. F. (1987). Neurobiological aspects of language in children. *Child Development, 58*, 653–688.

Wolf, A. (1995). *Sexual attraction and childhood association: A Chinese brief for Edward Westermark*. Stanford, CA: Stanford University Press.

Wolf, D., & Perry, M. D. (1988). From endpoints to repertories: Some new conclusions about drawing development. *Journal of Aesthetic Education, 22*, 17–34.

Wolff, P. H. (1966). The causes, controls and organization of behavior in the neonate. *Psychological Issues, 5* (1, Serial No. 17).

Wolff, P. H. (1969). The natural history of crying and other vocalizations in early infancy. In B. M. Foss (Ed.), *Determinants of infant behavior, IV* (pp. 81–115). London: Methuen.

Wolff, P. H. (1987). *The development of behavioral states and the expression of emotions in early infancy*. Chicago: University of Chicago Press.

Wolff, P. H. (2005). Sleep and wakefulness. In B. Hopkins (Ed.), *The Cambridge encyclopedia of child development* (pp. 378–382). New York: Cambridge University Press.

Wolfinger, N. H. (2001). Transmission of divorce: Do people replicate the patterns of marital instability they grew up with? *Journal of Family Issues, 21*, 1061–1086.

Wolfson, A., & Carskadon, M. (1998). Sleep schedules and daytime functioning in adolescents. *Child Development, 69*, 875–887.

Wong, I. C. K., Murray, M. L., & Camilleri-Novak, D., & Stephens, P. (2004). Increased prescribing trends of paediatric psychotropic medications. *Archives of Disease in Child, 89*, 1131–1132.

Wood, B. A. (1994). The oldest hominid yet. *Nature, 317*, 280–281.

Wood, D., Bruner, J. S., & Ross, G. (1976). The role of tutoring in problem-solving. *Journal of Child Psychology and Psychiatry, 17*, 89–100.

Woods, S. (2004). Untreated recovery from eating disorder. *Adolescence, 39*, 361–371.

Woodward, A. L. (2009). Infants' grasp of others' intentions. *Current Directions in Psychological Science, 18*, 53–57.

Woody-Dorning, J., & Miller, P. H. (2001). Children's individual differences in capacity: Effects on strategy production and utilization. *British Journal of Developmental Psychology, 19*, 543–557.

Woolley, J. D. (1997). Thinking about fantasy: Are children fundamentally different thinkers and believers from adults? *Child Development, 68*, 991–1011.

Woolley, J. D., & Boerger, E. A. (2002). Development of beliefs about the origins of controllability of dreams. *Developmental Psychology, 38*, 24–41.

Woolley, J. D., Boerger, E. A., & Markman, A. B. (2004). A visit from the Candy Witch: Factors influencing young children's belief in a novel fantastical being. *Developmental Science, 7*, 456–468.

Woolley, J. D., & Cox, V. (2007). Development of belief about storybook reality. *Developmental Science, 10*, 681–693.

Woolley, J. D., & Wellman, H. M. (1992). Children's conceptions of dreams. *Cognitive Development, 7*, 365–380.

Wright, V. C., Chang, J., Jeng, G., Chen, M., & Macaluso, M. (2004). Assisted Reproductive Technology Surveillance—United States, 2004. *Morbidity and Mortality Weekly Report, 6* (SS06), 1–22.

Wright, V., Schieve, L. A., Vahratian, A., Reynolds, M. A. (2004). Monozygotic twinning associated with day 5 embryo transfer in pregnancies conceived after IVF. *Human Reproduction, 19*, 1831–1836.

Wynn, K. (1992). Addition and subtraction by human infants. *Nature, 358*, 749–750.

Wynne-Edwards, K. E., & Reburn, C. J. (2000). Behavioural endocrinology of mammalian fatherhood. *Trends in Ecology & Evolution, 15*, 464–468.

Yakovlev, P. I., & Lecours, A. R. (1967). The myelenogenetic cycles of regional maturation of the brain. In A. Minkowski (Ed.), *Regional development of the brain in early life*. Oxford, UK: Blackwell.

Yarrow, M. R., & Waxler, C. Z. (1976). Dimensions and correlates of prosocial behavior in young children. *Child Development, 47*, 118–125.

Yeates, K. O., & Taylor, G. H. (2005). Neurobehavioral outcomes of mild head injury in children and adolescents. *Pediatric Rehabilitation, 8*, 5–16.

Yoon, J. M. D., & Johnson, S. C. (2009). Biological motion displays elicit social behavior in 12-month-olds. *Child Development, 80*, 1069–75.

Youngblade, L. M., & Dunn, J. (1995). Individual differences in young children's pretend play with mother and sibling: Links to relationships and understanding of other people's feelings and beliefs. *Child Development, 66*, 1472–1492.

Yunger, J. L., Carver, P. R., & Perry, D. G. (2004). Does gender identity influence children's psychological well-being? *Developmental Psychology, 40*, 572–582.

Yussen, S. R., & Levy, V. M. (1975). Developmental changes in predicting one's own span of short-term memory. *Journal of Experimental Child Psychology, 19*, 502–508.

Zahn-Waxler, C., Duggal, S., & Gruber, R. (2002). Parental psychopathology. In M. H. Bornstein (Ed.), *Handbook of parenting* (2nd ed.), Vol. 4: *Social conditions and applied parenting* (pp. 295–328). Mahwah, NJ: Erlbaum.

Zahn-Waxler, C., Iannotto, R. J., Cummings, E. M., & Denham, S. (1990). Antecedents of problem behaviors in children of depressed mothers. *Development and Psychopathology, 2*, 271–291.

Zahn-Waxler, C., & Radke-Yarrow, M. (1982). The development of altruism: Alternative research strategies. In N. Eisenberg (Ed.), *The development of prosocial behavior* (pp. 109–137). New York: Springer-Verlag.

Zahn-Waxler, C., Radke-Yarrow, M., & King, R. M. (1979). Childrearing and children's prosocial initiations toward victims of distress. *Child Development, 50*, 319–330.

Zahn-Waxler, C., Radke-Yarrow, M., Wagner, E., & Chapman, M. (1992). Development of concern for others. *Developmental Psychology, 28*, 126–136.

Zajonc, R. B., & Marcus, G. B. (1975). Birth order and intellectual development. *Psychological Review, 82*, 74–88.

Zani, B. (1991). Male and female patterns in the discovery of sexuality during adolescence. *Journal of Adolescence, 14*, 163–178.

Zarbatany, L., McDougall, P., & Hymel, S. (2000). Gender-differentiated experience in the peer culture: Links to intimacy in preadolescence. *Social Development, 9*, 62–79.

Zebrowitz, L. A., Kendall-Tackett, K., & Fafel, J. (1991). The influence of children's facial maturity on parental expectations and punishments. *Journal of Experimental Child Psychology, 52*, 221–238.

Zelazo, P. D., Carlson, S. M., & Kesek, A. (2008). The development of executive function in childhood. In C. A. Nelson & M. Luciana (Eds.), *Handbook of cognitive developmental neuroscience* (2nd ed., pp. 553–574). Cambridge, MA: MIT Press.

Zelazo, P. D., Carter, A., Reznick, J. S., & Frye, D. (1997). Early development of executive function: A problem-solving framework. *Review of General Psychology, 1*, 198–226.

Zelazo, P. D., Frye, D., & Rapus, T. (1996). An age-related dissociation between knowing rules and using them. *Cognitive Development, 11*, 37–63.

Zelazo, P. D., Kearsley, R. B., & Stack, D. M. (1995). Mental representation for visual sequences: Increased speed of central processing from 22 to 32 months. *Intelligence, 20*, 41–63.

Zelazo, P. D., Müller, U., Frye, D., & Marcovitch, S. (2003). The development of executive function in early childhood. *Monographs of the Society for Research in Child Development, 68* (Serial No. 274).

Zelazo, P. D., Sommerville, J. A., & Nichols, S. (1999). Age-related changes in children's use of external representation. *Developmental Psychology, 35*, 1059–1071.

Zelazo, P. R., Zelazo, N. A., & Kolb, S. (1972). Walking in the newborn. *Science, 176*, 314–315.

Zentner, M. R., & Kagan, J. (1996). Perception of music by infants. *Nature, 383*, 29.

Zeskind, P. S., & Ramey, C. T. (1978). Fetal malnutrition: An experimental study of its consequences on infant development in two caregiver environments. *Child Development, 49*, 1155–1162.

Zeskind, P. S., & Ramey, C. T. (1981). Sequelae of fetal malnutrition: A longitudinal, transactional, and synergistic approach. *Child Development, 52*, 213–218.

Zhou, X., Huang, J., Wang, B., Zhao, Z., Yang, L., & Zhengzheng, Y. (2006). Parent-child interaction and children's number learning. *Early Child Development and Care, 176*, 763–775.

Ziegler, J. C., & Goswami, U. (2005). Reading acquisition, developmental dyslexia, and skilled reading across languages: A psycholinguistic grain size theory. *Psychological Bulletin, 131*, 3–29.

Ziegler, J. C., & Goswami, U. (2006). Becoming literate in different languages: Similar problems, different solutions. *Developmental Science, 9*, 429–453.

Ziegler, J. C., Pech-Georgel, C., George, F., Alario, F.-X., & Lorenzi, C. (2005). Deficits in speech perception predict language learning impairment. *Proceedings of the National Academy of Sciences (USA), 102*, 14110–14115.

Zimmer-Gembeck, M. J., & Helfand, M. (2008). Ten years of longitudinal research on I.S. adolescent sexual behavior: Developmental correlated of sexual intercourse, and the importance of age, gender, and ethnic background. *Developmental Science, 28*, 153–224.

Zimmer-Gembeck, M. J., Siebenbruner, J., & Collins, W. A. (2001). Diverse aspects of dating: Associations with psychosocial functioning from early to middle adolescence. *Journal of Adolescence, 24*, 313–336.

Zimmerman, F. J., & Christakis, D. A. (2007). Associations between content types of early media exposure and subsequent attentional problems. *Pediatrics, 120*, 986–992.

Zimmerman, F. J., Christakis, D. A., & Meltzoff, A. N. (2007). Associations between media viewing and language development in children under age 2 years. *The Journal of Pediatrics, 151*, 364–368.

Zito, J. M., Safer, D. J., dosReis, S., Gardner, J., Boles, M., & Lynch, F. (2000). Trends in the prescribing of psychotropic medications to preschoolers. *Journal of the American Medical Association, 283*, 1025–1030.

Zito, J. M., Safer, D. J., dosReis, S., Gardner, J., Magder, L., Soeken, K., Boles, M., Lynch, F., & Riddle, M. A. (2003). Psychotropic practice patterns for youth. *Archives of Pediatric and Adolescent Medicine, 157*, 17–25.

Zivin, G. (1977). On becoming subtle: Age and social rank in the use of a facial gesture. *Child Development, 48*, 1314–1321.

Zuber, J., Pixner, S., Moeller, K., & Nuerk, H-C. (2009). On the language-specificity of basic number processing: Transcoding in a language with inversion and its relation to working memory capacity. *Journal of Experimental Child Psychology, 102*, 60–77.

Zucker, K. J., & Bradley, S. J. (1995). *Gender identity disorder and psychosexual problems in children and adolescents.* New York: Guilford.

Zucker, K. J., Bradley, S. J., Olovier, G., Brake, J., Fleming, S., & Hood, J. (1996). Psychosexual development of women with congenital adrenal hyperplasia. *Hormones and Behavior, 30*, 300–318.

Zukow-Goldring, P. (2002). Sibling caregiving. In M. H. Bornstein (Ed.), *Handbook of parenting*, Vol. 3: *Being and becoming a parent* (2nd ed., pp. 253–286). Mahwah, NJ: Erlbaum.

Name Index

Subject Index

"Back to Sleep" campaign, 131
Bacteria as teratogen, 108
Baldness, 89
Bandura, A. *See* Social learning
Bar/Bat Mitzvah, 648
Barometric self-esteem, 275
Baseline self-esteem, 275
Basic trust v. mistrust stage, 58
Bayley Scales of Infant and Toddler Development, 391–392, 395
Bedwetting and sexual abuse, 627
Behavior. *See also* Antisocial behaviors; Prosocial behaviors
  applied behavioral analysis, 50–51
  brain development and, 176–178
  communication and, 530
  describing, 23–25
  divorce and, 548, 549
  goal-directed behavior, 306
  media, influence of, 556–558
  natural selection and, 72
  neonate behaviors, 124–132
  premature infants and, 122
  of rejected children, 576
  remedies for problem behaviors, 530
  rewards and, 530
  Tinbergen's four questions, 80
  tools for changing, 530
Behavioral genetics, 97–104
  concordance rates and, 98–99
  family studies and, 97–99
  genotype→environment theory, 101–102
  heritability, 98, 99–101
  nonshared environment and, 100–101
  shared environment and, 100–101
  significance of, 103–104
Behaviorism, 48–49
Belief-desire reasoning, 285–286
Beliefs
  belief-desire reasoning, 285–286
  emotions and, 450, 451
  parenting beliefs, 527–528
Biases
  gist bias, 330–331
  hostile attributional bias, 598
  in-group bias, 27
  negativity bias, 449–450
  out-group discrimination and bias, 579
Bicultural identity, 285
Bidirectional relationships, 13, 20, 46
  and conscience, 609
  evolutionary developmental psychology and, 76–77
  and families, 522
  instructed learning and, 297
  in self-esteem, 276
Bilingualism. *See* Second language
Binocular vision, 196
Biological clock, 524
Biologically primary abilities, 414
Biologically secondary abilities, 414
Biological motion, 249–251
Biological sensitivity to context, 460
Biology, 7
  and culture, 59
  developmental psychology and, 12
  development of biological knowledge, 248–253
  gender development and, 621

gender identity and, 647–649
infant perception and, 222
language development and, 350–351
organismic theories and, 48
prosocial behaviors, biological bases for, 588–589
sexual orientation, perspective on, 637–638
social learning and, 298–299
Biophilia, 252
Biparental families, 520, 521–522
Birds
  ducklings, auditory imprinting of, 20–21
  imprinting on, 20–21, 483–484
  pecking orders, 583
Birth, 115–120
  assistance to mothers, 118–119
  cultural practices, 115–116
  history of, 118–119
  infections and, 118
  process of, 116–120
  stages of, 117
Birth canal, 116
Birth control, 522
  abstinence-only sex education and, 631
Birth order, 547
Bisexuality, 634
  congenital adrenal hyperplasia (CAH) and, 637
  effeminate boys and, 636
Bisocial theory of gender identity/sexual orientation, 637–638
Bitter taste, disgust for, 443
Black Americans. *See* African Americans
Black English, 372–373
Black-sheep effect, 27
Bladder control, 159–160
Blank slates, infants as, 220–222
Blastocysts, 105
Blended families, 551. *See also* Stepparents
Blindness. *See also* Vision-impaired children
  color blindness, 94
Blood-borne neurotransmitters, 143
Blood types, 89
BMI (body mass index), 147
Bodily aggression, 594
Bodily-kinesthetic intelligence, 402
Body fat distribution, 143
Body image and puberty, 157–158
Body mass index (BMI), 147
Body size
  changes, 139–140
  culture and, 146
Bonding, 487, 488–489
  monkeys, research with, 488–489
  romantic love and, 633
Bone age, 140
Bone mass and anorexia nervosa, 151
Bonobos. *See* Monkeys
Bottle-feeding neonates, 126
Brain. *See also* Brain damage; Broca's area; Frontal cortex; Hippocampus; Hypothalamus; Neurons
  adolescents, development in, 177–178
  behavior and development of, 176–178
  cell death and, 174
  declines in development of, 174–175
  developmental psychology and, 12
  development of, 172–176
  dyslexia and, 418
  evolution of, 172

face recognition and, 22
fMRI (functional magnetic resonance imaging) of, 171, 641
innate behavior and, 21–22
institutionalized children and, 409
language acquisition and, 351–353
lateralization and, 166–167
metabolism changes in, 175
neuroimaging techniques, 171
object permanence and, 176–177
plasticity and, 178–179
prosopagnosia, 197
rises in development of, 174–175
risk-taking and, 472
of savants, 405
sex differences in development, 175–176
SIDS (sudden infant death syndrome) and, 131
size of, 172
social complexity and, 271
social interactions and, 568–569
social play and, 580
techniques for studying, 171
Brain damage
  age and, 180
  deferred imitation and, 220
  in development, 180
  language development and, 355
  multiple intelligences theory and, 403
  prosopagnosia, 197
  savants and, 405
Brain stem, 170
Brainy Baby, 223
Breastfeeding
  attachment and, 487
  natural parenting and, 502–503
  neonates, 126–127
  SIDS (sudden infant death syndrome) and, 131
Breasts
  culture and development of, 154–155
  puberty and, 154
Breech position, 116
  Cesarean delivery and, 117
Broca's area, 171
  language acquisition and, 352
Bronfenbrenner, U. *See* Ecological systems theory
Brothers. *See* Siblings
Bulimia, 151
Bullying, 592–593
  child abuse and, 535
  guidelines for dealing with, 593
  reasons for, 592–593
By-products, 75

Cadmium and prenatal development, 112
Caffeine
  prenatal development and, 111–112
  as teratogen, 108
Cancer. *See also* HIV/AIDS
  DES (diethylstilbestrol) and, 110
  mitosis of cells, 92
Candy Witch, 264, 293
Canela Indians, 5–6
Capuchins. *See* Monkeys
Carbon monoxide and prenatal development, 111
Card sorting task, 318–319
Caregiver attunement, 497
Caretaking behaviors, 484
Cartilage, 140

Emotional self-regulation, 441–451, 452–454
  factors influencing, 453
  in infancy and childhood, 452–453
  strategies for promoting, 453
Emotional understanding, 441–451, 454
  components of, 450
  eyewitness memory and, 337
Emotions
  action tendencies associated with, 440
  adaptive goals associated with, 440
  in adolescence, 454–455
  affective neuroscience, 443
  ambivalent nature of, 450, 451
  continuity of function and, 439
  defined, 438
  discrepancies between emotions, 450
  discrete emotion theory, 440–441
  dynamic systems theory, 443
  evolutionary approach to, 442–443
  families of, 439
  functionalist approach, 439–441
  management of, 450
  memory and emotions, understanding, 450
  multiple emotions, 450, 451
  other-conscious emotions, 447
  parenting styles, emotional adjustment and, 531
  primary emotions, 441–443, 444–446
  regulating emotions, 438–439
  secondary emotions, 442–443, 446–448
  self-awareness, 447
  self-conscious emotions, 442
  separation distress, 446
  sex differences in, 641–642
  stranger distress, 446
  as universal, 440
Emotion talk, 451
Empathy, 585–586
  articulate empathy, 438
  friendship and, 572
  as secondary emotion, 447
Empiricism, 18–19
Empiricist position, 348–349
Employers and employment
  child labor laws, 10–11
  social network sites, checking on, 561
Emulation, 297
Encoding, 339–340
  multiple intelligences theory and, 403
Endocrine system
  glands of, 144
  physical growth and, 143–144
Endogenous smiles, 444
Enuresis and sexual abuse, 627
Environment
  ADHD (attention-deficit with hyperactivity disorder) and, 320–321
  attachment style and, 501
  of evolutionary adaptedness, 72, 74
  executive function and, 319–320
  genotype→environment theory, 101–102
  good-enough parents and, 541
  heritability and, 100–101
  IQ (intelligence quotient) and, 405, 406–412
  MAOA activity and antisocial behavior, 103
  physical growth, factors affecting, 144–146
  prenatal development, environmental risk factors and, 109–113

sexual orientation and, 635–636
  temperament and, 474–475
Environmental construal and temperament, 475
Environmental elicitation and temperament, 474–475
Environmental manipulation and temperament, 475
Environmental contaminants
  menarche and, 155
  as teratogens, 108
Environmental selection and temperament, 474–475
Envy, 447
Epigenesis, 19–20
Epilepsy, neuron migration and, 174
Episodic memory, 327
Equal distribution of resources, 608–609
Equipotential, 180
Erikson's psychoanalytic theory, 56–57
  identity formation in adolescents and, 280–281
  psychosocial stages, 58
Erogenous zones, 56
Essentialist position, 474
Estrogens, 144
  menarche and, 154
  and puberty, 152–153
Ethical Standards for Research with Children, 40
Ethic of autonomy, 610
Ethic of community, 610
Ethic of divinity, 610
Ethics of child research, 40
Ethnic constancy, 284
Ethnicity. See also African Americans; Latinos; Native Americans
  ethnic identity, development of, 283–285
  feelings and preferences on, 284
  graduation rates by, 552
  knowledge of, 284
  parenting styles and, 536–537
  role behaviors and, 284
  self-identification by, 284
  sexual intercourse in adolescence and, 630
  sexual-minority youth, acceptance of, 639
  single-parent families and, 524
Ethnology and naturalistic studies, 28
European Community, bilingualism in, 378
Evaluative embarrassment, 448
Event memory, 327, 333–334
  age and, 341
Event-Related Potentials (ERPs), 171
Evocative effects, 102
Evolution
  aggression, evolutionary patterns and, 76
  of brain, 172
  emotions, evolutionary approach to, 442–443
  gender identity and, 621
  group socialization theory and, 568–569
  human evolution, 73
  of morality, 600, 610
  slow growth and, 138
Evolutionary context for development, 46
Evolutionary developmental psychology, 71–79
  bidirectional gene-environment interactions and, 76–77
  constraints on development, 77
  deferred adaptations, 77–78
  extended childhood, need for, 77
  natural selection in, 76

ontogenetic adaptations, 78
  plasticity of children, 79
  principles of, 75–79
Evolutionary psychology
  misuses of, 76
  principles of, 72–75
  reproductive strategies and, 617
Evolutionary theory, 12, 13, 71–79
  of child-rearing, 504–514
  cooperative breeding hypothesis, 507
  natural selection, 71–72
  sex differences and, 640
Evolved cognitive mechanisms, 72, 73
Executive function, 312–321
  ADHD (attention-deficit with hyperactivity disorder) and, 320–321
  attention span and, 315–317
  brain development and, 177–178
  cognitive flexibility, 318–319
  defined, 313
  effortful control and, 463
  emotional self-regulation and, 453
  false-belief tasks and, 291
  inhibition and, 317–318
  key concept definitions, 322
  lying and, 606–607
  memory span and, 313–315
  origins of, 319–321
  physical fitness and, 319–320
  prospective memory and, 341
  resistance to interference, 317–318
  simultaneous bilingualism and, 379
  speed of processing, 313, 314
  training for, 320
Exercise. See also Athletics
  obesity and, 148, 149
  play, 253
Exhibitionist behaviors, 622–623
  in preschool children, 625
  in school-age children, 626–628
Exosystem, 68–70
Experience
  auditory imprinting and, 20–21
  consciousness and, 330
  face recognition and, 22
  self-esteem and, 276
  sensitive periods and, 22–23
Experience-dependent synaptogenesis, 179
Experience-expectant synaptogenesis, 179, 409
Experiential intelligence, 399
Experimental studies, 32, 35–36
Explicit memory, 327–328
  deferred imitation as, 220
  hippocampus and, 221
  implicit memory compared, 328–330
Explicit self, 272
Extended childhood, 77
Extended families, 521
  parenting and, 532
  single fathers and, 525
External causes and emotions, 450
Externality effect, 197
Externalizing
  authoritarian parents and, 529
  child maltreatment and, 535
  personality and, 466–467, 468
  rejected children and, 576

Rearing environment. *See* Families
Reasoning, 310–312
  analogical reasoning, 310–311
  belief-desire reasoning, 285–286
  fuzzy-trace theory and, 331
  scientific reasoning, 311–312
Receptive language, 364
Recessive genes, 88–89
  disorders transmitted by, 88–89, 90
  sex-linked genes as, 94
  traits associated with, 89
Reciprocal altruism, 585
Reciprocal determinism, 53
Reciprocal relationships, 571
  by parents, 577
Reciprocity and core knowledge, 210
Reconciliation and group cohesion, 583–584
Red hair, genes for, 88
Reflective abstraction, 242
Reflexes
  of neonates, 129–132
  in sensorimotor stage, 233
Reflexive sounds, 360, 362
Regulating emotions, 438
Regulatory systems and teratogens, 110
Rehearsal, 323–324
Rejected children, 573–574
  social competence of, 575
Relational aggression, 590–591
Relational theories, 57
Relationships, 571–573
  in microsystem, 68
Reliability, 25
  interobserver reliability, 25
  replicability, 25
Religion
  Bar/Bat Mitzvah, 648
  birth and, 115
  Catholic Church on children, 9
  Confirmation (Christianity), 648
  intuitive theists, children as, 294–296
  polygamous communities, siblings in, 545–546
Remarriage, 547–548. *See also* Stepparents
  serial monogamy and, 520
  sex difference in adjustment to, 548–549
Remembering, 327
  language and, 332
Removing children from problem areas, 530
REM sleep
  in fetuses, 107
  in neonates, 125–126
Renaissance, children in, 10
Replicability, 25
Reproductive strategies, 79, 616–617
  K strategies, 617
  natural selection and, 620
  parental investment theory, 617–621
  r strategies, 616–617
Research
  case studies, 26, 30–31
  data collection methods, 26–33
  development, research methods in, 23–40
  diaries and, 31
  ethics of child research, 40
  interviews, 26–27
  observational studies, 26, 28–29
  obtaining child research participants, 39

problems with child research, 39–40
  questionnaires, 26, 27–28
  on sexuality in childhood, 621–622
  standardized tests, 26, 27–28
  subject loss, problem of, 39
  theories directing, 47
Research designs
  correlational studies, 32, 33–35
  cross-sectional studies, 32, 36–38
  cross-sequential studies, 32, 37–38
  in developmental psychology, 32, 33–39
  experimental studies, 32, 35–36
  longitudinal studies, 32, 36–37
  microgenetic studies, 32, 38–39
Resiliency of children, 15
Resistance to interference, 317–318, 322
Resource distribution, 608–609
Respiratory distress syndrome, 122
Restrictive parenting and ethnicity, 536–537
Retention processes and observational learning, 52
Retrieval of information, 339–340
Retrospective memory, 340
Retrospective studies of childhood sexuality,
    622, 623
Reversibility, 238
Rewards
  and behavior, 530
  emotional self-regulation and, 453
  prosocial behaviors and, 589
Rh factor incompatibility
  prenatal development and, 113
  as teratogen, 108
Rh positive blood type, 89
Rhythmic stereotypes, 253
Right-hand preference, 166–167
Risk-taking, 468–470
  in adolescence, 469, 472–473
  conscientiousness and, 467
  factors influencing, 469–470
  genes and, 470
  peer pressure and, 470
  personal fable and, 470
  sex differences in, 468–469, 641–642
Ritalin, 321, 458
Rites of passage, 648
Rocking infants, 129
Roles
  confusion, 281
  in microsystem, 68–69
Romanian orphans, 407–408
  cortisol levels of, 459
Romantic love, 632
Rooting reflex, 130
Rough-and-tumble play, 253, 580
R strategies, 616–617
Rubella
  prenatal development and, 112
  as teratogen, 108
Rules
  cognitive flexibility and, 318–319
  play, 253
Rumors and aggression, 590
Running, 161

Sacrificing children, 8
Sadness, 440. *See also* Depression
  as primary emotion, 444

Safe sex, 631
Same-sex families. *See* Single-gender families
Santa Claus, 263, 293
SAT (Scholastic Aptitude Test), 28, 398
  Mathematics score for males or females, 427
Savants, multiple intelligences theory and, 403,
    404–405
Savant syndrome, 404–405
Scaffolding, 65
Scatter plots, 33–34
Schizophrenia, concordance rates for, 98
School-age children, sexual behaviors in,
    626–628
Schools. *See also* Academic performance
  bullying in, 592–593
  families and, 553
  formal schooling, 552–553
  graduation rates by race/ethnicity, 552
  IQ, attendance and, 392–393
  purposes of, 553
  sleep needs and, 160–161
  social function of, 553
  socialization and, 551–552
Science. *See also* Research
  of developmental psychology, 23–25
Scientific explanations, 25
Scientific reasoning, 311–312
  metacognition and, 326
Scribbling, 257–258
Scripts and event memory, 333–334
Secondary circular reactions, 234
Secondary emotions, 442–443, 446–448
  cultural variation and, 443
Secondary sexual characteristics, 152–153, 628
  in females, 154
  in males, 153–154
Secondary teeth, 141–142
Secondhand smoke and SIDS (sudden infant death
    syndrome), 131
Second language, 351–354
  benefits of bilingualism, 378–380
  brain and development of, 353
  children, acquisition by, 355
  costs of bilingualism, 378–380
  critical period effects in learning, 356
  multiple intelligences theory and learners, 402
  semilingualism, 379–380
  sequential bilingualism, 379
  simultaneous bilingualism, 379
Second order symbolism and writing, 421
Secure attachment, 491–492
  consequences of, 499–500
Sedatives as teratogens, 108
Selection. *See also* Natural selection
  in triarchic theory of intelligence, 400–401
Selective attention, 315–316
  resistance to interference and, 317
Selective cell death, 174
Self. *See also* Social cognition
  development of concept, 270–274
  understanding self, 269–270
Self-awareness, 447
  cognitive flexibility and, 319
  development of, 270–274
  early stages of, 272–273
  humanness and, 271
  theory of mind and, 286

Self-concept, 272
    autobiographical memory and, 333
    descriptions by children, 273–274
    early stages of, 272–273
    infantile amnesia and, 333
    milestones in development of, 277
Self-conscious emotions, 442
Self-directed learning, 322
Self-directed thinking, 305–306
Self-disclosure and friendship, 572
Self-efficacy, 272
    development of, 277–280
    optimistic child, 278–279
    overestimating one's abilities, 279–280
Self-esteem, 272
    development of, 274–277
    early-maturing girls and, 158
    milestones in development of, 277
    obesity and, 149
    overinflated sense of self, 276
    secure attachment and, 499
    sexual abuse and, 627
    sleep needs and, 160
Self-exploration, 559
Self-fulfilling prophecy, 394–395
Self-generated movement, 141
Self-image in adolescence, 454
Self-propelled motion, 249–250
Self-reflection
    in adolescence, 454
    social learning and, 52
Self-regulation. *See also* Emotional self-regulation
    aggression and, 596
    conscience and, 609
    instructed learning and, 297
    lying and, 606–607
    permissive parents and, 529
    social learning and, 52
Self-segregation into groups, 579
Self-touching behaviors, 622–623
    in preschool children, 625
    in school-age children, 626–628
Semantic memory, 327–328
Semantics, 348, 359
    constraints on word learning, 364–365
    development of, 362–365
    fast mapping, 363
    first words, 363
    humor and, 366
    overextensions, 364
    productive language, 364
    receptive language, 364
    underextensions, 364
    word spurt, 362–363
Semilingualism, 379–380
Seminal vesicles, 154
Sensation, 188–189
Sensation-seeking. *See* Risk-taking
Sensitive periods, 22–23
    for language acquisition, 351–352
Sensorimotor stage, 55, 58, 230–231
    locomotion and, 164
    substages of, 232–235
Sensory register, 53
Sensory systems of neonates, 127–128
Sentences
    interrogative sentences, 369
    negative sentences, 369

passive sentences, 369–370
Standard *vs.* Black English, 372
structure of, 350
Subject-Verb-Object (SVO) order, 368–369
Separation distress, 446, 486, 488–489
    child care and, 490
Separation protest, 488–489
Sequential bilingualism, 379
Serial monogamy, 520
Seriation, 240
Serotonin, 173
    depression and, 457
    romantic love and, 632
    SIDS (sudden infant death syndrome) and, 131
SES (socioeconomic status). *See also* Poverty
    affluence, perils of, 534
    at-risk children and IQ, 408
    gesture use and, 357
    IQ tests and, 393
    parenting goals and beliefs and, 527–528
    parenting styles and, 532–533
    sexual behavior of adolescents and, 630
    spanking and, 533
Sex cells. *See also* Ova; Sperm
    meiosis and, 92–93
Sex chromosomes, 93–94
    color blindness and, 94
    Turner syndrome, 96–97
Sex determination
    chromosomes and, 86, 94
    in Galápagos Islands turtles, 85–86
    genotypes and, 91
Sex differences, 638–643
    in aggression, 590–591
    in brain development, 175–176
    in bullying, 592–593
    in childcare, 506
    in cognition, 78, 643
    in dental development, 140
    divorce, reaction to, 548–549
    in emotional self-regulation, 454
    evaluating, 640–641
    in externalizing problems, 456
    in friendships, 572–573
    in gender stereotyping, 647
    in growth curves, 140
    in internalizing problems, 456
    in make-believe play, 581
    in mathematics ability, 427–428, 641–643
    in moral reasoning, 604–605
    in mortality rates, 641–642
    in motor development, 167–168, 641–642
    naturalistic fallacy and, 620
    origins of, 640
    parental investment theory and, 617–619
    patterns of, 641–642
    in prodigies, 405
    in reading abilities, 419–420
    in reconciliation, 584
    remarriage, adjustment to, 548–549
    in risk-taking, 468–469
    in self-esteem, 275
    SIDS (sudden infant death syndrome) and, 131
    in social play, 580–581
    stepparents, dealing with, 548–549
    in temperament, 463
    in tool use, 309–310
Sex education, abstinence-only, 631

Sex hormones. *See also* Androgens;
        Estrogens; Testosterone
    gender identity and, 638
    risk-taking and, 472–473
    as teratogens, 108
Sexism and evolutionary psychology, 76
Sex-linked inheritance, 88, 94
    color blindness, 94
Sex-ratios, 93–94
Sex segregation, 577–578
    in-groups and, 578
Sexting, 561
Sexual abuse, 533, 627
    eyewitness memory and, 339
Sexual behavior
    classification of behaviors, 622–623
    developmental differences in, 624–625
    development of, 621–634
    early-maturing girls and, 158
    emergence of, 623–624
    media and, 557
    preschool years, decrease after, 624–625
    sexual abuse and, 627
    sexual orientation and, 634
    siblings and, 618–619
    as social behavior, 620–621
Sexual development, 152–155. *See also* Puberty
Sexual fantasies, 629
Sexual intercourse
    in adolescence, 629–630
    age, rates by, 629
Sexuality, 616
    American culture and, 631
    childhood sexuality, 621–622
    continuum of, 634
    Freud's theories on, 56
    puberty and, 628
Sexual latency, 628
Sexually-transmitted diseases. *See* STDs (sexually transmitted diseases)
Sexual-minority youth, 639
Sexual orientation, 616, 634. *See also* Bisexuality;
        Heterosexuality; Homosexuality
    biology and, 637–638
    bisocial perspective, 637–638
    causes of, 635–637
    components of, 634
    development of, 634–638
    environment and, 635–636
    genes and, 636–637
    hormones and, 636–637
    as intentional choice, 638
    prenatal experience and, 637
    progression of, 639
    siblings and, 637
    single-gender families, children in, 526
    stability of, 638
Sexual reproduction, 616. *See also*
        Reproductive strategies
Sexual socialization, 557–558
Shame, 440, 448
Shaping in triarchic theory of intelligence, 400–401
"Shaq's Big Challenge," 150
Shared attention
    autistic children and, 292
    chimpanzees and, 294–295
    crawling and, 162
    emotional-self-regulation and, 452–453

language development and, 356–357
  social cognition and, 286–288
Shared environment, 100–101
Shared memory, 66, 67
Sharing, 586–587
  development of, 570
Short-term memory, 53
Shunning and aggression, 590
Siblings. *See also* Twin studies
  birth of sibling, conflict and, 543
  birth order, 547
  conflict and, 543–546
  cooperation and, 543–546
  differences among, 546–547
  favoritism by parents, 546–547
  genotype→environment theory and, 546–547
  homosexuality and, 637
  incest avoidance, 618–619
  learning from, 542–543
  living with, 542–543
  One-Child Policy (China), 542, 544–545
  polyandry, 520
  in polygamous communities, 545–546
  sexual relations between, 618–619
Sickle-cell anemia, 88, 89
  natural selection and, 90
Sickly children, abuse of, 535
SIDS (sudden infant death syndrome), 130, 131
  filicide and, 535
  motor development and, 169
  smoking and, 111
Sign language
  American Sign Language, 354
  Nicaraguan Sign Language, 354–355
Simple arithmetic in infants, 217–218
Simultaneous bilingualism, 379
Single-gender families, 526–527
  change in, 524
  differences in children from, 526–527
  sexual orientation of children and, 636
  statistics on, 526
Single mothers by choice, 524–525
Single-parent families, 522, 524–526
  increases in, 523–524
Sisters. *See* Siblings
Skeletal competencies and core knowledge, 210
Skeletal development, 140–142
Skipping, 161
  sex differences in, 168
Skulls of neonates, 120–121
Sleep. *See also* REM sleep
  divorce and sleep problems, 548
  need for, 160–161
  neonates, sleep-awake cycles of, 124–126
  postpartum depression and, 120
  sexual abuse and, 627
  SIDS (sudden infant death syndrome) and, 131
Sleep apnea and obesity, 149
Slow-to-warm-up babies, 461
Small-for-date infants, 122
Smell
  incest avoidance and, 619
  mother's smell, infant preference for, 498
  neonates and, 128
Smiling, 80
  endogenous smiles, 444
  evolutionary approach to, 442

as primary emotion, 444
  social smiling, 444
Smoking
  affluence and, 534
  early-maturing girls and, 158
  media and, 557
  menarche and teenage smoking, 158
  prenatal development and, 111
  SIDS (sudden infant death syndrome) and, 131
Snakes, fear of, 445
Sneeze reflex, 130
Social aggression, 590
Social cognition, 270
  humanness and, 271
  intentional agents and, 286
  perspective taking and, 286
  shared attention and, 286–288
Social cognitive theory, 51–52
Social comparisons and temperament, 475
Social compensation, 559
Social construction of mental functioning, 62, 63–67
Social Darwinism, 76
Social dissatisfaction of rejected children, 576
Social environment
  locomotion and, 164
  menarche and, 154–155
Social facilitation, 559
Social grooming, 588
Social information processing and aggression, 597–598
Social intelligence, 400
Social interactionism, 356–359
Social isolation. *See* Isolation
Socialization
  conscience development and, 609
  group socialization theory, 568–569
  Internet and, 558–559
  school and, 551–552
  sexual socialization, 557–558
Social learning, 296–300
  biological basis of, 298–299
  of chimpanzees, 294–295
  defined, 296
  emulation, 296–297
  imitative learning, 297
  instructed learning, 297
  mimicry, 296–297
  mirror neurons and, 298–299
  teaching, 297
  types of, 296–298
Social learning theory, 49–54
Social looking, 164
Social-moral infractions, disgust for, 443
Social perspective taking, 237–238
Social play, 580–581
Social preference, popularity and, 574
Social referencing, 449
Social skills
  and autistic children, 292
  modeling of, 577
  origins of poor social skills, 576–577
  of rejected children, 575
Social smiling, 444
Social status. *See also* SES (socioeconomic status)
  in peer groups, 573
  popularity and, 573–574

Social support
  for mothers, 508
  parenting and, 532
Society for Research in Child Development, 40
Sociocultural perspective, 12, 13, 61
Sociocultural theory, 62–68, 246
  cognitive development theory contrasted, 246–247
  major concepts of, 62
  social construction of mental functioning, 62, 63–67
  sociohistorical influences, 67–68
  tools of intellectual adaptation, 62, 63
Sociodramatic play, 253, 255
  culture and, 256
Socioemotional development, 7
Socioemotional network and risk-taking, 472
Sociohistorical influences, 13, 67–68
  development, contexts for, 46
Sociological meaning of childhood, 8
Sociometric techniques, 573
Soldiers, children as, 11
Solo mothers, 525
Sonagrams of fetus, 113, 115
Soothing techniques with infants, 128, 129
Source monitoring, 263
  eyewitness memory and, 337
South American street children, 11
Spanking, 530
  SES (socioeconomic status) parents and, 533
Spatial development
  and locomotion, 163
  sex differences in, 641–642
Spatial intelligence, 402
Species-specific, language as, 349–350
Species-uniform, language as, 349–350
Specific attachment stage, 487, 488
Specific language impairments, 377–378
  characteristics of, 378
Speech. *See* Language
Speech registers, 370, 371–374
Speed of processing, 313, 314, 322
Spelling
  deep orthography, 417
  writing and, 422–423
Sperm
  age of, 92
  conception, role in, 104
  meiosis and, 92–93
  puberty and, 154
Spermarche, 154
Spina bifida, 115
Spiritual/existential intelligence, 402
Spontaneous helping, 588
Sports. *See* Athletics
Spousal abuse, 76
Stability, 14–15
  and aggression, 594
  of attachment, 498–499
  divorce and, 550
  essentialist position, 474
  Five Factor Model of personality and, 474
  gender stability, 644–645
  of general intelligence (g), 396
  intelligence and, 14, 395–397
  parenting styles and, 532–533
  of personality, 464–465, 474
  plasticity *vs.*, 14–15
  of sexual orientation, 638